HISTORY

OF THE

INDIAN MUTINY,

1857-1858.

HISTORY
OF THE
INDIAN MUTINY,
1857-1858.

COMMENCING FROM THE CLOSE OF THE
SECOND VOLUME OF
SIR JOHN KAYE'S HISTORY OF THE SEPOY WAR.

BY

COLONEL G. B. MALLESON, C.S.I.
AUTHOR OF "HISTORY OF THE FRENCH IN INDIA,"
"HISTORICAL SKETCH OF THE NATIVE STATES OF
INDIA," ETC., ETC.

VOLUME I.

CONTEMPORANEOUS WITH SIR JOHN KAYE'S THIRD
VOLUME.

SECOND EDITION.

GYAN

Published by

Gyan Publishing House
5, Ansari Road
Daryaganj, New Delhi-110002
Phone: 011-47034999, 9811692060
E-mail: books@gyanbooks.com

Distribution Network
gyanbooks.com
India, USA, Canada, UK, Australia, France

ISBN : 978-81-212-3541-9 (Set)
ISBN : 978-81-212-4914-0 (PB)
First Published, 1878

2nd Impression 2020

Printed at: Gyan Press, Delhi.

History of the Indian Mutiny, Vol. I
1857-1858.
Author: Colonel G. B. Malleson

HISTORY

OF THE

INDIAN MUTINY, 1857–1858.

COMMENCING FROM THE CLOSE OF THE SECOND VOLUME OF SIR JOHN KAYE'S HISTORY OF THE SEPOY WAR.

BY

COLONEL G. B. MALLESON, C.S.I.

AUTHOR OF "HISTORY OF THE FRENCH IN INDIA," "HISTORICAL SKETCH OF THE NATIVE STATES OF INDIA," ETC., ETC.

VOLUME I.

CONTEMPORANEOUS WITH SIR JOHN KAYE'S THIRD VOLUME.

SECOND EDITION.

LONDON:
WILLIAM H. ALLEN AND CO.,
13 WATERLOO PLACE, PALL MALL, S.W.
1878.

TO

MAJOR-GENERAL

SIR VINCENT EYRE, K.C.S.I., C.B.

A FRIENDSHIP OF THIRTY YEARS
DURATION, THE VALUE OF WHICH I NEED NOT
HERE ESTIMATE, IS MY SOLE, BUT SUFFICIENT, REASON
FOR THE EXERCISE OF THE MOST GRACEFUL
PRIVILEGE OF AN AUTHOR, IN DEDICATING TO YOU THESE
PAGES, WHEREIN YOUR NAME OCCUPIES
A CONSPICUOUS PLACE IN CONNECTION WITH THE
MEMORABLE EVENTS WHICH I HAVE
ENDEAVOURED, FAITHFULLY AND IMPARTIALLY,
TO RECORD.

G. B. M.

PREFACE

TO THE SECOND EDITION.

The alterations which have been made in the seventh and eighth books, and in the first chapter of the ninth book of this volume, are almost entirely verbal, and in no way alter the sense of the text of the first edition. At page 295, a mistake in the name of the medical officer attached to the 2nd Cavalry, Gwáliár Contingent, has been rectified.

In the second chapter of the ninth book, a very gallant deed performed by Captain R. P. Anderson and Corporal Oxenham, assisted by four others, has been inserted; and in the third chapter of the same book I have endeavoured to render more complete justice to the gallantry of young Henry Havelock in one case, of Captain Olpherts in another, and of Captains Olpherts and Crump, and of Private Duffy, in a third.

Having carefully re-read and studied all the documents bearing on the Patná crisis, related in the second chapter of the seventh book, I have found it impossible to recede from the conclusion I deliberately recorded in the first edition. The opponents of the view I have taken have been forced to seek refuge in the assertion that in June and July 1857 Patná never was in danger. It can scarcely, however, be denied that but for the unanticipated success of Vincent Eyre—a success achieved with means far inferior to those which in the hands of another leader had failed—not only would Árah have fallen, but the whole of western Bihár, of which Patná was the capital, would have been overrun by the mutinous regiments, strengthened in numbers by the retainers of the landowners. It was in view of such a catastrophe, then impending, that Mr. Tayler, acting as a prudent general would have acted, issued to his subordinates the order to concentrate on Patná, there to oppose the enemy, where alone opposition could be effectual. Yet it is now gravely asserted that Patná never was in danger! It would be as true to affirm that in 1857–58 there was no mutiny in India. In no part of the country was the danger more imminent, more menacing to the safety of the empire, than in western Bihár in the month of July 1857. The danger was long warded off by the statesman-like action of Mr. Tayler; it was finally averted by the daring of Vincent Eyre. But for these two men it might have been necessary for the English to reconquer Calcutta.

G. B. M.

27, *West Cromwell Road,*
1st October 1879.

PREFACE

TO THE FIRST EDITION.

THE public has a right to demand why, a third volume of the late Sir John Kaye's history having already appeared, I should entirely ignore that volume, and should take up the story from the close of the second.

I now proceed to explain why I have done so.

The very day on which I returned to England from India, after my retirement from the service, I was asked to continue and complete Kaye's History of the Sepoy War.

Many reasons combined to induce me to accept the offer. I had been in India from the commencement of the mutiny till its force had been broken; I had collected on the spot, and had even thrown into shape, materials for such a work; not only was I acquainted with many of the actors, but I had had for years continuous opportunities of studying in India the points of controversy which had arisen after the mutiny had been quelled.

On the other hand it is always a disadvantage to continue the work of a writer from whom one may differ in essential points. This was, I felt, especially the case in the instance before me. For, whilst the first and second volumes of Sir John Kaye's work—not to speak of the political opinions they enunciated—had recounted in eloquent language the events of the earlier stages of the mutiny as they had happened, his third volume had, in the opinion alike of the actors and spectators of the drama, failed to render to those of whom it treated that impartial justice which their deeds, good or evil, had deserved.

I had read that volume in India. I do not wish to say a single word in depreciation of its style, of its brilliancy, of its literary merit. But I may simply observe that neither could the officers of the army, many in number, of all branches of the service, political and civil, as well as military; nor could I, accept it in many important particulars as history. The letters which appeared in the English newspapers, controverting many of its statements, and reflecting, I have since ascertained, but a fraction of the dissatisfaction and dissent felt regarding it, showed clearly that this opinion was not confined to India—that it was general.

When, therefore, I was asked to continue and complete the history I replied that I would do so only on the condition that the continuation should begin from the termination of Sir John Kaye's second volume, thus ignoring the third. This was agreed to.

In performing this task the plan of my narrative has been very much affected by the necessity of adhering as much as possible to the general scheme of Sir John Kaye's work. Naturally, I should have preferred to be free to form a grouping after my own taste. But this was impossible. I have, however, deviated from the arrangement sanctioned by Sir John Kaye in his third volume, in so far that I have left for the fourth volume the account of the storming of Dehlí, while I have included in the third the story of the first relief of Lakhnao.

It appeared to me that such an arrangement was absolutely essential to the harmony of the narrative. The first so-called relief of Lakhnao was not really a relief. It was in truth a reinforcement of the garrison. It did not deal, as did the capture of Dehlí, a deadly and a fatal blow to the rebellion. The siege of the Residency still continued after it had been effected. It seems therefore rightly included in a volume which records the progress of the mutiny. At the same time, the account of the storming of Dehlí being transferred to the fourth volume, that volume will be devoted mainly to the history of the downfall and crushing of the great rebellion.

It will be seen that I differ entirely from Sir John Kaye as to the wisdom of the action of the Government of India in the early days of the mutiny. I have given my reasons. They were formed on the spot twenty-one years ago. Further examination has confirmed them.

One word as to the authorities on which this history rests. It is based on letters, journals, and official documents, written at the time—in 1857. I have ever distrusted, and I distrust, documents penned from memory after a lapse of twenty-one years. To the dead, as well as to the living, justice must be rendered. Such justice can be dealt only by the historian who shall carefully peruse letters and journals—not meant for publication—written at the time; who shall subject these to a rigid examination; and who shall then conscientiously and impartially record the judgment formed upon that examination.

To do this I have devoted all my energies.

During the whirl of action, amid the distracting influences of the passing exigencies of the hour, it is not always possible to be impartial. The time has now arrived when the task of dealing out severe and strict justice to all may be attempted. In the process it is inevitable that men who may have been unduly exalted may be relegated to a lower place, whilst modest and neglected merit will be moved up higher. But my aim, my hope, my earnest desire, has been and is to render to all as they have deserved.

The fourth volume, containing the fall of Dehlí and the movements of the Dehlí force; the holding of the Residency and subsequently of the A'lambágh by Sir James Outram; the capture of Lakhnao and the crushing of the rebellion in Oudh by Sir Colin Campbell—afterwards Lord Clyde; the Central Indian campaign of Sir Hugh Rose (now Lord Strathnairn); and the daring achievements of Sir Robert Napier (now Lord Napier of Magdála),—will appear in the first quarter of 1879.

One word as to the spelling of proper names. I have adopted the modern system, that of spelling words in English as they are spelt in the language of Hindústán. When it is considered that by the barbarous method, or rather no-method, hitherto in force the sense of the names is utterly lost, I cannot think that the system I have adopted will be regarded as a harmful innovation. Take, for instance, the place usually known as Cawnpore. Spelt in that way the name is absolutely without signification. But spelt in the way in which it is written by the Hindús, Kánhpúr, the meaning becomes at once apparent. Kánh is a name for Krishna; Púr stands for a city. The entire word signifies "city of Krishna." For the convenience of those accustomed to the old method I append a glossary of the proper names I have employed, spelt according to both systems, and ranged in alphabetical order.

G. B. MALLESON.

27 West Cromwell Road.
1 May 1878.

GLOSSARY OF PROPER NAMES.

The mode of spelling now adopted.	The old mode of spelling.
Ágra	Agra.
Ajmír	Ajmeer.
Aligarh	Aligurh.
Alláhábád	Allahabad.
Alwar	Ulwur.
Ambálah	Umballa.
Arah	Arrah.
Árangábád	Aurungabad.
Ázamgarh	Azimgurh.
Badáon	Budown.
Balandshahr	Bolundshuhr.
Banáras	Benares.
Barélí	Bareilly.
Barhámpúr	Berhampore.
Bárrákpúr	Barrackpore.
Bharatpúr	Bhurtpore.
Bhopál	Bhopal.
Bihár	Behar.
Chambal	Chumbul.
Champáran	Chumparun.
Dánápúr	Dinapore.
Dehlí, or more correctly, Dihlí	Delhi.
Dehrá Dún	Deyra Dhoon.
Dhár	Dhar.
Dholpúr	Dholepore.
Dísá	Deesa.
Diwás	Dewas.
Etáwa, correctly Itáwa	Etawah.
Faizábád	Fyzabad.
Farrakhábád	Furruckabad.
Fathgarh	Futtehgurh.
Fathpúr	Futtehpore.
Fathpur-Sikri	Futtehpore Sekri.
Gayá	Gyah.
Ghágrá	Gograh.
Gorákhpúr	Gorruckpore.
Gúmtí	Goomtee.
Gwáliár	Gwalior.
Haidarábád	Hydrabad.
Hamírpúr	Humeerpore.

The mode of spelling now adopted.	The old mode of spelling.
I'ta	Etah.
Itáwa	Etawah.
Jabalpúr	Jubbulpore.
Jaipúr	Jeypore.
Jalpáigori	Julpigori.
Jamná	Jumna.
Jánpúr	Jaunpore.
Jhánsí	Jhansi.
Jodhpúr	Jodhpore.
Kánhpúr	Cawnpore.
Kotá	Kotah.
Láhor	Lahore.
Lakhnao	Lucknow.
Lalatpúr	Lullutpore.
Mathurá	Muttra.
Máu	Mhow.
Mewár	Meywar.
Mírath	Meerut.
Mirzapúr	Mirzapore.
Morádábád	Moradabad.
Motíhárí	Moteeharee.
Mozaffarnagar	Mozuffernuggur.
Mozaffarpúr	Mozuffarpore.
Náogong, or Naogaon	Nowgong.
Narbadá	Nerbudda.
Nasírábád	Nasseerabad.
Nímach	Neemuch.
Nipál	Nepaul.
Onáo	Oonao.
Panjáb	Punjaub.
Patná	Patna.
Pasháwar	Peshawar.
Rájpút	Rajpoot.
Rájpútáná	Rajpootana.
Rájsháhí	Rajshye.
Rángún	Rangoon.
Ságar	Saugor.
Sahāranpúr	Saharunpore.
Sái	Sye.
Sáran	Sarun.
Sháhábád	Shahabad.
Sháhjahánpúr	Shahjehanpore.
Sítápúr	Seetapore.
Súltánpúr	Saltanpore.
Tirhút	Tirhoot.
Udaipúr	Oodeypore.

CONTENTS

OF

THE FIRST VOLUME.

CONTEMPORANEOUS WITH

SIR JOHN KAYE'S THIRD VOLUME.

BOOK VII.

CHAPTER I.

CHAPTER II.

CHAPTER III.

BOOK VIII.

CHAPTER I.

CHAPTER II.

CHAPTER III.

CHAPTER IV.

CHAPTER V.

CHAPTER VI.

BOOK IX.

CHAPTER I.

CHAPTER II.

CHAPTER III.

HISTORY

OF THE

INDIAN MUTINY OF 1857.

BOOK VII.

CHAPTER I.

It is time now to return to Calcutta. The measures taken and the views entertained by the Government on receiving intelligence of the Mírath outbreak have been already recorded. It is evident that up to the end of the month of May they had not fully apprehended the gravity of the situation. "Everything," wrote the Secretary in the Home Department, Mr. Cecil Beadon, on the 25th of May, to the French Consul and the other French residents at Calcutta, who, with rare self-sacrifice, had placed their services at the disposal of the Government, "everything is quiet within six hundred miles of the capital. The mischief caused by a passing and groundless panic, has already been arrested; and there is every reason to hope that in the course of a few days tranquillity and confidence will be restored throughout the Presidency." Certainly the dis- 1857. May 25. Calcutta.

Book VII. Chapter I.

1857. May 25.

inclination of the Government to accept, to the extent to which they were proffered, the loyal and disinterested offers of the members of the Trades' Association, of the Masonic Fraternity, of the Armenians, and of the French residents, seemed to argue on their part a conviction that the resources at their disposal were equal to any emergency, and a belief that the measures already taken would suffice to put down the revolt. But, however that may have been, nothing could justify or even palliate the tone of the reply of the Home Secretary to the French residents. It seemed at the time difficult to affirm to whom Mr. Beadon, the mouth-piece of the Government, intended to impute "a passing and groundless panic." It could not apply to the citizens of Calcutta, for not only had they evinced no fear, but they had not caused the mischief. That mischief had been caused by the sepoys; but it was scarcely the result of panic. Nor, had it been so, was the panic, it would seem, altogether groundless, and certainly it was not passing.

It is clear, at any rate, that, on the 25th of May, the Government reckoned upon order being maintained throughout the country between Calcutta and Alláhábád, and upon the prompt repression of the rebellion.

They had, on the 20th of May, commenced, and they subsequently continued, the despatch by detachments of the 84th Regiment to the North-West Provinces. They had been cheered, on the 23rd of May, by the arrival from Madras of the 1st Madras Fusiliers, and with commendable

Book VII. Chapter I.

1857. May 25–30.

promptitude they had, at once, sent off that regiment in the same direction. They were expecting regiments and batteries from Persia, from Ceylon, and from Rángún.

Views of the Government.

The Government, then, felt tolerably secure regarding Bengal proper and the country south of Alláhábád. The news, however, from the districts north of the last-named city was calculated to alarm. Between the 25th and 30th of May, the native troops at Fírózpúr, at Aligarh, at Mainpúrí, at Itáwah, and at Balandshahr, had mutinied. Great fears were entertained regarding Lakhnao, Kánhpúr, A'gra, and the surrounding districts. On the other hand they were confident that the fall of Dehlí was imminent, and that the troops engaged in the capture of that place would be almost immediately available to secure the threatened districts north of Alláhábád. It is only fair to them to admit that this view was shared by the public, and, very generally, by soldiers. It was justified, moreover, by the records of the past. Neither to the invaders from the north, to the Maráthás, nor to the English under Lord Lake had the capital of the Moghols ever offered more than an ephemeral resistance. It was hardly, then, to be supposed that, garrisoned by native soldiers without a chief, it could successfully resist the trained and disciplined warriors of England.

Lord Canning's anxiety about the weak point of his position.

Secure, then, of his base, of the ground lying six hundred miles in advance of it, confident that the troops in the North-West would very soon be available for the repression of rebellion in the

Book VII. Chapter I.

1857. May 31.

central districts, and fearful only regarding the rising there of the native army before the Commander-in-Chief should detach a force to keep it under, the Governor-General, on the 31st of May, despatched the following telegram to General Anson :—"I have heard to-day that you do not expect to be before Dehli until the 9th. In the meantime Cawnpore and Lucknow are severely pressed, and the country between Dehli and Cawnpore is passing into the hands of the rebels. It is of the utmost importance to prevent this, and to relieve Cawnpore, but nothing but rapid action will do it. Your force of artillery will enable you to dispose of Dehli with certainty; I, therefore, beg that you will detach one European Infantry Regiment, and a small force of European Cavalry, to the south of Dehli, without keeping them for operations there, so that Allygurh may be recovered, and Cawnpore relieved immediately. It is impossible to overrate the importance of showing European troops between Dehli and Cawnpore. Lucknow and Allahabad depend upon it."

His view justified.

The instincts which dictated this telegram were undoubtedly true. The country between Dehlí and Alláhábád was the weakest and the most threatened part of the British position. The only error committed by the Governor-General was the error of believing that the force of artillery on the spot could dispose of the Moghol capital with certainty. But Lord Canning shared that belief with almost every other European, civilian and soldier, in British India.

Book VII. Chapter I.

1857. June 1.

On the 1st of June, then, all looked hopeful to the Government of India. They were so sanguine, that, having only two European regiments to guard Calcutta and the country between that city and Dánápúr, they dispensed with the aid which would have been afforded them by fifteen hundred armed European citizens; they allowed the three and a half native regiments at Bárrákpúr and the regiments at Dánápúr, Banáras, and the intermediate stations, to remain armed; knowing that the districts lying between Dehlí and Alláhábád were in imminent peril, they yet hoped, and even confidently hoped, that the catastrophe might be delayed until either General Anson should despatch a regiment from the North-West, or until they should be strong enough to send up troops from Calcutta.

Blindness of the Government with regard to the true character of the crisis.

If the Government of India had had no other resources at their disposal, the course they actually pursued would have been amply justified. But writing, not, so to speak, after the event, but in the spirit of those who were present in Calcutta at the time, I am bound to affirm that they had other resources, and that they neglected them. When the lives of thousands, when the *prestige* of one's country, when the very safety of the national position, are in danger, it is a crime to depend solely upon possibilities. If the Government of India did not know, every other man in India knew, that the mutiny of the 19th Native Infantry had been no isolated act. Conscious of this, as I must suppose they were, the Government of India most certainly knew that in the long

Book VII. Chapter I.

1857. June 1.

direct line between Dánápúr and Mírath there was but one European regiment. Yet, even in the first half of the first week of May, when fully aware that the condition of the native army was, to say the least, excited; and that the European soldiers were to the natives in the proportion of one to twenty-four, the Government of Lord Canning had, even then, actually ordered the return of the 84th Regiment to Rángún, and had only been deterred from this step by the opportune outbreak of mutiny at Lakhnao on the 3rd of that month.

The 84th Regiment remained, then, at Bárrákpúr to watch over, on the 6th of May, the disbandment of a mutinous portion of the 34th Native Infantry. That act accomplished, nothing further remained for it to do. Yet the first detachment of the 84th started for the North-West only fourteen days later (20th May). This delay not only remains unexplained, but it is inexplicable. So far as Bengal was concerned the Government of India had been content to dispense with the 84th Regiment on the 3rd of May, and to send it out of India. Yet though the occurrences at Lakhnao on that day disclosed the latent weakness in the centre of our line, the 84th was detained motionless near Calcutta! It is true it was used on the 6th, but subsequently to that date it wasted fourteen precious days,—days which, if profitably employed, might almost certainly have secured Kánhpúr!

Consequences of the blindness.

I cannot but think that a mistake, but little less important, was committed when the first offer of the Calcutta citizens, made on the 20th of May, was refused. The acceptance of that offer would have disengaged for immediate action the wing of a regiment. As events happened, the first batch of the 84th Regiment, leaving Calcutta the 20th of May, succeeded in reaching Kánhpúr early in June. Now, it cannot be questioned that the entire 84th Regiment, if despatched on the 6th of May, might have reached Kánhpúr during that month. Its presence would probably have prevented the outbreak which occurred there; and, in that case, it might certainly have been strengthened by a wing of the 53rd, leaving Calcutta the 21st, and by the Madras Fusiliers which actually left on the 23rd.

The reason why the Government did not act in the manner in which it might have acted is explained by Mr. Secretary Beadon in his letter already quoted to the French residents at Calcutta:— "Everything is quiet within six hundred miles of the capital. The mischief, caused by a passing and groundless panic, has fortunately been arrested; and there is every reason to hope that, in the course of a few days, tranquillity and confidence will be restored throughout the Presidency." This "reason to hope" had, I have shown, no solid foundation. The hope which existed was, in fact, without reason. It had sufficient vitality, however, to induce the Government to risk the weakest and most threatened point of their line, in order that they might appear strong to the world.

The week that followed the 1st of June disclosed to the Government their error, to the world the short-sightedness of the Government.

Book VII. Chapter I.

1857. June 1–7.

Their first awakening.

During that week intelligence reached Calcutta of the mutiny at Lakhnao, of the defection of all the regiments occupying Oudh, of revolts at A'zimgarh, at Banáras, and at Alláhábád, of the massacre of the Europeans at Jhánsí. This news increased the anxiety of the Government regarding the safety of their weak centre line; for Oudh was separated from Kánhpúr but by the river, and even before the defection of that province, the position of Kánhpúr, garrisoned by native troops and in close proximity to the stronghold of the discontented heir of a prince whom we had dispossessed, had inspired alarm. Counterbalancing, in a measure, the effect of this evil news the Government saw with satisfaction the arrival, during that week, in Calcutta of the 64th Foot and 78th Highlanders from Persia, of a wing of the 35th Foot from Múlmén, of a wing of the 37th Regiment, and of a company of Royal Artillery from Ceylon. Awake now to the danger before them they pushed on these regiments to the north with praiseworthy activity. The uncompleted state of the railway rendered the progress of the detachments slow. In default of this means of transit, single-horsed post-carriages—the quickest mode of travelling then available—bullock carriages, and steamers, were employed to the fullest possible extent. The Government, in fact, did then all that was possible to save the threatened line.

The awakening not complete.

I have said that the Government were awake to the danger before them in the north. It is strange, however, that their eyes were not yet opened to the full magnitude of the crisis; that they ignored the danger at their very door. At the time that they were despatching every available European soldier to protect a station in their centre line from the possible mutiny of the armed sepoys who garrisoned it, they allowed the sepoys close to Calcutta to remain armed; the native garrison of Dánápúr to remain armed. What is more, in spite of so many examples of disaffection, they believed in the loyalty of these men. Their policy at this period was to trust, or to seem to trust, every native regiment until it should revolt. Such a policy naturally greatly restricted the movements of the European troops, for it was often necessary to keep these inactive at a station to guard against a possible outbreak.

Thus, with the news of the revolt of many regiments stationed within the limits of the six hundred miles indicated by Mr. Beadon in his famous letter of the 25th of May ringing in their ears, the Government reported to the Court of Directors their belief that a public profession of loyalty made by the 70th Regiment of Native Infantry, then stationed at Bárrákpúr, would "have the happiest influence on the minds of all well-disposed men in the Native Army." They, therefore, allowed three and a half native regiments at that station to retain their arms. To the 6th Native Infantry at Alláhábád, on the eve of a revolt accompanied by marked barbarity, the Government sent, at the same time, their acknowledgment of a similar profession. They would not believe the fact which was patent to all

Book VII. Chapter I. 1857. June 1–7.

around them,—the fact that the entire native army was animated by but one feeling, and that the mutiny of a regiment was merely a question of time and of opportunity.

Their views regarding the possibility of an advance from Dehlí in the direction of their weak central line were encouraged by the receipt, at this period, of information of a victory gained by the Mírath garrison over the rebels issuing from Dehlí at the rivulet Hindan, near the town of Ghází-údín Nagar. This victory, in which the rebels lost five guns, was gained on the 31st of May. It encouraged the hope that almost any post might bring the intelligence of the fall of the great fortress.

Death of General Anson.

Another most important item of intelligence conveyed to the Government during this absorbing week was that of the death by cholera of the Commander-in-Chief, General Anson, at Ambála, on the 27th of May. This much to be lamented event did not occur until General Anson had prepared and set in action the measures which were to the end persistently carried out for the capture of Dehlí. His demise was a great—time

His character.

proved it to be a most sensible loss. A man of very remarkable natural talents, General Anson had, during a residence in India of more than five years, used those talents to master completely the necessities of Indian warfare. He was a perfect judge of character. No man ever more quickly detected the veneer of superficiality. He could not conceal his contempt for a man whom he discovered to be playing a part. Hence, probably, there swarmed up after his death enemies and detractors. They have not succeeded, however, in sullying his fair fame. For to him, as truly now as when death snatched him from the triumph which he had prepared, may be applied the immortal epitaph which the great historian of the Peninsular War composed for one of the most illustrious of English Generals:—"The honest loved, the dishonest feared him. For, while he lived he did not shun, but scorned and spurned the base, and, with characteristic propriety, they spurned at him when he was dead."

Consequent upon the death of General Anson the command of the force destined to besiege Dehlí devolved upon Major-General Sir Henry Barnard, commanding the Sirhind Division.

Summary of the mental range of the Government.

I have now given a picture—a severe but accurate picture—of the information possessed by the Government of India up to the end of the first week of June, of the deductions they drew from that information, of their hopes, their fears, and beliefs. It will have been observed that whilst, in the main, their view of the position was correct, they had not even then sounded the full depths of the disaster; and that as in May, so still, early in June, they preferred the upholding of their infallibility as a Government to throwing themselves frankly upon the loyalty of the only classes they could absolutely trust,—the Europeans and Eurasians living and settled in India.

The fortnight which followed was full of startling incidents, but incidents marked by the same general correctness of view regarding strategy,

Book VII. Chapter I.

1857. June 6.

The awakening almost complete.

the same weakness of political vision, and the same distrust of their own countrymen.

On the night of the 6th of June the native regiment at Alláhábád which, the previous day, had been thanked by the Government for its professions of unswerving loyalty, mutinied and murdered nearly all its officers, including some young boys just arrived from England. The fortress of Alláhábád, occupying a most commanding position on the Jamná, and considered the gateway to the North-West, escaped by a miracle. The telegraphic lines were cut or destroyed, and communication with the army before Dehlí became impossible except by way of Láhor or Bombay. The troops in Rájpútáná and in Central India were likewise reported to have risen. There had been a mutiny at Banáras, but thanks to the wise and statesmanlike conduct of Mr. Frederic Gubbins of the Civil Service, and the bold measures adopted by Colonel Neill and his Madras Fusiliers, the mutiny had been suppressed, and the disaffected of the great Hindú city had been overawed.

From the 7th of June, indeed, it may be truly affirmed that the outlook to the Government of India had become darkness intensified. Mr. Beadon's intact line of six hundred miles had been attempted in many places. Beyond it all was impenetrable.

Lord Canning's anxiety regarding his weak central line.

In this extremity the Government still clung to the army before Dehlí. On the 10th of June Lord Canning drafted to the Major-General commanding that army a letter in which he urged him to send southwards, with the least possible delay, an European force as large as he could spare.* He kept the letter by him for eleven days, and only despatched it when the chances of relieving the central line from Calcutta seemed almost desperate.

Book VII. Chapter I.

1857. June 10.

Mr. Grant's practical advice.

Two days after that letter had been penned Lord Canning yielding to the solicitations of the ablest of his councillors, Mr. J. P. Grant, resolved to avail himself of the aid which had been proffered him, three weeks earlier, by the citizens of Calcutta. But in order to induce the Governor-General to agree to this tardy concession, it was necessary for Mr. Grant to lay aside all gloss, to sacrifice the false confidence on which Mr. Beadon had laid so much stress three weeks previously, and to describe facts as they really

* The letter, in a more complete form, runs as follows:—"Benares has been made safe. So has Allahabad, I hope, but only just in time. Henceforward, the reinforcements will be pushed up still further—to Cawnpore; but the disorganised state of the country between Allahabad and Cawnpore may interpose delay; and both telegraph and dawk from any place north of Allahabad is now cut off from Calcutta. I cannot, therefore, speak so confidently of the time when help will reach Sir Hugh Wheeler. It may not be for four or five days, or even more. This makes it all the more urgently necessary that you should push down an European force immediately. When it reaches the Cawnpore division, it will, according to the instructions which have been sent to you, pass under Sir Hugh Wheeler's command. And with him will rest the responsibility of relieving Lucknow, and pacifying the country from Cawnpore downwards. It will be for you to judge what your own movements should be. All that I require is, that an European force as large an one as you can spare, should be sent southwards with the least possible delay, and that it should not be detained an hour for the purpose of finishing off affairs at Dehli after once the great blow has been struck."

Book VII. Chapter I.

1857. June 12.

were. "In reality," wrote Mr. Grant early in June, "in reality as well as in appearance we are very weak here, where we ought to be—and if we can't be should at least appear to be—as strong as possible. We have as enemies three Native Infantry regiments and a half, of which one and a half are the very worst type we know; one, two, three (for no one knows) thousand armed men at Garden Reach, or available there at a moment; some hundred armed men of the Scinde Ameers at Dum-Dum; half the Mahomedan population; and all the blackguards of all sorts of a town of six hundred thousand people. Against these we have one and a half weak regiments, most of whom dare not leave the Fort. There is no reason to expect real help in real danger from the Native Police. The insurrection is regularly spreading down to us. Is this an emergency or not? My conviction is that even a street row at the capital would give us an awful shake—not only in Bengal, but in Bombay and Madras—at this moment."

This remonstrance, vivid, true, and out-spoken, expressed in nervous, even in passionate language, the thoughts of the much maligned citizens of Calcutta. The daily newspapers had for a fortnight been pressing the same arguments on the Governor-General. These had failed to shake the reluctance of Lord Canning to take his own countrymen into his confidence, to admit that he had the smallest occasion for their aid. But now one of his colleagues, and incomparably the ablest of his colleagues, pressed upon him, in language more

Book VII. Chapter I. 1857. June 12.

clear and more forcible than any used by the Press, the dangers of persistence in the same policy of distrust. That even the weighty utterances of Mr. Grant would, in any case, have met the fate of the expressed opinions of the European community is scarcely probable. But he did not stand quite alone in his view. It happened that an examination of the records of the Home Office showed that the question of raising volunteers in India had been thoroughly discussed in the time of Lord Dalhousie; that a decision in favour of the measure had been recorded; and that that decision had received the endorsement of the Court of Directors. This discovery added force to Mr. Grant's argument. He clenched it further by recording his opinion that it was probable that, if a Volunteer Corps were not raised in the crisis then before them, the Home Government would ask the reason why. These arguments proved successful. Lord Canning, still retaining his opinion as to the practical uselessness of the measure, sanctioned, on the 12th of June, the enrolment of the citizens of Calcutta as volunteers.

Lord Canning sanctions the enrolment of volunteers.

The Calcutta citizens nobly responded to the call of the Government. In a very few days the three arms, Horse, Foot, and Artillery, sprang into vigorous life. Men of all classes and of all positions pressed forward to enrol themselves, and in less than three weeks a brigade was formed sufficiently strong to guard Calcutta, and to enable the Government, had they deemed it necessary, to send all the regular troops into the field.

Book VII. Chapter I. — 1857. June 13.

The day following that on which the Government had thus announced their intention to solicit the aid which three weeks previously they had rejected, they introduced and passed through the Legislative Council a measure calculated, above all others, to rouse the indignation of the community and to deaden the loyalty to which they had but just at the moment appealed.

The European and Native press.

It can well be imagiued that the events occurring all over the country had not been unnoticed by the public press. In India the fourth estate was represented by two distinct bodies of men. There was the English press advocating English interests, generally owned and entirely contributed to by Englishmen. Running parallel with this was the native press, the organ of native interests and owned and contributed to by natives. The two divisions were subject to the same laws and amenable to the same jurisdiction. So blended had become the interests of the native and the European that, as a rule, the two sections referred to advocated identical measures. It did happen indeed occasionally, though rarely, that they espoused opposite sides. Such had been the case when the legislature brought in a measure to introduce a native magistracy with power to try Europeans. Against this measure the European press had protested, whilst it was eagerly supported by the organs of native public opinion. But such occasions were not common. As traders, the interests of the European and of the native merchants were identical. The land question, which was to assume so great a prominence in later years, had then been but incidentally referred to. The two sections acted alike as critics on the conduct of the Government, and, as a rule, they performed this delicate duty with judgment, with temper, and with moderation.

It is true that, when dealing with individual officials, the press of India, native as well as European, was often extremely uncompromising. It certainly called a spade a spade. And as the Indian officials had experienced none of the rough training to which the statesmen of Europe are subjected, and were often men who owed their high positions to favour rather than to merit, this habit of plain speaking had been apt to engender, and often did engender, feelings of rancorous dislike in the breasts of the criticised.

When the early incidents of the mutiny occurred, that is, when the 19th Regiment of Native Infantry misbehaved at Barhámpúr, the English press had spoken out very plainly. It had urged the Government to adopt at once decided measures. More than one writer had pointed out that the Barhámpúr incident was a spark which, if not immediately crushed, would be speedily fanned into a flame. The native press was more deliberate and more reticent, but it offered no great opposition to vigorous action. The warnings of the press were disregarded. The Government did not act with promptitude, nor when it acted, did it act with vigour. When the spark had been fanned into a flame, when, that is to say, the outbreak at Mírath had disclosed to all who were not wilfully blind the gigantic extent of the

Book VII. Chapter I. 1857. June 13.

insurrection, whilst the European press clamoured more vehemently for prompt action, and urged the Government to throw themselves on the loyalty of the European community, the tone of the native press almost immediately changed. Possibly the supineness which they witnessed made them believe that the fatal day for the English had arrived, just as their fathers had seen that day overtake the Moghols, the Maráthás, and the Síkhs. Possibly the Bengálí portion of the native press, representing a highly educated people, unversed in arms, but alone capable of administering the country should it fall under native domination, possibly the Bengálí portion believed that their prospects would be greatly improved by the overthrow of the British power. Certainly many of them doubted our ultimate success. But whatever may have been the reason, it is at least undeniable that from the time of the arrival in Calcutta of the news of the Mírath outbreak the tone of the native press changed. It began to speak out against the Government, and to show very plainly that it had sympathy with the revolters.

This alteration in the tone of the native press was brought to the notice of Lord Canning early in June, and he was urged then to interfere, by legislative action, with its freedom. Unlike his colleagues, however, Lord Canning had been brought up in a free country. He had been accustomed all his life to the freedom of the press. He had seen in England that the law of the land was sufficient to put down license. He knew that

Book VII. Chapter I.

1857. June 13.

an honest Government had no better friend than a free and out-speaking public critic. To the solicitations of his councillors, then, he replied that "the remedy was worse than the disease."

The Gagging Act.

But a few days later the opinions of Lord Canning in this respect underwent a change. On the 13th of June he, for the first and only time during his tenure of office, went down to the Legislative Council, and declaring there that the incendiary tone of the native press had driven him to the conclusion at which he had reluctantly arrived, he brought forward and carried a measure to place the native press under restrictions so galling that, compared to them, the restrictions on the press of France during the darkest days of the reign of Napoleon III. were light and easy.

Had Lord Canning stopped there, he would have carried with him the voice of the public. The times were critical, the native press had encouraged sedition and rebellion, and it was necessary that authority should assert itself. But when Lord Canning proceeded to include in the same measure of stern repression the European press, in spite of "the loyalty and intelligence which marked their labours," on the ground, mainly, that he could not draw a line of demarcation between European and native publications,*

* The following are the exact words used by Lord Canning with respect to the European press:—"The remarks I have taken occasion to make with reference to the Native Press, I do not direct to the European Press. But I see no solid standing ground upon which a line can be drawn marking off one from the other, when the question is to prevent matter calculated to work mischief at a crisis

Book VII. Chapter I.

1857. June 13.

Indignation of the European community.

he evoked an outburst of opposition such as has been seldom witnessed in Calcutta. It was not only that the English community of that place resented the restriction of their liberties. Had such a restriction been proposed by a Government in which they had confidence they would have borne it patiently. But on this occasion they disbelieved in the sincerity of the Government. They had seen them slow to be convinced, slow to move, slow to avail themselves of the advantages forced upon them, confident where they should have been distrustful, and distrustful where they should have been confident. They had seen them arrogant whilst blundering, supercilious whilst courting disaster. They knew now that disaster had befallen them, that Mr. Beadon's line of six hundred miles had been broken, and that the central line beyond it was terribly endangered. And, yet, no sooner had they become aware of this than the Government shut their mouths. There was but one conclusion for them to draw. They believed then, and many believe still, that the action of the Government was

like this. For whilst I am glad to give credit to the conductors of the European Press for the loyalty and intelligence which mark their labours, I am bound by sincerity to say that I have seen passages in some of the papers under their management which, though perfectly innocuous as far as European readers are concerned, may, in times like the present, be turned to the most mischievous purposes in the hands of persons capable of dressing them up for the Native ear. I am glad to admit that the bill is not specially levelled at the European press, but I do not see any reason nor do I consider it possible in justice, to draw any line of demarcation between European and Native publications."

prompted by a determination to prevent, if possible, the transmission to England of any printed record of their mistakes.

That the Government was actuated by any such motive I am now far from thinking. But their action in muzzling the European press was undoubtedly a mistake. It severed the confidence which ought to exist in a great crisis between the rulers and the ruled, and increased the distrust which the tardiness of their measures had till then inspired.

The policy of feigning confidence.

This distrust was greatly augmented by an incident which occurred the day following. True to the opinion expressed by Mr. Secretary Beadon to the members of the Trades' Association, on the 21st of May, to the effect that it was most unfair to the Native Army of Bengal to assume that all its regiments were disaffected :—notwithstanding that Mr. J. P. Grant, a member of the Supreme Council, had, early in June, recorded his opinion that at Bárrákpúr, sixteen miles from Calcutta, the Government had "as enemies three Native Infantry regiments and a half, of which one and a half are the very worst type we know" :—in spite of the examples supplied by some stations in the upper provinces of the danger of allowing native regiments to retain their arms, and of the beneficial results which in others had followed their being disarmed :—Lord Canning had been resolute in allowing the regiments at Bárrákpúr, so graphically painted by Mr. Grant, to continue, armed, in the exercise of their duties. Before the Government had, on the 12th of June, accepted the

Book VII. Chapter I.

1857. June 13.

offers of the volunteers, Lord Canning was aware of the mutiny of the native troops at Banáras, at Alláhábád, at Lakhnao, in Rohilkhand, at the stations north of Kánhpúr; he knew that disarming at Láhor, at other stations in the Panjáb, and at A'gra, had been attended with beneficial results,—and yet he continued to permit the regiments quartered within sixteen miles of Calcutta to retain their arms!

State of Calcutta at the time.

What was the state of Calcutta at the time when the Governor-General persisted in this resolution? It cannot better be described than in the words, already quoted, of the ablest of Lord Canning's councillors, Mr. J. P. Grant. After recording in the language noted in the preceding paragraph his opinion of the native regiments quartered at Bárrákpúr, Mr. Grant added that the Government had, in addition to those "enemies," "one, two, or three (for no one knows) thousand armed men at Garden Reach" (a suburb of Calcutta), "or available there at a moment; some hundred armed men of the Scinde Ameers at Dum-Dum" (six miles from Calcutta), "half the Mahomedan population; and all the blackguards of all sorts of a town of six hundred thousand people." To encounter these enemies the Government had at their disposal, in Calcutta itself, a weak wing of an English regiment! A wing of another regiment, the 35th, was at Bárrákpúr, and a complete regiment, the 78th Highlanders, some miles beyond, at Chinsará. Those regiments were, in fact, detained near the seat of Government to guard the armed sepoys. For disarmed sepoys one-fourth of their number would have sufficed.

1857. June 13.

The natural result of the "feigning confidence" policy.

The fruits of this policy very soon showed themselves. Intended as a policy of conciliation,—to display confidence in quarters in which no confidence was felt,—it had the result of imparting boldness to those who had long been mutineers in heart, and who were watching only their opportunity. Lord Canning had accepted the offers to volunteer of the citizens of Calcutta on the 12th of June; he had passed the act, known thenceforth as the Gagging Act, on the 13th. The 14th was a bright, clear day, as bright as days are in India after the first rainy season has set in, and when no rain falls. It was a Sunday. That morning the church-goers attended service at the various churches at the ordinary hour of 11 A.M. In most of the churches nothing remarkable occurred. But those present at the garrison church in Fort William had their attention disturbed by the rolling sound of heavy *matériel* moving out of the Fort. One individual, who occupied a house in Chowringhee, the Park Lane of Calcutta, somewhat impressed by this unusual occurrence, thought he would endeavour to ascertain if anything had taken place to justify the movement. Accordingly, after the service was over, he, in accordance with the Sunday custom in Calcutta, went to make some calls. He called upon one of the Secretaries to Government. But nothing appeared out of its usual course, and he returned to his house with his curiosity unsatisfied. About two hours later, however, at 4 o'clock

Calcutta on the 14th of June.

Book VII. Chapter I.

1857. June 14.

in the afternoon, he received a note from a gentleman who was living in the same house with the Secretary on whom he had called. In this note he was informed that the native regiments at Bárrákpúr had mutinied, and were in full march on Calcutta; that the lives of the European inhabitants were in the greatest danger; that he (the writer) begged him and his wife to proceed at once to his (the writer's) house, where they had a stone staircase and five good rifles; further, that no time was to be lost.

The gentleman addressed declined to leave his own house. He even went outside to endeavour to ascertain the correctness of the information he had received. What he saw on that eventful afternoon he recorded on the spot. The impression the sight made upon him has never left him. The roof of his house commanded a view of the plain between Chowringhee and the Fort. Of the details which accompanied and which followed the scamper across the plain he had accurate knowledge, and, when he published his account of what occurred, he was prepared, as he is now prepared, to name, had he been called upon, the individuals to whom he referred. To the statement as he wrote it there is not a comma to add, nor from it is there a comma to be withdrawn. As an accurate picture of the events of that afternoon it is irrefutable.

The gentleman referred to thus painted the scene*:—"It has been said by a great writer that

* Red Pamphlet, page 105.

Book VII. Chapter I.

1857. June 14.

'there is scarcely a less dignified entity than a patrician in a panic.' The veriest sceptic as to the truth of this aphorism could have doubted no longer, had he witnessed the living panorama of Calcutta on the 14th of June. All was panic, disorder, and dismay. The wildest reports were in circulation. It was all but universally credited that the Bárrákpúr brigade was in full march on Calcutta, that the people in the suburbs had already risen, that the King of Oudh, with his followers, was plundering Garden Reach. Those highest in office were the first to give the alarm. There were Secretaries to Government running over to Members of Council, loading their pistols, barricading the doors, sleeping on sofas; Members of Council abandoning their houses with their families, and taking refuge on board ship; crowds of lesser celebrities, impelled by these examples, having hastily collected their valuables, were rushing to the Fort, only too happy to be permitted to sleep under the Fort guns. Horses, carriages, palanquins, vehicles of every sort and kind, were put into requisition to convey panic-stricken fugitives out of the reach of imaginary cut-throats. In the suburbs, almost every house belonging to the Christian population was abandoned. Half-a-dozen determined fanatics could have burned down three parts of the town. A score of London thieves would have made their fortunes by plundering the houses in the neighbourhood of Chowringhee which had been abandoned by their inmates."*

* Sir John Kaye quotes the following description, given by Dr. Mouat, residing at the time at Calcutta, of the events

Book VII. Chapter I.

1857. June 14.

Effect of the "feigning confidence" policy at Bárákpúr.

There was some reason for the alarm. There is not a shadow of doubt that the native regiments quartered at Bárrákpúr had long been watching their opportunity, and that, noting the successive arrival of European regiments from Persia, from Pegú, and from Ceylon, they had, on the night of the 13th of June, resolved to mutiny the following day. Fortunately, some of the well-disposed among them betrayed the secret that night. An express was at once despatched by the Major-General commanding the division to order down the 78th Highlanders from Chinsará, whilst permission to disarm the mutinous regiments without delay was urgently requested from Calcutta. The Highlanders set off that night from Chinsará. Misled, whether purposely or

here referred to. He says that the flight was "what might have been seen if a modern Herculaneum, had been evacuated in broad daylight on the approach of a visible eruption from a neighbouring volcano." Dr. Mouat adds, "The whole line of the ghauts was crowded with fugitives, and those who could find no shelter on the ships, took refuge within the Fort, of which the squares, the corridors, all the available space everywhere, indeed, were thronged by many, who passed the night in their carriages." Since writing the text I have seen Dr. Mouat. He tells me that his remarks apply to the Christian population of the suburbs, who were mostly Eurasians. In this I am in perfect agreement with Dr. Mouat. Nothing could exceed the courage and steadfastness of the members of the mercantile and trading community. In his journal, written at the time, and quoted by Sir John Kaye, Colonel Cavenagh, then the highest official in the Fort, recorded as follows:—"On my return home, I found my house besieged by all sorts of people wishing to obtain shelter in the Fort, and all full of rumours of the worst description from Dum-Dum and Barrackpore." Colonel Cavenagh, however, did not observe any unusual number of vehicles in the Fort.

otherwise may possibly be doubtful, by their guide, they wandered four miles out of their direct road, but recovering the track, a strong detachment of them arrived by daybreak in the station, weary and footsore, yet ready for any emergency. This prompt action entirely disconcerted the sepoys. They determined to defer the outbreak to a more convenient season. But the chance was not allowed them. The remainder of the 78th arrived during the day, and, the necessary permission having been received from the Government, the native regiments were at 4 P.M. paraded and disarmed in the presence of the wing of Her Majesty's 35th and of the 78th Regiment with loaded muskets, each on either flank, and of six 12-pounders in their front loaded with grape. They offered no resistance, but piled their arms in silence.

Book VII. Chapter I.

1857. June 14.

Arrest of the King of Oudh.

In Calcutta the night passed off tranquilly. But the following morning there was a new excitement. The list given by Mr. J. P. Grant in his famous minute of the enemies to public order in Calcutta will not have been forgotten. If prominently in this list figured the three and a half native regiments at Bárrákpúr, next in importance were enumerated the "one, two, three (for no one knows) thousand armed men at Garden Reach, or available there at any moment." Garden Reach was one of the suburbs of Calcutta, and the men alluded to were the followers of the deposed King of Oudh. Having, on the 14th, acted, so to speak, on Mr. Grant's first hint regarding the sepoys, the Government followed up that

Book VII. Chapter I.

1857. June 15.

vigorous action by taking up his second recommendation on the 15th. And it is due to them to state that they performed a distasteful, though necessary, task with great prudence and delicacy. They rightly deemed that the best mode of rendering powerless the followers of the King of Oudh would be to deprive those followers of their natural leader. On the morning of the 15th of June, therefore, the Foreign Secretary, Mr. Edmonstone, accompanied by a detachment of English soldiers, waited upon the King of Oudh and informed him that political necessities, and the fact that emissaries had made a mischievous use of his name, required that he should remove from Garden Reach and take up his residence in the Governor-General's house within Fort William. The King of Oudh behaved on the occasion with dignity and propriety. Having in the most solemn manner protested that, neither by word nor deed had he encouraged the mutineers, he declared himself ready to go wherever the Governor-General might think fit. He was then conducted to the Government House within the Fort. His late Prime Minister, Alí Nakí Khán, and a few other nobles were selected to bear him company. This action on the part of the Government excited no disturbance, and in its results it fully justified the ideas which prompted it. The unknown number of armed men at Garden Reach were by it rendered powerless for mischief.

Arrival of Sir Patrick Grant.

Two days later, the officer selected by Lord Canning to assume temporarily the command of the Bengal Army, vacated by the death of General

Book VII. Chapter I.

1857. June 17.

Anson, arrived in Calcutta. This was Lieutenant-General Sir Patrick Grant, K.C.B., Commander-in-Chief of the Madras Army. Sir Patrick Grant was an officer of the Company's service who had made his way through the regimental grades to the command of a regiment, and from the command of a regiment to the General Army Staff, rising eventually to be Adjutant-General of the Bengal Army. He had served on the staff during the first and second Sikh campaigns. Circumstances, to which it is unnecessary to refer, had made him unpopular with the majority of the officers of the Bengal Army, but his many and varied services seemed to justify Lord Canning in regarding him as the man for the situation, and certainly to few soldiers was a greater opportunity ever offered of vindicating the judgment of the Governor-General. The weak centre line I have so often referred to was known to be in imminent danger. It was believed that there was yet time to avert that danger. According to the latest reports received by the Government the Madras Fusiliers had reached Allháhbád; the 84th Regiment and a portion of the 64th had passed Banáras; a considerable number of the 78th had already left Calcutta, and the remainder, and a wing of the 37th, were to start on the 20th. These united would constitute a force sufficient, with the artillery available, to strengthen the weak central line. Could that line be strengthened before it were actually rent it seemed possible that direct communication with Dehlí might be re-opened. And the Govern-

His previous career.

Book VII. Chapter I.

1857. June 17.

ment had no information that the line had been rent.

To endeavour to execute this project, to reach Kánhpúr before our troops there had been overwhelmed, was a task sufficient to stimulate the energies and to satisfy the ambition of any man. And this task was open to Sir Patrick Grant to select.

His reasons for not taking the field.

Sir Patrick Grant did not select it. The reasons which he gave for his decision proved that, up to the date on which it was made, the 22nd of June, neither he, nor the Members of the Government who approved it, had comprehended the full extent of the calamity which had fallen on the country; that they still regarded the outbreak as partial in its effects and temporary in its nature. Those reasons were that "the Commander-in-Chief can most efficiently, and assuredly most expeditiously, control and direct all military movements now, *and the reorganization and regeneration of the Army hereafter*,* if he has the advantage of being in personal communication with the head of the Government, if he learns the views of Government with respect to the innumerable questions which must constantly arise, and, which is highly important, if he is made acquainted with the mass of intelligence which may be expected to reach the Government from every quarter of the empire."

It will be seen that, in the presence of actual and pressing danger, danger to be overcome at

* The italics are my own.

once if the empire was to be saved, the mind of Sir Patrick Grant was dreaming of "reorganization and regeneration." Surely the shortest way of accomplishing that dream was to act vigorously against the rebels who had rendered necessary the revision of the old system. The fact that the Commander-in-Chief himself was in the field would have increased the moral power of the army operating against the rebels, whilst in such a position the head of the Army would have exercised an authority such as could not be delegated even to the most trusted of his lieutenants.

Book VII. Chapter I.

1857. June 22.

As for the control and command of the army there was the fact that of the two armies, the Native and the European, the one had mutinied, the other was in the field. The presence of the Commander-in-Chief was naturally required with the latter. The routine work of ordering forward troops from Calcutta, of furnishing supplies and ambulances for the field force, could well be entrusted to the Deputy Adjutant-General of the Army and his subordinates, who were on the spot. There, too, remained the Indian War Office, represented by the Military Secretary to Government and his assistants.

Unsoundness of those reasons.

The reason given by the Commander-in-Chief for not placing himself at the head of the army in the field was, then, based upon premisses which were incorrect, and upon a general view of the situation which was erroneous. But another reason which Sir Patrick Grant recorded in the same State memorandum goes far to show that

Book VII. Chapter I.

1857. June 22.

he did well in coming to the conclusion which he adopted.

His further reasons.

"I may also observe," wrote Sir Patrick, "that it is quite impossible to conduct the multifarious duties of this large army without a numerous staff and extensive office establishment, requiring, when moving about the country, a complete regiment as an escort, and a large amount of carriage for their transport, neither one nor the other of which can be supplied under present circumstances."

Justify the decision to remain in Calcutta.

This reason is decisive. Sir Patrick Grant was in command of the army employed to crush the mutiny. If he thought that he could not leave details to the tried officers on the general staff at Calcutta, whilst he should be marching against the rebels; if he considered that he must attend personally to petty matters of promotion and appointments at the same time that he should be directing all his energies against the enemy, and that, at so grave a crisis, when every European soldier was an object of importance, he would need a complete regiment to escort his papers, he was certainly quite right to stay where he was, and to detach another officer to command the army in the field.

The officer whom he selected for the post was Major-General Havelock.

The achievements of this officer belong to another section of this history. I purpose to continue here the account of the state of Calcutta up to the date of his departure from Alláhábád to relieve or to reconquer the weak central line.

Book VII. Chapter I.

1857. June 22.

The false report of the capture of Dehlí

On the 17th of June,—the day of the arrival in Calcutta of Sir Patrick Grant,—the Government received intelligence that General Barnard had, on the 8th, beaten the rebels at Dehlí. For a short time there was a hope that Dehlí itself had fallen—a hope so vivid that it induced Lord Canning, four days later, to despatch to Dehlí the requisition he had penned to the general on the 10th, to send down southward as large an European force as he could spare, with the least possible delay. But it transpired in a few days that not the fortified city of Dehlí, but the cantonments on the ridge only, had fallen into British hands. The siege was to follow; and to conduct that siege with any prospect of success, General Barnard, far from being in a position to spare troops, urgently needed reinforcements.

Unfavourable news from other quarters.

From other parts of India the news was on the whole unfavourable. At the end of the third week of June the Government were without news from Kánhpúr and Lakhnao beyond the 4th. At Naogang, at Nímach, at Jhánsí, and at Jánpúr, they knew that mutinies had occurred; but they were without details. Dánápúr was safe; Banáras and Alláhábád had been made so in the manner already described. From A'gra they had good news up to the 10th. At A'zamgarh there had been an outbreak; and there were bad rumours from Rohilkhand.

The fourth week of the month, and the week succeeding, up to the 4th of July, added considerably to their knowledge. On the 3rd of July,

Book VII. Chapter I.

1857. July 3.

Government received information that the native troops at Kánhpúr had mutinied on the 4th of June; that they had been joined by Náná Dhúdú Pant, the adopted son of the last of the Peshwás, with all his armed following; that Sir Henry Lawrence, and the Europeans at Lakhnao, had been gradually hemmed in by the rebels until they retained only the Residency, the Machí Bhawan fort, and the cantonments, but that all was well there up to the 30th of June; that the troops of the Gwáliár Contingent had mutinied on the 15th of June; that an uneasy feeling prevailed at Haidarábád; that up to the 15th A'gra was safe, but that Bándah and other small stations had been occupied by the rebels. Such was the state of the intelligence up to the 3rd. The following day brought a letter from Sir Henry Lawrence, dated 10 P.M., the 28th of June. In that letter Sir Henry stated that "he had every reason to believe that the Kánhpúr force had been entirely destroyed by treachery." Details, which in the end turned out in the main to be true, were added. But it was further stated that the intelligence was not believed either at Alláhábád or Banáras.

Such was the information possessed in Calcutta when General Havelock set out from Alláhábád to re-cement the broken central line. I must add a few words as to the circumstances which attended his appointment.

General Havelock.

Major-General Havelock was Adjutant-General of the Queen's Troops in India. He had commanded a division during the Persian war, but on

Book VII. Chapter I. 1875. July 4.

its conclusion, ignorant of the demise of General Anson and of his replacement as Commander-in-Chief by General Somerset, he had come round by steamer to Calcutta, and had been a fellow-passenger from Madras with Sir Patrick Grant. General Havelock had seen a great deal of service in India. In Barmá, in Afghánistán, in Gwáliár, on the Satlaj, he had established the character of being a thorough soldier. Quiet and retiring in his manners, he was not calculated to make an impression on those who judge only by outward show, but he had read and thought much, and his acquirements were solid and profound. Thin and spare of frame, he was yet gifted with a vitality which was proof against fatigue. He was not a talker, and many, perhaps, before the campaign then about to ensue, might have doubted his ability to command. But in this respect he bore a strong resemblance to the most capable of the Marshals of the first Empire, the illustrious Masséna, of whom Napoléon thus wrote:—"His conversation gave few indications of genius: but at the first cannon-shot his mental energy redoubled, and when surrounded by danger his thoughts were clear and forcible."

Such was the officer to whom Sir Patrick Grant delegated the duty of commanding in the field the forces which the Government had been able to collect. To take command of those forces General Havelock left Calcutta on the 24th of June. What he accomplished with his army, and how he accomplished it, has been already related. It rests for me here only to say that

Book VII. Chapter I.

1857. July 4.

his position at Kánhpúr, even after his victories, was, in the presence of the rebels in Oudh on his right, and the revolted Gwáliár Contingent on his left rear, in a military sense unsound and dangerous. It was not the smallest proof of his skill and daring that, notwithstanding this, deeming it in a political sense essential, he maintained it; and this, too, at a time when Mr. Beadon's line of six hundred miles—the line which maintained his communications with Calcutta—had been rudely snapped in twain.

BOOK VII.

CHAPTER II.

Danger of Mr. Beadon's line.

WHILST the events recorded in the preceding chapter had been enacted in Calcutta itself, the state of affairs in Bengal and in Bihár had scarcely been of a nature to justify the jaunty confidence expressed by Mr. Beadon on the 25th of May. The first information that the line of six hundred miles was actually in danger of being broken was conveyed to Government on the 12th of June from Rohní, a station in the Santhál district, about three hundred miles from Calcutta. This station was the head-quarters of the 5th Irregular Cavalry, commanded by Major Macdonald, one of the best officers of the Bengal Army. This officer was taking tea in front of his bungalow on the evening of the 12th of June, in company with his Adjutant, Sir Norman Leslie, and the Assistant Surgeon of the regiment, Dr. Grant. During a pause in their conversation, Dr. Grant rose with the intention of entering the bungalow. In the act of rising, he noticed the stealthy approach of

Major Macdonald at Rohní.

Book VII. Chapter II.

1857. June.

three men, apparently strangers. As he turned to point them out to his companions, the intruders rushed upon them with drawn swords. Unarmed and taken by surprise, the Englishmen could defend themselves only with their chairs. But before he could do even this Sir Norman Leslie was cut down. Major Macdonald was scalped and received two other wounds on the head. Dr. Grant also was wounded. It would have gone hard with both had the assassins persevered; but suddenly and most unaccountably they turned and fled.

As no symptom of mutinous disposition had appeared in the 5th Cavalry, and as Major Macdonald believed in the loyalty of his men, it was at first conjectured that the assassins were discharged sepoys. A few days later, however, a sowar confessed that they belonged to the regiment. They were at once seized, tried, and sentenced to be hanged. This sentence, Major Macdonald, with a courage which was great, though not rare, carried out in the presence of the entire regiment. A moment's weakness on his part would have been the signal for a general rising. Subsequent events proved that there was at the time an organised conspiracy in the regiment; that many had been aware of the plot to assassinate the three officers, that they "waited its success to rise." They were deterred at this critical time solely by the courage and determination of Major Macdonald.*

* Major Macdonald thus related the circumstances at the time:—"To tell the truth, I never for a moment expected to leave the hanging scene alive; but, I determined to

Book VII. Chapter II.

1857. June.

Mutinous incident at Barhámpúr.

A comparatively trifling incident at Barhámpúr—caused by the action of a sowar of the 11th Irregular Cavalry, who not only released some deserters from the 43rd Native Infantry, apprehended by the police, but likewise incited the men of his regiment and of the 63rd Native Infantry to mutiny—influenced the Government to retain some European Infantry at that station. This measure would, I need scarcely point out, have been wholly unnecessary had the Government taken the precaution to disarm the native regiments.

Patná.

But it was at the great station of Patná, the Mahomedan capital of the country east of Banáras, that the strain was most severely felt. This city, containing 300,000 inhabitants, a large proportion of whom were Mahomedans, is

do my duty, and well knew the effect that pluck and decision had on natives. The regiment was drawn out. Wounded cruelly as I was, I had to see everything done myself, even to the adjusting of the ropes, and saw them looped to run easy. Two of the culprits were paralysed with fear and astonishment, never dreaming that I should dare to hang them without an order from the Government. The third said he would not be hanged, and called on the Prophet, and on his comrades to rescue him. This was an awful moment: an instant's hesitation on my part, and probably I should have had a dozen balls through me; so I seized a pistol, clapped it to the man's ear, and said, with a look there was no mistake about, "Another word out of your mouth, and your brains shall be scattered on the ground." He trembled, and held his tongue. The elephant came up, he was put on his back, the rope adjusted, the elephant moved, and he was left dangling. I then had the others up and off in the same way. And after some time, when I dismissed the men of the regiment to their lines, and still found my head upon my shoulders, I really could scarcely believe it."

Book VII. Chapter II.

1857. June.

situated on the right bank of the river Ganges, three hundred and eighty miles north-west of Calcutta, and ten miles east of the military station of Dánápúr.

Patná owed its importance partly to its traditions; partly to the fact that it was the capital of one of the richest provinces in the country; partly likewise to its being the head-quarters of the Wáhábís—the extreme Mahomedan party in India. It was ruled by a Commissioner, corresponding directly with the Lieutenant-Governor of Bengal. Subordinate to it and to its Commissioner were the districts of Gayá, to the south, with a chief town of the same name, fifty miles distant; of Sháhábád, comprising the country between the Ganges, the Karamnásá, and the Són, and having as its capital Arah, about thirty-five miles to the west of Patná; of Sáran, with Chaprá, forty miles to the north, as its capital; of Champáran, with Motíhárí, as its chief station; and Tirhút, between Nipál and the Ganges, represented by the civil station of Mozaffarpúr. In these stations the magistrate represented the executive power.

Garrison of Dánápúr.

The station of Dánápúr was garrisoned by three Native Infantry Regiments, the 7th, 8th, and 40th, by one company of European and one of Native Artillery, and by Her Majesty's 10th Foot. Dánápúr was the head-quarters of a division, and its divisional commander was Major-General Lloyd, an officer who had rendered excellent service in his day, and who, but four years before, had been selected by Lord Dalhousie to suppress the Sánthál insurrection—a task which he had accomplished with judgment and discretion. His command at Dánápúr was extensive in its range. To the north it included all the country to the foot of the Nipál hills; to the east it reached Barhámpúr; to the south Hazáríbágh and Rámpúr. The troops protecting this vast extent of country were, with one exception, massed at Dánápúr. That exception was the 12th Regiment of Irregular Cavalry, commanded by a most distinguished officer, Major Holmes. This corps was stationed at Sigaolí, about a hundred miles to the north of Dánápúr.

Book VII. Chapter II.

1857. June.

Peculiarities of the Patná division.

The province of which Patná was the capital, was, I have said, one of the richest in the possession of the English. It owed its importance partly to the fact that for several years it had been the chosen ground for the development of native industry by English landholders working with English capital; partly, and to a far greater extent, to the circumstance that the native landowners were, as a rule, men of ancient lineage and of large estates.

Before the arrival of reinforcements from Persia, Ceylon, and Barmá, the European regiment at Dánápúr was the only English regiment in the long line between Calcutta and Lakhnao. Having in view the extent of country it had to guard, its proximity to the influential city of Patná, to the fact that many of the native landowners of Bihár were men commanding a large following, it still seems strange that the expedient so successfully adopted at Láhor and other places—the expedient of disarming the native troops—was not early

Book VII. Chapter II.

1857. June.

resorted to here. The postponement of such a measure necessarily chained the European troops to the station of Dánápúr, leaving all the other districts in the Patná division to shift for themselves.

It was from no lack of knowledge of the danger of leaving arms in the hands of the sepoys, that the Government of India hesitated to give the order to disarm them. The Commissioner of Patná, Mr. William Tayler, had been unremitting alike in impressing his courageous spirit on the disaffected, and in keeping the Lieutenant-Governor of Bengal well informed of the general aspect of affairs. As this gentleman's name will figure somewhat conspicuously in the following pages, it is fit that I should introduce him here.

Mr. William Tayler.

Mr. William Tayler was a member of the Bengal Civil Service. He was a gentleman and a scholar, possessing great natural abilities which he had lost no opportunity of cultivating, an elegant mind, and a large fund of common sense. To these should be added the greater gifts, during a crisis such as that of which I am writing, of a nerve not to be shaken, a clear view, and a power to decide rapidly and correctly in difficult circumstances. In the prime of life, courteous in manner, loyal to his Government, ready to hear the opinions of all, yet resolved to act on those which best commended themselves to his understanding, he was just the man whom a Wellesley or a Napier would have detached as his lieutenant to command a difficult position.

Early detects the sore spot.

The mutinous spirit displayed early in the year

1857. June 7.

by the sepoys at Barhámpúr, and later by those at Bárrákpúr, had not been unnoticed by Mr. Tayler. As the pro-consul of a province which had as its capital the city of Patná, the head-quarters of the chiefs of the Wáhábís, it had devolved upon him to watch every vibration in the political system, so strangely agitated since the beginning of the year. Mr. Tayler, with a forecast surer than that of Mr. Secretary Beadon, had detected in the action of the 19th Regiment of Native Infantry and in the scarce-concealed sympathy with that action of the regiments stationed at Bárrákpúr, the germs of a very contagious political disease, and he had deemed it not at all improbable that, if not wholly eradicated by the measures of Government, the disease might gradually spread upwards. Never for a moment did he believe in the "passing and groundless panic" theory of Mr. Beadon. But not even Mr. Tayler, astute and far-seeing as he was, had imagined that the contagion would be communicated, as if by magic, to the upper provinces, passing over the intermediate divisions, to attack the body politic, suddenly, in its very heart.

When, therefore, the catastrophe of the 10th of May occurred at Mírath, it took not less by surprise the Commissioner of Patná than every other official in India. But Mr. Tayler was equal to the occasion. He summoned the European inhabitants of the place to deliberate on the means to be adopted to avert the crisis from Patná. Rejecting the timid counsel offered him shortly before by the judge, —who then, or a little later, took refuge in the

Book VII. Chapter II.

1857. June 7.

opium godown,—to despatch the Government treasure to Dánápúr and to be prepared on the first alarm to follow it thither, Mr. Tayler briefly stated to those present his information, his apprehensions, and his hopes, and then added that if they had confidence in him, he was prepared to assume the entire responsibility, and to act as he might consider necessary. In reply the Europeans present voted by acclamation confidence in their Commissioner. Thus armed, Mr. Tayler prepared for the inevitable emergency.

Is supported by the European community.

The first crisis.

On the 7th June the crisis seemed to arrive. Intimation was received that evening from Dánápúr to the effect that the native regiments were in a state of excitement, and that a rise was apprehended that very night.

Mr. Tayler meets it.

Mr. Tayler determined at once to make of his own house a fortress for the whole station. He drove to the nearest residents, and sent messengers to those further off, begging them to accept his hospitality during the crisis. In less than an hour his house was crowded by men, women, and children, from all parts of Patná. The house, however, was garrisoned by the Station Guards, who were all natives. Could they be trusted? Suddenly the discovery of a letter passing between them and the sepoys at Dánápúr showed Mr. Tayler that his guards were in league with the disaffected regiments.

Fortunately, a body of Sikhs newly raised by Captain Rattray, were then within forty miles of Patná. Mr. Tayler had sent expresses a day or two before to summon these men. They arrived at the early dawn. For the moment, then, Patná was safe. The several residents returned to their homes. Book VII. Chapter II. 1857. June 7.

A full report of this threatened outbreak made to the Lieutenant-Governor of Bengal had not the effect of inducing the Government of India to order the disarming of the men from whom the outbreak had been apprehended. Major-General Lloyd, then commanding at Dánápúr, had passed all his service in a sepoy regiment. He had witnessed the fidelity of the native soldier under trying and difficult circumstances, and, fortified by the opinion of the several commandants of regiments, he still clung to his belief in their loyalty. He shut his eyes too closely to the fact that of the three native regiments under his command two had already shown a mutinous disposition. Like so many officers, good honest men, who had spent their lives amid the sepoys, he could not bring himself absolutely to mistrust them,—to recommend their disarming, equivalent, in his opinion, to their dishonour. His confidence in his own judgment was increased by the fact that on the 7th of June—about the period when so many other regiments had risen; when he had been positively informed that his regiments would certainly rise; and when an opportunity had been offered them of seizing some £200,000 of money belonging to the Government, as they believed, but slightly guarded—those regiments had remained passive. On the 2nd of June he had reported to the Government his belief that the regiments would remain quiet, "unless some

Major-General Lloyd.

Trusts the sepoys.

Book VII. Chapter II.

great temptation or excitement should assail them," and five days later he reiterated the same opinion.

1857. June 7.

The Government trust Major-General Lloyd.

The Government, then, had before them the report of the Commissioner of the danger incurred at Patná on the 7th of June, and the opinion of the Major-General commanding the division that the native troops would remain quiet, "unless some great temptation or excitement should assail them." Having in view the composition of the native society at Patná, the isolation of the stations dependent upon it, the vast wealth of the province, the Government must, I think, be held guilty of fatuity in trusting, at such a crisis, to the chance that no great temptation or excitement would assail the sepoys. Neither at that time nor later would there have been any difficulty in disarming the sepoys at Dánápúr. The 10th Regiment was on the spot, and detachments of European troops were constantly conveyed past the station in steamers.

Defence of the action of the Government.

The only defence of the inaction of the Government with which I am acquainted, relating to this particular period, the first week of June, is to the effect that Lord Canning had "not merely to consider what was locally or individually best, but what was most generally conducive to the interests of those under his charge." It has been urged that the result of disarming might have been "dangerous in the extreme to our people in other parts of the country where sepoys abounded, and not a detachment of Europeans was to be seen": that the Governor-General "was looking anxiously for the arrival of fresh reinforcements when the

Book VII. Chapter II.

1857. June 7.

Its weakness.

game would be more in his own hands; but in the then destitute state of the Lower Provinces, it seemed to him and to the members of his Council to be sounder policy to temporise.* But these and similar arguments will not bear examination. Nothing that might have been done in the way of disarming could have produced results so disastrous as those which actually followed the inactive policy of the Government of India, and which I am now about to record. It may likewise be added that when Lord Canning had fresh reinforcements at his disposal, he still refused, in the manner hereafter to be described, to order the disarming of the sepoys.

Excitement of the people of Patná.

To return to Patná. The report brought by Captain Rattray of the reception accorded to his Sikh soldiers by the inhabitants of the city and the districts in its vicinity, was not of a nature to allay the apprehensions which his profound acquaintance with the province had excited in the mind of Mr. Tayler. Those soldiers, he was informed, had been constantly reviled on their march towards Patná, taunted with the part they were taking, accused of being renegades from their faith, and asked whether they intended to fight for the infidel or for their religion. When they entered Patná the high priest of the Sikh temple in the city refused to admit them to the sacred shrine, and wherever they were seen they met the most palpable evidences of the hatred and contempt of the population.

* Sir John Kaye, vol. iii. p. 65.

Book VII. Chapter II.

1857. June 7-11.

Private inquiries which Mr. Tayler instituted at this time soon brought to his mind the conviction that secret mischief was brewing. He learnt, too, that conferences of disaffected men were held at night, though in a manner so secret and so well guarded, that proof of meeting was rendered difficult, the capture of the plotters impossible.

Alarm in the districts.

The alarm meanwhile was increasing. The judge of Patná, the opium agent, and some others, left their houses with their families and took refuge in the opium godown. It spread likewise to the districts. Mr. Wake, the magistrate of Arah, afterwards so distinguished for his gallantry in the defence of that place, wrote to Mr. Tayler on the 11th, informing him that many of the railway *employés* and other Europeans had run away from his district in a panic, and had taken refuge in Dánápúr.

Splendid conduct of Mr. Tayler.

Under these trying circumstances Mr. Tayler acted with vigour, with judgment, and with decision. He stood out prominently amongst his compeers. He hid nothing from his superiors. The details of the crisis through which his division was passing were, therefore, well known in Calcutta. And when post after post brought to the capital accounts of the risings at Banáras, at A'zamgarh, in Central India and in the North-Western Provinces, the question rose naturally and involuntarily to the lips:—"How is it that Patná is quiescent?" Patná was quiescent simply because one man, Mr. William Tayler, the Commissioner of the Division, was a brave and deter-

1857. June 7-11.

mined man, ready to strike when necessary, and incapable, even under the darkest circumstances, of showing hesitation or fear.

The metal of which his character was formed was soon to be further tested. The disaffection among the Dánápúr troops, and in the districts, being daily on the increase, Mr. Tayler directed the removal of the moneys in the treasuries of Chaprá and Arah into Patná, thus bringing the coin under his own eye. He controlled with a firm hand the movements in his six districts of the officials, some of whom had actually left their stations under the conviction of an impending attack. Every day the post and messengers brought him intelligence of disaffection on the one side, of apprehension on the other; of plots to murder, of plots to burn, of plots to rise in revolt. He was informed, moreover, that Kúnwar Singh, a powerful landowner, whose estates in the vicinity of Arah were peopled by a martial tenantry devoted to their chief, was making secret preparations to seize the first opportunity to revolt.

Mr. Tayler did not, at the moment, credit the reports about Kúnwar Singh individually. He was well aware that to all the disaffected nobles and landowners of the districts only two opportunities, or one of two opportunities, would prove sufficiently tempting. These were, the mutiny of the native regiments at Dánápúr, and the rising of the population of Patná. It was clear that a successful mutiny at Dánápúr would be instantaneously followed by the rising of Patná; equally

Book VII. Chapter II.

1857. June 12–18.

so that a successful rising at Patná would precipitate the mutiny of the native troops. Mr. Tayler was, however, confident that if allowed by the Government unfettered action, he could maintain order in Patná so long as the native troops at Dánápúr should remain quiescent. Thus, in his view, all, for the moment, depended on the quiet attitude of the sepoys.

Fails to impress his views on Major-General Lloyd.

So many symptoms, amongst others intercepted correspondence, seeming to show that the native troops were only watching their opportunity, it appeared to Mr. Tayler imperatively necessary that they should be disarmed with as little delay as possible. He endeavoured to impress his views in this respect on Major-General Lloyd. But in this he was unsuccessful. Major-General Lloyd held to the views I have already quoted, and declared repeatedly to Mr. Tayler that he was in direct communication with Lord Canning on the subject, and that he would carry the province through the crisis without resorting to the supreme measure of disarming.

The enormous difficulties of his position.

Mr. Tayler's position was rendered a thousand times more difficult by the fact that in addition to a disaffected city under his very eyes, to disaffected districts within ranges varying from thirty to a hundred miles, to disaffected landowners controlling large portions of those districts, he had within eight miles of his own door three native regiments, pledged, as their correspondence showed, to mutiny, and only watching their opportunity. It is difficult to realise the enormous responsibility thus thrown upon the shoulders of one man. Other

Book VII. Chapter II.

1857. June 12–18.

positions in India were dangerous, but this was unique in the opportunities of danger which threatened it, in the number of the lives, in the amount of treasure, in the extent of country, devolving upon one man, almost unaided, to guard. Without a single European soldier, and with only a few Sikhs, at his disposal, Mr. Tayler was responsible for the lives of some hundreds of Europeans scattered over the province, for a treasury in his own city containing more than £300,000, and in the districts of still more, for opium of the value of millions, for his own good name, for the credit and honour of his country. And now all around was surging. Any moment might bring revolt and mutiny to his door.

I have said in my description of Mr. Tayler that he possessed great natural talents which he had cultivated. In the course of his reading he had not been slow to observe that in great crises, when two armies, or two political parties, are sitting armed opposite to each other, each watching its opportunity, success almost invariably inclines to the leader who struck the first blow. The time had now arrived for him to consider whether he was not himself placed in a position in which he would be justified in dealing at the disaffected chiefs a blow which would paralyze their movements—a blow not accompanied by bloodshed, but one strictly of self-defence. The measure he contemplated may, in one sense, be termed a measure of disarming. He was not strong enough, indeed, to disarm at the moment

Resolves to strike the first blow.

ᴏᴏᴋ VII. apter II. 1857. ˋune 19.

the inhabitants of Patná by depriving them of their weapons, but he could disarm their counsels of wisdom by apprehending and confining their trusted leaders. It was a bold and daring idea, requiring strength of nerve and resolution to carry through; but the necessities were pressing, the dangers were threatening, a general rising in Patná might be fatal. Mr. Tayler resolved to anticipate those dangers, to render impossible or fruitless that rising, by acting in the manner I have indicated.

The principal conspirators.

Accordingly he struck. Private information had satisfied Mr. Tayler that the chiefs of the disaffected natives were the Wáhábí Múlvís. These men were the leaders of the most bigoted Mahomedan party in the world, and as such commanded implicit obedience from the mass of Patná Mahomedans, holding in their hands the strings of the contemplated movement. Prominent amongst these Múlvís were three men, Sháh Mahomed Hussén, Ahmad U'llá, and Waiz-úl-Haqq. To seize these men openly would have provoked the outbreak which Mr. Tayler was careful to avoid. But it was necessary for the public peace that they should be secured. Mr. Tayler, therefore, requested their presence, and the presence of others, to consult on the state of affairs. When the conference was over he allowed the others to depart, but detained the three men I have named, informing them that in the then existing state of affairs it was necessary that they should remain under supervision. They politely acquiesced, and were conducted to a comfortable house near the

Mr. Tayler arrests them

Book VII. Chapter II.

1857. June 19.

Sikh encampment where suitable accommodation had been provided for them.

False criticism on this act.

The act of Mr. Tayler in arresting, without warning them that he intended to arrest them—in a word by enticing them to his house—men of whose guilt he had evidence amounting, in his mind, to certainty, and who, if left at large, would have so organized the outbreak that it should coincide with the rise of the sepoys—has been compared, in principle, to "the treacherous assassination of Sir William Macnaghten by Sirdar Mahomed Akbar Khan."* It is difficult to apprehend how the writer could have mistaken the striking difference between the two occurrences. Mahomed Akbar and Sir William Macnaghten were representatives of two nations, the one at war with the other: at the conference at which they met, Mahomed Akbar had guaranteed in the most solemn and sacred manner the life of his guest. Yet Mahomed Akbar shot Sir William Macnaghten dead. Mr. Tayler, on the other hand, represented the governing power of the land; the Múlvís were the avowed subjects of that power; they were not Mr. Tayler's guests; they went to his house to hear the voice of the Government they served; and that voice ordered them to remain in honorary confinement so long as the crisis might last. They were subjected to no humiliation: to no disgrace. Simply the power of endangering the lives of others was taken away from them.

Follows up the blow.

This act occurred on the 19th of June. It was

* Sir John Kaye, vol. iii. p. 84.

Book VII. Chapter II.

1857. June 20.

followed up by the arrest of Múlví Méhdi, the patroling magistrate of the city, strongly suspected of connivance with the disaffected. The next day, the 20th, the rank and file having been overawed by the seizure of their chiefs, Mr. Tayler issued a proclamation calling upon all citizens to deliver up their arms, within twenty-four hours, on pain of being proceeded against; and another, forbidding all citizens, those excepted who might be specially exempted, from leaving their homes after 9 o'clock at night.

Success of his bold action.

These several measures were to a great extent successful. The disaffected were deprived of their most trusted leaders; several thousand stands of arms were peaceably delivered up; nightly meetings of the conspirators ceased. As a first practical result, the judge, Mr. Farquharson, the opium agent, Mr. Garrett, and others, left their refuge at the opium godown, and returned to their houses. The second was the sudden diminution of the symptoms of disaffection throughout the districts under Mr. Tayler's orders.

Fresh discoveries of treason.

But the crisis was not over. Three days later a corporal of the native police, Wáris Ali by name, was arrested at his own station, in Tirhút, under most suspicious circumstances. Upon his person was found a bundle of letters implicating in the rebellious movement one Ali Karím, an influential Mahomedan gentleman, residing nine miles from Patná.

The chief criminal escapes—how?

Mr. Tayler at once despatched the magistrate of Patná, Mr. Lowis, to arrest this gentleman, placing at his disposal a party of Sikh cavalry.

1857. June 23.

But Mr. Lowis, listening to the voice of the native official who was to accompany him, resolved to act without the cavalry. The same friendly voice which had proffered this advice, warned Ali Karím of the magistrate's approach. When Mr. Lowis came in sight of his intended victim, the latter was mounted on an elephant. Mr. Lowis had at his disposal a small pony gig—and his legs. As Ali Karím turned at once into the fields, he was enabled easily to baffle his pursuer, and to escape.

The order which Mr. Tayler's bold measures had thus restored was maintained without interruption till the 3rd of July. The disaffected had been thoroughly cowed. In the interval, however, reports of the massacre at Sháhjahánpúr, of the fall of Kánhpúr, of Fathpúr, and of Farrakhábád, came to reanimate their hopes. The attitude of the sepoy regiments continued doubtful.

The Patná rising.

But on the evening of the 3rd of July the long threatened Patná rising occurred. Thanks, however, to the energetic measures already taken by Mr. Tayler, it occurred in a form so diluted that a continuation of the same daring and resolute policy sufficed to repress it. It happened in this wise. At the period on the 3rd already indicated, some two hundred Mahomedan fanatics, led by one Pír Ali, a bookseller, noted for his enthusiasm for his religion and his hatred of the English, unfurled the green flag, and summoning by beat of drum others to join them rushed, calling upon Allah, towards the Roman Catholic Church, situate in the very heart of the city. On the news of this movement reaching

Book VII. Chapter II.

1857. July 3.

Mr. Tayler, that gentleman directed Captain Rattray, attended by the magistrate, to march down with 150 Sikhs, whilst for the protection of the residents he put into operation the same precautions which had been adopted on the 7th of June, he himself going in person to the houses nearest to his own.

Murder of Dr. Lyall.

Meanwhile, and before the Sikhs had reached the spot, Dr. Lyall, the assistant to the opium agent, hearing the uproar, and thinking that his presence might overawe the rioters, had galloped to the scene of action. As he approached the crowd several shots were fired at him. By one of these he was killed.*

The sight of a fallen European stimulated the fanaticism of the crowd, and produced on them the effect which the taste of blood arouses in a hungry tiger. They pushed onwards with renewed enthusiasm, their numbers being augmented at every step. In a very few minutes, however, they found themselves face to face with Rattray's 150 Sikhs. Between the opposing parties, far from sympathy, there was the hatred of race, the hatred of religion; on the one side the newly aroused fanaticism, on the other the longed for opportunity to repay many a covert insult. It can well be imagined what followed. There was not a moment of parley. The rival parties instantaneously clashed, and, in a few seconds, the discipline and bayonets of the Sikhs suppressed the long threatened Patná rising.

The rising suppressed.

* His face was at once so mutilated that it could not afterwards be recognised.

Book VII. Chapter II.

1857. July 4–5.

Capture and trial of the ringleaders.

The next day, and the day following, the city was searched for the ringleaders of the outbreak. Thirty-one were apprehended. Amongst these were Pír Ali, the actual leader, and Shekh Ghasíta, the confidential servant of Lútf Ali Khán, the richest banker in the city.

Of the thirty-one men who were apprehended, fourteen were tried and executed without delay. With them likewise was hanged the Wáris Ali referred to in a previous page.* Two—the two above-named—were remanded for further examination.

Facts seemed to speak strongly against them. It was clearly proved that Pír Ali was a main agent for promoting a crusade against the English; that for months he and the Shekh Ghasíta above-mentioned had engaged and kept in pay numerous men who should be ready, when called upon, to fight for their religion and the Emperor of Dehlí. But these operations had required a large outlay. Pír Ali was poor. His associate, Ghasíta, was the hand of the great banker. But though it might have been fairly presumed that the great banker was implicated, no proceedings were, for the moment, taken against him.

Lútf Ali.

The two men, Pír Ali and Ghasíta, were tried and hanged. Lútf Ali, arraigned subsequently on the charge of harbouring a mutinous sepoy, and acquitted by the judge on the ground of insufficient evidence, was promptly released, and

* When taken to the gallows, this man called out in a loud voice, "If there is any one here who professes to be a friend of the King of Dehli, let him come and help me."

Book VII. Chapter II. — 1857. July 5–16.

shortly afterwards was welcomed and honoured as a martyr by the successor of Mr. Tayler!

But the outbreak was suppressed. It had been premature. As Pír Ali admitted, Mr. Tayler's strong measures had forced his hand and compelled him to strike before he was ready. But for those strong measures the conspiracy would have been silently hatched until the outbreak at Dánápúr should have given it the signal for explosion.

Major Holmes.

Whilst Mr. Tayler, thus, in spite of the all but superhuman difficulties in his path, maintained order in the most disaffected city still under British rule in India, and in the districts immediately contiguous, Major Holmes, commanding the 12th Irregular Cavalry, acting in concert with him and pursuing the same system, prevented an outbreak in the frontier district of Sigaolí. It is true, indeed, that Major Holmes still believed in his native soldiers, and equally true that up to the moment of their actual outbreak—almost simultaneous with that at Dánápúr—they had shown no symptom of disaffection. But this belief on the part of Major Holmes was so generally shared by the officers of the Bengal army, that it should attract no surprise. It was natural that the officers should believe in men with whom they had been associated twenty, thirty, and forty years; who had followed them unhesitatingly through the snows of Kábal; whose forefathers had served with goodwill in the expeditions against Egypt, and the isles of France and Bourbon; and who had protested against the indignity of being suspected. That was natural enough. But it

Book VII. Chapter II.

1857. July 5–16.

was not natural that the Government, raised above the passions and prejudices of regimental officers, should more than share their sympathies. With the far wider scope open to their view the Government possessed means, not available to the officers, of testing the truth of the lip-service so freely proffered by the men. It is impossible to say how much loss of life, how much misery, how much evil would have been avoided had the Government of India not refused to take from the native troops of the Dánápúr division the arms, which their own sepoy-trained Major-General had assured them, would be loyally used only if no great temptation or excitement should assail them!

Contrast between Mr. Tayler and Mr. Halliday.

Still, order was maintained. The means employed to assure that order, whilst they gained for Mr. Tayler the confidence of the English planters and traders throughout the province, were not at all to the taste of the Government of Bengal. Of that province, Mr. Halliday, of the Bengal Civil Service, was Lieutenant-Governor. It is scarcely to be doubted that if Mr. Tayler and Mr. Halliday could have changed places; if the former had been Lieutenant-Governor of Bengal, and the latter Commissioner of the Patná division, whilst the affairs of Bengal would not certainly have suffered, the nature of the rule at Patná would have been widely different. I am unwilling to re-open wounds which have partly closed, but no sane man who was in Bihár at the time doubts that whilst the policy of Mr. Tayler, condemned by Mr. Halliday, saved Patná; the policy of

Book VII. Chapter II. 1857. July 5–16.

concealing from the public view facts which it was of vital importance that the public should know,—of coquetting, so to speak, with armed rebels,—advocated by that gentleman, and employed so uselessly elsewhere, would, if followed, have played the game of the disaffected. The Patná rising, so easily suppressed by Mr. Tayler, would have been indeed a red day in the calendar of Mr. Halliday.

I repeat, under Mr. Tayler, order was maintained, under most difficult circumstances, in Patná. About Patná, then, so long as he should remain there, no apprehension was felt. But the case was not so with respect to Dánápúr. There, the sepoys remained armed and trusted. In spite of intercepted letters, of men occasionally caught in mutinous acts, the Government continued to trust to the chance that "no great temptation or excitement" would induce them to rise.

European interests in Bihár.

Far different was the feeling of the European community of Calcutta. These had important interests in Bihár, large districts of which were watered and fertilised by their capital. These interests seemed to depend entirely on the good behaviour of the sepoys. To many of them it was a question of wealth or poverty, to those on the spot of death or of existence. In Mr. Tayler they had absolute confidence. His measures had warded off one danger. But the other still remained, clear, vivid, threatening; ready to burst forth at any moment; safe to encounter no opposition capable of restraining it for an hour.

That the possibility of such an outbreak had

escaped the attention of the Government of India there is evidence to disprove. It may have been, as his latest apologist has asserted, that Lord Canning refrained at an earlier date from issuing a disarming order because he was waiting for "fresh reinforcements, when the game would be more in his own hands." But in the early part of July those fresh reinforcements arrived. Not only so, but those very reinforcements, consisting of a wing of the 37th Foot and of the 5th Fusiliers, had received orders to proceed towards the north-west in steamers, touching at Dánápúr on the way.

Favourable opportunity for disarming the Dánápúr sepoys.

Here then was the opportunity—the opportunity which would take from the Government the last excuse not to disarm the native regiments, unless they were prepared to avow that they would trust rather to the chance of the sepoys remaining quiescent.

The Government considered the question carefully and with attention. They arrived at a decision fatal alike to their prescience as statesmen, and to the true conception of the responsibilities of a great Government. They cast from their shoulders the entire responsibility. They would not order that the regiments should retain their arms; neither would they direct that they should be disarmed. They left the decision to Major-General Lloyd, commanding the Dánápúr division—the officer who had already reported his belief that the sepoys "would remain quiet, unless some great temptation or excitement should assail them, in which case, I fear, they could not be

The Government transfer their responsibility to Major-General Lloyd.

Book VII. Chapter II.

1857. July 5–16.

relied upon." The Government thus constituted Major-General Lloyd the sole judge as to whether such temptation or such excitement was likely to arise.*

This decision of the Government was not published, but was privately conveyed to the mercantile community of Calcutta. It failed to satisfy them. They saw that the responsibility had been only moved. It had been shifted from the shoulders of the Government to the shoulders of Major-General Lloyd. That officer was known to be opposed to disarming; to entertain a belief that he could carry those under his command through the crisis without having resort to any such means. In the opinion of the mercantile community, then, the decision arrived at by the

* The order of the acting Commander-in-Chief, Sir Patrick Grant, speaking the voice of the Government, runs thus: "The first detachment of H.M.'s 5th Fusiliers left Chinsurah this morning, on flats towed by steamers, in progress towards Benares, and the remaining portion of the regiment will follow by the same means of transit to-morrow and Friday. If, when the regiment reaches Dinapore, you see reason to distrust the native troops, and you entertain an opinion that it is desirable to disarm them, you are at liberty to disembark the 5th Fusiliers to assist you in this object; but, it is imperatively necessary that the detention of the regiment should be limited to the shortest possible period. If you decide on disarming, it should extend to all three regiments, and it should be carefully explained that it is merely a measure of precaution to save the well-disposed to be led to commit themselves by the machinations of designing scoundrels, some few of whom are always to be found, even in the best regiments. If resistance to authority is exhibited, the most prompt and decided measures for its instant repression should be adopted." The reader will observe that this letter contains no order, but simply throws the responsibility of ordering disarming on the Major-General.

Book VII. Chapter II.

1857. July 17.

The merchants of Calcutta remonstrate with Lord Canning,

Government seemed equivalent to a refusal to order disarming.

Impressed with the conviction of the certain evil which must follow a conclusion so adverse to their interests, to the interests of the province, and to public order, the merchants of Calcutta determined, as a last resource, to make, in the most temperate language, a personal appeal to Lord Canning. On the 17th of July, then, two days after they had been informed of the resolution at which the Government had arrived, the merchants solicited the Governor-General to receive from their body a deputation, charged with their ideas on the state of affairs in Tirhút and Bihár.

Lord Canning agreed to receive, and did on the 20th receive, the deputation. Its spokesman, a gentleman who carried with him the confidence of all Calcutta, began by pointing out how the mercantile interests were involved in the maintenance of peace and order; how both were threatened by the attitude of the native regiments at Dánápúr; how the disarming of those regiments would quiet the public mind and restore confidence; how that a most favourable opportunity for carrying out that measure then presented itself, inasmuch as the 5th Fusiliers, who had left Calcutta by steamer on the 12th, would reach Dánápúr on or about the 22nd; that they, disembarking, could very easily, in conjunction with the 10th Regiment on the spot, disarm the native regiments, and then, re-embarking, proceed on their upward journey. Such were the points submitted in respectful

Book VII. Chapter II.

1857. July 20.

language by the spokesman of the deputation. Lord Canning, in a curt and ceremonious speech, refused to accede to its prayer.

who is obstinate.

Summary of the action of the Government.

The events that followed can only be regarded as the consequence of the decisions of the Government of India. These decisions may be thus briefly stated:—1st, a refusal to order the disarming of the Dánápúr brigade at the period when the troops south of Dánápúr were being disarmed, when those north of it were mutinying, and when the greatest disaffection in the city and in the districts close to Dánápúr were daily being brought to light; 2ndly, the rejection of the request of the merchants of Calcutta to order the disarming when the strength in Europeans had been greatly increased; 3rdly, the transfer of responsibility to an officer who was known to be opposed to the disarming of the native troops under his command.

I now proceed to relate the consequences of these decisions.

Major-General Lloyd decides not to disarm the sepoys;

Major-General Lloyd was armed, we have seen, with the power, should he think fit, to detain the 5th Fusiliers at Dánápúr, and, acting with them and the 10th Regiment, to disarm the three native regiments of his command. Major-General Lloyd winced under this responsibility. He did not like it at all. He could not resolve to make use of the powers with which he was entrusted. When, therefore, on the 22nd of July, the main body of the 5th Fusiliers arrived off Dánápúr, he did not order them to disembark, he did not even detain them. They proceeded without delay on their way.

Book VII. Chapter II.

1857. July 22.

But no sooner had they left than Major-General Lloyd began to doubt whether he had acted rightly. He could not call them back. But it happened two days later, whilst the Major-General was half regretting, half doubting, that two companies of the 37th Regiment arrived off the station. Major-General Lloyd at once directed the disembarkation of these men.

But he had not even then brought himself to the point of ordering disarming. Nor could he, even with these new troops at his disposal, persuade himself to direct the necessary measure. The responsibility thrust upon him by the Government pressed him down. Like all weak men, weighted with a burden to which their intellect and their nerve are alike unequal, Major-General Lloyd hesitated. In the midst of his hesitation he bethought him of a half-measure—a measure which, he believed, would render the sepoys powerless and yet save their honour. He decided to leave them their percussion-muskets, but to deprive them of their percussion-caps!

but to deprive them of their percussion caps.

That the reader may clearly understand the danger with which such a measure was fraught, it is necessary that I should give a short description of the station of Dánápúr, and of its military plan.

The station of Dánápúr.

Dánápúr lies ten miles from the city of Patná, eight from the civil station in which reside the European officials. The native town occupies the easternmost point of the station, that nearest to Patná. Close to the town is a large square, tenanted mainly by European troops. Adjoining

Book VII. Chapter II.

1857. July 22.

this on its western side is a smaller square in which are the better quarters of the European officers. Beyond this a few detached houses, and beyond these again, the lines or huts occupied by the sepoys. Further on still, at the westernmost point of the station, was the magazine, in which were stored, amongst other items, the percussion caps for the use of the regiments. To remove these caps from this magazine into the square occupied by the Europeans, the whole length of the native lines would thus have to be traversed. It would not be possible to conceal from the sepoys the nature of the measure which should thus be carried out. They would most certainly divine its reason. Surely, then, in deciding to deprive the sepoys of their percussion caps, Major-General Lloyd was placing in their way that very temptation, and arousing in their minds that very excitement, which, he had reported to Government, would almost certainly incite them to mutiny!

Having received only the permission, not the order, to disarm, and not being able to nerve himself to a measure of a character so pointed, Major-General Lloyd directed the carrying out of a scheme far less decisive and infinitely more dangerous. A parade of the European troops was ordered for the morning of the 25th; and it was directed that whilst the troops should remain in the great square, already referred to, two carts should be sent to bring into that square the percussion cap cases from the magazine.

First consequences of

The order was obeyed. The 10th Foot, two

Book VII. Chapter II.

1857. July 25.

Major-General Lloyd's half-measures.

companies of the 37th Regiment, and the company of European Artillery were drawn up on the morning of the 25th in the great square, and the two carts were despatched to the magazine under the charge of an officer and a small guard. The carts reached the magazine, were loaded with the cap-cases, and set out on their return. As they passed the lines of the 7th Native Infantry, the sepoys showed the greatest excitement. Those who were being paraded for guard summoned their comrades to join them in preventing the carrying off of the caps. Their officers, however, succeeded in pacifying them. The men of the 8th Native Infantry were less demonstrative. Those of the 40th even showed a disposition to oppose the angry demonstrations of the men of the 7th. For the moment the difficulty was tided over; the cap-cases were brought safely into the square, and the parade was dismissed. The General, perfectly satisfied with the manner in which he had solved the difficult question, betook himself on board a steamer, which had that morning arrived, to take luncheon.*

Their apparent success.

Possibly the success which had attended this delicate operation, whilst the European troops were standing in their ranks ready for action, induced the belief in the mind of Major-General Lloyd that it would be equally easy, or I must suppose still easier, to carry out another measure,

The Major-General resolves to proceed further.

* It does not seem quite certain whether Major-General Lloyd went on board the steamer for the purpose of lunching, or because he had no horse at hand, and was unable, from gouty feet, to walk. But the point is immaterial. He was on board the steamer at luncheon time.

Book VII. Chapter II.

1857. July 25.

still more delicate, still more likely to cause opposition, whilst the European troops should be in the barracks eating their dinners, and he on board the steamer partaking of his luncheon. Not satisfied with a great victory he wished to turn it into a decisive triumph. Before, then, going on board the steamer, he issued orders to the commandants to parade their regiments without arms, and to take from the men the caps in the regimental magazines and those in their actual possession.

A more difficult operation than that entrusted to the regimental officers of the native regiments can scarcely be conceived. Nor, in the presence of the manifestation of the 7th Native Infantry in the morning, is it possible to imagine how the Major-General could have believed that the sepoys would calmly surrender the one thing still in their own hands which made their muskets valuable. However, the order of the Major-General had to be carried out, and the regiments were paraded at 1 o'clock.

Consequences of his resolve.

On the men falling in without arms the several commanding officers directed the native officers to collect the caps in pouch from each sepoy, explaining to them as they did so that the measure was one of precaution designed to save the well-disposed from being led away by the machinations of those bent on mischief. The native officers, who probably sympathised in a great measure with their men, might as well have spoken to the winds. The demand for the caps, was, in the 7th and 8th Regiments, the signal for mutiny. The men rushed tumultuously to the bells of arms, seized their muskets, and began to fire on their officers. The 40th showed some hesitation, but, after a short period of doubt, they too were carried away by the example of their comrades.

The mutiny,—and how it was not suppressed.

Whilst this was happening, Major-General Lloyd was at his luncheon, and the European soldiers were at their dinners. The Major-General had previously arranged, however, that in the event of any disturbance two musket-shots should be fired in quick succession by the European guard at the hospital—a large building between the smaller square and the native lines, and commanding a good view of the latter. At half-past 1 o'clock the report of those shots informed Major-General Lloyd and the Europeans that the native regiments had mutinied.

No sooner was the signal given than the "assembly" sounded in the large square. The 10th Regiment turned out under Lieutenant-Colonel Fenwick, two companies of the 37th under the senior captain present; the artillery under Lieutenant-Colonel Huyshe. But there was no one to take the command. Major-General Lloyd states that he had previously given instructions how to act on an emergency to Colonel Huyshe, and that he considered that these orders would ensure the attack and pursuit of the mutineers by the European infantry and artillery. Uneasy at the quiescent attitude of the troops, he, at a later period of the afternoon, despatched one staff officer to order the guns to advance, and another

Book VII. Chapter II.

1857. July 25.

to direct the officer commanding the detachment of the 37th Foot to place himself under the orders of Colonel Fenwick.

Whether the orders of the Major-General, given, it must be remembered, before the event, were sufficiently clear and precise, may be doubted. This at least is certain, that his absence from the parade-ground caused considerable delay in the advance of the troops. When at last they did move from their ground it was too late. No one knew where the Major-General was; neither the Commander of the 10th Regiment, nor the Commander of the battery of artillery, considered himself invested with power to act in the absence of the Major-General. And it was only when, after a prolonged delay, the two staff officers referred to hurried up from the steamer that the order to advance was issued.

The mutineers start for Arah.

Meanwhile, the mutineers, astonished at their easy triumph, and seeing that they were being disturbed only by some shots fired by the guard at the hospital, hastened to divest themselves of their red coats, to pouch all the caps in the regimental store, and to start off as fast as they could towards the river Sôn, in the direction of Arah. A few of them attempted to cross the Ganges; but the steamer, on board of which was the Major-General, effectually prevented this movement.

Are not pursued.

When, then, the European troops reached the native lines, they found that the sepoys had already disappeared. They set fire to their huts, and then halted for orders. No orders came.

Book VII. Chapter II.

1857. July 25.

Reflections on the event.

The Major-General was still on board the steamer, and no one cared to usurp his powers.

Such was the rising of Dánápúr,—a rising long foreseen, and yet managed as though it had been regarded as impossible. Who was to blame? First and principally, certainly, the Government of India, which, though warned in a manner compared to which the hand-writing on the wall at Belshazzar's feast after it had been interpreted was a mystery, not only persistently declined to take upon itself the responsibility of ordering the disarming of the sepoys, but thrust that responsibility upon an officer unfit, mentally and physically, to bear it. Secondly, and only to a less degree than the Government, Major-General Lloyd himself, who, under the weight of the responsibility thrust upon him, preferred to a decided, though simple and easy plan, a scheme elaborate and delicate, certain to wound whilst likely to fail; and who, further, deprived that scheme of all possibility of success by absenting himself from the parade-ground at the critical moment, and by leaving the European troops without orders. Had Major-General Lloyd mounted his horse and led on the European troops when the signal of mutiny reached him, the mutiny would have been crushed in the bud, and the terrible consequences which followed would have been averted.*

* General Lloyd states in a letter to Sir John Kaye, that he "had no horse in cantonments. My stable was two miles distant, and being unable at that time to walk far or much, I thought I should be most useful on board the steamer with guns and riflemen, &c." But surely, at such

Book VII. Chapter II.

1857. July 25.

Mutiny at Sigaolí.

Precisely on the day on which these events were taking place at Dánápúr, a bloodier tragedy was enacted at Sigaolí, the frontier station of the division. Here was quartered the 12th Irregular Cavalry, commanded by Major Holmes. I have said that Major Holmes trusted his men, and he showed the absolute trust that he felt in them. In dealing with a great crisis he went all the lengths of the great Lord Strafford. He was urgent for a "thorough" policy, for a prompt and sharp punishment for overt acts of treason and disaffection. Impressed with these views, he took the law into his own hands. He proclaimed, on his own authority, martial law in the five civil districts contiguous to his own station. Trusting absolutely, as I have said, his men, he sent them out in detached parties of from twenty to fifty all over these districts to overawe the disaffected and to maintain order. Every sepoy or mutineer caught in the act of rebellion he caused to be seized, tried by a court-martial, and, if found guilty, hanged. In all this he acted with the cordial approval of the Commissioner of Patná, for whom he had the highest admiration. It is probable that if the strain on his men had been eased a little earlier Major Holmes would have carried his district through the crisis. But the inaction of the Government with respect to the Dánápúr regiments, and probably the knowledge that a concerted movement between them and the native

a crisis, whilst a very delicate measure ordered by him was in operation, Major-General Lloyd ought at least to have taken care not only to have his horse in cantonments, but that it should remain saddled and accoutred at his very door.

1857. July 25.

landowners would soon come to maturity, were too much for his men. They determined to cast off the mask. On the evening of the 25th of July, then, four troopers suddenly attacked Major Holmes and his wife, a daughter of the heroic Sale, and killed them. The other Europeans in the station shared the same fate. The mutinous soldiers then plundered the treasury, and let themselves loose on the country, now at their mercy.

Murder of Major and Mrs. Holmes.

The fears of the mercantile community, expressed on the 20th of July to Lord Canning, were thus promptly realised. Lord Canning had on that date refused to order disarming. The troops, not disarmed, had mutinied, and on the 25th the richest province in India was at their mercy.

How Mr. Tayler met the danger.

I now return to Patná. The event so long dreaded, so long foreseen, to guard against the effects of which so many precautions had been taken by the Commissioner, had now occurred. The native troops had revolted; Bihár was without force to resist them. Early in the day of the 25th, Mr. Tayler had received from Dánápúr intelligence which left on his mind no doubt that the crisis there was imminent. He at once summoned the residents to the protection afforded by his house. The residents had scarcely arrived when the sound of the firing of the two guns announced that the outbreak had occurred. Later in this day of suspense intelligence arrived that the mutineers had left the station, and that the European troops had not followed them. The direction

Book VII. Chapter II.

1857. July 25.

taken by the native troops was unknown, but Mr. Tayler, guided by a true military instinct, determined at once to do all in his power to intercept them. He organized, therefore, a party of volunteers, and combining with them fifty Sikhs, fifty native police, and a small levy of horse, detached the party that night to Phúlwárí, about eight miles from Patná, there to bivouac for the night. He sent intimation of this movement to Major-General Lloyd, with a request that he would detach a small body of the 10th Foot to co-operate with this party, should he have reason to believe that the sepoys had taken that route.

The dawn of the following day, however, disclosed to Mr. Tayler the evil which, at the moment, appeared the more formidable of the two—the mutiny of the 12th Irregulars, and the murder of their commandant and others. This event gave to affairs a most serious aspect. A whole regiment of cavalry was thus let loose on the country, and it was difficult to say in what quarter they would strike their blow. An absolute necessity was thus created that all the available means of defence should be concentrated. The detachment, then, was at once withdrawn from Phúlwárí. The fate of Patná and of Bihár seemed now to depend upon the conduct of Major-General Lloyd. Should he have directed a rapid pursuit in force of the mutineers all might yet be well.

Uncertainty at Dánápúr.

But at Dánápúr affairs had taken a very different turn. The native troops had, we have already seen, been allowed time to march clean away with their muskets and their ammunition.

Book VII. Chapter II. 1857. July 25.

The European troops, after burning the native huts, had, in consequence of the absence of the Major-General, returned to their barracks. No one knew certainly the ultimate direction which the sepoys would take. It was believed, however, that their passage across the Ganges having been prevented, they would march on Arah.

Major-General Lloyd's opportunity.

Here was an opportunity such as a real soldier would have clutched at—an opportunity of repairing every mistake, of atoning for all shortcomings. Dividing the district of Sháhábád, of which Arah was the capital, from that of Patná, and some ten miles south-west of Dánápúr, is the river Sôn, swollen at that season by continuous rain, and traversable only by boats, not then collected. Had Major-General Lloyd, on landing from the steamer that evening, at once detached a strong force of infantry and artillery in pursuit of the mutineers, he must have caught them *in flagrante delictu*, with an unfordable river in their rear.

He will not take it.

But such action was far above the calibre of the mind of Major-General Lloyd. He has placed on record that probably a direct pursuit would not have been of much avail.* A dim idea of the use

* His words are: "It is perhaps to be regretted that some (European troops) were not sent that night or next morning, but only a small party, in comparison to the strength of the mutineers, could have been detached; no guns could have gone, and as the mutineers avoided the road and kept to the fields, where they could scarcely have been effectively followed by a small party of Europeans, they probably would not have been of much use." It is difficult to see the force of this argument. The high road to Arah was traversable by artillery. Though the sepoys might have spread over the fields they yet followed the line of that road.

Book VII. Chapter II.

1857. July 26.

which might be made of the Sôn river to stop the enemy prompted him, however, the following morning, to send some riflemen in a steamer up that river, but there was not sufficient draught of water, and the steamer and riflemen returned, having accomplished nothing. But before they arrived the Major-General had received information which diverted his thoughts entirely, for the moment, from an offensive movement, and directed them to the securing of the safety of his garrison by intrenching Dánápúr.*

The information referred to was to the effect that Kúnwar Singh, the great landowner mentioned in a previous page, whose estates lay in the vicinity of Arah, and along the banks of the Sôn, had raised his tenantry and was about to join the mutinous sepoys.

Kúnwar Singh.

Kúnwar Singh, a Rájpút chieftain of ancient lineage, had been made an enemy of the English rule by the action of our revenue system. The action of this system, which he imperfectly understood, had reduced his means so considerably that some short time before the outbreak of the mutiny his estates had been placed in liquidation. Still, there was one case pending which, if decided in his favour, would go a great way towards recouping his losses. After the mutiny had broken out, and when Kúnwar Singh was eagerly watching the turn of events, doubtful as to the course which

* "That afternoon the General wrote to tell me he proposed entrenching Dinapore, it was ascertained that the mutineers had gone off in a body towards Arrah, and it was apprehended by him that they might be joined by Koor Singh, and return to attack Dinapore."—W. Tayler's "Patna Crisis."

Book VII. Chapter II.

1857. July 26.

he should pursue, the law courts decided this case against him. About the same time the supporting hand of Government was withdrawn from the management of his case.* Thenceforward his mind was made up. Old as he was, and he had seen eighty summers, he resolved to seize the first opportunity of striking a blow for his freedom. When he learned, therefore, that the sepoys at Dánápúr had successfully risen and were marching towards Arah, he resolved to co-operate with them with all his power.

Mr. Tayler throws himself into the breach.

This was the information which influenced Major-General Lloyd to stop, for the moment, any further movement, and to intrench himself at Dánápúr. But the Commissioner of Patná, to whom he had imparted his resolve, deprecated it with all the fervour of his daring and energetic nature. He implored the General to pursue the rebels immediately. He pointed out that there might be yet time to catch them before they could cross the Sôn; that vigour and energy would yet retrieve the disaster.

* It would appear that Kúnwar Singh had engaged, when his estates were placed in liquidation, to raise a sum of £200,000 for the payment of his debts. Naturally some delay occurred in raising so large a sum; the money, however, was gradually coming in when the Board of Revenue informed him, through the Commissioner of Patná, that unless he should raise the whole sum within one month, they would recommend the Government "to withdraw all interference with his affairs, and to abandon the management of his estates." This decision of the Board of Revenue was regarded by Kúnwar Singh, and very naturally, as tantamount to the sequestration of his property. The course of the Board of Revenue was strongly objected to by Mr. Tayler,—who even went so far as to protest against it in a private letter to Mr. Halliday—but in vain.

Book VII. Chapter II.

1857. July 26.

Had Mr. Tayler been Major-General Commanding the Dánápúr division, the disaster would have been retrieved promptly and effectually. But, in that case, there would have been no disaster to retrieve. As it was he could only advise.

Further information, to which I am about to refer, added force to Mr. Tayler's recommendations, and at last determined the Major-General to detach a force in pursuit of the sepoys.

Troops are sent to relieve Arah.

July 27.

Intelligence that the sepoys had crossed the Sôn and were besieging Arah caused the Major-General to detach, on the evening of the 27th, a body of 193 men belonging to the 37th Regiment, in a steamer. The commander of this steamer was directed to steam up the Sôn, and to land the troops at the point where the road to Arah joins the river. The instructions given to the troops were that they should, on being landed, proceed to Arah, and bring away the civilians there besieged. It happened, however, that the steamer, running on after the moon had gone down, stuck fast on a sand-bank. Major-General Lloyd then resolved to recall his troops and attempt nothing more. But Mr. Tayler succeeded in inducing him to change his mind. The Major-General, then, in consultation with the captain of a river-steamer but just arrived, directed that a party of 250 men from the 10th Foot, with 70 Sikhs and some volunteers, should leave Dánápúr in the morning of the 29th, and, picking up on its way the flat attached to the steamer which had stranded, should convey the troops, the whole commanded

The Major-General resolves to recall them.

Mr. Tayler encourages him to persevere.

by Colonel Fenwick of the 10th Foot, up the Sôn, to the point previously indicated.

Book VII. Chapter II.

1857. July 29.

Some difficulties raised by the commander of the steamer caused the reduction of the European force by 100 men. The remainder constituting too small a command for an officer of high rank, Colonel Fenwick remained behind, and Captain Dunbar of the same regiment took the whole body under his orders. The steamer, with her 150 Europeans and 70 Sikhs, taking also a few gentlemen volunteers, left Dánápúr amid the enthusiasm of the European population, picked up the detachment of the 37th Regiment, reached the appointed spot in safety, and began to disembark the troops at 2 P.M. Before recounting their further movements I must return to the revolted sepoys.

The expedition sets out.

Those sepoys, leaving Dánápúr with their arms and accoutrements, had reached the banks of the Sôn on the morning of the 26th. For want of means to cross the river they did not reach the opposite bank till the evening. In the interval the servants of Kúnwar Singh had been busy in collecting boats for the mass, whilst as many as could be conveyed crossed by the ferry. Before night had set in every man was on the opposite bank. Short was the consultation that followed. Kúnwar Singh himself was on the spot, and, under the influence of the advice of this honoured Rájpút landowner, it was decided to march on Arah, massacre the residents, and plunder the treasury. The subsequent movements of the little army would necessarily depend on circumstances, but it was an

The mutineers cross the Sôn.

Book VII. Chapter II.

1857. July 29.

object with Kúnwar Singh to keep the sepoys, if possible, within the limits of Bihár.

A great portion of the expectations of the sepoys were realised almost at once. Having reached Arah, they released the prisoners from the jail (27th of July), plundered the treasury, and then set forth to slaughter the European residents. But in the attempt to prosecute this part of their scheme they met with an opposition on which they had not counted.

Arah.

The residents of Arah, in fact, had not awaited in idleness the visit which they had deemed always possible, and which, since the 25th, had been certain. One of their number, Mr. Vicars Boyle, a civil engineer connected with the railway, had, from a very early period, regarded it as quite a possible contingency that the station might be attacked by the mutineers. He, therefore, despite the jeers of some, and the covert ridicule of others, had fortified the smaller of the two houses in his compound in a manner which would enable it, if defended, to resist any sudden assault. This house was a small detached building, about fifty feet square, having one storey above the basement, and surmounted by a flat roof. As soon as a message from Dánápúr brought the information of the successful rise and departure of the sepoys, the residents resolved to take advantage of Mr. Boyle's prescience, and to defend themselves in his house against the enemy. Supplies of all kinds,—meal, wine, beer, water, biscuit, and sheep—had been gradually stored up by Mr. Boyle during the month.

Mr. Vicars Boyle.

Book VII. Chapter II.

1857. July 26.

Additional means of defence were now provided. Ammunition was collected; loopholes were drilled in the walls, and sand-bags were placed on the roof. At the same time, the front portion of the other and larger house in the same compound, about fifty yards distant from the improvised fortress, was entirely demolished, so as to prevent it from affording shelter to any possible assailants.

The European and Eurasian residents in Arah amounted in number to fifteen; but there was besides a Mahomedan gentlemen, whose fate was joined to theirs.* With so small a garrison, a successful defence of Mr. Boyle's house would have been impossible. But with the prescience which, in those trying days, marked every act of the career of the Commissioner of Patná, Mr. Tayler had, in anticipation of the crisis, despatched to Arah fifty of Rattray's Sikhs. These men were on the spot, and they too cast in their lot with the English. The united garrison thus numbered nearly seventy souls, and these, when information reached them of the crossing of the Sôn by the sepoys, threw themselves, armed with their muskets, their guns, and their rifles,

Prescience of Mr. Tayler.

* The garrison consisted of Mr. Littledale, the judge; Mr. Combe, the collector; Mr. Herwald Wake, magistrate; Mr. Colvin, assistant; Dr. Halls, surgeon; Mr. Field and Mr. Anderson of the opium department; Mr. Vicars Boyle; Syad Azimúdín Khan, deputy collector; Mr. Dacosta; Mr. Godfrey; Mr. Cork; Mr. Tait; Mr. Delpeison; Mr. Hoyle; and Mr. de Souza. The Sikh force consisted of a native lieutenant and two native sergeants, two corporals, forty-five privates, a water-carrier, and a cook. The charge of the defences was entrusted to Mr. Vicars Boyle, whilst Mr. Herwald Wake took the command in chief of the garrison.

Book VII. Chapter II.

1857. July 27.

into the house of refuge, resolved to defend it to the very last.

The mutineers reach Arah.

Great, then, was the surprise of the sepoys when, having released the prisoners and plundered the treasury, they set forth to slaughter the Europeans, they found that their progress was stayed by the occupants of one small house. Still confident in their numbers, and elated by the success which had attended all their movements, they advanced unhesitatingly, and in unbroken order, towards the last refuge of their enemy. The garrison reserved their fire till the sepoys came within range, but they then let fly with so sure an aim that the rebels fell back surprised and disconcerted. These, changing their tactics, then dispersed into groups, and taking possession of the larger house commenced from it and from behind the trees near it, a continuous fire on the garrison. The commanding position and the artificial defences of the smaller house enabled the latter to return the fire with terrible effect. Not a sepoy dare expose his person. If he chanced to do so, a bullet from a musket behind the sand-bags on the roof was certain to find out his weak point.

The defence.

Meanwhile, the sepoys had discovered that a portion of the garrison were Sikhs. They had some men of that nation in their own ranks. These were commissioned to use every possible argument to win over their countrymen. When the offer to share with them the plunder of the treasuries, of those sacked and of those still to be sacked, proved unavailing, threats of the doom

1857. July 27.

which hung over them were freely used. The most earnest appeals to their nationality and their religion were alike rejected. Rattray's Sikhs remained loyal to the Government which gave them their salt.

July 28.

During the next day the rebels brought two guns to bear on the besieged edifice. From these they fired every possible kind of projectile on which they could lay hands. They riddled the walls of the house, but they did not lessen the courage of the garrison. A musketry fire, carefully husbanded, yet used unsparingly whenever a chance presented itself, told them, in unmistakeable language, that they were still defied. This did not, however, prevent the rebels from offering terms. Possibly the sepoys were acquainted with the story of Kánhpúr. But this is certain that every evening a sepoy standing behind the pillar of the larger house, summoned the garrison, in the name of their general, a súbadár of the 8th Regiment Native Infantry, to surrender on conditions.

July 29.

The following day, the 29th, the same tactics were continued, the enemy's guns being shifted from point to point so as to bear on the weakest point of the besieged house, but with the effect only of increasing the damage effected in the outer wall.

At last the enemy succeeded in placing the largest of the two field-pieces on the top of the vacated house, and began to direct a fire on the smaller house as fast as they could collect or improvise cannon-balls. But nothing intimidated the gallant

Book VII. Chapter II.

1857. July 29.

men who formed the garrison. When the enemy raised a barricade on the roof of the adjoining house, the besieged raised one still higher on their own. When provisions began to fail, a sally procured more. In fact all the means that courage, labour, daring, and energy could suggest were used to the fullest extent to baffle the enemy.

At midnight on that day, the 29th, the garrison were aroused by the sound of repeated volleys of musketry about a mile distant, in the direction of the Sôn river. For a moment hope suggested the idea that the garrison of Dánápúr was about to relieve them. But the hope flickered and died almost as soon as it had received life. The sound of the firing became more and more distant:—at last it ceased altogether. It was clear that the relieving party had been driven back.

Captain Dunbar's march.

We left that party, consisting of 343 Europeans, 70 Sikhs, and a few gentlemen volunteers, having just succeeded in effecting their disembarkation, at 2 o'clock on the afternoon of the 29th, on the point nearest to the station of Arah. The order was at once issued for the men to dine, when suddenly firing was heard from the advance-guard. It was ascertained that this firing had been caused by the presence of a body of sepoys on the banks of a wide and deep rivulet, about two miles distant, and upon whom the advanced guard had opened. On receiving the fire the sepoys retreated. Then, though pressed to stop and bivouac for the night, Captain Dunbar determined to push on at once. It is true his men were fasting; but it was a fine moonlight night, and both

1857. July 29.

officers and men were cheered by the news brought by the villagers that the garrison was still holding out, whilst the sound of the booming of the guns in the direction of Arah showed that our countrymen were still hardly pressed. Fifteen miles lay before the men, through a well-wooded country, traversed by an unmacadamized road, and heavy from recent rain. The dinners, then, were left uncooked, the rivulet was crossed, and when, about 7 P.M., all had disembarked on the other side, the column started, led by a native guide. The force marched on for about eleven miles without seeing any traces of the enemy. A few minutes later, however, a body of horsemen appeared in front of the advancing column, but before they could be fired at they had galloped off. It was now 11 o'clock, and the moon went down. Still hopeful and confident, the column pressed on till within a mile of Arah, no enemy in sight. Here Captain Dunbar called in the skirmishers, and moved on in column of march. He suspected nothing, when, suddenly, as the column was marching along the length of a dense mango-grove on the right of the road, the grove was lighted up by a tremendous volley poured into the long flank of the column, whilst almost simultaneously a smaller volley from a group of trees in front struck down the leading files. Captain Dunbar and several officers were shot dead at the first discharge; the enemy was invisible; the firing was taken up from the other flank, and renewed from the quarters whence it had first proceeded. The Europeans, in their white summer clothing,

He is surprised by the rebels.

Book VII. Chapter II.

1857. July 29.

were splendid marks for the enemy. The confusion consequent upon the surprise was terrible; the men were bewildered, and there was no one to give the command. The natural consequences ensued. On recovering from their surprise the men formed into groups and began to fire wildly in all directions often, possibly, on each other.

It is hard to say how many minutes this fatal disorder lasted, but at last the only possible mode of restoring order was resorted to. An officer managed to find a bugler, and, taking him to an enclosed field at a short distance from the grove, sounded the "assembly." The men promptly rallied round him. They were fortunate enough to discover in this field a disused and half-empty tank, the hollows of which would suffice to protect them to a certain extent against the enemy's fire. From this the firing was kept up, returned, however, with interest. The white clothing of our men still operated greatly to their disadvantage, whilst the sepoys, in a state of semi-nudity, fired from behind trees and walls.

Under these difficult circumstances the surviving officers held a council of war. They felt that with their dispirited and diminished numbers it would be impossible to reach Arah; that they would be fortunate if they could fall back upon the Sôn. They resolved, then, to commence a retrograde movement as soon as the not then distant dawn should permit them to find the road.

The retreat.

As soon as it was daylight the men formed up in order, and marched out on the Arah road. But the enemy had been as vigilant as they. Every

1857. July 30.

point in their route—the ditches, the jungles, the houses—had been occupied in force. The British force marched straight onwards, returning, in a desultory manner, the fire which was poured upon them, but intent only on reaching the Sôn. The power of driving back the enemy was denied to them by the fact that no enemy was in sight. They were sheltered behind the trees, the copses, the bushes, the ditches, and the jungle. Occasionally, indeed, maddened by the sight of their comrades falling around them, the men constituting by accident the rear-guard formed up, faced about, and tried to charge. But there was no enemy to receive the charge. Five or six thousand men, the revolted sepoys and levies of Kúnwar Singh, kept themselves under the shelter offered by the natural obstacles of the country.

Confusion accompanying it.

At last, after losing many of their comrades, the main body of the British force reached the banks of the rivulet, to cross which the previous night they had found boats ready to their hand. The boats were still there. During the night, however, the water had run down, and of all the boats two only were floating. These were promptly seized by the men in advance and pushed off. Then ensued a scene which it is impossible to paint in living words. It was a scene to which the imagination alone could do justice. There were the stranded boats on the bank of the river, the defeated soldiers rushing at them to push them further into the stream, the musket fire from the victorious sepoys, the cries of the wounded and dying, the disorder and confusion

Book VII. Chapter II.

1857. July 30.

naturally associated with a military disaster. It was a scene to call forth all that was manly and heroic, all that was mean and selfish. But whilst the first-named qualities were markedly visible, the latter were conspicuous only by their absence.

The difficulties already enumerated were added to by the fact that some of the boats caught fire. The losses the British troops here sustained probably exceeded those they had suffered during the retreat. Order was impossible. To push a boat into the stream, to climb into it, to help others in, was the aim of every man's exertions. But when boats would not be moved the chance of drowning was preferred to the tender mercies of the sepóys. Many stripped and rushed in, until at last the majority of the survivors found themselves in safety on the opposite bank.*

The survivors reach Dánápúr.

When the remains of the party mustered there, it was found that out of four hundred and thirteen men, only fifty had not been hit, and out of

* Many acts of daring were performed during the retreat and crossing. Mr. Ross Mangles, of the Civil Service, one of the volunteers, supported and helped along for five miles of the retreat a wounded soldier of the 37th, who, but for that support, would have been left to die. For this act Mr. Ross Mangles received the Victoria Cross. Another of the volunteers, Mr. M'Donell, of the Civil Service, received the same distinction for cutting the lashings of one of the boats, full of men, amid a storm of bullets, to which he was exposed from the opposite bank. Private Dempsey and another man of the 10th carried one of their officers, Ensign Erskine, who had been mortally wounded, for five miles to the boats. Lieutenant Ingelby, who had volunteered to command the Sikhs, was the last man to leave the shore. He plunged into the water, and was shot in the act of crossing. These are a few amongst the many instances which occurred of combined courage and humanity.

Book VII. Chapter II.

1857. July 30.

fifteen officers only three were unwounded. Those survivors made their way sadly and disconsolately to the steamer. They were then conveyed back to Dánápúr.

There the European population were awaiting their return in triumphant expectation. The possibility of disaster had not crossed a single mind. But when, as the steamer approached, no signs of life on board were visible, when the very captain and his subordinates seemed cheerless, and the silence was the silence of the grave, it began to be felt that, at the least, our losses had been heavy. It was not, however, until the steamer had moored off the hospital that the full truth was realised, that the conviction rushed to the mind of every Englishman in Dánápúr, not only that our troops had suffered an overwhelming catastrophe, but that the little garrison of Arah was irremediably lost.*

The gallantry of the Arah garrison.

The Englishmen garrisoning Mr. Boyle's little house at that place had, then, rightly interpreted the reason for the gradual lessening of the sound of volley-firing which had reached their ears at midnight on the 29th. Even if they had had any doubts these would have been removed by the arrival under their walls of a wounded Sikh, a member of the relieving force, who had managed to crawl to the house to tell the story of the disaster. The intelligence was black indeed, but its only effect on the hearts of the gallant members of the garrison was to steel them to resist to the bitter end. They at least believed in their coun-

* Mr. Tayler's *Patna Crisis*.

Book VII. Chapter II.

1857. July 30.

trymen. The story of the "leaguer of Arah" had spread, they were well aware, as far as the means of communication would admit. Many detachments of Europeans were passing up country. By whom these detachments were commanded they knew not. But they did know that the several commanders were Englishmen, and they felt confident that amongst the Englishmen in authority to whom the story of their plight might be conveyed, there would be at least one who, bound though he might be by the red tape of regulations, would yet laugh at responsibility when he should learn that his countrymen were in danger; who would possess the brain to conceive and the nerve to carry out a plan for their relief. They judged rightly; and yet they were fortunate, for it is not every day that nature brings to maturity the mould of a Vincent Eyre.

The rebels renew their attack.

Meanwhile the sepoys returned to Arah, red with the slaughter of our countrymen. If their victory had not increased the courage which now, as before, recoiled from an assault in masses on the besieged mansion, it had yet had the effect of stimulating their inventive powers. At one time they attempted to smoke out the garrison. With this object they collected and heaped up during the night, beneath the walls of the house, a large quantity of combustibles, and surmounting these with chillies—the raw material of the famous red pepper of India—ignited the mass. The effect would have been most serious had the wind only favoured the enemy; but the element was against them, and before it had injured the garrison, the

Book VII. Chapter II.

1857. July 31.

pungent smoke was blown towards the hostile encampment. The same wind saved the garrison likewise from the putrid smell emanating from the rotting carcases of the horses, belonging to the garrison, which had been shot at the commencement of the siege. Mining was then attempted, but Mr. Wake met this device by a countermine. The gun raised to the roof of the larger house occasionally caused injury to a weak place in the beleaguered castle; but Mr. Wake and Mr. Boyle were there, and in a short time the place was made twice as strong as before.

The supplies of the garrison begin to fail.

After all these measures had failed, it seemed as though the garrison would be more likely to suffer from a deficiency of supplies than from the enemy's attacks. And, in truth, on the third day the supply of water began to run short. With unremitting vigour, however, the garrison within twelve hours had dug a well of eighteen feet by four. Four sheep rewarded one of their attempts at sallying out for supplies. The earth excavated from the well was used to strengthen the works on the roof. Cartridges were made from the powder which Mr. Boyle had been careful to store, and bullets were cast from the lead which he had laid in. Every means that energy could do, that skill could devise, and that valour could attempt, were successfully resorted to by that daring garrison, ably directed by Mr. Wake, Mr. Boyle, and Mr. Colvin.

But resources limited in extent must, sooner or later, come to an end. But for succour of an effective character the garrison would have been

Book VII. Chapter II. 1857. August.

eventually forced—not to surrender—the possibility of such a catastrophe never formed part of their calculations—but to endeavour to force their way to some ford on the river Sôn. Happily the necessity to have recourse to so desperate a chance was spared them. On the morning of the 2nd of August, just one week after they had been shut up in their improvised fortress, a great commotion amongst the enemy gave warning that something very unusual was taking place. The hostile fire slackened early, and almost ceased during the day. But few of the sepoys showed themselves. Suddenly, towards the afternoon the sound of a distant cannonade reached the ear. Minute succeeded minute, and yet the sound seemed neither to advance nor to recede. All at once it ceased altogether. Some hours later and the absolute discontinuance of the fire of the besiegers gave to the garrison a sure forecast of the actual state of affairs. A sally made by some of them after darkness had set in discovered the positions of the enemy abandoned; his guns unguarded; a canvassed tube filled with gunpowder lying unused close to the mine which had reached the foundations of their fortress. It was clear then to the tried and gallant men who had so successfully defended themselves against enormous odds, that a deliverer had driven away their enemies, and that before many hours they would be able to render honour to the name of him who had so nobly dared to rescue them.

August 2.

They are relieved.

Vincent Eyre.

Who was that deliverer? Amongst the many detachments which left Calcutta during the month

1857. August 2.

of July was one commanded by Major Vincent Eyre, of the Bengal Artillery. The detachment consisted of a company of European gunners, and a horse-battery of six guns. Major Eyre was an officer possessing natural ability improved by study, great determination, a clear head, and a lofty sense of duty. He had had great experience of men, had mastered all the details of his profession, was fit for any employment, but, like Dumouriez, he had reached the prime of life before the opportunity arrived which was to show the stuff that was in him. He had served during the first Afghánistán war, and had been one of those who had been selected by the British General as hostages* to be made over to Mahomed Akbar

His previous career.

* A little episode in Eyre's history at this period deserves to be recorded. On a previous occasion, the Afghán chiefs had required four married officers with their wives and children as hostages. Certain officers, of whom Eyre was one, were invited by the General, by an official circular, to undertake this risk. The following were the replies as given by Lady Sale in her journal:—"Lieutenant Eyre said, if it was to be productive of great good he would stay with his wife and child. The others all refused to risk the safety of their families. One said he would rather put a pistol to his wife's head, and shoot her; and another, that his wife should only be taken at the point of the bayonet; for himself he was ready to perform any duty imposed on him." On this incident the "Naval and Military Gazette" of the day thus commented:—"Channing, in his eloquent and philosophic analysis of the character of Napoleon, has felicitously defined three orders of greatness, in the last of which he assigns a place to the great conqueror of Europe. Following the spirit of that great thinker, we cannot but recognise in Lieutenant Eyre's noble reply a higher tone of feeling than can be traced in the answers of either of his gallant comrades. Therefore, while we may award to the latter niches in the same order with Napoleon, our acquiescence in the sentiments of Dr. Channing leads as to hail in Lieutenant Eyre's conduct on this

Book VII. Chapter II.

1857. August 2.

Khán. Subsequently he had been appointed by Lord Ellenborough to raise and to command a company of artillery for the newly formed Gwáliár Contingent. In 1855, Eyre had visited Europe. On his return to India, early in 1857, he had been sent to command a horse field-battery in British Barmá. Recalled thence with his battery, when the eyes of the Government of India were being opened to the gravity of the situation, Eyre arrived in Calcutta on the 14th of June. There he was kept for several days in a state of uncertainty, terminated only by his being ordered to leave with his battery in a steamer and flat, on the 10th of July, for Alláhábád.

July 25.

Steaming from Calcutta, on that date, Eyre arrived off Dánápúr on the afternoon of the 25th of July. Learning from a gentleman who had ventured in a small boat from the shore the catastrophe of that day, Eyre landed at 6 P.M., to offer his services to Major-General Lloyd. At his desire he disembarked three guns for the service of the Major-General until those sent after the mutineers should return,—an event which happened the same evening.

Arrives at Baksar.

Re-embarking his guns the following morning Eyre proceeded up the Ganges towards Baksar. On reaching that place at noon, on the 28th, Eyre was informed that the three revolted

occasion the lineaments of that *first* order—moral greatness—through which the soul defies all peril, reposes an unfaltering trust in God in the darkest hour, and is ever ready to be offered on the altar of his country, or of mankind." The reader will not be slow to recognise the same lineaments of that first order in the conduct of Major Eyre on the occasion I am now recording.

Dánápúr regiments were advancing by way of Arah, with the apparent intention of crossing the Ganges above Baksar, and that they had actually sent forward a party to secure the necessary number of boats. This information decided Eyre to detain the steamer and flat at Baksar to afford time to one of the detachments, which he believed to be steaming up behind him, to come up.

Book VII. Chapter II.

1857. July 28.

It must be borne in mind that Baksar was the head-quarters of a valuable Government stud, and that thirty miles above it lies Gházípúr, where was a branch of the same stud. There were no troops at Baksar, but Gházípúr was garrisoned by a strong native regiment held in check by only one weak company of the 78th Highlanders. Noting the importance of preventing the passage of the river by the mutinous sepoys, and observing no signs of the advance of the detachments he believed to be on their way, Eyre, on the morning of the 29th, hastened up with his battery to Gházípúr, landed two of his guns and his only subaltern for the protection of the place, and taking on board in their stead twenty-five men of the 78th Highlanders, returned that night to Baksar.

Resolves to attempt the relief of Arah.

On reaching Baksar, Eyre discovered to his intense satisfaction that one of the detachments he had expected, consisting of 160 men of the 5th Fusiliers, commanded by Captain L'Estrange, had arrived off that place. Information leading him to be confident that our countrymen were still holding out at Arah, Eyre at once despatched a note to L'Estrange, proposing to join forces for

Book VII. Chapter II.

1857. July 29.

an immediate attempt to relieve that station. L'Estrange promptly replied in the affirmative, stipulating only that Major Eyre should send him a written order to that effect, and should take upon himself the entire responsibility.

Assumes great responsibilities.

Eyre did not hesitate a moment. He despatched at once an official letter to L'Estrange, directing him to place himself and his men at his disposal. He took upon himself the further responsibility of requiring the captains of the steamers to place themselves unreservedly under his orders.

Early on the morning of the 30th, the guns and troops were disembarked, and arrangements were made for a march to Arah, about forty-eight miles to the eastward. At the same time one of the steamers was despatched to Major-General Lloyd with a letter informing him of the intended movement, and inviting his co-operation—for at that time Eyre was ignorant, not only of the defeat of Dunbar's force, but of the fact that any force had been sent to Arah.* The field

Strength of his force.

* Major Eyre's letter was dated the 30th. It reached Dánápúr that night. It elicited from Major-General Lloyd the opinion, dated midnight on the 30th, that "the advance from Baxar towards Arra would have been useful had the attack on the rebels succeeded; as it is, the Buxar force is too weak to venture far from Buxar, and it should occupy that place till further communication is sent from Dinapore." Two letters from the Assistant Adjutant-General of the division, both dated the 31st, and despatched by the same steamer, informed Eyre of the disaster at Arah; threw upon his own judgment and discretion the course he should adopt; warned him against expecting any co-operation from the Dánápúr side; and advised the utmost caution. A letter dated the day following reiterated the same arguments. Major Eyre did not receive these letters till after he had left Baksar.

rce thus extemporised consisted of forty artillery menand three guns, one hundred and fifty-four men of the 5th Fusiliers, six officers, including Major Eyre, two assistant surgeons, and eighteen volunteers, mostly mounted, of whom three were officers, one a veterinary surgeon, and one the joint magistrate of Gházípúr.* The twenty-five Highlanders, whose presence might at any time be necessary at Gházípúr, were left behind at Baksar, with orders to take the first opportunity of returning to their station. Eyre appointed as his staff officer Captain Hastings, an officer whose acquaintance he had made only two days before, but by whose energy and enthusiastic support he had been greatly impressed. Much required to be done. There were no horses for the guns, and bullocks from the plough had to be impressed. Carts for the reserve ammunition and commissariat supplies had to be secured. In this work Major Eyre found an able and willing coadjutor in Mr. Bax,† the district magistrate. This gentleman likewise used successfully his influence to borrow from the Dúmrao Rájá four elephants for the conveyance of tents and bedding.

Book VII. Chapter II.

1857. July 30.

At 5 o'clock in the afternoon, however, all preparations had been completed, and the column

Sets out.

* The names of the officers were; of the Artillery, Major Eyre and Assistant Surgeon Eleson; of the 5th Fusiliers, Captains L'Estrange and Scott, Ensigns Lewis, Oldfield, Mason, Assistant Surgeon Thornton; of the volunteers, Lieutenant Wild, 40th Regiment, Native Infantry; Captain the Hon. G. P. Hastings, Lieutenant Jackson, and Veterinary Surgeon Liddell; the Civil Magistrate was Mr. Bax.

† Now Mr. Bax Ironside.

Book VII. Chapter II.

1857. July 30.

set out. But the roads were very heavy from recent rain, and the bullocks, unused to drag guns and heavily laden carts, not only moved slowly, but required frequent halts to enable them to move at all. Owing to the delays thus enforced, the day broke before the first encamping ground was reached.

July 31.

Brief was the halt made here. The column pushed on after a short and hurried meal. When about twelve miles from Baksar a mounted scout was descried. Pursued, wounded, and taken prisoner, he proved to be a free lance in the service of Kúnwar Singh. As the presence of this man proved that the enemy was on the alert, Eyre pushed on as rapidly as he could, and did not halt for repose till he had reached Shahpúr, twenty-eight miles from Baxar.

First hears of Dunbar's defeat.

Whilst encamped at this place the tidings were brought to Eyre of the defeat and slaughter of Captain Dunbar's party. Here, too, he had further proof of the vigilance of the enemy, many of whose scouts were discovered. Eyre halted the early part of the day to refresh the cattle, but eager to rescue the garrison and to restore the *prestige* of our arms, he set out at 2 o'clock in the afternoon of the 1st, having now but twenty-two miles to traverse. After marching four miles, the column was checked by finding that the bridge over the nullah at Balaotí had been cut through and was impassable for guns and carts. In an hour, however, the mischief was sufficiently repaired, and the force pressed on to the village of Gújrájganj, on the further side of which it

August 1.

Presses on.

Book VII. Chapter II.

1857. August 2.

bivouacked for the night, posting a strong guard to protect the bridge over the nullah near it, and which Eyre had been delighted to find uninjured.

The mutineers come to meet him.

At daybreak the following morning (2nd of August) the force resumed its march. It had not, however, cleared a mile beyond its camping-ground before bugle-notes were heard sounding the "assembly" in a wood which bounded the view about a mile ahead, and through which lay the direct road to Arah. The road between the position occupied at the moment by our men and the wood was bounded on either side by inundated paddy fields. Eyre at once halted to reconnoitre. The enemy now began to show themselves in great force, and not content with occupying the wood in front, to send out large bodies on either flank with the evident object of surrounding the Europeans. This movement on their part decided Eyre. Judging, and rightly judging, that this double flank movement must weaken the enemy's centre, he boldly pushed forward his men in skirmishing order, his three guns opening out to the front and on either flank. Under the pressure of this fire, the enemy abandoned his flank movement, and fell back on the position in front. It was the object of Eyre to force this. He, therefore, massed his three guns, and opened a concentrated fire on the enemy's centre. This had the effect of driving them from the direct path. Eyre then rapidly pushed on his guns, covering their advance by a continuous fire from the Enfield rifles of his infantry, and succeeded in making way through the wood before the enemy

Eyre attacks them.

Book VII. Chapter II. — 1857. August 2.

could again close his divided wings. Emerging from the wood the road became an elevated causeway, bounded on either side by inundated rice-fields, across which the baffled enemy could only open a distant fire. Their intentions thus frustrated, the sepoys hurried round to oppose the advancing force at Bíbíganj, a village about two miles ahead, and situated on the opposite side of a river spanned by a bridge, which they had destroyed, and the approaches to which they had covered by breastworks.

The battle.

After driving the enemy from the wood, Eyre pushed on. When, however, within a quarter of a mile of the village of Bíbíganj he halted to refresh the men and cattle whilst he should reconnoitre the position. Finding that the bridge had been destroyed, that the direct approaches to the river had been covered by extensive earthworks, and that the sepoys were occupying in force the houses in the village, Eyre, unable through his scouts to find a ford, determined to make a flank movement to the nearest point of the railway embankment, distant about a mile, and along which there was a direct road to Arah. He endeavoured to mask this movement by the fire of his guns which opened on the village, whilst the infantry and carts pushed forward in the new direction. No sooner, however, did the enemy discover this manœuvre, than they hastened in great numbers to intercept the force at the angle of a thick wood which abutted on the embankment, and which it was necessary that Eyre should pass.

It was clear that the enemy would reach the wood first. But to increase the difficulties in the way of Eyre, they detached a portion of their force, the irregular levies of Kúnwar Singh, to harass his rear. They did this with such effect that when the British reached the wood they found it strongly occupied by the enemy, who opened at once from behind the trees a most galling fire. Eyre's position was now becoming critical. He must carry the wood or be lost. He halted his troops, formed them into skirmishing order, and opened fire from his infantry and artillery. But the numbers of the enemy and the cover afforded by the trees gave them a great advantage. During the hour which this combat lasted, the enemy twice charged our guns, exposed by the necessity of keeping the infantry in skirmishing order, but each time they were driven back by discharges of grape. At the end of the hour, Captain Hastings brought word to Eyre, who, having no subaltern, was compelled to remain with the guns, that the Fusiliers were losing ground, and that the position was becoming critical. Eyre upon this resolved to solve the question with the bayonet, and despatched Hastings with an order to L'Estrange to that effect. This order was promptly executed. The men hastily closing, rushed forward with a cheer—cleared the deep stream—here confined within narrow limits—at a bound, and charged impetuously an enemy twenty times as numerous as themselves. The enemy, taken completely aback, did not await the onslaught. They gave way

Severity of the fight.

Eyre orders a bayonet-charge, which decides it.

Book VII. Chapter II. 1857. August 2.

in the utmost disorder; the guns opened out on the retreating masses, and in a few minutes not a man of them remained to oppose the passage of the force.

An open road skirting the railway to within four miles of Arah was now available. Eyre marched along it. A little before nightfall, however, he came upon an impassable torrent. This forced him to halt. But he spent the night in endeavouring to bridge the torrent by casting into the stream large piles of bricks collected there by the railway engineers. In this way the stream was narrowed sufficiently to allow the construction across it of a rude sort of bridge formed from country carts. Over this, in the early morning, the infantry, guns, and baggage marched, and in little more than an hour afterwards the relief of the garrison of Arah was an accomplished fact. The sepoys, after their crushing defeat, had hastily abandoned their position in Mr. Boyle's larger house, and packing up their spoils, had fled precipitately to the jungle stronghold of their leader, Kúnwar Singh, at Jagdíspúr. Then it was that the gallant band, led with such skill and such daring courage, by the civilians Wake and Colvin, and by the engineer, Vicars Boyle—three names ever to be revered by Englishmen—discovered what manner of man he was who, serving a Government which up to that time had judged the conduct of its servants mainly by results, had assumed the responsibility of turning from his ordered course, of turning others from their ordered course, to endeavour, with a force

Relief of Arah. August 3.

The rebels flee to Jagdíspúr.

inferior in infantry by more than one-half to that which had already been ingloriously beaten back, to rescue his countrymen from destruction, to save Bihár and India from an impending great calamity.

Vincent Eyre and William Tayler.

To return to Patná. If the effect of the revolt of the Dánápúr sepoys, the mutiny of the 12th Irregular Cavalry, and the defeat of Dunbar's force, had been to neutralize all the prudent measures taken up to that time by the Commissioner of the Patná Division, the effect of Eyre's victory was to restore the confidence which the three events alluded to had so severely shaken. In taking, then, a comprehensive glance at the province of Bihár at this particular moment, we see, standing out from the mass, two prominent figures in whose presence all the others, the garrison of Arah alone excepted, are completely effaced. These two figures are Mr. Tayler and Major Eyre. In spite of unparalleled difficulties Mr. Tayler had, up to the 25th of July, saved Bihár. The Government of India and Major-General Lloyd then suddenly stepping in, neutralised to a great extent his stupendous exertions, and allowed the province to drift to the very verge of destruction. Major Eyre, dropping, as it were, from the clouds, warded off that impending destruction. Those who had caused the danger were thus blotted out from the public view. The wisdom and daring of Mr. Tayler, the energy and determination of Major Eyre, had atoned for the feebleness and timidity of the leaders who did not guide.

Book VII. Chapter II.

1857. July.

The interval at Patná.

But there was an intervening period which, for the right understanding of the subsequent action of the Governments of India and of Bengal, it is necessary that I should notice. I mean the period which elapsed between the mutiny of the native troops at Dánápúr and Sigaolí and the relief of Arah by Major Eyre.

The mutiny of the native troops had been an event to try to the utmost Mr. Tayler's hold on the province of which he was pro-consul. He had heard the Major-General commanding the division talking seriously of intrenching himself at Dánápúr. There was no assistance, then, to be looked for from that quarter. In the other direction, his right-hand man, Major Holmes, had been murdered by his own soldiers, and to those soldiers, about five hundred in number, the lives of the Europeans and the treasuries all over the province, might at any moment fall a prey. We have seen how Mr. Tayler behaved under these almost desperate circumstances; how he had posted to Major-General Lloyd to implore that officer to send out at once a force to attack the rebels. It certainly was not Mr. Tayler's fault that the force despatched at his earnest instigation should have been badly commanded and disgracefully beaten.

Enormous difficulties of Mr. Tayler's position.

But the fact that that force was disgracefully beaten added enormously to the difficulties of Mr. Tayler's position. The chances that Arah would almost immediately fall seemed reduced to a certainty. What could fifteen Europeans and fifty Sikhs effect against six thousand trained

Book VII. Chapter II.

1857. July.

sepoys and a large body of irregular troops?* Granted even—in itself, if Eyre had been beaten, an impossible assumption, for the rebels would then have captured the guns necessary for their purpose—that the position at Arah was impregnable, the supplies of food and of powder were very limited. But for Major Eyre, the fears of every one in the province regarding the Arah garrison must have been speedily realised; and it was not given to Mr. Tayler more than to any one else to feel assured that amid the detachments steaming up the Ganges one would certainly be commanded by the very man for the occasion, by the Dumouriez, who, in the silence and solitude of Gwáliár, had trained himself to be prepared for any emergency. The defeat of Captain Dunbar's force, then, seemed to leave the lives and the treasuries of Bihár more than ever at the absolute mercy of the revolted soldiery.

Great responsibilities devolving upon him.

Now, for those lives and for those treasuries, Mr. Tayler was responsible to the Government of which he was in Bihár the representative. The danger was great, the emergency was unparalleled. The rebel army led, as was known, by a powerful and influential landowner, flushed with victory, and provided to a certain extent with guns which had been exhumed from that landowner's estate, was awaiting only the fall of Arah to overrun the

* Amongst the sepoys slain in the battle, Major Eyre found men of nine different regiments, a sufficient proof that the three revolted Dáná-púr regiments had been largely reinforced from other quarters.

Book VII. Chapter II.

1857. July.

province. The recent defeat had reduced the Dánápúr garrison to absolute inaction.*

Rumours from the district were rife to the effect that the Dúmraon Rájá, whose estates extended along the line of road from Arah to Baksar, had joined or was about to join the rebels in Patná, the local police were distrusted, the Sikhs were for the most part employed on guard duties; very few even of them were available for any purpose outside the station.

Is devoid of the means to defend his extended line.

In four out of the five districts the means of defence were even less. These districts, as already stated, were known under the names of Sháhábád, Gayá, Sáran, Tirhút, and Champáran. Arah, the capital of the district of Sháhábád, was virtually in the possession of the rebels; at Gayá, also, the chief station of its district, there were indeed one hundred Sikhs and forty-five European soldiers; Mozaffarpúr, the chief station of Tirhút, was undefended, whilst Chaprá and Mótíhárí, the capitals respectively of the districts of Sáran and Champáran, had been abandoned by the European officials in consequence of the pressure of the mutineers.

It was at Gayá and Mozaffarpúr, then, that the greatest danger was to be apprehended. The position of these stations rendered them peculiarly liable to attack. They were exposed to the first

* On the 31st of July, the Assistant Adjutant-General of the Dánápúr division, in a letter to Major Eyre, warned that officer that he "must not depend upon the co-operation of a force from Dánápúr, of which the present amount of troops here does not admit."

brunt of the fury of the mutineers, and they had no sufficient means to resist them.

It must always be remembered that, at the period of which I am writing, the fall of Arah was considered certain. Equally certain, that a catastrophe of that nature would be promptly followed by a rising of all the disaffected through Bihár. The question which the Commissioner of Patná had to solve, then, was this: whether he should trust to the seemingly impossible chance of Arah being relieved, and, in that case, risk the lives of the officers under his orders, and the treasure under their charge; or, whether he should prepare himself to meet the coming danger, by drawing in his too widely extended line, and massing his forces in a central position.

The question he had to solve.

Had Mr. Tayler been a timid or a vain-glorious man, he would have shrunk from the responsibility of withdrawing his officers from the positions assigned to them by the Government. But being cool and resolute, ready to assume responsibility when the public weal was endangered, and endowed with a remarkably clear vision, Mr. Tayler adopted the sensible course of directing the officials at Gayá and Mozaffarpúr to retire upon the central position of Patná.

Mr. Tayler draws in his extended line.

Mr. Tayler well knew that, serving a Government which judged only by results, and which had already displayed a desire to judge him harshly, the responsibility which he was thus taking upon himself was enormous. But with the knowledge which he possessed, that Gayá was filled with men waiting only their opportunity

Book VII. Chapter II. 1857. July.

to rise; that the jail there alone contained eight hundred prisoners ready to commit any enormity; that the fall of Arah would certainly prove the signal for an attack on Gayá, he felt that but one course was possible, and that course he adopted.

The order to the officials at Gayá and Mozaffarpúr authorised them to withdraw their establishments to Patná, bringing with them the coin in the treasury, unless by doing so their personal safety should be endangered.*

July 31.

This order was transmitted on the 31st of July, after Mr. Tayler had become cognisant of the disaster which had befallen Captain Dunbar's expedition.

Results at Mozaffarpúr.

Mr. Tayler's order was acted upon with the best results at Mozaffarpúr. The residents there, utterly unprotected, and endangered further by the presence of a detachment of the 12th Irregular Cavalry, had been very apprehensive of a rising, and had some days before vainly implored Major-General Lloyd to detach a few European soldiers for their protection. They, therefore, hailed Mr. Tayler's order as their sheet-anchor. Having no troops to form an escort, they were

* The purport of Mr. Tayler's order could not be mistaken. It was clear that, in the presence of danger of an attack from an overwhelming body, with which their small force should be unable to cope, Mr. Tayler took upon himself the responsibility of saving the lives of his subordinates, even at the risk of abandoning the money, if the attack should take place, or if, in the opinion of his subordinates, it should be so imminent as not to admit of taking the usual measures for removing the treasure. In a word he relieved his subordinates of the responsibility of uselessly sacrificing their lives in attempting to defend money-bags which they could not save.

unable to take the public money with them. They left it, therefore, in the treasury, and moved upon Patná. During their absence the detachment of the 12th revolted, and attacked the public buildings. The rebels were, however, driven away by the native officials and the police, who encouraged by the wealthy and influential Hindu traders and bankers of the place, the safety of whose property depended on the maintenance of British authority, remained loyal to the hand that fed them. When, a few days later, the European officials returned to the station, they found that order had been maintained in all the public buildings, and that the mutineers, baffled in their attempts upon the treasury, had vented their fury upon one or two private houses.

Book VII. Chapter II.

1857. August.

At Gayá.

Mr. Alonzo Money.

The case was far different at Gayá. The magistrate of that district was Mr. Alonzo Money. This gentleman had, three days before, recorded his opinion that, whilst nothing was to be feared from the townspeople, two causes of apprehension yet existed, viz., the inroad of any large number of the Dánápúr mutineers, and the approach of the 5th Irregular Cavalry. In any case he declared his intention to defend the station and the treasure to the utmost.

Two days subsequently to the despatch of this letter Captain Dunbar's detachment was surprised and beaten by the mutineers. Mr. Money received a letter informing him of this catastrophe the following day; but the messenger who brought that letter conveyed to him likewise an order from his Commissioner, Mr. Tayler, to fall

Book VII. Chapter II.

1857. August.

back with the European residents and troops upon Patná, bringing with him the treasure, unless by so doing the personal safety of the European residents should be endangered.*

Mr. Money resolves to abandon the Government treasure.

On receiving these instructions Mr. Money summoned the European civil officers of the station to advise him as to the course he should follow. Unfortunately timid counsels prevailed, and there was no Tayler present to override them. In vain did some of the residents entreat Mr. Money to remain at the station till carts could be procured to convey the treasure. He would not. But, acting as he considered the emergency required, he decided to obey that portion of Mr. Tayler's order which directed a retirement on Patná,—but to abandon the treasure.

The abandonment not warranted by circumstances.

No sufficient explanation has ever yet been afforded as to this extraordinary abandonment. The station was not then threatened. Mr. Money had previously recorded his conviction that the forty-five Europeans, the hundred Sikhs, and the new police at his disposal, were more than sufficient to ward off danger on the part of the townspeople.† A company of the 64th Regiment was within a few miles of the place. Mr. Tayler's order had been written, Mr. Money could not fail to see, solely with reference to

* "Everything," wrote Mr. Tayler, "must now be sacrificed to holding the country, and the occupation of a central position."

† Mr. Money's words, dated 28th of July, were: "There is nothing, however, to be apprehended from the townspeople. They are surrounded by a new and strong police, and have a wholesome dread of the forty-five English, and one hundred Sikhs."

danger to be apprehended from without—to the inevitable consequences of the fall of Arah. The instructions not to abandon the treasure unless the personal safety of the Europeans should be endangered, would justify its abandonment in case an attack should be made upon that treasure by irresistible force. It certainly conveyed no authority to abandon the treasure when it was yet unthreatened, when no danger was to be apprehended from the townspeople, before any attempt had been made to remove it, and when a sufficient body of troops to escort it was at hand.

He sets out.

However, Mr. Money, in consultation with the members of the station he had summoned, arrived, after due deliberation, at this decision. He and they and their escort started at 6 o'clock that very evening, leaving behind them a jail filled with prisoners, and eighty thousand pounds of Government money.

Some idea of the un-English character of this step would seem at a very early period of the retreat to have struck one of the members of the party. This was Mr. Hollings, of the opium department. As this gentleman rode further and further from Gayá the conviction continued to gain strength in his mind that he and his fellow-countrymen were committing a very disgraceful act. At last he could bear it no longer. He rode up to Mr. Money and imparted to him his doubts and his misgivings.

Mr. Money was the officer directly serving under the Commissioner of Patná, and the re-

Book VII. Chapter II.

1857. August.

sponsibility of the retreat from Gayá, however much he may have acted upon the opinions of others, really lay with him. He had moved off the troops and the other residents, leaving behind him the Government money. But, now, the arguments of Mr. Hollings seemed to convince him that in so acting he had acted wrongly. Instead, however, of ordering back the troops—an act which lay entirely within his competence—Mr. Money determined to return to Gayá with Mr. Hollings, leaving the troops and the others to pursue their way.

He repents and returns.

No greater condemnation of the part he had taken in leaving the station could be pronounced than this thus passed by Mr. Money upon himself. His return, too, would appear, at first glance, a very Quixotic proceeding. If the money could not be saved, and the station could not be maintained, when Mr. Money had under his orders a force of one hundred and fifty Europeans and Sikhs, what could he expect to accomplish when aided solely by Mr. Hollings?

Remarks on Mr. Money's vacillation.

But Mr. Money after all risked but little. He was well aware that within easy call of Gayá there was a detachment of the 64th Regiment, and almost his first act after his return was to summon that detachment to join him. The question might perhaps be asked, why he had not summoned it before he abandoned the station?

Summons a detachment of the 64th Regiment.

Mr. Money found the station still quiet, but he was by no means at his ease. He distrusted the men who surrounded him. The distrust, however, did not inspire him with prudence. The following morning he showed his hand to every native official by openly burning the Government stamped paper, thus proving to the natives of Gayá that he had returned solely to baulk them of their anticipated plunder.

Book VII. Chapter II.

1857. August 1.

Fortunately for Mr. Money before any open manifestation of the public discontent had taken place the company of the 64th returned (2nd of August). Mr. Money then feeling himself strong, collected carts upon which to load the treasure. On the 4th the treasure was loaded, and sent off under the guard of the 64th detachment. Mr. Money intended to accompany the party, but returning to his own house to save a few things of value he was suddenly startled by hearing the yells of the prisoners whom the native station guards had just then let loose from the jail. Mr. Money had but just time to mount his horse, fortunately kept saddled, and to join the detachment.

The question had arisen as to the direction which the convoy should take. Had Mr. Money decided to march upon Patná, he would yet, though in a clumsy and vacillating manner, have obeyed the instructions he had received from his official superior. But he would appear to have been misled by false reports as to the danger of traversing the short distance which lay between Gayá and that station. He decided, therefore, to move the Europeans, so urgently required in the north-west, from the field of action, and to undertake the far longer journey to Calcutta.* The

Resolves to proceed to Calcutta.

* Mr. Money reported to Government: "The next day (August 3), brought a letter to Captain Thompson" (com-

Book VII. Chapter II.

1857. August 4.

detachment, after repulsing outside Gayá the hap-hazard onslaught of the released prisoners, reached Calcutta unmolested.

Mr. Money's conduct from first to last inexplicable.

It is clear from the above plain story that whilst the conduct of Mr. Tayler in directing a general concentration of his subordinates on Patná, in the face of the blow delivered at British *prestige* on the banks of the Sôn, was marked by a statesman-like prudence and a thorough comprehension of the vital interests at stake, the action of Mr. Alonzo Money was dictated by a vacillating spirit, and by an unstable and impulsive nature. It is clear that, if Mr. Alonzo Money had carried out literally the orders of his official superior, though he might have gained no sensational triumph, he would have brought the treasure from Gayá safely into Patná. Indeed it may be confidently asserted that, in saving the treasure even as he did save it, he carried out, though in a style peculiarly his own, Mr. Tayler's orders. To himself, as a free agent, history will accord no peculiar merit. He imperilled the success of his superior's schemes by abandoning the treasure when he quitted the station, in the face of the

manding the company of the 64th), "written by an officer at Dinapore of his own corps. It contained these words in pencil, 'For God's sake look out. The 8th N. I. mutineers have marched upon Gya, they say, with one gun.' The news of martial law proclaimed in all the Bahar districts reached us the same morning. I called another council, and told Captain Thompson he was now the principal authority in the district. I gave him my opinion that, encumbered with treasure, we were too weak to run the risk of meeting so large a body of mutineers, and recommended falling back on the Grand Trunk Road." In such a case, the opinion of the chief civil officer was naturally decisive.

Book VII. Chapter II. 1857. August.

orders he had received to bring it with him if he could do so without endangering the lives of his coadjutors; he imperilled the success of his superior's schemes by returning with one companion to the station, after having advisedly denuded it of the European and Sikh troops; and, finally, he disobeyed his superior's orders and risked the whole policy of the Government by taking down the treasure to Calcutta, instead of moving it to the adjoining station of Patná. Fortune greatly befriended him; for Fortune changed a gross dereliction of duty, a disobedience to orders which would have subjected a soldier to a court-martial —into a sensational triumph almost unparalleled. For a very brief space, and in the eyes of a very small, though a very influential body of men, Mr. Alonzo Money became the hero of Bihár.*

Is wonderfully favoured by Fortune.

Let us see now how it was that he became so.

The Government of India and the Government of Bengal had been terribly frightened by the story of the successful revolt of the Dánápúr sepoys, and of the defeat of Captain Dunbar's detachment. The Government of India, mistaking severity for vigour, showed the extent of their terror by at once directing that their agent—the man upon whom they had cast the responsibility properly belonging to themselves—that Major-General Lloyd should be tried by a court-martial. That Government had their scape-goat handy. Mr. Halliday, representing the Government of Bengal, was in a different position. He had, in-

* For his conduct on this occasion, Mr. Money was made a Companion of the Bath.

Book VII. Chapter II.

1857. August.

deed, a score to settle with Mr. Tayler, because Mr. Tayler had maintained a bold and resolute front, and had preserved order in his province by measures not altogether approved of by the Lieutenant-Governor. But Mr. Tayler had been too successful to be touched. He had saved Patná. To remove him now, when Bihár apparently was at the mercy of the victorious mutineers, was not to be thought of—even by Mr. Halliday.

Mr. Halliday before Eyre's victory.

After.

Suddenly, however, the scene changed. A God-like mortal shone through the mist, dispersed the black cloud, annihilated the revolted sepoys, removed all apprehension at once and for ever regarding the safety of Bihár, and left it free to Mr. Halliday to exercise to the fullest extent his undoubted right of patronage—and of revenge.

Major Eyre virtually reconquered lost Bihár. He restored the province to the position in which Mr. Tayler, unaided, had maintained it, until the Government of India and Major-General Lloyd had contrived to plunge it into danger. But in the short interval the Gayá episode had occurred. Whilst Arah was yet trembling on the verge of destruction, Mr. Tayler had issued the withdrawal order. Eyre saved Arah. But before the results of Eyre's great feat of arms had become known, Mr. Alonzo Money, first disobeying then half obeying the directions of his Commissioner, was, by his vacillating and impulsive action, converting a plain act of duty into a sensational drama, of which he, for a few brief moments, was the star-bespangled hero.

After.

For to Calcutta, immediately after the news of

Book VII. Chapter II. 1857. August.

Eyre's great triumph, came, in a distorted and inaccurate shape, the intelligence of Tayler's withdrawal order. The danger was now over; the tears in the council-chamber of Belvedere* were dried up; a feverish exaltation followed. It was necessary that some proof should be given that energy had not died out in Bengal. Mr. Tayler's withdrawal order furnished the opportunity. Forgetting, or choosing not to remember, his transcendent services, the fact that he had never despaired of the safety of his division, that he had baffled the counsels of the mutineers, and had suppressed, unaided, the rising of Patná; that he had been the rock on which every hope in Bihár had rested; that he had cheered the despairing, stimulated the wavering, roused to action even the faint heart of the soldier; forgetting, or choosing not to remember, these great achievements, the Government of Bengal, acting in concert with the Government of India, seized upon his withdrawal order to dismiss Mr. Tayler from his post, to consign the saviour of Bihár, in the very morning dawn of the triumph which he had prepared, to signal and unmerited disgrace.

Dismisses from his post the man who saved Bihár.

The Government of Bengal added insult to injury. Not content with suppressing the fact that Mr. Tayler had coupled with the order for the withdrawal of the officials from Gayá a direction that they should bring with them the treasure under their charge, unless by so doing their personal safety should be endangered, Mr. Halliday did not scruple to charge with being actuated by

* The seat of the Lieutenant-Governor of Bengal.

Book VII. Chapter II.

1857. August.

panic* the man whose manly bearing had been throughout an example to the whole of India. It would be difficult to produce, in the annals of official persecution, rife as they are with perversions of truth, a statement more gratuitous.†

* Mr. Halliday wrote on the 5th of August: "It appears from a letter just received from Mr. Tayler, that, whilst apparently under the influence of a panic, he has ordered the officials at all the stations in his division to abandon their posts and fall back on Dinapore. * * * * Under these circumstances I have determined at once to remove Mr. Tayler from his appointment of Commissioner of Patna." It was on Mr. Halliday's report that Mr. Tayler was subsequently described by the Governor-General as "showing a great want of calmness and firmness"; as "issuing an order quite beyond his competency"; as "interfering with the military authorities." Mr. Halliday subsequently "explained" officially, that "panic was apparent on the face of Mr. Tayler's order, and specially from his urgent and reiterated advice, if not order, to Major Eyre, not to advance to the relief which saved Arah." With respect to this last charge it may be as well to state, once for all, that Mr. Tayler never addressed Major Eyre on the subject of the advance on Arah. What he did do was simply this. On the evening of the day on which Mr. Tayler learned the defeat of Captain Dunbar and his detachment of upwards of 400 men, he received a letter from Mr. Bax, the magistrate with Major Eyre, informing him that Eyre at the head of 150 men was about to attempt the task in which Dunbar had failed, and asking his opinion. Mr. Tayler thereupon wrote to Mr. Bax, telling him of Dunbar's defeat, and expressing his opinion that it would be prudent if Major Eyre were to drop down in his steamer to Dánápúr, take up reinforcements there, and advance thence on Arah. Mr. Tayler did not even send this letter to Mr. Bax. He sent it *open* to Major-General Lloyd, that the General might forward it with such instructions as he might think fit to give. Who will deny that in thus expressing his opinion Mr. Tayler performed only a clear and imperative duty?

† Sir John Kaye has thus ably summarised the arguments on this point:—"On the whole, it appears to me, on mature consideration, that the orders issued by Mr. Tayler were not of such a character as to merit the condemnation which Government passed upon them. It is not to be questioned that up to the time

Book VII. Chapter II. 1857. August.

But the fiat had gone forth. Mr. William Tayler was dismissed from his post. His career of the mutiny of the Dinapore regiments, the whole bearing of the Patna Commissioner was manly to a point of manliness not often excelled in those troubled times. He had exhorted all his countrymen to cling steadfastly to their posts. He had rebuked those who had betrayed their fears by deserting their stations. His measures had been bold; his conduct had been courageous; his policy had been severely repressive. If he had erred, assuredly his errors had not leaned to the side of weakness. He was one of the last men in the service to strike his colours, save under the compulsion of a great necessity. But when the Dinapore regiments broke into rebellion—when the European troops, on whom he had relied, proved themselves to be incapable of repressing mutiny on the spot, or overtaking it with swift retribution—when it was known that thousands of insurgent Sepoys were over-running the country, and that the country, in the language of the day, was "up"—that some of the chief members of the territorial aristocracy had risen against the domination of the English, and that the predatory classes, including swarms of released convicts from the gaols, were waging deadly war against property and life—when he saw that all these things were against us, and there seemed to be no hope left that the scattered handfuls of Englishmen at the out-stations could escape utter destruction, he deemed it his duty to revoke the orders which he had issued in more auspicious times, and to call into Patna such of our English establishments as had not already been swept away by the rebellion or escaped without official recall. In doing this he generously took upon himself the responsibility of withdrawal, and absolved all the officers under him from any blame which might descend upon them for deserting their stations without the sanction of superior authority. It was not doubted that if there had been any reasonable ground of hope that these little assemblies of Englishmen could hold their own, that they could save their lives and the property of Government by defending their posts, it would have been better that the effort should be made. But their destruction would have been a greater calamity to the State than their surrender. It was impossible to overvalue the worth of European life at that time, and the deaths of so many Englishmen would have been a greater triumph and a greater encouragement to the enemy than their flight. It was the hour of our greatest

Book VII. Chapter II. 1857. August.

in the Indian Civil Service was ruined by one stroke of the pen.

And yet this man had accomplished as much as any individual man to save India in her great danger. He had done more than Mr. Halliday, who recalled him; more than the Government which supported Mr. Halliday. With a courage as true and a resolution as undaunted as that which he showed when dealing with the Patná mutineers, Mr. Tayler has struggled since, he is struggling still, for the reversal of the unjust censure which blighted his career. Subsequent events have singularly justified the action which, at the time, was so unpalatable to Mr. Halliday. Mr. Tayler's denunciation of the Wáhábí leaders, treated as a fable by his superiors, has been upheld to the full by the discoveries of recent years.* It has

darkness and our sorest need. We know now how Wake and Boyle and Colvin and their comrades in the 'little house' held the enemy in check, and how Vincent Eyre taught both the Sepoy mutineers and the Shahabad insurgents that there was still terrible vitality in our English troops. Of this William Tayler knew nothing. But he had palpably before him the fact of Dunbar's disaster, and he believed that nothing could save the little garrison at Arrah. The probabilities at the time were that the Dinapore regiments, with Kower Singh and his followers, having done their work in that direction, would move, flushed with conquest and gorged with plunder, upon Gya and other stations, carrying destruction with them wheresoever they might go. What the Commissioner then did was what had been done and what was being done by other authorities, civil and military, in other parts of the country; it was held to be sound policy to draw in our scattered outposts to some central point of safety where the enemy might be defied. In this I can perceive no appearance of panic. If Tayler had not acted thus, and evil had befallen the Christian people under his charge, he would have been condemned with a far severer condemnation for so fatal an omission."

* *Vide* Appendix A.

been abundantly shown that, to his energetic action alone was it due that Patná escaped a terrible disaster. The suppressed words of the withdrawal order have been published to the world, and the charge of panic has been recognized everywhere as untrue.

Recantation of Mr. Tayler's judges.

It is a curious and a very remarkable fact that of the members of the Council of the Governor-General who supported at the time Mr. Halliday's action, two have, in later years, expressed their regret that they acted hastily and on incorrect information. "Time," wrote, in 1868, one of the most prominent amongst them, Mr. Dorin, "time has shown that he (Mr. Halliday) was wrong and that you were right."* Another, the then Military Member of Council, General Sir John Low, G.C.B., thus, in 1867, recorded his opinion: "I well remember my having, as a Member of Lord Canning's Council, concurred with his Lordship in the censure which he passed upon your conduct . . . but it has since been proved—*incontestably* proved—that the data on which that decision was based were quite incorrect! . . . I sincerely believe that your skilful and vigorous management of the disaffected population of Patná was of *immense* value to the Government of India,

* "I can, of course, have no sort of objection to repeat," wrote, in 1868, the gentleman who was Lord Canning's private secretary in 1857, "what is a very *sincere conviction*, that if Lord Canning had seen the papers which you have now to produce, and been made acquainted with the subsequent progress of events, he would most likely have changed his opinion as to the treatment you have experienced; and if he had changed his opinion, a man of his noble character would have been forward to say so, and to do you justice."

Book VII. Chapter II. — 1857. August.

and that in the last few months of your Commissionership, commencing with the arrest of the three Wáhábí conspirators, and the disarming of the greater portion of the inhabitants of Patná city, your services were of more vital importance to the public interests than those of many officers, both civil and military, during the whole period of their Indian career, in less critical times, who have been rewarded—and justly rewarded—by honours from the Queen; while your services, by an extraordinary combination of unlucky circumstances, have hitherto been overlooked." It is not less remarkable that three ex-Governors and two ex-Lieutenant Governors of the presidencies and provinces of India have recorded similar opinions, whilst one gentleman, decorated for his distinguished conduct in the province of which Mr. Tayler was the pro-consul, has not hesitated to inform him that until Mr. Tayler should be rewarded for the conduct which saved the province, it would be too painful for him "to wear in your presence the decoration which I have so gratefully received from Her Majesty."

Justice still denied him.

His comrades in India, then, and the public generally, have rendered to Mr. William Tayler the justice which is still denied him by the Government which he served so truly and with such signal success. The ban of official displeasure still blights his declining years. Whilst his rival, decorated by the Crown, has been awarded a seat in the Council of India, he "who was right when that rival was wrong," still remains in the cold shade of official neglect. Although with a

Book VII. Chapter II.

1857. August.

Can the lapse of time sanction a wrong?

pertinacity which is the result of conscious rectitude Mr. Tayler has pressed upon each succeeding Secretary of State his claims for redress, that redress has still been, up to the latest date, denied him. It seems to be considered that the lapse of years sanctions a wrong, should that wrong in the interval remain unatoned for. We English not only boast of our justice, but, in the haughtiness of our insular natures, we are apt to reproach the French for the manner in which they treated the great men of their nation who strove unsuccessfully to build up a French empire in India. We taunt them with having sent Lally to the block, and allowed Dupleix to die in misery and in want. But, looking at our treatment of Mr. William Tayler, can we say that, even with the advantages which a century of civilization has given us, our hands are more clean? This man saved a province. In saving that province it is possible that he saved with it districts outside his own. Yet is he not, I ask, looking at the treatment he received, is he not entitled to use, if not the very words, yet the sense of the very words employed by Dupleix in 1764: "I have sacrificed," wrote three months before he died that greatest of Indo-French administrators, "I have sacrificed my youth, my fortune, my life, to enrich my nation in Asia . . . . My services are treated as fables; my demand is denounced as ridiculous. I am treated as the vilest of mankind." To this day the treatment of Dupleix is a lasting stain on French administration. I most fervently hope, for the credit of my country, that our children and our children's

Book VII. Chapter II. — 1857. August.

children may not be forced to blush for a similar stain resting on the annals of England; that the French may never have it in their power to return the reproach which our historians have not been slow to cast at them. In the history of the mutiny there is no story which appeals more to the admiration than the story of this man guiding, almost unaided, a province through the storm, training his crew and keeping down the foe, whilst yet both hands were at the wheel, and in the end steering his tossed vessel into the harbour of safety. Character, courage, tact, clearness of vision, firmness of brain, were in him alike conspicuous. May it never descend to posterity that in the councils of England services so distinguished were powerless in the presence of intrigue!

BOOK VII.

CHAPTER III.

Arah after the relief.

We left Major Eyre enjoying, on the early morn of the 3rd of August, the triumph of his decisive victory. It is difficult even to imagine a position more gratifying to a high-minded soldier than that which he then occupied. Of the dangers he had incurred in attempting the relief of Arah that to his life had been the least. He had risked his reputation as a soldier, his very commission as an officer; for he had turned aside without authority from his course. And now, he could scarcely exaggerate to himself the importance of the results of his daring. To have saved his fellow-countrymen was a great thing; but, for the interests of India it was greater still to have dealt a staggering blow at victorious rebellion, to have saved all Bihár from the fate which, but for him, would have overtaken Arah.

But even in that hour of triumph Eyre must have felt, and Eyre did feel, that his task was but half accomplished. A "staggering blow" may

Book VII. Chapter III.

1857. August 3.

baffle a murderous onslaught, but unless the recipient of it be thoroughly disabled a renewal of the attack is always possible. So reasoned Eyre. The rebels whom he had baulked of their prey were still strong enough to return. His very departure would invite them. He felt, then, that he must follow up his victory and pursue the sepoys to the stronghold of the great landowner whom they had recognised as their leader.

Eyre resolves to follow up the blow.

The task was not easy. The roads were reported to be almost impassable; the country surrounding the stronghold of Kúnwar Singh was described as inaccessible. But the events of the previous eight-and-forty hours had told their tale. The mental courage which had dared, the skill and gallantry which had carried to success, the march on Arah, had been marked and appreciated by the Englishmen who had followed Eyre. No men are more quick to discern noble qualities in a leader than the private soldier. It was a striking testimony to the hold which Eyre's conduct and character had taken on the minds of the men of the 5th Fusiliers, that when they heard that he was about to lead them across those impassable roads to an inaccessible stronghold, they were loud in their expressions of the confidence with which they would hail the order to move onwards.*

* In his report to Army Head-quarters, Captain L'Estrange, commanding the detachment of the 5th Fusiliers, after describing the reported difficulties of the march, added: "Under all the circumstances, a feeling of doubt, if not of apprehension, as to the success of our expedition might easily have pervaded troops less confident than ours were in the judgment, talent, and courage of our leader."

Book VII. Chapter III.

1857. August 3–7.

But before setting out on this expedition something yet remained to be done at Arah. The townspeople had unmistakeably sympathised with the revolted sepoys. Not a single voice had warned Captain Dunbar of the ambush into which he was leading his detachment. Some of the more prominent men of the city had even taken an active part against our countrymen. As a preliminary measure, then, Eyre disarmed the population. Men whose active aid on behalf of the rebels was indisputable were brought to trial. Throughout the district order was restored. At the same time Eyre communicated his intentions to the military authorities at Dánápúr, and solicited reinforcements of at least two hundred more European troops and a supply of ammunition. He took advantage, likewise, of the number of volunteers flocking to his camp, to organise a corps of European volunteer cavalry, the command of which he conferred upon Captain Jackson, of the Stud Department. His wounded he sent in to Dánápúr.

Receives reinforcements and sets out.

On the 8th of August Eyre was joined by two hundred men of the 10th Foot and five officers. Three days later a hundred of Rattray's Sikhs joined him. His total augmented force then consisted of three hundred and thirty European Infantry, thirty-six European Cavalry, one hundred and forty Sikhs, forty of whom were the Arah garrison commanded by Mr. Wake, and sixteen Volunteer Cavalry. With this force Eyre set out on the afternoon of the 11th, in the direction of Jagdíspúr, the hereditary stronghold of Kúnwar Singh.

August 11.

Book VII. Chapter III.

1857. August 11.

Kúnwar Singh.

Meanwhile the troops under the orders of Kúnwar Singh had to a great extent recovered heart. The halt of eight days duration made by Major Eyre at Arah had inspired them with the belief that no further advance was intended by the English, and that they would be left unmolested in their stronghold. Impressed with this idea, Kúnwar Singh detached small parties in the direction of Baksar, to feel their way and to intercept any small bodies of Europeans whom they might meet. In this they were partially successful, and this success would probably have incited their leader to make a little later a movement in force in the same direction. But Kúnwar Singh was well served by the country-people. He was informed, almost as soon as they arrived, of the reinforcements which reached Eyrc. He felt certain, then, as to the next move of the British force, and he resolved with the energy which formed so strong a feature of his character to meet it with his remaining available strength.

Calling in, then, all his detachments within reach he occupied, in considerable force, the village of Dálaor, about a mile and a half in advance of Jagdíspúr, and covered by a river. This village he caused to be entrenched. It was connected with Jagdíspúr by a very thick jungle, with the intricacies of which, however, his men were well acquainted.

His faulty tactics.

Not content with occupying a position presenting difficulties to an assailant, and capable of being in a great measure masked, Kúnwar Singh was so ill-advised as to send a strong body of cavalry and infantry across the river to occupy a village, Tolá Náráinpúr, on its left bank. It was this cardinal error which made his defeat certain. He had in the field altogether about five thousand two hundred men, of whom twelve hundred were sepoys.

Book VII. Chapter III.

1857. August 11.

Eyre's victory and capture of Jagdíspúr.

Eyre had advanced towards Jagdíspúr the afternoon of the 11th. He marched eight miles, passing over *en route* his late battle-field, and encamped for the night on the banks of the Gaggar rivulet. Resuming his march with the early dawn he halted at 9 o'clock to refresh his men. At 10 o'clock he again advanced, and in half-an-hour detected the presence of the enemy in Tolá Náráinpúr. He at once sent forward his skirmishers, supported by a fire of grape. This fire forced the enemy in and about the village to discover themselves. Eyre then sent at them with the bayonet the detachment of the 10th, eager to avenge their comrades. The main body of the enemy stood their ground with great obstinacy, but were in the end driven across the river. Meanwhile the 5th Fusiliers, assisted by a field howitzer, had held in check the enemy's left, consisting of irregulars, horse and foot. These now simultaneously gave way. The river was crossed by our men, and an impetuous attack on the intrenchments of Dálaor placed that village almost immediately in their power.

August 12.

Still there lay a mile and a half of thick jungle to be traversed. Eyre gave the enemy no time to recover themselves; but sending on his infantry in skirmishing order, forced his way through the

Book VII. Chapter III. — 1857. August 12.

thicket, driving the sepoys before him. In their retreat the enemy left behind them two of their guns. Completely disheartened by the continuous advance of our men they scarcely attempted to defend their leader's stronghold, but fled, taking Kúnwar Singh with them, in the direction of Sahasrám. The battle had begun at half-past 10 o'clock. At 1 o'clock Eyre and his force were in possession of Jagdíspúr. The enemy lost three hundred men. The loss of the British amounted to six wounded.

August 14.

On the morning of the 14th Eyre detached a force to Jataorá, about eight miles from Jagdíspúr, to beat up the quarters of Kúnwar Singh,—but the wily chieftain had had good information, and had retired early. The house he had occupied there was, however, destroyed. A similar fate befell the palace and other buildings, notably the property of rebels, at Jagdíspúr and in its vicinity.

The campaign terminated with the victory at Jagdíspúr. Two days after it had been achieved, the Assistant Adjutant-General of the Dánápúr division wrote to inform Eyre that Havelock, then

Is ordered to Alláhábád.

attempting to relieve Lakhnao, had been compelled to fall back; that the cry at Kánhpúr was still for troops; and that he and those under his command were required to join a force then being collected at Alláhábád.

Eyre had accomplished his mission. His work was done. The mutineers had been driven from Bihár. He and his gallant comrades were then not at all unwilling to proceed to the part of India for which they had originally been destined, and where they might hope to render fresh services to their country. Eyre, therefore, bade adieu to Arah on the 20th, and on the following day set out for Baksar *en route* for Alláhábád.* Book VII. Chapter III. 1857. August 20.

Meanwhile events had been occurring in Calcutta calculated greatly to increase the means at the disposal of the Government for the suppression of the revolt.

Sir James Outram.

On the 1st of August, Major-General Sir James Outram landed in Calcutta. The varied services of this distinguished officer at once marked him out for high command. The name of Outram had for years been a household word in India. A keen and successful sportsman, a quick-witted and energetic political officer, a hater and exposer of corruption, Outram had but recently figured as

* I may be pardoned for extracting in this place a summary of this three weeks campaign taken from an article on Sir Vincent Eyre which appeared in the *Calcutta Review* for April, 1867. "On August 21, the gallant little Arah field force was finally dispersed, having terminated its brief and adventurous career in a campaign of three weeks' duration, fruitful in important consequences to the Government of British India. When this force was first improvised by Eyre at Baksar, on his own responsibility, the entire province of Bihár was in open insurrection, having proclaimed Kúnwar Singh as their Rájá and ruler; the civilians of Arah were besieged by the mutinous regiments of Dánápúr without a hope of relief; our river communication between Bengal and the Upper Provinces was in danger of being interrupted—a danger which imperilled the very existence of Havelock's small isolated force in the Doáb; and Bengal itself showed symptoms of a general rising. What a change had Eyre's little campaign effected! Arah relieved; the Dánápúr mutineers twice defeated and dispersed; Kúnwar Singh in full flight to the north-west; the district of Shahábád restored to order and tranquillity; and the route of the Ganges open for the safe transit of our steamers and troops."

Book VII. Chapter III.

1857. August.

commander-in-chief of the expedition despatched in 1856 to the Persian Gulf. His success there had been prompt and complete. When, on the conclusion of peace with Persia, the regiments which had composed his expeditionary force had been detached rapidly to India, Sir James Outram had followed to Bombay. It would seem to have been the original intention of the Governor-General to re-employ him in the political post which had been bestowed upon him before the mutiny, that of agent to the Governor-General in Rájpútáná. The mutinies at Indúr, at Nasírábád, at Nímach, and the outbreaks in other parts of Central India had thrown that part of the country into disorder, and Lord Canning felt that a strong hand controlling a strong force would be required to re-establish authority. The state of the country, however, rendered it impossible for Sir James Outram to proceed alone from Bombay to his post in Rájpútáná; and he felt, moreover, that in the actual state of affairs his presence might be more useful to the Government in some other part of India. On arriving at Bombay, then, he at once telegraphed to the Governor-General for orders. Receiving no reply—for Lord Canning could not at the moment make up his mind—Outram cut the Gordian knot by steaming round to Calcutta. He arrived there, as already stated, on the 1st of August.

Meanwhile, Lord Canning had, on the 15th of July, determined to employ Sir James Outram in the command of an expeditionary force in Central India, and he telegraphed to Bombay to that effect. But again he changed his views, and resolved to use his services to restore order in the country between Patná and Kánhpúr. Sir James Outram's arrival in Calcutta on the 1st of August coincided then with the latest wishes of the Governor-General.

The reader must remember that, on the 1st day of August, the only information possessed by the Government regarding Bihár was that Captain Dunbar's detachment had been beaten, that Arah was besieged, that the grand trunk road was unsafe, and that the entire province might at any moment be lost to them. From Kánhpúr they had information that Havelock was about to cross the Ganges with his small force, and to march on Lakhnao. Having regard to the fact that an entire province was arrayed in arms against him, his attempt did not seem promising. Altogether the look-out on the 1st of August was gloomy in Calcutta.

Is appointed to command the force destined to relieve Lakhnao.

No sooner, then, had Sir James Outram landed, than Lord Canning felt that the man for the occasion had arrived. Four days later he appointed him to command the united Dánápúr and Kánhpúr divisions of the army, thus placing him in supreme military command of the country between the first of those stations and Lakhnao. Outram eagerly clutched at the offer. Like every true soldier, he was of opinion that "action, not counsel," was required. He started to assume his command the very day after he had been nominated to it, taking with him a mountain train of artillery, but no gunners to work it.

Book VII. Chapter III.

1857. August.

Mr. Grant is appointed to administer the central districts.

The day prior to Sir James Outram's nomination, Lord Canning, feeling the extreme inconvenience of leaving the civil divisions of Banáras, Alláhábád, Kánhpúr, and other outlying districts, without a supreme administrative officer to control them—the Lieutenant-Governor of the North-West Provinces being at the time shut up in A'gra—had given effect to a resolution at which he had arrived, to detach one of his councillors to Banáras to take up the lapsed authority in that part of India. His selection had fallen upon Mr. J. P. Grant. I have already alluded to this gentleman as the ablest member of the Council of the Governor-General. Mr. Grant was, indeed, a man of very remarkable ability. He had a clear and sound understanding, a quick and subtle brain, great independence, and great decision of character. If he had a fault it may have been that he did not always make sufficient allowance for men whose intellect was less vast and whose views were less sound than his own. He failed thus to rate at their full influence on the multitude opinions firmly advocated by others, but which he knew to be untenable. His prescience came thus to be mistaken for dogmatic assertion, his keen insight for conceit. But this slight defect, arising from want of European training, was overborne by the powerful intellect, the high and lofty ideas of one of the greatest members of the Indian Civil Service.

The despatch of an administrative officer of the first order to the civil districts north of Bengal had been further rendered advisable by the action of the Government of India at the very end of July. On the 31st of that month there appeared in the Official Gazette a resolution of the Governor-General in Council directing the course to be pursued in dealing with mutineers who might be captured or who might surrender to the authorities. This resolution was much criticised at the time, and in England as well as in India it was very generally condemned. After a lapse of twenty years it is, perhaps, possible to bring to its consideration a calm and unbiassed judgment.

Book VII. Chapter III.

1857. July 31.

Resolution in Council regarding the treatment of mutineers.

Its object.

The avowed object of the resolution was to prevent the civil officers of the country from hastily resorting to and carrying too far measures of severity against the revolted sepoys, some of whom might, possibly, have been unable to withstand the influence of their comrades; some might have endeavoured to protect their officers; some might have merely revolted without murdering their officers; and some might have simply taken their way to their homes on the general revolt of their regiment.

Its provisions

To carry out this object, it was ruled in the resolution, first, that no native officer or soldier belonging to a regiment which had not mutinied should be punished, even as a deserter, unless he were found with arms in his hand. Such men, it was directed, should be made over to the military authorities, or, when such a step were impossible, should be kept in prison pending the orders of Government.

The second section provided for native officers and soldiers, being mutineers or deserters, belong-

Book VII. Chapter III.

1857. July 31.

ing to regiments which had mutinied, but who had not murdered their officers. Such native officers and soldiers, when apprehended without arms in their possession, were to be sent to a certain fixed place, to be dealt with by the military authorities.

The third section dealt with mutineers or deserters who belonged to regiments which had killed a European officer, or who had committed some sanguinary outrage. Such offenders were to be judged by the civil power. In the event, however, of extenuating circumstances transpiring, the case was to be reported to the Government before the carrying out of the sentence.

These were the three principal provisions of the resolution. In the remaining portion of it Lord Canning dwelt very much upon the evil certain to arise by continuing to punish indiscriminately after a district or division had been brought into order, and after a sufficient impression had been made upon the rebellious and the disorderly.

Objections made to it at the time.

It was objected to this resolution that it was ill-timed; that, issued when the struggle was still undecided, when the enemy still held Dehli, when our countrymen were besieged in Lakhnao, on the morrow, as it were, of the massacres of Fathgarh and Kánhpúr, and whilst the fate of Bihár was trembling in the balance, it was calculated to encourage the rebels, to show them that, through fear of them, we were anxious to entice them back to their allegiance. It is possible that the strong dislike with which the resolution was regarded at the time was in a great measure attributable to

Book VII. Chapter III.

1857. July 31.

the want of confidence felt in the Government. Certainly, the provisions I have quoted were not only not objectionable, but the spirit in which they were conceived was worthy of the highest praise. They are not fairly liable to the condemnation that was passed upon them at the time. They do not condone mutiny or desertion. But—the public had no confidence in the Government. The order that, in certain circumstances, an appeal lay from the civil magistrate to the highest authority, roused suspicion. It was considered, moreover, that the very publication of such a resolution was a tacit rebuke to those who had carried out severe measures of retribution.

Objections combated.

Examining the order after a lapse of twenty years all the objections to it made at the time fade away. The provisions it contained are wise and statesman-like.

The disarming order.

Another measure contemplated by Lord Canning about this time filled to overflowing the measure of his unpopularity. The danger arising from allowing an entire population to carry arms had not been unremarked by the citizens of Calcutta. It was a danger obvious, and in many cases most pressing. On the 13th of July, then, the Grand Jury in their presentment suggested the disarming of the native population of Calcutta and its suburbs as a measure required for the preservation of peace and the prevention of crime. A disarming bill had for some time been under the consideration of the Government. The presentment of the Grand Jury stimulated their action regarding it. But the indignation of the

Book VII. Chapter III. — 1857. July 31.

Calcutta public was intense when it was found that the measure of the Government applied the order to disarm to Europeans as well as to natives.

Objections to it at the time.

It was in vain that it was pointed out that the act of the Government contained a proviso under which it was possible for any man to apply for a license to carry arms, and that it was not to be credited that such permission would be refused to an European. So profound was the mistrust of the Government that all argument was wasted. Again I have to record my conviction that the measure of the Government, accompanied by the proviso referred to, was a statesman-like measure. Any other, partial or one-sided in its limitations, would have been wrong in principle and might have been mischievous in action.

Lieutenant-Colonel G. M. Sherer.

Whilst in these terrible months of June and July the Government of India had had to encounter dangers at a distance from their own door, they were being preserved by the commanding officer of a native infantry regiment from a peril close at hand, and which, but for him, might have been serious indeed. The station of Jalpaigorí, about three hundred miles from the capital, and in the direct route to the station of Ɖarjíling, was garrisoned by the 73rd Regiment Native Infantry. The commanding officer was Lieutenant-Colonel G. M. Sherer. This officer had passed nearly the whole of his Indian career in the Stud Department. His knowledge of horses was profound. In managing the quadruped he had learned, too, how to deal with his master. Transferred, according to the orders then in force, on his promotion to a Lieutenant-Colonelcy, from the superintendence of the stud at Baksar to the command of a native infantry regiment, having in the intervening period of thirty years forgotten all his drill, he very soon showed his officers that great natural ability is universal in its practical application, and that, whatever be the sphere assigned to him wherein to labour, a really capable man will always come to the front.

Colonel Sherer had not been long in command of his regiment when the mutiny broke out. His position was full of peril. His men were, so to speak, masters of the situation. There were no Europeans within easy reach of them. There were, too, traitors in their ranks. But there were also men who still trusted to the fortune of the British. It must be remembered, moreover, that to this regiment the new cartridge, regarded by others as the symbol of the Christianising intentions of the Government, had not been served out. The station, likewise, was far from the high road. Still, rumours, detailed reports, letters, emissaries, found their way from time to time into the regimental lines. Alarm succeeded alarm. Still Sherer and his officers were calm. They maintained a careful watch over the movements of their companies. At last there could be no doubt but that mischief was intended. Four of the most influential men in the regiment were indicated to Sherer as the heads of a conspiracy which would inevitably break out that or the following night. Sherer had them seized and tried. They were condemned to death. The sen-

Book VII. Chapter III.

1857. July.

tence, however, required the confirmation of the Major-General commanding the Presidency Division. It reached him when all was *couleur de rose* at Bárrákpúr and at Calcutta. The hearts of the Major-General and of the Commander-in-Chief were merciful. An order was transmitted to Sherer to "dismiss the offenders from the service." Before this order could reach Sherer the horizon had darkened. The sepoys at Dánápúr had revolted; the Arah catastrophe had occurred. To temporize at such a crisis would be fatal. But Sherer had the order. He obeyed it—after his fashion. Commanding a parade for the following morning, he brought out the condemned sepoys and had them blown away from guns. The same day he wrote officially to the Major-General commanding the Presidency Division to inform him that, in obedience to his orders to dismiss the four condemned sepoys from the service, he had that morning dismissed them—from the muzzles of four loaded guns.*

Dismisses four mutineers—from the service.

This act of vigour had its effect. The rising was postponed. Two days later Eyre's victory deprived the disaffected of all hope of success, and Sherer, continuing a combined policy of watchfulness, conciliation, and firmness, brought his regiment safely through the crisis, their arms maintained, and their reputation unstained.†

Lord Elgin.

Very shortly after this episode, Lord Elgin, then the British Plenipotentiary in China, arrived

* I received these details from Sir George Sherer himself.

† Colonel Sherer was rewarded by receiving the order of a Knight Commander of the Star of India.

in Calcutta (8th of August). He was conveyed by H. M.'s ship *Shannon*, Captain William Peel, having on board three hundred marines and one hundred of H. M.'s 90th Regiment. Three days later, the consort of the *Shannon*, the *Pearl*, Captain Sotheby, brought besides her crew two hundred more men of the 90th. From that moment the arrival of reinforcements was continuous, and the country south of Alláhábád was for ever out of danger.

Book VII. Chapter III.

1857. August 8. Captain William Peel. Captain Sotheby.

But the arrival of the *Shannon* and the *Pearl* had a result more practical than the mere announcement that they had brought to Calcutta Lord Elgin and some three or four hundred soldiers would seem to imply. In the month of July, Major-General Thomas Ashburnham, who commanded the China expedition, and who had proceeded by way of Calcutta on his way to his destination, had written thence to Lord Canning to express his great desire to send him a naval brigade to keep open under all circumstances his communications with Alláhábád. In the same letter General Ashburnham had likewise expressed his conviction that Captain Peel would be a most admirable coadjutor in carrying to perfection a scheme of that nature. Lord Canning clutched at the idea thus propounded; Lord Elgin assented to it, and, as we have seen, he arrived at Calcutta on the 8th of August, prepared not only to give moral aid to the Government, but "to place Her Majesty's ships *Shannon* and *Pearl*, with their respective crews," at the disposal of Lord Canning.

The Naval Brigade.

Book VII. Chapter III.

1857. August 10.

Lord Canning, as I have said, clutched at the offer. On the 10th the two vessels were officially placed at his disposal. On the 18th Captain William Peel started for Allahábád with a naval brigade composed of four hundred men, six 68-pounders, two 24-pound howitzers, and two field pieces.

Arrival of Sir Colin Campbell.

I must chronicle one more important arrival, and then quit Calcutta for the scenes of turmoil and action. In the last week of July the new Commander-in-Chief, Sir Colin Campbell, arrived in Calcutta. Lord Canning had recommended that the post he came to fill should be bestowed upon Sir Patrick Grant. But the Prime Minister of the day, Lord Palmerston, strongly held the opinion enunciated by Sir James Outram, that to suppress the Indian Mutiny action rather than counsel was required in a General. He, therefore, selected a plain blunt soldier, and sent him to Calcutta to assume the supreme direction of military affairs in India. The selection was extremely popular with the army, for Sir Colin had served on the North-West frontier, and had won the confidence and affection of officers and men.

The men who preserved Mr. Beadon's line of six hundred miles.

Calcutta may now safely be quitted. Numerous reinforcements had made her secure. The crisis which had menaced Mr. Beadon's line of six hundred miles had been successfully surmounted. Many dangers had been overcome. Banáras had been threatened and restored to order; Alláhábád had been snatched from destruction; Patná, Dánápúr, and Bihár, after a terrible trial had been brought again under the ægis of British protection. Who had saved that line? Not the Supreme Government, for the action of the Government in refusing to disarm the native troops had fomented the disorder. Not the Local Governments—the one shut up in A'gra, the other hair-splitting in Calcutta. No,—four names indicate the men who saved that line to the British. North of Bihár, Mr. Frederic Gubbins, of the Civil Service, the judge who virtually administered the great Hindú city, and Colonel Neill, whose prompt and resolute action stamped out rebellion whenever and wherever it raised its head. South of Banáras, Mr. William Tayler and Major Eyre. These are names to be honoured,—these are the subordinates who won the battle; the untitled upholders of the honour, the glory, and the fair name of England. They were alike the heads that devised, the hands that executed. Associated for ever with theirs, too, in their undying glory, as supports who maintained the over-burdened structure, will be the names of those whose sphere of action, though confined, was of vital importance,—the names of the members of that Arah garrison, most fitly represented by their three leaders, by Wake, by Boyle, and by Colvin.

BOOK VIII.

CHAPTER I.

In the preceding chapters allusion has been made to the fact that the Lieutenant-Governor of the North-West Provinces had been debarred from the execution of his administrative functions by the circumstance that he was shut up in A'gra. It has now to be shown what constituted the North-West Provinces, who and what kind of man was the Lieutenant-Governor, and how it had come about that he had been forced to take refuge in the famous fortress which had been one of the glories of the Moghol rule.

The North-West Provinces.

The provinces, named before the annexation of the Panjáb in 1849, North-West, and continuing subsequently to bear that title, comprehended the country lying between the western part of Bihár, the eastern boundary of Rájpútáná and the Cis-Satlaj States, and the northern line of the provinces comprised in the Central Indian Agency. They touched the Himálayas, included Rohilkhand, and ran into the Central Provinces below Jhánsí.

Within their limits were the imperial cities of Dehlí and A'gra, the great Hindú city Banáras, the important station and fortress of Allábábád, the flourishing commercial centres of Mírzápúr and Kánhpúr. The rivers Ganges and Jamná rolled in majestic rivalry through their length. They were peopled by a race the majority of whom we had rescued from the sway of the Maráthás, and whose prosperity under our rule had enormously increased. Here, too, the descendants of the courtiers of Akbar and of Aurangzíb still continued to live, if not to flourish. For them, as for the landowners in Bihár, the action of our revenue system had been fatal. Their doom had been signalled when the Maráthá supplanted the Moghol. It had been pronounced when the Frank ousted the Maráthá.

Book VIII. Chapter I.

1857. May.

Benefits arising to the cultivators of the soil from British rule.

But the change which had been fatal to the descendants of the men who had gained their position at the Moghol court partly by the sword, but more often by intrigue, had been extremely beneficial to the toiling masses. From the time when Mahmúd of Ghazní had introduced the crescent as a sign of rule and domination in the country of the Hindús until the period when Lord Lake conquered the imperial city in 1803, the cultivators of the soil of the North-West Provinces had been in very deed hewers of wood and drawers of water. Gradually, under the fostering rule of the English they had been emancipated from this serfage, until, under the reign of Mr. Thomason, the immediate predecessor of the Lieutenant-Governor who ruled in 1857,

10

Book VIII. Chapter I.

1857. May.

they had attained a flourishing position; the rights of every village, and of every man in that village, being thoroughly understood and entirely respected.

Political arrangement of the North-West Provinces.

The government of the North-West was divided into eight commissionerships, those of Banáras, Alláhábád, Jabalpúr, Jhánsí, A'gra, Rohilkhand, Mírath, and Dehlí. The provinces were but poorly garrisoned by European troops. In fact, when the mutiny broke out there was but one European infantry regiment, and one battery, at A'gra. The only other European troops were at Mírath.

Mr. John Colvin.

The Lieutenant-Governor of the North-West Provinces was Mr. John Colvin. Mr. Colvin was a man of considerable ability; conscientious, painstaking, courteous, and amiable. He was animated by a thorough sense of duty, gave all his energies to the public service, and never spared himself. It is not too much to affirm that had his lot been cast in ordinary times his reputation as Lieutenant-Governor would have rivalled that of the most eminent of those who, before and subsequently, have held that office. But with all his ability, his experience of affairs, his devotion to duty, Mr. Colvin lacked that one quality, the possession of which is absolutely necessary to enable a man to buffet successfully against the storms of fortune. Mr. Colvin wanted, in a word, that iron firmness—that rare self-confidence—which enables a man to impress his will upon others. Supreme at A'gra, his was not sufficiently, during the mutiny, the directing mind. Surrounded by civilians of high standing, men of

Book VIII. Chapter I.

1857. May.

ability and of consideration in the service, but holding, and tenaciously holding, theories regarding the mutiny diverse from his, although differing widely amongst themselves, Mr. Colvin allowed himself to be swayed too much by the views of others. It often happened that the course he had proposed to follow was a wiser course than that which he ultimately pursued. Owing possibly to the fact that the circumstances of the time differed widely from those to which he had been accustomed he almost always renounced his own ideas, and accepted the opinions pressed upon him by one or other of his advisers. Yet,—the responsibility of every action fell upon him.

Mr. Colvin's earlier career.

It is possible that Mr. Colvin's earlier career was to a certain extent answerable for this defect in his character as a ruler in troublous times. He had been private secretary to Lord Auckland, when Lord Auckland was Governor-General of India. In all the arrangements which led to the Afghánistán war, with its delusive triumphs and its disastrous results, Mr. Colvin shared the responsibility with the Governor-General, of whom indeed he was believed to be the intimate adviser.* Up to the hour of the catastrophe he was jubilant regarding the success of the policy. But when the catastrophe did come, with its loss of human life, its lowering of British *prestige*, its humiliation

* Sir John Kaye states that Mr. Colvin was supposed to exercise over Lord Auckland, "an influence far greater than has been exercised by any officer in the same subordinate position."

Book VIII. Chapter I.

1857. May.

to the national arms, it was a blow sufficient to destroy the convictions of a life-time, to change a man's nature. It is probable that, thenceforward, Mr. Colvin became less inclined to trust entirely to his own opinion, more ready to accept the suggestions of others.

The Mírath mutiny a surprise to Mr. Colvin.

The disaffection displayed by the 19th Regiment of Native Infantry at Barhámpúr in the early part of the year, and the events at Bárrákpúr which followed, had not apparently been regarded by Mr. Colvin as indicative of any general plan of insurrection on the part of the native army. The rising at Mírath, then, on the 10th of May, took him entirely by surprise.

Mr. Colvin received intelligence of the Mírath

May 11.

outbreak on the 11th of May. Further information leading him to believe that the mutineers had sacked Dehlí and were marching on A'gra, he summoned a council of war. As the seat of the North-West Government A'gra was the residence of many notabilities. There were members of the Board of Revenue, judges of the Court of Appeal, a brigadier, colonels, majors, and officers of lower grades. The scientific corps were well represented. Besides these were commissioners, magistrates, civil servants of degrees covenanted and uncovenanted, a Roman Catholic bishop, and two Pro-

He summons a general council,

testant chaplains. The chiefs of this large society responded to Mr. Colvin's summons to what might be termed, without any decided misuse of its natural signification, a general council. Pro-

at which the opinions are discordant.

bably in the whole annals of the mutiny there never assembled a body of men whose opinions

Book VIII. Chapter I.

1857. May 11.

were so discordant, so distracted, so baseless of any fixed principle of action. Mr. Colvin himself was in favour of abandoning the station of A'gra and taking up a position within the fort. Indeed, he not only announced this as his intention, but intimated that he had already issued the order for the native regiments to evacuate the fort, that the Christian population might take refuge within its walls. Against this course of action many of those present, notably Mr. Harington—an ex-judge of the Court of Appeal, but just then nominated member of the Legislative Council of India—and Mr. Drummond, the magistrate, loudly protested. As to the actual policy to be followed there were nearly as many opinions as counsellors. The information that the mutineers were marching on A'gra—information proved that same evening to be untrue—clouded the intellects of many. At last, however, a definite decision was arrived at. It was resolved to show a bold front to the enemy, to secure the fortress by a detachment of Europeans, to raise a volunteer corps, cavalry and infantry, and to hold a general parade of the troops the following morning, when the Lieutenant-Governor should deliver an address to the European and native regiments.

Resolves to show a bold front.

The troops stationed at A'gra consisted of one battery of Bengal Artillery, the 3rd European Regiment,* the 44th and 67th Native Infantry. On the morning of the 14th,† these were brigaded

Harangues the Europeans,

* Now the 107th Foot.

† Mr. Colvin in his report to Government gives the date as the 13th; but that is evidently a mistake. The general council was held on the 13th.

Book VIII. Chapter I.

1857. May 14.

on their own ground. The Lieutenant-Governor, and the principal civil officers of the station were present. Mr. Colvin addressed the European soldiers first. He told them not to distrust their native fellow-soldiers, but with an inconsequence scarcely in keeping with his recommendation, added: "the rascals at Delhí have killed a clergyman's daughter, and if you have to meet them in the field, you will not forget this." He then turned to the sepoys. He told them that he fully trusted them, asked them to come forward if they had any complaints to make, and offered to discharge on the spot any man who might wish to leave his colours. "Prompted by their officers to cheer," records a civilian of high rank, who was present on the occasion,* "the sepoys set up a yell; they looked, however, with a devilish scowl at us all."

and the sepoys.

Mr. Colvin does not yet recognise the magnitude of the crisis;

That yell, and that "devilish scowl," should have opened the eyes of the Lieutenant-Governor. He might have read in the symptoms thus displayed that the sepoys of those two regiments, like the sepoys of all the other regiments of the Bengal army, were but watching their opportunity. There were not wanting at the elbow of the Lieutenant-Governor men animated by the conviction that the rebellious movement had been concerted, that the sepoys as a body were involved in it, that the time had passed by when phrases however neatly turned, and expressions of confidence however sonorous, could avail anything.

* *Notes on the Revolt of the North-West Provinces of India,* by Charles Raikes, Judge of the Sadder Court of Agra.

1857. May 14.

The Chief Engineer, Colonel Hugh Fraser, noting the signs of the times, had advised Mr. Colvin to distrust everybody and to recognise the emergency. In plain language he counselled a removal into the fort,—a removal not only of the treasure, the records, the women and children, but likewise of the Lieutenant-Governor and his staff. But Mr. Colvin, who but the previous morning had been led by his own instincts to order an identical action, had at this time fallen under the influence of other advisers. He saw not the significance of the "devilish scowls," and regarded not the counsel of the engineer. He reported to Government his confident expectation that quiet would be maintained at A'gra; his opinion, that it was not by shutting themselves up in forts that the British could maintain their power in India.

believes in the possibility of maintaining order.

But there was a potentate whose capital lay some seventy miles from A'gra who had taken a more accurate view of the situation. This was Mahárájá Jyají Rao Sindia, ruler of the Maráthá kingdom called generally after the name of its capital, Gwáliár.

Mahárájá Sindia.

Mahárájá Jyají Rao Sindia has afforded throughout his career a living example of the wisdom exercised by the paramount power in dealing generously with native princes. The history is remarkable. It happened in 1843, when the Mahárájá was a minor, that Gwáliár, worsted in a war which the intriguers who conducted its government had provoked, lay at the feet of the British. Many courses lay open to the then Governor-General, Lord Ellenborough. He might

Wise action of Lord Ellen-

Book VIII. Chapter I.

1857. May 14.

borough regarding Gwáliár in 1844.

annex it, as Lord Dalhousie, under precisely similar circumstances, did, six years later, annex the Panjáb. He might confiscate a portion of it, just as four years later Lord Hardinge acted with regard to Jálandhar. He might lay upon it a heavy contribution in the shape of money. But Lord Ellenborough was a prescient statesman. He did none of these things. On the contrary, he conceived that it might be possible by a generous treatment of the fallen State so to bind it to the British that it might become a source of strength to our empire. To the minor Mahárájá, of whose infancy his counsellors had taken advantage to provoke the war, Lord Ellenborough restored, then, the whole of his patrimony. But his army he disbanded. In place of it he raised another army, to be administered by British officers, but to be at the charge of the State of Gwáliár. He placed at the same time near the person of the Mahárájá a Resident, whose duty it should be to watch over and counsel the youthful monarch.

Excellent results of his policy.

This generous policy produced all the results which had been hoped for it by its author. The Mahárájá, as he grew up and studied the history of the past, recognised in the British Government the Suzerain to whom he was bound by considerations alike of gratitude and of interest. He resolved frankly to recognise their supremacy, and to take up the position assigned to him—that of being one of the main pillars of the British Empire of Hindústán. When, therefore, the Mírath revolt became known at Gwáliár, the

Sindia resolves to cast in his lot with the British.

Mahárájá unhesitatingly resolved to cast in his lot with his Suzerain. The very fact of his being a native of India had given him a more complete insight into the secret reasons which prompted the revolt than could be claimed by any European. He was conscious that the dominant power was about to encounter a shock, which would tax all their resources, and which might terminate fatally for them.

Book VIII Chapter 1

1857. May 14.

At the very time, then, when the Lieutenant-Governor of the North-West Provinces was congratulating himself, and was assuring the Supreme Government of his belief that the two native infantry regiments stationed at A'gra would remain quiescent, Sindia, well assured that the entire native army was undermined, was warning the political agent at his court that the disaffection was universal, and that the men of his own contingent would, sooner or later, follow the example of the regular army.

He recognises the gravity of the crisis.

The ideas which Mr. Colvin had apparently imbibed at this time regarding the mutiny had taken the shape of a conviction that, far from being caused by the spontaneous action of the sepoys, it was a movement prompted by the Court of Dehlí. He considered it, then, very important to enlist on the side of the British those races which, in former times, had been most antagonistic to the representative of the Moghol dynasty, and whose timely support might, at this critical moment, influence the sepoys. Of these there were two in close proximity to A'gra—the Maráthás represented by Gwáliár; the Játs, enthroned at Bha-

Mr. Colvin applies to Sindia and to Bharatpúr for aid,

Book VIII. Chapter I.

1857. May 14–20.

which is given.

ratpúr. To both of these, then, Mr. Colvin applied at once for material assistance. The replies were favourable. Sindia at once despatched to A'gra a battery of six guns, commanded by Captain Pearson, and Captain Alexander's regiment of cavalry,—followed, a little later, by Captain Burlton's regiment. On the part of Bharatpúr Captain Nixon was sent to occupy the station of Mathurá with a detachment of infantry.

But this timely assistance in no way retarded the quick approach of the evil which had been fore-shadowed.

News arrives of the revolt at Aligarh.

On the 21st news reached A'gra that the native troops at Aligarh had mutinied. By this revolt direct communication with Mírath was cut off. It deserves, therefore, to be recorded in full detail.

Aligarh.

The station of Aligarh lies on the grand trunk road, not quite midway between the cities of A'gra and Mírath, being distant about eighty miles from the latter, and fifty from the former. It possesses a bastioned fort, well capable of defence, and memorable in Indian history as having been the scene of the first of the many effective blows dealt by Lord Lake at the Maráthá power in 1803. In May 1857, the fort was not occupied, but the station was garrisoned by four companies of the 9th Regiment of Native Infantry—a regiment which bore a very high character, and which, it was pretty generally believed, would prove faithful, even should all the others mutiny.

Effect produced there by the Mírath revolt.

The events of the 10th of May, at Mírath, had naturally been reported at Aligarh; but the story had had no effect on the outward behaviour of the

1857. May 14–20.

men of the 9th. Rumours of disorder in the district having subsequently reached the commanding officer a detachment of the regiment was sent out to ascertain the truth. The detachment returned at the end of two days, having found the rumours greatly exaggerated. And although it was stated that as they marched through the town to the regimental parade-ground the butchers had endeavoured to work upon the minds of the sepoys and to induce them to revolt and shoot their officers, still the fact remained that they had not revolted, and that they had not shown the smallest sign of disaffection. On the contrary, both at that time and subsequently, the sepoys delivered up to their officers men who had entered their lines to seduce them from their allegiance.

Apparent calm attitude of the sepoys.

Incident of the Brahman.

It happened, however, that one of the men thus delivered over to justice was a Brahman who had acted as the agent of some villagers in the neighbourhood. This man had imagined a plot, whereby, under cover of the noise and excitement of a simulated marriage procession, the European officers might be murdered, and the money in the treasury, amounting to about £70,000, secured for the revolters. The Brahman, caught in the act, was tried by native officers, and condemned to be hanged on the evening of the same day, the 20th. On that evening the native troops were drawn up, and in their presence the sentence was read to the condemned prisoner. The latter was then taken to the gallows, the rope was adjusted, the cart was taken away. During the whole of

Book VIII. Chapter I.

1857. May 20.

The spark which ignited the powder.

these proceedings the sepoys had maintained their usual passive demeanour. Suddenly, however, one of their number, bolder than his comrades, stepped forth from the ranks, and pointing to the dangling corpse, exclaimed: "Behold a martyr to our religion!" This exclamation touched in the heart of the sepoys a chord which had till then lain dormant. As if struck by the wand of a magician, these men—who had passed the sentence and had assisted at the execution—broke out into open mutiny. They dismissed their officers, unharmed; but they compelled them and all other Europeans at the place to quit Aligarh.* They then plundered the treasury, opened the gates of the jail, and went off bodily to Dehlí.

Balandshahr.

This occurred on the 20th of May. There were detachments of the same regiment, the 9th Native Infantry, at Balandshahr, at Etáwá, and at Mainpúrí. To these stations information of the revolt at Aligarh, promptly conveyed, produced the natural result. At Balandshahr, the outbreak was attended by no violence. The sepoys simply plundered the treasury and went off. The case was different at Mainpúrí and at Etáwá.

Mainpúrí.

Mainpúrí lies seventy-one miles to the eastward of A'gra. The detachment of the 9th Native

* Amongst these were Lady Outram, wife of Sir James Outram, and their son, Mr. Francis Outram, of the Civil Service. Lady Outram succeeded in reaching A'gra in safety, and without molestation. Mr. Outram, and other Europeans, led by Mr. Watson, C.S., took the road to A'gra, escorted by a party of the cavalry of the Gwáliár Contingent. Their adventures belong to a part of this history yet to be related.

Infantry at this place was commanded by Lieutenant Crawford. Information of the revolt at Aligarh reached the station the evening of the 22nd. Mr. Power, the magistrate, who received it, at once consulted the Commissioner, Mr. Arthur Cocks, as to the course to be followed. These two gentlemen decided to send all the ladies and children into A′gra and meanwhile to march the sepoys out of the station in the direction of Bhaogaon. The detachment of non-combatants set off very early the following morning under charge of the assistant magistrate, Mr. J. N. Power. This gentleman escorted the ladies and children one stage. There he placed them under charge of a faithful Mahomedan who saw them safely into A′gra. Mr. J. N. Power, on their departure, returned to Mainpúrí.

Book VIII. Chapter I.

1857. May 22.

Mr. J. N. Power escorts the non-combatants towards A′gra, May 23.

and returns.

Meanwhile, the officers of the 9th Native Infantry, Lieutenants Crawford and de Kantzow, were endeavouring to induce their men to march out of the station. The sepoys set out, but on reaching the limits of their parade-ground, they refused to proceed further; and breaking out into mutiny, warned their officers with menaces to depart—some even going so far as to fire at them. In the confusion that followed the officers were separated from each other. De Kantzow dismounted, and Crawford, unable to see him for the tumult and believing he had been killed, galloped back to warn the civilians of the mutiny, and to announce his own intention of riding for A′gra.

The sepoys at Mainpúrí mutiny.

Crawford found assembled Mr. Arthur Cocks

Book VIII. Chapter I.

1857. May 23.

the Commissioner, Mr. Power the magistrate, Dr. Watson the civil surgeon, and Mr. Kellner a missionary. After a short consultation, Mr. Cocks, declaring that no one was bound under the circumstances to remain at Mainpúrí, started off.

Devotion of the two Powers, of Mr. Kellner, of Dr. Watson, three serjeants, and a clerk.

Mr. Kellner, Mr. Power, and his brother,—who just then returned from escorting the non-combatants,—refused, with a noble devotion to duty, notwithstanding the reports of musket-firing which reached them from the parade-ground, to quit the station. In this resolve they were joined by Dr. Watson, as well as by three serjeants of the Road and Canal Departments, Mitchell, Scott, and Montgomery, and by a clerk, Mr. Glone.

Loyalty of Rao Bhowání Singh.

The first cousin of the Rájá of Mainpúrí, Rao Bhowání Singh, with a small force of horse and foot, agreed at the same time to stand by Mr. Power.

Daring and presence of mind of de Kantzow.

Meanwhile, de Kantzow, dismounted, had been opposing to the mutinous sepoys a firm and courageous will. He implored them, he upbraided them, he threatened them. Muskets were levelled at him in vain. The courageous attitude of the solitary officer, endeavouring to recall to duty men whose hearts told them they were doing wrong, overbore for the moment physical force. Not, indeed, that he entirely mastered the sepoys. But they did not kill him. They still rushed on madly towards the treasury, bearing with them their earnestly gesticulating, madly imploring lieutenant. Arrived at the iron gates of the treasury de Kantzow made one last appeal. Turning suddenly from his own sepoys, he threw himself on the loyalty of the civil guard of thirty men, posted to protect the Government money. They responded; they rallied round him; the officials of the jail added their efforts; and for the first time since the actual outbreak on the parade-ground the torrent was stemmed.

Book VIII. Chapter I.

1857. May 23.

He checks the mutineers.

Even more,—it was stopped. Not, indeed, at the instant. De Kantzow, with a wisdom beyond his years, avoided precipitating a conflict. He forbade the civil guard to fire, but drew it up to oppose a resolute front to the halted sepoys, whilst with all the energy of an excited nature he again implored these not to add plunder and murder to mutiny. For three hours his arguments, backed by the physical efforts of the civil guard, kept the rebels at bay.

and keeps them at bay.

The iron gates to the last resisted all the efforts made to force them. It is possible that, unaided, de Kantzow might even have persuaded the mutineers to withdraw. But help, not in numbers but in influence greater than his own, brought about this coveted result. When almost exhausted by his efforts he was joined by Rao Bhowání Singh, deputed by the magistrate, Mr. Power.* The arguments of this gentleman added to those of de Kantzow were successful. The sepoys agreed to withdraw provided that the Rao should accompany them. He did this, and the Treasury was saved. The sepoys, after plunder-

Is opportunely joined by Rao Bhowání Singh.

They save the treasure.

* Mr. Power was anxious to join de Kantzow, but he was assured by that officer, in a few lines he managed to convey to Mr. Power, that the sepoys were yelling for his life, and that he, de Kantzow, was gradually quieting them.

Book VIII. Chapter I.

1857. May 23.

ing their lines and other buildings, left the station Their repulse and departure restored order and confidence throughout the city and district of Mainpúrí.

Lord Canning gracefully acknowledges the service rendered by de Kantzow.

The gallantry, the devotion, the cool daring of Lieutenant de Kantzow were not allowed to pass unnoticed by the Government. Lord Canning wrote to the young subaltern an autograph letter in which in vivid and touching language he described the impression which his conduct had made upon him. "Young in years," he added, "and at the outset of your career, you have given to your brother soldiers a noble example of courage, patience, good judgment, and temper, from which many might profit." None will deny that the encomium was well deserved; that an act such as that I have recorded merits to be treasured up in the archives of a nation's history!

It remains to be added that the revolted sepoys went off to Dehlí, and that de Kantzow, left by their departure without employment, was at once placed in command of a body of police for special service in the district.

Etáwá.

The scene at Etáwá was more tragic and bloody than that just recorded. Etáwá lies seventy-three miles south-east of A'gra, and about a hundred miles north-west of Kánhpúr. It was garrisoned by one company of the 9th Regiment of Native Infantry. The chief civil officer was Mr. Allan Hume, the magistrate and collector. The assistant magistrate was Mr. Daniell. On receiving intelligence of the events at Mírath and at Dehlí Mr. Hume had organised patrolling parties to watch

Mr. Hume organises

1857. May 16.

Patrolling parties.

the roads, to intercept, if possible, any small detached parties of mutineers, and at all risks to debar them free access to the station. On the night of the 16th of May the patrols fell in with, and brought in as prisoners, seven troopers of the 3rd Cavalry, a regiment which had mutinied. They had, however, omitted to deprive these men of their arms, and the troopers, brought face to face with the native infantry drawn up at the quarter-guard, suddenly levelled their carbines or drew their swords, and assaulted the European officers on duty. The guard instantly turned out, and in the *melée* that followed five of the mutineers were killed. Of the two who escaped one was shortly afterwards captured.

The want of caution displayed brings on the crisis.

Three days later, the patrols stopped at Jaswantnagar, ten miles from Etáwá, a large cart containing several revolted troopers, all belonging to the 3rd Cavalry, and well supplied with sabres, pistols, and carbines. This time the patrols attempted to disarm their captives; but attempting it without due precaution they paid dearly for their rashness. Pretending to deliver up their arms the troopers fell suddenly upon their captors and shot them down. Having done this they took up a position in a Hindú temple near at hand, small, but of great strength, the approach to which lay along a grove with walls on either side.

Mr. Hume and Mr. Daniell attempt to meet it,

Prompt intelligence of this untoward event was conveyed to Mr. Hume. That officer, accompanied by Mr. Daniell, proceeded to the spot, followed by some troopers and foot police. A glance at the

Book VIII. Chapter I.

1857. May 19.

temple showed Mr. Hume the strength of the position. The approach to it was thoroughly commanded by the carbines of the enemy. The inhabitants of the neighbouring village showed likewise a strong disposition to aid the troopers, for they not only opened communications with them, but sent them a supply of food and ammunition. To storm the temple by a front attack was dangerous, but it was the only possible course, unless the honour of the day were to be conceded to the troopers. This was not to be thought of, so Mr. Hume and Mr. Daniell, summoning the police to follow them, advanced boldly to the assault. But one man answered to their call. He was killed, Mr. Daniell was shot through the face, and Mr. Hume thought it then advisable to renounce an undertaking which never had a chance of success. Supporting his wounded friend, he gained his carriage, and returned to Etáwá. That night, the troopers, fearing lest a more formidable attack should be made upon them, evacuated their position.

but unsuccessfully.

The mutineers, however, retire.

The detachment at Etáwá, mutinies, May 23.

The fourth day subsequent to this event the detachment of the 9th Native Infantry at Etáwá mutinied. The ladies and children, accompanied by the civilian officers, and by some native officers who had remained staunch, retired in safety to Barpúra, a police station on the road to Gwáliár. Etáwá was sacked, the treasury was plundered, the prisoners were released from the jail, anarchy was inaugurated. The reign of terror, however, was not of long duration. On the evening of the 24th, a regiment of the Gwáliár contingent, the 1st

Book VIII. Chapter I.

1857. May 25.

Grenadiers, reached Barpúra. The following morning this regiment marched on Etáwá, and restored order. For the moment, British authority was again supreme, though no one dared conjecture how soon or how late the restorer might become the persecutor!

but order is soon restored.

Mr. Colvin determines to offer a golden bridge to the well-disposed sepoys.

Whilst the spirit of disaffection was thus spreading from station to station Mr. Colvin was cherishing the hope that even a majority of the sepoys might still be amenable to reason. He believed that whilst the ringleaders had deliberately set the Government at defiance, others had been induced to follow them solely by fear of the consequence of not following them; that to inaugurate a policy of general severity towards all, because of the misconduct of a few, would precipitate a general insurrection of the native army. But if, he argued, means of escape, by a proclamation of pardon, should be opened to all who could properly be admitted to mercy, it would gladly be seized by those who had no heart in the business. Impressed with these views, which, it would appear, were shared by all about him, by soldiers as well as by civilians, Mr. Colvin, without awaiting the sanction, for which he applied, of the Supreme Government, issued, on the 25th of May, a proclamation giving effect to the views just stated. He was catching at a straw, but, in the sea of difficulties in which he was struggling, there was positively nothing more tangible at which the hand could grasp!

Issues a proclamation giving effect to his views.

Mr. Colvin's proclamation was disapproved of, on several grounds, by the Government of India,

Book VIII. Chapter I.

1857. May 25.

who substituted for it another of their own composition. There was really little substantial difference between the two, and both were useless. In point of fact, the time had not arrived to issue proclamations of pardon. Mr. Colvin's offer was well meant, but, though the proclamation was sown broad-cast over the province it failed to bring in a single penitent sepoy. The straw at which he had clutched crumbled in his hand.

It has no effect.

Events which followed on its issue.

Mr. Colvin's proclamation was issued on the 25th of May. On the 30th, three companies of native infantry which happened to be at Mathurá, only thirty-five miles from A'gra, belonging to the two regiments stationed at A'gra, suddenly mutinied, shot down one officer, wounded another, plundered the treasury, fired the houses of the English, released the prisoners from the jail, and went off to Dehlí. This was the first practical answer given by the sepoys to Mr. Colvin's proclamation.

The Bharatpúr troops mutiny,

But the Rájá of Bharatpúr had, as I have shown, despatched a detachment of his troops, under Captain Nixon, to aid the British at Mathurá. When the three companies at that station mutinied on the 30th, the Bharatpúr detachment was occupying a position at Hódal, a small town lying between Mathurá and Dehlí, thirty-seven miles north of the former and only sixty from the latter. Being on the high road, it was the place of all others to be occupied with advantage by a body of men wishing to intercept troops marching from Mathurá on Dehlí. So at least reasoned, on the morning of the 31st, Mr.

Book VIII. Chapter I.

1857. May 31.

Harvey, the Commissioner of A'gra, who was with the Bharatpúr troops; so reasoned Captain Nixon, who commanded them. A position was accordingly marked out and the troops were ordered to take it up. But here occurred an unexpected difficulty. The sepoys of the Rájá of Bharatpúr not only refused to obey, but they warned the British officers to depart. The rebellion, then, was not confined to sepoys in British pay. It was becoming hourly more national.

and drive away their British officers.

Remonstrances, threats, entreaties, were alike useless. It was not, however, until the guns were turned upon the group of some thirty Englishmen, who were present, that these yielded reluctantly to the mutineers. A few minutes after their departure, the shouts of the sepoys, and huge bonfires caused by the burning of their tents and the few bungalows built for Europeans, showed that the mutiny had been consummated. The officers escaped with difficulty and after many perils to Bharatpúr.

Effects of the mutiny at Mathurá on Mr. Colvin.

The intelligence of the mutiny at Mathurá disturbed the calculations and destroyed the hopes of Mr. Colvin. That mutiny had been the act of the men whom he had harangued on the 14th, and amongst whom his proclamation had been most freely circulated. It had been their own unadulterated work; conceived by their own brains, neither prompted from outside, nor produced by contact with other regiments. It became evident then, even to Mr. Colvin, that other means than those which he had employed

Book VIII. Chapter I.

1857. May 31.

would be necessary to put down "this daring mutiny."

The intelligence of the mutiny at Mathurá reached Mr. Colvin at midnight of the same day on which it occurred. The bearer of it was Mr. Drummond, the magistrate. At the time when the first "general council" was held at A'gra Mr. Drummond had been of opinion that the disaffection was partial, and that our policy should be to appear to trust everyone. It was Mr. Drummond who had most strenuously opposed Mr. Colvin's policy of retiring within the fort. But Mr. Drummond's views were altered now. Far from endeavouring to restrain the action of the Lieutenant-Governor he had now to stimulate it. Mr. Drummond, then, when he woke Mr. Colvin with the news of the Mathurá disaster, pointed out to him the necessity it had created of at once disarming the regiments at A'gra. And when Mr. Colvin, only half-convinced, seemed inclined to hesitate, the magistrate called attention to the fact that any sudden outbreak on the part of the sepoys would probably result in the liberation of the prisoners from the jail, with its consequent disorder and possible disaster. Then Mr. Colvin hesitated no longer. The order was at once issued for a general parade the following morning.

He resolves to disarm the A'gra brigade.

At dawn of day on the 31st of May the troops were drawn up on the A'gra parade-ground. There was Captain D'Oyley's battery, the 3rd Europeans, and the two native regiments—these so posted as to be under the fire of the Europeans. The Brigadier—Brigadier Polwhele—an officer of the Indian army—then directed the commandants of the native infantry regiments to order arms to be piled. The order was given. "There was a moment of hesitation, a look of discontent. The officers sternly reiterated the order. Silent and sullen, the sepoys obeyed—piled their arms, and marched off to their lines. The 44th and 67th Regiments, whose colours had waved from the Indus to the Brahmapútra, were no more." *

Disarms them.

Fuller effect was now given to the carrying out of the resolution passed at the general council regarding the organisation of volunteers, horse and foot. The class appealed to, composed of clerks in the public offices, pensioned soldiers, Eurasians, tradesmen, independent gentlemen, responded freely to the call. A body of infantry was formed for the protection of the station itself, whilst Horse Volunteers were enrolled to guard and escort to the fort the women and children in case of a sudden rising, and to afford aid to fugitives from neighbouring stations.

Raises volunteers.

Notwithstanding the disarming of the sepoys the mind of Mr. Colvin was far from easy. The country around A'gra was in a blaze. Direct communication with the districts to the north-

Difficulties of Mr. Colvin's position.

* Raikes's *Notes on the Revolt*. Mr. Raikes adds: "On examining the musquets, many were founded loaded with ball. It was afterwards well known, that on this very Sunday morning, the sepoys had conspired to overpower the European regiment when in church, to rush upon the guns, and then to shoot, plunder, and burn, from one end of Agra to the other."

Book VIII. Chapter I.

1857. May 31.

west had been cut off in the last week of May; that with Calcutta was severed the first week in June. In the capital of his own provinces the Lieutenant-Governor was isolated. One by one the towns and districts around him fell away from his grasp. The disbanding of the sepoys, and the presence of a regiment of European infantry and of a battery of European artillery, had for the moment saved A′gra. But A′gra was within seventy miles of the capital of the greatest of the Maráthá rulers, faithful himself to the British, but whose troops, levied in the recruiting ground which had supplied the British native army, were not to be perfectly trusted. A′gra again was the natural and historical point of attack for the contingents of the native princes of Central India,—and, however favourable might have been Mr. Colvin's opinion of the native princes, the example of Bharatpúr had led to the inference that their contingents sympathised with the mutineers.

Mr. Colvin's position, then, even after he had, by disbanding his two native regiments, removed the immediate danger, was extremely critical.

The initiative passes into the hands of the rebels.

Every day events were passing beyond his control; his power to initiate was disappearing; it was becoming more incumbent upon him to shape his action so as to meet the manœuvres of others. The initiative in fact had passed into the hands of the rebels.

The Gwáliár contingent.

The danger nearest to him was that which might come from the Gwáliár contingent. I have stated in a preceding page that immediately after

Book VIII. Chapter I.

1857. May 31.

the outbreak at Mírath Sindia had placed a considerable body of troops of his contingent, commanded by British officers, at the disposal of the Lieutenant-Governor. But these men were the brothers of our sepoys, allied to them by caste, by religion, by sympathy. Sindia not only did not trust them, but he had warned the British political agent at his Court, Major Charters Macpherson, that they would inevitably seize their opportunity to follow the example set them at Mírath and Dehlí. Major Macpherson, an officer of a stamp especially fostered by the East India Company, thoroughly acquainted with the natives of India and trusted by them, pointed out then to the Maháráj́á, that, holding the convictions he had expressed regarding the men of his contingent, it would become him to show the sincerity of his attachment to his Suzerain by placing his body-guard, Maráthás of his own kindred or caste, at the disposal of the Lieutenant-Governor. To this proposal Sindia had acceded, and the body-guard had been sent off to A'gra. Later events were to show that not even the comrades and kinsmen of the Maháráj́á had been able to escape the infection.

Sindia sends his body-guard to A'gra.

The Gwáliár contingent was composed of four field batteries of artillery, a small siege train, two regiments of cavalry, and seven of infantry, aggregating eight thousand three hundred and eighteen men. The greater portion of the force was stationed at Gwáliár, under the command of Brigadier Ramsay, with outposts at Siprí and A'gar.

Policy of having the

The cantonment at Gwáliár was occupied by

Book VIII. Chapter I.

1857. May.

ladies at Gwáliár.

the officers of the contingent, their wives and families. It may excite surprise that with the avowed conviction of the Mahárájá regarding the degree of confidence that could be placed in the soldiers of the contingent—convictions shared by his Prime Minister, Dinkar Rao; by the Resident, Major Macpherson; and communicated, it must be presumed, to the Lieutenant-Governor—the ladies and children should not have been placed in security, whilst yet there was time to remove them. The subject had not been neglected.

They are sent to the Residency,

The Mahárájá himself had, so early as the last week of May, suggested the removal of the ladies and children from cantonments to the Residency, which was beyond the city, and about five miles from the cantonments. It so happened that, on the 28th of May, in consequence of a strong impression that the sepoys would rise that night, the ladies did actually spend a night there, protected by a portion of the Mahárájá's own guard. Well would it have been if they had been allowed to remain, or if they had been sent to A'gra! But on receiving a remonstrance from the native officers, affirming the excellent disposition of their men, and protesting against the slur which had been cast upon them by the transfer to the protection of the Mahárájá of the ladies and children, the Brigadier recalled the latter to the station.

but ordered back to cantonments.

Forebodings of disaster.

Though confidence had disappeared the illusion was maintained. Almost every post brought in vain to Gwáliár convincing proofs that of all possible illusions this was the most baseless.

Book VIII. Chapter I.

1857. June.

With rumours of the wildest character from the North-West there came from places nearer at hand accounts in detail the truth of which was apparent. Now it was that the troops at Ajmír and at Nasírábád had mutinied, and had made their way to Dehlí; now, that their example had been followed by the Nímach garrison; now, that the province of Rohilkhand had risen; now, that there had been a massacre at Jhansí; and now, that the panic had even reached Calcutta. From Kánhpúr, from Alláhábád, and from the stations in their vicinity, the absence of news gave birth to even more sinister forebodings.

The terrible suspense.

Such was the life from day to day in Gwáliár during the first fortnight of June 1857. It was a life of terrible suspense, of pressure on the nervous system, difficult to endure.* "Suspense," has declared a great writer, "suspense is agony, but decision may be despair." There were some of our countrywomen at Gwáliár, one certainly of the fairest and most gifted amongst them, to whom it was allotted to pass through the suspense to succumb in the end to the ruthless and too cruel decision. At one time during that fortnight it had been almost resolved to send the ladies in

* "We live in a state of dreadful uncertainty," writes Mrs. Coopland (*A Lady's Escape from Gwalior*). "My husband seldom undressed at night, and I had a dress always ready to escape in. My husband's rifle was kept loaded (I learned to load and fire it), as we were determined not to die without a struggle. Oh! the misery of those days! None but the condemned criminal can know what it is to wait death passively; and even he is not kept in suspense, and knows he will be put to a merciful end."

Book VIII. Chapter I.

1857. June 12.

Reaches the verge of despair.

to A'gra, and a proposal to that effect had been made to the Lieutenant-Governor. The idea that he would accede to this plan kindled some hope in the minds of those most interested. But on the 12th that hope was blighted. A telegram from Mr. Colvin directed that the ladies were not to be sent into A'gra until mutiny should have broken out at Gwáliár.*

The crisis at Gwáliár.

June 14.

At last the crisis came. It was Sunday, the 14th of June. The Europeans in Gwáliár had attended the service of the Church in the morning, passing on their way many sepoys loitering about the road. During the day fuller details of the Jhánsí massacre had been received—details but ill-calculated to dispel the gloom that hung over the station. The prevailing idea in the minds of the residents as they read those details was that the same fate was reserved for themselves,—"for now they were more than ever isolated, revolted provinces on three sides of them, and the telegraphic communication with

* *A Lady's Escape from Gwalior* by Mrs. Coopland. With admirable good sense Mrs. Coopland indicates the fatal error of thus keeping ladies and children in a dangerous position. "Before this," she adds "my husband had often wished to send me to Agra; but he would not desert his post and I would not leave him. I have often thought since that had I done so he might have escaped, by riding off unimpeded by me; many unmarried officers having escaped in this way. When the mutinies first began, if all the ladies and children at the numerous small stations had been instantly sent away to Calcutta or some place of safety before the roads were obstructed, their husbands and fathers would probably have had a better chance of escape. Instead of which, the lives of men, women, and children were sacrificed, through the efforts to avoid arousing the suspicion of the troops."

Book VIII. Chapter I.

1857. June 14.

A'gra severed." * Suddenly, about midday, the alarm was given that one of the bungalows was on fire. This circumstance, the unvarying precursor elsewhere of a rising, warned the residents that their hour had arrived. But they had prepared themselves for a crisis of that character. Waterpots had been stored up in readiness. On the alarm then being given the occupiers of the several thatched houses had their roofs well saturated. But the wind was high, incendiaries were creeping about, and there were some houses not at the moment occupied. The fire speedily spread to the Mess-house and thence to a large swimming bath-house adjoining it. These and the bungalow first attacked by the flames were burnt to the ground. But the further progress of the fire was then arrested. The wind fell, precautions had been taken, every European was on the look out, and the day had not waned.

Begins by an act of incendiarism.

Few, however, doubted as to the course events would take as soon as darkness should set in. A little incident confirmed the already too certain conviction. Mrs. Coopland, the wife of the

* "My husband laid down and tried to get a little sleep, he was so worn out. He had just before been telling me the particulars of the Jhansi massacre, too frightful to be repeated; and we did not know how soon we might meet the same fate ourselves.

"I hope few will know how awful it is to wait quietly for death. There was now *no* escape; and we waited for our death-stroke. The dread calm of apprehension was awful. We indeed drank the cup of bitterness to the dregs. The words 'O death in life, the days that are no more,' kept recurring to my memory like a dirge. But God helps us in all our woes; otherwise we could not have borne the horrible suspense."—Mrs. Coopland.

Book VIII. Chapter I.

1857. June 14.

chaplain of Gwáliár, relates* that on that afternoon she and her husband went for a drive. "We saw scarcely anyone about, everything looked as it had done for days past; but as we were returning, we passed several parties of sepoys, none of whom saluted us. We met the Brigadier and Major Blake, who were just going to pass a party of sepoys, and I remember saying to my husband, 'If the sepoys don't salute the Brigadier the storm is nigh at hand.' *They did not.*"

Keen insight of Mrs. Coopland.

The instincts of Mrs. Coopland were true. The storm was nigh at hand. That night, immediately after the firing of the evening gun—9 P.M.—the sepoys of the Gwáliár contingent rose in revolt. They fired the lines, sounded the alarm, and rushed from their huts in tumultuous disorder, discharging their loaded muskets. The officers, as in duty bound, galloped down to the lines in the vain endeavour to recall their men to order. They were met by murderous volleys directed at them. Captain Stewart commanding a battery of artillery was severely wounded, and afterwards when a prisoner was deliberately shot dead. The return of his riderless horse to the house-door conveyed the sad news to his wife. She herself, fair and bright as the Morning Star, did not long survive him. She, too, was shot dead, and her boy with her. The sepoys spared her little girl. Major Hawkins, also commanding a battery, Majors Shirreff and Blake, commandants of infantry regiments, shared the same fate.

The mutiny breaks out.

* *A Lady's Escape from Gwalior.*

Book VIII. Chapter I.

1857. June 14.

Dr. Kirk, the superintending surgeon, was discovered in the place in which he had sought refuge and was killed before the eyes of his wife.* Mr. Coopland, violently separated from his wife, who was spared, was murdered.† Others managed to escape; but of the fourteen British officers present that morning at Gwáliár one half were slain. With them likewise, three women and three children, and six sergeants and pensioners.‡

Its fatal results.

* Then poor Mrs. Kirke, with her little boy joined us. She had that instant seen her husband shot before her eyes; and on her crying: 'Kill me too!' they answered, "No; we have killed you in killing him. Her arms were bruised and swollen; they had torn off her bracelets so roughly; even her wedding ring was gone. They spared her little boy, saying, "Don't kill the butcha (child); it is a missie baba (girl)." Poor child; his long curls and girlish face saved his life. He was only four years of age."—Mrs. Coopland.

† "We all stood up together in the corner of the hut" (to which they had been conveyed by Mr. Blake's faithful Mahomedan servant, Mírza); "each of us took up one of the logs of wood that lay on the ground, as some means of defence. I did not know if my husband had his gun, as it was too dark in the hut even to see our faces. The sepoys then began to pull off the roof; the cowardly wretches dared not come in, as they thought we had weapons. When they had unroofed the hut they fired in upon us. At the first shot we dropped our pieces of wood, and my husband said, 'We will not die here, let us go outside.' We all rushed out; and Mrs. Blake, Mrs. Raikes, and I, clasped our hands and cried, 'Mut maro, mut maro (do not kill us).' The sepoys said, 'We will not kill the mem-sahibs (ladies) only the sahib.' We were surrounded by a crowd of them, and as soon as they distinguished my husband, they fired at him. Instantly they dragged Mrs. Blake, Mrs. Raikes, and me back; but not into the bearer's hut; the mehter's (sweeper's) was good enough for us, they said. I saw no more; but volley after volley soon told me that all was over."—Mrs. Coopland.

‡ Mrs. Stewart was the only lady killed; but with her her boy and her European nurse. The wife of a warrant officer was also killed. The officers murdered were Dr. Kirk, Ma-

Book VIII. Chapter I.

1857. June 14.

The survivors find their way to A'gra.

Those who escaped, men, women, and children, made their way as best they could, some in parties, one or two almost singly, into A'gra.* Their sufferings were great. The agony of that terrible night weighed upon them long afterwards. The widowed wife, the orphaned child, the bereaved mother, were indeed bound to each other by the sympathy of a common sorrow. But until A'gra was reached danger seemed still to threaten them all. They, the survivors, could derive little satisfaction from the fact that their dear ones had been shot down solely because the Government had been afraid to show mistrust of the sepoys. Their present condition was the result of that simulated reliance. They felt, then, as they had felt before, that the timely withdrawal of the ladies and children would have at least given the officers a chance of escape. But now all was over. The murdered husbands had died in the performance of rigorous duty. The wives, the children, who had perished, had been the holocausts of a policy, timid, irrational, even provocative of disaster. In deciding to have recourse to such a policy the impress of a strong character had been painfully wanting.

Intelligence of the Gwáliár mutiny reached A'gra on the 15th. Following it came likewise the information that the Mahárájá, and his able minister, Dinkar Rao, still loyal and true, would

jors Shirreff, Blake, Hawkins, Captain Stewart, Lieutenant Proctor, and the Reverend Mr. Coopland.

* Many of them came through the Dhólpúr country, the Rájá of which was prodigal in his attentions and in his provision of conveyances and escort.

Book VIII. Chapter I.

1857. June 15.

Risings all about A'gra.

use every means in their power to restrain the over-charged aspirations of their followers and their sepoys. But graver events were at hand. Central India had risen; Rohilkhand had risen; and it was soon seen that the safety of A'gra was imperilled from without. It will be my duty now to recount the nature of these perils, and then to describe the mode in which they were met by the ruling powers of the North-West Provinces.

BOOK VIII.

CHAPTER II.

The events which were occurring at the period at which we have arrived at Alláhábád, Kánhpúr, Banáras, and in the Mírath division have been already related. From those quarters there came no light to A'gra. From others, within and without the circle of the North-West Provinces, issued those menacing demonstrations which forced at last a decisive policy on the Government. These have now to be noticed.

Three central points in the North-West.

In writing the history of the mutiny in the North-West Provinces, it has to be borne in mind that three central positions stand out, each distinct from the others, and each attracting to itself separate attacks, unconnected with the others. These three central positions were A'gra —the point aimed at by the mutineers on the right bank of the Jamná—by those, in a word, issuing from Central India :—Kánhpúr, connected henceforth intimately with Oudh :—and Dehlí, attracting the rebels from Rohilkhand and the northern part of the Doáb. To preserve, then, unbroken the narrative of the events affecting A'gra as a main central point, it is necessary that I should leave for a future chapter the stations and districts on the left bank of the Jamná, and endeavour to concentrate the attention of the reader on Bandalkhand, Central India, and on Rájpútáná.

Jhánsí.

The town of Jhánsí lies one hundred and forty-two miles south of A'gra. It is the capital of the province of the same name. The history of this province has been peculiar. Amid the general plunder and robbery which accompanied the break-up of the Moghol empire under the successors of Aurangzíb, a portion of Bandalkhand belonging to the dominions of the Rájá of Urchá had been appropriated by one of the Maráthá officers serving under the Péshwá, and to him confirmed by *sanad.* The territory so appropriated, containing nearly three thousand square miles and a population of about a quarter of a million, was called after the chief town within its borders, Jhánsí. As long as the power of the Péshwá lasted the Maráthá officer and his successors ruled Jhánsí as vassals of that prince. But on the downfall of the Péshwá in 1817 the territories possessed by him in Bandalkhand and elsewhere were ceded to the British. Amongst these territories was Jhánsí, the ruler of which, known under the title of Súbádár, accepted the protection of the British, and agreed to pay an annual tribute of seventy-four thousand rupees of the currency of his State. In return the British

Its early history

Book VIII. Chapter II.

1857.

Government declared him hereditary ruler of the country. The name of the Súbádár with whom this arrangement was concluded was Rám Chand Rao. Fifteen years later the British Government, to mark their approval of his rule, exchanged his title of Súbádár for the higher rank of Rájá. Rám Chand Rao enjoyed his new dignity for three years and then died without issue (1835).

The Rájá had died, and had left no direct heir, natural or adopted. But in the guarantee given eighteen years before the State had been declared to be hereditary in his family. It was, therefore, incumbent upon the British Government to acknowledge as Rájá the member of that family nearest in relationship to the deceased. Ultimately the choice fell upon Rao Ragonáth Rao, his uncle.

This man was incapable and a leper. After three years of unpopular rule he died, and the throne became again vacant.

Disputes regarding the succession.

There were several claimants to succeed him. Their pretensions were examined by a commission appointed by the Governor-General of India, and after a long interregnum all but one were pronounced invalid. The excepted claim was that of Bábá Gangádhar Rao, brother of the deceased. He, therefore, was nominated Rájá.

Meanwhile the revenues of the country had been falling. During the reign of the leper there had been practically no government. Everywhere disorder had been rampant. Bábá Gangádhar Rao was not the man to remedy this state of things. He, too, was an imbecile, and it was conjectured that under his sway, disorder, far from being checked, would be increased tenfold.

British agency introduced.

Under these circumstances, the British Government stepped in as the paramount power and resolved to carry on the administration of the country by means of British agency. To the Rájá an annual allowance was granted, and he was informed that the government of the country would only be made over to him when it should appear that he was fit to conduct it properly.

The Rájá restored.

That happy period arrived in 1843. By the exertions of the British officers the country had been restored to more than its former prosperity. It was then made over to the Rájá, subject to a small cession of territory in commutation of the annual payment previously made for the support of the Bandalkhand legion.

He dies without heirs.

Bábá Gangádhar Ráo ruled Jhánsí for eleven years neither very wisely nor very well. He died in 1854 without heirs. He was the last male descendant of the family to which the British Government in 1817 had guaranteed the right of succession. The Governor-General of the day, Lord Dalhousie, was of opinion that the treaty of 1817, whilst it did guarantee the right of succession to the members of a certain family, gave no right of adoption, after the disappearance of that family, to the widow of its latest representative. He was fortified in this view by the opinion of the commission appointed by Lord Auckland in 1848, and which had unanimously rejected the pretensions of all the claimants excepting one. And now that one had died, childless. Lord

Book VIII. Chapter II.

1857.

Dalhousie, therefore, in spite of the protestations of the widow of the deceased Rájá, declared the State of Jhánsí to have lapsed to the paramount power.

Jhánsí is declared a lapse. Anger of the Rání.

This happened in 1854. The three years which had passed between that date and the period of which I am writing had in no way reconciled the Rání to a policy which she regarded as unjust to herself, and insulting to the family of her late husband. On the contrary, the year 1857 found her brooding over her griefs and panting for revenge.

The British Government regarded her anger and her remonstrances with careless indifference. They did what was even worse, they added meanness to insult. On the confiscation of the State, they had granted to the widowed Rání a pension of £6000 a year. The Rání had first refused, but had ultimately agreed to accept this pension. Her indignation may be imagined when she found herself called upon to pay, out of a sum which she regarded as a mere pittance, the debts of her late husband.

The British Government takes no pains to mollify her.

Bitter as was her remonstrance against a course which she considered not less as an insult than as a fraud, it was unavailing. Uselessly she urged that the British had taken the debts of the late ruler with the kingdom of which they had despoiled her. Mr. Colvin insisted, and caused the amount to be deducted from her pension. Other grievances, such as the slaughter of kine amid a Hindú population, and the resumption of grants made by former rulers for the support of Hindú

Book VIII. Chapter II.

1857. May.

temples, whilst fomenting the discontent of the population with their change of masters, formed subjects for further remonstrance; but the personal indignity was that which rankled the most deeply in the breast of this high-spirited lady, and made her hail with gratitude the symptoms of disaffection, which, in the early part of 1857, began to appear amongst the native soldiers of the hated English.

Garrison of Jhánsí in 1857.

The garrison of Jhánsí was composed entirely of native troops. There was a detachment of Foot Artillery, the left wing of the 12th Regiment of Native Infantry, the head-quarters and right wing of the 14th Irregular Cavalry. Jhánsí is a walled town, overlooked by a stone fort surmounted by a round tower. The cantonments lay outside, and at a little distance from the town. Within their limits was comprehended a small fort, occupied by the artillery and containing the treasure-chest, called the Star Fort. The troops were commanded by Captain Dunlop, of the 12th Native Cavalry. The political and administrative officer was Captain Alexander Skene.

The Rání is encouraged by the Mírath revolt.

The account of the events at Mírath on the 10th of May produced the effects which might have been expected on the mind of the Rání of Jhánsí. Her hopes at once revived. From the doors of her palace there started at once confidential servants towards the sepoy lines. These returned with reports fully responding to her highest hopes. The time so eagerly longed for was approaching. Her task, then, was to lull the English into security. It would appear that in

Book VIII. Chapter II.

1857. May.

Throws dust into the eyes of the officials,

the political officer, Captain Skene, she had soft material to work upon. She succeeded so well in impressing the mind of this gentleman with a conviction of her loyalty, that she obtained from him permission to enlist a body of armed men for her own protection from any attack from the sepoys! This permission obtained, she rapidly invited the old soldiers of the State to rally round her, at the same time that she secretly caused to be unearthed heavy guns which had been buried at the time of her husband's death.

who trust her, and the sepoys.

Meanwhile, Captain Skene, utterly unconscious of the impending danger, was reporting to his Government his confidence in the state of affairs at Jhánsí. Neither from the native soldiers of the Company, from the levies of the Rání, nor from the nobles of Jhánsí, did he apprehend the smallest disturbance. Captain Dunlop and his brother officers were almost equally trustful. Reports were made to them from time to time regarding the difficulty felt by spies in their attempts to enter the lines of the men. The fact that difficulty should have been experienced was, in their eyes, a sufficient proof of the fidelity of the sepoys. Besides, Captain Dunlop trusted the irregular cavalry, and he felt satisfied that with their aid he could suppress in the bud any outbreak on the part of the other native soldiers.

Incendiarism at Jhánsí.

The burning of the bungalows occupied by the English officers at Jhánsí, the invariable precursor of a rising, did not disturb the serenity of Captains Skene and Dunlop. A fire, which occurred on the 1st of June, was attributed to accident. But

1857.
June 5.

on the afternoon of the 5th of June an event occurred the bearings of which it was impossible to mistake. A company of the 12th Regiment of Native Infantry, led by one of its native sergeants, and cheered on by the native gunners of the battery, marched straight into the Star Fort, and announced their intention to hold it on their own account. Captain Dunlop rushed instantly to the parade-ground, accompanied by his officers. The remaining four companies of the regiment professed themselves highly indignant at the conduct of the rebellious company, and they and the cavalry declared they would stand by their officers. The following morning they were paraded. They repeated their protestations. Captain Dunlop was then proceeding to prepare measures to bring the revolted company to reason. Whilst engaged in these preparations at the quarter-guard of his regiment he was visited by Captain Skene, and by his assistant, Captain Gordon. After these had left him, Dunlop wrote some letters and posted them himself. But on his way back from the post office he was shot dead by his own men.

The sepoys seize the Star Fort.

In fact the preconcerted day had arrived. The capture of the Star Fort on the 5th had simply been a feeler to test the officers. Finding on the following morning that these were as credulous as they had been the preceding day the sepoys resolved to strike at once. The afternoon of the 6th, then, the Rání, escorted by her new levies, came from her palace, and went in procession towards the cantonment. As she issued from the town, a Múlla called all the true

The affair develops into mutiny.

Book VIII. Chapter II.

1857. June 6.

believers to prayers. This was the signal. The cavalry and infantry at once rose in revolt.

The mutineers kill their officers.

They met Captain Dunlop, as already stated, on his return from the post office, and shot him dead. With him, another officer, Ensign Taylor. The Irregular Cavalry scoured the plain with loaded carbines in pursuit of others. The sergeant-major, Newton, was their next victim. Then Lieutenant Turnbull, of the Survey, an officer of the highest promise, who, however, did not succumb until he had made his assailants pay dearly for their treachery. Lieutenant Campbell, the only officer with the irregular cavalry, was wounded, but being well mounted, he succeeded in reaching the larger fort in safety.

Some officers occupy the larger fort,

Meanwhile, Captains Skene and Gordon had returned to that larger fort. There also were the wife and two children of the former; Lieutenant Burgess, of the Survey Department; Dr. McEgan, 12th Regiment of Native Infantry, and his wife; Lieutenant Powys, of the Canal Department, his wife and child; Mr. W. S. Carshore, collector of Customs, and his family; Mr. T. Andrews; Mr. R. Andrews and family; Mrs. Browne and her daughter; Mr. Scott and family; Messrs. Purcell, two brothers; two brothers Crawford; Mr. Elliot, Mr. Fleming, and others in the subordinate departments of the Government, chiefly Eurasians, and whose names I have been unable to ascertain. The total number, including women and children, was fifty-five.

The sepoys having killed all the officers on whom they could lay hands marched with loud

1857.
June 6.

shouts towards the fort overlooking the town. But Captain Skene and his comrades had not been inattentive spectators of the scene in cantonments. They had bestirred themselves with the instinct of self-preservation to defend their position. Rifles had been distributed; the ladies told off to cast bullets and to cook; piles of stones had been heaped up behind the gates, and positions allotted to each member of the garrison. When, therefore, the rebels approached the fort, they were received with so well directed a fire that they fell back in confusion to prepare renewed efforts for the morrow.

which they prepare for defence,

and repulse the sepoys.

The resource now available to the besiegers lay in the guns which the Ráni had unearthed. During the night these, and the smaller *matériel* from the cantonment, were placed in position. On their side, too, the English had held a council of war. A successful defence seemed impossible. Guns, provisions, a continued supply of water, were all wanting. It was decided, then, at that council to send three of the garrison under a safe-conduct to treat with the Ráni for the retirement of the men, women, and children within the fort, to a place of security in British territory.

Send three envoys to treat with the Ráni,

On the morning of the 7th, Messrs. Andrews, Scott, and Purcell, issued from the fort. They were almost immediately seized by the rebels, and conveyed by them to the palace. The Ráni by this time had become thoroughly intoxicated with the success that had been achieved. Declaring that "she had no concern with the English swine," she ordered the three prisoners to be taken to the Rissaldar, commanding the Irregular Cavalry, for

Book VIII. Chapter II.

1857. June 7.

orders. This was equivalent to their death-warrant. The Englishmen were then dragged out of the palace. Mr. Andrews was killed before its gates by a native who was supposed to harbour a grudge against him; the two others were despatched beyond the walls of the town.

who has them killed.

The rebels then renewed their attack on the fort but again without success. The guns had not been brought up. On the following morning (the 8th) this operation was attempted, and soon after daybreak a brisk cannonade was opened against the walls. But whether from want of skill, or from defect in the guns, not a single brick was displaced by the fire.* A stray shot, however, carried off Captain Gordon. The fire of the musketry from the fort did, meanwhile, a great deal of execution, and the rebels were deterred from approaching too near to its gates.

The rebels renew their attack,

but are repulsed.

Hope was now beginning to dawn upon the fated garrison, when, as if the overwhelming force outside was not a sufficient foe to contend against, they discovered treachery within the fort. Certain native servants had been admitted for the performance of menial offices. Two of these men, in concert with the rebels outside, were found in the act of opening the door of a secret passage communicating with the town. Lieutenant Powys, who discovered them, shot one man dead, but was himself cut down by the other. Captain Burgess avenged him in a second and the two traitors were laid prone side by side in a ditch.

The garrison discover traitors within.

* Narrative of a native of of the Collector of Customs Bengal attached to the office at Jhánsí.

1857. June 8.

This attempt frustrated, the garrison attempted to open communication with Nagód and Gwáliár. But the bold men (Eurasians) who attempted to carry out this resolve were intercepted and killed. Provisions now began to fail; ammunition was becoming scarce—assistance from outside seemed impossible. Despair seemed to clutch at the smallest chance of escape. Just at the moment one seemed to present itself. The Rání and the sepoys had been baffled by the unexpected resistance offered. What if it should continue? What if these Europeans had supplies of which they knew nothing? Their own guns had failed: assault was dangerous; would it not be advisable to get these bold men into their power by soft promises, and then to make away with them?

The Rání offers terms,

This idea, so consonant to the principle of Asiatic warfare, had no sooner been entertained than it was acted upon. The Rání sent messengers to the fort under a flag of truce, demanding a parley. Captain Skene responded. The native messengers then declared that the Rání wanted only the fort; that if the Europeans would lay down their arms and surrender the position they held they should be escorted to some other station. These terms having been affirmed by the most solemn oaths, Captain Skene, on behalf of the garrison, acceded to them. They seemed indeed to offer the only chance of life. The members of the garrison then laid down their arms, and walked out of the fort.

which are accepted.

Then commenced the last act of the drama. No sooner had the Europeans issued from the

Massacre of the garrison.

Book VIII. Chapter II.

1857. June 8.

fort than the rebels fell upon, bound them, and carried them to a garden, called the Jókan Bágh. Arrived there, they were halted near a cluster of trees. The word then passed that the Ressaldar had ordered them to be massacred. The prisoners, disarmed and bound, were then ranged in three lines, the first containing the adult males, the second the adult females, the third the children. Then, suddenly, the head native official of the jail raised his sword and cut down Captain Skene. This was the signal. The murderers then went to work, each armed with a lethal weapon. The captives were pitilessly hewn down. Not a man, woman, or child, survived that afternoon's butchery.

Such was the massacre of Jhánsí. A doubt has been raised as to the complicity of the Rání in the atrocious deed. But it must be remembered that not only was it the Rání who had instigated the slaughter of the three envoys sent by Captain Skene the morning after the investment, but it was she who profited by the slaughter. She wished to be rid of the English that she might seize the principality which she considered to be rightfully her own, and she hesitated not at the means by which they were moved from her path. What followed the massacre? For a moment it seemed very doubtful whether the Rání and the revolted sepoys would not quarrel about the division of the spoil. The latter even threatened to bring upon the scene an illegitimate relation of the late Rájá as a rival. But the Rání was a very clever woman. The sepoys had their price, and she

The Rání bribes the sepoys,

was prepared to pay it. She wanted the title,—they the coin. She gave them the coin. Whereupon they proclaimed her Ráni of Jhánsí. She proved herself a most capable ruler. She opened a mint, fortified the strong places, cast cannon, raised fresh troops. Into every act of her government she threw all the energy of a strong and resolute character. Possessing considerable personal attractions, being young, vigorous, and not afraid to show herself to the multitude, she gained a great influence over the hearts of her people. It was this influence, this force of character, added to a splendid and inspiring courage, that enabled her some months later to offer to the English troops, under Sir Hugh Rose, a resistance which, made to a less able commander, might even have been successful.

and is proclaimed Ráni of Jhánsí.

Her great abilities.

The right wing of the 12th Regiment of Native Infantry, the left of the 14th Irregular Cavalry, and a detachment of native Artillery,—constituting in fact a moiety of the force located at Jhánsí—were, during this period, stationed at Naogáng, about two hundred miles eastward of Jhánsí. The station was commanded by Major Kirke, of the 12th Native Infantry. At Naogáng perfect confidence reigned up to the 23rd of May. On that day, however, a sepoy reported the presence in the lines of a suspicious character. The report of the sepoy caused considerable excitement. It related to natives of Bandalkhand, men not connected with the sepoys, who were supposed to harbour a design to massacre the British officers. By some the story was credited,

Naogáng.

Book VIII. Chapter II.

1857. May.

by others it was disbelieved. It had, however, this apparently most gratifying result that the sepoys manifested towards their officers a warmth of affection which touched to the quick those who were the objects of it.

Precautions taken by the authorities.

During the week that followed, although many circumstances occurred well calculated to rouse suspicion, the confidence of the British officers never wavered. They slept every night in their lines, and took every opportunity of showing unlimited trust in their men. But on the 30th of May reports of intentions expressed by the native gunners to rise were again rife. Four men, proved to be implicated in this plot, were dismissed from the station, and subsequently to that night Major Kirke took the precaution to have the guns of the battery brought in front of the quarter-guard of the 12th Regiment.

Quiet now seemed to be restored. On the morning of the 5th of June the men of four companies of the 12th even volunteered to serve against the rebels. Those of the 5th company were about to express a similar wish, when suddenly an express arrived from Jhánsí, written by Captain Dunlop, with the information that the artillery and infantry at that place had mutinied. This intelligence caused great excitement amongst the native soldiers, but it elicited from them, especially from the infantry, enthusiastic expressions of fidelity to their officers.

News arrives from Jhánsí.

Quite assured regarding his men, Major Kirke at once took steps to open communications with Jhánsí and Lalatpúr. For four days nothing occurred to disturb public order. On the 9th, however, the news of the mutiny of the four companies of the 12th at Jhánsí and of the murder of Captain Dunlop and Ensign Taylor reached the station. The following day brought tidings still more disastrous. The native magistrate of Maoránpúr wrote that morning to Major Kirke to inform him of the murder of every European in Jhánsí, and that he had received an official order to the effect "that the Rání of Jhánsí was seated on the throne, and that he was to carry on business as hitherto."

Book VIII. Chapter II.

1857. June 9.

Further intelligence from that place.

The effect of this news was electric. At sunset of that day as the guards were being paraded three Sikhs of the 12th Regiment came to the front, shot the native sergeant-major through the head, and seized the guns. The English sergeant-major, fired at ineffectually, fled to the mess-house to warn the officers. The latter hurried down to the lines. But by this time the farce of loyalty had been played out. The officers arrived in time only to see their sepoys, the cavalry troopers, and the artillerymen, in full revolt.

The sepoys at Naogáng mutiny.

In vain were these adjured to remain faithful. The *furor* was on them. There was nothing, then, for the Europeans and their families to do but to retire, if retirement were still possible. They attempted it, accompanied by a number, increased ultimately to eighty-seven, of their men who still remained faithful.

The story of that retirement has been written by four of the survivors. It is a story of misery and suffering hardly to be surpassed. First it was

The British leave the station.

Book VIII. Chapter II.

1857. June 9.

decided to move on Chatarpúr, but in the darkness of the night the fugitives took by mistake a road which branched off to Garáolí. This mistake saved them. The mutineers, counting upon their choosing the Chatarpúr road, followed the fugitives, after they had plundered the station, in that direction. Other rebels had been sent to occupy different points in the main line of retreat, and they, too, were waiting for the disheartened Europeans. The mutineers, finding these men on the road, and learning that our countrymen had not passed, retraced their steps. The fugitives, meanwhile, making mistake after mistake as to the road, still pressed onwards, and were fortunate enough to reach Chatarpúr by a circuitous route, unmolested, by daybreak the following morning.

Are well received at Chatarpúr.

Chatarpúr was the capital of a small State governed by a Ráni. This lady behaved well and loyally. Though pressed by her Mahomedan advisers to follow the example set at Jhánsí, she rejected their counsel, and showed her intention to defend the English to the utmost of her power.

The fugitives halted at Chatarpúr the 11th and 12th. On the last named day, two officers, Captain Scott and Lieutenant Townshend, were sent into Naogáng to reconnoitre the state of affairs there. Strange to say these two Europeans succeeded, by the simple discharge of their guns, in re-asserting British authority there for the few hours they remained. They returned, however, the same evening.

1857. June 16.

Their sufferings after leaving Chatarpúr.

The fugitives left their hospitable quarters at Chatarpúr on the night of the 12th, and marched in the direction of Alláhábád. Hearing, however, on the 16th, of the mutinies at Bandá and Hamirpúr, they changed the route on the 17th to Kalingarh. That night they found their progress stopped by bandits who occupied a pass it was necessary they should traverse. The bandits demanded money. The British officers wished to force the pass. The faithful sepoys, assenting at first, recommended in the end that the money should be paid. It was paid. But next morning before daybreak, as our party was preparing to move on, the bandits commenced a fire upon them. The faithful sepoys began to fire wildly in return, but with the exception of ten or twelve, they speedily dispersed. All attempts to rally them were vain. The fugitives were now deserted. One of their number, Lieutenant Townshend, fell shot through the heart. The others, returning the bandits' fire, moved as best they could in one direction—whither they knew not. Fortunately the road they had taken led to the hospitable territory of Chatarpúr. Across the border the bandits did not follow them, and though some villagers fired at them, they reached the village of Kalrai at 3 P.M.

Their losses.

Not all of them, however. Townshend had been shot through the heart; Major Kirke and Mrs. Smalley, and a native, had succumbed to sunstroke or apoplexy. The women and children had been brought on with the greatest difficulty. The officers had given up their horses, and on these the

Book VIII. Chapter II.

1857. June 17–18.

non-combatants had been laden like so many sacks. On that day and on those that followed many of these poor creatures perished, and had to be left by the wayside.

Are terribly reduced in number.

There was no safety for the English at Kalrai. The majority of them—for some, and all the Eurasians, elected to remain behind—pushed on to Mahóba. By this time the party was reduced to seven officers, one sergeant, two civilians, three women, two children,*—with nine horses amongst them. The other Europeans had either been killed, had died, or had stayed behind at Kalrai.

The fugitives moved on again on the 20th of June; but they were attacked on their way and dispersed. The subsequent sufferings which some of them endured were extraordinary. Dr. Mawe, Lieutenant Barber, Lieutenant Ewart, and Mrs. Smalley's child, died of sunstroke or fatigue. Sergeant Kirchoff, assaulted by the villagers, was left for dead, but ultimately escaped. Captain Scott saved Mrs Mawe's child, carrying it in front of him whilst Mrs. Smalley sat behind. The villagers, especially those in British territory, were found generally most hostile. But for the generous kindness of the Nawáb of Bandá and of the Ráni of Azigarh not one of the fugitives would have escaped. The Nawáb and the Ráni did more than protect them in their States,—they used every means in their power to assuage the hostility of the villagers. To them alone was it

Further sufferings.

Reach Bandá.

* Their names were, Captain Scot, Lieutenants Ewart, Barber, Jackson, Remington, and Franks, Dr. Mawe, Mrs. Mawe and child, Mr. Harvey Kirke, Mrs. Smalley and child, Sergeant Kirchoff and wife.

due that a remnant of the party which had fled from Naogáng succeeded ultimately in reaching territory still possessed by the British.*

Generous conduct of the Nawáb of Bandá.

Reference has been made in the preceding narrative to the generous conduct of the Nawáb of Bandá. But Bandá was itself a military station. There was quartered a detachment of the 56th Regiment of Native Infantry. These men, in correspondence with their brethren of the 12th, were equally tainted. Learning betimes of the successful outbreak at Naogáng they followed its example. Rising on the 14th of June, and making common cause with the troops of the Nawáb, they plundered the treasury and went off to join their comrades. The Nawáb was able to save the lives of the officers. He extended the same protection to the Europeans who had escaped from Hamirpúr, and to those likewise who had fled across the Jamná from Fathpúr. The time, however, was to arrive when the Nawáb, like Sindia and the Hindú princes of Rájpútáná, would find himself unable to contend any longer against the excited passions of his followers. True, however, to his liege lord, he extended hospitality and protection to every European fugitive as long as he could do so, and when the insubordination of his troops rendered it impossible for him to afford them further protection, he had his guests safely escorted to territory still owning the British rule.

* There are most interesting narratives of these events by Captain Scott, Mrs. Mawe, Lieutenant Jackson, Sergeant Kirchoff, and Mr. Langdale. Of the men left behind at Kalrai, forty-one persons, drummers, buglers, and their families, ultimately reached Bandá in safety.

Book VIII. Chapter II.

1857. June.

Fidelity of the 50th N.I.

There was one station in Bandalkhand, and only one, in which the native troops stationed did not mutiny. This was the station of Nagód. The regiment there quartered, the 50th Native Infantry, stood firm to the last, fourteen men in the whole regiment having alone shown symptoms of disaffection. Nor was the misconduct of these men displayed until a later period (27th of August).

BOOK VIII.

CHAPTER III.

More important in their results on the general situation were the occurrences taking place about the same time in the States of the native princes in Central India and Rájpútáná. I have narrated a portion of these under the head of Gwáliár. It is necessary now to invite the attention of the reader to the larger remainder as yet untold.

Colonel Durand.

The acting representative of the Governor-General at Indúr, the capital of the dominions of Holkar, and the head-quarters of the Central Indian Agency, was Colonel Henry Marion Durand. Colonel Durand was one of the most remarkable of the remarkable men for the production of whom the East India Company was famous. Endowed with a clear head, a comprehensive grasp of affairs, a quick and keen vision, a singularly retentive memory, and an energy that nothing could tire, Durand could not escape distinction. Anywhere, and under any circumstances, he would have attained it. Seldom has

Book VIII. Chapter III.

1857.

there served in India a man who could do all things so well; who could successfully apply to so many diverse subjects his vast talents. He was equally at home in planning a campaign, in giving, as he did give, the soundest advice to a Commander-in-Chief, after an indecisive action, such as that of Chillianwálá, and in devising schemes for the improvement of the complicated revenue system of the North-West Provinces. Nor did his private character belie his conduct as a public officer. Large hearted, full of sympathy for the suffering and the oppressed, he had unsparing scorn and contempt for those only whom he believed to be false, to be treacherous, to be corrupt, to be time-serving. For a man of that class, when once he had found him out, Durand had no pity. But the true man, however poor, however neglected by Fortune he might be, always received from Durand support, encouragement, and sympathy. This remark applies alike to Colonel Durand's relations with natives and with Europeans. It is not true that he had a scorn for Asiatics as Asiatics. He had scorn for corrupt Asiatics, as he had scorn for corrupt Europeans. But in his mind the colour of the skin weighed not at all. With him honesty was honesty, falseness was falseness; and wherever he detected these opposite qualities, he loved or despised the possessor, whether he were Asiatic, or whether he were European.

His character.

His constant struggle with Fortune.

It is a remarkable fact that throughout his long career in India—a career extending over forty years—Durand owed nothing to Fortune. On the contrary, his life was a constant struggle against the efforts of the blind goddess. She made his path hard and difficult. He rose to one of the highest positions in India,—the Lieutenant-Governorship of her most important province—in spite of envy, in spite of calumny, in spite of the thousand and one indirect obstacles which can be and are used to thwart the upward career of an able and honest man, who, connecting himself with no party, dares to have the courage of his opinions. There have been epochs in Indian history when it has been possible for men without brains to rise very high indeed. Servility, complaisance, a cautious reticence, a suppression in fact of one's inner consciousness, are sometimes found useful and are often rewarded. But Durand scorned the backstairs path. He always spoke exactly what he thought, always acted as he believed to be right, regardless of consequences. This manly action made him many enemies, and these enemies thwarted him, as enemies in high places can thwart a man true to his own convictions. That he succeeded in spite of them was due partly to his indomitable strength of will, partly to the fact that in times of pressure and adversity Governments find themselves forced to replace the smiling sycophant by the skilled workman.

His hatred of intrigue.

His manliness.

Colonel Durand belonged to the Engineers. Yet, so great had been his capacity, and so comprehensive his intellectual range, that he, then a Lieutenant of Engineers, had been selected in 1838 for the post of Secretary to the Board of

His earlier career.

Book VIII. Chapter III.

1857.

Revenue of the North-West Provinces. He had accepted this post when he was invited to accompany the army which was to march under Sir John Keane into Afghánistán. He threw up his civil appointment, joined that force, and was one of the two officers who blew in the gates of Ghazní thus admitting the storming party. His health requiring a change to England, he had returned to India with Lord Ellenborough in 1841 in the capacity of aide-de-camp. Before landing in Calcutta Lord Ellenborough had promoted the aide-de-camp to be private secretary. Durand held this office during the brilliant Indian career of Lord Ellenborough. On the recall of the latter by the Court of Directors he was appointed Commissioner of the Tenasserim Provinces. Then came into play those arts which incompetent rulers employ to get rid of men, subordinate to them in position, but in every other respect their superiors. Charges, frivolous in themselves, and subsequently proved to be utterly unfounded, were trumped up against Durand. He was removed from his Commissionership. He returned to England with the justificatory pieces in his pocket; convinced the Court of Directors, convinced the Board of Control, and went back to India with an order from the President of that Board that he was to receive an appointment equal to that of which he had been unjustly deprived. But Lord Dalhousie was then Governor-General of India. Lord Dalhousie did not like Durand. He offered him an appointment in the Panjáb so inferior to that he was

Cabal against him.

How he met it.

Returns to India.

entitled to expect that Durand unhesitatingly refused it. He re-entered upon his duties as a military Engineer, joined the army then fighting in the Panjáb, was summoned to the councils of war held by Lord Gough after Chillianwálá, and aided by his practical advice in ensuring the victory of Gújrát. An account of this campaign from his pen enriched shortly afterwards the pages of the *Calcutta Review*. After the annexation of the Panjáb Durand accepted from Lord Dalhousie the post of political agent at Bhopál. His labours of years here were most useful. He formed the mind of the Bégam; taught her those golden lessons of true and honest dealing as a ruler, from which she profited so much afterwards; and showed her, from the examples of the Mahomedan rulers of India, the material advantage a sovereign reaped from the prevalence of the knowledge that he was to be believed on his own word. Severe illness drove Durand to England in 1854. His appointment at Bhopál lapsed to another, and he returned at the end of 1856 to the corps of Engineers. But shortly afterwards, Sir Robert Hamilton, the agent for the Governor-General at Indúr, having decided to take furlough to Europe, Lord Canning sent Durand to act for him. Thus it happened that when the Mutiny broke out in 1857, Colonel Durand was the representative of the Government of India at the court of Holkar, and had political charge of Central India.

Book VIII. Chapter III.

1857.

Joins the army in the field.

Becomes political agent at Bhopál.

Is forced by ill-health to visit England.

Appointed the Governor-General's Agent for Central India.

Colonel Durand took up his office at Indúr on the 5th of April. At that time all was quiet in

Book VIII. Chapter III.

1857. April 25.

Earliest warnings of the mutiny.

Central India. The excitement which had prevailed in Bengal regarding the greased cartridges had not penetrated to Máu,* nor even to Indúr. On the 25th of April, however, a sepoy of the 30th Native Infantry was apprehended in the act of conveying a treasonable message to the Darbár of Ríwá. There is no doubt that he was one of many sent by the several regiments to ascertain the temper and sentiments of the native courts. From this time an uneasy feeling began to prevail throughout Central India—a feeling brought to a climax by the mutiny of the 10th of May at Mírath.

To understand the position of Colonel Durand when the news reached him of the revolt at Mírath it is necessary to define the nature of the territory of which he had political charge, its extent, its resources, and its position with regard to other States, Native as well as British.

Central India.

Central India comprised the Native States in subsidiary alliance with the British Government of Holkar, of Sindia, of Bhopál, of Dhár, of Diwás, and of Jaorá.

Its geographical position.

The dominion of Sindia may be roughly stated to comprise the territory bordered by the river Chambál to the north and north-west, severed on the east by the river Sind from Bandalkhand, and, further south, by the Bétwá, from the British possessions. Between it and the British territories due south, lies Bhopál, divided from the

* Máu is the British military station between thirteen and fourteen miles, by the then existing road, south-west of Indúr.

latter by the river Narbadá. To the west of Bhopál is the dominion of Holkar, comprising likewise a portion of the country south of the Narbadá, and reaching nearly to the Táptí. This dominion is, so to speak, pressed in by its neighbours. Its capital, Indúr, lies in a tract of country separated from the remaining part of the dominion by the independent State of Diwás to the north and north-east, and by the independent State of Dhár to the west. On the north it is hemmed in by the south-western limits of the dominion of Sindia, whilst, separating it again from its northernmost districts, is Jaorá, nominally a fief of Holkar, but really independent. To the north of Jaorá, again, the dominion of Holkar thrusts its head into Rájpútáná, by which it is surrounded on three sides.

Book VIII. Chapter III.

1857. May.

Military occupation of Central India.

It will thus be seen that of all the dominions under the Central Indian Agency, that of Holkar was the least compact. Hemmed in on three sides by Native States, its various component portions were isolated from each other, likewise by Native States. Each of these had its own troops. First in order may be named Gwáliár, possessing a force of 8,000 men, disciplined and led by European officers. The main body of this force was at Gwáliár itself, but it had detachments at Siprí; further south still, at Gúna; and, on the very borders of Holkar's territory, at A'gar. Thirty miles from A'gar was Méhidpúr, the head-quarters of the Málwa contingent, a small force comprising a regiment of infantry, a battery of artillery, and some cavalry, likewise officered by

Book VIII. Chapter III.

1857. May.

British officers. Immediately to the north of Méhidpúr lies Jaorá, and to the north of that again, and on the high road to Dehlí, are the stations of Nímach and Nasírábád, garrisoned by troops of the regular army.

The purely native force there.

The purely native force in the dominions of Jaorá, of Dhár, and of Diwás, was contemptible in point of numbers and efficiency, but to the east of Indúr, and about a hundred miles from it, was the Bhopál contingent, a body of infantry, cavalry, and artillery, commanded by British officers, and stationed at Síhor. To the east and north-east of this, again, were native troops of the regular army, in the Ságar and Narbadá territories and in Bandalkhand.

Its position with respect to British territory.

It will thus be seen that Indúr was completely cut off on three sides from the British territory by native troops and native contingents. On the south, indeed, rather more than thirteen miles distant from it, and about five-and-twenty miles north of the Narbadá, lay the British station of Máu, garrisoned by the 23rd Regiment of Native Infantry, commanded by Colonel Platt, a wing of the 1st Cavalry, under Major Harris, and Captain Hungerford's battery of Artillery, having European gunners but native drivers. Thus, if Indúr was isolated, Máu was still more so. For while, to the north of it, Indúr was occupied by a large native force under the personal direction of Holkar himself, to the south it rested, so to speak, in the air, no British troops intervening between it and the military stations in the Madras and Bombay Presidencies.

Garrison of Máu.

Book VIII. Chapter III.

1857. May.

Political considerations which affected Central India.

It is clear, then, that, in the event of the mutinous contagion spreading to Central India, the maintenance of order in the country north of the Narbadá depended entirely on one of two contingencies. The first of these was, naturally, the early fall of Dehlí; the second, the advance of reinforcements from the south. In view of the latter contingency, the paramount importance of maintaining, at all risks, the line of the Narbadá will at once be recognised.

The line of the Narbadá.

Crossing the Narbadá below Indúr, and running right through the territories under the Central Indian Agency to a point on the Chambál directly north of Gwáliár, ran the direct road from Bombay to A'gra. Not only was this road invaluable as a postal and telegraphic line,* but it was absolutely necessary as a military road, constituting, as it did, the direct route by which troops from the south could advance. The importance of maintaining this line, more especially the portion of it south of the Narbadá, cannot be over-rated.

Weak points of that line.

Its weak points were those where it was commanded by the troops stationed at Méhidpúr and at A'gar, and where it passed through stations held by troops belonging to the Gwáliár Contingent, such as Siprí and Gwáliár, and where it traversed Dholpúr.

The troops at Indúr.

At Indúr, for the protection of the treasury and other public buildings, was a detach-

* There was, in 1857, no direct telegraphic line between Madras and Calcutta, and the only circle by which telegraphic communication with the Madras and Bombay presidencies could be effected was that by Agra and Indúr.—*Central India in* 1857.

Book VIII. Chapter III.

1857. May.

ment of the Málwa contingent, two hundred strong. These were the only troops stationed there when the news of the mutiny of the 10th of May at Mírath reached the Residency.

Policy of Colonel Durand.

Colonel Durand received this intelligence on the 14th of May. He comprehended at a glance its importance. He saw that it was but the first act of a very tragic drama. But his duty was clear to him. To maintain his own position at Indúr as long as it could be maintained; to sever all intercourse between the native troops of the regular army and the soldiers of the native contingents; to secure the Narbadá, and the important road I have described; to re-assure the native princes under his superintendence:—these were his first considerations, and he set himself at once to act upon them.

Summons troops from Sirdárpúr and Bhopál.

It happened that, in addition to the troops I have mentioned, there was a regiment of Bhíls at the station of Sirdárpúr, near Mandlésar, about forty miles from Indúr. The Bhíls are men who have no caste prejudices, and who, reclaimed from a wild life by the British, had always proved good soldiers. Durand sent at once to Sirdárpúr for two hundred and seventy of these men. Believing, too, that of all the contingents, those who had been raised at Bhopál were the least likely to waver in their fidelity, he ordered up a strong detachment of cavalry and infantry and two guns from that place. These troops, using every expedition, reached Indúr on the 20th of May. Colonel Durand being precluded, as an officer in political employ, from exercising military duties, the command of these detachments, and the arranging for the protection of the Residency, devolved upon Colonel Stockley of the Bhíl corps.

Mutinous disposition of the troops at Máu.

They arrived just in time. The native troops in Máu had not escaped the contagion of the disease by which the entire native army had been infected. Not only were they, at this very time, ripe for revolt, but they had even debated whether it would not be advisable to make at once a dash for the scene where their brethren were fighting, by way of Indúr. Conscious that such a move was possible, that, under certain circumstances,—such, for example, as the presence in the ranks of the native troops of a master mind,—it was certain, Durand had made every preparation to meet the contingency. In consequence of his requisition Mahárájá Holkar had supplied him with cavalry * to form pickets on the roads. From the same source he had received half a battery of guns and three companies of infantry. These had been posted so as to command the approaches to the Residency. A certain number of troopers were kept always in the saddle. Yet, after all, if the attempt had been made, the chances of the English at Indúr would have been poor. For the question *quis custodiet ipsos custodes* had not then been solved. A few days later it was solved, not exactly to the credit of the *custodes*.

Durand accepts a guard of Mahárájá Holkar's troops.

* The cavalry furnished by Holkar were never considered trustworthy. When, therefore, Colonel Travers arrived at Indúr, the Mahárájá was requested to remove them, and to send them on distant duty. This was done.

Book VIII. Chapter III.

1857. June.

Colonel Travers arrives and assumes command at Indúr.

In the middle of June a further detachment of cavalry from Bhopál, under their commandant, Colonel Travers, arrived at Indúr. The command of the entire force round the Residency devolved, then, on Colonel Travers, as the senior officer. This onerous duty could not have fallen to a more gallant soldier or to a truer-hearted man. To him was then committed the military care of the Residency, and it is only just to record that not a single precaution was neglected to ensure the safety of its occupants against the effects of a sudden rising.

Gloomy intelligence from the outer world.

For some short time prior to the arrival of Colonel Travers affairs had appeared to move more smoothly. From the outer world, however, there came intelligence which more than ever convinced Durand that, unless a decisive blow should be struck speedily at the heart of the rebellion, the drain upon his resources would be hard to meet. Thus, disquieting rumours from Nasírábád and Nímach; the more than doubtful behaviour of detachments of the Gwáliár contingent; the receipt of a letter from the officer commanding that contingent expressive of his distrust of their loyalty; intelligence that emissaries from the native regiment at Máu had been discovered tampering with the men of the Bhopál contingent:—these reports, the one following the other in quick succession, were more than sufficient to satisfy Durand that, literally, he and his were standing on a quicksand. It is true that their feet still rested on the treacherous surface, but every wave of the tide, every effort of the feet to extricate themselves,

Durand is perfectly conscious of the danger of his position.

made the position more perilous, the danger more apparent.

1857. June.

Possibility that the disastrous news might affect the troops at Máu.

This, in fact, was the case when, on the 1st, Durand received intelligence of the mutiny at Nasírábád; on the 6th, of that at Nímach. The information which reached Durand could not be hidden from the regular troops at Máu. The head-quarter wing of the cavalry regiment there stationed had just mutinied at Nímach. How would the men of the other wing, and the men of the infantry regiment, receive the news? Should they revolt, would the European battery be able to disperse them? Should they make a rush for Indúr, would the troops of Holkar oppose them or unite with them? These were questions on the solution of which depended, not only the lives of the Europeans, but the maintenance of British authority in Central India.

but they are apparently not affected by it.

For a moment it seemed as though the native troops at Máu were about to prove an exception to their comrades, that amid the faithless they would be faithful. Reports, indeed, to their discredit were rife. It was openly stated that they were in league with the troops of Holkar, and that, strong in that alliance, they intended to master the guns at Máu, and then march on Indúr. But they showed no outward sign of ill-will or of disaffection. Never were they more respectful; never more fervent in their protestations of loyalty.

Durand is not taken in.

Durand was not taken in. He saw through it. As he wrote to Lord Elphinstone, "it was all moonshine." But to him there was still a glimmering

Book VIII. Chapter III.

1857. June.

of hope. Though the news of the revolt at Nímach was followed by that of the mutiny of the cavalry of the Malwá contingent—pushed up, contrary to Durand's orders, into contact with the mutineers—accompanied by the murder of their officers; though reports arrived of the massacre of the Europeans at Jhánsí, with its accompanying horrors; and though, last and most fatal of all, intelligence was received of the revolt of the bulk of the Gwáliár contingent at Gwáliár itself, Durand still hoped. There was a chance, and apparently a good chance, that he might yet override the storm, that a ray of sunshine might yet harden the treacherous soil.

The one hope on which he depends.

This chance lay in the march of a column despatched to Máu from the Bombay Presidency under Major-General Woodburn. It was the approach of this column, consisting of five troops of the 14th Dragoons, a battery of artillery, a company of sappers, and a native regiment, that had caused hesitation in the minds of the native garrison at Máu. It was the approach of this column that gave a degree of confidence to Durand. Had it only pushed on Central India would have been saved from a great calamity.

General Woodburn's column.

It happened, however, that General Woodburn's column was suddenly diverted to another point. Disturbances had broken out at Arangábád. It was believed that on the suppression of those disturbances depended the fidelity to British interests of the troops of the Nizám, and that, therefore, at any sacrifice, they must be suppressed. General Woodburn, then, turned off to

The column is diverted to Arangábád.

Book VIII. Chapter III.

1857. June.

Arangábád. He suppressed the disturbances there, but, having suppressed them, did not move forward. He remained at Arangábád, halted, I must suppose, in deference to superior orders. To compensate, as far as he could, for the alienation of this force, the Governor of Bombay, Lord Elphinstone, ever zealous for the public service, was seeking the means of equipping another column for the relief of Central India.

Durand's one hope is thus disappointed.

The hope, then, so promising, apparently so well grounded, was destined to prove delusive. Even before it had utterly flickered away there had come tidings sufficient to daunt the most stout-hearted, but which did not daunt Durand. The northern portion of the great road between A'gra and Bombay had, he knew, been lost when the troops at Jhánsí, and when, subsequently, the Gwáliár contingent had mutinied. But now he learned that his communications were still further threatened; that the troops at Jabalpúr, at Lalatpúr, and at Ságar, were on the verge of mutiny; that throughout Bandalkhand the natives were rising, and that the temper of the troops in Máu was becoming daily more uncertain.

Another hope glimmers on the horizon.

But in these desperate circumstances there suddenly appeared in the north-west the reflection of a light sufficient, had it been real, to calm all apprehensions. Just at the time when Durand received information that General Woodburn had crushed the rising at Arangábád the report reached him that Dehlí had fallen. This was the blow at the heart which would have paralysed

Book VIII. Chapter III.

1857. June.

intending mutineers—this the light which would have diffused its cheering ray into every corner of the Empire. It was not Durand alone who heard the report. It had crept into the counting-houses of the native bankers and been whispered in the furthest recesses of the bazaars. The quieter demeanour of the lower classes of the population showed how markedly the confirmation of the rumour would have affected the course of events.

The hope proves delusive,

But it proved to be a will o' the wisp—to be premature—to be untrue. Not to Durand, in the first instance, came the denial of the rumour. Certain information that the intelligence was false reached a banker of the city. He refused to disclose to Durand the nature of the information it was known he had received. But a little later it came to Durand direct. On the morning of the

July 1.

1st of July a letter from A'gra, dated the 20th of June, was handed to him. From this he learned for the first time that the previous report regarding the fall of Dehlí was untrue, that, up to the 17th, the British, forced to remain on the defensive, had been repeatedly attacked; that they had with difficulty held their own; and that the General commanding had determined to suspend all offensive movements pending the arrival of reinforcements.

even worse than delusive.

The consequence.

The communication from A'gra was placed in Colonel Durand's hands about 8 o'clock on the morning of the 1st of July. About half an hour later he sat down to condense its contents into a letter to be despatched to the Governor of Bombay when he was startled by the sudden discharge of

Book VIII. Chapter III.

1857. July 1.

the three guns in the Residency enclosure.* A second later and one of his official servants rushed in to report that the whole place was in an uproar. Durand rose and walked hastily to the steps of the Residency. The scene that met his gaze left no doubt upon his mind. The crisis, so long and so skilfully averted, had come upon him.

Before I recount the measures taken by the Agent and the Commander of the force round the Residency to avert this sudden danger, I propose to describe that place and its environs, and to show how the troops under the orders of Colonel Travers had been posted.

The Indúr Residency.

The Indúr Residency is a double-storied house built of stone,† in an open enclosure, about four hundred yards to the north of the Khán river, flowing in a north-westerly direction towards the city of Indúr, from which the Residency is two miles distant. In the same enclosure are

* In his letter to Holkar, dated the 3rd of August, Durand stated that the attack began at twenty minutes to 9.

† Major Evans Bell (*Last Counsels of an Unknown Counsellor*) implies that the Residency was not made defensible. But the following description of that building will show how impossible it was to make it proof against cannon shot. Not only was the Residency built of stone, but in the lower storey it is entered by from twenty-four to thirty glass and Venetian doors, incapable of resisting even a kick. The chief entrance to the upper storey is from outside, by a handsome flight of stone steps. The glass and Venetian doors on this storey are as numerous as those below, but are larger.

It was impossible to throw up earthworks in front of the Residency, for the simple reason that there was no earth wherewith to make the works. The Residency stands upon ground not having an inch of soil in depth. Even for the small flower-beds in front of the building, earth had to be brought from a considerable distance.

Book VIII. Chapter III.

1857. July 1.

bungalows for the assistants to the Agent and other buildings and bazaars. Within its circumference, in fact, was comprised the entire civil station of Indúr. It is an open park-like place surrounded by groves aud gardens. Immediately on its western front runs the road to Máu. This, passing the Residency, crosses the Khán river about four hundred yards to the west by south-west of that building. To the south-east of this road are thickly wooded groves and gardens; but immediately to the west of it, and, in some instances, bordering it, were bazaars and a number of native buildings of various sorts. These extended for a considerable distance on either side of the road leading to the city. Not more than a hundred yards intervened between the easternmost of these buildings and the Residency. In and about these were located the native troops, three companies of infantry, and three field guns, sent by Holkar to protect the Residency.

Its situation with respect to the city, the bazaars, the river, and the road to Máu.

The location of the troops.

To the north of that building, and still nearer to it, was the stable square, in the immediate vicinity of the post-office, the telegraph office, and the treasury. Here was the cavalry picket. Round about it were the camps of the Bhopál cavalry, one hundred and fifty strong, the infantry of the Bhopál and Méhidpúr contingents, numbering about four hundred men, and the detachment of Bhíls, two hundred and seventy strong. Of all these detachments the cavalry was the most remote from the Residency.

They are engaged in

On the morning of the 1st of July neither were these men nor their officers under the smallest

Book VIII. Chapter III.

1857. July 1.

apprehension of a rising. The men were scattered about in undress; some were bathing; some were cooking their food. The native officers and non-commissioned officers had just come up to transact their morning business at the orderly-room. Colonel Travers himself, in conversation with some of them, was on the point of entering that room. Suddenly they were all startled by the same artillery fire and the same tumult which had drawn Durand to the steps of the Residency. A moment's glance sufficed to show them that the rebels were upon them.

their ordinary occupations,

when they are suddenly attacked,

Who were these rebels, and who set them on? The rebels were the men of the three companies of Holkar's army, and the gunners of Holkar's three guns, posted for the protection of the Residency in the buildings between it and the city, and distant from it, at the nearest point, only a hundred yards. To these men, a little after 8 o'clock, a man named Saadat Khán,* an officer in

by the troops of Mahárájá Holkar,

headed by Saadat Khán.

* In a work recently published, *Last Counsels of an Unknown Counsellor* (Major Evans Bell), Saadat Khán is described as "a sort of half-pay officer, with no men under his command." Again, "a man of good family, considering himself to have some claim to be hereditary Bukshie of Holkar's army, but out of employ and in disgrace." But the Governor-General's Agent —who then was Sir Robert Hamilton—describes him in 1858, in his official letter to Government, as a "Durbar officer of cavalry." Major-General Sir Henry Daly, subsequently and still the Governor-General's Agent at Indúr, thus described him officially in 1874: "Saadat Khan was a man of weight in Indur in 1857; his father was commandant of cavalry, in which he was known as Ressaldar. The Customs Department was also under his control." The fact is that Saadat Khán, although influential with the Mahomedans, did not occupy a position of authority, nor was he in favour with the Darbár.

Book VIII. Chapter III.

1857. July 1.

Holkar's cavalry, followed by eight troopers, coming from the direction of the palace, galloped, shouting: "Get ready, come on to kill the sáhibs; it is the order of the Mahárájá." Saadat Khán was followed at a distance by the rabble of the town, eager for blood and for plunder; for the word had gone forth that Durand was about to remove into Máu the treasure,* amounting to £150,000 in silver, which he had guarded in a strong building, erected by the Government for the purpose, close to the Residency.

Murder of the Christians not in the Residency.

Others of the same class mingling with Darbár soldiers had rushed to seek out the Christian population who had remained in their own homes or in their offices, unprepared for and not expecting the sudden murderous onslaught which was to lay them low.†

* Major Evans Bell states, as I understand him (*Last Counsels of an Unknown Counsellor*, page 89), that Durand had given orders for the removal of the treasure to Máu on the 1st of July. But there are reasons for believing that no such order was issued. The Tréasury Guard was under the orders of Colonel Travers. On Colonel Travers it would have devolved to furnish the escort for the treasure. Now Colonel Travers received no order whatever on the subject. Not a cart, not even a camel had been obtained. The Treasury was closed. Had Durand intended to remove the treasure, the fact could not have been kept secret from the officers, nor could he have overlooked communication with Colonel Travers.

† Lieut-General Travers, V.C., C.B., states (*The Evacuation of Indore*), that the number of the English population, men, women, and children, murdered by these ruffians amounted to thirty-nine. In a work recently published, *Last Counsels of an Unknown Counsellor* (Major Evans Bell), it is stated that this statement is erroneous, that the murdered were only twenty-five in number, and that of these only two were Europeans. But the Agent to the Governor-General in 1874, Major-General Sir Henry Da-

Book VIII Chapter III.

1857. July 1.

The troops sent to guard the Residency join in the revolt.

The Darbár troops thus appealed to by Saadat Khán turned out at once. They were not taken by surprise. Their commandant, Bans Gopál, admitted subsequently that his men had been demoralised. Certainly neither he nor any other officer made the smallest attempt to check the outbreak. On the other hand, no men could have shown themselves more ready and eager for mischief. They at once began to shout vociferously as they formed up, whilst the gunners placed their three guns in position, and opened fire on the picket of cavalry.

Colonel Travers.

Such was the sight and such were the sounds that met Durand and Travers about half-past 8 o'clock that morning. Sudden as was the outbreak it found the two men cool and collected. Travers, who, I have said, was at the moment talking to his native officers, hastened to the picket in the stable-square, ordered the troops to turn out and the guns to be placed in a position to open fire on the rebels. The men, surprised,

ly, K.C.S.I., writing officially to the Government in that year (10th of September), reports as follows (para. 5): "It was recorded in the Durbar Diary of July 1857, that Saadat Khan, after the attack on the Residency on 1st of July, which resulted in the slaughter of British subjects, European and native, women and children, in all, 39," &c. It would thus appear that the only mistake made by Lieut.-General Travers is in the use of the adjective "English." That thirty-nine persons were massacred by the rebels is clear. Not less so, that these thirty-nine persons were British subjects. It is no exculpation of the brutality of the assassins to state that of the total number only two were full-blooded Europeans and the remainder half-breeds, or Eurasians. The numbers given by General Travers are those attested to by the Durbar records, and quoted as indisputable by the highest British authority on the spot.

Book VIII. Chapter III.

1857. July 1.

half-stupified by the suddenness of the attack, showed at first no hesitation. But while they were turning out, Travers, having caused the men of the picket to mount, rapidly conducted them to a point whence they could most advantageously charge the enemy's battery. He then attempted to form them up to charge. But here, likewise, treason had done its work. The native officer of the picket had been "got at." And though the picket was three times formed for attack, three times did this man break the formation from the rear. This action threw the men into confusion. Two opposite feelings seemed to contend in them for mastery. But to stand still was fatal. Travers felt this, and feeling it, notwithstanding that success seemed hopeless, he gave the order to charge. Gallantly leading, he charged home, and though followed by but five of his men, he drove away the gunners, wounded the inciter of the mutiny, Saadat Khán, and for a few moments had the guns in his possession. Had he only been properly supported this charge would have been decisive. But not only was he not supported, but he and his five men were exposed to the fire of the enemy's infantry, now drawn up in order. For a moment, indeed, that infantry seemed inclined to waver; but when they recognised the small number of the men who had followed Travers, they re-gathered heart and continued, formed up, their musketry fire.

Turns out the men.

Traitors in his ranks attempt to baulk him,

but notwithstanding he leads a gallant charge on the enemy's guns.

which he captures;

but is not supported.

His charge, however, is opportune and useful.

The gallant charge of Travers had not, however, been useless. It had given time to Durand to make hasty preparations for the defence of the

Residency, to the gunners to place the guns in position, to the officers to turn out and form up their men. Durand, too, had utilised the few minutes at his disposal to write a letter to Colonel Platt, commanding at Máu, telling him that he had been attacked, and requesting him to send Captain Hungerford's battery to his aid.

Book VIII. Chapter III.

1857. July 1.

Durand writes to Máu for Hungerford's battery

Durand had just come out with this note in his hand when he met Travers returning from his charge. He gave Travers the note, with a request to forward it at once. Travers entrusted the important missive to a trooper on whom he believed he could depend. But he felt even then that absolute confidence was to be placed in no native soldier, and he more than doubted whether the letter would be delivered.

The enemy recover from the effect of the charge of Travers:

Meanwhile the enemy, recovering from the effect of the spirited charge of Travers, moved their guns round the left flank of the barracks into the open ground, with the intention of taking up a position for a front attack on the Residency. To meet this, Travers pushed forward his two guns two hundred yards to the right front of the Residency, and directed the gunners to open a concentrated fire on the enemy's supports. The guns, well served by two serjeants, Orr and Murphy, and by fourteen native gunners, who had remained faithful, at once opened out with effect, disabling one of the rebels' pieces, and forcing their infantry to retire. Again was a splendid chance offered to the garrison. A charge in force now would have decided the day. The Head was there to see the opportunity, the Hands

who, however, again forces them back.

Book VIII. Chapter III.

1857. July 1.

A golden opportunity of deciding the day,

were there that might have seized it, but the Hearts that should have animated those hands were cold and lifeless. In a word, the cavalry, who could have gained the victory, would not. They came up in excellent formation, but despite the efforts of their officers and of Durand they melted away. Twenty-five or thirty of them galloped off at once to Sihor, filling the air with cries that the Europeans were being massacred.

is frustrated by the refusal of the native troops to act.

The greater number remained helpless, panic-stricken, afraid of each other. The Hindús and Sikhs amongst them suspected the Mahomedans, and the Mahomedans suspected the Hindús and Sikhs. Divided into parties they scattered themselves over the enclosure, seeking the best available shelter from the enemy's fire, passive spectators of an assault which with union and heartiness they might have prevented.

Travers renews his attempt to charge,

Still conscious of the possibilities before him, and maddened by the refusal of the Bhopál men to seize them, Travers ordered Captain Magniac to ride after the men and to do his utmost to bring up a dozen or even half a dozen to attack the battery still lying defenceless in the open.

but in vain.

But again he was disappointed. The men would not respond to his call.

Baulked by the behaviour of the cavalry, Travers turned to the infantry feeling, like Eyre at Arah, that a bayonet-charge would yet save the day. But here again he was disappointed.

The infantry also refuse to fight.

The two hundred men of the Méhidpúr contingent absolutely refused to fight. Of the two hundred and seventy men of the Bhopál contingent only about twelve showed signs of obedience. The rest levelled their muskets at their officers, and drove them off. They declined even to lift a finger on behalf of the British. The Bhíls allowed themselves to be formed up but would not act.

Book VIII. Chapter III.

1857. July 1.

Still the defence was not abandoned. It was determined to bring the Bhíls—the only troops not in open mutiny—under cover. They were accordingly brought inside the Residency in the hope that they might be prevailed upon to discharge their pieces at the enemy when sheltered by stone walls. But, meanwhile, the rebels, finding that no advantage had been taken of their first check and rightly conjecturing that our troops had refused to fight them, had completed their artillery movement, and were pouring in many directions a fire of round shot and grape. Under the influence of this fire the Bhíls were completely cowed, refused even to discharge their pieces, and abandoning their posts at the outer windows, crowded into the centre rooms. The rebel infantry was forming up, evidently with the intention of taking advantage of the effect of the fire of their guns. To defend the Residency there now remained, besides the fourteen faithful native gunners, eight combatant officers, two doctors, two sergeants, and five Europeans * of the telegraph department. Under their charge were eight

Even the Bhíls refuse to discharge their pieces.

The number of defenders is reduced to a handful,

* One of them was Postmaster. All, however, were unable, either from alarm or from being unnerved by the slaughter which they had escaped, to use their arms. They did not fire a single shot.

Book VIII. Chapter III.

1857. July 1.

too few to continue the contest.

ladies and three children. The forces were too disproportionate for the contest to continue longer, unless succour should arrive. The enemy's officers were calling on their men to assault, and their ranks were rapidly filling. The position seemed desperate.

The "loyal" cavalry determine to retire.

At this crisis, the few cavalry who had remained huddled up, passive and inactive, behind the Residency, sent a message through their officer, Captain Magniac, that they were about to consult their own safety, further defence being hopeless; that if they did not then move, their retreat would be cut off, and they begged that this last chance might be taken of saving the women and children.

Summary of the situation.

I pause for a moment to ask the reader to take a glance at the position. Let him imagine a large stone house, occupied by seventeen Englishmen and fourteen faithful natives, with two guns for its defence, attacked by about six hundred trained sepoys, swelled by the constantly augmenting rabble of the city*:—the besieged embarrassed, moreover, by having eleven women and children to protect, and encumbered and threatened by having nearly five hundred mutinous troops within the range of their defence—troops who, if they acted at all, would act against them. But this is not all. The assailants occupied the buildings and roads all about the Residency. But

* The six hundred trained sepoys were composed of about two hundred of all ranks of Holkar's men, and the contingent infantry who, just about this time, fairly went over to the rebels.

1857. July 1.

there was besides a body of native cavalry, willing to protect the Europeans from actual assault if they would abandon the Residency and retreat, but unwilling to stir hand or foot in defence of that building. But now this body of cavalry was being out-flanked. It was threatening to ride off. Should it go, its place would inevitably be occupied by the enemy, and the Residency would be attacked on four sides.

Courses which might be open to Durand and Travers.

This was the position. How was Durand to act? Could he cut his way through the enemy? He and the other men might have done so; but they would have exposed to certain death the women and the children. As a body, the civil portion of the Europeans were unarmed. They had escaped to the Residency with their bare lives. No valid assistance then was to be looked for from these. To remain was impossible. Could the attack be resisted there were no supplies—even water would have failed the garrison. Could Durand wait for Captain Hungerford's battery from Máu? He had written for it at a quarter to 9 o'clock. It was then half-past 10, and there was no sign of its approach. In any case it was impossible it could arrive before half-past 12,—and then the enemy would be concentrated to receive it, whilst the last hope of saving the women and children would have been lost. Under these circumstances there was really but one course to pursue. On this all were agreed, Durand as well as Travers; all the other officers as well as Durand and Travers. They collected then the little garrison, and placing the ladies on

Of these only one really feasible.

Book VIII. Chapter III.

1857. July 1.

They evacuate the Residency.

gun-wagons, moved out of the Residency, covering their rear with the cavalry, ready to follow the Europeans though not to fight for them. It was then half-past 10 o'clock.*

Maháráјá Holkar.

But where, all this time, it may be asked, was Holkar? Where was Captain Hungerford's battery? These are the questions I now propose to answer.

Was he loyal or disloyal?

Few matters have been more debated than the conduct of Holkar at this critical period. There are those who believed then that he was disloyal, who believe still that he was a watcher of the atmosphere. There are those, on the other hand, who consider that his loyalty was unimpeachable, and that the doubts cast upon that loyalty, culminating as they have in the denial to him of a practical expression of the complete satisfaction

* Major Evans Bell (*Last Counsels of an Unknown Counsellor*, page 99), has laid some stress on the fact that no one was killed during the withdrawal from the Residency. I have communicated on this subject with Lieutenant-General Travers, V.C., C.B., and I append his reply. "The Residency," writes General Travers, "stands upon the shoulder of slightly rising ground which falls away towards the enemy's position and the river, and, rounding the shoulder, slopes in the other direction for some distance. The ground is open and smooth, and by keeping the building as long as possible between the fugitives and the enemy's artillery, a considerable advantage was gained. Indeed, by holding the cavalry as an additional screen, the enemy's attention was withdrawn, and he was delayed in bringing his guns into action. What damage was done by his fire I cannot say. We could not possibly know what natives composed our mixed party. I myself can only speak to one man, an European or Eurasian—a clerk, I believe—whose head was taken off by a round shot. He fell in a little jungle, and might not have been discovered had not his horse stood by the corpse."

Book VIII. Chapter III.

1857. July 1.

of the paramount power, similar to that bestowed upon his compeers, are a standing insult to his family and to his name.

Considerations not germane to the question.

In writing history, sentiment is, or ought to be, excluded. The historian has to deal only with facts. It is not very germane to the point at issue to inquire whether Durand disliked Holkar, or Holkar disliked Durand. It may even be admitted that Durand did not admire the character of Holkar; and that Holkar, regarding Durand as a *locum tenens* only, as one who would shortly make way for the man whom he really cared for, took no special pains to conciliate Durand. But there is unquestionable evidence to prove that up to the 1st of July Durand did believe in the loyalty of Holkar. I have been assured by a distinguished officer,* present with him throughout this critical time, and who enjoyed his confidence, that up to the time of the outbreak Durand constantly insisted that Holkar must know the strength of England too well to be other than loyal. That there was cordiality between the Agent and the Prince may well be doubted; but Durand gave a positive proof † that he trusted Holkar when he accepted from him, for the protection of the Residency, three companies of his troops and three of his field-guns. That he should withdraw that confidence pending ex-

* Lieutenant-General Travers, V.C., C.B.

† I may mention another proof. A very few days before the mutiny, Holkar represented to Durand that his magazine was almost empty of artillery ammunition. Without inquiry or question Durand had him supplied from the Máu magazine at once.

Book VIII. Chapter III.

1857. July 1.

planation, when those troops and those guns fired on him, without any apparent prohibition on the part of Holkar, was, to say the least, a very natural proceeding.

But to return to the region of facts. What was Holkar's conduct on the eventful 1st of July?

It is only due to the Mahárájá to state the explanation which he himself gave.

The explanation of his conduct given by the Mahárája himself,

For some time past Mahárájá Holkar had felt the control of his troops slipping out of his hands. Only the day before the 1st of July some of his men had assumed so mutinous an attitude that he provided them with carriage and supplies in order to rid Indúr of their presence. It is not at all surprising that this should have been so. Under the trying circumstances of that trying period the most popular sovereigns could not command the obedience of their followers when they called upon these to act against their strong inner convictions. The loyalty of Mahárájá Sindia, in 1857–58, has never been questioned. Yet his own clansmen turned against him rather than fight for the British. There can be no question but that the troops of the native princes did sympathise deeply with the mutinous sepoys, and did regard their cause as their own. At Indúr, moreover, in 1857, there was a strong Mahomedan faction, scarcely less hostile to Holkar than to the British. Holkar, himself, prior to the 1st of July, had shown that he was well aware of the disorder fomenting around him. He had candidly told Durand that he mistrusted his own troops. Taking the above facts into consideration, the circumstances, that the day prior to the mutiny he had sent away from Indúr his most uncontrollable troops, that the leader of the assault on the Residency was a prominent member of the Mahomedan faction, I think it sufficiently established that on the 1st of July his mutinous soldiers took the bit into their mouths, and acted without his knowledge and in spite of him.

makes it clear that his troops acted in spite of him.

But the part of Holkar's conduct, which, up to the present time, has seemed the most to require explanation, is that which relates to his action whilst the attack on the Residency was proceeding. In the explanation which he offered at the time the Maháráját stated that the confusion had been too great to allow of any communication being made to the Residency; that on learning what had happened, he was preparing to set out for that place, when he was stopped by the intelligence that all was over. Now, the first discharge of grape into the Residency took place between 8 and 9 o'clock; the garrison evacuated the Residency at half-past 10. What was Holkar doing during those two hours? There is no doubt but that he was aware of the nature of the events which were taking place. Before 9 o'clock, Saadat Khán, blood-stained and wounded, had ridden into his presence to report that he had attacked the Residency, and wounded a *sáhib*. What, then, was he doing?

Why did not Holkar come to the Residency?

Here again we are met with opposite opinions. On the one side it is hinted, if not asserted, that he was watching the turn of events, not caring to

The supposition that he was watching the turn of events.

Book VIII. Chapter III.

1857. July 1.

interfere on behalf of the British, until it was certain that their sun had not set. On the other, it is declared that in acting as he did, he was unswerving in his loyalty to British interests; that had he mounted his horse and ridden to the scene of action, his presence would have sanctioned the mutiny, and given stability of action to the revolted soldiery; that in any case he would have been powerless to control them.*

is combated by his supporters

successfully.

I cannot but consider that there is force in this argument. Having regard to the fact that his army had slipped from his control, it is certainly possible, I think, that Holkar's presence on the scene might have been misinterpreted by the soldiery, and might have inspired them with the moral force of which, actually, they were in want. It is certainly true that Durand sent a letter to Holkar. But it is not less an ascertained fact that Holkar did not receive it. The messenger who carried it, alarmed, made for his own house, taking the letter with him. The passive attitude of Holkar, then, certainly proves nothing against him. It is perfectly reconcilable with absolute want of sympathy with the mutineers. To gauge what were his real wishes, it is necessary to inquire into his conduct subsequent to the evacuation of the Residency.

His conduct subsequent to the evacuation.

On this point, I find a general agreement as to the facts combined with a marked difference with respect to the conclusions. It is not denied that Saadat Khán rode up, wounded, to Holkar's

* *Last Counsels of an Unknown Counsellor*, Major Evans Bell.

Book VIII. Chapter III.

1857. July 1.

palace whilst the conflict was going on, and told Holkar that he had wounded a *sáhib* and had attacked the Residency. It is not denied that, though Holkar managed at the time to place that rebel leader in confinement, Saadat Khán was free a few hours later, and actually entered with his family into occupation of the Residency. It is asserted on the one side, and I cannot find it denied on the other, that Holkar remained in his palace till the third day in constant communication with the mutineers; that he then visited the Residency, and conversed with Saadat Khán, with Bans Gopál—the commandant of the infantry which had led the attack—and with the Súbadár of the 23rd Native Infantry, whose hand was red with the blood of his commanding officer.

Suspicious elements in that conduct,

Of these three facts, the only one apparently incriminating Holkar is the last. And his conduct here has been explained. It is but fair to the Mahárájá to state that explanation in the very words of his advocate.* "On the 4th of July, mounted, and spear in hand, he (Holkar) confronted the mutineers boldly at the Residency. They received the Mahárájá at first respectfully, but afterwards reminded him of the martial character of his ancestor, Jeswant Rao, and reviled him as a degenerate Holkar. He absolutely refused his countenance, and rejected all their demands." The visit of Holkar to the Residency is, therefore, entirely consistent with

have been satisfactorily explained.

* *Last Counsels of an Unknown Counsellor,* Major Evans Bell.

Book VIII. Chapter III.

1857. July 1.

the theory that he had lost control over his troops, and that they acted without his orders and in spite of him.

It is clear that he protected European fugitives,

It is, too, in my opinion, clearly made out that the Mahárájá, on the day following the assault, refused the threatening demands of the mutineers from Máu to deliver up the Europeans and other Christians who had taken refuge in his palace.*

at the risk of his life.

He states himself that he offered to them his own person rather than the heads of those under his protection. It may be said that this proves only that Holkar had not fully decided to go against us, that he was aware that the European battery held Máu. But in judging his conduct as a person accused of complicity with the mutineers this action is a strong point in his favour.

His further conduct on the day of the mutiny.

Another point, not less strong, perhaps even stronger, is the fact, that on the 1st of July, the very day of the mutiny, Holkar sent in to Máu, by the hands of Ganpat Rao, his agent at the Residency, a letter addressed to Colonel Platt to inform him of the mutiny, and stating that his own troops had refused to act against the mutineers. On the same day he wrote also to the Governor of Bombay, Lord Elphinstone, telling him of what had occurred. He wrote also that evening to Durand, protesting his innocence, and begging that the march of General Woodburn's force might be hastened as much as possible. It deserves further to be stated that none of the

The members of his Darbár

influential members of the Darbár, none of

* This protection was acknowledged by three Europeans, seven Eurasians, and some native Christians.

the Mahárájá's kinsmen or associates, joined in the attack on the Residency.

are free from complicity.

Looking at the question as a whole, I am of opinion that Holkar was free from complicity with the mutineers; that his soldiers had slipped out of his hands; that his presence amongst them on the 1st of July would have been misinterpreted; and that subsequently he did his best to serve the British interests. But it must be admitted that, at the time, his conduct bore a very suspicious appearance. It must not be forgotten that, although Durand sent him a letter by the hands of a messenger, that messenger never appeared at the Palace; that his own troops, led by his own officer, Bans Gopál, attacked the Residency; that Durand had reason to believe that his retreat on Mandlésar was prevented by the occupation by Holkar's troops of the Simrol pass. These circumstances could not but seem most suspicious to the Agent on the spot, thus attacked and thwarted. Whilst, then, Holkar must be acquitted of complicity with the rebels, the conduct of Durand in refusing to hold confidential intercourse with him until the Government of India should clear him from the suspicions attaching to his conduct must be upheld and justified.

The decision must be favourable to Holkar.

Though the facts justified the conduct of Durand at the time.

Máu.

It is time now to turn to Máu. Colonel Durand's letter to Colonel Platt, the commandant of the 23rd Native Infantry and of the station, despatched from Indúr at a quarter to 9, reached Colonel Platt about 10 o'clock. Colonel Platt instantly gave orders to Captain Hungerford,

Captain Hungerford's battery,

Book VIII. Chapter III.

1857. July 1.

commanding the battery, to set out for the relief of the Residency at Indúr. The battery,—why, has not been explained,—was not ready to leave Máu before noon. It then advanced on the Indúr road at a trot. It had reached the village of Rao, half-way between the two stations,* when Captain Hungerford learned that Colonel Durand and the British residents had left Indúr, and had not taken the road to Máu. Hungerford at once turned about, and galloped or cantered back to Máu, arriving there at 3 o'clock in the afternoon.†

leaves at noon.

Hungerford hears of the evacuation,

and returns.

Futility of its proceeding further.

It is clear from this statement that Captain Hungerford's battery could not have reached Indúr, if it had continued the journey at the rate at which it was going, before 3 P.M.—equally clear from the narrative I have given of the events at Indúr, that Colonel Durand and the garrison could not have held out for the four and a half hours which would have elapsed between his departure and the arrival of Captain Hungerford. Further, it is tolerably certain that Captain Hungerford's battery, arriving at any hour after the complete investment of the Residency, driven by native drivers, unsupported by cavalry or infantry, would have been unable to hold its own against the large force of all arms, which it would have found at Indúr. However, Captain Hungerford returned to Máu. The same evening he took his battery within the fort. That night, the regular

The troops at Máu mutiny.

* Major Evans Bell speaks of the distance between the Residency and Indúr as being ten miles. It is so now by the new road. But by the road which existed in 1857, it was more nearly fourteen than thirteen miles.

† Colonel Durand to Lord Canning's Private Secretary.

troops in Máu, in conformity with the arrangement made with their brethren in the service of Holkar, broke out into revolt. They began, as usual, by firing the mess-house. Their colonel, Colonel Platt, and their adjutant, Captain Fagan, having gone down to the lines to reason with them, they shot them both dead. The cavalry troopers, likewise, killed their commandant, Major Harris. The other officers escaped with their lives.

Book VIII. Chapter III.

1857. July 1.

On the first sound of the mutiny, Colonel Platt had called upon Captain Hungerford to turn out with his battery. Captain Hungerford proceeded to respond to the call, but by the time he arrived on the parade-ground the mischief had been done and no enemy was to be seen. Nothing fell upon his vision but the blazing bungalows till then occupied by the officers. In this perplexity Hungerford directed fire to be opened on the lines. Then poured forth the sepoys, liberated from restraint. They pushed on to Indúr, effected a junction with the mutineers at that place, and subsequently made their way to Dehlí.

Hungerford drives the mutineers from Máu,

Hungerford then held the chief authority at the station. Occupying the fort which commands the military road from Bombay and the low country to the highlands of Central India, he was able to render excellent service. During the absence of Durand, he assumed the post of representative of the Government of India at the court of Holkar. The real authority, however, still remained with Durand whose course I now propose to follow.

and assumes charge of the Central Indian Agency.

Book VIII. Chapter III.

1857. July 1.

The evacuation of the Residency.

We left Durand with the garrison, the women, and children, evacuating the Residency at half-past 10, on the memorable 1st of July. Travers made a last effort to induce the infantry of the two Contingents to make but one charge. These men, however, had by this time become so infused with the mutinous spirit that the attempt proved dangerous and useless. He managed, however, to collect the greater portion of the Bhopál cavalry, and though these refused to charge, they assumed an attitude sufficiently threatening to prevent pursuit. The next point to be considered was the direction in which they were to retire.

Considerations regarding the line of retreat.

The natural line of retreat was on Máu. By that road alone was it likely that assistance could come. A letter had been despatched for that assistance at a quarter to 9. That letter could scarcely have reached Colonel Platt before 10. It was just possible that Hungerford might be starting.* But it was equally possible, and more probable, that the letter might not have reached Máu. At a time when the native cavalry all over India were falling away by hundreds, it would have been hazardous to carry out a military manœuvre, the safe execution of which depended on the fidelity of one solitary trooper.

Insurmountable difficulties in the way of a retreat on Máu,

Still in war something must be risked, and Durand and Travers were alike prepared to accept the chance that Hungerford had started to meet them. But there was an insurmountable difficulty to the retreat on Máu. In my description of the Residency, I have shown that the road

* In point of fact he did not leave Máu till noon.

to Máu passed near that building on its western front, and at a distance of about four hundred yards from it crossed the Khán river. I have shown, likewise, that it passed by the cluster of buildings occupied by Holkar's troops. When the Residency was evacuated, not only was the entire length of that road in their possession, but their right rested upon it, a few yards in front of the bridge and completely covering it. Had the men of our Contingents made one charge the enemy's right might have been forced back and the bridge secured. But—as has been already stated—the cavalry refused to act; the infantry, when appealed to by Travers, threatened his life. The timely devotion of a sepoy alone saved him. To move artillery without supports close to and in face of an enemy flanking the moving body is, in war, impossible. For four hundred yards the retreating party would have been exposed to the fire of an enemy elated by victory. The attempt to cross that bridge would, then, have been fatal to the entire party. Nor was it possible to cross the river itself above the bridge—for it had steep banks and was not fordable. I may add, with confidence, that even had the bridge been forced, the difficulties of the retreating party, harassed by a formidable enemy, would not have been lessened.

by the regular road.

But there was another bridge across the Khán, higher up, and beyond the Residency garden. This might certainly have been crossed. But having crossed it where would the party have been? To gain the Máu road they would have had to move for about six hundred yards by the

The other road equally out of the question.

Book VIII. Chapter III.

1857. July 1.

road on the left bank of the Khán—the only other traversable road. To the point where that road meets the Máu road the rebels were nearer by three parts of the whole distance to be traversed than were the ladies and the garrison. That is to say, the rebels, crossing by the lower bridge, were about a quarter of a mile distant from that point, whilst the garrison, leaving the Residency, would have to traverse more than a mile to reach it. Surely to attempt that road by the upper bridge would have been to draw rather too large an order on the blindness of an enemy reeking in slaughter, and flushed with victory!

Disinclination of the native troops to go to Máu.

Another reason for not attempting the Máu road was based on the disinclination of the remaining cavalry to follow it. Their hearts were in their homes and with their families. Their homes and their families were at Sihor—and Sihor was the goal of their hopes.

Durand and Travers renounce the idea of Máu.

Durand and Travers were forced then, most unwillingly, to renounce the idea of a retreat on Máu. The impossibility of reaching that station being clear to them it devolved on Durand to decide the direction in which to retire. In connection with this point a plain duty, he conceived, lay before him.

Reasons which actuated Durand in his choice of a line of retreat.

I have already alluded to the Bombay column halted at Arangábád. Under the circumstances of the case, attacked by Holkar's troops, with, as he undoubtedly believed at the time, the sanction and concurrence of Holkar, driven out of Indúr, cut off from Máu, it seemed to Durand to be his plain duty, at any and every sacrifice,

Book VIII. Chapter III.

1857. July 1.

to make his way to that column and urge its immediate advance. He could not help believing Central India to be in the utmost peril; nor that the only mode of saving, or of promptly recovering it, lay in the immediate advance of Woodburn's column. He resolved then to push on towards that column by way of Mandlésar.

Attempts to move on Mandlésar.

The party started then on the Mandlésar road. But, after proceeding some distance, Travers found it might be within the range of possibility to communicate with Hungerford. It had occurred alike to Durand and himself that it was just possible that Hungerford's battery had started; that it would push on to Indúr, and that Hungerford, embarrassed by native drivers, might find himself in difficulties. To relieve Hungerford, then, Travers wrote to him two notes, stating that Durand had evacuated Indúr, and was endeavouring to effect a retreat by the Simrol pass. The notes were despatched, each by the hand of a trooper, in the hope that, finding his way across country, one at least would reach Hungerford.

The Simrol pass is reported occupied by Holkar's troops.

The troopers had not long started when reports from many quarters reached Durand that the Simrol pass was occupied by the cavalry and artillery of Holkar. These were, he was told, the very cavalry and artillery whom Holkar, to be rid of, had furnished with carriage and supplies. Durand, nothing daunted, resolved to force this pass. But again he was baffled by his following. The Bhopál cavalry were willing enough to follow the English residents to their own homes at Sihor, and to protect them from

The Bhopál cavalry refuse to attempt to force it.

Book VIII. Chapter III.

1857. July 1.

assault on the road; but they were not prepared to run any risk to escort them anywhere else. They positively refused to attempt the Simrol pass. They declared that they would go only to Sihor, in the first instance—thence to any station that might be named. No resource was left, then, to Durand but to retire upon Sihor. It was a bitter alternative, for it removed him from the line by which General Woodburn would have to advance. The distance, too, was long and wearisome for the ladies and children. More than that, it appeared to be surrounded by danger. The reception of the fugitive party at Sihor was by no means assured. Durand could not be certain that the Bégam of Bhopál would be able to withstand the severe pressure that he well knew was put upon her, or that she would be able to restrain her excited Mahomedan subjects.* But there was no help for it. Could he have seen his way to the Bombay column, *viâ* Máu, it is obvious he would have taken it. He could then have left his wife, then suffering, and the other ladies, in safety at Máu, whilst he should proceed on his journey to the south. But the evidence is overwhelming that such a movement was impossible. Forced, then, to take the road to Sihor, he proceeded by rapid marches to that

Durand compelled to retire on Sihor,

* General Travers, V.C., thus writes:—"When we reached Ashta" (in Bhopál territory), "on the 3rd of July the guard drawn up on the banks of the Párbatti, and across our road, and the crowd with it, made many think their last hour had come. The women and children were dismounted from the limbers, and the guns got ready for action, when a messenger arrived to announce it was the Guard of Honour! It *was* a relief."

place, and arrived there on the 4th of July with the guns and the Europeans who had left the Indúr Residency on the morning of the 1st of July.

Book VIII. Chapter III.

1857. July 4.

which he reaches the 4th of July.

I have occupied many pages in treating this interesting episode in the great Indian mutiny, but the widely diverse views disseminated, since his decease, regarding the conduct of the principal actor, have imposed upon me the necessity of making my narrative of the events which happened at Indúr as clear and as precise as possible. It has been more than insinuated that Durand needlessly abandoned his position; that he might have retired on Máu; that he was quite unequal to the occasion. Such charges, if made anonymously, might have been left to be disposed of by the judgment of those who knew Durand in India. But they have assumed the garb and the title of History. It was necessary, therefore, that their baselessness should be made clear by History. And no one will assert that, for such a purpose, the narrative of the events at Indúr in these pages is too long.

Reason why the story of Indúr has occupied so much space, will be generally accepted as sufficient.

What, in fact, in a few words, was the conduct so carped at, but, in reality, so noble and meritorious, of Colonel Durand, in those dark days which intervened between the 14th of May and the 4th of July 1857? That conduct has been clearly, fairly, and briefly summed up in a manner which cannot be improved upon. "Without the aid of any European force," summarises the writer of *Central India in* 1857, "he had succeeded in maintaining himself at Indúr for six weeks after

Summary of Durand's conduct.

Book VIII. Chapter III.

1857. July 4.

the outbreak at Dehlí, by isolating the contingent troops, and playing them off against the regulars. When, contrary to his wishes, the two were allowed to come into contact, the fidelity of the contingents gave way, and, gradually, the circle of insurrection closed upon Indúr. At last, driven out of the Residency by a combination of treachery and cowardice, he made a good, soldierly retreat, in the face of overwhelming masses, veiling his weakness by a show of force, and marched into Sihor without the loss of gun, standard, or trophy."

He proceeds to Hoshangábád,

Such was the conduct of this noble representative of the English race up to the 4th of July. His subsequent action neither belied his reputation, nor conduced less to the security of British interests in Central India. Arriving at Sihor, Durand stayed there but one day, and then started off for Hoshangábád, on the southern bank of the Narbadá, in the hope of being able to communicate with General Woodburn. At Hoshangábád he heard of the mutiny of the regular troops at Máu, and of their departure from that station, held, thenceforward, in security by Hungerford's battery. Secure, then, of Máu, Durand was anxious that Woodburn's force should make safe the line of the Narbadá, and thus interpose a barrier "between the blazing north and the smouldering south." But here he met with an unexpected difficulty. Mr. Plowden, the Commissioner of the Central Provinces, under the impression that the rising at Máu had been fatal to all the Europeans stationed there, was urging

urges the advance on Máu of Woodburn's column.

General Woodburn to throw up the line of the Narbadá, and to march on Nágpúr. Durand strongly protested against the adoption of a course of action which would have roused Central India against us. He wrote to the Government of India; he wrote to Mr. Plowden; he wrote to General Woodburn. He even authorised the officers commanding military posts to disregard any orders they might receive to abandon their positions on the Narbadá. But he did more. Keenly sensible of the necessity for prompt action, of the delays entailed by correspondence, and of the value of enforcing his arguments by his personal presence, Durand started for Arangábád, where he believed Woodburn's column still to be. On his way, the gratifying intelligence reached him that his urgent requisitions for the advance of the column had been successful; that General Woodburn had returned to Púna in bad health; that Brigadier Stuart had succeeded him, with orders to push on at once, and that the column was on its way to Máu *viâ* Asírgarh. To Asírgarh, then, Durand hurried. His presence was a tower of strength. He impressed his own energy on every one present with the force. There were no further delays. Pressing onwards, the column traversed the pass of Simrol on the 1st of August, and entered Máu on the following day, just in time to escape the difficulties the rainy season, which began that night, would have entailed upon them. The line of the Narbadá was saved.

Book VIII. Chapter III.

1857. July.

Joins that column at Asírgarh,

and accompanies it to Máu.

In this rescued position, for the present, I

Book VIII. Chapter III. 1857. July.

must leave Central India, to glance at the condition of affairs in the bordering States of Rájpútáná, and then to record how the action in the Native States affected Mr. Colvin and A'gra.

BOOK VIII.

CHAPTER IV.

RA'JPU'TA'NA'—the country of the Rájpúts—comprises eighteen native states,* seventeen of which were ruled by Hindús of the purest blood—the eighteenth, Tonk, by the Mahomedan descendant of the famous freebooter, Amír Khan. To most of these States was assigned a political officer, but the chief of all these, the Governor-General's Agent for the general control of Rájpútáná, was Colonel George St. Patrick Lawrence, brother of Sir Henry and of Sir John Lawrence. **Rájpútáná.**

To Colonel George Lawrence had been allotted many of the great qualities of his famous brothers. He was high-spirited, conscientious, decided, a lover of truth and justice, frank, and straightforward. He had seen a great deal of service. As a cavalry officer he was much appreciated. As **Colonel George Lawrence.**

* These states are Udaipúr or Mewár, Jaipúr, Jodhpúr or Márwár, Búndí, Kotá, Jháláwar, Tonk, Karaulí, Kishngarh, Dholpúr, Bharatpúr, Alwar, Bikanír, Jaisalmír, Siróhí, Dongarpúr, Banswárí, and Partábgarh.

Book VIII. Chapter IV.

1857.

a political he had greatly distinguished himself during the arrangements which followed the conquest of Afghánistán. After the murder there, which he witnessed, of the envoy, and the annihilation of our army, he had shared the captivity of Eyre, of Colin Mackenzie, and of the last survivors of General Elphinstone's army. Employed in the most responsible position at Pasháwar after the first Sikh war he was taken prisoner by the Afghán allies of the Sikhs during the second. Released after the peace conquered at Gújrát he continued to give to the Government able and conscientious service in the political department, latterly at Méwar in Rájpútána. In March 1857, on the transfer of his brother Sir Henry to the higher post of Chief Commissioner of Oudh, Colonel George Lawrence was appointed to act for Sir James Outram as political agent to the Governor-General for the whole of Rájpútáná.

His earlier career.

Is appointed to act as Agent for Rájpútáná.

In conformity with the prevailing custom Colonel Lawrence moved in the month of April to Abú, a mountain in the Siróhí territory about five thousand feet above the sea. All was quiet then in Rájpútáná. Under the fostering suzerainty of the British the Rájpút dynasties had been, during the preceding forty years, gradually recovering from the wounds inflicted upon them by the House of Taimúr, and from the severer gashes they had suffered from the Maráthá marauder and Pindárí plunderer. They were now protected, and they and their subjects were gradually reaping the benefits of that most efficient protection. If any of the officials holding high political and

The Rájpút dynasties favourable to British supremacy.

Book VIII. Chapter IV.

1857. April.

administrative office under the Government of India had reason to regard with a light heart the future as affecting his duties and his charge that official was the Agent to the Governor-General in Rájpútáná.

Colonel Lawrence hears of the mutiny at Mírath.

Colonel Lawrence went to Abú in April, then, with serenity and confidence, nor had he any reason to feel uneasy until the account of the mutiny of the 10th of May at Mírath roughly startled him. The intelligence of this event reached Abú the 19th of May. Colonel Lawrence at once comprehended its importance in all its bearings. His long connection with the native army had not mastered a judgment naturally keen and searching. He saw that the Barhámpúr mutiny, the Bárrákpúr outbreak, the Mírath rising, were no isolated acts due to some local grievance, but that each of these constituted a scene in one and the same tragedy. He saw at a glance, in fact, that the whole army was contaminated.

The condition of Rájpútáná.

His first thought directed itself naturally to the province under his charge. What, in fact, was the condition of Rájpútáná? Its population numbered ten millions of men subject to protected kings: it comprised an area of a hundred thousand square miles; within that area were five thousand native troops of all arms, belonging to the British army, all of whom, Colonel Lawrence, in his inmost heart, knew, would take the first favourable opportunity to mutiny: within that area, excluding some twenty sergeants attached to the native infantry regiments, there was not a

Book VIII. Chapter IV.

1857. May.

single European soldier fit for duty. The nearest station held by English troops was the station of Dísá, in the Presidency of Bombay, about a hundred and fifty miles from Abú.

The troops at the disposal of Colonel Lawrence.

Such then was the position—a province inhabited by ten million natives, guarded by five thousand ill-disposed soldiers, presided over by a Colonel in the British army with some twenty or thirty British officers at his disposal, watching the certain approach of the wave of mutiny! It was a position to test the stuff that was in a man! How did Colonel Lawrence meet it?

The arsenal at Ajmír,

One of the first thoughts that occurred to him was that the arsenal at Ajmír must at all hazards be secured. Ajmír is a strip of British territory in the heart of Rájpútáná having as its capital the ancient and famous city of the same name. Close to this city, and commanded by the heights outside it, was an old and dilapidated fort, and within the fort was an arsenal capable of furnishing a siege train of great strength, guns, muskets, and ammunition; and containing a large quantity of specie.* This arsenal was, when the mutiny broke out, under charge of the light company of the 15th Regiment of Native Infantry, a regiment notoriously disaffected. But, after the bad news from Mírath, the military authorities at Nasírábád, acting on a curious principle, somewhat analogous to that of setting a thief to catch a thief,† had strengthened the light

is garrisoned by disaffected troops.

Is now reinforced by other disaffected troops.

* *The Mutinies in Rajpootana*, by Iltudus Prichard.

† "When the excitement began, in consequence of the news from Meerut, the grenadier company of the 15th

1857. May.

company by adding to it the grenadier company of the same regiment. The arsenal at Ajmír, containing the *matériel* for the whole of Rájpútáná was, then, when the news of the Mírath outbreak reached Colonel Lawrence, under the protection of two companies of a native regiment which all but its own officers knew to be disaffected.

Colonel Lawrence summons European troops from Dísá.

It was most important to place this arsenal as soon as possible in secure hands. As quick as thought, then, Colonel Lawrence despatched a requisition to the officer commanding at Dísá to despatch a light field force to enable him at the same time to assure the safety of the arsenal and to overawe the regular native troops at Nasírábád. The force was despatched, but before it could arrive, the Commissioner of Ajmír, Lieutenant-Colonel Dixon, acting on the inspiration of a dying man—for he survived but a few days—had made the arsenal safe. This officer, feeling, as Colonel Lawrence felt, that the caste question was a most important factor in the movements of the native army—that it was in fact the question of the hour—bethought him of the regiment, of which, in fact, he was

Colonel Dixon's happy inspiration,

Native Infantry was sent, ostensibly to reinforce the light company in the foot, in reality to act as a check upon it. This may appear a curious arrangement to some of my readers, as, if the protection of the fort was the object aimed at, it could scarcely be attained by doubling the strength of a traitorous garrison; but the grenadier company was generally supposed to be less tainted, or rather, I should say, more free from suspicion than the rest, and, in those days, we were all deceived alike."—*The Mutinies in Rajputana.* The author belonged to the 15th Native Infantry.

Book VIII. Chapter IV.

1857. May.

commandant, raised for civil duties and appertaining exclusively to Rájpútáná, composed entirely of low-caste men, of men who had no sympathy with the Brahmanical prejudices of the regular army. This regiment was the Mairwárá battalion, quartered at Bíáor, a little place south-west of Nasírábád on the Dísá road. Without the delay of a single day Dixon ordered Lieutenant Carnell, his second in command, to march at once with a hundred men of his battalion upon Ajmír. Carnell replied by acting with the most praiseworthy promptitude. Making a forced march of thirty-seven miles, he surprised the sepoys before they had concerted their plans with their comrades at head-quarters. The new arrivals at once took charge of the arsenal, and the regular troops were sent back to Nasírábád.

and Carnell's promptitude, save the arsenal.

This movement saved Rájpútáná.* The low-caste Mairs continued to the end faithful to their European lords. To show his appreciation of their good service and their loyalty Colonel Lawrence raised on his own authority a second battalion from the men of their tribe. Subsequently he did even more. He recommended that both battalions should enjoy all the privileges of regular native regiments, and this recommendation was agreed to.

Colonel Lawrence raises a second battalion of Mairs.

To return. Colonel Lawrence, secure, on learning of Colonel Dixon's successful action,

* It cannot be doubted that if the arsenal at Ajmír had fallen into the hands of the mutineers, and with it, the city, Rájpútáná would have been lost for the time. —Prichard's *Mutinies in Rajpootana*, pages 39, 40.

1857. May 23.

He addresses the native princes of Rájpútáná.

regarding the arsenal and important position of Ajmír, turned his attention to the native princes with whom he was officially connected. Feeling that it was above all thing necessary to maintain before their eyes a sovereign position, and to insist upon their fulfilling the duties which protected princes owed to the paramount power, Colonel Lawrence on the 23rd issued to them a proclamation. In this proclamation he called upon them to preserve peace within their borders, to concentrate their troops on the frontiers of their respective States, so that they might be available to aid the British, to show zeal and activity in dealing with any body of rebels who might attempt to traverse their territories. Whilst thus requiring the co-operation of the native princes Colonel Lawrence warned the commandants at the several stations to act with promptness and vigour, and he made the request to the Government of Bombay, that any European troops, returning to Persia, who might be required for service in the North-West Provinces, should be sent to A'gra *viâ* Gújrát and Rájpútáná.

Nasírábád and Nímach are garrisoned wholly by native troops.

The two military stations garrisoned by the native regular army, in the province under Colonel Lawrence's control, were Nasírábád and Nímach. The regiments and batteries at these stations being entirely native it was not to be expected, and Colonel Lawrence did not expect, that they would escape the general infection. Hence the precaution he had taken to send to Dísá for troops. It was a wise and prudent precaution, but unfortunately the troops could

Book VIII. Chapter IV.

1857. May 23–28.

not march so quickly as the rumour which heralded their approach. Before they could arrive the mischief had been accomplished. They were able, however, to a great extent to repair it.

The disposition of the Nasírábád garrison.

The garrison of Nasírábád consisted of the 15th and 30th Regiments of Native Infantry, a battery of native Artillery, and the 1st Bombay Lancers. Reports regarding the bad disposition of the men of the 15th had been circulated in the station very soon after the arrival of the news of the Mírath outbreak. But their officers considered these reports greatly exaggerated, believing that although their men might follow the lead of others, they would not show the way. The result showed that they were mistaken.

Precautions there taken.

In consequence of the prevalent rumours every possible precaution for the safety of the station had been taken. The cantonment was patrolled every night by parties of the 1st Lancers—believed to be faithful—the guns were kept limbered up and loaded with grape. But about 3 o'clock on the afternoon of the 28th of May some men of the 15th suddenly rushed to the guns, with loaded muskets, and declared themselves in revolt. The guns almost simultaneously opened fire. The officers galloped down to the lines and attempted to bring their men to reason, but in vain. Muskets were pointed, in some cases fired, at them, and they were warned to be off. The 30th Regiment, which till then had remained quiescent, apparently in a state of hesitation, joined the revolters about 4 o'clock. There still remained the Lancers. These at least would remain true.

The sepoys there mutiny.

1857. May 28.

Disaffection of the cavalry.

In this belief the infantry and artillery officers joined them, hoping with them to charge the rebels. They did charge. But the guns loaded with grape opened upon them. The men had no heart in the business. I have said that they charged. But it would have been more correct to state that they made several feints to charge. They never rode home. One of the officers, Newbery, who did charge home, was cut down and hacked to pieces, Captain Spottiswoode also was killed, and two officers, Captain Hardy and Lieutenant Lock, were badly wounded. Then it was that, feeling all their efforts useless, the officers resolved to retreat and accompany the ladies to Bíáor. These had been sent outside the cantonments when the first shot was fired. There the officers found them, and escorted them all that night and till 11 o'clock the next morning to their destination. There was but one casualty —Colonel Penny of the Lancers dying of heat apoplexy on the road.

The officers, ladies, and children are forced to evacuate the station.

Nímach.

Nímach lies about a hundred and fifty miles south of Nasírábád. The troops at this station consisted of the 72nd Regiment of Native Infantry, the 7th Regiment of the Gwáliár contingent, and a wing of the 1st Bengal Cavalry. Sudden firing of houses, reports from the lines, and the unwonted presence of strangers, had foreshadowed for some time past a rising at this station. Yet the men loudly protested their fidelity and their indignation at the conduct of their brethren. All remained quiet till the 3rd of June. That day full information was received of

Book VIII. Chapter IV.

1857. June 3.

The rising there.

the events at Nasírábád on the 28th. That night about 10 o'clock the firing of two guns announced to the officers that the men had risen. Fortunately at Nímach there was a fortified square which had been prepared as a place of refuge in case of an emergency. Its defence, however, had been entrusted to the men of the 7th Regiment of the Gwáliár contingent. The officers on the first sound of the mutiny rushed to this square, and found the left wing of that regiment entering it, whilst the men of the right wing were lining the ramparts. The officers spoke cheerfully and encouragingly to the men. These promised fidelity, many declaring that they would rather die than surrender. Delusive were their promises. At 4 o'clock in the morning the sepoys guarding the fort mutinied, despite the protestations of their officers, and filed out to join their comrades in the plunder of the station. No officers lost their lives, but there were some hair-breadth escapes. The wife of a serjeant and her three children were murdered before they could reach the fort. Ultimately the Europeans succeeded in making their way to Udaipúr. The rebels burned all the houses in the station but one, plundered the treasury, and made, by way of A'gra, for Dehlí. Their operations on the rear of our force there, and their sudden assault on A'gra, will be related presently.

The officers escape to Udaipúr.

Colonel Lawrence starts for Bíáor.

Intelligence of the mutiny at Nasírábád reached Colonel Lawrence at Abú on the 1st of June. He started at once for Bíáor so as to be close to the scene of action. On his arrival at Bíáor he found

He is nominated Brigadier-General.

Book VIII. Chapter IV.

1857. June 1–12.

himself nominated Brigadier-General in command of all the troops in Rájpútáná. Almost his first act was to direct the repair of the dilapidated fort* of Ajmír, and to store it with provisions. But a general can do nothing without an army, and at the moment of receiving his grade General Lawrence had not fifty European soldiers at his disposal. The native regular troops had mutinied and had taken themselves off. The contingent corps attached to several of the native courts were, as a rule, not to be trusted. Unlike the men of the Mairwárá battalion they were composed of Hindús—with whom food is a religion.

His scanty resources.

But very soon the results of the earlier inspirations of General Lawrence began to manifest themselves. On the 12th of June there arrived at Nasírábád the force for which he had made a requisition on Dísá. This force consisted of four hundred men of Her Majesty's 83rd; the 12th Bombay Native Infantry; and a troop of European Horse Artillery. He at once ordered a hundred men to Ajmír to reinforce the Mairs stationed there. General Lawrence then made that

Troops from Dísá arrive.

Re-occupation of Nasírábád,

* It should be stated that on the summit of the hill commanding Ajmír, and commanding the magazine and the city was another and a smaller fort, close to a shrine held in veneration by the Mahomedans. Not having at his disposal a sufficient number of men to guard the fort, General Lawrence entrusted the defence of this post to the Mahomedans of the shrine, the chief priests of which had satisfactorily proved that it was their interest as its guardians to remain faithful to the British. They were true to the end, performing the garrison duties with zeal and fidelity till the danger had passed away.

Book VIII. Chapter IV.

place his head-quarters, making constant visits, however, to Bíáor and Nasírábád.*

1857. June 12.

and of Nímach,

After the revolt of the native troops at Nímach, General Lawrence had caused that place to be occupied by detachments from the contingents of Méwa, Kotá, and Búndí. He had no choice, for at the moment no other troops were available. A few indications, however, soon showed him that these men were as little to be trusted as were their brethren in the line. He took, then, an early opportunity of replacing them by a detachment from the troops but just arrived from Dísá.

by European troops.

The lieutenants of General Lawrence.

But it was impossible for General Lawrence to be everywhere; it was impossible that he should be able to demonstrate personally to all the native sovereigns and chieftains with whom he was officially connected that the knell of British rule had not sounded; it was impossible for him to enact at each native capital the policy which had been so successful at Ajmír. And the effect of all these impossibilities ultimately made itself felt. A narration of these events belongs to a subsequent period of this history. It will be suffi-

* "During June and July I resided alternately between Ajmír, Bíáor, and Nasírábád as I deemed my presence necessary at each place with reference to my military as well as civil and political duties. My head-quarters were, however, at Ajmír, where I resided in the Daolat Bágh, close to the city, with a native officer's party of the Mairwárá battalion as my only guard. When at Ajmír I never once allowed the routine of civil duties to be interrupted, but held open court, almost daily visiting the city, where, although fierce and sullen faces were always to be seen, I was always treated with the greatest respect."—*Forty Years Service in India*, by Lieutenant-General Sir George Lawrence.

cient here to state that whilst General Lawrence by his personal exertions and prompt action saved the great arsenal of Ajmír and recovered the two military centres of Nasírábád and Nímach, his lieutenants at Jaipúr, at Jodhpúr, and at Bharatpúr, nobly seconded his efforts. It will be necessary to devote some lines to their action.

Book VIII. Chapter IV.

1857. June.

Major William Eden.

The agent at Jaipúr was Major William Eden, an officer possessing ability, firmness, and discretion. The reigning Rájá of Jaipúr, Mahárájá Rám Singh, owed his throne, his education, it might almost be said his life, to the British. He had been extremely well educated, was naturally intelligent, and, being well acquainted with the history of Rájpútáná during the later days of Moghol sway and the entire period of Maráthá oppression, he was profoundly convinced that his own safety, the permanence of his rule, and the prosperity of his subjects, were bound up in the maintenance of the British suzerainty. The tale of the oppressions and tyrannies suffered by his ancestors and their subjects during the short period which had elapsed between the withdrawal of that suzerainty and its restoration—the period between 1804 and 1818—was still fresh in the minds of the prince and of his people. Major Eden then experienced no difficulty with the Mahárájá. He was as eager to show his loyalty as Major Eden was to demand it. The same spirit animated his people generally. Unhappily it was not so with his army. The sepoys composing it had come, for the most part, from the recruiting grounds which had supplied the British native

Rám Singh, Rájá of Jaipúr.

His reasons for being attached to British over-rule.

Book VIII. Chapter IV.

1857. June.

His loyal feeling is not shared by his troops;

army, and they were influenced by the same feelings of distrust and hostility. Here, too, as at Gwáliár, as at Indúr, it was plainly shown that when the fanaticism of an oriental people is thoroughly aroused, not even their Rájá—their father as all consider him, their god as some delight to style him—not even their Rájá can bend them against their convictions. Five thousand of the Mahárájá's troops were indeed put into the field:—they even marched towards the districts of Mathurá and Gúrgaon with the avowed mission to maintain order and re-establish civil government. But it quickly appeared that if the maintenance of order and the re-establishment of civil government were to involve the necessity of fighting the revolted sepoys, the Jaipúr troops would neither maintain the one nor re-establish the other. Like the Sihor cavalry, they were prepared to defend European fugitives, but they would not wage an aggressive warfare. Their views in this respect having been practically established, the five thousand Jaipúr troops were recalled to their own territory.

who refuse to wage war for the English.

Jódhpúr.

At Jódhpúr, the agent was Captain Monck-Mason, highly-gifted, energetic, daring, and possessing tact and judgment. The position of Jódhpúr was peculiar. Its Rájá, Takht Singh, transferred in 1843 from the throne of I'dar to that of Jódhpúr, on the failure of hereditary issue in the family of the deceased ruler of the latter State, had not succeeded in conciliating the respect or the affections of his subjects. He had shown himself avaricious, careless of affairs,

Rájá Takht Singh.

His misgovernment.

difficult of access. Many of his thákúrs, or nobles, were extremely ill-disposed towards him; some were in veiled, others even in open rebellion. The Mahárájá himself had no love for his Suzerain. Still he was not blind to the fact that, in the state of ill-feeling that existed between him and his nobles, it behoved him to cling to the British as his surest anchoring ground. He placed, therefore, a small contingent—two thousand men and six guns—at the agent's disposal. Up to the end of June, then, matters looked well in Jódhpúr. The events that succeeded belong to a subsequent period of this history.

Book VIII. Chapter IV.

1857. June.

Places a small contingent at the disposal of the British.

At Bharatpúr, the agent was Major Nixon. The prompt action of the Darbár of the minor Rájá, and the mutiny of the troops of this principality, have been already related.*

Bharatpúr.

At Alwar there was no political agent. The Ráo Rájá, Bénéi Singh, at once placed a small contingent at the disposal of the British. His death, however, almost immediately afterwards, and the complications that ensued in his own State, rendered the proffered aid for all practical purposes nugatory.

Alwar.

There remains to be noticed Udaipúr, the most ancient and the most venerated of all the States of Rájpútáná. The name of theRáná was Sarúp Singh. He, like the Rájá of Jodhpúr, was not on good terms with his nobles. The British agent at this court was Captain Showers. When the news of the Mírath mutiny reached Rájpútáná, Captain Showers was at Abú, with other officers,

Udaipúr.

Captain Showers.

* *Vide* page 154.

Book VIII. Chapter IV.

1857. June.

the guest of Colonel Lawrence. Captain Showers was ordered to leave Abú and to return to his post at Udaipúr. In the opinion of his chief, however, his movements in that direction were not sufficiently rapid. Nor did his subsequent proceedings meet more with General Lawrence's approval, and at a later date that officer was under the necessity of reporting to the Government Captain Showers's "repeated acts of disobedience and defiance of his authority." The ultimate result was the removal of Captain Showers from political employment; the immediate consequence, a jar in the communications which it was necessary that the Agent for the Governor-General in Rájpútáná should maintain with the staff of officers through whom he worked with the native princes.

Disapproval of his conduct by Colonel Lawrence,

and its consequences.

Summary of Colonel Lawtence's conduct in Rájpútáná,

I have endeavoured thus briefly to describe the condition of Rájpútáná up to the end of June, 1857. We see the shock of the mutiny broken, the great arsenal saved, the principal native chiefs confirmed in their loyalty, by the vigorous and decided action of Colonel Lawrence. It is true that the regular regiments located in the two military centres had revolted. But Colonel Lawrence had recovered those centres. In Rájpútáná, in a word, defiance had been met by defiance, force by force. Events proved this principle to be a sound one. Compare the instant relief of the regular garrison at Ajmír by troops who could be trusted, with the hesitation to show doubt evinced at A'gra, Alláhábád, Banáras,

Dánápúr, and Bárrákpúr. The first-named policy saved British interests without imperilling a single life; the second led through a sea of slaughter to the same results. Had Rájpútáná risen, it is difficult to see how A'gra could have held out, how our force before Dehlí could have maintained its ground. And that Rájpútáná did not rise is due to the prompt, decided, and far-seeing action of Colonel George St. Patrick Lawrence.

which was saved by his promptness, decision, and foresight.

The mutinous regiments are hurrying out of Rájpútáná. It is time now that I should bring back the reader to the fortress which they are hoping to surprise and capture.

BOOK VIII.

CHAPTER V.

A'gra in the last fortnight of June.

THE events recorded in the three preceding chapters affected, more or less intensely, the situation at A'gra. That situation was becoming, towards the latter end of June, difficult to maintain. During that month the entire country on the right bank of the Jamná, on which the city stood, had pronounced against the British.

Its gradual isolation.

Nor were any reassuring signs visible on the left bank. There, where the light of day was not entirely shut out, the lurid flame of insurrection alone was visible. In a word, towards the fourth week of June, the capital of the North-West Provinces had become entirely isolated. But her worst days had not even then dawned upon her.

Reception of the fugitives from Gwáliár.

The mutiny at Gwáliár had occurred on the 14th of June. During the following days the fugitives had been gradually arriving at A'gra. They were received there with all the kindness and consideration due to suffering humanity, their wants were supplied, and their comforts were attended to. Up to this time the idea of retiring within the Fort had not again been mooted. The defence of the station had been entrusted to the volunteer levies, and these had latterly been placed under the command of an officer in active service, Major Prendergast. Besides these were the regular European troops before alluded to, numbering altogether about six hundred and fifty fighting men.

Disposable troops at A'gra.

In addition to these defenders was another body in whom the Lieutenant-Governor, Mr. Colvin, and the magistrate, Mr. Drummond, were unhappily disposed to place confidence. These were the native police, the leading spirits of whom were, to a man, Mahomedans.* If the evidence of those who were at A'gra, and who enjoyed opportunities of noting the conduct of these men, is to be trusted, the confidence reposed in them was entirely misplaced. They were in communication with the several bodies of mutinous men on the right bank of the Jamná. It was in response to their entreaties that these latter turned their steps towards A'gra. They harassed and opposed the officers who were engaged in victualling the fort; they intercepted communication with the world outside A'gra; and they showed in various ways, unmistakeably to all except to Mr. Drummond and the Lieutenant-Governor, that they too were waiting their opportunity.†

Mr. Colvin and Mr. Drummond place confidence in the native police, who are untrustworthy.

Meanwhile, towards the end of the third week

Rumours from outside.

* Raikes's *Notes on the Revolt.* † *Ibid.*

Book VIII. Chapter V.

1857. June.

of June, the rumour gradually filled the air that the regular troops who had revolted at Nímach and at Nasírábád, recruiting their strength by taking up stray revolted bodies in their course, were marching direct upon A′gra. Every item of ascertained information pointed to the conclusion that the rumour was true. The strength of the force was then estimated to be about two thousand six hundred men with twelve guns.

Mr. Colvin authorises retirement within the fort,

The confirmation of this rumour decided Mr. Colvin. Certain now that the rebels were approaching A′gra, with the intention of attacking it, the Lieutenant Governor felt how his position would be hampered by the necessity of defending the non-combatant population of a large and straggling station. At the end of June, therefore, he authorised the retirement within the fort of the helpless members of the Christian population. But, whilst he did this, he, with a fatuity which is inexplicable, forbade the transfer to the place of refuge of "any property beyond the sort of allowance which a French Customs' House officer at Calais or Marseilles passes under the term of a *sac de nuit*."* This extraordinary prohibition entailed subsequently "the loss and destruction of books, furniture, archives, records, public and private, and the ruin of hundreds of families."† The victualling of the fort was, however, pushed on from this time with greater earnestness than before.

but limits the amount of property to be stored there.

The rebels reach Fathpúr-Sikrí.

It was but time that measures of precaution

* Raikes. † *Ibid.*

should be taken. On the 2nd of July the rebel army had reached Fathpúr-Sikrí, only twenty-three miles from A'gra. Further measures now became necessary. I shall endeavour to describe, as clearly and succinctly as I can, those which were adopted.

Book VIII. Chapter V.

1857. July 2.

Disposition of the native troops and levies at and near A'gra.

I have already stated* that native troops from Gwáliár had been despatched to A'gra by Mahárájá Sindia, on the requisition of Mr. Colvin, as soon as the intelligence of the Mírath outbreak had been received. These troops had been sent out to endeavour to restore order in the A'gra and Aligarh districts and were no longer at A'gra.† Subsequently a detachment of the Kótá contingent had arrived and had been retained at the capital. Besides these there was at the same place, under the command of Saifúlla Khán, a native civil officer of high character, a body of about six hundred Kiráolí matchlockmen and three hundred Bharatpúr horse, with two nine-pounder guns. Lieutenant Henderson of the 10th Foot acted as the agent of the Lieutenant-Governor with this force.

Changes made on the approach of the rebels.

As soon as it was known that the rebel army was at Fathpúr-Sikrí a disposition was made of these two bodies of men by which they should command the flanks of a force marching on A'gra from the west. The detachment of the Kótá contingent was brought into the cantonment, whilst Saifúlla Khán's levies were ordered to the neighbourhood of Sháhganj, four miles on the

* Page 154.

† Their operations will be detailed in the next chapter.

Book VIII. Chapter V.

1857. July 3.

road to Fathpúr-Sikrí. This disposition took effect on the 2nd of July.

Mr. Colvin is forced by sickness to resign temporarily his office.

On the following morning there happened an event which took the supreme power out of the hands of the statesman who had up to that time directed it. Mr. Colvin was threatened with an apoplectic attack. If his measures had not been successful, his task, it must be admitted, had been most difficult. He had at least maintained his post at the helm and had done his best. Throughout a most trying period he had displayed great personal courage, an unselfishness not to be surpassed, whilst his kindness of heart and sympathy with suffering had endeared him to all with whom he had come in contact. Feeling himself, for the time, incapable of the direction of affairs Mr. Colvin made over charge of the Government, by warrant, the same day, to three officers—Mr. E. A. Reade, Brigadier Polwhele, and Major Macleod.

Mr. E. A. Reade.

Mr. Reade was the senior member of the Board of Revenue. He was a man of considerable capacity, and possessed judgment and energy.

Major Macleod.

Major Macleod of the Engineers, Mr. Colvin's Military Secretary, had served with credit in the first Afghánistán campaign, and had a high character in the army.

Brigadier Polwhele.

Brigadier Polwhele was the officer commanding the station. As it is action which is the truest test of the stuff which is in a man, and as the action of Brigadier Polwhele against the mutineers is now about to be recorded, I prefer that the reader should draw his own conclusions regarding his character from that action.

Book VIII. Chapter V.

1857. July 4.

Active measures of the new Council.

The day following the nomination of this Council active measures were taken for the defence of the place. Feeling that the prisoners in the large jail might in the impending attack be released, and that their presence within our defences would be most undesirable, the Council had the able-bodied men removed from the prison to the opposite side of the river and there set free. The pontoon bridge close to the fort, by which rebels from that side might cross was broken down; the native Christians were all brought into the fort; the two nine-pounder guns with Saifúlla Khán's force were removed to the magazine; at the same time, orders were transmitted to the officer commanding the Kótá contingent to march out and attack the advancing rebels.

The native levies not to be depended upon.

The first three of these measures were carried out successfully and with good effect. The two last produced a crisis—a crisis, which, whilst it materially diminished the number of fighting men at the disposal of our countrymen, yet cleared the air. When Lieutenant Henderson, for instance, reached the camp of the Kíráolí and Bharatpúr levies and required that the guns should be returned to the magazine, great excitement was manifested. But no open opposition was shown, and by a mixture of tact and firmness the guns were brought in. That night, however, Saifúllá Khán reported that he could no longer depend upon his levies; that the Bharatpúr horse had deserted, and that the Kíraólí men were discouraged by the removal of the guns, and would

Book VIII. Chapter V.

1857. July 4.

not fight. Prompt action followed this report. Saifúlla Khán and his levies were ordered to leave Sháhganj, and to start at once for Kíráolí. They obeyed that night.

Mutiny of the Kótá contingent.

Even before the guns had been taken from these levies the Kótá contingent had mutinied. The order to them to advance had been designedly a tentative order—a test of their fidelity. It did test it—and to some purpose. No sooner had the men received the order to march than the leading spirit amongst them, a native sergeant, shot down the European sergeant in charge of the stores. This was the signal. Firing hastily at their European officers, happily without effect, the men rushed off to join the rebels. They were in such a hurry that a loyal gunner, by name Mathurá, had time to spike the guns, whilst their European medical officer, Dr. Mathias, aided by his servants and others, strewed in the sand their powder, ammunition, and case shot.* The most serviceable portion of their armament was thus rendered useless. A party sent out from A'gra brought the guns to the fort.

Mr. Colvin enters the fort and resumes his authority.

On the evening of that day, the 4th of July, Mr. Colvin entered the fort. An improvement in his health enabled him to resume his authority. The movement into the fort had become absolutely necessary, the behaviour of the native troops who formed the two wings of the British force having left the station quite exposed. Still

* *Official narrative of events attending the outbreak of disturbances and the restoration of authority in the Agra district in* 1857-58 by A. L. M. Phillipps, Magistrate of Agra.

Book VIII. Chapter V.

1857. July 4.

Mr. Colvin changed his residence with great reluctance and under the pressure of his advisers. He could not but see, however, that the advance of the enemy had made Brigadier Polwhele, for a time, master of the situation. And Brigadier Polwhele wished to have his hands entirely free.

Approach of the rebels.

The time for military action had indeed arrived. A strong picket of the volunteer cavalry, posted at Sháhganj, notified to the Brigadier, on the morning of the 5th, the approach of the enemy. The question as to whether the British force should wait to receive the rebels in A'gra, or whether it should go out and meet them, had previously been debated. Brigadier Polwhele had had to consider whether, having under his orders the only European force available between A'gra and the Bombay Presidency on the one side, and between A'gra and that forming at Alláhábád on the other, he would be justified in courting an engagement with an enemy about eight times as strong in numbers as he was, and in which defeat might be fatal. He felt that with his European force he could maintain the fort of A'gra against all comers. To attempt to defend the station, without advancing, was impossible. Was he justified in risking his force, and possibly the loss of the fort, by advancing to meet the enemy in order to save the station of A'gra from destruction?

Considerations before Brigadier Polwhele.

He decides to meet the enemy.

Brigadier Polwhele was a brave man. Beset by advisers, he had seemed at first to incline to a policy of defence, but when, on the morning of the 5th, he received the information that the

Book VIII. Chapter V.

1857. July 5.

enemy was advancing upon A'gra, his soldierly instincts at once asserted themselves. He determined, on his own responsibility, to go and meet them.

Wisdom of his resolve.

It was a wise and prudent resolve. The history of India shows us that there is but one plain and simple mode of beating Asiatics, and that is to move straight onwards. Their numbers may overwhelm a general if he tries to manœuvre, but a steady advance is irresistible. It will be seen that Polwhele lost the battle of Sassiah because he did not sufficiently bear in mind the truth of this radical principle.

Numbers of the opposing forces.

The enemy's force had received considerable reinforcements at Fathpúr-Sikrí. It consisted now of about four thousand infantry, fifteen hundred cavalry, and eleven guns.* To meet these Brigadier Polwhele could dispose of five hundred and sixty-eight men of the 3rd European Regiment, one battery with sixty-nine Europeans, including officers, and fifty-four native drivers, fifty-five mounted militia, and fifty officers and civilians who had taken refuge in A'gra. The European Regiment was commanded by Colonel Riddell; the Artillery by Captain D'Oyly. In the disposition of battle, however, the battery was divided,—Captain D'Oyly taking three guns on

* In his official report, Brigadier Polwhele states that, from the most accurate information he was able to gather, the enemy's force consisted of the 72nd Native Infantry; the 7th Regiment Gwáliár contingent; 4th and 6th troops 1st Light Cavalry; four troops of cavalry of Méhidpúr contingent; part of the Kótá contingent; one troop of horse artillery; and one horse field-battery; altogether more than five thousand men.

the right flank—an equal number on the left being commanded by Captain Pearson.

1857. July 5.

The British force advances to Sháhganj.

The British force left the A'gra parade-ground about 1 o'clock. It took the road to Fathpúr-Sikrí and moved along it till it reached Bégam Samrú's walled gardens. On arriving at the village of Sháhganj, a halt was sounded to wait the return of the reconnoitring parties. These came in about half-past 2 o'clock with the information that the enemy were in strength at the village of Sassiah, about a mile distant. The force then advanced, but, after clearing the village of Sháhganj, it quitted the road, and forming up in the order indicated, the infantry in line in the centre, with the guns and a handful of cavalry covering either flank, inclined to the right over a sandy plain. Marching across this the enemy were descried. Their infantry appeared to be posted in and behind the village of Sassiah. Their artillery likewise was on either flank, but their guns were screened by rising ground, forming natural breastworks, and by thickly planted trees. Their cavalry was massed in considerable strength behind both flanks.

The enemy are descried.

They open fire,

The English force continued to advance to within half a mile of the enemy's position when the latter opened out with a fire from their left battery. Brigadier Polwhele then, halting his men, ordered the Europeans to lie down and the guns on either flank to return the fire. Owing to the screened nature of the enemy's position it soon became evident that their guns could not be silenced without an advance being made. In a

Book VIII. Chapter V.

1857. July 5.

short time they acquired the exact range and made such excellent practice that they exploded two tumbrils, and dismounted one of the guns in the half battery on the left, besides inflicting severe loss amongst the horses and drivers.

and make excellent practice.

Captains D'Oyly and Pearson urge an advance,

All this time our infantry were lying down. Captains D'Oyly and Pearson finding that their ammunition would soon be running low had sent repeated messages to the Brigadier reporting the fact, and urging him to attack the village with his infantry. The enemy, far from being checked, had been encouraged by the success of their guns to throw out skirmishers and to threaten our flanks with their cavalry. It had been for some time evident that if we were to confine ourselves to an artillery duel we could not beat them. Still, for two hours, the Brigadier seemed content to hold his own with the guns.

but without success.

Probable reasons influencing the Brigadier.

And yet, in continuing stationary, he was simply courting disaster. At any period within those two hours Brigadier Polwhele was in a more favourable position than Eyre had enjoyed in his fight near Arah. On that occasion Eyre, after pounding his enemy until he found that pounding alone would not win the day, had let loose his infantry upon him. He did not wait till his caissons had been exhausted, till every shot had been fired away! But this is just what Brigadier Polwhele did do! The fact is, that, tenderness for the lives of the only European infantry available for the defence of A'gra had made him over-cautious. His men were comparatively safe, there, lying down. He could not make up his mind to give, in sufficient time, the order to advance! Fatal caution! Lamentable oblivion of the history of former wars! It needed but an onward movement of that thin red line to drive the enemy out of the village. The guns would then have completed their discomfiture. But minute succeeded minute, and our infantry still lay, prone and motionless, on the ground.

Book VIII. Chapter V.

1857. July 5.

Inaction of the infantry,

Brigadier Polwhele was yet considering whether the time had arrived to give the order to advance, when the explosion of another tumbril in the half battery on our left warned him that it had all but passed. That explosion was greeted by the enemy with a frantic shout of joy. Their cavalry, emerging in order from behind the village, swept round the left flank to the rear of our force, and from that point made a desperate charge at the disabled guns. Calm and collected, Captain Pearson wheeled round one of his guns and awaited their approach. The company of the 3rd Europeans nearest him rose likewise, and wheeled to face them. A volley of grape and musketry greeted then the enemy as they charged through the guns shouting and waving their swords. They did not stop to complete their work.

till too late!

Charge of the enemy's cavalry,

but are driven off.

Almost immediately after the incident just related one of the enemy's horsemen was seen to approach our right flank, as if to ascertain our condition there. The horseman returned and made his report. At once about two hundred of the enemy's cavalry advanced with the evident intention of charging Captain D'Oyly's half-battery. At this sight Captain Prendergast, who

They attack the right flank.

Book VIII. Chapter V.

1857. July 5.

commanded eighteen mounted volunteers, could not contain himself, but with his small following charged the two hundred. As a manœuvre to stop the enemy's advance this gallant charge was effective, but in other respects it was disastrous. In the hand to hand conflict which followed, our horsemen lost more than one-third of their number. Had the enemy not shown abject cowardice not one of our men would have escaped.

Gallant charge of Prendergast.

The artillery-ammunition is exhausted,

More than two hours had elapsed. Captain D'Oyly now reported that his ammunition was all but exhausted. Then, and then only, did the Brigadier give the order to advance. The result showed how decisive would have been the movement had it been made earlier. Our infantry started to their feet, moved forward, and though suffering severely from the enemy's guns and from the fire of marksmen stationed on the roofs of the houses, gallantly forced their way into the village. One of the enemy's guns was captured and spiked. But our loss in this advance had been severe. The gallant D'Oyly, whose horse had been shot under him early in the day, was mortally wounded by a grape-shot whilst endeavouring to right one of his guns. Lifted on to a tumbril he still continued to direct the fire of his battery. The spirit of the soldier was still strong within him. Careless of his own sufferings, his duty to his guns, his corps, his country, mastered every other thought. Overcome, at last, by intense pain he turned to the man nearest him and said; "They have done for me now; put a stone over my grave and say that I

when the Brigadier orders the advance.

D'Oyly's splendid conduct.

Book VIII. Chapter V

1857. July 5.

died fighting my guns."* He died the second day after in the fort.

Our losses in the village.

In the village itself Major Thomas of the 3rd Europeans, a brave and accomplished officer, was mortally wounded. Many men fell with him. Every house, lane, and gateway was disputed. At last the enemy were driven out. It required now but the support of artillery to complete the victory. But here the fatal result of the delay in the advance became apparent. There was not a single round of ammunition left.

Fatal consequences of the delay in advancing.

To continue the contest with small arms was useless, for the enemy, though driven out of the village itself, still occupied detached houses whence they continued to pour a heavy fire on our men. D'Oyly was mortally wounded; Pearson, with the other half battery a complete wreck, had lost his only subaltern, Lamb, early in the action, and had suffered so severely in men and horses, and by the desertion of his native drivers with the spare horses, that he could not make a pretence of assisting. Meanwhile the enemy attributing to the right cause the silence of our guns, and gathering courage, began to make a strong demonstration with all three arms. For all practical purposes we had only infantry to oppose to them. The village could not be held by infantry alone. It would have been easy to cut off our communications with the fort. Our object besides was to defeat the rebels:—failing that—to guard the fortress of A'gra. A retreat then seemed

* "If glory be a distinction, for such a man death is not a leveller." — Napier's *Peninsular War.*

Book VIII. Chapter V.

the only possible course, if indeed even this were possible.

1857. July 5.

The force retires on A'gra,

The retreat was ordered. It was a keen disappointment to all. There was not one, even amongst the privates, who did not feel that the day had been lost by bad generalship; that an early advance would have gained the victory. They showed the stuff that was in them when the enemy's horsemen seemed disposed to contest their retreat. Waiting calmly till the enemy approached, somewhat hesitatingly, within musket range, they then delivered a volley which made

in good order.

many a horse riderless. Again and again the rebel cavalry tried the same manœuvre, but always with a similar result. The fire from the rebel guns, which had been at first alarming, now gradually slackened, and from the fact that in the last round they fired copper coins, it was inferred that they too had run short of ammunition.

Pearson tries to save his gun.

Meanwhile Pearson had made superhuman exertions to mount and get away his disabled gun. But horses, drivers, men, and time alike failed him. It did not, however, adorn the enemy's triumph, for it remained on the ground and a day or two later was brought into the fort.

The enemy, wanting ammunition, move on Dehlí.

Baffled by the result of their attempts to charge, and, probably, by the failure of their ammunition, the rebels as they followed marked their triumph by setting fire to every building they reached. Returning then to Sháhganj, they took there a hasty meal, and set off that very night on the road to Dehlí. They reached the imperial city on the 8th of July, and were received there with a grand salute in honour of their victory of Sassiah.

1857. July 5.

The villagers "improve" our defeat.

The beaten little army reached the fort as the day was closing. They had lost in killed forty-five, in wounded and missing, one hundred and eight of their number. Before the survivors entered, the blaze, advancing from house to house in the cantonments and civil station, had told the non-combatants and ladies within the fort how the battle had been appreciated by the natives. Hordes of villagers who had watched the contest from afar had at once dispersed to burn and to plunder. The previously released prisoners, and their comrades, now set at large, joined in the sport. All night the sky was illuminated with the flames of burning houses, and a murmur like the distant sea told what passions were at work. It was a magnificent though sad spectacle for the dispirited occupants of the fort.

The city and the station are plundered,

During the two days following disorder was rampant in and outside the fort. The city, the cantonments, the civil lines were ruthlessly plundered. Of all the official records those only of the revenue department were saved. Even these were secured by the unauthorised action of a high official—Mr. E. A. Reade. The others were burned with the buildings in which they were stored. At the same time the King of Dehlí was proclaimed in the city.* The rabble,

and the King of Dehlí is proclaimed.

* "On the morning after the battle the town crier, at the order of Morád Ali, Kótwál, proclaimed the reign of the King of Dehlí through the city. The armed procession that accompanied the crier was composed of most of the leading Mahomedan police officers attached to the Kót-

Book VIII. Chapter V.

1857. July 7.

who had at first wondered at our inaction after a battle which, if we were beaten in it, had at least caused the enemy to move off to Dehlí, soon began to attribute it to fear, and to take advantage of it accordingly.

Loyalty of Rájárám.

But there were men amongst them of a higher stamp who knew us better. One of these, by name Rájárám, a resident in the city, managed on the evening of the 7th to have conveyed to the magistrate within the fort a note in which he informed him that there were no rebel troops in A'gra; that the confusion which reigned was the work of the rabble; and that the entry of the magistrate into the city with a sufficient force would restore order.

Mr. Drummond restores order in the station.

An intimation of this nature was quite sufficient to stir to action a man possessing the energetic character of Mr. Drummond. The following morning he issued from the fort, escorted by a company of Europeans and some guns, made a circuit of the principal streets and of the station, and proclaimed the restoration of order and British rule. Then, too, he became for the first time aware of the manner in which the rabble had vented their fury upon the Christian population who had hesitated to avail themselves of the protection of the fort. It happened that whilst the great bulk of the European and Eurasian inhabitants had taken advantage of that protection,

wálí headed by the Kótwál himself, and followed by a crowd of inferior grades and rabble: there is no reason to suppose that a single Mahomedan of any respectability was in any way engaged or accessory to this proceeding."—Mr. Phillipps's *Narrative*, already referred to.

there had been men of the latter class, born in India, natives in habits, in modes of thought, in everything save religion, who preferred to confide in the friendship of their native friends. These had been sought out and slaughtered. At the same time too some Europeans on their way to the fort had been intercepted and murdered. The number of both these classes who thus fell outside the fort amounted to twenty-two.*

Order also revives in the fort.

The restoration of order in the fort followed Mr. Drummond's action in the town. The natives of the lower class, prompt to appreciate decision, returned as if by magic to their duties. Prior to Mr. Drummond's triumphant tour through the city, there had been a great dearth of servants in the fort; but the day following small shopkeepers flocked in with provisions; domestics of every

* Of these fifteen were men, four were women, and three were children. Most of them were slaughtered by our own rebellious police. Amongst them were Mr. Hubbard, Professor of literature, Ágra College; Mr. Hare, an old and paralytic man, and his son; Mr. Christie; Major Jacobs; Mr. and Mrs. Dennis; Mr. and Mrs. Derridon and their three children. A curious circumstance is related in connection with the murder of these last, illustrative of the fidelity, so often evinced during the mutiny, of native servants to their masters. Mr. and Mrs. Derridon and three children were murdered at the door of their house by a gang of Mahomedans. They had three other children and a Mahomedan nurse. Whilst her master and mistress were being killed this nurse was severely wounded. But with rare fidelity she carried two of the other children to the Kótwálí, and watched over their safety there. They were made over to Mr. Drummond as he rode through the city on the 8th. The third surviving boy, aged twelve, escaped by creeping through the legs of the assassins, and alone traversed the city in safety till he arrived at the fort.—Phillipps's *Narrative.*

Book VIII. Chapter V.

1857. July 9.

grade we.. eager to renew or proffer service. The battle of Sassiah had at all events cleared the air. The natives had seen the utmost the rebel troops could accomplish; and their faith in British ascendancy revived.

Life in the fort.

Now began that long life in the fort of A'gra, —so tedious for soldiers, so conspicuous for the display of those splendid qualities which render a noble woman in very deed a ministering angel. The story has been told in graceful and touching language by one, herself a widowed fugitive from Gwáliár,—from whose account of the tragedy there I have already quoted*—and whose own sufferings never made her forget the griefs and necessities of others. There are some points in it which demand a place in History.

Difficulties which had at first to be overcome.

As soon as the restoration of order outside the fortress had been completed arrangements were made to provide for the necessities of the Christian population within. In addition to the residents of A'gra there were congregated there fugitives from many stations. The majority of these had lost all their property. Some had reached A'gra only with the clothes which they wore. A not inconsiderable proportion were children. It was difficult to provide for these all at once. For, it must be remembered, the non-combatant population of A'gra had been prohibited, prior to the mutiny of the Kótá contingent, to take with them into the fort more than the contents of a small hand-bag. Nor had this

* *A Lady's Escape from Gwalior*, by Mrs. Coopland.

state of things been wholly remedied by the removal of Mr. Colvin and the civilians to the same protection. No one had seriously contemplated the defeat of our troops at Sassiah. Our force had marched out of the station the better to defend the station. No one had anticipated the actual result. The blaze of the burning bungalows which announced it gave to many, then, the first intimation that the bulk even of their wearing apparel had been lost to them for ever.

But notwithstanding these and other more serious losses the love of order, of arrangement, and of comfort so characteristic of the British nation quickly manifested itself.

Preparations for the reception of the sick and wounded,

The first necessity had been to set apart one of the buildings as a hospital for the sick and wounded. At first a barrack was selected for this purpose. At a later period the Motí Masjid, or Pearl Mosque, was also appropriated to the same object. This building, built entirely of a beautiful creamy white marble, was well fitted to be used as a hospital on account of the cloisters and cells by which its inner court was surrounded. These, formerly inhabited by priests and devotees, were now made over to those suffering from their wounds, their privations, or the climate. The civilians of A'gra were lodged in the small apartments ranged along three sides of the beautiful garden near the Díwán-i-Khláss, or the hall of nobles. For others, fugitive ladies and children, huts, separated the one from the other by grass screens, silky, strong, and flexible, were arranged in the stone gallery, twelve feet wide, the roof supported

of the civilians,

the ladies and children,

Book VIII. Chapter V.

1857. July.

on arches, which runs round the Díwán-i-A'm, the hall of audience of Akbar.* To the senior officers and their families were allotted small tiled houses near the Mótí Masjid. Separate houses were also made over to fugitives of distinction. For officers of a lower rank tents were pitched on a large green plot near the same building. The Roman Catholic Archbishop and his ecclesiastical staff were similarly accommodated. To the nuns and their numerous pupils were assigned the sheds or store-rooms where the gun-carriages had stood.† The Protestant chaplains had comfortable quarters, and the missionaries lived in the Palace garden. To the unmarried soldiers were assigned one set of barracks, whilst the married with their families occupied another set. These latter had saved their furniture and lived in comparative comfort. Those of the Europeans most to be pitied, in point of accommodation, were the merchants and shopkeepers. They had to content themselves with erecting small grass huts on the archways and tops of buildings. The Eurasians were still less comfortably provided for. They had to find an abiding place "anywhere."‡

(Margin notes: the officers, — the priests and nuns, — the soldiers, — the shopkeepers, — and the Eurasians.)

* The officers who had the allotting of the quarters (a task that was no sinecure) had appointed to us each one arch, which we divided as I have before described. The temporary partitions of grass were so thin you could hear every word uttered in the next division."—*A Lady's Escape from Gwalior.*

† "They turned one large room or storehouse into a chapel and fitted it up marvellously well with crucifixes, altars, and candlesticks."—*A Lady's Escape from Gwalior.*

‡ I have taken these details from Mrs. Coopland's book. Regarding the Eurasians she writes: "The half-caste, or 'Kala Feringhees,' as the natives call them, who are uncharitably said to have the

The total number of Europeans in the fort in July amounted to one thousand nine hundred and eighty-nine. Of these one thousand and sixty-five were men, the rest women and children. In addition there were three thousand eight hundred and fifty-six Eurasians and Natives.

The total number in the Fort.

So much for the accommodation. In the course of a few days the various habitations came to be classified as "blocks" alphabetically arranged. This was the first dawn of order and arrangement. Several of the archways or vestibules within the fort were about the same time converted into shops; one into a post office. In the shops were sold the European stores which had escaped the savage instincts of the rabble. For some days no butcher's meat was procurable; but after the restoration of order in the city this defect was partly remedied, and the residents were supplied by the Commissariat Department. As time went on the natives began to bring in from outside fowls, eggs, and butter.

Further arrangements for supplies.

But if the accommodation was rough and the privations were for a long time great, there were those who were prevented by no personal suffering from devoting themselves to the wants of others. Before even the men wounded at the battle of Sassiah had been deposited in the first improvised hospital, mattresses, pillows, and quilts,

Devotion of the ladies to the sick and wounded.

vices of both different races and the virtues of neither, were in immense swarms and had to accommodate themselves anywhere. A large number of them lived in our 'square' just beneath our balcony:" (the balcony of the Díwán-i-A'm) "the rest lived in holes, tyrconnels, or on tops of buildings all over the fort."

Book VIII. Chapter V. 1857. July.

which the ladies had been preparing for the event, had been arranged on hastily manufactured wooden cots. The ladies then formed themselves into a committee to assist the doctors in ministering to the wounded. At the request of the senior medical officer, Dr. Farquhar, one lady, Mrs. Raikes, undertook to preside over this committee. The ladies were then divided into watches, and to these watches certain hours during the day and night were apportioned. To avoid teasing the men by too much nursing a small separate room was made up for the lady nurses. From this, at stated times, they issued and went their rounds distributing tea, jelly, soda-water, coffee, and soup, or helping to dress the wounds of the patients under the orders of the medical officers.*

Meanwhile the Government stores within the fort were opened for the supply of clothing to those who most needed it. By degrees tailors were admitted from outside, and though the demeanour of these and other domestics was not

* Raikes's *Notes on the Revolt.* Mr. Raikes adds the following tribute to the feeling and conduct of the British soldier. "For weeks that the ladies watched over their charge never was a word said by a soldier which could shock the gentlest ear. When all was over, and when such of the sick and wounded that recovered were declared convalescent, the soldiers, in order, as they expressed it, to show their gratitude for the conduct of the ladies, modestly asked permission to invite their nurses and all the gentry and society of A'gra to an entertainment in the beautiful gardens of the Taj. There, under the walls of the marble mausoleum, amidst flowers and music, these rough veterans, all scarred and mutilated as they were, stood up to thank their countrywomen who had clothed, fed, and visited them when they were sick."

always respectful, they showed yet the same regard as of yore for the punctually paid monthly stipend.

Book VIII. Chapter V.

1857. July.

Charity knows no creed.

It is gratifying to be able to record that the charity and devotion to the cares and sorrows of others displayed in the A'gra fortress knew no differences of religion. There was no place for the display of narrowness on the one side or of bigotry on the other. I have been particular in the inquiries I have made on this subject and the result of these has been to convince me that in their several spheres Catholic and Protestant strove to their utmost to do their duty to their neighbour.

Brigadier Polwhele is removed.

The Civil Government all this time existed, but for all purposes of defence and provisionment the administration was in the hands of the military. Subsequently to his defeat at Sassiah Brigadier Polwhele had, by express orders from the Governor-General, been removed from command.* His place was taken by Colonel Cotton. Vigorous measures were speedily inaugurated. The defences of the fortress were strengthened and increased; numerous guns were mounted on the ramparts; the want of garrison artillerymen was supplied by the enlistment of promising Eurasians to form gun detachments; from the same class volunteers were called and selected and trained to serve as drivers; the powder magazines were covered by mud ramparts to protect them alike against treacherous attack and against the chances

Measures taken by his successor.

* This order, dated 26th of July, was received in A'gra on the 5th of August.

Book VIII. Chapter V.

1857. August.

Dangers to which the garrison were exposed.

of being shelled. It must be recollected that all this time the Gwáliár contingent, possessing numerous field guns and a heavy battering train, was within seventy miles of A'gra; that its leaders were constantly boasting that they would attack A'gra; and that they were with difficulty restrained by Mahárájá Sindia. Inside the fortress was Major C. Macpherson, the agent for the Governor-General at Sindia's court. His communications with Sindia were daily. The nature of them led the garrison to believe that they were always liable to an attack from that formidable contingent. They could not be certain that the loyalty of the Mahárájá and his minister would for ever be able to restrain the soldiers. And this uncertainty, whilst it added no little to the difficulties of the garrison, hastened the completion of defensive preparations.

The Commissariat Department.

Amongst these was the provisionment of the fortress. The cares of the Commissariat Department in this respect were greatly lightened by the influence exerted by a character well known in Indian history, Lálá Jotí Pershád, a contractor whose successful provisionment of the army during the Afghán, the Sikh, and the Gwáliár wars had gained him a great and deserved reputation. A bazaar was established immediately outside the fortifications and quickly assumed the proportions of a regular market.

An expedition organised and sent to Aligarh.

By degrees it began to be considered possible to organise an expedition for the relief of the neighbouring districts. Of these Aligarh, commanding the direct road to Dehlí, was the most important. Colonel Cotton, accordingly, equipped a small force composed of three companies of Europeans, three guns, thirty of the volunteer cavalry, and a few trustworthy native mounted levies. Major Montgomery, the Brigade Major, commanded the force, whilst the volunteer cavalry were led by the gallant de Kantzow, famous for his conduct at Mainpúrí. Leaving A'gra on the 20th of August the force reached Aligarh on the 24th. They found the rebels, consisting of a large body of Gházís or fanatics, and a detachment of the 3rd Cavalry, in the occupation of a walled garden. It was difficult to ascertain the precise position of their main body, but some of their cavalry having been noted outside and on the left of the enclosure, de Kantzow was directed to dislodge them. De Kantzow did not require more explicit instructions. Addressing a few words to the volunteers he placed himself at their head and led them straight at the enemy. The rebels watched the approach of this handful of Europeans without flinching till they were within shot. They then raised their carabines and fired. A second later, and without waiting to ascertain the result of their volley, they turned their horses heads and fled. Meanwhile the Gházís emerging from the enclosure had attacked our infantry. A considerable number of them, dressed in garments white as the driven snow, suddenly dashed from the enclosure, flourishing their scimitars aloft, and crying out "Religion!" "Victory!" rushed on the advanced skirmishers of the Europeans. They fought with so furious a desperation and with so

Book VIII. Chapter V.

1857. August 20.

August 24.

The rebels there are defeated.

Book VIII. Chapter V. — 1857. August 24.

frantic a rage that it became necessary to bring up the guns to bear upon them. Then they retired, and our infantry, dashing after them completed the overthrow. The Gházís and their allies were driven out of Aligarh.

This was the last operation on anything like a large scale in which the A'gra force was engaged until after the fall of Dehlí. But before relating the manner in which that "crowning mercy" was achieved it is necessary to turn to the events which were happening during this period in the districts on the left bank of the Jamná—events less affecting A'gra than the operations in the vicinity of Lakhnao and of Dehlí.

Mr. Colvin's health fails.

During a great portion of this period Mr. Colvin still continued to administer the duties attaching to his high office. But he was no longer the strong man hoping for the prompt repression of the rebellion that he once had been. It was not alone the revolt that had broken him. The uprooting of convictions deeply held and long clung to was indeed a blow hard to bear. But it was rather the sense of his inability to restore order in his own provinces; the forced isolation to which events condemned him; the compulsory inaction; that preyed most deeply upon him. Of the fine courage, the devotion to duty, the earnest consideration for others which had characterised his career there never was the smallest abatement. These noble qualities shone brightly to his very last hour. Warned by his medical advisers that continued attention to the details of office would be fatal,

Book VIII. Chapter V.

1857. August.

that he required perfect rest of body and mind, Mr. Colvin refused, nevertheless, to relinquish the smallest of the duties attaching to his high office. He felt that it would ill become the captain to leave the deck of his ship when she was drifting on to a lee shore, the breakers almost in sight; that ill as he was, it was his duty to set an example; and that as he must die some day, it was better that he should die in the performance of duties for which he yet had strength rather than seek to prolong his existence by casting his cares upon another.

He continues, nevertheless, to perform the duties of his office.

Few will question the nobility of soul which prompted Mr. Colvin to direct the course of the State-vessel to the very last. It has been thought that he might perhaps have advantageously consented to leave some of the minor details to his subordinates. But when Mr. Raikes, a judge of the Court of Appeal at A'gra, writes, so late as July, that if he wanted a sword or pistol from the magazine Mr. Colvin's counter-signature was necessary, he only exposes the red-tape system of administration which flourished then, and which probably flourishes still, in other countries as well as in India. He exposes a system which was then ingrained in the country. It was but a brick in the wall of Indian administration. The reform of the system was necessary but it could scarcely have been undertaken during the mutiny. It was not routine duties of this nature that affected Mr. Colvin. The real pressure which broke him down has been already indicated.

Faults of the red-tape system.

Book VIII. Chapter V.

1857. September.

Mr. Colvin dies.

"Early in September," writes Mr. Raikes in his journal, "Mr. Colvin asked me to prepare a plan for the restoration of the Police in the North-Western Provinces, and I submitted a note on the subject; on the 7th I called to talk over the matter, but found the Lieutenant-Governor too ill to attend to business. On Wednesday, the

September 9

9th, to our great sorrow he died, and on the next day I, as pall-bearer, paid my last tribute of respect to his memory. After ruling over the fairest provinces of India in her palmiest days he died without secure possession of an acre of ground beyond the Fort, and his body was interred within the walls."

Tributes to his memory.

Thus died in the performance of his duty, before the dawn of the triumph of which he never despaired, the brave, true-hearted, and noble Lieutenant-Governor of the North-West Provinces. Whatever failings or prejudices he may have had they are all obliterated by the recollection of the earnestness, the single-mindedness, the devotion to duty that characterised him in a most critical period. He was sustained to the last by the consciousness that "he had not shrunk from bearing the burden which God had called upon him to sustain;" by the conviction that he had performed his duty to his God and to his country, and that he had ever striven to have a conscience void of offence towards God and Man. His demise was deeply felt by all with whom he was connected by private friendship or by official ties; and the Government of India only gave utterance to a feeling that pervaded all classes when by a notification in the Official Gazette it paid a just tribute to his name and memory.*

Book VIII. Chapter V.

1857. September.

* The following is the text of the notification referred to: "It is the melancholy duty of the Right Honourable the Governor-General in Council to announce the death of the Honourable John Russell Colvin, the Lieutenant-Governor of the North-West Provinces.

"Worn by the unceasing anxieties and labours of his charge, which placed him in the very front of the dangers by which, of late, India has been threatened, health and strength gave way; and the Governor-General in Council has to deplore with sincere grief the loss of one of the most distinguished amongst the servants of the East India Company.

"The death of Mr. Colvin has occurred at a time when his ripe experience, his high ability, and his untiring energy, would have been more than usually valuable to the State.

"But his career did not close before he had won for himself a high reputation in each of the various branches of administration to which he was at different times attached, nor until he had been worthily selected to fill the highest position in Northern India; and he leaves a name which not friends alone, but all who have been associated with him in the duties of Government, and all who may follow in his path, will delight to honour.

"The Right Honourable the Governor-General directs that the flag shall be lowered half-mast high, and that seventeen minute guns shall be fired at the seats of Government in India upon the receipt of the present notification."

BOOK VIII.

CHAPTER VI.

In the first chapter of this Book I have described the mutiny of the 9th Regiment of Native Infantry cantoned in detachments at the stations of Aligarh, Mainpúrí, Etáwá and Balandshahr. It remains now to give an account of the subsequent occurrences in the districts represented by those stations, and in the districts adjoining, and of the action of the mutinous feeling in the important province of Rohilkhand.

I propose in the first instance to take the reader back to the station of Aligarh. The mutiny at that station, occurring on the 20th of May, has been already related.* Intelligence of this disaster had reached the Lieutenant-Governor on the 21st. Mr. Colvin at once organised an expedition to hold the line. Acting under his orders, Captain Alexander, commanding 1st Irregular Cavalry Gwáliár contingent, sent by Sindia to aid

Despatch of Sindia troops to the districts.

* Page 155.

in maintaining order, detached Lieutenant Cockburn, with two hundred and thirty-three troopers, on the 13th, to Aligarh. Cockburn, making forced marches, reached that place on the 26th.

Book VIII. Chapter VI.

1857. May 26.

He arrived in time to protect and to escort to Hátrás, a walled town twenty-two miles distant, the Europeans who had till then maintained their position in the vicinity of Aligarh. At Hátrás, however, about a hundred of his men, principally Mahomedans, rebelled, and after having vainly attempted to invite their comrades to join them, rode off to stir up the villagers in the districts. But Cockburn, though his party was reduced to one hundred and twenty-three men, resolved to be even with his revolted troopers. Receiving information that they had been joined by about five hundred villagers, and that these were organising a system of plunder and murder, Cockburn formed a plan by which to entrap them. He procured a curtained bullock cart, such as native women generally travel in. Inside this cart he placed four troopers with loaded carbines, and drew the curtains. He then sent the cart on the road towards the rebel camp, he following with his main body under the shade of some trees. No sooner did the rebels see the cart than they dashed forward to secure the lady whom they imagined to be inside. The troopers behind the curtains waited till the foremost men approached, when they discharged their carbines with fatal effect. Hearing the discharge, Cockburn and his men dashed forward, killed forty-eight of the surprised foe, and dispersed the remainder.

Some of them mutiny at Hátrás.

Cockburn outmanœuvres the rebels.

Book VIII. Chapter VI.

1857. June.

The detachments of the Gwáliár contingent mutiny.

An action like this was, however, but a transient gleam of sunshine. To aid in pacifying the districts, Mr. Colvin had ordered thither, likewise, detachments of the 2nd Cavalry, under Captain Burlton and Lieutenant Salmond, and Captain Pearson's battery, of the Gwáliár contingent. Lieutenant Cockburn's detachment had also been strengthened by the main body of his regiment, the 1st, under Captain Alexander. Up to a certain point, the men belonging to these several arms and detachments behaved perfectly well. Gradually, however, as the villagers rose on every side, the pressure became too much for them. On the 1st of July, the 1st Cavalry, then at Hátrás, mutinied. The men showed no ill-feeling towards their officers, but simply told them they must go. When hundreds with arms in their hands issue orders to units, the units must obey. Alexander and the officers with him had, then, nothing for it but to ride for A'gra, a journey they successfully accomplished. The following day, the men of the Artillery, under Pearson, and those of the 2nd Cavalry, commanded by Burlton, and then stationed at Sánsí, seven miles beyond Hátrás, incited by letters from their comrades at that place, likewise rose in revolt, and intimated to their officers that they no longer required them. Pearson, Burlton, and Salmond did all that men could do to keep their men true, but in vain. The men insisted on joining their comrades at Hátrás. The cavalry started off the following morning for that place, their officers still accompanying them. There they effected a junction

July 1.

with the 1st Cavalry, and once again, and in a peremptory manner, insisted that their officers should leave them. Burlton, Salmond, and the surgeon, Dr. Dalzell, at once then took the road to Ágra. Shortly afterwards, Pearson, who had clung to his battery, arrived with his mutinous gunners. The only other European with him was his staff-sergeant. Pearson found the two regiments of cavalry drawn up as if on parade. He rode up to them, received their salutes, questioned them about their officers, and was told they had left for A'gra. He then calmly and coolly rode down their ranks, speaking to the men he knew, and exchanging greetings with the native officers. His position was full of peril. At any moment he might have been shot down. An imprudent gesture, a sign of alarm, would have been fatal to him. But Pearson was equal to the occasion. He continued his ride down the ranks coolly, followed by his sergeant, mounted on his second charger; nor did he change his pace till the line had been well cleared. He and the sergeant then put spurs to their horses. A little beyond the village they overtook the cavalry officers. The whole then rode on, hiding by day, and reached A'gra in time to share in the disaster of the 5th.

Book VIII.
Chapter VI.

1857.
July 3.

Courage and coolness of Captain Pearson.

The officer escape to A gra.

It is remarkable that the men made no attempt to molest them! Most remarkable when the fact is taken into consideration that the foot-soldiers of the same contingent evinced the most bloodthirsty feelings towards their officers! Can there be any significance in the fact that the cavalry

Were the Mahomedans less blood-thirsty than the Hindús?

Book VIII. Chapter VI.

1857. July 3.

soldiers were mostly Mahomedans, whilst nineteen-twentieths of the infantry men were Hindús?

The district volunteers.

Meanwhile, some well-mounted volunteers had been doing good service in the districts. Composed of civilians, of officers whose regiments had mutinied, of clerks in public offices, of planters, of shopkeepers, all animated by but one feeling, their first act had been to relieve a body of six or seven of their countrymen, besieged by the rebels in an indigo factory. They then pushed on to Aligarh, where they were joined by Mr. Watson, the magistrate, a man of remarkable courage, and by others. But they were not strong enough to dominate the rebellious villages, and gradually fell back on Ágra. Twelve* of them, however, disdaining a retreat so rapid, remained behind occupying a factory about five miles from Aligarh. But resolute as were these men, they, too, were forced to retreat when the Gwáliár cavalry had mutinied. On the concentration of the volunteers at A'gra, they were employed as pickets on the Mathurá road to watch the approach of the Nímach brigade. How they behaved towards that brigade has been already related.

They fall back on A'gra.

It will thus be seen that the efforts of the Government of the North-West Provinces to stay the plague in the districts lying on the left bank of the Jamná, between Dehlí and A'gra, had signally failed. In the more northerly districts, and in

* Cocks, Watson, and Outram, C.S.; Saunders and Tandy, planters; Stewart Clarke, surgeon; Castle, Hine, Burkinyoung, and Harington; Ensigns Marsh and Oliphant.

Rohilkhand, rebellion had been even more rampant and more successful. Book VIII. Chapter VI.

1857. June.

Although the troops in Rohilkhand rose in revolt a few days earlier than did those in the more northerly districts, the plan of the narrative, leading southwards to Kánhpúr and Lakhnao, renders it necessary that the latter should in the first instance be considered. I therefore propose to carry the reader with me to the districts known as Sahàranpúr and Mozaffarnagar, to descend thence through Rohilkhand to Fathgarh.

Sahàranpúr.

The station of Sahàranpúr was, before the mutiny, essentially a civil station. It was situated on the bank of a small stream, about two miles from the city of the same name, and which was the capital or chief town of the district, also called Sahàranpúr. The population of the town amounted to about forty thousand—many of them Mahomedans, with rather a bad character for turbulence. In the earlier portion of the present century Sahàranpúr had been one of the frontier stations of the British territories. To guard it a rather strong fort had been built on its northern face. But to such an extent did confidence in their star override in those days all suggestions of prudence in the British mind, that on the extension of our frontier the fort had been converted into a civil jail, whilst the Stud Department had been allowed to run up the ditches and mud walls of their paddocks so close to its ramparts that it would have been easy from their cover to pick off the defenders of the place.

Description of the civil station.

Book VIII. Chapter VI.

1857. May.

and of its population.

When the mutiny broke out at Mírath the European male population of Sahàranpúr, including clerks, numbered only six or seven persons. The Eurasians were scarcely more numerous. There was over the treasury a native guard of some seventy or eighty sepoys, commanded by a native officer, and furnished by the 29th Native Infantry at Morádábád. The civil jail guard, numbering about a hundred men, in addition to their duties over the jail, furnished guards to the civil officers' houses. Throughout the district, likewise, was scattered the ordinary police force, amply sufficient in times of peace * to repress the disorder of a population numbering even nearly a million souls.

Importance of its situation.

The situation of Sahàranpúr was still important. It was the point whence the road led to Dérá and to the hill stations of Masúrí and Lándáur; it was contiguous to Rúrkí, from the canal establishments of which the army before Dehlí was largely supplied with men and materials for forwarding the siege; and it was the seat of one of the Government studs. Yet now the entire district, comprising likewise the Engineers' College, the canal workships and costly aqueducts, seemed to be at the mercy of the sepoys and the disaffected natives, for there were no European troops who could be summoned with any hope that the call would be responded to. There were indeed European troops at Mírath, some seventy miles distant. But, until after the fall of Dehlí, timidity bordering upon panic, selfishness utterly neglect-

* Robertson's *District Duties during the Revolt.*

ful of the general public weal, ruled with fatal effect the military counsels at that station.

Mr. Robert Spankie.

Fortunately there were men at Sahấranpúr whose bold spirit and ready resource supplied the place of soldiers. The magistrate, Mr. Robert Spankie, was an able public servant, full of energy and mental power. His lieutenant, Mr. Dundas Robertson, joined to a manly and energetic nature a clear head and a coolness not to be surpassed. A fit associate with these was Lieutenant Brownlow, of the Engineers, cool, daring, enterprising, and resolute. With such men at Sahấranpúr there was yet a glimmering of hope that the crisis might be surmounted.

Mr. Dundas Robertson.

They send the non-combatants to Masúrí.

The news of the outbreak at Mírath reached Sahấranpúr on the evening of the 14th of May; that of the massacres at Dehlí on the following day. At a meeting convened by Mr. Spankie it was decided to hold the station, but to despatch the women and children to Masúrí. This arrangement was carried out at once. As soon as possible after the departure of the ladies, those of the gentlemen of the station who had remained behind * determined to unite and occupy one house. The clerks and Eurasians, invited to join them, showed at first some disinclination, but in a day or two they changed their minds and acceded to the proposal.†

Dangers that threatened Sahấranpúr.

Space will not permit me to detail in full the preliminary dangers which threatened these few bold men. Now, it was the mutiny at the not

* Two quitted it, ostensibly to escort the ladies.

† *District Duties during the Revolt*, page 25.

Book VIII. Chapter VI.

1857. May.

distant station of Mozaffarnagar; now, it was the approach of two mutinous companies of the sappers and miners; now, a combination of the villagers to attack them. This last-named danger, a very serious one, was warded off by acting on the principle, so conspicuous during the mutiny, that "boldness is prudence." Instead of waiting for the intended onslaught, Mr. Robertson, enlisting in his cause some influential and well disposed landowners, anticipated it, attacking and capturing the conspirators. Continuing to pursue this policy, Mr. Robertson, taking with him a few of the 4th Lancers (native); a detachment of the 29th Native Infantry, and some police; proceeded to the most important and the most disaffected parts of the district to assert British authority. By a combination of tact and daring Mr. Robertson accomplished a great deal. He soon ascertained, however, that the landowners sympathised with the rabble, and that the fact that rebellion, not plunder, was their object, would make his task extremely difficult. Further success, he felt, would depend on the fidelity of the sepoys. But soon amongst these appeared the usual symptoms of disaffection. On the 30th of May, Mr. Robertson had been joined by two companies of the 5th Regiment of Native Infantry. These mutinied on the 3rd of June. But Mr. Robertson still continued his noble efforts in the cause of order; nor, though the detachment of the 29th Native Infantry revolted on the 11th of July, did he, or his superior, once relax their hold on the district. This was still virtually British

Zeal and energy displayed by Mr. Robertson.

Disaffection amongst the sepoys.

Mr. Robertson holds his ground notwithstanding.

when the fall of Dehlí removed from the native mind the calculations which till then had inspired them to resist.

Mozaffarnagar.

At the civil station of Mozaffarnagar, about midway between Saháranpúr and Mírath, the native guard over the treasury was furnished by the 20th Regiment of Native Infantry, quartered at Mírath. This regiment took a prominent part in the famous outbreak of the 10th of May. It was not to be expected, therefore, that the detachment would abstain from following the example thus set. For three days, however, it did abstain. Nor did the sepoys composing it make any demonstration until the British magistrate on the spot had given a signal proof of his belief in the collapse of British rule. That official, Mr. Berford, with a precipitancy as unworthy as it was rare, closed the public offices on the receipt of the bad news from Mírath. He subsequently took refuge in a small house in the town, withdrawing the guards posted over the jail for his own personal protection. The consequence of this abnegation of authority was the rise of the district. Landowners and peasants alike believed that the sun of British rule had set, never to rise again. Every man who had a grievance, the plunderers by profession, the plunderers by opportunity, seized the golden chance. Nor were the sepoys then backward. They broke open the treasury, carried away all they could convey away, and marched for Morádábád. The balance fell to the townspeople and district revolters. There was no one to prevent or to

Mr. Berford.

The population rises,

and the sepoys mutiny.

Book VIII. Chapter VI.

remonstrate with them. Authority had disappeared with Mr. Berford.

1857. May.

Rohilkhand.

But the risings in the northerly portions of the North-West Provinces were trifling compared with those in Rohilkhand. The principal station in Rohilkhand was Barélí. Here were cantoned the 8th Irregular Cavalry, the 18th and 68th Native Infantry, and a native battery of Artillery. The brigade was commanded by Brigadier Sibbald.

The garrison of Barélí.

Barélí was likewise the chief civil station in Rohilkhand, being the head-quarters of the Commissioner. The Christian population, including Eurasians, somewhat exceeded one hundred in number.

Excitement at that station.

The uneasy feeling amongst the native troops, which had manifested itself so strongly in Bengal in the month of March, gradually travelling up country, had reached Barélí in April. During that month the men of the infantry regiments there stationed questioned their officers regarding the new cartridges, and asked pointedly whether it were true that those cartridges were greased with the fat of the cow and of the pig. The reply given by the officers was apparently satisfactory, for the excitement created by the rumour almost at once subsided. But the introduction into the regiments of the new musket drill again roused suspicion. The natives of India are essentially conservative in their views. The case for innovation must be very clearly put to con-

The reasoning of the sepoys.

vince them. The sepoys at Barélí, their minds prone to suspicion, could not then understand the reason why, for any military purpose, a new

Book VIII. Chapter VI.

1857. May.

musket or a new musketry drill should be necessary. "We and our fathers," they said, "have conquered Hindústán with the present musket; what is the use of a new one?" They continued, however, to practise the new drill, and, when taught singly, even touched the cartridges, though with evident dislike.

Up to the beginning of the second week of May the men when drilled together, by companies, had been taught only the new bayonet exercise. But in the second week it was deemed advisable to instruct them in the new system of ball-practice. The experiment began with the grenadier company of the 18th Native Infantry. But only one round per man was served out.

It happened that an arrangement previously considered—by which the guns of the battery were to be moved from their actual position to another close to the practice-ground*—had taken effect early on the very morning on which it had been decided that the men of the grenadier company of the 18th Native Infantry should make their first experiment with the new ammunition. To the minds of the sepoys, already over-excited, this change in the position of the guns was a

Their minds prone to suspicion.

* The real object was to place the guns under the charge of the 8th Irregular Cavalry. They were in fact regularly confided to that corps. It will be seen in the text that subsequently they were withdrawn, and restored to their own men. This restoration was a part of the feigning confidence policy which it was considered advisable to adopt. The Súbadár of the Artillery, whose tearful protestations in favour of this measure excited the sympathy of many, subsequently assumed the command of the rebellious brigade. His name was Bakht Khán. He eventually commanded in chief at Dehlí.

Book VIII. Chapter VI.

1857. May.

new revelation. The conviction flashed upon their minds that the guns had been shifted with the sole object to coerce them into using the obnoxious cartridges. This, too, accounted for the fact, which at the time had seemed so strange to them, that only one round of balled ammunition had been served out to each man. They would thus be formed up on the practice-ground, they argued, practically defenceless, commanded by the guns. The suspicion, equal to conviction, spread to the entire regiment. The Grenadier company had already set out. A considerable number of the men of the other companies ran then to the artillery lines to upbraid the gunners with thus aiding the attempt to take away their comrades' caste; but the bulk of them, gloomy, anxious, but determined, waited in their lines the booming of the guns, or the return of the grenadiers. When these appeared, unharmed, the excitement for the moment cooled.

Panic caused by the change in position of the guns.

News of the Mírath mutiny.

Only, however, for the moment. The same day brought to the station news of the mutiny at Mírath, of the disaffection of the districts round Barélí, and of evil dispositions manifested by the native regiment stationed at Morádábád.

Colonel Colin Troup

This was on the 14th. The Brigadier, Sibbald, was absent on a tour of inspection. His place was temporarily occupied by Colonel Colin Troup, a gallant and distinguished officer. Colonel Troup had not been an indifferent spectator of all that had been going on in the native army during the preceding two months. But experienced as he was, shrewd, clever, and discerning beyond most of the old officers of the Company's army, even Colonel Troup had not detected the radical cause of the disease he was called upon to combat. He believed that it could be cured by persuasion, by an unbounded display of confidence, by, in fact, treating the sepoys as one would treat naughty children, by assuring them that all previous offences would be condoned, if they would behave well for the future. In a word, he was a believer in Mr. Beadon's theory of "a passing and groundless panic."

is in favour of persuasive measures.

But Colonel Troup did not the less take every possible measure to meet an emergency which he foresaw might at any moment arrive. Of all the regiments under his command he believed most implicitly in the 8th Irregular Cavalry. The antecedents of that regiment gave him reason for his belief. Not only was it a splendid regiment, well manned, well horsed, and well commanded, but it had but a very short period before come forward at a critical period to show its readiness to proceed wherever the interests of the British service might demand its presence. When, in 1852, the 38th Regiment of Native Infantry had refused to proceed to Pígú, on the ground that the caste of the men would be ruined by a sea voyage of eight days, the 8th Irregulars had volunteered to sail thither. Taken at their word, they marched from Hánsí to the port of embarkation, a distance of a thousand miles, without losing a single man from desertion. Proceeding by sea to Pígú, they not only rendered there most excellent service, but made themselves remarkable

The 8th Irregular Cavalry;

their favourable antecedents.

Book VIII. Chapter VI. 1857. May.

for their discipline and their intelligence. Their native officers were men of good family, given to manly and intellectual pursuits, and proud of their regiment and their service.

Captain A. M. Mackenzie.

The acting commandant of this regiment was Captain Alexander Mackenzie. Captain Mackenzie had been some years with the 8th. He had served with it as adjutant and as second in command. He was devoted to his regiment, gave to it his undivided care, and was unsurpassed in all the qualities of a commanding officer. He was well supported by his second in command, Lieutenant Becher.

Up to the period at which my narrative has arrived the conduct of this regiment had been most exemplary. Colonel Troup, then, looking at its antecedents and at its actual behaviour, had reason to regard it as his mainstay in case of an outbreak.

Colonel Troup doubles the strength of the 8th Irregulars,

It was, I have said, on the 14th of May, that the evil news from the outer world reached Barélí. Colonel Troup at once directed that the strength of the regiment he most trusted should be doubled; he wrote to the civil authorities requesting them to place under his orders all the sowars, or horse patrols, in their districts; he recalled all officers from leave; and he recommended that the ladies and children, in fact all the European women and children, should be sent off to the hill station of Nainí Tál.* Large cavalry pickets were thrown out, and the Ir-

sends the ladies to the hills,

* The ladies, women, and children were sent off to Nainí Tál escorted by a detachment of the 8th Irregular Cavalry.

Book VIII. Chapter VI.

1857. May 15.

regulars were kept ready to turn out at any moment. At the same time Colonel Troup paraded the brigade, and addressing the men assured them that they had nothing to fear as long as they continued to behave themselves; that no new cartridges were coming, and that if any should come, he would destroy them on the parade-ground in their presence. On the following day, the 16th, further to allay the suspicions of the men, he had the guns moved back to their former position.

and endeavours to remove the suspicions of the sepoys.

Causes working against him.

But the evil was too deeply rooted. Notwithstanding all Colonel Troup's efforts the suspicions were not allayed and confidence did not return. For some days, indeed, the sepoys continued to perform their duties with precision, but they were, whether in the lines or on guard, always in a state of excitement. This excitement was fed by the evil-disposed of the city, by sepoys from Mírath, from Dehlí, from Firózpúr, and especially by intriguers from the districts instigated by one Khán Bahádur Khán, a pensioner of the Government, and the heir of the famous Rohilla chief, Háfiz Rahmat.*

Brigadier Sibbald returned to Barélí on the 19th. From that date till the 29th, no material change occurred in the state of affairs. The brigadier confirmed and carried out all Colonel

* Háfiz Rahmat was the last independent Mahomedan ruler of Rohilkhand. He was defeated and slain in 1774 in a battle against the British, fought at Kattrá. Khán Bahádur Khán received one pension as the descendant and heir of the last ruler of the Rohillas, another as a retired civil officer of the British Government.

Book VIII. Chapter VI.

1857. May 20.

Troup's arrangements. The attempts at "management" on the part of the British, the suspicions, the excitement, the sullen determined mien, combined with rigid performance of duty, on the part of the sepoys, continued. But on the morning of the 29th, Colonel Troup received a note from Mr. Alexander, the Commissioner, informing him that it had come to his knowledge that his, Colonel Troup's regiment, the 68th Native Infantry, intended to mutiny that day. Colonel Troup had but just perused that note when the native sergeant-major of his regiment ran breathless into his presence to tell him that whilst bathing in the river that morning, the men of both regiments, the 18th and 68th, had sworn to rise at 2 P.M. and murder their European officers.

Forewarnings of mutiny.

Colonel Troup prepares for the crisis.

Colonel Troup acted at once as the emergency required. He warned the officers of the three regiments and of the artillery; informed the brigade major, Captain Brownlow, of the notices he had received, and recommended him to ride off at once to report the information to the brigadier, fixing the lines of the 8th Irregular Cavalry as the place of rendezvous for all.

Loyal spirit of the 8th Irregulars.

It was about 1 o'clock in the day when Captain Mackenzie received the order to turn out his regiment. In a very few minutes the men were in their saddles, and certainly, as far as appearances went, no men could have displayed a more loyal spirit, or a greater readiness to do their duty, than did the men of the 8th Irregulars. The regiment continued mounted for two hours.

1857. May 29.

In the interval, whether from the attitude of the cavalry, or from some other reason, the men of the infantry changed their plans. The rising was postponed.

The behaviour of the 8th Irregulars had justified Colonel Troup's confidence. On this apparently crucial day not a symptom of disaffection had been manifested by a single trooper. Yet—curious fact—on the evening of that day, Colonel Troup received from a sure authority information that the men of that regiment were not absolutely to be relied upon; that they had sworn not to act against the infantry and artillery, though they would not harm or raise a hand against any European. The horizon was becoming darker.

Colonel Troup receives a private warning that the 8th are not to be relied upon.

The night of the 29th, the day and night of the 30th, were passed in excitement on the one side, in watchfulness on the other. Colonel Troup did not doubt now but that the outbreak was a question, not of days, but of hours. Few of the other officers shared his opinions. The brigadier, the brigade-major, the officer commanding the 18th, the officer commanding the battery, all believed that the storm would pass over. Captain Mackenzie, whilst sharing Colonel Troup's opinions regarding the other regiments, had still faith in his own men. It would have been strange had it been otherwise, for up to the 31st of May the fidelity and devotion of the 8th Irregulars and their officers had alone kept down revolt.

He feels the crisis upon him.

On the morning of the 31st the crisis came. It was heralded by the usual attempt at incendiarism, Captain Brownlow's house having been

The crisis comes.

Book VIII. Chapter VI.

1857. May 31.

fired in the small hours of the morning. The only other warning given was that conveyed by the behaviour of the men on the treasury guard, who had snatched from a native official a letter he was carrying to the fort, torn it up in his face, and abused him. This was the first serious impropriety committed by the native soldiers at Barélí. These two occurrences put many on their guard. Still all continued quiet in the lines, when just at 11 o'clock, the report of one of the battery guns, followed by a volley of musketry and the yells of the sepoys, warned everyone in the station that the crisis was upon them.

First manifestation of the sepoys.

Their actual preparations and resolves.

The rising in fact had been thoroughly organised by the sepoys. Parties had been told off to murder each officer. The hour fixed was 11 o'clock on that Sunday, the 31st. No sooner had the regimental gongs struck eleven strokes than some sepoys of the 68th rushed to the guns and poured in a volley of grape into the houses nearest to their lines. Small parties carrying with them their muskets went off to each separate bungalow; the remainder rushed out in a mass to burn, to kill, to destroy.

They mutiny.

The warning of which I have spoken had induced many officers to have their horses saddled, and to hold themselves ready for immediate action. The rendezvous was the lines of the 8th Irregulars. To reach those lines some had to gallop across the infantry parade-ground exposed to volleys of grape and musketry. Others, ignorant of the previous occurrences of the morning, and, therefore, not warned, were forced to

The officers make for the rendezvous.

1857. May 31.

take refuge in the city. The brigadier, mounting his horse on the first discharge of the battery guns, rode off at once, but was shot in the chest as he was making for the rendezvous. Other officers shared the same fate, some at the time, some later.

Brigadier Sibbald is shot.

But whilst all are hastening to the rendezvous, the reader must outstrip them, and see what Captain Mackenzie and his regiment were doing there.

Action of Captain Mackenzie.

At 10 o'clock that morning a Hindú Rissaldar of his regiment had reported to Mackenzie that some of the Hindús of his troop, while bathing, had heard the sepoys of the 18th and 68th say that they intended to rise that day at 11 o'clock, murder every European—man, woman, and child—in the place, seize the treasury, and open the jail. Similar reports had been so prevalent during the preceding fortnight that Mackenzie was justified in not giving implicit credence to this. But, as a measure of precaution, he sent orders to his native adjutant to warn the native officers commanding troops to have their men ready to turn out at a moment's notice. He also imparted the information by letter to Colonel Troup. Then Mackenzie, Becher, and the surgeon, Dr. Currie, had their horses saddled; they breakfasted; and then donned their uniforms so as to be ready for immediate action. These operations had scarcely been completed, when the brigade-major, Captain Brownlow, rushed in with the information that the row had begun. Almost simultaneously the fire of

He and his officers prepare for action.

Book VIII. Chapter VI.

1857. May 31.

the battery guns and the discharge of musketry came to confirm his story. Colonel Troup followed almost immediately. Mackenzie and Becher at once mounted their horses and rode down to their lines to turn out the men. The 1st, 2nd, and 3rd troops of the 8th, forming the right wing, were soon drawn up in front of their lines facing the station. But it seeming to Mackenzie that the troops of the left wing showed unusual delay, he proceeded amongst them to hasten their movements. Meanwhile, the confusion was every moment increasing. From all parts of Barélí officers, civilians, and others, were running and riding into the lines for protection. The artillery and infantry were keeping up a constant and rapid fire on the fugitives, whilst all around bungalows were beginning to smoke and blaze. Keeping his head cool all this time, Mackenzie, gallantly aided by Becher, had turned out the troops of the left wing, and was getting them into order, when happening to look round, he saw the troops of the right wing go "Threes right," and move off at a trot to the right and rear of the lines. Digging his spurs into his horse Mackenzie quickly headed the wing, halted it, and asked by whose order they had moved. The Rissaldar, commanding the 1st squadron, replied that Colonel Troup had given the order. Upon this, Mackenzie rode on to Colonel Troup, who had moved ahead in company with some officers and civilians, and asked what he proposed to do. Troup, who by the death of the brigadier had become the senior officer in the station, replied that he proposed to

He turns out his men;

rides to hasten the movements of the left wing;

sees the right wing go off;

gallops after hem;

Book VIII. Chapter VI.

1857. May 31.

retire on Nainí Tál. Mackenzie, still feeling sure of his men, earnestly requested permission to be allowed to take his regiment back and try and recover the guns. Troup replied that it was useless; but yielding at last to Mackenzie's urgent pleadings he consented in these words: "It is no use, but do as you like."

obtains Colonel Troup's permission to attack the mutineers.

Diversity of the influences operating upon Troup and upon Mackenzie.

The fact was that Colonel Troup, influenced by the information he had received on the night of the 30th of May and the impression then formed having been strengthened by the delay of the left wing to turn out, entirely mistrusted the 8th Irregulars. Mackenzie, on the other hand, whilst thoroughly believing in them, felt satisfied that the order given to them by Colonel Troup to follow the Europeans to Nainí Tál was the one order which would try their fidelity to the utmost, as the carrying it out would impose upon them the necessity to leave all their property, and, in some instances, those for whom they cared more than for their property, at the mercy of the rebels. There can be no doubt now that the information on which Colonel Troup acted was partly true. There were traitors amongst the 8th Irregulars. Prominent amongst these was the senior native officer, Mahomed Shaffí. This man had been gained over by Khán Bahádur Khán, and had in his turn done his best to gain the men. Yet it is to be regretted, I think, that Mackenzie's arrangements were interfered with before the temper of the men had been actually tested. The movement to the right, and the remonstrance

Mahomed Shaffí.

Book VIII. Chapter VI.

1857. May 31.

with Colonel Troup, lost many precious moments at a most critical period.

Mackenzie betrayed by Mahomed Shaffí.

The value of a few moments was never more clearly demonstrated than on this occasion. Whilst Mackenzie had been talking to Colonel Troup, the left wing had been drawing up in line. The moment they were quite ready, the traitor, Mahomed Shaffí, watching his opportunity, gave the order to the men of the wing to follow him, and at once rode towards the cantonment. Mackenzie heard the tramp of their horses' feet the moment after he had received Colonel Troup's permission to do as he liked. He did not at once realise the cause of their action, for almost simultaneously with it arose the cry that they had gone to charge the guns. Mackenzie at once addressed the men of the right wing, and told them he was going to take them to recover the guns. The men received the intelligence with apparent delight, and followed Mackenzie—accompanied by Mr. Guthrie, the magistrate, and some officers *—at a steady trot to the parade-ground. On arriving there they found the left wing drawn up, apparently fraternising with the rebels. It was necessary to bring them back, if possible, to their allegiance, so Mackenzie leaving his right wing under charge of Becher, rode up to them and addressed them. Whilst, however, in the act of speaking, and after the men had shown a

Does not at once realise his perfidy.

Brings up the right wing.

* Their names were Captain Kirby and Lieutenant Fraser of the Artillery; Captain Paterson and Lieutenant Warde, 68th Native Infantry, Lieutenant Hunter, 18th Native Infantry.

Book VIII. Chapter VI.

1857. May 31.

disposition to follow him, there arose from the magazine of the 18th Native Infantry—the point where the mutinous sepoys were massed, and where a gun had been placed—a cry summoning all the sowars to rally round the Mahomedan flag and to uphold their religion, "otherwise," shouted the speaker, "the Mahomedans will be forced to eat pork, and the Hindús beef." At the same time a green flag was hoisted. The cry and the sight of the flag arrested the favourable disposition of the men of the left wing, and Mackenzie finding his efforts with them hopeless, rode back to the right. Here, however, a new disappointment awaited him. The men of this wing had felt the influence acting on the left, and had begun to steal off. By the time Mackenzie returned men to the number of about one troop alone remained. Amongst these were most of the native officers. With so small a body it was hopeless to charge, and it was almost certain that an order to that effect would not have been obeyed. Mackenzie retired then in the direction taken by Colonel Troup and the others. As he passed his regimental lines more men dropped away, and before he had gone half a mile, the number of the faithful was reduced to twenty-three, of whom twelve were native officers!* They overtook Colonel Troup, and

Passionate appeal of the mutineers to the 8th Irregulars:

who all go over to the rebels,

except twenty-three.

* It is due to these twenty-three men to place on record that though every possible temptation was held out to them to desert the Europeans not one of them yielded to it. Amid many trials they remained faithful, and managed to do excellent service. The Rissaldar, Mahomed Nazím Khán, not only left all his property, but three children

Book VIII. Chapter VI.

1857. May 31.

his party twenty-three miles from Barélí. Troup was warm in his acknowledgments. In truth he never expected to see them. "Thank God," he exclaimed to Mackenzie, as the latter rode up, "I feared you had gone to certain death." The retiring party now united, proceeded without a halt to Nainí Tál, accomplishing the distance, sixty-six miles, in twenty-two hours.

The Europeans reach Nainí Tál.

The rebel rule is inaugurated at Barélí

On the departure of the fugitives for Nainí Tál the rebel rule was inaugurated at Barélí. Every European house but one had been burnt down. Khán Bahádur Khán was proclaimed

behind, to obey the call of duty. Mackenzie's orderly, a Mahomedan, rode throughout the retreat of sixty-six miles Mackenzie's second charger, a magnificent Arab, on which it would have been easy for him to ride off. But he was faithful, and when the horse Mackenzie was riding dropped dead, the orderly at once dismounted and came on on foot. These men had their reward when the regiment was re-organised, and they redeemed, on the 6th of April 1858, the good name of their regiment, being commended for the "marked gallantry" they displayed at Harhá in Oudh under the command of Captain Mackenzie.

In the text I have recorded a plain and unadorned statement of the conduct of Captain Mackenzie and Lieutenant. Becher on this trying occasion It is but just to both those officers that the opinion of the officer commanding the brigade to which they belonged should be added. In his report on the events recorded in the text Colonel Troup thus wrote: "In justice to Captain Mackenzie and Lieutenant Becher I consider it my duty, however much they like others may have been deceived by their men, to state that in my opinion no two officers could have behaved better towards, or shown a better or more gallant example to their men than they did. I was in daily, I may say hourly communication with them, and I have great pleasure in stating that from the very first to the last they were unremitting in the performance of the many harassing duties required of them." Colonel Troup further recommended them to the favourable notice of the Commander-in-Chief.

1857. May 31.

Viceroy of Rohilkhand. His vice-royalty was baptised with blood. The two judges, Messrs. Robertson and Raikes; the deputy-collector, Mr. Wyatt; Dr. Hay, Mr. Orr, Dr. Buck, and three other civilians; all the merchants, traders, and clerks, and all the women and children who had not quitted the station, were murdered. Most of these were judicially slaughtered—slaughtered, that is to say, by the express order of the new viceroy, and many of them after having been brought into his presence. Exposed to this terrible ordeal, cast by ruffians at the feet of this greater ruffian, the English race still asserted itself. The new viceroy was told to his face that though he might water his new throne with their blood, it would yet take no root in the ground; that though he might find it easy to slaughter unarmed men, women, and children, British power would yet assert itself to crush him.

by the slaughter of the English.

Khán Bahádur Khán.

The better to assure the mastery and to rid himself of all rival claimants Khán Bahádur Khán took the earliest opportunity to persuade Bakht Khán, the súbadár of artillery before alluded to, and who had assumed the title of Brigadier, to lead the sepoys to Dehlí, furnishing him with a letter to the king. He even made a show of accompanying him. But it was only a show. He returned from the first stage to Barélí, fortified his house, and, adding sacrilege to murder, destroyed the tomb of Mr. Thomason, whilom Lieutenant-Governor of the North-West Provinces, to build with the materials, after the manner of the princes of the House of Taimúr, a

Book VIII. Chapter VI.

1857. June.

mausoleum for himself. He at the same time enlisted all the Mahomedans who would carry arms, and with their aid, began to oppress and plunder the rich Hindús. The latter began very soon to regret the overthrow of the British rule.

Causes the British rule to be regretted.

On the very same day on which the tragedy I have recorded was being enacted at Barélí, events not less startling were taking place at Sháhjahánpúr, but forty-seven miles distant. There was but one native regiment at Sháhjahánpúr, the 28th Regiment of Native Infantry. The news of the Mírath outbreak, arriving about the 15th of May, had not caused less excitement at this station than elsewhere. But whilst the residents, and especially the officers, continued to trust the sepoys, they looked for an outbreak on the part of the notoriously turbulent population. Little, however, occurred at the time to cause apprehension. But as day after day passed and rebellion seemed to be gathering head unchecked all about them, the sepoys began to display a behaviour not entirely consistent with duty. Still, however, their officers believed that the bulk of them were loyal.

Sháhjahánpúr.

The sepoys there are not distrusted.

This belief was roughly and suddenly dispelled. The 31st of May was a Sunday. Many of the residents and officers had gone to church. They were still at their prayers when the sepoys of the 28th rushed upon them.

But they mutiny,

On hearing the tumult the chaplain went to the door of the church to meet the mutineers. He was at once attacked, but escaped for the moment with the loss of his hand severed by a

and attack the English when at church.

1857. May 31.

sword stroke. He was subsequently killed by some villagers. Mr. Ricketts, the magistrate, whose vigilance had attracted towards him the peculiar hatred of the mutineers, received a sword cut. He then attempted to escape to his house but was cut down about thirty-five yards from the vestry door. Mr. Labadoor, a clerk, was killed in the church. His wife, his sister-in-law, and the bandmaster of the regiment, escaped for the moment, but eventually met a worse fate. Another clerk, a Mr. Smith, stole away, but was tracked out and killed.

The English barricade themselves.

The scuffle at the door of the church and the attack upon those who first presented themselves to the mutineers had given time meanwhile to the other officers and ladies present there to improvise a defence. Captain Lysaght, Mr. Jenkins, and others, succeeded in barring the chancel doors against their assailants. These, happily, had brought with them no muskets, only swords and clubs, and so mistrustful were they, that on observing the approach of one solitary officer, Captain Sneyd, armed with a gun, they made at once for their lines to get their muskets.

The gentlemen had, before this, placed the ladies in security in the church turret. Hardly had they done this when the sepoys went off in the manner described, and almost immediately afterwards their domestic servants, faithful in this extremity, arrived at the church, bringing with them their masters' guns and rifles. The English then ventured to open the doors. They found not only the horses and carriages, which

Book VIII. Chapter VI.

1857. May 31.

had brought them to church, still at the door, but clustering round about a hundred sepoys, principally Sikhs, who had hastened up to rally round and to defend their officers. For the moment they were safe.

Slaughter in the cantonment.

Meanwhile the cantonments had been a scene of tumult and bloodshed. When one party of the mutineers had rushed to the church another had fired the bungalows and sought out the Europeans. The assistant magistrate was killed in the verandah of his court whither he had fled for refuge. Captain James, in temporary command of the 28th, was shot on the parade-ground whilst trying to reason with his men. In reply to his arguments they asserted that they were not after all such great traitors, inasmuch as they had served the Government faithfully for twenty years. As he turned away in disgust they shot him. The mutineers allowed Dr. Bowling, the surgeon of the regiment, to visit the hospital unmolested, but, on his return, after he had taken up and placed inside his carriage his wife, his child, and his English maid, they shot him dead and wounded his wife. She managed, however, to reach the other fugitives at the church.

There, now, were assembled all the Europeans remainiug alive. What were they to do? It was a terrible extremity. But desperate situations require desperate remedies, and the only sensible course seemed to be to make for the residence of the Rájá of Powáin—across the Oudh frontier, though but a few miles distant. Thither accord-

The fugitives take refuge with the Rájá of Powáin.

ingly they proceeded, and there they arrived the same day. But their reception was unfavourable. The Rájá declared his inability to protect them and refused them shelter. Mr. Jenkins, the assistant magistrate, who was one of the party, wrote at once to Mr. Thomason, the Deputy Commissioner of Móhamdí, in Oudh, to inform him of the events at Sháhjahánpúr, and to beg him to send all the available carriage to enable the fugitives to reach Móhamdí. Mr. Thomason received the letter that night and complied, as far as he could, with the request. At Móhamdí the fugitives arrived, in a terrible plight,* two days later. But they were not saved. Their subsequent adventures form one of the saddest episodes in the Indian mutiny.

Badáon.

Midway between Barélí and Sháhjahánpúr, though not in a direct line, and some thirty miles from the former, lies the civil station of Badáon. The magistrate and collector of this district, which took its name from the station, was Mr. William Edwards. Mr. Edwards had served as Under Secretary in the Foreign Department during the rule of Lord Ellenborough. A man of observation and ability he had marked how, during the fifteen years preceding the mutiny, the action of our revenue system had gradually ruined the landowners of the country and broken up the village communities. Under the action of that revenue system landed rights and interests, sold

Mr. William Edwards.

* "Sad was the appearance of the poor Shajahanpore fugitives on their arrival at Mohundi; weary and with naked feet did they with much difficulty and toil reach thus far."—*Narrative of the Shajahanpur Mutiny and Massacre.*

Book VIII. Chapter VI.

1857. May.

for petty debts, had been bought by strangers who had no sympathy with the people. The dispossessed landowners, irritated and discontented, smarting under the loss of their estates, looked upon the British Government as the author of their calamities; whilst the peasantry, connected with these landowners for centuries, bestowed upon them all their sympathy, reserving their hatred for the strangers—and for their patrons, the British.

Effect of our revenue system.

The social state in Rohilkhand having been gradually growing to this point it can easily be conceived that when the mutiny broke out in the North-West Badáon was ripe for revolt.

Isolated position of Mr. Edwards.

Mr. Edwards was well aware of the dangers which awaited him in his isolated position. He was alone at Badáon. As soon as the revolt at Mírath had disclosed to him the nature of the impending catastrophe he had sent his wife and child to Nainí Tal. He remained alone—well aware that the population all around him was discontented, that the company of sepoys who guarded his treasury was not to be trusted, that the police would join in the scramble which a signal from Barélí would inaugurate. To oppose an insurrection on the part of these men Mr. Edwards had no resource beyond his brave and resolute heart.

His solitary resource.

On the 29th of May Mr. Alfred Phillipps, the magistrate of I'tá, a station in the A'gra districts on the right bank of the Ganges, rode into Badáon. He was on his way to Barélí to demand help from thence, his own districts being in a state

Mr. Phillipps rides into Badáon.

1857. May.

Edwards asks help from Barélí.

of insurrection. Mr. Edwards told him that help was not to be looked for from Barélí as he had himself asked it in vain. But two days later information reached Edwards that the important town of Bhilsia was about to be attacked by the rebels. To allow this place to fall without an effort was not to be thought of. Edwards decided then to make another appeal to Barélí. The answer was favourable. He was promised a company of sepoys under a European officer. Joyfully he was expecting these, when, on the 1st of June, he received information that the entire Barélí brigade had mutinied, and that revolt reigned at that station.

June 1.

News arrives of the mutiny at that station.

Mr. Edwards received this information early in the morning. He imparted it to Mr. Phillipps, who, realising at once the failure of his mission, started at once to return to his district before the roads should be barred by the rebels. Very soon after Mr. Phillipps's departure Mr. Edwards was joined by two indigo planters, the Messrs. Donald, and by a patrol, Mr. Gibson. These expressed their resolution to accompany him whithersoever he might go. But at the moment Mr. Edwards had no mind to go anywhere. The sepoys had not yet broken into revolt, and their commandant, on receiving the intelligence from Barélí, had voluntarily assured Mr. Edwards that he and his men would defend the treasury confided to them to the last man. That very evening, however, they rose, and being joined by a party from Barélí and by the released jail-birds of the place, began to plunder and destroy.

The troops and population rise in revolt.

Book VIII. Chapter VI.

1857. June 1.

Mr. Edwards and three others flee.

There was now nothing for the four Englishmen but flight. Their numbers, far from being a protection, were an embarrassment, for, with the districts all around them surging, concealment, difficult for one or two, would be almost impossible for four. But there was no help for it. The four Englishmen, accompanied by an Afghán servant of Mr. Edwards and by an orderly—a Sikh, Vazír Singh—both true men, rode at once for their lives. During the first few days, they galloped from village to village, quitting it, or remaining, as they found the natives hostile or the reverse; often forced to flee when most in need of food and rest. They crossed the Ganges two or three times, tracing out a zig-zag path in the hope of avoiding danger. Ultimately, with the loss of one of their number, they reached Fathgarh. But Fathgarh, on the eve of revolt, was no abiding place for fugitive Europeans. Mr. Edwards himself wished to make for Kánhpúr, or even for A'gra. Both these routes having been pronounced impracticable, he and his companions determined, in pursuance of the advice of his friend, Mr. Probyn, the Collector of Fathgarh, to join Mrs. Probyn and her children, then at Dharampúr, the fortified residence of a friendly native, Hardéo Baksh. Mr. Edwards reached that place on the 10th of June and found collected there many Europeans. Most of these, however, returned to Fathgarh. Mr. Edwards, Mr. and Mrs. Probyn and their children, remained at Dharampúr, and ultimately—after the party had undergone terrible troubles and privations, the weaker and more

Their wanderings.

They reach Fathgarh.

Mr. Edwards takes refuge at Dharampúr.

delicate of its members having been forced to lie for weeks concealed "in a wretched hovel, occupied by buffaloes, and filthy beyond description, the smell stifling, and the mud and dirt over our ankles,"—they reached Kánhpúr. They arrived at that goal of safety on the 1st of September, just three calendar months after Mr. Edwards had left Badáon.

Book VIII. Chapter VI.

1857. June.

Shares the fortunes of the Probyns.

Meanwhile at that place rebel rule had been inaugurated. The authority of Khán Bahádur Khán was acknowledged, and the sepoys, after having rifled the treasury, were persuaded to march to Dehlí. Thanks to the prevision of Mr. Edwards, the rifling of the treasury was unusually unproductive, that gentleman having refused, with a view to possible eventualities, to receive the instalments of revenue due from the land-holders.

Rebel rule is inaugurated at Badáon.

Morádábád lies forty-eight miles north-west of Barélí. In 1857 it was garrisoned by one native regiment, the 29th Native Infantry, and by half a battery of native artillery. It was likewise the seat of a civil district, with judge, magistrate and collector, assistant magistrate, and civil surgeon.

Morádábád.

The news of the mutiny at Mírath reached Morádábád on the 16th of May. No immediate result was apparent; but on the evening of the 18th intelligence reached the authorities in the station that a small party of the 20th Regiment of Native Infantry—one of the regiments which had mutinied at Mírath—was encamped, fully equipped and with a large quantity of treasure,

Rebels arrive in its vicinity.

Book VIII. Chapter VI.

1857. May 18.

in the jungle, on the left bank of the Gorgan river, about five miles from the station.

The temper of the 29th Native Infantry is tested;

The opportunity was considered a good one for testing the loyalty, always loudly professed, of the men of the 29th Native Infantry. Accordingly, a company of that regiment, commanded by Captain Faddy, was ordered for duty that night. The night was pitch dark, but as a surprise was intended that circumstance was in favour of the British. At 11 o'clock, Captain Faddy set out, preceded by thirty horsemen and accompanied by his subaltern and some civilians. On approaching the Gorgan river Faddy halted his infantry, and ordered the cavalry to take up a position to cut off the enemy's retreat. As soon as this movement had been satisfactorily accomplished he dashed on to the enemy's encampment with his infantry, overpowered their sentries, and roughly woke them from their slumbers. The darkness was so great that friend could only be distinguished from foe by the flash of the fire-arms. Owing to this the bulk of the insurgents managed to steal off, with the loss, however, of all their arms and horses, ten thousand rupees in coin, eight prisoners, and one man killed.

apparently satisfactorily.

Possible doubts are not entertained.

So far the men of the 29th would seem to have stood the test well. It has indeed been asserted that they did not exert themselves as much as they might have done, and that had their heart been in the struggle, they might have prevented the escape of so large a number of the insurgents. Such was not, however, the opinion of their officers at the time. At the best it can only be conjecture, for the pitchy darkness of the night was quite sufficient to account for the escape of the dark-skinned mutineers, roused suddenly from slumber.

Book VIII. Chapter VI. 1857. May.

They stand a second test.

It would appear, however, that the mutineers themselves did not consider that the hearts of the men of the 29th Native Infantry were very much incensed against them. For, the very morning following the surprise just narrated a few of them, escaped from that surprise, came into the station and boldly entered the lines of the 29th! But, again, the 29th displayed a loyal resolution. The native sergeant who was leading the rebel sepoys was shot down and the remainder were taken prisoners. It being considered unsafe to lodge the prisoners in the quarter-guard they were sent to the jail. It happened, however, unfortunately, that the native sergeant who had been shot had a near relation in the 29th, and that this near relation was a man of some influence in the regiment. No sooner had this man discovered who it was who had been slain than he collected about a hundred men, the worst characters in the regiment, led them to the jail, stormed it, and released not only the men of the 20th but the six hundred prisoners lodged there!

Some evince a mutinous spirit.

But the main body continues loyal.

But the bulk of the regiment was still true. On hearing of the raid against the jail the officers turned it out, and the men displayed the greatest alacrity in responding to the call made upon their loyalty. A number of them followed the Adjutant, Captain Gardiner, in pursuit of the rioters and the escaped convicts,

Book VIII. Chapter VI.

1857. May 19.

and actually succeeded in bringing back a hundred and fifty of them. The civil authorities co-operated with the military in this well-timed expedition, and are entitled to share in the credit due to its success. Subsequently more of the insurgents were caught. Some even returned of their own accord. But this was only the 19th of May. The crisis, far from having been surmounted, was still looming in the future. On the 21st the authorities discovered that a number of Mahomedan fanatics from Rámpúr* had collected on the left bank of the Rám Gangá, opposite the town of Morádábád, had hoisted the green flag, and were in communication with the evil-disposed men of the town. In the town itself the threatening effect of this demonstration was manifest at a glance. The shops were all shut, the streets were deserted, the doors of the houses were barred.

Another crisis arrives.

Mr. Cracroft Wilson's energetic measures

It was patent to all that unless this demonstration were encountered with a firm and resolute hand the British cause was lost. The judge, Mr. Cracroft Wilson, called upon the military authorities to aid him. The aid was given. Setting out then with some sowars and with two officers and a company of the 29th he attacked and dispersed the fanatics. One of the latter, levelled at Mr. Wilson's head a blunderbus loaded with slugs. Mr. Wilson seized it in time. The fanatic then drew a pistol from his belt; but before he

carry the station hrough it.

* Rámpúr, the capital of a mediatized Afghán chief, Mahomed Yúsúf Ali Khán, lies eighteen miles to the east of Morádábád.

could discharge it a sepoy of the 29th knocked him down. That night the chief of the evil-disposed party within the town was killed by the police.

A third crisis

Two days later, the 23rd, another incident came to try alike the English and the sepoys. On that day intelligence arrived that two companies of sappers and miners, laden with plunder and fully equipped, were approaching the station. Instantly two companies of the 29th Native Infantry and sixty sowars were warned for duty. Captain Whish, who commanded the party, took with him two guns and marched out on the road by which the enemy were to advance. But intelligence of his march had preceded him. The rebels, not caring to encounter him, crossed the river and made for the Terai. The joint magistrate, however, tracked them with four sowars, and kept them in sight till the detachment came up, when, without the semblance of a struggle, they laid down their arms. Previous experience having demonstrated the impolicy of bringing any prisoners into Morádábád, these men were deprived of their arms their ammunition their money and their uniform and were turned loose.

is successfully encountered.

Causes which were working on the sepoys.

The good conduct of the men of the 29th Native Infantry in these expeditions had nursed the hope that they might remain staunch and loyal to the end. But it is easy now to perceive how, in the times that were approaching, it was all but impossible that this should be so. The districts around them were surging. Every day they were seeing and talking with men who

Book VIII. Chapter VI.

1857. May.

appealed to the sentiment lying nearest to their heart—to their religion and their caste; who told them how it was the deliberate intention of the British Government to violate the latter; who pointed to the sufferings and privations their brethren were enduring in the sacred cause; and who appealed at the same time to the baser passions of cupidity and ambition. Morádábád was but forty-eight miles from the larger station of Barélí, and we have seen what was passing at Barélí during the last two weeks of May!

News arrives of the mutiny at Barélí.

Until the 2nd of June, however, the sepoys of the 29th Native Infantry performed their duty loyally and well. But early on the morning of that day it was known throughout Morádábád that rebellion was triumphant at Barélí. The judge and the magistrate had received that intelligence at 2 o'clock in the morning by the hands of a special messenger from the Nawáb of Rámpúr.

Effect of the news on the sepoys.

The effect of this intelligence upon the sepoys of the 29th Native Infantry and upon the towns-people was prompt and significant. No one doubted but that a crisis was at hand. The men were sullen, sarcastic, and even rude in their manner; the towns-people defiant and disrespectful. Mr. Wilson's energetic proposal to them to follow their officers to Mírath with their colours flying, taking guns and treasure with them, was met with derision. They had decided for themselves the part to be taken.

They throw off all disguise.

The following morning they threw off all disguise. They began by refusing to all but the Europeans admission to the building in which the public moneys were deposited, on the ground that the fanatics from Rámpúr might return to attack it.

Book VIII. Chapter VI.

1857. June 3.

The civilians seeing the treasure thus beyond their control, thought it would prevent a general disturbance if it were so disposed that the sepoys could take possession of it without opposition. They accordingly had it placed, the sepoys quietly acquiescing, upon tumbrils, and formally made it over to the treasury guard. The magistrate, Mr. Saunders, seized the opportunity to destroy as many as possible of the Government stamps in store as he could lay hands upon. The amount of the money made over to the sepoys was but £7,500. They were greatly disappointed at the smallness of the amount. In the first burst of their fury they seized the native treasurer, dragged him to the guns, and threatened to blow him away unless he would disclose the place where the remainder had been concealed. Captain Faddy and Mr. Saunders rescued the man from his impending fate. But when Mr. Wilson and Mr. Saunders were about to ride off a few of the disaffected men levelled their pieces at them and ran round to prevent their escape. Some of the native officers, however, reminding the men of the oath they had taken to spare the lives of the Europeans, induced them to lower their muskets and to desist.

They take possession of the money in the treasury,

Simultaneously with the seizure of the rupees the sepoys deliberately appropriated the opium, and all the plate-chests and other property consigned for security to the Government treasury.

and the other property of the Government.

Book VIII. Chapter VI.

1857. June 3.

The police had ceased to act. The rabble were beginning to move. There was but one course to pursue, and that was to save for future service lives which, at Morádábád, would have been uselessly sacrificed.

The English evacuate Morádábád.

The English started, then: the civilians and their wives, accompanied by a native officer and some men of Irregular Cavalry, who happened to be there on leave, for Mírath; the officers and their families for Nainí Tál. Both stations were reached without loss of life.

Fate of those who remained.

Those who chose to remain behind, principally Eurasians, clerks in offices, were not so fortunate. An invalided officer, an Englishman, Lieutenant Warwick, and his wife, a native Christian, were killed. Mr. Powell, a clerk, was wounded. But he, and some thirty-one others, purchased immunity from further ill-treatment by embracing the Mahomedan faith. Their subsequent fate is uncertain; but it is believed that but few lived to hear of the fall of Dehlí.

Rohilkhand under Khán Bahádur Khán.

With the mutiny of the troops at Morádábád Rohilkhand passed nominally under the sway of Khán Bahádur Khán, the descendant of its last independent ruler, and a pensioned civil officer under the British. I say, nominally, for his authority was never thoroughly established. His sway, in fact, was the sway of disorder. It can best be described by using a proverb familiar to the natives: "The buffalo was the property of the man who held the bludgeon." A social condition was inaugurated, not dissimilar to that which prevailed throughout Maráthá India at the close of the last century. Unarmed sepoys, if in small parties, were certain to be set upon by villagers armed with clubs, and plundered—often murdered. Pious Brahmans, telling their beads, were suddenly assaulted and murdered by Mahomedan stragglers, for the sake of the brass vessels in which they cooked their food. The landowners, dispossessed under the action of the British revenue system, resumed their lands, but in many cases, they, and the farmers generally, especially the Mahomedans, exercised the authority they thus acquired, or of which they were possessed, with so much severity that no peaceably disposed man would dare to venture beyond the limits of his village, even in the daytime. If he travelled at night the greatest secrecy and precaution had to be observed.

The social life was insecure.

Such was the social life in Rohilkhand under native sway in 1857. Nor was the political condition of the province more flourishing. Over the Thákurs, or barons, the authority of Khán Bahádur Khán was for a long time disputed. These Hindús were just as greedy of plunder as had been the sepoys, and they rejoiced for the moment at the sudden acquisition of power to attack villages and towns. But from some cause or other they and their followers were very badly armed—their weapons consisting mainly of bludgeons and matchlocks, antique in form, and rusty from long disuse. Their power, then, was not equal to their will. Badáon, thrice threatened, successfully resisted them. They had no guns. They were, therefore, unable to combat the trained

The political life

Book VIII. Chapter VI.

1857. June.

troops of the native viceroy. Whenever these trained levies marched against them and beat them, they, their relatives, and their followers, experienced no mercy. Mutilation and murder followed defeat, and confiscation followed mutilation and murder. Sometimes stories of these atrocities induced several Thákurs to combine, but never successfully. Badly armed and untrained, the peasantry whom they led, even when they obtained a transient success, dispersed for plunder. In the end they were always beaten.

was unsatisfactory.

The people long for the return of the British.

It is scarcely surprising, if under these circumstances, the hearts of the rural population began after a time to yearn for their old rulers. It was in vain that, in a boastful proclamation, Khán Bahádur Khán denounced the English as liars, as destroyers of the creeds of others, as confiscators of property. In the recesses of their own houses the peasantry replied that at least the English were truth-tellers; at least, they did not war on women and children; at least, they were a moral race, above treachery and deceit. The longer the rule of the Mahomedan viceroy lasted the more these opinions circulated. His misgovernment begat contrast. Contrast begat a longing desire for the old master, until at last the victory of the English came to be the hope of every peasant's hut, the earnest desire of every true working man in the province.

Fathgarh.

The course of events now takes us down to Fathgarh, a station in the A´gra division, on the right bank of the river Ganges, twenty-five miles south of Sháhjahánpúr.

Fathgarh was the seat of a gun-carriage manufactory—the works connected with which were carried on in a dilapidated fort—and the headquarters of the 10th Regiment of Native Infantry and a native battery. Three or four miles to the west of it, lies the native city of Farakhábád, the seat of a pensioned Patáu Nawáb. The inhabitants of the district numbered upwards of a million. About one-tenth of these were Mahomedans, but Mahomedans of a peculiarly turbulent character, given to murder and rapine beyond their co-religionists in other provinces. They had been under English rule since the year 1802, but the characteristics of their race had long secretly rebelled against the system of order and care for life and property then imposed upon the district in which they lived.

Turbulent character of the Mahomedans of the district.

The events at Mírath on the 10th of May had awakened in the minds of the men of the 10th Native Infantry sentiments analogous to those which had been produced elsewhere. They resolved to temporise and to bide their time. In this way the month of May was tided over. But on the 3rd of June intelligence was received of the mutinies at Barélí and at Sháhjahánpúr and of the rising of Rohilkhand. It happened that Colonel Smith, commanding the regiment, was a man of energy and decision. He at once summoned a council of the leading residents, and announced to them his intention of despatching that night the women and children by boat, down the Ganges, to Kánhpúr. It was known that Kánhpúr was then safe; that Euro-

Colonel Smith sends away the non-combatants;

VIII. pter VI. 1857. June 4. pean soldiers had arrived there; that more were on their way thither. It seemed in every respect eligible as a place of refuge.

some of whom proceed to Kánhpúr; At 1 o'clock on the morning of the 4th of June, then, about one hundred and seventy non-combatants, a large proportion of whom were women and children, started off in boats. The next day, all sorts of contradictory reports reaching the fugitives, it was resolved to divide into two parties. One hundred and twenty-six continued to prosecute their journey to Kánhpúr, only to be seized there by the order of Náná Sáhib, and by his order to be foully murdered; the other party, amongst whom were the wife and family of Mr. Probyn, preferred to accept the hospitality of a native landowner, Hardéo Baksh, at Dharampúr. This party was afterwards joined by Mr. Probyn and by Mr. Edwards. They remained, whilst the majority, about forty in number, after some hesitation, returned to Fathgarh (13th of June).

others return; some stay at Dharampúr.

Meanwhile, affairs in Fathgarh had not progressed very favourably. On the very day of the despatch of the boats Colonel Smith had attempted to move the Government treasure into the fort. But the sepoys had flatly refused to allow this. With strange inconsistency, and although they were corresponding with the mutinous regiments in the province of Oudh, the same men cheerfully obeyed their Colonel's order to destroy the bridge of boats, the sole link between the district of Farakhábád and that province. They seemed to evince a true and loyal feeling, when, on the 16th of June, they handed to their Colonel

Contradictory demeanour of the sepoys.

1857. June 16.

a letter written to them by the Súbádár of the 41st Native Infantry—a regiment which had recently mutinied at Sítápúr, in Oudh—in which that Súbádár announced that he and his regiment had arrived within a few miles of Fathgarh, and that he and they now called upon the 10th to murder their officers, to seize the treasure, and to join them. The native officer who communicated to Colonel Smith the contents of this letter added that he and the men had replied that they had served the Company too many years to turn traitors; that they were resolved to remain true to their salt, and to oppose by force the 41st if they should march that way. It was after this correspondence that the men of the 10th aided in breaking down the bridge of boats across the Ganges. Yet the very next day, the 18th of June, they warned Colonel Smith that they would no longer obey the British, and that he and his officers had better retire within the fort.

Culminates in mutiny.

It would appear from this warning and this action that the men of the 10th had no desire to kill their officers; that they cared only for the coin. The day following the 41st crossed the river in boats and joined them. Bloodier counsels then prevailed.

The mutinous 41st arrives.

Colonel Smith and the European population had not, meanwhile, been slow to avail themselves of the opportunity given them. To the number of upwards of one hundred* they entered the fort. Of that number only thirty-three were able-bodied

Other fugitives arrive.

* They had been joined by fugitives and travellers from other parts of the country.

Book VIII. Chapter VI.

1857. June 19.

men: the remainder consisted of women, children, and infirm non-combatants. The first care was to mount guns on the ramparts. A 6-pounder was at once placed in position to command the gateway. By strenuous exertions a 3-pounder, a 9-pounder, a 12-pounder, an 18-pounder, and a 24-pounder, were likewise mounted. The last three however were howitzers. A small brass mortar, and three hundred muskets were also unearthed and made ready for use.

Preparations of the garrison.

The next care was to search for ammunition. The supply of this was, however, extremely defective. The garrison could not lay hands on more than a few muster round shot and shells; six boxes of balled, and an equal number of blank cartridges. These latter were at once broken up, and the powder was put by for the use of the guns—a lot of nuts, screws, hammer-heads and such-like articles being collected to be used as grape. At the same time the garrison were told off into three parties, each under an officer, and to these distinct watches were assigned.

Paucity of ammunition.

All these arrangements had been happily completed before the sepoys showed any sign of molesting our countrymen. The fact was that perfect union did not reign among the mutineers. The 10th Regiment, on dismissing its officers, had placed itself unreservedly at the disposal of the Nawáb but had refused to hand over to him the treasure. The 41st, meanwhile, crossing the Ganges in boats, had entered the city, and demanded from the men of the 10th their share of the plunder. The 10th refused to part with

Disunion amongst the mutineers.

1857. June 19–24.

their spoils, whereupon the 41st reproaching them with having spared the lives of their officers, went tumultuously to the Nawáb and implored him to order the 10th to join them in an attack on the fort. The Nawáb, it is believed, gave the required order; but the 10th had, in the interval, divided the treasure amongst them. Then the greater number of them seized the first opportunity to cross the river into Oudh, and to make their way to their homes. The few who remained were set upon by the men of the 41st. In the contest which ensued many on both sides were killed. It ended only by the survivors of the 10th agreeing to follow the counsels of the 41st.

Bloody counsels prevail.

The 41st were now masters of the situation, and the object of the 41st was European blood. The Nawáb threw himself heartily into their cause, and supplied them with provisions and all the munitions of war at his disposal. But the mutineers still delayed the attack. They were awaiting, they said, an auspicious day. This delay was of no small advantage to the besieged as it enabled them, by means of the natives who still adhered to them, to store the fort with provisions.

The mutineers attack the fort.

June 25.

The auspicious day was the 25th of June. But it was not till the evening of the day following that the first alarm was given. This was caused by the opening of a musketry fire upon some coolies employed by our people to pull down some walls outside, but contiguous to, the fort. It led to nothing. Before daybreak the following morning, however, the mutineers opened fire from

Book VIII. Chapter VI.

1857. June 25.

their only two guns, but, finding it ineffectual, they soon caused it to cease. A little later, taking up their position behind trees, bushes, and any wall that afforded cover, they opened out a heavy musketry fire. It was, however, positively ineffective, whereas many of them were hit by the English marksmen.

They are foiled,

The only incident which made the following day differ from its predecessor was the display by the enemy of escalading ladders. But not one of these could be planted against the walls of the fort. The aim of our countrymen was too true.

again and again.

They change their tactics,

For four days similar tactics were pursued, varied only by ineffectual attempts to escalade. The enemy suffered severely from the guns and muskets of the besieged, whereas the loss sustained by the latter was extremely slight. On the fifth day the rebels changed their tactics. Ceasing direct attack a body of them went to occupy a village called Húsénpúr, the roofs of the houses in which commanded a portion of the interior of the fort. From these roofs they opened a deadly and effective fire, speedily productive of casualties amongst the garrison. At the same time another body took possession of a small outhouse about seventy yards from the fort and commanding the rampart, loopholed it, and opened a destructive fire on the gunners, rendering the service of the guns impossible. The garrison suffered a good deal from this fire, Colonel Tucker being amongst the slain. The enemy then began mining operations, and at the end of two days sprung the mine. The explosion shook the whole fort but blew away only five or six yards of the outer wall, leaving the inner half standing. They made two attempts, then, to storm. But the first was defeated by the vigilance of one of the garrison, Mr. Jones, who noticing their assembling below the breach, poured into them, unaided, "the fire of two double-barrels and eight muskets, and again discharging them as they were reloaded by a native;" the second, by the excellent aim of Mr. Fisher, the chaplain, the leader of the storming party falling dead by a shot from his rifle.

but are again baffled.

The situation of the garrison was nevertheless sensibly deteriorating. They had lost some of their best men. Many of their defences were commanded. Ammunition was running short. The enemy, too, were daily devising fresh schemes of attack. The day following the repulse just recorded they managed to hoist one of their guns in a position to command the building in which the women and children were located; the other to bear against the main gateway. The firing from these was effective. The building was struck, the gate was pierced, and worse than all two of the garrison guns were disabled. Still, however, damages were repaired with a will, and the enemy were again baffled. Under these circumstances they once more had recourse to mining.

Difficulties under which the garrison labour.

New attacks.

Up to this point the garrison had shown a spirit, an energy, and a resolution not to be surpassed. But their losses had been severe. Their effective number, originally small, had considerably diminished. Excessive work had thus been

Losses of the garrison.

Book VIII. Chapter VI.

1857. July.

thrown upon the survivors, and they were now fairly worn out by fatigue and watching. They could still have repelled a direct attack, but when they witnessed a second attempt to mine their position, despair of a successful defence began to steal over their minds. It would have been strange had it been otherwise. It was evident that after the firing of the second mine two breaches would be available for the assault, and the garrison were not sufficiently strong in numbers to defend more than one. The case was desperate. Effective defence had become impossible.

Their prospects deteriorate.

Possibility of evasion.

But there remained to the garrison still one chance of escape. The rainy season had set in, and under its influence there had been a considerable rise in the waters of the Ganges. Three large boats had been kept safely moored under the fort walls. It might be possible, starting at night, to descend the rapidly flowing river to a point where they would be far from the reach of the murderous sepoys. Such a course, at all events, offered, or seemed to offer, a better chance of escape than a continuance of the defence of the fort with numbers diminished and ammunition all but exhausted. So thought, after due consideration, Colonel Smith and the garrison. They resolved then to evacuate the fort and steal away in the boats. On the night of the 3rd of July the attempt was made. The ladies and children were divided into three parties and at midnight were stowed away in the boats. Meanwhile the pickets and sentries still remained at

The garrison attempt it.

their posts. But as soon as the non-combatants had been embarked they were called in. They first spiked the guns, destroyed the small amount of ammunition that remained, and then made their way to the boats. It was 2 o'clock in the morning before they had all embarked. The order was then given to let go. The boats started in good order, but the clearness of the night betrayed their movements to the sepoys. These at once guessed the truth. Raising the cry that the Franks were running away, they fired wildly at the boats, and then followed, still discharging their pieces, along the bank. But Fortune for the moment favoured our countrymen. The banks were unfavourable for running and the current was strong. The hostile missiles all fell short.

Book VIII. Chapter VI.

1857. July 3.

Favourable commencement of the enterprize.

I have already stated that the boats were three in number. They had been apportioned respectively to the commands of Colonel Smith, Colonel Goldie, and Major Robertson. But Colonel Goldie's boat was soon found to be too unwieldy and was abandoned, its occupants being removed to Colonel Smith's boat. The delay caused by the transhipment enabled the sepoys to bring down one of their guns to bear on the boats, but the balls still fell short. At length the fugitives resumed their journey and reached without accident the village of Singhirámpúr. Here they stopped to repair the rudder of Colonel Smith's boat. But the villagers turned out, opened fire upon it, and killed one of the two boatmen. The villagers still continuing to turn out, five of our

One boat is abandoned.

Attack by the villagers.

Book VIII. Chapter VI.

1857. July.

officers* jumped into the water, waded to land and charged and drove back the enemy, numbering now about three hundred, killing some of their leaders. They then returned to the boat, the rudder of which had been repaired. They had scarcely gone a few yards, however, before Major Robertson's boat grounded on a soft sandbank. Notwithstanding every effort, and that the fugitives jumped into the water to push her off, she remained there immovable. Colonel Smith's boat, meanwhile, had gone down with the stream.

Major Robertson's boat takes the ground.

The rebels approach in two boats,

The grounded boat had been in the helpless position above recorded about half an hour when its occupants descried two boats coming towards them down the stream apparently empty. These boats approached to within twenty yards of them, when suddenly they became alive with armed sepoys. These opened upon our countrymen a murderous and continued fire. Before the fugitives had time to recover from their surprise, many of them, including Major Robertson, had been wounded, and some sepoys had already boarded the boat. Major Robertson, despite his wound, still retained his cool courage. He implored the ladies to throw themselves into the water and trust to the current rather than to the sepoys. Many of them did so. But the sepoys

and attack Major Robertson's boat.

* These were, Major Munro, Lieutenants Eckford, Sweetenham, and Henderson of the 10th Native Infantry, and Captain Edmund Vibart, 2nd Cavalry. The writer gladly takes this opportunity to offer his tribute of regret to the untimely end of the last-named officer, who to the form of an Antinous united the noblest and most manly sentiments and a ripe and brilliant intellect.

Book VIII. Chapter VI.

1857. July.

were upon them. Some of the men aiding the ladies, some alone, succeeded in swimming down the stream. But many of these were drowned; many were killed. The rest were taken prisoners and carried to the Nawáb.*

Colonel Smith's boat

Meanwhile, Colonel Smith's boat had been carried down by the stream. Its occupants received authentic intelligence of the fate of their friends from Mr. Jones, who, after having defended himself as long as defence was possible, and received a bullet-wound in the right shoulder, had struck out into the stream. Mr. Jones states in his narrative that on board that boat he found "everything in confusion," some having been killed, some wounded by the villagers of Singhirámpúr. Shortly afterwards Mr. Fisher was picked up. The boat continued to drop down without pursuit, molestation, or intercourse with the natives, till on the evening of the following day it reached a village opposite Kúsúmkhor, in the Oudh territories. Here the villagers offered the fugitives assistance and protection. These at first feared treachery, but becoming convinced of the friendly intentions of the peasants, they put to shore for the night, and were refreshed by a

reaches a friendly village.

* Amongst those who succeeded in swimming to the other boat were Mr. Jones, whose narrative I have mainly followed; Mr. Fisher, the chaplain, whose gallantry had endeared him to everyone, and who, on this occasion supported his wife and child till they died in his arms. Mr. David Churcher, supporting Major Robertson, by means of an oar, succeeded in reaching the village of Kalhúr. Here the villagers sheltered them. Mr. Churcher remained here tending Major Robertson for two months. The latter then died. Ultimately Mr. Churcher succeeded in reaching Kánhpúr, then occupied by the British.

Book VIII. Chapter VI.

1857. July.

meal consisting of unleavened bread and buffalo milk.

The fugitives pursue their way, one of their number excepted.

Well would it have been if our countrymen had remained with these kind-hearted villagers. One of them, Mr. Jones, whose wound had become most painful, decided on doing so. The others all set out that night. They set out to meet their death. The precise form in which that death was meted out to them may not be certainly known. Some believe that the boat was stopped near Kánhpúr, its occupants dragged out, and there murdered. There is, on the other hand, some ground for believing that as the boat passed Bithúr,* the stronghold of Náná Sáhib, it was fired upon by the sepoys, and all on board were killed. This, however, is certain, that they all met their death at or near Kánhpúr, on the order of Náná Dhúndú Pant.

Fate of the remainder.

The gains of the Nawáb.

Thus had the Nawáb, Tafúzal Húsén Khán, triumphed at Farakhábád. He inaugurated his accession by the slaughter of some forty Europeans taken in various parts of the district. The prisoners brought back from Major Robertson's boat were kept for about a fortnight in confinement, and then murdered, under most atrocious circumstances. But the blood thus spilt failed to cement his throne. It failed to win for him the

* "The boat left. I heard nothing more of it for several days till their Mánjí (boatman) who took her down returned and gave out that Nana Sahib had fired upon them at Bithúr, and all on board were killed."—*Mr. Jones's Narrative.* Mr. Jones himself succeeded in joining Mr. Probyn, and ultimately in accompanying him to Kánhpúr.

Book VIII. Chapter VI.

1857. July.

affection of the Hindús, constituting nine-tenths of the population of the district. It failed to give him a sense of security. In a few short months, it was this blood which choked his utterances for pardon, and which, when the penalty he had incurred had been remitted by the unauthorised action of a subordinate official, condemned him to an existence more miserable than death. The Government could not recede from the plighted word of their officer, but though the Nawáb was allowed to live, he lived only to see the utter annihilation of his own schemes, the complete restoration of the authority he had insulted and defied, to be made conscious every day of the contempt and disgust he had brought upon his person and his name.

BOOK IX.

CHAPTER I.

WHATEVER may be the justification offered for the annexation of Oudh, it cannot be questioned that, having regard to the manner in which that policy was carried out, it not only failed to conciliate—it even tended to alienate from the British every class in India. Under any circumstances the absorption of an independent Mahomedan kingdom would have afforded to the already disaffected section of the Masalmáns throughout India, especially in the large cities, not only a pretext, but a substantial cause of discontent and disloyalty. But the annexation of Oudh did far more than alienate a class already disaffected. It alienated the rulers of Native States, who saw in that act indulgence in a greed of power to be satiated neither by unswerving loyalty nor by timely advances of money on loan to the dominant power. It alienated the territorial aristocracy, who found themselves suddenly stripped, by the action of the newly introduced

Effects of the annexation of Oudh,

Book IX. Chapter I.

1857.

British system, sometimes of one half of their estates, sometimes even of more. It alienated the Mahomedan aristocracy—the courtiers—men whose income depended upon the appointments and pensions they received from the favour of their prince. It alienated the military class serving under the king, ruthlessly cast back upon their families with small pensions or gratuities. It contributed to alienate the British sepoys recruited in Oudh,—and who, so long as their country continued independent, possessed, by virtue of the privilege granted them of acting on the Court of Lakhnao by means of petitions presented by the British Resident, a sure mode of protecting their families from oppression.* It alienated alike the peasantry of the country and the petty artisans of the towns, who did not relish the change of a system, which, arbitrary and tyrannical though it might be, they thoroughly understood, for another system, the first elements of which were taxation of articles of primary necessity. In a word, the annexation of Oudh converted a country, the loyalty of whose inhabitants to the British had become proverbial, into a hotbed of discontent and of intrigue.

in alienating every class from the British.

Sir Henry Lawrence arrives.

On the 20th of March 1857, Sir Henry Lawrence had assumed the Chief Commissionership of Lakhnao. His clear and practical eye saw at a glance that the new system was not working

* When it is considered that there was scarcely a peasant family in Oudh unrepresented in the British army the immense importance of this privilege may be conceived.

Book IX. Chapter I.

1857.

satisfactorily; that his predecessor had thrust it *en masse* on the province, and that its effect had been—alienation. Of all the men who have ever attained a prominent position in India, Sir Henry Lawrence was, perhaps, the most qualified to remove a discontent engendered by action on the part of the Government too fast, too hard, and too reckless. He had great sympathies with the people. He thoroughly understood them. He knew that their feelings, their instincts, were thoroughly conservative; that they distrusted change in the abstract; that if one thing more than another would rouse their long-suffering and docile nature, it would be change coming upon them suddenly, harshly, unaccompanied either by warning or argument. Sir Henry Lawrence noted, then, not only that there was discontent, but that there was reason for that discontent; and he at once made it his business to lessen, as far as he could, the oppressive action of the newly imposed regulations.

His fitness for the office.

He at once detects the discontent,

The correspondence of Sir Henry Lawrence with the Governor-General and with his family shows clearly not only how the discontent of the people had impressed him, but how deeply he regretted the too hasty and too zealous action of the officials who had unwittingly fomented the ill-feeling. Suddenly to introduce a system which will have the immediate effect of depriving the territorial aristocracy of a country of one half of its estates is not a policy consistent with the diffusion of a spirit of loyalty,—and yet within a month of his installation in Lakhnao Sir Henry

Which he regards as justifiable,

Book IX. Chapter I.

1857.

Lawrence wrote to Lord Canning to inform him that in the Faizábád division of Oudh the Talúkdárs had lost half their villages—that some had lost all! Nor did he find that the peasantry had benefited. Heavy assessments, increased duties, had driven them frantic, whilst the large towns were inundated by the disbanded adherents of the late *régime*, all in a state of discontent and disaffection!

on the grounds which he assigns.

The "caste question."

Amongst the population thus seething the dangerous spark of the caste question was suddenly thrown. Who threw it? Was it, as some have asserted, the ill-judged order of a thoughtless official? Was it, as others maintain, the angry retort of a low-caste lascar? Or was it, rather the eager grasp, the clever appropriation of a clique thirsting for an opportunity? That is a question on which perfect agreement is perhaps impossible. This, at least, seems clear to me that the hold which this question took of the minds of the sepoys was due mainly to the fact that they were for the most part men of Oudh, and that annexation and its consequences had prepared the minds of the men of Oudh to accept any absurdity which might argue want of faith on the part of the British. That the sepoys believed that the greased cartridges were designed to deprive them of their caste is, I think, not to be questioned. But they believed that calumny mainly because the action of the British Government, with respect to their own province, had so shattered their faith in the professions of the ruling power, that they were ready to credit anything against it.

Was it an original cause, or a pretext, of discontent?

Reasons for believing that there was a cause of discontent independent of the caste question;

Book IX. Chapter I. 1857.

Mr. Beadon called the action of the sepoys "a passing and groundless panic." But, as I have said elsewhere, if it was a panic, it was not a groundless panic. In a greater degree the annexation of Oudh and the measures which followed that annexation; in a lesser degree the actual employment of animal fat in the composition of the cartridges, constituted ample grounds for the distrust evinced by the sepoys.

which, though a cause, was only a secondary cause.

Sir Henry studies the position,

In the earlier hours of his arrival in Oudh the attention of Sir Henry Lawrence had been mainly occupied by the condition and the discontent of the people he had come to govern. He felt that, could peace be maintained, there was yet time to remedy the main evil. In a very few days he had weighed the higher officials in Lakhnao and had satisfied himself that he could manage them. The question to be solved was whether the little cloud rising in the horizon near Barhámpúr would not develop into a tempest, fierce enough to disturb the tranquillity of the entire country, before he should have time to instil confidence in the minds of the people of the newly annexed province.

and fears the evil is too far advanced.

The reason why the danger in Oudh was likely to be excessive.

This question was unhappily solved in the negative. The feeling which had animated the sepoys at Barhámpúr, in the month of March, was more widely spread in Oudh than in any other province in India. For Oudh was the home of the sepoys. Oudh supplied three-fifths of the recruits annually enlisted in the Bengal army. Every feeling engendered in the ranks permeated through Oudh, whilst the notions imbibed in the homesteads of the peasants found an echo in every regiment of the native army.

Book IX. Chapter I. 1857.

Sir Henry Lawrence was not slow to detect the increasing feeling of mistrust in the very class on whose loyalty the British empire in India seemed to depend. Reports reached him from every corner of the province, all conveying the same story. He could not conceal from himself that the spirit of the people was deeply excited, and excited on the one subject on which to be excited was to be dangerous. He saw that credit was very generally accorded to the whisper that the British Government was bent on destroying the caste of the sepoys, and he knew that to maintain that caste inviolate the Hindú would risk his property, his homestead, all that he valued in this world; that he would gladly sacrifice his life.

The surging of the storm.

In the wars waged by Aurangzíb against the princes of Rájpútáná, to maintain the *jézia* or poll-tax upon infidels, the Emperor possessed the advantage of counting upon the religious bigotry of his Mahomedan subjects. But Sir Henry Lawrence was not blind to the fact that in any contest which might be impending with the Hindús the sympathies of that class would be denied him. Amongst the original fomenters of the rising disaffection many certainly were Mahomedans. The desire to recover their lost over-lordship, the ambition to revive their vanished empire, the longing to avenge themselves on the conqueror, were the motives which prompted them. But the Mahomedan customs have so much in common with the Christian

The secondary cause enables the Mahomedan leaders to work on their followers.

Book IX. Chapter I.

1857.

customs, the food partaken of by the two communities is, with one exception, so similar, that they would have found it difficult under ordinary circumstances to persuade their brethren in the ranks of the army that their religion was in danger. The opportune discovery of the use of lard in the manufacture of the cartridges came to these conspirators as an inspiration from heaven. They used it with an effect that was decisive. The Mahomedan rank and file, disaffected on other grounds, determined from the moment of that revelation to cast in their lot with their Hindú comrades.

The one slight chance in favour of a peaceful issue.

That a crisis of no ordinary magnitude was approaching became apparent, then, to Sir Henry Lawrence very soon after he had assumed the reins of office at Lakhnao. He did not despair. His intimate acquaintance with the natives of India had satisfied him that there were no people in the world more tractable when once their reason had been satisfied. Fanatics, it is true, never reason. But there might, he thought, be some chance of enlisting on his side that divine faculty, if an opportunity of appealing to it before the stage of fanaticism had been arrived at could be secured. On these slender grounds he built such hopes as he entertained.

Almost from the very moment of his arrival, Sir Henry Lawrence had laid himself out to remedy the most pressing material grievances complained of by the various classes of the population. The evil already effected had been too great to admit of his being perfectly success-

Book IX. Chapter I.

1857.

ful. The aristocracy of the Court, indeed, who, as I have already stated, had been ruined by the abrupt action which followed annexation, were propitiated by the immediate payment to them of the pensions which had been promised, but till then had been withheld. An early opportunity was likewise taken of assuring the officials, who had served under the previous *régime*, that their claims to employment would receive prior consideration, and that as a rule the natives of Oudh would be preferred to immigrants from the British provinces. The case of the disbanded soldiers was more difficult. These men were promised preference in enlistment in the local corps and in the military police. Only a comparatively small number of the cavalry availed themselves, however, of this privilege. In many cases they did not hesitate to state the reason of their refusal. "I have eaten the king's salt, and will not touch that of another." * With the small traders in Lakhnao itself Sir Henry succeeded better. They were pacified by the personal interest displayed by the new Chief Commissioner in their welfare, and by the practical measures he took before their eyes to put a stop to the seizures and demolition of houses in the city, which had formed one staple of their grievances. With the territorial magnates, Sir Henry, in spite

Sir Henry Lawrence tries to repair the faults of his predecessors;

and partially succeeds.

* This was especially the case with respect to enlistments in the regular regiments, and in the military police. The disbanded soldiers accepted service more readily in the district police, in which a like amount of drill and descipline was not enforced.

The district police were under the civil authorities alone.

Book IX. Chapter I.

1857.

of no slight opposition, dealt in the same enlightened spirit. He held Darbárs to receive them, to listen to their views, to remedy their just complaints. And he did greatly pacify them by the ennunciation of a policy, by the action of which they would be reinstated in the position they had occupied at the time of the annexation.

Would probably have wholly succeeded if he had, in the first instance, been sent to Oudh.

In this way, in a few weeks, the material evils complained of were placed in a fair way of being remedied. It was a more difficult and a more delicate task to remove the rising religious discontent. The mischief had been virtually accomplished before Sir Henry Lawrence reached Lakhnao. I think it quite possible that had he succeeded Wájid Ali Sháh it would never have arisen. But in all such questions prevention is easier than cure. I repeat—fanatics never reason. And before Sir Henry Lawrence had reached Lakhnao the religious question had assumed all the proportions of fanaticism.

The first practical intimation that the contagion of the cartridge question had reached Oudh was manifested early in April. Before adverting to it, it is necessary that I should state the troops by whom the newly annexed province was garrisoned.

Garrison of Lakhnao.

At Lakhnao itself were quartered Her Majesty's 32nd Regiment, about seven hundred strong; a weak company of European artillery; the 7th Regiment Light Cavalry (native); the 13th, 48th, and 71st Regiments of Native Infantry. Besides these, there were at Lakhnao, or in its immediate environs, two regiments of Irregular Native Infantry, raised for local service in Oudh, the 4th,

Book IX. Chapter I.

1857. April.

and the 7th; one regiment of Military Police, the 3rd; a large proportion of the mounted Military Police;* one regiment of Oudh Irregular Cavalry; and two batteries of Native Artillery. Thus the native armed troops were in the proportion of nearly ten to one, the actual numbers being seven thousand to seven hundred and fifty. At Sítápúr, in addition to local troops, was stationed the 41st Native Infantry, having a detachment at Maláon; at Sultánpúr the 15th Irregular Cavalry. The other stations, Dariábád, Faizábád, and Baraitch were garrisoned only by local corps.

And of the districts.

First symptoms of disaffection at Lakhnao.

The intimation that the caste contagion had reached Lakhnao occurred in this wise. The surgeon of the 48th Regiment had incautiously applied his mouth to a bottle of medicine. The sepoys attributed the surgeon's action to design, and, although the bottle which had been tasted was broken in their presence, they seized an early opportunity to burn down his house. The authors of this outrage, though known to belong to the 48th, escaped detection.

In ordinary times the incident of the bottle would have had little significance. But the vengeance wreaked on the surgeon showed the importance attached to it, in the month of April 1857, by the men of the 48th. Further indica-

* The Oudh Military Police consisted of one thousand cavalry and three regiments of infantry. This force was commanded by Captain Gould Weston, who, prior to the annexation of the province, had been engaged for some years in the suppression of Thagí and Dakaití in Oudh, and had done good service as Superintendent of the Frontier Police, and as one of the Assistants to the Resident.—Sir William Sleeman's *Journey through Oudh.*

Book IX. Chapter I.

1857. April.

tions soon intimated very plainly to the authorities that the feeling which had manifested itself in Barhámpúr was not less strongly rooted in Oudh.*

Sir Henry makes earnest appeals to the native officers and soldiers.

Sir Henry Lawrence, I have said, whilst not insensible to the extreme difficulty of the task, had deemed it might just be possible to dispel, by plain appeals to reason and to facts, the cobwebs from the minds of such men as had not become absolutely fanatical on the subject of the alleged attempt on their caste. He made an earnest appeal, then, to the loyalty of the men. He pointed out to the native officers how contrary it was to the experience of a century that the English should attempt to produce by fraud a result which they would consider only valuable if brought about by conviction. He explained to them the danger which threatened them—the danger of being persuaded by evil-disposed men to become false to their salt. He warned them at the same time of the consequences. He would not palter with mutiny. Sharp and summary should be the punishment of those who should fail in their duty. "It is impossible," writes one† who was at his elbow at this period, "it is impossible here to mention the various steps taken

* "Not long after it became known that the regiment was disaffected. Some of the native officers were reported by the police to be intriguing with relatives of the Ex-King of Oudh, residing in the city . . . . . Not long after Captain Adolphus Orr, commanding one of the regiments of military police, the 3rd, reported that an attempt had been made by some sepoys of the 48th to tamper with a native guard of his regiment."—Gubbins, *The Mutinies in Oudh.*

† *Narrative of the Mutinies in Oudh*, by Capt. G. Hutchinson, Military Secretary to Sir H. Lawrence.

1857. April.

by Sir Henry Lawrence to preserve the soldiery in their duty and the people in their allegiance. Every conciliatory measure was adopted consistent with the dignity of the British Government; and there is no doubt that by his untiring energy, discretion, ability, and determination, he *did* fan into a flame for awhile the wavering loyalty of many of the native officers and men, and that the army and people generally felt that his was a firm and experienced hand." This is most true. All that it was possible to do to check the mutiny was done in Oudh. Firmness combined with conciliation, fairness of speech with fairness of action, prompt punishment with prompt reward. Yet this policy—in the circumstances a model policy—though not wholly fruitless, though checking the outbreak for awhile, did not stop it in the end. The reason is not difficult to find. Oudh had been undermined—the point of fanaticism had been very generally reached before Sir Henry Lawrence arrived there. He came too late indeed to repair the mischief, though not too late to save the British honour—not too late to preserve from the hands of the despoiler the plot of ground which constituted the seat of Government, and which will be referred to in future ages as the monument of his sagacity and of the prowess of his countrymen.

Partial success of the appeals.

Too late.

For he did not confine himself solely to the work of pacifying and of reasoning with the people. He realised almost at a glance the danger that threatened India. He felt that at any moment the handful of Englishmen in the

He sees the full extent of the coming danger.

Book IX. Chapter I.

1857. April.

country might have two hundred millions on their hands. Whilst, then, he used every persuasive argument, and put into action every precautionary measure to avert a crisis, he prepared to meet one.

He takes early precautions.

He began his preparations in April. His own head-quarters were at the Residency situated in the city, close to the river Gúmtí, and upwards of a quarter of a mile from the iron bridge leading to the Mariáon cantonments. At Mariáon were the native infantry regiments, a light horse battery of European artillery and a battery of native artillery. At Múdkipúr, a mile and a half further still from the Residency was one native cavalry regiment. In an opposite direction, in a line in fact forming a right angle with the road to Mariáon and at a distance of a mile and a half from the point of the angle, the Residency, was H. M.'s 32nd Regiment, about seven hundred strong. Nearly a mile and a half directly north of the barracks of the British Regiment, and on the opposite bank of the river Gúmtí, was the only remaining regiment of native cavalry. South of the river again, at or near Músá Bágh three miles from the Residency, were two irregular native regiments, and between them and the Residency was a magazine containing a considerable stand of arms.

The Residency.

About the Residency itself were clustered several substantial buildings of solid masonry occupied by the higher European officials. Here also were the Treasury, the Hospital, and a jail. A detachment of native troops guarded the Residency and the Treasury. One company occupied a curved line of buildings outside the principal gate leading to the Treasury. The whole of the Residency buildings were known to the natives throughout Oudh by the name Baillie Guard.*

Rather less than one mile from the Residency, on the same side of the river Gúmtí, and close to the brick bridge spanning it is a castellated and picturesque stronghold called the Machhí Báwan—the fortress of the rebellious Shékhs in the time of the vice-royalty of Asúf-ud-dáola, but for many years used only as a depositary of lumber—occupying a very commanding position.

Sir Henry prepares to meet any possible emergency.

The attention of Sir Henry was, in the first instance, directed to the making the Residency defensible, and to a better location of the European troops. With this end in view he began to clear away the huts and other obstructions which occupied the ground close to the Residency: to lay in supplies of grain of all sorts and European stores: to accumulate powder and small ammunition and to dig pits for their reception: to arrange for a constant water supply; by degrees to send for the treasure from the city and outlying stations; and to form outworks in the ground encompassing the Residency. At the same time he moved up to the vicinity of the barracks of the 32nd Foot four guns of the native battery stationed at Mariáon.

His preparations had not been made a moment too soon. On the 30th of April the storm threatened. On the 3rd of May it broke.

* The Guard in question, commanded by a Súbádár, was first stationed at this gate by Colonel Baillie, whilom resident at the Court of Oudh. Hence the name.

Book IX. Chapter I.

1857. April 30.

The 7th Oudh Irregulars mutiny.

It happened in this wise. The 7th Regiment of Oudh Irregular Infantry was stationed at Músá Bágh about three miles from the Residency. The adjutant of the regiment was Lieutenant Mecham of the Madras Army, a cool, determined, and resolute officer. On the 30th of April when he took his men to ball-practice, these suddenly showed a disinclination to use the new cartridge. Mecham pointed out to them that the cartridge was similar to that which they had been using the previous fortnight. This seemed to satisfy the men and they proceeded with the practice. But the next morning the sergeant-major reported that the men positively refused to bite the cartridge, that many even declined to receive or even to touch it.

They are induced to return to their lines.

The day following was spent by the men in brooding over their grievances. They worked themselves to the state of fanaticism which will not hear reason, and at 10 o'clock, on the 3rd, they had arrived at the conclusion that they must kill their European officers. The latter, warned in time by the quartermaster-sergeant of the disposition of their men, nobly did their duty, and succeeded after a time in inducing the sepoys to return to their lines,* though they refused to surrender their arms.

* It was related at the time of Lieutenant Mecham that he owed his life on this occasion to his coolness and presence of mind. Taken unawares by the mutineers and told to prepare to die, he replied: "It is true you may kill me but what good will my death do to you? You will not ultimately prevail. Another adjutant will take my place and you will be subjected to the same treatment you receive from me." The mutineers did not injure him.

Book IX. Chapter I.

1857. May 3.

Sir Henry Lawrence deprives them of their arms.

But Sir Henry Lawrence was not content with this doubtful triumph. Having made preparations to suppress any attempt which the sepoys might make to display insubordination he sent that afternoon two officers with instructions how to act. The men of the 7th were paraded. The question was put to them whether they would continue to bite the cartridge or whether they would refuse. The men, in an insolent and sullen manner, promised to obey. The force organised by Sir Henry, consisting of the 32nd Foot, an European battery, three regular native regiments of infantry and one of cavalry, arrived soon after on the ground. Darkness had now set in. The 7th were at once formed up and ordered to lay down their arms. In the presence of this imposing force and of the lighted portfires of the gunners they had no option but to comply. Most of them indeed fled stricken by panic, but on being assured that no violence would be used if they would obey orders they returned, and before midnight all their muskets were secured. The next day the ring-leaders were seized, and it transpired from their admissions that a treasonable correspondence with the view to a general rising had been going on for some time between them and the men of the 48th Regiment of Native Infantry.

The Darbár at Lakhnao.

In the events which immediately preceded, and immediately followed the affair of the 7th Oudh Irregulars, Sir Henry Lawrence had received valuable information from native officers and others. In the crisis which he saw advancing

Book IX. Chapter I.

1857. May 3-12.

with rapid strides he considered that rewards should go hand in hand with punishment, that the justice,—the truth in action—which had always been the maxim of the British Government, should at all hazards be maintained. He considered it advisable, moreover, that the bestowal of the rewards should be made the occasion for a solemn ceremony, at which he might speak the mind of the Government. With this view he invited the native aristocracy, the European and native civil officials, the European and native officers, and others to a Darbár on the evening of

May 12.

the 12th of May. Every arrangement had been made to give solemnity to the scene. At 6 P.M. Sir Henry Lawrence entered, followed by his staff. Near him were deposited in trays the presents and rewards to be bestowed upon the loyal

Touching address of Sir Henry Lawrence.

native officers and soldiers. But before distributing these Sir Henry addressed in Hindustani the assembled company. He went straight to the point; spoke of the fears for their religion entertained by the Hindús; reminded them how, under the Moghol rule, that religion had never been respected; how Aurangzíb had imposed the *jézia*; and how the flesh of the cow had been thrust down the throats of unwilling converts. Turning then to the Mahomedans he reminded them that Ranjít Singh would never tolerate their religion at Láhor. Passing on from that he begged them to recall to mind the toleration which for a century the English Government had afforded to both religions. He adverted next to our power, to our exploits in the Crimea, to our

Book IX. Chapter I.

1857. May 12.

ships, our resources; pointed out how hopeless of ultimate success would be a crusade against the English. He next dwelt on the long and intimate connection between the sepoys and their officers, on the community of danger and the community of glory between them, and begged the men to cherish as their most precious heirlooms the deeds of their ancestors. He concluded an eloquent speech, delivered in the language of the people, by warning his listeners against becoming the dupes of designing men, and of the fate which would inevitably follow the neglect of his advice. He then caused the deserving native officers and soldiers to be brought up to him, and, in the name of the Government, delivered to them the rewards they had merited.*

Its effect passing and transitory.

The speech of Sir Henry Lawrence had, undoubtedly, some effect at the moment. His earnest manner, his character so trusted and so respected, added weight to his words. When the Darbár broke up there was not probably a man present who was not loyal. But the opposite feeling was too deeply rooted to be dissipated by a passing sensation. The listeners went from the Darbár into the society of the plotters and intriguers against whom Sir Henry had warned them. The whispers, constantly repeated, of these men at first weakened, and ultimately deadened the effect which had been produced by the scene at the Darbár.

* Strange contradiction! Some of the men who were thus rewarded for loyalty were shortly afterwards hanged for proved disloyalty!

Book IX. Chapter I.

1857. May 13.

News of the Mírath revolt arrives.

That Darbár was held on the 12th of May. The Mírath mutiny had broken out on the 10th. A telegram conveying information that something serious had happened in the North-West reached Sir Henry on the 13th. A second telegram giving fuller details of the Mírath revolt and an account of the seizure of Dehlí reached him on the 14th. Averse as he was from any measures which might show premature distrust of the sepoys Sir Henry felt that a crisis had come upon him which must be met by prompt action. His plans had been arranged before-hand. During the 16th and 17th they were carried out. The morning of the last-named day saw a moiety of the 32nd Foot occupying the ground about the Residency and commanding the iron bridge. The second moiety were brought up from the city into the cantonments of Mariáon. The bridge of boats was moved nearer to the Residency and brought under control, whilst a selected body of sepoys was detached to occupy the Machhí Báwan, not yet sufficiently cleansed to be fit for occupation by European troops.

Prompt measures taken by Sir Henry.

A central position was thus secured for the Chief Commissioner, for his officials, and his European soldiers. Sir Henry had by one movement prepared himself to meet any emergency. But whilst prepared he had not altogether abandoned the hope that the emergency might not arise. He apprehended danger less from the native population than from the native troops. But with time he hoped that the difficulty might

He still longs for "time."

Book IX. Chapter I.

1857. May 18.

still be surmounted. "Time," he wrote in a memorandum dated the 18th of May, "time is everything just now. Time, firmness, promptness, conciliation, prudence . . . . . A firm and cheerful aspect must be maintained; there must be no bustle; no appearance of alarm, still less of panic; but at the same time there must be the utmost watchfulness and promptness; everywhere the first germ of insurrection must be put down instantly."

Sir Henry is nominated to supreme military command in Oudh.

Immediately on receiving information of the occurrences at Mírath and Dehlí Sir Henry Lawrence telegraphed to the Governor-General a strong recommendation to send for European troops from China, Ceylon, and other places, and for the Gúrkhás from the Hill Stations and from Nipál. Feeling, moreover, that at such a crisis it was necessary that the Chief Commissioner of the province should be invested with plenary military authority he asked the Governor-General to confer such power upon him. Lord Canning promptly replied. On the 19th he conferred upon the Chief Commissioner the plenary power asked for, and on the 22nd he gave him authority to apply to Jang Bahádur for his Gúrkhá troops.

Sir Henry Lawrence assumed the military command on the 19th. To understand the military arrangements which had been carried out two days previously under his instructions, it will be advisable to give an outline sketch of the city of Lakhnao.

The city of Lakhnao.

The city of Lakhnao, about fifty miles distant from Kánhpúr, extends for about three miles on the

Book IX. Chapter I.

1857. May.

right bank of the river Gúmtí. All the principal palatial buildings, the Residency and the Machhí Báwan, are between the city and the river bank. South of these buildings, and covering an immense space, is the city. This is intersected by a canal which falls into the Gúmtí close to the Martinière College, about three miles south-east of the Residency. A little to the south of this is the Dilkhúsha, a hunting-box or palace, within an enclosed park. The space between the Residency and the Martinière is occupied by palaces, among which the Motí Mahal, the Sháh-Manzal, the Sikandra Bágh, and Farrabaksh-kí-kothí, are the most conspicuous. South of the city, about four miles from the Residency on the southern side of the road leading to Kánhpúr, is the A'lam Bágh, a large walled garden with a high and pretentious gateway.

Sir Henry's military arrangements.

Not counting the position of the native cavalry at Múdkipúr, Sir Henry possessed now three military posts. Two of these—the Residency and the Machhí Báwan—he made as strong as he could. Having regard to possible eventualities he removed the spare ammunition from the magazines, into the Machhí Báwan. He seized the earliest opportunity of garrisoning that place with Europeans, of storing supplies there, and of mounting on the ramparts guns of sorts. Many of these were taken from the King's palaces, and were useful only to make a show. In the Residency compound, over the Treasury, he posted a mixed guard of two hundred sepoys, one hundred and thirty Europeans, and six guns—the guns being

Book IX. Chapter I. 1857. May.

so placed that they could, at the first alarm, be brought to bear on any mutineers. The third post was at the old cantonment of Mariáon. It was garrisoned by three hundred and forty men of the 32nd Foot, fifty European artillerymen, and six guns; the three native regiments and a battery of native artillery. Here Sir Henry, for the time, took up his quarters.

The ladies and children are brought into the Residency.

Having made these preparations Sir Henry Lawrence took an early opportunity to move the ladies and children into the houses within the Residency enclosure. Here also were brought the families and the sick men of the 32nd Regiment. At the same time the clerks, copyists, section-writers, and others of that class were armed and drilled. On the 27th of May he was able to write to Lord Canning, "both the Residency and the Machhí Báwan are safe against all probable comers." Whilst thus preparing to meet the possibilities Sir Henry betrayed none of the anxieties which he felt, but went freely amongst the people, endeavouring to calm their minds, to reason with them, to lay bare to them their folly. It was however too late, and he was made every day to feel it. "I held," he wrote to Lord Canning early in May, "I held a conversation with a Jemadár of the Oudh artillery for more than an hour, and was startled by the dogged persistence of the man, a Bráhman of about forty years of age, of excellent character, in the belief that for ten years past Government has been engaged in measures for the forcible, or rather fraudulent, conversion of all the natives.

Mistrust shown by a native officer.

Book IX. Chapter I.

1857. May 27.

. . . . . My interview with him was occasioned by his commanding officer having specially mentioned his intelligence and good character."

Towards the end of May the long smouldering discontent of the turbulent Masalmáns of the Malhiábád district burst into a flame, and on the 27th of that month Sir Henry Lawrence detached Captain Gould Weston, the Superintendent of Military Police, in the hope of restoring order. That officer's escort consisted of a troop of his own cavalry and a company of the mutinous 7th Oudh Irregular Infantry, under the command of the gallant Mecham. In the midst of an insolent Mahomedan population, to whom everything was a grievance, and from whom Captain Weston could elicit no real tangible cause of the rebellion, these two officers were in imminent danger.* Their lives depended not less upon their own coolness and daring before their avowed foes than upon the personal influence they might exercise on the wavering fidelity of their escort. Happily these essential qualities were not wanting; had it been otherwise, neither Weston nor Mecham would have fought his way back to Lakhnao with the detachments when recalled by Sir Henry Lawrence the day after the mutiny of the troops at Mariáon.

Mutinous feeling in the districts.

On the same day, the 27th, Captain Hutchinson of the Engineers, Military Secretary to the Chief

* Hutchinson's *Narrative of Events in Oudh,* published by authority. Captain Hutchinson adds: "Nothing but the bold determined firmness of Captain Weston over-awed the 3,000 fanatic wretches who surrounded him."

Commissioner, an officer of great talent and daring, was ordered by Sir Henry Lawrence to accompany into the district, as political officer, a column composed of two hundred men of the 7th Cavalry, and two hundred men of the 48th Native Infantry. The object of sending this column was to rid Lakhnao of the presence of men who might there be dangerous, but who, posted on the northern frontier of Oudh, might be employed with advantage to restrain the turbulence of the inhabitants. The idea emanated from Mr. Christian, through whose districts the column would pass.

Book IX. Chapter I.

1857. May 27.

Marching from Lakhnao on the 27th, the column passed through Malhiábád on the 28th —scowled upon by the armed villagers—and reached Sandila the 1st of June. There Hutchinson received accounts of the mutiny of the 30th of May at Lakhnao. The sepoys heard of it by the same post. It became at once apparent that they were biding their time. Hutchinson endeavoured to calm them by the disbursement of almost the entire contents of the treasure chest in the shape of pay. For the moment they seemed pacified. Their own senior officers, Captains Burmester and Staples, believed in them implicitly. Meanwhile the column was pressing on towards the Ganges. Hutchinson, who noted the increasing insolence of the men, urged the officers not to allow themselves to be taken in the net which was preparing for them on the other side of the river. But they were deaf and would not hear. The regiment crossed. On the 7th or 8th the

Mutiny of detached parties of the 48th Native Infantry and 7th Light Cavalry.

Book IX. Chapter I.

1857. May 30.

men rose, massacred all but one, Lieutenant Boulton, who fled to perish elsewhere, and went off to Delhí. Hutchinson, accompanied by the paymaster of pensioners, Major Marriott, who with him had declined to cross the river, returned in safety to Lakhnao.

Sepoys at Lakhnao mutiny.

The precautions I have before referred to had not been taken at that city at all too soon. On the night of the 30th of May the insurrection broke out. At 9 o'clock the evening gun fired as usual. The men of the 71st Regiment, previously told off in parties, started off at this signal to fire the bungalows and murder their officers. A few men only of the other infantry regiments, and some men of the 7th Cavalry, joined them. Their further proceedings will be related presently.

Warning given to Sir Henry.

Sir Henry Lawrence was dining that night at the Residency bungalow at Mariáon. An officer of his staff had informed him that he had been told by a sepoy that at gun-fire (9 P.M.), the signal to mutiny would be given. The gun fired; but all for the moment seemed quiet. Sir Henry leaned forward and said to the officer, "Your friends are not punctual." The words were scarcely out of his mouth when the discharge of muskets proved that his staff officer had been well informed, and that his friends were punctual.

A strange incident happened a few minutes later. Sir Henry Lawrence, surrounded by his staff, was standing on the steps of the Residency bungalow, waiting for the horses which had been ordered up from the stables. They were in the full glare of Mr. Couper's house, which, fired by the mutineers, had burst almost instantaneously in a blaze. Suddenly the Súbádár of the sepoys on duty at the Residency brought up his guard, and halted it facing Sir Henry and his staff at a distance of about forty paces. The Súbádár then came up to Captain Wilson, and saluting him said, "Shall I order the guard to load with ball?" Wilson referred the question to Sir Henry, who replied, "Yes, let them load." The loading then began—Sir Henry and the officers still standing in the glare of the fire. The thud of ramming down the leaden balls was distinctly heard. The sepoys then brought up their muskets to the capping position. The caps were adjusted. The next movement of the sepoys was eagerly waited for. They had the *élite*—the chiefs—of the British force at their mercy. One disaffected man bold enough could, then and there, have decided the fate of Lakhnao. The group standing on the steps of the Residency bungalow felt this in their inward hearts. But not an action, not a gesture, showed that they felt it. Yet they must have been relieved when the shouldering of arms followed the capping. The next moment the horses were brought up, and Sir Henry followed by his staff started for the lines.

Danger of Sir Henry and staff.

On his way he found three hundred men of the 32nd, four guns, Major Kaye's battery, and two of the Oudh force, posted in a position on the extreme

Sir Henry's movements to suppress the mutiny.

Book IX. Chapter I.

1857. May 30.

right of the 71st lines, and contiguous to the road leading from cantonments to the city. Recognising the necessity of preventing as far as possible communication between the mutineers and the evil-disposed in the city Sir Henry took with him two guns and a company of the 32nd to occupy the road leading from the cantonment to the bridge. He sent back shortly for the remainder of the Europeans, and for two more guns. Meanwhile, the officers of the native regiments had hastened to the lines to endeavour to reason with the men. Many of these, however, had already begun the work of plunder. A considerable body had marched straight on the 71st mess, and failing to find the officers—who had but just left—they fired it. Very soon after a musketry fire from the 71st lines opened on the Europeans. This was replied to with grape, and with such effect that the sepoys made a rush to the rear. In their hurried course they passed the infantry picket, composed of natives, and commanded by Lieutenant Grant, 71st Native Infantry. Some of his own men tried to save this officer by placing him under a bed. But a sepoy of his own regiment, who was on guard with him, discovered the place of concealment to the mutineers, and by these he was brutally murdered.

Action of the mutineers.

The main street patrolled.

Meanwhile, Lieutenant Hardinge, taking with him a few of the Irregular Cavalry, had been patrolling the main street of cantonments, in the endeavour to maintain order and to save life and property. He was not, however, in sufficient force to prevent the burning and plundering of

1857. May 30.

the officers' houses and the bazaars. The mutineers were prowling about in all directions. One of them fired at Lieutenant Hardinge, and when his shot missed fire he came at him with his bayonet and wounded him in the arm. All this time there was great excitement in the lines. But gradually some satisfactory symptoms evinced themselves. First, about three hundred of the 13th Native Infantry, with their British officers, their colours, and the regimental treasure, marched up and enrolled themselves with the British. They were followed by a very few of the 71st, without, however, their colours or their treasure. Of the 48th nothing was heard that night. The Europeans still remained formed up in the position assigned to them in case of alarm by Sir Henry Lawrence, their front flanking that of the several native regiments. About 10 P.M. some of the mutineers crept up to and occupied some empty lines bearing on that position, and opened a musketry fire. Brigadier Handscomb, riding from his house straight into the 71st lines, was immediately shot. The fire, however, soon ceased, and arrangements having been made to protect the Residency bungalow and the part of the cantonment next the city road, and strong guards having been posted, the force piled arms and waited for the morn.

Many sepoys prove loyal.

The mutineers baffled,

At daylight next morning, Sir Henry placed himself at the head of the force, and learning that the rebels had retired on Múdkipúr, followed them thither. Crossing the parade ground our men came upon the body of Cornet

Book IX. Chapter I.

1857. May 31.

Raleigh, a newly joined officer, who, left sick in his quarters, had been murdered by the rebels. At the same moment the mutinous regiments were discovered drawn up in line. On sighting them, hesitation was at once noticed in the ranks of the, till then loyal, 7th Cavalry. Their attitude appeared to an officer of Sir Henry Lawrence's staff to betoken an intention to charge the guns. That officer consequently at once directed the guns to open fire on the distant line. This prompt action decided the matter. The 7th Cavalry, with the exception of about thirty, raising a fearful yell, galloped over to the enemy, who turned and fled. Our troops followed them up for about ten miles and took sixty prisoners. In this pursuit Mr. Gubbins greatly distinguished himself, capturing several of the enemy with his own hand. By 10 A.M. our force had returned to cantonments, the heat being excessive.

pursued, and dispersed.

In announcing the suppression of this rising to Lord Canning Sir Henry Lawrence wrote: "We are now positively better off than we were. We now know our friends and enemies. The latter have no stomach for a fight though they are capital incendiaries." In the respect to which he referred he was indeed better off. He was rid of doubtful friends. Nearly the whole of the 7th Cavalry, a few men of the 13th, more than two-thirds of the 71st, a very large proportion of the 48th, and almost all the irregular troops, had shown their hand and departed. He could now concentrate his resources. But in

The position is improved by the mutiny.

Book IX. Chapter I.

1857. May 31.

other respects the day was full of foreboding. Intelligence received from the districts soon made it clear that the entire province was in arms against British rule.

Sítápúr. May 27.

Three days indeed prior to the rising at Lakhnao an incident had occurred at Sítápúr which showed very plainly that the train was laid at that station and that a single spark would ignite it. Sítápúr is the head-quarters of the Khairábád or north-west division of Oudh. It lies about fifty-one miles from Lakhnao. In 1857 it was garrisoned by the 41st Regiment of Native Infantry, commanded by Lieutenant-Colonel Birch, and by the 9th and 10th Regiments of Oudh Irregular Infantry. The Commissioner of the Division, Mr. Christian, resided there, together with Mr. Thornhill and Sir Mountstuart Jackson, civil officers of the Oudh Commission.

Precursors of the mutiny.

About noon of the 27th of May the vacant lines of the 2nd Regiment of Military Police, commanded by Captain John Hearsey,* were fired. It had not then become generally recognised that incendiarism was the invariable precursor to rebellion. Although, therefore, the firing of the lines caused some uneasiness, no absolute suspicion was directed to any particular body of men. The sepoys aided in extinguishing the fire, and the incident was not immediately followed by any overt act of mutiny.

Incendiarism.

It would appear that the firing of the lines had

* Captain Hearsey was most amiable and excellent offi-
formerly of the Oudh service, a cer much respected by his men.

Book IX. Chapter I.

1857. May 27.

been a tentative measure. The sepoys were anxious to feel their way, to test the credulity of their officers, before acting decidedly. They proceeded then by degrees.

June 2.

Plea that the flour has been adulterated.

Of all the regiments I have mentioned the 10th Oudh Irregulars were regarded as the most trustworthy. Great, then, was the surprise in Sítápúr when, five days later, the 2nd of June, it became known that the sepoys of that regiment had rejected the flour sent from the city for their consumption, on the plea that it had been adulterated for the purpose of destroying their caste. They insisted that the flour should be thrown into the river. The flour was thrown into the river.

The gardens plundered.

They now became bolder. The same afternoon the men of the same regiment plundered the gardens of the European residents of the ripe fruit growing in them. Their officers checked them, and, after some time, with success.

Confidence in regiment of Lieutenant-Colonel Birch.

It was now evident that the men were getting out of hand. Still, strange infatuation! the officers, whilst suspecting the other regiments, believed in their own. Lieutenant-Colonel Birch, commanding the 41st Native Infantry—a regiment which showed itself as truculent as any which mutinied—had the most absolute confidence in the loyalty of his men. He put that loyalty to the test by marching his regiment out on the 1st of June on the Lakhnao road to meet the mutineers advancing along it from the capital, and his men had justified his confidence by firing on their comrades and forcing them to alter their

Book IX. Chapter I.

route! After such behaviour it was treason in Sítápúr to doubt the loyalty of the 41st.

1857. June 2.

Mr. Christian prepares to meet the coming danger.

Yet Mr. Christian, a man of intellect and intelligence, did not feel secure. The idea of abandoning his post never crossed his mind. Like all the members of the noble service to which he belonged he felt that his place was where the Government had sent him. For himself he had no care; but reading rightly the signs of the times he had deemed it his duty to invite all the ladies of the station to occupy his house with their children. All responded except four who preferred to remain with their husbands. The house was well situated for defence, being cut off on one side from the adjoining ground by a rivulet. In front of it, and between it and the lines of the 41st, were posted four guns. The flanks were guarded by the irregular regiments, in whom Mr. Christian was inclined to place confidence.

Major Apthorp reports the disaffection of the 41st.

The incidents of the flour and of the fruit robbery on the 2nd of June had been sufficient to warn the residents that a crisis was approaching. But Lieutenant-Colonel Birch still believed in the loyalty of the 41st. At sunrise on the morning of the 3rd, however, Major Apthorp of that regiment satisfied himself that the sepoys were no longer to be trusted. He communicated his suspicions to Mr. Christian and his Colonel. They were soon verified. At 8 o'clock, a company of the regiment went off to the treasury to seize the public money, whilst the others, forming up, advanced in a menacing attitude against the guns

Book IX. Chapter I.

1857. June 3.

and against the irregular regiments on either flank of them.

They mutiny and murder Colonel Birch.

The safety of the Europeans seemed now to depend on the fidelity of the irregulars and native gunners. But before this could be tested Colonel Birch determined to make one effort to recall his men to duty. Accompanied by Lieutenant Graves he galloped towards the treasury. Mr. Christian, having strengthened the garrison of his house by a small party of military police, about twenty, started to follow the colonel, when Captain John Hearsey, who had preceded him, rode hurriedly back with the information that that officer and Lieutenant Graves had been shot by their men. It was clear now that the sepoys were bent on the blood of their officers. The 9th Irregulars almost immediately followed the example of the 41st, killing their officers; the 10th were not slow to imitate them. They suddenly rushed with yells against the bungalow, bent on slaughter.

The Irregulars mutiny also.

Slaughter of the English.

It is not easy to describe the scene that followed. The only possible safety lay in flight, and flight was difficult. The rivulet Saraián, which protected the rear of the bungalow against attack, was now an obstacle to the fugitives. However it was an obstacle that must be attempted. Mr. Christian, who had boldly started, rifle in hand, to meet the mutineers, seeing that all was lost, returned to his house to flee with his family. Preceded by his wife with an infant in her arms, he succeeded in crossing the rivulet, but he had scarcely reached the opposite bank when he was shot dead by the pursuing rebels. A similar fate befell his wife, her baby, and the nurse. The elder child, a girl taken across the river by Sergeant-Major Morton, was conveyed by him to the estate of the Mitholí Rájá and ultimately to Lakhnao where she died. Mr. and Mrs. Thornhill were shot dead either crossing the stream or just after. Sir Mountstuart Jackson, his sister, Captain Burnes, and some others likewise reached the estate of the Mitholí Rájá. There Mrs. Orr had already found shelter, and thither Captain Patrick Orr escaped from the Mohamdí party to be presently referred to. The Mitholí Rájá afforded to the fugitives only a half-hearted protection. Timid and fearing for himself he allowed them to remain in the jungles in the vicinity of his fort unmolested—and he provided them with food. They stayed there till the end of October, when, as will be told, the rebel troops took the survivors prisoners into Lakhnao.

Book IX Chapter I.

1857. June 3.

Some escape, to Mitholí.

Of the other fugitives from Sítápúr one party guided by Lieutenant Lester, who was intimately acquainted with the country, made straight for Lakhnao, which they reached. Another party, consisting of nine ladies, ten children, and three men, reached the same place, by circuitous paths, concealing themselves in the daytime, and indebted very much to the zamíndár of Rámkót, on the 28th of June. A third party, composed of Mrs. Phillipps and a few friends, found shelter in a village, and remained in concealment there for ten months, when they were rescued by a column of Lord Clyde's army. A fourth party escaped to Makápúr, and proceeded thence with

Some to Lakhnao.

Some lie concealed.

Book IX. Chapter I.

1857. June.

Some reach Makápúr.

the residents of that place and fugitives from Sháhjahánpúr to Mathurá, the estate of the Dhaorérá Rájá. Here they remained in safety till discovered by a party of rebel sepoys, who took them prisoners towards Lakhnao. But escaping on the road some fled into Nipál. The majority remained for some time in concealment, but were ultimately discovered by the rebels and taken into Lakhnao. A fifth party found their way to the estate of the Mitholí Rájá as already related.

Results of the mutiny at Sítápúr.

But if many thus escaped, some of them only for the moment, many too succumbed. On that terrible day twenty-four English, men, women, and children, were murdered by the sepoys. This slaughter but whetted the appetite of the loyal 41st. How they proceeded from Sítápúr to Farakhábád, and how there they incited the 10th Regiment to mutiny and murder has been told in the preceding Book.

Malaon.

One detachment of that loyal regiment, and a detachment of the 4th Oudh Irregulars, were, however, stationed at Malaon, also in north-west Oudh, but considerably to the south of Sítápúr. Here the only civil officer was Mr. Capper the Deputy Commissioner. His position had been long full of peril, for Malaon was on the high road to Farakhábád, and the population of that district was the most disorderly in India. Long before the mutiny at Sítápúr Mr. Capper had felt the loneliness and the danger of his position. The natives round about his station had intimated in the plainest manner possible, short of actual speech, that they knew that the sepoys were watching

Book IX. Chapter I.

1857. June.

their opportunity. But Mr. Capper did not flinch from his duty. He was at his post when the sepoys at Sítápúr mutinied. He remained there after they had mutinied. Nor did he entertain the idea of leaving it until the detachment at Malaon had shown unmistakeably that they, too, were about to take the law into their own hands. He then mounted his horse and rode into Lakhnao.

Mr. Capper reaches Lakhnao.

The third district in North-West Oudh is Mohamdí. The Deputy Commissioner there was Mr. Thomason: his assistant Captain Patrick Orr.*

Mohamdí.

In a previous page† I have recorded how some of the fugitives from Sháhjahánpúr reached Mohamdí. I propose now to recount the condition of that station before, and the events which happened subsequently to, their arrival there.

Neither Mr. Thomason nor Captain Orr had been blind or deaf to the signs of the times. The position of Mohamdí, almost on the frontier

Its position.

* Captain Patrick Orr was the second of three brothers, all, prior to the annexation, in the service of the King of Oudh.

The eldest brother, Alexander, had then rendered excellent service as Assistant to the Superintendent of Frontier Police. After the annexation he was made an Assistant Commissioner. He was as able as he was hard-working.

The second brother, Patrick, commanded originally one of the King's regular regiments of infantry. On the annexation he, too, was made an Assistant Commissioner. He was a brave, zealous, and able officer.

The youngest brother, Adolphus, was, under the King, adjutant of one of his infantry regiments. On annexation he was appointed to command the 3rd Regiment of Oudh Military Police, which, on the outbreak of the mutiny, was stationed in the Motí Mahal, Lakhnao.

† Book VIII. Chapter V. page 321.

Book IX. Chapter I. 1857. May.

of Rohilkhand and but a short distance from Sháhjahánpúr, rendered it peculiarly sensitive to the insurrectionary feeling of the population in our own provinces. The garrison consisted of a detachment of the 9th Oudh Irregulars, a regiment formerly raised and commanded by Captain Patrick Orr, under the King of Oudh, before the annexation; two companies of military police, and about fifty troopers.

Its garrison.

Mr. Thomason hears of the mutiny at Sháhjahánpúr,

Alive as were both Mr. Thomason and Captain Orr to the gravity of the crisis they were yet hopeful that so long as Rohilkhand should remain quiet they would manage to weather the storm. Nor was it until a letter written by Mr. Jenkins from Sháhjahánpúr, reaching Mr. Thomason on the evening of the 31st of May, revealed the catastrophe at that station, that the two Englishmen felt that every faculty they possessed was about to be tried to the utmost.

receives a letter from the fugitives thence.

The letter from Mr. Jenkins informed Mr. Thomason that the troops at Sháhjahánpúr had mutinied, that he and a body of fugitives, amongst whom were ladies and children, had reached Powaen, that the Rájá of that place had refused them shelter, and it begged that all the available carriage might be sent out to bring in the fugitives to Mohamdí.

He scents the coming storm.

Mr. Thomason complied with Mr. Jenkins's request. At the same time, he and Captain Orr, feeling that the crisis was upon them, determined to take active measures for the safety of their own belongings and of the expected fugitives. Their first step was to despatch Mrs. Orr and child to Mithaolí, a distance of twenty-six miles. The Rájá of that place was under considerable obligations to Captain Orr, and he was indebted to Mr. Thomason for many acts of kindness and courtesy. Thither, therefore, Mrs. Orr and her child were sent under the guard of some sepoys of Captain Orr's old regiment, the native officer commanding which swore fidelity. He kept his word. Marching all night Mrs. Orr and the party reached Mithaolí at 8 o'clock on the morning of the 1st of June. The Rájá, however, was asleep and would not be disturbed. When, at the end of two hours, he did awake, he sent a message to Mrs. Orr that he could not receive her in his fort, but that she must proceed to a place called Katchiání in the jungles, where she would be safer—less likely to attract the notice of roving mutineers.

Book IX. Chapter I.

1857. June.

Mrs. Orr is sent to Mithaolí,

To Katchiání accordingly Mrs. Orr proceeded. After a weary journey of two hours she found herself and child in a mud fort, desolate and dreary, devoid of all furniture—the very picture of discomfort. There she had to remain. There too the Rájá visited her that evening, and swore to protect her. He did not disguise from her that troublous times were upon them, and that the sepoys all over Oudh were pledged to revolt.

thence to Katchiání.

To return to Mohamdí. Having sent off Mrs. Orr and her child, Mr. Thomason and Captain Patrick Orr turned to provide for their own safety and for that of their expected guests. They first caused the treasure to be moved into the fort of Mohamdí. They then moved with their troops

Book IX. Chapter I.

1857. June.

The fugitives reach Mohamdí.

into that fort. This occurred on the 1st of June. The day following the Sháhjahánpúr fugitives arrived from Powáen. Weary, with naked feet, all exhausted, some badly wounded, they had with difficulty reached the place, which was not to be a place of refuge. Mohamdí was too close to the borders of Rohilkhand to be secure. It was considered certain that the mutinous regiments of that province would soon be upon the fugitives. On the other hand up to that date no mutiny had, to their knowledge, broken out in Oudh. Sítápúr was regarded as safe. To Sítápúr then Mr. Thomason wrote for carriage for the party. His letter reached Mr. Christian before mutiny had broken out at that place. Mr. Christian sent the carriage—under charge of an escort of sepoys of the Oudh Irregulars.

They resolved to retire on Sítápúr.

The terrible tragedy which ensued began with the arrival at Mohamdí of this carriage—and of this escort. The escort brought infection with them. Immediately on arrival they disseminated the report that their brethren had been cut up at Lakhnao for refusing to become Christians, and that they were resolved to be revenged. Captain Orr reasoned with the native officers. They knew him as an old servant of the King of Oudh, and his influence with them was not wholly extinct. After some conversation they announced their intention of marching back to Sítápúr, swearing that they would spare the lives of the Europeans, taking with them Mr. Thomason and Captain Orr, and allowing the others to go away unmolested. They took a solemn oath that they would do this.

An escort arrives.

Book IX. Chapter I.

1857. June 4.

Their first proceeding was to take possession of the treasure; their next to release the prisoners. Then, at half-past 5 o'clock on the afternoon of the 4th of June they started. The Europeans accompanied them, two or three ladies crammed into a buggy, the remainder prone on baggage-carts. The first march of ten miles was accomplished without incident. Of the second march only about three miles had been walked when the halt was sounded, and a trooper told the Europeans they were at liberty to go where they liked. They pushed on at once towards the nearest town, Arangábád. They had arrived within half a mile of that place, when the mutineers, regardless of their oaths, set upon them, and began the work of butchery. Of the whole party, one alone was spared to tell the tale, and it is from his narrative that I am able to collect this story of perjury and murder.* It remains to

The fugitives are all murdered,

but one.

* Captain Patrick Orr. The following is his account of the slaughter. "Next morning, Friday, the 5th, we marched towards Arangábád. When we had come about two koss the halt was sounded and a trooper told us to go on ahead where we liked. We went on for some distance when we saw a party coming along. They soon joined us, and followed the buggy which we were pushing on with all our might. When within half a mile of Arangábád a sepoy rushed forward and snatched Key's gun from him and shot down poor old Shiels who was riding my horse. Then the most infernal struggle ever witnessed by man began. We all collected under a tree close by, and put the ladies down from the buggy. Shots were firing in all directions amidst the most fearful yells. The poor ladies all joined in prayer coolly and undauntedly awaiting their fate. I stopped for about three minutes amongst them, but thinking of my poor wife and child here, I endeavoured to save my life for their sakes. I rushed out towards the insurgents and one of our men Gúrdín, 6th company, called

Book IX. Chapter I.

1857. July.

add that Captain Orr after some adventures, and communicating by the way with one of the fugitive parties from Sítápúr—that led by Sir M. Jackson—succeeded in joining his wife and child at Katchiání. On arriving there he received a communication from the Rájá that the mud fort at that place was required for the Sítápúr fugitives; that it would not be safe for so many to be together; and that it was advisable that he and his wife and child should migrate to and live in the jungles about Mithaolí. This they did. By this term, jungles, the reader must not understand an ordinary forest, the noble trees of which would have afforded a grateful and necessary shade; but he must picture to himself a vast and dreary extent of land, covered with thorny brushwood, and where it was necessary to light fires at night to scare away tigers, wolves, and other wild animals. Only the coarsest food was provided for them. The other fugitives were then sent from Mithaolí to occupy Katchianí.†

Fugitives from Sitápúr reach Mithaoli.

out to me to throw down my pistol and he would save me. I did so, when he put himself between me and the men, and several others followed his example. In about ten minutes more they completed their hellish work . . . . . They killed the wounded and the children butchering them in the most cruel way. With the exception of the drummer boy every one was killed of the above list, fugitives from Shájehánpúr, besides poor good Thomason and our two clerks. They denuded the bodies of their clothes for the sake of plunder." The list above referred to comprised one civilian, three captains, six lieutenants, three ensigns, a sergeant, a bandmaster, eight ladies, and four children. Of the drummer, who was not an European, I can find no further mention.

† They consisted of Sir M. Jackson and his sister; Lieutenant Barnes; Sergeant-Major Morton and Mr. Christian's little girl. Joined after a time

Book IX. Chapter I.

1857. April.

Bahráich.

Adjoining the Khairábád division is the northern, or Bahráich division of Oudh, bounded on the south by the river Ghágrá, separating it from the Faizábád division, on the west by the Sardá dividing it from Khairábád, and on the north by Nipál. The principal civil station, and the head-quarters of the Commissioner of the division, Mr. Charles Wingfield,* was close to the town which gave its name to the division—the town of Bahráich. The other stations were Mathápúr to the west, Sikrorá to the south, Gondah to the south-east. Of these, Sikrorá was the principal military station. In the month of April 1857, it was garrisoned by the 1st Regiment of Oudh Irregular Cavalry, commanded by Captain Daly; by the 2nd Oudh Infantry, under Captain Boileau; and by a local horse battery, under Lieutenant Bonham.

Sikrorá.

by the party from the jungle, the fugitives remained in this fort suffering great privations and subject to repeated attacks of jungle-fever, till the 25th of October. They were then ordered to depart, no one knew whither, under a guard furnished by the Rájá of Mithaolí. With scant clothing, bare-footed, the men loaded with chains, they were taken to Lakhnao, and imprisoned in the Kaisar-bágh, one of the regal palaces, then strongly occupied by the rebels. The sufferings of the men did not last long. On the 16th of November the men were taken out and shot by a party of sepoys of the 71st Native Infantry. A few days later the surviving daughter of Mr. Christian died. There remained then Mrs. Orr, Miss Jackson, and the child of the former. To save the child her death was simulated, and she was conveyed in safety to the house of Mán Singh, and ultimately to the British camp. The ladies remained in confinement till the 19th of March, when they were rescued by a party of Gúrkhás commanded by two British officers, and conveyed safely to the camp of Sir James Outram.

* Now Sir Charles Wingfield, K.C.S.I.

Book IX. Chapter I.

1857. April.

Mr. Wingfield.

During the month of April Mr. Wingfield had been driven by circumstances entirely unconnected with the rising storm to remove his head-quarters to Sikrorá. A man of ability, of culture, and of large views, he had not sympathised with the sweeping change of system which had inaugurated the transfer of Oudh from its Mahomedan king to British rule. He had ever been in favour of dealing gently with the territorial aristocracy. A system, roughly, even rudely introduced, which scarcely veiled its animating principle of raising the peasantry and small proprietors to a position which would enable them ultimately to oust the great landowners, was not in accordance with his ideas. He had done, then, all that lay in his power to make the transfer easy, to smooth down the rough edges, to mitigate the worst effects of the process. The appointment of Sir Henry Lawrence as Chief Commissioner, coming even when it did, was a great support to him. It would have been still greater, still more weighty, had it been made earlier.

His sound views.

Early foresees the tendency of the policy adopted.

Like his chief at Lakhnao, like that chief's brother at Láhor, like Durand at Indúr, like William Tayler at Patná, Mr. Wingfield had never been a partisan of the "passing and groundless panic" theory of Mr. Cecil Beadon. He had fully appreciated the events at Barhámpúr and at Bárrákpúr. The revolt at Mírath he regarded as the practical answer of the sepoys to the policy of the Government. He felt, then, than an outbreak at the military station of Sikrorá was a mere question of time; that, given all the circumstances of the case—the composition of the native army, the annexation of Oudh—the province, a portion of which he was administering, would not be the last to feel the shock of mutiny.

Book IX. Chapter I. 1857. April.

Impressed with this belief, and having absolutely no faith in the men who composed the garrison of Sikrorá, Mr. Wingfield had endeavoured to enlist on the side of the British the members of that territorial aristocracy whom the annexation of Oudh had done so much to injure. Chief among these was Dirg Bijéh Singh, Rájá of Balrámpúr, a town in the north-east corner of his division, and close to the Nipál frontier. Rájá Dirg Bijéh Singh was a man of character and sense. He entertained towards Mr. Wingfield friendly—even grateful—feelings. He had not been innoculated with the poison that pervaded the atmosphere. He received, then, Mr. Wingfield's advances with courtesy; he responded to them; and even engaged to afford refuge, in case of necessity, to him and to the officers serving in his division.

Gratitude felt towards him by the landowners.

The views entertained by Mr. Wingfield regarding the general untrustworthiness of the sepoys, were fortunately shared by many other officers at Sikrorá. Neither he nor they, therefore, thought that either wisdom or courage required that the ladies and children should be left in a position, defenceless and incapable of being defended, until an actual outbreak should occur. It happened that an officer of Daly's Horse, Captain Forbes, was in Lakhnao early in June. He knew that his own men would mutiny, and he

Captain Forbes escorts the ladies and children to Lakhnao.

Book IX. Chapter I. 1857. June.

knew that at Sikrorá there was no place of refuge in case of an outbreak. Anxious, therefore, for the safety of his wife, his children, and his countrywomen, he set out from Lakhnao with a party of Sikh and volunteer cavalry, reached Sikrorá, mounted the ladies on elephants and in doolies, and conveyed them safely to the capital. Mr. George Lawrence, the Deputy Commissioner, by the express order of his uncle, Sir Henry, accompanied them. This move was accomplished on the 9th of June.

Mr. Wingfield scents the mutiny at Sikrorá.

The same day the temper of the troops manifested itself in a way not to be mistaken. Intelligence had reached Sikrorá of the revolt of the troops at Faizábád on the previous day. Mr. Wingfield accordingly, mounting his horse, rode to the neighbouring station of Gondah, where was stationed the 3rd Oudh Irregulars, commanded by Lieutenant Miles. There I must leave him for a moment, whilst I narrate the occurrences at Sikrorá after his departure.

It breaks out.

The day of the 9th of June was a day of great excitement at that station. So violent was the manifestation that early the following morning the officers of the infantry regiment,—Boileau, Hale, and Kendall,—mounted horse and rode straight for Balrámpúr. Lieutenant Bonham, of the artillery, refused to accompany them. He believed in his men; he certainly possessed great influence over them; and he still hoped that they would stand by him in the cause of order. He elected, therefore, to remain at Sikrorá, alone of

Book IX. Chapter I.

1857. June 9.

all the officers, and supported only by two farrier sergeants and the quartermaster-sergeant of the infantry regiment. Had there been no other native troops at Sikrorá his courage and his influence might have prevailed. But the men of the cavalry and infantry had broken out; they had plundered the treasury, and they were thirsting for blood. Even over these men Bonham attempted to assert authority. But it was in vain. His own men would save his life, but they would not fire on his comrades. They told him at last that he must go. They brought him at the same time money and a horse, and warned him not to pursue a certain road which they knew to be occupied by the rebels. Forced to leave, Bonham started with a heavy heart, accompanied by his three sergeants, crossed the Ghágrá by an unfrequented ferry, and reached Lakhnao the next day.

Devotion of Lieutenant Bonham.

Strong feeling towards him of his men.

Meanwhile Mr. Wingfield had arrived at Gondah. He brought the intelligence that the troops at Faizábád had mutinied, and that those at Sikrorá were on the verge of mutiny. He found the troops at Gondah scarcely behind their comrades in that respect. They, too, had heard the news; they, too, were aware of all that had happened at Faizábád. Before the night fell they had received accounts of the mutiny at Sikrorá. In vain were they harangued by their commanding officer. Their demeanour showed that they, too, were preparing for action.

Mr. Wingfield at Gondah.

The next day they mutinied. Mr. Wingfield had not waited for the overt act, but had started

He takes refuge with the

Book IX. Chapter I.

1857. June 10.

Rájá of Balrámpúr.

for Balrámpúr. The officers and the women* who remained at the station started as soon as the outbreak had pronounced itself, and reached the same place in safety. The number of individuals who thus received the protection of the Rájá was nineteen, exclusive of children. They all succeeded in crossing into British territory, and in reaching Gorákhpúr.

The station of Bahráich.

At Bahráich, the head-quarters of the division, were cantoned two companies of the 3rd Oudh Irregulars, commanded by Lieutenant Longueville Clarke. The Deputy Commissioner was Mr. Cunliffe and his assistant was Mr. Jordan. The main body of the 3rd Oudh Irregulars mutinied, as we have seen, at Gondah, on the 10th of June. As it was very clear that the two companies of the same regiment would at once follow their example, the three officers I have named wisely resolved to take advantage of their earlier information, and to escape. They started off at once, then, northward, in the direction of Nánpárá, the seat of a minor Rájá. There, however, admission was refused them, and they were forced to retrace their steps. Returning to Bahráich, they started for Lakhnao by way of Bairámghát. This was the road against which the native gunners of Sikrorá had warned Bonham. The fugitives, who had disguised themselves as natives, found the passage over the Ghágrá occupied here by the mutineers. Trusting to their disguise, however, they embarked on the ferry-boat with their horses. The

The officials scent the mutiny and leave it.

* The ladies had been sent to Lakhnao, *viâ* Sikrorá, on the 5th of June.

ferry-boat started. At first the fugitives appeared to attract no attention, but they had crossed scarcely one-third of the river when the cry arose that Europeans were escaping. Instantly there was an uproar. The sepoys crowding into other boats, made for the ferry-boat, opening at the same time a fire of musketry. The boatmen at once abandoned the ferry-boat. Exposed to a concentrated fire, our three countrymen were unable effectively to work the boat, thus left to itself, nor to prevent it from being borne back by the current to the bank whence it started. Before it reached that bank Cunliffe and Clarke had been shot dead. Jordan, taken alive, shared the same fate a few days later.

They are murdered crossing by the ferry.

Malápúr.

At Malápúr there were no troops,—consequently there was no open mutiny. The general disorganisation of the country soon, however, spread even here, and the civil officers, prominent amongst whom was the Deputy Commissioner, Mr. Gonne, were forced to leave. Having been joined by other fugitives, they first attempted to make their way down the Sarjú river by boat. But warned that all the landing-places were occupied, they abandoned this attempt; they set off northward and gained the fort of Mathiárí, belonging to the minor Rájá of Dhorairah. Thence Mr. Gonne made more than one unsuccessful attempt to reach Lakhnao. At last even the resource of remaining at Mathiárí failed them. The adherents of the minor Rájá proved faithless. In imminent danger of their lives they had to flee. Three of the party were seized. The

The officials leave,

and eventually all perish,

Book IX. Chapter I.

1857. July.

but one.

remainder gained the Nipál hills, where they found shelter till, gradually, with one exception only,* they yielded to the deadly climate of the Tarai.

Faizábád.

Faizábád is the eastern division of Oudh. It lies immediately south of the Bahráich division, and is divided into the three districts of Faizábád, Sultánpúr, and Saloní. The Commissioner was Colonel Philip Goldney.

Its garrison.

Colonel Goldney, and the Deputy-Commissioner of the district, Captain Reid, were at the head-quarter station of Faizábád. The troops here consisted of a horse battery of native artillery, the 22nd Regiment of Native Infantry, the 6th Oudh Irregular Infantry, and a squadron of the 15th Irregular Cavalry—the whole commanded by Colonel Lennox, of the 22nd Native Infantry.

Precautions taken by the officials.

The officers at Faizábád suffered from no delusion regarding the intentions of the mutineers. The events that had taken place during the second week in May at Mírath and at Dehlí had made it clear to them that their turn would come. They took precautions then, at an early date, to prepare for the rising storm. With this

May.

view they began in May to store supplies in a house occupied by Captain Thurburn, Special Assistant Commissioner. This house was chosen because it was surrounded by a walled enclosure. This walled enclosure was now fortified. So far the authorities at Faizábád acted with wisdom and forethought. But they counted like-

* Captain John Hearsey, commanding 2nd Regiment Oudh Military Police.

Book IX. Chapter I.

1857. May.

wise upon resources which were certain to fail them. They counted upon the aid of the pensioned sepoys and of the landholders of the district. To count upon both these classes proved they had not fully gauged the depth of the crisis.

Value of reliance placed on the pensioners;

It would seem that it was but natural to count upon the aid of the pensioned sepoys. The yearly stipends drawn by these men were paid by the British Government, and their continuance depended on the existence of the British Government. The material interests of this class were, therefore, bound up in the maintenance of British authority. Old associations too, in many cases stronger than caste, bound them to the British. In its proper place it will be related how these men responded to the appeal made to them by Sir Henry Lawrence. But at Faizábád their numbers were too small, their influence was too slight, to weigh much in the balance against the rising discontent.

on the talúkdárs.

The case with respect to the landowners was different. It must not be forgotten that Faizábád was the division regarding which Sir Henry Lawrence wrote thus to Lord Canning in April 1857: "the talúkdárs have also, I fear, been hardly dealt with. At least, in the Faizábád division, they have lost half their villages. Some talúkdárs have lost all." It may be said that the remark of Sir Henry applied only to the higher order of the territorial aristocracy. But in reality it referred to the assessment as it touched every class connected with the soil. It could not have been seriously expected that the men who had suffered most from our rule would risk their lives

Book IX. Chapter I. — 1857. June.

to maintain it. No surprise, then, ought to be felt at the laconic record of the Deputy Commissioner: "we found that the zamíndárs, however well-disposed, would not fight against disciplined troops, with guns."

The plan of defending Captain Thurburn's house was, then, on the 5th of June, abandoned. For a moment, Colonel Goldney entertained the idea of sending the ladies and children into Lakhnao. But it was too late. The road to Lakhnao passed through Dariábád, a station in the Lakhnao division; and disorder reigned in Dariábád.

Rájá Mán Singh,

But another plan had a little before been presented to Colonel Goldney. The principal talúkdárs of the Faizábád division, prominently amongst whom may be named Rájá Mán Singh, Udrés Singh, Thákúr Narain, Mír Bákir Húsén, and Nádir Sháh, had scented the mutiny from afar, and had warned Colonel Goldney of its approach. At this time the most considerable of these men, Rájá Mán Singh, was in disgrace. He was even under arrest. It happened that one of the assistant commissioners at Faizábád was Captain Alexander Orr. Captain Orr had well and truly served the old *régime* when Oudh had her king, had known intimately Mán Singh, and had conceived for him a great regard. When, then, the Rájá fell into disgrace Captain Orr earnestly begged his release from arrest. Mán Singh was released from arrest, and in return for Captain Orr's efforts in his behalf, he offered protection to his wife and children in his fort of Sháhganj

is communicated with by Captain Alexander Orr.

He agrees to protect the civil officers and their families;

and finally those of the officers generally.

during the troublous times that were coming. Captain Orr communicated the offer to the Commissioner. Colonel Goldney received it just about the time when the journey of the ladies to Lakhnao had been pronounced impracticable. He, in consultation with the other officers, determined to ask the Rájá so to enlarge his offer as to include all the ladies in the station. Rájá Mán Singh was communicated with by Captains Reid and Orr. He agreed to receive the wives and families of the civil officers, but demurred to a larger number on the ground that secrecy would thus be rendered futile. Finally, however, he agreed to receive all, provided that due caution were observed in movement.

Some take advantage of his offer.

With one exception the wives of the regimental officers decided not to accept the offer of Mán Singh. Not only did they distrust him, but they and their husbands considered that the movement would serve as a signal to the sepoys to mutiny. On the night of the 7th of June, however, the wives and children of the civil officers, and the wife and children of the Executive Engineer, Captain Dawson, started for and reached Sháhganj. They were followed to the same place, the following morning, by the wives and children of the staff-sergeants.

The sepoys rise in revolt,

That night the sepoys rose in revolt. More audacious than their comrades elsewhere they did not pretend a grievance, but loudly asserted that, feeling they were stronger than the English, they intended to turn them out of the country. The senior Rissaldár of the 15th Irregular Cavalry

Book IX. Chapter I.

1857. July 7.

took command of the brigade, and endeavoured to induce the men to murder their officers. But the sepoys had not then wound themselves up to the pitch of blood-thirstiness. They were anxious to rid themselves of their officers, but not to take their lives. Keeping them under restraint all night in the quarter-guard, they procured four boats for them, and in the morning gave them money and told them to be off. The boats were unprovided with boatmen, but they had oars.

but procure boats for their officers.

Faizábád is on the river Ghághrá, navigable thence to Bhaliá, where it joins the Ganges. Four boats containing the fugitive Europeans, and propelled by them, started before sunrise on the morning of the 9th of June. The mutineers who had plundered the treasury, and sacked the houses, did not interfere with them. But—strange contradiction—whilst protecting them against the more blood-thirsty of their own clan, whilst aiding them to depart, they sent a messenger begging the men of the 17th Regiment of Native Infantry to slay them on their way. The 17th, stationed at A'zamgarh, a station in British territory near the eastern frontier of Oudh, had arrived within a few miles of Faizábád on the 8th of June. Their line of march lay along the right bank of the Ghághrá. Their hands were already red with blood. They were willing to shed more.

The boats set out.

The sepoys send intimation to their brethren of the 17th Native Infantry,

The men of the 17th responded then to the call. They intercepted the two first boats at Bégamganj, about twelve miles by the road from Faizábád, though far longer by the river. Here, at a point where the stream was the most narrow,

who intercept the boats.

Book IX. Chapter I.

1857. June.

they opened fire on the fugitives. A few moments later, and from the opposite bank, there started boats full of armed men to attack their left flank. Recognising the impossibility of resistance Colonel Goldney counselled a run for life. The Colonel, too old to run himself, remained to die. Seven, however, including, curious to relate, a Mahomedan sepoy of the 22nd, Téz Alí Khán, who had linked his fate to that of the British, followed the recommendation and ran across country. Two of the party were drowned endeavouring to cross a stream. The remaining five reached Amorah in safety. Here they were joined by the three officers, who had formed the crew of the fourth boat, and who had abandoned her on account of her slowness of pace before she had reached the point where the men of the 17th had been lying in wait. The party, thus augmented to eight, pushed on across country. Betrayed at Mohádaba by two policemen whom they had trusted they were attacked by the villagers. Crossing a rivulet waist-deep, hotly pursued, they lost first Lieutenant Lindsay, then Lieutenants Thomas, English, Ritchie, and Sergeant Edwards. There now remained only Lieutenant Cautley, Sergeant Busher, and Téz Alí Khán. In the chase that followed Lieutenant Cautley was caught and killed. Sergeant Busher escaped for the moment but was captured the next day. His life, however, was spared, and at the end of ten days he was released. He ultimately joined Captain Lennox at Captainganj, where he found also his fellow fugitive, Téz Alí

Of the Englishmen in three boats one only escapes.

Book IX. Chapter I.

1857. June.

Khán. The fugitives who had remained in the first and second boats, numbering eight, were massacred to a man.

Fate of those in the remaining boat.

Three boats have now been accounted for, the first, the second, and the fourth. But there was another manned by five officers, headed by Colonel O'Brien. This boat, following the first and second, had put in at the town of Ayodhya,* the birthplace of Rám—the town that gave its name to the province. Here they exchanged their boat for a larger one, and hired native rowers to row it. They then lay down hidden by the thatch and matting from the gaze of inquiring eyes, whilst the natives pulled away singing a national air. The boat thus passed unsuspected through the hostile array, and the fugitives reached Dánápúr in safety.

Sufferings of Mrs. Mills and her children.

But some had remained at Faizábád. Amongst these were Mrs. Mills, wife of Major Mills, of the Artillery, and her three children. Mrs. Mills had refused to accept the hospitality offered by Mán Singh. When the mutiny broke out, she attempted to conceal herself in the city; but sinking for want of food she was obliged to discover herself to the leader of the mutineers. He sent her and her children across the Ghághrá into the Gorákhpúr district. Here she wandered for eight or ten days from village to village. A tender and delicate lady, her sufferings were terrible. Her youngest child died from the exposure. At last Rájá Mán Singh hearing that there was an

* The name *Ayodhya*, has *Avadh*, and *Avadh* to *Audh* or been gradually corrupted to *Oudh*.

Book IX. Chapter I.

1857. June.

English lady in distress, fetched her in to Sháhganj, provided for her wants, and after a few days rest, sent her and the sergeants' wives into Gorákhpúr. Her husband was one of those murdered in the second boat.

Escape of Colonel Lennox and family.

Colonel Lennox and his family had not started with the other officers in the boats. At 2 P.M., however, finding the sepoys becoming riotous and insolent for plunder he and they set out. They soon came upon the blood-thirsty 17th. But it was night. Realising their danger, they crept, unobserved, from their boat, and made their way into the Gorákhpúr district. They were soon, however, taken prisoners, and confined in the fort of Názim Mír Mahomad Húsén Khán. The Názim was disposed to be friendly. Threatened by the mutineers, he concealed the fugitives in a reed hut in rear of his zanána, and kept them there for nine days. He then made them over to an escort sent for them by the Collector of Gorákhpúr. On their way to that station, they picked up Sergeant Busher, and the sepoy, Téz Alí, as already related.

The civil officers of Faizábád.

There is still a party of the officials of Faizábád whose fate has to be recorded. I allude to the civil officers who had not started in the boats. These were Captain Reid, Captain Alexander Orr, Captain Thurburn, and Mr. Bradford. The wives and children of these gentlemen were under the protection of Mán Singh at Sháhganj, where also were Captain Dawson, Executive Engineer, Corporal Hurst of the Sappers, and a clerk named Fitzgerald.

Book IX. Chapter I.

1857. June.

They take refuge with Mán Singh.

When the mutiny broke out the four gentlemen just mentioned were together. Momentarily separated from, but soon rejoined by, Mr. Bradford, they reached Sháhganj on the 11th. Mán Singh was not there. He had gone to Ayodhya, probably to watch the course of events. Thence he had sent a message to say that he had made a compromise with the mutineers, by virtue of which he would be able to afford protection to the women and children, but not to the men; that these must depart instantly, as his house was to be searched the day following.

That day a boat was secured, and that night the party including ladies and children, and consisting of thirty-eight souls, set for the river. Twenty-nine of them reached its bank, eight miles below Faizábád, just before sunrise. The carriage containing the remaining nine had broken down.* It was impossible to wait for them. The country, especially that in the vicinity of the river-bank, was swarming with mutinous cavalry. The twenty-nine then started. Their boat proceeded for some time with only occasional alarms; but on the second day it was lured by the agent sent with it by Mán Singh into a position between two forts by both of which it was commanded. Here the fugitives were forced to give up their money, their arms, and their valuables. There was no help for it. After suffering much from hunger, from exposure, and other causes, and

* This contained the sergeants' wives and children. They returned to Sháhganj and were ultimately sent into Gorákhpúr with Mrs. Mill, as already related.

Book IX. Chapter I.

1857. June.

after constant detention, the fugitives reached Gópálpúr on the 21st of June. By the loyal Rájá of that place they were cordially received, hospitably entertained, and provided with the means of proceeding to Dánápúr, where they arrived the 29th of June.

Loyalty of the Rájá of Gópálpúr.

Sultánpúr.

Sultánpúr, the chief town of the district of that name, lies on the right bank of the river Gúmtí, almost in a direct line between Faizábád and Alláhábád. The principal civil officer was Mr. Block, C.S. Sultánpúr was the head-quarters of the 15th Regiment of Irregular Cavalry, commanded by Colonel S. Fisher, one of the most gallant and daring officers in the service.

Symptoms of mutiny.

On the 5th of June, Mr. Blook received intimation from a native official, a Mahomedan, whom he had sent on duty to Chandah, that mutinous sepoys from Jánpúr in British territory had arrived at that place, professing themselves to be in correspondence with the troops at Sultánpúr, and declaring their resolve to kill all the Europeans. This intimation was repeated the following day. Mr. Block at once ordered the man back to Sultánpúr, and communicated the intelligence he had received to Colonel Fisher, who at once despatched all the ladies in the station in the direction of Alláhábád under charge of two officers. The Mahomedan returned to Sultánpúr the 8th of June, saw Colonel Fisher and Mr. Block, told them that the Jánpúr sepoys had plundered Chandah and were on their way to Sultánpúr, that their own men were not to be depended

Book IX. Chapter I.

1857. June 8.

upon, and advised them, whilst there was yet time, to leave the place. This Colonel Fisher and Mr. Block decided not to do.

Early next morning the 1st Regiment of Military Police, commanded by Captain Bunbury, rose in revolt. Colonel Fisher rode down to their lines, followed by his men, to endeavour to recall them to order. Whilst he was addressing them, a policeman came round and shot him in the back. He fell mortally wounded from his horse. His own men had been passive spectators of the deed. They would not now approach him, although they allowed the adjutant, Lieutenant Tucker, to tend him in his last agony. Whilst they permitted this, however, they turned upon the second in command, Captain Gibbings, shot him, and then shouted to Lieutenant Tucker to be off. By this time Colonel Fisher's last agony was over, and Tucker, having nothing more to do, mounted, and, riding for his life, succeeded in reaching the fort of Rústam Sáh, on the banks of the Gúmtí. By this chief he was sheltered. He eventually reached Banáras in safety.*

Murder of Colonel Fisher,

of Captain Gibbings,

and of Messrs. Block and Stroyan.

Meanwhile, the Mahomedan already referred to had conveyed to Mr. Block and Mr. Stroyan news of Colonel Fisher's death, and of the mutiny of the troops. The two gentlemen started off to flee, and reached a small house in the vicinity of the station. Imprudently stopping here, whilst their guide was sent to ascertain how matters were pro-

* Captains Bunbury and Smith, Lieutenant Lewis and Dr. O'Donel also received hospitality from the same chieftain. They all reached Banáras.

gressing in the station, they were attacked and murdered.

Book IX. Chapter I.

1857. June 9.

Thus did Sultánpúr pass into the hands of the rebels. These, after plundering the houses and securing the treasure, started off in the direction of Lakhnao.

Salóní.

The other district station in the division of Faizábád was Salóní. The Deputy-Commissioner here was Captain L. Barrow.* The troops consisted of six companies of the 1st Oudh Irregulars, commanded by Captain Thomson. By the exertions of the officers tolerable order was maintained here for the first nine days in June. On that day intelligence arrived of the mutinies at Sultánpúr and elsewhere, and of the approach of mutineers from other stations. The next day the troops threw off the mask and revolted. The officers succeeded in leaving the station in safety, and in reaching the fort of Daraopúr, possessed by a talúkdár, Rájá Hanmant Singh of Kálá Kankar,†

Generosity of Rájá Hanmant Singh.

* Subsequently Chief Commissioner of Oudh.

† This noble Rájpút had been dispossessed, by the action of the revenue system introduced by the British, of the greater part of his property. Keenly as he felt the tyranny and the disgrace, his noble nature yet declined to regard the fugitive chiefs of the nation which had nearly ruined him in any other light than as people in distress. He helped them in their distress. He saw them in safety to their own fortress. But when, on bidding him farewell, Captain Barrow expressed a hope that he would aid in suppressing the revolt, he stood erect, as he replied: "Sáhib, your countrymen came into this country and drove out our king. You sent your officers round the districts to examine the titles to the estates. At one blow you took from me lands which from time immemorial had been in my family. I submitted. Suddenly misfortune fell upon you. The people of the land rose against you. You came to me whom

Book IX. Chapter I. — 1857. June 10.

who not only sheltered them, but escorted them to the ferry opposite Alláhábád. It deserves to be recorded that ten of Captain Thomson's sepoys continued faithful and never left him.

We come round now to the division from whose capital we started—the division of Lakhnao. The other two district stations here were Púrwá and Dariábád.

Dariábád.

At Dariábád, on the high road from Faizábád to Lakhnao was quartered the 5th Oudh Irregular Infantry, commanded by Captain W. H. Hawes. This officer was zealous, active, and much liked by his men. It is scarcely possible that even had no extraordinary temptation assailed them they would have remained faithful, for they were bound by the ties of blood and caste to the men who all around them were rising in revolt. But they were tempted beyond the ordinary temptation. In the public treasury of Dariábád lay stored £30,000 in silver—and they knew it. Captain Hawes knew it too, and knowing that fact, and the inevitable consequences which would ensue were the money to remain at Dariábád, he had made an effort, in the early part of the last week of May, to escort it into Lakhnao. In this attempt he was baffled by the ill-will of some of the men of his regiment. But Captain Hawes was a man who did not lightly resign a well

Mutiny of the sepoys.

you had despoiled. I have saved you. But now,—now I march at the head of my retainers to Lakhnao to try and drive you from the country." It is satisfactory to be able to add, that after the suppression of the mutiny his lands were restored to this true-hearted gentleman.

1857. June 9.

digested idea. On the 9th of June, he made a second effort. On this occasion he succeeded, amid the cheers of his men, in escorting the money outside the station. But he could not persuade them to take it further. A portion of them suddenly mutinied, gained the upper hand, and drove their officers away. Captain Hawes escaped by a miracle. "He was repeatedly fired at, sometimes a volley being directed at him, and, at others, single deliberate shots."* But he escaped, and not only he, but, after various adventures, all the other officers, civil and military, with their wives and children, belonging to Dariábád. After the departure of the Europeans, the mutineers proclaimed Wájid Alí Sháh, ex-King of Oudh, as their king.

Escape of Captain Hawes.

Púrwá.

Púrwá is about twelve miles from the Ganges, not far from the high road between Kánhpúr and Lakhnao. There were no troops there. The Deputy-Commissioner there, Captain Evans, maintained his position in his district till the end of June, sending in all the information he was able to glean regarding affairs at Kánhpúr. His own wife and children, his assistant, Mr. Arthur Jenkins, were at that ill-fated station. Captain Evans, loyally assisted by his Mahomedan officer of police, Mansab Alí by name, was able to keep open communications till Sir Hugh Wheeler's force had succumbed. After that catastrophe, it was impossible for him to remain at his post. He, therefore, retired on Lakhnao.

* Gubbins's *Mutinies in Oudh.*

Book IX. Chapter I.

1857. June 12.

Lakhnao on the 12th of June.

To that city we must now return. We left it on the 31st of May, just after the outbreak there had been suppressed by the vigour and energy of the Chief Commissioner. We return to it on the 12th of June. In the interval every station in the province had been lost to the British. Writing on that day to the Lieutenant-Governor of the North-West, Sir Henry Lawrence thus expressed his sense of the situation:—"We still hold the cantonment, as well as our two posts, but every outpost (I fear) has fallen, and we daily expect to be besieged by the confederated mutineers and their allies. The country is not yet thoroughly up, but every day brings it nearer that condition . . . . . All our irregular cavalry, except about sixty Sikhs of Daly's corps, are either very shaky or have deserted . . . . . The irregular infantry are behaving pretty well, but once we are besieged it will be black against white, with some very few exceptions. More than a hundred police deserted last night, and since I began this page I have received the report of the military police post having deserted the great central gaol over which they were specially placed . . . . . Then, again, we ought to have only one position. I put this question to some sixteen officers five days ago, but all stood out for the two positions. I am convinced they were wrong, and the best of them now think so, but we are agreed that, on the whole, the Residency is the point to hold . . . . . The talúkdárs have all been arming, and some have already regained possession of the villages of which Mr. Gubbins dispossessed them." On

Book IX. Chapter I.

1857. June 12.

The situation.

the day following he expressed a similar opinion in a letter to Lord Canning. After enumerating the native troops still faithful, about five hundred and thirty, he added: "few of them can be expected to stand any severe pressure. We, however, hold our ground in cantonment, and daily strengthen both our town positions, bearing in mind that the Residency is to be the final point of concentration." These extracts will suffice to show how fully Sir Henry Lawrence appreciated the situation. I propose to describe in the next chapter the manner in which he met the storm when it actually burst over his head.

BOOK IX.

CHAPTER II.

Illness of Sir Henry Lawrence.

The repression of the mutiny of the 30th and 31st of May at Lakhnao had, at least, rid the cantonments of the least trustworthy of the sepoys. But the incessant labour, mental and bodily, the deprivation of sleep, the constant anxiety, had told on the already overtasked strength of the Chief Commissioner. His spare frame daily became still sparer, physical strength diminished under mental toil. His medical advisers insisted then that he should rest for a time from the labours of his office. Sir Henry Lawrence, I have already stated, had been on the point of proceeding to Europe for the benefit of his health when he was summoned by Lord Canning to Oudh. Regarding that summons as a call of duty, with characteristic forgetfulness of self, he had obeyed it. But the fatigues, the excitement, the anxiety had now made his state worse than it had been when his medical advisers had ordered him home from Rájpútáná. It was necessary that he should rest.

No one had felt less confident as to his power to stand the wear and tear of work in trying times than Sir Henry himself. His strength he knew might utterly fail him at any moment. Under ordinary circumstances he might, and probably would, have felt satisfied that the Government would on his demise provide a fit officer as his successor. But the circumstances were not ordinary. In the then state of the country the Government had not the means to send to the province a successor from outside its borders. They might not even have the power of communicating with those in the province itself. In that case the succession would, by right of seniority, devolve upon a civilian in whose judgment and capacity for the post Sir Henry Lawrence had no confidence.

His views regarding his successor.

To prevent the possibility of an occurrence which he could not regard in anticipation in any other light than as a public misfortune, Sir Henry Lawrence, feeling his strength daily failing, despatched to Lord Canning on the 4th of May a telegram in which he earnestly recommended that, in the event of anything happening to himself, the office of Chief Commissioner might be conferred on Major Banks, and the command of the troops on Colonel Inglis. "This," he added, "is no time for punctilio as regards seniority. They are the right men, in fact the only men for the places."

Recommends Major Banks and Colonel Inglis.

The Major Banks referred to was the Commissioner of the Lakhnao division. He belonged to

Major Banks.

Book IX. Chapter II. 1857. June.

the Bengal Army. He was distinguished by the wide range and the depth of his acquirements, by his thorough knowledge of the natives of India, by administrative talents of the highest order, by a large fund of humour, and by his large-hearted sympathies. He was the most promising political officer who had not actually attained the highest grade in that branch of the Indian Service. For languages he had a remarkable talent. He was familiar alike with Persian, with Hindí, and with Sanskrit. Major Banks had filled several appointments with distinction; had gained the esteem of men so opposed to each other as were Sir Charles Napier and Lord Dalhousie; and, on the annexation of Oudh, had been selected by the latter to be Commissioner of one of the four divisions of the kingdom. Installed as Commissioner of Lakhnao Banks speedily justified Lord Dalhousie's opinion. How he had impressed a man not easily deceived is apparent from the recommendation made by Sir Henry Lawrence to Lord Canning that Banks should succeed him.

Lieutenant-Colonel Inglis.

Lieutenant-Colonel Inglis, the other officer referred to, commanded the 32nd Foot. He was in the prime of life, an excellent soldier, active, energetic, and quick-sighted. The native army having mutinied, and the only remaining reliable troops being European troops, it was practically necessary that the officer commanding the European regiment should have the chief military authority. It was, to repeat Sir Henry Lawrence's remark, "no time for punctilio" as regarded seniority. The recommendation, then, was characterised by practical good sense.

Book IX Chapter I

1857. June 9

Five days after the despatch of this telegram, the health of the Chief Commissioner seemed to give way entirely. On the 9th of June, "an alarming exhaustion came on, and the medical men pronounced that further application to business would endanger his life."* In consequence of this sudden illness, a provisional council was formed of Mr. Gubbins, the Financial Commissioner, Mr. Ommaney, the Judicial Commissioner, Major Banks, Colonel Inglis, and the Chief Engineer, Major Anderson. Of this council, Mr. Martin Gubbins was the President.

Sir Henry resigns his authority to a council of five.

The President—Mr Martin Gubbins.

The character of Mr. Gubbins has thus been sketched by Sir Henry Lawrence: "He is a gallant, energetic, clever fellow, but sees only through his own vista, and is therefore sometimes troublesome." Now at this particular period, the "vista" of Mr. Gubbins showed him the danger of retaining the armed remnants of the native regiments, the necessity of trusting the native military police. As president of the Council of Five he insisted, then, that the sepoys who still remained in the lines should be disarmed and dismissed. In vain was it pointed out to him that these men had stood the test; that they had been tried in the fire; that they had not only resisted temptation, but had acted with spirit against their comrades on the 30th and 31st of May. Mr. Gubbins would listen to no argument. Opposed

* Gubbins.

Book IX. Chapter II.

1857. June 11.

in the Council, he yet step by step carried out his favourite measures, until, on the 11th of June, he actually started off to their homes all the sepoys belonging to the province. This act had upon Sir Henry Lawrence an effect more decisive than the prescriptions of his medical advisers. It roused him to action. Shaking off his weakness, he immediately dissolved the Council, resumed authority, the following day recalled the sepoys, and "had the satisfaction of seeing numbers return to their post, with tokens of delight, the honesty of which was verified by their loyalty during the siege."*

Sir Henry resumes authority.

His views regarding the native troops;

Sir Henry Lawrence was particularly desirous to retain the services of a large portion of the native troops. He believed that those who had stood the ordeal of the 30th of May would thenceforth remain faithful. He believed that without the aid of native troops his position at Lakhnao would not be tenable. And he believed, likewise, that by judicious arrangement, it would be possible to ensure loyalty and good service from those who still remained. On resuming office, then, he directed his energies at once to this matter. He collected all the Sikhs from the three native regiments, and formed them into one battalion; the Oudh men he likewise banded together, rejecting those only who had given evidence of disloyalty. Sir Henry had recourse likewise to men of another class. Confident that many of the men who had served in the Company's

* MS. Memorandum, quoted by Merivale. *Life of Sir Henry Lawrence.*

Book IX. Chapter II.

1857. June 11.

army prior to the annexation had carried with them to their homes their military pride and their fidelity to their masters, he summoned by circular to Lakhnao all of their number who would care to re-enlist for the cause of order. The response to this summons was very remarkable. About five hundred pensioned sepoys hastened to Lakhnao. Amongst them were the gray-headed, the halt, the maim—even the blind—some on crutches, —all anxious to evince their loyalty. Sir Henry gave them a kind and cordial reception. He selected about a hundred and seventy of them for active service, and placed them under separate command. The number of the native brigade was thus brought to nearly eight hundred.

and the pensioners.

That night the whole of the cavalry of the military police remaining at their head-quarters at Lakhnao broke into revolt. The cavalry were under the special command of Captain Gould Weston, and he at once rode down to their lines, situated near the Dil A'rám Kothí on the left bank of the Gúmtí, followed only by his two native orderlies. He came upon them as they were starting and exhorted them to listen to the voice of duty and of honour. But his efforts proved unavailing, and they galloped off into darkness.

The military police cavalry revolt;

The next morning (the 12th of June) the 3rd Regiment of Infantry of the Military Police mutinied at the Motí Mahal about a mile and a half from the Baillie Guard. Captain Adolphus Orr, who, although he had removed his family into safety at the Residency continued to occupy

and the infantry.

Book IX. Chapter II.

1857. June 12.

his house near his men, fortunately escaped uninjured, and riding in hot haste to the superintendent reported that the regiment had gone off in the direction of the Dil Kúsha Park, and was in full march towards Kánhpúr. Weston was engaged at the time with Mr. Ommaney, the Judicial Commissioner, but on hearing the evil tidings he instantly, without one moment's hesitation, rushed from the house, mounted the first horse he could find from the picket of the 7th Cavalry, and galloped after the mutineers. He overtook them about five miles from the Residency. It is impossible to over-estimate the danger of his position. There he was—a solitary European—in the presence of about eight hundred men who had mutinied, and who fully intended to join in the attempt to drive the English out of India. One shot would have sufficed to lay low the daring Frank. But it was that very daring that saved Weston. The bolder spirits were captivated by it. Dashing aside the muzzles already pointed towards their English commander they declared in reply to his appeal to them to return to their duty that they must go—they were committed to it—but that his life should not be taken. They then fell in and marched onwards. A few men of the 2nd Regiment of Military Police who had been on guard at Weston's house but who had joined the mutinous 3rd Regiment, determined to remain with him, and they returned to the Residency that night to tell of Weston's escape from death, which, bearing in mind the force of evil example, and the fact that scores of officers had already

Captain Gould Weston.

Owes his life to his daring.

fallen victims to their men, was well nigh miraculous.*

Book IX. Chapter II

1857. June 12.

On their way back they were met by the cavalry and the two guns of the little force despatched in pursuit, under Colonel Inglis, and which had far outstripped the two companies of Her Majesty's 32nd intended for their support. But the ground was broken and difficult, and although the artillery did some execution and the native troopers cut up a few stragglers, a fair blow was not struck at the main body. Meanwhile a considerable number of the mutineers had occupied a village on the further side of some ravines, our infantry had not come up, and the day was fast closing. Colonel Inglis, therefore, wisely determined to desist from further pursuit, and brought back his men much exhausted after a long and trying march in an exceptionally hot day. The enemy lost about twenty killed and had many more wounded, whilst some ten prisoners were captured. Two of our troopers were killed, and others were wounded, including their gallant native officer; two of the Europeans succumbed to sun-stroke, and Mr. Thornhill of the Civil Service, a man of great, even remarkable, daring, was twice seriously wounded.

The mutinous police followed up

Mr. Thornhill, C.S.

Since the mutiny of the 30th of May efforts to make the Residency defensible had been pushed on with extraordinary vigour. The outer tracing had been connected by breastworks; ditches had

Attempts made to render the Residency defensible;

* Hutchinson's *Narrative;* see also Rees's *Siege of Lucknow.*

Book IX. Chapter II. — 1857. June 12.

been excavated in front of them, and parapets erected behind them; at certain points ramparts had been thrown up and embrasures had been pierced; slopes had been scarped; stakes and palisades fixed; some houses had been demolished; the roofs of others had been protected by mud walls; windows and doors had been barricaded; walls had been loop-holed. All the ordnance belonging to the ex-King of Oudh that could be found in the city was brought within the defences. Some houses outside the walls of the Residency were left solely because time had not remained to level them, as had been intended. They thus afforded shelter to the enemy, who not only made them points of observation to watch the garrison, but kept up from them a heavy fire on the defences.

and the Machhí Báwan.

Nor was the Machhí Báwan neglected. Sir Henry Lawrence had originally resolved to hold this post in conjunction with the Residency, only to concentrate on the latter when threatened in overwhelming force. With this view he had strengthened it and made it habitable for Europeans. He then stored it with food and ammunition. On the 13th of June, Sir Henry Lawrence was able to write to Lord Canning in the words already quoted: "We hold our ground in cantonment, and daily strengthen both our town positions, bearing in mind that the Residency is to be the final point of concentration." Sir Henry continued to strengthen the Machhí Báwan till the very last, believing that the preparations made would be greatly noised abroad, and would affect the *morale* of the enemy.

Book IX. Chapter II.

1857. June 13.

Sir Henry's anxiety about Kánhpúr.

A terrible anxiety which preyed upon Sir Henry Lawrence about this time, was caused by his inability to assist Sir Hugh Wheeler, then beleaguered at Kánhpúr. The scission of communication with that station on the 6th of June had made it clear that the native troops there had mutinied. That they had gone further, and, under the leadership of Náná Sáhib had besieged the British general in his barracks, had been shortly afterwards made known. Then there came from General Wheeler earnest appeals for help. Mr. Gubbins, generous, sympathetic, strong-willed, and eager, urged him to comply with these appeals. But it was, in point of fact, simply impossible. How it was so cannot more fitly be expressed than in Sir Henry's own words.

His reasons for not moving to its aid.

Writing to Sir Hugh Wheeler on the 16th of June the Chief Commissioner said: "I am very sorry indeed to hear of your condition, and grieve that I cannot help you. I have consulted with the chief officers about me, and, except Gubbins, they are unanimous in thinking that with the enemy's command of the river, we could not possibly get a single man into your intrenchment. I need not say that I deeply lament being obliged to concur in this opinion, for our own safety is as nearly concerned as yours. We are strong *in* our intrenchments; but by attempting the passage of the river, should be sacrificing a large detachment without a prospect of helping you. Pray do not think me selfish. I would run much risk could I see a commensurate prospect of success. In the present scheme I see none." A week

Book IX. Chapter II. — 1857. June 16.

later he wrote to Lord Canning; "It is deep grief to me to be unable to help Kánhpúr; I would run much risk for Wheeler's sake, but an attempt, with our means, would only ruin ourselves, without helping Kánhpúr." No military critic will question the soundness of these views.

Soundness of those reasons.

To cross the Ganges, even with the entire force at the disposal of Sir Henry Lawrence, in the face of the army serving under Náná Sáhib, would have been impossible.

A few days later a letter reached Sir Henry with the information that Wheeler had agreed to treat with Náná Sáhib. He then knew that all was over. His forebodings were confirmed by the receipt of details of the massacre on the 28th of June.

Learns the fate of the Kánhpúr garrison.

"If Kánhpúr holds out I doubt if we shall be besieged at all." Thus had Sir Henry Lawrence written to Lord Canning on the 23rd of June. But five days later he learned that Kánhpúr had fallen. Prior to that date, and with more certainty every day, had come the intelligence that the mutinous troops of the Oudh Irregular force —the troops who had revolted in the provinces— were gradually collecting at a place called Nawábgánj Bárá Bánkí, only twenty miles from Lakhnao. The subsequent movement of these troops, whose numbers were not inconsiderable, obviously depended on the result of the leaguer of Káhnpúr.

Hears that the enemy are moving on Chinhat.

It was known on the 28th that that place had fallen. The following morning the advanced guard of the enemy's force marched on Chinhat, a village on the Faizábád road, within eight miles of the Residency.

This gave Sir Henry an opportunity at which he clutched. With the foresight of a real general opposed to Asiatics he felt that for him to await an attack would be to invite a general insurrection, whereas, an effective blow dealt at the advanced troops of the rebels would paralyse their movements, and spread doubt and hesitation amongst them. He hoped and believed, in fact, that it might not be impossible to reply to Kánhpúr by Chinhat. To say that because he did not succeed his plan was bad and impolitic is not a logical argument. His plan was justified alike by military science and by political considerations. Whilst he fought a battle in which victory would have been decisive, he lost nothing by defeat. He did not, in a word, risk part of his general plan, nor was he in a worse position after his defeat than that which he had occupied before he went out to fight. In some respects, indeed, his general position became more assured, because more clearly defined.

Book IX. Chapter II.

1857. June 29.

His reasons for determining to strike a blow.

Those reasons sound.

Sir Henry's first step was to withdraw the troops from the cantonments and to bring them within the Residency. He then ordered that a force composed of three hundred men of the 32nd Regiment; two hundred and thirty men of the regular native infantry; the small troop of volunteer cavalry, thirty-six strong; one hundred and twenty troopers of the Oudh Irregulars; ten guns and an 8-inch howitzer, should assemble at the iron bridge at daylight the following morning to march thence at once in the direction of Chinhat. It deserves here to be remarked that of the ten

Concentrates his forces.

Book IX. Chapter II. 1857. June 30.

guns six were manned by natives and four only by Europeans. The howitzer was on a limber drawn by an elephant driven by a native.

Marches on Chinhat.

The force had been ordered to march at dawn, but the necessary arrangements caused unavoidable delay, and the sun was already high—it was past 6 o'clock—when it marched from the iron bridge across the Gúmtí in the direction of Chinhat. After marching three miles along the metalled road it reached the bridge spanning the rivulet Kúkrail. Here a halt was ordered whilst Sir Henry with his staff, and a few cavalry, rode in front to reconnoitre. From the summit of a rising ground under some trees he could see nothing. He then and there decided to return to Lakhnao, and sent the Assistant Adjutant-General to countermarch the force, in view to its marching back. This order was carried out, when suddenly fresh instructions arrived for the force to move on towards Chinhat. The men then advanced along "a newly raised embankment, constructed of loose and sandy soil, in which every now and then gaps occurred, indicating the positions of future bridges."* The force was formed in regular order. An advanced guard of cavalry, with vedettes thrown out, led. This was followed, first, by the 8-inch howitzer, then by the four guns manned by Europeans, then by four manned by natives. An hundred and fifty men of the 13th Native Infantry came next, followed by two guns manned by natives, then by three hundred

* Gubbins.

men of the 32nd Foot, and then by the remaining native troops, eighty in number. After marching in this order for about a mile and a half they descried the enemy drawn up at a distance of about twelve hundred yards, their right covered by a small hamlet, their left by a village and a lake, their centre resting on the road. Simultaneously the enemy saw them and at once opened a heavy round-shot fire.

Descries the enemy.

Sir Henry immediately halted his column and deployed the infantry into line. Then placing his European guns in position, and ordering the infantry to lie down, he returned the enemy's fire. A continuous cannonade from both sides was now kept up. Then, after something of a lull, which induced many officers to believe that the British were getting the best of the day, the enemy suddenly divided, and menaced both flanks in considerable force. That on the British left was made not only in overwhelming numbers, but from the cover of the village of Ishmáilganj—a village which ran parallel to that part of our line occupied by the 32nd. The fire from this village caught that regiment in flank, and in a very few minutes nearly half of its number present, with a large proportion of officers, including the commanding officer, Lieut.-Colonel Case, were lying dead or disabled on the ground. Meanwhile every effort had been made to bring the native artillery into action but with very indifferent success. The native artillerymen were traitors. Two of the guns had been upset in the ditch, and the traces of some of the others had been cut.

Battle of Chinhat.

The enemy gain our left flank.

Book IX. Chapter II.

1857. June 30.

The British retreat.

Elated with their first success, the enemy pressed heavily on, and a retreat became necessary if any of the force were to be saved. A retreat was then commenced, the 32nd necessarily, from the position they had occupied near the road, leading; the native infantry protecting the rear. The retreat once begun, the enemy galloped their guns on either flank of our force, and continued to pound it with grape all the way to the Kúkrail bridge. So heavily was the column pressed, that few of those who were hit were saved, a fact borne out by the extraordinary proportion of killed to wounded—in the 32nd alone one hundred and fifteen to thirty-nine. As the retiring force approached the bridge over the Kúkrail a large body of the rebel cavalry was descried immediately in their line of retreat. They were in considerable force. But on our side there was no hesitation. Captain Radcliffe's trumpet sounded the charge, and instantly our thirty-six horsemen dashed at the enemy. A more gallant charge was never made. It appalled the rebels. They did not wait for it but turned and fled. The line of retreat was secured.

Gallantry of Captain Radcliffe and his companions.

The danger, however, was not over. The enemy's infantry was pressing on. All our gun-ammunition was exhausted. In this dilemma Sir Henry showed a nerve and decision not to be surpassed. He placed the guns on the bridge and ordered the portfires to be lighted. The feint had all the hoped-for effect. The enemy shrunk back from a bridge apparently defended by loaded guns. They at once relaxed their pursuit, and

The pursuit is checked at Kúkrail;

Book IX. Chapter II. — 1857. June 30.

our little army succeeded in gaining the shelter of the city and in retiring in some sort of order on the Machhí Báwan and the Residency. Their losses, however, had been most severe, and they had left the howitzer and two field-pieces behind them.*

Immediately after crossing the Kúkrail bridge Sir Henry Lawrence made over the command to Colonel Inglis, and, followed by his staff officer, Captain Wilson, and by his secretary, Mr. Couper, —who, acting throughout the day as his aide-de-camp, had displayed equal coolness and courage— galloped, unattended by any escort, through the city to the Residency. Arriving there, Sir Henry ordered out fifty men of the 32nd, under an officer, Lieutenant Edmonstone, to the iron bridge over the Gúmtí, with a view to their being posted in the two houses on either side of the bridge, to defend it. Towards this bridge the elated enemy surged in crowds, but they never forced it. The fifty Englishmen, covered by a fire from two 18-pounders in the Redan battery, held it successfully, though not without loss, till noon. The enemy then desisted, and crossed the river by another bridge. Our men were then finally withdrawn. This defence was a very gallant affair.

again at the Gúmtí.

That the loss of the battle of Chinhat should precipitate the crisis was certain. But the crisis

Advantages derived by the loss of the battle.

* These two field-pieces were, however, spiked by Captain Wilson, the Assistant Adjutant-General, before they were left. The heroic efforts made by Lieutenant Bonham of the Artillery to save the howitzer would most assuredly, had Sir Henry Lawrence lived, have gained for that officer the Victoria Cross.

Book IX. Chapter II.

1857. June 30.

would have equally come had there been no battle. And the battle, unfortunate in its immediate results though it proved to be, had at least this advantage,—it removed from Sir Henry's mind any doubt he might have had as to his ability to hold two positions. Brigadier Inglis states, in his despatch, that, had both posts been held, both must have fallen; and he ascribes the concentration of the troops on the better position of the two to Chinhat.

Calmness in combat of Sir Henry.

Of the behaviour of Sir Henry Lawrence on that day but one opinion has been recorded. That opinion is ably summarised in the record of a gallant soldier, the Assistant Adjutant-General throughout the siege. "Throughout that terrible day, during the conflict," records Captain Wilson, "and when all was lost, and retreat became all but a rout, and men were falling fast, he displayed the utmost calmness and decision; and as, with hat in hand, he sat on his horse on the Kúkrail bridge, rallying our men for a last stand, himself a distinct mark for the enemy's skirmishers, he seemed to bear a charmed life."

The first consequence of the defeat was the occupation of the city by the rebels and the uprising of the discontented spirits within it. That very afternoon they began to loop-hole many of the houses in the vicinity of and commanding the Machhí Báwan and the Residency. They even succeeded in bringing a six-pounder to bear on the outer verandah of the post afterwards known as Anderson's post. Subsequently, about

Book IX. Chapter II.

1857. June 30.

half-past one, they brought another gun into position, and soon demolished the outer defences, including a loop-holed mud parapet but recently erected. The post, however, was so important, that orders were sent to its garrison to hold it to the last extremity. Shortly afterwards a circumstance happened, the precursor of many deeds of gallantry on the part of the defenders of Lakhnao.

Anderson's post is attacked.

The house which was thus being defended was the residence of Mr. Capper, C.S. Mr. Capper had volunteered to aid in its defence, and was standing for that purpose under the verandah, behind one of the pillars, when the enemy's fire brought down the verandah, and buried him under six feet of wood and masonry. Captain Anderson, 25th Native Infantry, though not the senior officer present, at once called upon the garrison to assist in rescuing the buried gentleman. The work was one of no ordinary danger, for there was no protection against the concentrated fire of the enemy, and one at least of those present expressed the opinion that the act would be useless, as Capper would probably be dead. Anderson was not discouraged by these doubts. Announcing his intention to rescue Capper at all risks, he called on those around to aid him, and set to work with a will. He was speedily joined by Corporal Oxenham, 32nd Foot, Monsieur Geoffroi, a Frenchman, Signor Barsotelli, an Italian, and two Englishmen, Lincoln and Chick, from the Post Office garrison. The enemy's round shot continued to pour over the place where

Mr. Capper is buried in the ruins of the verandah.

Anderson gallantly sets to work to extricate him,

Book IX. Chapter II.

1857. June 30.

and succeeds.

Capper lay, and, to be able to work, the six men I have mentioned were forced to lie on their stomachs, and grub away in that position. At length they succeeded in extricating Capper's body, but his legs still remained buried. The situation for him was now replete with danger, for to stand up was almost certain death. In this dilemma, Oxenham, obeying a signal from Anderson, who was supporting the head, dashed round to the other side, and extricated by a supreme effort the buried legs. This done, Capper was hauled in by the other five, and was saved.*

The Machhí Báwan is abandoned.

The following morning the enemy opened a heavy musketry fire upon the Machhi Báwan and the Residency. Sir Henry had foreseen this action and had prepared for it. Resolved to con-

* For this act Oxenham received the Victoria Cross; but Mr. Capper ever considered that he owed his life mainly to Anderson, who alike suggested the attempt, and, by his example, carried it to a successful issue. Anderson was recommended for the Cross in 1868, but it was not bestowed upon him. On this occasion Mr. Capper wrote as follows: "My former letters clearly acknowledge that it was to the gallantry of Colonel Anderson that I owe my life: that had he not, by word and example, shamed the others to action, no effort would have been made to save me. . . . It is clear that Colonel Anderson must have voluntarily exposed himself to imminent danger for the long period of three-quarters of an hour—contrary to the advice of his superior officer—with the object of rescuing a comrade from a terrible and lingering death. At the moment when Corporal Oxenham (at the call of Colonel Anderson) went forward to extricate my legs and feet, Colonel Anderson was supporting my head and shoulders; and whilst all three of us were exposed to the cannonade, the head and upper part of Anderson's body must have been exposed to the same heavy musketry fire as was risked by Oxenham. The risk of life accepted by Anderson was continuous; and if the question is, to whom (under God) I am chiefly indebted for the preservation of my life, the answer is—Colonel Anderson."

centrate all his defensive efforts on the Residency he signalled the following night to the garrison of the Machhí Báwan to evacuate and blow up that fortress. These orders were admirably carried out by Captain Francis, 13th Native Infantry, then commanding at that post. A quarter of an hour past midnight the garrison of the Machhí Báwan entered the Residency with their guns and treasure, without the loss of a man. Shortly afterwards the explosion of two hundred and forty barrels of gunpowder and of five hundred and ninety-four thousand rounds of ball and gun ammunition announced the complete destruction of that post.

Book IX. Chapter II. 1857. July 1.

A singularly good fortune attended the time chosen for this operation. The enemy had determined, before they commenced in earnest to besiege the Residency, to devote a preliminary night to the plunder of the shops of the town. They were engaged in this congenial work when the explosion of the Machhí Báwan signified to them that they had missed a great chance.

The time for the evacuation fortunately chosen.

The troops of the garrison, consisting of nine hundred and twenty-seven Europeans* and seven hundred and sixty-five natives, were now concentrated in the Residency. To all appearances the situation was desperate. Not only were the fortifications incomplete, but the enemy had at once occupied and loop-holed the houses which had been left standing outside and close to those

The garrison.

The weakness of the defences.

* These were composed as follows:—32nd Foot, 535; 84th Foot, 50; Artillery, 89; officers, not with English regiments or Artillery, 100; Civil and Uncovenanted, 153.

Book IX. Chapter II. 1857. July 2.

fortifications. The west and south faces of the enclosure were practically undefended, the bastion which had been commenced at the angle of the two faces having been left unfinished. Looking at the weakness of our resources and the comparative numbers of the besiegers and the besieged it is not wonderful that Sir Henry himself, at the first moment, scarcely expected to hold out, without relief, for more than ten or fifteen days.*

The mode in which they might have been forced.

And if the enemy had possessed as leader a real soldier, such was the advantage of their position, so great was their superiority in point of numbers, it is possible that the earlier forebodings of Sir Henry might have been realised. A general who would have freely sacrificed his men, and whose men would not have flinched from his summons, might well have taken advantage of the disaster of Chinhat. The Residency was not, in a military sense, defensible, and must have succumbed to the determined onslaught of determined men, vastly superior in numbers to the garrison.

Comparison between the English and Asiatic soldier.

But it is a remarkable fact that the mutiny produced no general amongst the mutineers—not a single man who understood the importance of time, of opportunity, of dash, in war. It is, too, worthy to be noted, that whilst no men in the world have a greater contempt of death than the natives of India, they yet almost always shrink from a hand to hand encounter with Europeans. Still more are they averse from an attack on a fortified position defended by Europeans. If carelessness

* His letter to General Havelock, dated 30th of June.

Book IX. Chapter II

1857. July 2.

of life be courage no people in the world are braver than the natives of India. But the courage which is required to make a man a real soldier is something more than mere carelessness of life. Such a man must be anxious to affront death, to court it. He must be indifferent to pain; must be capable of enjoying the delirium of battle; must be animated by a love of glory, and above all by a confidence in his superiority to his enemy. None of these qualities are possessed by the native soldier to the same extent as by our own countrymen; whilst, with respect to the last, it is conspicuous by its absence. Perhaps it is mainly because the native soldier opposed to the British soldier, far from feeling the confidence I have referred to, is imbued with the conviction of the enormous superiority of his enemy, that his moral nature is cowed, and he cannot fight him as he can and does fight a fellow Asiatic.

Certainly in the case of Lakhnao this moral power was a strong factor on the side of the British. There they were, few in numbers, occupying a position, not, in a military sense, defensible; two sides of it, indeed, practically undefended. To attack them came an army enormously superior in numbers, flushed with victory, and occupying positions which commanded a great portion of the defences. To all appearance the victory of the attacking party was assured. It was not gained, simply because the inferior moral nature of the Asiatic, shrinking involuntarily from actual contact with the European

Effect of the superior *morale* of the English.

Book IX. Chapter II.

1857. July 2.

The Residency enclosure. What was it?

behind defences, neutralised the superiority of numbers.

What was the position? Let the reader imagine a number of houses, built for ordinary domestic purposes, originally separated from each other by small plots of ground, but now joined together by mud walls and trenches—the mud walls for defence from outer attack, the trenches for protection against the enemy's shells! Such in a few words was the enclosure known to the world, from the principal building within it, as the Residency. It is true that the walls of the houses were thick, that the bricks were of that small class peculiar to India during the last century, and that they were cemented by well-tempered mortar. But even the strongest houses constitute but a poor military position. This position, moreover, was blockaded and attacked by the enemy before, as I have said, a single part of it had been made really defensible. As the blockade progressed, and whilst the enemy were erecting batteries, mounting guns, throwing up barricades, and loop-holing the empty houses outside of, but close to the enclosure, the garrison had time, notwithstanding the fierce and continuous fire maintained upon them, to repair, and in some cases even to strengthen their defences. These defences were naturally rough, run up under enormous difficulties, and never in their most finished state deserving the names of regular fortifications. The houses of the several occupants, and the batteries erected along the line of intrenchments came to be regarded as posts, and

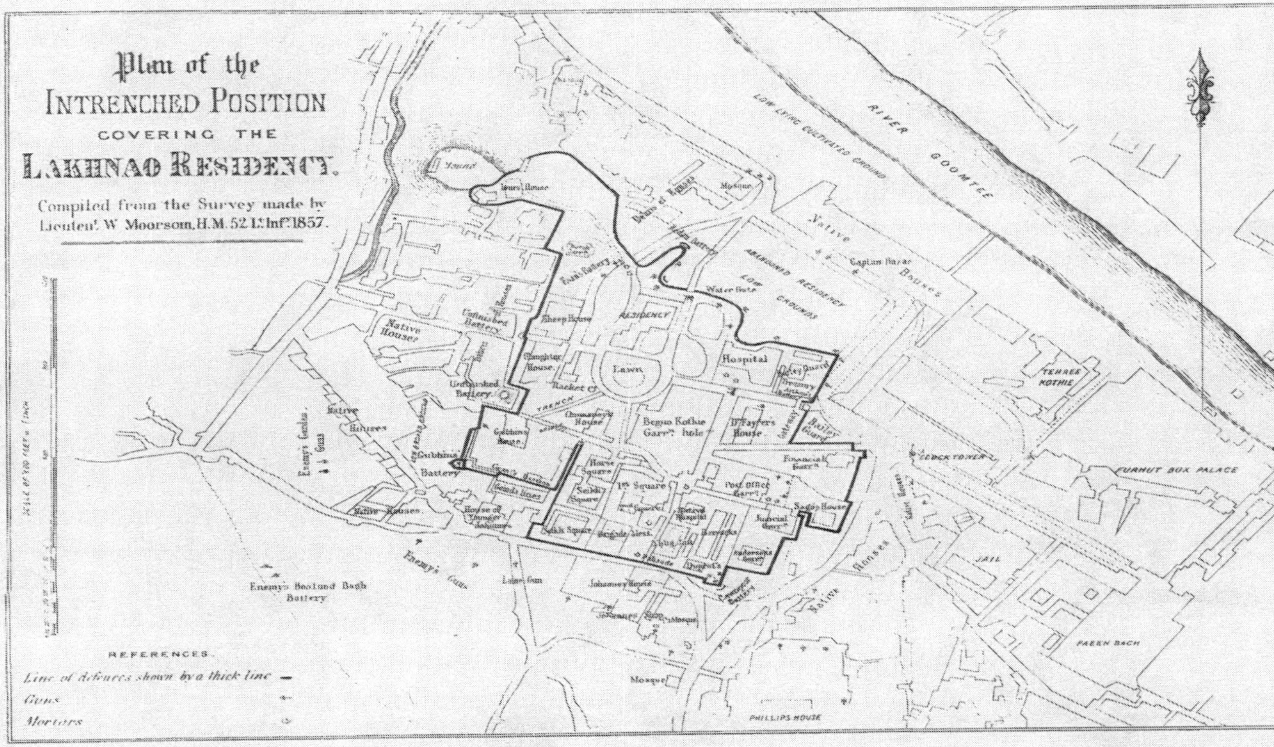
Plan of the
INTRENCHED POSITION
COVERING THE
LAKHNAO RESIDENCY.
Compiled from the Survey made by
Lieutenᵗ. W. Moorsom, H.M. 52 Lᵗ. Infʸ. 1857.
RIVER GOOMTEE
LOW LYING CULTIVATED GROUND
Native Houses
Captain Bazar
ABANDONED RESIDENCY
LOW GROUNDS
Water Gate
Mosque
RESIDENCY
Hospital
Lawn
Sheep House
Slaughter House
Racket Ct.
TRENCH
Begum Kothie
Dr. Fayrer's House
Bailey Guard
Financial Garrⁿ.
Post Office Garrⁿ.
Sago House
Judicial Garrⁿ.
Barracks
Sikh Square
1st Square
Gubbins' House
Gubbins' Battery
Unfinished Battery
Native Houses
Enemy's Garden
Enemy's Guns
Enemy's Boolund Bagh Battery
House of Thunder Johnson
Johannes' House
Mosque
PHILLIPS HOUSE
CLOCK TOWER
FURHUT BOX PALACE
TEHREE KOTHIE
JAIL
PAEEN BAGH
REFERENCES.
Line of defences shown by a thick line
Guns
Mortors

Book IX. Chapter II. — 1857. July 2.

each of these posts was commanded by an officer. What these posts and who these officers were will be related in due course. At present, I have to do with the earliest and most regrettable incident of the siege.

Proceedings of the enemy after Chinhat.

Since the retirement of our force within its lines of defence the fire of the enemy upon it had been continuous. Night and day, from the tops of surrounding houses, from loop-holed buildings, from every point where cover was available, they had poured in a perpetual fire of round shot, of musketry, and of matchlock balls. Many of the garrison who were in places considered before the siege perfectly safe were hit. But no place was so exposed as the Residency itself, and on it a well directed fire was constantly maintained. Moreover, the enemy had recourse to digging deep approaches to their batteries and guns, and these effectually concealed them from our sharp-shooters.

But long before the cautious system of attack thus described had attained its full development, the garrison sustained an irreparable loss.

A shell penetrates Sir Henry Lawrence's room.

Sir Henry Lawrence occupied in the Residency a room convenient for the purpose of observing the enemy, but much exposed to their fire. There, the day after the defeat at Chinhat, he was seated conversing with his secretary, Mr. Couper. Suddenly an 8-inch shell, fired from the very howitzer we had lost at Chinhat, fell into the room, close to them. It burst, however, without injury to either. The whole of the staff then implored Sir Henry to remove to a less exposed

Book IX. Chapter II.

1857. July 2.

position. But this he declined to do, remarking with a smile that another shell would never be pitched into the same room. Later in the day, when it was evident the enemy's round-shot were being directed at the Residency and were striking the upper storey Captain Wilson and Mr. Couper again pressed Sir Henry to go below and to allow his things to be moved. He promised to comply on the morrow. The following morning he went out to post and arrange the force which had come in from the Machhí Báwan and to place the field-pieces in position. He returned tired and exhausted about 8 o'clock. He lay down on his bed, and transacted business with the Assistant Adjutant-General, Captain Wilson. He was engaged in this work when suddenly a howitzer shell entered the room, and bursting, wounded him mortally. He lingered in extreme agony till the morning of the 4th, when he died. Captain Wilson's account of the event is as follows:—

A second strikes and kills him.

Captain Wilson's account of the event.

"During the first day the enemy threw an 8-inch shell from the howitzer they had captured from us into the room in which Sir Henry and Mr. Couper were. It burst close to both, but without injury to either, and curiously enough did little damage. We now urged Sir Henry to leave the Residency and go elsewhere, or at least go down below into the lower storey. This, however, he then declined to do, as he laughingly said he did not believe the enemy had an artilleryman good enough to put another shell into that small room. Later in the day some round shot came into the top storey of the Residency; and in the evening Mr. Couper and I both pressed him to go below, and allow his writing things and papers to be moved; and he promised that he would the next day." . . . . . . "Towards 8 a.m." (on the 2nd) "he returned, greatly exhausted (the heat was dreadful), and lay down on the bed with his clothes on, and desired me to draw up a memorandum as to how the rations were to be distributed. I went into the next room to write it, but, previous to doing so, I reminded him of his promise to go below. He said he was very tired, and would rest a couple of hours, and that then he would have his things moved. In about half an hour I went back into the room with what I had written. His nephew, Mr. George Lawrence, was then lying on a small bed parallel to his uncle's, with a very few feet between them. I went between the beds, and stood on the right hand side of Sir Henry's, with one knee resting on it. A native servant was sitting on the floor pulling the punkah. I read what I had written. It was not quite in accordance with his wishes, and he was in the act of explaining what he desired altered, when the fatal shot came; a sheet of flame, a terrific report and shock, and dense darkness, is all I can describe. I fell on the floor, and, perhaps for a few seconds, was quite stunned. I then get up, but could see nothing for the smoke and dust. Neither Sir Henry nor his nephew made any noise, and, in alarm, I cried out, 'Sir Henry, are you hurt?' Twice

Book IX Chapter I.

1857. July 2.

Book IX. Chapter II.

1857. July 2.

I thus called out without any answer. The third time he said, in a low tone, 'I am killed.' The punkah had come down with the ceiling, and a great deal of the plaster, and the dust and smoke were so great that it was some minutes before I could see anything; but as they gradually cleared away I saw the white coverlet of the bed on which Sir Henry was laid was crimson with his blood. Some soldiers of the 32nd now rushed in and placed Sir Henry in a chair. I then found that the back of my shirt was all blown off (I had on only a shirt and trowsers), that I was slightly wounded by a fragment of the shell, that our chief was mortally wounded; and that the servant pulling the punkah had had one of his feet cut off by another fragment of the shell. Mr. George Lawrence was alone of the four in the room unhurt."

Character of Sir Henry Lawrence.

Sir Henry Lawrence was one of those rare characters which it is difficult to over-praise. The adjective "noble" expresses most nearly what he was. His thoughts and his deeds were alike noble. In one of the eloquent and effective speeches which he who was then Mr. Disraeli delivered when in the cold shade of opposition "justice" was most felicitously described as being "truth in action." The life of Sir Henry Lawrence was a witness to the soundness of this aphorism. The nobleness of his nature, the honesty of his mind, his unqualified love of justice, displayed themselves in his every act. He was just to others because he was true to himself. Than his, it is difficult to imagine a

His noble nature.

purer, a more unselfish, a more blameless, and at the same time a more useful life. He, at least, did not live in vain. Great as were his services to his country those he rendered to mankind were still greater. The establishment of the Lawrence Asylum—an institution which provides, in the healthy mountainous ranges of India, food, lodging, and instruction, for the children of our European soldiers, was not the least important of those services. To it Sir Henry gave his time, his savings, the energies he could spare from his duties. He inoculated his friends and the Government of India with his ardour. For more than thirty years that institution has borne testimony to the practical nobility of the spirit which founded it.

His human passions.

It must not be imagined that because he possessed great virtues Sir Henry Lawrence was fashioned after the manner of the monks of the middle ages. There could not be a greater mistake. He was essentially human with strong human passions. His passions, indeed, had been brought gradually and by long training very much under control.* Yet, even when they burst the bonds, there was something noble about them too. He never concealed the annoyance which had been caused him by having been "cavalierly elbowed out of the Panjáb." He felt that he had been wronged, that injustice had been done him, that

* He did not admit this. Writing of Mr. Coverly Jackson, he says: "He is an able and energetic man, but, like us Lawrences, has strong passions not under much control."

Book IX. Chapter II.

1857. July 2.

advantage had been taken of his generosity, and he showed that he felt it. This wrong, he admitted, had caused him to fret even to the injury of his health. Yet how hearty was his forgiveness of those who had so wrung him when the stain on his reputation, as he regarded it, was removed by Lord Canning. "I can now," he writes, "more freely than ever forgive Lord Dalhousie."

Faculty of gaining respect and affection.

In his personal dealings with other men the nobleness of his nature is reflected by the love, the respect, the affection, he drew towards himself. "Few men," wrote Brigadier Inglis, when commenting on his demise, "few men have ever possessed to the same extent the power which he enjoyed of winning the hearts of all those with whom he came in contact, and thus ensuring the warmest and most zealous devotion for himself and for the Government which he served." The deep affection with which he was regarded when living survives to the present day. Of no man is the recollection more warmly cherished. Nor is this to be wondered at, for no man ever excited so much enthusiasm in others. When he arrived at a decision those to whom he communicated felt that the subject had been thoroughly considered in all its bearings, and that the order was final. His elevation excited no envy. His nature and his policy alike incited him to trust. He believed in the honour, the right feeling, the public spirit of those with whom he was brought in contact until they actually showed themselves unworthy of his

Trust reposed in him

confidence. He gained, to a greater extent than

Book IX. Chapter II.

1857. July 2.

by the natives.

any Englishman of the present century, the trust of the natives. He gained this trust by his absolute frankness. Far from flattering them, far from simulating a regard which he did not feel, his frankness was carried to the extremest limit. But they believed in him. They had a saying that "when Sir Henry looked twice up to Heaven and once down to earth, and then stroked his beard, he knew what to do." He devoted all his energies to the country he served so well. In a word, he was a striking type of that class, not a rare one, of the public servants of England, who give themselves without reserve to their country. That Sir Henry Lawrence felt to the last the inner conviction that he had so given himself wholly and without stint, is evidenced by the expression of his dying wish, that if any epitaph were placed on his tomb, it should be simply this: "Here lies Henry Lawrence who tried to do his duty."

Credit due to Sir Henry for the ability to defend the Residency with success.

The credit of the successful defence of the Residency at Lakhnao is due, in the first place, to Sir Henry Lawrence. He alone made it possible successfully to defend it. Three weeks before any one else dreamed of the chance even of a siege he began to lay in supplies. He did more. To ensure the prompt provisionment of the place he paid for the supplies so stored considerably in excess of their market value. It is a fact, not perhaps generally known, that he did this in spite of the written protests of men so highly placed that they might almost be called his colleagues. He caused to be brought into the Residency the

Book IX. Chapter II.

1857. July 2.

treasure from the city, and, whenever feasible, from out-stations. The treasure amounted to a very large sum. To obviate the necessity of placing a guard over it, he buried it, and made it the site of a battery in the Residency enclosure. He collected there the guns, the mortars, the shot and shell, the small arms, the ammunition, and the grain. A great portion of the latter he caused to be stored under-ground. He strengthened the fortifications, formed outworks, cleared away the obstructions close up to the Residency. He did all this before the siege commenced. And it was owing to his care, his energy, his determination, his foresight in respect of these things, that the gallant men who survived him were able to offer to the foe a successful resistance.

Lakhnao the Plevna of India.

The value of that successful resistance to the general interests of England in India has never publicly been sufficiently appreciated. It appears to me that this is the proper place, dealing as I am with the character of the man who made that successful resistance possible, to estimate it. An event which occurred nearer to us in the autumn and winter of last year will bring more vividly before the reader than any description the value of the successful defence of Lakhnao. I allude to the defence of Plevna by the Turks. That splendid feat of arms neutralised for four months two Russian armies, and gave time to Turkey to organise whatever means she might have to prolong the contest. Now the Lakhnao Residency was the Plevna of India. It is not too much to assert that the siege of the Residency

Book IX. Chapter II.

1857. July 2.

kept in Oudh for five months immense masses of the regular army*—troops who but for that defence would have been employed either in overrunning the North-West or in reinforcing the garrison of Dehlí. It was the splendid defence of the Residency that kept those troops from harming us, that gave time to England to send out reinforcements. That defence was, in a word, necessary to the maintenance of the hold of England on India. That that hold was preserved sums up, briefly, the amount of one portion of the debt incurred by England to Sir Henry Lawrence.

Major Banks succeeds him.

Sir Henry died, I have said, on the 4th of July. In consequence of his death-bed instructions Major Banks assumed the chief civil authority, whilst the command of the troops devolved upon Brigadier Inglis.

The "posts" of the Residency.

The ground on which were built the detached houses now about to be attacked was an elevated plateau, the surface of which was rough and unequal. The defences traced around it had the form of an irregular pentagon. A glance at the accompanying plan will show that regarding the point indicated as "Innes's house" as the northern-most point, its eastern face ran irregularly parallel with the river Gúmtí as far as the Baillie Guard. From that point to "Anderson's garrison" constituted the south-eastern, and from

* Besides the regular troops were many thousand men belonging to the ex-king's army, and many of whom had been drafted into the local and police force of the country; also the numerous retainers of the talúkdárs.

Book IX. Chapter II. 1857. July 4.

Anderson's garrison to "Gubbins's battery," the south-western face. The western face comprehended the line between Gubbins's battery and Innes's garrison.

Innes's garrison occupied a long, commodious lower roomed house, containing several rooms, two good verandahs, and having a flat roof. It was commanded by Lieutenant Loughnan of the 13th Native Infantry, a most gallant officer.

Overlooking this post on the eastern face was the Redan battery, at the apex of the projecting point of high level ground. This battery was armed with two 18-pounders and a 9-pounder. It was commanded by Lieutenant Samuel Lawrence of the 32nd Foot.

The line of intrenchments between the Water Gate and the Banqueting hall, transformed into a hospital, was commanded by Lieutenant Langmore of the 71st Native Infantry. It was entirely without shelter.

Passing over the Residency and the Banqueting hall, we come to the Treasury buildings situated below and to the eastward of the latter known under the name of the Bailey Guard. This was armed with two 9-pounders and an 8-inch howitzer, commanded by Lieutenant Aitken, 13th Native Infantry. Following the outer tracing we come to Fayrer's house with one 9-pounder, commanded by Captain Gould Weston, late Superintendent of the Military Police; to the Financial garrison post commanded by Captain Sanders, 13th Native Infantry; and to Sago's house, commanded by Captain T. T. Boileau, 7th Cavalry. The two last-named buildings were commanded by the Post office armed with two 18-pounders and a 9-pounder, and whose garrison was under the orders of Lieutenant Graydon. Book IX. Chapter II. 1857. July 4.

Following the line of outer-works we arrive at the Judicial post, an extensive upper-roomed house, commanded by Captain Germon 13th Native Infantry. Next to that, and forming the south-eastern angle of the position, was Anderson's post,—a two-storied house surrounded by a wall, with two good verandahs, and intrenched and loop-holed. No battery was attached to this post. It was commanded by Captain R. P. Anderson, 25th Native Infantry.

The Káhnpúr battery, constructed of earth and palisades, was the next post. This was armed with an 8-pounder and two 9-pounders. This was the only post the commandant of which was constantly changed. The reason was that it was so entirely commanded by the enemy's works, that when they concentrated a heavy fire upon it, no man could live in it. But neither could the enemy occupy it, for it was entirely commanded by the house behind it. It thus remained to the end a part of our defences. The Thug jail, occupied by the boys of the Martinière College, and commanded by their principal, Mr. Schilling; the Brigade Mess, a high and convenient building, commanded by Colonel Master, 7th Light Cavalry; and the Sikh squares; led to Gubbins's post, armed with two 9-pounders and an 18-pounder, and commanded by Major Apthorp, 41st Native Infantry. Be-

Book IX. Chapter II.

1857. July 4.

tween this post and the Church garrison were the Bhúsa intrenchments and sheep pens, slenderly defended by the officers and soldiers of the Commissariat Department. The Church garrison consisted of about a dozen Europeans. It was stored with grain. This leads us back to Innes's house, whence we started.

Of the garrisons within the line of defence may be mentioned Ommaney's post, connected by a lane with Gubbins's post and supported by the residents of the Bégam Kótí, few in number and principally on the staff.

Difficulties in the way of the defence.

It must always be remembered that on the morrow of Chinhat this plateau was, in a military sense, indefensible. In many places barricades of earth constituted the only defence against the enemy. Nor was it easy to repair the want. "It is difficult," wrote a staff officer, "to chronicle the confusion of those few days, for everywhere confusion reigned supreme." The same authority gives a little further on examples of this confusion. After mentioning the severe wound received by the commissariat officer, Lieutenant James, at Chinhat, and the consequent disorder in that department, he paints in graphic terms how the bullocks, deserted by their attendants and wandering about in search of water, fell into wells; how fatigue parties of civilians and officers, after having been engaged many hours in repelling the enemy's attacks, had to spend six or seven more in burying the dead cattle; how the horses of the troopers of the 7th Cavalry who had deserted, maddened for want of water, broke loose and fought with each other, unheeded by the over-worked garrison.

Book IX. Chapter II.

1857. July 4.

Why the enemy took no advantage of those difficulties.

The enemy was not ignorant of the confusion that reigned behind those weak ramparts. Why did they not take advantage of it? They had guns, they had position, they had over-whelming numbers. One determined rush, or an unceasing succession of determined rushes, and though their losses would have been enormous, the position must have been carried. The reader will have already answered the question. They did not attempt those rushes because they were entirely Asiatics and the defenders were mainly Europeans!

The defence—as described by Brigadier Inglis.

The course which they pursued, and the means adopted by the garrison to baffle that course, have been described in immortal language by the Brigadier who commanded the defence.* It would be difficult to add to the grandeur of that simple and expressive story. Regarded from a literary point of view it is a model of despatch-writing. But it is far more than that. Its greater merit lies in the fact that it records with unsurpassed modesty, untinged by a shadow of self-laudation, a long deed of heroism, unsurpassed and unsurpassable, to be spoken of with reverence so long as the pulse of the English heart beats high in appreciation of what is brave, of what is manly, of what is noble.

Tactics of the mutineers.

Far from taking of their victory at Chinhat that prompt advantage at which an English army

* *Despatch of Brigadier Inglis to the Secretary to the Government of India, Military Department,* given at full length in Appendix B.

Book IX. Chapter II.

1857. July 1–20.

would have clutched, the rebels, for nearly three weeks, did everything but assault those slight defences. They did indeed occupy the houses which commanded them; they erected batteries; they placed guns in position; they dug trenches to protect their men from our shells; and for the entire period I have mentioned, that is from the 1st to the 20th of July, they kept up a terrific and incessant fire day and night, not less than eight thousand men, and probably a larger number, firing at one time into our position. Their fire was very effective. The mosques, the houses which from want of time to destroy them had been allowed to stand, the not very remote palaces, afforded them commanding positions. Their shells penetrated into places before considered absolutely secure. Many succumbed to this incessant rain of projectiles. Mrs. Dorin was killed in an inner room of Mr. Gubbins' house; Mr. Ommaney, of the Civil Service, was mortally wounded on the 4th of July; Major Francis, of the 13th Native Infantry, a very gallant officer, on the 7th; Mr. Polehampton, the chaplain, the same day, severely. Before the 20th of July dawned, the list of casualties had been increased by Mr. Bryson, at one time Sergeant-Major, 16th Lancers, shot through his head on the 9th; by Lieutenant Dashwood, 48th Native Infantry, who succumbed the same day to cholera; by Lieutenant Charlton, 32nd Foot, shot through the head on the 13th; by Lieutenant Lester, mortally wounded on the 14th; by Lieutenants Bryce and O'Brien, wounded on the 16th; by Lieutenant Harmer wounded, and Lieutenant

Casualties in the early part of the siege.

Arthur killed, on the 19th. That day also, Mr. Polehampton, wounded on the 7th, died of cholera. In addition to these officers, many privates, Europeans and natives, succumbed. A few of the latter deserted to the enemy.

Further effect of the enemy's fire.

Upon the improvised defences the effect of the enemy's fire was even greater. Thus on the 15th Anderson's house was entirely destroyed by round shot, though still nobly held by the garrison; on the 18th, many round shots were fired into the Post office, Fayrer's house, Gubbins's, and the Brigade mess-house. At one time the rebels succeeded in setting the Residency on fire by firing carcasses into it. At another they threatened an assault on Gubbins's post. In fact they had recourse to every possible expedient excepting one, and when they did attempt that one it was met gloriously and successfully.

Proceedings of the garrison.

The garrison during these three weeks had their work cut out for them. The order, so conspicuous by its absence in the first hours of the siege, was gradually restored. By the 10th arrangements had been made for securing and feeding the bullocks, whilst the surviving horses, after scores had been shot down, had been got rid of by turning them loose over the intrenchment in the dark of the night. A strong element of disorder was thus removed. These animals, however, had previously perished in great numbers, and the interring of them was no slight addition to other labours.*

* Numbers of horses and bullocks died, and their burial at night by working parties, in addition to nightly fatigue

Book IX. Chapter II.

1857. July 1–20.

Difficulties they had to contend with.

The heat during this time was excessive. Cholera was busy. The stench from putrid animals was most offensive. Few officers had a servant. The real work of the garrison, in fact, took place in the night time. Then, stores had to be dug out and carried, guns to be shifted, trenches to be dug, shafts for mines sunk, the dead buried, and the thousand and one necessities devolving upon men so situated attended to. Still the garrison showed no signs of faltering. The necessity for having the mind constantly on the stretch, however, whilst, perhaps, it added to the bodily capacity to bear fatigue, told in the long run upon many.

The first sortie.

On the 7th of July a sortie was made. The party consisted of fifty men of the 32nd and twenty Sikhs. The object was to examine Johannes house, a building outside, and close to the line of defence, near the Brigade mess, as it was believed that the enemy were mining. The sortie was successful. The enemy were driven out of the house, and fifteen or twenty of their number were killed. On our side three men were wounded.

Daring of Lieutenant Sam. Lawrence.

I cannot quit the account of this sortie without making special reference to the gallantry of

parties for the purpose of burying the dead, carrying up supplies from exposed positions, repairing intrenchments, draining, and altering the position of guns, in addition to attending on the wounded, caused excessive fatigue to the thin garrison, who had but little rest, night or day. In all duties the officers equally shared the labours with the men, carrying loads, and digging pits for putrid animals, at night, in heavy rain. All exerted themselves to the utmost, alternately exposed to a burning sun and heavy rain."—*Journal of a Staff Officer.*

Book IX. Chapter II. 1857. July 1–20.

the officer who led it, Lieutenant Sam. Lawrence, of the 32nd Foot. The cool daring he displayed obtained for Lieutenant Lawrence the Victoria Cross.*

For some time subsequently the garrison confined themselves strictly to defence. But on the 20th the enemy changed their tactics. They determined then to try the rush which they should in the first instance have attempted.

July 20.

At midnight, on the 20th of July, the enemy's fire almost ceased, nor was heavy firing resumed in the early morning. About half-past 8 o'clock, however, a considerable movement on their part was noticed. The garrison in consequence were well on the alert. A little after 10 o'clock they sprung a mine inside the water-gate, about twenty-five yards from the inner defences, and close to the Redan. Immediately after the explosion the enemy opened a very heavy fire on the defences near which the mine had been sprung. Under cover of this fire, as soon as the smoke and dust

The first assault.

* It may be interesting to the reader to peruse the words in which the bestowal of this honour was notified. In the *London Gazette* of the 22nd of November 1859, the following announcement appeared:—"Lieutenant, now Brevet-Major, S. Lawrence, 32nd Foot.—Date of act of bravery, 7th July 1857.—For distinguished bravery in a sortie on the 7th of July 1857, made, as reported by Major Wilson, late Deputy Assistant Adjutant-General of the Lucknow garrison, 'for the purpose of examining a house strongly held by the enemy, in order to discover whether or not a mine had been driven from it.' Major Wilson states that he saw the attack, and was an eye-witness to the great personal gallantry of Major Lawrence on the occasion, he being the first person to mount the ladder and enter the window of the house, in effecting which he had his pistol knocked out of his hand by one of the enemy."

Book IX. Chapter II.

1857. July 21.

had cleared away, they advanced in heavy masses against the Redan. The garrison, however, received them with so heavy a fire that they reeled back sorely smitten; nor, although they made a second attempt, and penetrated to within a very few yards of the English battery, could they effect a lodgment. Again they fell back, baffled.

Simultaneously a heavy column advanced against Innes's house. The garrison here consisted only of twelve men of the 32nd Foot; twelve of the 13th Native Infantry; and a few non-military servants of Government;—the whole commanded by Ensign Loughnan, 13th Native Infantry. Against this handful of men, the enemy pressed in large numbers, and made their way to within ten yards of the palisades. A rolling fire sent them back. They came, however, again,—and again;—and again;—but always with the same result. The officer who commanded the post, young in years, but cool, wary, determined, and resolute, covered himself with glory. His name, I repeat, was Loughnan. He at last forced the enemy to desist from their attempts to storm the post, and to content themselves with a heavy musketry fire from a safer distance.

Gallantry of young Loughnan.

But the enemy's attack was by no means confined to the two points I have noted. They made a desperate and very determined attempt on the Kánhpúr battery, their standard-bearer, who led them on, jumping into the battery ditch. But a well-directed bullet having stopped his further progress the enemy became disheartened and fell back. Very soon afterwards they advanced with

The attack repulsed at all points.

scaling ladders against Anderson's and Germon's posts. But their reception at both was so warm that they retreated, not to renew the attack.

Book IX. Chapter III. 1857. July 21.

It was now 2 o'clock. The enemy continued for two hours to pour in a heavy fire, and even attempted to effect a lodgment in one of the brick-built cook-houses close to the outer defences. But the real attack was over. Made in great force and with considerable resolution it had been defeated by the British with a loss of but four killed and twelve wounded. By sharp experience the garrison had learned the wisdom of not too much exposing themselves.

Moral aspects of the repulse;

This attack and this repulse deserve to be considered under two aspects—the material and the moral. As a feat of arms it is scarcely to be surpassed by any feat in history. It was the triumph of British coolness and pluck over Asiatic numbers and swagger; of the mind over matter. But in a moral point of view it was more important still. It showed the mutineers that they had miscalculated their chances; that if it had ever been possible for them to storm the intrenchment, that time had gone by; that, unless famine should come to aid them, they and their associate Asiatics would never triumph over that handful of Europeans.

on the Asiatics,

Nor did they, the Europeans who formed that garrison, feel less the moral exaltation of that victory. After three weeks of incessant pounding with shot and shell the enemy had tried to overwhelm them by an assault. In making that assault they had been singularly favoured. Their mine

on the Europeans.

Book IX. Chapter II.

1857. July 21.

had been sprung in accordance with their calculations; they had covered the advance of their infantry by a fierce artillery fire; their infantry had penetrated to within a few yards of the defences! And yet the garrison had repulsed them,—and repulsed them with a loss so small that it did not visibly affect their numbers. The garrison were immensely elated at the results of the day, and, when their posts were visited in the evening, they could talk of nothing but of the heavy losses they had inflicted on the enemy as shown by the numerous corpses in front of their posts. Well might they, from that day, look forward with more hope to the future!

Death of Major Banks.

But the day following this inspiring victory the garrison sustained a loss which it could ill afford. Major Banks, who had succeeded Sir Henry Lawrence as Chief Commissioner, was shot through the head whilst reconnoitring from the top of an out-house. It is true that the functions devolving upon Major Banks were purely civil functions. But his great knowledge of the natives, his noble and cheery nature, his accurate perception of the situation, had rendered him invaluable as a colleague to Brigadier Inglis. His fearlessness, his courage, and his sympathy with suffering had endeared him greatly to the garrison. His place was not filled up.

This arrangement did not take place, however, without a protest. Mr. Gubbins at once intimated his intention of assuming the position of Chief Commissioner. But Brigadier Inglis and his advisers felt that the time for divided authority

Brigadier Inglis holds in abeyance

Book IX. Chapter II.

1857. July 21.

had passed; that under the circumstances it was necessary that there should be but one chief, and that that chief should be a soldier. The Brigadier then issued an order intimating that the office of Chief Commissioner would be held in abeyance until such time as the Government of India could be communicated with.*

the post of Chief Commissioner.

The three weeks following the first assault.

From the 20th of July to the 10th of August the enemy contented themselves mainly with keeping up an unremitting fire upon the garrison, loop-holing more houses and bringing the attack closer and closer. They made no general assault. The garrison were so fully occupied in repairing damages, in countermining, often successfully, and in replying to the enemy's fire, that they could not find sufficient time to remove the carcases of horses and bullocks. The stench from these and from others only partially buried became almost unbearable, and possibly aided in fomenting the pest of flies, the spread of fever, of cholera, of dysentery, of scurvy, and of small-pox amongst the garrison. Perhaps the most fatal cause was the badness and insufficiency of the food, the want of cooks, and consequently the indifferent cooking.

Letter from Colonel Tytler.

But in the midst of these troubles and trials a spark of hope of aid from outside glimmered in the horizon. Many letters had been despatched by messengers believed to be faithful, but up to the 25th of July no reply had been received to any of them. Early in the morning of the

* This arrangement subsequently received the entire approval of the Governor-General.

Book IX. Chapter II. 1857. July 22.

22nd, the pensioner Angad came in from Kánhpúr, but without a letter. Angad was a very remarkable character. He had been a sepoy, but he must have proved a very bad bargain, for he had quitted the military service, when still young, smooth-faced, and wiry. He was the only messenger sent out from the intrenchment who ever brought back a letter. On this occasion he did not carrv one with him for fear of being detained by the enemy; but he stated that the English had been victorious; that he had seen two European regiments at or near Kánhpúr; that one of them had square buttons and the other light blue caps. This description greatly puzzled Brigadier Inglis and his staff who could not call to mind any regiment in the British army which wore square buttons or whose heads were adorned with light blue caps. But it was perfectly accurate. The square buttons belonged to the 78th Highlanders,—the blue caps, covers, to the 1st Madras Fusiliers.*

At 11 o'clock on the night of the 25th the same pensioner, who had been sent out again on the night of the 22nd to General Havelock's camp returned with a reply to that letter from that officer's Quartermaster - General, Lieutenant-Colonel Fraser-Tytler. The letter stated that "Havelock was advancing with a force sufficient to bear down all opposition, and would arrive in five or six days." † Brigadier Inglis at once resolved to smooth the way for the relieving force by transmitting by the same channel to General

* Now the 102nd. † Brigadier Inglis's despatch.

Book IX. Chapter II. 1857. July 25.

Havelock a plan of his position and of the roads approaching it. Angad accordingly took advantage of the first dark night to leave the intrenchment with the plan, drawn up by Major Anderson, and two memoranda partly written in the Greek character. He delivered these to General Havelock at Mangarwár on the 28th of July. They satisfied him as to "the extreme delicacy and difficulty of any operation to relieve Colonel Inglis."* Meanwhile the occasional sound of heavy firing on the road between Kánhpúr and Lakhnao, continued to confirm the hopes raised by the opening of this communication in the minds of the garrison.

The second grand assault.

Four days later,—the ominous 10th of August,—the enemy made their second assault. About 10 o'clock that morning a body, numbering perhaps sixteen hundred, were observed by the garrison massed behind their trenches, opposite the southern face of the defences. Very soon after, a large force was noticed approaching the bridge of boats from the Mariáon cantonments. Brigadier Inglis was not slow to mark the significance of these movements. The word was passed that an assault was impending. Instantly all the occupants of the posts were on the alert. Half an hour later the enemy fired a shell into the Bégam Kótí, a building in the centre of the intrenchment. This was apparently a signal, for immediately after they sprang a mine between Johannes house and the Brigade mess. The effect of the

Effect of the mine sprung by the enemy.

* Havelock's *Despatch to the Commander-in-Chief*, 28th of July 1857.

Book IX. Chapter II.

1857. August 10.

explosion was terrible. The greater portion of the Martinière house was blown in; the palisades and defences for the space of thirty feet were destroyed. On the smoke and dust clearing away, a breach was discovered through which a regiment might have marched in unbroken order. The enemy advanced with great resolution, occupied Johannes house and garden and the buildings close to the Kánhpúr battery, and made a desperate effort to take that post. But they were met, not only by a withering front fire from its defenders, but the garrison of the Brigade mess, composed of a large proportion of officers, many of them excellent shots, and armed with their sporting guns and rifles, poured upon their flank from its roof a well directed and continuous fusillade. This front and flank fire quite paralysed them. Some thirty of their number, however, more daring than their comrades, penetrated into the ditch of the battery within a few feet of our guns. But hand-grenades freely rolled into the midst of them speedily caused them to run back, under a heavy musketry fire, to their comrades under cover. Their losses were enormous.

The attack repulsed,

This attack then was repulsed. But whilst it was progressing, another had been attempted on the adjoining face. The explosion of a mine in front of Sago's house was the signal for the assault. But it was repulsed as bravely and as successfully as had been the other, just described.

everywhere.

They make a final effort; but in vain.

It was now about noon. The losses of the enemy had been very severe. Repulsed at all the points they had attempted, he kept up, however,

Book IX. Chapter II.

1857. August 10.

for two hours a steady and continuous fire of round shot and musketry. This then subsided into the ordinary routine fire which never ceased. But about 5 o'clock they made a sudden and formidable rush on Captain Sanders's post (the Financial garrison). So determined were those who led the assault, that one of them actually seized the bayonet on the musket of a man of the 84th and tried to wrench it off. He was shot, and the attack was repulsed.

At 9 o'clock the assault was renewed on this post, on Innes' house, on Anderson's post, and on Gubbins' post. But at each and all these places they met a reception which caused them to repent their audacity. By 10 o'clock the comparative quiet all around the intrenchments was a confession that the second general assault had failed.

Effect of the assault on both parties.

On this occasion our losses scarcely exceeded those sustained on the 21st of July. They amounted to three Europeans and two sepoys killed, and about double that number wounded. It was remarked by many of the garrison that the attack was neither so persistent, nor so energetic, as on the previous occasion—a proof how the *morale* of the enemy had been lowered by their first repulse.

The British soldier during the siege

Still, to achieve that victory, the garrison had been terribly tried. The reader must never forget how the paucity of their numbers told against them. There were men enough, it is true, to man the posts, to work the guns, to repulse the enemy. But to do all this every man was required. Reliefs were impossible. The same

Book IX. Chapter II.

1857. August 10.

men who had fought all day, had to continue under arms, working and watching all night. It was the exposure, the fatigue, the want of rest, the inferior nourishment, that combined to constitute an enemy more formidable than hostile bullets; an enemy wearing to the constitution, undermining the health, though never affecting the moral or the animal courage of the soldier. The illustrious French general, Foy, once wrote that "the British soldier is not brave at times merely; he is so whenever he has eat well, drunk well, and slept well." Sir William Napier rightly denounced this estimate as being a "stupid calumny." At Lakhnao the British soldier had to contend against want of sleep, against bad food, and latterly against an entire want of liquor and tobacco. Yet who will deny that at the defence of that place, "every helmet caught some beams of glory"? True it is, that even there "no honours awaited his daring, no despatch gave his name to the applauses of his countrymen; his life of danger and hardship was uncheered by hope, his death unnoticed." But cold must be the blood, dull and clouded the spirit of the man, whose heart does not throb as he peruses the lines which follow, as applicable to the defenders of Lakhnao as they were when penned by the immortal historian,* to the tried soldiers of Wellington. "Did his heart sink therefore? Did he not endure with surpassing fortitude the sorest of ills, sustain the most terrible assault in battle unmoved, and

* Sir William Napier.

with incredible energy overthrow every opponent, at all times proving that, while no military qualification was wanting, the fount of honour was still full and fresh within him!" Who will say that this eloquent record of the stamp and character of the unlettered men who beat the choicest soldiers of Napoleon does not literally and accurately pourtray the moral and physical qualities of their successors in the ranks of the British army, who, at the defence of Lakhnao, sustained to the full even the lofty measure of their imperishable renown?

Book IX. Chapter II. 1857. August 10.

a worthy successor of the warrior of the Peninsula.

The Kánhpúr battery.

The next day, and the day following, the enemy continued a heavy cannonade. They appeared to concentrate their fire on the Kánhpúr battery, which had already suffered so severely. The position of the garrison here was really critical. The battery was completely commanded by the enemy. It was quite impossible to hold it against an assault. Yet with a splendid audacity, the defenders would not withdraw their guns, lest such an act should give the enemy confidence!* In the evening of that day a strong working party did their utmost to repair damages in that battery and to remove from it one disabled gun. Three days later the battery was again rendered untenable, but again that night, and the following, were the damages repaired and the defences strengthened. Brigadier Inglis, always at hand whenever danger was to be encountered, having heard that the officers and men of the

* This post (the Kánhpúr battery) was so dangerous that the commanding officer had to be changed every day.

Book IX. Chapter II.

post believed that it had been successfully mined, went to it and remained there the night of the 16th.

1857. August 12.

A sortie made and repulsed.

In the interval, the 12th of August, the garrison, made a sortie in order to find out the intentions of the enemy in digging close to Sago's house. The party consisted only of twelve men of the 32nd Foot, under Lieutenant Clery, accompanied by Captain Hutchinson of the Engineers. The enemy, however, were well on the alert, and their covering party, strong in numbers, compelled our troops to retire without effecting their object.

The third grand assault.

On the 18th, the enemy delivered their third general assault. This time the usual preliminary mine had been dug under one of the Sikh squares. Exploded at daylight its effect was electric. Two officers and two sentries on the top of the house were blown into the air and fell among the *débris*. The guard below, consisting of six drummers and a sepoy, were buried in the ruins and lost their lives. Of those on the roof, the officers and one of the sentries escaped with a few bruises. The other sentry was killed.

Success of the explosion of the enemy's mine.

In other respects the explosion was most successful. A clear breach, some twenty feet in breadth, had been made in the defences. The enemy, stimulated and excited, were not slow to take advantage of this opening. One of their officers, a very gallant fellow, sprang at once to the top of the breach, and waving his sword called on his men to follow. Before, however, his summons was responded to, a bullet had laid him low. His place was instantly occupied by another but he

Book IX. Chapter II. 1857. August 18.

was as instantly killed. Simultaneously the head of the column was sorely smitten by the flank fire from the top of the brigade mess. The *morale* of the sepoys was greatly affected by these casualties, and the attacking force seemed suddenly to melt away. By means of some barricaded lanes, however, they managed shortly after to take possession of the right flank wall of the Sikh square. But the garrison, admirably commanded, not only drove them from this, but succeeded in capturing one of the houses previously held by them, between the Sikh square and Gubbins's house. It was from this house that the enemy had most annoyed that face of the defences. Consequently it and others contiguous to it were blown up that evening.

The assault repulsed,

The third assault was thus not only less formidable than its two predecessors; it resulted in a positive advantage to the besieged. And yet never had the latter been taken more completely by surprise, the presence of a mine in that spot not having been suspected. Notwithstanding the vigilance exercised by the garrison of the Sikh square they had not heard the slightest sound of the working of the mine which exploded.* No precautions had, therefore, been taken. The enemy then had the opportunity most coveted by an assailing army—an open breach, an unprepared

with advantage to the garrison.

* The officers at this post were Lieutenant Mecham and Soppett, and Captain Orr (unattached). One of them thus wrote, the day after the occurrence: "The new mine, which occasioned the calamity of yesterday, must have been worked by the enemy with sharp and noiseless tools, as . . . . not the slightest sound . . . . . . ever reached us."

Book IX. Chapter II.

1857. August 18.

garrison, their own troops massed, their leaders bold and resolute. And yet they were foiled. Who will assert that the result would have been the same if the defenders had been the assailants, and the assailants the defenders?

Reason for specially dwelling on the four great assaults.

In a history of the great Indian mutiny, and especially in the history of a prolonged siege, it is impossible to record every act of heroism, to describe every isolated attack, and every individual defence, however noble, and however gallant. I have selected, therefore, for more particular description the four general assaults made upon the defences of the Residency as affording the most striking examples of the conduct of the hostile parties. In this third assault I have shown how, with every advantage before them, the assailants were not only beaten back but actually lost ground. The inquiry naturally arises—to what particular action on the part of our troops were they indebted to their victory? It is due to those gallant men to answer this question somewhat in detail.

A glance at the sketch* will show that the outer Sikh square was commanded by the Brigade Mess. The explosion of the mine found the officers on the roof of that house ever watchful and ready and with a large reserve of loaded muskets. It was their fire which struck down the two daring leaders who in succession mounted the breach. It was their fire, taking an advancing enemy in the flank, which made the enemy's formed masses

* Facing page 442.

Book IX. Chapter II.

1857. August 18.

Detailed action of the garrison in the repulse of the 18th of August.

shrink from the assault. But that was not all. At the first sound of the explosion the entire garrison were on the alert at their allotted post. The Brigadier ordered down the reserve, consisting of only eighteen men, to the threatened point, and placed them in a position which commanded the breach from the right. At the same time boxes, doors, planks, etc. were rapidly carried down to make as much cover as possible to protect our men against musketry; a house, also, was pulled down and a road made for a gun; and, after incredible exertions, a 9-pounder was got into a position which commanded all the breach, and was loaded with a double charge of grape. I may leave this simple description without comment. It is typical of the garrison and its commander. Threatened with a great calamity, every resource to meet it was brought at once into play. The history of war does not show a brighter example of coolness and courage. The conduct of the assailants and the assailed on that 18th of August marks emphatically the fathomless distinction between the European and Asiatic in the qualities of a real soldier!

Peculiarities which distinguished this garrison from ordinary garrisons.

It may not be out of place to point out here some of the peculiarites which distinguished this garrison from ordinary garrisons of besieged places—peculiarities which, strange though the assertion may at first sight appear,—account to a certain extent for their success. One of these was the paucity of their numbers. One effect of this was that the garrison of a post at the begin-

Book IX. Chapter II. 1857. August 18.

ning of the siege remained the garrison of that post to the end. The men were never relieved, because there were no others to relieve them. So great was the necessity to be for ever on the alert that the member of one garrison was unable to visit the member of another garrison. The only man who quitted his post was the man who went in the morning to fetch the day's rations. Even when the post was knocked down by the enemy's fire the garrison of that post built up fresh defences from the *débris*. It was thoroughly understood by all that there was no retreat; that all must die at their posts; and that whatever casualties might occur vacant places could not be filled. One consequence of this was that the defenders of a post on the western face knew nothing during the day of what was going on on the eastern face. It is true that every evening the Assistant Adjutant-General, Captain Wilson, visited every post, generally accompanied by Mr. Couper, and whilst examining its state, noting its wants, and receiving the reports of the commander, encouraged the soldiers with accounts of success achieved in other parts. It is true also that there was a reserve—but its numbers from casualties had diminished very considerably. This reserve, and the Brigadier and his Staff,

The reserve.

were the only members of the garrison who had no fixed post to defend. The men of the reserve were posted in the centre of the position, with the strictest orders that they were not to move thence except under the personal orders of the Brigadier or his Staff. Summonses from other persons were on no account to be attended to. It was their business to rush wherever the Brigadier might consider their presence to be most needed. Nobly did they perform this dangerous duty. The others lived or died where they had been originally posted.

Book IX. Chapter II.

1857. August 18.

One consequence of this permanency of location, of this knowledge that they could neither be reinforced nor relieved, was to sharpen the wits of the defenders, to make them take precautions which otherwise they might have overlooked. Thus they had always a considerable reserve of loaded muskets: they were careful never to expose themselves unnecessarily; when boring loop-holes they made sure that the background should be dark. The subject of loop-holes was, indeed, so thoroughly mastered that it deserves a paragraph to itself.

Precautions taken by the garrison.

It must never be forgotten that the assailants and assailed were quite close to each other. The distance that separated them was, in many points, not greater than the average width of a street such as the Strand. No man on either side dared, therefore, expose himself in the open to discharge his musket. Unless at the time of a general assault the muskets were fired through loop-holes. Now, when two hostile parties are so close to each other it is very easy to discover the bearings of particular loop-holes—and to avoid them. Having found a point out of their range the besieging party would be naturally encouraged to post men at that point to fire on any defender who might expose his person. The garrison

Loop-holing.

Book IX. Chapter II.

1857. August 18.

came gradually to encourage the assailants to occupy such a point and to have confidence in occupying it. But they marked well the direction; and during the night they bored holes in that direction. In the morning the enemy would come up by twos and threes to occupy their chosen post; or the garrison would do something to attract them there. Then the muskets would be discharged from the new loop-holes. The result was almost always successful. This method of out-witting the enemy was tried again and again, and generally with success.

Correction of prodigality of fire.

At the commencement of the siege officers and men were prodigal of their fire. Even on the darkest night they discharged their pieces at an enemy they could not see. But, at the end of about ten days, this evil corrected itself. The fatigue was too great, the constant recoil of the piece too painful, to permit it to continue. After that the men husbanded their resources and never fired but when they could cover a foe. The garrison learned after the siege that nothing had tended more to daunt the enemy than the perfect stillness which used to prevail in the intrenchment during the night.

The look-out system.

Another most important matter in the defence was the mode adopted to obtain information of the enemy's movements. To procure this information, an organised system of "look-out" was established at a very early date. It was carried out in this way. At daybreak an officer, accompanied by a sepoy, was detailed to take post in the highest tower on the roof of the Residency.

From holes made in this tower the officer watched all the movements of the foe. He had slips of paper with him, and one of these he sent down by the sepoy whenever necessary. They were relieved every two hours. A precisely similar watch was maintained from the roof of the Post office. In this manner the Brigadier was kept acquainted with the movements which came within observation. These duties were by no means devoid of danger. During the defence two officers were severely wounded while so employed.

The British flag.

As I am writing of the roof of the Residency this may be a fitting place to record that on the highest point of that roof the British flag waved gloriously throughout the long siege. Whilst the members of the garrison felt a noble pride in thus displaying to their assailants their resolute confidence, the sight of that symbol of British predominance filled the hearts of those assailants with fury. The flag was a constant aim of their sharpshooters. Again and again were the halyards severed; the flag was riddled; the staff cut through, by bullets. But, as soon as darkness permitted, a new staff, new halyards, were supplied. Patched up though it might be, the flag continued to the last to float defiance to the enemies of England.

Mining.

Perhaps no mode of foiling the enemy was more practised by a portion of the garrison than mining and counter-mining. To enable the general reader to understand how this was effected I will briefly describe the process carried on in the defences as described to me by one of those who

Book IX. Chapter II.

1857. August 18.

was present. A shaft some four feet in diameter was sunk in the interior of the defences, as near as possible to the point to be assailed, to a depth of from twelve to twenty feet, according to circumstances. From this the gallery was run out in the direction and to the distance required.

The method adopted.

Now the real toil began. One man—an officer or soldier as the case might be—worked with a short pickaxe, or crowbar, to loosen the earth in front of him—to make a burrow just sufficiently high to clear his head when seated, and wide enough to allow of his working. Close behind this first worker sat another with an empty wine case. This he filled with loose earth. When filled he jerked a cord as a signal, and the box was drawn to the shaft, where another individual again gave notice to two at the top holding a rope attached to either side of the case. These pulled it to the surface, emptied, and returned it. Thus five men worked at once. Two in the mine, one at the bottom of the shaft, two above it.

There were usually ten men thus employed on one mine, relieving each other at intervals agreed upon by themselves. The usual spell was half an hour, but was not unfrequently less. As the gallery progressed, it was visited by an officer of Engineers, who gave all necessary instructions.

These mines were not always made for offensive purposes. Frequently they were used to cut off the subterraneous advance of the enemy. In such cases they were run out a short distance, and then carried on laterally.

The fatigue and labour of constructing such

works with indifferent tools and scant and impromptu appliances in a hot night in India, after fighting and working all day on an insufficiency of indifferent food, and without stimulants of any kind, cannot easily be imagined.

Book IX. Chapter II.

1857. August 18.

The officers and men share alike.

It deserves to be remarked that throughout the siege officers and men equally stood sentry. There were no exemptions. No place within the defences was absolutely safe. Even the building used as a hospital was constantly under artillery fire. In August a shell exploded there, killing one sepoy and wounding two others. On the 5th of September an 18-pounder shot traversed the building, wounding again Lieutenant Charlton and a soldier of the 32nd. In fact, both attendants and patients were always under fire.

The hospital no place of safety.

But to return. The defeat of the 18th of August had a depressing effect on the mutineers. They kept up, it is true, during the next day, a heavy fire, but they made no serious attempt to prevent the further demolition of houses and buildings outside the defences which had, up to that time, afforded them excellent cover. This demolition was effected by a small party under Captains Fulton, Hutchinson, and Anderson, supported from within the defences by a covering fire.

Houses outside the intrenchment demolished.

The day following, however, the rebels had recovered their spirits, and, covered by the heaviest cannonade the garrison had till then sustained, made an attempt to burn down the gates at the Baillie Guard, but without result. They soon had to learn that mining was an art which

Book IX. Chapter II.

1857. August 19.

The garrison successfully mine Johannes' house.

could be practised by defenders as well as by assailants. Johannes' house, held by the enemy, was a dominant position, and, as the siege wore on, the fire from it had become intolerable. It could no longer be taken by a sortie, for the enemy, warned by the previous successful sally, held it in such force as to render impossible any further attempt of the kind. There was only one resource, and that was to mine under it. Many nights of terrible toil, sustained almost exclusively by the officers, were spent in the work. At last the Engineer officer reported that the mine was, he believed, well advanced under the building. It was then heavily charged. To entice as many of the enemy as possible within the building, the garrison, on the 21st, opened upon it a heavy musketry fire. The enemy, regarding this fire as the prelude to another sortie, crowded into the house to assist in its defence. No sooner did the garrison note this than they fired the mine. The result was most successful. Johannes' house played no further part in the siege of Lakhnao.

Occurrences between the third and fourth assault.

In the interval between this date and the fourth and last assault on the 5th of September the losses of the garrison alike from the fire of the enemy and from sickness were very heavy. I find Captain Wilson, the Assistant Adjutant-General, thus writing in his journal on the 23rd of August:—"A heavy cannonade from the enemy from daylight till about 10 P.M. when it slackened. Their principal efforts were against the Brigade Messhouse and Kánhpúr battery: the former they

Book IX. Chapter II.

1857. August 23.

seriously damaged, and succeeded in entirely levelling the guard-houses on the top, both of which had fallen in and there was no longer any cover for our musketry to fire from. Our ranks were rapidly thinning." The following extract from the same diary on the same day will show the enormous difficulties which beset the garrison even in the matter of labour absolutely necessary and of the repair of damages from the enemy's shot. "We had work nightly," writes Captain Wilson, "for at least three hundred men; we had the defences to repair daily, supplies to remove from godowns which were fallen in from the effect of the enemy's shot, mines to countermine, guns to remove, barricades to erect, corpses to bury, and rations to serve out; but with our weak, harassed, and daily diminishing garrison, we could seldom produce as working parties more than three fatigue parties of eight or ten men each relief." Other difficulties too were overtaking them. It was the rainy season. And the grass and jungle outside the defences had grown in the prolific manner natural to grass and jungle during the rainy season in India. This extreme growth rendered it possible for the mutineers to steal up, unobserved, close to the intrenchment. The heavy rain had likewise greatly injured many of the defences. Many of the supplies had been expended; the supply of tobacco was exhausted; flour had become scarce.

The supplies diminished.

In place of flour wheat was now issued to all who could find time to grind it. The stench from decaying and decayed offal had become, in many

Book IX. Chapter II.

1857. August 23.

places, scarcely endurable. Mortality from sickness had, too, become very prevalent especially amongst the children.

Hopes of relief.

There was, however, during this period one great counterpoise to the mental and bodily wear and tear. The garrison were still buoyed up by hope from outside. On the 22nd and 23rd reports of distant firing were heard. These had been often noticed before, and now caused but little excitement. But on the 28th, the messenger Angad returned within the intrenchment conveying a letter from General Havelock, dated the 24th, with the information that he had no hope of being able to relieve them for twenty-five days. They had a certainty then of three weeks' continuance of this life, probably of more. One result of this letter was a further reduction in the amount of rations!

The fourth grand assault.

On the 5th of September the enemy tried their fourth grand assault. The morning was fine, with a late moon giving a clear light before day had broken. The enemy, however, waited for the dawn to commence a cannonade severer, if possible, than the last referred to. As the sun rose about eight thousand rebel infantry were descried preparing for an assault. It is needless to add that the garrison were ready—waiting for it. About 10 o'clock the enemy exploded two mines, one—the larger—close to the 18-pounder battery; the other at the Brigade Messhouse. Fortunately they had miscalculated their distance and in each case the explosion did little harm. But as soon as the smoke had cleared away they were seen advancing with great resolution—their attack specially directed against Gubbins's post. Planting an enormous ladder against the bastion they essayed to mount it. Several reached the top but they encountered so heavy a fire of musketry and hand-grenades from the defenders that not a man could gain a footing. They came on again and again, however, with extraordinary courage,—not only against this point but against the Sikh square and the Brigade Mess-house; nor was it until they had lost an enormous number of men that they fell back, beaten, baffled, and dispirited. The British loss amounted to but three killed and one wounded.

Book IX. Chapter II.

1857. September 5.

Repulsed.

It deserves to be recorded that in this attack eight sepoys of the 13th Native Infantry, assisted by three artillerymen, loaded and worked the 18-pounder in the 13th battery, and after three or four rounds, succeeded in silencing the 18-pounder opposed to them. This battery was entirely under charge of those sepoys. It had been constructed solely by them under the superintendence of the Engineers, and they were very proud of it.

The "eight" of the 13th Native Infantry.

Similar attacks, though in less force, were made the same day at other points, but they were all repulsed. The 5th of September was, in fact, the worst day the assailants had experienced. They had lost more men than on any previous occasion, and they appeared to those of the garrison who occupied positions commanding a view of their retreat to be more thoroughly

The assailants are dispirited by their repulse.

Book IX. Chapter II.

1857. September.

beaten than ever. Certainly they were more thoroughly dispirited, for they never tried a general assault again.

Sickness increases within the defences.

Still for twenty days the garrison remained cut off from the outer world, exposed day and night to a heavy fire of musketry and guns, to mines, to surprises, to attacks on isolated parts. The most unhealthy month of the year, the month in which the stagnant water caused by the abundant rainfall of July and August dries up, emitting miasmatic smells bearing with them fever, dysentery and cholera, had now come to find a congenial field for its ravages within the intrenchments. The live stock, too, was sensibly diminishing, the small stock of rum and porter,* reserved only for the sick and wounded, was running low. As the numbers of the garrison diminished the labours of the survivors naturally augmented. Added to this, scarcely a day passed but some portion of one or other of the posts crumbled under the weight of the enemy's fire. Now it was two sides of Innes's house, steadily cannonaded daily with 18-pounder shot, that fell in;† now the verandah of the Residency

* Some idea of the scarcity may be conceived from the prices realised at auction and at private sales. On the 10th a bottle of brandy realised at auction £1 14s.; on the 12th, £2 were given for a small chicken; £1 12s. for a bottle of Curaçoa, whilst the same price was offered for two pounds of sugar. A new flannel shirt fetched £4, whilst five old ones realised £11 4s. On the 19th the price of a bottle of brandy had risen to £2.

† The post was, however, still nobly held, and preparations made for some kind of defence out of the *débris*. —*Diary of a Staff Officer*.

that succumbed to incessant battering; now the wall of the building occupied by the boys of the Martinière. Some idea of the incessant nature of the hostile fire may be gleaned from the fact that on the 8th of September two hundred and eighty round shot, which had lodged there during the siege, varying in size from a 24 to a 3-pounder, were gathered from the roof of the Brigade Mess-house alone!

Book IX. Chapter II.

1857. September.

At 10 P.M. on the 16th the pensioner Angad was again sent out with a letter rolled up in a quill for General Havelock. He evinced no reluctance. The risk was great, certain death if discovered, but the reward promised him was enormous—not less than five hundred pounds a trip. He was absent just six days. He returned at 11 P.M. on the 22nd bringing with him a letter containing the gratifying intelligence that the relieving force had crossed the Ganges and would arrive in three or four days! To guard against that depression amongst his men apt to be engendered by disappointed hope, the Brigadier put on ten days to the time, and announced to the garrison that help from outside would arrive certainly within the fortnight. The effect was electric. The garrison were greatly elated by the news, and on many of the sick and wounded the speedy prospect of a possible change of air and security exercised a most beneficial effect. As to Angad—whatever may have been his adventures, they had satisfied him for his life. "Live or die," he exclaimed, "I have made the trip three times in safety;

Sept. 16.

Angad again sent out.

Angad brings glad tidings.

Book IX.
Chapter II.

I'll go no more, but come life or death I'll remain with you." *

1857.
Sept. 23.

The approach of the relieving force heralded.

On the 23rd—the day following Angad's return—a smart cannonade was heard in the direction of Kánhpúr: some even fancied they heard musketry fire. A considerable movement of troops was also observed in the city, but the object was not apparent. A similar sound of distant firing and a similar movement of troops in the city was noticed likewise on the 24th. The night that followed was very unquiet, two alarms keeping the whole garrison under arms. It subsequently transpired that the enemy, aware of the near approach of the relieving force, were determined to use all possible means to prevent communication between that force and the garrison. Sounds indicating great disturbance reached them from the city. At 10 o'clock the following morning a messenger arrived bringing an old letter from General Outram dated the 16th. The messenger could only add of his own knowledge that the relieving force had reached the outskirts of the city. The anxiety of the garrison was now intense. It was not lessened by the gradual cessation of the fire about an hour later (11 A.M.). The sounds of disturbance still continued, however, to reach them from the city. At noon the sound of musketry and of cannon close at hand gladdened their ears, whilst the smoke from the discharge of the latter showed that their friends were within the limits of the city. The excitement now almost

Intense excitement of the garrison.

* Angad had made four trips; but the three last of these only had been undertaken by order of the Brigadier.

passed the power of endurance. But it had to be borne. For an hour and a half it was evident that a fierce struggle was going on. But then it became evident that the European had asserted his superiority. At 1.30 P.M. many of the people of the city commenced leaving with bundles of clothes on their heads and took the direction of the cantonments across the different bridges. At 2 P.M. armed men and sepoys began to follow them, accompanied by large bodies of Irregular Cavalry. Whilst the struggle in the city had been progressing a blockading party of the enemy's troops had continued to keep a heavy fire on our defences. They continued it, now that their comrades were retreating, more vigorously than ever. But the garrison, leaving them to do their worst, brought every gun and mortar to bear on the foe fleeing from the city. They were able to do this with the more effect as the bridge of boats had been carried away, and many of the enemy's cavalry had to swim the river Gúmtí. The cannonade on these men lasted an hour and a half, a proof that their numbers must have been considerable.

Signs of the enemy's defeat.

The scene that followed cannot be better told than in the words of one to whose diary* I am so largely indebted. "At 4 P.M." writes Captain Wilson in his journal "report was made that some officers dressed in shooting coats and solah hats, a regiment of Europeans in blue pantaloons and shirts and a bullock battery were seen near

The relief.

* *The Defence of Lucknow,—a Diary by a Staff Officer.*

Book IX. Chapter II. 1857. Sept. 25.

Mr. Martin's house and the Motí Mahal. At 5 P.M. volleys of musketry, rapidly growing louder, were heard in the city. But soon the firing of a Minié ball over our heads gave notice of the still nearer approach of our friends, of whom as yet little or nothing had been seen, though the enemy had been seen firing heavily on them from many of the roofs of the houses. Five minutes later, and our troops were seen fighting their way through one of the principal streets; and though men fell at almost every step yet nothing could withstand the headlong gallantry of our reinforcements. Once fairly *seen*, all our doubts and fears regarding them were ended: and then the garrison's long pent-up feelings of anxiety and suspense burst forth in a succession of deafening cheers. From every pit, trench, and battery—from behind the sandbags piled on shattered houses—from every post still held by a few gallant spirits, rose cheer on cheer. Even from the hospital many of the wounded crawled forth to join in that glad shout of welcome to those who had so bravely come to our assistance. It was a moment never to be forgotten.

The meeting.

"Soon," continues the journal, "soon all the rear-guard and heavy guns were inside our position; and then ensued a scene which baffles description. For eighty-seven days the Lakhnao garrison had lived in utter ignorance of all that had taken place outside. Wives who had long mourned their husbands as dead were again restored to them. Others, fondly looking forward to glad meetings with those near and dear to them, now for the first time learned that they were alone. On all sides eager inquiries for relations and friends were made. Alas! in too many instances the answer was a painful one."

Was it relief or reinforcement?

But relief had come. Communication with the outer world had been opened. By whom had this gallant dash through the beleaguering force been accomplished? This is a question which I shall answer fully in the next chapter. In this place I will only add that when the delirium of joy at the sight of old friends, and of receiving intelligence from outside had given place to sober considerations, it was recognised that the garrison had been not relieved, but reinforced; that the losses sustained by the incoming force had been so great that, combined with the garrison, they still could not thoroughly master the enemy. In some respects, even, the position of the garrison had been rendered worse. There were more mouths to feed, and there was no increase of food to supply them; more accommodation to be provided only to be obtained by extending the position; and withal the uncertainty as to the period when it would be possible for the Government to equip another force sufficiently large to attempt a real relief.

Summary.

But with the arrival of that force concludes the episode of the first siege of the Lakhnao Residency. If in the course of my narrative of that unsurpassed trial of courage and endurance I have not more markedly referred to individuals by name it is because, where all fought so nobly,

Book IX. Chapter II.

1857. Sept. 25.

where all showed such a devotion without stint and a valour that was dauntless, I have thought it becoming to accept the judgment—the keen and decisive judgment—of the man who was in all respects the best qualified to form an opinion. In his admirable report to the Government of India* Brigadier Inglis has specially mentioned those to whom he considered himself most indebted. In that report the members of the staff; the commandants of outposts; the officers of the artillery, of the 32nd, of the 84th, and of the native regiments; the gentlemen of the Civil Service, covenanted and uncovenanted; of the medical service, and those unconnected with the Government, are specially mentioned. Omitting necessarily the names of the class regarding which Sir William Napier wrote: "no honours awaited his daring, no despatch gave his name to the applauses of his countrymen" —the private soldier—all, who in the opinion of the Brigadier deserved special mention, have been mentioned. But there is one exception—an important though necessary exception. Brigadier Inglis could say nothing regarding the conduct of Brigadier Inglis. I may be allowed to fill up the vacuum.

Honour to whom honour is due.

Brigadier Inglis.

To command a small party defending a weak intrenchment against an overwhelming force, certain sterling qualities are necessary. A man need not be a strategist or a tactician. But, whilst confident in bearing, unyielding in temper, he

* *Vide* Appendix B.

Book IX. Chapter II.

1857. Sept. 25.

must be bold, determined, and resolute in action. He must likewise possess the valuable quality the existence of which displays itself in the capacity to weigh correctly the professional opinions of the officers about him. Now by the testimony of all with whom I have conversed on the subject Brigadier Inglis fulfilled all these conditions. His daring obstinacy in resisting, his confident mien, his cool courage, gained him the respect and affection of officers and men. What he might have accomplished in the field I cannot say. But it may with confidence be affirmed that for the actual duties devolving upon him—for the defence of a weak post with a small force—few men were better qualified than Brigadier Inglis, and certainly no one more merited than he the honours and promotion by the bestowal of which a grateful country showed its sense of the eminent service he had rendered.

Captain Wilson.

But it is impossible to allude to the qualities of Brigadier Inglis without paying a special tribute to the man who was his right hand—a man to whose untiring watchfulness, great decision, and unceasing exertions, the prolonged and successful defence of the Residency was in no small measure attributable. This is not my opinion only. It was the opinion of Brigadier Inglis: it is the opinion of every man of the garrison with whom I have spoken. I allude to Captain Thomas Fourness Wilson, now Colonel Wilson, C.B., of the Bengal Staff Corps, and A.D.C. to the Queen.

Captain Wilson had been nineteen years in the army when the mutiny broke out. He had no inte-

Book IX. Chapter II. 1857. Sept. 25.

rest, and was still but a regimental captain when Sir Henry Lawrence came to Lakhnao. On being nominated brigadier-general Sir Henry was naturally anxious to have as his assistant adjutant-general a perfectly competent officer. He selected Captain Wilson, unknown to him before, but whom he had specially marked from the time of his first conversation with him. Brought at once into confidential relationship with Sir Henry Wilson speedily gained his admiration and esteem. His activity, his prudence, his cool daring, his stern and inflexible nature, the determination with which he carried out orders, marked him as the man for the occasion. And when, after Sir Henry's death, Wilson served under Inglis in the same capacity, he won his confidence by the display of the same qualities which had gained for him the esteem of his predecessor.

It is impossible, indeed, to over-estimate the "splendid conduct," of this officer during the long siege. Brigadier Inglis, from whom I have taken this expression, wrote of him at the time that he "was ever to be found where shot were flying thickest;" and he bore emphatic testimony alike to "his untiring physical endurance and bravery," and to "his ever ready and pertinent counsel and advice in moments of difficulty and danger." Every night throughout the siege he visited the several posts, ready with advice, with assistance, with encouragement. His determined nature, his prompt decision, were invaluable to all, from the Brigadier to the meanest private. Nor will it be possible to speak of the gallant defence of the beleaguered Residency without associating it in the mind with the name of Thomas Fourness Wilson.

Book IX. Chapter II.

1857. Sept. 25.

Captain Fulton.

Brigadier Inglis was fortunate in his Engineers. Captain Fulton, who, to the grief and dismay of every one in the garrison, was killed on the 14th of September. Captain Fulton was a man unsurpassed in his profession, supremely daring, and ever courting danger. No one than he more fertile in resource, more ready, more eager. He was peculiarly happy in the devices he adopted to foil the cunning of the enemy. A short experience had convinced him that when he had detected the enemy mining the wisest plan was to meet him with a countermine. Often would he proceed, pistol in hand, descend into the burrow which formed his countermine, and wait listening to the progress of the hostile pickaxe on the same level. The enemy hearing no sound would continue to work confidently. Suddenly the ground would give way to the pick. A lantern would be shown behind the leading man. Instantly Fulton's pistol would lay that man low. The others unable to pass him would turn and run. Before they could come back the mine would be filled and exploded. His death, occurring but eleven days before the relief, was most acutely felt and lamented by all. It even caused a feeling akin to dismay.

Lieutenant James.

Amongst others who are gone a tribute must be paid here to Lieutenant James, the Commissariat officer. It would be difficult, indeed, to add a word to the glowing eulogium of Brigadier

Book IX. Chapter II.

1857. Sept. 25.

Inglis. "It is not too much to say that the garrison owe their lives to the exertions and firmness of this officer." Wounded as he was at Chinhat by a ball in the knee, causing him immense suffering, he refused to be placed on the sick list, and never ceased to pay the strictest attention to his onerous duties. His determination and his courage were alike conspicuous. His peculiar temperament fitted him exactly for the position he held. Lieutenant James lived to justify to the full the high opinion entertained of him by all his comrades. He met his death in the prime of life when pigsticking in Bengal. As a tribute—though a feeble tribute—to his daring nature and manly qualities he was buried in the scarlet hunting coat which he wore when he met his fatal accident.

Mr. Couper, C.S.

I have spoken of Mr. Couper. This gentleman deserves more than a passing mention. A civilian, he was ever ready to descend into the mine, to visit the posts, to assist in interring the dead animals, to dig trenches, to carry stores, and to fight. He was ever cheery and buoyant. His subsequent career has not belied the early promise. For at the present moment he is Sir George Couper, Lieutenant-Governor of the North-West Provinces.

The honoured dead.

These men were types of their class in devotion to duty, and to their country. There were many others. Prominent amongst those who fell during the siege, nobly fighting, or who died of wounds, or from other causes, were Radcliffe of the 9th Cavalry, daring, ready-witted, full of energy; Francis of the 13th Native Infantry, "a brave, good officer, respected by all, and in whom Sir H. Lawrence had much confidence"; Anderson, the Chief Engineer, to whose able counsel Brigadier Inglis felt deeply indebted; Simons, of the Artillery, distinguished at Chinhat; Case, of the 32nd, who fell when gallantly leading on his men at that battle; Shepherd and Arthur, of the 7th Cavalry, killed at their posts; Hughes, of the 57th Native Infantry; Mansfield and McCabe, of the 32nd—all three foremost in danger; Lucas, a gentleman volunteer, and Boyson of the uncovenanted service, both conspicuous for their coolness and courage. These were among the honoured dead. To mention with them the survivors who rivalled them, men of whom Master, Langmore, and Aitken were the types, it would be necessary to recount the story of the siege in every minute detail.

The native troops.

It is difficult to praise too highly the fidelity and gallantry of the remnants of the 13th, the 48th, and the 71st Native Infantry, and the daring and bravery of their officers. Of those regiments the 13th counted the greatest number of loyal men. They were chiefly posted at the Baillie Guard. This position was described by Brigadier Inglis as "perhaps the most important in the whole line of defences." Here, led by the most gallant of men, Lieutenant Aitken, they rendered the most splendid service. "They were exposed," reported Brigadier Inglis, "to a most galling fire of round shot and musketry, which materially decreased their numbers. They were so near the enemy

Book IX. Chapter II.

1857. Sept. 25.

that conversation could be carried on between them; and every effort, persuasion, promise, and threat, was alternately resorted to, in vain, to seduce them from their allegiance to the handful of Europeans, who, in all probability, would have been sacrificed by their desertion." They vied with their European comrades in the work of the trenches, in the ardour of their courage, in their resolution to defend to the last the spot of ground assigned to them. True it is that they were led by their own officers, and it would be impossible to overpraise men such as Germon, Aitken, and Loughnan, of that regiment. But the sepoys did more than fight. They risked even their caste for the English. On an occasion when it had become necessary to dig new intrenchments, and to erect a new battery on the spot where sepoys had been previously buried, the highest Bráhmans of the 13th responding to the call of the gallant Aitken, themselves handled the putrid corpses to throw them into the outer ditch.

The pensioners.

A few words must here be devoted to the native pensioners who replied to the call of Sir Henry Lawrence. I have stated in a previous page that about one hundred and eighty of these men were enrolled. It is difficult to write in too high terms of the conduct of these men. Most of them were old, the vision of some was impaired. Yet they bore themselves most bravely. Unable to work much, they yet manned the loopholes, and the least capable amongst them were ever ready to load and pass to their countrymen the spare muskets always at hand. Notwithstanding the facts that throughout the siege these men received no tidings from their family or their relations; that they were on reduced rations and entirely deprived of the condiments so highly prized by a native of India in his advanced years; not a single instance of desertion occurred amongst these men. Some died, many were killed, yet no one heard a grumble from the survivors. They continued to the last to abuse the rebels, and to declare that having for so many years eaten the salt of the State, the State had a right to their lives.

The ladies.

Imperfect as is this story of this first siege, it would be still more so were it to contain no reference to those who, despite their own sufferings and their own privations, used every effort to assuage the sufferings and the privations of others. "Many," wrote Brigadier Inglis referring to the ladies, "among whom may be mentioned the honoured names of Birch, of Polehampton, of Barber, and of Gall, have, after the example of Miss Nightingale, constituted themselves the tender and solicitous nurses of the wounded and dying soldiers in the hospital." The word "many" might be held to include all whose attention was not absorbed by their own children, or who were not held down by sickness and ill health. They were exposed to a danger of no ordinary kind, to privations almost unparalleled. When the siege began the number of ladies amounted to sixty-eight, and of children sixty-six. Of the former seven, of the latter twenty-three succumbed to the want of suitable food, to the fire of the enemy, and to

Book IX. Chapter II. 1857. Sept. 25.

privations. It has rarely happened that ladies have been placed in a position so trying—never that they have displayed qualities more worthy of respectful homage.

The losses sustained.

One word regarding the losses sustained by the defenders. I have already stated that at the beginning of the siege the strength of the garrison amounted to nine hundred and twenty-seven Europeans, and seven hundred and sixty-five natives. Of the Europeans, one hundred and forty were killed or died of their wounds; one hundred and ninety were wounded; this does not include sixteen non-military men killed and fourteen wounded. Of the natives, seventy-two were killed and one hundred and thirty-one were wounded. There were deaths from other causes, and a few of the natives deserted. This is certain that on the 25th of September the number of the European defenders, including sick and wounded, had been reduced to five hundred and seventy-seven; that of the natives to four hundred and two. In eighty-seven days the garrison had thus been reduced, in various ways, by three-eighths.

But they are now in the first delirium of the long-expected relief. They are welcoming with enthusiastic delight Outram, Havelock, and their gallant following. It remains for me now to relate how it was that Outram and Havelock accomplished the great feat of arms with which their names will for ever be associated.

BOOK IX.

CHAPTER III.

July 16.

Brigadier-General Neill, pressed by the Commander of the Forces, Sir Patrick Grant, to hasten to Kánhpúr to join General Havelock as soon as possible, in order that he might be on the spot to take command of the force should Havelock from any cause become unfit for the duty, left Alláhábád on the 16th of July, and proceeding with all possible expedition, reached Kánhpúr on the 20th.

Brigadier-General Neill arrives at Kánhpúr.

On his way he had received a note from General Havelock telling him that he was anxiously awaiting his arrival, as immediately on that occurring, he intended "to strike a blow that will rebound through India." Neill, as I have said, arrived on the 20th. He dined that evening with Havelock, and was informed that he intended to begin the passage of the Ganges on the morrow, leaving Neill in command at Kánhpúr with about two hundred men, the majority of whom were sick and wounded. In this arrangement, Neill,

Havelock announces his intention to march to relieve Lakhnao.

Book IX. Chapter III.

1857. July 20.

anxious that Havelock should take with him every available man, entirely concurred.

He traces out a position on the Kánhpúr side.

Before deciding on making a desperate effort to relieve Lakhnao General Havelock had traced out a position resting on the river, which it would be easy for a small force to hold against very superior numbers. The work was being intrenched and some guns were being mounted there at the time of Neill's arrival. He was to complete and to hold it.

Havelock crosses into Oudh.

The morning of the 21st set in rainy—the heavy rain of the Indian monsoon—but the preparations had been made the evening before, and, in the presence of Havelock's determination to push on, nothing would have stayed them. That day the artillery and a portion of the 78th Highlanders passed over to the opposite bank. To cross the Ganges in the height of the rainy season is no easy matter. The breadth of the swollen river, the rapidity of the current, alone present formidable obstacles. Fortunately, the General had at his disposal a small steamer. To this steamer he caused to be attached five or six of the boats peculiar to the country, and these she towed across —with difficulty; for it was all she could do to hold her own against the current.

Takes no *impedimenta* with him.

It will easily be understood that, under the circumstances stated, and although the force destined for the expedition numbered little more than fifteen hundred men, and although they took with them no tents of any kind, the operation should be tedious. It occupied just four days. On the afternoon of the 24th, General Havelock crossed likewise, and marched the force about five miles on the Lakhnao road, halting for the night at the little village of Mangalwár.

Book IX. Chapter III.

1857. July 21.

Constitution of his force.

The force which was now starting on an expedition, which, however desperate it was, seemed at the time to present, under so daring a leader as Havelock, some chance of success, consisted of artillery—ten guns, imperfectly equipped and imperfectly manned; of infantry—the remnants of the 64th, the 84th, the 78th, the Madras Fusiliers, and of Brasyers' Sikhs; and of cavalry, some sixty volunteer horse. Small as were their numbers they were animated by the best spirit, and had unbounded confidence in their General.

His first bivouac at Mangalwár.

On the night of the 24th of July this force bivouacked at Mangalwár. It remained halted at that village four days, to enable the General to complete his dispositions for carriage and supplies. On the 28th these had been made so far as, in the disorganised state of the country, it was possible to make them. At 5 o'clock on the morning of the 29th the force began its onward movement.

Makes a decided advance.

After marching three miles the advanced pickets of the enemy were discerned. These fell back as our men still pressed on, and disclosed the enemy occupying a very strong position. Their main force rested on the town of Onáo, a straggling place, extending about three-quarters of a mile, and which the heavy rains and the nature of the soil rendered it impossible to turn on either side. In advance of this town, and between it and the British force, was a succession of walled enclosures, filled with skirmishers. These joined

Finds the rebels occupying Onáo.

Book IX. Chapter III.

1857. July 29.

themselves on to a village, united with Onáo by a narrow passage, and all the houses in which were loop-holed and occupied. The narrow passage referred to was also commanded by loop-holed houses on either side of it, whilst the enemy had placed their batteries so as to pour a concentrated fire on troops advancing against the town.

Strength of the position.

Havelock is forced to attack it in front.

It was impossible to turn such a position; it was murderous work to attack it in front. But if he was to get on at all Havelock had no option. The simple motto of "move straight forward," embodying a principle which has never failed when tried by British troops against Asiatics, must be adopted. After a steady reconnaissance, then, Havelock gave his orders. Covering his main body with skirmishers, armed with the Enfield rifle, he opened a heavy fire from them and from his guns on the more advanced positions of the enemy. This fire drove them from those positions and forced them to take refuge in the loop-holed houses. At these Havelock then sent the 78th Highlanders and the Madras Fusiliers. Gallantly did they advance. But to dislodge an enemy from loop-holed houses, singly, one after another, is deadly work. So our men found it. Havelock, therefore, ordered up the 64th. Their advance decided the day. The enemy were either bayoneted in the houses or sought refuge in flight.

His first success.

He manœuvres to be attacked.

But the town of Onáo was still in the enemy's possession, and, what was of more consequence, fresh troops were observed hastening down the Lakhnao road in its direction. Havelock at once

Book IX. Chapter III.

1857. July 29.

made preparations to meet them. Drawing off his force on to a spot of dry ground between the village and the town, he placed his guns in a position to command the high road, by which alone he could be attacked, and waited for the movement of the enemy further to develop itself. In a short time it was manifest he would be attacked. They were marching in dense masses upon him. Havelock's joy was great. He felt that he had them. Restraining his impatience till they were well within distance, he suddenly opened upon them from both arms a withering fire. It stopped them. They attempted to deploy. But on either side of them were swamps and marshes. Consequently, their horses and their guns stuck fast, their infantry floundered. All this time they were exposed to a continuous fire. Being what they were they did not then make the one movement, a straight rush, which might have saved them. Meanwhile, some of our men, wading in the marshes, made their presence perceptible on either flank. That was the final blow. The rebels gave way, and fled precipitately, leaving in our possession fifteen guns.

Success of his manœuvre.

In one of his letters written during his advance on Kánhpúr, I think it was just after the battle which gave him that place, Havelock remarked that viewing his position, he suddenly recollected "old Frederic at Leuthen," and acted accordingly. Probably no man had more completely studied the campaigns of that great master in the art of war, as well as those of his immediate successor in the roll of Fame. If he had learned from

He determines to follow up the blow.

Book IX. Chapter III. 1857. July 29.

Frederic the mode in which to turn to his own advantage a false position occupied by himself he ever adhered strictly to the Napoleonic maxim of promptly following up a victory. He could not at Onáo put into execution this maxim in the manner which would have gladdened his heart—for to carry it out efficiently a general has need of cavalry, and Havelock had but sixty sabres. But he could and he did work it in the only way open to him. Notwithstanding that he and his men were under the terrible July sun of India, he determined to push on after the enemy as soon as his men should have satisfied the cravings of exhausted nature. He ordered, then, a halt; and while the cooks prepared the food, and the doctors attended the wounded, he caused to be disabled the fifteen guns he had captured, for want of cattle to take them with him!

Gives his men their food;

At the end of three hours the men again fell in, and pushed forwards—always towards Lakhnao. They had marched six miles, when suddenly they came in sight of a walled town, situated in the open, and intersected by the road which they must traverse. This was the town of Bashíratganj. It looked very formidable. In front of it was a large pond or tank, swollen by the surrounding inundation to the form of a river. On the Lakhnao side of it was another pond or lake, traversed by a narrow causeway. It possessed besides a wet ditch, and its main gate was defended by an earthwork and four guns, and flanked on either side by loop-holed turrets. Havelock halted his men, while he rode to reconnoitre. The scheme that

and pushes forwards.

Finds the enemy in force at Bashíratganj.

1857. July 29.

his brain then conceived was very daring. But it had this great merit that, if successful in every detail, the enemy would be destroyed. He conceived in a word the idea of amusing the enemy with a cannonade, whilst he should send the 64th to cut off the enemy from the causeway. When he should consider that movement sufficiently pronounced, he would storm the town with the 78th and the Madras Fusiliers, and catch the enemy between two fires. He succeeded in all, except in the most decisive of his combinations. He poured a tremendous fire on the town, whilst the 64th made a flank movement to his right; then, when he deemed the moment to have arrived, he sent on his remaining infantry at the main gate. But—one of the chains in his scheme had snapped. The 64th had not reached the causeway—and the main body of the enemy escaped across it.

Endeavours, while attacking in front, to cut them off.

Forces the position, but fails to cut them off.

Still their loss that day had been severe. It was computed that not less than four hundred of them had been killed or wounded. On the British side eighty-eight had been placed *hors de combat*—but two battles had been gained!

Result of the day's fighting.

But the thoughts of the General that night were not consoling. It was not alone, or even mainly, that his losses in the fight had been heavy. Sickness also had done its work. On the morrow of the two battles he could not, deducting the necessary guards, place in line more than eight hundred and fifty infantry. He knew that in front of him were places to be traversed or stormed, the means of defence of which exceeded those of

Considerations which forced themselves upon his notice.

Book IX. Chapter III. — 1857. July 30.

the places he had already conquered. Then, he had no means of carrying his sick. He could not leave them. He could not leave behind a sufficient force to guard them. But perhaps his strongest difficulty lay in the fact that every step forwards would take him further from his base, and he had information that that base was threatened. Náná Sáhib, in fact, had no sooner heard of the onward move of the British, than he sent a considerable body of cavalry across the river to cut off their communications with Kánhpúr.

Such arguments as these were sufficient to make even Havelock hesitate. But with them came the other consideration,—the possibility, notwithstanding all these obstacles, of success.

Dominating force of those considerations.

But he could not help putting to himself this pertinent question:—What sort of success would it be? If, on the morrow of his first march he could bring only eight hundred and fifty infantry into line, how many would he be able to muster on the morrow of the fourth? This question was answered by the General's own Quartermaster-General in a telegram sent to the Commander-in-Chief. "We could not hope to reach Lakhnao," telegraphed Lieutenant-Colonel Fraser Tytler, on the 31st, "with six hundred effective Europeans; we had then to pass the canal, and force one and a half mile of streets"—and this in face of some thousands of trained and disciplined soldiers, and an armed and countless rabble!

Havelock falls back on Onáo.

I do not think the soldier lives who would fail to justify the resolution at which Havelock arrived

Book IX. Chapter III.

1857. July 30.

the following morning, to fall back on Mangalwár, and to ask for reinforcements. From Mangalwár it would be possible to send the sick and wounded to Kánhpúr without permanently weakening his force. He effected this movement the following day without haste, and in the most perfect order. He did not march before 2 P.M. and then retired only to Onáo. The following morning (31st) he fell back on Mangalwár. Thence he despatched his sick and wounded into Kánhpúr, and a letter to General Neill, stating that he had been forced to fall back, and that to enable him to reach Lakhnao it was necessary that he should receive a reinforcement of a thousand men and another battery of guns.

Neill at Kánhpúr.

Neill received this letter the same day. He had assumed command at Kánhpúr on the 24th, and in a few hours the troops there had felt the effect of his vigorous and decided character. Neill was a very remarkable man. By the law of desert he stands in the very front rank of those to whom the Indian mutiny gave an opportunity of distinction. It is impossible to put anyone above him. Not only did he succeed in everything he undertook, but he succeeded when the cases were all but desperate. He succeeded because he dared; because he threw into all he attempted the energy of one of the most determined characters ever bestowed on man. Such a man could not fail and live. His whole soul was in his profession. He had made his regiment, the Madras Fusiliers, equal to any in the world. At Banáras he had, by his vigour and decision,

Character of Brigadier-General Neill.

Book IX. Chapter III. 1857. July 24.

crushed an outbreak, which, had it been successful, would have raised all the country to the north-west and to within a hundred miles of the capital. The same qualities displayed at Alláhábád had saved that important fortress. In the moment of success, when men had begun to stake all their hopes on his advance to Kánhpúr, he was suddenly superseded by Havelock. And now, second to that general, he was at Kánhpúr commanding there a few invalids, with the commission to finish the fortified work on the river, to erect *têtes de pont*—so that on the subsiding of the waters a bridge of boats might be established—and to send on to his senior officer all the reinforcements in men and material he might receive.

It displays itself in vigorous action.

Neill, I have said, assumed command on the 24th of July. He had been but ill-satisfied with the state of affairs, as he found them, at Kánhpúr. The location of the troops appeared to him faulty; the camp pitched without method or arrangement; no effectual steps taken to put a stop to the plundering in the city—a plundering carried on by our European and Sikh soldiers.* But on the 24th he was master and could remedy these evils. His first act on the 25th was to appoint a superintendent of police; to re-establish authority and order in the city and bazaars; to put a stop to plundering. He announced his assumption of command, and notified the carrying out of the measures above stated in a telegram the same

* *Private Journal of Brigadier-General Neill*, unpublished.

Book IX. Chapter III.

1857. July 25.

day to the Commander of the Forces, Sir Patrick Grant. The spirit of the man showed itself in the all but concluding words of this telegram: —"All well here. I will hold my own against any odds."

Boldness of his resolves.

He was a bold man who would thus write under existing circumstances. Not only was Neill aware that Náná Sáhib, distant from him but twenty-four miles, was threatening to cross the river and to attack him, but he had received information that the mutinous 42nd Native Infantry were within eight miles of the station, and that other native regiments were gradually collecting on the right bank of the Jamná with the avowed intention of making a dash on Kánhpúr. But Neill was not disturbed. "If the 42nd are within reach," he recorded in his journal on the 30th, "I will deal them a blow that will astound them." With the levies of Náná Sáhib he did deal. On the 31st he despatched a party of fifty Fusiliers and twenty-five Sikhs, with two 6-pounders and a $5\frac{1}{2}$-inch mortar, manned by six gunners, under the command of his aide-de-camp, Captain John Gordon, of the 6th Regiment N. I., in the steamer to Jájamao, to seize the boats in which it was reported Náná Sáhib intended to cross the river. The party destroyed several boats, carried off six or eight, and returned to Kánhpúr the next day.

Sends Captain John Gordon to clear the river.

Neill meanwhile had been receiving small reinforcements. He was daily expecting half a battery (Olpherts's), with which to reinforce Havelock; but unfortunately there was a deficiency of gunpowder—and no gunpowder could be ex-

Book IX. Chapter III.

1857. July 30.

Considerations which influenced Neill;

pected for a week. Under these circumstances, and in view of the one fact that on the 30th he received from General Wilson, commanding before Dehlí, a letter intimating that it might be necessary for him to retire on Karnál, and of the other that his own position was threatened from the west, it became more than ever necessary to show a bold front, and even, whenever feasible, to strike a blow. The one thing necessary for the success of Neill's views in this respect was that Havelock should continue to move successfully on to Lakhnao.

and which made him regard with dismay the retirement of Havelock on Onáo.

This being the case, and the character of the man being considered, some idea may be conceived of the fury which seized him when he received, on the night of the 31st, a letter from General Havelock, informing him of his retrograde movement, and that he could not advance until he should receive a reinforcement of a thousand European infantry and another battery of guns. A second letter merely asked for all the infantry that could be spared and half a battery. With the demand for guns came, too, the information that of the fifteen pieces taken from the enemy every one had been destroyed. "Our *prestige* here is gone," records Neill in his journal. The letter from General Wilson was bad enough,—but that was only a possibility—it might not happen. But this retirement, the death-blow to all his hopes, had actually occurred. Who, he asked himself, was to blame for it? He did not take long to answer. He had no love for Havelock. He had felt deeply the slight, as he considered it, that he, the second in

Book IX. Chapter III.

1857. July 31.

command, had not been invited to assist at the councils of war which had been held; that although asked to communicate unreservedly with Havelock, he had been told to address his Adjutant-General. These things had chafed him. And now this retreat had come to upset all his calculations. He could not restrain himself. He had been asked to communicate "unreservedly" with Havelock through his staff. He determined to write "unreservedly" direct. He did so.*

Communicates his opinions to Havelock,

* The following is the text of the most salient part of Neill's letter:—"I late last night received yours of 6 p.m. yesterday. I deeply regret you have fallen back one foot. The effect on our prestige is very bad indeed. Your camp was not pitched yesterday before all manner of reports were rife in the city—that you had returned to get more guns, having lost all you took away with you. In fact, the belief amongst all is that you have been defeated and forced back. It has been most unfortunate your not bringing any guns captured from the enemy. The natives will not believe that you captured one. The effect of your retrograde movement will be very injurious to our cause everywhere, and bring down upon us many who would otherwise have held off, or even sided with us. The troops at Gwáliár have marched, whether to this or Ágra is not yet known. The troops collected at Fathgarh will very soon follow. They are now joined by the 42nd N. I., which have passed on. I could not move out and intercept them. . . . You talk of advancing as soon as reinforcements reach you. You require a battery and a thousand European infantry. As regards the battery, half of Olpherts's will be in this morning; the other half started yesterday or to-day from Alláhábád. This will detain you five or six days more. As for the infantry you require they are not to be had, and if you are to wait for them Lakhnao will follow the fate of Kánhpúr. Ágra will be invested: this place also: the city will be occupied by the enemy. I have no troops to keep them out, and we will be starved out. You ought not to remain a day where you are. When the iron guns are sent to you, also the half battery, and the company of the 84th escorting it, you ought to advance again, and not halt until you have rescued, if possible, the garrison of Lakhnao. Return

Book IX. Chapter III.

1857. August 2.

and is rebuked and makes an *amende*.

Havelock replied in the indignant tone which might have been expected. By this time the first burst of Neill's anger was over, and the rejoinder he sent to Havelock's reply was pronounced by the high authority to which it was referred—the acting Commander-in-Chief, to be "perfectly unexceptionable." The matter was then allowed to drop, but the correspondence had produced between the two generals a coolness which, whilst it did not interfere with co-operation for the good of the State, could yet never be forgotten.

Havelock receives a small reinforcement,

On the 3rd of August Havelock was reinforced by Olpherts's half-battery and a company of the 84th. Hopes had been held out to him that the 5th Fusiliers and the 90th Light Infantry would reach Kánhpúr early in August. Had the Government of India only taken the precaution to disarm the native regiments at Dánápúr early in June, this might have been possible. But the fatal trust in men known to be untrustworthy had kept the 5th Fusiliers in Bihár and had

here sharp, for there is much to be done between this and Ágra and Delhí." In his reply, Havelock described this letter as "the most extraordinary letter he had ever perused." "There must be an end," he went on to say, "to these proceedings at once. I wrote to you confidentially on the state of affairs. You send me back a letter of censure of my measures, reproof and advice for the future. I do not want and will not receive any of them from an officer under my command, be his experience what it may. Understand this distinctly, and that a consideration of the obstruction that would arise to the public service at this moment alone prevents me from taking the stronger step of placing you under arrest. You now stand warned. Attempt no further dictation. I have my own reasons, which I will not communicate to anyone, and I alone am responsible for the course which I have pursued."

Book IX. Chapter III.

1857. August 4.

stopped the onward progress of the 90th.* This culpable weakness made itself felt in Lakhnao as well as in Bihár. But the disappointment only roused Havelock to renewed exertion. On the 4th of August, having then about fourteen hundred effective men under his command, two heavy guns (24-pounders), two 24-pounder howitzers, and a battery and a half of guns, he started a second time in the direction of the besieged Residency. Having heard that the town of Bashíratganj had been re-occupied in force he bivouacked that night at Onáo. Leaving that place early the following morning he found the enemy occupying a position very similar to that from which he had dislodged them on the 29th of July. This time he determined there should be no mistake; that if the enemy would only wait the completion of his turning movement, they should not escape. Havelock then ordered the advance by the road of the heavy guns, supported by the 1st Madras Fusiliers and the 84th Foot; whilst the 78th Highlanders, the Sikhs, and Maude's battery, should turn the village on its left. The heavy guns, commanded by Lieutenant Crump of the Madras Artillery, a very able and gallant officer, speedily dislodged the enemy from the outer defences. As they retreated our infantry advanced. Meanwhile the turning movement greatly disquieted them. They saw that if carried out it would entrap them. Bewildered by the

and renews his advance into Oudh.

He finds the enemy strongly posted at Bashíratganj.

Again attempts to annihilate them.

They flee in a panic,

* "So great is the alarm," wrote a journalist at the time, "that H.M.'s 90th and 5th Fusiliers have been retained, though grievously required to reinforce Káhnpúr."

Book IX. Chapter III.

1857. August 5.

progress it was making and much embarrassed by the firing in front of them they were stricken by panic and fled across the causeway. This flight saved them from certain and entire destruction. The turning movement had not been completed. Still it had advanced so far that in their flight across the causeway the enemy came under the fire of the guns of Maude's battery and were mown down in numbers. The heavy guns continued all this time their destructive fire, silencing the guns of the enemy and forcing them back. The rebels did indeed for some time longer hold villages to the right and left of the town, but in the end they were forced out of these.

and their position is gained.

Still, though the enemy was beaten, "the whole transaction," to use the language employed by Lieutenant-Colonel Tytler to Sir Patrick Grant, "was most unsatisfactory, only two small iron guns, formerly captured by us, and destroyed, in our ideas,* being taken."

Considerations which weighed at this conjuncture with Havelock.

The loss of our force had not been large. Two had been killed and twenty-three wounded. The loss of the rebels was estimated at three hundred. But there were weighty considerations to stay further advance. Cholera had broken out in the camp. This disease and fever had placed seventy-five men on the sick list. In the action at Bashíratganj one-fourth of the gun ammunition

* These were the guns captured on the 29th of July. General Havelock reported regarding them that they had been "dismantled by the Commandant of Artillery; so imperfectly, however, that the enemy again fired out of them."

1857. August 5.

had been expended. Between that town and Lakhnao, was a deep river, the Sái, and three strong places, guarded it was believed by 30,000 men. The zamíndárs, too, had risen on every side in bodies of five hundred or six hundred, independent of the regular troops. "All the men killed yesterday," wrote Colonel Tytler, "were zamíndárs." But even were the force able to reach Lakhnao what could it effect, enfeebled and worn out, against the myriads who would oppose it in the streets? On the morrow of the fight at Bashíratganj it was impossible to parade nine hundred infantry. To what extent would this number be reduced in fighting its way to the Residency?

Had he continued to advance his numbers would have been greatly reduced.

These were potent reasons against an advance, but there were others still stronger. Intelligence reached Havelock on the 5th that the men of the Gwáliár contingent had successfully mutinied against their own Mahárájá, and were threatening to move on Kalpí. Kalpí was a position which would threaten Kánhpúr, and menace the communication with Alláhábád. It is true that had it been possible to strike a decisive blow at Lakhnao the striking of it would have been the best reply to any demonstration on Kalpí. Not less true that a defeat involving a heavy loss to the force in an attempt on Lakhnao would precipitate any such demonstration. The intelligence regarding the Gwáliár force then brought home to Havelock for immediate decision the question of advance or retreat. The advance could scarcely be successful, and yet failure in it

Other considerations which influenced him.

Book IX. Chapter III. — 1857. August 5.

involved, in Havelock's opinion,* the destruction of his force, and with it, possibly, a disaster at Kánhpúr. Retreat only risked Lakhnao. But did not an unsuccessful advance subject Lakhnao to a risk even greater?

The action of Havelock justified.

No sensible man will deny that, under the circumstances of the case, Havelock exercised a wise judgment in deciding to retire and wait for reinforcements. He fell back on Mangalwár. He lay there for four days recruiting his men. On the 11th he purposed to recross into Kánhpúr. But learning that the rebels had established themselves in considerable force at Bashíratganj, with advanced parties at Onáo, prepared to disturb him while crossing, he resolved to anticipate them. For the third time, then, he advanced along the Lakhnao road, pushed the advanced parties of the enemy out of Onáo, and bivouacked near that town for the night. At dawn the following day, the 12th, he set out and found the enemy strongly intrenched behind earthworks in a village in advance of Bashíratganj. Covered by his artillery and skirmishers Havelock advanced in echelon of battalions from his right. The swampy nature of the ground delayed the advance of the heavy guns, and our troops suffered somewhat meanwhile from the enemy's fire. Our guns when in position opened on the earthworks, with-

He falls back on Mangalwár, but again advances in order to cover his passage of the river.

* "The only three staff officers in my force whom I ever consult confidentially, but in whom I entirely confide, are unanimously of opinion that an advance to the walls of Lucknow involves the loss of this force. In this I concur." —*Brigadier-General Havelock to the Commander-in-Chief*, August 1857.

out, however, making much impression. An infantry charge was, therefore, resolved upon. The 78th Highlanders precipitated themselves, without firing a shot, on the earthworks in front, while the Madras Fusiliers, to whom the turning movement had been entrusted, took them in flank. The result was decisive. Two of the enemy's guns were captured and turned on them. They fled in disorder, leaving about two hundred killed and wounded. Our loss amounted to thirty-five.

Book IX. Chapter III.

1857. August 12.

Beats the enemy at Bashíratganj and recrosses.

Having thus scared away the enemy Havelock leisurely fell back on the 13th, and by 2 o'clock of that day had recrossed into Kánhpúr without a casualty. His troops were taken over in the steamer and in country boats towed by the steamer, the current being still too strong to permit the putting together of the bridge of boats, materials for which had been prepared.

Action of Neill at Kánhpúr.

In his absence the gallant Neill had not been idle. The night of the 5th of August intelligence had reached him that a party of the mutinous 42nd Native Infantry, aided by some disaffected villagers, had plundered part of Bithor, and had sacked the house, and carried off the two daughters of Súbádár Narain Rao, a relative of Náná Sáhib, but who, throughout the mutiny, had been staunch in his allegiance to the British, and had suffered much persecution in consequence. Neill at once ordered a party, commanded by Captain J. Gordon, and accompanied by the Súbádár referred to, to set out at daybreak the following morning in the steamer for Bithor. Gordon started at 4 o'clock on the morning of the 6th, having under him forty

Again despatches Captain J. Gordon to clear the river.

Book IX. Chapter III.

1857. August 6.

men of the Madras Fusiliers, twenty-five Sikhs, and six gunners, in charge of two 6-pounders, and a $5\frac{1}{2}$-inch mortar. Passing Bithor, the roof of one of Náná Sáhib's houses was observed to be crowded with men. These were speedily put to flight. A party was then sent on shore to endeavour to recover the daughters and property of the Súbádár—the latter accompanying it. In both attempts success attended its efforts. The steamer, whose guns had meanwhile effected considerable damage on the houses and shipping of the rebels—sixteen boats having been sunk—picked up the Súbádár,* his daughters, and property—and reached Kánhpúr at 6 o'clock that same evening.

And again.

A third steamer expedition under the same officer, Captain Gordon, was organised for the 8th. The object this time was to intercept the troops of Náná Sáhib, who had begun the previous evening to cross the Ganges three miles above Bithor. The steamer, having on board the same number of troops as on the 6th, set out again at 4 A.M. Passing Bithor, a shot was directed at her from the shore. This was followed by a heavy musketry fire, and it soon became evident that the place was occupied by a strong body of the mutinous 42nd. The steamer returned the fire from guns and Enfields as she slowly moved

* "We then took on board the Súbádár and the Sikhs. The Súbádár was looking quite happy, having recovered his two little daughters. One of them (the eldest) is really a beautiful little creature, about eight years old. Some of the Súbádár's plundered property was also recovered, so he was in high glee altogether."—*Manuscript Journal of an Officer present.*

Book IX. Chapter III.

1857. August 8.

on, the sepoys following her, taking advantage of every scrap of cover for three miles. At this point the current was so strong that the steamer could proceed no further. The sepoys then took possession of a house on the bank and opened a heavy fire; but they were speedily shelled out of it. Captain Gordon, unable to make further way against the current, ascertained by other means that no troops were crossing, and then turned the head of the steamer down stream. But after passing Bithor, she struck heavily on a sand-bank. Fortunately this sand-bank was beyond musketry range. There the steamer remained all night. The following morning the enemy brought some guns to bear upon her, but the great strength of the current had enabled her to cut her way through the sand-bank during the night, and at daybreak she dropped down to Kánhpúr.

Neill parades his troops.

Captain Gordon had ascertained that the number of mutineers, regular troops, at Bithor, amounted to about two thousand. He made his report accordingly to Brigadier Neill. With a soldier's true instinct, Neill the next morning, marched about two hundred men and four guns about three miles on the Bithor road, passing the city on the way. This movement had the best effect. It gave confidence to our well wishers, and discouraged the rebels and their friends. It was repeated the following day and the day after.

Havelock re-assumes command at Kánhpúr.

I have already stated that General Havelock recrossed on the 13th. He at once assumed com-

Book IX. Chapter III.

1857. August 13.

mand. The meeting between the two generals was outwardly friendly; but it was impossible after the correspondence I have alluded to that there should be any real cordiality between them. At an interview on the following day Neill expressed to Havelock his opinion that his men were not then in a fit state to march on Lakhnao; that they required rest, and not to be unnecessarily exposed; that it was indispensable that the rebels at Bithor should be dealt with first. The private journal of Neill shows that he still held to his previous opinion, that in retiring after his first victory on the 29th of July, Havelock had committed an error which could not be redeemed until he had received large reinforcements. I cannot concur in this view. Subsequent events prove, I think, that it was not well founded. Indeed—considering the immense temptation to Havelock to advance, the pain which the issue of the order to retreat caused him, I cannot but regard his resistance to that temptation as the most heroic act even of his heroic career.

Havelock's resistance of the temptation to advance on Lakhnao justified by subsequent events.

Havelock allowed his troops to rest on the 14th and 15th. At 4 o'clock on the morning of the 16th, leaving only a hundred men under Neill in the intrenched camp, he marched against Bithor. The rebels at that place, now augmented to nearly four thousand, were composed of sepoys from the 17th, 28th, 31st, 34th, and 42nd Native Infantry; of the 2nd Regular and 3rd Irregular Cavalry; of Náná Sáhib's retainers and two guns. Havelock found them drawn up in advance of the castle of Bithor. Their position was strong, being defended

Book IX. Chapter III

1857. August 16.

Havelock marches against the rebels at Bithor.

by intrenched mud quadrangles filled with sepoys, and sheltered by plantations of sugar-cane rising high above the head. Two villages, one on either flank, and connected by earth-works, formed the supports of this position. The villages were strongly occupied. The enemy looked so formidable that Havelock resolved to avail himself of his great superiority in guns. He made his men lie down, whilst for twenty minutes he poured on the enemy a heavy fire from the artillery and Enfield rifles. The guns made, however, little impression on the quadrangles, and Havelock saw he must effect his purpose with the bayonet. Covering his infantry with the Madras Fusiliers, he gave the order for an advance. The quadrangles were rapidly approached, but when our men were within twenty yards of them, the men of the 42nd Native Infantry, dressed in their red coats, started up, and met them. Bayonets were actually crossed, and it was not till sixty of the 42nd had fallen that they retired on their supports between the two villages. Havelock cannonaded this position for a time, but the enemy's guns were so well served that he again sent on the infantry. Another desperate contest ensued. The enemy defended their guns with great spirit and were only driven from their position by hard fighting. Meanwhile a body of their cavalry, some two hundred strong, had made a raid on our rear, killed twenty or thirty camp followers, and carried off the mess property of the volunteers. This raid did not, however, affect the action. That was decided in front of Bithor by the defeat of the

The 42nd Native Infantry cross bayonets with our men,

and fight with great gallantry,

but are beaten.

Book IX. Chapter III.

enemy, the capture of his position, and the loss of his two guns.

1857. August 16.

the victory dearly bought.

Still, victory as it was, it was in every sense of the word most exhausting to the victors. In the 84th Regiment seven men died from sunstroke alone. The Madras Fusiliers lost five from the same cause. In killed and wounded we lost between fifty and sixty. The men were much knocked up from fatigue. They could not pursue the enemy, but bivouacked where they had fought. The next morning they returned to Kánhpúr.

Havelock, on return from his victory, finds himself superseded.

This was on the 17th. General Havelock found awaiting him on his return a copy of the *Calcutta Gazette*, dated the 5th of August, containing the nomination of Major-General Sir James Outram to the military command of the country in which he was operating. He learned, in fact, that he was superseded. He received this information from the *Gazette* alone. It was accompanied by no communication to break the news. He had the harsh and bald announcement only.

Reflections on the policy of judging only by results.

This, then, was the result of his splendid daring, of his victories against Náná Sáhib, of his strenuous efforts to reach Lakhnao! Supersession! A hard word to a victorious soldier! For though Havelock had failed to reach Lakhnao he had ever been victorious. Supersession! The first thought of a feeble Government when their hopes have not been entirely fulfilled! With what confidence could any man serve a Government which acted in this manner towards one who had shown, by his daring, his self-negation, his devotion, by his success wherever success was possible, that he had never despaired of the safety of his country. It was not in this way that Rome treated her generals. Terentius Varro carried rashness to its extreme when he fought Hannibal, yet, recognising the patriotism of his motives, Rome received Varro with applause. She thanked him for not having despaired of the fortunes of the republic. Havelock was opposed to no Hannibal, but he had fought against an enemy exceeding him in numbers, occupying chosen and well fortified positions, and animated by the energy of despair. Circumstances had forced him to emulate even Varro in rashness. He had been compelled to risk much, to put aside the prudent part of the regulations of the military science, to dare and to dare greatly. He had won all his battles. And if in the ultimate aim he had not entirely succeeded, it was to a great extent because the fatuous action of the Government of India with respect to the sepoys at Dánápúr had hindered the onward progress of the reinforcements by whose aid alone complete success would have been possible!

The policy of judging by results.

And he was superseded—without a word—by a simple announcement in the *Gazette*. Again was it apparent that success was the sole standard by which, in those troublous times, the Government judged their servants. Mark their action in this respect. At Dánápúr they threw on Major-General Lloyd the responsibility of disarming or of not disarming the sepoys. That officer took thereupon certain measures which were not successful. In consequence, the Government super-

Examples of the effect of that policy as pursued, without discrimination, by the Government of India.

Book IX. Chapter III.

1857. August 17.

sede him and announce their intention to bring him to a court-martial. At A'gra, Brigadier Polwhele fights a battle with the enemy, and though one result of that battle was the retirement of the enemy from A'gra, yet in the actual conflict he was beaten. The Government of India promptly remove him from his command. Mr. William Tayler saves the province of Bihár. Then, in the dire extremity to which that province is again brought by the action of the Government he issues an order which in its operation might, under certain circumstances, expose the Government to the chance of losing a few thousand pounds. Fortune brings on the spot a heaven-born soldier to avert that chance. Yet, because it had been incurred, Mr. Tayler is removed from his post and professionally ruined. Neill starts from Calcutta, achieves great things at Banáras and at Alláhábád. The Government of India are impatient for him to march on Kánhpúr. But the mutiny has caused confusion in every department. Supplies have to be stored; carts to be collected; elephants, camels, and bullocks, to be brought in—and this when the whole civil organisation of the country is out of gear. Neill, aided nobly by the civil authorities, completes all his arrangements. At last he is on the point of moving. But there has been some delay—necessary delay—yet delay. The very day he telegraphs he is about to move on he learns that he has been superseded by Havelock. He, labouring, perspiring, taking no rest night or day, displaying an energy that acts as inspiration to all around him, has not yet been sufficiently expeditious for the occupiers of the gilded saloons of Calcutta. Again, the test of results is applied. Neill makes way for Havelock. And now, under the influence of the same test, Havelock gives way to Outram.

The distinguishing characteristic of Englishmen,

It is one of the glories of our countrymen that, however acutely they may feel a disappointment of this nature it never affects their public conduct. It is this recognition of, and this devotion to, duty that stamp the Englishman. He subordinates to it all private feelings. He may be keenly sensible of the injustice perpetrated towards himself, but above himself is always his country. He may have his own views as to how that country may best be served —but when the Government which represents it has other and different views he feels bound to devote all his energies to make possible of success the orders of the Government. Thus acted Neill. And now, thus also acted Havelock. Superseded as he regarded himself to be, he was as active, as daring, as devoted, as when he ruled the unfettered commander of an independent force. Never indeed was the exercise of the great qualities of resolution and energy more necessary than after his return from the expedition against Bithor. Out of seventeen hundred English troops whom he had had altogether under his order from the time of his quitting Alláhábád but six hundred and eighty-five remained effective. Not only was he now compelled to abandon for the moment all idea of

is eminently conspicuous in Havelock.

Difficulties and dangers of his position.

Book IX. Chapter III.

1857. August 17.

recrossing into Oudh, but the action of the Gwáliár contingent threatening Kalpí rendered it doubtful whether he could even hold Kánhpúr. Kalpí once occupied by this force, consisting of five thousand disciplined men with thirty guns, and his communications with Alláhábád might at any moment be cut off. To the north, the Nawáb of Farrakhábád was ready with thirty thousand men—some sepoys, some raw levies—to take advantage of any difficulty which might threaten Kánhpúr. It was, too, in the power of the rebels in Oudh to cross the Ganges at any point below Kánhpúr, and acting singly, or co-operating possibly with the Gwáliár troops, to endanger his communications. Of all these dangers Havelock had the fullest cognizance. Yet his judgment was never clouded. To remain at Kánhpúr was undoubtedly a risk, but to fall back on Alláhábád would have been a calamity. Not only would he have lost by such a movement the *prestige* and the material advantages his victories had gained, but such a movement would have had the effect of uniting against him the now divided enemies, and of placing them, with more means at their disposal, in a position stronger than that from which he had dislodged Náná Sáhib. His central position, faulty as it was in a military sense, gave him an immense moral power. He resolved to hold it as long as possible. He announced, then, to the newly-arrived Commander-in-Chief, Sir Colin Campbell, that if hopes of reinforcements were held out to him, he would, in spite of the very threatening aspect of affairs, continue to hold

He faces them with calmness and resolution.

Book IX. Chapter III.

1857. Aug. 17–20.

Kánhpúr; that otherwise he should be forced to retire on Alláhábád. The reply of Sir Colin on this head was re-assuring. Reinforcements were on their way. Havelock resolved to await them at Kánhpúr.

He resolves to hold Kánhpúr.

The month that intervened between the battle of Bithor and the arrival of Sir James Outram was rich in events, which, if not showy, were important. On the 20th of August, the indefatigable Captain Gordon had again been sent on an expedition in the steamer. This time he was to proceed down the river and destroy some sixty-two boats belonging to the Oudh rebels, said to have been collected opposite Rájghát, in the Fathpúr district. The operation was one most necessary to be carried out, for it was by these boats that the Oudh rebels might hope to cross the river and operate on our communications with Alláhábád. Gordon, taking with him one hundred men of the Madras Fusiliers, twelve artillery-men, twelve Sikhs, and three pieces, started on the 19th. On the way down the river, hundreds of horse and foot were noticed collected on the Oudh side opposite the intrenched camp of the British. The steamer was fired at from more than one fort on the way down. The expedition may be pronounced successful, for the party on board the steamer managed in four days to destroy thirty-five boats of various sizes.

Captain Gordon again sweeps the Ganges.

Arrangements meanwhile were made and carried out for sending all the sick and wounded who could bear the journey to Alláhábád. Reinforcements gradually arrived in small parties; the

Preparations at Kánhpúr.

Book IX. Chapter III.

1857. August 20.

troops were allowed to rest after their fatigues; the regulations for the maintenance of public order were rigorously enforced; the works at the intrenchment were pushed on. In all these works the co-operation of the civil authorities, at the head of whom was Mr. Sherer, C.S., was of inestimable value. Our countrymen had the gratification likewise of welcoming fugitives from various parts of the country. On the 1st September, Mr. and Mrs. Probyn and family, Mr. Edwards and Mr. Jones, came in from Oudh. "They looked so joyous and happy after their sufferings."* On the 4th, eleven more (Eurasians) came in from Kalpí, their release having been negotiated some time before by General Neill with the Rájá of that place. To keep the men in spirits, games and races were instituted every evening; there were occasional theatrical performances, and a band constantly played.

Neill is appointed to command the right wing of the relieving force.

The feeling entertained by Neill towards Havelock had never been very cordial. The two men were not formed to act together. Neill had chafed much under the inaction to which since Havelock's arrival he had been subjected, and he had greatly feared that in the advance which was to take place, he would again be left behind. His gratification then may be imagined when, on the eve of Outram's arrival, Havelock informed him that the command of the right wing of the relieving force had been conferred upon him.

Sir James Outram arrived at Kánhpúr on the

* Brigadier Neill's Journal.

1857. August 20.

Sir James Outram.

15th of September. If there were anything in the world which could reconcile a successful soldier to supersession it would be to be superseded by such a man as Outram. Sir James Outram bore the highest character. He was a paladin of the days of chivalry and romance. To a fearlessness which never recognised danger, to a nerve that never trembled, to a coolness that never varied, he added a generosity without stint, a forgetfulness of self rarely paralleled, a love of the soul's nobility for its own sake alone. Not idly had he been called the Bayard of the Indian army. He was without fear and without reproach. Engaged in many contests, he never fought for himself—he fought always the cause of those whom he believed to have been wronged. When a man so acts—when he gives himself, as it were, to others—the thought of self always flies. So it was with Sir James Outram. He gave all his energies to his clients. On their behalf he staked his prospects, his position, his future. He was appalled neither by the power, the talent, the interest, of the side to which he was opposed. He had emphatically the courage of his opinions, and, convinced of their soundness, he fought for them to the end.

In an earlier part of this volume * I have stated that Sir James Outram had arrived in Calcutta on the 1st of August. Four days later he was re-appointed Chief Commissioner of Oudh, and nominated to the joint command of the Dánápúr

* Page 133.

Book IX. Chapter III.

1857. Sept. 2.

and Kánhpúr divisions—a command including practically the entire country between Calcutta and A'gra. General Outram left Calcutta at once by river steamer, and after a tedious voyage up the Ganges, reached Alláhábád on the 2nd of September. He devoted three days to the necessary preparations. These made, he sent off on the morning of the 5th the 5th Fusiliers, some detachments of the 64th and the 1st Madras Fusiliers, and Major Eyre's battery of artillery—the same which, with a detachment of the 5th, had relieved A'rah—following himself the same evening with the 90th Light Infantry.

He arrives at Alláhábád,

and sets out for Kánhpúr.

Learns that the rebels are attempting to cut him off.

For the first three days the progress of the troops was uneventful. But on the fourth day, on arriving at the camping-ground of Kalógan, definite information reached Outram that a party of insurgents from Oudh, in number from three to four hundred, with four guns, had crossed the Ganges, near the village of Kúndanpati, on the trunk road between Fathpúr and Alláhábád. The object of this party was evident. It was to sever the communications between Outram and Alláhábád.

Despatches Vincent Eyre against them.

Outram at once sent orders to the advanced guard of his force to halt where it was. On joining it, he directed Major Eyre to march against the enemy. For this purpose, he placed at that officer's disposal one hundred men of the 5th Fusiliers, sixty of the 64th, all mounted on elephants, and two guns. Forty men of the 12th Irregulars were directed to join this detachment on its march.

Book IX. Chapter III.

1857. Sept. 10.

Eyre marches on the enemy,

Eyre set out on the 10th. On reaching, that same evening, the village of Hatgaon he was joined by Captain Johnsou and his forty horsemen (the 12th Irregulars). As these men had made a forced march of twenty-four miles to join him Eyre prudently resolved to halt for a few hours. By so doing he would refresh his men, and still be able to reach his destination by daybreak. He set out again at half-past one in the morning and came in sight of Khúndanpati at early dawn. The villagers whom he met reported the rebels to be close at hand, if not actually within the walls of the village, and that their boats were moored about a mile off. Eyre at once ordered his cavalry to gallop at once to the gates of the town,—to guard them should the rebels still be there—to pursue and hold them in check should they have evacuated it. Meanwhile he pressed on the infantry.

and crushes them.

The prudence of these dispositions was quickly justified. The rebels, learning almost at the same time of Eyre's approach, had already commenced a hasty retreat towards the river, and were entering their boats when the cavalry came upon them. The latter were just in time to prevent the unmooring of the boats. The infantry and artillery came up very soon after. Eyre at once gave orders to board. The enemy, crowded in their boats, made for some time an obstinate resistance. Seeing then that the day was going against them, they made a desperate attempt to blow up the boats and all therein. In one boat only was the attempt partially successful. Noting their failure, and resolved not to ask for quarter, they threw their

Book IX. Chapter III.

1857. Sept. 11.

guns overboard, and precipitated themselves into the river. Eyre at once drew back his men, and opened upon the enemy a grape and musketry fire the effect of which was decisive. Not a man surrendered—but only three escaped.

Eyre's decisive action defeats the plans of the rebels.

The effect of this decisive movement completely paralysed the plans of the mutineers. It was felt all over the Doáb. Another, and, it was estimated, a larger party, had landed some four miles higher up with the intention of co-operating with the men against whom Eyre had marched. But so great was the terror caused by his victory that they re-embarked and re-crossed into Oudh before the cavalry could intercept them. The movement, so skilfully planned and so vigorously carried out, had, in fact, relieved Sir James Outram from the danger, no light one, of having his communications cut off during the contemplated operations in Oudh.*

Outram arrives at Kánhpúr.

Thus secure regarding his communications, Outram continued his march, and reached Kánhpúr on the 16th of September. His very first act was of a nature so noble, so generous, so disinterested, that had it been the solitary glorious act of his glorious life, it would have sufficed to

* That this was the view taken by the General himself is clear from the despatch to the Commander-in-Chief, dated the 11th of September: "The importance of this success will, I am sure, be appreciated by your Excellency and the Governor-General. I now consider my communications secure, which otherwise must have been entirely cut off during our operations in Oudh. A general insurrection, I am assured, would have followed throughout the Doáb had the enemy not been destroyed, they being but the advanced guard of more formidable invaders."

1857. Sept. 16.

surround his name for ever with a halo of veneration and respect—an act so rare, so striking in its self-abnegation, that lesser and ignoble natures, unable to comprehend it, endeavour to seek for it a motive congenial to the temper of their own minds,—but yet an act essentially genuine — pertaining to the nature of the man — consistent with every previous act of his life.

He generously leaves to Havelock the glory of relieving Lakhnao.

Sir James Outram had been sent to Kánhpúr to command the force which was to relieve Lakhnao. In accepting that command he superseded the man whose daring efforts with an inferior force to effect that relief had won for him the applause and admiration of his countrymen. To the generous nature of Outram it seemed revolting that he should reap where another had sown; that he should obtain the glory where another had endured the trials and the dangers. He could not do it. He was determined that it should not be done. Availing himself of the circumstance that whilst, in a military point of view, he was commander of the forces about to march into Oudh, he would also enter that country in a civil capacity as its Chief Commissioner, he published, the day of his arrival at Kánhpúr, the following order:—

The order which he issued on the occasion.

"The important duty of relieving the garrison of Lucknow had been first entrusted to Brigadier-General Havelock, C.B., and Major-General Outram feels that it is due to that distinguished officer, and to the strenuous and noble exertions which he has already made to effect that object,

Book IX. Chapter III.

1857. Sept. 16.

that to him should accrue the honour of the achievement.

"Major-General Outram is confident that this great end for which Brigadier-General Havelock and his brave troops have so long and gloriously fought, will now, under the blessing of Providence, be accomplished.

"The Major-General, therefore, in gratitude for, and admiration of, the brilliant deed of arms achieved by Brigadier-General Havelock, and his gallant troops, will cheerfully waive his rank in favour of that officer on this occasion, and will accompany the force to Lucknow in his civil capacity, as Chief Commissioner of Oudh, tendering his military services to Brigadier-General Havelock as a volunteer.

"On the relief of Lucknow, the Major-General will resume his position at the head of the forces."

Sir Colin Campbell appreciates Outram's noble self-abnegation.

Rare and noble act of generosity! Only a soldier can appreciate the full extent of abnegation of self which it involved. Well might the illustrious warrior who then commanded in chief in India—well might Sir Colin Campbell, when announcing to the army this deed of real glory, write these glowing words: "Seldom, perhaps never, has it occurred to a Commander-in-Chief to publish and confirm such an order as the following one, proceeding from Major-General Sir James Outram, K.C.B.

Sir Colin Campbell's order to the army.

"With such a reputation as Major-General Sir James Outram has won for himself, he can well afford to share glory and honour with others.

But that does not lessen the value of the sacrifice he has made with such disinterested generosity in favour of Brigadier-General Havelock, C.B., commanding the field force in Oudh.

Book IX. Chapter III.

1857. Sept. 16.

"Concurring as the Commander-in-Chief does, in everything stated in the just eulogy of the latter by Sir James Outram, His Excellency takes this opportunity of publicly testifying to the army his admiration for an act of self-sacrifice and generosity, on a point, which, of all others, is dear to a real soldier."

Reflections on the act.

I cannot believe that there will be one amongst my readers who will grudge the time and the space I have devoted to the complete elucidation of this "act of self-sacrifice and generosity." The incidents of war often harrow the imagination. They bring to the surface many of the darker and the baser emotions of human nature. They show men to the world with their passions excited often beyond control, their worst feelings rampant and raging. This was especially the case with the mutinous sepoys, and with the rebellious population generally. It is a relief to turn from the contemplation of such incidents to a noble deed—a noble deed of a noble man—unsurpassed and unsurpassable of its kind—and which will have its record eternal as the language in which it has been chronicled.

General Havelock then remained commander of the force that was to relieve Lakhnao. He issued the same day an order acknowledging "the kind and generous determination of Major-General Sir James Outram, G.C.B., to leave to him the

Book IX. Chapter III.

1857. Sept. 16.

task of relieving Lucknow, and rescuing its gallant and enduring garrison," and expressing "his hope that the troops will strive, by their exemplary and gallant conduct in the field, to justify the confidence thus reposed in them."

Numerical strength of the relieving force.

The force now at Havelock's disposal consisted of three thousand one hundred and seventy-nine men of all arms.* He divided it into three brigades:—two of infantry, the third of artillery. The first brigade consisted of the 5th Fusiliers, the 84th Regiment, and, attached to it, two companies of the 64th, the 1st Madras Fusiliers. It was commanded by the gallant Neill.

The 2nd Brigade, composed of the 78th Highlanders, the 90th Light Infantry, and the Sikh regiment of Firozpúr, was commanded by Brigadier Hamilton, 78th Highlanders.

The 3rd Brigade comprehended Captain Maude's battery, Captain Olpherts's battery, Major Eyre's battery of heavy 18-pounders, the whole commanded by Major Cooper.

Besides these there were a hundred and nine volunteers, and some fifty-nine of the 12th Irregulars, believed to be faithful, under the command of Captain L. Barrow. Major-General Outram was one of these volunteers. To defend Kánh-

* The numerical strength of the component portions of the force was as follows:—

European Infantry - - - - -	2,388
Ditto Volunteer Cavalry - -	109
Ditto Artillery - - - - -	282
Sikh Infantry - - - - - -	341
Native Irregular Cavalry - - -	59
Total -	3,179

Book IX. Chapter III.

1857. Sept. 16.

púr during the advance on Lakhnao there remained the Head-Quarters of the 64th Regiment, under the command of Colonel Wilson.

The whole of the reinforcements had reached Kánhpúr by the morning of the 16th of September. It was decided, however, not to attempt the passage of the river till the bridge of boats should be completed.

Measures taken to en- the passage of the Ganges

The enemy, meanwhile, were on the alert. On the afternoon of the 17th, a party of their cavalry and infantry, with three guns, came down to the opposite bank to reconnoitre. Their appearance was the signal for the withdrawal to our side of a party of Sikhs who had been sent across to cover the formation of the bridge. Emboldened by this, a portion of their infantry crossed to an island, and under cover of the long grass found there opened a fire on the men working at the bridge. But a few round and shrapnell shot from our heavy pieces soon drove them away.

The bridge head on the opposite side was covered by a detachment of our men during the night, and on the 18th the bridge had so nearly approached completion, that it was resolved to make arrangements at once to effect a successful passage. On the 18th no enemy was to be seen on the opposite bank. That morning four guns of Maude's battery were crossed over to the island above referred to, and the 78th Highlanders and the 90th Light Infantry were marched to a position en the river bank to be ready to take immediate advantage of the completion of the bridge. Subsequently, part of the 90th and three

Book IX. Chapter III. — 1857. Sept. 18.

guns of Maude's battery crossed the river. At 11 o'clock the enemy brought down their heavy guns and opened fire on our men. Our guns answered. The cannonade lasted three hours, when it ceased almost as suddenly as it had begun.

The passage.

On the 19th the bridge was ready. Our troops crossed in the following order. The 78th Highlanders led. They were followed by the Sikhs of the regiment of Firozpúr, by the remainder of the 90th Light Infantry, by Olpherts's battery, by the 1st Madras Fusiliers, then Her Majesty's 84th and two companies of the 64th, the Volunteer Cavalry and Irregulars, then half of Maude's battery, in the order named.

First movements after the passage of the main body had been effected.

As soon as they had crossed the troops were formed into contiguous columns at quarter distance, and the 84th were ordered to lie down as they were in the line of the enemy's fire. Skirmishers from the 78th Highlanders were sent out at once to cover the line. General Neill's brigade was then ordered to take up a position on the right of the line and to drive the enemy from some sand-hills occupied by them about six hundred yards in advance. Neill immediately moved forward his brigade and attacked the enemy. They made a firm resistance but were driven from their position. Whilst the infantry fight was going on Olpherts brought up a half battery in splendid style and silenced the enemy's guns. The enemy slowly retired, and the cavalry having followed them up to observe, the force piled arms and laid themselves out for breakfast, pending the

Book IX. Chapter III.

arrival of the camp equipage. This did not reach the ground till past 3 o'clock.

1857. Sept. 20.

Passage of the heavy guns.

The next day was devoted to the crossing of Eyre's heavy guns. They were brought into camp by noon. The arrangements for the advance were then complete.

The advance on Lakhnao.

At half-past 5 o'clock on the morning of the 21st the force started on its arduous task. The second brigade, having Olpherts's battery attached to it, and with the volunteer cavalry on its reverse flank, led; the first brigade, with Maude's battery, followed; then came Eyre's heavy battery, escorted by the 5th Fusiliers, one wing leading, the other covering the rear; last of all, the 12th Irregulars under Captain Johnson. The pickets of the previous night formed the baggage and rear guards.

The enemy driven from Mangalwár.

On approaching the village of Mangalwár it became evident that the enemy were massed there in great strength. Havelock upon this took ground to the left, and deployed into line, having the volunteer cavalry on the extreme left. This manœuvre had scarcely been accomplished before the enemy's guns, five in number, opened fire. They had playing on the road one heavy gun defended by a breastwork. Our three batteries at once replied, whilst our infantry marched through the swamp to the hard ground from which they could act on the rear of the enemy. Just at this moment the rain came down in torrents. This did not affect our men, but before they could reach the road behind the village the enemy had evacuated it. A rapid pursuit ensued. It was most successful.

Book IX. Chapter III.

1857. Sept. 21.

The volunteer cavalry captured two guns, a set of colours, and an elephant, and killed about a hundred and twenty men. It was said in camp that five men had fallen to the sword of Lieutenant Havelock alone. Olpherts's battery, though newly horsed with but half trained horses, pushed on splendidly, doing great execution. As our infantry advanced they found the road strewed with shoes which the rebels had cast off to facilitate their flight. But fast as they ran our men followed to within musket-shot. This close pursuit drove the enemy helter-skelter through the village of Onáo without their making even an effort to defend it.

Our troops make a momentary halt at Lakhnao,

Our men halted for breath and a mouthful of food at Onáo. They stayed there but half an hour. Then, pushing on, they reached Bashírat-ganj—likewise abandoned by the enemy in their flight—and put up for the night in the *serai* or travellers' resting place—a very large building, capable of accommodating nearly the whole of the force. There was not a man not wet to the skin, for the rain had been of the pelting nature peculiar to the break-up of the rainy season. The baggage was some distance behind, but it came up two hours later, and afforded then to our men the luxury of dry clothes and a dinner.

and bivouac for the night at Bashírat-ganj.

The force had thus reached with but a skirmish the furthest point of Havelock's three brilliant inroads into Oudh. This time there was no talk of retreat. Yet, excited with victory, proud of their day's work as they were, the men were not unconscious that their greatest difficulties lay

Temper of the men.

Book IX. Chapter III.

1857. Sept. 21.

before them. But had those difficulties been ten times greater they were in the mood to overcome them. The end to be attained was the relief of their beleaguered countrymen—of those countrymen who for more than eighty days had held out against the hosts of the enemy. It was that enemy who now barred their onward progress. The pent-up determination of every heart found vent that night in the expressions of firm resolve that, be the resistance of the enemy what it might, it should bar the way no longer.

They recommence the onward movement.

The rain fell heavily next morning as Havelock's force left its night quarters at half-past 7, the first brigade leading. Every one was in the highest spirits, and, in spite of the pelting downpour, wetting to the skin, all stepped out gaily. No enemy was seen in front—a few cavalry only, at a safe distance, on the flanks. After a march of sixteen miles they reached the village of Baní. Baní was a strong and defensible position. To reach it a force coming from Kánhpúr had to cross the river Saí, here spanned by a long bridge built of masonry. After passing the bridge the road takes a turn to the right. The river was not fordable. Strong as was the position, the enemy neither used the advantages it offered to them nor opposed to our troops the smallest opposition. They even neglected to break down the bridge. Nor, although they had constructed two half-moon batteries on the Lakhnao side of it had they the spirit to use them. In a word, panic-stricken by our rapid advance, they abandoned the best chance they had of stop-

The rebels, panic-stricken, abandon defensible positions.

Book IX. Chapter III.

1857. Sept. 22.

The troops bivouac for the night at Baní.

ping us and evacuated their strongest position before even it had been attacked. Baní was but sixteen miles from Lakhnao. Havelock, then, in the hope of giving information of his approach to the garrison of the Residency, fired that evening a Royal salute. His men lay there for the night, their indignation aroused and their slumbers troubled by the constant sound of the booming of the cannon fired against their beleaguered countrymen.

The events of the following day, the 23rd, were certain to be crucial. Breakfast, then, was served out to the men before they started. But by half-past 8 o'clock they were on their way marching in column of subdivisions right in front. The rain had cleared off but it was very close and steamy, without a breath of wind.

They start again the following morning,

Since 6 o'clock that morning the booming of the cannon discharged against the Residency had ceased. This silence seemed to indicate that the enemy were massing their big guns to oppose the relieving force. Our men, however, unawed by the silence, pressed on with determined step. For some time no enemy was visible. But as they approached the A'lambágh infantry began to show themselves on their flanks, and it soon became apparent that the enemy were prepared to receive them at that walled garden. A party of cavalry was sent on to reconnoitre. They returned to report the enemy had six guns in position; that their left rested on the A'lambágh, their centre and right being drawn up behind a chain of hillocks.

but meet no enemy till they approach the A'lambágh.

Book IX. Chapter III.

1857. Sept. 23.

Havelock's dispositions for attack.

Havelock then halted his force, changed the order of the column from right to left in front, and brought up the 78th Highlanders and Eyre's heavy guns. These changes having been effected the British force moved on. No sooner, however, were they within range than the enemy's guns opened with round and grape shot. They must have studied the distance very carefully for their first shot knocked over three officers of the 90th, all of whom subsequently died. The casualties amongst the men and camp followers were likewise considerable. But these losses did not check the advance. Whilst the 78th, the 90th, and the remainder of the 2nd Brigade pushed quickly on to gain the open ground on which it could deploy, Neill, with the 1st Brigade, took ground to the left, passing through deep ditches, through swamps, and over heavy ground. On reaching the open he deployed his men in a position causing them to overlap the enemy's right. Meanwhile Eyre's battery on the road, and Olpherts's on the right, had opened out on the enemy. Maude's quickly followed. This fire had the effect of dispersing the rebel cavalry and cleared the way for the advance of our men. By this time the two brigades had reached open ground, had deployed, and were advancing, the 2nd on the front, the 1st enveloping the enemy's right. Neill led his men over very heavy ground and drove the enemy from several villages in succession. The key of the enemy's position, however, was the A'lambágh and the upper-storied buildings adjacent to it.

He drives the enemy from the A'lambágh,

Book IX. Chapter III.

1857. Sept. 23.

These the rebels defended with great resolution; but they could not withstand the assault made by the 5th Fusiliers. Advancing with the bayonet the men of this splendid regiment cleared the houses and stormed the position. The rebels then fell back to resume the contest on the morrow. Of the guns they had brought into action five were captured by the Volunteer Cavalry. One of these, however, in the darkness and confusion of the night, they recovered.

Having driven the enemy from the A'lambágh the force advanced to within sight of the domes, the minarets, and the gardens of Lakhnao. But the day's work had been hard—much still remained to be effected, and the General prudently determined to halt for the night. Accordingly he took up a position, placing the 1st brigade on the right, the 2nd on the left, of the road, Eyre's heavy battery on the road itself. Our men, however, had scarcely taken up the ground assigned to them and had halted, when the rebels who, up to that time, had been fleeing in desperate haste, suddenly stopped, brought up fresh guns, and opened a heavy fire on the regiments as they stood or lay in line. They occupied also in considerable strength a two-storied house, subsequently known as the Yellow house, and from it began a fusillade on our line. Just at this time the rain came down in torrents and our men were soon wetted to the skin. Havelock met this action of the enemy by drawing back his line out of fire, throwing his right on the A'lambágh and refusing his left. The movement was a difficult

advances, then halts for the night.

The enemy turn upon him.

Book IX. Chapter III.

1857. Sept. 23.

one, as darkness had set in, and the road was jammed with horses, elephants, bullocks, guns, and men. However, it was carried out. The 5th Fusiliers occupied the A'lambágh. The other regiments were more or less provided for, some occupying hamlets, some lying in the open. The Madras Fusiliers bivouacked in mud ankle deep; but they and the rest of the force "were as merry and jolly as possible.* The rain had ceased. The men had been greatly cheered by the news that reached them that day that Dehlí had been captured, and were in a humour to bear up against evils far greater than those they were encountering. They had shown their enthusiasm by loudly cheering Olpherts's battery as, led by that most daring officer, it had passed in front of the infantry line at a gallop to charge the enemy.

He contents himself with occupying a strong position for the night.

Fine temper of the men.

The force halted throughout the day of the 24th to prepare for the desperate deed of the morrow. During the day the position was further changed so as to remove the men entirely from the range of the enemy's guns, which nevertheless continued their cannonade. The enemy's cavalry likewise, creeping round to the rear, made an attempt on our baggage, but, after killing, by surprising them, some ten or twelve of our men, they were driven off. That night all the baggage of our men was stored in the A'lambágh and a guard of two hundred and fifty men was placed there.

The force halts during the 24th.

At last the day of trial dawned. General Have-

The advance on the 25th.

* MSS. Journal kept at the time.

Book IX. Chapter III. — 1857. Sept. 25.

lock, in consultation with Sir James Outram, had resolved to advance, not by the direct route to the Residency, but by another and more circuitous road skirting the Chárbágh canal. At half-past 8 o'clock on the morning of the 25th, the 1st brigade, headed by Maude's battery, with two companies of the 5th Fusiliers leading, moved off in column of sections, right in front. They had advanced but a short distance when a tremendous fire opened upon them. From the A'lambágh to the Yellow house before alluded to the advancing troops had to encounter a perfect storm of round and grape shot and a sharp fire of musketry. Vigorously pushing on they approached the enclosure called the Chárbágh and a village, both filled with the enemy. From these the musketry fire was very galling. Our men, however, dashed at the enemy, and expelled them.

The Chárbágh bridge.

The next point to be reached was the Chárbágh bridge, the only opening left into Lakhnao. This bridge was barred by an earthen parapet about seven feet high, stretching completely across it, and having in the centre an opening, overlapped on both sides by the walls of the parapet, through which it was possible for only one man to pass on foot. On this parapet were mounted six guns, two of them 24-pounders. To the right of the bridge, on the side by which the British were advancing, were some enclosures occupied by the enemy. On approaching the position the force halted; Maude brought two guns to the front and opened fire, whilst Outram, taking with him the 5th Fusiliers and the Sikhs, proceeded to drive the enemy from the enclosures on the right, with the view of bringing a reverse fire on the guns defending the bridge.

Book IX. Chapter III.

1857. Sept. 25.

An artillery duel ensues there.

The enemy, on their side, had not been slow to reply to the challenge given them by Maude, and for some time the artillery duel raged with great fury. In this the enemy had the advantage of numbers and position. They had heavy guns, and those guns were under cover. Maude had but two light guns, and they were in the open.

Maude appeals to young Havelock.

When the duel had lasted half an hour, it became evident that Maude could make no impression on the enemy. He had lost twenty-one men at the Yellow House, and others had fallen in front of the bridge. In his despair he appealed to young Henry Havelock, then standing by his side, to "do something." Havelock rode at once to Neill, who was standing on the opposite side of the road, and suggested to him that he should charge the bridge. But, in the absence of Outram, Neill conceived that he would not be justified in giving such an order until that general's turning movement should have made itself felt. Fraser-Tytler made a similar attempt, and with the same result.

Havelock's daring ruse.

Something, however, had to be done. Under these circumstances, young Henry Havelock, always bold, daring, and adventurous, imperilled his commission to carry out an idea which had flashed through his brain. Turning his horse's head, he galloped off in the direction of the post occupied by his father. After making the turn

Book IX. Chapter III.

1857. Sept. 25.

of the road, he halted, waited for three or four minutes, then galloping back to Neill, saluted him and said—as if bringing an order from the general, whom he had not seen—"You are to charge the bridge, Sir." Neill at once issued the order. Tytler and Havelock carried it across the road, formed up the men, and gave the order to advance.

Havelock and Private Jakes on the Chár-bágh bridge.

Arnold of the Madras Fusiliers dashed on to the bridge with the advance of twenty-five men, Tytler and Havelock accompanying them mounted. Tytler's horse was shot dead, and he was pierced through the groin. Every other man of the twenty-five, the mounted Havelock and a private named Jakes excepted, was shot down by a discharge from the enemy's six guns loaded with grape. Havelock, unable to pass the overlapping barrier of which I have spoken, sat in his saddle, his sword in his hand, calling on the men to come on. Jakes stood by his side loading and firing as fast as he could. The interval between their first touching the bridge and the arrival on it of the storming column was, probably, not more than two minutes, but it seemed an hour. Standing alone on the bridge, the two Englishmen—the daring officer and the gallant private—were exposed to a fire from all the neighbouring houses, every wall loop-holed, every window fortified by sand-bags, and every roof occupied. In the language of Outram, "they were the target for many muskets." Just at this moment, when the storming party was coming on, a rebel sepoy jumped on the parapet, within ten yards of Have-

Book IX. Chapter III.

1857. Sept. 25.

lock, and took at him a deliberate aim. The direction was true, but the musket threw high, for the bullet passed through the centre of the top of his hat. Havelock paid him back in truer coin. Returning his sword to the scabbard, he drew his revolver and shot him, as he was reloading, through the body.

The Chárbágh bridge is carried.

A few seconds later the Madras Fusiliers came up with a rush, swarmed over the parapet and through the gap, and carried all before them. The 78th Highlanders belonging to the 2nd brigade followed; and the captured guns were spiked.* The entry into Lakhnao was won!

Havelock determines not to force the main streets, but to turn them.

On the whole of the 2nd brigade closing up, the whole force advanced, but, in pursuance of the resolution already referred to, instead of moving straight on through the city, they took a turn to the right at the bridge, and pushed on by a very bad and narrow road along the outskirts. The troops pressed along this road, subjected here to but little opposition.

Two regiments detached to cover the rear.

The enemy, however, having made a demonstration on the rear of our force, two regiments were detached to cover the advance of the remainder, as well as to protect the heavy guns, the dragging of which over the heavy road was found both tedious and difficult.

* For his gallant conduct on this occasion, Havelock was recommended by Sir James Outram for the Victoria Cross. He had previously received it for his conduct at Kánhpúr. Maude also received the Cross for the persistent gallantry he displayed this day. "But for his nerve and coolness," wrote Outram, "the army could not have advanced." Private Jakes was killed later in the day.

Book IX. Chapter III.

1857. Sept. 25.

Progress of our men through the city.

This road gradually led into the outskirts of the city, and our men were forced to penetrate through narrow streets and lanes, every one of which seemed alive with the enemy's fire. Still the one way to win the day was to press on, and the men continued to dash forward, overcoming or disregarding every obstacle. Suddenly, however, they found their progress impeded by a most formidable obstacle. Before them lay a narrow bridge over a nullah with high banks on the opposite side. This bridge lay under the lee of the Kaisarbágh, partially commanded by the two guns posted there and by the muskets of the numerous enemy occupying it. Our infantry and our guns were forced to cross that bridge, and to cross it almost singly. The fire opened from the Kaisarbágh was tremendous. It happened, however, that a sheltered position was attainable on the other side from which the enemy might be fired at with advantage. Our troops, then, as they ran across the bridge took up this position, and opening a fire, to some extent covered their comrades. But the ordeal was a terrible one and many men fell at this point. Having passed this obstacle, the force re-united and halted under cover of some deserted buildings near the Chattar Manzil and Farídbaksh palaces.

Terrible obstacles in their way.

They gallantly surmount them.

Olpherts gains the Cross.

It was before this—before, indeed, the Chárbágh bridge had been carried—that Olpherts performed the gallant deed which gained for him the Victoria Cross. The 90th Light Infantry, led by Colonel Campbell, had been ordered to charge and carry a battery of two guns, strongly posted at the end

Book IX. Chapter III.

1857. Sept. 25.

of a street. They charged and carried it. Whilst they held the guns, Olpherts, who had charged with them, galloped back, under a severe fire of musketry, and brought up limbers and horses to carry off the captured ordnance. This was, in round numbers, the thirtieth time that this gallant officer had deserved the Cross he so nobly wears!

Outram proposes to halt at the Chattar Manzil till the rear-guard should rejoin;

To return. Darkness was now coming on. The rear-guard, with the heavy guns, the wounded, and the baggage, was behind, exposed to the fury of the enemy. In a consultation with General Havelock Sir James Outram proposed that the force should occupy the Chattar Manzil palace for a few hours to permit the junction with the rear-guard. The proposition showed judgment and prudence, for the Chattar Manzil was a strong position easy to hold, and virtually communicated, by means of intervening palaces, with the Residency. Had the suggestion been adopted the safety of the rear-guard would have been assured, and the entrance into the Residency enclosure could have been effected with comparatively little loss. But General Havelock considered that the importance of letting the beleaguered garrison know that succour was at hand outweighed every other consideration.

but accedes to Havelock's earnest desire to push on.

The troops again push on.

The troops, re-formed, accordingly pushed on. The houses in Khás Bazaar were thronged with the enemy. As our men approached the archway, a tremendous fire opened upon them. Neill, who was leading them, passed through the archway, then, suddenly pulling up his horse, he directed his Aide-de-camp, Gordon, to gallop back and recall a half-battery which had taken a wrong

Book IX. Chapter III.

1857. Sept. 25.

road. He remained there sitting on his horse, his head turned in the direction from which he expected the half-battery to emerge, when a sepoy, who had taken post on the arch, discharged his musket at him over the parapet on the top. The bullet entered his head behind the left ear, and killed him.

The death of Neill.

James Neill.

Thus fell one of the bravest and most determined men in the British army. Neill had only required opportunity to become great. Hating pedantry, cant, and circumlocution, he was essentially a man of action. In the early days of the mutiny, when everyone from highest to lowest seemed utterly abroad, Neill suddenly appeared on the scene, and by his prompt decision and quick energy had in a moment stayed the plague. He was a born warrior, very cool, very keen-sighted, and very determined. His military capacity must not be judged by his condemnation of Havelock's retreat from his first advance. He, I believe, under similar circumstances, would have acted similarly. But his judgment was clouded on this occasion by his personal feelings. He had felt deeply his supersession by Havelock, and he disliked him. Every one of his acts was marked by judgment, by a keen appreciation of the end to be attained. In a word, he was a noble type of the northern land that owned him. Though twenty-one years have elapsed since he fell the memory of him still lives, fresh and green, in the hearts of those who knew him—and who, knowing, loved and respected him—alike in India and in England.

1857. Sept. 25.

Undeterred by the loss they had sustained our troops pressed on through the Khás Bazaar, fiercely assailed by a musketry fire. Emerging from this, the sounds of cheering from the Residency enclosure suddenly gladdened the ears of the Highlanders and their comrades. Others of the advancing force, who had forced their way through other streets, appeared on the scene almost immediately afterwards, and took up the cheers most vociferously. Well, indeed, might their hearts swell within them! Those cheers were but the natural outburst of the sweetest feelings of which the nature of man is capable—the pleasure of aiding those in dire distress.

Our men, still pushing on, overcome every obstacle,

But they are not yet within the enclosure. The night was dark, and before our troops could enter it was necessary to make a way for them and for the guns. To displace the impediments at the gate of the Baillie Guard which had so long resisted the enemy's assaults caused some delay. But at last they were removed, and many of the victorious troops entered. Then ensued the scene which I have endeavoured faintly to describe in the last chapter.

and reach the gate of the Baillie Guard.

I have said that many of the victorious troops entered. The bulk of them, however, lay all that night on the ground between the Baillie Guard gateway and the Farídbaksh palace and rejoined their comrades early the next morning. There still remained the rear-guard, Of them, even in the morning, there were no tidings. At noon, consequently, a party was ordered out to support or to disengage them. This detachment, con-

They enter, some that night, some the following morning.

Sept. 26.

Book IX. Chapter III.

1857. Sept. 26-27.

The rear-guard.

sisting originally of two hundred and fifty men of the 5th Fusiliers, and Sikhs of the Firozpúr regiment, and subsequently reinforced by a hundred men of the 78th Highlanders under Captain Haliburton, and a hundred of the 32nd under Captain Lowe, the whole commanded by Colonel Napier, R.E.,* effected their junction that night with the rear-guard, who had forced their way to, and were holding, the walled passage in front of the Motí Mahal palace. The junction having been effected, the surviving sick and wounded were transported on the morning of the 27th along the river bank into the intrenchment.

The losses of the rear-guard.

A 24-pounder gun is recovered.

It then became a great object to extricate from the exposed position in which it had been left on the 26th, a 24-pounder gun, used the previous day against the enemy. It was scarcely possible to approach this gun, so heavy was the fire maintained on it. The attempt, however, was made by three daring men, Olpherts of the Bengal, Crump of the Madras, Artillery, and Private Duffy of the Madras Fusiliers. Crump, an officer of the most brilliant promise, was killed; but Duffy, by a display of combined daring and ingenuity, managed to fasten a rope to the gun in such a manner as to ensure its withdrawal.†

The gun recaptured, earnest endeavours were made to open out a road for the whole of the ordnance through the palaces to the Residency. At 3 o'clock on the morning of the 27th, the

* Now Lord Napier of Magdála.

† For this act, Duffy, on the recommendation of Olpherts, received the Victoria Cross.

whole force proceeded undiscovered through the enemy's posts, and succeeded in packing the heavy guns and waggons in the garden of the Motí Mahal. The garden adjoining, and which was held in force by the enemy, was then attacked and carried by detachments of the 90th, 32nd, and 5th Fusiliers, led by Colonel Purnell and Captain McCabe. From this point measures were taken to open a road for the guns through the palace, and by the 1st October every gun and waggon was safely lodged in the intrenchment.

Book IX. Chapter III.

1857. Sept. 27.

Such an operation as the relief of Lakhnao by so small a force could not indeed be effected, save at a heavy sacrifice of life. The actual loss, up to the 26th of September inclusive, in killed and wounded, amounted to five hundred and sixty-four officers and men. This does not include the casualties sustained by the rear-guard up to the morning of the 27th, amounting to sixty-one killed and seventy-seven missing. As the missing were sick or wounded men who had been intercepted or slain, the number of killed of the rear-guard may be counted as the total of the two numbers, or one hundred and thirty-eight. This would raise the entire losses of the relief operation to seven hundred and two, officers and men. Amongst the former was Major Cooper, commanding the artillery brigade. By his death the command of that brigade devolved upon Major Eyre.

The garrison are reinforced—not relieved—by

The force which had thus with such daring and persistent bravery reached the beleaguered Residency discovered in a few hours that they had

Book IX. Chapter III.

1857. Sept. 27.

Havelock's success.

reached that spot only to increase the number of the garrison. Means of transport for the combined force were absolutely wanting. Even had they the transport, was that force strong enough to escort the ladies and children in safety to Kánhpúr? These were considerations which pressed themselves on Sir James Outram, who had, on the 26th, resumed command. For the moment the result of the successful advance on Lakhnao was that more mouths were required to be fed—more lodgment had become necessary for the garrison. These were difficulties. But to meet and overcome difficulties is one of the natural tasks of a real man. How Sir James Outram met and conquered them I shall describe in the next volume.

Reflections on the defence—and on the successful advance.

There remained meanwhile to him, to Havelock, and to their gallant comrades the inspiring conviction that by greatly daring they had accomplished a feat unsurpassed in the history of war. The English traveller who shall visit Lakhnao may well pause, struck with wonder and admiration, as contemplating the narrow streets and lofty houses of the city, the size of the palaces, the extent of the walled enclosures surrounding them, he calls to mind that they were a handful of his countrymen who forced their way through those narrow streets, the houses filled with armed enemies; who beat down the opposition offered them by the foe in those walled enclosures;—to rush to the succour of other men, also countrymen, who, beleagured in a weak position—a position in a military sense not defensible

—had repulsed, during eighty-seven days, the incessant attacks of countless foes. Contemplating in turn the city and the enclosure he will be unable to resist the conviction that the relievers and the relieved were in very deed worthy each of the other. If he wonder at the possibility of a small force maintaining itself in the battered enclosure of the Residency he will equally doubt the power of repeating a feat such as that which Havelock and his soldiers accomplished. Both the one and the other were impossible had they not been done. That both were achieved was due to a combination of qualities which, on another field and on a different occasion, exposed our countrymen to the taunt that they never knew when they were beaten. The spirit that had animated Raleigh, that had inspired Drake, that had given invincible force to the soldiers of Cromwell, that had dealt the first deadly blow to the conqueror of Europe, lived in these men—their descendants. It was that spirit, born of freedom, which filled their hearts with the conviction that, being Englishmen, they were bound to persevere, bound to dare every danger, every discomfort,—to conquer. It was not simply the joy of battle—the *certaminis gaudia* which incited Attila* to con-

Book IX. Chapter III.

1857. Sept. 27.

* At the battle of Chalons Attila, observing the repulse of the attack of his troops on a hill which the enemy had succeeded in occupying before him, sent for the commanders of his divisions and thus addressed them: "After having conquered under my orders a great part of the world, you ought to know what sort of a man I am, and I cannot forget what you are. Let us leave to generals accustomed

Book IX. Chapter III. 1857. Sept. 27.

quest — that animated their hearts. Rather was it the conviction that they were struggling

to slumber on the bosom of peace encouragements of an ordinary character. War is your natural condition; vengeance your sweetest passion. For you a battle is a holiday; let us celebrate this one with joy. Behold your victims; sacrifice them to your glory; to the manes of your companions whom they surprised and killed. Here, courage has nought to fear from wile and artifice. These open plains can give cover to no ambush. All is open; all is assured to valour. And what is this army that you are about to fight? It is a confused mass of weak and effeminate nations, afraid of each other, hating each other, and who were tearing each other to pieces when the fear of your arms united them. Already, before the battle, they tremble. It is terror which has lent them wings to fly to that height. They repent already of having offered battle in the plains. They seek elevated ground to be out of reach of your missiles; they would like to hide themselves in the clouds. As for the Romans we know them already. I only fear the promptitude of their flight. Without awaiting even the first blow they are accustomed to fly before the dust raised by our horses' feet. Give them, then, no time to arrange themselves in battle array. Cast yourselves on their squadrons; then, without stopping to pursue your victory over them, charge the Alans, the Franks, and the Visigoths. They are those alone whom we have need to conquer; they are the nerves of the army; all the rest will fall with them. Think not that your individual fate depends on the enemy. No dart can reach him who is reserved by Mars to sing the song of victory. No dart can touch him who has to conquer, whilst he who has to die would meet his fate even in inglorious ease. Why should Fortune have given the Huns victory over so many nations unless it were to prepare them for the joys of this battle? Why should she have opened to our ancestors the Mæotic marsh closed and unknown for so many ages? . . . . If circumstances do not deceive me—here—here before us—is the field of which so many exploits have been the promise and the forerunners. For myself, I will be the first to launch my javelin against the enemy —let him die who shall refuse to follow Attila! (Si quis potuerit Attila pugnante otium ferre, sepultus est)." —Jornandès, *de Rebus Geticis*, c. 12.

for the right, that they were combating treacherous foes, that England looked to them for the vindication of her honour and for the safety of the trust she had confided to them, that inspired the defenders with dogged resolution—the soldiers who followed Havelock with an *élan* that was irresistible. The men whose great achievements, reflecting an eternal glory on their country, I have but faintly pourtrayed, all lived but twenty-one years ago. Some of them are with us still. Outram and Havelock and Inglis and Neill have passed away, but there are those why remain who emulated their example, and on whom the inspiration of their great deeds has not been cast away. There survive at least a Napier of Magdála, then the chief of Outram's Staff, and whose name and reputation have since become European; a Vincent Eyre, who carried into Oudh the daring and resolution that had saved Bihár; a Wilson who was the right hand of General Inglis at Lakhnao; a Lowe, who commanded the 32nd during the defence, and a Bassano who succeeded him, when wounded, in that command; a Havelock who gained his Victoria Cross at Kánhpúr, and who accompanied his father in all his great exploits; a Gordon, who was the trusted staff-officer of Neill. And there are many others. These men have been tried in the fire. They are representatives of those gallant soldiers from whose minds neither the assaults of an overwhelming enemy, the privations of scanty food, incessant watching, nor the terrible trials of climate, could obliterate the fact that

Book IX. Chapter III.

1857. Sept. 27.

they were Englishmen, and as such were bound to conquer—and who did conquer.

I leave them now, and with regret. But I leave them for a field not less noble. For I have to narrate now how it was that the imperial city of Dehlí succumbed to the army which had so patiently and so persistently assailed it.

APPENDIX A.

THE entire proceedings of the Bengal Government, in respect of the Wahábí fanatics of Patná in 1857, are so extraordinary that they merit distinct and special notice.

The principal facts are now matters of history, as Dr. Hunter, who had free access to the Government archives, has given a detailed and accurate account of these remarkable men in his work on "Our Indian Mussulmans."

From his pages it may be learned "that some years ago the great Wahábí prophet, Syad Ahmad, organised a regular system of apostolic successors; that two of the khalifs or vice-regents, Inayat and Wilayat Ali, had early established a character for themselves on the frontier as fanatical firebrands; and so far back as 1847 Sir Henry Lawrence sent them as dangerous characters to their homes at Patná, where security was taken from them for their future good conduct."

In 1850 they were again found "preaching sedition in the Rájsháhí district of Lower Bengal, and were twice turned out of the district"; and in 1851 the vice-regents, though bound by bond and security to remain at their homes in Patna, "were found disseminating treason on the Panjáb frontier."

And finally, in 1852, they "had established a regular organisation for passing up men and arms from Bengal to the rebel camp at Sittána."

But the most significant fact connected with this history

is that on the 9th of August 1852, only five years before the mutiny, the magistrate of Patná reported that "the rebel sect was on the increase in that city; sedition was openly preached by the principal inhabitants of this capital of a British Province. The police had leagued themselves with the fanatics, and one of their leaders, "Maulvi Ahmedoola (Ahmad Ullá), assembled 700 men in his house, and declared his resolve to resist any further investigation of the magistrate by force of arms."

Dr. Hunter then proceeds, "The British Government could no longer shut its eyes to the existence of a great treasonable organisation within its territories for supplying money and men to the fanatical camp on the frontier. During the autumn of 1852 Lord Dalhousie recorded two important minutes on the subject, and by the first he directed the internal organisation to be closely watched."

The above brief extracts from Dr. Hunter's able work, written under the most favourable auspices for the accurate ascertainment of the facts, is, I imagine, sufficient to prove to the satisfaction of the most incredulous that a dangerous confederation existed in the country; that the city of Patná was the head-quarters of the sect of Wahábís, and contained not only the two notorious vice-regents or khalifs, but at least one determined and desperate leader, even in the time of peace, sufficiently bold and powerful to defy the power and authority of the British Government.

And if it be inquired who this resolute traitor was, I may reply that he is the identical man whose arrest and precautionary confinement in 1857 by Mr. Tayler I have described at page 52 of this volume.

Such, then, briefly sketched, was the known and recorded state of Patná at the commencement of the mutiny and rebellion.

Lord Canning had only recently arrived, and was necessarily dependent on the Lieutenant-Governor of Bengal and his own secretaries for all important information.

It is fair, therefore, to assume that he was in ignorance of the character and antecedents of the Wahábí fanatics, their connection with Patná, the intrigues in which they had been detected, and, doubtless, of the open defiance with which Ahmad Ullá had resisted the warnings of the magistrate.

But what can be said to excuse, what can be imagined to explain, the ignorance, or, if not ignorance, the infatuation of the Bengal Government?

Mr. Halliday had been appointed Lieutenant-Governor of Bengal about 1853, but for years prior to his appointment he had been secretary under ex-officio Governors, and, as well is known, exercised all the powers, though not bearing the responsibilities, of Governor. Is it conceivable that he was ignorant of all the strange and important incidents above noticed?

Was not he well aware that the prophet's vice-regents had their homes at Patná, that security for their good conduct had been taken, that Lord Dalhousie, as ex-officio Governor of Bengal, had placed on record a minute regarding them?

There had been, as related in the first volume of this history, an organised attempt at Patná in 1845 to tamper with the British sepoys, which, had the Panjáb campaign ended in failure, would doubtless have been carried out.

And it must have been evident to Mr. Halliday, as it was to all intelligent observers, that Patná was the centre of intrigue and dangers.

In the face of these facts, when Mr. Tayler, from information received, and from his own observation of certain suspicious incidents, quietly arrested and placed under precautionary surveillance the notorious Ahmad Ullá and two other leaders of the Wahábí sect, Mr. Halliday, instead of even then admitting that he had at least directed his precautionary measures towards individuals of suspected character whose names were in the black books of the Government, coldly calls for the "proofs on which the arrest had been made," designating these men as the "Wahábí gentlemen," a complimentary appellation never before used in such a case, and evidently implying, though not openly expressing, disapprobation of the act of arrest.

Not even at that crisis did Mr. Halliday condescend to consult his records, or to communicate to Mr. Tayler the significant incidents regarding these men.

Though the archives of Government would have shown him that these very men had for years been under suspicion, bound by sureties not to leave Patná, and compelled to give security for good conduct; that Ahmad Úllá, their leader, had openly defied the authorities, not one word of warning or caution did he vouchsafe to the officers responsible for the safety of the province and the lives of the Christian residents.

But strange as was this neglect on the part of the Lieutenant-Governor, it might be overlooked or excused as an oversight, or, at worst, unintentional negligence, but for what subsequently occurred.

Not only did Mr. Halliday fail to give intimation to his representative of these elements of danger in the great city of Patná, but, with the palpable fact before him of the outbreak at Mírath, he endeavoured to lull the Commissioner of Patná into a state of false and dangerous security by officially informing him that he could not bring himself to believe that there was "any danger in Patná"; that the mutiny of the Dánápúr sepoys in the face of the European force was "*inconceivable.*"

And this opinion was recorded with respect to a city where eight years before a plot had been hatched by a band of conspirators; when cash had been distributed to the sepoys; a scroll discovered containing the names of one hundred of the principal families:—a city which was the head-quarters of the two notorious vice-regents of the great Prophet—in which Mr. Tayler himself two years before represented the existence of dangerous excitement.

But the acmé of delusion, if delusion, indeed, it was, which thus induced Mr. Halliday to cast aside the lessons of experience and deny the existence of danger where all the worst elements of danger notoriously existed, has not yet been reached. But some short time after Mr. Tayler's removal, when Mr. Tayler's successor, in a personal attack on Mr. Tayler himself, in which he endeavoured to distort and disparage that gentleman's measures, actually recorded his opinion that the Wahábí leaders, whom Mr. Tayler had placed under surveillance, were "innocent and inoffensive men," mere "bookmen," against whom there was "no cause of suspicion"; and again, that he was inclined to believe that Mr. Tayler had been induced by two native gentlemen, Dewán Mawla Baksh, the Deputy Magistrate, and Syud Wiláyut Ali Khán, a wealthy banker in the city, to arrest the Wahábís, because, from their special loyalty, they (the Wahábís) stood in the way of their own treasonable designs; Mr. Halliday, in spite of all his means of information as to the real facts, actually endorsed these fatuous opinions with his official approval, sent the letter of Mr. Samuels for publication in the newspaper, and circulated it to all the Commissioners in Bengal for their information and guidance, refusing at the same time to give publicity to Mr. Tayler's refutation.

What was the issue of this controversy? That the mutiny which Mr. Halliday held to be inconceivable took place I need hardly mention, but the exposure of the incorrectness of his opinions regarding the Wahábís was reserved for a future day. The story is like a novel. Seven years had elapsed; Mr. Tayler, driven by relentless persecution, had resigned the service, but was still in India. The Wahábí leaders, who had been released when the crisis had passed, were in high favour with Government; Ahmad Ullá had been honoured with official appointments, specially introduced by the Lieutenant-Governor to the new Viceroy in Calcutta, and was basking in the sunshine of official favour.

Suddenly, and with no previous notice or intimation, an officer arrived at Patná from the Panjáb. A clue had been discovered. With a warrant in his pocket he walked into Sadikpúr, the quarter of the Patná city where the Wahábís had their abode, entered, without being suspected, into Molwí Ahmad U'llá's house, and with the help of the police arrested the happy family all unprepared either for flight or resistance.

A series of judicial trials was then held by the distinguished Commissioner of the Panjáb, Sir Herbert Edwardes.

The result of these deliberate and impartial investigations confirmed in every respect Mr. Tayler's estimate of these dangerous and intriguing characters.

Ahmad-U'llá himself was subsequently tried at Patná.

The innocent and inoffensive bookmen, upheld by Mr. Samuels with the concurrence and approval of Mr. Halliday, were proved to be confirmed and deadly traitors; the injured Ahmad-U'llá was shown to be their chief leader.

It was proved that they had for years been deliberately plotting against the British Government, supplying our enemies on the frontier with men and money, and publicly preaching at Patná a crusade against the infidel.

They were convicted and sentenced to be hanged. The sentence was commuted by the High Court to imprisonment for life, principally on the ground that the Government, by its laxity, had in some sense encouraged their treason. They were banished to the Andaman Isles, where Ahmad-U'llá was under nominal confinement when Lord Mayo was murdered.

It is difficult to exaggerate the important character of this strange episode.

At a crisis of national peril we find two high officers both in different degrees responsible for the safety of a great province, the Lieutenant-Governor of Bengal and the Commissioner of Patná.

It was, I need hardly say, of the utmost importance that each should form an accurate estimate of the character and purposes of the people by whom he was surrounded and with whom he had to deal.

Mr. Halliday, the Lieutenant-Governor, with all the means of information on record before him sufficient to establish with certainty the dangerous character of the Patná Wahábís, deliberately endorsed the recorded opinion that they were innocent men, above suspicion, and officially circulated this declaration throughout his Government.

Mr. Tayler, the Commissioner, forming his opinions with difficulty, without any information supplied or hinted at by the Government, acting on his own observation of passing events, his acquaintance with Mahomedan character, and the special tenets of the Wahábí sect, came to the conclusion that they were dangerous characters—that their influence would probably be exerted against the Government, and, if so exerted, would be fraught with danger. Arriving at this conclusion, he at once acted wisely; avoiding opposition or resistance, he quietly and unostentatiously placed them under safe *surveillance*.

And how were the services of these two officers rewarded? Mr. Halliday, who by his ignorance, neglect, or want of judgment thus imperilled the Empire, is honoured by the marked approval of the Crown, and obtains a seat in the Council of India.

Mr. Tayler, whose judgment was correct, whose action was prompt, is removed from his post, and driven by persecution to resign the service.

And if this was the case with respect to those dangerous traitors, I find the same misconception and the same ignorance in regard to the loyal and the good.

Mr. Tayler received active and disinterested support from two (among other) respectable natives.

One, a deputy-magistrate named Maola Baksh, and the other a banker, unconnected with Government, named Wiláyut Ali Khán.

Both these men did important service at great risk to themselves, and both were specially recommended by Mr. Tayler for honour.

Both were disparaged, and Mr. Samuels and Mr. Halliday endorsing the disparagement, officially upheld the recorded suspicion that these loyal men had hood-winked Mr. Tayler and induced him to arrest the Wahábís because of their exceptional and unprecedented loyalty.

Since then Dewan Mowla Baksh has been honoured with the Star of India, and Wiláyut Ali Khán has been recommended for the same distinction, and was especially introduced to the Prince of Wales during his visit to Patná, and congratulated for his service in 1857.

Thus, both for good and evil, Mr. Halliday was totally, even dangerously, wrong, though possessing all the means of correct judgment.

Mr. Tayler, with no assistance but his own vigilance and discernment, was, in every respect and on every point essential to the safety of the province, right.

I needly hardly dwell on the deep importance of this state of things, which is perhaps unparalleled in history.

But I cannot close this strange tale without adverting to some later incidents which give almost a dramatic character to the picture.

I have shown Mr. Tayler struggling against the ignorance and infatuation of Mr. Halliday, accused of persecuting innocent and inoffensive men (afterwards sentenced to death as deadly traitors), and his entire administration denounced as causing "public scandal and discontent."

I have also shown how entirely his views, opinions, and actions were vindicated by subsequent events, and the recorded testimony of many of the most able and distinguished Indian statement.

But it was left to a still later day to add a sad and tragical verification of Mr. Tayler's warnings.

In 1871, the Chief Justice of Calcutta was stabbed by a Wahábí fanatic on the steps of his own court, and the following year Lord Mayo, visiting the Andaman Islands, was assassinated also by a Mahomedan.

Official optimism held the murder to have been actuated by private vengeance, without any political purpose. Mr. Tayler, however, in a memorandum which he submitted to the Secretary of State, gave cogent reasons for concluding that whatever the personal character of the actual murderer, the deed had been contrived and aided by the notorious Ahmad-Ullá, whose open defiance of the authorities I have noticed, and whose treason was established in the trials before Sir Herbert Edwardes.

This man, a fact but little known, was in the Andamans at the time of the murder, and had been exerting as much influence from his prison cell as in his house at Patná.

These are the facts of the case. They appear to me equally to justify the conduct of Mr. Tayler towards the Wahábís, described in the text, and to condemn the action of the Government towards Mr. Tayler.

APPENDIX B.

"FROM BRIGADIER INGLIS, *Commanding Garrison of Lucknow,* TO THE SECRETARY TO GOVERNMENT MILITARY DEPARTMENT, *Calcutta.*

Dated, Lucknow, 26th September 1857.

"SIR,—In consequence of the very deeply-to-be-lamented death of Brigadier-General Sir H. M. Lawrence, K.C.B., late in command of the Oude Field Force, the duty of narrating the military events which have occurred at Lucknow since 29th June last, has devolved upon myself.

"On the evening of that day several reports reached Sir Henry Lawrence that the rebel army, in no very considerable force, would march from Chinhut (a small village about eight miles distant on the road to Fyzabad) on Lucknow on the following morning; and the late Brigadier-General therefore determined to make a strong reconnoisance in that direction, with the view, if possible, of meeting the force at a disadvantage, either at its entrance into the suburbs of the city, or at the bridge across the Gokral, which is a small stream intersecting the Fyzabad road, about half-way between Lucknow and Chinhut.

"The force destined for this service, and which was composed as follows, moved out at 6 A.M. on the morning of the 30th June :—

Artillery.—Four Guns of No.—Horse Light Field Battery.
Four ditto of No. 2 Oude Field Battery.
Two ditto of No. 3 ditto ditto ditto.
An eight-inch Howitzer.

Cavalry.—Troop of Volunteer Cavalry.
120 Troopers of Detachments belonging to the 1st, 2nd and 3rd Regiments of Oude Irregular Cavalry.
Infantry.—300 Her Majesty's 32nd.
150 13th Native Infantry.
60 48th Native Infantry.
20 71st Native Infantry (Sikhs).

"The troops, misled by the reports of wayfarers—who stated that there were few or no men between Lucknow and Chinhut—proceeded somewhat further than had been originally intended, and suddenly fell in with the enemy, who had up to that time eluded the vigilance of the advanced guard by concealing themselves behind a long line of trees in overwhelming numbers. The European force and the howitzer, with the native infantry, held the foe in check for some time, and had the six guns of the Oude Artillery been faithful, and the Sikh Cavalry shown a better front, the day would have been won in spite of an immense disparity in numbers. But the Oude artillerymen and drivers were traitors. They overturned the guns into ditches, cut the traces of their horses, and abandoned them, regardless of the remonstrances and exertions of their own officers, and of those of Sir Henry Lawrence's staff, headed by the Brigadier-General in person, who himself drew his sword upon these rebels. Every effort to induce them to stand having proved ineffectual, the force, exposed to a vastly superior fire of artillery, and completely outflanked on both sides by an overpowering body of infantry and cavalry, which actually got into our rear, was compelled to retire with the loss of three pieces of artillery, which fell into the hands of the enemy, in consequence of the rank treachery of the Oude gunners, and with a very grievous list of killed and wounded. The heat was dreadful, the gun ammunition was expended, and the almost total want of cavalry to protect our rear made our retreat most disastrous.

"All the officers behaved well, and the exertions of the small body of Volunteer Cavalry—only forty in number—under Captain Radcliffe, 7th Light Cavalry, were most praiseworthy. Sir Henry Lawrence subsequently conveyed his thanks to myself, who had, at his request, accompanied him upon this occasion, Colonel Case being in command of H. M.'s 32nd. He also expressed his approbation of the way in which his staff—Captain Wilson, Officiating Deputy Assistant Adjutant-General; Lieutenant James, Sub-Assistant Commissary-General; Captain Edgell, Officiating Military Secretary; and Mr. Couper, C.S.,—the last of whom had acted as Sir Henry Lawrence's A.D.C. from the commencement of the disturbances,—had conducted themselves throughout this arduous day. Sir Henry further particularly mentioned that he would bring the gallant conduct of Captain Radcliffe and of Lieutenant Bonham, of the Artillery, (who worked the howitzer successfully until incapacitated by a wound), to the prominent notice of the Government of India. The manner in which Lieutenant Birch, 71st N. I. cleared a village with a party of Sikh skirmishers, also elicited the admiration of the Brigadier-General. The conduct of Lieutenant Hardinge, who, with his handful of horse, covered the retreat of the rear-guard, was extolled by Sir Henry, who expressed his intention of mentioning the services of this gallant officer to His Lordship in Council. Lieutenant-Colonel Case, who commanded H. M.'s 32nd Regiment, was mortally wounded whilst gallantly leading on his men. The service had not a more deserving officer. The command devolved on Captain Steevens, who also received a death-wound shortly afterwards. The command then fell to Captain Mansfield, who has since died of cholera. A list of the casualties on this occasion accompanies the Despatch.

"It remains to report the siege operations.

"It will be in the recollection of His Lordship in Council that it was the original intention of Sir Henry Lawrence to occupy not only the Residency, but also the fort called Muchhee Bhowun—an old dilapidated edifice, which had been hastily repaired for the occasion, though the defences were even at the last moment very far from complete, and were moreover commanded by many houses in the city. The situation of the Muchhee Bhowun with regard to the Residency has already been described to the Government of India.

"The untoward event of the 30th June so far diminished the whole available force, that we had not a sufficient number of men remaining to occupy both positions. The Brigadier-General, therefore, on the evening of the 1st July, signalled to the garrison of the Muchhee Bhowun to evacuate and blow up that fortress in the course of the night. The orders were ably carried out, and at 12 P.M. the force marched into the Residency with their guns and treasure without the loss of a man; and shortly afterwards the explosion of 240 barrels of gunpowder and 6,000,000 ball cartridges, which were lying in the magazine, announced to Sir Henry Lawrence and his officers—who were anxiously awaiting the report—the complete destruction of that post and all that it contained. If it had not been for this wise and strategic measure, no member of the Lucknow garrison, in all probability, would have survived to tell the tale; for, as has already been stated, the Muchhee Bhowun was commanded from other parts of the town, and was moreover indifferently provided with heavy artillery ammunition, while the difficulty, suffering, and loss which the Residency garrison, even with the reinforcement thus obtained from the Muchhee Bhowun, has undergone in holding the position, is sufficient to show that, if the original intention of holding both posts had been adhered to, both would have inevitably fallen.

"It is now my very painful duty to relate the calamity which befel us at the commencement of the siege. On the 1st July an 8-inch shell burst in the room in the Residency in which Sir H. Lawrence was sitting. The missile burst between him and Mr. Couper, close to both; but without injury to either. The whole of his staff implored Sir Henry to take up other quarters, as the Residency had then become the special target for the round shot and shell of the enemy. This, however, he jestingly declined to do, observing that another shell would certainly never be pitched into that small room. But Providence had ordained otherwise, for on the very next day he was mortally wounded by the fragment of another shell which burst in the same room, exactly at the same spot. Captain Wilson, Deputy Assistant Adjutant-General, received a contusion at the same time.

"The late lamented Sir Henry Lawrence, knowing that his his last hour was rapidly approaching, directed me to assume command of the troops, and appointed Major Banks to succeed him in the office of Chief Commissioner. He lingered in great agony till the morning of the 4th July, when he expired, and the Government was thereby deprived, if I may venture to say so, of the services of a distinguished statesman and a most gallant soldier. Few men have ever possessed to the same extent the power which he enjoyed of winning the hearts of all those with whom he came in contact, and thus ensuring the warmest and most zealous devotion for himself and for the Government which he served. The successful defence of the position has been, under Providence, solely attributable to the foresight which he evinced in the timely commencement of the necessary operations, and the great skill and untiring personal activity which he exhibited in carrying them into effect. All ranks possessed such confidence in his judgment and his fertility of resource, that the news of his fall was received throughout the garrison with feelings of consternation only second to the grief which was inspired in the hearts of all by the loss of a public benefactor and a warm personal friend. Feeling as keenly and as gratefully as I do the obligations that the whole of us are under to this great and good man, I trust the Government of India will pardon me for having attempted, however imperfectly, to pourtray them. In him every good and deserving soldier lost a friend and a chief capable of discriminating, and ever on the alert to reward merit, no matter how humble the sphere in which it was exhibited.

"The garrison had scarcely recovered the shock which it had sustained in the loss of its revered and beloved General, when it had to mourn the death of that able and respected officer, Major Banks, the Officiating Chief Commissioner, who received a bullet through his head while examining a critical outpost on the 21st July, and died without a groan.

"The description of our position, and the state of our defences when the siege began, are so fully set forth in the accompanying Memorandum, furnished by the Garrison Engineer, that I shall content myself with bringing to the notice of His Lordship in Council the fact that when the blockade was commenced only two of our batteries were completed, part of the defences were yet in an unfinished condition, and the buildings in the immediate vicinity, which gave cover to the enemy, were only very partially cleared away. Indeed, our heaviest losses have been caused by the fire from the enemy's sharp-shooters stationed in the adjoining mosques and houses of the native nobility, the necessity of destroying which had been repeatedly drawn to the attention of Sir Henry by the staff of Engineers; but his invariable reply was, 'Spare the holy places, and private property too, as far as possible;' and we have consequently suffered severely from our very tenderness to the religious prejudices and respect to the rights of our rebellious citizens and soldiery. As soon as the enemy had thoroughly completed the investment of the Residency, they occupied these houses, some of which were within easy pistol shot of our barricades, in immense force, and rapidly made loop-holes on those sides which bore on our post, from which they kept up a terrific and incessant fire day and night, which caused many daily casualties, as there could not have been less than 8,000 men firing at one time into our position. Moreover, there was no place in the whole of our works that could be considered safe, for several of the sick and wounded who were lying in the Banqueting hall, which had been turned into an hospital, were killed in the very centre of the building, and the widow of Lieutenant Dorin and other women and children were shot dead in rooms into which it had not been previously deemed possible that a bullet could penetrate. Neither were the enemy idle in erecting batteries. They soon had from 20 to 25 guns in position, some of them of very large calibre. These were planted all round our post at small distances, some being actually within fifty yards of our defences, but in places where our own heavy guns could not reply to them, while the perseverance and ingenuity of the enemy in erecting barricades in front of and around their guns, in a very short time rendered all attempts to silence them by musketry entirely unavailing. Neither could they be effectually silenced by shells, by reason of their extreme proximity to our position, and because, moreover, the enemy had recourse to digging very narrow trenches about eight feet in depth in rear of each gun, in which the men lay while our shells were flying, and which so effectually concealed them, even while working the gun, that our baffled sharpshooters could only see their hands while in the act of loading.

"The enemy contented themselves with keeping up this incessant fire of cannon and musketry until the 20th July, on which day, at 10 A.M., they assembled in very great force all around our position, and exploded a heavy mine inside our outer line of defences at the water gate. The mine, however, which was close to the Redan, and apparently sprung with the intention of destroying that battery, did no harm. But as soon as the smoke had cleared away, the enemy boldly advanced under cover of a tremendous fire of cannon and musketry, with the object of storming the Redan. But they were received with such a heavy fire, that, after a short struggle, they fell back with much loss. A strong column advanced at the same time to attack Innes' post, and came on to within ten yards of the palisades, affording to Lieutenant Loughnan, 13th N.I., who commanded the position, and his brave garrison, composed of gentlemen of the Uncovenanted Service, a few of Her Majesty's 32nd Foot, and of the 13th N.I., an opportunity of distinguishing themselves, which they were not slow to avail themselves of, and the enemy were driven back with great slaughter. The insurgents made minor attacks at almost every outpost, but were invariably defeated, and at 2 P.M. they ceased their attempts to storm the place, although their musketry fire and cannonading continued to harass us unceasingly as usual. Matters proceeded in this manner until the 10th August, when the enemy made another assault, having previously sprung a mine close to the Brigade Mess, which entirely destroyed our defences for the space of twenty feet, and blew in a great portion of the outside wall of the house occupied by Mr. Schilling's garrison. On the dust clearing away, a breach appeared, through which a regiment could have advanced in perfect order, and a few of the enemy came on with the utmost determination, but were met with such a withering flank fire of musketry from the officers and men holding the top of the Brigade Mess, that they beat a speedy retreat, leaving the more adventurous of their numbers lying on the crest of the breach. While this operation was going on, another large body advanced on the Cawnpore battery, and succeeded in locating themselves for a few minutes in the ditch. They were, however, dislodged by hand grenades. At Captain Anderson's post they also came boldly forward with scaling ladders, which they planted against the wall; but here, as elsewhere, they were met with the most indomitable resolution, and the leaders being slain, the rest fled, leaving the ladders, and retreated to their batteries and loop-holed defences, from whence they kept up for the rest of the day an unusually heavy cannonade and musketry fire. On the 18th August the enemy sprung another mine in front of the Sikh lines with very fatal effect. Captain Orr (unattached), Lieutenants Mecham and Soppitt, who commanded the small body of drummers composing the garrison, were blown into the air, but providentially returned to earth with no further injury than a severe shaking. The garrison, however, were not so fortunate. No less than eleven men were buried alive under the ruins from whence it was impossible to extricate them, owing to the tremendous fire kept up by the enemy from houses situated not 10 yards in front of the breach. The explosion was followed by a general assault of a less determined nature than the two former efforts, and the enemy were consequently repulsed without much difficulty. But they succeeded, under cover of the breach, in establishing themselves in one of the houses in our position, from which they were driven in the evening by the bayonets of H.M.'s 32nd and 84th Foot. On the 5th September the enemy made their last serious assault. Having exploded a large mine, a few feet short of the bastion of the 18-pounder gun, in Major Apthorp's post, they advanced with large heavy scaling ladders, which they planted against the wall, and mounted, thereby gaining for an instant the embrasure of a gun. They were, however, speedily driven back with loss by hand grenades and musketry. A few minutes subsequently they sprung another mine close to the Brigade Mess, and advanced boldly; but soon the corpses strewed in the garden in front of the post bore testimony to the fatal accuracy of the rifle and musketry fire of the gallant members of that garrison, and the enemy fled ignominiously, leaving their leader—a fine-looking old native officer—among the slain. At other posts they made similar attacks, but with less resolution, and everywhere with the same want of success. Their loss upon this day must have been very heavy, as they came on with much determination, and at night they were seen bearing large numbers of their killed and wounded over the bridges in the direction of the cantonments. The above is a faint attempt at a description of the four great struggles which have occurred during this protracted season of exertion, exposure, and suffering. His Lordship in Council will perceive that the enemy invariably commenced his attacks by the explosion of a mine, a species of offensive warfare for the exercise of which our position was unfortunately peculiarly situated, and had it not been for the most untiring vigilance on our part in watching and blowing up their mines before they were completed, the assaults would probably have been much more numerous, and might, perhaps, have ended in the capture of the place. But by countermining in all directions, we succeeded in detecting and destroying no less than four of the enemy's subterraneous advances towards important positions, two of which operations were eminently successful, as on one occasion not less than eight of them were blown into the air, and twenty suffered a similar fate on the second explosion. The labour, however, which devolved upon us in making these countermines, in the absence of a body of skilled miners, was very heavy. The Right Honourable the Governor-General in Council will feel that it would be impossible to crowd within the limits of a despatch even the principal events, much more the individual acts of gallantry, which have marked this protracted struggle. But I can conscientiously declare my conviction that few troops have ever undergone greater hardships, exposed as they have been to a never-ceasing musketry fire and cannonade. They have also experienced the alternate vicissitudes of extreme wet and of intense heat, and that, too, with very insufficient shelter from either, and in many places without any shelter at all. In addition to having had to repel real attacks, they have been exposed night and day to the hardly less harassing false alarms which the enemy have been constantly raising. The insurgents have frequently fired very heavily, sounded the advance and shouted for several hours together, though not a man could be seen, with the view, of course, of harassing our small and exhausted force, in which object they succeeded, for no part has been strong enough to allow of a portion only of the garrison being prepared in the event of a false attack being turned into a real one. All, therefore, had to stand to their arms, and to remain at their posts until the demonstration had ceased; and such attacks were of almost nightly occurrence. The whole of the officers and men have been on duty night and day during the eighty-seven days which the siege has lasted, up to the arrival of Sir J. Outram, G.C.B. In addition to this incessant military duty, the force has been nightly employed in repairing defences, in moving guns, in burying dead animals, in conveying ammunition and commissariat stores from one place to another, and in other fatigue duties too numerous and too trivial to enumerate here. I feel, however, that any words of mine will fail to convey any adequate idea of what our fatigue and labours have been—labours in which all ranks and all classes, civilians, officers, and soldiers, have all borne an equally noble part. All have together descended into the mines, all have together handled the shovel for the interment of the putrid bullock, and all, accoutred with musket and bayonet, have relieved each other on sentry, without regard to the distinctions of rank, civil or military. Notwithstanding all these hardships, the garrison has made no less than five sorties, in which they spiked two of the enemy's heaviest guns, and blew up several of the houses from which they had kept up their most harassing fire. Owing to the extreme paucity of our numbers, each man was taught to feel that on his own individual efforts alone depended in no small measure the safety of the entire position. This consciousness incited every officer, soldier, and man to defend the post assigned to him with such desperate tenacity, and to fight for the lives which Providence had entrusted to his care with such dauntless determination, that the enemy, despite their constant attacks, their heavy mines, their overwhelming numbers, and their incessant fire, could never succeed in gaining one single inch of ground within the bounds of this straggling position, which was so feebly fortified that had they once obtained a footing in any of the outposts the whole place must inevitably have fallen.

"If further proof be wanting of the desperate nature of the struggle which we have, under God's blessing, so long and so successfully waged, I would point to the roofless and ruined house, to the crumbled walls, to the exploded mines, to the open breaches, to the shattered and disabled guns and defences, and, lastly, to the long and melancholy list of the brave and devoted officers and men who have fallen. These silent witnesses bear sad and solemn testimony to the way in which this feeble position has been defended. During the early part of these vicissitudes, we were left without any information whatever regarding the posture of affairs outside. An occasional spy did, indeed, come in with the object of inducing our sepoys and servants to desert; but the intelligence derived from such sources was, of course, entirely untrustworthy. We sent our messengers daily, calling for aid and asking for information, none of whom ever returned until the 26th day of the siege, when a pensioner named Ungud came back with a letter from General Havelock's camp, informing us that they were advancing with a force sufficient to bear down all opposition, and would be with us in five or six days. A messenger was immediately despatched requesting that on the evening of their arrival on the outskirts of the city two rockets might be sent up, in order that we might take the necessary measures for assisting them while forcing their way in. The sixth day, however, expired, and they came not; but for many evenings after officers and men watched for the ascension of the expected rockets, with hopes such as make the heart sick. We knew not then, nor did we learn until the 29th August—or thirty-five days later—that the relieving force, after having fought most nobly to effect our deliverance, had been obliged to fall back for reinforcements; and this was the last communication we received until two days before the arrival of Sir James Outram, on the 25th September.

"Besides heavy visitations of cholera and small-pox, we have also had to contend against a sickness which has almost universally pervaded the garrison. Commencing with a very painful eruption, it has merged into a low fever, combined with diarrhœa; and although few or no men have actually died from its effects, it leaves behind a weakness and lassitude which, in the absence of all material sustenance save coarse beef and still coarser flour, none have been able entirely to get over. The mortality among the women and children, and especially among the latter, from these diseases and from other causes, has been, perhaps, the most painful characteristic of the siege. The want of native servants has also been a source of much privation. Owing to the suddenness with which we were besieged, many of these people who might, perhaps, have otherwise proved faithful to their employers, but who were outside the defences at the time, were altogether excluded. Very many more deserted, and several families were consequently left without the services of a single domestic. Several ladies have had to tend their children, and even to wash their own clothes, as well as to cook their scanty meals entirely unaided. Combined with the absence of servants, the want of proper accommodation has probably been the cause of much of the disease with which we have been afflicted. I cannot refrain from bringing to the prominent notice of His Lordship in Council the patient endurance and the Christian resignation which have been evinced by the women of this garrison. They have animated us by their example. Many, alas! have been made widows, and their children fatherless, in this cruel struggle. But all such seem resigned to the will of Providence, and many, among whom may be mentioned the honoured names of Birch, of Polehampton, of Barbor, and of Gall, have, after the example of Miss Nightingale, constituted themselves the tender and solicitous nurses of the wounded and dying soldiers in the hospital.

"It only remains for me to bring to the favourable notice of His Lordship in Council the names of those officers who have most distinguished themselves, and afforded me the most valuable assistance in these operations. Many of the best and bravest of these now rest from their labours. Among them are Lieutenant-Colonel Case and Captain Radcliffe, whose services have already been narrated; Captain Francis, 13th N.I.,—who was killed by a round shot—had particularly attracted the attention of Sir H. Lawrence for his conduct while in command of the Muchhee Bhowun; Captain Fulton, of the Engineers, who also was struck by a round shot, had, up to the time of his early and lamented death, afforded me the most invaluable aid; he was, indeed, indefatigable. Major Anderson, the Chief Engineer, though, from the commencement of the siege, incapable of physical exertion from the effects of the disease under which he eventually sank, merited my warm acknowledgments for his able counsel; Captain Simons, Commandant of Artillery, distinguished himself at Chinhut, where he received two wounds, which ended in his death; Lieutenants Shepherd and Arthur, 7th Light Cavalry, who were killed at their posts; Captain Hughes, 57th N.I., who was mortally wounded at the capture of a house which formed one of the enemy's outposts; Captain McCabe, of the 32nd Foot, who was killed at the head of his men while leading his fourth sortie, as well as Captain Mansfield, of the same corps, who died of cholera—were all officers who had distinguished themselves highly. Mr. Lucas, too, a gentleman volunteer, and Mr. Boyson, of the Uncovenanted Service —who fell when on the look-out at one of the most perilous outposts—had earned themselves reputations for coolness and gallantry.

"The officers who commanded out-posts—Lieutenant-Colonel Master, 7th Light Cavalry; Major Apthorp, 41st

N. I.; Captain Gould Weston, 65th N. I.*; Captain Sanders, 41st N. I.; Captain Boileau, 7th Light Cavalry; Captain Germon, 13th N. I.; Lieutenant Aitken, and Lieutenant Loughnan, of the same corps; Captain Anderson, 25th N. I.; Lieutenant Graydon, 44th N. I.; Lieutenant Langmore, 71st N. I., and Mr. Schilling, Principal of the Martinière College—have all conducted ably the duties of their onerous position. No further proof of this is necessary than the fact which I have before mentioned, that throughout the whole duration of the siege the enemy were not only unable to take, but they could not even succeed in gaining one inch of the posts commanded by these gallant gentlemen. Colonel Master commanded the critical and important post of the Brigade Mess, on either side of which was an open breach, only flanked by his handful of riflemen and musketeers. Lieutenant Aitken, with the whole of the 13th N. I. which remained to us with the exception of their Sikhs, commanded the Bailey Guard—perhaps the most important position in the whole of the defences; and Lieutenant Langmore, with the remnant of his regiment (the 71st,) held a very exposed position between the hospital and the water gate. This gallant and deserving young soldier and his men were entirely without shelter from the weather, both by night and by day.

"My thanks are also due to Lieutenants Anderson, Hutchinson and Innes, of the Engineers, as well as to Lieutenant Tulloch, 58th N. I., and Lieutenant Hay, 48th N. I., who

* G. G. O., No. 1546, dated, *Fort William, 15th November* 1858: "Major-General Sir J. E. Inglis, K.C.B., formerly commanding Lucknow Garrison, having brought to notice that the name of Captain G. Weston, 65th Regiment Native Infantry, was inadvertently omitted in his despatch of the 26th September 1857, the Hon. the President of the Council of the Right Hon. the Governor-General of India in Council, with the concurrence of his Lordship, desires to rectify that omission, and is pleased to direct that that officer's name be added to the paragraph commencing with the words 'the officers who commanded the outposts,' and inserted after the name of Major Apthorp, 41st Native Infantry. Order Books to be corrected accordingly."

were placed under them to aid in the arduous duties devolving upon that department. Lieutenant Thomas, Madras Artillery, who commanded that arm of the service for some weeks, and Lieutenants Macfarlane and Bonham rendered me the most effectual assistance. I was, however, deprived of the services of the two latter, who were wounded, Lieutenant Bonham no less than three times, early in the siege. Captain Evans, 17th B. N. I., who, owing to the scarcity of Artillery officers was put in charge of some guns, was ever to be found at his post.

"Major Lowe, commanding H. M.'s 32nd Regiment; Captain Bassano, Lieutenants Lawrence, Edmonstoune, Foster, Harmar, Cook, Clery, Browne, and Charlton, of that corps, have all nobly performed their duty. Every one of these officers, with the exception of Lieutenants Lawrence and Clery, have received one or more wounds of more or less severity. Quartermaster Stribbling, of the same corps, also conducted himself to my satisfaction.

"Captain O'Brien, H. M.'s 84th Foot; Captain Kemble, 41st N. I.; Captain Edgell, 53rd N. I.; Captain Dinning, Lieutenant Sewell, and Lieutenant Worsely, of the 71st N. I.; Lieutenant Warner, 7th L. C.; Ensign Ward, 48th N. I.; (who, when most of our Artillery officers were killed or disabled, worked the mortars with excellent effect); Lieutenant Graham, 11th N. I.; Lieutenant Mecham, 4th Oude Locals; and Lieutenant Keir, 41st N. I., have all done good and willing service throughout the siege, and I trust that they will receive the favourable notice of his Lordship in Council.

"I beg particularly to call the attention of the Government of India to the untiring industry, the extreme devotion and the great skill which have been evinced by Surgeon Scott (superintending surgeon) and Assistant-Surgeon Boyd, of H. M.'s 32nd Foot; Assistant Surgeon Bird, of the Artillery; Surgeon Campbell, 7th Light Cavalry; Surgeon, Brydon, 71st N. I.; Surgeon Ogilvie, Sanitary Commissioner;

Assistant Surgeon Fayrer, Civil Surgeon; Assistant Surgeon Partridge, 2nd Oude Irregular Cavalry; Assistant Surgeon Greenhow; Assistant Surgeon Darby, and by Mr. Apothecary Thompson, in the discharge of their onerous and most important duties.

"Messrs. Thornhill and Capper, of the Civil Service, have been both wounded, and the way in which they, as well as Mr. Martin, the Deputy Commissioner of Lucknow, conducted themselves, entitles them to a place in this despatch. Captain Carnegie, the Special Assistant Commissioner, whose invaluable services previous to the commencement of the siege, I have frequently heard warmly dilated upon, both by Sir H. Lawrence and by Major Banks, and whose exertions will probably be more amply brought to notice by the Civil authorities on some future occasion, has conducted the office of Provost Marshal to my satisfaction. The Reverend Mr. Harris and the Reverend Mr. Polehampton, Assistant Chaplains, vied with each other in their untiring care and attention to the suffering men. The latter gentleman was wounded in the hospital, and subsequently unhappily died of cholera. Mr. McCrae, of the Civil Engineers, did excellent service at the guns, until he was severely wounded. Mr. Cameron, also, a gentleman who had come to Oude to enquire into the resources of the country, acquired the whole mystery of mortar practice, and was of the most signal service until incapacitated by sickness. Mr. Marshall, of the Road Department, and other members of the Uncovenanted Service, whose names will, on a subsequent occasion, be laid before the Government of India, conducted themselves bravely and steadily. Indeed, the entire body of these gentlemen have borne themselves well, and have evinced great coolness under fire.

"I have now only to bring to the notice of the Right Hon'ble the Governor-General in Council the conduct of several officers who composed my Staff;—Lieutenant James, Sub-Assistant Commissary-General, was severely wounded by a shot through the knee at Chinhut, notwithstanding which he refused to go upon the sick list, and carried on his most trying duties throughout the entire siege. It is not too much to say that the garrison owe their lives to the exertions and firmness of this officer. Before the struggle commenced, he was ever in the saddle, getting in supplies, and his untiring vigilance in their distribution after our difficulties had begun, prevented a waste which otherwise, long before the expiration of the eighty-seven days, might have annihilated the force by the slow process of starvation.

"Captain Wilson, 13th N. I., Officiating Deputy Assistant Adjutant-General, was ever to be found where shot was flying thickest, and I am at a loss to decide whether his services were most invaluable owing to the untiring physical endurance and bravery which he displayed, or to his ever-ready and pertinent counsel and advice in moments of difficulty and danger.

"Lieutenant Hardinge—an officer whose achievements and antecedents are well known to the Government of India—has earned fresh laurels by his conduct throughout the siege. He was officiating as Deputy Assistant Quarter-master-General and also commanded the Sikh portion of the cavalry of the garrison. In both capacities his services have been invaluable, especially in the latter, for it was owing alone to his tact, vigilance, and bravery, that the Sikh horse-men were induced to persevere in holding a very unprotected post under a heavy fire.

"Lieutenant Barwell, 71st N. I., the Fort Adjutant and officiating Major of Brigade, has proved himself to be an efficient officer.

"Lieutenant Birch, of the 71st N. I., has been my A.D.C. throughout the siege. I firmly believe there never was a better A.D.C. He has been indefatigable, and ever ready to lead a sortie, or to convey an order to a threatened outpost under the heaviest fire. On one of these occasions he received a slight wound on the head. I beg to bring the services of this most promising and intelligent young officer to the favourable consideration of His Lordship in Council.

"I am also much indebted to Mr. Couper, C. S., for the assistance he has on many occasions afforded me by his judicious advice. I have, moreover, ever found him most ready and willing in the performance of the military duties assigned to him, however exposed the post or arduous the undertaking. He commenced his career in Her Majesty's Service, and consequently had had some previous experience of military matters. If the road to Cawnpore had been made clear by the advent of our troops, it was my intention to have deputed this officer to Calcutta, to detail in person the occurrences which have taken place, for the information of the Government of India. I still hope that when our communications shall be once more unopposed, he may be summoned to Calcutta for this purpose.

"Lastly, I have the pleasure of bringing the splendid behaviour of the soldiers, *viz.*, the men of H. M.'s 32nd Foot, the small detachment of H. M.'s 84th Foot, the European and Native Artillery, the 13th, 48th, and 71st Regiments N. I. and the Sikhs of the respective corps, to the notice of the Government of India. The losses sustained by H. M.'s 32nd, which is now barely 300 strong; by H. M.'s 84th and by the European Artillery, shew at least that they knew how to die in the cause of their countrymen. Their conduct under the fire, the exposure, and the privations which they have had to undergo, has been throughout most admirable and praiseworthy.

"As another instance of the desperate character of our defence and the difficulties we have had to contend with, I may mention that the number of our artillerymen was so reduced that on the occasion of an attack, the gunners—aided as they were by men of H. M.'s 32nd Foot, and by Volunteers of all classes, had to run from one battery to another wherever the fire of the enemy was hottest, there not being nearly enough men to serve half the number of guns, at the same time. In short, at last, the number of European gunners was only twenty-four, while we had including mortars, no less than thirty guns in position.

"With respect to the native troops I am of opinion that their loyalty has never been surpassed. They were indifferently fed and worse housed. They were exposed—especially the 13th Regiment—under the gallant Lieutenant Aitken, to a most galling fire of round shot and musketry, which materially decreased their numbers. They were so near the enemy that conversation could be carried on between them; every effort, persuasion, promise, and threat was alternately resorted to, in vain, to seduce them from their allegiance to the handful of Europeans, who, in all probability, would have been sacrificed by their desertion. All the troops behaved nobly, and the names of those men of the native force who have particularly distinguished themselves, have been laid before Major-General Sir James Outram, G.C.B., who has promised to promote them. Those of the European force will be transmitted in due course for the orders of his Royal Highness the General Commanding-in-Chief.

"In conclusion, I beg leave to express on the part of myself and the members of this garrison, our deep and grateful sense of the conduct of Major-General Sir J. Outram, G.C.B., of Brigadier-General Havelock, C.B., and of the troops under those officers who so devotedly came to our relief at so heavy a sacrifice of life. We are also repaid for much suffering and privation by the sympathy which our brave deliverers say our perilous and unfortunate position has excited for us in the hearts of our countrymen throughout the length and breadth of Her Majesty's dominions.

"I have, &c.,

"(Signed) J. INGLIS, *Colonel*,

"*H. M.'s* 32*nd Brigadier.*"

HISTORY
OF THE
INDIAN MUTINY, 1857-1858.

HISTORY
OF THE
INDIAN MUTINY,
1857-1858.

COMMENCING FROM THE CLOSE OF THE
SECOND VOLUME OF
SIR JOHN KAYE'S HISTORY OF THE SEPOY WAR.

BY

COLONEL G. B. MALLESON, C.S.I.
AUTHOR OF "HISTORY OF THE FRENCH IN INDIA,"
"HISTORICAL SKETCH OF THE NATIVE STATES OF
INDIA," ETC., ETC.

VOLUME II.

GYAN

Published by

Gyan Publishing House
5, Ansari Road
Daryaganj, New Delhi-110002
Phone: 011-47034999, 9811692060
E-mail: books@gyanbooks.com

Distribution Network
gyanbooks.com
India, USA, Canada, UK, Australia, France

ISBN : 978-81-212-3541-9 (Set)
ISBN : 978-81-212-4915-7 (PB)
First Published, 1879

2nd Impression 2020

Printed at: Gyan Press, Delhi.

History of the Indian Mutiny, Vol. II
1857-1858.
Author: Colonel G. B. Malleson

HISTORY

OF THE

INDIAN MUTINY, 1857–1858.

COMMENCING FROM THE CLOSE OF THE SECOND VOLUME OF SIR JOHN KAYE'S HISTORY OF THE SEPOY WAR.

BY

COLONEL G. B. MALLESON, C.S.I.

AUTHOR OF "HISTORY OF THE FRENCH IN INDIA," "HISTORICAL SKETCH OF THE NATIVE STATES OF INDIA," ETC., ETC.

VOLUME II.

LONDON:
WILLIAM H. ALLEN AND CO.,
13 WATERLOO PLACE, PALL MALL, S.W.
1879.

IN THE HOPE THAT THIS BOOK MAY LIVE,

I DEDICATE IT

TO THE MEMORY OF MY BROTHER-IN-LAW,

Quintin Battye,

OF THE CORPS OF GUIDES,

ONE OF THE FIRST OF THE MANY GALLANT MEN WHO GAVE THEIR LIVES FOR THEIR COUNTRY ON THE RIDGE BEFORE DEHLI.

THE WORDS WHICH HE UTTERED,

WHEN, ON THE 9TH JUNE, 1857, HE RECEIVED THE WOUND WHICH HE KNEW TO BE MORTAL,

DULCE ET DECORUM EST PRO PATRIA MORI,

WERE CHERISHED

AS A MOST PRECIOUS INHERITANCE BY HIS BROTHER,

Wigram Battye,

WHO, ENTERING THE SERVICE AFTER HIS DEATH,

WAS APPOINTED TO THE SAME REGIMENT, THE CORPS OF GUIDES,

AND BY UNFLINCHING GALLANTRY AND DEVOTION

WON FROM THE STERN FRONTIER MEN WHO COMPOSED IT THE ESTEEM AND AFFECTION

WHICH THEY HAD BORNE TO QUINTIN.

FOLLOWING THROUGHOUT HIS NOBLE LIFE

IN THE FOOTSTEPS OF HIS BROTHER,

HE EMULATED HIM IN THE MANNER OF HIS DEATH,

FOR HE TOO DIED LEADING THE GUIDES IN A GALLANT CHARGE

AGAINST THE ENEMIES OF ENGLAND,

AT FATHABAD, NEAR JALLALABAD, THE 2ND APRIL, 1879.

SIMILAR AS WAS THEIR LIFE,

SIMILAR AS WAS THEIR DEATH,

I WOULD NOT SEPARATE IN THIS DEDICATION

THE TWO GALLANT BROTHERS.

PAR NOBILE FRATRUM.

PREFACE.

In the preface to my last volume I expressed my intention of publishing the volume which should conclude the history of the Indian Mutiny in the early part of the current year.

But after writing the six hundred pages which form the volume I now offer to the public, I found that the stirring events in the Western Presidency, including a review of the administration of Lord Elphinstone; the occurrences in southern and central India, and in Bandalkhand, including the campaigns of Sir Hugh Rose, of Sir Robert Napier, and of Whitlock; and the campaign which terminated in the pacification of Oudh, had still to be recorded. I had, too, to write a review of the policy inaugurated by Lord Canning in the later phases of the revolt.

Compelled, as I have been, to confine to the smallest space the notice of events not germane to the main threads of the story, and conscious that even with the greatest possible compression the history of the mutiny up to the point it has reached in the present volume had occupied nearly six hundred pages, I felt that were I to condense in the same volume the occurrences still remaining to be told, either I should be forced to write them on a scale much smaller than that which their intrinsic importance demanded; or, the volume would attain an exceptional bulk, extremely inconvenient to the reader.

Under these circumstances I could not hesitate. I decided to publish the second volume at once.

The division which by these means is produced seems in other respects to be convenient. Whilst the present volume deals with the storming of Dehlí; with Sir Colin Campbell's campaigns of 1857 in Oudh, and of 1858 up to the end of May of that year in Oudh and Rohilkhand; with the movements of the several columns and detachments in north-western India, in the Ázamgarh district, in Bihar, in eastern Bengal, and on the south-western frontier; whilst, in fact, it deals generally with the Bengal Presidency and Rajpútáná, the volume which is to follow, and which I hope to offer to the public in the first month of the coming year, will narrate the occurrences in the sister presidencies, in Haidarábád, and in central India. I propose, too, to devote one chapter of that volume to a comprehensive review of Lord Canning's later policy; and another to a consideration of the action of the civil officers in many of the districts which came, more or less, under the influence of the great wave of the revolt.

In the present volume I have endeavoured to render justice not less to the generals entrusted with the suppression of the mutiny than to those officers of less exalted rank whose splendid exertions enabled the generals to conquer. In the instances in which the conduct of a general has seemed to me to be open to criticism I have endeavoured to state the case with fairness and impartiality. There is not a published official document, there is not a document, relating to the events I have recorded, to which it was possible for me to have access, which I have not carefully read and noted.

Whilst expressing my acknowledgments to those who have, in this way, rendered me invaluable aid; to others who have placed at my disposal journals and letters written at the time, it is fit that I should admit the special obligation under which I lie to the writer of an article on Lord Clyde's Indian Campaign which appeared in *Blackwood's Magazine* for October 1858. If the author of that article, who, I understand, is Major-General Sir Archibald Alison, C.B., had continued his story in the same graphic and nervous style, and with the same attention to correct detail which characterises the article to which I refer, this history would never have been written. Having traversed the same ground in Blue-books and private documents, I have shown my opinion of that writer's historical power and impartiality by the copious extracts I have made from his article, and I am desirous to place here upon record my admiration of its vigour, its truth, and its vivid reality.

I am anxious, before I conclude, to acknowledge the generous reception which the first volume of this work has met with in this country, in the colonies, and in America. It was not possible, writing of events, many actors in which survive, and to some of whom a record of their performances cannot be palatable, that I should absolutely escape hostile criticism. But the bulk of opinion in England, in Australia, and in America has been sufficiently out-spoken to encourage me to believe that with the course of time the history I have written of the occurrences of a very memorable period will meet with universal acceptance.

G. B. MALLESON.

27, *West Cromwell Road,*
9th August 1879.

GLOSSARY OF PROPER NAMES.

The mode of spelling now adopted.	The old mode of spelling.
Ágra	Agra.
Ájmír	Ajmir.
Álambágh	Alumbagh.
Áligarh	Aligurh.
Allahábád	Allahabad.
Árah	Arrah.
Ázamgarh	Azimgurh.
Baksar	Buxar.
Balamgarh	Ballumgurh.
Balandshahr	Bolundshuhr.
Banáras	Benares.
Bandalkhand	Bundelkhund.
Banni	Bunnee.
Barhámpúr	Berhampore.
Bhágalpúr	Bhagulpore.
Bhútán	Bhootan.
Bihár	Behar.
Bilúchi	Beloochee.
Chaibása	Cheybassa.
Chátgáon	Chittagong.
Chattra	Chuttra.
Chutiá Nágpúr	Chota Nagpore.
Dákhá	Dacca.
Dánápúr	Dinapore.
Dárjíling	Darjeeling.
Dehlí, or Dihlí	Delhi.
Dilkúsha	Dilkoosha.
Faizábád	Fyzabad.
Farrakhábád	Furruckabad.
Fathgarh	Futtehgurh.
Fathpúr	Futtehpore.
Firozpúr	Ferozpore.
Gandak	Gunduck.
Ghághrá	Gogra.

The mode of spelling now adopted.	The old mode of spelling.
Gházipúr	Ghazipore.
Gorákhpúr	Gorruckpore.
Gúmti	Goomtie.
Gwáliár	Gwalior.
Imámbárá	Emambarah.
Itáwa	Etawah.
Jagdispúr	Jugdispore.
Jaipúr	Jeypore.
Jajhar	Jujjhur.
Jalpáigorí	Julpigori.
Jamná	Jumna.
Jánpúr	Jaunpore.
Jodhpúr	Jodhpore.
Kálpi	Calpee.
Kánhpúr	Cawnpore.
Kánúj	Canouj.
Katak	Cuttack.
Kúsi	Koosi.
Lakhnao	Lucknow.
Mainpúri	Mynporie.
Manghir	Monghyr.
Mathurá	Muttra.
Múltán	Mooltan.
Naddi	Nuddee.
Nasírábád	Nusseerabad.
Nímach	Neemuch.
Nipál	Nepaul.
Orisá	Orissa.
Panjáb	Punjaub.
Patná	Patna.
Púrniá	Purnea.
Rajpútáná	Rajpootana.
Rohilkhand	Rohilkhund.
Rúrki	Roorkee.
Silhat	Sylhet.
Són	Soane.
Tirhút	Tirhoot.
Tísta	Teesta.

CONTENTS

OF

THE SECOND VOLUME.

BOOK X.

CHAPTER I.

CHAPTER II.

BOOK XI.

CHAPTER I.

CHAPTER II.

CHAPTER III.

CHAPTER IV.

CHAPTER V.

CHAPTER VI.

CHAPTER VII.

CHAPTER VIII.

CHAPTER IX.

BOOK XII.

CHAPTER I.

CHAPTER II.

CHAPTER III.

CHAPTER IV.

CHAPTER V.

HISTORY

OF THE

INDIAN MUTINY OF 1857.

BOOK X.

CHAPTER I.

Book X. Chapter I.

1857. Sept. 1.

The siege of Dehlí.

I TAKE up the history of the siege of Dehlí from the 1st September. Nicholson's great victory at Najafgarh, gained the 25th August, had not only forced the enemy within their defences, but had ensured the safety of the siege-train then in progress from Fírozpúr. From that moment, then, preparations were set on foot for carrying out active operations for the capture of the place.

It was not, indeed, without much misgiving that the commander of the besieging army, Major-General Archdale Wilson, had given his consent to the carrying out of a measure the success of which, he considered, would depend on accident.* In an elaborate letter, addressed on the 20th of

* His own words were: "It is evident to me that the results of the proposed operations will be thrown on the hazard of a die."

Book X. Chapter I.

1857. Sept. 1.

Doubts and fears of General Wilson.

August to the chief engineer, Major Baird Smith, General Wilson, dwelling with considerable emphasis on the difficulties that had attended the progress of the siege—on the fact that he and his army had in reality occupied the position of a besieged force—had announced his intention of commencing offensive operations against the city on the arrival of the siege-train from Fírozpúr, though with no "hope of being able to take the place until supported by the force from below." He concluded his letter—the contents of which he intended to send to the Governor-General as a justification of his conduct—with a request that Major Baird Smith would favour him with such remarks and emendations as his experience as Chief Engineer might suggest.*

* The entire letter, a perusal of which will make clear the position before Dehlí at the date on which it was written (20th August 1857), runs as follows: "A letter has been received from the Governor-General urging our immediately taking Dehlí, and he seems angry that it was not done long ago. I wish to explain to him the true state of affairs: that Dehlí is seven miles in circumference, filled with an immense fanatical Músalmán population, garrisoned by full 40,000 soldiers armed and disciplined by ourselves, with 114 pieces of heavy artillery mounted on the walls, with the largest magazine of shot, shell, and ammunition in the Upper Provinces at their disposal, besides some sixty pieces of field artillery, all of our own manufacture, and manned by artillerymen drilled and taught by ourselves; that the Fort itself has been made so strong by perfect flanking defences erected by our own engineers, and a glacis which prevents our guns breaking the walls lower than eight feet from the top, without the labour of a regular siege and sap—for which the force and artillery sent against it has been quite inadequate; that an attempt to blow in the gates and escalade the walls was twice contemplated, but that it was considered,

Who and what sort of a man was he to whom the commander of the besieging army, at this

Book X. Chapter I.

1857. Sept. 1.

from the state of preparation against such attack on the part of the rebels, such an attempt would inevitably have failed, and have caused the most irreparable disaster to our cause; and that, even if we had succeeded in forcing our way into the place, the small force disposable for the attack would have been most certainly lost in the numerous streets of so large a city, and have been cut to pieces. It was, therefore, considered advisable to confine our efforts to holding the position we now occupy, which is naturally strong, and has been daily rendered more so by our engineers, until the force coming up from below could join to co-operate in the attack. That since the command of the force has devolved on me I have considered it imperatively necessary to adopt the same plan as the only chance of safety to the Empire, and that I strongly urge upon his Lordship the necessity of his ordering General Havelock's or some other force marching upon Dehlí as soon as possible. The force under my command is, and has been since the day we took our position, actually besieged by the mutineers, who, from the immense extent of suburbs and gardens extending nearly to the walls of the town, have such cover for their attacks that it has been very difficult to repel them, and at the same time to inflict such a loss as would deter a repetition of them. They have frequently been driven back with loss, but they immediately take refuge under the grape fire of their heavy guns on the city walls, and, on our retirement, reoccupied their former positions; every such attack upon them has entailed a heavy loss upon our troops, which we can ill spare, and has done us little good. I shall be reinforced by a siege-train from Firozpúr by the end of this or the beginning of next month, when I intend to commence more offensive operations against the city; but I cannot hold out any hope of being able to take the place until supported by the force from below. As an artillery officer, I have no hesitation in giving my opinion that the attack on Dehlí, garrisoned and armed as it now is, is as arduous an undertaking as was the attack on Bharatpúr in 1825-26, for which 25,000 troops and 100 pieces of artillery were not considered too large a force. I enclose a return of the original force which was sent down to capture this strong place, and also a return of the

Book X. Chapter I. 1857. Sept. 1. Baird Smith.

important conjuncture, made this earnest appeal? Major Baird Smith was an honour even to the Corps of Engineers. To a knowledge founded on extensive reading, to a mind which had thought out the several problems pertaining to Indian administration, he added a power of prompt and decisive action rarely bestowed except upon the senior wranglers of the University of Nature. He had travelled much, had mastered the several methods in which, in the countries of continental Europe, science, and especially the engineering science, had been laid under contribution to develop the latent forces of nature; and in India, had, as the administrative agent to whom was entrusted the completion of the Ganges Canal, applied the experience thus acquired to the perfection of that great work. The genius which could grasp great schemes of administrative reform, was equally at home in the performance of those duties with which the military side of his profession brought him into contact. Chief Engineer of the army before Dehlí, he had brought to the performance of his

present effective force, including sick and wounded, from which his Lordship will see how desperate would have been any attempt to take the city by assault, more especially as the mutineers keep a large portion of their force encamped outside the city walls, who, on our assaulting the city, could easily attack and capture our camp, with all our hospitals, stores, and ammunition, unless a strong provision was made against it. Something of this sort I intend forwarding to the Governor-General, and shall be glad if you will return this with such remarks and emendations as your experience as Chief Engineer suggests."

Book X. Chapter I.

1857. Sept. 1.

duties the large mind, the profound knowledge, the prompt decision which had characterised him in his civil work. Neither the shock and pain caused by a wound, nor the weakness and emaciation produced by a severe attack of camp scurvy, aggravated by diarrhœa, depressed his spirit or lessened his energies. Refusing to be placed on the sick list, though assured that mortification would be the consequence of a continued use of his wounded leg, Baird Smith clung to the last to the performance of his duty. The advice which he gave to General Wilson proved that never was his courage higher, never were the tone and temper of his mind more healthy, than when, bowed down by two diseases and suffering acutely from his wound, he seemed a livid wreck of the man he once had been.

The reasons which influenced Baird Smith to advise immediate action.

It was to such a man that Wilson appealed. The answer was clear, emphatic, decisive. Baird Smith was for action, for prompt and immediate action. True it is, he reasoned, the besieged are more numerous than the besiegers; true it is their resources are greater, their position is formidable, their defences are strong. But in war something must be risked. In his opinion the risk of a repulse in a well-contrived and well-organised assault was infinitely less than the risk which would attend the waiting during a long and uncertain period for reinforcements from below. The waiting for reinforcements involved inaction —an inaction which might last for weeks. Such inaction, at a time when the Panjáb, denuded of its last troops, was quivering in the balance, in-

Book X. Chapter I.

1857. Sept. 1.

volved a risk greater even than the risk of a repulse before the walls of the city. Nor was this last danger so great, in Baird Smith's estimation, as the General seemed to consider. He believed that it would be possible by skilfully preparing and effectively delivering an assault, to reduce it to a small proportion. He gave the fullest expression, in his reply, to these convictions, and concluded by urging the General to prepare for and to deliver that assault without delay—before the enemy should have time to strengthen his position within and without the beleaguered city.

These arguments, forcible, clear, based on logic and reason, had their natural effect on General Wilson. Though he did not share to the full Baird Smith's opinions as to the probable result of an assault, he was brought to regard the risk which would thus be encountered as considerably less than the risk which would be involved by inaction. He yielded * then, and directed the Chief Engineer to prepare a plan of attack.

Wilson yields, though without being convinced.

The reluctant assent of General Wilson threw upon the shoulders of his Chief Engineer the responsibility for the assault. Far from shrinking from the burden, Baird Smith eagerly seized it.

* General Wilson wrote thus on Baird Smith's memorandum: "It is evident to me that the results of the proposed operations will be thrown on the hazard of a die; but under the circumstances in which I am placed, I am willing to try this hazard—the more so as I cannot suggest any other plan to meet our difficulties. I cannot, however, help being of opinion that the chances of success under such a heavy fire as the working parties will be exposed to, are anything but favourable. I yield, however, to the judgment of the Chief Engineer."

1857. Sept. 1.

Baird Smith and Taylor prepare a plan of assault.

In conjunction with his second in command, Captain Alexander Taylor, a most able and indefatigable member of the same corps, one of those men who, once tried in difficult circumstances, are found to be indispensable, he submitted a plan —previously prepared, but subject to alteration resulting from daily-gained experience—simple, bold, and effective—easily workable, on the sole condition of hearty and zealous co-operation and obedience on the part of his subordinates. The result showed how well placed was the confidence bestowed by the Chief Engineer in the officers serving under his orders.

Before adverting to that plan, I propose to lay before the reader a short description of the defences of, and the approaches to, Dehlí.

The fortifications of Dehlí.

The characteristic features of the place were, at the time, thus officially described by Baird Smith: "The eastern face rests on the Jamná, and during the season of the year when our operations were carried on the stream may be described as washing the base of the walls. All access to a besieger on the river front is therefore impracticable. The defences here consist of an irregular wall, with occasional bastions and towers, and about one half of the length of the river face is occupied by the palace of the King of Dehlí, and its out-work, the old Mogol fort of Sélimgarh. The river may be described as the chord of a rough arc formed by the remaining defences at the place. These consist of a succession of bastioned fronts, the connection being very long, and the out-works limited to one

Book X. Chapter I.

1857. Sept. 1.

crown-work at the Ajmír gate, and martello towers mounting a single gun at such points as require additional flanking fire to that given by the bastions themselves. The bastions are small, generally mounting three guns in each face, two in each flank, and one in the embrasure at the salient. They are provided with masonry parapets about twelve feet in thickness, and have a relief of about sixteen feet above the plane of site. The curtain consists of a simple masonry wall or rampart sixteen feet in height, eleven feet thick at top, and fourteen or fifteen at bottom. This main wall carries a parapet loopholed for musketry, eight feet in height and eight feet in thickness. The whole of the land front is covered by a berm of variable width, ranging from sixteen to thirty feet, and having a scarp wall eight feet high. Exterior to this is a dry ditch, of about twenty-five feet in width, and from sixteen to twenty feet in depth. The counterscarp is simply an earthen slope easy to descend. The glacis is a very short one, extending only fifty or sixty yards from the counterscarp. Using general terms, it covers from the besiegers' view from half to one third of the height of the walls of the place. The defences, in a word, are 'modernised' forms of ancient works that existed when the city fell before Lord Lake's army in 1803. They extend about seven miles in circumference, and include an area of about three square miles. On the western side of Dehlí there appear the last out-lying spurs of the Aravelli mountains, and represented here by a low ridge, which dis-

1857. Sept. 1.

appears at its intersection with the Jamná, about two miles above the place. The drainage from the eastern slope of the ridge finds its way to the river along the northern and the north-western faces of the city, and has formed there a succession of parallel or connected ravines of considerable depth. By taking advantage of these hollow ways admirable cover was constantly obtained for the troops, and the labour of the siege was materially reduced. The whole of the exterior of the place presents an extraordinary mass of old buildings of all kinds, of thick brushwood, and occasional clumps of forest trees, giving great facilities for cover, which, during the siege operations at least, proved to be on the whole more favourable to us than to the enemy."

Such being the place, the plan for assaulting it traced by Baird Smith and Taylor may thus be described.

Plan of the attack.

It was inevitable that the attack should be made on the northern face of the fortress—the face represented by the Morí, Káshmir, and Water bastions, and the curtain walls connecting them. These connecting curtains were merely parapets, wide enough only for musketry fire. It had been in the power of the enemy greatly to strengthen these defences by pulling down the adjacent buildings, and on their ruins erecting a rampart, from which a continued fire of heavy guns should be concentrated on an attacking force. In neglecting, as a rule, to use the advantage thus open to them the rebel leaders added another example to many preceding it, of the absence from their

Book X. Chapter I. 1857. Sept. 1.

councils of a really capable commander. The neglect was likely to be fatal to the defence, for it enabled the besiegers to concentrate on the curtains a fire sufficient to crush the defenders' fire and to effect breaches through which the infantry could be launched against the town.

The plan of the Chief Engineer, then, was to crush the fire of the Morí bastion at the north-west corner of the city. That fire silenced, the advance on the extreme left, which was covered by the river, would be secure, and there the assault would be delivered.

Its simplicity and wisdom.

The simple wisdom of this plan will be at once recognised. In the first place the advance was effectually covered by the river on one flank, and partially so by trees and brushwood in front. The assault delivered, our men would not be at once involved in narrow streets, but there would be a space comparatively open in which to act.

Effective number of the besieging force. Sept. 6.

On the 6th September all the reinforcements which could be expected, together with the siege-train, had arrived in camp. The effective rank and file, of all arms, amounted to eight thousand seven hundred and forty-eight men, of whom three thousand three hundred and seventeen were Europeans. In line with, and acting with them, were two thousand two hundred native levies from Káshmir, and some hundreds from Jhínd.

Sept. 7.

The evening of the 7th was fixed upon for the commencement of the tracing of the batteries which were to assail the northern face of the city. On that day General Wilson issued to

1857. Sept. 7.

General Wilson announces to the troops his intention to assault.

the troops an order, in which he announced to them that the time was drawing near when he trusted their labours would be over, and they would be rewarded for all their past exertions, and for the fatigue still before them, by the capture of the city. Much, he reminded the infantry, still remained to be accomplished. They had to aid and assist the engineers alike in the erection of the batteries and in acting as covering parties; and when the way should be smoothed for them by the scientific branches of the service, they would have to dare death in the breach. When it should come to that point it would be necessary for them to keep well together, to push on in compact and unbroken masses.

His appeal to the infantry,

As for the artillery, their work, General Wilson warned them, would be harder than any they had till then encountered. He expressed, at the same time, his confidence that the members of that branch of the service would bring to the performance of that harder work the same cheerfulness and the same pluck which had characterised their labours up to that time.

to the artillery,

Reminding the troops of the cruel murders committed on their officers and their comrades, as well as on their wives and children, General Wilson declared that whilst the troops should spare the women and children who might fall in their way, they should give no quarter to the mutineers.

regarding quarter to the foe,

Upon the regimental officers was impressed the necessity of keeping their men together, of preventing plunder, of carrying out the directions of

to the regimental officers.

Book X. Chapter I.

1857. Sept. 7.

the engineers. The Major-General concluded by asserting his confidence that a brilliant termination of their labours would follow a zealous enforcement of his directions.

Before detailing the work which, on the evening of the 7th, followed the issue of this order, it is necessary to inform the reader that at the suggestion of Major Charles Reid,* who commanded on the ridge, a light battery had been erected on the night of the 6th upon the plateau of the ridge close to the Sammy house. The object of this battery, known as Reid's battery, was to keep the ground clear and to protect the contemplated new heavy battery, No. 1, during its construction. Reid's battery contained eight light pieces, six 9-pounders, and two 24-pound howitzers, and was commanded by Captain Remmington.

Reid's battery.

To return.—On the evening of the day on which General Wilson's order was issued the engineers commenced their work. In pursuance of the resolve to trace out a battery, the fire from which should crush the Morí bastion, Captain Alexander Taylor, assisted by Captain Medley, proceeded at sunset, accompanied by half-a-dozen sappers, to Hindú Ráo's house. A site had previously been selected to the left of the Sammy House, below the ridge on the open plain, and within seven hundred yards of the Morí bastion. Sand-bags had been taken down on the night of the 6th and covered over with grass and brushwood. These were found untouched by the enemy. The two engi-

Taylor and Medley trace No. 1 battery.

* Now General Sir Charles Reid, K.C.B.

Book X. Chapter I.

1857. Sept. 7.

neers at once set to work to trace a battery on this spot. The battery, styled No. 1 battery, was divided into two sections. The right section, commanded by Major Brind,* intended to receive five 18-pounders and one 8-inch howitzer, was to silence the Morí bastion, and to prevent it from interfering with the real attack on the left; the left section, and armed with four 24-pounders, under the command of Major Kaye, was designed to keep down the fire from the Káshmir bastion until the order to assault it should be given. These two sections were to be connected by a trench which, carried on beyond the left section, would communicate with the deep nullah close to the rear, and form a sort of first parallel, giving good cover to the guard of the trenches.

Its right section.

Its left section.

The tracing completed.

The tracing of this battery had but just been completed when a strong covering party of Reid's Gúrkahs arrived. Camels with fascines and gabions followed, and the work progressed rapidly during the night. The working parties were but little disturbed by the enemy, three well-directed showers of grape from the Morí alone reaching them.

In order to draw off the enemy's attention as much as possible, Major Reid, who was with

* Now General Sir James Brind, K.C.B. General Wilson's orders in writing, and verbally given by the Assistant Adjutant-General of Artillery, Edwin Johnson, were to the effect that Major Brind, commanding the Foot Artillery of the Delhi Field Force, was to command the Key, or No. 1 battery; Majors Frank Turner and Edward Kaye being attached for the subordinate command of the right and left wings. Major Turner being struck down by serious illness, the left wing was placed under charge of Major Kaye, supervised throughout by Major Brind.

Book X. Chapter I.

1857. Sept. 7.

Reid diverts the fire from the Morí bastion.

Taylor and Medley, sent directions to Captain Remmington to keep up a constant fire on the Morí bastion. This had the desired effect, for the Morí at once opened on Reid's battery and the Sammy House, and did not again molest the working parties. Indeed the enemy did not discover till the day dawned this fresh work upon which the besiegers had been engaged. Much to their dismay they beheld Brind's battery all but completed. Though great efforts had been made, however, all was not ready in it, and but one gun was in position as the morning of the 8th dawned. The rebels on the Morí bastion were not slow to notice the results of the work of that long night. Instantaneously they took measures to demolish it. With the daylight there poured on the barely armed battery showers of grape and round shot. So terrible and so incessant was the fire, that almost every man who ventured from the protection of the battery was knocked over. To this storm the defenders of the battery had but one gun to reply. Major James Brind, one of the heroes of this long siege, who, as already stated, commanded the entire No. 1 battery, noting this, dragged, by great exertion, a howitzer to the rear, and fired over the parapet at the Morí. The fire of the enemy still poured in, however, fierce, incessant, relentless. Emboldened by the weakness of the British reply, they even thought it might be possible to carry by assault the newly made battery. With this object they despatched a body of cavalry and infantry from the Láhor gate. This little

Sept. 8.

At dawn of day the enemy discover the new batteries.

Brind's splendid exertions.

The enemy's attempt to carry the

force, emerging from the gate with resolution, took at once the direction of the battery. But they had not gone far when they encountered a hot fire from the 18-pounder and howitzer in the right section of No. 1 battery, from the guns on the ridge, and the light guns on the plateau. This threw them into confusion—a confusion changed into a rout by the opportune discharge of a volley of grape from Brind's battery. The volley sent them back faster than they had come. All this time the men in this battery had been working hard, and though pelted incessantly from the Morí bastion, they soon succeeded in finishing a second platform, then a third, soon after a fourth and a fifth. On the completion of each platform the gun placed on it opened at once on the enemy. The effect of the fire, thus gradually increasing, was soon felt on the Morí. In Major Brind the officers and men possessed a commander of great perseverance, rare energy, a strong will, and a thorough knowledge of his profession. Under his skilful direction the shot from the battery told with tremendous and unceasing effect on the masonry bastion. Gradually the fire from it diminished; by the afternoon it ceased altogether. The bastion was then a heap of ruins, and although the enemy, displaying rare courage, managed to replace the heavy guns in succession to those knocked over, and to discharge them at the battery, the want of cover made it deadly work, and their fire soon languished. One part of the Engineer's plan had thus been carried out. The Morí bastion had been made harmless.

battery is baffled.

The right section is armed.

Major Brind renders the Morí harmless.

Book X. Chapter I.

1857. Sept. 8.

Heavy fire was, however, continued upon it from the right section and from the ridge until the night before the assault was delivered.

The left section

Whilst the right section of the battery had thus been blazing away at the Morí, the 24-pounders in the left section under Major Kaye had been doing their work well, their fire directed on the Káshmir bastion. This fire was continued day and night until noon on the 10th, when the battery caught fire from the constant discharge of our own guns. The sand-bags first caught the flame, then the fascines, made of dry brushwood, and at length the whole battery was in a blaze, which it was feared might extend to the right section and expense magazine.

is destroyed by fire on the 10th.

Gallantry of Lieutenant Lockhart.

Lieutenant Lockhart, now Colonel Lockhart, commanding 107th Foot, who was attached to Reid's Gúrkahs, was at the time on duty with two companies of the regiment in the connecting trench between the two sections. The necessity to extinguish the fire was so apparent to him, that he at once suggested to Major Kaye whether it might not be possible to save the battery by working from the outside and top of the parapet. Kaye replied that he thought something might be done if a party were to take sand-bags to the top, cut them, and smother the fire with the sand. Lockhart instantly jumped on to the parapet, followed by six or seven Gúrkahs, and began the work in the manner suggested. The enemy were not slow to discover what had happened, and, determined that the flames should not be extinguished, they at once brought every gun to bear on the blazing

Book X. Chapter I.

1857. Sept. 10.

battery and poured in a deadly fire of grape and musketry. Two of the Gúrkahs fell dead, and Lockhart rolled over the parapet with a shot through his jaw. The shot penetrating through the right cheek, passed under his tongue, and went out through the left cheek, smashing the right jaw to pieces.* The fire was eventually extinguished by means of the sand from the sand-bags, but the section was destroyed.

* The noble example set by Lockhart was witnessed by Major Reid, and mentioned as a case worthy, he considered, of the Victoria Cross. Unfortunately Reid's pencil reports, like many more despatches of his written daily from the ridge in pencil and under fire, were destroyed by General Wilson, as, being written in pencil and not in the regulated form, they were not considered "official." It thus happened that when General Wilson penned his final despatch, he had none of Reid's pencil notes and reports to refer to. Reid subsequently represented that his recommendations had not been attended to; that he had again and again brought to notice the gallant conduct of officers of the 60th Rifles and others who had served under him; and at length he himself sent in a supplementary despatch, through Colonel Norman, then Acting Adjutant-General. The reply he received was that in Lord Clyde's opinion "the time had altogether passed for publishing any further despatches relative to services of officers at Delhi, which, however meritorious, are now of old date." This was in February 1859. Prior to this Reid had been urging General Wilson to take notice of his recommendations. But it was in vain. Neither his pencil notes written under fire, nor his reports after the siege, were ever properly attended to, and many deserving officers were consequently left unrewarded. Among these was Captain John Fisher, second in command of the Sirmúr Battalion, who was on the ridge with the regiment throughout the siege, who commanded it during the assault, and who was the only officer out of nine who escaped being wounded. This officer did not even receive a brevet. For the same reason Major Reid's appreciatory mention of the services of the Engineer and Artillery officers, expressed in the strongest language, remained unpublished.

Book X. Chapter I.

1857. Sept. 7.

To return to the 7th. At the same time that the batteries just referred to were traced on the right, preliminary arrangements for the real attack had been made on the left. On the evening of the 7th, Kúdsia Bágh and Ludlow Castle were occupied by strong pickets. No opposition was offered to this occupation, the mutineers being impressed with the idea that the real attack would be made on the Morí. With these two posts strongly occupied as supports, the engineers were able, on the evening of the 8th, to trace out battery No. 2. This trace was made in front of Ludlow Castle, and five hundred yards from the Káshmir gate. Like battery No. 1—called, after the commandant, Brind's battery—it was divided into two portions, the right-half being intended for seven heavy howitzers and two 18-pounders; the left, about two hundred yards distant, for nine 24-pounders. The fire from these two portions was intended to silence the fire from the Káshmir bastion, to knock away the parapet right and left that gave cover to the defenders, and to open the main breach by which the place was to be stormed.*

Tracing of battery No. 2.

Sept. 8.

Warned by the experience of Brind's battery,

* These and the other details describing the plans of the engineers have been taken chiefly from a work entitled *A Year's Campaigning in India*. This book—written by Captain, now Lieutenant-Colonel, Julius George Medley, R.E., himself a distinguished actor in the scenes he describes—gives an account of the proceedings at this memorable epoch of the siege, which may be almost styled authoritative, confirmed as it has been by the testimony of distinguished officers who took part in the preliminaries to the assault.

no attempt was made to complete battery No. 2 in one night. On the 8th the tracing alone was completed. The wisdom of this cautious mode of proceeding was made clear the following day, when a sharp fire of shot, of shell, and of musketry was opened from the Káshmir and Water bastions and the Sélimgarh, on the positions newly occupied. Little damage, however, was effected, and the work was pushed forward during the nights of the 9th and 10th. Before dawn of the 11th the battery had been completed and armed, and it was then unmasked. Major Campbell commanded the left section of it, and Major Kaye—transferred from the ignited left section of Battery No. 1—the right, but the former officer having been wounded on the evening of the 11th, Captain Edwin Johnson,* Assistant Adjutant-General of Artillery, then serving in the battery, succeeded to the command, and held it to the moment of assault, when he resumed his place on General Wilson's staff.

Book X. Chapter I.

1857. Sept. 8. The enemy open fire upon it.

Sept. 9-11.

The third battery was not completed before that night. This battery was traced by Captain Medley the evening of the 9th. With a boldness which was not rare, but the display of which, in this instance, testified to remarkable negligence on the part of the enemy, the engineers traced this battery within one hundred and sixty yards of the Water bastion. Seeking for a fit site for the battery, the director of the attack, Captain Medley, discovered a small ruined building, an

Battery No. 3.

* Now Lieutenant-General Sir Edwin Johnson, K.C.B.

Book X. Chapter I.

1857. Sept. 9–11.

out-office of the Custom House—a large edifice within one hundred and sixty yards of the Water bastion, and totally unoccupied by the enemy. Captain Medley took possession of the Custom House, and determined to trace the battery inside the small ruined building referred to, the outer wall of which would conceal the work and give cover to the workmen. This daring measure completely succeeded. Though the enemy, suspecting something though not the actual truth, peppered our workmen incessantly, these never flinched. When one man fell another would take his place.* Working in this way the battery was finished and armed by the night of the 11th.

Battery No. 4.

Another battery, No. 4, for four heavy mortars, commanded by Major Tombs, was traced and armed on the night of the 10th, in a safe spot in the Kúdsiabágh itself, ready to open fire when required.

The enemy detect the point from which the attack is to be made,

The mutineers had by this time become alive to the fact that it was not from the right but from the left that the real attack was to issue. With an alacrity worthy of the highest praise, they at once decided upon measures which, if

* "Pandy did not know what we were at, but at any rate he knew the people were working in that direction, and he served out such a liberal supply of musketry and shell that night that the working party lost thirty-nine men killed and wounded. It was wonderful indeed to see with what courage the men worked.

"They were merely the unarmed Pioneers I have described above, and not meant to be fighting men. With the passive courage so common to natives, as man after man was knocked over, they would stop a moment, weep a little over their fallen friend, pop his body in a row along with the rest, and then work on as before."—*Medley*.

commenced but forty-eight hours earlier, would have effectually baffled the attack. Seeing the effect which the fire from the still masked batteries must produce, they set to work to mount heavy guns along the long curtain. In other convenient nooks, out of reach of the fire of the attack, they mounted light guns. Taking advantage, too, of the broken ground before them, they made in one night an advanced trench parallel to the left attack, and three hundred and fifty yards from it, covering the whole of their front. This trench they lined with infantry.

Book X. Chapter I.

1857. Sept. 10–11.

and take measures to repel it.

The heavy guns could not be mounted behind the long curtain in time to anticipate the attack; but at daybreak, on the morning of the 11th, the light guns above alluded to opened an enfilading attack from the right, whilst the muskets from the infantry in the new trench began a hot and unceasing fire. For a time there was no answer. But at 8 o'clock the two sections of No. 2 battery, unmasked, replied. They began with a salvo from the nine 24-pounders—a salvo greeted by cheers from the men in the battery. The effect was marked and decisive. As the site of the breach was struck, huge fragments of stone fell, and the curtain wall disappeared in the ditch. The defenders on the Káshmir bastion attempted to reply, but in ten minutes their fire was silenced. For the rest of the day the guns of No. 2 battery continued to pound away at the walls. It was an exhilarating sight to watch the stone-work crumbling under the storm of shot and shell, the breach getting larger and larger, and the 8-inch

They open fire on the new batteries.

Effective reply from No. 2 battery.

Book X. Chapter I.

1857. Sept. 11.

shells, made to burst just as they touched the parapet, bringing down whole yards of it at a time.*

During the night the mortars from No. 3 battery kept the enemy on the alert with incessant fire. But the rebels were by no means idle. The light guns already alluded to, reinforced by a heavy one, playing from martello towers and from holes in curtain walls, maintained a constant and most effective front and enfilading fire on Nos. 1 and 2 batteries. The batteries were constantly raked from end to end. So terrible and so effective was this fire, that, at last, one of the guns of No. 1 battery was withdrawn from playing on the breach and placed in the epaulment to keep down, if possible, the enfilading fire. But even this did not prove very effectual. At one time General Wilson was inclined to make a rush at these guns from the right† and spike or capture them. But their position, within grape-shot of the curtain wall, rendered an attack on them difficult, and certain to be attended with loss. On the other hand, No. 3 battery would be completed on the morrow, and it was hoped that the effect of the full power of the artillery would be decisive.

The enemy's fire works destruction in No. 1 and 2 batteries.

Sept. 12.

At 11 o'clock on the morning of the 12th,

* Medley.

† In fact, Major Reid actually was instructed to make a night attack on the position, and four companies of Guides and Gúrkahs were told off supplied with spikes for the purpose. At the same time the battery near the Sammy House received orders from Major Reid to cover the attack and draw off the enemy's fire. Just then orders arrived from General Wilson countermanding the attack.

Book X. Chapter I.

1857. Sept. 12.

Greathed, of the Engineers, aided by some native sappers, unmasked the embrasures. The battery was commanded by Major Scott, with the gallant Fagan as his second in command. In another minute the six guns of the battery opened fire. The effect was tremendous. The enemy's guns were dismounted or smashed; the Water bastion was beaten into a shapeless mass, and in a few hours the breach seemed almost practicable. But the rebels showed no faint heart. Though their guns were silenced, they continued to pour in so heavy and continuous a musketry fire that the air seemed alive with bullets. The loss of life was consequently severe. Fagan, who, in his over-anxiety to see the effect of the first salvo, had raised his head above the parapet, was shot dead. Still further to embarrass the attack, the enemy opened from the other side of the river an enfilading fire, which, though not so effective or so destructive as that carried on from martello towers, was still sufficiently annoying. But our gallant artillerymen never flinched. Throughout the day all the batteries poured in a fire from fifty guns and mortars on the devoted city. The heat was intense, the labour was severe, the danger was enormous. But during the long hours of the day, and of the night which slowly followed, those unflinching officers and men, sustained by the conviction that to their unflagging energies was entrusted a task necessary for the triumph of the British cause, stood firmly to their guns, resisting every weakness of the flesh, their hearts joined in one firm resolve, re-

No. 3 battery opens fire,

with tremendous effect.

Splendid exertions of the Bengal Artillery.

Book X. Chapter I.

1857. Sept. 12–13.

Their continued fire effects breaches in the defences.

joicing in the sight of the destruction made by their guns, their mortars, and their howitzers on the walls which had so long bade them defiance.* The fire continued that day, that night, and the day following, the enemy still responding, and with considerable effect. On the afternoon of the 13th, General Wilson, in consultation with Baird Smith, thought that two sufficient breaches had been made. He accordingly directed that they should be examined.

Four engineers sent to examine the breaches.

For this dangerous duty four young engineer officers were selected, Medley and Lang for the Káshmir bastion, Greathed and Home for the Water. The two first-named officers made one attempt as soon as it was dusk, but they were discovered and fired at. They determined, therefore, to postpone the examination till 10 o'clock. To facilitate the accomplishment of his task,

Medley and Lang

Medley requested the officers commanding the batteries to fire heavily on the breach till 10 o'clock, then to cease firing. He then arranged that six picked riflemen of the 60th Rifles should accompany himself and his companion, and that an officer and twenty men of the same regiment should follow in support, halting at the edge of

* "At different times between the 7th and 11th," wrote Major Baird Smith in his despatch, "these batteries opened fire with an efficiency and a vigour which excited the unqualified admiration of all who had the good fortune to witness it. Every object contemplated in the attack was accomplished with a success even beyond my expectations; and I trust I may be permitted to say, that while there are many noble passages in the history of the Bengal Artillery, none will be nobler than that which will tell of its work on this occasion."

the jungle while they went on to the breach. Should the officer see that the two engineer officers and party were being cut off, he was to bring his men to their support, sounding his whistle for them to fall back. Should, on the other hand, one of the examining party be wounded, or should the party require support, they were to whistle for him.

Book X. Chapter I.

1857. Sept. 13.

The night was a bright starlight, and there was no moon. Just before the two officers and their party started, an 8-inch shell from the enemy buried itself deep in ground close to them, burst, and covered them with earth. A minute later and the gongs sounded 10. The firing suddenly ceased. The explorers were at once on their feet, and, drawing swords, and feeling that their revolvers were ready to hand, began to advance stealthily into the enemy's country.

set out for the Káshmir bastion.

Safely, and without discovery, the two officers and their six followers reached the edge of the ditch. Not a soul was to be seen. The counterscarp was sixteen feet deep, and steep. Lang slid down it; Medley then passed down by the ladder, and with two of the men descended after Lang, leaving the other four to cover the retreat. In two minutes more they would have reached the top of the breach. But careful and stealthy as had been their movements, they had not been quite noiseless. Just at that moment they heard several men running from the left towards the breach. They, therefore, reascended, though with some difficulty, and throwing themselves on the grass, waited for events. Prone in the deep

They reach the edge of the ditch;

descend into it;

find the enemy on the alert;

return to the edge;

Book X. Chapter II. — 1857. Sept. 13.

shade, they could see, without being seen, against the clear sky, not twenty yards distant, a number of dusky forms. They watched them as they loaded their muskets. The moments were exciting, but the excitement did not prevent Medley and his comrade from carefully examining, from the ground where they lay, the longed-for breach. They saw that it was large, that the slope was easy of ascent, and that there were no guns in the flanks. They had had experience that the descent was an easy one. It would be desirable, they felt, to reach the top, but the dusky figures would not move, and any attempt to surprise them would be uncertain, and would involve possibly the loss of some of their party. Besides, they had really gained the knowledge they had come to acquire. Medley, therefore, determined to be satisfied and to fall back. But how to fall back? There was but one way. Medley suddenly gave a preconcerted signal. At once they all started up and ran back. A volley followed them, but ineffectively. Untouched they gained their own batteries in safety.

find the breach practicable;

and run back in safety.

Greathed and Home had not been less successful in their expedition. They had examined the Water bastion; and although they had found that the musketry parapets had not been so sufficiently destroyed as they would be were the cannonade to be prolonged, they reported the breach practicable.

Greathed and Home report the breach at the Water bastion practicable.

With these two reports before him, Baird Smith did not hesitate. The dangers of delay, the worn-out state of the men in the batteries, far

Baird Smith advises Wilson to deliver the

Book X. Chapter I.

1857. Sept. 13–14.

outweighed any consideration which the condition of the musketry parapets in the Water bastion might suggest. He at once, then, advised General Wilson to deliver the assault at daybreak the following morning.

assault at once.

In such a matter the General commanding could not but act on the advice thus tendered him. General Wilson immediately issued the necessary orders. To Brigadier-General Nicholson, of the Bengal Army, whose triumphant march through the Panjáb and subsequent victory at Najafgarh had made him the hero of the campaign, was assigned the command of the first column, destined to storm the breach near the Káshmir bastion, and escalade the face of the bastion. This column was composed of three hundred men of H.M.'s 75th Regiment under Lieutenant-Colonel Herbert; of two hundred and fifty men of the 1st Fusiliers * under Major Jacob; and of four hundred and fifty men of the 2nd Panjáb Infantry, under Captain Green; in all, one thousand men. The engineer officers attached to this column were Lieutenants Medley, Lang, and Bingham.

Wilson accepts the advice and assigns the commands of the several assaulting columns.

First column, Nicholson.

The second column was commanded by Brigadier William Jones, C.B., of H.M.'s 61st Regiment. It was formed of two hundred and fifty men of H.M.'s 8th Regiment, under Lieutenant-Colonel Greathed; of two hundred and fifty men of the 2nd Fusiliers,† under Captain Boyd; of three hundred and fifty men of the 4th Sikh

Second column, Brigadier William Jones.

* Now H.M.'s 101st Royal Bengal Fusiliers.

† Now H.M.'s 104th Bengal Fusiliers.

Book X. Chapter I. — 1857. Sept. 13-14.

Infantry, under Captain Rothery; in all, eight hundred and fifty men. This column was to storm the breach in the Water bastion. The engineer officers attached to it were Lieutenants Greathed, Hovenden, and Pemberton.

Third column, Colonel Campbell.

The command of the third column was confided to Colonel Campbell, H.M.'s 52nd Foot. It was composed of two hundred men of the 52nd, under Major Vigors; of two hundred and fifty men of the Kamáon Battalion, under Captain Ramsay; of five hundred men of the 1st Panjáb Infantry, under Lieutenant Nicholson; in all, nine hundred and fifty men. The duty assigned to it was to assault by the Káshmir gate after it should have been blown open. The engineer officers attached to it were Lieutenants Home, Salkeld, and Tandy.

Fourth column, Major Reid.

The fourth column was commanded by Major Reid of the Bengal Army. It consisted of the Sirmúr Battalion,* the Guide Corps, and such of the pickets, European and native, as could be spared from Hindú Rao's house; in all (of these) eight hundred and sixty men. But, in addition, there was a portion of the contingent of the Maháráj́á of Káshmir, commanded by Captain Richard Lawrence, and consisting of twelve hundred men. The task assigned to this column was to attack the suburb Kishanganj, and to enter the Láhor gate.† The engineer officers attached to

* Now the Prince of Wales's Own Gúrkahs.

† This was the plan laid down by General Wilson. Had Reid attempted to follow it literally, that is, to enter by the Láhor gate, his troops would have been exposed to

this column were Lieutenants Maunsell and Tennant.

1857. Sept. 13-14.

Fifth column, Brigadier Longfield.

The fifth, or reserve, column was commanded by Brigadier Longfield of H.M.'s 8th Regiment. It was composed as follows: two hundred and fifty men, H.M.'s 61st Regiment, under Lieutenant-Colonel Deacon; four hundred and fifty men, 4th Panjáb Infantry, under Captain Wilde; three hundred men, Bilúch Battalion, under Lieutenant-Colonel Farquhar; three hundred men of the Rájá of Jhind's auxiliary force, under Lieutenant-Colonel Dunsford; in all, one thousand three hundred men. To these were subsequently added two hundred men of the 60th Rifles, under Lieutenant-Colonel John Jones of that regiment, detailed in the first instance to cover the advance. This column, acting as a reserve, was to follow the first column. The engineer officers attached to it were Lieutenants Ward and Thackeray.

The commanders of the assaulting columns.

The officers appointed to the command of the five assaulting columns were, then, Nicholson, Jones, Campbell, Reid, and Longfield. They were all picked men, fitted alike by nature and

the fire of the left face of the Láhor bastion, of the right face of the Burn bastion, and to the musketry fire from the loop-holed curtain connecting both bastions, which had been untouched by our artillery. Reid wrote to General Wilson to say that his column would be destroyed if he attempted anything of the sort, and proposed that, after taking Kishanganj and the suburbs, he should leave the Jammú contingent in the fortified serai, and follow the dry bed of the canal, where his troops would be under cover the whole way to the Kábul gate, which, he had arranged with Nicholson, should be opened for him from the inside.

Book X. Chapter I.

1857. Sept. 13-14.

Nicholson.

by training for the task devolving upon them. Of Nicholson it is unnecessary to say much. His exploits in the Panjáb, and but a few days before at Najafgarh, had made him the paladin of the army. The commander of the second column,

Jones.

Brigadier William Jones, had served at Chilianwála and at Gújrát; had co-operated in the destruction of the enemy after that crowning victory by pursuing them, at the head of his regiment and a troop of artillery, to the Khaibar pass; and, during the siege of Dehlí, had distinguished himself as brigadier of the 3rd In-

Campbell.

fantry Brigade. Colonel Campbell, commanding the third column, was the colonel of the 52nd. He had commanded his regiment with distinguished gallantry at Siálkôt, where it formed part of Nicholson's force.

Reid.

Major Reid, of the fourth column, belonged to the Bengal Army. Major Charles Reid had served in Sind under Sir Charles Napier, throughout the Satlaj and Barmese wars, and had ever distinguished himself not less by energy and daring, than by readiness of resource and presence of mind. During the siege, whilst the remainder of the attacking force had occupied the old parade ground, covered by the ridge, Reid alone had held the ridge. All the pickets detached from the main force to various points on the ridge had been under his orders, and his only. The posts thus under his command had included the main picket at Hindú Rao's house, the Observatory, the Sammy House, the Crow's Nest, and the Sabzimandi. On the positions so indicated he had, between the 8th June* and the 14th September, repulsed no less than twenty-six attacks, displaying a daring, a coolness, and a presence of mind not to be surpassed. On the 17th June, with a small force of four companies of the 60th Rifles, his own regiment, the Sirmúr Battalion, and twenty-five sappers, he had stormed the strong position of Kishanganj, destroying the enemy's batteries stationed there, and returning the same evening to his position on the ridge. Brigadier Longfield, commanding the reserve column, was brigadier of the second brigade during the siege. His conspicuous services fully entitled him to the post which was assigned him on this memorable occasion.

Book X. Chapter I.

1857. Sept. 13-14.

Longfield.

It was 3 o'clock in the morning. The columns of assault were in the leash. In a few moments they would be slipped. What would be the result? Would the skill and daring of the soldiers of England triumph against superior numbers defending and defended by stone walls; or would rebellion, triumphing over the assailants, turn that triumph to a still greater account by inciting by its means to its aid the Panjáb and the other parts of India still quivering in the balance? That, indeed, was the question. The fate of

Sept. 14.

The enormous stake dependent on the result of the assault.

* Major Reid's services in the mutiny commence from even a prior date. He marched with his regiment from Dehrá on the 14th May 1857, and by his vigorous action in the disturbed district of Balandshahr, opened communications with Mírath and Álígarh, and with the seat of Government in Calcutta, a service of vital importance, for which he received the thanks of the Governor-General in Council.

Book X. Chapter I. — 1857. Sept. 14.

Dehlí was in itself the smallest of the results to be gained by a successful assault. The fate of India was in the balance. The repulse of the British would entail the rising of the Panjáb!

The order of assault.

It had been decided that whilst the first and second columns should direct their attack against the breaches near the Káshmir and Water bastions, an explosion party should steal ahead and blow up the Káshmir gate, through which the third column should then effect an entrance into the city. The explosion party consisted of Lieutenants Home and Salkeld of the Engineers; of Sergeants Smith, Carmichael, and Corporal Burgess, *alias* Grierson, of the Sappers and Miners; of Bugler Hawthorne, H.M.'s 52nd Light Infantry; and of eight native sappers. It was covered by two hundred men of the 60th Rifles, under Lieutenant-Colonel Jones of that regiment. The duty devolving on the Sappers and Miners and their officers, was, it is almost needless to state, to blow up the Káshmir gate; that of Bugler Hawthorne was to announce, by means of his bugle, to the storming party, that the explosion had done its work completely.

The first, second, and third columns set out.

Though preparations had been made to advance to the assault a little after 3 in the morning, some slight delay occurred, and the day was dawning ere the columns were in motion. All this time the besiegers' batteries were pouring in a heavy and continuous fire—a fire which the enemy, always on the alert, answered with rockets, shells, and round shot. It was amid the din and tumult caused by this artillery duel that, just

Book X. Chapter I.

1857. Sept. 14.

after dawn, the first, second, and third columns started on their tremendous errand. General Nicholson had the general management of the attack. He looked quiet but anxious. General Wilson rode up just as the columns were advancing, evidently full of anxiety.* No wonder, knowing, as he did know, the enormous issues at stake on the result of the day's work before his men.

Their progress to the ground opposite Ludlow Castle.

The columns advanced as far as the ground opposite Ludlow Castle. There they halted. The first column then moved sharply to the left to take up its position in Kúdsia Bágh, there to wait for the signal; the second went further to the left, and formed up behind No. 3 battery; the third remained on the high road, to await there the bugle-sound which was to summon them to the Káshmir gate. The signal for the assault of the first and second columns was to be the sudden advance of the skirmishers of the 60th Rifles.

Nicholson gives the signal to push on.

The columns having taken up their positions, Nicholson gave the signal. The Rifles at once dashed to the front with a cheer, extending along and skirmishing through the low jungle—which at this point extends to within fifty yards of the ditch—and opening at the same time a fire on the enemy on the walls. At the sound of their advance, the engineer officers attached to the first column, previously posted on the edge of the jungle whence the column was to advance towards the breach, waved their swords to show the way

* Medley.

Book X. Chapter I.

1857. Sept. 14.

to the stormers. The fire from our batteries had ceased, whilst that of the enemy, now thoroughly alive to the nature of the contest, continued incessant. Through this fire Medley and Lang and the ladder-men advanced at a quick walk till they reached the edge of the cover. Then, forming their ladder-men into a sort of line, they rushed to the breach, closely followed by the storming party, and in a minute gained the crest of the glacis. They were here in the open exposed to a terrific and unceasing fire from the breach and the open parapet walls, which told with fatal effect. So hot was the fire that for ten minutes it was impossible to let down the ladders. "Man after man was struck down, and the enemy, with yells and curses, kept up a terrific fire, even catching up stones from the breach in their fury, and, dashing them down, dared the assailants to come on."* But, undaunted by these cries and by the fire by which they were accompanied, the British soldiers did push on. They succeeded at length in getting two of the ladders into the ditch, and instantly the officers led their men down them†. Once in the ditch, to mount the escarp and scramble up the breach was the work of an instant. But the enemy did not wait

The engineers of the first column reach the breach.

The assailants are met by a terrible fire,

but by desperate valour gain the breach.

* Medley, who is my chief authority for all the details of the assault.

† "The storming parties pushed on, two ladders were thrown into the ditch, and a brave officer, Fitzgerald, of H.M.'s 75th Regiment, who was killed directly afterwards, was the first to mount. As soon as I saw my first ladder down, I slid down into the ditch, mounted up the escarp, and scrambled up the breach, followed by the soldiers."—*Medley.*

for them. The insulting yells and curses ceased as the whilom utterers hurriedly vacated their position. "The breach was won, and the supporting troops pouring in fast, went down the ramp into the main-guard below."* Book X. Chapter I. 1857. Sept. 14.

Whilst the first column was thus carrying out, with daring and success, the work assigned to it, the second, under Brigadier William Jones, C.B., had not been less occupied. Led by its engineers, Greathed and Hovenden, the column advanced towards the breach in the Water bastion. By some mistake the supporting party of the stormers pressed forward on the right of the party, and, rushing to the counterscarp of the curtain, slid into its ditch, climbed its breach, and won the rampart. The stormers of the 8th,† however, most of them carrying ladders, followed the engineers to the Water bastion. They had to make a slight detour to the right to avoid some water in the ditch, and being in the open, they were exposed to the full fury of the enemy's fire, which, at this point, was incessant and well directed. The two engineer officers fell, severely wounded, and of the thirty-nine ladder-men, twenty-nine were struck down in a few minutes. But here, as at the Káshmir gate, British valour was not to be daunted. The ladders were at length placed and the breach was carried by the survivors, twenty-five in number, the senior of whom was a colour-sergeant.

The second column.

The bulk of it turn off to the right and gain the rampart.

The stormers of the 8th King's gain the breach of the Water gate.

Meanwhile the remainder of the column, which

* Medley.

† Captain Baynes, Lieutenants Pogson and Metge, and seventy-five rank and file.

Book X. Chapter I.

1857. Sept. 14.

had entered by the curtain breach, had done wonders. Their entrance into a vital point of the defences, where an attack had not been expected, for the moment paralysed the enemy.

Brigadier Jones presses forward to the Kábul gate.

Brigadier Jones, who, in command of the column, had displayed great gallantry, took advantage of the disorder into which they had been thrown by clearing the ramparts as far as the Kábul gate, on the top of which he planted the column flag,* carried by a private of the 61st, Andrew Laughnan.

Before recording the proceedings of the third column, I propose to follow the explosion party, on whose action the movements of that column were to depend.

The explosion party.

The composition of this party has already been given. Posted in front of the third column, it advanced straight on the Káshmir gate, in the face of a very hot fire.

Splendid audacity of Home.

Undeterred by this fire, Lieutenant Home and four men, each carrying a bag of twenty-five pounds of powder, pushed on through a barrier gate, which was found open, across the ditch, to the foot of the great double gate. So great was the audacity of this proceeding, that it completely paralysed the enemy. Firing only a few straggling shots, they closed the wicket with every appearance of alarm, and Home, after laying his bags, had time to jump into the ditch unhurt. Salkeld was not so for-

* This flag was presented by Sir William Jones to Her Majesty the Queen on the 1st January 1877, the day of the proclamation of Her Majesty's title of Empress of India.

Book X. Chapter I. 1857. Sept. 14.

tunate. Before he could reach the gate the enemy had recovered from their panic, and, divining his object, had resolved to do their utmost to thwart it. From either side of the top of the gateway, and from the open wicket close by, they poured upon him and his party a deadly fire. Salkeld, nevertheless, laid his bags, but was almost immediately after shot through the arm and leg, and fell back disabled on the bridge. He handed the portfire to Sergeant Burgess, bidding him light the fusee. Burgess, trying to obey, was shot dead. Sergeant Carmichael then seized the portfire, lighted the fusee, but immediately fell, mortally wounded. The other sergeant, Smith, thinking that Carmichael had failed, rushed forward to seize the portfire, but noticing the fusee burning, threw himself into the ditch. The next moment the massive gate was shattered with a tremendous explosion. Home at once ordered Hawthorne to sound the bugle-call.* Fearing that in the noise of the assault the sound might not be heard, he had it repeated three times. The 52nd, anxiously awaiting the signal, did not hear it; but their colonel, the

Salkeld lays his bags, but is wounded.

Burgess and Carmichael are killed.

Wonderful escape of Smith.

Home orders the advance to be sounded.

* A more daring and gallant achievement than that of the officers and non-commissioned officers mentioned in the text has never been recorded. Their subsequent fate cannot but inspire interest. Burgess and Carmichael were killed on the spot; Salkeld, Home, Smith, and Hawthorne were recommended by General Wilson for the Victoria Cross. But Salkeld succumbed in a few days to the severe wounds he had received; Home met his death shortly afterwards at Málagarh; Smith and Hawthorne survived, to receive the honours that they had so nobly earned.

Book X. Chapter I.

1857. Sept. 14.

Campbell does not hear the sound, but orders the advance on hearing the explosion.

gallant Campbell, who also commanded the column, in front of which he had posted himself, noticing the explosion, and expecting the call, asked, not hearing it himself, whether it had reached the ears of any of those about him. Though no one had heard it, Campbell felt that at so critical a moment action was better than standing still. He at once ordered the advance. The column responded eagerly. The 52nd gallantly led the way, and in less than a minute after the bugle had sounded, they dashed on over the bridge, and entered the city just as the other columns had won the breaches.*

Campbell pushes on to within sight of the Jamma Masjid.

Colonel Campbell, on gaining the main-guard inside the gate, at once re-formed his column, and pushed on with the intention of occupying the Kótwáli, and, if possible, the Jamma Masjid. He cleared the Water bastion, within which some of the enemy were still lurking, the church, and the enclosure known as the "Delhi Gazette compound," and forced his way through the Káshmir Gate bazaar. A gun which commanded the line of advance was carried by a rush of a party of the 52nd, under Lieutenant Bradshaw, who, however, paid with his life on the spot the penalty of his daring. Still pressing forward, Campbell reached the gate opening on the Chándni Chók. Forcing this, he advanced without much opposition, except from a musketry fire from a few houses. A sudden turn of the road

* Lieutenant Home's *Report*; Bugler Hawthorne's *Statement*; Medley; Bayley's *Assault of Dehlí.*

Book X. Chapter I.

1857. Sept. 14.

brought him within sight of the Jamma Masjid, its arches and gates bricked up, incapable of being forced without powder-bags or guns, rendered safe against assault from mere infantry. Unwilling to forego the chance of storming this formidable position, Campbell remained in front of it for half an hour, under a fire of musketry from the houses, in the expectation of the successful advance of the other columns. But as time went on, and there were no visible signs of the approach of the one or the other, Campbell deemed it advisable to retire on the Bégam's Bágh, a large enclosure. He held this place for an hour and a half, exposed to a heavy fire of musketry, grape, and canister. Here I must leave him whilst I trace the progress of the fourth column.

For want of support retires on the Bégam Bágh.

Much depended on the success of its attack. Commanded by Major Reid, it was designed to move from Hindú Rao's house, on the right, against the suburbs of Kishanganj and Pahári-púr, with a view of driving the enemy thence and effecting an entrance at the Kábul gate after it should be taken by General Nicholson. The successful advance of the first, second, and third columns depended, then, very much on the result of this flank attack.

Attack of the fourth column.

Major Reid's column,* composed of detachments of eight different regiments, eight hundred and sixty men in all, with a reserve of one thousand two hundred infantry of the Jammú contingent,

His column deficient in guns.

* *Vide* Appendix A.

Book X. Chapter I.

1857. Sept. 14.

formed up at 4.30 A.M. on the Grand Trunk Road, opposite the Sabzi Mandi picket. Before 5 A.M. all was in readiness, but the four horse artillery guns which were ordered to accompany the column had not arrived. Presently the guns came up, but the officer reported that there were only sufficient gunners to man one gun. Reid had no intention of taking one gun into action contrary to the rules of the service, so he directed the officer to obtain the full complement of gunners as soon as possible. It was now broad daylight, and he was anxiously listening for the explosion (the blowing in of the Káshmír gate), which was to have been his signal to advance, when he heard musketry fire on his right, and soon discovered that the party of the Jammú troops, four hundred infantry and four guns, which he had ordered to proceed direct from the camp at 3.45 A.M., for the purpose of making a diversion by occupying the Ídgar, had become engaged with the enemy. No time under these circumstances was to be lost, so he at once pushed on with the column without the horse artillery guns, and more than half an hour before the attack of the other columns.

The Jammú troops, sent by Reid to make a diversion, become engaged with the enemy.

Reid advances.

The detachment of the 60th Rifles, under Captain Muter, was thrown out in skirmishing order to the right of the road, while a feeling party of the Guides was sent a short distance ahead of the column. When within sixty yards of the canal bridge, Reid discovered that the enemy had manned their breast-works across the road, as also one running parallel to the road, and that

Book X. Chapter I.

1857. Sept. 14.

both of them had been considerably strengthened during the night. The head of the column approached the first line of breast-works, within fifty yards, when the enemy opened with a tremendous volley. The 60th Rifles meanwhile closed to the left, and with the Sirmúr Gúrkahs, made a dash, and instantly drove the enemy from his first line of defence. They at once retreated on their second line. Meanwhile a steady fire was kept up by the enemy from the loop-holed wall of Kishanganj, eighteen feet high, which completely commanded the position now gained by the head of Reid's column, and many of his men fell. Reid, who was standing on the parapet of the canal bridge, now observed that the enemy had been reinforced from the city. They came in thousands down the dry bed of the canal over which Reid was standing, and a large body appeared on the road, hesitating apparently whether they should drive our men from the breast-work already gained, or attack the detachment of the Jammú troops on the right, which had never approached the Ídgar—a result of their starting from the camp nearly an hour after the time laid down. Guns at this time, whilst the enemy stood in a mass on the road, would have been invaluable, and would have proved of the greatest service to Reid, but, though the guns had been sent, no gunners, through some unaccountable mistake, were available to man them.

Embarrassment felt by Reid from the want of artillery.

Reid is struck down.

Reid was just about to feign an attack in front of the Kishanganj heavy batteries, whilst he should direct a real one in their flank and rear, when he fell over the parapet of the bridge with a musket-

Book X. Chapter I. 1857. Sept. 14.

shot wound in the head, his engineer officer, Lieutenant Maunsell, who was standing near him, being also hit in the head. Up to this time, Reid states in his dispatch, "all was going on admirably, the troops were steady, and well in hand, and I made sure of success." How long he lay on the ground insensible is not known—all thought he was dead—but when he came to his senses he found himself on the back of one of his Gúrkahs. He then saw the party of the Jammú contingent on his right hard pressed. He sent for Captain Lawrence, who was his second in command, and, presently meeting him, directed him to take command and to support the right. The reserve, under Captain Lawrence, consisting of one thousand two hundred infantry of the Jammú contingent, was in rear of the column. The detached party of four hundred infantry destined for the Ídgar, became perfectly disorganised after Reid's fall. They rushed into the main column, and caused the greatest confusion, making it difficult to distinguish friend from foe.

On reviving he makes over command to Richard Lawrence.

Fatal effect of the fall of Reid.

The fall of Major Reid was an irreparable blow to the success of the fourth column. He knew every inch of the ground thoroughly: he knew the officers, he knew the men; and every officer and every man felt in his leading the most absolute confidence. The first effect of his fall showed itself in the confusion which was thereby caused in the command. Next in seniority to Reid was Captain Richard Lawrence, brother of the Chief Commissioner of the Panjáb. Captain Lawrence was in command of the body of the Káshmir

Book X. Chapter I.

1857. Sept. 14.

contingent, one thousand two hundred strong, which formed the reserve to that part of the fourth column which was attacking Kishanganj. Major Reid had been stunned by his wound; but, as I have already stated, on recovering his senses, he called out for Captain Lawrence, and personally made over the command to him. But before this had happened, many of the officers who had been conducting the attack under Major Reid, feeling the absence of a commander, and seeing that the attack had failed, had resolved to fall back. Falling back, they came upon Captain Lawrence, to whom they reported themselves, and who approved their conduct. Meanwhile Captain Muter of the 60th Rifles, who was with the attacking column, seeing Major Reid fall, and apparently regarding Captain Lawrence in the light only of a political officer attached to the Káshmir force, assumed the command of the portion of the column with which he was serving. This caused considerable confusion; Captain Lawrence and Captain Muter each regarding himself as commandant of the column, and each giving his own orders. As reinforcements of artillery which had been applied for failed to arrive, and as the enemy, pressing forward on the right flank of the column, seemed to threaten his rear, Lawrence retired leisurely on the batteries behind Hindú Rao's house. The attack on the Ídgar, conducted by a portion of the Káshmir troops under Captain Dwyer, was still more unfortunate. The Káshmirians, greatly outnumbered, were not only repulsed, but lost four guns.

Captain Muter assumes the command of a portion of the column,

the attack of which is repulsed.

Book X. Chapter I.

1857. Sept. 14.

Disastrous effect on the other columns of the repulse of the fourth column.

The repulse of the fourth column greatly aggravated the difficulties of the assault. I left the first and second columns, to which I must now return, victorious inside the breach. Nicholson at once collected the great body of his column on the square of the main-guard, then turning to the right, pushed forward along the foot of the walls towards the Láhor gate. The second column, under Brigadier Jones, had previously cleared the ramparts, and passing the Móri bastion, had planted their flag, in the manner already indicated, on the summit of the Kábul gate. Nicholson advanced beyond this in the hope of feeling the support of the fourth column. But we have seen that the attack of this column had failed, and it was this failure which now rendered the position of the advanced assailants difficult and dangerous in the extreme.

In pushing along the foot of the walls towards the Láhor gate our troops had been assailed by musketry fire from the houses in the place, and by grape and round shot from the Sélimgarh and the palace. This, however, had not impeded the advance. But when the column had reached the eastern extremity of the town and ascertained that, by the failure of the fourth column, the defences there were still in the hands of the enemy, they saw that their entire position was altered, and that they had before them another struggle at least as serious as that which they had but just then overcome.

Position of the Láhor gate.

The Láhor gate of the city was the gate which led to the Chándni Chók or principal street of the city. This gate was commanded by a bastion about two-thirds of the way between it and the Kábul gate. But to reach this bastion not only had narrow streets, the houses in which were strongly manned, to be forced, but the left of the attacking party would be exposed to a very heavy fire from the enemy now concentrating there. It was a prospect such as to make the boldest leader pause. Nicholson was a man of great daring, but there were men with him at the time, not less brave, who pointed out to him that under the circumstances in which he found himself it would be wise to be content with establishing himself in the houses which dominated the position, and await intelligence before advancing further. Seymour Blane of the 52nd, who acted as his brigade-major, strongly pressed this advice upon him. Major Jacob of the 1st Fusiliers, a most able and gallant officer, and who commanded the regiment on the occasion, supported this view. But Nicholson was impatient to press on. He believed that delays were dangerous, that the fullest advantage should be taken, at the moment, of the successful storm. More than two hours had already elapsed since his men had stood triumphant on the breach. A firm footing in the city had been gained. But this was not in itself sufficient. The repulse of the fourth column had renewed the hopes of the enemy. To destroy these it was necessary, in the opinion of Nicholson, to penetrate into the city.

Book X. Chapter I.

1857. Sept. 14.

The enemy concentrate in the narrow streets leading to it.

Nicholson is anxious to force them, despite of remonstrances to the contrary.

In front of the column was a lane, tolerably

Description of the posi-

Book X. Chapter I. 1857. Sept. 14. tion occupied by the enemy.

straight, about ten feet wide, but narrowed in places by projecting buttresses or towers with parapets. Where these buildings existed the roadway was narrowed to about three feet.* The city side of the lane was bounded by houses with flat roofs and parapets. Not only were all these buildings strongly occupied by the enemy, but the lane was further defended by two brass guns; one about a hundred and sixty yards from its opening, pointed in the direction of the advance; the other, about a hundred yards in its rear, commanding it. Behind both was a bullet-proof screen, whilst projecting as it were from the wall was the bastion commanding the Láhor gate, armed with heavy pieces, and capable of holding a thousand men.

The assault.

It was this formidable position that Nicholson decided to attack whilst yet the enemy might still be under the influence of their defeat at three out of the four points attacked. On receiving the order, his men dashed gallantly up the lane, took the first gun with a rush, and then pushed on to the second. But within ten yards of this they were assailed by a fire of grape and musketry, and volleys of stones and round shot, thrown by hand, so severe that they recoiled under the terrible and ceaseless shower. There was no shelter for them, and they were forced to retire. It would be difficult to paint in colours too bright the exertions of their officers. Con-

Gallantry of the assailants,

* "The 1st Bengal European Fusiliers in the Delhi Campaign," an article contributed to *Blackwood's Magazine* for January 1858.

Book X. Chapter I.

1857. Sept. 14.

spicuous amongst these was Lieutenant Butler of the 1st Fusiliers. This officer penetrated up to the bullet-proof screen already mentioned. How he escaped with his life was a marvel. At the screen two bayonets were thrust at him which pinned him between them as if he were between the prongs of a fork. There he stood, unable to advance or to retire, until, firing his revolver down the loop-holes, he forced the men who were thrusting at him to withdraw their weapons.*

who are driven back,

The assailants were, I have said, forced to retire. Only, however, for a few moments. Re-formed, they again advanced. Again they captured the first gun, which was spiked by Captain Greville, 1st Fusiliers; again they dashed at the second. As they rushed on, their leader, Major Jacob of the 1st Fusiliers, a cool, daring, and accomplished officer, was mortally wounded. Lying there on the ground, knowing his hour had come, the gallant Jacob called to his men to press onward. But the fire was tremendous. Wemyss, Greville, Caulfield, Speke, Woodcock, Butler, all officers belonging or attached to the 1st Fusiliers, were in turn struck down. The men, greatly discouraged, were falling back a second time, when Nicholson rushed to the front. His voice never rang more nobly, his presence was never more inspiring, than when, waving his sword, he summoned the men to follow where their general led. But the broken order could

again.

Jacob is struck down, and with him many officers of the 1st Fusiliers.

Nicholson then rushes to the front,

* "The 1st Bengal Fusiliers in the Delhi Campaign."

Book X. Chapter I. 1857. Sept. 14.

not be restored in a moment, and before a sufficient number of men could respond to the call, John Nicholson was struck down by a bullet which pierced his body.

but is pierced by a bullet.

The wound was mortal, and Nicholson knew it to be so. But neither the agony of the pain, nor the certain approach of death, could quench the ardour of that gallant spirit. He still called upon the men to go on. He insisted on lying there till the lane should be carried. But he was asking dying, as he had asked living, that which was all but impossible. Without artillery, the enemy's position was too strong to be carried. Soldiers not accustomed to be baffled, the same men who that morning had carried the walls by escalade, had recoiled twice before it. In that lane alone eight officers and fifty men had fallen. There was nothing for it but to retire. The fallen hero was then carefully removed to the hospital on the ridge, and the men fell back on to the Kábul gate. Nicholson still lived, and the lungs being uninjured by the ball, the doctors had some hope of his life. He alone had the certainty that the triumph for which he had prepared would escape his grasp.

He still urges the men on.

But the men are ultimately forced to retire.

By the fall of Nicholson the command of the first and second columns, now established at or near the Kábul gate, devolved on Brigadier Jones, C.B.

Nicholson is succeeded in command by Jones.

Whilst the infantry were thus contending with alternate success and mishap to establish themselves in the imperial city, the cavalry were not less actively employed outside the walls. It had

Action of the cavalry.

never been absolutely certain that all the four columns would succeed in their attack, whilst it was tolerably clear that the failure of any one of them would entail a counter assault from the victorious enemy. It was necessary likewise that the flanks of the assaulting columns should be efficiently covered. With wise prevision, then, General Wilson had directed Brigadier Hope Grant to move with the greater part of his cavalry and a troop and a half of Horse Artillery at the time of the assault to the vicinity of No. 1 battery, to check any attempt to take our storming columns in flank by sortie from the Láhor and Ájmir gates, and to hold himself in readiness to act as circumstances might require.

Book X. Chapter I.

1857. Sept. 14.

Hope Grant and Tombs.

Hope Grant, taking with him two hundred men of the 9th Lancers, four hundred of the Sikh horsemen, and a troop and a half of Horse Artillery, under Major Tombs, moved to the point indicated. Handling his men skilfully, he effectually covered the assaulting columns. Moving onwards as the columns advanced, he took up a position under the walls of the city, covering the batteries. Here he remained, ready for further action, till the moment when the movement of the enemy on his right showed him that the fourth column had been repulsed. In fact the enemy following up that column had thrown themselves into the houses and gardens near Kishanganj, and now opened a heavy musketry fire on the cavalry. Hope Grant at once ordered the Horse Artillery to the front. Tombs galloped up, unlimbered, opened fire, and compelled the enemy to fall back.

Book X. Chapter I.

1857. Sept. 14.

Their presence produces a material effect on the enemy's movements.

But as they did so, the guns on the Burn bastion opened out on the cavalry. At a distance of five hundred yards, drawn up for action, though compelled to remain inactive, their presence on the spot constituted a material aid to the infantry then endeavouring to make good their position within the city. For two hours they stood to receive. General Wilson, alive to their danger, promptly despatched Captain Bourchier's battery to aid them. But the round shot from the Burn bastion continued to empty saddle after saddle, or to dismount officer after officer. Nine officers of the Lancers had their horses shot under them. Conspicuous on either side of this gallant regiment were the scarlet-clad horse of Dighton Probyn, and the Panjábis of John Watson in their slate-coloured garments. Gallantly they stood, conscious that thus exposing their lives without the power of retaliating they were serving the common cause. At the end of about two hours the cavalry were further reinforced by about two hundred of the Guides and Gúrkahs. Then shortly afterwards came the intelligence that the infantry had established their positions within the town. Then, and then only, did Hope Grant withdraw leisurely to Ludlow Castle, satisfied that he had not only prevented the enemy from following up their victory over the fourth column, but had occupied their attention with a very considerable result on the main operations.

The gallantry displayed the greater because of the compulsory inaction.

The reserve column.

We have now to consider the operations of the reserve column.

The commander of this column, Brigadier Longfield, having previously detached the wing of the Bilúch battalion, three hundred strong, to the right of No. 2 battery, followed No. 3 column through the Káshmir gate, and cleared the College gardens. One portion of the column, consisting of the 4th Panjáb Rifles and some of the 61st Regiment, occupied these gardens; whilst another, composed of the Jhind Auxiliary Force and some of the 60th Rifles, held the Water bastion, the Káshmir gate, Colonel Skinner's house, and the house of Ahmad Áli Khán, a large, commanding building.

Book X. Chapter I.

1857. Sept. 14.

Results of the day's work.

The position of four out of the five columns of the attacking force as the evening set in may thus briefly be described. The entire space inside the city from the Water bastion to the Kábul gate was held by the first, second, and fifth columns. The fourth column, repulsed in its attack on Kishanganj, was holding the batteries behind Hindú Rao's house. We have still to account for the third column. I left that column, gallantly led by Colonel Campbell, holding a large enclosure parallel with the Chándni Chók, called the Bégam Bágh, anxiously expecting assistance from the other columns, and exposed to a heavy fire of musketry, grape, and canister.

Reason for the want of support accorded to the third column.

The failure of the first column in its attempt to master the lane leading to the Chándni Chók, and the repulse of the fourth column, account for the unsupported position in which Colonel Campbell was left. In advance of, and without communication with, the other columns; in the vicinity of a position strongly occupied by the

Book X. Chapter I. — 1857. Sept. 14.

enemy; liable to be cut off from the main body; the position was eminently dangerous. But Colonel Campbell knew himself, and he knew the men he commanded. They were eager to dare, anxious to press on. But the Jamma Masjid had been made impregnable to an attack from infantry, and the Brigadier had neither artillery to beat down, nor powder-bags to blow up, the obstacles in the way of his men. Under these circumstances, taking a soldierly view of the situation, he had occupied the Bégam Bágh, resolved to hold it till he could communicate with head-quarters. Whilst occupying this position he was rejoined by the Kamáon Battalion, belonging to his column, but which had in the advance diverged to the right, and had occupied the Kótwáli. An hour and a half elapsed, however, before he was able to communicate with head-quarters. Then, for the first time, he learned that the first and second columns had not been able to advance beyond the Kábul gate, and that he could not be supported.

Campbell, towards evening, falls back on the church.

A glance at the plan of Delhí will make it evident, even to non-military readers, that with the main body unable to penetrate beyond the Kábul gate, it would be injudicious for the third column to attempt to hold the Bégam Bágh during the night. Colonel Campbell, then, leisurely fell back on the church, the nearest point at which he touched the reserve column. Placing the 52nd in the church, he occupied Skinner's house with the Kamáon Battalion, and posted the 1st Panjáb Infantry in the houses at the end of the two streets

Book X. Chapter I.

1857. Sept. 14.

that lead from the interior of the city into the open space around the church.* At the head of those streets guns had previously been posted.

Notwithstanding heavy losses a solid base for further operations had been gained.

A review of the work of the 14th September 1857, will show that though the British loss had been heavy, though all had not been accomplished which it had been hoped to accomplish, yet not only had great obstacles been overcome, but a solid base had been obtained whence to continue and complete the work. In less than six hours the army had lost sixty-six officers, and eleven hundred and four men in killed and wounded. Four out of five of the assaulting columns were within the walls, but the position which they held was extensive, and owing to the failure of the fourth column, their right flank was threatened. The enemy were still strong in numbers, strong in guns, strong in position. They, too, had had success as well as reverses, and they had not yet abandoned all hope of ultimate victory.

The positions gained are secured during the night.

The first care of the assailants was to secure as best they could the posts that had so dearly gained. That night the engineers who were still fit for duty—they were but few, for out of seventeen ten had been struck down during the assault—were sent to fortify the advanced positions. Here they threw up barricades, and loop-holed and fortified the houses commanding the approaches. To maintain the flank communications between the heads of the several columns,

* Major Norman's *Narrative* in the Blue Book, No. 6, 1858.

Book X. Chapter I.

1857. Sept. 14.

in the shape of strong pickets, throwing out vedettes, were established.*

Review of the losses of the day.

Such was the result of the assault of the 14th September. At the cost of a very heavy loss of life a firm lodgment had been gained. The five assaulting columns numbered, exclusive of the Káshmir Contingent, five thousand one hundred and sixty men. Of these, one thousand one hundred and four men and sixty-six officers, or about two men in every nine, had been killed or wounded. Amongst the brave men who were killed or died of their wounds, were Nicholson, of whom I shall write further on; Jacob of the 1st Fusiliers; Speke, 65th Regiment Native Infantry; Salkeld, Engineers; Roper, 34th Foot; Tandy, Engineers; Fitzgerald, 75th Foot; Bradshaw, 52nd Light Infantry; Webb, 8th Foot; Rempay, 4th Panjáb Infantry; Pogson, 8th Regiment; MacBarnett, Davidson, and Murray, doing duty respectively with the 1st Fusiliers, the 2nd Panjáb Infantry, and the Guides. The number of wounded officers amounted to fifty-two, of whom eight were Engineers. All these officers were but a type of the unreformed British army. They were men in whom their soldiers had confidence, whose physical energies had not been neutralised by a premature absorption of the powers of the brain, who had learned their duties in the practical life of camps, who were ever to the fore in manly exercises in cantonment, ever as eager as able to lead their men

* Medley.

Book X. Chapter I.

1857. Sept. 14.

on the battle-field. Honour to their memory! However limited their acquirements might have been regarded by examiners, they at least knew how to lead their men to victory!

General Wilson is inclined to withdraw from the position he had gained.

The determination not only to hold the ground already won, but to continue further operations, was not arrived at by General Wilson without considerable hesitation. The success achieved, important as it was, had not corresponded—I will not say to his anticipations, for he had never been very confident—but to his hopes. The repulse of the first and fourth columns, the mortal wound of Nicholson, the tremendous loss in killed and wounded, the conviction he personally acquired that evening that the city had yet to be taken,—all these considerations combined to work on a nature never very sanguine or self-reliant, and now enfeebled by anxiety and ill-health. The General's first thought had been to withdraw the assaulting columns to the positions they had so long held on the ridge.

But is deterred by the remonstrances of Baird Smith and Neville Chamberlain.

From this fatal determination General Wilson was saved by the splendid obstinacy of Baird Smith, aided by the soldierly-like instincts of Neville Chamberlain. What sort of a man Baird Smith was, I have recorded in a previous page. Neville Chamberlain had been cast in a mould not less noble. A soldier almost from the hour of his birth, Neville Chamberlain united to the most complete forgetfulness of self, a courage, a resolution, a coolness equal to all occasions. The only fault that the most critical could find with his action was that he was too eager to press forward. If

Neville Chamberlain.

Book X. Chapter I.

1857. Sept. 14.

a fault, it was a noble fault—a fault which the critics carefully avoided. But, warring against Asiatics, to go forward is never a fault, and I have been assured, not by one but by many, that Chamberlain's personal daring had contributed greatly to inspire with confidence the soldiers he commanded.

Chamberlain was Adjutant-General of the Army. He had been a consistent counsellor of bold and daring measures, and he had more than once, after repulsing a sally of the enemy, led the counter-attack which had driven him headlong within the city. In one of these daring pursuits he had been severely wounded, and it was this severe wound which had prevented him from taking an active part in the actual assault. But from the summit of Hindú Rao's house he had witnessed all the events of that memorable day. The repulse of the fourth column, and the demonstration made by the enemy to pursue that column, seemed for a moment indeed to imperil his position, and he had summoned the native guard to the roof to defend the threatened magazine. This danger was averted by the action, already recorded, of Hope Grant and the cavalry. But this episode in no degree diverted the attention of the Adjutant-General from the other events. He noticed the first successes of the other columns; then the check—the apparently insurmountable check—evidently a bar to further progress on that day. To Chamberlain its significance was clear and unmistakeable. There was but one course to pursue. To hold, at any

Book X. Chapter I.

1857. Sept. 14.

cost, the positions taken, to fortify them, and to make them the base of a fresh attack at the earliest moment. Unable to move himself, he sent to the General a record of his convictions, accompanied by an earnest request that he would hold the ground for the night.

Would the written request of the Adjutant-General, not actually on the spot, have alone sufficed to turn the General from the course which a personal inspection had at once suggested to him? It is doubtful. The General undoubtedly believed that the safety of the army would be compromised by the retention of the positions they had gained. Fortunately, Baird Smith was at his elbow. Appealed to by General Wilson as to whether he thought it possible for the army to retain the ground they had won, his answer was short and decisive, "We *must* do so." That was all. But the uncompromising tone, the resolute manner, the authority of the speaker, combined to make it a decision against which there was no appeal. General Wilson accepted it.*

Baird Smith's resolute answer to Wilson.

The following day, the 15th, was devoted to the securing of the positions gained, to the esta-

Sept. 15.

* Many other officers gave the General the same advice. Amongst others, prominently, his Assistant Adjutant-General of Artillery, Captain Edwin Johnson, who shared his tent. This officer not only constantly urged General Wilson to see the matter through to its bitter end, but sustained him in his hours of depression, and by his tact, judgment, and practical ability, contributed to bring his mind into a state willing to accept the advice of Chamberlain and Baird Smith. All the foremost officers of the army, Nicholson, Jones, Reid, and others, had been all along in favour of decisive action.

Book X. Chapter I.

1857. Sept. 15.

Proceedings on the 15th.

blishing and making use of mortar batteries to shell the city, the palace, and the Sélimgarh, to the restoring of order, and to the arranging of means for putting a stop to indiscriminate plundering. That our troops were permitted to carry out this programme with but slight disturbance from the enemy, shows how truly Baird Smith and Chamberlain had judged the position. It is not too much to affirm that a retrograde movement on the 15th would, for the time, have lost India. As it was, whilst a mortar battery, established by our engineers in the College gardens, effected considerable damage in the enemy's defences, and our men, under the cover of that fire, were able to occupy and fortify some houses in front of the position taken the previous evening, the enemy's fire from Sélimgarh and the magazine was comparatively ineffective. Already the depression of failure, which our retirement would have changed into the joy of triumph, was beginning to weight their efforts very heavily.

Temptations placed in the way of the Europeans.

I have said that measures were taken on the 15th to restore order and to put a stop to indiscriminate plundering. The fact is, that the part of Delhí which our troops had occupied was the part which abounded in stores containing intoxicating liquors. What a temptation this would be to men faint from work of the severest character, and subjected for months to deprivations on the ridge, may easily be conceived. The indulgence in half an hour's unchecked impulse might paralyse the force. The danger was imminent, for the advanced guards fell victims to the snare.

But it was met promptly and with energy. The General ordered that the whole of the liquor should be destroyed, and the order was, to a very great extent, carried out.

Book X. Chapter I.

1857. Sept. 15.

The morning of the 16th dawned hopefully. During the night and in the early morning the enemy evacuated the suburb of Kishanganj, whence they had, on the 14th, repulsed the fourth column. Our men at once occupied the position, and captured five heavy guns which had been left there by the enemy. They were immensely impressed with the great strength of the place. The fire from our batteries, also, having effected a breach in the magazine, a party, consisting of H.M.'s 61st Regiment, a part of the 4th Panjáb Rifles, and the wing of the Bilúch Battalion, was detached, personally directed by the General, to storm it. The position was carried with but slight loss to the stormers—three men only being wounded—another proof of the growing depression of the enemy. The capture was of the highest importance, the magazine containing one hundred and seventy-one guns and howitzers, most of them of the largest calibre, besides ammunition of every kind.

Sept. 16.

Kishanganj is evacuated by the rebels,

and the magazine is stormed.

On the afternoon of the same day, the enemy made an attempt to recapture the magazine, as well as the workshops adjoining it. They advanced under cover of the fire of some guns in front of the palace gate, carried the workshops, but were driven back from the magazine, and ultimately from the workshops also. On this occasion, Lieutenant Renny of the Artillery dis-

Gallantry of Renny.

Book X. Chapter I.

1857. Sept. 16.

played great coolness and contempt of death. For, mounting on the roof of the magazine, he pelted the enemy with shells which were handed to him with their fuses burning!

Continued despondency of Wilson.

It would be natural to imagine that the fact that the army could not only hold its own, but make an impression upon the enemy so formidable as that implied by the abandonment of Kishanganj, and the feeble defence of the magazine, would have inspired the General with a confident hope as to the ultimate issue. But he was still desponding, and with Nicholson dying and Chamberlain unable to take an active part in his operations, it needed all the exertions of the engineers, than whom it would have been impossible to have collected a more daring and energetic set of men,* to carry out the necessary forward movement.

* Pre-eminent amongst these were Alexander Taylor, of whom Baird Smith thus wrote: "He was, throughout, my most able and trusted subordinate;" George Chesney, at a later period author of the *Battle of Dorking*; Fred Maunsell and Henry Brownlow, both shot down in the assault; Julius Medley, who to ability and daring added a genius for organization of no common order.

The tone of General Wilson's mind, at this particular period, may be gathered from his correspondence. "We took possession," he wrote at 2 o'clock on the afternoon of the 16th, "of the magazine this morning with the loss of only three men wounded. This advances us a little, but it is dreadfully slow work. Our force is too weak for this street fighting, when we have to gain our way inch by inch; and of the force we have, unfortunately there is a large portion, besides the Jummoo troops, in whom I place no confidence. . . I find myself getter weaker and weaker every day, mind and body quite worn out. The least exertion knocks me down. I walk with difficulty, and fully expect in a day or two to be laid altogether on my bed. . . We have a long and hard struggle still before us; I hope I may be able to see it out."

On the 17th and 18th the advance was pushed still further. The brain-task fell to the engineers, it having been decided to avoid the line of the streets and to sap through the houses. In this way the bank, Major Abbott's house, and the house of Khán Muhammad Khán were taken, and our posts brough close up to the palace and the Chándni Chók. During these days, too, the positions on the right and left, indicated by the Kábul gate and the magazine, were brought into direct communication by a line of posts.

Book X. Chapter I.

1857. Sept. 17–18.

The advance pushed on on the 17th and 18th by the engineers

Nor were the artillery silent. Whilst the steady progress of sapping was going on, the heavy mortars and guns in the magazine, and the recovered and re-armed batteries of the enceinte bastions and gates, were at work, pouring a continuous flight of shells into the city and palace. Of the enemy's resistance it may be said that, though continuous, it was not characterised by the determination which had marked their conduct on the 14th. They had read their doom, and though they still fought, their hearts were elevated neither by the hope of victory nor by the energy of despair. Many had abandoned the city. The courage of those who remained was still undaunted, but hopelessness of success had weakened their powers. Owing partly to this, and in a great measure to the skill of the attack, the British losses on those days were small.

and by the artillery.

The resistance slackens.

The position of the attacking force on the evening of the 18th has thus been described: "The line of the canal may be said to have been our front; on its bank some light mortars were

Sept. 18.

Book X. Chapter I. 1857. Sept. 18.

posted, to clear the neighbourhood of the Láhor gate; while light guns were posted at the main junction of the streets, and sand-bag batteries erected to prevent the possibility of a surprise."* The establishment of communications between the extreme right and left has been already mentioned. In the rear everything was our own.

Greathed's attack on the Láhor gate fails.

Still all was not *couleur de rose.* On the morning of that day an attack on the Láhor gate had been directed, and failed. Greathed, who directed that attack at the head of a column composed of detachments from the 8th, the 75th, and a Sikh Regiment, and supported by fifty men of the 1st Fusiliers, had to advance up a narrow lane leading into the Chándni Chók through a gate at the end of it. This gate had been closed, and behind it dwelt the unknown. Greathed had led his men up the narrow lane, but as he approached the end leading into the Chándni Chók the gate was suddenly thrown open and displayed to his astonished gaze a 24-pounder turned on the assailants. This gun opened suddenly with grape on the column, whilst simultaneously from the houses on either flank poured a smart and continuous fire of musketry. No wonder that the men recoiled. They were enormously outnumbered, and occupied a cramped position, which gave no play for manœuvring. Greathed drew them back, and, bringing a 6-pounder to the front, ordered a charge under cover of the smoke. But all was in vain. For a moment indeed the hostile gun

* *Eight Months' Campaign against the Bengal Sepoys,* Bourchier.

Book X. Chapter I.

1857. Sept. 18.

appeared to be in the possession of our men;* but the odds were too great, the position too confined; the enemy being thoroughly on the alert, surprise had become impossible. No one saw more clearly than Greathed that the attack on the Chók had failed. He therefore gave the order to retire. The retreat was effected in good order and without loss, the enemy not venturing to enter the lane.

Its lowering effect on General Wilson.

The repulse of Greathed's column had filled the mind of General Wilson with despair. "We are still," he wrote, that same day, "in the same position in which we were yesterday. An attempt was made this morning to take the Láhor gate, but failed from the refusal of the European soldiers to follow their officers. One rush, and it would have been done easily; but they would not make it. The fact is, our men have a great dislike to street fighting; they do not see their enemy, and find their comrades falling from shots of the enemy who are on the tops of houses and behind cover, and get a panic, and will not advance. This is very sad and, to me, very disheartening. We can, I think, hold our present position, but I cannot see my way out at all. I have now only three thousand one hundred men (infantry) in the city, with no chance or possibility of any reinforcements. If I were to attempt to push on into the city, they would be lost in such innumerable streets and masses of houses,

* *Blackwood's Magazine,* January 1858. The writer of the article is known to the author.

Book X. Chapter I. 1857. Sept. 18.

and would be annihilated or driven back." The reader will remark that, desponding as are these words, they mark a step in advance of those uttered on the evening of the 14th. Then, General Wilson was inclined to retire to the ridge to save his army. On the 18th, though he still doubted of ultimate success, he felt he could hold his own.

Sept. 19.

On the 19th action of a different character was taken. A glance at the plan will show the position, previously described, attained on the evening of the 18th. Immediately in front of our right was the Burn bastion, no longer supported by the presence of a strong hostile force in Kishanganj and Táliwári. Now the Burn bastion commanded the Láhor gate, and with it the Chándni Chók; and, though from our advanced post in the Bank that important street could be occupied, it would be difficult to maintain it and to push on operations against the palace and the Jamma Masjid until the remaining strongholds on the enemy's left should be occupied.

The Burn bastion.

Alexander Taylor is authorised to work through to the Burn bastion.

To the clear minds of the Chief Engineer and of his principal coadjutor, Captain Alexander Taylor, the requirements of the position were apparent. With the concurrence, then, of the former, Captain Taylor obtained from the General an order to the Brigadier commanding at the Kábul gate to place at his disposal, for operations on the following morning, a body of men to work through the intermediate houses, and thus to gain the Burn bastion. Whilst this gradual and necessarily somewhat slow process was being

Book X. Chapter I.

1857. Sept. 19.

adopted, a column of about five hundred men, taken from the 8th and 75th and the Sikh regiment, proceeded, under Brigadier William Jones, to attack the Láhor gate.

Its capture by Brigadier Jones.

The sapping party, directed by Captain Taylor, gradually made their way through the detached houses situated between the Kábul gate and the Burn bastion, annoyed only by a constant musketry fire maintained by the enemy upon such of their number as were forced to show themselves. Making their way, as it were, step by step, they succeeded, as night fell, in occupying a house which completely overlooked the Burn bastion. From this place they were able to pour a commanding fire upon the occupants of the latter, and they did this with so much effect that the enemy, convinced of the impossibility of holding it, evacuated it during the night. Brigadier Jones then pushed forward his men, and found it deserted. But his men were in a very unruly condition. Much brandy had fallen into their hands, and it was difficult to keep them steady.*

The immense gain of the capture.

The news brought to the General that night (19th) by Captain Taylor of the capture of the Burn bastion, could not fail to revive his spirits.

* The men were in a very unruly state . . . Much brandy, beer, and other intoxicating liquors were left so exposed by the enemy, that it would seem they had almost been left about purposely; and though the officers endeavoured to persuade their men that the liquor was poisoned they did not succeed. . . One old soldier, a thirsty soul, taking up a bottle of brandy, and looking at it, said: "Oh no, Sir, the capsule is all right—Exshaw and Co.—no poison that."—*Blackwood's Magazine*, January 1858.

Book X. Chapter I. 1857. Sept. 19.

It was an immense gain; for the possession of that bastion was the certain key to the capture of the Láhor gate. So impressed was General Wilson with the importance of the conquest that he sent some officers of his staff to spend the night in the bastion, and to take measures for its retention. The precaution, wise though it was, was not needed. The enemy by this time were thoroughly cowed, and, far from thinking of recovering the place, were hurrying out of the city as fast as their legs could carry them.

Sept. 20.

Jones carries the Láhor gate,

The capture of the Burn bastion was the beginning of the end. Early the following morning (the 20th) Brigadier Jones's column, pursuing the advantage of the previous evening, carried the Láhor gate with a rush; the Garstin bastion fell also to their prowess. The Brigadier then received instructions to divide his force, and, whilst detaching one portion up the Chándni Chók to occupy the Jamma Masjid, to proceed with the remainder towards the Ájmir gate. The opportune arrival of Major Brind and his artillery caused the Brigadier to confide to him the command of the first portion.

and Brind the Jamma Masjid:

Brind, having under his orders, in addition to his own men, the 8th Regiment and the 1st Fusiliers, marched at once to the Jamma Masjid, and carried it without difficulty. He had no sooner occupied it than he perceived that the one thing wanting to assure the complete capture of the city was to assault the palace, promptly and without delay.

he then invites Wilson to attack the palace.

He, therefore, on the spot, wrote a pencil note to the General reporting his success, and urging him to an immediate attack on the royal residence.

Book X. Chapter I.

1857. Sept. 20.

Completion of the occupation of the gate.

Meanwhile Jones had penetrated to the Ájmír gate. Almost simultaneously the main body of the cavalry, going round by the Ídgar, found the camp of the mutineers outside Dehlí evacuated, and secured the clothing, ammunition, and plunder left by the rebels in the precipitation of their flight.

Wilson sends a force against the palace,

General Wilson responded to Brind's note by ordering the advance of the column at the magazine to attack the palace. The decreasing fire from the battlements of the residence, famous in history, famous in romance, of the descendants of Bábar, had made it abundantly clear that the last representative of the family which had for so long ruled in Hindustan had, with his family and attendants, sought refuge in flight. When the British troops (the 60th Rifles), pressing forward, reached the walls, a few fanatics alone remained behind, not to line them, for their numbers were too few, but, careless of life, to show to the very last their hatred of the foe they had so long defied. Powder-bags were promptly brought up, the gates were blown in, and our troops entered, and hoisted the British flag. The Sélimgarh fort had been occupied even a little earlier. Its capture was effected in a manner which demands a separate notice.

which is captured.

Some short time before the assault on the palace gate, Lieutenant Aikman, with a small party of Wilde's Sikhs, had been directed to feel his way to the left. Aikman, the most daring and intrepid of men, knew the ground thoroughly; and having

Aikman captures the Sélimgarh.

Book X. Chapter I.

1857. Sept. 20.

received, as he imagined, permission to act on his own judgment, he resolved to effect an entrance into the Sélimgarh from the rear, and hold the enemy as in a trap. Accordingly he doubled round to the Calcutta gate, forced it open, and pushed on to the Sélimgarh. The few men in that fort fled on his appearance, and escaped across the river. Aikman's attention was then turned to the gateway at the narrow passage from the Sélimgarh into the rear of the palace. This passage connected the rear gate of the palace with an arched gate over the fort, over which was a parapet. Were he able to gain possession of this he could stop the escape of multitudes till the storming party should reach them from the front. Thus thinking, he acted without hesitation, shot the sentry at the gate opening on to the drawbridge leading into the rear of the palace, and placed his men in the best position to defend it. He then, with the assistance of the Sergeant-Major of Renny's troop or battery, set to work to spike the heavy guns directed against the Water bastion. He was in possession of the gate and drawbridge when the gates of the palace were blown in. The rush of the fugitives was not so great as had been anticipated, so extensive had been the flight on the two preceding days. But some at least were kept back. A more gallant or well-thought-out act was not performed even during that long siege.*

* Official report of Major Wilde, commanding 4th Sikh Infantry.

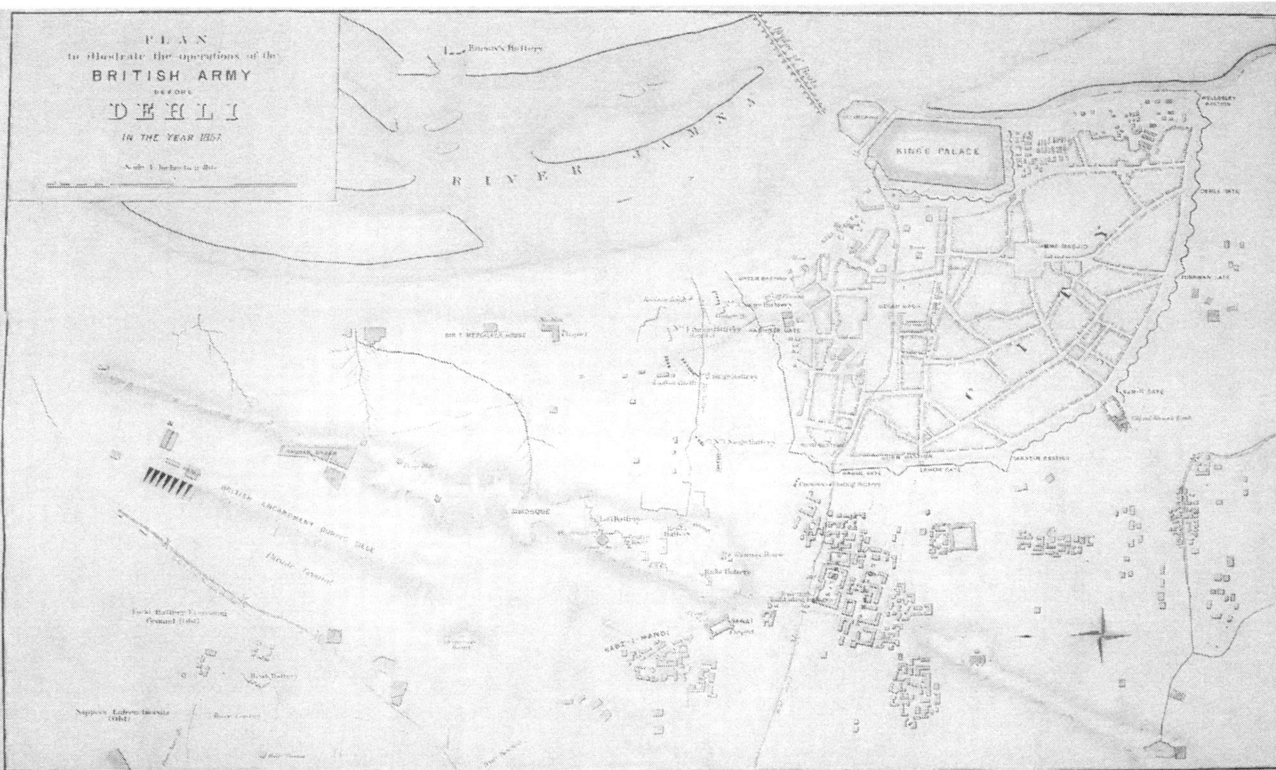
PLAN
to illustrate the operations of the
BRITISH ARMY
BEFORE
DEHLI
IN THE YEAR 1857
Hindu Rao's House
Rumbold's Battery
Bridge of Boats
RIVER JAMNA
KING'S PALACE
WELLESLEY BASTION
DEHLI GATE
TURKMAN GATE
JUMMA MUSJID
CITY
CABUL GATE
LAHORE GATE
AJMIR GATE
MOORE BASTION
BURN BASTION
WATER BASTION
CASHMERE GATE
SIR T. METCALFE'S HOUSE
IDGAH
BRITISH ENCAMPMENT DURING SIEGE
SUBZI MANDI
KISHENGUNJ
SERAI
Flagstaff Tower
Ludlow Castle

In the afternoon of the same day General Wilson, having given directions for the establishment of posts at the various gateways and bastions, took up his quarters in the imperial palace.

Book X. Chapter I.

1857. Sept. 20.

Appearance of Dehlí after the capture.

The appearance of Dehlí after the capture of the palace, the Sélimgarh, and the Jamma Masjid had placed it in the hands of the British, has thus been graphically described by a gallant officer who took part in the assault and in the subsequent operations.*

"The demon of destruction," writes Colonel Bourchier, "seemed to have enjoyed a perfect revel. The houses in the neighbourhood of the Mori and Káshmir bastions were a mass of ruins, the walls near the breaches were cracked in every direction, while the church was completely riddled by shot and shell. . . . In the Water bastion the destruction was still more striking. Huge siege-guns, with their carriages, lay about seemingly like playthings in a child's nursery. The palace had evidently been hastily abandoned. The tents of Captain de Teissier's battery, stationed at Dehlí when the mutiny broke out, were left standing, and contained plunder of all sorts. The apartments inhabited by the royal family combined a most incongruous array of tawdry splendour with the most abject poverty and filth. The apartments over the palace gate, formerly inhabited by Captain Douglas, who commanded the palace guards, and Mr. Jennings the clergy-

* *Eight Months' Campaign against the Bengal Sepoys*, by Colonel George Bourchier, C.B., R.A.

Book X. Chapter I. 1857. Sept. 20.

man, were denuded of every trace of the unfortunate party which had inhabited its walls, and with whom, not many months before, I had spent a happy week. It was with a sad and heavy heart that I paced its now empty rooms, which could tell such terrible tales of the scenes there enacted."

Dehlí was now virtually our own. But though the strong places had been occupied by our troops thousands of the mutineers were still in the vicinity, armed, and ready to take advantage of any slackness of discipline. The very relief of guards and batteries was still a matter of danger and difficulty, nor did the event of the following day, which deprived the rebels of their nominal leader, lessen in any material degree the magnitude of the risk.

The King of Dehlí.

The King of Dehlí, his family, and his personal adherents had shown themselves as easily depressed by adversity as they had been cruel and remorseless when Fortune had seemed, in the early days of the revolt, to smile upon them.

Sept. 14.

The result of the events of the 14th September had produced upon the mind of the King effects precisely similar to those which had, for the moment, mastered the cooler judgment of the British commander. We have seen that General Wilson, surveying his position on the evening of the 14th, declared that a prompt retreat to his original position could alone save the army. Baird Smith and Neville Chamberlain forced him, so to speak, to remain. On the other side, the King and his advisers, deeply impressed by the

Book X. Chapter I. 1857. Sept. 14.

successful storm of the assailants, and not considering that success outweighed, or even balanced, by the repulse of the first and fourth columns, rapidly arrived at the conclusion that, unless the British should retire, the game was up. There was no Baird Smith at the right hand of the King to point out to him how many chances yet remained in his favour if he would but profitably employ the small hours of the night; no Neville Chamberlain to urge him, above all things, to dare. When the morning of the 15th dawned, and the British were seen to have retained their positions, to be making preparations for a further advance, the hearts of the King and his advisers fell, and they began even then to discount the future.

Sept. 15. The persistence of the British depresses the adherents of the King.

Still, as long as the Sélimgarh, the palace, the Jamma Masjid, and the Láhor gate were held, no active measures for retreat were taken. But when, on the night of the 19th, the Burn bastion, virtually commanding the Láhor gate and the Chándni Chók, was captured, the thought that had been uppermost in every heart found expression. That thought was flight.

Sept. 19. Their success completes the despondency.

The commander-in-chief of the rebel army, the Bakht Khán, whom we have seen exercising so strong an influence at Baréli,* evacuated the city that night, taking with him all the fighting men upon whom he could depend. Ways of egress, that by the bridge of boats, and those by the Khairáti and Dehlí gates were still open to

Bakht Khán urges the King to accompany the army in its flight.

* Vol. i., page 303, *note*.

Book X. Chapter I. 1857. Sept. 19.

them; and of these they availed themselves. Bakht Khán exerted all his eloquence to induce the King to accompany him. He represented to him that all was not lost, that though the English had gained their stronghold the open country was before them, and that, under the shadow of his name and presence, it would be still possible to continue the war, always with a chance of success.

The King vacillates.

Had Bahádur Khán possessed a spark of the persistent nature or the vigorous energy of his ancestors, of Bábar, of Humáyun, or of Ákbar, that appeal had not been made in vain. But he was an old man—one of that class of old men who have exhausted youth in their teens, and who become, with increasing years, more and more nerveless and irresolute. It is probable that throughout the mutiny the King had been a mere puppet in the hands of others. Whilst the siege lasted the chiefs of the army had sustained their power over him by promises of ultimate victory. But with impending defeat their influence vanished; and the old King, acted upon by events, was in the humour to fall under any spell which might seem to promise him immunity for his misdeeds.

The secret thoughts of Mirza Iláhi Bakhsh.

Such a spell was at hand. Of all the nobles about him the wiliest was Mirza Iláhi Bakhsh, whose daughter was the widow of the eldest son of the King. It is probable that in the early days of the mutiny the counsels of Iláhi Bakhsh had been strongly in favour of vigorous action. But he had a keen eye for probabilities. The

Book X. Chapter I.

1857. Sept. 19.

events of the 14th and 15th September had read to him no doubtful lesson. He foresaw the triumph of the English—a triumph fraught with ruin to himself and his family unless he could turn to account the few days that must still intervene.

He moulds the King to his purpose.

He did turn them to account. Having made all his plans, he listened, without speaking, to the eloquent pleadings made to the King by the commander-in-chief, Bakht Khán. When all was over, and when Bakht had departed with a promise from the King that he would meet him the following day at the tomb of Humáyun, Iláhi Bakhsh persuaded the Moghol sovereign to accompany him to his house for the night. Having brought him there, he moulded him to his purpose. He pointed out to him the hardships which would follow his accompanying the army, assured him of its certain defeat, and then, showing the other side of the shield, indicated that a prompt severance of his cause from the cause of the Sepoys would induce the victorious English to believe that, up to that moment, he had acted under compulsion, and that he had seized the first opportunity to sever himself from traitors.

Sept. 20.

The King refuses to accompany the army.

These arguments, urged with great force upon one whose brain power, never very strong, was waning, had their effect. When, next day, the King of Dehlí, his zenana, his sons, and his nobles, met the rebel commander-in-chief at the tomb of Humáyun, he and they declined to accompany them. Rather than undergo the fatigues, the

Book X. Chapter I. 1857. Sept. 20.

perils, the uncertainties attendant on the prolongation of a contest which they had encouraged, they deliberately preferred to trust to the tender mercies of the conqueror. What those tender mercies were likely to be did not seem to trouble much the degenerate Moghols. They promised, at all events, a quick decision—a decision preferable to the agony of suspense.

The rebel army leaves Dehlí.

Bakht Khán and the rebel army, then, went their way, leaving behind the royal family and a numerous crowd of emasculated followers, the scum of the palace, men born never to rise above the calling of a flatterer or a scullion. So far had the plans of Mirza Iláhi Bakhsh succeeded. The next step was more difficult. It involved the betrayal of his master.

The intrigues of Mirza Iláhi Bakhsh.

Difficult, it was not insurmountable. Chief of the native agents maintained by the English to obtain correct information regarding the movements of the enemy during the siege, was Múnshí Rajab Áli, a man possessing wonderful tact, cleverness, assurance, courage—all the qualities which go to make up a spy of the highest order. He possessed to the full the confidence of the English administrators, and he was true to his employers. With this man Iláhi Bakhsh opened communications. Rajab Áli requested him simply to detain the royal family for twenty-four hours after the departure of the rebel army, at the tomb of Humáyun, and to leave the rest to him.

Their nature communicated to Captain Hodson.

Rajab Áli communicated the information he had received to Hodson of Hodson's Horse; Hodson at once rode down to the General's head-

Book X. Chapter I.

1857. Sept. 20.

quarters, communicated the news, and requested permission to take with him a party of his men to bring in the King. With some reluctance—for he knew Hodson's nature—General Wilson accorded the permission, but solely on the condition that the King should be exposed to neither injury nor insult. Hodson, taking fifty of his troopers with him, galloped down towards the tomb.

Hodson.

Who was Hodson? Some men are born in advance of their age, others too late for it. Of the latter class was Hodson. Daring, courting danger, reckless and unscrupulous, he was a *condottiere* of the hills, a free-lance of the Middle Ages. He joyed in the life of camps, and revelled in the clang of arms. His music was the call of the trumpet, the battle-field his ball-room. He would have been at home in the camp of Wallenstein, in the sack of Magdeburg. In him human suffering awoke no feeling, the shedding of blood caused him no pang, the taking of life brought him no remorse. The *certaminis gaudia* did not entirely satisfy his longings. Those joys were but preludes to the inevitable consequences—the slaughter of the fugitives, the spoils of the vanquished.

Hodson rides to capture the King.

Hodson rode off, full of excitement, towards the tomb of Humáyun. As he approached that time-honoured structure he slackened his pace, and making way cautiously to some ruined buildings near the gateway, posted his men under their shade. Having taken every precaution, he then sent to announce to the King his arrival, and to invite him to surrender.

Book X. Chapter I.

1857. Sept. 20.

The scene within the tomb of Humáyun.

Within the tomb despair was combating with resignation. The favourite wife of the last of the Moghols, anxious above all for the safety of her son, a lad not old enough to be implicated in the revolt, and yet not too young to escape massacre, was imploring the old man to yield on the condition of a promise of life; the mind of the old man, agitated by a dim recollection of the position he had inherited and forfeited, by despair of the present, by doubts of the future, was still wavering. Why had not he acted as Ákbar would have acted, and accompanied the troops to die, if he must die, as a king? What to him were the few years of dishonour which the haughty conqueror might vouchsafe to him? Better life in the free plains of India, hunted though he might be, than life in durance for him, a king! But then rushed in the fatal conviction that it was too late. He had decided when he dismissed Bakht Khán! The Frank and his myrmidons were at his door!

The King surrenders on condition that his life be spared.

Yet still the difficulty with him was to act on that decision. His mind was in the chaotic condition when everything was possible but action. For two hours, then, he hesitated, clutching at every vague idea only to reject it; his wife, his traitorous adviser, his surroundings, all urging upon him one and the same counsel. At last a consent was wrung from him to send a message to Hodson that he would surrender provided he should receive from that officer an assurance that his life should be spared.

Hodson receives the

On receiving this message, Hodson gave the

Book X. Chapter I.

1857. Sept. 20.

promise. Then, issuing from his cover, he took post in the open space in front of the gate of the tomb, standing there alone to receive the royal prisoner. Preceded by the Queen and her son in palanquins, the King issued from the portico, carried in a similar conveyance. Hodson spurred his horse to the side of the palanquin and demanded of the King his arms. The King asked if his captor were Hodson Bahádur. Receiving an affirmative reply, the King asked for a promise from the Englishman's own lips of his life and of the lives of his wife and her son. The promise given, the arms were surrendered and the cortége moved towards the city. The progress was slow, and for a great part of the journey the palanquins were followed by a considerable number of the King's retinue—men never dangerous and now thoroughly cowed. These gradually dropped off as the Láhor gate was approached. By that gate Hodson entered, and traversing the Chándni Chók, made over his captives to Mr. Saunders, the principal civil officer in the city. He then went to report his successful achievement to the General, carrying with him the arms of the last sovereign of the imperial house of Bábar.

King as a captive

and makes him over to the civil authorities.

So far Hodson had acted as a chivalrous officer of the nineteenth century. But the spirit of the *condottiere* now came into play. The same active agents who had informed him of the whereabouts of the King, now came to tell him that two of the King's sons and a grandson, men who were reported to have taken part in the massacre of May,

Hodson learns that the King's sons and a grandson could be captured.

Book X. Chapter I.

1857. Sept. 20.

had not accompanied the rebel army but were concealed in the tomb of Humáyun or in its vicinity. The information excited all the savage instincts of Hodson. These men could not stipulate for mercy. He might himself "rid the earth of those ruffians." He rejoiced in the opportunity.* The following morning, then, having obtained permission from the General to hunt down the princes, he started, accompanied by his second in command, Lieutenant McDowell, one hundred troopers, and his two spy-informers, Múnshí Rajab Áli and Mirza Iláhi Bakhsh, and rode for Humáyun's tomb. The three princes, Mirza Kházar Sultán, Mirza Moghol, and Mirza Abú Bakht, were in the tomb attended by a considerable number of the scum of the people—the same who, the previous day, had seen, without resistance their king carried off, and who were not more prepared to resist now. It is true that the more daring among them, seeing the approach of Hodson, implored the princes to resist, offering to defend them to the last. Better for the princes, ten thousand times better for Hodson's reputation, if the offer had been accepted. At least, then, the Englishman would have been able to aver that he killed his enemies in fair fight. But with the example of their father before them, the princes hoped to gain the promise of their lives by

Sept. 21.

He starts with a hundred troopers to capture them.

Refuses to promise to spare their lives.

* "In twenty-four hours I disposed of the principal members of the House of Timour the Tartar. I am not cruel, but I confess that I did rejoice in the opportunity of ridding the earth of these ruffians."—Letter from Hodson, 23rd September 1857.

Book X. Chapter I.

1857. Sept. 21.

They surrender to his mercy and generosity.

negotiation. For two hours they implored that promise. Hodson steadily refused it. Their spirits weakened by the useless effort, the three princes then surrendered to the mercy and generosity of the conqueror.

They came out from their retreat in a covered cart. Similar carts conveyed the arms of which Hodson, in the meanwhile, had deprived the crowd. Hodson placed troopers on either side of the cart which bore the princes, and directed it towards the Láhor gate. The people, the same miserable population who had previously followed the King, followed this cortége also. Between them and the cart containing the princes were a hundred of Hodson's far-famed horsemen. There was no real danger to be apprehended from them. They were too cowed to act. Hodson would have rejoiced had they displayed the smallest intention to resist. He wanted blood. His senses were blinded by his brutal instincts. He had completed five-sixths of his journey from the place of capture to Dehlí without the display of the smallest hostility on the part of the crowd. Despairing, then, of any other mode of gratifying his longings, he made the pressure of the mob upon his horsemen a pretext for riding up to the cart, stopping it, and ordering the princes to dismount, and strip to their under garments. Then, addressing the troopers, he told them in a loud voice, so as to be heard by the multitude, that the prisoners were butchers who had murdered our women and our children, and that it was the will of the Government that they should die.

He shoots them when within a mile of Dehlí.

Book X. Chapter I.

1857. Sept. 21.

Then, taking a carbine from the hands of a trooper, he shot dead his three unresisting captives!

Comments on Hodson's act.

A more brutal or a more unnecessary outrage was never committed. It was a blunder as well as a crime. It is true that the gossip of the camp had accused the princes of the imperial house of having instigated the massacre of our countrymen and countrywomen in the month of May, but not a single item of evidence had been adduced to substantiate the charge. It is quite possible that a fair trial might have cleared them; or, had it convicted them, the British public would have enjoyed the satisfaction of knowing that they deserved the fate which would then have befallen them. The princes surrendered, prisoners of war. It is idle to say that unless they had been shot they would have been rescued. No attempt was made by the crowd to wag a finger on their behalf. Its undisciplined and unarmed component parts had lost the only fair chance of resistance when they assented to the surrender of the princes. They made no sign when Hodson ordered his intended victims to descend from the cart and to strip. It is possible, indeed, that a man deficient in nerve might have been so far daunted by the sight of the number of men following his troopers as to lose his presence of mind, and, in sheer desperation, end the matter by murdering his captives. But Hodson had nerves of iron. He had all his wits about him. He had regretted that his instructions forbade him to kill the King. His savage instincts required to be satisfied, and he satisfied them by this cowardly murder. Book X. Chapter I.

1857. Sept. 21.

It is to be regretted on every ground that he gave way to the promptings of his nature. On the grounds of justice, because it was a base and unnecessary act; on the grounds of public interest, because the trials of the princes would probably have elicited much curious information regarding the revolt; on the grounds of his own reputation, for though whilst men's blood was still hot the deed might have been overlooked, their better feelings would have asserted themselves in the end, and Hodson would have been a marked man for ever. In the history of the mutiny there is no more painful episode than that connected with his name on this occasion.

It is now time to return to the city. I left it on the evening of the 20th, its strong places fully occupied by our troops. On the following morning began the work of securing the city. To Major James Brind—known in the camp, for his gallantry, for his untiring energy, for the earnest and persistent manner in which he had pounded the enemy, as Brind of the batteries—was allotted the task, in conjunction with the Chief Engineer, of ensuring the safety of the gateways and posts.

A more high-minded, a more gallant, or a more merciful officer than Major James Brind never lived. Every soldier knew, and every soldier loved him. He brought to his task all the characteristics which had gained for him respect and affection. But that task was no light one. The

Book X. Chapter I.

1857. Sept. 21.

scum of the rebel army still lurked in the place, hiding in mosques or burying themselves in underground receptacles. As Major Brind went about it he was again and again startled by reports of cold-blooded murder of our soldiers, of their being enticed by a promise of drink into the dark corners of the city and there basely murdered. He found that numerous gangs of men were hanging about, prepared to interfere with the reliefs of the batteries and posts, and that it was even possible they might attempt to surprise the garrison. The time was critical. It was necessary to show the rebels that we were prepared for them.

Brind clears the city of murderers and incendiaries.

Major Brind, therefore, determined to make an example of the first gang of murderers who might be caught. Just at the moment a murder of an atrocious character was reported to him. Collecting a few artillerymen, Brind hastened to the spot, stormed the mosques and houses where the murderers and their associates were assembled, ordered the perpetrators to be executed, and made over the remainder to the authorities. This act of vigour, combined with acts of the same nature carried out by other commanding officers, had a wonderful effect. The remainder of the rowdy element quitted the city, and from that day forth there was neither murder nor disturbance. Major Brind was then able to continue, in comparative freedom from alarm, his task of making the gate-ways and other military posts as secure as possible from attack. Colonel Burn, an officer not attached to the force, but who, being on leave at the time, had joined it, was, on the 21st, nominated military governor of the city. Book X. Chapter I.

1857. Sept. 21.

One sad event remains yet to be chronicled—the death of the heroic man who, sweeping across the Panjáb, had come down to reinforce the besieging army, to inflict a deadly blow on the enemy at Najafgarh, and to command the storming party on the 14th. After lingering for eight days, John Nicholson died. As fortunate as Wolfe, he lived long enough to see the full success of the attack he had led with so much daring. At the age of thirty-seven he had achieved the highest rank alike as an administrator and as a soldier. There never lived a man who more thoroughly exemplified the truth of the maxim that great talents are capable of universal application. Whatever the work to which he had applied himself, he had succeeded. His mastery over men was wonderful. His penetrating glance never failed in effect. It was impossible to converse with him without admitting the spell. With all that, and though he must have been conscious of his power, he was essentially humble-minded. "You must not compare me with Herbert Edwardes," he said to the writer in 1851. In appearance, especially in the eye and the contour of the face, he bore a striking resemblance to Lord Beaconsfield, as Lord Beaconsfield was when, as Mr. Disraeli, he first became leader of the opposition. The resemblance had been remarked by many when he visited England in 1850. What he might have become it is difficult to guess. It is difficult because it would be hard to put a limit to his career. Look-

Sept. 22.

John Nicholson dies.

Book X. Chapter I.

1857. Sept. 22.

ing at the point whence he started, at the reputation he had acquired at the age of thirty-seven—the reputation of being the most successful administrator, the greatest soldier, the most perfect master of men—in India, it is impossible to believe that he would have fallen short of the most famous illustrations of Anglo-Indian history, for to all the military talents of Clive he united a scrupulous conscience, and to the administrative capacity of Warren Hastings he joined a love of equal justice for the rights of all.

Remarks on the siege.

The stronghold had fallen, "the first great blow struck at the rebel's cause." * The total loss of the army, from the 30th May to the final capture on the 20th September, had amounted to nine hundred and ninety-two killed, two thousand seven hundred and ninety-five wounded, and thirty missing, out of a force never numbering ten thousand effective men. But in addition to these, many died from disease and exposure.

"In the history of sieges," wrote at the time an officer, in words the truth of which the lapse of twenty years has confirmed,† "that of Dehlí will ever take a prominent place. Its strength, its resources, and the prestige attached to it in the native mind, combined to render formidable that citadel of Hindustan. Reasonably might the 'Northern Bee' or the 'Invalide Russe' question our ability to suppress this rebellion if they drew their conclusions from the numerical

* Medley. † *The Red Pamphlet.*

strength of the little band that first sat down before Dehlí. But the spirit that animated that handful of soldiers was not simply the emulative bravery of the military proletarian. The cries of helpless women and children, ruthlessly butchered, had gone home to the heart of every individual soldier and made this cause his own. There was not an Englishman in those ranks, from first to last, who would have consented to turn his back on Dehlí without having assisted in meting out to those bloody rebels the retributive justice awarded them by his own conscience, his country, and his God. It was this spirit that buoyed them up through all the hardships of the siege, that enabled them for four long months of dreary rain and deadly heat, to face disease, privation, and death, without a murmur." Book X. Chapter I. 1857. Sept. 22.

The British soldier.

It was indeed an occasion to bring out the rare qualities of the British soldier, to show how, under the untoward circumstances of climate, of wet, of privation, he can be staunch, resolute and patient whilst waiting for his opportunity, daring when that opportunity comes. With him, too, can claim equal laurels the splendid Gúrkah regiment of Charles Reid, the magnificent frontier warriors of the Guide Corps, the cavalry regiments of Probyn, Watson, and Hodson, the levies from the various parts of the Panjáb. These men were worthy to vie with the British soldier. Their names, unfortunately, do not survive for the advantage of posterity; but their commanders live to speak for them. They, in their turn, will leave the scene of this world. But when the tale

His native comrades.

Book X. Chapter I.

1857. Sept. 22.

The heroes of the siege.

is told to our children's children, the names of Nicholson, of Chamberlain, of Charles Reid, of Baird Smith, of Edwin Johnson, of Alec Taylor, of James Brind, of Seaton, of Daly, of Jacob, of Probyn, of Watson, of Medley, of Quintin Battye, of Speke, of Greville, of Aikman, of Salkeld, of Home, and of many others—for the list is too long—will be inquired after with sympathy, and will inspire an interest not inferior to that with which the present generation regard the achievements of their forefathers in Spain and in Flanders.

BOOK X.

CHAPTER II.

Deeply sensible of the fact that a victory not followed up is a victory thrown away, General Wilson prepared, as soon as he felt his hold upon Dehlí secure, to detach a force in the direction of Balandshahr and Aligarh to intercept, and, if possible, cut off the rebels.

Wilson follows up the capture of Dehlí

Had Nicholson lived, it had been the General's intention to bestow upon him the command of this force. On his demise it was thought that it would be offered to the commandant of the cavalry brigade, Brigadier Hope Grant. The presence of this gallant and able officer was, however, still thought necessary at Dehlí. The officer selected was Lieutenant-Colonel Edward Greathed, commanding the 8th Foot.

by sending a force towards A'gra.

The force consisted of two thousand seven hundred and ninety men, composed as follows:—

Book X. Chapter II.

1857. Sept. 21.

	Europeans.	Natives.
Captain Remmington's Troop of Horse Artillery, five guns .	60	—
Captain Blunt's Troop of Horse Artillery, five guns . .	60	—
Major Bourchier's Battery, six guns	60	60
Sappers	—	200
H.M.'s 9th Lancers . . .	300	—
Detachments, 1st, 4th, and 5th Panjáb Cavalry, and Hodson's Horse	—	400
H.M.'s 8th and 75th Regiments	450	—
1st and 4th Regiments Panjáb Infantry	—	1,200
	930	1,860

Glad sensations of officers and men on leaving Dehlí.

"Never," wrote a distinguished member of the force,* "never did boys escape from the clutches of a schoolmaster with greater glee than we experienced on the 21st September, when we received our orders to proceed on the following morning to the plain in front of the Ájmír gate, where a column was to be formed under the command of Colonel Greathed, H.M.'s 8th Foot, destined to scour the Gangetic Doab." With the exhilarating feelings sufficiently indicated in the above extract, the force I have detailed marched on the morning of the 24th by way of the Hindan in the direction of Balandshahr.

Sept. 24.

* *Eight Months' Campaign against the Bengal Sepoy Army during the Mutiny of* 1857, by Colonel George Bourchier, C.B.

Book X. Chapter II.

1857. Sept. 26–27.

Greathed destroys Dádri and comes on the track of the rebels.

Crossing the Hindan, and passing through Ghazi-ú-dín Nagr, the force reached Dádri on the 26th. The Gújar inhabitants of this place having been convicted of having sacked the loyal town of Sikandarábád, their town was destroyed. Pushing on, Greathed reached Sikandarábád on the 27th. Here he found himself upon the track of the enemy, a body of their cavalry having evacuated the place only on the day preceding. The distance from Sikandarábád to Balandshahr is about eight miles. Five miles from the latter is the fort of Málagarh, a place which had been held for upwards of three months by Walidád Khán, a partisan of the royal family of Dehlí, and connected with it, it was said, by ties of blood. To expel Walidád Khán from Málagarh was then the first object of Greathed's mission.

Sept. 28.

Moves on Balandshahr.

Starting in the early hours of the 28th, the column reached at daylight four cross roads within a mile and a half of Balandshahr. One of these cross roads led to Málagarh. Balandshahr was immediately in front of the column.

A picket of the enemy's cavalry, stationed at the cross roads, falling back before the advanced cavalry of the British force on Balandshahr, made it clear to Greathed that that station was the true point of attack. He at once prepared to avail himself of his knowledge. Strengthening the advanced guard with two Horse Artillery guns, and forming a reserve under Major Turner for the protection of his baggage, he advanced, his troops well in hand, towards the town.

Book X. Chapter II.

1857. Sept. 28.

Position of the rebels.

The rebels had occupied a position in front of the town, at a point where two roads leading to it converged. The position was well-wooded, abounding in high crops, and in gardens, the walls of which were lined with infantry. Their guns were in the centre, concealed by the crops.

Greathed's order of attack.

On this position Greathed marched, four guns of Remmington's troop moving on by the main road; Bourchier's battery, supported by a squadron of the 9th Lancers and the squadron of the 5th Panjáb cavalry, advancing on the right, the remainder of the cavalry with the other two guns of Remmington's troop under Lieutenant Cracklow, on the left; the 8th and 75th Foot and the 2nd Panjáb Infantry being at the same time pushed forward through the gardens and houses of the civil station. Remmington's guns pounded the enemy in front, while Bourchier advanced till he could gain a position to open a cross fire on the enemy's flank. The moment this position was gained, the enemy gave in, and the British centre and left advancing, drove them headlong into the town.

The cavalry turn the enemy's right.

Meanwhile the cavalry under Major Ouvry and Cracklow's guns had circled round to the left, and though exposed in their progress to a severe fire, from a serai* which the enemy had fortified and from the jail, which momentarily checked them, they carried all before them. Their loss was heavy,—not, however, out of proportion to the results obtained by their dash. The advan-

* A traveller's resting-place.

Book X. Chapter II.

1857. Sept. 28.

tage they had gained was followed up by the infantry and the remainder of the cavalry, who penetrated into or turned the place. The rout then became general. Four hours after the halt at the cross roads, the town, three guns, a quantity of baggage and ammunition, were in the hands of our troops. The enemy lost about three hundred men, the victors forty-seven in killed and wounded.

The infantry come up and complete the defeat of the enemy.

The wisdom of forming a reserve to cover the baggage was justified by the results. For no sooner had the main column advanced to attack the town than a flying party of the enemy made a dash at the baggage. Major Turner, however, beat them off, and Lieutenant Probyn with the squadron of the 2nd Cavalry following them up killed several of them.

An attack on the baggage repulsed with loss.

Lieutenant Watson, 1st Panjáb Cavalry, and Lieutenant Blair, 9th Lancers, greatly distinguished themselves in this action. Of Lieutenant Roberts, of the Artillery, so distinguished during the present year as General Roberts for his conduct in Áfghánistán, and who, a few months later, gained a Victoria Cross, Captain Bourchier writes that he "seemed ubiquitous."

Málagarh was, however, the main object of Greathed's hopes, and he at once reconnoitred with a view to attack it. But the blow inflicted at Balandshahr had penetrated to Málagarh. The rebels evacuated it in a panic, leaving behind them all the plunder they had collected there.

Sept. 28–Oct. 2. Greathed pushes on to Málagarh.

Málagarh was occupied, and orders were given to destroy its fortifications. In carrying out this

Book X. Chapter II.

1857. Sept. 28–Oct. 2.

Accidental death of Lieutenant Home.

operation an accident happened, by which the engineer, Lieutenant Home, was unhappily killed on the spot. Home was an officer of great distinction and greater promise. He was the sole surviving officer of the gallant band who had blown up the Káshmir gate on the morning of the 14th September. For that act, one of many deeds of skill and daring, he had been promised the Victoria Cross. To die by accident after having survived the storming of the Káshmir gate was a hard dispensation, but though Home did not live to reap the fulness of his reward, he had at least known how his former splendid service was appreciated by his comrades.

Oct. 3–9.

Kúrjah and its skeleton.

From Balandshahr the column marched, 3rd October, to Kúrjah. On entering this town the soldiers were greeted by a sight calculated above all others to excite their feelings of resentment to boiling pitch. "As we entered Kúrjah," writes Colonel Bourchier, "a skeleton was stuck up on the road-side, exposed to public gaze, against a wall. The head had been severed from the body, and cuts in the shin-bones were apparent, inflicted by some sharp instrument; and, in the opinion of a medical committee, this skeleton was that of a European female."

Kúrjah was on the high road to Aligarh. It was a place of some importance, for it paid a considerable revenue. The civil officer attached to the column was, therefore, strongly opposed to the prosecution of any measures of retaliation against the townspeople. To the indignation, then, of the soldiers, Kúrjah was spared, and

Greathed pushed on for Áligárh, two marches in advance, where he believed he should meet a considerable force of the rebels.

Book X. Chapter II.

1857. Oct. 3-9.

The column gains A'ligarh and pushes on to Akbarábád.

Áligarh, however, was found substantially undefended, the enemy having evacuated it and taken to the open. Pursued and overtaken in headlong flight, about two hundred and fifty of them fell to the British troopers, whose loss amounted only to three men wounded. Leaving here a garrison, Greathed pushed on to Akbarábád, and was fortunate enough to surprise it with two notorious rebel chiefs within its walls. The two chiefs, Mangal Singh and Maitáb Singh, were tried and summarily executed.

Oct. 9.

An instance of the forbearance of the rebels.

Greathed now pushed forward in the direction of Ágra, from which place "epistles, imploring aid, in every language, both dead and living, and in cypher, came pouring into camp."* On the 9th October he was at Bijégarh, forty-eight miles distant. Near this place, a contrast to the general destruction of European property by the mutineers, was found a house belonging to an indigo factory, containing all its furniture uninjured, and having servants in attendance. The owner, a European, had fled to Ágra. From Bijégarh, in consequence of the urgent entreaties he received from Ágra, Greathed sent forward at midnight the cavalry and horse artillery by forced marches. Four hours later he followed with his infantry, using the utmost speed, mounting his men on elephants, carts, and

* Bourchier's *Eight Months' Campaign.*

Book X. Chapter II. — 1857. Oct. 9-10. Greathed receives urgent prayers for assistance from A'gra.

camels. The despatches he received on the way were more and more urgent. "His credit was at stake," he was told, "if Agra were attacked and he so near." Thus implored, he pressed on with the utmost expedition, overtook his artillery and cavalry, and with them crossed the Jamná at the bridge of boats under the walls of the fort of Ágra on the morning of the 10th.

To account for the urgent requisitions of the Ágra garrison it is necessary to give a brief narrative of the occurrences at that place from the time we left it.

Sept. 9. The condition of A'gra

We left Ágra on the 9th September. The death of Mr. Colvin had left Mr. E. A. Reade the senior civil officer in the North-west Provinces. To great capacity for work, a clear brain, and a large understanding, Mr. Reade added the rare virtue of absolute disinterestedness. Conscious that *inter arma silent leges*, Mr. Reade at once wrote to the Supreme Government, recommending that until order were restored the administration should be vested in the hands of a military chief, and promising his hearty co-operation in any capacity. Pending the orders of Government, Mr. Reade, though the senior officer, retained only his office of Financial Commissioner.

Even before Mr. Colvin's death Ágra had been agitated by the rumour of another attack. The 23rd Native Infantry, which, it will be recollected, had mutinied at Máu on the night of the 1st July—joining itself to the mutinous contingents of Central India—those of Méhidpúr, of Málwa, and of Bhopál—and to the

Book X. Chapter II.

1857. Sept. 9.

rabble of the Native States, had reached Gwáliár. There, by the loyal exertions of Mahárájá Sindia, in active correspondence with the political agent, Major Charters Macpherson, residing in the fortress of Ágra, they had been detained the whole of the month of August. To detain them so long the Mahárájá had strained his authority, and was at times in imminent personal danger. To keep them longer was impossible. Early in September, then, this force of Central Indian mutineers, joined by a number of Gwáliár malcontents, though not, it is believed, by any of the regular army of that State, broke loose from the capital, and marched on Dholpúr. This place lies nearly midway beween Gwáliár and Agra, being distant but thirty-four miles from the latter. The presence, then, of a large force of the three arms at Dholpúr constituted an undoubted threat to the fortress of Ágra.

threatened by the mutineers of Central India,

So much was known at the time of Mr. Colvin's death. It was impossible to attempt to disturb the intruders by detaching from the fortress of Ágra any portion of the small garrison upon whom the safety of so many thousand lives depended. Emboldened by the silent attitude of the English, the rebels began then to feel their way towards Ágra. Sending out detachments from Dholpúr about the 11th September, they spread over the districts of Khairagarh, Fathpúr-Sikri, Irádatnagar, and Fathábád, expelling from them the native officials in the pay of the British Government.

who are emboldened by the compulsory silent attitude of the garrison.

Sept. 11.

The storming of Dehli, instead of lessening, aggravated for the moment the difficulties of the

The difficulties of the Ágra garrison

Book X. Chapter II.

1857. Sept. 14–17.

momentarily aggravated by the fall of Dehlí.

British authorities in Ágra. For, although the result of the 14th September at Dehlí had been partial, yet the persistence of General Wilson on the 16th and 17th, had had the effect of inducing the more soft-hearted of the rebels to leave the town. A considerable body of these men, led by a Shahzádeh named Firozshah, bent their way from Dehlí towards Mathurá, reached that place

Sept. 26.

on the 26th September, and joining there the rebel Sepoys of the regular army, mainly of the 72nd Native Infantry, led by one Híra Singh, a subadár of that regiment, effected a junction with the rebels from Central India.

Measures taken in consequence by the Ágra authorities.

Sept. 19.

To combat the facts and rumours surging about him, Mr. Reade, in conjunction with Lieutenant-Colonel Cotton, commanding the garrison, issued orders on the 19th September, to set to work at once to level some obstacles which interfered with the free play of the guns mounted on the fort, and to mine some of the more prominent buildings, including the great Mosque, which were in dangerous proximity to the walls.

Sept. 30.

Colonel Hugh Fraser, C.B., is appointed Chief Commissioner.

On the 30th September an order from Calcutta was received at Agra nominating Colonel Hugh Fraser, C.B., of the Engineers, to act as the Governor-General's Chief Commissioner for Ágra and its dependencies.

Three days prior to the installation of Colonel Fraser, official intelligence had been received in Ágra of the complete success of the British arms in Dehlí, of the capture of the king, and the slaughter of his two sons and grandson. It was then anticipated that a column of the Dehlí force, released from its siege operations, would at once be despatched to Ágra by Gúrgáon and Mathurá on the right bank of the Jamná.

Reason for the urgent applications sent to Greathed.

Great then was the consternation in the fortress when the news arrived that though a column under Colonel Greathed had been despatched southwards, it had crossed the Jamná and had taken the route of Kúrjah and Aligarh. To the minds of the British within the fortress there was present always the possibility that Greathed's force, regarding Agra as secure in the strength of the fortifications, might push on towards Kánhpúr or Baréli, leaving the Ágra garrison threatened by the incongruous mass of rebels of whom I have spoken. Hence it was that the urgent applications I have referred to were sent to Colonel Greathed,—applications imploring him to make the best of his way to Ágra, to relieve the garrison there from their unpleasant predicament, and to re-establish the Government of the North-west Provinces.

Reason why these applications caused merriment in Greathed's force.

That these urgent applications should have been misunderstood, and have been the cause of some merriment among the officers of Greathed's force, is scarcely surprising. The officers and men of that column had for more than three months occupied a position before Dehlí, exposed to the fire of the enemy, to rain, and heat, and privations of every sort. They were fresh from the storming of the imperial city, and worn by exposure, by fatigue, by watchings,*

* "We went," writes Mr. C. Raikes (*Notes on the Agra Revolt*) "to the royal bastion this morning, to see Colonel

Book X. Chapter II.

1857. Sept. 30– Oct. 10.

their minds were scarcely tuned to listen to entreaties for help from men who, however anxious and wearisome their position, seemed to have enjoyed comparative ease in the shelter of the fortress.

Greathed reaches A'gra and is informed that the enemy have retreated.

We have already seen how Colonel Greathed, responding to the entreaties pressed upon him with so much urgency, turned off the Grand Trunk Road and hurried by forced marches to the threatened capital. When at sunrise on the morning of the 10th he marched his force over the bridge of boats, cheered by the 3rd European Regiment on the bastions, to the gates of the fort, he was informed that the enemy, alarmed at his approach, had retired beyond the Kári Nadi, a stream about nine miles distant.*

Greathed's movable column cross the bridge. Sikhs, Lancers, three batteries of Horse Artillery, and skeletons of two Queen's regiments. This column came in by long forced marches, owing to an express sent out by Colonel Fraser. From the bastion we went down to the Dehli gate. The Queen's 8th passed within three yards of us. 'Those dreadful-looking men must be Afghâns,' said a lady to me, as they slowly and wearily marched by. I did not discover they were Englishmen till I saw a short clay pipe in the mouth of nearly the last man. My heart bled to see these jaded, miserable objects, and to think of all they must have suffered since May last, to reduce fine Englishmen to such worn, sun-dried skeletons."

* An attempt has been made to deny this. In his official report, Mr. Phillips, Magistrate of A'gra, quotes a memorandum by Mr.—now Sir William—Muir, that "there was no intimation given to Colonel Greathed, by any of the authorities, on the morning of the 10th, that the enemy were re-crossing." But the presence of the enemy was either unknown or misbelieved, for I find it stated in a manuscript journey of a very high official: "Major Hennessy, Commandant of the Agra Militia, had been on picket duty during the previous night (9th) with militia-men, mounted

Book X. Chapter II.

1857. Oct. 10.

Difference of opinion as to the encamping ground.

The force halted on the public road in front of the fortress, whilst the Ágra authorities and Colonel Greathed were debating about an encampment ground. Two hours were spent in this discussion—a dreary two hours for men who had just completed a forced march of forty-eight miles. The "local executives," touched doubtless by the sun-burnt appearance of the troops, were all for encamping them "in a series of gardens overgrown with brushwood, where the guns would not have had a range of fifty yards, and where the cavalry could not possibly act," but Greathed was too much of a soldier to accede without urgent remonstrance, to such a proposition.

Greathed gains the point and encamps on the parade ground.

In the end, however, Greathed's proposal that

and foot, at the Metcalfe Testimonial and the cemetery beyond it. *His warning of the approach of the enemy, though some of his scouts had been fired upon, was disregarded. Such was the confidence that the arrival of Colonel Greathed's force would deter any attempt, that his repeated remonstrances led to his being summarily remanded to the Fort. The same information, given by one of Mr. Muir's spies, was scornfully rejected.*" Rejected—by whom? Certainly by the Ágra authorities. Mr. Muir himself, writing the same day to Sir Hope Grant, says, "It was a most complete surprise in one sense to us, but a greater one to them (the rebels)." Major Norman, now Lieutenant-General Sir H. Norman, K.C.B., wrote in 1858, "The head authorities at Ágra informed Colonel Greathed that the insurgent force from Dholpúr was beyond the Kari Naddi, ten miles from cantonments, across which they would find difficulty in passing . . . This information was given in positive terms." It is clear, then, that convinced in their own minds that the enemy had crossed the Kári Naddi and were ten miles distant, the Ágra officials conveyed their convictions on this point to Colonel Greathed. It was, perhaps, unwise in him to trust to this.

Book X. Chapter II.

1857. Oct. 10.

his men should encamp on the parade ground, a magnificent grassy plain, with not an obstacle within three or four hundred yards of it, and then only a few high crops, was allowed to prevail. The camp was marked out, the horses were picketed, and the men went to their breakfasts. Some of the officers hastened into the fort, others from the fort poured into the camp, followed or accompanied by men of all sorts, who seized the long wished for opportunity of communicating with their friends of the outside world.

Greathed's camp.

The men in the camp, having swallowed a hasty meal, were variously occupied. Some, pending the arrival of the baggage, now slowly coming up, had thrown themselves on the ground and were fast asleep; some were talking to their friends; some were assisting to pitch the few tents that had reached the ground. The long march had caused the camp to be pervaded by an air of listlessness and languor, common to men who have but just completed an undertaking of more than ordinary labour. Not a sign betokened an enemy. As far as the eye could reach, the horizon was clear. The high crops and trees which shut in the view at no great distance were stirred only by the breeze. After their long fatigues it seemed as though the weary soldiers were to enjoy at last a day of repose.

The soldiers prepare to rest after their toil.

This sense of security was scarcely justified by the certain proximity of the enemy, and by the absence of any effort being made to ascertain whether the conjectures of the Ágra officials were correct. It was soon disturbed in a very sudden

Book X. Chapter II.

1857. Oct. 10.

and remarkable manner. Four natives, apparently conjurors, and beating tom-toms, came strolling up to the advanced guard of the 9th Lancers. On the sergeant in charge ordering them off, one of them drew a sword from under his clothes and cut him down. Another sergeant moving up to the rescue was also wounded. These men were soon despatched by the troopers, but, before the alarm had reached the rear, round shot "from out the blue" came pouring into the camp. The familiar sound was sufficient for the soldiers of Dehlí. The assembly was sounded, though the call was scarcely needed. To start to their feet, seize their muskets, mount their horses, and man the guns, was the work of an instant. But while this was doing the cannonade spread terror among the camp-followers, and as great among the visitors.*

They are surprised by the enemy;

but promptly form up.

The enemy's horse, taking advantage of the surprise, had charged our artillery and had sabred the gunners of one gun, when a dashing charge made upon them by a squadron of the 9th Lancers, drove them back in disorder. It cost the squadron dear, for Captain French, the squadron leader, was killed, and Lieutenant

Gallant charge of the 9th Lancers.

* "Such was the terrible panic among the latter," writes Colonel Bourchier, C.B., an eye-witness and actor in the drama, "that those officers who had gone into the fort and were eager to get back to their posts could not stem the torrent of affrighted beings; an officer of the Dragoons in attempting it was fairly carried off his legs and borne back with the crowd. Not satisfied with legitimate means of escape, the gun horses in many cases were seized as they were being led to the guns, and were found next morning in the fort."

Book X. Chapter II.

1857. Oct. 10.

Greathed deploys his line.

Jones, his subaltern, was dangerously wounded and cut up when dismounted. Greathed, who was on the spot a few minutes after the attack had begun, lost not a moment in taking the necessary measures. He deployed his line and directed Watson to move off with a portion of his irregular cavalry to turn the enemy's left flank.

Pearson brings his battery to the ground,

The line when advancing was joined by Pearson's 9-pounder battery, which had been despatched from the fort on the first arrival of the column. This gallant officer, whose distinguished conduct has already been mentioned,* had brought this battery again into a state of efficiency by substituting for the native drivers, who had wholly deserted after the disastrous affair of the 5th July, volunteers from the Eurasian fugitives in the fort.† He now arrived at an opportune moment on the right of the line where there was no artillery, and where the infantry were giving ground under the fire of some heavy guns of the enemy which commanded the road along which their centre was advancing. Three of these having had their limbers blown up, and been captured in succession by Pearson's advance; and the cavalry under Ouvry, with all the guns on the left under Turner, having also made a forward

and, checking the enemy, drives back his left.

* Note, vol. i. pages 272–276.

† It is but justice to these men to record that in consequence of their admirable behaviour on this and other occasions, Lord Canning asked Captain Pearson if he would undertake to raise a battery of them. But there were several reasons why it was deemed inexpedient to repeat the experiment in a permanent form.

movement, the enemy were soon seen to be giving way on all sides. A well-timed charge by Watson and Probyn completed the disorder; nor though, with their usual tactics, their cavalry attempted to make a diversion by threatening the camp, were they successful. A second charge of the Lancers and two squadrons of Hodson's Horse sent them back more quickly than they came.

Book X. Chapter II.

1857. Oct. 10.

The enemy's disorder is completed by the cavalry.

Colonel Cotton had by this time arrived from the fort with the 3rd Europeans, and, as senior officer, had assumed the command. Detaching two companies of this regiment to strengthen the Panjáb infantry on the right flank, where the enemy were still contesting the ground under shelter of some high crops, he urged the whole line forward in pursuit. The rebels fell back in hasty disorder by the Gwáliár road, nor did they make a halt even at their camp, which was found standing about midway between Ágra and the Kári Naddi. Here the infantry were done up and halted, but the pursuit was continued with great vigour and success by the artillery and cavalry. "Once only," says Colonel Bourchier, "did they make a stand. A few rounds of grape, however, scattered them in all directions, and the cavalry were soon among their flying ranks, doing great execution. For seven miles the road was one continued line of carts, guns, ammunition waggons, camels rushing about without their drivers, and baggage of every description—all of which fell into our hands. Not a gun or a cart recrossed the stream; all became prize owing to the rapidity with which the victory was followed

Colonel Cotton arrives with the 3rd Europeans and assumes command.

The enemy defeated and pursued.

Book X. Chapter II.

1857. Oct. 10.

Their guns and ammunition taken.

up on the opposite bank. A few cavalry troopers made their appearance, but soon disappeared after a few rounds from the Horse Artillery. Thirteen pieces of ordnance, with an enormous quantity of ammunition, were brought into camp. Much that was useless was destroyed; and the enemy's camp, with the villages on which it abutted, was burnt."

Merit due to the troops who won it.

No victory could have been more rapid or decisive. It was especially creditable to the troops who had that morning marched into Ágra, and whom neither fatigue nor hunger, nor want of sleep, could stop when an enemy was within their grasp. Bourchier's 9-pounder battery had marched thirty miles without a halt before the action began. From first to last Greathed's cavalry and artillery had marched at least over sixty-four miles, and the infantry fifty-four miles of road, in less than thirty-six hours, besides moving through the fields, and fighting a general action. It was a splendid performance—well marched, well fought, well followed up. The force did not return to their camp before 7 o'clock in the evening.

The surprise as great to the rebels as to the British.

But it was a surprise! Yes—but a surprise also to the rebels. They were not aware, until the sleeping camp had been startled into activity by the fire of their guns, that it was Greathed's force which lay before them. They believed they had to do only with the garrison of Ágra. In adjusting the balance, then, of surprises, it must be admitted that the rebels had more reason than the British to regret the want of a careful look-out.

Book X. Chapter II.

1857. Oct. 10-13.

The column halts three days to refit.

The column halted at Ágra the three days following the battle. A supply of ammunition was obtained from the fort, and the wounded were sent into the hospital which had been improvised in the Moti Masjid. Here they were attended not only by the medical officers but by the ladies, whose zealous and tender exertions have been recorded in a previous volume.*

Whilst the column lay halted at Ágra a change in the command of it was inaugurated.

Hope Grant

Brigadier Hope Grant was Lieutenant-Colonel of the 9th Lancers. Left behind at Dehlí in command of the cavalry, he had felt keenly his separation from his splendid regiment. He could not, however, devise, nor could General Penny—commanding at Dehlí, in the absence of General Wilson, who on the fall of the place had proceeded on sick certificate to the Himalayas—devise any plan by which he could serve with the column to which his regiment was attached. For he was senior to Greathed, and General Penny did not possess the power to supersede that officer. One morning, however, when ruminating over the sad fate which compelled him to be inactive, he received a letter from Mr. (now Sir William) Muir, the Secretary to the Government of the North-west Provinces—a letter dated the 10th October, and concluded while Greathed was beating the rebels—in which occurs the following passage: "You are to come on as sharp as you can. . . . You are to come on at

* Vol. i. page 284.

Book X. Chapter II.

1857. Oct. 10-18.

is directed to proceed to A'gra and assume command of the column.

once in the mail-cart if possible." Grant, doubting the authority of Mr. Muir to confer upon him the command of a moveable column, showed the letter to General Penny, who, reading through the lines, directed Grant to proceed to Ágra, and gave him a written order to assume command of the column.

He assumes command,

Oct. 19-29.

reaches Kánhpúr,

crosses the Ganges,

The column had left Ágra for Kánhpúr before Grant, hurrying night and day, reached that place. He overtook it, however, at Firozábád, the third march out of Ágra, and at once assumed command. Pushing onwards, he reached Mainpúri, evacuated by its rebel Rájá, on the 19th, and arrived at Kánhpúr on the 26th October—a skirmish of a squadron of the 9th Lancers and two of the Panjáb cavalry with some five hundred rebels, on the Káli rivulet, near Kánúj, on the 23rd, ending in their complete defeat, their pursuit by Lieutenant Probyn as far as the Ganges, and the capture of four guns and a large quantity of ammunition and two store carts, alone breaking the monotony of the march. At Kánhpúr arrangements were made whereby the strength of the column would be increased, by additions principally to its infantry, to about five

Oct. 30.

and encamps in the plain beyond the Banni bridge.

thousand men. On the 30th, Grant crossed the Ganges for the Álambágh, but in consequence of orders from the Commander-in-Chief, he halted within a few miles of it, near the village of Banthíra, situated in a fine plain four miles on the Lakhnao side of the Banni bridge, there to await the arrival of the Commander-in-Chief, Sir Colin Campbell, on his way to commence operations

Book X. Chapter II.

1857. Oct. 30.

for the final relief of Lakhnao. To gain this position Grant had a skirmish with the rebels who had occupied the village of Banthíra. He drove them out of it, however, without loss, and captured the only gun they possessed—a 9-pounder, the property of the East India Company.

Van Cortlandt,

Simultaneously with the advance of Greathed's column to relieve Ágra, a considerable body of native levies, raised and commanded by Van Cortlandt—an officer of foreign extraction who had served under Ranjit Singh, and had subsequently to the campaign of 1845–6 accepted civil office under the British Government—proceeded to restore order in the districts to the north-west of the imperial city. Van Cortlandt was well qualified for the task. He had had great experience of native soldiers, and he had shown on many an occasion, notably when he assisted Herbert Edwardes in that gallant officer's campaign of 1848, that he could make them fight. On this occasion his work was comparatively easy. The large villages all over the district submitted without a blow; many mutinous soldiers surrendered to him; the roads were opened; and on the 26th September he had so far reduced the large district of Rohtak to submission, that it was possible to re-establish the civil authorities, and even to collect revenue.

reduces the districts to the north-west of Dehlí.

Another column, under Brigadier Showers, the commanding officer of the 2nd European Regiment, was despatched on the 2nd October to clear the districts to the west and south-

Brigadier Showers proceeds to the west and south-west.

Book X. Chapter II.

1857. Oct. 2–17.

west. This column consisted of portions of the Carabineers, of a portion of Hodson's Horse, and the Guide Cavalry, of a field battery and two or three heavy guns, and mortars, of the 2nd European Regiment, the 2nd Gúrkahs, and a regiment of Sikh infantry. The first destination of this column was the fort of Jajhar, on the way to which place it had to march within a few miles of Balamgarh.

The Rájá of Balamgarh

The Rájá of this place had certainly admitted the authority of the King of Dehli. It is more than possible, it is probable, that he had to choose between such a course and destruction. Certain it is that when he heard that the British force was in the vicinity of his capital, he drove out in

submits.

his carriage to meet it. The British officer with whom he came in contact was the notorious Hodson. Hodson has recorded his opinion that the Rájá and his followers deserved to be exterminated; but the orders not to interfere with the native chief of Balamgarh had been so positive that he was constrained to allow him to return, and the force, striking away from the road to Balamgarh, marched through the Riwári

Showers takes Riwári, Jajhar, and Kanáund.

district in the direction of Jajhar. The fort overlooking the town of Riwári was taken without opposition. Jajhar was next reached and occupied, the Nawáb having made his submission, on

Oct. 18.

the 18th. The still stronger fort of Kanáund in the same district, armed with fourteen guns, and containing five lakhs of rupees, surrendered the following morning to the Carabineers and Hodson's Horse, both having marched forty-one

Book X. Chapter II.

1857. Oct. 19.

miles in fifteen hours. Being then on the borders of the sandy desert, Showers returned to Dehli. In the course of his expedition he had occupied four forts, burnt many villages, and taken about seventy guns and £80,000, besides much ammunition and many horses. He had captured or forced to surrender, two princes, the Nawáb of Jajhar, and the Rájá of Balamgarh,* and one notorious partisan, Hákim Abdúl Hak, chief of Gúrgaon. The last-named was hanged immediately after the return of the column to Dehlí.

Showers returns.

Results of his expedition.

Showers's column had scarcely returned to Dehlí when intelligence reached General Penny that the rebels, reinforced by the mutineers of the Jodhpúr legion, had beaten the troops of the loyal Rájá of Jodhpúr, and reappeared in great force in the districts which had but just been traversed, reoccupying Riwári. It became necessary, therefore, to organise and despatch a second force to restore order. A column composed of the 1st Fusiliers, under Captain Caulfield, the 7th Panjáb Infantry, under Godby, a troop of Horse Artillery—the 3rd Brigade—under Colin Cookworthy, a heavy battery of 8-inch howitzers and 18-pounders, under Gillespie, a portion of the Corps of Guides, under Kennedy and Sandford, and the Múltání horse under Lind, was ordered on this duty. The direction of it was bestowed upon Colonel Gerrard, an officer of merit and distinction, trained in the 1st Fusiliers, and who then commanded that regiment.

The rebels, reinforced by the Jodhpúr legion, renew their excesses.

A column is sent under Gerrard to repress them.

* The unfortunate Rájá was subsequently tried and hanged at Dehlí.

Book X. Chapter II.

1857. Nov. 10-13.

Gerrard marched from Dehlí on the 10th of November, reached Riwári on the 13th, and re-occupied the fort without opposition. Here he was joined by two squadrons of the Carabineers. At Kanáund, which he reached two days later, he was met by a detachment of the Hariáná Field Force—of the three arms, including, in addition to the police and native levies, the 23rd Panjáb Infantry—under Captain Stafford. Thence he pushed on over a very sandy plain difficult to traverse to Nárnúl, where, it was understood, the enemy had mustered in force.

Gerrard joined by detachments under Stafford.

The rebels meanwhile had occupied Nárnúl.

Nov. 16.

It was true that on the morning of that very day, the 16th November, the rebels had occupied the village of Nárnúl in considerable force. They occupied it, however, only to prove, for the fiftieth or sixtieth time in this memorable year, that neither strong positions, nor numbers, nor personal courage, are of any avail when there is no leader able to take full advantage of those positions, of those numbers, or of that valour. Never was there a stronger exemplification of the harmlessness of lions, when the lions are led by asses. Nárnúl was a very strong place. It lay under a hill about four hundred feet high, which formed part of a ridge extending some miles to the south-east. It was covered in front—the front facing the road by which the British force would have to advance—by low walls, forming admirable defensive cover. A large and well-filled tank with steep banks, standing much above the surrounding plain, distant only about two hundred yards from the village, and commanding the

Their splendid position—and the folly which prevented their keeping it.

Book X. Chapter II.

1857. Nov. 16.

road to it, afforded another strong position, which infantry might advantageously have occupied. The ground to the left was broken and uneven, but the plain in front was level and broad, admirably adapted to the movements of cavalry, in which arm the rebels were very strong.

The rebel leader learns that the English are marching against him.

Such was the position occupied early on the morning of the 16th November by the rebel army, flushed with recent victory over the Rájpút levies of Jaipúr. It was clear that their leader, Sannand Khán, a near relative of the Nawáb of Jajhar, was well aware that a British force was moving against him, for he had specially selected the strong position of Nárnúl as one against which that force would spend its strength in vain. But with the country people well disposed towards him, he made no effort to procure information regarding his enemy's movements. He posted no vedettes, he sent out no scouts. Wielding a numerous cavalry, he trusted entirely to his own eye-sight to learn when and in what manner the British would advance.

Notwithstanding this information he posts neither vedettes nor scouts.

As up to 10 the English had not come in sight he vacates his splendid position.

It would appear that he expected the British early on the morning of the 16th. But when the clock struck eight, then nine, and when then the hands began to point towards ten, and not a single speck of dust was visible on the horizon, he gave them up for the day, and retiring to his camp, near a dilapidated fort of the same name, about two miles in the rear, there gave orders to his men to dismount and eat. He thus deliberately abandoned, though for the short space of only

Book X. Chapter II.

1857. Nov. 16.

one hour, a position which it would have required all the dash, all the energy, all the exertions of the small British force, numbering altogether about two thousand five hundred men, to carry. That hour was fatal to him.

Causes which had fortunately retarded the British.

The fact was, that the impediments in the road between Kanáund and Nárnúl had terribly—though owing to the incompetence of the rebel leader, fortunately—delayed Gerrard's advance. The distance to the fort of Nárnúl was but fourteen miles, and Gerrard had started at 1 o'clock in the morning. Yet, in the first instance, the enormous difficulty experienced by the artillery in traversing the narrow and sharp-angled streets of Kanáund, and, in the second, the depth of the sand in the road which followed, so hindered the advance, that in ten hours they were only able to accomplish twelve miles! At 11 o'clock Gerrard reached the village of Nárnúl, now guiltless of the presence of an enemy.

The delay smooths away great difficulties.

How he and his officers grumbled at the inevitable delay, may well be imagined. Not one of them could imagine that Fortune was working for them—that the blind goddess was really removing the difficulties in front and plotting to spare the lives of many—to give them in the plain the easy victory which, though still certain, would have been difficult and bloody in the village.

At Nárnúl, I have said, Gerrard saw no signs of the enemy. The difficulties of the march had greatly fatigued his men. He therefore halted while a dram was served out, and the men devoured the small store of food which each had

Book X. Chapter II.

1857. Nov. 16.

carried with him. They had hardly finished this frugal meal when "a slight cloud of dust was seen to rise over a gentle swell of the ground to the left in front."* Another smile from Fortune! Sannand Khán had withdrawn his men for an hour that they might break their fast at the encampment near the ruined fort: he was now returning, hoping to reoccupy his strong position!

The enemy return to occupy their position.

In a moment the British infantry stood to their arms, the cavalry were in the saddle. A trooper belonging to the Corps of Guides rode to the front to reconnoitre. As he nears the rising ground a bullet strikes the ground close to him. But prior even to that evidence of the presence of the enemy he had seen enough. He turned to report to his commanding officer, but before he could reach him the rebel horsemen showed themselves in numbers moving from left to right along the crest of the rising ground. Meanwhile Gerrard had ordered an advance, the Carabineers and the Guides on the right, linked to the centre by a wing of the 7th Panjáb Infantry, and six light guns. In the centre the 1st Fusiliers, the heavy 18-pounders, which it had cost so much trouble to drag across the sand, a company of the Guide Infantry, and the 23rd Panjáb Infantry. To connect the centre with the Irregular Cavalry and Múltáni Horse on the left, and protected by the Sikh Infantry, were four light Sikh guns. In front of all rode Gerrard, a handsome man, with wavy grey hair, his red coat covered with decorations,

A Guide trooper reconnoitres.

The enemy show themselves in numbers.

Gerrard advances.

* *Blackwood's Magazine*, June 1858. The writer of the article was present at the affair.

Book X. Chapter II.

1857. Nov. 16.

conspicuous on his white Arab, surrounded by his staff. So steady were the movements, it might have been an ordinary field-day.

The cavalry of the rival hosts join.

The trooper of whom I have spoken had scarcely rejoined his regiment when the enemy's guns opened with grape on our right. There reply to them first our light guns, next the big eighteens and an 8-inch howitzer. Many hostile saddles are emptied, so the rebels, thinking this poor work, mass their cavalry on their left, and come down with a shout. But the movement has been foreseen, and the Carabineers and Guides, moving up at the same moment, gallop to meet them. About midway between the two lines the rival hosts join.

The cavalry conflict.

It was a gallant conflict. Never did the enemy fight better. There was neither shirking nor flinching. Both sides went at it with a will. The Guides were commanded by Kennedy,* "the worthy son of a worthy sire," and he led them with a skill and a daring which could not be surpassed. The Carabineers, splendidly led by Wardlaw, who commanded the entire cavalry, equalled, if they did not surpass, their former splendid achievements. Never was there a charge more gallant, and certainly, never were the British cavalry met so fairly or in so full a swing by the rebel horse. As the rival parties clashed in deadly shock, the artillery fire on both sides was suspended as it were by instinct, the gunners gazing with outstretched necks at the converging horsemen.

* Now Colonel Kennedy, commanding a cavalry regiment in Afghánistán.

Book X. Chapter II.

1857. Nov. 16.

The result was not long doubtful. Though the enemy fought with the courage of despair, though they exposed their lives with a resolution which forbade the thought of yielding, they were fairly borne down. The Carabineers and the Guides forced them back, cleaving down the most stubborn foemen, till the remainder, overpowered, sought safety in flight. Then Wardlaw and Kennedy, mindful of the mistake of Prince Rupert, gathered up their men, and, instead of pursuing the routed horsemen of the enemy, wheeled suddenly round to the left, and came down with a swoop on the enemy's guns. The shock was irresistible; the gunners who stood were cut down. Leaving the guns, the cavalry then went on to prevent any rally on the part of the enemy's horse.

The infantry conflict.

But that had long since been cared for. Meanwhile the enemy's infantry and gunners, recovering from their panic, had, after our horsemen had swept by, pushed forward, and recovering the guns, opened fire on our advancing infantry. Not for long did they continue this hazardous game. The 1st Fusiliers, coming up with a run, reached the guns after two rounds had been fired, and recaptured them.

The conflict on the left.

On our left the cavalry movement had not been so successful. The Múltáni Horse, new levies, had not displayed the alacrity to come to close quarters which their comrades on the right had so conspicuously manifested. In vain did their gallant commander, Lieutenant Lind, dash amongst the foe. But few followed him, until the Field Engineer, Lieutenant Humphrey, who that day

Book X. Chapter II.

1857. Nov. 16.

acted as Aide-de-Camp to Gerrard, riding up to the still hesitating mass, called upon them to follow him, and charged single-handed the rebel horse. Then the Múltánis followed, not, however, before the gallant Humphrey had been unhorsed and cut down, receiving a severe wound in his right arm, another, slighter, on the left side of his body, "while a third entirely divided his leather helmet and thick turban which covered it, fortunately without injuring his head." He subsequently recovered.

The enemy completely defeated.

But the action was over. The right and the centre had won it, and the charge of the Múltánis tardy though it was, completed their good work. The enemy, beaten and in disorder, fell back through the gardens and broken ground on their left, in full retreat to their camp. The British followed them up with vigour, each arm vying with the other. It was on this occasion that the Horse Artillery performed a feat unsurpassed even in the annals of that splendid regiment. It is thus recorded by an eye-witness:* "On turning up from the left, the Artillery got into a ploughed field, which was separated from the road by a mud wall fully three feet high. At this, Dawes's troop, this day commanded by Captain Cookworthy,† rode at full gallop. On they come—over go the leaders, nicely both together, next follow the centre pair, and lastly the wheelers take the leap; then, with a sort of kick and a bump, over goes the gun on to the hard road.

Cookworthy's gallant feat.

* *Blackwood's Magazine*, June 1858.

† Now Major-General Colin Cookworthy.

Book X. Chapter II.

1857. Nov. 16.

The Fusiliers were so delighted that they gave a willing cheer, while the Sikhs, who witnessed the feat, said nothing for some time, but looked on with open mouths and eyes; at last 'Truly that is wonderful!' burst from their lips spontaneously." Of such was the old Bengal Artillery, unsurpassed and unsurpassable!

The old Bengal Artillery!

Colonel Gerrard, the commander of the column, had ridden in front the whole time. He was the only man of the force—his orderly officer, Captain Osborn alone excepted—dressed in red, the infantry wearing the khâki, or dust-coloured uniform, then authorised for service in the field. As in the fight, so in the pursuit, Gerrard maintained his prominent position. He pushed forward, directing the men, till he reached a rivulet with partially wooded banks. On these banks he drew in his horse, whilst he directed the movements of the troops to the other side. To him, thus sitting on his white Arab and giving directions calmly, one of his staff officers, Lieutenant Hogg, suddenly pointed out a man on the opposite bank taking deliberate aim at him. Just then the man fired, but missed. Hogg entreated the Colonel to move back. Gerrard replied that he would move in a minute, but that he must see what was going on. But before he did move, the man had reloaded and fired. This time his aim was true. Gerrard fell mortally wounded, and died in two hours.

Gerrard, directing the pursuit, is killed.

By the death of Gerrard the command devolved upon Captain Caulfield, then commanding the 1st Fusiliers. But before the intimation of his pro-

Caulfield takes command.

Book X. Chapter II.

1857. Nov. 16.

motion reached him, the troops, carrying out Gerrard's plan, had crossed the rivulet, and had stormed the enemy's camp. The action, however, was by no means over. The rebel horse, rallying on the right, made a sudden charge on Lind's Múltánis and recaptured two of their lost guns. Their success, however, was but momentary. Two companies of the Fusiliers, under Lieutenant Warner, charged and recovered the guns, whilst the main body of the regiment, under McFarlane, expelled the rebel infantry from the still remaining buildings in the fort of Nárnúl. The rebels then dispersed, leaving in the hands of the victors eight guns, their camp, and the fort.

The enemy make a sudden stroke for victory, but are foiled.

Nov. 17-23.

The next day Caulfield gave the force a rest, only sending out parties of horse to ascertain the direction in which the enemy had fled. This direction proving to be to the south-east, towards the dominions of the Rájá of Alwar, Caulfield set off on the 19th to follow them. The rebels were, however, invisible. On the 23rd the force reached Paltaóli. Here it was joined by its new commander, Lieutenant-Colonel Seaton, C.B., sent for that purpose from Dehlí. To that place Seaton marched the force to prepare it to escort to the camp of the Commander-in-Chief at Kánhpúr a large convoy of grain and stores—covering above eighteen miles of road. Here I must leave him, to return once more to Calcutta, there to note how the Commander-in-Chief selected by Lord Palmerston to crush the mutiny was preparing to carry out his rôle.

Seaton is sent to replace Gerrard; he returns to Dehlí preparatory to marching towards Kánhpúr.

BOOK XI.

CHAPTER I.

State of affairs throughout India on the arrival of Sir Colin Campbell.

Sir Colin Campbell had arrived in Calcutta on the 13th August. At that moment affairs were seemingly at their worst. The North-west Provinces, Dehlí, Rohilkhand, and Oudh were lost. The Panjáb was fermenting. Central India was in a state of veiled rebellion. The very existence of the English in India was depending upon the early capture of Dehlí, and Dehlí still held out.

The latest accounts received from the districts occupied by the rebels were far from re-assuring. The British force before Dehlí was believed to be more besieged than besieging. The British garrison in Agra was known to be isolated and cut off from communication with the outer world. All that men knew of Lakhnao was that the small British force, having sustained a defeat in the field, was shut up in an enclosure, not, in a military point of view, defensible, charged with the care of a large number of women and children; that Havelock, after two heroic efforts to re-

Book XI. Chapter I.

1857. Aug. 13–Oct. 26.

lieve them, had been forced to fall back upon Kánhpúr.

But if these accounts were sufficient to dishearten, the private information received was scarcely calculated to console. Every day made the loyalty of the Sikhs more questionable. Every day increased the difficulty of Sindia to restrain his troops from a movement against Ágra, or, more to be dreaded still, upon Kánhpúr. Every day relaxed our hold upon the princes of Rajpútáná and of Bandalkhand, whilst from the Western Presidency there came unmistakable symptoms that order in the southern Maráthá country could be maintained only by a strong and vigorous hand.

The British hold on the country decreasing every day.

Sir Colin finds that though certain centres are held, there has been a great dissemination of troops east of Allahábád.

What was Sir Colin Campbell's position? What were his means? Thanks to the skill, the energy, the daring of a few men who had come to the front in the heart of the crisis—to Neill, to Frederic Gubbins, to Vincent Eyre, and to William Tayler—the British held Allahábád, and the important cities between that fortress and Calcutta, of Banáras, of Gh$\acute{\text{a}}$zipúr, and of Patná. The retention of these three salient points enabled them to hold four others of lesser though of great importance, and by their means to command the great river artery between Calcutta and Allahábád. But the holding of these posts involved the occupation of them by troops, whose services were urgently needed in the field. This, too, at a moment when the reinforcements from England were only beginning to arrive.

The distance by river between Calcutta and

Book XI. Chapter I.

1857. Aug. 13–Oct. 26.

Allahabad is eight hundred and nine miles. When Sir Colin Campbell arrived, no troops were available for active purposes. Two regiments indeed, the 5th and 90th, had been despatched to join Havelock's force at Káuhpúr. All the others were employed in keeping open the river communication between Calcutta and Allahabad.

He has no troops available for active purposes.

It is true there was the grand trunk road—Mr. Beadon's famous line of six hundred miles—though in point of fact the distance was somewhat less. But along this road the railway extended only to Ránigauj, one hundred and twenty miles. Thence it was necessary to march, and the route was not only long, but as events proved, in spite of Mr. Beadon, it was liable to be traversed by the rebels. The troops marching upon it, therefore, might at any moment be diverted for other duties.

Mr. Beadon's line still, and always, in danger of being broken.

The refusal of Lord Canning's Government in the month of July to order the disarming of the native regiments at Dánápúr had added still further to the difficulties of the new Commander-in-Chief. Two regiments of foot and a battery of artillery were thus diverted from the general plan—the plan which had made Lakhnao the point at which the first great blow was to be dealt—in order to quell a rebellion which, had the members of the Government of India been unfettered by sophisms and theories, would never have occurred—the rebellion in western Bihár.

The results of Lord Canning's refusal to disarm the Dánápúr native regiments still felt.

But if Sir Colin Campbell had no men with whom to operate, it might be imagined that the Government had at least provided for him resources to be

Book XI. Chapter I.

1857. Aug. 13–Oct. 26.

Want of foresight of the Supreme Government.

made available for the troops expected from China and from England. There could not be a greater delusion. Dreaming of reorganisation, sanguine that the coming troops would at once settle the business, the members of the Government had opened wide their mouths in expectancy. They had done nothing, and nothing had fallen into their mouths. They had prepared no means of transport; they had no horses, either for cavalry or artillery; Enfield rifle ammunition was deficient; flour was even running out; guns, gun-carriages and harness for field batteries were either unfit for service or did not exist.* Sir Colin Campbell's first care was to supply these deficiencies. He moved the Government to the purchase of horses on a large and necessarily an expensive scale; to indent on England for Enfield rifle ammunition whilst stimulating the manufacture of it on the spot; to procure flour from the Cape; to cast field guns at the Kásipúr foundry; to manufacture tents; to make up harness; to procure English-speaking servants for the expected European regiments from Madras. Before the end of August Sir Colin had quintupled the activity of the "departments," and had infused even into the Government a portion of his own untiring energy.

Sir Colin Campbell has "to organise victory."

Nor was his attention confined to the preparations necessary for the troops before they could stir one foot from Calcutta. Those troops were

* *Blackwood's Magazine*, October 1858; also personal experience and observation.

Book XI. Chapter I.

1857. Aug. 13–Oct. 26.

He moves the Government to organise a bullock train to convey troops to Allahábád.

to move forward—but how? I have given a description, in outline, of the two routes which were open to them—the river route and the land route. But useful, and in some respects superior, as the river route had been in the months of June, July, and August, Sir Colin could not but feel that with the cessation of the rainy season the river would fall, and the way by it would become tedious and uncertain. He therefore resolved to do all in his power to improve the land route and to quicken the means of transport. With this view, under his inspiring pressure, the Government established the bullock train. This train was composed of a number of covered waggons, in each of which a fixed number of European soldiers could sit at ease. To draw these, a proportionate number of bullocks were posted at stages all along the road. The starting-point of the bullock train was the railway terminus at Ránigani, one hundred and twenty miles from Calcutta. The soldiers, leaving the train, were supposed to enter the bullock-carriages and to travel in them all night and in the early hours of the morning and evening, resting for food during the heat of the day. This scheme was soon brought to perfection, and was made to work so as to land daily in Allahabad two hundred men fresh and fit for work, conveyed in the space of a fortnight from Calcutta.

The scheme is soon brought to perfection.

Dangers which threatened the line to be traversed by the bullock train.

But, I have said, Mr. Beadon's famous line of six hundred miles, once already rent in twain, was still far from safe. Constant revolts rendered it less and less so every day. The Rámgarh battalion, stationed at Ránchi, on the left of the road,

Book XI. Chapter I.

1857. Aug. 13–Oct. 26.

breaking the bands of discipline, menaced all the salient points running within easy distance of that station; on the right the remnants of the Dáná-púr garrison, of the 5th Irregular Cavalry, and subsequently the mutinous portion of the 32nd Native Infantry, uniting themselves with the bands of Kúnwar Singh, threatened the districts in the neighbourhood, and spread consternation amongst the local authorities. These mutinous bands constituted the great difficulty of Sir Colin Campbell. Not that they were sufficiently formidable to check a British force. Could they have been found collected, a few companies of Europeans would have annihilated them. But spreading over a vast tract of country, they harassed every district and threatened every post. For the moment Sir Colin's one care was to ensure the safety of the small parties travelling along the Trunk Road in the bullock train. To secure this he formed moveable columns, of about six hundred men each, infantry and artillery, to patrol the road. This measure, successful in so far that it secured the passage of the troops, was less so in another. It afforded to the civil authorities the temptation of diverting some of the troops to small and comparatively unimportant local operations on the flanks, "So that," says a well-informed writer, "at one period, out of about two thousand four hundred men who were proceeding by the different routes to Allahábád, one thousand eight hundred were, on one pretence or other, laid hold of by the civil power, and employed for the time being in opera-

Sir Colin orders patrol parties to secure it.

The temptation thus afforded to the civil authorities to use these troops for local purposes sometimes irresistible.

tions extraneous to the general plan of the campaign."*

Troops of the China Expedition reach Calcutta.

The efforts made by the Government to produce resources and to ensure the safety of the road were beginning to bear good fruit when most of the troops diverted by Lord Elgin from the China Expedition arrived. These consisted of the 93rd Highlanders, the 23rd Fusiliers, three companies of the 82nd Foot, two companies Royal Artillery, and one company of Sappers. About the same time also, that is during September and in the first week of October, there arrived from the Cape of Good Hope a company of Royal Artillery with fifty-eight horses and about five hundred of the 13th Light Infantry. To hurry forward these troops had now become a matter of the greatest necessity. In the interval before their arrival Dehlí had, it is true, fallen, but Lakhnao had not been relieved; so far from it, the British force that had reached our garrison in the Residency, besieged itself by the rebels, had been thus withdrawn from active operations, and left a gap on which an enterprising enemy might act with fatal effect.

The gap left by the retention of Outram's troops in Lakhnao,

The rebel troops of Gwáliár were displaying unwonted activity, and it certainly was in their power at this particular period to cut the British line in two, and sever communications between Calcutta and Kánhpúr. To press on troops quickly to Allahábád, where equipments were being prepared, became then an imperative duty. To this end every exertion was made. Horses

necessitates prompt and active measures.

* *Blackwood's Magazine*, October 1858.

Book XI. Chapter I. — 1857. Aug. 13– Oct. 26.

were taken bodily from regiments which had mutinied, and were pressed into service. The Military Train Corps, composed to a great extent of old dragoons, was formed, by means of some of the horses so become available, into a cavalry regiment, and they, too, were sent on with the rest.

The *Shannon* and *Pearl*.

But before a single man of the China expeditionary Corps had left Calcutta, there had set out from that city in river steamers a gallant body of men, gallantly commanded, destined to cover themselves with glory in a series of actions for which they had no special training. In another part of this history I have alluded to the arrival in Calcutta of H.M's ships *Shannon* and *Pearl*, and of the offer made by Lord Elgin to place those vessels with their respective crews at the disposal of the Governor-General. The offer was accepted, and, on the 18th August, Captain William Peel had started for Allahábád in the river steamer *Chunar* with a flat in tow, conveying four hundred and fifty men, six 68-pounders, two 24-pound howitzers, and two field-pieces. Captain Peel took with him also a launch and cutter belonging to the *Shannon*.*

Aug. 18.

* The following officers accompanied Captain Peel: Lieutenants Young, Wilson, Hay, and Salmon, R.N.; Captain Gray and Lieutenant Stirling, R.M.; Lieutenant Lind, of the Swedish Navy; the Rev. G. L. Bowman; Dr. Flanagan; Mr. Comerford, Assistant Paymaster; Messrs. M. Daniel, Garvey, E. Daniel, Lord Walter Kerr, Lord Arthur Clinton, and Mr. Church, midshipmen; Messrs. Brown, Bone, and Henri, engineers; Mr. Thomson, gunner; Mr. Bryce, carpenter; Mr. Stanton, assistant-clerk; and Messrs. Watson and Lascelles, naval cadets.—*The Shannon's Brigade in India.*

Book XI. Chapter I.

1857. Aug. 18.

Captain William Peel.

Captain William Peel was a man who would have made his mark in any age and under any circumstances. To an energy that nothing could daunt, a power that seemed never to tire, he added a freshness of intellect, a fund of resource, which made him, in the expressive language of one of his officers, "the mainspring that worked the machinery." Bright and joyous in the field, with a kind word for every comrade, he caused the sternest duty, ordered by him, to be looked upon as a pleasant pastime. "The greatness of our loss we shall in all probability never know," wrote Dr. Russell, on learning of his untimely death from small-pox. And, in truth, that reflection of the genial correspondent represents the exact measure by which to gauge the value of Peel's services. Starting from Calcutta on an expedition unprecedented in Indian warfare, he conquered every obstacle, he succeeded to the very utmost extent of the power to succeed. He showed eminently all the qualities of an organiser and a leader of men. Not one single speck of failure marred the brightness of his ermine. His remarkable success in a novel undertaking, on an untried field—a success apparently without an effort—was in itself a proof that had he survived, his great powers might have been usefully employed in larger and more difficult undertakings. There must be something in the man who, not exercising supreme command, is able to stereotype his name in the history of his native land. Yet William Peel accomplished this. To the chaplets of fame placed by his father on the altar of his

Book XI. Chapter I.

country, he, still young, added another not less immortal.

1857. Sept. 2–20. The *Shannon* brigade reaches Allahábád.

Peel reached Allahábád on the 2nd September. There he was joined on the 20th of the following month by the two parties from the *Pearl* and *Shannon*,* which came to complete his brigade, bringing its numbers to seven hundred and twenty men, exclusive of officers. Here for the present I must leave him.

More troops reach Calcutta. Sept.–Oct. 26.

We left Sir Colin Campbell in Calcutta engaged in "organising victory." We have seen how in September and the first week of October he had been gladdened by the arrival of troops from China and the Cape, how he had at once sent them to the point of rendezvous in batches of two hundred daily. During the next fortnight there had arrived the remainder of the 82nd Foot, one hundred and ninety-eight men of the 38th, H.M.'s 34th, and one hundred and forty-four men of the 42nd Highlanders, and one hundred and two recruits for the local European regiments. These were quickly followed by six hundred and twelve men of the Royal Artillery, nine hundred and three of the Rifle Brigade, 2nd and 3rd battalions, two hundred and ninety of the 42nd Highlanders, three hundred and fifty-two of the 54th Foot, six hundred and twenty-seven of the 88th, and

* The contingent from the *Pearl* was composed of one hundred and fifty-five men, commanded by Captain Sotheby, R.N.; the second detachment from the *Shannon* of one hundred and twenty men, under Lieutenants Vaughan and Wratislaw; Mr. E. H. Verney, mate; Mr. Way, midshipman; and Mr. Richards, naval cadet.

Book XI. Chapter I.

1857. Oct. 27.

eight hundred and eighty-three recruits. Having placed upon a thoroughly well organised basis the scheme for despatching these reinforcements as expeditiously as possible to the front, Sir Colin Campbell, with the Army Headquarters and Staff, set out, on the 27th October, by post, for Allahábád.

The narrative clears the road behind Sir Colin Campbell.

The operations of Sir Colin Campbell demand an entire chapter to themselves. It will be advisable that, before entering upon them, I should clear the road behind him, and place before the reader a general view of the transactions in Bengal and Bihár since Vincent Eyre's splendid gallantry had redeemed the *laches* of the Government in those important provinces.

Bhágalpúr.

The large division of Bhágalpúr, comprising the districts of Bhágalpúr, Manghyr, Púrnia, Santhália, and Rájmahal, was governed by Mr. George Yule as Commissioner. The division constituted the eastern moiety of the province of Bihár. The headquarters were at the station of Bhágalpúr, on the Ganges, two hundred and sixty-six miles westward of Calcutta.

Mr. George Yule.

Mr. George Yule* was a good specimen of a manly, true-hearted gentleman. He was essentially a man of action. His even-handed justice had gained for him—what was rare in those days—the confidence alike of the native ryot and the European planter. Both classes alike trusted him, and both were prepared to obey his orders without hesitation or murmur.

* Now Sir George Yule, K.C.S.I.

Book XI. Chapter I.

1857. June.

The native troops in eastern Bihár.

Up to the time when the native garrison of Dánápúr broke out into revolt, there had been no signs of disaffection in the Bhágalpúr division. The troops quartered there—the 5th Irregular Cavalry, with their headquarters at Bhágalpúr, the 32nd stationed at Báosi, and the 63rd at Barhámpúr, had, with the exception noted in the preceding volume,* displayed no inclination to follow the example of their mutinous brethren. The conduct of Major Macdonald on the occasion in question had greatly impressed the men of the 5th, and the strong will of that courageous man had repressed the smallest inclination on the part of his soldiers to manifest the sympathies which, subsequent experience proved, they held in secret. The men of the corps had, subsequently to the event of the 12th June, been detached to various stations in the division, as well to divide them as to overawe the turbulent classes.

Mr. Yule, at the outset, tries to maintain order without European troops,

Although ruling over a native population numbering, besides the Santháls, about six millions, Mr. Yule had considered it unnecessary to ask for, or to accept, the services of a European detachment, however small. He believed that if the districts contiguous would but remain loyal, he would be able, with the assistance of his assistants and the planters, to maintain order in Bhágalpúr. He did so, successfully, till the third week of July. But when, during that week, the mutiny of the 12th Irregular Cavalry and the native regiments quartered at Dánápúr threatened the loss

* Vol. i. page 37.

of western Bihár, he deemed it prudent to detain at Bhágalpúr ninety men of the 5th Fusiliers, then being towed up the river, and to despatch fifty men of the same regiment to garrison the important fortress of Manghír.

but the threatening aspect of affairs forces him to detain a few.

The proceedings of the native soldiers of the Dánápúr garrison, almost invited to mutiny by the supine action of the Supreme Government, combined with the immediate rising of Kúnwar Singh to render the condition of eastern Bihár dangerous in the extreme. Not only was it impossible any longer to rely upon the native soldiers in that province, but it had become necessary, for the security of life and property, to prove to the disaffected that the hand wielding executive power was thoroughly aware of the danger, and thoroughly ready to meet it.

Effect on eastern Bíhar of the Dánápúr mutiny.

Mr. Yule, as a practical man, accustomed to command, was well aware that occasions may arise when an active demonstration is the best defence. Such an occasion had, in his opinion, arisen in eastern Bihár, and he prepared to act accordingly.

Fore-warned, it was necessary to be fore-armed. His first act, then, had been to press into his service the detachment of the European troops passing by, and secured Bhágalpúr and Manghír. The importance of this precautionary measure can scarcely be over-rated. The occupation of those two stations, both salient points on the Ganges, was absolutely essential to the free navigation of that river, and it must be remembered that in July, when Mr. Beadon's line of six hundred miles had been broken, the Ganges consti-

The securing of two salient points in his division assures the navigation of the Ganges,

Book XI. Chapter I.

1857. July.

tuted the only safe highway between Calcutta and Allahábád.

and stops communication between the disaffected of eastern and western Bihár,

Great as was the advantage thus gained, another, second only to it in importance, naturally followed. The native troops stationed at Barhampúr had not, up to that time, thanks to the timid policy of the Government, been disarmed. Had Bhágalpúr and Manghír not been occupied by Europeans, the armed mutinous soldiers scattered over western Bihár would have held uninterrupted communication with their brethren on either side of them, and a general insurrection would probably have ensued.

who now wait for the result of the siege of A'rah.

But the occupation of those stations cowed the disaffected for the time. They were content to wait. The fate of eastern Bihár now depended on the result of the siege of Árah. To that the eyes of the natives were turned with an excitement daily increasing.

The natives not always inclined to trust the news they receive.

One rather remarkable circumstance deserves to be noticed. Ill news generally, it is said, flies quickly. But it is a fact that throughout the troubled times of the mutiny, news betokening evil to the rebels did not fly surely to their friends. It was not that the rebels failed to transmit to them a true record of events. But that record came, not written on paper, but by word of mouth. The result was that when the news was bad, the men who received it, impatient of inaction, and confident of ultimate success, refused to believe it. Their sanguine natures induced them to imagine that the Europeans had invented the bad news and had caused it to be conveyed to them by men whom they had suborned. They proceeded to act then, in very many cases, as though the bearing of the news were exactly contrary to the actual meaning of the words in which it was conveyed.

Book XI. Chapter I.

1857. August.

So it happened on this occasion. The 5th Irregular Cavalry in the districts round Bhágalpúr had, in common with the other native soldiers in the province, waited long for the result of the leaguer of Árah. Had they not waited, but broken out, the difficulties of the British position in Bihár would have been enormously increased. But they waited to hear of its fall. On the 14th August information reached the men of the 5th that Árah had been relieved by Eyre. They believed this story to be a weak invention of the enemy—that the contrary had happened. That night, therefore, they deserted, and pushed with all speed for Báosí, where the 32nd Native Infantry were stationed.

The 5th Irregular Cavalry in eastern Bihár mutiny.

They try to reduce the 32nd,

But before the mutineers of the 5th Irregulars reached the 32nd Native Infantry, the men of that regiment had received positive proof of the utter and absolute defeat of their brethren at Árah and at Jagdispúr. Mr. Yule, too, with an energy worthy of the occasion, had despatched to their commandant, Colonel Burney, a special messenger, warning him of the departure in his direction of the 5th. Burney was a capable man, a splendid linguist, and thoroughly conversant with the native character. He harangued his men, and made it palpably clear to them that whether they should march eastward or westward, they would march to destruction. He spoke

who, under the influence of Colonel Burney, repel them.

Book XI. Chapter I.

1857. August.

eloquently and with effect. When the 5th Irregulars then, on the 16th, presented themselves at Báosí, they were received by the 32nd with bullets and bayonets. The 5th, baffled in their hopes, continued their course *viâ* Rohni to Árah.

For the moment the active measures of Yule had conjured from eastern Bihár all danger. It was, however, otherwise in the neighbouring district of Chutiá Nágpúr. This mountainous district lies between southern Bihár, western Bengal, Orisá, and the Central Provinces. It is called Chutiá Nágpúr from Chutiá near Ránchi, the residence of the Rájás of Nágpúr. It is chiefly inhabited by aboriginal tribes, such as Kóls, Oráons, Mundás, Bhúmij, Korwás, and others. Its chief military stations were Hazáríbágh, Ránchi, Chaibásá and Parúliá.

Chutiá Nágpúr.

July.

At Hazáríbágh there was quartered in July 1857 a detachment of the 8th Native Infantry; at Ránchi, the headquarters and artillery of the local Rámgarh battalion; and at Chaibásá and Parúliá, detachments of that battalion. The acting Commissioner of the district was Captain Dalton.

Effect in Chutiá Nágpúr of the mutiny at Dánápúr.

The news of the mutiny of the native garrison at Dánápúr and of the rising of Kúnwar Singh, reached Hazáríbágh on the 30th July. The detachment of the 8th Native Infantry at once mutinied, driving their officers and the civil authorities from the station.

Those were still the days of confidence. Almost every officer of the native army, whilst admitting and deploring the disaffection of other

The troops in the province generally mutiny

regiments, believed implicitly in the loyalty of his own men. When, then, intelligence reached Dúranda, the civil station adjoining Ránchi, that the troops at Hazáríbágh, only sixty miles distant, were shaky, the officer commanding at that station despatched Lieutenant Graham with thirty horsemen of the Rámgarh Irregular Cavalry, two companies of the Rámgarh battalion, and two guns, to Hazáríbágh, to disarm them. Graham marched, but he had not reached the second stage before Captain Oakes met him with the information that the detachment of the 8th Native Infantry had mutinied the previous day. That same night his own infantry mutinied, seized, in spite of his protestations, the guns and ammunition, as well as four elephants, the property of Captain Dalton, and marched back to Ránchi, breathing hostile imprecations against the Europeans there stationed. The cavalry remained staunch.

Captain Dalton abandons Ránchi and proceeds to Hazáríbágh.

Captain Dalton and a few European officers were at Ránchi. They received timely information of the revolt. The defence of the place was impossible. They remained there, however, till the latest safe moment, and then proceeded to Hazáríbágh, now abandoned by the rebels, and whither Lieutenant Graham with a few horsemen who had remained faithful had preceded them.

The plunder of Ránchi and Dúranda.

The stations of Ránchi and Dúranda fell into the hands of the rebels, who plundered the treasury, fired cannon at the church, released the prisoners, and destroyed private property.

Meanwhile, Dalton, ably seconded by the offi-

Book XI. Chapter I.

1857. August.

Efficient measures taken by Dalton to restore order.

cers of the Rámgarh battalion and the cavalry, by his own civil officers, Captains Davies and W. H. Oakes, was exerting himself to restore order in Hazáríbágh. In this he was loyally assisted by the Rájá of Rámgarh. This petty chief placed at the Commissioner's disposal some forty or fifty armed men. With the aid of these men, and of the few native horsemen and foot soldiers who had remained faithful, Dalton not only tranquillised Hazáríbágh, but he recovered a large quantity of the property seized by the rebels, and captured many of them. In a few days the courts were re-opened, and business proceeded as usual.

Parúliá and Chaibásá.

At Parúliá and at Chaibásá, the other posts in Chutiá Nágpúr occupied by native troops, scenes had taken place similar to those enacted at Ránchi and Hazáríbágh. On the 5th August, the sepoys of the Rámgarh battalion, stationed at those places, mutinied, plundered the treasury, released the prisoners, and sacked the private houses of the Europeans. These, few in number, fell back upon Ráníganj.

Loyal conduct of the Rájá of Rámgarh.

The Rájá of Rámgarh, at the time that he afforded to the Commissioner of Chutiá Nágpúr the aid in armed men of which I have spoken, had expressed his strong conviction that it would be difficult to hold Hazáríbágh against the surging influences around it, unless European troops should be sent to occupy it. He had therefore pressed upon Captain Dalton the necessity of asking at once for a European regiment.

Captain Dalton asked for a European regiment.

Book XI. Chapter I.

1857. August.

It was but natural and proper that he should do so. But how was it possible for the Government to comply? Dehlí had not fallen. The districts below Kánhpúr were in the state which I have endeavoured to describe in the opening pages of this chapter. Sir Colin Campbell had just arrived, but Sir Colin Campbell had not a soldier to dispose of. When an army was urgently required at Kánhpúr, it was not in his power to do more than to organize transport for the troops which were to come, but which had not arrived.

Dalton applies for European troops.

None are available.

It happened, however, that the Government had other resources at its disposal, and that it was possible to use these for the double purpose of tranquillising Chutiá Nágpúr *en route* and of then lending a hand to the force which was concentrating at Allahábád.

Other resources at the disposal of the Government.

The native soldiers of the army of the Madras Presidency—those of one regiment, the 8th Light Cavalry alone excepted—not been tainted by the mutinous spirit which had disgraced their brethren in the Bengal army. Inheritors of the fame of the men who had fought the French soldiers of Lally, who had helped to wrest Southern India from the grasp of Haidar Ali, the Madras sepoys had come forward, on the first bursting of the storm, to offer their services, had begged—to use their own touching language—"to be granted an opportunity of proving their faithful attachment to the Government which had cherished them." After some hesitation, the Government of India responded favourably to the request thus pressed upon them. On the 5th

The Madras army.

Book XI. Chapter I.

1857. August.

August, the 27th Regiment Madras Native Infantry, and a wing of the 17th Regiment Native Infantry, landed in Calcutta. They were speedily followed by the remaining wing of the 17th Regiment, some native artillerymen, a company of sappers, half of the E Troop Horse Artillery, and a little later by a Rifle battalion composed of the rifle companies of the 1st, 5th, 16th, 24th, 36th, 49th, and 34th Regiments of Native Infantry, the whole under the command of Brigadier M. Carthew.

Brigadier Carthew.

Of Brigadier Carthew I shall have to speak more in detail further on. It will suffice here to state that to a thorough knowledge of his profession he combined great quickness of military vision, the capacity and the nerve to strike at the right moment. All that he did, he did thoroughly and well. With larger opportunities it cannot be doubted that he would have achieved great things.

The Madras troops constitute the other resources at the disposal of the Government.

Besides the troops of the Madras Army already enumerated, there were others marching by land from Katak in eastern Bengal. Among these was the 18th Madras Native Infantry, under the command of Lieutenant-Colonel Fischer.

These Madras troops constituted the further resources at the disposal of the Government of India to which I have alluded, and which enabled them to reply with effect to Captain Dalton's requisition for European troops.

Reply of the Government to Dalton's requisitions.

They pointed out to him, in effect, that the moment the artillery, then daily expected from Madras, should arrive, a considerable force would

Book XI. Chapter I. 1857. August.

be sent to restore order; that one column would proceed along the grand trunk road to Barhí and Hazáríbágh, the other direct to Parúliá and Ránchi. The Government expressed a hope that until these reinforcements should arrive Captain Dalton would be able to maintain himself at Hazáríbágh.

Difficulties of Dalton.

But this was just what Captain Dalton could not do. Matters became so threatening that he, accompanied by his few adherents, was forced, on the 13th, to fall back on Bagoda. Here he remained for a few days, when he was joined by one hundred and fifty of Rattray's Sikhs, under Lieutenant Earle. With these men, Dalton re-occupied Hazáríbágh.

Difficulties of the Government

But the mutineers were still at large, and although the Government, grown wise by experience, had endeavoured to prevent any augmentation of their forces by the disarming, on the 2nd August, of the 63rd Native Infantry, the 11th Irregular Cavalry, and the troops of the Nawáb Názim at Barhámpúr, yet the presence of a considerable body of revolted soldiers of all arms in the vicinity of the grand trunk road—the line of six hundred miles—constituted a danger which it was necessary to meet, and meet quickly. The danger was increased by the sudden mutiny, accompanied by the murder of their officers, of two companies of the 32nd Native Infantry at Déogarh in the Sánthál districts.

enhanced by further mutinies.

Fischer is ordered to march direct on Hazáríbágh.

The Government therefore revised their plans. Countermanding their intention of working on two lines, they directed Colonel Fischer, command-

Book XI. Chapter I.

1857. September.

ing a detachment of Madras troops, to mass them, and march by way of Dorandá on Hazáríbágh.

Fischer received this message at Barhí on the night of the 13th September. He had with him his own regiment, a few Sikhs, a detachment of the 53rd, and two guns.

Fischer despatches a detachment, 53rd, under English towards Dorandá.

Before the message arrived, he had ascertained that the mutineers had left Chutiá Nágpúr, probably for Rhotásgarh: he submitted that instead of marching on Hazáríbágh, he should move to intercept them in their retreat. This was agreed to in principle, but other contradictory telegrams from headquarters disarranged Fischer's plans. When at length he received the orders to carry out his own ideas, he had already despatched Major English with one hundred and fifty men of the 53rd and one hundred and fifty Sikhs towards Dorandá.

Fischer is directed to protect the trunk road,

Whilst English was marching on Dorandá, Rattray, with two hundred Sikhs, was intrenched at Dehri, and Fischer, with the main body, was moving towards Jalpa. No one knew where the enemy was. "It is incredible, but a fact," wrote Colonel Fischer, on the 24th September, to the Chief of the Staff at Calcutta, "that the Rámgarh mutineers, with their guns, are moving about in a small province, and not an official, civil or military, can tell where they are to be found." A careful consideration of probabilities induced Fischer, however, to think that Chattra would prove to be their place of refuge. He informed the Chief of the Staff of his opinion. But in reply, Fischer was relieved from the charge of

Book XI. Chapter I.

1857. October.

the operations against the insurgents, and directed to protect the trunk road. The small campaign in Chutiá Nágpúr was confided to Major English, under the direct orders of the Commander-in-Chief.

English to operate against the insurgents.

English attacks the enemy at Chattra,

Major English marched then on Chattra, reached that place at 9 o'clock on the morning of the 2nd October, and encamped on the west side of the town. That officer's force now consisted of one hundred and eighty men of the 53rd Foot, one hundred and fifty Sikhs, and two guns, in all about three hundred and fifty men. The rebels amounted to three thousand. Nothing daunted, English attacked them, and after a resistance lasting over an hour, completely defeated them. The survivors fled in great disorder, hotly pursued for some distance, leaving in the hands of the victors four guns and waggons complete, forty carts laden with ammunition, ten elephants, twenty-nine pair of ordnance bullocks, and several boxes of treasure. The loss of the British amounted to forty-two killed and wounded: that of the enemy was never accurately known.

and completely defeats them.

The province is then left to the protection of Rattray.

This action removed the greatest danger from the grand trunk road. Though English's detachment, in the pressing circumstances of the times, was not allowed to remain in the province, Rattray's Sikhs were left there, and these excellent soldiers, under the guidance of their active and energetic commander, proved themselves fully competent to make head against the insurgents in Chutiá Nágpúr and in the districts immediately to the north and east of it.

BOOK XI.

CHAPTER II.

Sir Colin starts for the seat of war,

I RETURN to Sir Colin Campbell. That gallant officer left Calcutta for Allahábád on the 27th October. The insecurity of the road was almost illustrated by his capture. The two revolted companies of the 32nd Native Infantry had pushed northwards, travelling on the elephants they had purloined. Sir Colin and his staff travelled without an escort. They reached Sherghiti in safety. Again setting out, they had proceeded ten or twelve miles, when a turn of the road revealed to the driver of the foremost carriage the fourteen elephants laden with native soldiers, and escorted by some twenty-five sowars. Fortunately, the bullock train with a British detachment was some short distance behind. On this train the carriages at once fell back. But for the good look-out and prompt action of the drivers, the Commander-in-Chief could not have escaped capture—and worse.

and runs a risk of being captured.

Book XI. Chapter II.

1857. Nov. 1.

The troops as they reach Allaháblád are sent on in strong detachments to Kánhpúr.

On the evening of the 1st November, Sir Colin arrived at Allahábád. The troops of the Line and the Naval Brigade, pushed to that station by the energy of the Commander-in-Chief, had, under his instructions, left it in strong columns or detachments for Kánhpúr. Some of these had reached that place without encountering an enemy on the road. The case was otherwise with the column of which a detachment of Peel's Naval Brigade, under Peel himself, formed a considerable portion.

The Naval Brigade and 53rd detachment,

One detachment of the Naval Brigade, consisting of a hundred men and four officers, escorting the siege-train, had left Allahábád for Kánhpúr on the 23rd October; the second detachment, under Peel himself, followed on the 28th. Accompanying this second detachment, were a wing of the 53rd Regiment, a company of the 90th, drafts for different regiments, and a company of Royal Engineers, the whole under the command of Colonel Powell, C.B., of the 53rd. It is with this last detachment that I have at present to deal.

commanded by Colonel Powell.

Powell learns at Fathpúr that the rebels are close at hand.

This column reached Fathpúr, about midway between Allahábád and Kánhpúr, at midnight of the 31st October. That afternoon, information had reached Powell that the revolted regiments of the Dánápúr garrison, the same whom Eyre had driven out of Bihár, their ranks swollen by other mutineers, were then occupying a strong position at the village of Kajwá, some twenty-four miles north-west of Fathpúr. Their numbers were estimated at, in round numbers, two thousand

Book XI. Chapter II.

sepoys, and about the same number of untrained adherents.

1857. Nov. 1.

Kajwá.

Kajwá is rather a famous place in Indian history. Here it was, in January 1659, that Aurangzíb gained the empire of Hindustán by a decisive victory over his brother Shúja. Close to the town is a spacious garden, walled and turreted, flanked by enclosures, capable, when held by good soldiers, of offering a solid resistance to an advancing foe. Moreover, troops occupying this place barred the road to any column marching from Fathpúr to Kánhpúr.

Colonel Powell, C.B.

Powell possessed the truest instincts of a soldier. He had been in Fort William in command of his regiment when the mutiny broke out. He had watched every turn it had taken, and throughout, when our fortunes seemed lowest, had proclaimed his certain confidence in the ultimate success of our arms. He had panted for action. Now, unexpectedly, the opportunity came to him. He marched on at once to Fathpúr and arrived there at midnight. That night he made all his preparations for a forced march and an attack on the following morning.

He marches against the rebels at Kajwá.

At half past 5 o'clock on the morning of the 1st November, Powell set out with a detachment, increased before coming into action to five hundred and thirty men. It consisted of a hundred and three officers and men of the Naval Brigade under Peel, one company of Royal Engineers, under Captain Clarke, two companies (one hundred and sixty-two men) of the 53rd, under Major Clarke, one company of the 90th, under Captain

Cornwall, and a company made up of the men of different detachments, under Lieutenant Fanning. It had two 9-pounder guns, under Lieutenant Anderson. Captain William Peel was the second in command.

Book XI. Chapter II.

1857. Nov. 1.

It was not till 3 o'clock on the afternoon of the following day that Powell came in sight of the enemy. He saw at a glance that he had them. Instead of taking advantage of the walled garden and the buildings in Kajwá, they had placed their right on open ground, covered by some sand hillocks, forming a sort of embankment; their left on higher ground on the other side of the road. They had three guns posted in the road, two somewhat in advance, the third on a bridge near the village behind. A field of standing corn in front of their position concealed their skirmishers.

False position of the enemy.

Nov. 2.

Powell attacked at once. Pushing the enemy's skirmishers out of the corn-fields, he made a dash at the two foremost guns, the fire of which had done great execution amongst his men. He had just secured these when he fell dead with a bullet through his forehead. The command then devolved on Peel.

Powell attacks them;

is killed just as he had captured two guns.

Whilst the 53rd, under Powell, had been marching on the guns, the Naval Brigade, on the right, had forced back the enemy's left. The position of the battle was then changed. The enemy, driven back on the left, now faced the road, and the British, whose right had been thrown forward, faced them. Peel gave them no time to rally. Posting a strong force to secure his new position, he carried his troops round the upper end of the

The Naval Brigade force back the enemy's left;

Peel then cuts their force in two, and defeats them.

Book XI. Chapter II.

1857. Nov. 2.

embankment, cut the enemy's force in two and drove them from their positions, capturing their camp, two of their guns, and a tumbril.

Result of the action.

Pursuit was impossible. The infantry had marched seventy-two miles in three days, and Peel had no cavalry. His losses, too, had been severe, amounting in killed and wounded to ninety-five. That of the enemy was estimated at three hundred. The captured guns and tumbril, as well as a third gun and three tumbrils, abandoned by the rebels in their flight, were brought into camp the same evening. Peel then regained the high road and pursued his march to Kánhpúr.

Sir Colin reaches Allahábád,

This successful action was fought the day Sir Colin Campbell arrived at Allahábád. It made the way clear for his further progress. Sir Colin stayed at Allahábád only one day. He did not leave, however, until he had perfected all the arrangements for the districts he had left, those especially by which a force under Colonel Longden, of the 10th Foot, was to clear of rebels the district of Ázamgarh and its neighbourhood. The movements of this force will be referred to hereafter.

and pushing on,

arrives at Kánhpúr. Nov. 3.

The Commander-in-Chief reached Kánhpúr on the 3rd November. Rejecting the counsels which conceited men attempted to thrust upon him, he had resolved, before doing anything else, to relieve Lakhnao. Oudh was the ulcer which had up to this time swallowed up all the reinforcements which had been pushed up from Calcutta, which was attracting to it the hardened warriors released by the fall of Dehlí. At all costs the heart of Oudh must be pierced: Lakhnao must be

His resolve to march on Lakhnao justified.

Book XI. Chapter II.

1857. Nov. 3-8.

really conquered before a single step could be taken to subdue enemies still rising up on many sides.

The immediate effect of the fall of Dehlí is to add to the enemies of the British.

I use the expression, "still rising up," advisedly. It had been very generally believed that the fall of Dehlí would terminate the revolt. It did nothing of the sort. It is true that it saved India: that is, occurring when it did, it prevented the insurrection of the Panjáb. On the other hand, it added greatly to the number of our enemies in the field. The rebellious sepoys, cooped up till its fall in Dehlí, spread in detachments over the country. But, perhaps, its most important result was the manner in which it affected the trained soldiers of the Mahárájá of Gwáliár.

Its effect on Sindia and on the Gwáliár contingent.

In the preceding volume I have narrated how whilst the troops of Sindia had mutinied, Sindia himself had remained loyal to his British overlord. Sindia continued loyal to the end. When, on the 22nd September, he received certain tidings of the complete conquest of Dehlí, his joy could not contain itself. At last he was free from the tension that had almost killed him. He could breathe: he could talk: he could even laugh. It often happens that sudden transition from anxiety to its opposite can find relief only in exaggerated expressions of pleasure. It was so in this instance. Sindia's joy was so unmistakeable, that the trained soldiers, whom till then he had succeeded in detaining at Gwáliár under various pretences, broke loose from his grasp, and sought a chief who would lead them against the English. After brief negotiation they agreed to the terms offered by

Book XI. Chapter II. — 1857. Nov. 3-8.

the Ráni of Jhánsi and her confederate, Tántia Topi, the Maráthá chief, who, under the orders of Náná Sáhib, had superintended the massacre of Kánhpúr. Tántia at once assumed command of them. A wary, capable, astute man, he alone of all the natives brought by the mutiny to the front —Kúnwar Singh and the Oudh Moulvi alone excepted—showed any great qualities of generalship. Tántia was a man to be feared. Fortunate was it for the British that the Gwáliár soldiers had not earlier placed themselves under his orders, for his first act on taking up his office was to march them southwards to occupy a position which should threaten Kánhpúr.

Reasons which prompted Sir Colin to march, in the first instance, on Lakhnao.

A weaker mind than that of Sir Colin Campbell might have been deterred, by the action of Tántia Topi, from leaving Kánhpúr with a small garrison and marching to a contest which must be desperate, and might be doubtful at Lakhnao. But, in war, something must always be risked. The information from Lakhnao was to the effect that the store of provisions could not well last to the end of the month. There we had our soldiers, our women, our prestige. That was the decisive point—and Sir Colin had a way of always striking at the decisive point.

Hope Grant's position beyond the Banni bridge.

Before he reached Kánhpúr, then, he had made all his arrangements for an advance on Lakhnao. I have already stated that Hope Grant's column had reached Kánhpúr on the 26th October, and had been there increased to an effective strength of five thousand five hundred; that he had crossed the Ganges on the 30th, and pushing forward, had encamped on the plain between Banni and the Álambágh, to await there the arrival of Sir Colin. In this position Grant formed the *point d'appui* upon which all the detachments and store carts, as they came up, were to mass themselves. Daily there arrived something in the way of provisions and carriage—for the certainty of having to carry back with him the women and children had not been lost sight of by the Commander-in-Chief.

Book XI. Chapter II.

1857. Nov. 3-8.

Sir Colin Campbell joined Hope Grant on the 9th. The interval—from the 3rd to the 9th—had been spent by the Commander-in-Chief in arranging for the protection of his base—that base being Kánhpúr. He left behind him at that station about five hundred Europeans. These consisted of four companies of the 64th Regiment, strengthened by men belonging to other regiments to four hundred and fifty men; forty-seven men of the Naval Brigade; and some eighteen or twenty artillerymen. There were besides a few Sikhs, who, with the artillerymen, manned a field battery of four guns, which had been hastily improvised. This garrison was placed under the command of Major-General Charles A. Windham, C.B., of Redan celebrity. Windham was directed by the Commander-in-Chief to place his troops within the intrenchment which, on the reoccupation of Kánhpúr by Havelock in July, had been hastily constructed on the river; not to attack any enemy unless by so doing he could prevent the bombardment of the intrenchment; to send into Oudh, by wings of regiments, the detachments of European infantry which might arrive; on no

Nov. 9.

The force left at Kánhpúr

commanded by Windham.

Book XI. Chapter II.

1857. Nov. 9.

Instructions given to Windham.

pretext to detain them unless he should be seriously threatened, and, even in that case, to ask for instructions from the Commander-in-Chief. Windham was authorised, however, to keep back the brigade of Madras native troops, expected the following day, the 10th November, until the intentions of the Gwáliár contingent should become developed.

Sir Colin joins Hope Grant.

Having, by these instructions, secured, as he believed, his base, Sir Colin Campbell started on the 9th, accompanied by his staff, to join Hope Grant's camp in the sandy plain four miles beyond Banni. He reached it that afternoon, had a cordial meeting with Hope Grant and his old friends of the Dehlí force, and, after a short conversation, gave his orders for the following day. In pursuance of these orders, Colonel Adrian Hope was sent forward to the Álambágh, the following day, in charge of a large convoy of provisions. The provisions were to be left there, and the carts laden with sick and wounded to be sent back to Kánhpúr. That same day a portion of the siege-train, escorted by the Naval Brigade, arrived in camp. This had been expected. But it had been preceded by an arrival which was not altogether anticipated. Suddenly, in the early morning of the 10th, there presented himself to the astonished gaze of Sir Colin Campbell, an European gentleman, disguised as a native, and who, in that disguise, had managed to make his way through the beleaguring forces, carrying on his person important despatches. His name was Kavanagh. To understand thoroughly the nature of the information he brought, I must ask the reader to return with

Kavanagh joins Sir Colin from the Residency.

Nov. 10.

me to Lakhnao, and to view the Residency on the morrow of the arrival of the relieving force under Outram and Havelock.

Book XI. Chapter II.

1857. September.

Outram and Havelock in the Residency.

On the night of the 25th September, the advanced portion of Havelock's force had entered the Residency. They were followed the next morning by all but the rear-guard. Thanks to the splendid exertions of Colonel Napier, R.E., and the valour and skill of Crump, of Olpherts, of Fraser, of Private Duffy—of the artillery—of Lowe of the 32nd, who covered the movement, of Dodgson and of others, the wounded men and the guns were brought safely to the new ground occupied by the British, and to which reference will be presently made, on the 27th. It had been already discovered that the advent of Outram's force constituted not a relief but a reinforcement; that means of transport for the ladies and children, the sick and the wounded, were wanting; that an enormous addition had been made to the hospital list; and that even had the transport been available, the combined force was scarcely strong enough to escort it to Kánhpúr. But one course, then, remained open to Outram, and that was to hold the Residency until he should be effectively relieved by Sir Colin Campbell.

The manner in which Outram provides accommodation for the increased force.

Outram's first care was to provide accommodation for the largely increased force. With this view, he at once caused the palaces extending along the line of the river, the Tára Koti, the Chattar Manzil, and the Faríd Baksh, to be occupied, the enemy's works and guns in the vicinity being at the same time destroyed.

Book XI. Chapter II.

1857. September.

The palaces extending along the river are taken

These posts were taken on the morning of the 26th September. One party, composed of one hundred and fifty men of the 32nd Regiment, under Captain Lowe, commanding that regiment, attacked the rebels in the Captain Bazaar, drove them into the Gúmti with loss, and captured three large and four small guns. Another, composed of the 13th Native Infantry, under Lieutenant Aitken, assaulted the gateway leading to the Farid Baksh palace, and carried it with considerable loss to the enemy. It was mainly in consequence of these sorties that the palaces above mentioned fell into the hands of the British.

and occupied.

These new posts were held by the troops forming Havelock's command, and were under his personal orders. The old garrison, reinforced by the Madras Fusiliers, continued, under Brigadier Inglis, to occupy their posts in the Residency.

The Álambágh.

There remains to be mentioned the Álambágh. The reader will remember that this place had been occupied by Havelock on the 23rd September, that he had stored there the baggage of the force, and left in it a guard of two hundred and fifty men. This small party had under its charge many of the wounded, several of whom speedily became convalescent and able to bear arms. Separated from the Residency as was the Álambágh by the city, which was still and was likely to remain in the hands of the rebels, it was very defensible. A fortified enclosure, the garrison brought to defend it two heavy guns and two 9-pounders, besides others taken from

Book XI. Chapter II.

1857. September.

the enemy. They had ammunition and water, every necessary of life except a large store of provisions. It was very desirable to maintain the position as a touching point for a relieving army. But the want of provisions constituted a difficulty. Outram therefore instructed Major McIntyre, 78th Highlanders, the senior officer at the post, to hold it as long as he could do so, and only in case of absolute necessity to fall back on Kánhpúr.

He attempts to get rid of the native cavalry,

To rid himself entirely of his native cavalry, useless inside a fortified enclosure, Outram, at an early period after his arrival, directed Lieutenant Hardinge to endeavour to arrange so that they should all leave the enclosure in the dark of the night, and, if successful in this, should make at once for Kánhpúr. Hardinge got his men under arms and endeavoured to lead them out. But the sound of his horses' hoofs was the signal for a heavy and concentrated fire upon them from the loop-holed houses of the streets through which they had to pass—a fire so heavy and so concentrated that the attempt had to be abandoned. It was clear that the enemy were well on the alert. The result was that the horses, reduced in the absence of grass to feed on the bark and branches of the trees, died in great numbers, and those that survived to get out were utterly unfit for service.

but the enemy baffle him.

Difference between the period prior, and that subsequent, to the relief.

The six weeks which followed the arrival of Outram's force have not been inaptly described as the blockade. That arrival had terminated the siege. The danger of being overwhelmed by the

Book XI. Chapter II.

1857. September.

masses of the enemy had in a great measure passed away. But, in spite of this change in their condition, events were of frequent occurrence which served to keep up the soldierly excitement of the garrison. There was only this difference in the feeling. Before the reinforcements had reached it, it had generally been the excitement of defence; it had now become the more stirring excitement of attack.

Sortie of the 27th September.

On the 27th September, for instance, a party of the 1st Fusiliers, and some men of the 32nd Regiment, under the command of Major Stephenson, made a sortie for the purpose of taking some guns in the enemy's Kánhpúr battery. The British troops were met by a very heavy fire from the enemy, and although they succeeded in spiking three of the enemy's guns, they were unable to bring them back within the defences. On their return, they were exposed to so destructive a fire from the tops of houses and loopholes that they found it most difficult to carry in their killed and wounded. One sergeant, severely wounded, must have been left on the ground, had not a private of the 32nd, in the most gallant manner, and with the assistance of Captain Galway 1st Madras Fusiliers, carried him to a place of safety. Lieutenant Huxham, of the 48th Native Infantry, was wounded.*

The 32nd Foot.

The unexampled losses which the 32nd Regiment had suffered, may be gathered from the

* For his conduct on this occasion, following on previous acts of distinguished gallantry, Private William Dowling, of the 32nd Foot, received the Victoria Cross.

fact that, on this occasion, they were commanded by Lieutenant Warner, of the 7th Light Cavalry, solely because there were no regimental officers available. Tried as this gallant regiment had been during the siege, its men were yet detailed for every sortie and for every attack.

Subsequent sorties and their results.

Thus on the 29th September, three sorties were made simultaneously. One of these proceeded from the left square of the Brigade Mess; the second from the Sikh Square; the third from the Redan. The last named, composed of two hundred men, with a reserve of one hundred and fifty, from the 32nd and 5th Fusiliers, drove the enemy from their guns, and advanced till they came to a lane commanded by an 18-pounder. In this advance they lost Captain McCabe of the 32nd, a most distinguished officer, who was then leading his fourth sortie. Major Simmons of the 5th Fusiliers was also shot dead; and, it being ascertained that no further advance could be made without considerable loss, the party was recalled. The second party, from the Sikh Square, commanded by Lieutenant Hardinge, was composed of men from the 32nd, 78th, and 1st Madras Fusiliers, two hundred in all, and supported by some men of the 13th Native Infantry, under Lieutenant Aitken. They succeeded in demolishing several houses and batteries. The first-named party, commanded by Captain Shute, and composed of men from the 32nd, 64th, and 84th, succeeded in destroying a 24-pounder gun, and in spiking two mortars, and four native guns of small calibre. Their loss was very severe,

Book XI. Chapter II.

1857. September.

quite disproportionate to the service rendered. On the 2nd November Lieutenant Hardinge again led a party composed of the 32nd, 84th, 1st Madras Fusiliers, and seven artillerymen, to destroy some guns on the Kánhpúr road. This was done effectively and almost without opposition.

The officers and men of the Indian army.

To write a detailed account of these operations would require a volume devoted wholly to the siege of Lakhnao. Dealing with a large subject I unwillingly confine myself to a simple statement of deeds in which every man was a hero. In these the officers of the Indian army were not one whit behindhand. Constantly recurring are the names of Wilson, Aitken, Ouseley, Apthorp, Forbes, Graham, and Cubitt; the Engineers, McLeod Innes, Anderson, and Hutchinson; there were, too, many others. Some, not less prominent, and whose names will be found mentioned further on, were killed. With them, too, Thornhill of the Civil Service, one of the most daring of men.*

* As a proof of the fidelity and gallantry of the native troops, I may mention that every native officer of the 13th Bengal Native Infantry was either killed, wounded, or died during the siege. The subadár-major of the regiment, Amar Singh, a gallant old Rájpút, received two wounds at Chinhat, but struggled back into the Residency with the beaten troops from that fatal field, and served throughout the siege and for many years afterwards as subadár-major of the Regiment of Lakhnao.

Débidín Misr, the drill havildár of the 13th, got through the siege without a wound, in spite of his conspicuous gallantry, and was for many years subsequently subadár-major of the Regiment of Lakhnao.

Hírá Lál Misr, a sepoy of the 48th, at the commencement and throughout the siege was the right-hand man of Captain James, the head of the Commissariat. He dis-

Book XI. Chapter II.

1857. October.

On the 2nd October, Outram, finding that the garrison were greatly annoyed by a fire from a very strong battery—known as Phillips' Garden battery, on the Kánhpúr road—ordered out a party formed of detachments from several regiments under Colonel Napier to storm it. Napier conducted the attack with his usual combination of science and daring, and took the battery—a very strong one—with the loss of two men killed and eleven wounded. He captured three guns—two 9-pounders and a 6-pounder. There was nothing strange in this: but it was remarkable that he should have rescued a private soldier of the Madras Fusiliers, who had been three days in the power of the enemy, without their knowing it. The man had fallen down a well, and had remained there, undiscovered by the rebels who were occupying the place.

Napier attacks Phillips' Garden battery,

and captures three guns.

Remarkable rescue of a soldier.

Outram had been very much impressed with the advantage which must accrue from adopting

Outram endeavours to open out the Kánhpúr road,

played the greatest gallantry and intelligence, and died a few years ago a subadár of the Regiment of Lakhnao. He, like many of the distinguished native officers, who served throughout the Defence, received a village in perpetuity.

Many other gallant sepoys, especially of the 13th, may be mentioned. Séoráj Singh (severely wounded on the 20th June under Loughnan, defending Innes's post,) and Indra Singh, both sepoys of the 13th when the siege commenced, and native officers when Sir Colin Campbell came to the relief of the Residency, are worthy of mention, as are Anúka Singh and Híra Singh, both Sikhs; Rámnarain Pándé, who greatly distinguished himself, under Lieutenant Aitken, in the sortie of the 26th September. All ranks of this gallant regiment, the 13th, as well as of the 48th and 71st Native Infantry, received the Order of Merit.

Book XI. Chapter II. — 1857. October.

the direct Kánhpúr road as the mode of communication with the Álambágh. To carry out this idea, he directed Major Haliburton, of the 78th Highlanders, to extend the position in that direction, working from house to house. This operation, which was full of danger, was begun on the 3rd. The next day Haliburton was mortally wounded. Stephenson of the Madras Fusiliers, who succeeded him, shared the same fate on the 5th. Still the work was persevered with. Several houses were pierced through. At last, on the

but is baffled.

6th, a large mosque was reached. This place was of great strength in itself, and was occupied in considerable force. To reduce it would have required more extensive operations than, in the state of the garrison, would have been convenient. The operations, therefore, were relinquished, but the intermediate houses were blown up and the 78th were located in the garden, in which rested the battery captured on the 2nd. This became an important permanent outpost, and not only protected a considerable portion of the old intrenchment, but connected it with the palaces which had been occupied on the 26th and 27th.

Development of the work of mining and countermining.

The work of mining and countermining, so remarkable during the siege, was, during the blockade, still further developed under the superintendence of Colonel Napier. Ably seconded by the engineer officers, Crommelin, Anderson, McLeod Innes, Hutchinson, Russell, Limond, and by others, all the efforts of the enemy in this direction were frustrated. The post to which I have alluded as occupied by the 78th Highlanders,

Book XI. Chapter II.

1857. October.

and called Phillips' garden, from its situation outside the intrenchment, offered temptations to their miners which were irresistible. But Hutchinson successfully countermined them. The Sikhs of the Firozpúr regiment (Brasyer's) became very skilful in this work, and always baffled the enemy. Some of the 32nd, trained during the siege, likewise made themselves remarkable for their dexterity. For general purposes, a company of miners was formed of volunteers from the several corps, and placed under the orders of Captain Crommelin. These "soon gave him the ascendancy over the enemy, who were foiled at all points, with the loss of their galleries and mines, and the destruction of their miners in repeated instances." *

The limits of the British position are extended.

The occupation of Phillips' garden by the 78th Highlanders formed a part of the plan conceived by Outram for relieving the old garrison from all molestation on its east, north-east, and south-east faces; that is from the Kánhpúr road to the commencement of the river front. The plan was completed by the occupation as outposts of three strong positions commanding the road to the

* Sir James Outram's official report. "I am aware," wrote Outram in the same report, "of no parallel to our series of mines in modern war. Twenty-one shafts, aggregating two hundred feet in depth and three thousand two hundred and ninety-one feet of gallery, have been executed. The enemy advanced twenty mines against the palaces and outposts; of these they exploded three which caused us loss of life, and two which did no injury; seven have been blown in, and out of seven others the enemy have been driven and their galleries taken possession of by our miners."

Book XI. Chapter II.

1857. October.

iron bridge. Whilst these posts and that held by the 78th received the brunt of the enemy's attacks, the defences of the original intrenchment were thoroughly repaired, and new batteries to mount thirteen guns were constructed.

Altered tactics of the rebels.

The effect of the occupation of these outposts on the enemy was remarkable. During the siege they had occupied positions within a few yards of our intrenchments. From these they were now driven back to a distance so great, that their musketry fire had no chance of doing mischief inside the old position. They accordingly, with considerable skill, altered their tactics. They withdrew their guns to a point whence the balls would clear the outer defences and fall within the intrenchment. The plan was ingenious, and was so far well worked that the point of fire was constantly shifted. But for one defect it might have been very damaging. That defect consisted in want of confidence in the success of the plan, which produced, therefore, want of continuity in the working of it. It was fatal.

The garrison hear of the complete success at Dehlí and of Greathed's march.

On the 9th of October, the garrison were cheered by news that Dehlí was completely in our power; that the King was a prisoner; and that Greathed had set out to lead a brigade to Kánhpúr. This news was confirmed the following day by the further intelligence of the victory gained by Greathed at Balandshahr.

From this date the chief enemy to combat was impatience. Relief was a question of time, and if relief would but arrive before the 20th November, Outram felt that all would be well. He ought to

Book XI. Chapter II.

1857. November.

Mistake regarding the quantity of provisions in stock.

have known that his stock of provisions would last much longer. But on this point an utterly mistaken impression prevailed. Outram believed, from the information officially given him, that, even on the reduced scale of rations allowed, the supplies in the Residency would not feed the force longer than the 20th. In reality they would have lasted much longer. The error might have had evil consequences. For it was mainly the belief that Outram's supplies were nearly exhausted that induced Sir Colin Campbell to march to Lakhnao before disposing of Tántia Topí and the Gwáliár troops. And the non-disposal of them almost landed us in disaster.

Some casualties of the siege.

Still, though the greatest enemy was impatience, the efforts of the enemy outside the walls never slackened; nor were they wholly without effect. Between the 25th September and the 10th November, Lieutenant Graydon of the 44th Native Infantry, an excellent officer, in command of Innes's post, was shot dead while superintending the works beyond that post. I have noticed the death of McCabe whilst gallantly leading his fourth sortie. Captain Hughes of the 57th Native Infantry, doing duty with the 32nd, was mortally wounded at the attack of a house which formed one of the enemy's outposts. Captain Lowe, commanding the 32nd, was severely wounded. Wounded also were Browne, Edmonstone, and Assistant-Surgeon Darby, of the same regiment. On the south side of the intrenchment, the fire continued to be specially galling, several bullets entering the loop-holes. Complete exposure on this

Book XI. Chapter II.

1857. November.

side was certain death. On the 4th November, Dashwood, of the Bengal army, lost both his legs by a round shot, whilst sketching in the Residency compound. He had been warned by a first shot passing near him, but he would not stir.

The garrison hears of the advance of Hope Grant.

On the 6th November, news reached the garrison that Hope Grant had encamped on the ground on the Lakhnao side of the Banni bridge, and that he was to wait there for Sir Colin Campbell, whose arrival at Kánhpúr was also announced.

Outram devises a plan of communication with the Commander-in-Chief.

It now became a point with the generals to devise some plan of communicating with the Commander-in-Chief. Sir James Outram had previously forwarded to the Álambágh a despatch for Sir Colin, in which were contained plans of the city and its approaches, and his own ideas as to the best mode of effecting the junction of the relieved with the relieving forces. He had advised the Commander-in-Chief to make a *détour* from the Álambágh to the right of the Dilkúsha, and to advance thence by the Martinière and Sikandar Bágh. By a means of a preconcerted signal, he ascertained that his despatch had safely reached the Álambágh. The success of this mode of communication suggested the improvising of a semaphore telegraph, and the idea was no sooner conceived than it was carried out.*

* "All necessary particulars," writes Mr. Martin Gubbins, "being fortunately found under the head 'Telegraph,' in the *Penny Cyclopædia* in my library, the General ordered the immediate erection of a semaphore on the top of the Residency, and copies of the necessary instructions were sent to the Álambágh."

Book XI. Chapter II.

1857. November.

But though written descriptions might be useful to the Commander-in-Chief, their value could in no respect equal that which might be conveyed by an intelligent member of the garrison, by one who had undergone the siege and withstood the blockade, and who could cast the light of personal experience on the insufficient description of a despatch. But where was a man to be found who would dare the risk—who would undertake to penetrate the serried lines of the enemy, knowing that death was synonymous with discovery? Disguise was necessary, an almost impossible disguise, for the fair skin of the European, the light hair, the northern accent, could scarcely escape detection. To ask a man to attempt this, was to ask him to encounter something worse than death in its ordinary aspect, to expose himself to the ignominious fate of the spy!

Necessity felt in the garrison for personal communication with Sir Colin Campbell.

To ask a man to dare this risk was, everyone felt, impossible. But everyone felt, at the same time, that it was a risk which it was most desirable should be undertaken. Such was the common thought: such the whisper of the garrison. It has often been found, amongst Englishmen, that the occasion produces the man. It produced him, even on this, when the risks of death were enormous, and when the death would be an ignominious death. A clerk in one of the civil offices, by name Thomas Henry Kavanagh, caused General Outram to be informed, some time on the 9th November, that he was prepared to traverse in disguise the hostile lines, and to convey a letter to the Commander-in-Chief in his camp

Thomas Henry Kavanagh,

Book XI. Chapter II.

1857. November.

notwithstanding his thoroughly European characteristics,

near Banni. Mr. Kavanagh's offer was the more heroic, inasmuch as, of all the garrison, he was perhaps the most difficult man to disguise. Tall, taller than the ordinary run of natives, he was very fair—fair of a freckly fairness—and his hair glittered as gold. But, perfectly cognisant of these drawbacks to disguise, Mr. Kavanagh offered himself. General Outram loved a gallant deed: but, brave as he was, and loving bravery in others, he yet shrunk from exposing a man blindly to the consequences of a deed such as that which Kavanagh proposed. He told him frankly the risks he ran, the almost certain fate that would befall him. But Kavanagh had made up his mind. Dangers there were, he knew. But, having in view the all-important consequences of his mission, he would brave them.

volunteers to traverse the enemy's lines in disguise.

Having made up his mind, and received his commission, Kavanagh proceeded to disguise himself. He chose the garb of a Badmásh—a native "swashbuckler"—a soldier for plunder, of the sort which abounded in the ranks of the rebels. He put on a pair of tight silk trousers, fitting close to the skin, a tight-fitting muslin shirt, and over this a yellow silk short jacket. Round his waist he bound a white waistband, over his shoulders he threw a coloured chintz cloth, on his head he placed a cream-coloured turban, his feet he inducted into the slipper-like shoes affected by the natives of India. His face down to the shoulders and his hands down to the wrist, he caused to be stained with lamp-black dipped in oil. His hair he cut short. Thus disguised, and wearing the

The garb he chose.

shield and sword peculiar to the swashbuckler, Kavanagh, at 9 o'clock on the evening of the 9th November, accompanied by a faithful native spy, by name Kanáojí Lál, set out. Nov. 9. He sets out,

His journey, though not without its alarms,* proved that Mr. Kavanagh had not counted vainly on his brave and resolute heart. He could not, indeed, reach the Álambágh, but, passing by it, he fell in, on the morning of the 10th, with a party of Panjáb Cavalry, by whom, after receiving their warm greeting and hearty congratulations, he was escorted to Sir Colin Campbell. Nov. 10. and succeeds.

The information thus received by that gallant commander supplied the one link which, till then, had been wanting to his complete mastery of the position. The following morning his engineer park arrived, and orders were issued for an advance the next day. Nov. 11. But that afternoon Sir Colin devoted to an inspection of the men with whom he was to accomplish the relief of the long beleaguered garrison—to deal the first deadly blow at the revolters of Oudh. Who and what were those men? They were composed mainly of the remnants of regiments which had already fought and bled against the mutineers. Sir Colin Campbell's force. There were, of the Line, the 8th, a wing of the 53rd, the 75th and 93rd Regiments; of Sikhs, the 2nd and 4th Panjáb Infantry; of Cavalry, the 9th Lancers, and detachments of the 1st, 2nd, and 5th Cavalry, and

* Mr. Kavanagh has written an account of this journey, "*How I Won the Victoria Cross*," Ward and Lock.

Book XI. Chapter II.

1857. Nov. 11.

of Hodson's Horse; of Artillery, sixteen guns, all tried at Dehlí; a few Bengal sappers, and some Panjábi pioneers; and of the Naval Brigade, two hundred and fifty men, with eight heavy guns, and two rocket tubes, mounted on light carts. The total number of fighting men, European and Native, was estimated at three thousand four hundred men.

Sir Colin inspects them.

Such were the men whom Sir Colin Campbell inspected on the afternoon of the day prior to the advance. "The scene," writes one who was present on the occasion,* "was striking. The small army was drawn up in quarter-distance columns in the centre of a vast plain, surrounded by woods. On the edge of these the pickets were posted. A mere handful it seemed. The guns of the troops and batteries who came down from Dehlí, looked blackened and service-worn, but the horses were in good condition, the harness in perfect repair, the men swarthy, and evidently in perfect fighting trim. The 9th Lancers, with their blue uniforms and white turbans twisted round their forage caps, their flagless lances, lean but hardy horses, and gallant bearing, looked the perfection of a cavalry regiment on active service. Wild and bold was the carriage of the Sikh cavalry, riding untamed-looking steeds, clad in loose fawn-coloured robes, with long boots, blue or red turbans and sashes, and armed with carbine and sabre. Next to them were the worn and wasted remains of the 8th and 75th, clad entirely

Their different costumes and appearance.

* *Blackwood's Magazine*, October 1858.

in slate-coloured cloth. With a wearied air, they stood grouped round their standards — war, stripped of its display, in all its nakedness. Then the 2nd and 4th Panjáb Infantry, tall of stature, with eager eyes overhung by large twisted turbans, clad in short sand-coloured tunics—men swift to march and forward in the fight—ambitious both of glory and of loot. Last stood, many in numbers, in tall and serried ranks, the 93rd Highlanders. A waving sea of plumes and tartans they looked, as, with loud and rapturous cheers, which rolled over the field, they welcomed their veteran commander, the chief of their choice. It was curious to mark the difference between the old Indian troops and the Highlanders in their reception of Sir Colin. Anxious and fixed was the gaze of the former as he rode down their ranks—men evidently trying to measure the leader who had been sent to them from so far. Enthusiastic beyond expression was his reception by the latter. You saw at once that to him was accorded their entire confidence—that, under him, they would go anywhere and do anything."

Book XI. Chapter II. 1857. Nov. 11.

Reception of Sir Colin by the 93rd;

by the veterans of Dehlî.

At sunrise the following morning, the troops advanced. The plan upon which Sir Colin Campbell, well-instructed by Sir James Outram and possessing the advantage of the presence by his side of Mr. Kavanagh, had determined, was to move on the Álambágh; to store within that enclosure all the tents, and having drawn to himself the detachments still in rear, to make, with a wide sweep, a flank march to the right, on the Dilkúsha Park and the Martinière; starting afresh

Nov. 12.

Plan of operations.

Book XI. Chapter II.

1857. Nov. 12.

from these points, to force the canal close to its junction with the Gúmti; then, covered by that river, to advance, up its right bank, on the Sikandar Bágh. This point once secured, a portion of the force would make a dash southwards on the barracks north of Hazratganj, and having seized them, would erect there batteries to play on the outworks of the Kaisarbágh. The main body, meanwhile, forcing the Shah Najíf and the Motí Mahal, would open out the way for a junction with Outram. To support this operation, Outram would co-operate by a heavy fire on the intermediate positions held by the enemy from all the guns in the Residency; having forced these, he would move out, with all his sick and wounded, women and children, and treasure, between the Gúmti and the Kaisarbágh, and effect a junction with the Commander-in-Chief. It was, in all essential points, the plan which had been submitted by Outram to Sir Colin, and the authorship of which has been publicly attributed, I believe, with justice, to Colonel Napier.*

The army advances.

To carry out this plan, the little army set out, as I have said, at sunrise on the morning of the 12th November. It had marched barely three miles when the advanced guard, headed by a squadron of Hodson's Horse, commanded by Lieutenant Gough, striking the road leading to the little fort of Jallálábád, came at once under the fire of some light guns, covered by a line of field-works. The moment the sound was heard,

* Now Lord Napier of Magdála.

Captain Bourchier brought up his field battery, and opened out a fire which soon silenced the hostile guns. The rebels then attempted to remove them, but Gough, dashing forward, was amongst them like lightning, and drove them from the field with the loss of two of their pieces.

Book XI. Chapter II.

1857. Nov. 12.

Bourchier silences, and Gough pursues the rebels.

No further opposition was offered to the progress of the force to the Álambágh. That same evening the camp was pitched close to that enclosure: but as it thus came under the fire constantly directed by the enemy on that place, its position had to be changed to another, which brought it under cover of the Álambágh. Here the force halted for the following day.

The force encamps near the A'lambágh.

The Álambágh was, at this time, held by Major McIntyre of the 78th Highlanders, nine hundred and thirty Europeans, a few Sikhs, and eight guns. McIntyre's original garrison of two hundred and eighty men had been from time to time augmented by parties from Kánhpúr, escorting the provisions which had maintained his garrison. It is a proof of Major McIntyre's skill, energy, and good arrangement, that although from his first occupation of the post, on the 25th September, to the date of his relief—a period of forty-nine days—he had been incessantly annoyed by the fire of the batteries erected by the enemy about the place, he had only lost one European soldier, and that two only had been wounded. The native camp-followers and the cattle had, however, suffered severely.

The A'lambágh and Major McIntyre.

On the evening of the 12th he was, I have shown, relieved. The following day was devoted

Book XI. Chapter II.

1857. Nov. 13.

by Sir Colin Campbell to making arrangements for a decisive advance on the 14th. First he despatched a small brigade, under the command of Colonel the Hon. Adrian Hope of the 93rd Highlanders—an officer of great attainments and brilliant promise—to take possession of the fort of Jallálábád, in the right rear of the position at the Álambágh. Hope found that the fort, which might have been advantageously defended, being constructed of thick mud with good flanking defences, had been evacuated. He therefore rendered it useless by blowing in one of its faces, and returned.

Adrian Hope carries the fort of Jallálábád.

Whilst one brigade was engaged in this operation, Sir Colin caused to be stacked within the enclosure all the camp equipage not required for the hard work in prospect. He directed, also, that whilst supplies for fourteen days for himself and the troops in Lakhnao should accompany him, every soldier should carry in his haversack provisions for three days' consumption. Then, too, he received his last reinforcements from Kánhpúr, distributed to their several regiments the men brought up by various detachments he found in the Álambágh, and made a fresh division of his force into brigades. By successive reinforcements, and the junction with the Álambágh garrison, the force had now been augmented to about five thousand men of all arms,* with forty-

Preparations made on the 13th for an advance the following day.

* Naval Brigade and Artillery, four hundred and fifty; cavalry, nine hundred; infantry, three thousand five hundred and fifty; sappers, two hundred; heavy guns, twelve; mortars, ten; light field guns, twenty-seven.

nine guns. The force was thus re-arranged. The 75th Regiment, not three hundred strong, and which had suffered much from previous service, was directed to occupy the Álambágh, aided by fifty Sikhs of the regiment of Firozpúr, and a detachment of artillery under Captain Moir. The detailing of these troops for the purpose indicated reduced the force effective for field operations to about four thousand seven hundred men.

Re-arrangement of the force; the A'lambágh detachment,

The naval brigade, commanded by Captain William Peel, consisted of two hundred and fifty men of the crew of the *Shannon*, seamen and marines, having with them eight heavy guns and howitzers, drawn by bullocks, and two rocket tubes mounted on light carts. Vying with these in zeal and ardour was the artillery brigade, composed of Travers's 18-pounder battery, Remmington's and Blunt's troops of Horse Artillery, half a troop of Madras Horse Artillery under Captain Bridge, and Bourchier's battery. This brigade was commanded by Brigadier Crawford, R.A.

the naval brigade and artillery,

The cavalry brigade, commanded by Brigadier Little, was composed of two squadrons of the 9th Lancers, and one each of the 1st, 2nd, and 5th Panjáb Cavalry, and of Hodson's Horse.

the cavalry,

The Engineers' Department, commanded by Lieutenant Lennox, R.E., was composed of a company of Royal Engineers, a company of Madras Sappers, a few Bengal Sappers who had served at Dehlí, and two companies of newly raised Panjáb Pioneers.

the engineers,

The infantry brigades were the third, the

the infantry.

Book XI. Chapter II. 1857. Nov. 13.

fourth, and the fifth. The third, commanded by Brigadier Greathed, was composed of the remnant of the 8th Regiment; of a battalion of detachments of three regiments shut up in Lakhnao; and of the 2nd Panjáb Native Infantry. The fourth, led by Brigadier Adrian Hope, was the strongest of all. It was composed of the 93rd Highlanders, and a wing of the 53rd, the former fresh from England, the latter from Calcutta; of the 4th Panjáb Infantry, and a weak battalion of the regiments shut up in Lakhnao. The fifth brigade, commanded by Brigadier Russell, was composed of the 23rd Fusiliers and a detachment of the 82nd Regiment. Hope Grant, with the rank of Brigadier-General, had the general direction of the force under the supervision of the Commander-in-Chief.*

Hope Grant has general supervision of the force.

On the evening of the 13th Sir Colin rode out to reconnoitre. The following morning at 9 o'clock, the troops having first partaken of a good breakfast, he gave the order to march. The advance was made from the right, through the fields, crossing the several roads leading from the city at right angles. The enemy had not evidently anticipated this circuitous movement, as whilst their scouts watched the route of the British from the tops of trees, small bodies of them were seen hastily endeavouring to throw up cover at the several points by which it was likely that the head of the advanced column would turn towards the city.

Nov. 14.

The order to advance is given;

* Sir Hope Grant's *Sepoy War*, page 179.

Book XI. Chapter II.

1857. Nov. 14.

and carries the Dilkúsha.

The turning movement having been completed, the advance, bringing forward their right shoulders, moved directly on the wall of the Dilkúsha park. Up to this moment no opposition had been offered by the rebels, but as the advance neared the enclosure a heavy matchlock fire was opened upon it from the left. Reinforcements were at once sent to the front, and the British guns opened upon the group whence this fire proceeded and silenced it. A body of rebel skirmishers then showed themselves emerging from the park, but the British skirmishers, horse, foot, and artillery, advancing, drove them speedily back and pushed them through the grounds of the Dilkúsha park, over the crest of the plateau, to the Martinière, about a mile below it, on the banks of the Gúmti. The Dilkúsha was thus carried, almost without a blow.

This operation, described though it be in a few lines, had occupied two hours. The loss on both sides had been inconsiderable, as the enemy did not stand to receive, but retreated after discharging their pieces. The work had been easy for the assailants, and they were ready for more.

The British skirmishers dash at the Martinière,

They did not halt then in the Dilkúsha, but, running and cantering across the park, pressed on to the Martinière. The rebels were in advance of them, and the sight of these men running in panic had inspired their comrades, entrusted with the defence of the Martinière, to do something to check the pursuit. They succeeded, by considerable exertions, in turning two guns on the advancing cavalry; but before they could

Book XI. Chapter II. — 1857. Nov. 14.

produce any perceptible effect, Bourchier and Remmington opened upon them. Their fire was quickly followed by discharges from Travers's 18-pounders, and from a heavy howitzer brought up by Captain Hardy, R.A. Many rounds had not been fired when the infantry, composed of a battalion made up of companies from the 5th Fusiliers, the 64th and 78th Foot, and the 8th Foot, commanded by Lieutenant-Colonel Hamilton of the 78th, came up, dashed down the slope, and carried the Martinière, the enemy not waiting to receive them, but retreating across the canal with all speed, followed by our cavalry. In the course of the pursuit, Lieutenant Watson* of the Bombay army, commanding the squadron of the 1st Panjáb Cavalry, encountered and slew in a hand to hand encounter the leader of the enemy's party, a native officer of the 15th Irregular Cavalry. Watson had a narrow escape, his opponent having discharged his pistol at him within a few feet of his body.

Which they carry.

Watson's hand to hand encounter.

Sir Colin Campbell makes arrangements for holding the ground up to the edge of the canal.

Both these important places having been carried, and the ground up to the edge of the canal being held by our troops, it devolved upon the Commander-in-Chief to make arrangements for holding it. He accordingly brought up Adrian Hope's brigade (the 4th), and arranged it in position in the gardens of the Martinière. Remmington's troop of horse artillery was located there likewise. Russell's brigade (the 5th) was posted on the left in front of the Dilkúsha; whilst

* Now Colonel Watson, C.B. and V.C.

on the plain in front of the Martinière, occupying a line drawn from the canal on their right to the wall of the Dilkúsha park on their left, were Little's brigade of cavalry and Bourchier's battery. Somewhat later in the afternoon, in pursuance of orders issued by Sir Colin, with a view to guard his communications with the Álambágh from being cut off by a turning movement on his left, Brigadier Russell pushed forward several companies of his infantry to occupy two villages on the canal, covering the left of the British position.

Book XI. Chapter II.

1857. Nov. 14.

These arrangements had not been made one moment too soon. They were hardly completed, when it became evident from the massing of troops on their centre, that the enemy were contemplating an aggressive movement. To gain information as to its probable nature, Captain Grant of the 9th Lancers galloped forward to reconnoitre. He was received by a crashing musketry fire, which, however, left him unscathed. Little at once ordered Bourchier to the front, supporting him with his cavalry. It was then seen how wise had been the occupation of the two villages already referred to; for the enemy, creeping down to the bed of the canal, had opened upon them a heavy and continuous fire. But as soon as Bourchier's guns opened upon their supporting masses, they fell back very rapidly to the city. A few more discharges cleared the canal bed.

The enemy prepare to attack him;

but the attack had been previously discounted.

Little, having accomplished his mission, withdrew to the Martinière compound, and orders were at once issued for a night bivouac. But

They make a second attempt;

Book XI. Chapter II. — 1857. Nov. 14.

scarcely had the horses been untraced, than the enemy, regathering courage, made a second and more desperate attempt to turn the British position. About four hundred yards to the proper right of the wall of the Dilkúsha park, as one faces the canal, is the bridge connecting the Martinière plain with the Hazratganj main street. It was on this bridge that the rebels now came down in great numbers and with several guns.

but are baffled by Adrian Hope,

It was now nearly 5 P.M., and our men were ready for them. Adrian Hope brought up his brigade with an alacrity not to be surpassed. The 93rd he placed lining a mud-wall opposite the bridge. On either side of them were the 53rd and the 4th Panjábis. Remmington's troop galloped at once to the front, closely followed by the remainder of the artillery, and opened fire on the enemy. The cavalry were handy. As each successive regiment came up it lined the banks of the canal.

aided by William Peel and Bourchier.

Bourchier's battery and Peel's 24-pounders occupied a position on some high ground on the left of the bridge, whence they were able to direct a concentric fire on the angle formed by the canal near the bridge, and where the enemy were massed in large numbers. Their fire speedily "crushed"* the enemy out of this position. Then Adrian Hope, forming up his brigade, pushed across the bridge, drove back the enemy with heavy loss, and secured a lodgment on

* *Blackwood's Magazine*, June 1858.

the other side. The attack of the rebels had failed.*

1857. Nov. 14.

The bivouac for the night.

Then did the British troops bivouac for the night, Adrian Hope's brigade, flanked by Bourchier's battery, two guns of the naval brigade, and a troop of cavalry, on the canal; Russell's brigade on their right; Greathed's in the rear; the bulk of the artillery on the high ground to the left, and the cavalry on the summit of the plateau round the Dilkúsha house behind the centre. The men slept with their arms by their side, ready for prompt action.

Nov. 15.

The following day, the 15th, was spent in making preparations for the grand advance. The Dilkúsha palace was to be made a second depôt for the stores and baggage which would have needlessly encumbered an army which had to fight in the streets. The heavy baggage, consisting of everything pertaining to the officers and soldiers, had been placed in charge of a strong rear-guard, commanded by Lieutenant-Colonel Ewart, H.M.'s 93rd Highlanders. This officer, whose splendid gallantry was soon to be displayed in a position more advanced and still more dangerous, had had no easy time of it. Getting under arms on the morning of the 14th at the same time as the rest of the army, his progress, charged with a large

Ewart, 93rd Highlanders, commands the rear-guard.

* In this action our force lost two very promising officers, Captain Mayne, of the Bengal Artillery, and Captain Wheatley, of the Carabineers, doing duty with the 9th Lancers. A few hours before, Wheatley, talking with some comrades of the approaching Christmas, had remarked, "I wonder how many of us will then be alive." He was a very gallant officer.

Book XI. Chapter II.

1857. Nov. 15.

convoy, had necessarily been slow. The enemy, hovering about the main force, but afraid to attack it, had singled out the rear-guard as their prey. The attacks which they made upon it were incessant. But, well aided by Blunt of the Bengal, and Crawford of the Royal, Artillery, Ewart beat back every assault. But the attacks had necessarily delayed him, and he was unable to bring his convoy into camp before the 15th. But he brought it then, having accomplished, skilfully, a difficult and harassing task.

Aided by Blunt and Crawford, he repulses every attack.

Arrangements made at the Dilkúsha.

Then did Sir Colin make his final arrangements. The whole of his heavy baggage, his supplies for fourteen days, he stored in the Dilkúsha. Into the palace all the sick and wounded were conveyed. Defences were thrown up round that building, and a force was detailed to guard it. This force consisted of five field guns, half the 9th Lancers, the Military Train, a squadron of Panjáb Cavalry, and the remnant of the gallant 8th, about three hundred strong—the whole under the command of Brigadier Little of the 9th Lancers.

The afternoon and night prior to the advance.

But though the 15th was a day of preparation, the enemy did not leave the fighting qualities of our soldiers untested. About mid-day, huge masses of infantry, supporting two horse artillery guns, made a strong demonstration against the extreme right of the British position. Their pickets, however, were on the alert, and the guns (two guns of the Madras Native Horse Artillery) speedily opening fire, the enemy fell back. As the point thus threatened was that from which it was intended to made the advance the following morning, Sir Colin deemed it advisable to draw the enemy's attention to another quarter. He accordingly a little later in the day made a strong reconnaissance in front of our extreme left, and subsequently massed all our artillery on that point. He further directed that, during the night, a fire of mortars should be directed on the point opposite our left, so as to keep the enemy's attention fixed there, whilst silence should be preserved at the other end of the line.

Book XI. Chapter II.

1857. Nov. 15.

Sir Colin signals to Outram his intention to advance.

Having made all the arrangements which skill and foresight could suggest, Sir Colin signalled to Sir James Outram, by a code previously arranged, that he would advance on the morrow.

Nov. 16.

Early on the morning of the 16th the heavy guns were withdrawn from the advanced pickets on the canal, and the detachments of Adrian Hope's brigade which had been sent to the front, rejoined their regiments. The men first breakfasted. Then, a strong body of cavalry, with Blunt's troop of horse artillery and a company of the 53rd, forming the advance guard, moved forward from the extreme right. The way crossed the canal, then dry; followed then for about a mile the bank of the Gúmti, led then through a narrow line, through thickly wooded enclosures, and then made a sharp turn to the left on to a road which, turning again, runs between low mud houses, for about one hundred and twenty yards parallel to the Sikandarbágh. Following the advance guard marched Adrian Hope's brigade; then Russell's; then the ammunition and engineers' park. Greathed's brigade, now reduced

The advance on the 16th.

Book XI. Chapter II.

1857. Nov. 16.

by the retention of the 8th at the Dilkúsha, remained till mid-day occupying the position on the canal, so as to protect the left rear of the main body. It then followed the remainder of the force as its rear-guard.

The precautions taken by Sir Colin the preceding afternoon and evening had been successful, for the enemy's attention had been completely diverted from the line of advance he had contemplated. His advanced guard, then, marched along the bank of the Gúmti, through the lane and enclosures, without meeting an enemy. Suddenly it made the sharp turn to the left already described. Then the enemy for the first time took the alarm. First from men occupying huts and enclosures in advance of the building, then from the mass of men in the Sikandarbágh* itself, poured an overwhelming fire on the troops forming the advance. Their position was, in a military point of view, desperate, for they were exposing their flank to the enemy. For a distance of a hundred and twenty yards to the walled enclosure of Sikandarbágh, they were broadside on to the enemy's fire. Our officers saw the position clearly. Before a shot had been fired a staff officer remarked to his right-hand comrade, "If these fellows allow one of us to get out of this *cul de sac* alive, they deserve every one of them to be hanged."†

The British advance comes in contact with the enemy.

Danger of its position.

* The Sikandarbágh is a high-walled enclosure about one hundred and fifty yards square, with towers at the angles.

† *Blackwood's Magazine*, October 1858. The writer of the article quoted either made or heard the remark. He was himself a distinguished actor in the campaign.

Book XI. Chapter II. 1857. Nov. 16.

The situation was indeed critical. The gallant 53rd (one company only), in skirmishing order, lined indeed the enclosures bordering on the lane; but their numbers were few, and the fire of the enemy was concentrated; the cavalry were jammed together, unable to advance, and the high banks on either side seemed to offer an impassable barrier to artillery.

The splendid gallantry of

But only "seemed." Up the steep bank the daring Blunt led his gallant troop, and "conquering the impossible," brought them, guns and all, into an open space between the Sikandarbágh and another large loop-holed building, exposed as he galloped on to a terrific cross-fire. Here unlimbering, with remarkable coolness and self-possession, he opened with his six guns on the Sikandarbágh. Never was anything done better.

Adrian Hope's brigade.

Whilst Blunt was engaged on this gallant deed, Adrian Hope's brigade, disengaging itself, had come up with a rush and driven the enemy first from the enclosures bordering the lane, and then from the large building of which I have spoken opposite the Sikandarbágh. This gave it access to the open space on which Blunt had unlimbered.

Travers and his heavy battery.

Travers followed with his heavy battery, and the sappers and miners having demolished a portion of the high bank, he too was able, by the aid of the infantry, to bring two of his 18-pounders into position and to open fire against the angle of the enclosure. In less than an hour their fire opened a hole in the wall which might be practicable for stormers.

Meanwhile the infantry of Adrian Hope's bri-

Book XI. Chapter II.

1857. Nov. 16.

The assault of the Sikandarbágh.

gade, after the achievement already related, had been ordered to lie down, covered by a small bank and some trees. But the moment the breach was considered practicable the bugle-sound gave the signal for assault. It was made by the 93rd Highlanders and the 4th Panjáb Rifles, supported by the 53rd and a battalion of detachments. Springing to their feet the Highlanders under Lieutenant-Colonel Ewart, and the Sikhs under Lieutenant Paul, dashed forward. "It was," writes an eye-witness,* "a glorious rush. On went, in generous rivalry, the turban of the Sikh and the dark plume of the Highlander. A native officer of the Sikhs"—Subadár Gokal Singh, specially mentioned by the Commander-in-Chief in his despatch—"waving his tulwar above his head, dashed on full five yards in front of his men. The Highlanders, determined not to be left behind, strained nerve and limb in the race. Their officers led like gallant gentlemen, shaking their broad swords in the air. Two young ensigns springing over a low mud wall gave the colours of the regiment to the breeze. Paul with voice and accent urged on his wild followers." All ran towards the hole—a small hole in a bricked-up doorway, about three feet square and about the same distance from the ground. A Sikh of the 4th Rifles reached it first, but he was shot dead as he jumped through. A similar fate befell a Highlander in his track. A young officer of the 93rd, Richard Cooper by name, outstrip-

Richard Cooper,

* *Blackwood's Magazine*, October 1858.

ping the remainder of his comrades, was more fortunate. Flying, so to speak, through the hole, he landed unscathed. "His jump into it," wrote the gallant Blunt, who witnessed it, "reminded me of the headlong leap which Harlequin in a pantomime makes through a shop window, and I thought at the time that if he was not rushing to certain death life would be very uncertain to those first making entrance by that ugly blind hole." Cooper was almost immediately followed by Colonel Ewart of the 93rd, Ewart by three privates of his regiment, they again by eight or nine men, Sikhs of the 4th Panjáb Rifles and Highlanders. Altogether, besides the two officers, about a dozen men, Sikhs and Highlanders, had jumped within the enclosure, when, from some reason yet undiscovered, the supply from outside suddenly stopped. The enclosure in which these fourteen men found themselves was one hundred and fifty yards square, with towers at the angles, and in the centre of the eastern face a building, consisting of a room opening out into a courtyard behind it. The grass growing all over the ground of the enclosure sufficiently high to conceal the enemy from view. There were, however, two pathways—the one to the left leading to the gate; the other, to the right, to the building in the centre of the eastern face.

Book XI. Chapter II.

1857. Nov. 16.

Ewart, and twelve Sikhs and Highlanders jump into the enemy's walled enclosure.

Losing not a moment after he had daringly jumped in, Cooper dashed along the path to the right, closely followed by Ewart and the soldiers, one of whom had almost immediately been shot down. Following the path, they reached an angle

Cooper, Ewart, and their followers

Book XI. Chapter II.

1857. Nov. 16.

of the enclosure, turned it, and in three seconds more found themselves in front of the square building I have already described. There were rebels in front of it, rebels within it, rebels in the courtyard behind it. But on this occasion, as on so many others, boldness was prudence. The rebels outside, astonished by the sudden appearance of the two British officers and their following, ignorant of their numbers, and believing, it may be presumed, that the main entrance had been forced, ran hurriedly into the building, and attempted to make their way through a small door into the courtyard behind. The two officers and their men dashed after them, and a hand-to-hand encounter ensued. Cooper, after greatly distinguishing himself and laying many low with a sword wielded by an arm of more than ordinary strength, was singled out by a native officer of the regiment of Lúdhiáná, and received from him a slash across the forehead at the same moment that he laid his antagonist dead at his feet. Ewart, forcing his way into the courtyard, pushed forward with his following against the men at the other end of it. Some of these men had muskets, some swords and shields. They allowed Ewart to approach within ten yards of them, when those who had muskets fired a volley. Fortunately they fired high. One ball pierced Ewart's bonnet. Our men then rushed at them, and a desperate hand-to-hand encounter ensued. One tall rebel, armed with sword and shield, singled Ewart out for destruction, but that gallant officer was beforehand with him, and shot him, and five others who

come face to face with the enemy's masses.

Cooper is slashed across the head.

Notwithstanding the splendid achievement of Ewart, the contest is doubtful,

Book XI. Chapter II.

1857. Nov. 16.

followed him, dead with his revolver. Still in the end numbers might have prevailed when at the critical moment the Highlanders, the Sikhs, and the 53rd poured in to the rescue.

when the remainder of the storming party arrive.

How they had been delayed.

How these had forced their way remains now to be told. Impatient of the delay which would be caused by jumping singly through a narrow hole, the bulk of the storming party had turned to the left to force a way by the gate of the enclosure. This gate was locked and barred; and although the men used all their efforts, firing their pieces at the lock, some time elapsed before it gave way. But at last it yielded, and the 93rd and Sikhs dashed through it. Almost simultaneously the 53rd forced a barred window to the right of it and joined in the rush to the rescue of Ewart, of Cooper, still fighting in spite of his wound, and their comrades.

The splendid gallantry of Ewart and Cooper unnoticed and unrewarded.

I have been particular in describing in full detail the services of these two gallant officers, both belonging to the 93rd Highlanders, not only because they and the ten or twelve men who followed them were the first to penetrate within the enclosure of the Sikandarbágh, nor because their action had a direct effect on the ultimate issue, holding, as they did, the rebels in check while the main body of the storming party were engaged in endeavouring to force an entrance by the main gate, but because whilst many officers were mentioned in the despatch,* the splendid services of

* "The attack on the Sikandarbágh had now been proceeding for about an hour and a half when it was determined to take the place by storm through a small open-

Book XI. Chapter II.

1857. Nov. 16.

these two gallant men did not receive even a bare notice. It is fit that, even after the lapse of twenty years, history should atone, as far as atonement is possible, for official neglect.

The stormers drive back the rebels.

To return. I have already stated that whilst Ewart and Cooper and their small following were making fierce head against the mass of rebels opposed to them, a considerable body of the 93rd and the 4th Panjáb Rifles, outside the enclosure, had, by strenuous exertions, succeeded in forcing the main doorway, whilst the 53rd had driven in the window on its right. Through these, and through Cooper's hole, which the

ing which had been made. This was done in the most brilliant manner by the remainder of the Highlanders, the 53rd and 4th Panjáb Infantry, supported by a battalion of detachments under Major Barnston."—*Official Despatch of Sir Colin Campbell,* dated 18th November 1857. It will be observed that neither Ewart nor Cooper is mentioned. Yet Cooper's splendid deed was well known in camp. I have seen letters from distinguished officers stating that he was pointed out to them as the man "who had leapt into the breach." When, a little later, the officers of the 93rd were called upon to elect from among themselves one member whom they considered entitled to receive the Victoria Cross for distinguished conduct and bravery under fire in the field, although the majority of the officers voted for Captain W. D. Stewart, many voted for Ewart and Cooper. No other officer was voted for. "On that occasion" wrote three years later one, not the least distinguished amongst them, "I, for one, gave my vote in Cooper's favour, conscientiously considering that he had justly earned the distinction. . . . I know that this was the opinion of others besides myself. . . . . . Cooper and Ewart both deserved to receive the Victoria Cross." Yet their gallant deeds were not even mentioned. It is true that Colonel Ewart was subsequently made a Companion of the Bath and Aide-de-Camp to the Queen, but Cooper was left out in the cold—where he still remains.

sappers had succeeded in enlarging, the stormers poured as fast as they could make their way. As they entered, the rebels fell back into the towers at the angle of the enclosure, and opened a heavy and continuous musketry fire on our men, occasionally diversifying this mode of fighting by descending to a hand to hand encounter. In one of these, Colonel Ewart succeeded in cutting down two native officers who guarded a colour, and in capturing the colour,* which he presented with his own hand to Sir Colin Campbell.

Ewart captures a colour, cutting down its defenders.

The contest for the possession of the enclosure was bloody and desperate, the rebels fighting with all the energy of despair. Nor did the struggle end when our men forced their way inside. Every room, every staircase, every corner of the towers was contested. Quarter was neither given nor asked for, and when at last our men were masters of the place more than two thousand rebel corpses lay heaped upon each other. It is said that of all who garrisoned it only four men escaped, but even the escape of four is doubtful.

After a desperate slaughter, the Sikandarbágh is gained.

Meanwhile, whilst a portion of the 93rd, of the 53rd and the 4th Panjáb Rifles were gra-

The "Barracks" captured.

* This was another splendid deed buried till now in silence. Ewart had observed the colour in question in one of the rooms into which the rebels had retreated. He determined to get possession of it, and made a dash, quite unassisted, at the room. He found the entrance to it defended by two native officers armed with tulwars, each on either side of the doorway. He fought them both and killed them, receiving himself two sabre cuts.

Book XI. Chapter II.

1857. Nov. 16.

dually overcoming resistance in the enclosure, some companies of the 93rd and 53rd, supported by two guns of Blunt's battery, had pushed forward through the opening, and following the plain, nearly southwards, for almost half a mile, had attacked and effected a lodgment in a large building called "The Barracks," and which formed at about half the distance the angle of the rectangular road, used in contradistinction to the direct road which connected the Sikandarbágh with the Kaisarbágh. In this attack Captain Stewart of the right wing of the 93rd greatly distinguished himself by capturing two guns which commanded the approaches to the Barracks.

Captain Stewart, 93rd.

But the shorter road from Sikandarbágh to the Residency ran directly westward between the large loop-holed building, stormed in the first instance by Adrian Hope's brigade and the Sikandarbágh itself, across an open plain about twelve hundred yards broad. "About three hundred yards along this road there is a small village, with garden enclosures round it; while about two hundred and fifty yards further on, and one hundred yards to the right of the road stood the Shah Najíf, a large mosque, situated in a garden enclosed by a high loop-holed wall. This wall is nearly square and very strong. Between it and the plain is a thick fringe of jungle and enclosures, with trees, and scattered mud cottages, which make it impossible to get a distinct view of the place until you come close on it. Between it and the Sikandarbágh, amidst jungles and enclosures, to the right of the little plain,

The Shah Najíf.

was a building on a high mound called the Kaddam Rasúl."*

1857. Nov. 16.

Sir Colin determines to carry the Shah Najíf.

The afternoon was now waning, and Sir Colin Campbell deemed it essential to carry the Shah Najíf. The operation was dangerous and most difficult. Success, to most men, would have seemed uncertain. Failure was ruin. Of all the actions in the campaign this was the most critical. How it was done has been described by an actor in the scene, with a vigour of touch and with a life-like freshness which it is impossible to surpass. I have read nothing which conveys the scene more vividly to the mind. I am sure, then, I shall be pardoned, if, instead of using my own language, I borrow the account of the daring action from one who saw it, and who wrote what he saw.†

Preliminaries to the attack.

"Hope," says the writer, taking up the story from the point where I left it, "having now drawn off his brigade from the Sikandarbágh, led it against the village, which he cleared and occupied without much difficulty; while Peel brought up his 24-pounders, mortars, and rocket frames, and placed them in battery against the Shah Najíf in an oblique line, with their left resting on the village. The musketry fire which streamed unceasingly from that building and the surrounding enclosures, was most biting and severe; and after nearly three hours battering it was still unsubdued. An attempt, made with great gallantry by Major Barnston with his battalion of detachments, to drive the

* *Blackwood's Magazine*, October 1858.

† *Ibid.*

Book XI. Chapter II.

1857. Nov. 16.

enemy from the fringe of jungle and enclosures in front, by setting fire to the houses, proved unsuccessful; but on the right the Kaddam Rasúl was assaulted and carried by a party of Sikhs.

The confusion in the lane communicating with the rear.

"In the narrow lane leading up from the rear, meanwhile, the utmost confusion prevailed. The animals carrying the ordnance and the engineer supplies, unable to advance from the enemy's fire in front—unable to get out on either side, and pressed forward by those in rear—got completely jammed, insomuch that an officer, sent to bring up ammunition and all Greathed's disposable infantry to the now hard-pressed front, had the utmost difficulty to get the men on in single file; whilst some houses having been wantonly set on fire by the camp-followers, the passage was for a time entirely blocked up; and it was only when the flames were abating that a string of camels, laden with small-arm ammunition, which was urgently required by the troops engaged, could with great risk and toil be forced through the narrow and scorching pass. Even then, however, the confusion near the Sikandarbágh had got to such a pitch, that all passage had become impossible; and had it not been that a staff officer discovered a by-path leading into a broad road, which abutted on the Sikandarbágh, neither men nor ammunition could have been brought up.

The battle makes no way against the Shah Najíf.

"In front of the Shah Najíf the battle made no way. The enemy, about 4 o'clock, got a heavy gun to bear upon us from the opposite bank of the river, and their very first shot blew up one of Peel's tumbrils, whilst their deadly musketry had obliged him to withdraw the men from one of his pieces and diminished the fire of the others. The men were falling fast. Even Peel's usually bright face became grave and anxious. Sir Colin sat on his white horse, exposed to the whole storm of shot, looking intently on the Shah Najíf, which was wreathed in volumes of smoke from the burning buildings in its front, but sparkled all over with the bright flash of small arms. It was now apparent that the crisis of the battle had come. Our heavy artillery could not subdue the fire of the Shah Najíf; we could not even hold permanently our present advanced position under it. But retreat to us there was none. By that fatal lane our refluent force could never be withdrawn. Outram and Havelock and Inglis, with our women and children, were in the front, and England's honour was pledged to bring them scatheless out of the fiery furnace. What shot and shell could not do the bayonets of the infantry must accomplish. But the crisis was terrible. Even as the fate of the French empire hung at Wagram on the footsteps of Macdonald's column, so did the fate of our Indian dominions depend that day on the result of the desperate assault now about to be undertaken.

Sir Colin harangues the 93rd,

"Collecting the 93rd about him, the Commander-in-Chief addressed a few words to them. Not concealing the extent of the danger, he told them that he had not intended that day to employ them again, but that the Shah Najíf *must be taken;* that the artillery could not bring its fire under, so they must win it with the bayonet. Giving

Book XI. Chapter II. 1857. Nov. 16.

them a few plain directions, he told them he would go on with them himself.

and determines to win it with the bayonet.

"To execute this design Middleton's battery of the Royal Artillery was ordered to pass Peel's guns on the right, and getting as close as possible to the Shah Najíf, to open a quick and well sustained fire of grape. Peel was to redouble his, and the 93rd to form in column in the open plain, close to the village, ready to rush on.

Middleton.

"Middleton's battery came up magnificently. With loud cheers, the drivers waving their whips, the gunners their caps, they galloped forward through that deadly fire to within pistol-shot of the wall, unlimbered, and poured in round after round of grape. Peel, manning all his guns, worked his pieces with redoubled energy, and, under cover of this iron storm, the 93rd, excited to the highest degree, with flashing eyes and nervous tread, rolled on in one vast wave. The grey-haired veteran of many fights rode, with his sword drawn, at their head. Keen was his eye, as when in the pride of youth he led the stormers of St. Sebastian. His staff crowded round him. Hope, too, with his towering form and gentle smile, was there, leading, as ever was his wont, the men by whom he was loved so well. As they approached the nearest angle of the enclosure the soldiers began to drop fast; but, without a check, they reached its foot. There, however, they were brought to a stand. The wall, perfectly entire, was nearly twenty feet high, and well loop-holed; there was no breach, and there were no scaling-ladders. Unable to advance,

William Peel. *Sir Colin.* *Adrian Hope.*

Book XI. Chapter II.

1857. Nov. 16.

unwilling to retire, they halted and commenced a musketry battle with the garrison. But all the advantage was with the latter, who shot with security from behind their loops, and the Highlanders went down fast before them. At this time nearly all the mounted officers were either wounded or dismounted. Hope and his aide-de-camp were both rolling on the ground at the same moment, with their horses shot under them: his major of brigade had just met with the same fate: two of Sir Colin's staff had been stricken to the earth: a party, which had pushed on round the angle to the gate, had found it so well covered by a new work in masonry, as to be perfectly unassailable. Two of Peel's guns were now brought up to within a few yards of the wall. Covered by the fusilade of the infantry, the sailors shot fast and strong; but, though the masonry soon fell off in flakes, it came down so as to leave the mass behind perpendicular, and as inaccessible as ever.

The Shah Najíf baffles them all.

"Success seemed now impossible. Even Hope and Peel, these two men, iron of will and ready of resource, could see no way. Anxious and careworn grew Sir Colin's brow. The dead and wounded were ordered to be collected and carried to the rear. Some rocket frames were brought up, and threw in a volley of these fiery projectiles, with such admirable precision, that, just skimming over the top of the rampart, they plunged hissing into the interior of the building, and searched it out with a destroying force. Under cover of this, the guns were drawn off. The shades of evening were falling fast—the

Success seems impossible.

Book XI. Chapter II.

1857. Nov. 16.

As a last resource Adrian Hope attempts a flank movement,

assault could not much longer be continued. Then, as a last resource—the last throw of a desperate game—Adrian Hope,* collecting some fifty men, stole silently and cautiously through the jungle and brushwood away to the right, to a portion of the wall on which he had, before the assault, thought he perceived some injury to have been inflicted. Reaching it unperceived, a narrow fissure was found. Up this, a single man was, with some difficulty, pushed. He saw no one near the spot, and so helped up Hope, Ogilvy (attached to the Madras Sappers), Allgood, the Assistant Quartermaster-General, and some others.

which succeeds.

The numbers inside soon increased, and as they did so they advanced, gradually extending their front. A body of sappers, sent for in haste, arrived at the double: the opening was enlarged, the supports rushed in. Meanwhile, Hope's small party, pushing on, to their great astonishment, found themselves almost unopposed. Gaining the gate, they threw it open for their comrades. The white dresses of the last of the garrison were just seen gliding away amidst the rolling smoke into the dark shadows of the night. Panic-stricken apparently by the destruction caused by the rockets, and the sudden appearance of some of the assailants within the walls, they fled from the place and gave up the struggle just when victory was secure.

* I believe that, in point of fact, Adrian Hope's attention was drawn to this portion of the wall by Sergeant Paton, 93rd, who was the first to discover its weakness. For this act Paton received the Victoria Cross.

Book XI. Chapter II. — 1857. Nov. 16.

"Never had there been a harder-fought day,* but never was a result gained more satisfactory."

A lodgment had been gained for the night. Every man felt now that the work was virtually accomplished. It is true that between their position and that occupied by Outram there were still buildings which the rebels would fight to maintain. But those buildings taken all together did not equal one Shah Najíf. The men who had, under the circumstances narrated, stormed that mosque, might justly feel confident that the difficulties of the morrow could not be insuperable. No wonder that "there was joy now in every heart—there was light in every eye."

The order then was given to bivouac for the night. The main body of the 93rd garrisoned the Shah Najíf: another portion of that regiment, under Colonel Ewart, occupied the barracks, already adverted to. The troops not occupying these two posts lined the roads, maintaining the communications between the three points—the Barracks, Sikandar Bágh, and the Shah Najíf. The field hospital for the wounded was established in some huts opposite the Sikandar Bágh, which might be regarded as the central point of the position taken up for the night. The men lay down in line with their arms in their hands.

How justice is not done to deserving officers in despatches.

Whilst they are sleeping I may advert, I fear too briefly, to some of the deeds of gallantry

* "It was an action almost unexampled in war."—*Sir Colin Campbell's Despatch*, 18th November, 1857.

Book XI. Chapter II.

1857. Nov. 16.

accomplished during that eventful day. Not all the brave actions performed on the battle-field can come under the notice of a commander; nor, coming under his notice, are they always mentioned. The stereotyped form of despatch writing prevailing in, if not peculiar to, the British army, necessitates the mention of all officers on the staff of the commander, of the divisional and brigade commanders and their staffs, of the officers commanding regiments and batteries, of all heads of departments. Not to mention any one of these officers is to disgrace him. It follows that such stereotyped mention is without real value. This hard and fast rule is unjust. It may sometimes happen that a particular staff officer or a particular regimental commander fails to distinguish himself, that he makes serious blunders. Such matters are at once known in the camp. But when the despatch appears, the capable finds himself bracketed in one chorus of praise with the incapable, the clear-headed with the dullard, and the general public knows no difference between them. Hence, I repeat, the stereotyped praise of despatches is really without value.

How justice might be done.

But there is some praise which is not stereotyped. Such is the praise, for instance, awarded for special deeds of daring. Applause of this sort is real and genuine. Yet whilst its genuineness when applied cannot be questioned, it is undeniable that many greatly distinguish themselves whose names are never brought forward. No stranger can be sure, when addressing an officer of the British army, that he is not speaking to an undecorated hero.* Book XI. Chapter II.

1857. Nov. 16.

The heroes of the day.

I have mentioned, in the proper place, the splendid achievements, in the early part of the day, of Ewart and of Richard Cooper. Those "undecorated heroes" were undoubtedly the men who made the first entrance into the Sikandar Bágh. But on a day when so many distinguished themselves they were not the only heroes. One non-commissioned officer and two privates of the 93rd, Dunley, Mackay, and Grant, effected their entrance into the Sikandar Bágh by the hole through which Cooper had leapt, though after him, and gallantly supported their officers. More fortunate than these they received the Cross for their daring. Sergeant Munro of the same regiment received the Cross for distinguished conduct in the same enclosure. In the 53rd Regiment, Lieutenant Ffrench, and Privates Kenny and Irwin, and in the 84th, Captain the Hon. H. A. Anson,† deservedly received the Cross for conspicuous daring in the capture of the Sikandar Bágh. Later in the same day, Captain Stewart of the 93rd secured the Cross for the capture of two of the enemy's guns at the Barracks. I have already mentioned Sergeant Paton of the 93rd.‡ The Cross was given to this daring non-commissioned officer "for distinguished personal gallantry in proceeding alone round the Sháh Najíf under an

* Vide Appendix B.

† Captain Anson's gallant conduct at Balandshahr, already mentioned, had previously entitled him to the Cross.

‡ Page 194, note.

Book XI. Chapter II.

1857. Nov. 16.

extremely heavy fire, discovering a breach on the opposite side, to which he afterwards conducted the regiment, by which means that important position was taken." There were many others, not less deserving even than this man. What could exceed the gallantry of Blunt of the Bengal Horse Artillery, taking his guns over an "impossible" wall, and calmly unlimbering on the plain between a heavy fire on either side of him; the imperturbable coolness of William Peel, the daring of Travers, of Middleton, of Bourchier, of Longden, of Walker, of Hardy—killed fighting with his guns,—of Ford, of Brown, and of Bridge—all gunners, Royal and Bengal? "It is impossible," wrote Sir Colin Campbell, "to draw any distinction between any of these officers. They all distinguished themselves under very arduous circumstances." Of Adrian Hope I have already spoken. The bare statement of his action is sufficient. Not less deserve to be mentioned the two Alisons, sons of the historian, Paul, MacQueen, Biddulph, Oldfield, Barnston, Wood, Keen, Welsh, McNamara, Lumsden—killed at the Sikandar Bágh,—all of whom were spoken of in the camp. But the list is too long, for there are many others.

Outram, during this day, is endeavouring to effect a diversion.

Whilst the men are still sleeping on their arms, it is fit, too, that I should state that, during the hours employed by the troops under Sir Colin Campbell in attacking the Shah Najíf, the Residency garrison, under Sir James Outram, were using all their efforts to effect a diversion. They captured some of the positions to the east of the Residency, and from these maintained a continuous fire of guns and mortars on the rebels. I shall give a more detailed account of their proceedings in the proper place.

The action of the rebels during the day.

Nor must I omit to record the fact that whilst our men had been struggling onwards, winning with difficulty those important posts, the enemy had threatened their flanks and their communications. They had attacked, fortunately without result, the Martinière and the Dilkúsha, and had even shown themselves in force on the road to the Álambágh. They were seen, too, in numbers on the opposite bank of the Gúmti. What would have been the position of the army, with the enemy all about it, and the lane by which it had advanced completely blocked up, had the attack on the Sháh Najíf failed, the reader may imagine. Happily, it did not fail.

indicates a resolve to wait for the failure of the direct attack.

The night of the 16th,

The British and Sikh troops, lying in unbroken order, their arms by their sides, slept the sleep of men who had earned their rest that sixteenth night of November. They were awakened early in the morning of the 17th, not by their own bugles, but by the bells of the city and the beating of the enemy's drums. It seemed as though an attack were imminent. The British soldiers sprang up with alacrity, each man in his place, ready for action. But the enemy did not come on. Sir Colin Campbell was, therefore, able to carry out his own plan and to choose his own time.

and morning of the 17th.

Nov. 17.

Sir Colin's plans for the 17th.

His plan was, first, to carry the Mess-house, a large masonry building, defended by a ditch twelve feet broad, surmounted by a loop-holed wall behind, about midway between the Shah

Book XI. Chapter II.

1857. Nov. 17.

Najíf and the Kaisarbágh. The Mess-house carried, the Moti Mahal, lying due north of the former, and on the direct road from the Shah Najíf to the Residency, would be the next point of attraction. Could the Moti Mahal be carried, a junction with Outram would be the certain consequence. That alone would be a good day's work. Much would still remain to be accomplished. The strong positions of the Kaisarbágh —covered by the Tára Koti—and of the Bégam's palace, covering the vast city behind them, would still remain in the occupation of some 30,000 unsubdued foes, and it was in the face of these that Sir Colin would have to withdraw the women and the children, the sick and the wounded.

The difficulties before him.

Sir Colin secures his left flank;

Knowing all this—that absolute success on the 17th would be the prelude to difficulties of a new kind on the 18th and the days following the 18th —Sir Colin marked the commencement of his operations on the first-named day with great caution. First, he deemed it advisable to secure his left flank. It was true that he had a force at the Barracks, connected with the Sikandar Bágh, but as the enemy commanded all the massive buildings south of the Barracks, and even to the eastward of them, it would not be difficult for them to make a détour, avoiding the Barracks, and to act on our left rear. To prevent this, Sir Colin detached the 5th Brigade under Brigadier Russell to carry the house called Banks's house and four bungalows close to the Barracks, to convert them into military posts. To make the plan clear to the reader, I may state that Banks's house occu-

determines to attack Banks's house and the bungalows.

pied a position on the edge of the city, on the city side of the canal, directly south of the Barracks, and somewhat south of an imaginary straight line, from west to east, drawn from the Kaisarbágh to the canal. The four bungalows were to the north of it, close to the Barracks. A direct road led from Banks's house across the canal to the Dilkúsha. It will thus be seen that, possessing now the Barracks and the Dilkúsha, the occupation of Banks's house and the bungalows would sever the communication between the Kaisarbágh and the Dilkúsha, and would cover the left rear of the attacking force.

William Peel cannonades the Mess-house.

Having thus made arrangements to secure his communications, Sir Colin directed William Peel to open fire with his heavy guns on the Mess-house—formerly the Mess-house of the 32nd Foot. He "was determined to use his guns as much as possible in taking it." * The fire continued from the early morning till 3 o'clock in the afternoon. At that hour, the musketry fire of the enemy having been almost completely silenced, it appeared to Sir Colin that the Mess-house might be stormed without much risk. He ordered on this duty a company of the 90th Foot, under Captain Wolseley,† and a picket of the 53rd, under Captain Hopkins, supported by Major Barnston's battalion of detachments under Captain Guise of the 90th,‡ and some of the 4th

Garnet Wolseley ordered to storm it.

* Sir Colin Campbell's Despatch, dated 18th November.

† Now Sir Garnet Wolseley, K.C.B.

‡ Major Barnston had been severely wounded the previous day in the attack on the Shah Najíf.

Book XI. Chapter II. 1857. Nov. 17.

Panjáb Rifles, under Captain Powlett. The actual leader of the storming party was Captain Wolseley.

The feat of arms Wolseley was about to attempt was no light one. The Mess-house, a building of considerable size, was surrounded by a loop-holed mud wall, covering a ditch about twelve feet broad, scarped with masonry. The ditch was traversed by drawbridges, but whether these were down or up, was unknown to the storming party.

He storms it,

Never was a daring feat of arms better performed. Leading his men at the double across the intervening space, exposed to a hot fire from the neighbouring buildings, Wolseley reached the mud wall of which I have spoken. Here he halted for a moment to recover breath, then clambered through the breach into the garden. Pushing forward, despite the fire of the enemy's matchlockmen, he reached the ditch. Fortunately, the enemy, with the carelessness that had so often characterised their proceedings, had left the drawbridges down. Wolseley and his men crossed them, entered the house, which the enemy had abandoned at their approach, and climbing to the roof, planted on its summit the British flag. Twice was the flag struck down by the enemy's bullets, and twice was it replaced. At length, however, the severity of the fire forced the stormers to seek cover. Just then came up a company of supports, commanded by Captain Irby. Wolseley sent him to clear the houses to the left, whilst he himself attacked those on the right. Both attacks were successful, and the rebels, driven out, fled in panic to the Moti Mahal.

Book XI. Chapter II.

1857. Nov. 17.

The victorious stormers followed the fleeing enemy, and Wolseley, far from checking them, determined to push his advantage to the utmost. He had, it is true, no orders to attack the Moti Mahal, but the inborn instinct of the soldier had taught him that nothing tended so much to bloodless victory as immediate pressure upon a defeated foe. He pressed on therefore to the wall of the Moti Mahal, but the opposition offered was great, and the wall was solid, and the gateway had been blocked up. He had, therefore, to send back for the sappers. These promptly came up, and succeeded after a time in making narrow openings in the wall. Through these Wolseley and his men eagerly rushed, and attacked the network of buildings within. The resistance they encountered was, however, stout and even desperate, every room being contested. At length the enemy were expelled, and the Moti Mahal, the last building held by the rebels on the line communicating with Outram and Havelock, came completely into British possession.*

and follows the enemy to the Moti Mahal,

which, after a keen resistance, he storms.

* "It will be allowed that Wolseley had good reason to anticipate the congratulations and thanks of the Commander-in-Chief for his conduct, but what was his astonishment on learning from his Brigadier, the Hon. Adrian Hope, that Sir Colin was furious with him for having exceeded the letter of instructions in that, when he was only ordered to take the Mess-house, he actually of his own motion had driven the enemy out of the Moti Mahal! The Brigadier advised him to keep out of the way, as the Chief was asking for him, and he never saw a man more enraged

Book XI. Chapter II. 1857. Nov. 17.

An open space, nearly half a mile in width, still intervened between the assailants and the advanced positions of Outram and Havelock. This space was exposed to a heavy musketry fire from the Kaisarbágh and could not be crossed without imminent risk. But the risk did not prevent the two gallant generals and their staff from crossing the space to meet the Commander-in-Chief. They started—eight officers and one civilian. They were Outram, Havelock, Napier (now Lord Napier of Magdála), Vincent Eyre, young Havelock (now Sir Henry Havelock), Dodgson, the Deputy Adjutant-General, the aide-de-camp Sitwell, the engineer Russell, and the gallant Kavanagh. They had not gone many paces before they were seen by the enemy, and the musketry fire from the Kaisarbágh redoubled. Napier was struck down, young Havelock was struck down, Sitwell and Russell were struck down. Outram, Havelock, Eyre, Dodgson, and Kavanagh, alone reached the Moti Mahal uninjured. Then, to borrow once again the appropriate language of Sir Colin Campbell, "the relief of the garrison had been accomplished."

Outram, Havelock, Dodgson, and Kavanagh return.

The conversation between the Commander-in-Chief and his four visitors, though animated and joyful, was not long. The visitors had to return across the terrible space. They set out at a run.

in his life."—Low's *Life of Sir Garnet Wolseley*.

It is due, however, to Sir Colin, to add, that although when he met Wolseley the following morning he wigged him severely, he almost immediately cooled down, congratulated him on his courage and ability, and promised to recommend him for promotion.

Outram and Kavanagh were able to keep it up. But Havelock, weak and ill, soon tired. Turning to Dodgson, he exclaimed, "I can do no more, Dodgson, I can do no more." Dodgson, than whom no braver, no more modest, and no more deserving soldier ever lived, at once supported the gallant veteran. Resting on Dodgson, then, the illustrious soldier traversed, at a slow and measured pace—the only pace of which his strength was capable—the ground still remaining to be gone over, the enemy's balls striking all around them, at their feet, just short of them, just before them, just behind them, but all missing their mark.

Book XI. Chapter II.

1857. Nov. 17.

Havelock and Dodgson.

I propose now to devote a few moments to explain in detail the manner in which Outram and Havelock had accomplished their portion of the allotted task. I left Outram on the 9th November, sending off the devoted Kavanagh, disguised as a native, to the camp of the Commander-in-Chief. From that date Outram was made aware, by means of preconcerted signals, of each move of Sir Colin Campbell's force; of his successive arrivals at the Álambágh and the Dilkúsha, and of his movement against the Sikandar Bágh and the Shah Najíf on the morning of the 16th.

The proceedings of Outram and Havelock.

The time, so long and eagerly looked for, had now arrived when it would be possible for the troops pent up in the Residency and the adjoining buildings to co-operate actively with the relieving force. With his usual self-denial, Outram once again assigned to the illustrious Havelock the honour of conducting this critical operation.

Havelock assumes command of the advance. Nov. 16.

Book XI. Chapter II. 1857. Nov. 16.

In pursuance of his instructions, Havelock selected from his division a body of about one thousand two hundred men, and held them in readiness on the first signs of the successful storming of the Sikandar Bágh, to drive the enemy from the strong positions which would still intervene between him and the advancing columns of the Commander-in-Chief.

Composition of the advance.

The force selected by Havelock consisted of one hundred and sixty men of the 5th Fusiliers, under Lieutenant Mara; of forty-eight of the 64th Regiment, under Captain Shute; of one hundred and sixty of the 84th, under Captain Wills; of one hundred and forty-two of the 78th Highlanders under Captain Lockhart; of one hundred and eighty-one of the 90th Light Infantry, under Lieutenant-Colonel Purnell; of one hundred of the Regiment of Firozpúr, under Lieutenant Cross. Of artillery, he had three batteries of heavy guns, howitzers, and mortars, commanded respectively by Vincent Eyre (with the rank of Brigadier), Olpherts, and Maude, R.A. Each column was likewise accompanied by a party of miners, with tools and powder-bags, under the command of an engineer officer. The engineer officers were Russell, Hutchinson, and Limond. To these also was attached Captain Oakes. The reserve was composed of two hundred men from the 5th Fusiliers, 78th Highlanders, and Regiment of Firozpúr.

Havelock's plan.

Havelock had occupied the Faríd Baksh palace. It was his intention, as soon as the attack on the Sikandar Bágh should be pronounced, to blow up, by means of mines previously prepared, the outer wall of the Faríd Baksh palace, and open a heavy fire upon the enemy from the heavy batteries which had been constructed behind it. As soon as that fire should produce a certain effect, the infantry would rush forward and storm two buildings between Faríd Baksh palace and the Moti Mahal, known as the Harn-khána and the steam-engine house. Under these, mines had been constructed. It may be convenient to state that, on the two batteries constructed behind the outer wall of the the Faríd Baksh were mounted four 18-pounder guns, one 8-inch iron howitzer, four 9-pounder field guns, and two 24-pounder field howitzers. In position behind these were six 8-inch mortars, under Captain Maude, R.A.

He gives orders for action,

At about 11 o'clock Havelock learned that the advancing force was operating against Sikandar Bágh. He at once gave orders for the explosion of the mines under the outer wall of the Faríd Baksh. It happened, unfortunately, that the result of the explosion was not nearly so effective as he had hoped, and it devolved upon the batteries to complete the work which the mines had only very partially accomplished. Vincent Eyre and the officers serving under him were, however, in no way discouraged. A continuous fire lasting over three hours, not only demolished the remaining obstacles of the wall, but produced a very considerable effect on the buildings beyond it. So great was it, indeed, that at 3 o'clock Havelock formed his columns of assault in the square of the

Book XI. Chapter II.

1857. Nov. 16.

Chattar Manzil—outside the battered wall of the Faríd Baksh—and ordered his engineers to fire the mines laid under the two buildings beyond.

and carries the enemy's position as far as the engine-house.

At a quarter past 3, two of the mines of the Harn-khána exploded with good effect. A quarter of an hour later the signal for assault was given. "It is impossible," wrote Havelock in his despatch, "to describe the enthusiasm with which this signal was received by the troops. Pent up in inaction for upwards of six weeks, and subjected to constant attacks, they felt that the hour of retribution and glorious exertion had returned." Their action corresponded to the feelings which swayed it. Dashing forward with a cheer, they carried the Harnkhána, then the engine-house, and were thus in a position to extend their hands to their friends of the advancing force as soon as these should have captured the Moti Mahal. I have already shown how this was done.

The difficulties that yet remained.

"The relief of the garrison was accomplished." Yes—but to quote once again from the gallant writer whose account of Lord Clyde's campaign is a masterpiece of description of military movements,* "a most difficult and dangerous task still remained. The garrison, with women and children, sick and wounded, guns and stores, had to be withdrawn; and to effect this in the face of the vast force of the enemy was no easy task. One narrow winding lane alone led to the rear, and through it the whole force had to be filed.

* *Blackwood's Magazine*, October 1858.

To protect the march of the convoy, the whole of the immense line, extending from the ruined walls of the Residency to the wooded park of the Dilkúsha, required to be held, and this gave a most hazardous extension to our forces—far too weak for the maintenance of so extended a position. To keep any considerable reserve in hand was impossible." Book XI. Chapter II. 1857. Nov. 17.

The circumstances were indeed such as to merit the earnest care and consideration which the Commander-in-Chief devoted to them. Fortunately, Sir Colin Campbell was a man of iron nerves, of splendid resolution. He could act promptly and steadfastly even when confronted by so great a difficulty as that which now presented itself. His plans were quickly formed. The enemy still occupied the Kaisarbágh in great force. From the Kaisarbágh they threatened the flank and the left rear of the British army. To permit an enemy so numerous to occupy a position so strong and so threatening whilst carrying out the delicate operation which it had now devolved upon Sir Colin Campbell to attempt, was more than any prudent commander could permit. Sir Colin's first object, then, was to silence the fire from the Kaisarbágh. This silenced, two lines of retirement might be open to him. Sir Colin Campbell is equal to cope with them.

I have already stated* that on the 17th November Sir Colin had detached the 5th Brigade, under Brigadier Russell, with some artillery and rockets, to carry the house called Banks's house His plans.

* Page 200.

Book XI. Chapter II.

Nov. 17,

Brigadier Russell carries Banks's house and the bungalows.

and four bungalows, adjacent to the Barracks, with the view of converting them into military posts covering his left rear. Russell found the positions well fortified, and strongly garrisoned. But he was equal to the occasion. The four bungalows were first stormed. A detachment of the 2nd Panjáb Infantry, led by a gallant subaltern, Lieutenant Keen, was then pushed forward to Banks's house. This officer occupied that house without difficulty and remained there with fifty Sikhs, during the remainder of the operations for the relief of Lakhnao. His position was extremely dangerous, for the enemy were in great numbers, and in his comparatively isolated position, he might at any moment have been overwhelmed before assistance could reach him. But he showed a bold front which daunted the enemy.

Russell's position

The chain of posts covering the British left rear was now complete. The proper right of this chain was the Barracks occupied by Lieutenant-Colonel Ewart and three hundred of the 93rd, its proper left Banks's house; the right centre was formed of the four bungalows referred to, the left centre by gardens. But precisely at the moment when Russell's brigade had succeeded in occupying the right centre and left of the position, there rose in the minds of the rebels the conviction that such occupation barred to them the road by which they had intended to operate, and that they must at any cost expel the British.

is fired upon by the rebels.

Throughout the night of the 17th and during the whole of the 18th, then, they kept upon the right and right centre of the position, a vigorous and unceasing fire from muskets and from an 18-pounder. Had it been Sir Colin Campbell's intention simply to occupy these posts whilst his large convoy was being withdrawn by the line he had advanced, this incessant fire, however annoying, would have had no important result. But Sir Colin Campbell having resolved, as I have shown, to dominate in the first instance the fire of the Kaisar Bágh, and thus to secure properly a second line of retirement by the Barracks and Banks's house, the line of posts had become a base from which to attack and occupy certain buildings between them and the Kaisar Bágh. In this view the heavy fire kept up by the enemy during the 18th possessed a far greater importance.

Book XI. Chapter II.

1857. Nov. 18.

Reasons why the retention of the post was important.

The first building Russell had decided to attack was the hospital, the nearest important post to the four bungalows and the Barracks. But before he could move, it was necessary to silence the enemy's fire. This could only be done by means of artillery. Early on the morning of the 18th, then, Sir Colin directed Colonel Biddulph of the Bengal Army, head of the Intelligence Department, to proceed in company with Major Bourchier, to reconnoitre the roads leading to the Barracks and the canal, with the view of discovering whether guns could not be taken down to co-operate with Russell.

Russell reconnoitres the roads.

To no nobler and more zealous men could this dangerous task have been entrusted. Bourchier, to whose splendid services I have already referred, was one of the most daring officers of his unsurpassed regiment—the Bengal Artillery.

Bourchier and Biddulph.

Book XI. Chapter II.

1857. Nov. 18.

Biddulph was cool, intelligent, and a thorough soldier. They quickly found a road, and then with the utmost speed brought down a 9-pounder and a 24-pound howitzer, and four 5½-inch mortars. The gun and the howitzer were placed in position in front of the bungalow, on the extreme right, the mortars behind the bungalow.

Russell is wounded.

The fire then opened. Brigadier Russell was almost immediately placed *hors de combat* by a contusion.* Colonel Biddulph then assumed the command. The fire continued with great effect, and the rebels withdrew their 18-pounder. Biddulph then organised a column for an attack on the hospital. But as he was explaining his plans to the officer next to him in command, Lieutenant-Colonel Hale of the 82nd, a bullet, which had previously traversed the cap of the latter, penetrated his brain.

Biddulph is killed.

Hale assumes command,

Hale then assumed command. At 4 o'clock in the afternoon, he led his column to the assault, covering it with a quick fire from the 24-pound howitzer. Traversing some intermediate gardens, he attacked the hospital. The resistance, how-

* The story is thus told by Colonel Bourchier (*Eight Months' Campaign against the Bengâl Sepoys*): "The 18-pounder (rebels') was not above one hundred and twenty yards distant, and to avoid giving notice to the enemy of our intentions by opening an embrasure, the muzzle of the 9-pounder was crammed through a hole that a shot had just made. The riflemen declared they had not been able to load again. As we fired, so did they. A cloud of dust is all I remember. Brigadier Russell, Captain Ogilvy, and I were on our backs. Poor Russell had just been grazed on the back of the neck: the clods broken from the wall had knocked us over."

ever, was obstinate, nor did he drive out the enemy until they had inflicted a severe loss on his column. Nor, unfortunately, was he able to maintain himself in the hospital after it had been stormed. Its thatched roof was kindled by the enemy, and the heat of the flames alone forced him to retire. He withdrew, then, in perfect order, to his original position.*

Book XI. Chapter II.

1857. Nov. 18.

but can make no progress.

Whilst the struggle, followed by the retirement, had been going on at the hospital, the rebels, thinking that the central position, that between the Barracks and Sikandar Bágh, must have been thereby weakened, attacked the pickets in considerable force. But Sir Colin Campbell, attentive to every detail, was no sooner cognisant of the situation, than he himself brought up Remmington's troop of Horse Artillery, a company of the 53rd, and a company of the 23rd, to meet the attack. These were absolutely the only troops of which he could dispose, but they were sufficient. The conduct of Remmington's troop elicited the admiration of the whole army.

The enemy attack the centre pickets.

Splendid conduct of Remmington's troop.

* Colonel Bourchier thus mentions a gallant deed, performed on this occasion, which deserves a permanent record in history. "Lieutenant Harrington, Bengal Artillery, and another officer (whose name I regret I never knew) belonging to H. M.'s service, with a gunner of artillery and a drummer of infantry, did most gallant service. A man of the storming column had been wounded and left in the garden for an hour and a half. The drummer stuck by him, and dashed into the picket to report the fact. The little party above mentioned, under a very hot fire, rushed out and brought in the wounded man. As they left the picket a round shot struck the ground under their feet." Lieutenant Harrington received the Victoria Cross.

Book XI. Chapter II.

1857. Nov. 18.

"Captain Remmington's troop of Horse Artillery," wrote Sir Colin, "was brought up, and dashed right into the jungle with the leading skirmishers, and opened fire with extraordinary rapidity and precision. Captain Remmington distinguished himself very much. I superintended this affair myself, and I have particular pleasure in drawing your Lordships' attention to the conduct of this troop on this occasion as an instance of the never-failing readiness and quickness of the horse artillery of the Bengal Service." The attack was repulsed.

The roads on the left again reconnoitred,

Thus ended the 18th. The British had maintained the position covering their left rear, but had made no substantial progress towards gaining a second line of retirement. The difficulties experienced in gaining the posts which would command such a line rendered it advisable once more to reconnoitre the ground between the positions actually held and the canal, to ascertain whether it was possible, abandoning the projected line of retirement by the direct road from Sikandar Bágh to Banks's house, to withdraw the guns and the troops by one of the unmetalled roads behind the bungalows already occupied. The reconnaissance showed that the roads in that locality, though heavy, were practicable for artillery. On receiving a report to this effect, Sir Colin determined to withdraw his force by the road by which he had advanced. He therefore directed Colonels Ewart of the 93rd, Hale of the 82nd, and Wells of the 23rd, commanding the posts covering the left rear, simply

and are found practicable for guns.

Book XI. Chapter II.

1857. Nov. 19–22.

to maintain their positions, whilst he would himself personally superintend the delicate operation of the withdrawal by the road already traversed of the sick and the wounded, the women and the children. The order was simple, comprehensible to the meanest capacity, and was carried out to the letter.

Sir Colin's plan of retirement.

On the morning of the 20th, whilst Captain Ogilvy, already mentioned in these pages, was, under the direction of Colonel Hale, engaged in entrenching the positions covering the left rear, Sir Colin Campbell began to carry out the withdrawal. As a preliminary measure, William Peel, on the morning of that day, opened on the Kaisar Bágh a tremendous fire from his heavy guns. This fire continued during that day, the day following, and the 23rd, increasing every hour in intensity. It gradually assumed the character of a bombardment. The enemy suffered enormous losses, and on the evening of the 22nd three breaches in the walls of the Kaisar Bágh invited assault. They expected it. Such, however, was not the intention of Sir Colin. The bombardment had in fact been used to cover the withdrawal of the women and children, sick and wounded. Long before it concluded, these had reached the Dilkúsha in safety. The effecting of the three breaches on the evening of the 22nd was used to carry out the retreat of the glorious garrison of Lakhnao. Whilst the rebels passed that night in devising measures to meet the assault which they expected on the morrow, the garrison which had so long held them at bay, the veterans of

The retirement.

William Peel opens fire on the Kaisar Bágh with signal effect.

The rebels expect an assault, under cover of which expectation Sir Colin withdraws,

Book XI. Chapter II.

1857. Nov. 22-23.

Inglis's force, the victors in many fights of Havelock's and Outram's, began, at midnight, their retirement. The guns which they could not carry away they rendered useless. Then, "behind the screen of Campbell's outposts, Inglis's and Havelock's toilworn bands withdrew. Then these began also to retire; the pickets fell back through the supports, the supports glided away between the intervals of the reserve—the reserve, when all had passed, silently defiled into the lane—thick darkness shrouded the movement from the gaze of the enemy—and, hours after the position had been quitted, they were firing into the abandoned posts. Hope's brigade, which had so nobly headed the advance, had also covered the retreat. Before daylight on the 23rd, the last straggler had quitted the camp at Dilkúsha." *

without being molested.

How Hale covered the left rear.

Whilst the Commander-in-Chief was thus effecting the well-planned retirement, in the security gained by his skilful operations against the Kaisar Bágh, his lieutenants, Hale, Ewart, and Wells, covering his left rear, had remained occupying the positions they had gained and intrenched. During the three days of the bombardment of the Kaisar Bágh, the rebels had never relaxed their musketry fire against those positions. But they had attempted no assault. The fact that they made no attempt at all is another remarkable proof, added to the many already cited, of the scarcity of military ability amongst their leaders. For Banks's house was not only entirely sepa-

* *Blackwood's Magazine*, October 1858.

Book XI. Chapter II.

1857. Nov. 23.

rated from the other posts, but it was garrisoned only by fifty Sikhs, who might have been overwhelmed ere succour could have reached them.

Hale rejoins Sir Colin at the Dilkúsha,

But no such attempt was made, and Hale and his lieutenants, as soon as he had ascertained that the Commander-in-Chief had advanced far enough on his line of retreat, evacuated the Barracks and bungalows, and fell back on the Dilkúsha by the road which had been selected after the reconnaissance of the 19th. They rejoined the main force at this place early on the morning of the 23rd.

where the army halts, but does not rest.

The re-united force remained at the Dilkúsha during that day and the ensuing night. But there was no rest for officer or private. The detachment parties who had come up with the relieving force had to be distributed to their several regiments; carriages had to be allotted; arrangements for the formation of the convoy of the women and children under responsible officers, had to be made. In a word, there was made on this day a reorganisation of the whole force to remain in operation as far as the Álambágh.

The cavalry.

Looking back from this place—the first halt—after the successful relief, I find a sincere pleasure in paying the tribute of the historian to the splendid exertions of one arm of the service, whose place on the field of action has not yet been specifically mentioned. The storming of the Sikandar Bágh, of the Shah Najíf, of the Moti Mahal, of the bungalows adjacent to the Barracks, was the united work of the artillery and the infantry; the bombardment of the Kaisar Bágh, of the artillery and the sailors. During

Book XI. Chapter II.

1857. Nov. 23.

this time, the cavalry, ever ready, always on the alert, prompt to take advantage of every opening, had been engaged in covering advanced movements, in keeping up the long line of communications, and in repelling the counter attacks of the enemy on the extreme right.

Their leaders.

Such services were necessary to the safety of the force, and, though they might be less prominent, they were not inferior in value to those of the other arms. The names of Little, and of Ouvry, of Probyn, of Watson, of Younghusband, and of Gough, still live in the memory of those who served under them.

Havelock dies.

Nor, when writing of the halt at the Dilkúsha, dare I omit to chronicle the one mournful event which tinged the joy of the relief. That day, Havelock, who had been long ailing, passed away to his last home. He had lived long enough to hear that his Queen and his countrymen had appreciated his noble qualities, that his name had become a household word among the homes and the hearths of England.

Havelock.

The life of Havelock had been a life devoted to his profession. He had made the strict performance of duty his polar-star. Gifted with military abilities of a very high order, and conscious that he possessed those abilities, he had borne without repining the sapping torment of slow promotion and its inevitable results—employment in positions below his capacity. But every trial of Fortune had found Havelock cheerful, resolute, and devoted. To the smallest office he gave his best abilities. And, whilst thus labouring, he had striven also to prepare himself for the eventualities which were to follow. Book XI. Chapter II.

A story is told of the famous Scot-Austrian Marshal, Loudon, that when he was a major on frontier duties in Croatia, he used to spend his leisure in studying an enormous map of the Austrian dominions. This map he had placed on the floor of one of his rooms. His wife, jealous of this devotion, burst open one day the door of his study, and seeing Loudon on his knees tracing a particular route on the map, exclaimed, in a pet, "I wonder what pleasure you can find in eternally studying that map?" Loudon, turning to her, replied, "Leave me alone, my dear, the knowledge I am now acquiring will be useful to me when I become a Marshal of the Empire." Not only did Loudon become a Marshal of the Empire, but he came also to be recognised as the one Austrian general whom the great Frederic respected.* 1857. Nov. 23.

Similar was the course pursued by Havelock. He studied all his life for the future. Similar, too, was the result. When the opportunity did come, he used it in a manner which electrified his contemporaries, which gained for him the confidence and devotion of his soldiers. His daring march from Allahábád to Kánhpúr against enemies

* On one occasion after the seven years' war, when Joseph II. entertained Frederic at Neustadt, in Moravia, Loudon had modestly taken a seat towards the end of the table on the side opposite to that on which Frederic was seated. "Come up here and sit near me," called to him the latter. "I would rather see you by me than opposite to me."

Book XI. Chapter II.

1857. Nov. 23.

excited by the slaughter of our countrymen; the splendid defiance of rule which he showed by, to effect a great end, fighting the battle of Kánhpúr with a river in his rear; the skill with which he gained it; the inspired audacity which characterised his marches into Oudh; the confidence with which he resolved at all risks to hold on to the position he had taken up at Kánhpúr—a position in a military sense false, inasmuch as his communications were liable to be severed: all these deeds stamp him as a general of the very first order. He was bold and daring in conception, prompt and sudden in execution, persistent and unshaken in his resolves. The jealousy of men in whose hands the opportunities granted to Havelock would have shattered, has attempted, since his death, to diminish his glory. But the poisoned darts have rebounded, blunted, from the iron cuirass of the warrior. His deeds speak for themselves. The incidents of that Kánhpúr campaign will live, an imperishable record of his glorious qualities. The statue which adorns Trafalgar Square, whilst it will show his outward form to the generations which shall have known him not, will whet their curiosity to inquire regarding the early training and later deeds of one who, in a short and glorious campaign, illustrated all the qualities which combine to form a commander of the first rank.

Havelock buried at the Álambágh.

Havelock died on the 24th. On the morning of the 26th, his remains were consigned to a humble grave in the Álambágh. His gallant son, the leaders who had been associated with him,

Book XI. Chapter II.

1857. Nov. 24.

Campbell, Grant, Outram, Inglis, and others, and a crowd of officers, followed him to his last resting place. He had fought a good fight: he had died, as he had lived, in the performance of duty.

Sir Colin and his convoy reach the A'lambágh.

To return. On the afternoon of the 24th, Sir Colin, having made all his arrangements, marched with his men and the train of women and children whom they guarded, leaving Outram's divison, in front of the Dilkúsha, to cover his retirement. That evening Sir Colin, with his long convoy, reached the Álambágh. The rebels had made no demonstration against Outram, and that officer, having received a supply of carriage from Sir Colin, fell back and rejoined his chief on the 25th. As Outram was preparing to fall back, the rebels showed themselves for a moment—only, however, to disappear. They had not forgotten the rough lessons of the preceding days.

Nov. 25.

Fresh distribution of the force at the A'lambágh.

With the junction of the divisions of the army at the Álambágh came the necessity for making a new distribution of it. Three matters pressed themselves particularly on Sir Colin's attention, viz. the safe transport of the ladies and children to Kánhpúr, the necessity of dealing with the Gwáliár mutineers, and the occupation by a sufficient force of the Álambágh. The second of these matters was a cause of considerable anxiety, inasmuch as Sir Colin had for many days received no communication from General Windham, commanding at Kánhpúr, and it was impossible to say how circumstances had gone with him subsequently to the 9th November.

The third matter was, naturally, that first settled.

Book XI. Chapter II.

1857. Nov. 26.

Outram ordered to remain at the A'ambágh.

Sir Colin decided on the 26th that Sir James Outram should remain at Álambágh with a force augmented to about four thousand men of all arms, twenty-five guns and howitzers, and ten mortars. Outram would thus occupy a position threatening Lakhnao, and would retain it till the Commander-in-Chief, having placed his convoy in safety and disposed of the Gwáliár mutineers, should return, to act offensively against the city of Lakhnao. To maintain the communication with Kánhpúr, a post at the Banni bridge, up to that time occupied by the wing of a Madras native regiment and two guns, was strengthened by a detachment of European troops.

Sir Colin and the remainder of the force start for Kánhpúr;

Nov. 27.

Having made this disposition on the 26th, Sir Colin set out for Kánhpúr at 11 A.M. on the 27th. He had with him about three thousand men, including the wasted remnant of the 32nd Regiment, and the few survivors of the native pensioners who had responded to the call of Sir Henry Lawrence. Under the convoy of the troops, were the ladies, the children, the sick, and the wounded, numbering altogether about two thousand, and the treasure which had been rescued from Lakhnao. That same evening Sir Colin encamped at the Banni bridge. In reply to an inquiry as to whether any communication had been received from Kánhpúr, the officer there commanding reported that not only had he heard a cannonade during that day, but during the day previous also.

reaches Banni,

but can hear nothing of Windham.

His position should Windham have

This information was of an alarming nature. If Windham had been overwhelmed, the rebels

Book XI. Chapter II.

1857. Nov. 28.

been overwhelmed.

A cannonade is heard in the distance.

Receives news of an impending disaster to Windham, unless he were speedily relieved.

would certainly have destroyed the bridge of boats, and the British army would be cut off from its own provinces, which for the moment would be in the power of the rebels. There was nothing for it but to press on with the utmost expedition. Early on the following morning, the force pressed onward. "At every step the sound of a heavy and distant cannonade became more distinct; but mile after mile was passed over, and no news could be obtained." * Just before noon, however, a native who had been concealed behind a hedge, ran forward, and delivered a missive to the Staff at the head of the advance guard. "He had a small rolled-up letter in the Greek character, addressed 'Most urgent, to General Sir Colin Campbell, or any officer commanding troops on the Lakhnao road.' The letter was dated two days previously, and said that unless affairs shortly took a favourable turn, the troops would have to retire into the intrenchment; that the fighting had been most severe; and that the enemy were very powerful, especially in artillery. It concluded by expressing a hope that the Commander-in-Chief would therefore see the necessity of pushing to their assistance with the utmost speed."†

The information contained in this note converted into certainty the impressions which the sound of the cannonade had produced. It deepened

* *Blackwood's Magazine.*

† *A Lecture on the Relief of Lucknow*, by Colonel H. W. Norman, C.B. Sir Colin stated that he received three notes in succession, *vide* Bourchier's *Eight Months' Campaign.*

Book XI. Chapter II.

1857. Nov. 28.

The scene that followed described by an eye-witness.

the anxiety of the leaders, the impatience of the troops. The scene that followed has thus been painted by an eye-witness:—* "The impatience and anxiety of all became extreme. Louder and louder grew the roar—faster and faster became the march—long and weary was the way—tired and footsore grew the infantry—death fell on the exhausted wounded with terrible rapidity—the travel-worn bearers could hardly stagger along under their loads—the sick men groaned and died—but still on, on, on, was the cry."

The tension too great for Sir Colin;

After progressing in the usual order for a short time, the tension became too great for Sir Colin. Leaving the infantry to march on with the convoy, he pressed forward with the cavalry and horse artillery. On reaching Mangalwár, about five miles on the Lakhnao side of the Ganges, he halted his troops, directed the artillery to fire

he announces his approach by salvoes;

salvoes to announce the approach of assistance, and galloped forward with his staff, in mingled hope and fear regarding the condition in which he might find the bridge of boats. As he approached the river, a glance dissipated every doubt on this

then gallops on with his staff;

head. Through the glimmering light, for evening had set in, the bridge was seen to be intact. Flames rising in every direction, mingling with the light of the setting sun, showed that the enemy must have taken the city and a large part of the cantonments; that the tents intended for the ladies and children, the sick and wounded from Lakhnao, and the stores of clothing intended for the de-

* *Blackwood's Magazine*, October 1858.

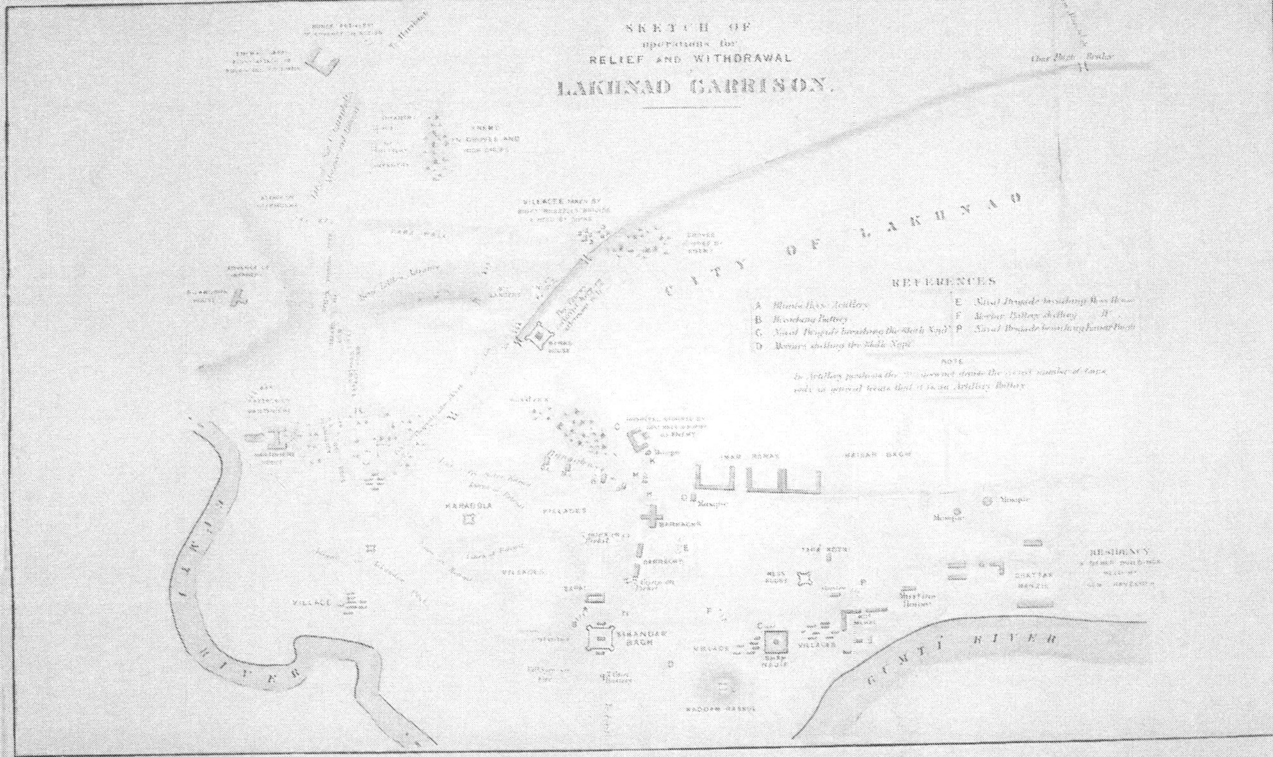
SKETCH OF
operations for
RELIEF AND WITHDRAWAL
LAKHNAO GARRISON.
CITY OF LAKHNAO
REFERENCES
NOTE
KAISAR BAGH
SIKANDAR BAGH
VILLAGES
VILLAGE
BARRACKS
MESS HOUSE
CHATTAR MANZIL
RESIDENCY
GUMTI RIVER

Book XI. Chapter II.

1857. Nov. 28.

fenders of the Residency, must have been destroyed; whilst the artillery fire occasionally directed at the bridge, and the musketry fire near the river bank, proved that a sharp crisis was impending. In a word, to use the language of an officer on Sir Colin's staff, "the veil which had so long shrouded us from Windham was rent asunder, and the disaster stood before us in all its calamity." *

has a glimpse of the disaster

What that disaster was, and how it came about, will form the theme of the next chapter. I leave Sir Colin and his staff galloping, on the dusky evening of the 28th November, across the bridge, the preservation of which might yet enable him to repair the evil that had been accomplished.

as he gallops across the bridge into Kánhpúr.

* *Blackwood's Magazine*, October 1858.

BOOK XI.

CHAPTER III.

In the preceding chapter I mentioned that when, on the 9th November, Sir Colin left Kánhpúr to join his army in the plain beyond Banni, he had left at that station about five hundred Europeans and a few Sikhs under the command of Major-General C. A. Windham. On the 6th November, in a memorandum addressed to that officer, he had directed him to occupy and improve the intrenchment which had been constructed on the river; to keep a careful watch over the movements of the Gwáliár force; to send into Oudh, unless he should be seriously threatened, by detachments of wings, any European infantry that might arrive; but to detain, if he should think fit, the brigade of Madras native troops, expected the following day, until the intentions of the Gwáliár contingent expected to arrive at Kálpi on the 9th, should become developed. In case of any pronounced movement towards Kánhpúr on the part of that force General Windham was directed to make as great a show as possible of

Kánhpúr.

Detailed instructions given to General Windham,

Book XI. Chapter III.

1857. Nov. 9–28.

the troops at his disposal by encamping them conspicuously and in extended order in advance of the intrenchment, which, however, was to be sufficiently guarded. On no account was he to move out to attack, unless compelled to do so by force of circumstances, in order to save the intrenchment from being bombarded.

It is a proof alike of the careful supervision which Sir Colin Campbell exercised over the generals subordinate to him, but placed in independent command, and of the anxious attention which he devoted to that particular position, that, two days later, he sent to General Windham a second memorandum, in which he entered in full detail into the possibilities before that officer. Every movement of the Gwáliár troops was provided for; the corresponding action of General Windham was defined; and the retention of certain troops and the despatch into Oudh of others were again insisted on.

supplemented by a second memorandum still more in detail.

General Windham prepared at once to carry out the directions of the Commander-in-Chief in their most essential point. The rendering the intrenchment secure against any attack was that point. The intrenchment guarded, though it did not absolutely protect, the passage of the river, the commissariat stores, and two of the hospitals. Windham, then, at once took measures to clear the glacis and the country beyond it, to extend and strengthen the works, and to train men to work the guns. For the intrenchment he had nine guns worked by a detachment of the Naval Brigade. Six field guns were to arrive with

Windham takes steps to carry out Sir Colin's orders.

Artillery at his disposal.

Book XI. Chapter III. 1857. Nov. 9–28.

the Madras force on the 10th. He had, besides, two 9-pounders and one 24-pounder howitzer, with ammunition in their waggons. But there being no gunners attached to these guns, Windham set to work to train some Sikh soldiers for that purpose.

Tántia Topi arrives at Kálpi.

Meanwhile, Tántia Topi was preparing to establish his claim to generalship. Well served by his agents, Tántia had received very minute and very timely information regarding the movements of Sir Colin Campbell. He arrived with the revolted Gwáliár contingent at Kálpi on the 9th November. Kálpi lies on the right bank of the river Jamná, forty-six miles south-west from Kánhpúr. The direct road between the two places ran through the villages of Bhognipúr and Suchandi. From Suchandi to Kánhpúr the distance is fourteen miles, the road being intersected at the fourth milestone by the Pándu rivulet, at the eighth by the Ganges canal. Another line, which led to positions a little to the north-east of Kánhpúr, must now be referred to. Leaving Kálpi, and passing through Bhognipúr, this road, just about midway from the latter to Suchandi, branches off to Akbarpúr. Thence, running nearly north, it touches the Pandú rivulet at Sheoli, and then, taking a turn to the north-west, crosses at a distance of four miles the Ganges canal, and prolonging itself for two miles, reaches the village of Sheorájpúr on the grand trunk road about three miles from Serai Ghát on the Ganges, and twenty-one miles north-west of Kánhpúr.

The country between Kálpi and Kánhpúr.

To march on Kánhpúr, Tántia had first to cross

Book XI. Chapter III.

1857. Nov. 9-28.

Plans and hopes of the rebel commander.

the Jamná. There was no one to oppose the passage. He had left at Jaláon his treasure and *impedimenta*. Kálpi he garrisoned with three thousand men and twenty guns. Then, on the 10th, he crossed the Jamná. The passage effected, Tántia, determined not to make too decided a demonstration until Sir Colin Campbell should have absolutely committed himself to the relief of Lakhnao, and hoping that the rebel troops there would find means to detain him at least the time necessary for the perfect carrying out of his own scheme, moved slowly forward with about six thousand men and eighteen guns to Bhognipúr. Leaving here one thousand two hundred men and four guns, he advanced by Akbarpúr to Sheoli and Sheorájpúr, occupying the first-named place with two thousand men and six guns, Sheoli with the same number and four guns, and Sheorájpúr with one thousand men and four guns.

He occupies the salient points between Kánhpúr and the Jamná;

These operations, beginning about the 10th November, were completed about the 19th. Their effect was completely to sever the communications between Kánhpúr with the west and north-west—the country on which it had been mainly dependent for its supplies.

thus severing the communications between Kánhpúr and its supply-country.

Effect of Tántia Topi's movements on Windham.

Windham had been neither blind nor indifferent to the movements of the enemy. He was duly informed of the passage of the Jamná and the occupation of positions reaching to the Ganges, some twenty miles to the north-west of his position. What did this movement forebode? Some thought that the march on the Ganges at a prudent distance from Kánhpúr indicated an intention

Book XI. Chapter III.

1857. Nov. 9–28.

He divines the reasons which actuate the rebel leader.

to cross unmolested into Oudh to act there on the rear of Sir Colin Campbell. Windham was not of this opinion. Crediting Tántia Topi with merely natural acuteness, he could not believe that he had any other intention but that of taking advantage of Sir Colin's absence to crush him at Kánhpúr. He believed, in fact, that Tántia would act as a general in his position ought to act.

Communicates to Sir Colin the enemy's movements.

Yet, believing this, convinced of it, he had still those positive and reiterated orders of the Commander-in-Chief which required him to forward into Oudh by detachments of wings of regiments the European troops as they should arrive. General Windham, whilst obeying these instructions, made an urgent representation to Sir Colin Campbell, informing him of the disquieting reports he was daily receiving regarding the movements of the Gwáliár contingent, and requesting permission to retain such troops as he might consider absolutely necessary for the defence of the place. Pending a reply, he continued to forward the arriving detachments towards Lakhnao.

Receives permission to detain European troops.

Brigadier Carthew arrives;

On the evening of the 14th November the required permission arrived. On the morning of that day the Madras brigade, commanded by Brigadier Carthew, had marched into Kánhpúr. It was but a shadow of its former self. One of the regiments of which it had been composed, the 17th Native Infantry, had been left, by superior orders, at Fathpúr, to maintain the communication between Allahábád and Kánhpúr. Carthew brought with him, then, only the wing of one native regiment, the 27th, four 9-pounders, manned by natives, and two manned by Europeans. Between this date and the 26th the force was increased by successive companies or drafts of the 34th, 82nd, 88th Regiments, of the Rifle Brigade, and by the remaining wing of the 27th Madras Native Infantry. But the course of the narrative will show that not all of these were retained.

Book XI. Chapter III.

1857. Nov. 9-28.

is followed by detachments of European regiments.

Windham was now more at ease. On the 17th, following the instructions he had received, he took up a position beyond and to the west of the town, near the junction of the Dehlí and Kálpi roads, and encamped there. This camp, composed of detachments from the 34th, 82nd, 88th, and Rifle Brigade, and of the right wing of the Madras Native Regiment, the 27th, with six guns, was placed under the command of Brigadier Carthew. Windham thus entirely followed out his orders, making a show of his troops, encamping them conspicuously, at the same time that he covered the town and with it the buildings between the town and the intrenchment, some of which had been prepared for the reception of the Lakhnáo ladies, and in others of which supplies had been stored.

Windham takes up a position west of the town,

and displays his troops.

Matters so continued till the 20th. On that date Windham had become aware of the movement of the Gwáliár contingent I have already described, and of their occupation of strong positions stretching from Kálpi to Sheorájpúr. Nor was this all. Up to the 19th he had received in-

Communication with the

Book XI. Chapter III.

1857. Nov. 9–28.

Commander-in-Chief ceases.

Windham learns that the Banni bridge has been surprised.

telligence of the successful attacks made by the Commander-in-Chief on the Sikandarbágh and the Shah Najíf. But from that date all communications from Lakhnao, even from the Álambágh, ceased; while, to add to his perplexity, he received, on the 22nd, information that the enemy had surprised and defeated the police force stationed to guard the Banni bridge, on the high road to Lakhnao!

He despatches troops to re-occupy that bridge.

The occupation of the Banni bridge by the rebels might, if permitted to continue, lead to fatal consequences; for Windham could not know how, since the 19th, it had fared with Sir Colin Campbell. It was quite possible, with thirty thousand still unconquered rebels in Lakhnao, that he might yet have to fight hard for it. Under these circumstances the conduct of Windham was marked by great judgment and great self-denial. Not caring to consider, in the presence of this possibly great danger, that Tántia Topi and his trained soldiers were pressing upon him, he deliberately diminished his force to re-open the communications with Lakhnao. At 3 o'clock on the morning of the 23rd the right wing of the 27th Madras Native Infantry, with two 9-pounder guns manned by Europeans, marched, by his orders, to re-occupy the Banni bridge.

Windham is thoroughly aware of the difficulties and danger of his position.

Notwithstanding the permission he had received, and on which he had acted, to detain at Kánhpúr the European troops who might arrive, Windham had felt from the first that the showy position he had, in obedience to orders, taken up beyond the city, would in no way defend Kánhpúr in case of

Book XI. Chapter III.

1857. Nov. 9–28.

a serious attack. Under no circumstances could he prevent the enemy from bombarding the bridge with their heavy guns. The extent of the position, too, would prevent its proper defence with even the larger number of troops at his disposal, while, in the event, almost certain were he attacked seriously, of having to fall back on the intrenchment, the city and the houses I have spoken of would fall into the enemy's hands. With respect to the intrenchment, it should be borne in mind, that though Windham had done much to strengthen it, it was not, in a military sense, defensible.

He transmits to Sir Colin a plan of aggressive defence.

Windham was a brave and adventurous soldier. His position not being, in point of fact, defensible, he asked himself whether an aggressive defence might not present better chances of success. Thinking the matter over, he devised a scheme which he was prepared to carry out, and, on the very day on which he had taken up the position at the junction of the Dehlí and Kálpi roads—the 17th November—he transmitted this scheme to Lakhnao to obtain for its execution the sanction of the Commander-in-Chief.

Nature of the scheme.

This scheme was based on the honoured principle of taking advantage of the separation from each other of the enemy's posts and of destroying them in detail. The enemy had taken up positions, as already stated, at Bhognipúr, Akbarpúr, Sheoli, and Sheorájpúr. Between the two last-named villages at the distances of three miles and two miles flowed the Ganges canal. Windham conceived the idea of transporting one thousand

Book XI. Chapter III. 1857. Nov. 9–28.

two hundred men in the night by this canal, taking his guns along the towing-path, and falling upon one or other of the positions (Sheoli or Sheoráj-púr), overwhelming it, always able to fall back on Kánhpúr before the enemy from Akbarpúr could reach it.

Receiving no reply from Sir Colin,

To the request containing this plan Windham received no answer. The roads were closed. Meanwhile he had simply maintained his position and had sent off troops, as already mentioned, to regain the Banni bridge. But he had every day fresh causes for disquietude. The very day that he had heard of the defeat of the police force at the Banni bridge information reached him that rebels were crossing over from Oudh to swell the ranks of Tántia Topi's force. It was necessary to take some decisive step. He hesitated to attempt a plan so opposed to his instructions as the canal-plan without special sanction. But something must be done. Windham knew, from his reading, from his instincts, from conversation with officers experienced in Indian warfare, that the most certain mode of defeating an Asiatic enemy is to march straight against him. At half past 8 o'clock on the morning of the 24th, then, he broke up his camp, and marching six miles south-westward, took up a position close to the bridge by which the road to Kálpi crosses the canal. The position was comparatively strong, for his entire front was covered by the canal, and he was still nearer to the intrenchment than the enemy.

he takes up a position on the Kálpi road.

The Gwáliár troops, noting Windham's forward movement, regarded it as a challenge. They ac-

The rebels accept his challenge,

cepted it. That very day the detachment at Akbarpúr set out for Suchandi. Between this village and the canal, about midway, runs the Pándu rivulet. The rebels reached Suchandi on the 24th; the banks of the Pándu on the 25th. As soon as information of this movement reached Brigadier Carthew he despatched a special messenger with it to the General. Windham at once galloped to the camp, and reached Carthew's tent a little after midnight—during the first hour of the 26th.

Book XI. Chapter III.

1857. Nov. 9-28.

and march to the Pándu.

Windham prepares to attack them.

Windham at once made his plans. Dividing his force into two brigades, he placed Carthew at the head of the first, composed of the 88th Connaught Rangers, four companies of the 2nd battalion Rifle Brigade, and four 6-pounder guns, manned by natives. The second brigade, consisting of the 34th Regiment, four companies of the 82nd, and four 9-pounder guns, drawn by bullocks and manned by Europeans and Sikhs, he gave to Colonel Kelly of the 34th. Windham had also at his disposal one hundred native troopers and ten men of the 9th Lancers. With this force he determined to take the initiative the following morning. His plan was to deal the most advanced division of the enemy a heavy blow; then, returning to his base, repeat, should occasion offer, the same tactics on another portion of their force.

He reconnoitres,

Before daylight of the 26th, Windham, having taken precautions to guard his baggage, to protect the canal bridge, and to observe the enemy on the side of Sheorájpúr, rode forward to reconnoitre. He found the rebels posted beyond the

Book XI. Chapter III.

1857. Nov. 9–28.

and advances to the attack.

Pándu rivulet, then nearly dry. They numbered about two thousand five hundred infantry, five hundred cavalry, and they had six guns of large calibre. Windham at once sent back orders for his troops to advance. The order was at once obeyed.

Carthew silences the enemy's fire,

Carthew led forward his brigade from the right, the men of the Rifle Brigade leading in skirmishing order. The enemy were seen in masses in front of a large tope of trees, but as the skirmishers approached they moved to their right. This movement completed, their guns in the tope opened a very heavy fire. The balls passed over the skirmishers and fell right into the 88th, who were following them, knocking over many officers and men. Carthew brought his guns into position as quickly as possible, and opening upon the enemy, silenced their fire, whereupon Kelly, from the position on the left, led the 34th at the guns, and captured three of them (two 8-inch iron howitzers and one 6-pounder gun). Such, in brief, was the story of the main fight. I may add, that prior to Colonel Kelly's attack, a portion of his regiment had repulsed a charge of the enemy's cavalry. These did not appear again until later in the day, but it will be seen that they then made their presence felt.

and Kelly, pushing on the 34th, captures their guns.

Windham marches back to the city, but threatened by the enemy's cavalry,

The capture of the guns was followed by the flight of the enemy, who were pursued for some distance. Windham then drew off his troops and marched back towards the city. This retrograde movement inspired the enemy with courage, and their cavalry, coming to the front, became so insolent that Windham halted and deployed his troops. It was no part of their game, however, to attack our men in the open, so they again drew off. Windham then marched his force to a new position near the town across the Kálpi road, immediately in front of some brick-kilns. A letter from the Commander-in-Chief's camp had reached him to the effect that all was well, and that the army was marching towards Kánhpúr. Windham hoped, then, that the blow he had inflicted that day might serve as a deterrent to the enemy at least till the Commander-in-Chief should arrive. Their loss had been severe; his own amounted to ninety-two killed and wounded.

Book XI. Chapter III.

1857. Nov. 9-28.

takes up a new position across the Kálpi road.

But the leader of a rebel army was no fool. The blow dealt by Windham, far from frightening him, had disclosed to his astute mind the weakness of the British leader. A force, completely victorious, does not as a rule fall back beyond even the position it had occupied before the action had commenced; nor, in falling back, does it allow itself to be threatened with impunity by the troops it had defeated. But these things had happened to the little army of Windham. It had been victorious on the field—a fact proved by the capture of three of the enemy's guns. But the necessities of his position had forced Windham, after his victory, to fall back, threatened by the enemy's horse, to a position nearer to the city than that he had occupied before the battle. Tántia Topi read the necessities of Windham's position as he would have read an open book, and, with the instincts of a real general, he resolved to take advantage of them.

Tántia Topi, perceiving Windham's weakness, resolves to attack him,

Book XI. Chapter III.

1857. Nov. 9–28.

in front and in flank.

Far, then, from allowing Windham the respite of twenty-four hours which would, that general hoped, bring the Commander-in-Chief to his aid, Tántia Topi directed that portion of his force which had engaged at Suchandi the previous day to stand at their arms at daybreak, ready for a forward movement, but to withhold that movement until the detachments at Sheoli and Sheorájpúr, which would march in the night, should open fire on the right flank of the British. That fire was to be the signal for a general attack.

Windham, standing on the defensive,

Meanwhile, Windham, hoping much from the blow he had delivered the previous day, had not the less prepared for possible eventualities. His troops stood to their arms at daybreak. But, as there were neither signs of an enemy, nor any certain information as to his movements, they were dismissed, at 9 o'clock, to their breakfasts. The General, after partaking of his morning meal, ordered up two 24-pounder guns, drawn by bullocks, and manned by seamen of the *Shannon*, and then went to reconnoitre. The aspect of affairs evidently did not satisfy him, for at 11 o'clock he sent down to the camp an order for the whole force to stand to their arms. An hour later, just as the British gun in the intrenchment fired the mid-day signal, he rode into camp. He had scarcely arrived when a heavy cannonade was opened on the right flank of the British. Almost simultaneously a shell exploded over the trees in their front. It was evident that an attack in force had begun on all points.

is attacked at noon.

Cool and prompt in action, Windham at once

directed Brigadier Carthew, with the 34th, two companies of the 82nd, and four 6-pounder guns, to take up and hold a position on the right, defending the approaches to the town by the Bithor road. Carthew at once moved off, detaching the 34th to occupy some gardens on the left of his position, throwing some fifty men of the 82nd into some ruined huts on its right, and covering the guns in the centre with the remainder of the two companies of that regiment. As his brigade, so to call it, was marching to the points indicated, the enemy opened fire upon it at a long range. But so effective was the reply from the 6-pounders and Enfields, so steady and continuous their fire, that the rebels ceased their attack on that side.

Book XI. Chapter III.

1857. Nov. 9–28.

He detaches Carthew to repulse the enemy on his right.

Carthew succeeds.

In the front, forming the extreme left of his position, Windham had not been so fortunate. He had there five companies of the 2nd battalion Rifle Brigade, the 88th Regiment, two 9-pounder guns, and two 24-pounder howitzers, and two 24-pounder guns manned by seamen of the *Shannon*. To the right of this position, in a wood midway between it and that occupied by Carthew, was posted the main body of the 82nd.

Windham's front, or left, position.

Windham placed the guns in the centre of his position, supporting them by the Rifle Brigade and the 88th on either flank. Before the first gun had been fired, he proceeded himself to the right to watch the attack in that quarter, leaving the left brigade in charge of Colonel Walpole of the Rifle Brigade. The 24-pounder guns were then

Book XI. Chapter III.

1857. Nov. 9-28.

pushed to the front to within sight of the enemy.* The enemy on sighting them, fired the first shot from a gun they had placed on the road. The British guns at once replied, but they had not fired two rounds when the rebels opened fire with grape and canister from batteries in front and on the right flank of Windham's position.

The great superiority of the rebels in artillery makes itself felt.

So superior, from their immense superiority in the number of guns, was their fire, that Windham, on his return, an hour later, from the right brigade, found that his men were getting all the worst of it. The rebel leader, with great judgment, kept back his infantry, and fought Windham with his artillery alone. The advantage he derived from his greatly superior numbers was enormous, for they enabled him to form a semicircle round the British position. Any attempt on the part of Windham to break through this semicircle at any point would have placed it in the power of the rebel leader to lap over and overwhelm his far inferior force.

Finding his position untenable, Windham falls back on the brick-kilns,

Windham used all the means in his power to make head against the enemy. Their flanking fire he attempted to silence by turning upon it one of the 24-pounders worked by the men of the *Shannon*. But all would not do. The position was not tenable against an enemy superior in number and who fought only with their guns. To add to his misfortunes, the bullock-drivers, not liking the prospect, deserted as fast as they could, and, as a final blow, ammunition began to run short. Orders were accordingly given to fall back

* *The Shannon's Brigade in India*, page 36.

on the brick-kilns, a little to the left of the position Windham had taken up on the night of the 26th. Windham at the same time sent for the 34th to reinforce him, and directed Carthew, by an order twice repeated, to fall back also on the brick-kilns.*

and orders Carthew to do the same.

Carthew, meanwhile, had held the position on the right, and with the force at his disposal he probably could have held it. But, at this moment, Windham, to protect his retiring movement, sent for the bulk of the 34th. This regiment, which had covered itself with glory by its repulse of the enemy, was accordingly sent to reinforce the left brigade. It found that brigade in considerable disorder. The two big guns had been for the moment abandoned, and the men were falling back disheartened. The 34th came up in time to take the initiative in dashing at the big guns, and, with the aid of the sailors, in bringing them on with the retreating column.

Before this, Windham had reinforced his left with the 34th, taken from Carthew.

Windham falls back.

But the retiring movement had served as a signal for the enemy to advance. They crowded on in numbers, firing their guns. The English fell back, confused and in disorder, on the brick-kilns. Here it was hoped a stand might be made. It was now 5 o'clock, and Windham, thinking the position now reached might be held, and anxious for the condition of the right brigade, weakened by the withdrawal of the 34th, left General Dupuis,

The enemy follow.

Windham gallops to the right.

* Windham stated subsequently that he afterwards countermanded that order, but the countermand never reached Carthew.

Book XI. Chapter III.

1857. Nov. 9-28.

R.A., in command, with orders to hold the brick-kilns, if possible, and galloped to the right.

Fatal effect of Windham's reiterated order to Carthew to fall back.

But before he could reach the right brigade, the order to retire, which he had sent to it, had had its fatal effect. It is true that, weakened by the withdrawal of the 34th, the brigade could with difficulty hold its ground against the enemy pressing on it. But, coping bravely with the difficulty, Carthew did hold it. So convinced was he of the value of the position, that he did not act on the first order which he received. The second order was imperative. He was forced to obey his general, and he fell back.*

Great confusion at the brick-kilns.

When Carthew reached the brick-kilns, confusion seemed worse confounded. The carriage cattle had been driven off, whilst the tents of the encampment had been struck, and, with most of the heavy baggage, were lying in disorder on the earth. Just then, an order reached Dupuis to fall back on the intrenchment. Windham, as he was riding to look after his right brigade, had received intelligence that the rebels, turning the extreme right of his extended position had occupied the lower part of the city,

* Captain Drury, who was Brigadier Carthew's brigade-major on this occasion, thus described the situation in a letter to a friend at Madras: "The other position" (Windham's) "of the force had not fared so well, and the General sent for the 34th to strengthen the encampment. Shortly afterwards we were ordered to return to the encampment and occupy some brick-kilns immediately in its rear. This order was repeated, and it was not until the second time that we commenced falling back to the place directed. This order was a grave error. General Windham says he sent a countermand afterwards. *That* never came."

and were then attacking his last stronghold. Fortunately, at the moment a detachment of the 2nd battalion Rifle Brigade arrived opportunely from Fathpúr. Windham, placing himself at their head, drove the enemy from the lower part of the town, at the same time that he sent the order to Dupuis to fall back on the intrenchment. This movement had been just begun when Windham, riding towards the force after the exploit just recorded, personally directed Carthew to take two companies of the 88th and his four 6-pounders, to return to the position he had vacated on the right, and on reaching the Bithor road, to fall back on and occupy the theatre. This building lay about a quarter of a mile south of the intrenchment, and was filled with stores and clothing for the troops.

Book XI. Chapter III.

1857. Nov. 9-28.

The rebels attack the intrenchment,

but are driven back.

Windham orders a retreat on the intrenchment,

but directs Carthew to defend his right.

Whilst the main body, abandoning tents and the soldiers' kits, fell back on the intrenchment, "pursued by the enemy and harassed by musketry," * Carthew moved to the right to execute Windham's latest order. Between the suburb through which he had to pass and the Bithor road were the abandoned lines of a native regiment. On debouching from the suburb, he saw the enemy's skirmishers feeling their way down the road toward the intrenchment. They were exposing their right flank to Carthew, but the moment they saw him they fell back in soldier-like

Carthew moves to the right,

* *The Shannon's Brigade in India*, page 36. A private letter from a soldier of the 34th says: "They took all our kit and encampment, which we saw burning during the night."

Book XI. Chapter III.

1857. Nov. 9-28.

style and occupied the abandoned lines I have spoken of. But Carthew, sending his men at them with the bayonet, drove them out in fine style, and as far as the Bithor road. Here he came upon their guns, which at once unlimbered and opened fire. But Chamier's four 6-pounders were at hand. They had had to make a short detour to avoid the narrow streets, but they came up with all possible haste, and, worked magnificently by the swarthy gunners of the Madras army, they silenced and drove back the guns of the enemy. Had Carthew had four companies instead of two, he would have captured the enemy's guns. But it was growing dark, and his few men were dispersed in skirmishing order. He could not rally in time a sufficient number for a rush.

and drives back the enemy

Carthew had, however, completely fulfilled his instructions. He had gained the Bithor road. Here he halted, alike to collect his men and show a front to the enemy. But the enemy had had enough of it. He then fell back, unmolested, on the theatre—the one officer in high command who had been victorious in every encounter on that eventful day!

and occupies the theatre.

The theatre constituted now the centre of a chain of outposts, forming a semi-circle about a quarter of a mile in front of the intrenchment. The left of this semi-circle rested on the canal, the right in an outwork on the river Ganges. This outwork was occupied by the 64th. Carthew's small force, having just barricaded a bridge in their front over a narrow but deep nullah,

He halts here for the night, barricading a bridge over a deep nullah in his front.

bivouacked on the road near the theatre. The 88th occupied the road leading from the canal to the town. The remainder of the force and the guns were withdrawn within the intrenchment.

Remarks on the events of the day.

The laurels of the day rested certainly with the rebels. They had driven back the British force, had compelled it to renounce the defence of the town. With a little more enterprise they might probably have cut it off altogether. The fact is, Windham occupied with one thousand seven hundred men a very extended position, and he attempted to defend this position against an enemy computed, erroneously, I think, at twenty-five thousand trained soldiers, but who probably numbered at least fourteen thousand. It is possible, however, that if he had been content with holding the position he had taken up on the night of the 26th, near the brick-kilns, he could have maintained it. For the right flank of that position was covered by Carthew's brigade and by the linking detachments of the 82nd and 34th. But, by pushing his own brigade forward on the Kálpi road to a position in which its whole front and right flank were exposed to the enemy's fire, he virtually invited defeat. When he at last ordered Dupuis to fall back on the brick-kilns it was too late. His ill-judged order to Carthew, resisted as long as possible by that officer, to abandon the position he had successfully defended, gave an opening to the enemy to penetrate on his right. When, after the evil had so far worked its effect as to necessitate the order to Dupuis to fall back, Windham attempted to repair it by

Book XI. Chapter III.

1857. Nov. 9-28.

sending back Carthew to his old position, Carthew did, indeed, by a display of skill and daring, prevent the mischief from becoming irremediable. But the position at the brick-kilns, which might have been maintained, had to be abandoned and the town to be sacrificed.

The night that followed.

The night passed quietly. The British, that is to say, were not assailed. But the glare of the flames, and the tumult outside their position, proclaimed the triumph of the rebels. A great anxiety reigned within the British lines. Windham passed the night in consultation with the officers he most trusted. At one time he hoped to be able to redeem the past by a night attack on the rebels, but he could obtain no trustworthy information as to the locality of the enemy's guns. Nothing remained to him, then, but to make the best preparations to repel the renewed attack to be expected on the morrow.

Windham issues instructions for the morrow.

That night Windham issued to the senior officers of his force the instructions for carrying out the plan upon which, after mature consideration, he had decided. To Colonel Walpole—commanding five companies of the Rifle Brigade under Lieutenant-Colonel Woodford, two companies of the 82nd Regiment under Lieutenant-Colonel Watson, and four guns—two 9-pounders manned by Madras gunners, and two 24-pounder howitzers manned by Sikhs, under Lieutenant Green, R.A.—he confided the defence of the advanced portion of the town on the left bank of the canal, that is, the portion in the left rear of the brick-kilns separated from them and from the rest of the

Line of defence entrusted to Walpole,

town by the canal; to Brigadier Carthew—having under him the 34th commanded by Lieutenant-Colonel Kelly, the flank companies of the 82nd, and the four Madras 6-pounders under Lieutenant Chamier—the defence of the Bithor road, in a position more advanced than, and a little to the right of, that occupied the previous day. The intrenchment was entrusted to the care of the 64th under Brigadier N. Wilson, who was also to guard against a turning movement on the right by establishing a post at the Baptist Chapel; whilst Windham himself, having under him the 88th Regiment commanded by Lieutenant-Colonel Maxwell, should defend the portion of the town nearest the Ganges, on the left bank of the canal.

to Carthew, to Wilson, to Windham himself.

Disproportionate force allotted to guard the key of the position.

Before the action has begun, the impartial reader cannot but be struck by the disproportionate force allotted to Brigadier Carthew. That officer had to defend the key of the position. He had proved his capacity the day before; and yet to him, occupying the post which was certain to draw upon him the weight of the enemy's attack, a force was assigned not larger than that given to Walpole, whose position was far more defensible.

Carthew, after advancing, is ordered to fall back and defend the bridge.

At daylight on the 28th the several movements indicated took effect. Carthew pushed across the bridge he had barricaded the previous evening with the 34th and guns, covering his flanks with the two companies of the 82nd. He had just reached the point at which the road turned off to the position he was to occupy a little to the right, when the Assistant Quartermaster-General,

Book XI. Chapter III.

1857. Nov. 9-28.

Captain M'Crea, brought him an order from the General to fall back on to the bridge. This position, then, Carthew took up, covering his left with two companies, occupying with three the ruined houses in the front and on the flanks of the bridge, and keeping the remainder at the bridge. The detached party on the right consisted of one company of the 34th commanded by Captain Stewart. The house it occupied was a lofty building with a flat roof, and from this roof Stewart noticed the advance of the enemy's artillery to a position whence their guns could bear with decisive effect on the bridge. A zealous, intrepid officer, beloved by the regiment, Stewart posted his men in positions whence they could pick off the enemy's gunners. They succeeded in this task beyond their hopes, in spite of the grape and round shot which came pouring upon them. This state of things continued for more than two hours, from half-past 9 o'clock till noon, the enemy pouring in shot and shell, the 34th and 82nd replying with musketry, and Chamier's two small guns* doing all the mischief of which they were capable. The enemy made no way, but their artillery fire did considerable execution, and though they, too, suffered severely from the British fire, their immense superiority in numbers enabled them to fill up vacancies as they occurred.

Captain Stewart.

Successful defence offered by Carthew.

This was the state of affairs on the right at 12 o'clock. On the left Walpole had received the

* The other two had been withdrawn, most unnecessarily, to defend the Alláhábád road.

Book XI. Chapter III.

1857. Nov. 9–28.

Success of Walpole on the left.

attack of the enemy. But the enemy's attack on the left bank of the canal, though made in force and with great resolution, was but the adjunct to his main attack on the right. The left advanced position was not the decisive point of the scene of action, yet on this point the British were posted in numbers sufficient to beat back the enemy; and though Windham from his post to the rear of them sent and brought up supports, those supports were not required to ensure the repulse of the enemy, for Walpole had achieved that result without them.* A real general, having under his command in reserve a fine British regiment such as was the 88th, seeing that Walpole was able to hold his own, would at once have hurried to the scene of action, which the lay of the ground and the importance of the position to be gained there must have shown him to be the decisive scene. The stores, clothing, and impedimenta of all sorts were on the side which Carthew was defending—not where Walpole was successfully fighting.

Criticisms on Windham's conduct at this conjuncture.

He sends an order to Carthew to advance,

But Windham did not possess the *coup d'œil* of a general. Instead of hurrying to the support of Carthew, he despatched to him, at 12 o'clock, his Assistant Quartermaster-General, Captain M'Crea, to direct him to advance once again up

* "On the left advance, Colonel Walpole, with the Rifles, supported by Captain Greene's battery, and part of the 82nd Regiment, achieved a complete victory over the enemy, and captured two 18-pounder guns. *The glory of this well-contested fight belongs entirely to the above-named companies and artillery.*"—General Windham's Despatch, 30th November 1857. The italics are mine.

Book XI. Chapter III.

1857. Nov. 9–28.

the road, and promising him that the 64th Regiment under Brigadier N. Wilson would make a parallel advance on his right. To cover this movement of the 64th, M'Crea took with him to strengthen that regiment, forty men of a company of the 82nd, till then under Carthew's orders.

and to Wilson.

The ground on which they were to act.

That the reader may more clearly comprehend the movements which followed, I may here state that after crossing the bridge the road runs up the centre of a parade-ground about six hundred yards long and two hundred yards wide, traversed by a watercourse, and having houses on both sides of it. On the advance being sounded, the three companies which till then had occupied the ruined buildings in front and on the flanks of the bridge pushed across the plain in skirmishing order, in spite of a continual shower of grape from three guns posted at the further end of it. When within about one hundred yards of these, Captain Stewart, who was leading his men in splendid style, was shot through the thigh. The adjutant of the 34th, Leeson, at once supplied his place, but the fire from the front and from the buildings on either side was so hot that it was impossible to reach the guns.

Carthew advances.

Impossibility of further progress without cavalry.

To gain breath the men lay down in the watercourse of which I have spoken, whilst Carthew, mounted, in the middle of the parade-ground, endeavoured to collect a sufficient number of men to make a rush at the enemy. But, crippled by the paucity of his numbers—a paucity caused by the necessity of guarding his left flank—his efforts in this respect were fruitless. He was

Book XI. Chapter III.

1857. Nov. 9–28.

more successful, however, in causing Chamier's two guns to be brought to the front. These, unlimbering, replied to the enemy's fire; and, splendidly served by the Madras gunners, in the course of twenty minutes not only silenced it, but compelled the enemy to withdraw their pieces. Then was the chance if Carthew had but had one squadron of horse at his disposal. He had not a single trooper; and just at the moment he discovered that Wilson's attack on his right had failed and that his right rear was threatened by the rebels.

Wilson, being repulsed,

Captain M'Crea, taking with him forty men of the 82nd, had directed Brigadier Wilson to move to the front parallel with Carthew. The two companies covered the advance, harassed by a fire from six guns in position in their immediate front.* When within about a hundred yards of these guns the skirmishers charged them and for a few minutes had them in possession. Unfortunately the main body were too far behind, and the rebels, recovering from their first panic, came on in overwhelming numbers, and cut to pieces many of the heroic band of skirmishers. There fell here Brigadier Wilson, Captain M'Crea, Captain Morphy, Major Sterling, Lieutenant McKenna,

exposes Carthew's right.

* General Windham writes thus in his despatch: "Brigadier Wilson thought proper, prompted by his zeal for the service, to lead his regiment against four guns placed in front of Brigadier Carthew." Brigadier Wilson did nothing of the sort. The guns upon which he advanced were nearly half a mile from the guns in front of Carthew's troops. They were, as stated in the text, covering the line upon which Windham himself had, by the mouth of M'Crea, ordered Wilson to advance.

Book XI. Chapter III.

1857. Nov. 9-28.

Lieutenant Gibbins, all nobly fighting. The supports came up only in time to cover the retreat of the few survivors.

Criticisms on Windham's conduct at this conjuncture.

Windham had thus engaged, without supports, his entire right wing on the decisive point of the scene of action. The available supports were in his own hand on a side part of action, never intended by the enemy to be the decisive scene. The advance in parallel lines on the right, ordered by himself, had, owing to one of those accidents always likely to occur in war, failed. Carthew had indeed repulsed the enemy, but he had no men to follow him up. The 64th had been repulsed, and their repulse endangered Carthew's right. Now was the moment when supports would have been invaluable. They might even have changed the face of the day.

Carthew falls back to his old position,

His right rear threatened—for the 64th had been gradually forced back on the intrenchment—Carthew very gradually, and showing a bold front to the ever-increasing enemy, fell back on the bridge. But how different was his position here to what it had been in the morning! Then, the bridge was the centre of a chain of posts, both flanks being guarded, and his front covered. Now the flanking parties had fallen back and he was isolated.

now scarcely defensible,

but which he still bravely defends.

Still, Carthew knew the importance of the position, and he resolved to hold it as long as he could. But the enemy's attacks became more and more furious, the number of his guns increased and their fire became more concentrated. Still

Carthew did not move. He had but two guns with which to reply, but the gallant Chamier and the sturdy Madrásis worked them with a will.

Book XI. Chapter III. — 1857. Nov. 9-28.

But every moment was pregnant with some new danger for him. The rebels, climbing to the roofs of the houses which the retirement of the 64th and of the detachment which connected him with that regiment had left empty, poured upon the gallant soldiers of the 34th a stream of fire. But the unconquered soldiers of that splendid regiment still held on. Twice did they clear the streets in their front, twice the Church compound on their right. But the continuous stream of fire of which I have spoken would not allow them to hold the positions they had gained at the point of the bayonet. More than that, the enemy shifted their position so that Chamier's guns could no longer bear on any vital point, whilst the fire from the roofs caused the defenders to drop fast.

Gallantry of the 34th; and increasing numbers of the enemy.

A strong reinforcement might still have saved the position. Carthew sent for it. Pending its arrival this gallant leader went amongst the men, cheering them, and keeping them to their work. Even when the position had become practically untenable, when the enemy had all but turned his flanks, and when the party he had sent under Colonel Simpson of the 34th to keep open his communications was forced back, he still held on. Still the reinforcements did not come. At last, when it was absolutely certain that unless he were to retire he would be cut off, Carthew reluctantly gave the order—to give which when he could no longer hold out he had

In spite of Carthew's splendid tenacity, he is at last compelled to fall back.

Book XI. Chapter III.

1857. Nov. 9-28.

Carthew and Windham.

the authority of Windham—to fall back on the intrenchment.*

All this time where was Windham? Windham was with the victorious left wing, where his presence was not needed. What he was precisely doing, or why he did not hasten to strengthen the key of his position, may never be known. He never attempted to explain his action. In his despatch he endeavoured, in the most ungenerous manner, to cast, by implication, the blame of the defeat on Carthew. "Brigadier Carthew," he wrote, "of the Madras Native Infantry, had a most severe and strong contest with the enemy from morning till night; but I regret to add that he felt himself obliged to retire at dark." This passage conveyed to the mind of Sir Colin Campbell the impression that Brigadier Carthew had, at a critical period, retired from his post without orders; and, on the 9th December, he animad-

* "I have not the slightest hesitation," wrote, on the 11th December 1857, Lieutenant-Colonel Simpson of the 34th to Brigadier Carthew, "in giving my opinion about the brigade retiring from the position we held on the bridge on the evening of the 28th November. It is my firm conviction that you had no other alternative—that if you had not retired the brigade would have been cut off, as the enemy were completely outflanking us on our left. By your orders I sent round two companies of this regiment to check them, which they did for the moment, but could not make a stand, as they in turn were quite outflanked on their left. When the two officers commanding those companies (officers in whom I have the greatest confidence) came back and told me what was going on, and from what I saw myself, I spoke to Colonel Kelly, Colonel Gwilt, and one or two more of the regiment, and I myself, and I think others, told you that if we did not retire we should be cut off. You then, *reluctantly*, gave the order to retire."

Book XI. Chapter III.

1857. Nov. 9-28.

verted very severely in an official memorandum on such conduct. When Carthew received the memorandum he took it at once to Windham, who—it will scarcely be credited—advised him not to reply to it. But Carthew had too nice a sense of his own honour to act upon such advice. He not only replied to it, but forced from Windham an acknowledgment that he himself had given the Brigadier authority to retire when he could no longer maintain his position. Upon this, Sir Colin Campbell not only withdrew his censure, but expressed his regret that under an "erroneous impression" he should have given pain to a meritorious officer.

As he is falling back Carthew receives reinforcements,

But,—to return to the question,—where was Windham? I have already stated that Carthew had sent for reinforcements. He received them in the shape of two companies of the Rifle Brigade, as he was falling back, just in time to cover his retreat. Had Carthew not begun his retreat the reinforcement was too small to be of much avail. Windham states that he himself took down this reinforcement, and, returning, ordered up two companies of the 82nd. But it was too late—the mischief had been done; a strong reinforcement an hour earlier might have saved the position. It was not to be saved by sending on small supports in piecemeal. Under cover of the riflemen Carthew fell back in good order within the intrenchment. It was then quite dark.

too few in number,

too late in time.

Carthew, the 34th, and the rest of his brigade.

He and his officers and men had been for thirty-six hours almost without food and sleep. He had

Book XI. Chapter III. — 1857. Nov. 9-28.

exposed himself to the hottest fire throughout the day. His cool and calm courage had been the admiration of everyone. His efforts had been splendidly supported by all under his command. In the 34th alone three officers had been killed and eight wounded. The total number of killed and wounded in Windham's operations up to the night of the 28th amounted to three hundred and fifteen. Carthew brought back with him all his guns.

Windham's aggressive defence probably saved Kánhpúr.

The plain account I have given of the day's proceedings requires little comment. That Windham was justified in deciding to make an aggressive defence cannot, I think, be questioned. It is the opinion of those best qualified to form an opinion that, regard being had to the enormous superiority of the rebels in artillery, a purely defensive system would have ensured the destruction of his force, and the occupation of Kánhpúr by the rebels, with consequences—Sir Colin and the women and children of the Lakhnao garrison being on the other side of the river—the evil extent of which it would be difficult to exaggerate. Windham, by his military instincts, saved the country from this disaster, and he is entitled to all the credit due to a daring initiative. That the action might have been more skilfully fought is certain; but the aphorism of Napoleon, that in war victory is to the general who makes the fewest mistakes, must never be forgotten. Mistakes will be made; and it should be remembered that this was the first time that Windham had held an independent command in the field.

Book XI. Chapter III.

1857. Nov. 9-28.

Destruction consequent on the British defeat.

Both wings fell back that evening into the intrenchment. The town of Kánhpúr, the theatre and the houses, full of clothing and stores, or prepared for the reception of the Lakhnao ladies, fell into the hands of the rebels.

But before the right wing had reached the intrenchment, whilst Carthew, nobly daring, was still holding on to the Baptist Chapel, an event full of importance had occurred. Sir Colin Campbell had arrived, the precursor by a few hours of his army.

BOOK XI.

CHAPTER IV.

THE second chapter of this book left Sir Colin Campbell, followed by his staff, crossing the bridge of boats into Kánhpúr. The shades of evening were falling, and the light was the short twilight following the setting of the sun. Ascending at a gallop the road leading to the gate, some men of the Rifle Brigade, posted on the rampart, recognised their general, and repeated cheers at once announced his arrival alike to Windham's soldiers and their enemy. Windham was within the intrenchment, and Sir Colin had hardly reached him when a demand for reinforcements arrived from the Baptist Chapel—a proof that even then Carthew was still, with the small means at his disposal, attempting the impossible. The reinforcements were sent, but they arrived too late, and Carthew fell back in the manner already related. With

Sir Colin reaches the intrenchment.

Book XI. Chapter IV.

1857. Nov. 29.

his arrival within the intrenchment the fighting for the night ceased.

After conversation with Windham, returns to his camp.

Sir Colin remained some time with Windham, listening to his report and asking questions. He then communicated to him his plans. He would recross the river to his camp; as soon as possible the next morning drive the enemy with his guns from the positions he had taken up near the bridge, and then send over his infantry. Sir Colin then rode back to his camp, "into which, all night, the guns, stores, women, and sick, continued to stream."*

The rebels attempt to break the bridge of boats.

Early the following morning Sir Colin proceeded to execute his plans. Peel's heavy guns had reached the ground, from their march of thirty miles, only an hour before sunrise. The astute leader of the rebel army had noticed with the early light of the morning the mass of soldiers filling the plain on the Oudh bank of the river, and that sight had told him that unless he could break the bridge his chances of ultimate victory would melt away. But there was yet time to break the bridge. He had therefore brought down his heaviest guns to the positions on the banks of the river whence he had the previous day driven the 64th, and had opened upon it a heavy, but fortunately an ill-directed fire. Sir Colin Campbell had foreseen that the rebels would try this last chance. Allowing, then, the men of the Naval Brigade but one hour for rest and food, he despatched them at sunrise to a point above the bridge of

Sir Colin, foreseeing the attempt, baffles them.

* Norman's *Relief of Lucknow.*

Book XI. Chapter IV.

1857. Nov. 29.

boats whence they could play on the enemy's guns. The artillery fire from the intrenchment was directed to the same point. For some time the artillery combat appeared not unequal, but gradually the guns of the British asserted their superiority. Then commenced the passage of the cavalry, the horse artillery, and of Adrian Hope's brigade. As they crossed, dark masses of smoke mingled with sheets of flame, arising from the store-laden buildings so well defended by Carthew the previous day, proved that the enemy had given up the contest for the bridge, and that they had set fire to the stores to cover his change of position. But it was yet possible that they might attempt a counterstroke on the weakened camp, crowded with non-combatants, on the Oudh bank of the river. The upper course of the river was in their possession; they had numberless boats at their command. What could be easier than to take advantage of the divided state of the British force and overwhelm the weaker portion? But the contingency had entered into the calculations of Sir Colin. By 9 o'clock he had crossed the troops I have already mentioned. On reaching the Kánhpúr bank these were instructed to take up a position facing the city, their right resting on a point near the intrenchment, their left stretching towards the grand trunk road. Their passage effected, Sir Colin crossed and established his headquarters on the Kánhpúr side, leaving Brigadier Inglis to protect the convoy until all the troops should have crossed. At 3 o'clock in the afternoon the passage of the convoy commenced.

The enemy fire the captured stores.

Sir Colin takes measures to meet every eventuality and every attack.

The passage of the troops continues without a break till the evening of the 30th.

Book XI. Chapter IV. 1857. Nov. 30.

During that afternoon, during the ensuing night, and till 6 o'clock on the evening of the 30th, the passage of the convoy and of the troops forming the rear-guard continued. Practically it was not interrupted by the rebels, and by the hour I have mentioned it was accomplished. The ladies and children, sick, and wounded were taken across the canal to a camp on the plain near "the mouldering remains and riddled walls of the position Wheeler had held so long."

Confidence of the rebels.

The rebels still continued to hold the town and the line of the canal passing through it to the westward. They were in considerable numbers, had a strong force of artillery, were flushed with victory, and they had as their leader a man of very great natural ability. They were evidently resolved to try conclusions with Sir Colin, and they had perhaps some reason for believing that even Sir Colin might find it a very difficult, perhaps an impossible, task to drive them from the position they had occupied.

Great strength of their position.

That position was, indeed, extremely strong. "Their left," to quote from the actor in the scene whose graphic journal I have so largely used,* "was posted among the wooded high grounds, intersected with nullahs, and thickly sprinkled with ruined bungalows and public buildings, which lie between the town of Kánhpúr and the Ganges. Their centre occupied the town itself, which was of great extent, and traversed only by narrow winding streets, singularly sus-

* *Blackwood's Magazine*, October 1858.

Book XI. Chapter IV. 1857. Nov. 30.

ceptible of defence. The portion of it facing the intrenchment was uncovered; but from the camp of our army it was separated by the Ganges canal. . . . Their right stretched out behind this canal into the plain, and they held a bridge over it, and some lime-kilns and mounds of brick in its front. The camp of the Gwáliár contingent was situated in this plain, about two miles in rear of the right, at the point where the Kálpi road comes in." The reader will be able the better to picture to himself the position if he will bear in mind that the right of the enemy was in the position whence they had dislodged Windham on the 27th; the left, that whence they had driven Carthew and Wilson on the 28th; and that the town, between the two, and up to the Ganges canal, formed the centre. This position was held by an enemy whose numbers were computed at twenty-five thousand men, with forty guns. It is probable that, even granting the correctness of this computation, the number of trained soldiers did not exceed fourteen thousand.

Their numbers.

As a preliminary to attacking them,

To attack a position so strong, and so numerously guarded, Sir Colin felt that he would require the services of every man of whom he could dispose. It was then, obviously, a main condition to despatch to Allahábád the ladies and children, the sick and wounded, before engaging in an action. Victorious though he felt he would be, the presence of the convoy near the battle-field, whilst constituting a danger to its members, would deprive him of the troops necessary to protect it against contingencies. His first care,

Book XI. Chapter IV.

1857. Dec. 1–3.

then, was to arrange for the despatch of the convoy.

Sir Colin arranges to despatch the ladies and children to Allahábád.

I have already stated that by 6 o'clock on the evening of the 30th November, every man, woman, and child had crossed into Kánhpúr. The days of the 1st, 2nd, and 3rd December were devoted to the perfecting of arrangements for the despatch of the convoy to Allahábád. The rebels did not fail occasionally to remind the Commander-in-Chief of their presence. On the 1st they attacked the British outposts. Although they were not in great force, and were easily repulsed, they managed nevertheless to effect some damage. Ewart, of the 93rd, whose gallantry at the storming of the Sikandar Bágh will be remembered, had his left arm carried away by a round shot, his regiment being at the time under cover of the unfinished barracks. On the 2nd they opened a very brisk cannonade, apparently pointed at the tents occupied by Sir Colin Campbell and the head-quarter staff. The cannonade became so pronounced, that the Commander-in-Chief detached a body of riflemen to occupy some houses near the canal, commanding the position occupied by the battery which was annoying him. This movement compelled the enemy to withdraw.

The enemy try to interrupt him.

At length the arrangements for the transport of the convoy were completed. The communications between Kánhpúr and Allahábád, interrupted during Sir Colin's absence, had been restored, and, on the night of the 3rd December, the convoy, composed of the women and children who

The convoy starts on the night of the 3rd December.

Book XI. Chapter IV.

1857. Dec. 3.

had survived the dangers and trials of the siege of Lakhnao, of the wounded who had shared those dangers and trials, or who had bled to relieve them, started for Allahábád. If for them war ceased thenceforth to be an affair of personal concern, inasmuch as they were no longer exposed to the fire of the enemy, the memory of its dread effects could not fail to accompany them. The sufferings of more than a lifetime had for many of that gentle cohort been crowded into the brief period of three months. There were few amongst them who had not experienced the loss of someone near and dear to them, of a husband, a child, a relation; and, rescued though they were, many were still leaving behind to the chances of death from a ruthless enemy the one dear companion, without whom the burden of life would be indeed hard to bear.

The attack delayed till the convoy should be out of distance.

Relieved from the anxiety which the presence of such a convoy within his lines could not fail to produce, Sir Colin Campbell prepared to attack the enemy. One strong reason moved him to delay still for a few days. For, whilst the convoy was near, it was always possible for the rebels, though beaten in action, to double round and destroy it. He wished, too, to arrange for the disposition of those slightly wounded men whom it had not been considered necessary to despatch to Allahábád. These were brought within the intrenchment.

The rebels still endeavour to harass Sir Colin.

In spite of the check given to them on the 2nd, the rebels still continued their attacks on the British position. On the 4th, they floated a number

Book XI. Chapter IV.

1857. Dec. 4–5.

of fire-boats, which, carried by the current against the bridge of boats, should set it on fire. This attempt was detected in sufficient time to cause it to be frustrated. On the afternoon of the 5th, they opened a heavy fire of artillery on the left pickets, whilst they threatened, or seemed to threaten, to turn that flank with infantry. The enemy's artillery fire gradually extended along their whole front. It needed a considerable display of troops and a continuous fire from the British guns to force them to cease their attack. Sir Colin Campbell determined it should be their last. He would himself take the initiative the next day.

The one weak point of the position of the rebels

I have already described the position held by the rebels. The reader will not have failed to perceive that whilst it was strong, and, in a military sense, unassailable in the centre and on the left—as whilst that left rested on the Ganges, both it and the centre and part of the right were enormously strengthened by the possession of buildings, bridges, narrow streets, and winding lanes—the extreme right was comparatively weak. It was weak because it rested almost without cover on a broad plain, intersected only by the canal. This canal, whilst it covered the centre and right, could be crossed in front of the latter only by two bridges. Whilst assailable with difficulty in front, the right was thus liable to be turned and driven in on its centre. This turning movement promised, moreover, another advantage. The troops executing that movement would naturally seize the Kálpi road—which

Book XI. Chapter IV.

1857. Dec. 5.

formed, so to speak, a prolongation of the ground occupied by the enemy's right wing; and the seizure of that road, by depriving the Gwáliár troops of their natural line of retreat, would drive them, were the execution to correspond with the design, into the British net. This idea decided Sir Colin's plans. He resolved to mass the largest number of troops on his left—the decisive point—to attack and defeat the enemy's right before it could receive assistance from the centre; then, taking possession of the Gwáliár camp, establish himself on the Kálpi road, and striking at the enemy's communications, compel him to renounce the strong positions occupied by his centre and left.

is detected by Sir Colin.

Reasons for limiting the number of the trained soldiers of the enemy.

One word as to the number and composition of the enemy's force. I have already said that it has been computed at twenty-five thousand men with forty guns. But, I repeat, it is difficult to believe that more than one half of these, or, at the outside, fourteen thousand, were trained soldiers. The Gwáliár contingent was composed of four companies of artillery, two regiments of cavalry, and seven regiments of infantry, a total of about seven thousand men. There may have been in addition an equal number of trained sepoy regiments, some of which had attached themselves to Náná Sáhib—who commanded on the left—in the earlier period of the mutiny, others which had come in from Bandalkhand and Central India. The remainder of the force consisted of the adherents of the Ráni of Jhánsi, attached to the Gwáliár troops on the right; and of the undisciplined and irregular followers of Náná Sáhib and of other discontented landowners on the left.

Book XI. Chapter IV.

1857. Dec. 5.

Number and composition of the British force.

Sir Colin Campbell's force consisted of about five thousand infantry, six hundred cavalry, and thirty-five guns. His infantry were divided into four brigades. That called the 3rd, commanded by Brigadier Greathed, consisted of the wasted remnant of the 8th, of the 64th, and of the 2nd Panjáb Infantry; the 4th, under Adrian Hope, was composed of the 53rd Foot, the 42nd and 93rd Highlanders, and the 4th Panjáb Rifles; the 5th, commanded by Inglis, counted the 23rd Fusiliers, the 32nd Regiment, and the 82nd; the 6th, led by Walpole, was formed of the 2nd and 3rd battalions Rifle Brigade, and a detachment of the 38th Regiment. The cavalry was the same as that which we have already seen doing such good service at the relief of Lakhnao—the 9th Lancers, and detachments of the 1st, 2nd, and 5th Panjáb Cavalry, and Hodson's Horse, commanded by the same gallant leader, Brigadier Little. The artillery consisted of the guns of the Naval Brigade, led by William Peel, of the troops of Blunt and Remmington, of the batteries of Bourchier, Middleton, Smith, Longden, and Bridge, commanded in chief by Dupuis. The engineer brigade, the same as that which had served in Oudh, was commanded by Colonel Harness. To Windham was consigned the command of the intrenchment—a command, it will be seen, of considerable importance. Hope Grant acted, nominally, in command of the whole force, but his real position was that of second to Sir Colin Campbell.

Book XI. Chapter IV.

1857. Dec. 5.

Position occupied by the British force.

The advanced positions of the British force occupied the suburb called Generalganj, an old bazaar of very considerable extent along the canal, facing the centre of the enemy. This post had been held since the 30th by Greathed, and upon him and his brigade had fallen the brunt of the skirmishing of the subsequent days.

Sir Colin's plan of attack.

Sir Colin's plan of attack was simple. Whilst Greathed should continue to occupy his position facing the enemy, Windham was to open on the enemy's left from the intrenchment a very heavy fire, so as to draw the attention of the rebel leaders to that point. The rest of the infantry, meanwhile, were to be massed in contiguous columns behind, and covered from view by, the old cavalry lines, buildings to the left rear of Greathed's position, and communicating by a cross road running immediately in their rear, at a distance of rather less than half a mile, with the grand trunk road. As soon as Windham's fire should produce the intended effect, the turning movement would be attempted. To facilitate this, certain orders were given to Greathed and to the other brigadiers, the purport of which the narrative of the action will disclose.

Sir Colin begins the action at 9 o'clock on the 6th December with a fire of artillery.

Early on the morning of the 6th December, Sir Colin Campbell struck his camp, and, to avoid the slightest risk of accident, despatched it to the river side under a guard. This having been accomplished, and the men having breakfasted, Windham, at 9 o'clock, opened fire. The enemy promptly replied, and in a few moments the earth shook with the noise of a terrific artillery com-

Book XI. Chapter IV. 1857. Dec. 6.

bat. Under cover of this fire, the infantry were massed in the position I have indicated, whilst the cavalry and horse artillery were held in readiness, at the same time, to cover the turning movement and to make a detour to the left, and crossing the canal by an unguarded bridge about a mile and a half further up, to threaten the enemy's rear, and to cut him off or intercept him when defeated.

Greathed makes a false attack on the centre,

The artillery duel continued about two hours. It then gradually slackened, and Greathed, in pursuance of his instructions, moved forward on to the canal, occupying the houses near it and from them opening a severe musketry fire on the enemy's centre. At the same time, the main body proceeded to carry out the plan confided to them.

whilst Walpole, Hope, and Inglis prepare to turn the right.

The position assigned to each brigade may thus be stated. Walpole, with the sixth, immediately on Greathed's left, was to cross the canal above the town, and advancing along its face, was to mask every gate, and prevent the enemy from affording assistance to their right wing. Meanwhile, on his left, which was the extreme left, Adrian Hope would debouch with the fourth brigade, supported by Inglis with the fifth, and carry out the turning movement.

Walpole crosses the canal.

When, then, the fire of the artillery slackened, and the rattle of Greathed's musketry was heard, Walpole, assisted by Smith's battery, dashed with his riflemen at the bridge, crossed the canal, and moved along the outskirts of the western face of the town. As he did this, a strong fire opened

Book XI. Chapter IV. — 1857. Dec. 6.

from the heavy guns of the Naval Brigade, and from Bourchier's and Longden's batteries massed on the left.

Adrian Hope turns the right of the rebels.

The fire had scarcely opened when Adrian Hope brought his brigade into the open, supported by that of Inglis, and covered by the cavalry and horse artillery. The dust raised by the progress of the latter effectually concealed from the enemy the movements of the infantry. They marched to the left, in the direction given by the cross road already indicated. Suddenly, when they reached a point rather beyond a line parallel with the brick-kilns which played so prominent a part in Windham's fight of the 27th, the infantry brigades brought forward their left shoulders—the cavalry and horse artillery still continuing their forward movement parallel with the canal. Hope had covered his advance with the Sikhs of the 4th Panjáb Rifles in skirmishing order, supported by the 53rd. As these gallant men pushed forward, there opened upon them a very heavy fire of shot and shell from the enemy's guns posted behind the canal. At the same time masses of the rebel infantry, protected by the brick-kilns and by mounds formed by the operation of brick-making, poured in a rattling fire of musketry. But our men were not to be baulked. The Sikhs, splendidly supported by the 53rd, rushed on at the double, and driving the enemy from the mounds, gained for themselves a momentary shelter. Only momentary, however. Obeying an order conveyed to them, they rushed at the bridge over which the rebels had fallen back. But the bridge

Splendid conduct of the 4th Panjáb Sikhs and the 53rd.

Book XI. Chapter IV.

1857. Dec. 6.

had been well cared for by the enemy. Upon it guns were pointed, whilst the rallying infantry of the enemy, recovering heart, again poured upon the skirmishers incessant volleys. For a moment the struggle seemed doubtful, when a rumbling sound was heard, and William Peel and his sailors, dragging with them a heavy 24-pounder, came up with a run, dashed through the skirmishers, planted the gun on the bridge, and opened fire. The effect of this splendid deed was electric. Whilst it roused our men to the wildest enthusiasm, it completely cowed the enemy. Highlanders, Sikhs, and 53rd, dashing by the gun, or fording the canal, rushed on the enemy, and capturing their guns, drove them back in the wildest disorder. The Gwáliár camp was now almost within their grasp. But, before the infantry could reach it, the battery of the gallant Bourchier, always in the front, passed them at a gallop, and, unlimbering, opened fire. In a few minutes the infantry had repassed them, and the Gwáliár camp was their own.*

Firm resistance of the enemy at the canal.

William Peel brings up a 24-pounder and opens fire.

The canal is forced,

and the enemy are beaten.

Sir Colin Campbell joined his two left brigades at the enemy's camp. His measures had been completely successful. Windham's bombardment of the rebels' left had concentrated their attention

General view of the action.

* "So complete was the surprise, so unexpected the onslaught, that the chuppathes were found heating upon the fires, the bullocks stood behind the hackeries, the sick and wounded were lying in the hospitals; the smith left his forge, and the surgeon his ward, to fly from the avenging bayonets. Every tent was found exactly as its late occupants had sprung from it."—*Blackwood's Magazine*, October 1858.

Book XI. Chapter IV.

1857. Dec. 6.

on that quarter; then Greathed's threatened attack on their centre so far imposed upon them, that they made no attempt, as a really capable general assuredly would have done, to pierce that —the weakest point of our line; Walpole had successfully prevented the centre from debouching by the western faces of the town to support their right. Adrian Hope and Inglis, Peel, Bourchier, and the gallant officers with their brigades and batteries, had done the rest. There was but one drawback to his complete satisfaction. The guide sent with the cavalry and horse artillery had misled them, and they were not on the spot when the camp fell into our hands. They came up shortly afterwards, however, in time to join in the pursuit which Sir Colin at once directed along the Kálpi road, and which was continued by Sir Colin in person to the fourteenth milestone.*

The enemy are pursued along the Kálpi road.

Completeness of the victory over the Gwáliár troops.

It was a great victory. The most formidable portion of the enemy's army, the Gwáliár contin-

* "For two miles without a check the pursuit was carried on by the battery alone" (Bourchier's), "accompanied by Sir Hope Grant and his staff. Four times in that distance did we come into action, to clear our front and flanks, until General Grant, thinking wisely we were too far from our supports, determined to wait until the cavalry arrived. A halt was called; not until it was required, for the horses, though in the condition of racers, had felt the pace. A small cloud coming nearer and nearer is seen on the left. The head of the cavalry column debouches from a grove. The order for a further pursuit is given. The cavalry spread like lightning over the plain in skirmishing order. Sir Colin takes the lead. The pursuit is continued to the fourteenth milestone, assuming all the character of a fox-hunt."—Bourchier's *Eight Months' Campaign against the Bengal Sepoys.*

Book XI. Chapter IV. 1857. Dec. 6.

gent, had been completely defeated; their camp, with all their stores, magazines, and a part of their *matériel*, had been captured. In a word, the right wing of the rebel army, its head, its brain, had been severed from the body.

The centre and left still shut up in Kánhpúr.

The centre and left of the enemy were thus cut off, shut up in Kánhpúr. They had but one line of possible retreat, that by the Bithor road.

Their line of retreat.

On the Bithor road, due north of the city, and immediately in rear of the enemy's left, was a large tank, known as the Subadár's Tank. As the Commander-in-Chief had cut them off on the right, and Greathed and Windham had imposed upon them in front, the occupation of this position would, Sir Colin Campbell felt, force the surrender of the entire force of the enemy. Before, then, he had started to pursue the beaten right wing, he ordered a force to occupy it at once. Whether he felt his presence more necessary with the pursuers, or whether, in the generosity of his heart, he desired to give a chance to one of his generals, I know not. But, considering the regard, almost amounting to affection, he felt for the officer whom he did select for this duty, it is, I think, probable that he was anxious to give him an opportunity of distinguishing himself as a commander. This officer was the Chief of the Staff, Major-General William Mansfield.

Sir Colin, before pursuing the Gwáliár troops, sends Mansfield to occupy that line of retreat.

General Mansfield.

General Mansfield was, in many respects, a remarkable man. Tall, and soldierly in appearance, it was impossible for anyone to look at his face without feeling certain that the man before whom he stood possessed more than ordinary

Book XI. Chapter IV.

1857. Dec. 6.

ability. Conversation with him always confirmed this impression. Mansfield was a man of more than ordinary ability. He could write well, he could speak well, he was quick in mastering details, he possessed the advocate's ability of making a bad cause appear a good one. He had that within him to procure him eminence in any profession, excepting one. He was not, and could never have become, a great soldier. Possessing undoubted personal courage, he was yet not a general, at all, except in name. The fault was not altogether his own. Nature, kind to him in many other respects, had denied him the penetrating glance which enables a man to take in, on the instant, the exact lay of affairs in the field. His vision, indeed, was so defective that he was forced to depend for information regarding the most trivial movements upon the report of others. This was in itself a great misfortune. It was, in the case of Mansfield, made irreparable by a haughtiness and innate reserve which shrank from reliance upon anyone but himself. He disliked advice, and though swayed, perhaps too easily, by those whom he loved and trusted, he was impatient of even the semblance of control from men who were brought in contact with him only officially and in a subordinate position. Hence it was that, when in independent command, unable to take a clear view himself, he failed to carry out the action, which, to so clever a man, would undoubtedly have recommended itself, had he had the leisure to study it over a map, in the solitude of his closet.

Book XI. Chapter IV.

1857. Dec. 6.

The troops with Mansfield.

General Mansfield took with him the whole of the infantry with which Sir Colin had turned the enemy's right wing, with the exception of the 23rd and a wing of the 38th, which he left to guard the captured camp.

He advances towards the Subadár's Tank.

It was about 2 o'clock in the afternoon. Mansfield advanced, the Rifles skirmishing in front, the heavy guns following, then the main body, the 93rd Highlanders in reserve. The position on which Mansfield was ordered to march—and which, if properly occupied, would completely cut off the enemy—was one to the north of and close to the Subadár's Tank. Driving the enemy before him, he marched to this point, and there halted.

Consequence of his defective vision.

He then ordered the infantry to lie down. He could not see, and would not believe that he had placed them in a position where they could not act, and in which, if the enemy had had any audacity, they might easily have been cut off from the rest of the force. But the enemy had but one idea, that of escaping. The troops were held back, apparently to facilitate their escape. Their indignation was unbounded. More than one senior officer pointed out to Mansfield the golden opportunity he was losing. But he could be persuaded to do no more than to withdraw his infantry from the false position in which he had placed them. He still insisted on keeping back his men, whilst the horse and the foot and the artillery of the rebels filed down the road to Bithor.

Indignation of the troops.

The enemy are emboldened,

This passive action not only rendered the movement to the Subadár's Tank useless, but, in

Book XI. Chapter IV.

1857. Dec. 6–7.

and carry off their guns to Bithor.

accordance with the invariable rule of warfare of India, it emboldened the enemy to venture an artillery attack upon the stationary British. This, indeed, was repelled, but Mansfield still allowed the enemy to carry off all their guns without let or hindrance.*

The left wing and centre of the enemy thus succeeded in making good their retreat on Bithor. The victory, though great, was not absolutely decisive, for Mansfield's inaction had made it necessary to follow it up with another blow.

Dec. 8.

Sir Colin rests his troops,

Giving his men one clear day's rest, Sir Colin detailed a body of troops for this duty on the 8th. The officer he selected this time to command was Hope Grant—a tried, daring, noble-hearted soldier.

then detaches Hope Grant to follow up the escaped rebels.

At 1 o'clock in the afternoon of the 8th, Hope Grant set out on his mission. He had with him Adrian Hope's brigade, composed of the 42nd and 93rd Highlanders and 4th Panjáb Rifles; five hundred and fifty-one cavalry; Middleton's field battery, Remmington's troop of horse artillery, and one hundred sappers, or about two thousand seven

* "Their guns might have been taken," wrote Mansfield, in his despatch, "but I refrained from giving the necessary order, being aware that it was contrary to your Excellency's wish to involve the troops among the enclosures and houses of the new cantonments," &c. Whether Sir Colin Campbell was satisfied with this explanation may be doubted. Let the reader contrast the notice in his despatch, without comment, of Mansfield's inaction, with his laudatory remarks in the same despatch on Hope Grant's operations two days later. With respect to the absolute correctness of the account in the text of Mansfield's operations, I appeal with confidence to the surviving officers of the 93rd and of the other regiments present on the occasion.

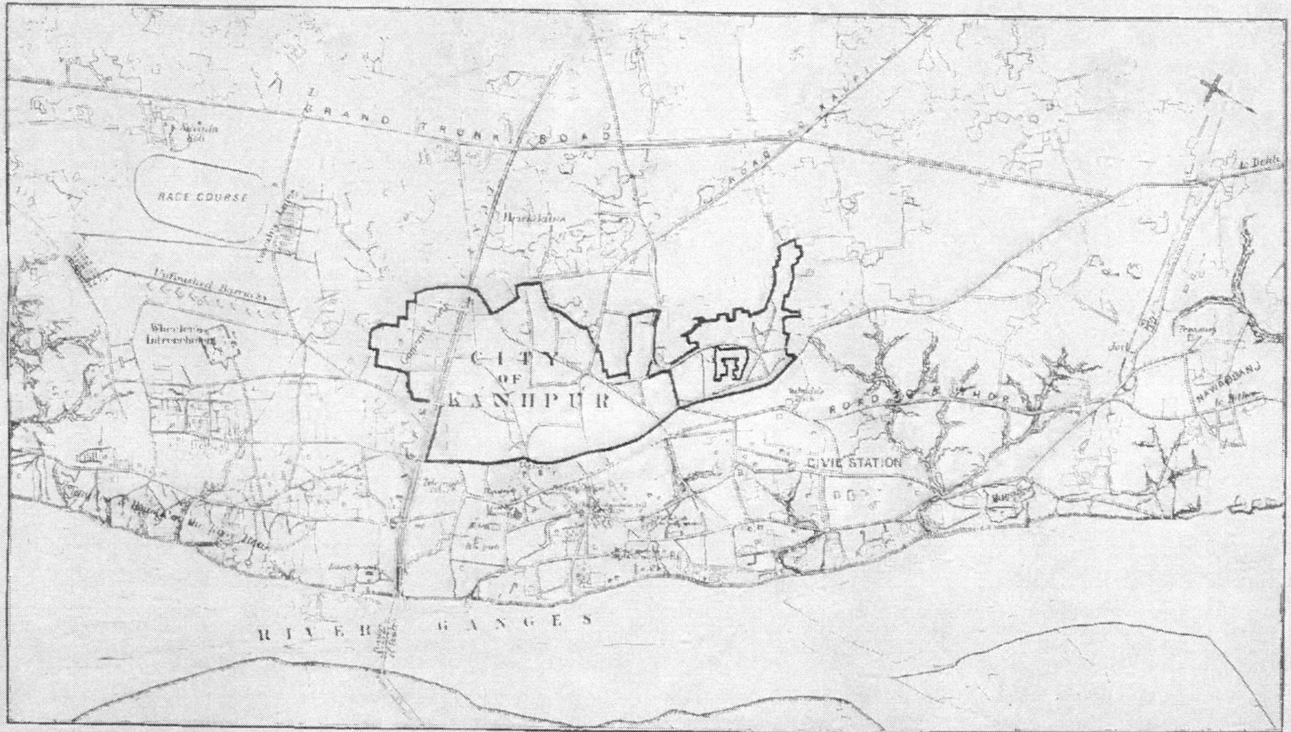

GRAND TRUNK ROAD
RACE COURSE
CITY OF KANHPUR
CIVIL STATION
RIVER GANGES
NAWABGANJ

Book XI. Chapter IV.

1857. Dec. 8.

hundred men of all arms. It was known that the rebels had retreated by the Bithor road, but as it was considered far from improbable that they might attempt to cross into Oudh by the Serai ferry, about three miles from Sheorájpúr, Grant had received discretionary power to change his route in that direction.

He traces the route they had taken.

In the course of his march Grant, careful to examine the traces of the retreat, satisfied himself that the rebels had taken the road leading to the ferry. He therefore continued his march, halting only at sunset for a light meal, direct to Sheorájpúr. He reached that place a little before daylight. Leaving here, under a small guard, the impedimenta not absolutely necessary for combat, Grant dashed across country with the bulk of his force for the ferry. When within about a mile of it he galloped to the front to reconnoitre. Whilst thus engaged, the men of his escort were fortunate enough to capture alive a trooper of the rebel force. From this man Grant learned that he had arrived in time; that the rebel guns were on the banks of the river, and that the crossing was to take place that day. Having satisfied himself that the man had told the truth, Grant sent back orders for the cavalry, guns, and infantry to come on with all speed. The remainder of the story is best told in the words of the noble and gallant soldier who commanded.* "The narrow road ran sometimes parallel to, and sometimes through, a sort of quicksand. Under a

He finds them,

* *Incidents in the Sepoy War*, compiled from the private journals of General Sir Hope Grant, G.C.B.

Book XI. Chapter IV.

1857. Dec. 8.

high bank, and close to the river, we found the long-sought-for 24-pounder * embedded up to its axle-trees. We had great difficulty in getting our guns over this bad ground; but at last we reached sounder soil, and then we advanced rapidly. As soon as we came within one thousand yards of the enemy, a tremendous fire opened upon us; but Lieutenant Warren, a fine young fellow, who commanded the leading guns, never stopped until within five hundred or six hundred yards of the rebels, when he opened fire on them. In a few minutes Captain Middleton joined him with the remainder of the battery. Captain Remmington now galloped up with his troop, and came into action in an excellent position behind a bank, at a range of two hundred yards or less. This concentrated artillery-fire told with such terrible effect upon the enemy, crowded into a mass, with their guns, bullocks, baggage, that they gave way and retreated as fast as possible along the river bank, where it would have been difficult to pursue them in force, owing to the marshy state of the ground. However, the irregular cavalry managed to overtake and to cut up some of them. My gallant regiment, the 9th Lancers, was in support of our batteries. We captured fifteen of the enemy's guns, with the finest bullocks I ever saw, belonging to the Gwáliár contingent. We were only just in time; for as we came up to the ferry, we

and defeats them,

capturing their guns.

* This was one of the two 24-pounders captured in the Kálpi road on the 6th, but which mysteriously disappeared whilst our troops were continuing the pursuit.

found the rebels preparing to embark the guns in some boats which they had collected for the purpose." A gallant and effective deed of arms, told in the modest language eminently characteristic of the chief actor in the scene! But Hope Grant was as modest as he was daring, as careless of self as he was prodigal of his zeal. His forced march of twenty-five miles, and the prompt movement which followed it, enabled him to repair the mismanagement at the Subadár's Tank on the 6th.

Book XI. Chapter IV.

1857. Dec. 8.

Character of Hope Grant.

The rebel army was now utterly crushed. In the two days' fight, the 6th and the 8th, it had lost thirty-two guns, a strong position, and a vast number of killed. The two parts of which its army was composed had been for ever separated; the one driven headlong to Kálpi; the other, prevented from crossing into Oudh, had fled without its guns to Bithor, there still within our reach. These great results had been accomplished by the British with a loss to them of only ninety-nine killed and wounded! *

Results of the fighting on the 6th and 8th.

The battle established the right of Sir Colin Campbell to be regarded as a great commander. In attacking with five thousand men an army of fourteen thousand regular troops, in addition to some odd thousands of irregulars, occupying a very strong position, it was necessary to run some risk; and there can be no doubt that in leaving

Sir Colin Campbell as a general.

* The official return was: two subalterns, one sergeant, ten rank and file, killed; two field officers, three captains, four subalterns, one staff-sergeant, five sergeants, seventy-one rank and file, wounded.

Book XI. Chapter IV.

1857. Dec. 8.

Greathed's weak brigade, not exceeding one thousand men, to guard his centre whilst he massed the rest of his army against the extreme right of the enemy, Sir Colin did leave an opening of which a Napoleon or a Frederic would have taken advantage. But the great thing for a general is to know when to dare. Sir Colin knew that the opponents' general was neither a Napoleon nor a Frederic, and that the soldiers he commanded were neither Frenchmen nor Prussians. He felt that with his actual opponents he could take liberties which they would not resent. It is true that he risked his centre, but the false attack which it made reduced all danger in that quarter to a *minimum*. Knowing his enemy, as he did, it was a sound and daring policy, a policy certain to obtain the end he was aiming at—that of preventing an attack—to order Greathed to feign an onslaught on the enemy's position at the moment he was about to hurl the bulk of his forces against their right wing. This movement would appear to the enemy the necessary corollary of the heavy artillery fire to which they had been subjected from the intrenchment. The plan succeeded, as it eminently deserved to succeed. Completely imposed upon, the enemy's centre and left remained quiet whilst their right was being destroyed. They allowed the centre to be hemmed in in front by Greathed's weak brigade, and on the right by Walpole—and why? Simply because Greathed and Walpole played offensive and not defensive parts. Sir Colin understood Indian warfare well, and he knew that attack supplied inferiority in numbers.

Book XI. Chapter IV.

1857. Dec. 9-11.

The theoretical weakness in his plan of attack was, then, under the circumstances of the case, no weakness at all. The plan was admirably adapted to the occasion, and the execution was worthy of the general. It was no barren victory. One section of the rebel army did indeed escape, though with heavy loss, to Kálpi, but the other, forced to evacuate the town, was pursued to the Ganges, and deprived of its power for mischief on the banks of that river.

Bithor is destroyed.

Nor did Bithor itself escape. Sir Colin Campbell, on receiving from Hope Grant a report of his success, directed that officer to march at once on the residence of Náná Sáhib and destroy it. Grant set out on the 11th. He found the place evacuated. He carried out his orders by blowing up the temple and burning the palace. Amongst the booty discovered in a large well contiguous to the palace were "some curious pots, lamps which seemed of Jewish manufacture, and spoons of a barbaric weight. All were of the purest metal, and all bore an appearance of antique magnificence."

Two parts of Sir Colin's plans have been accomplished.

Of the large programme Sir Colin Campbell had sketched out for his operations in the North-west Provinces and Oudh, the two first had now been accomplished. He had relieved Lakhnao, and he had utterly defeated the rebel army threatening Kánhpúr. His way was now clear for the performance of the third act of the drama—the opening communications between Kánhpúr and the Panjáb. This accomplished, he would be free to take vengeance on Lakhnao, and to reconquer Rohilkhand.

Book XI. Chapter IV.

1857. Dec. 9–11.

Minor parts of the great scheme to be considered.

It is necessary that the reader should bear in mind that whilst the main action of the campaign rested with the army led by the Commander-in-Chief, there were other actors who contributed effectively, though on a smaller scale, to bring to a perfect conclusion the general scheme which had been sketched out. In a previous chapter* I have referred to the order given to Colonel Seaton to escort a convoy from Áligarh to the south-west. His movements, which would also serve to reopen completely communication with the north-west, will be noticed in the next chapter. I shall then have to transport the reader to the east and north-east, to witness the other operations, conducted by columns under Brigadiers Franks and Rowcroft, and by the Nipalese force under Jang Bahádur, having for their object to co-operate with the fourth great movement contemplated by Sir Colin Campbell—the reconquest of Lakhnao.

* Page 118.

BOOK XI.

CHAPTER V.

Sir Colin's movements hampered by want of carriage

After the decisive actions of the 6th and 8th December, Sir Colin Campbell was naturally desirous to push onwards whilst the memory of the defeat of the rebels should be yet fresh in the minds of the combatants and their sympathisers. But there was one material difficulty in the way of his progress. His means of transport were restricted. It had taxed his energies to the utmost to procure carriage in sufficient abundance to serve for the transit of the ladies and children, sick, and wounded he had rescued from the Residency. These, to the number of at least two thousand, had been sent to Allahábád. In leaving Outram with four thousand men at the Álambágh, he had supplied him with the means of moving his troops in case of necessity. For his own entire army, forced to march rapidly a distance of fifty miles, he had not retained the wherewithal to enter upon a harassing campaign. He could

Book XI. Chapter V.

1857. December.

equip a column, but not an army. The supply of camels from northern and central India was cut off. He was forced, then, to remain inactive until the carriage conveying the convoy of ladies should return from Allahábád.

The carriage arrives,

This carriage did not reach Kánhpúr till the 23rd December. Meanwhile Sir Colin had been maturing his plans. Fathgarh—the Fathgarh whose Nawáb had cast in his lot with the rebels, and had aided the mutinous sepoys in the destruction of our countrymen *—Fathgarh was the first point to be attacked. The occupation of this place, about midway between Allahábád and Dehlí, would complete the command over the Doáb, which had been secured only partially by the reconquest of Dehlí and the maintenance of Agra and Allahábád. That point regained, Rohilkhand would still remain to be conquered and Lakhnao to be regained. To quench the embers of the insurrection in the minor places on the left bank of the Jamná, and to the east of Allahábád, flying columns would, it was hoped, prove sufficient.

and Sir Colin detaches Walpole to Mainpúri.

Sir Colin Campbell's movements against Fathgarh were planned with his usual caution. Availing himself of Seaton's march from Aligarh, he directed Walpole to make a semicircular sweep by the Kálpi road *viá* Ákbarpúr to Itáwa and Mainpúri, at once threatening the Kálpi force and clearing of rebels the districts dependent upon Ágra. At Mainpúri Walpole would effect a junc-

* *Vide* volume i. pp. 335 to 346.

tion with Seaton, who was to wait for him there. These, uniting their forces, were then to march on Fathgarh, upon which place the Commander-in-Chief would move by the direct road from Kánhpúr. In recounting these separate movements, I propose to follow first Walpole, then Seaton; then, leaving the two combined, to proceed to the leader, who had the shortest distance to traverse, and upon whom it devolved to fight the decisive battle.

Walpole marches on Itáwa.

Walpole, taking with him the 2nd and 3rd battalions Rifle Brigade, a detachment 38th Foot, Bourchier's battery, Blunt's troop of horse artillery, and one company of sappers, set out on the morning of the 18th December. The column marched by Ákbarpúr to Itáwa without adventure of any kind. Itáwa had been plundered in the early days of the mutiny.* It was now a wreck; the church, the court-house, the private residences were in ruins; but it was now held by the rebels.

A few fanatic rebels bar his way.

On learning of Walpole's approach the majority of these men evacuated the place. A few fanatics, however, occupying a covered, square, loop-holed enclosure, determined to hold out to the last. Few in number, armed only with muskets, they were animated by a spirit fiercer even than the spirit of despair—by a determination to die martyrs to their cause. Walpole reconnoitred the place. It was, for a place to stop an army, insignificant. It could easily be stormed. Yet to

* Volume i. pp. 160 to 163.

Book XI. Chapter V. 1857. December.

storm it in the face of its occupants would cost valuable life, and it seemed that easier and less costly means were available.

The place they occupy is blown up.

These easy means were at first tried. Hand grenades were thrown in; an attempt was made to smoke them out with burning straw. But all in vain. Through their loop-holes the rebels poured in a constant and effective fire on the assailants, and for three hours kept them at bay. At last it was resolved to blow up the whole place. For this purpose Bourchier, aided by Scratchley of the Engineers, made a mine, with a number of his gun cartridges, in the roof. The explosion conferred on the defenders the martyrs' honours they coveted. It buried them in the ruins.

Walpole reaches Mainpúri.

This happened on the 29th December. The column marched without further adventure to Mainpúri, and the following day, the 3rd February, joined Brigadier Seaton's force at Béwar, fifteen miles distant, on the road to Fathgarh.

Composition of Seaton's force.

Meanwhile Seaton, appointed to the command of the force ordered to escort to Kánhpúr a large convoy of grain and stores,* had set out on the 9th December for Áligarh. He had under him, of artillery, two hundred and thirty-three men, manning six 9-pounder guns, two 6-pounders, two 18-pounders, one 8-inch howitzer, and two 5½-inch mortars; of cavalry, a squadron of the Carabineers, and a few of the 9th Lancers, one hundred and forty in all, and Hodson's Horse, five hundred and fifty strong, led by Hodson; of

* *Vide* page 118.

Book XI. Chapter V. 1857. December.

infantry, the 1st Fusiliers, three hundred and seventy-six strong; the 7th Panjáb Infantry, five hundred and forty strong; of sappers, one hundred and twenty. He was joined on the march by Wales's Horse and some Sikhs.

Seaton, learning that the rebels are in the Áligarh district,

The night before Seaton left Dehlí he was informed that a considerable body of rebels had assembled in the Áligarh district, and that they were threatening to attack the small force with which Colonel Farquhar held it. With characteristic vigour, Seaton, in spite of his convoy, proceeded to Áligarh by forced marches. Arriving there, he placed his convoy under the guns of the Áligarh fort, made arrangements for a field hospital, rid himself of every ounce of extra baggage, and taking with him a small portion of the fort garrison (one hundred men of the 3rd Europeans) under Major Eld, set out to join Farquhar.

marches against them,

He found him encamped at a place called Gangarí, close to the suspension bridge over the Káli river. The enemy were believed to be some thirteen miles distant. Seaton at once, then, crossed the river, marched a mile and a half, encamped in some fields, and sent Hodson to the front to reconnoitre.

and sends Hodson to reconnoitre.

Seaton and his soldiers are breakfasting, or about to breakfast,

Whilst Hodson, accompanied by Major Light of the Bengal Artillery, a very gallant and skilful soldier, were galloping to the front to reconnoitre, Seaton and the other officers sat down to their breakfasts, whilst the men, hungry after their march, watched the cook-boys as they prepared for them the same stimulating meal. The officers had breakfasted, the men were about to sit down

Book XI. Chapter V.

1857. December.

when the alarm is sounded.

to their breakfasts, already placed, smoking hot, before them, when the alarm called them, fasting, to their posts. Half a minute before, Light, galloping at full speed, had brought the information that the enemy was advancing on both flanks. At once all was bustle and animation. The infantry, without waiting to put on their coats, turned out, as in the Dehlí days, with their muskets and side-arms. The cavalry were in their saddles in less than three minutes. The gunners, always on the alert, were not a whit behindhand. In less time than it has taken to describe it, all arms of the force, thus suddenly alarmed, were in their places. On the extreme right were the Carabineers and Lancers; on the extreme left Hodson's Horse; the 1st Fusiliers and one hundred men of the 3rd Europeans were in the centre behind the guns; on the left of the 1st Fusiliers were the Sikhs and Rifles.

The troops turn out, fasting.

Seaton advances against the rebels.

Seaton moved forward to meet the enemy. He had scarcely set his troops in motion when Hodson rode up and reported to the Brigadier that he had seen the enemy some miles in front filing through a village with guns; that having watched their further proceedings, he had sent on Light to make his report. Hardly had he finished speaking when the heads of the enemy's columns appeared in sight—two large bodies, one on each flank. Their infantry soon followed, filling up the gap between the two. Seaton at once ordered the guns to the front. These at once opened on the enemy. The hostile guns replied, and though the reply was feeble, yet from the position they

Book XI. Chapter V.

1857. December.

had taken up they were able to rake the British line. Seeing this, Wardlaw of the Carabineers, who had received discretionary orders, charged the enemy's battery. The guns turned at once upon the gallant soldiers led most gallantly. But nothing stopped them. Out of the five officers with the Carabineers three, Wardlaw, Hudson, and Vyse, fell dead; the lieutenant of the handful of Lancers charging with them, Head, was dangerously wounded, whilst of the men six were killed and eleven wounded; but the guns were captured! The cavalry were then led by the only surviving officer, Lieutenant Russell, along the fields, and his men, making good use of their carbines, cleared out the enemy without further loss.

Gallant charge of the Carabineers, who, in spite of losses, capture the guns.

Whilst this was happening on the left, Hodson on the right had dashed with his regiment against the enemy's horse, and had overthrown them.

Hodson overthrows the enemy on the right.

The infantry did not pause to receive. Throwing away their arms, they ran to hide themselves in the fields and ravines, or to continue their flight over the country. They had lost all their guns, one 9-pounder and two 6-pounders, and—what was of greater importance—had received "great discouragement." It appeared that they had no idea that Seaton had come up; they hoped to have to do only with Farquhar's small force of Bilúchis. The discovery that a considerable European force was marching through the districts was a warning to them that from that time forth their occupation was gone!

The enemy completely defeated.

Their mistake!

This fight received from the name of the town

Book XI. Chapter V. 1857. December.

near which it was fought the title of combat of Khásganj. That town was occupied the following morning. It was a strong place, filled with brick houses, and surrounded by old gardens, encompassed with strong mud walls, and, if well-defended, would have been hard to take. Seaton then pushed on to Sahávar, and the next day, the 17th, to Pattiáli. When, however, passing through a village about two miles of this place, a few shots were heard, and Hodson, who was with the advanced guard, sent word that the enemy's outposts had fired their muskets, and galloped off. On receiving this report, Seaton brought all his men through the village, then halted, and served out bread and grog to the men, whilst Hodson and the engineers went to the front to reconnoitre.

Seaton occupies Khásganj, and pushes on to Pattiáli, where, hearing of the rebels, he sends Hodson to reconnoitre.

In about twenty minutes Hodson returned to report that the enemy had formed across the road, barring the entrance to Pattiáli; that their right and right centre were resting on some large ravines, on the right face and front of which earthworks had been thrown up; that their left centre and left were posted in front of gardens and enclosures, covered on the extreme left by their cavalry, posted in an open country. In front of the centre of their position, and about half a mile from it, was a small village, through which, they had calculated, the British force would advance. They had laid their plans accordingly.

Hodson reports the position occupied by the enemy.

On hearing this report Seaton disposed his force for action. On the right he massed Hodson's Horse, the Carabineers and Lancers, and

Seaton forms his plan.

Book XI. Chapter V. 1857. December.

some light guns; in the centre the Europeans; on the left the native infantry, and the heavy guns. His plan was to turn their left flank.

Begins the battle with an artillery duel;

Occupying, then, the small village of which I have spoken with a few men, and thus constituting that village the left of his position, he brought four guns to the front on the extreme right, and sent four more to take up a position almost enfilading the enemy's position from left to right. But before these could unlimber, the enemy opened fire from a battery of twelve guns. In a few minutes, however, the British guns replied, and the duel commenced in earnest. The artillery contest lasted about thirty minutes, the cavalry and infantry meanwhile being halted. But as the fire from the British guns had, during those thirty minutes, been gradually gaining on the enemy, when that time had elapsed, Seaton could contain himself no longer. Giving the order to the infantry to advance, he charged himself at the head of the cavalry. The enemy did not await that charge. They broke and fled, and when the infantry, which had advanced on receiving the order, reached the spot, they found that their efforts were not required: they had been forestalled by their gallant Brigadier.*

then, charging, gains it with his cavalry.

* "On we move, and, to our surprise, without receiving a shot from the enemy, whose guns, we found, on reaching their position, had been captured by Colonel Seaton, who had led the Staff and horse artillery, with some few of Hodson's Horse. In fact, seeing the enemy wavering, this bold charge, led by Seaton, decided matters, so far as the guns were concerned." — The 1st

Book XI. Chapter V.

1857. December.

The rebels are pursued and slaughtered;

The gallant charge of Seaton decided the day; but it did not stop the slaughter. The Carabineers, the Lancers, Hodson's Horse, and the artillery "got in" among the fleeing enemy, and pursued them for seven miles, taking blood for blood. It is computed that not less than six hundred of the rebels succumbed in this pursuit. On the side of the British the loss was singularly small, one man only having been killed and three wounded. The number of guns taken amounted to thirteen. Amongst the trophies captured on this occasion were the elephant, the silver howdah, and the sword of the Hakím, hereditary commander-in-chief of the Nawáb of Farrakhábád. The Hakím himself had been killed by Hodson. In the choice of an open position in front of one very defensible, he had clearly demonstrated that the qualities which go to form an efficient commander-in-chief are not hereditary.

among them their hereditary commander-in-chief.

Great effect on the country of this victory.

Seaton halted three days at Pattiáli, chiefly to give time to the administrative officers to reorganise their establishments and settle the country. This halt showed him the marvellous effect which his triumphant march had produced. On all sides the rebels were falling back, terrified, on Fathgarh, or endeavouring to cross the Ganges into Oudh. Some bodies of them, of whose movements he heard, and against whom he despatched a small force, fled on the appearance even

Bengal Fusiliers after the fall of Delhi (*Blackwood's Magazine*). The writer of the article was at the time attached to the 1st Fusiliers.

Book XI. Chapter V. — 1857. December.

of a reconnoitring party!* Seaton thought, then, that he might fairly return for his convoy.

Hodson disposes of two noted rebels.

Accordingly on the 21st he retraced his steps. On the 22nd, when within a few miles of Khásganj, he was met by Mr. Cocks, the Civil Commissioner of the division, with the information that a notorious rebel, named Jawáhir Singh, who had fought against him at Pattiáli, had doubled round, and had returned with one son, wounded in that engagement, to Khásganj. Hodson was at once sent to the front to dispose of the question. He disposed of it in his own manner. He killed the son; the father, taken prisoner, was tried by a military commission and blown from a gun that evening. He deserved his fate, for not only was he in receipt of a pension from the British Government as a native officer, but he was receiving also the emoluments attaching to the Order of British India, of which he was a member.

Seaton arranges for the convoy,

From Khásganj Seaton sent Major Eld to escort the captured guns to Áligarh and to despatch the convoy thence under charge of the escort with which he furnished him. He then resumed his march to Íta. There he received information that the Rájá of Mainpúri, a debauchee, named

and marches on Mainpúri.

* "On the appearance in the distance of the reconnoitring party they had fled precipitately. The officer went over the ground on which they had been encamped, and found their food still cooking on the fire, their pots and pans, and all their baggage standing apart. The fear of us had fallen on all the district round about."—*From Cadet to Colonel*, by Sir Thomas Seaton, K.C.B.

Book XI. Chapter V.

1857. December.

Téj Singh, had raised a force with the intention of barring the road to him. Upon Mainpúri, then, Seaton marched, *viâ* Karáoli.

Learns on his march that the rebel Rájá is in his path, to oppose his progress.

At Karáoli, fourteen miles from Mainpúri, Seaton learned from his scouts that the young Rájá had drawn up his little force in position across the road from Karáoli just above the junction with the grand trunk road leading to Ágra, and that he had occupied walled gardens on either side of the road, and had covered the road itself with field-works.

Seaton out-manœuvres,

Seaton's plan was instantly made. When within a mile of the enemy's position, he turned off from the main road by a path to the right, hiding his movement, as far as possible, by the dust made by the cavalry, until he had gained a position whence he could rake the enemy's line from left to right. In vain did the enemy bring their guns to bear on him. Seaton continued his movement until he had reached the point he was aiming at. The British guns then opened. Two rounds were sufficient. The enemy fled in disorder, abandoning on the field and in the fort, which they did not attempt to defend, eight guns. Their loss cannot be properly estimated; it did not probably exceed one hundred. Seaton's amounted to two wounded!

and defeats him.

Seaton halts at Mainpúri. Hodson proposes to open communication with the Commander-in-Chief.

The action near Mainpúri was fought on the 27th December. Seaton halted in the vicinity of that place till the 31st, whilst Hodson of Hodson's Horse made a daring and most successful effort to open communications with the Commander-in-Chief. Many gallant deeds were performed during the mutiny, but not one exceeded this in cool and deliberate courage.

Book XI. Chapter V.

1857. December.

My opinion of Hodson has been already recorded. He was a free-lance of the Middle Ages. But if his action towards the unarmed and captive princes of the House of Taimúr proved that the instincts of the natural savage reigned strong within him, his fearlessness, his contempt of danger, his joy in the battle, his ever cool brain, made him invaluable as a partisan leader. When a risk for the general good was to be undertaken, Hodson always came forward to undertake it. In matters affecting, or likely to affect, him physically, he never counted the cost. He was invaluable to a commander. Was information regarding the enemy's movements required, Hodson would get it. Was a delicate movement at a particular period of a battle considered essential, the execution of it was entrusted to Hodson. Always in the position where his presence was needed, always the first to detect a false movement, always with his life in his hand ready to risk it, Hodson could not fail to be the right-hand man of his general. "He is indefatigable," said Seaton, to General Penny, when asking for his services—"a soldier of the highest class; I have unbounded confidence in him, and would rather have him than five hundred more men."

Hodson invaluable as a partisan leader.

The undertaking to which he now devoted himself was one requiring nerve, intelligence, and activity of the highest order. Seaton's camp was at Mainpúri. The Commander-in-Chief was reported to be at Gúrsahaiganj, about forty miles

Danger of the undertaking he proposed to accomplish.

Book XI. Chapter V.

1857. December.

from Mainpúri, marching for Fathgarh. But the country between the two places was the country into which the rebels, so often beaten, had been driven, and though some, doubtless, had reached Fathgarh, others had lingered on the road. The rebels beaten at Mainpúri must of necessity be there.

Hodson and M'Dowell start on their dangerous errand.

Still, it was very advisable to attempt to open out communications with the Commander-in-Chief, and, the task being difficult and dangerous, Hodson naturally volunteered to execute it. His offer was accepted, and on the morning of the 30th he set out, taking with him his second in command, M'Dowell, a very gallant officer, and seventy-five of his own men. He carried on his person Colonel Seaton's despatches.

Hodson rode straight to Béwar, fourteen miles distant. There he left all his escort except twenty-five men. With these and with M'Dowell he continued his course to Chibramáo, another fourteen miles, where he made another halt.

Leaving their escort behind, they reach their destination to find the Chief still distant from it.

From this point he determined to push on to Gúrsahaiganj accompanied only by M'Dowell. The distance was about twelve miles. Leaving, then, the twenty-five native troopers in Chibramáo, the two officers rode on alone. They reached Gúrsahaiganj in safety, only to find, however, that the Commander-in-Chief's camp was at Míran-ká-serai, some fifteen miles further off.

Alarming nature of the situation;

The situation was alarming. The villagers reported that the rebels, seven hundred strong with four guns, were within two miles of the place. But hesitation never entered into the calculations

Book XI. Chapter V.

1857. December.

of Hodson. He and his comrade continued their journey, and reached the headquarter camp, without adventure, at 4 o'clock in the morning. They had ridden fifty-five miles in ten hours, without change of horse.

but they push on, and gain the Chief's camp in safety.

It happened that on the road between Chibramáo and Gúrsahaiganj, Hodson had bestowed alms upon a native. A very short time after he had left the former place, it had been entered by a party of two thousand rebels on their way to Fathgarh. These men overpowered and killed the troopers, and having gathered from the villagers that Hodson and his companion would return, they resolved to lay wait for them. Meanwhile, Hodson had been splendidly received by Sir Colin Campbell, had been closeted with him the greater part of the day, and had dined with him. At 8 o'clock in the evening, he and M'Dowell set out on their return journey. They proceeded without adventure till within five or six miles of Chibramáo. Here they were stopped by the native whom Hodson had befriended in the morning, with the information that Chibramáo was occupied by the rebels, who were on the look-out for them. It was near midnight, the moon was bright, and the wind cold. It was neither the time nor place for deliberation, nor did Hodson require it. He determined to push on. Dismounting, then, from their horses, he and his companion led them to the soft unmacadamised strip which forms the border to an Indian road, and followed by the native, walked on. They gradually approached Chibramáo, they entered it,

While he is there the road he traversed is occupied by the rebels.

Hodson and M'Dowell start to return;

they are warned of the danger threatening them.

By prudent boldness they escape the danger.

Book XI. Chapter V. 1857. December.

they saw the camp of the enemy, they heard the hum of voices; but they reached unseen the further end of the village. On emerging from it, they dismissed their guide, with a promise from him to join them in their camp, remounted, and rode on. At Béwar they were met by a party which Seaton, hearing of the surprise at Chibramáo, had sent out to look for them.

and return.

Seaton, indeed, alarmed at the reports brought in by the troopers left at Béwar, had moved on to that place on the 31st. Here he remained with his convoy till the 3rd January, when, as already related, Brigadier Walpole marched into Béwar. Seaton's force came at once under his orders.

Seaton effects a junction with Walpole.

BOOK XI.

CHAPTER VI.

It is time now to return to the Commander-in-Chief.

The carriage necessary for his movements returned from Allahábád on the 23rd December. Sir Colin marched from Kánhpúr on the 24th. Clearing the country lying between the main road and the road by which he had despatched Walpole with his left brigade, and stripping the Ganges of boats with a brigade on his right, Sir Colin reached Míran-ká-serai on the 30th. It was at this place that he met Hodson in the manner I have related in the preceding chapter. The following day he reached Gúrsahaiganj. Here a road branches off from the main road, and leads the traveller over the Káli Naddi, traversed by a suspension bridge at a distance of five miles from the junction of the roads to Fathgarh.

Sir Colin Campbell sets out for Fathgarh.

The advance of the Commander-in-Chief had been acting on the various detachments of rebels

The rebels driven from all sides to-

Book XI. Chapter VI. — 1857. Dec. 30-31. wards Fathgarh.

in the manner of a loaded net sunk in a stream and drawn upwards by men on both banks. Walpole and Seaton prevented escape on one side, Sir Colin drove his victims up on the other. There was one outlet, however, which neither commanded, and for this the harassed tribe was now making. The outlet was Fathgarh.

They determine, too late, to destroy the bridge over the Káli Naddi.

The Káli Naddi barred the entrance of a hostile force into Fathgarh. But I have said that it was spanned by a suspension bridge. The rebels, jammed into the place from all sides, some fleeing from Seaton, some from Walpole, some from the Commander-in-Chief, began, recovering from their panic, to reflect that their last chance of safety lay in the removal of the suspension bridge. Like so many of their reflections, it came too late.

They begin their work of destruction.

However, on the 31st they sent down a party to destroy the bridge. Had they worked with a will they might have succeeded. But though they effected some damage that night, they left the piers and the main chains intact, hoping, it may be supposed, to deal with them on the morrow.

But are checked by Adrian Hope.

But for the destruction of the bridge there was to be no morrow. Early on the morning of the 1st January, Sir Colin detached Adrian Hope's brigade, reinforced with two 24-pounders and one 8-inch howitzer, under Lieutenant Vaughan of the Naval Brigade, and some engineers, sappers, and cavalry, to the Káli Naddi, with orders to drive away the enemy and to repair the bridge in case it should be found damaged.

Book XI. Chapter VI.

1857. Jan. 1–2.

On the approach of Adrian Hope the rebels fled, and the engineers and sappers at once set to work to repair it, covered by a strong infantry picket. They laboured with so much earnestness that day and through the night, that by half-past 7 o'clock the next morning the bridge was in a fit state to be traversed.

Sir Colin comes up and reconnoitres the ground beyond the bridge.

The labours of the British troops had but just been completed, and the sailors, who had helped in the work, were on the river-bank washing their garments, when the Commander-in-Chief and his staff arrived to examine the position. Halting, he noticed a large village, facing the bridge, at a distance of about three hundred yards, flanked on its right by some tall trees. In front of the village was a small square building, which proved afterwards to be a toll-house. The road from the river-bank gradually ascended to a point beyond the village, which it intersected.

The rebels open fire upon him.

Sir Colin had had barely time to make these observations when the rebels, who till then had kept out of sight, poured into the village, and opened a heavy musketry fire upon the group of which the Commander-in-Chief was the centre. Under cover of this fire, they brought up two guns, and opened out on the pickets sent across to guard the bridge-head, and on the bridge itself. Sir Colin at once sent orders to the main body of his troops, then about four miles in rear, to push on. Till they could come up, he directed Adrian Hope to hold the bridge, but on no account to attack the enemy.

Adrian Hope keeps them in check.

Adrian Hope at once detached the 53rd across

Book XI. Chapter VI.

1857. Jan. 2.

the bridge to reinforce the pickets, directing them to extend under cover of the bank, and to keep up a brisk musketry fire on the enemy. One wing of the 93rd he kept in hand, ready, if necessary, to support the skirmishers, the other wing being posted three miles lower down guarding a ford.

The 53rd lie down beyond the bridge and open fire.

The 53rd, crossing the bridge, found a partial though inadequate cover from the mounds and ridges of earth and the tall grass covering the bank. Lying down here, they opened on the enemy a very effective fire. Meanwhile, Vaughan's three guns crossed the bridge, and taking up a position close to a yellow bungalow near its northern end, opened fire on the village.

Vaughan dismounts one of the enemy's pieces.

Still the rebels continued their fire, and their leader, noting that a gun placed under cover of the toll-house would sweep the bridge, brought up one of his pieces to that position between 2 and 3 o'clock, and opened from it. The effect was most damaging to our men, one shot alone killing or wounding eight of them. This practice continued for some time, when the guns of the Naval Brigade, splendidly directed by Vaughan, succeeded in dismounting the piece and blowing up the tumbril.*

* The manner in which this work was done reflects so much credit on all who were concerned in it, that it merits a notice more detailed than that which I have given in the text. "Lieutenant Vaughan now pointed and fired one of our guns at the small gun of the enemy, which was concealed behind the corner of a house, and annoying us much. His first shot struck the roof of the house; his second struck the angle of the wall about half-way down; and a third dismounted the gun and destroyed the carriage. Captain Peel, who was standing

Book XI. Chapter VI.

1857. Jan. 2.

The gun which had caused so much destruction had scarcely been dismounted when the 53rd, disregarding their orders to remain where they were, made a simultaneous rush to the front on the toll-house, clearing out the enemy. Sir Colin was furious at this disobedience, but he vainly tried to check it.* The men of the 53rd had heard that they were to be relieved, and they were determined to be in the front. There was nothing for it but to support them. Fortunately, the heads of the main column were now at hand. The 93rd crossed the bridge in support of the 53rd, whilst Greathed's brigade, following, advanced up the slope to the left, flanked on the extreme left by the cavalry led by Hope Grant. As the infantry advanced on the village, the enemy abandoned it. Upon this, Hope Grant, taking on his men round at a trot, caught the enemy as they were emerging from the other end, and, charging in echelon of squadrons, completely broke them. "Then despair seized upon the rebel mass; breaking their ranks, throwing aside their

The 53rd rush to the front.

Complete defeat of the rebels.

by, said: 'Thank you, Mr. Vaughan; perhaps you will now be so good as to blow up the tumbril.' Lieutenant Vaughan fired a fourth shot, which passed near it; and a fifth, which blew it up and killed several of the enemy. 'Thank you,' said Captain Peel, in his blandest and most courteous tones; 'I will now go and report to Sir Colin.'"—*The Shannon's Brigade in India.* E. H. Verney.

* "The Commander-in-Chief was terribly annoyed, and, riding up to the regiment, pitched into it well. But these wild Irishmen were incorrigible. Whenever he began to speak, a lot of them exclaimed, as loud as they could, 'Three cheers for the Commander-in-Chief, boys!' until at length he himself was obliged to go away, laughing."—Hope Grant's *Incidents.*

Book XI. Chapter VI.

1857. Jan. 2.

arms, they fled in wild confusion; but the horsemen were upon them and amongst them, and the slaughter was terrible; for several miles they rode along spearing and cutting down at every step; and the progress of their swift advance might be marked by the smoke of exploded tumbrils curling up amidst the dark-green trees." *

The rout of the enemy was complete. Eight guns, several colours, palanquins, and ammunition waggons fell into the hands of the victors.

They flee into Rohilkhand.

The rebels did not cease their flight even when they reached the fort of Fathgarh, but, hastily seizing on all that was portable in their camp outside that fort, hurried in panic and dismay across the same river which many of them had crossed but six short months before, arrogant with the pride of revolt, thirsting for the blood of the officers whom whilom they had sworn to obey! They fled into Rohilkhand.

Ovation given by the soldiers to Sir Colin.

The ovation the Commander-in-Chief received from his soldiers that evening is thus described by an eye-witness, one of the gallant actors in that stirring scene. "Their return from this" (the return of the cavalry from the pursuit) "was a stirring sight of war. In front came the 9th Lancers, with three captured standards at their head; the wild-looking Sikh horsemen rode in the rear. As they passed the Commander-in-Chief he took off his hat to them, with some words of praise and thanks. The Lancers shook their lances in the air and cheered; the Sikhs

* *Blackwood's Magazine*, October 1858.

took up the cry, waving their sabres above their heads. The men carrying the standards gave them to the wind; the Highland brigade, who were encamping close by, ran down and cheered both the victorious cavalry and the veteran Chief, waving their bonnets in the air. It was a fair sight, and reminded one of the old days of chivalry. When Sir Colin rode back through the camp of the Highlanders, the enthusiasm of the men exceeded description." *

Book XI. Chapter VI.

1858. Jan. 2.

Sir Colin's losses amounted to four men killed, two officers and eight men wounded. Those of the enemy were naturally much greater.

Gallantry of Roberts.

I have mentioned the skilful conduct of Vaughan of the Naval Brigade at this action, but I cannot quit the subject without referring to the gallantry of Roberts, the same Roberts who so distinguished himself recently in Afgháhistán. In pursuing the rebels, this officer, then a lieutenant, came suddenly upon and engaged two sepoys with a standard, cut one of them down, and captured the standard. He subsequently cut down another sepoy who was keeping a trooper at bay. For these acts Roberts received the Victoria Cross.

Sir Colin re-occupies Fathgarh,

Sir Colin halted for the night some twelve miles from Fathgarh. Early the next morning he marched for that place, blew open the gate of the fort, and entered without opposition. So great had been the previous confidence, and so complete the present panic of the rebels, that they had left in it uninjured a valuable stock of timber, stored for the purpose of making gun-carriages, steam

* *Blackwood's Magazine*, October 1858.

Book XI. Chapter VI.

1858. January.

engines, guns of all sorts, and a large quantity of soldiers' clothing. They had even neglected to cut the bridge of boats communicating across the Ganges with the opposite bank. This was at once secured.

and there concentrates his flying columns.

Jan. 4.

The next day Walpole's column, strengthened by Seaton's, and escorting the convoy, marched into Fathgarh. The army thus concentrated amounted to more than ten thousand men, well supplied with camp equipage and means of transport.

The third portion of his programme accomplished.

Thus was accomplished successfully the third portion of the original programme of the Commander-in-Chief. Communication with the north-west had been re-established: the Doáb had been cleared of rebels. Those rebels had escaped into Rohilkhand. That province and the province of Oudh still remained in open revolt. The dealing with them was to constitute the fourth scene of the drama.

Sir Colin Campbell is in favour of dealing with Rohilkhand before reconquering Oudh.

It was the opinion of Sir Colin Campbell that the three months of cold weather which yet remained to him might be most profitably employed by following the enemy into Rohilkhand. Stamping out the rebellion in that province the submission of the whole of the north-west would be assured. The separate forces then operating, as will be hereafter described, in western and central India, in Rájpútáná and in Bandalkhand, would at the same time restore order and tranquillity throughout those parts of India. Oudh alone would remain; and Sir Colin was of opinion that Oudh, hemmed in by the Gúrkahs

Book XI. Chapter VI.

1858. January.

in one extremity, and by troops whom he would dispose in summer quarters from that extremity to the further border, might wait his pleasure—might remain, that is to say, for some months longer in the hands of the rebels, until the ensuing cold season would permit his troops to operate more effectually in that country. His European troops he regarded as the mainstay, the backbone of his army, and he was unwilling, if it could be avoided, to expose them to the exhaustion and loss inseparable from a hot-weather campaign—a campaign carried on under circumstances which would often require the employment of small detachments, hurried and forced marches, exposure to the mid-day sun, and possibly to the heavy autumnal rains.

Lord Canning prefers that the reconquest of Lakhnao should first be attempted.

But, in the opinion of the Aulic Council of the Government of India, the political exigencies of the time were so pressing, that they overbore considerations which, if prompted partly by sound rules of military science, were dictated in the main by regard for the health and preservation of the European soldier. Lord Canning and the members of his Council were guided in the views they propounded by two great principles: the one, that no rest should be given to the rebels—that they must be attacked and pursued until they should submit; the other, that the main object of the next movement should be the recapture of Lakhnao. These were cardinal points with the Government. They were supported, too, by another, which, if a minor, was yet not an unimportant consideration. I allude to the co-operation of the

Book XI. Chapter VI.

1858. January.

Gúrkahs, led by the Prime Minister of Nipál, Jang Bahádur. These troops, ten thousand in number, were occupying a position from which they could co-operate effectively with the British in Oudh. Were Sir Colin to deal immediately with Oudh, they would join in the action. But it could not be expected, if the Oudh campaign were adjourned, that these men, natives of the Himalayas, would remain during the hot and rainy seasons in the plains exposed to a climate with which they were naturally unfitted to cope.

Arguments in favour of the course adopted by Lord Canning.

There are few, I think, who would be disposed now to question the wisdom of the course recommended by the Government of India. It seems to me that every consideration favoured its adoption. Alike in war and in politics, it is always advisable to strike a decisive blow at the most important point of the enemy opposed to you. In this case Lakhnao was that point. Lakhnao taken, the heart of the rebels would be broken. No other great rallying-place would remain to them. So long, on the other hand, as that regal city should remain in their possession, their adherents would continue to nourish hope, and it would require more than ordinary tact and care to prevent the outbreak of rebellion in parts which had been already over-run.

Again, of the two provinces, Rohilkhand and Oudh, the latter was by far the most formidable, the most important. The pacification of Rohilkhand would produce little or no effect on the men of Oudh. On the contrary, the re-conquest of Lakhnao would be felt in every village and in

Book XI. Chapter VI.

1858. January.

every corner of Rohilkhand. To this must be added the important consideration that whilst Outram was, with some difficulty, holding the Álambágh with nearly four thousand men, rebels from all parts of India were daily crowding into Lakhnao. This fact alone would show that the case of Lakhnao was the more pressing.

The Commander-in-Chief adheres to Lord Canning's views.

The necessity of dealing in the first instance a deadly blow at Lakhnao was insisted upon with so much force by Lord Canning that it became a law to the Commander-in-Chief. It devolved, then, upon him to make his preparations to carry into effect the settled plan.

Advantageous position occupied by Sir Colin at Fathgarh.

At Fathgarh, situated on the Ganges, at the south-western extremity of the border-line between Oudh and Rohilkhand, Sir Colin was occupying a position of no small advantage. It effectually barred the entrance into the reconquered districts of mutineers from the capital of Rohilkhand—Barélí—seventy-seven miles distant; from the north-western division of Oudh; and from Lakhnao. The river-line between Fathgarh and Kánhpúr was strongly held, there being intermediate posts at Bithor and Miran-ka-Serai. It was impossible for Sir Colin Campbell to undertake the contemplated measures against Lakhnao without the aid of a siege-train. Now, the siege-train was at Ágra. The distance between Ágra and Kánhpúr, the point whence the advance on Lakhnao must be made, is one hundred and seventy-nine miles. The road passed through Itáwa, whence Walpole had but recently expelled the rebels, and in the vicinity of districts cleared by Seaton. The

The road between Kánhpúr and A'gra protected on the left flank,

Book XI. Chapter VI.

1858. January.

victory near Fathgarh and the occupation of that place by Sir Colin protected it against attacks from the left during its progress.

and on the right.

It was scarcely less secure on its right. For, although the broken remnant of the Gwáliár contingent was supposed to be at Kálpi or in its vicinity, the men forming it could scarcely have recovered from the heavy blow and sore discouragement inflicted upon them on the 6th December. It seemed almost certain, too, that they would feel in their rear the effects of the superhuman efforts which it was known were being made by the British troops in Central India and in Bandalkhand to get at them; whilst the fact that Kánhpúr was guarded by a brigade under Inglis, that the communications with Allahábád were preserved by a Madras brigade under Carthew, and that those between that place and Banáras were protected by another brigade under Franks, left them, in reality, but one line upon which they could act against the siege-train—the line by Akbarpúr, and that was the line which Walpole had but very recently cleared, and along which no force could march from Kálpi without exposing its right to Kánhpúr and Bithor.

Sir Colin makes preparations for Lakhnao.

The siege-train was then ordered from Ágra. Whilst it was on its way, Sir Colin had time to organise the measures he considered necessary to secure his conquests and to facilitate his movements. To guard the position at Fathgarh and the districts to the west and south-west of it, including Itáwa, Mainpúri, and Miran-ka-Serai, he required an officer of more than ordinary intelli-

Book XI. Chapter VI. 1858. January.

gence and decision, well-acquainted with the natives, and capable of arriving at and acting on a decision. For this command he selected Colonel Seaton. What Seaton was may be gathered from the account I have given of his march from Dehlí to Béwar. A gallant soldier, shrinking from no responsibility, always ready to give his life for his country, he was just the man to hold a position full of difficulty and danger. The post that was offered him came emphatically within that category. For, to hold Fathgarh and the districts which Fathgarh covered, Sir Colin proposed to leave him only two weak English regiments,—one of which only, the 82nd, was at Fathgarh—the 7th Panjáb Infantry, a 9-pounder field battery, and three hundred and fifty newly raised native horsemen; this, too, when fifteen thousand rebels were within seven miles of Fathgarh! But, difficult as was the occasion, Seaton was equal to it.

Sir Colin manœuvres so as to induce a belief that Rohilkhand is his object.

Meanwhile, Sir Colin had endeavoured to amuse the Rohilkhand rebels. His great object was to mislead them—to impress them with the idea that Barélí was the object of his attack. Immediately after occupying Fathgarh, he had sent Adrian Hope's brigade to scour the country in the vicinity. On Hope's return, learning that a force of fifteen thousand men had assembled at the town of Allahganj on the banks of the Rámganga river, some seven or eight miles distant, Sir Colin sent Walpole's brigade, with guns, cavalry, and sappers, to make a demonstration against them. Walpole's orders were to make as much display as possible, but not to commit himself to an en-

Book XI. Chapter VI. — 1858. January.

gagement across the river. He carried out these orders to the letter; he made as though he would repair the bridge, which the rebels had broken down, across the Rámganga; and to add to the delusion, Sir Colin rode out himself and made a careful reconnaissance of the spot. The ruse succeeded admirably, for the rebels were completely deceived, and, for a time, became rooted to the left bank of the river.

Adrian Hope defeats the rebels at Sútia.

Whether suspicion gradually dawned upon them, or whether they were well served by their spies, I do not know. But it is certain that after remaining in this position ten or twelve days, they detached a body of five thousand men to attempt an incursion into the reconquered districts. These men, crossing the Rámganga at a point above that watched by Walpole, marched to a ferry on the Ganges, called Surájghát, about twelve miles above Fathgarh, crossed that river, and occupied the village of Shamsábád. At ten o'clock on the evening of the 26th January, Adrian Hope's brigade, consisting of the 42nd, the 93rd, the 4th Panjáb Rifles, Remmington's and Blunt's troops of Bengal Horse Artillery, two squadron's of the 9th Lancers, and half of Hodson's Horse, was sent to attack them. Marching all night, Adrian Hope found the enemy at 8 o'clock in the morning posted at the village of Sútia, half a mile from Shamsábád. As soon as the rebels saw the English their guns opened fire. Hope did not reply till well within distance; but when he did reply, it was with considerable effect. At the fifth discharge the rebels broke and fled.

Hodson and the 9th Lancer squadrons were amongst them at once, and though the rebel cavalry fought well, the slaughter of them was great. The British loss did not exceed five or six killed and about twenty wounded. Amongst those wounded mortally was M'Dowell, the gallant second in command of Hodson's Horse, the companion of Hodson in many a daring enterprise. Hodson himself was wounded in two places. The enemy were pursued eight or nine miles. Those who escaped recrossed the Ganges into Rohilkhand, leaving four guns in the hands of the victors.

Final preparations before marching on Lakhnao.

Meanwhile, in order the better to relieve pressure on Seaton's small brigade, Sir Colin Campbell had arranged with the Chief Commissioner of the Panjáb, Sir John Lawrence, that a force should be organised at Rúrki for the purpose of entering Rohilkhand from the north-west. This column, he had reason to believe, would be ready to set out on this expedition on the 1st February. It was now approaching that date; Hope's victory at Sútia had been severe enough to impose prudence on the rebels for a few days; the siege-train was well on its way to Kánhpúr; Seaton had had a week to examine the lay of the districts committed to his care and prudence; there was no reason for further delay. Sir Colin was anxious to return to the place which was to be his base in the new campaign, to see how the works he had ordered to cover the bridges were progressing, to be present there to receive the siege-train, and to despatch it across the Ganges

Book XI. Chapter VI. 1858. January.

to the first advanced position on the Lakhnao road—the station of Onáo. He left Fathgarh, then, on the 1st February, followed by the cavalry and the horse artillery, and making forced marches, reached Kánhpúr on the 4th. Hope's brigade and the artillery park started the same day by regular marches, whilst Walpole's brigade, strengthened by a portion of that which Seaton had brought down, stayed a few days longer, to cover to the last the communications with Ágra. But by the 23rd February all had crossed the Ganges into Oudh. On the sandy plains between Oonao and Banni were massed engineers, artillery, horse, foot, commissariat waggons, camp-followers, the most efficient European army ever ranged in the plains of India. It counted seventeen battalions of infantry, fifteen of which were British; twenty-eight squadrons of cavalry, including four English regiments; fifty-four light and eighty heavy guns and mortars. They are there on the eve of their departure. The morrow will see them start for the rebellious city, the capture of which will be so fatal to many among them. I must leave them for the moment; for before I describe their deeds it is fitting that I should narrate the manner in which Jang Bahádur and Franks had been co-operating from the south-east, and how Outram and his gallant companions were bearing up in the A'lambágh.

BOOK XI.

CHAPTER VII.

Jang Bahádur offers at an early date to aid to suppress the revolt.

Among the offers of assistance which, in the early days of the revolt, had been made to the Governor-General was one of peculiar significance. Jang Bahádur, the virtual ruler of the independent Hill State which, touching the British territory at Kamáon, extends all along the north-east border of Oudh, then rejoining British territory at a point in the Gorákhpúr district due north of the station of the same name, continues the touch to within a few miles of Dárjiling—Jang Bahádur had, in the month of May, placed the whole military resources of Nipál at the disposal of the Governor-General. The independent position occupied by Nipál, the known ability of the man, who, though only Prime Minister, wielded all real authority in the country, the certainty that the overthrow of the British could scarcely fail to offer great opportunities to an able general commanding a compact and well-disciplined army,

Book XI. Chapter VII.

1857. May–July.

gave to Jang Bahádur's proposal the appearance of being inspired by a pure and generous friendship. Few untravelled independent rulers would have acted in a similar manner. But Jang Bahádur had but a few years previously visited Europe. This visit had enlightened him on many points, and on one point in particular. It had convinced him that, under all circumstances, England would be able to maintain her hold on India. It became therefore with him a matter of interest to support the stronger combatant.

The offer, after some delay, is accepted;

Lord Canning thanked Jang Bahádur for his offer, but it was not till some time in the month of June that he accepted it. In pursuance of the agreement between the contracting parties, Jang Bahádur in July despatched three thousand Gúrkahs from Khátmándu. These, entering the British territory at a point north of Gorákhpúr, marched on that place, and reached it at the end of the month. Their arrival was the signal for the disarming of the sepoys stationed there (1st August). The neighbouring stations of Ázamgarh and Jánpúr were then in the throes of anarchy. Vainly had the heroic Venables, the indigo-planter, who had been steadfast among the faint-hearted, struggled and fought for order. It is true that on the 16th July, after a gallant fight of the few against many, he had repulsed them in an attack on Ázamgarh. But, after the victory, his own followers had shown symptoms of mutiny, and he and the few Europeans who followed him had been forced, on the 30th July, to retreat on Gházipúr. To restore order, then,

and a few Gúrkah troops are sent to the A'zamgarh district.

in Ázamgarh and its vicinity, the arrival of the Nipálese troops was opportune. They occupied Ázamgarh on the 13th August, and Jánpúr on the 15th. Meanwhile, on their evacuating it, Gorákhpúr was taken possession of by rebels from Oudh, commanded by one Muhammad Husén.

Book XI. Chapter VII.

1857. Aug.-Sept.

British officers sent to represent the Government with the Nipál troops.

The Government of India, to ensure concert between these allies and its own troops, had transmitted orders to the military authorities at Banáras to appoint certain officers, left unemployed by the mutiny of their regiments, to join and act with the Nipálese. In obedience to these orders, Captain Boileau and Lieutenants Miles, Hall, and Campbell, came to Jánpúr and took up the duties assigned to them. Two or three weeks elapsed before an opportunity offered of testing the quality of the allied troops, but in the third week of September the approach to Ázamgarh of a large body of rebels gave an occasion of which they eagerly availed themselves.

Ázamgarh is again threatened.

Ázamgarh was the point threatened. Lieutenant-Colonel Wroughton, commanding at Jánpúr, deemed it advisable then to detach the Shér regiment of Nipálese, one thousand two hundred strong, and two guns, to reinforce that station.

The Nipálese left Jánpúr at 10 A.M. on the 18th September, marched forty miles that day, and reached Ázamgarh at 6 o'clock in the evening. It was known when they arrived that the rebels were encamped at or near a village called Mandori, ten miles distant; and as they would probably be ignorant of the arrival of the Nipál reinforcement it was determined to surprise them.

Book XI. Chapter VII.

1857. September.

The Nipál troops and Mr. Venables surprise and defeat the rebels.

Accordingly, at half past 1 o'clock the next morning, the Shér regiment again set out, accompanied by Captain Boileau as English officer in charge of the force, by Mr. Wynyard the judge, by Mr. Venables, the gallant planter whose recent services I have just referred to, and by three other officers. Mandori was reached a little after sunrise. The rebels were found strongly posted, their centre covered by the village, and their flanks protected by fields of sugar-cane, then at their full height. Nothing daunted, the Nipál colonel, Shamshér Singh, formed his men up in five columns, and dashed at the enemy's position. Their onslaught was so fierce, that in ten minutes the rebels were in full flight, leaving on the field three brass guns. They lost about two hundred men killed and wounded. On the side of the Nipálese two were killed and twenty-six wounded. Mr. Wynyard, in his report of the action to his civil superiors, alluded in the highest terms to the conduct of the Nipál troops. Regarding Mr. Venables, who commanded the cavalry, he wrote: "He was always where fighting was hardest; he was first up at the first gun taken, and killed three men with his own hand."*

The victory is followed up.

This victory had an excellent effect on the conquerors. Up to that time some hesitation had been shown in employing our allies against the rebels, but with the victory of Mandori all uncertainty vanished. To march fifty miles in two

* So sensible were the rebels of the immense service rendered by Mr. Venables to his country that they offered a reward of five hundred rupees for his head.

days and then to win a battle in an unknown country would have reflected credit on veteran soldiers. Their success on this occasion filled the English officers with confidence, and caused the step already taken to be followed up by others. On the 27th September, another party of Nipál troops from Jánpúr, commanded by Colonel Wroughton, and accompanied by the civil officers, marched against and occupied Mubárakpúr—the stronghold of a rebel Rájá, Irádat Khán. He was captured and hanged. Proceeding onwards, the Nipál troops pacified the entire district. On the 29th, a similar demonstration was made from Ázamgarh, and with similar success. Atráolia, the stronghold of the rebel leader Béni Mádho, was occupied, its fortifications were destroyed; and although Béni Madho escaped, he quitted the district, and up to the borders of Oudh order was for the time restored.

A detachment of British troops sent from Banáras under Longden.

To support the Nipál troops, the Government had, in September, directed the despatch from Banáras of a small force, consisting of three hundred and twenty men of the 10th Foot, two 9-pounder guns, a small detachment European artillery, and one hundred and seventy of the 17th Madras Native Infantry, under the command of Lieutenant-Colonel Longdon of the 10th Foot. But before this small force could reach the scene of action, the Oudh rebels had again crossed the frontier, and had encountered and been beaten by the Nipálese at Kúdúa on the 19th October, and at Chánda on the 30th of the same month. The last-named action was severe enough to

Book XI. Chapter VII.

1857. Oct.-Nov.

merit a separate record. The rebels, numbering from four to five thousand men, were strongly posted and had seven guns. The Nipál troops counted only one thousand one hundred with two guns. The battle, obstinately contested, terminated in the complete defeat of the rebels, with a loss on their side of three hundred killed. Four of their guns were taken. But the victory was dearly purchased. Lieutenant-Colonel Maddan Mán Singh, and eleven men were killed, and fifty-nine were wounded. But the gallantry of the Nipál troops had been conspicuous. Of one of them, Lieutenant Gambhír Singh, it is related in the official account of the action that "single-handed, he took a gun, cutting down five of the artillerymen, and wounding and driving away two others." This gallant ally was covered with wounds but eventually recovered.

Longden captures Atráolia.

Longden reached Jánpúr just after the action of Chánda. Three days after his arrival (4th November) the Oudh rebels, to the number of one thousand, with two guns, again crossed the Oudh frontier, and seized the fort of Atráolia. The attention of Longden was at once called to the fact. Uniting his force to that of the Nipálese, he marched out at once, and, on the 9th, cannonaded the place so vigorously, that the enemy evacuated it during the night.

The Government concludes an arrangement with Jang Bahádur

But the fact that the British territory was still liable to invasion, and that the British troops, though strong enough to repel an isolated attack, were not strong enough to defend the whole frontier, and might be forced, under certain circum-

Book XI. Chapter VII.

1857. Nov.-Dec.

stances, to fall back on Banáras, induced the Government of India to conclude with the Nipál Government a new arrangement. In virtue of this, it was arranged that Jang Bahádur should proceed himself to the scene of action with a force of nine thousand picked troops, and that to this force Colonel MacGregor should be attached with the rank of Brigadier-General. At the same time measures were taken greatly to increase the British force on the eastern frontier of Oudh. Large reinforcements were likewise sent to the Jánpúr force, and that force so strengthened was placed under the command of one of the ablest officers in the British army, Brigadier-General Franks, C.B. Similarly, another mixed force was organised by Colonel Rowcroft to move from Tirhút along the Gandak towards Gorákhpúr. These three separate *corps d'armée* had but one primary object, to clear the British districts to the north of Banáras and east of Oudh; these once cleared, whilst one corps would remain in observation, the other two would march to co-operate with Sir Colin Campbell in his attack on Lakhnao. It will be necessary to deal with them separately.

For assistance led by himself.

The British force is likewise strengthened.

Rowcroft's force was composed of thirty men of the Royal Marines, one hundred and thirty of the Naval Brigade under Captain Sotheby, three hundred and fifty Nipál troops, fifty men of the Bengal Police Battalion, and four 12-pounder howitzers, two of which were mountain-train guns. It occupied an intrenched camp at Mirwá, about forty-nine miles from Chaprá. Seven miles distant, at Sobanpúr on the west bank of the little

Colonel Rowcroft's force

Book XI. Chapter VII.

1857. December.

beats the rebels at Sobanpúr,

Gandak, lay a small rebel army, computed to consist of twelve hundred regular sepoys, and four thousand armed adventurers, of whom one hundred were mounted, with four guns. On the morning of the 26th December, Rowcroft, who had waited for the arrival of the Gorákhnáth Nipál regiment from Sigáoli, marched to attack them. The enemy's position was strong. They occupied a village, covered in front by a tank with high banks, and on the right by a tope of trees. Rowcroft halted within half a mile of the place and rode forward to reconnoitre. He resolved to render useless the enemy's strong positions in the centre and on the right by turning his left. He did this with great coolness and success. The Nipál troops behaved splendidly under fire. Sotheby of the Naval Brigade managed the artillery with great skill. The Minié rifles of the Royal Marines, directed by Lieutenant Pym, produced a striking effect. The result was that the enemy, attacked a little after 10 o'clock, were completely beaten by half past 1, forced back from Sobanpúr, and followed six miles further to Majáoli, and thence driven across the Gandak, with the loss of one large iron gun. Rowcroft followed up his victory the next day by crossing the river and destroying the homesteads of the leading rebels.

and halts on the Ghághrá for orders.

Then, in pursuance of instructions he had received from Brigadier-General MacGregor, under whose orders he had been placed, he marched to Burhat Ghát on the river Ghághrá, there to await further instructions.

Jung Bahádur enters

Jang Bahádur's little army, meanwhile, setting

out from Nipál, had crossed the British frontier. On the 23rd December, it reached Bhetiá, eighty-two miles east of Gorákhpúr. Here it was joined by MacGregor. Continuing its march, it crossed the river Gandak on the 30th, and arrived in the vicinity of Gorákhpúr on the 5th January. Gorákhpúr was occupied by the rebels, but by rebels disheartened, divided in purpose, and hopeless of success. When attacked, then, the following morning by the Nipál army, they made but a feeble resistance, but fled across the Ráptí, leaving seven guns in the possession of the conquerors. These lost but two men killed. Seven were wounded. The loss of the rebels amounted to about two hundred.

Book XI. Chapter VII.

1857-8. Dec.-Jan.

British territory,

and beats the rebels at Gorákhpúr.

The civil administration was at once re-established in Gorákhpúr. The British districts were cleared of rebels. At the same time, awaiting the time when the Nipál force at Ázamgarh should cross the Oudh frontier in co-operation with that under General Franks, MacGregor transmitted orders to Rowcroft to embark his little force in boats and ascend the river.

Civil administration restored in Gorákhpúr.

Before Rowcroft came up, the moment referred to had arrived, and Jang Bahádur, starting from Gorákhpúr on the 14th February, reached Barári, on the left bank of the Ghághrá, on the 19th. On the evening of that day, Rowcroft's force anchored within four miles of that place, and landed on the right bank. There, on the morning of the 20th, he was joined by a brigade of the Nipál force, with six guns. Rowcroft's boats were ordered to be brought up to allow the rest of the

Rowcroft approaches the Nipál force,

Book XI. Chapter VII.

1858. Feb.-March.

and defeats the rebels at Phúlpúr.

Nipál force to cross over at Phúlpúr. But meanwhile, Rowcroft, discovering that place to be in the occupation of the rebels, marched on it, attacked, and dispersed them, capturing three guns. A bridge was then formed of the boats, and the entire Nipál force crossed. It was arranged that Rowcroft, with the Naval Brigade, the Yeomanry Cavalry, which had joined him, and two Nipál regiments, should occupy Gorákhpúr, to keep open the communications, whilst Jang Bahádur should march *viâ* Súltánpúr on Lakhnao.

Jang Bahádur enters Oudh,

Crossing the Ghághrá, Jang Bahádur marched to Ambarpúr on the 25th February. The road to that place was commanded by a small fort, having a triple line of defence within a bamboo jungle, and defended by thirty-four men. It was necessary to storm this post, for though it might be turned, yet its occupation by the rebels would enable them to act on the communications of the advancing force. The Nipál troops, then, were sent against it. It was defended with so much vigour and resolution, that the assailants lost seven men killed and forty-three wounded before they gained possession of it. The defenders died, all, at their posts.

and storms a strong fort.

The effect of this capture was great, for two days later the rebels evacuated a larger fort occupied by two hundred men, towards which the Nipálese were advancing. Neither their passage across the Gúmti near Súltánpúr, nor their further progress to Lakhnao, was disturbed by the enemy. They reached the vicinity of that city on the 10th March, and moved into line with the British army on the 11th, in full time to take an efficient part in the capture of that city.

1857. November.

General Franks:

I propose now to turn to General Franks. On the 29th November that officer had been appointed to command the troops in the A'zamgarh and Jánpúr districts. The force at his disposal consisted of about five thousand five hundred men—of whom three thousand two hundred were Nipálese—and twenty guns. His own brigade was composed of the 10th, 20th, and 97th Foot, the 6th company 13th battalion, and 8th company 2nd battalion Royal Artillery; detachments of the 3rd battalion Madras, and of the 5th battalion Bengal, Artillery, and a detail of native artillery. The Assistant Adjutant-General of the force was Captain H. Havelock, son of the famous general, and who had served under Franks, as adjutant of the 10th Regiment, for six years. This gallant officer, on learning the nomination of his old colonel to the command of the force, had at once applied to serve with it; and on the application being granted, though still suffering from severe wounds, had hastened to join. Franks was officially informed that his main duties would consist in protecting Banáras against attack, in preventing the rebels from crossing the Ganges into Bihár, in recovering British districts occupied by them. It was at the same time impressed upon him, in a memorandum, that the safety of Banáras was the prime, the main consideration, to which every other was to be subordinated.*

his force; his Assistant Adjutant-General; his instructions.

* Lord Canning's Memorandum, dated 29th November 1857, addressed to Colonel Franks.

Book XI. Chapter VII.

1857. December.

Supplementary instructions given to him by Mr. Grant.

Nevertheless, the Lieutenant-Governor of the Central Provinces, Mr. J. P. Grant, in communicating this memorandum to Colonel Franks, wisely supplemented it with a description of the state of the frontier, of the rebel chiefs, of their following, of the positions they had taken up, as well as of the probable means of offence and defence at their disposal. This memorandum, written clearly and with accurate knowledge, proved of inestimable value.

He shows a bold front to the invader.

By end of December, Franks had organised his force, and had placed it in strong defensive positions, showing a bold front to the invader. His right column was near Ázamgarh, his centre some miles in front of Jánpúr, and his left at Badlapúr. Though the attitude taken up imposed on the rebels so far as to prevent them from hazarding an attack, it did not hinder them from pillaging and plundering the districts about one hundred and twenty miles to the west of Jánpúr.

The rebel leader

The leader of the rebels was called Mehndi Husén. He called himself Názim of Súltánpúr. Like many men who rise to the surface in a period of riot and disorder, he was an adventurer, whose main object in life was to secure for himself something tangible out of the general wreck. He had under him about fifteen thousand men, mostly

and his army.

matchlock-men, of whom not more than a third could be depended upon to fight. The rebel leader had his headquarters at Chánda, a town thirty-six miles from Jánpúr, on the direct road from that station to Súltánpúr; but his lieutenant, Fazal A'zím, occupied a strong position at Saríon, just

Book XI. Chapter VII.

1858. January.

fourteen miles north of Allahábád. His outposts were within four miles of that place.

How Franks's want of cavalry

Franks had no regular cavalry. He had, indeed, thirty-eight mounted policemen, known as the Banáras Horse, commanded by Captain Matheson. To compensate as far as possible for the deficiency, he had mounted twenty-five men of the 10th Foot, and placed them under the command of Lieutenant Tucker, of the Bengal Cavalry. The services rendered by these men can scarcely be exaggerated, but their numbers were insufficient to effectively follow up a victory. It would have been easy for him, with the force at his disposal, to beat the pseudo-Názim or his lieutenant; but a barren victory—a victory which could not be efficiently followed up—would be useless. The Government and the Commander-in-Chief were equally alive to the necessity that Franks should be supplied with this arm in sufficient numbers, and they did all that seemed to them possible under the circumstances. But the supply could only proceed by detachments. The first of these, composed of two squadrons of the Bays, and four horse artillery guns, was despatched from Allahábád on the 20th of January to reinforce him.

was attempted to be supplied.

Franks moves forward.

As soon as he heard that cavalry were on their way to join him, Franks (21st January) moved forward with his left column, numbering fourteen hundred men, of whom eight hundred were Nipálese, and six guns, to Sikandra, seven miles from Saráon. He found that Fazal Ázím, with eight thousand men and fourteen guns, was still at that place. Fazal Ázím heard at the same time

Book XI. Chapter VII.

1858. January.

The enemy advance to a strong position.

of the arrival at Sikandra of General Franks. The country all about Saráon being open, he broke up his camp that night and advanced to Nasratpúr, a very strong position, held then by an ally, an influential talúkdár, Béni Bahádur Singh. In this position, extremely strong by nature, and the approach to which had been rendered more difficult by art, the two friends hoped to be able to give a good account of any assailant, even though that assailant should be British.

Franks waits for his cavalry,

Franks learned next morning of the retreat of the rebels. He could not attack them at once, for his cavalry had not come up, and he had directed them to join him at Sikandra. The day of the 22nd, then, was devoted to preparing for the move, which he thought would scarcely be delayed beyond the morrow. Franks gathered all the information possible regarding the enemy's position, and whilst receiving this, he erected a kind of stockade, or fortified enclosure, there to leave his baggage whilst he should march on the enemy.

which arrives.

In this way the day passed, anxiously towards the closing hours, for the cavalry did not appear. At last, about 8 o'clock, they arrived, accompanied by four horse artillery guns. There was no more hesitation. Next morning Franks sent his men in two columns against the enemy. The strength of the position did not stop them; Nipálese rivalled European. With the loss of only six men slightly wounded, the stronghold was captured; the rebels hastily fleeing to save as many of their guns as possible. Two of these were captured; but the density of the jungle, first,

Franks attacks and beats the rebels.

Book XI. Chapter VII. 1858. Jan.–Feb.

and the difficult nature of the ground, afterwards, greatly impeded the action of the cavalry, and the rebels were able to carry the remainder across the Oudh frontier.

The cavalry sent back to Allahábád.

After the action, Franks was forced, to his regret, but in obedience to orders, to send the cavalry back to Allahábád.

Franks moves to the Oudh frontier at Singramáo,

Having destroyed the rebel stronghold, Franks moved to Saraón, re-established the civil authorities in the districts bordering on Allahábád, and then returned to Badlapúr, preparatory to an advance by Súltánpúr on Lakhnao. Thence he moved eight miles in advance to Singramáo, close to the frontier, there to await the action of Jang Buhádur, on his right, at Gorákhpúr.

and advances to Súltánpúr.

We have seen how the arrival of Rowcroft at Gorákhpúr on the 19th February loosed the hands of the Nipál Mahárájá. Franks set out the same day for Súltánpúr. The distance was thirty-three miles, but the greater portion of it was occupied by the rebels. Their advanced post, Chánda, thirteen miles from Singramáo, was guarded by eight thousand men, of whom two thousand five hundred were sepoys trained by British officers and another strong corps of ten thousand men lay within a few miles of them.

He reaches Chánda.

Franks, I have said, marched on the 19th from Singramáo. His plan was to move rapidly and defeat the enemy's forces in detail, and he carried out his programme to the letter. Reaching Chánda about 8 o'clock in the morning, he found the place occupied by the rebel corps I have already mentioned. This corps, eight thousand strong, had

Book XI. Chapter VII.

1858. February.

Proceedings of the enemy.

eight guns, a good position, and every incentive to make a sturdy resistance. Its commander, a civil officer, named Banda Húsén, had despatched very early that morning express messengers to his chief, the pseudo-Názim, Mehndi Husén, informing him of the approach of the British, and begging him to move up with his following of ten thousand men to his support. Could he resist but for three hours, that support was assured to him.

Franks attacks and defeats Banda Husén

But the impetuous onslaught of the British and Nipálese was not to be withstood even for three hours. Sepoys from four trained regiments were there, but they were there only to give way, almost without a serious effort. After a contest, which did not cost the allies a single man, Chánda was occupied, and the enemy were pursued three miles further to Rámpúra.

At Rámpúra Franks halted—only for two hours. He had become aware that the reinforcements under Mehndi Husén were on their way, and he was resolved to deal with them before they should recover from the panic which the defeat of the Chánda force would certainly inspire. He took ground, then, to the left, and occupied the village of Hamirpúr. Mehndi Husén had been in full march for Chánda when he learned from some fugitives of the defeat of his lieutenant. Surprised as he was, he still hoped to retrieve the day. After a short halt for reflection, he made a circuit, and, as the shades of evening were falling, he appeared on the left rear of Franks's position. But Franks was not so to be caught. At once changing front, he dashed at the rebels. Surprised, when they had

and Mehndi Husén.

hoped to surprise, they made but the semblance of resistance, and then fled in disorder. Owing to the lateness of the hour, Franks pursued them but a short distance: he then bivouacked on the ground he had occupied before the action.

Losses on both sides.

The loss of the allies in these two actions amounted to only eleven wounded—a proof of the slightness of the resistance. That of the enemy cannot be accurately computed; but the speed of their flight and the paucity of cavalry with the victors would induce the belief that it was not considerable.

Importance to both parties of the fort of Budhayan.

The pseudo-Názim rallied his forces at Wári, intent on renewing the struggle. Between the contending armies and Súltánpúr was a very strong fort, surrounded by a jungle, and completely commanding the approaches to that town—the fort of Budhayan. The Názim was thoroughly well aware of the importance of this position, and he resolved to secure it. But Franks possessed a knowledge not inferior and a determination at least equal. He possessed, too, this advantage, that at Hamirpúr he occupied a position from which he could deal a blow at an enemy who should attempt to attack Budhayan from Wári. The Názim did, nevertheless, make the attempt, and in a manner which entitled him to some consideration as a general. It was far from his desire to encounter the English in the plain. The recollection of the battle of the previous day was strong within him. But he was anxious to mislead his enemy, and gain a post from which he could defy him.

Book XI. Chapter VII.

1858. February.

Franks outmanœuvres the Názim,

But he failed. Do what he would, Franks always put himself in his way. After a long day of manœuvring, it came to this,—that the army which was ready to fight a battle would gain Budhayan. The Názim would do everything but that. Franks would do everything including that. The greater daring gained the day, and on the afternoon of the 21st Franks occupied Budhayan. The Názim, baffled, though not discouraged, made a long detour, and turning the town of Súltánpúr, took up a position at Bádshahganj, two miles beyond it, ready there to dispute the further progress of the allies. On this point, rallied all his scattered partisans, and the troops of Banda Husén. Here, too, he was joined by Mirza Gaffúr Bég, a general of artillery under the ex-king of Oudh, who had been sent from Lakhnao for the express purpose of assuming the command and of driving back Franks. He assumed the command, but he did not drive back Franks.

who takes up a strong position near Súltánpúr.

Franks is constrained to act without cavalry.

Franks had halted at Budhayan on the 22nd to await the arrival of the Láhor Light Horse and the Pathán cavalry, urgently required and anxiously expected. But as these had not arrived on the early morning of the 23rd, he felt constrained to act without them. He set out, then, at 6 o'clock in the morning of that day, to attack the enemy.

The position of the rebels at Súltánpúr.

The position which Gaffúr Bég occupied was very formidable. It may thus be described. His whole front was protected by a deep and winding nullah, which ran into the Gúmti. The main body extended in a line of a mile and a half in the plain behind that nullah, the left resting on the Súltánpúr bazaar, the centre placed behind the ruined lines of the police battalion; the right covered by a range of low hillocks in advance of the village and strong masonry buildings of Bádshahganj. The nullah which covered his front was crossed by the road leading to Lakhnao, and which Franks must traverse. To prevent such a movement, Gaffúr Bég placed his principal battery on this road. The rest of his guns were distributed along his front, three being posted in the village near the bazaar on his extreme left, six in the masonry building of Bádshahganj on his right.

Book XI. Chapter VII.

1858. February.

Its defects.

Formidable though the position was, it had one great fault. It could be turned on its right. The road from Allahábád to Lakhnao, to the south-west, crossed the nullah at a point out of reach of the enemy's fire, and led to ground behind their right. Gaffúr Bég had forgotten this, for he had pushed neither cavalry nor scouts in that direction.

Franks detects the weak point of the rebels' position.

Franks marched, as I have said, at 6 o'clock in the morning. At about 9 o'clock, or a few minutes after, his advance guard, composed of the twenty-five mounted men of the 10th Foot, and thirty-eight men of the Banáras Horse, which constituted his only cavalry, caught sight of the enemy's outposts on the nullah. Franks at once halted his force. He had detected the weak point in the position of the enemy, and had resolved to profit by it.

Battle of Súltánpúr.

Feigning a front attack, occupying the enemy by a demonstration which had all the appearance

Book XI. Chapter VII.

1858. February.

of being real, he moved his infantry and light guns obliquely to the left, and seized the Allahábád road. The feigned attack so completely concentrated upon it all the attention of the enemy, that the movement of the infantry brigades remained unmolested, and those brigades had reached a position completely in rear of the enemy's right before the latter had the smallest suspicion that they were not in front of them. The surprise when the Anglo-Indian force deployed and attacked may be surmised. In vain did the rebels attempt to rectify the error, to bring their guns round to the new front—it was too late. The English pushed forward with a decision that allowed no time to repair mistakes. In advance even of the skirmishers, a gallant officer of engineers, who had during the siege of Lakhnao rendered the most splendid service, Macleod Innes, secured the first hostile gun, as the rebels were abandoning it. Falling back from this, the rebels rallied round another gun further back, from which the shot would, in another instant, have ploughed through the advancing columns. Macleod Innes noticed the danger. He never stopped to consider, but galloping up, alone and unsupported, he shot the gunner as he was about to apply the match, and remaining undaunted at his post, the mark for a hundred matchlockmen who were sheltered in some adjoining huts, kept the artillerymen at bay till assistance reached him.*

Macleod Innes.

His splendid gallantry.

* For this splendid act Macleod Innes received the Victoria Cross.

The British line then swept on. Its left soon reached the high road to Lakhnao. The rest of the enemy were enclosed between the British and the nullah. The latter, which had covered his front, now held in his rear. Soon after, the central battery was captured. Franks himself, cap in hand, led the skirmishers of the 10th Foot right up to the guns, which the enemy's gunners served to the last, dying at their posts. After this, the battle was over. The plain was covered with fugitives who had left behind them twenty guns (one 32-pounder, two 24-pounders, two 18-pounders, four 12-pounders, one 9-pounder, and ten smaller pieces), their camp, their baggage, and their ammunition. It is probable that a considerable number of them were killed and wounded. "Had the Láhor Light Horse and Patháns reached me six hours sooner," wrote Franks, "when the whole plain was covered with fugitives, whom the utmost efforts of my infantry could not overtake, their loss would have been considerably heavier." The casualties on the side of the British amounted to two killed and five wounded. The cavalry referred to—augmenting the cavalry force under Franks to six hundred sabres—arrived on the ground shortly after the action was over.

The enemy totally defeated,

but not efficiently pursued for want of cavalry,

The next morning Franks was joined by the Jalandhar Cavalry.* This body of horse, raised on the Guide principle under the auspices of Lake, Deputy Commissioner of Jalandhar, only a few

who arrive after the action.

* This regiment was subsequently absorbed into the 3rd Sikh Cavalry.

Book XI. Chapter VII.

1858. Feb.-March.

Aikman joins with the Jalandhar cavalry.

months before, and equipped and drilled by Lieutenant Aikman, had marched from the Satlaj to join Franks in an incredibly short space of time—the last march covering forty miles. "I did not expect you for a fortnight," exclaimed Franks, as he welcomed Aikman: "had I known you would have been here, I would at any cost have postponed the action." It will be seen that, though too late to share in the battle of Súltánpúr, Aikman was to inaugurate the arrival of his new levies by an action not yielding in brilliancy to any performed in the campaign.

Gallant deed of Aikman.

The road to Lakhnao was now apparently open, and there seemed little chance of any further opposition being offered. But on the early morning of the 1st March, Aikman, who had been posted for the night three miles in advance of the camp with a hundred of his men, learned that a body of five hundred rebel infantry, two hundred cavalry, and two guns, under a noted rebel chief, Mansab Ali, who had long evaded pursuit, was occupying a position three miles off the high road, on the banks of the Gúmti. This was quite enough for Aikman. Despatching a trooper to Franks, begging him to send up in support the cavalry and the guns, he led his men to the spot, charged the enemy, totally defeated them, killed more than one hundred of them, and drove the survivors into and across the Gúmti, capturing the two guns. This most gallant and successful charge was made under every disadvantage of broken ground, and partially under the flanking fire of a hostile fort. Nothing could exceed the

Book XI. Chapter VII.

1858. March.

splendid daring displayed by Aikman on this occasion. For some time he was at sword's point with several rebels at the same time, and from one of them he received a severe sabre-cut across the face. The cool and resolute courage with which he continued to fight inspired his men with the supreme resolution which caused the combat to terminate in the successful manner I have described.* The cavalry and the guns arrived after the fight was over.

After this splendid achievement, Franks pushed on, and, on the morning of the 4th, reached a mosque a mile beyond the town of Améthi, eight miles from Lakhnao. He had received orders from the Commander-in-Chief to advance. Learning, however, that the fort of Dhaorára, two miles to the right of the road, was occupied by a large body of the rebels with two guns, Franks, apprehensive that that body, if unmolested, might annoy his long train of baggage, resolved to drive them out.

The repulse at Dhaorára.

The resolution in itself was perfectly sound, but the mode in which it was carried out left much to be desired. Against the fort Franks detached, with a body of cavalry, only two horse artillery guns. In vain did Havelock protest, as far as he could protest, urging the general to use the two 24-pounder howitzers which were available. Franks was obstinate. The result was that the two horse artillery guns, moved up succes-

* Lieutenant, now Lieutenant-Colonel, Aikman received the Victoria Cross for this gallant act.

Book XI. Chapter VII.

1858. March.

sively to four hundred, three hundred, and even two hundred yards of the fort, failed to breach the walls or to silence the matchlock fire of the rebels. Subsequently the 24-pound howitzers were brought up, the outer defences were forced, and the hostile guns were captured; but the rebels barricaded themselves in a house guarded by a massive gate, and still bade defiance to the British. The shot from one of their own guns which had been turned against this making no impression upon it, and a fire kindled against it producing no effect, and the only engineer officer, Macleod Innes, having been severely wounded while trying to burst the gate open, Franks determined to withdraw. The force then resumed its march and joined Sir Colin the same evening.*

Results of Franks's campaign.

This was the last action which signalised Franks's successful march from the borders of eastern to central Oudh. He joined Sir Colin on the night of the 4th March, having, in thirteen days, marched one hundred and thirty miles, beaten an enemy immensely superior in four general actions, and captured thirty-four pieces of ordnance with the small loss of thirty-seven officers and men killed and wounded. Such leading needs no comment. Franks was known as one of the best regimental officers in the British

* It was believed that this check had important consequences for Franks. He had been selected by Sir Colin to command the *corps d'armée* which was to act on the left bank of the Gúmti; but when, it is said, Sir Colin heard of the slap on the face he had received at Dhaorára, he struck his name out and substituted that of Outram.

Book XI. Chapter VII. 1858. March.

army. This short campaign stamped him as qualified to take very high rank among its generals. The repulse at Dhaorára was little more than an accident, arising from over-confidence.

Havelock.

It is true he was well supported. In Captain, now Sir Henry, Havelock, he had an Assistant Adjutant-General, who combined to a vigorous frame an ardent love of his profession and a clear head, able to detect the weak points of an enemy's position and to devise the means of profiting by his faults. Havelock was a born general, and, possessing as he did the entire confidence of Franks, his intuition may be discerned in every action but one of this short campaign. That one was the last. Against the attack with insufficient means, when sufficient means were available, Havelock protested with all the energy of his nature. Had his advice been followed, the great opportunity which had been in the grasp of Franks would not have been denied him.

Patrick Carnegy.

But there was another gentleman attached to Franks's staff, whose services deserve special mention. I allude to Mr. Patrick Carnegy, of the uncovenanted service. The son of a general officer in the service of the Company, Patrick Carnegy had wanted the interest which in those days was required to obtain for a man a commission in the military service. Forced to become a civilian in the uncovenanted grade, Carnegy had brought to the performance of his duties an intelligence, an industry, and a zeal which would have won his spurs in any profession. He worked his way up steadily. He gained the confidence

Book XI. Chapter VII. 1858. March.

of the Government and the affection of the people. His tact and judgment enabled him to steer clear through every crisis. In Franks's camp he had charge of the intelligence department, and in this office his knowledge of the people, their language and their customs, made him invaluable. Brought constantly into connection with Havelock, who was scarcely less distinguished as a linguist, a desire to attain the same ends in the same plain straightforward manner brought about an intimate friendship, in itself most advantageous to the public service.* "His information regarding the enemy has proved so correct," wrote General Franks, "that on it alone the whole of my operations might have been planned: he has always accompanied me in the field, and assisted in carrying orders under the heaviest fire."

Venables.

Another non-military gentleman, Mr. Venables, whose services will be more specially referred to further on, rendered splendid service in this campaign;

Longden.

Colonel Longden, of the 10th Foot, showed, too, special qualifications for the service in which he was employed, that of commanding the advanced guards of marksmen and light guns.

The troops led by these men from the eastern side of the province have at last been brought to the scene of action, their part in which is to be so brilliant. But before I narrate their deeds, or

* In subsequent years Mr. Carnegy rose as high in the service as it was possible for an uncovenanted officer to rise. Had he had a commission, or had he entered the Civil Service, there is scarcely any position in India to which he might not have attained.

Book XI. Chapter VII.

1858. March.

The story reverts to Outram.

the deeds of their comrades now marching from Kánhpúr, it is fit that I should briefly tell how Outram had borne his part in the period which had elapsed since the Commander-in-Chief, on the 26th November, had entrusted to his safe keeping the Álambágh, and to his watchful eye a supervision over Lakhnao.

BOOK XI.

CHAPTER VIII.

In the second chapter of this book,* I stated that on the 26th November Sir Colin Campbell, marching with his large convoy to Kánhpúr, had left to occupy the Álambágh and to threaten Lakhnao, until he should return, Major-General Sir James Outram, with a force of between three and four thousand men of all arms, and twenty-five guns and howitzers.† As the period of Sir Colin Campbell's return is now approaching, it is fit that I should relate how Outram and his

* Page 222.

† The European force consisted of three hundred and thirty-two artillerymen, two hundred and ninety-two cavalry, two thousand seven hundred and seventy-one infantry; the Native, of one hundred and eight artillery, seventy-seven cavalry, and eight hundred and sixty-two infantry, or in all four thousand four hundred and forty-two. But, of these, five hundred and forty were detached to the Banni bridge. The infantry regiments were the 5th, the 95th, the 84th, the 98th, the 90th, the 1st Madras Fusiliers, the Firozpúr Regiment, the 27th Madras Native Infantry, and the Madras Sappers.

gallant warriors had comported themselves during the more than three months which intervened between the departure and the return of the Commander-in-Chief.

Book XI. Chapter VIII.

1857. December.

The Álambágh was one of the royal gardens, being a square of five hundred yards, enclosed by a wall about nine feet high, and entered by a handsome gateway. In the centre was a double-storied garden-house of masonry. The garden had been full of fruit trees; but these had been cut down, and all traces of them had disappeared. The wall, on the city side, had been strengthened by a strong ramp of earth; and an interior earthen ramp or traverse had been thrown all round the centre building to protect it from the enemy's fire. Well-formed earthen bastions had been erected at each angle, and the face of the enclosure next the road was protected by a ditch. It lay on the right of the high road coming from Kánhpúr, at a distance of about two miles from the outskirts of the city of Lakhnao.*

The A'lambágh.

Outram did not occupy the Alambágh with his main force. Holding it with a small detachment and a few guns, he pitched his camp in the open, about half a mile behind it. He then occupied a position across the road, extending to the right and left on either side; on the right as far as the fort of Jallálábád, and covered on all points by batteries, trenches, and abattis; on one or two by some happily situated swamps.

Position taken up by Outram.

The artificial defences I have indicated were

The enemy greatly dis-

* Gubbins's *Mutinies in Oudh*.

Book XI. Chapter VIII.

1857. December.

not thrown up at once, they were developed as the energy of the enemy showed them to be required. But that enemy had received a lesson so severe in the storming of the Sikandar Bágh and of the Shah Najíf, and in the bombardment of the Kaisar Bágh, that several days elapsed ere he ventured to show himself on the track of the conqueror who had robbed him of his prey. Nor was it till the early days of December that any indications of life or movement whatever were visible on his part. But on the 2nd December it became apparent that he had recovered heart, and that he was preparing an attempt to dislodge Outram.

heartened by the successful withdrawal.

Their leader devises a skilful plan to expel Outram.

The British right, resting on the fort of Jallálábád, was tolerably secure. The leader of the rebels, the famous Moulvi, known as Ahmad Shah, far from meditating an attack in that quarter, had devised a plan, not at all despicable had it been carried out with sufficient force and with energy, whereby, amusing the whole front of the British, he should suddenly turn their left, and pouncing on the Banni bridge, hem them in between two fires.

Recovering confidence, they begin to work out their plan.

The manner in which the rebels began to work out this plan indicated a return of confidence. They began, in the first week of December, to throw up batteries in front of the British left. When these were completed, they began to extend them towards their proper left, opposite the right centre of the British. Whilst these were in progress, they threatened the British position, skirmishing up to within grape distance, but always making their attacks in front. They repeated these until the gunners of Outram's force came to look forward to a daily visitation as a matter of course.

The rebels make their attack.

At length, on the 22nd December, the rebels threw off the mask, and attempted to carry out the programme they had drawn up. They sent a detachment of four thousand infantry, four hundred cavalry, and four guns, to march by the villages of Gaili and Badrúp to Banni, and there, in the rear of the British force, to intrench themselves, severing the communications with Kánhpúr.

Their plan had been betrayed to Outram.

Skilful as was this plan, it yet laboured under a fatal defect. Two days before it was executed it had been betrayed to Outram by his spies. Possessing the inestimable advantage of complete acquaintance with his enemy's designs, Outram determined to play their own game against them; and, whereas they were trying to sever his communications with Kánhpúr, he determined to cut them off from Lakhnao.

The rebels try to sever Outram's communications.

The rebels set out on the night of the 21st December, reached the village of Gaili, and, occupying a position between that village and Badrúp, encamped for the night. In that position they were not quite cut off from Lakhnao, for the left of their position was but half a mile from the Dilkúsha, which had, since Sir Colin's departure, been strongly reoccupied by the insurgents.

Outram attacks them,

Against the rebels so encamped, Outram started very early on the morning of the 22nd, with a force consisting of one thousand two hundred and

Book XI. Chapter VIII. 1857–8. Dec.–Jan.

twenty-seven infantry, under Brigadier Stisted, one hundred and ninety cavalry, under Major Robertson, and six 9-pounder guns, under Captain Olpherts. At daybreak he came upon them. Sending his centre against their main position, with his left he drove them from Gaili, doubling them back on Badrúp. Surprised, the rebels scarcely attempted resistance as these manœuvres were being carried out. They lost their four guns and an elephant. They were then again attacked and driven from Badrúp. Changing their line of retreat, they then fell back on the Dilkúsha. The pursuit then ceased, and in sufficient time. For the detachments from the main rebel army, hearing the uproar, were crowding from the Dilkúsha to retrieve the day. They arrived in time only to receive their beaten comrades. The loss of the rebels exceeded fifty killed. That of Outram amounted to two killed and some eight or ten wounded.

And drives them back on the Dilkúsha.

After three weeks' comparative rest, the courage of the rebels returns

This repulse considerably checked the enemy's ardour, and during the three weeks that followed they but once made a manifestation of attack. On this occasion they confined themselves to a long cannonade, ineffective against our position, but too successful in killing a most prominent artillery officer, Lieutenant D. Gordon. Nothing further occurred till the 12th January. But on that day the rebels made a supreme effort for victory.

on learning that Outram has weakened his force.

Circumstances seemed to favour them. They, too, were well served by their spies, and they had learned that on the 8th January Outram had weakened his force by four hundred and fifty infantry, eighty cavalry, and four guns, detached to protect a convoy of empty carts—to be laden and returned—he was sending into Kánhpúr.

Book XI. Chapter VIII.

1858. January.

Reasons for weakening the force.

A rebel partisan, named Mansúb Áli, was at this time in the district, in communication with the main body of the Lakhnao rebels. The task had been assigned to him to hover about the main line of British communication, and to harass and, when possible, to cut off small detachments and convoys. It had become known to Outram that early in January this man had received considerable reinforcements from Lakhnao. Hence it was that he had detached a large covering party with the convoy I have alluded to.

The Lakhnao rebels waited till they believed that the convoy and its escort had reached Kánhpúr. They then, on the morning of the 12th January, made their long meditated attack.

The rebels make their supreme effort.

They came out in force—to the number, it was estimated, of thirty thousand. Massing this large body opposite the extreme left of Outram's position, they gradually extended so as to face his front and his left flank, thus covering nearly six miles of ground. Threatening only with their left, their right centre and right advanced to the attack.

Outram develops his plans.

Outram waited till the enemy s movement should take some ascertainable form. He allowed them, therefore, to extend—even round his left flank. But the moment he began to advance he dealt, with rapidity, the counter blow he kept ready for delivery. Forming up his two brigades, the one consisting of seven hundred and thirteen, the

Book XI. Chapter VIII. — 1858. January.

other of seven hundred and thirty-three European troops, to face the front attack of the enemy, he directed the ever-daring Olpherts to take four horse artillery guns, and, supported by a detachment of the Military Train, to dash at the overlapping right of the enemy. The protection of the rear of the position in case it should be threatened, was confided to the volunteer and native cavalry.

Olpherts foils the enemy's right.

With the dash and energy eminently characteristic of the man, Olpherts took out his guns at a gallop, and pushing to the front, opened fire on the rebel masses just as they had begun the second overlapping movement, to gain the rear of the British position. The vigorous assault made by Olpherts completely disconcerted them. Renouncing their turning efforts, they fled in confusion and dismay.

Down foils their centre.

Whilst Olpherts was thus delivering a decisive blow on the extreme right, a repulse, scarcely less signal, had been inflicted upon the rebel troops opposed to the British left centre. These advanced with considerable spirit into a grove of trees in front of the picket commanded by Captain Down of the Madras Fusiliers, and usually occupied by him. Down allowed them to come rather near; then dashing at them with the bayonet, drove them back with loss. Whilst the enemy's attacks were thus being repulsed on the left and the left centre, they had not been idle on the British right. This part of the British line was covered by the fort of Jallálábád, upon which some rough repairs had been executed, and it was

Book XI. Chapter VIII.

1858. January.

considered comparatively unassailable. Acting upon the probability that it was, therefore, weakly defended, the enemy, whilst threatening, as we have seen, the left, and making on that side a noisy demonstration, had quietly massed a large body of infantry against the picket connecting the right with Jallálábád, and, bringing three guns to the front, opened upon that picket a heavy fire. But here, too, Outram was equal to the occasion. Bringing to the front, from the left of the right brigade, detachments of the 5th Fusiliers and Brasyer's Sikhs, and two guns of Moir's bullock battery, he took up a position which gave him the right flank of the enemy, and then opened upon that flank. The effect was instantaneous. The rebels abandoned the advanced position, evacuated the village they had occupied, and though for a time they continued the fire from their guns, their practice was bad, and caused no damage.

Outram foils their left,

Simultaneously with the attack just described, the enemy advanced against the Álambágh, and established themselves in a thick cover close to that enclosure. From this, about 12 o'clock, they advanced into the open. Here, however, they became exposed to a heavy fire from Maude's guns and riflemen, and they were soon driven back.

and they are driven back from the A'lambágh,

By 4 o'clock in the afternoon the rebels were in full retreat on all sides. Their losses must have been considerable. Outram's amounted, on that day, to only three wounded.

and the rebels fall back.

The serious manner in which the rebels were affected by their repulse and their losses was manifested in a very curious manner. The natives of

Religious influences affecting the natives.

Book XI. Chapter VIII. — 1858. January.

India are peculiarly influenced by religious influences. They believe in fortunate days and periods—days and periods peculiarly auspicious for producing certain results. It happened that the most learned pandit in Lakhnao had declared on the 12th January that unless the British were driven from their position within eight days from that period, they never would be expelled; and, moreover, that the period in question, from the 12th to the 20th inclusive, was peculiarly favourable to effecting their expulsion. In consequence of this prophecy it had been resolved by the rebels to give the British no rest throughout the period indicated.

But when the attack, prepared with so much foresight, and delivered with all the skill of which they were capable, failed, their spirits sank to zero; and, in spite of the pandit, they remained quiescent on the 13th and two following days. Nor was it till the 16th that they made their second attempt.

But though they made no attack on the British position, they did attempt to intercept the convoy.

The Moulvi's oath,

The active and determined Moulvi had sworn that he would capture the convoy and ride back into Lakhnao through the British camp. He left Lakhnao with a considerable force without baggage, on the night of the 14th, turned the British camp, and took up a position from which he could advantageously pounce on the convoy. Everything seemed to favour him. A violent dust storm was blowing towards the direction whence the convoy was approaching, and its leader had no warning. But again did Outram's prescience baffle him. Reports as to the Moulvi's movements had reached that general, and he, noting how the weather seemed to favour an attack, ordered out Olpherts with two guns and a detachment of the Military Train, on the road to Banni. He subsequently supported this small body with the rest of the battery and the Military Train, a detachment of Wale's Horse, and the 90th Light Infantry.

and Olpherts's performance.

Olpherts revelled in danger. He possessed the *coup d'œil* of a dashing leader, was ready in resource, and quick to act as circumstances might require. He waited for the enemy till he came in the open, and then opened on them and killed or dispersed them. The Moulvi was wounded, and narrowly escaped capture.

The British convoy safely arrives in camp.

Early on the morning of the 16th, between 1 and 3 o'clock, the convoy returned with supplies to the camp. The force was thus increased again by about four hundred men. No attack was anticipated, and many officers were about to unpack and distribute some of the private stores arrived, when, about 9 o'clock, the enemy made a sudden and very formidable attack on a picket guarding a battery in the process of erection, between Jallálábád and the camp. No guns were mounted here, and the picket had to fall back on the intrenchment; but the alarm had no sooner been given than Brasyer's Sikhs, ready for any emergency, rushed to the front, and rallying the picket, put the enemy to flight and captured their leader, attired in the imaginary costume of the

An attack on the right is repulsed by Brasyer's Sikhs.

Book XI. Chapter VIII. — 1858. Jan.-Feb.

god Hanumán. He turned out to be a Brahmin, very influential with his countrymen. The enemy's loss was severe.

That on the left

On the left the rebels confined themselves for several hours to a cannonade on the position. Their attack, though it ranged along the whole front, seemed specially directed against the picket occupying a village on the extreme left. Their grape and round shot came in very thick at this point, but beyond sending their cavalry within one thousand yards of the British front, only to be driven back, they made no demonstration with the other arms till evening had set in. But as soon as it was dark they pushed forward masses of infantry against the village. The officer commanding at this point was Major Gordon, 75th Regiment. Gordon allowed the enemy's masses to approach within eighty yards, when he opened out upon them with three guns and musketry, and drove them off immediately. The left rear was guarded by Olpherts with four horse battery guns and a detachment of the Military Train. With these he beat back the cavalry demonstration above indicated. The British loss from the enemy on this occasion amounted to one killed and seven wounded.

is driven back by Gordon and Olpherts.

Thenceforward till the 15th February the enemy cease to attack in force.

The failure on this occasion completed the discouragement of the rebels. From that time forth until the 15th February they confined themselves to demonstrations, to attempts to excite alarm—and to incessant bugling. Outram's spies announced attacks for given dates, but the dates passed by and the attacks were not made. Mean-

Book XI. Chapter VIII.

1858. Jan.-Feb.

while the conviction seemed to be stealing into their minds that they were bound to a losing cause. They heard of the loss of Fathgarh, and rumours even reached them of the capture of Baréli. This conviction was not slow in producing discord in their councils, and blows between rival chieftains. On the 22nd January the troops led by the Moulvi and those obeying the orders of the Bégam came to a sharp encounter, resulting in the slaying of about one hundred men. All this time the advance portion of Sir Colin's force was approaching, and on the 23rd January Outram received a reinforcement of ten guns escorted by a party of the 34th Regiment. To counterbalance this, the remnants of the heroic 75th, of Dehlí renown, left on the 14th February for the Himalayas.

Contentions among the rebels.

Outram receives reinforcements.

At last, goaded by the Moulvi, who, after a brief imprisonment by the Bégam's party, had escaped and assumed an ascendancy in the rebel councils, the enemy hazarded an attack on the 15th. They attempted their favourite plan of turning the left. But Outram was ready for them. The 90th turned out, and Olpherts, always full of zeal, galloped to the front with his guns, accompanied by the cavalry of the Military Train. When within four hundred yards of the rebels, Olpherts unlimbered and poured in round after round. The rebels could not stand it, but broke and fled. The British lost one man killed and one wounded.

The Moulvi attacks on the 15th,

but Olpherts drives him back.

On the morning of the 16th they threatened to renew the attack, but after a great deal of show, they retired; in the evening, however, they

Further vain manifestations of the rebels.

Book XI. Chapter VIII.

1858. Feb. 16.

came on against the whole British front as though they were in earnest. They made four separate advances, and retired as often, coming under musketry fire only on one point, the extreme left of the British. But finding the picket on the alert, they made no serious attack even here. Their advances were accompanied by yells and shouts and the clang of brass instruments. This day they admitted to a loss of sixty killed and wounded.

The rebels determine to attempt one last assault.

Stores were now coming in daily from Kánhpúr, and the movements of the various brigades of Sir Colin Campbell's force had become so pronounced as to spread conviction amongst the rebel leaders that unless they could, within the next five or six days, succeed in their projects against Outram, they would be for ever baffled. They determined, therefore, to try one last grand assault—an assault better planned, on a larger scale, and more sustained than any of its predecessors. Having ascertained from their spies that it was the custom of the General and a large proportion of officers and men to attend church parade early on Sunday morning, they fixed upon an early hour on the following Sunday, 21st February, for their great blow.

Sunday, 21st February.

They had calculated correctly. The men of the right brigade were attending a Church parade, the General being with them, when masses of the enemy began to concentrate opposite the extreme right and left of the British position. Captain Gordon, whom we have known as aide-de-camp to General Niell, and who was now on the Staff,

Book XI. Chapter VIII. 1858. Feb. 21.

noticed the movements of the enemy from No. 2 battery, and rode down to report the fact to the General. Outram at once sent down the Assistant Adjutant-General, Captain Dodgson, to turn out the left brigade, whilst the batteries opened all along the line. For the enemy, originally massing their forces on both flanks, had gradually extended inwards, and were threatening the whole position. They had advanced, in fact, within five hundred yards of the British position before the troops were turned out ready to receive him. But then the old story was repeated. On the right the enemy, advancing against Jallálábád, were checked by an artillery fire, whilst Captain Barrow, with two hundred and fifty of the volunteer cavalry and two guns, coming up from behind that fort, dashed upon a party sent to turn the British position, and drove them back to their main body. On the left Olpherts and a squadron of the Military Mounted Train, under Major Robertson, carried out the same plan, with the same success. Forced now to make a front attack, and threatened in turn on their left, the enemy did not long persevere. Once indeed they made as though they would try and overwhelm the left turning party, but at the decisive moment some well-directed rounds of shrapnel and round shot induced them to pause. "He who hesitates is lost" is a truth more applicable even to warfare than to the ordinary affairs of life. They did not renew their design, but, at a quarter past 10 o'clock, fell back, beaten, baffled, and humiliated,

The rebels fell back beaten.

Book XI. Chapter VIII.

1858. Feb. 25.

to the city. They admitted to a loss of three hundred and forty men killed and wounded. That of the British amounted to nine men wounded.

Outram receives reinforcements.

The last, the most desperate, and the best-fought attack was made on the 25th February. During the few days immediately preceding, troops from Kánhpúr had been gradually pouring in, and up to that date the force under Outram's orders had been strengthened by the arrival of Remmington's troop of horse artillery, of the 7th Hussars, of Hodson's Horse, and of the 1st Bengal Fusiliers. Hence he was now able, should he think fit, to retaliate more effectively on the enemy in the open plain.

The rebels make a final attack in sheer desperation.

The despairing attack of the rebels was made with all the pomp and circumstance of war. For the first time the royal Bégam, mounted on an elephant, attended by the Prime Minister and principal nobles, similarly mounted, accompanied the assailants. The proceedings began by a violent cannonade directed against the Álambágh at 7 o'clock in the morning. This lasted an hour. A little later, about 10 o'clock, a strong force was sent to threaten the British left, whilst the main body began to march along the right front, to the right, and out of the range of the guns. Of this force, which consisted of between twenty and thirty thousand men, a moiety, after passing the extreme point of the British right, made a sharp turn to the right again, and continued this until they had gained a position, sheltered by trees, in the right rear of the fort of Jallálábád. The other moiety, with which was the Bégam, halted at the turning angle, so as to support the attack, or to maintain communications with the main posts, as might be required. The advanced portion began at once to shell the fort of Jallálábád.

Book XI. Chapter VIII.

1858. Feb. 25.

Outram attempts to cut off the rebels from their base.

The movement of the rebels to the right rear of the British position had been so pronounced that, at last, Outram thought he had them. Taking with him his right infantry brigade, four of Olpherts's guns, four of Remmington's, a squadron of the 7th Hussars, the Military Train, and detachments of Hodson's Horse and Graham's Horse, he started, a little before 10 o'clock, to the right, to cut off the advanced moiety of the rebels, whilst Barrow's Volunteers and Wale's Horse, making a detour, should take them in rear.

He first drives back their supports.

The line taken by Outram naturally brought him in sharp contact with the second or reserve moiety of the rebel army. The cavalry with this reserve, numbering nearly a thousand, supported by infantry, came up to within seven hundred yards of Outram's left flank, and threatened to come nearer. But the ubiquitous Olpherts, always ready, at once wheeled his four guns to the left, and advancing a short distance, unlimbered and opened fire. The effect was remarkable. The Bégam left the field, the Prime Minister followed in attendance, and the courtiers accompanied to guard the Prime Minister. The consternation caused by the fire of Olpherts's guns had not abated—for the enemy had begun to fall back—when Remmington came up at full gallop, and

Book XI. Chapter VIII.

1858. Feb. 25.

taking up a position about four hundred yards to the left and in advance of Olpherts, opened fire on the retreating enemy; the squadron of the 7th Hussars and Brasyer's Sikhs advanced with them, and kept the enemy in check.

Brigadier Campbell charges and captures two guns.

Made secure of his left by the action of these gallant men, Outram pushed forward with the remainder of his force to deal with the first or advanced moiety of the enemy's army. Acting under his orders, Brigadier Campbell of the Bays took with him the Military Train and detachments of Hodson's Horse and Graham's Horse, and advanced beyond Jallálábád. Turning then to the right, he came in full view of the enemy. Alarmed by the sound of Olpherts's and Remmington's guns, the rebels, sensible of the presence of danger, were forming up hurriedly when they caught sight of Campbell's horsemen. Campbell gave them no time for reflection, but at once charged the two guns which had been playing on the fort. The sepoys, surprised as they were, did not flinch. They met the charge with courage, and though, as its result, the two guns remained in the hands of the Military Train, fifty corpses about them testified to the desperate valour of the defenders.

The rebels succeed in falling back,

The enemy's infantry meanwhile had fallen back on a tope of trees, from the upper branches of which some of their marksmen kept a constant fire on Outram's force as it approached. The defence of this tope was so sustained as to give time for the main body of the rebels to fall back and recover their line of retreat. They even once again threatened the fort, but gave way before the persuasive powers of Olpherts and Remmington.

Book XI. Chapter VIII.

1858. Feb. 25.

It was now half-past 2. The fighting for the day was apparently over. But the rebels were resolved to make one final effort. Strengthening their right with the troops who had fought in the morning, they made a desperate attack, about 5 o'clock, on the village forming the left front of the British position. Never had they fought with greater determination. They took possession of the tope of trees in front of the village, and then pressed on, encouraged by the fact that the British picket, just then short of ammunition, was falling back. But their triumph was short. A reinforcement came up, and forced them to retire. All that night, however, they continued their endeavours to take that village, threatening at the same time the entire left front of the position. Nor was it till the dawn of the following day that they gave up the task as hopeless.

and then make a final effort,

but are baffled.

With this attack the defence of the Álambágh may be said to merge into the more exciting drama of Lakhnao. It is, however, impossible to leave the gallant defenders of that important position without endeavouring, however inadequately, to indicate the great service which their prolonged occupation of it had rendered to the country. For more than three months Outram, with a force originally nearly four thousand strong, and subsequently often smaller, had kept in check the main army of the rebels. That army, known in November to count thirty thousand men, most of them trained soldiers, under its banners, had been

Service rendered to the country by the successful occupation of the A'lambágh.

Book XI. Chapter VIII.

1858. Feb. 28.

gradually augmented after the fall of Dehlí to more than treble that strength.* Between that augmented army and the Ganges lay Outram and his four thousand men—his right, his left, his rear, equally exposed. His nearest base was the Ganges; but between him and that base lay forty miles of road, guarded only at one point, the Banni bridge, and which, if sometimes occupied by the British, was occupied only by long convoys. He was, so to speak, in the air, liable to meet attacks on all sides. In point of fact, he was attacked on all sides—in front, on his flanks, and in his rear. If there be any who might be inclined to make light of the service rendered by his successful defence, I would ask them to consider what the state of affairs would have been had Outram succumbed to the attacks made upon him on all sides. He had no line of retreat but that leading to the Ganges. Driven from the Álambágh, he would have fallen back, hotly pursued, on that river. In the face of such pursuit, could he have crossed by the frail bridge of boats? No one will affirm that to

* Outram ascertained, on the 27th January, that the strength of the enemy on that date was as follows:—

37	trained regiments of sepoys	27,550
14	regiments of new levies	5,400
106	Najib, or irregular regiments	55,150
26	regiments of cavalry	7,100
	Camel corps	800
		96,000

This did not include artillerymen, the number of whom was unknown, nor the armed followers of the Talúkdars, estimated at 20,000. Altogether there could not have been less than 120,000 men in Lakhnao on that date.

Book XI. Chapter VIII. 1858. Feb. 28.

have been possible. He would have been lost; Kánhpúr would have been reoccupied; Sir Colin's communications would have been severed; the rebels might have captured Allahábád, and—the Ázamgarh district and Bihár being in revolt—they could then have penetrated to Calcutta. All this would have been possible, but all this Outram and his gallant followers prevented by their gallant defence.

The men who aided Outram.

Of Outram himself I have often spoken; but who were his followers? First, deserving a large meed of praise, comes Colonel Berkeley, of the 32nd Regiment, occupying virtually the position of chief of his staff. Than Berkeley it would have been difficult to find a more competent officer. To great activity of body he joined a head to devise the most complicated movements, and skill and coolness to carry them into execution. "He possesses," wrote Outram, after bearing testimony to his services, "to an extent I have rarely seen equalled, the power of securing the confidence, acquiring the respect, and winning the personal regard of those with whom he is thrown in contact." He was, in very truth, the right hand of his chief; and the relations between them, founded on mutual respect, were of the most cordial character.* Fit to be bracketed with Berkeley may be mentioned Vincent Eyre, Brigadier of the artillery force, who sustained to the full the reputation he had gained at Árah. In

* This most gallant officer did not long survive the campaign in which he was so gloriously engaged.

Book XI. Chapter VIII.

1858. Feb. 28.

Olpherts and Maude he had lieutenants of more than ordinary skill and daring, always to the front, and always full of fight. Dodgson, the Assistant Adjutant-General—the most modest, the least pushing, but the bravest of men; always cool, calm, self-possessed, and yet always in the place where his services were most required; Macbean, the able and energetic commissariat officer, without whose fertility of resource the army could not have been fed; Moorsom, the Assistant Quartermaster-General, uniting to the finest qualities of a fighting soldier the skill of the accomplished draughtsman;—it was to his skill, indeed, that Outram and Havelock were indebted for the plan which enabled them to penetrate so skilfully to the Residency; Gould Weston, who had served throughout the long defence of that Residency in command of Fayrer's house, and of whom, now attached to the Intelligence Department, Outram wrote in the despatch he penned after the capture of Lakhnao, that "he has signalized himself by the spirit and gallantry which he displayed on several occasions, and has been of much use to me"; Chamier and Hargood, most efficient as staff officers; Alexander Orr and Bunbury, useful from their knowledge of the country and the people; Barrow and Wale, daring cavalry leaders; Brasyer, of Brasyer's Sikhs—whose name in those stirring times was a household word; Nicholson, of the Royal Engineers, unsurpassed in his profession;—these are but a few names amongst the many of the gallant men who contributed to that splendid defence.

Book XI. Chapter VIII. — 1858. March 3.

But it has become a thing of the past. On the 1st March the Commander-in-Chief visited the Álambágh, and on the 3rd his troops were seen marching past that post. To the Commander-in-Chief, then, I must now return.

BOOK XI.

CHAPTER IX.

The force at Sir Colin's disposal.

THE force at the disposal of Sir Colin Campbell for the capture of Lakhnao amounted, inclusive of the division under the command of Outram, to twenty thousand men and one hundred and eighty guns. With such a force, four times as large as that with which he had relieved the Residency in November, Sir Colin was able to act on a scientific plan, at once effective and exposing to no unnecessary risk the lives of his soldiers.

This plan, drawn up in consultation with Colonel R. Napier, now Lord Napier of Magdála, may thus briefly be described.

Description of the defences of Lakhnao.

The city of Lakhnao on the right bank of the Gúmti cannot be strange to my readers. On that bank was the Residency; on that bank the Kaisar Bágh, the Moti Mahal, the Shah Najíf, the Barracks, the Sikandar Bágh, the Dilkúsha, and those other strong places described in the first chapter of this Book. On this side also was the city. On

Book XI. Chapter IX.

1858. March 1.

the left bank of the river were few buildings of strength. Some gardens indeed there were, such as the Bádshah Bágh, the direct road to which traversed the bridge of boats, but the ground was mainly covered by small earth-built houses, forming nominally a suburb, but reaching almost the dimensions of a town. Through this suburb ran the road across the iron bridge connecting the Residency with the old cantonment of Mariáon.*

The inner line of defence.

The city and the strong buildings on the right bank of the Gúmti were occupied by the rebels. They occupied an irregular parallelogram, covered on its northern side by the Gúmti; and on its eastern face by the canal, which, running into the Gúmti, forms a junction at right angles to it near the Nawáb ki Kothi. The third side of the figure was formed by an imaginary line running from the Chárbágh† bridge on the canal along the southern face of the city, and was guarded by an interior line of very strong posts, thus enumerated in their proper order: Banks's house, the fortified mosque which played an important part in November, the Bégam Koti, Hazrat Ganj, the Imámbára, and the Kaisar Bágh. The fourth side was partly open, but as it approached the Gúmti it had strong defences in buildings such as the Músa Bágh and the Great Imámbára. The city, I have shown in the preceding volume, was formed of narrow streets flanked by tall houses, and capable of a very strong defence. This position, naturally strong, had, during the three months which had clapsed since November,

* Vol. i. page 360.

† Vol. i. page 536.

Book XI. Chapter IX.

1858. March 1.

The canal.

been made infinitely stronger. The canal, from the Chárbágh bridge to its junction with the Gúmti, had been deepened in some parts, and at its lower end a new and straight cut had been dug to supersede the shallow and tortuous bed near that point. All the bridges over it had been broken down, and, regarding it as a wet ditch, the rebels had built a strong earthern rampart, with strong bastions at intervals, on the city side of it.

The second line of defence.

A second line of defence started from the Gúmti in front of the Moti Mahal, covered the Mess-house, the Imámbára, and the Hazratganj. A third line covered the river face of the Kaisar Bágh. This place, as well as the other places I have named, had been so strongly fortified as to constitute small citadels. The streets and main roads, too, had been blocked up at various points, the houses loop-holed and strengthened, and isolated batteries had been constructed in commanding positions.*

Such was the fortified camp, extremely strong on two sides of the parallelogram,† covered by works on which were mounted not less than one hundred and twenty guns and mortars of various calibres, and garrisoned by from sixty thousand to a hundred thousand armed men.

This camp possessed outworks beyond the canal —the Dilkúsha and the Martinière—both described in a previous chapter.

* Medley's *A Year's Campaigning*.

† I call it a parallelogram, as it more nearly approaches that figure than any other, but it was very irregular; the vast extent of the city and suburbs would violate the limits of any regular figure.

Book XI. Chapter IX.

1858. March 1.

But strong as was the fortified camp on the eastern and southern sides of the parallelogram, on the northern it was weak. There it had only the river Gúmti; and it was quite within the power of an enemy, by advancing on that face, to take all his defences in reverse. The western face had strong defences only near the Gúmti; elsewhere it was open.

The out-works of the defence.

The weak face of the defence.

Why the rebels should have neglected to throw up defences on the northern side seems, at the first glance, most strange. The real reason affords an additional proof to the many already cited of the absence of original thinking power from their ranks. The natives of India are essentially creatures of habit, of custom. When set to repeat a task already once accomplished they follow implicitly the lines previously trodden. So it was now. Havelock and Outram, in their attempt to relieve Lakhnao, had advanced by the Chárbágh bridge; Sir Colin Campbell, in November, had crossed the canal and attacked the Sikandar Bágh. Neither the one nor the other had approached the Gúmti. Hence, drawing the conclusion that the courses pursued before would be followed again, the rebels neglected the Gúmti, and concentrated all their energies on the lines previously attacked.

Reasons why this face was neglected.

Sir Colin Campbell detected at a glance the error they had committed, and he resolved to profit by it. He had men enough at his disposal to risk a division of his forces. He determined, then, to send across the Gúmti a strong *corps d'armée*, which, marching up that river, should

Sir Colin detects the weak point.

Book XI. Chapter IX. — 1858. March 1.

take the enemy's position in reverse, and, by the fire of artillery, render it untenable. At the same time, advancing with his main force across the canal, he would turn the enemy's position, and move by the Hazrat Ganj on the Kaisar Bágh.

His plan of attack.

Whilst a strong force should hold the base of the triangle Outram's force would occupy one side of it. Rather more than one half of the opposite side would be held by the Álambágh force and the Nipálese. Neither the remaining part of that side nor the western side could, with the troops at his disposal, be hemmed in, but it was to be hoped that as Sir Colin advanced his base, Outram might move round the angle on one side, whilst the Álambágh force and the Nipálese might close up round the corresponding angle on the other. Should the execution equal the design the entire rebel force would be reduced to extremities.

March 2. Sir Colin advances

Early on the morning of the 2nd March, Sir Colin Campbell began to execute his plan. Taking with him the headquarters of the Artillery Division (Sir A. Wilson and Colonel Wood, C.B.) and three troops of horse artillery (D'Aguilar's, Tombs's, and Bishop's), two 24-pounders, and two 8-inch howitzers of the Naval Brigade, and two companies of sappers and miners; the headquarters of the Cavalry Division (Hope Grant), and Little's Cavalry Brigade (9th Lancers, 2nd Panjáb Cavalry, detachment 5th Panjáb Cavalry, 1st Sikh Irregulars); and the 2nd Division of Infantry (Sir E. Lugard), comprising the 3rd and 4th Brigades: (3rd Brigade (Guy), 34th, 38th, and 53rd; 4th Brigade (Adrian Hope),

42nd and 93rd Highlanders and 4th Panjáb Rifles); he marched on the Dilkúsha park. Passing the fort of Jallálábád within sight of the Álambágh force, Sir Colin drove in the advanced pickets of the enemy, and captured a gun. The palace was then seized and occupied as an advanced picket on the right—a small garden, known as Muhammad Bágh, fulfilling the same purpose on the left. It was found impossible to bring up the main body of the infantry, for the enemy's guns, in position along the canal, completely commanded the Dilkúsha plateau. Sir Colin therefore drew back his infantry as far as was practicable, while he issued orders to erect batteries with all convenient haste at the Dilkúsha and the Muhammad Bágh to play on the enemy and keep down their fire. Until the batteries could be established—and they were not established till late on the night of the 2nd—the British troops were greatly annoyed by an unremitting fire, directed with precision on a point the range to which was thoroughly well known.

Book XI. Chapter IX.

1858. March 2.

on the Dilkúsha, which he captures,

and erects batteries there to keep down the fire of the rebels.

But when, on the morning of the 3rd, the batteries established at the Dilkúsha and Muhammad Bágh opened their fire, that of the rebels began perceptibly to decline. They were, in fact, forced to withdraw their guns, and though, from the further distance whence they directed a new fire, the shot occasionally ranged up to and into the British camp, it caused but a trifling loss. On that day and the day following, then, the remainder of the siege-train, together with the 3rd Division (Walpole's), comprising the 5th and 6th

March 3.

The batteries open

and silence the enemy's guns.

Book XI. Chapter IX.

1858. March 4.

More troops are massed on the Dilkúsha.

Brigades (5th Brigade (Douglas), 23rd Fusiliers, 79th Highlanders, 1st Bengal Fusiliers; 6th Brigade (Horsford), 2nd and 3rd battalions Rifle Brigade, 2nd Panjáb Infantry); closed up on the Dilkúsha.

New line occupied by the British.

The line now occupied by the British force touched the Gúmti on its right at the village of Bibiapúr, then stretching towards the left intersected the Dilkúsha, and proceeding towards Jallálábád, stopped at a point about two miles from that fort. The interval was occupied by one native regiment of cavalry, Hodson's Horse, nearly sixteen hundred strong. Outram's force, from which three regiments had been withdrawn, still occupied its old position.

Franks and his troops arrive.

To complete the position necessary to be occupied, if the complete success at which Sir Colin Campbell aimed were to be ensured, another strong division of troops was yet required. This want was supplied on the morning of the 5th by the arrival of Brigadier-General Franks with the gallant force of Europeans and Nipálese whose gallant deeds have already been imperfectly recorded.

Sir Colin orders the conquerors to bridge the Gúmti.

But before complete communication with Franks had been established, that is, on the evening of the 4th, Sir Colin had directed that two pontoon bridges should be thrown across the Gúmti near Bibiapúr. It was across those bridges that he would despatch the division of the army intended to march up the Gúmti and take the enemy's position in reverse.

A picket is thrown across

The engineers worked at the bridges all that

night with so much energy and effect that before the morning of the 5th dawned they had completed one of them. Across this was at once despatched a strong picket, which began without a second's delay to throw up a small earthwork to defend the bridge-heads. As the enemy showed shortly in some force in a village at a distance of about a thousand yards, some guns were brought down to the river-bank close to the bridges to silence the enemy's fire whenever it should become annoying. The precaution enabled the engineers to continue their work throughout that day and during the following night.

Book XI. Chapter IX.

1858. March 5.

One of these on the 5th.

By midnight on the 5th the two bridges and the embankments connecting them with the level on both sides were completed. Sir Colin, having counted on this, had directed Outram to cross to the left bank with a strong *corps d'armée* at 2 o'clock in the morning to carry out the plan I have already detailed. Outram had with him Walpole's division of infantry, the 2nd Dragoon Guards, the 9th Lancers, the 2nd Panjáb Cavalry, detachments from the 1st and 5th Panjáb Cavalry, D'Aguilar's, Remmington's, and Mackinnon's troops of horse artillery, and Gibbon's light field battery. Hope Grant accompanied him as second in command. It had been intended that he should cross at 2 o'clock in the morning; but the night was dark, the ground broken and full of watercourses, and the troops had much difficulty in finding their way. Outram, who had ridden on in front to the bridges,

Both completed on the night of the 5th.

Outram is ordered to cross.

March 6.

The difficulties of the ground delay him.

Book XI. Chapter IX.

1858. March 6.

dismounted, and knowing that nothing that he could do would hasten the arrival of his corps, sat on the ground and lighted a cigar. It was close upon 4 o'clock when the 2nd Panjáb Cavalry, leading the way, reached the ground. Then the crossing began. Sir Colin, angry at the delay, anxious that the troops should cross before the dawn should discover them to the enemy, came down to stimulate their movements.* His presence, due to a natural anxiety, really added nothing to the effect. The staff officers were in their places, doing their work calmly and efficiently, and before the day broke the whole force had completed the passage of the Gúmti. The place which it had left vacant on the right bank was at once occupied by Franks's division, the fourth.

Sir Colin's anxiety for the prompt crossing.

Importance of the position on the left bank of the river.

The reader will not fail to see that Outram, on the left bank of the river, was in a position to execute the first move in the game. He was to push up the left bank of the Gúmti, and turn and render untenable the strong positions of the enemy on the other side of it. When it should become apparent that he had turned the first line of those works, then, but not till then, would the second move be made by Sir Colin himself with the troops waiting for Outram's success in the position of which the Dilkúsha may be called the centre.

* "Sir Colin, being anxious to get his men across before the enemy could discover our intention and open upon us, rode down to the river-side and pitched into everybody most handsomely, I catching the principal share."—Hope Grant.

In pursuance of this plan, Outram, drawing up his force in three lines, marched up the left bank of the river for about a mile. The river there made a turn; so Outram, throwing forward his right, and leaving the sinuosities of the river, moved straight on in the direction of the city. A party of the enemy's cavalry which shortly afterwards appeared on his left was charged, routed, and pursued, though with the loss of Major Percy Smith of the Queen's Bays, described as an excellent officer. No further interruption to the progress of the force was offered, and it encamped that evening about four miles from the city, which it faced, its left resting on the Faizábád road, about half a mile in advance of the village of Chinhat.

Book XI. Chapter IX.

1858. March 6.

Outram pushes forward to the Faizábád road.

The following day and the 8th were spent mainly in skirmishing—the enemy advancing and being invariably repulsed. Outram, whilst maintaining his position, threw his pickets gradually much more forward. On the 8th, in obedience to instructions from Sir Colin, he sent back D'Aguilar's troop of horse artillery and the 9th Lancers, receiving in exchange twenty-two siege guns. That night he constructed two batteries, armed with heavy guns, within six hundred yards of the enemy's works on the old racecourse.

He advances his pickets and constructs batteries. March 7–8.

At daybreak the following morning, the 9th, he made his attack. Preluding it with a heavy fire from the newly constructed batteries, he detached a column of infantry under Walpole to attack the enemy's left, and, after forcing it back,

His plan of attack on the 9th.

Book XI. Chapter IX.

1858. March 9.

to wheel to the left and take them in the rear. He designed, meanwhile, to lead in person the left column across the Kokrail stream to a point whence, on the success of the right column being pronounced, it could attack and occupy a strong building known as the Yellow House—the Chakar Kothi—the key of the position of the rebels, and the occupation of which would turn and render useless the strong line of intrenchments erected by them on the right bank of the Gúmti.

Walpole beats the enemy's left

The result corresponded entirely to Outram's soundly based hopes. Walpole drove the enemy's left through the jungles and villages covering their position, and then bringing his right forward, debouched on the Faizábád road, in rear of their most efficient battery, which, however, was found empty. The left column, meanwhile, which had marched at 2 o'clock in the morning to take up the position assigned to it, as soon as it learned that Walpole had reached the Faizábád road, attacked the Yellow House. The rebels were there in numbers, but, with the exception of nine, they did not show fight, but made so rapid a flight along the banks of the river that before the guns could open upon them they were out of reach. The "nine," however, clung to the building, and killed or wounded more than their own number. Amongst them were Anderson of the Sikhs, and St. George of the 1st Fusiliers. It was only by firing salvoes from the horse artillery guns that they were eventually dislodged.*

and Outram their right.

* Hope Grant. They killed or wounded three officers and nine men.

The success of the column was notified to Sir Colin Campbell by the hoisting of the colours of the 1st Fusiliers on the roof of a small room erected on the second storey of the Yellow House.

Book XI. Chapter IX.

1858. March 9.

The column then pressed forward, following the rebels, drove them rapidly through the old irregular cavalry lines and suburbs to the Bádshah Bágh, and thence to the river, where they effected a junction with the right wing. The whole line then halted, and, occupying the houses and breastworks on the banks of the stream, opened and maintained a heavy fire on the rebels who lined the walls and occupied the gardens. Under cover of this fire three heavy guns and a howitzer were placed in position to enfilade the works in rear of the Martinière. Another battery of two 24-pounder guns and two 8-inch howitzers was likewise erected near the river to keep down the fire from the town.

Pressing the rebels,

Outram establishes a battery enfilading the enemy's works.

The first battery I have mentioned—that composed of three heavy guns and a howitzer—occupied the extreme left of Outram's line. It was commanded by Major Nicholson, R.E., of whose services at the A'lambágh I have already spoken, and protecting the guns was a party of the 1st Fusiliers under a very gallant and capable officer, Captain Salusbury. The guns had been unlimbered when Nicholson remarked that the hostile lines seemed abandoned by the rebels. Salusbury proposed to cross with a party of his men and ascertain the fact, but Nicholson considered it would be too hazardous to leave the guns without protection. At this conjuncture a young lieutenant of the 1st

The extreme left of Outram's line.

Book XI. Chapter IX.

1858. March 9.

Butler volunteers to signal to the Highlanders on the right bank.

Fusiliers, named Thomas Butler, and four privates, volunteered to go down to the river-bank and signal their presence to the Highlanders of Adrian Hope's brigade, who were discerned at a distance of about six hundred yards on the other side of the river. They ran down accordingly; but shouting and signalling were alike useless—they could attract no attention. It was very important to open the communication, and, all other means having failed, Butler did not hesitate an instant to try the last and the most hazardous. It was about 3 o'clock in the afternoon; the river was some sixty yards wide, its depth was considerable, the stream was strong. But Butler, caring for no consequences, heedless of the chance that the batteries on the other side might be occupied, took off his coat and swam across. He landed in rear of the batteries, which he found unoccupied. Mounting the parapet of one of the works, he quickly attracted attention, and after some delay caused by the stupidity of a staff officer, who considered it would not be correct to occupy the abandoned works without special orders, the Highlanders and 4th Panjáb Rifles relieved him. During the time that Butler, wet, cold, and unarmed, occupied the works, he was twice fired at by the distant enemy, but he did not leave them to swim back until he had made them over to the men of Adrian Hope's brigade. For his cool gallantry on this occasion Butler received the Victoria Cross.

Unable to attract their attention, Butler swims the river,

and attracts the attention of the 93rd.

Outram's movement on the 9th had thus answered every expectation. He occupied the left bank of the Gúmti as far as the Bádshah Bágh; the hostile batteries on the other side of the river were enfiladed. The enemy were completely taken in reverse. I propose now to show how, on that same day, the 9th, Sir Colin Campbell profited by Outram's manœuvres.

Result of Outram's operations on the 9th.

The Commander-in-Chief had waited patiently in his position at the Dilkúsha whilst Outram, on the 6th, the 7th, and the 8th, was executing the manœuvres which were the necessary preliminaries of the attack on the 9th, just described. Early on the morning of that day the guns and mortars, which, by Sir Colin's orders, had been placed in position on the Dilkúsha plateau during the preceding night, opened a very heavy fire on the Martinière. This fire was maintained until, about 2 p.m., the hoisting of the British ensign on the roof of the litttle room on the second storey of the Yellow House, made it clear to Sir Colin that Outram's attack had succeeded. Then, without the slightest delay, he launched Adrian Hope's brigade (the 4th), supported by the 53rd and 90th Regiments, the whole commanded by Lugard, against the Martinière. The effect of Outram's work that afternoon then became quickly apparent. The enfilading fire from the batteries which he had erected had caused the abandonment of a post which otherwise would have offered a strenuous resistance. It fell, so to speak, without a blow. The rebels, who had withdrawn their guns, fled precipitately across the river. The British loss was extremely small; and but for the fact that the returns re-

Sir Colin, in his turn, advances,

and carries the Martinière.

Book XI. Chapter IX.

1858. March 9.

cord a dangerous wound inflicted by a musket ball on the gallant William Peel,* they would be too slight to be specially recorded.

Adrian Hope occupies the works

Not content with the capture of the Martinière, Adrian Hope's brigade pushed onwards. The 4th Panjáb Rifles, gallantly led by Wylde, supported by the 42nd Highlanders, climbed up the intrenchment abutting on the Gúmti, and proceeded to sweep down the whole line of hostile works till close to the vicinity of Banks's house. It was to this brigade that the men belonged who occupied the fortified place which the gallant Butler had stormed single-handed. This and the works forming a line from the Gúmti to a point not far from Banks's house were occupied during the night by Adrian Hope's brigade and the 53rd Regiment.

from the Gúmti to the vicinity of Banks's house.

Total result of the fighting on the 9th.

The work of the 9th had, then, resulted in success on both the lines of operation. Outram, establishing himself on one side of the parallelogram, had made it possible for Sir Colin to push up the other side of it—and this he had effectively done.

Outram strengthens his position during the 10th.

The next day, the 10th, Outram intended to be a day of preparation rather than of conflict. The rebels being in considerable force in the suburbs in his front, he wished to strengthen the position he had already gained. But the rebels, fully aware now of the danger threatening them from across the Gúmti, came on in considerable force

* "He went out with his usual nonchalance to find a suitable place for some guns to be posted to breach the outer walls of the Martinière, when he was shot in the thigh by a musket ball." — *The Shannon's Brigade in India.*

Book XI. Chapter IX.

1858. March 10.

and attacked a picket held by the 79th Highlanders. They were, however, repulsed with loss, and the work designed by Outram proceeded thenceforward undisturbed. To ensure its rapid execution, the cavalry under Hope Grant patrolled the vicinity of the camp. This patrolling produced occasional conflicts with detached parties of the rebels, and in one of these Major Sandford of the 5th Irregular Cavalry, an officer of much promise, was killed. Throughout this day Outram's batteries at the mosque west of the Chakar Kothi played on Hazratganj and the Kaisar Bágh.

Sir Colin storms Banks's house.

The same day the Commander-in-Chief contented himself by completing the work of the previous evening by the storming and occupation of Banks's house. This was accomplished by Lugard with the troops already indicated, and with but trifling loss.

Total result of the fighting on the 10th,

By the evening of the 10th two sides of the parallelogram were all but completely occupied. The attempt to pierce its centre—to force the line stretching from Banks's house to a point beyond the Kaisar Bágh—was now to be made. Strong as were the buildings which constituted the value of that inner line, the position of Outram on the opposite bank of the Gúmti, and of Sir Colin Campbell now firmly established across the canal, having in Banks's house a post strong for attack, caused the chances to be very much in favour of the assailants. For whilst Outram enfiladed the enemy's works on one side, Sir Colin was now able to turn them on the other.

and prospects of the morrow.

Book XI.
Chapter IX.

1858.
March 10-11.

Outram is directed to attack the positions covering the iron and stone bridges.

In pursuance of the plan already indicated, Outram was directed to employ the evening and night of the 10th in establishing batteries which should rake the enemy's works, and annoy the Kaisar Bágh with a fire vertical and direct. He was also instructed to resume his offensive movement on the morning of the 11th by attacking the positions covering the iron and stone bridges—the former leading to the Residency, the latter to the Machi Báwan—and, by carrying them, to command the iron bridge from the left bank of the river.

He carries the positions leading to the iron bridge.

Outram carried out these instructions to the letter. He established during the night batteries which bore, in the manner prescribed, on the Mess-house and on the Kaisar Bágh. On the 11th, shortly after daylight, he led Walpole's column—the right—(79th Highlanders, 2nd and 3rd battalions Rifle Brigade, 1st Bengal Fusiliers, Gibbons's light field battery, and two 24-pounders) to gain a position commanding the iron bridge. The column, covered by the Rifles, worked its way through the suburbs till it reached a mosque within an enclosure at the point where the road from the Bádshah Bágh joins the main road to cantonments, about half a mile from the iron bridge. The place being very defensible, Walpole left there the 1st Fusiliers, and proceeded towards the stone bridge. On his way to this bridge he surprised and captured the camp of Hashmat Ali Cháodri of Sandíla, with that of the mutinous 15th Irregulars, took two guns and their standards, and killed many of those soldiers faithless to their salt.

1858. March 11.

Sending Gould Weston with a troop of the Bays to cut off the fugitives from Makkaganj—a service efficiently performed—Outram pushed on, without serious opposition, to the head of the stone bridge. Finding, however, that it was commanded by the enemy's guns, as well as by musketry fire from several high and stone-built houses from the opposite side of the river, he deemed it more prudent to retire to the mosque at the cross roads, there to remain till the operations I am about to record had been completed. He then fell back on his camp behind the Bádshah Bágh.

Pratt establishes batteries near the iron bridge.

Meanwhile the left column (23rd Fusiliers, 2nd Panjáb Infantry, two 24-pounder guns, and three field battery guns), commanded by Lieutenant-Colonel Pratt, starting twenty minutes after the right column, had met with considerable opposition, and, being exposed to the fire of a hostile battery from the right side of the river, suffered considerable loss. It succeeded, however, in occupying all the houses down to the river's bank and the head of the iron bridge, to the right of which the two 24-pounder guns were placed in battery. It was a difficult and dangerous operation, and though it succeeded, it cost Outram the lives of two of his most gallant officers, Captain Thynne of the Rifle Brigade, and Lieutenant Moorsom, Deputy Assistant Quartermaster-General, a soldier of remarkable talent and promise. He was guiding the column, and was killed whilst reconnoitring in front of it.

It may be convenient, for the sake of clearness, here to add that the positions taken up by Out-

Book XI. Chapter IX. — 1858. March 11–15. ram on the 11th continued to be occupied by him on the 12th, 13th, 14th, and 15th. During those days he carried out, with vigour and accuracy, the purpose he had in view—the maintenance of an enfilading fire, raking the positions which the Commander-in-Chief was assailing on the other side of the river. Having been reinforced on the 12th by four 18-pounder guns, two 10-inch howitzers, and five 10-inch and four $5\frac{1}{2}$-inch mortars, he erected, in addition to the batteries already enumerated, three more to play on the Kaisar Bágh; and when that strong place fell, as I am about to recount, on the morning of the 14th, he turned the fire of those batteries against the Residency and the buildings to the right of the bridge. It can easily be conceived the enormous assistance rendered to the main attack by this heavy enfilading fire, maintained without the slightest intermission. It had been possible to do even more, but he was hampered, as I shall show in its proper place, by restrictions to action placed on him by the Commander-in-Chief.

March 10. I now return to Sir Colin. I left him, on the evening of the 10th, established on the city side of the canal on a line stretching from the Gúmti to Banks's house. Whilst the Chief Engineer, Brigadier Robert Napier, maintained a heavy fire from Banks's house on the works in front—especially on the block of palaces known as the Bégam Kothi—Lugard, bringing forward his right, occupied, without opposition, the Sikandar Bágh—famous in Sir Colin's first advance for the splendid gallantry

The Sikandar Bágh occupied.

Book XI. Chapter IX. — 1858. March 10.

of Ewart and Cooper and their dozen followers, Highlanders and Sikhs—and then prepared to work his way to the Shah Najíf. His operations were greatly facilitated by the noble daring of three engineer officers attached to his column, Medley, Lang, and Carnegy.

The happy audacity of three engineer officers

From three to four hundred yards to the right front of the Sikandar Bágh stood an isolated building high on a mound overlooking the river, called the Kaddam Rasúl. Beyond this again, but in close vicinity to it, was the Shah Najíf, the building which, in Sir Colin's first advance, had almost made him falter, and the capture of which was due to the keen observation and happy audacity of Sergeant Paton* and Adrian Hope. Both these posts were immediately outside the enemy's third line of works, which ran in front of the Moti Mahal, the old Mess-house, and the Tárá Kothi. Lang, noticing that the two posts I have referred to, the Kaddam Rasúl and the Shah Najíf, were very quiet, proposed to his companions that they should reconnoitre, and possibly occupy, them. The three officers at once set out, followed by four native sappers. Creeping quietly up to the Kaddam Rasúl, they found it abandoned. Entering it and ascending the little winding staircase, they looked down into the garden of the Shah Najíf. This seemed also abandoned. But not liking to make, with four men, an attack, which, if the interior of the place were occupied, would certainly fail, the engineers, leaving the four

gains the Kaddam Rasúl

* *Vide* page 194.

Book XI. Chapter IX.

1858. March 10.

sappers to guard their conquest, returned to the Sikandar Bágh to ask for men to take the Shah Najíf. The officer commanding at that post declined, however, to take upon himself a responsibility from which, in the case of the Kaddam Rasúl, the engineers had not flinched, whereupon Medley rode to Banks's house to obtain an order from Lugard. This was at once granted, and Medley, returning, had placed at his disposal one hundred men. With these and fifty sappers, the engineers entered the place and found it abandoned. As it was but two hundred yards from the line of intrenchments already spoken of, the engineers at once set to work to make it defensible on the side nearest the enemy, and, at Medley's suggestion, one hundred men were thrown into the place.*

and the Shah Najíf.

Lugard effects a breach in the Bégam Kothi.

Whilst this operation was successfully conducted on the right, the guns from the heavy batteries on the left were pouring shot and shell on the Bégam Kothi. The contiguous palaces known under this designation were extremely strong, capable, if well defended, of resisting for a very long time even the fighting power sent against them by Sir Colin Campbell. But in warring against Asiatics, the immense moral superiority which assault gives to an assaulting party is an element which no general can leave out of con-

* This deed of happy audacity was not mentioned in the despatches. It was, however, well known in camp. My account of it is taken almost *verbatim* from the statement of one of the actors, to whom it is unnecessary further to refer.

Book XI. Chapter IX.

1858. March 10.

sideration. It is true that on this occasion, about half-past 3 o'clock in the afternoon, a breach was effected which opened a way to stormers; but the breach was so narrow, and the defences behind it were so strong, that if the men who lined them had been animated by a spirit similar to that which inspired the assailants, no general would have dared to attempt an assault.* As it was, though unaware of the extreme strength of the inner defences, Lugard, on the breach being pronounced, gave, without hesitation, the order to storm.

and sends Adrian Hope's brigade to storm it.

The storming party consisted of those companions in glory, the 93rd Highlanders and the 4th Panjáb Rifles. It was indeed fit that to the men who, in the previous November, had stormed the Sikandar Bágh and carried the Shah Najíf should be intrusted the first difficult enterprise of Sir Colin's second movement on Lakhnao. Fortunate in their splendid discipline, in their tried comradeship, in their confidence each in the other, the 4th Panjáb Rifles and the 93rd Highlanders enjoyed the additional privilege of having as their leader one of the noblest men who ever wore the British uniform, the bravest of soldiers, and the most gallant of gentlemen. Those who had the privilege of intimate acquaintance with Adrian Hope will recognise the fitness of the description.

Description of the Bégam Kothi.

The block of buildings to be stormed consisted

* "At the Bégam's palace the defences were found, after the capture of the place, so much stronger than could be observed or had been believed, that the General said that had he known what lay before the assaulting column he should have hesitated to give the order for advance."—*Twelve Years of a Soldier's Life in India*, page 393, note.

Book XI. Chapter IX.

1858. March 10.

of a number of palaces and courtyards, one within the other, surrounded by a breastwork and deep ditch. The artillery fire had breached the breastwork and the wall of the outer courtyard, but some of the inner walls had not been seriously injured. They were occupied by a considerable body of sepoys, probably exceeding rather than short of five thousand.

The assault.

At 4 o'clock in the afternoon Adrian Hope led his men to the assault, the 93rd leading, the 4th Panjáb Rifles in support. The sepoys, not yet daunted, met their assailants in the breach, and for a short time their greatly superior numbers offered an obstacle difficult to pierce. But individual valour, inspired by a determination to conquer, was not to be withstood. The Adjutant of the 93rd, William McBean, cut or shot down eleven of the enemy with his own hand. His example was followed by many others. The Panjábis, pressing on from behind, added to the weight of the attack. Their behaviour excited the admiration of everyone. When a Highlander chanced to fall, his native comrades rushed forward to cover his body and avenge his death. The splendid rivalry of the two soon made itself felt. Forced back from the breach, the sepoys scarcely attempted to defend the strong positions yet re-

The Bégam Kothi is gained.

maining to them. They seemed to have but one object—to save themselves for a future occasion. But the Highlanders and the Panjábis pressed them hard. Quarter was neither asked for nor given, and when the Bégam Kothi was evacuated by the last survivor of the garrison, he left be-

Book XI. Chapter IX.

1858. March 10.

hind him, within the space surrounded by the deep ditch of which I have spoken, six hundred corpses of his comrades! It was "the sternest struggle which occurred during the siege." *

Robert Napier proceeds by the sap and heavy guns.

The capture of the Bégam Kothi opened to the Chief Engineer, Brigadier Napier, the means of dealing destructive blows against the remaining positions of the enemy. It brought him inside the enemy's works, and the enclosures the assailants had stormed now served as a cover from the enemy's fire. "Thenceforward," says Sir Colin, in his report, "he pushed his approach, with the greatest judgment, through the enclosures by the aid of the sappers and of heavy guns, the troops immediately occupying the ground as he advanced, and the mortars being moved from one position to another as ground was won on which they could be placed."

Death of Hodson.

The storming had been effected with comparatively small loss on the side of the British. But amongst those who fell was one who had made a name for himself as a most daring and able soldier. Hodson, of Hodson's Horse, was mortally wounded on this day. He had joined the storming party, had entered the breach with Robert Napier, and had been separated from him in the *mêlée*. He was not wounded during the storm; but, after the breach had been gained, he rushed forward to hunt for sepoys who might be concealed in the dark rooms and corners of the palace. Coming suddenly upon a party of these,

* Sir Colin Campbell's Official Report.

Book XI. Chapter IX.

1858. March 10-11.

he was fired at and mortally wounded. The Highlanders avenged his death, for they bayoneted every man of the group which had fired at him.

My opinion of Hodson has been recorded in an early page of this volume. I have little to add to it. His abilities were great. As a partisan soldier he was not to be surpassed. But the needless slaughter of the princes of the House of Taimúr would seem to indicate that he was born more than a hundred years after the era when all his qualities would have obtained recognition. Trenck and his Pandours were too bloody and too savage for the civilisation of 1756; and Trenck was never accused of shooting unarmed prisoners.

Position of the assailants the evening of the 11th.

The position of the assailing force on the evening of the 11th was in considerable advance of that it had occupied in the morning. It was now pushed forward to the Shah Najíf on the right, and it held the Bégam Kothi on the left. Before the Kaisar Bágh could be assailed, the Mess-house, the Hazrat Ganj, and the Imámbárá had first to succumb.

The Nipál troops arrive.

On that day the Nipál troops, led by the Mahárájá Jang Bahádur, were brought into line. This reinforcement enabled Sir Colin Campbell, as I shall show, to extend the plan of his operations on the succeeding days.

Franks's division comes to the front on the 12th.

The following day, the 12th, was a day chiefly for the engineers. Their work proceeded steadily and surely. Some changes, however, were made in the disposition of the troops. Lugard's division, the 2nd, which had hitherto been in the

Book XI. Chapter IX.

1858. March 12-13.

front, was relieved by Franks's, the 4th. The Nipál troops, too, were brought into line, and ordered to advance on the British left, so as to hold the line of the canal beyond Banks's house.

Napier presses forward with the sap.

The 13th was likewise an engineer's day. Avoiding the main road, which was well defended by the enemy's batteries, Napier pressed forward on a line about one hundred and twenty yards to its left and parallel to it, sapping through the houses, out of the line of the enemy's fire. When necessary, the heavy guns opened breaches for his advance, and the sappers, supported by the infantry, pushed on slowly but steadily, enlarging the breaches communicating with the rear, so as to have a way ready for supports, should they be required. The overwhelming superiority of the British artillery fire, supported as it was by Outram's enfilade and cross fire from the other side of the Gúmti, effectually prevented any serious annoyance from the enemy's guns. The rebels maintained, however, from the neighbouring houses, a hot fire of musketry on the advance, to which the men forming the latter replied effectively.*

The Nipálese operate on the extreme left.

This day, too, the Nipál force, crossing the canal, moved against the suburb considerably to the left of Banks's house. This operation drew the attention of a portion of the rebel force to that quarter at the same time that it covered the left of the British army.

* *A Year's Campaigning in India.*—Medley.

Book XI. Chapter IX.

1858. March 13-14.

Position on the evening of the 13th.

By the evening of the 13th the task assigned to the engineers had been completed. All the great buildings on the left up to the Imámbárá had been sapped through. The battery which had been playing on the massive walls of that building had effected a breach, and it was hoped that it would be sufficiently practicable on the morrow to permit an assault.

The morning of the 14th.

Early on the morning of the 14th, the heavy guns, at a distance of thirty yards, were still pounding at the breach—"the 8-inch shot, at this short distance, walking through three or four thick masonry walls in succession as if they had been so much paper."* The enemy were replying from the walls with musketry fire. At length, about 9 o'clock in the morning, the breach was reported practicable; and the stormers, who had been drawn up, awaiting the signal, received the order to assault.

Franks storms the Imámbárá.

The storming party was composed of sixty men of Brasyer's Sikhs and two companies of the 10th Foot, supported by the remainder of the two regiments. These men, gallantly led, dashed at the breach with all the impetuosity of their pent-up energies. The defenders waited to receive them; nor was it until after a very sharp struggle that they were forced back in disorder. Once forced back, they fled as though panic-stricken, and in a few minutes the Imámbárá was in the possession of the stormers. The support and reserve followed, completing the lodgment. In

* Medley.

Book XI. Chapter IX.

1858. March 14.

the assault there fell a very gallant officer of the regiment of Firozpúr, Captain Da Costa, who had volunteered for this special service. He had lived a life which had brought him many enemies, but the hostility of the bitterest of them would have changed to admiration had they witnessed the heroic manner in which he led his men to the assault.

The stormers gain a position commanding a portion of the Kaisar Bágh.

The gain of the Imámbárá did not quench the zeal of the stormers. The rebels were in such haste to save themselves that, emerging from the Imámbárá through the great gateway into the road, they ran as fast as they could to the Kaisar Bágh. Brasyer's Sikhs, burning to avenge Da Costa's death, dashed after them as they fled, and a few men of the 10th joined in the pursuit. Following in a parallel line, a portion of the 90th, guided by the Deputy Assistant Adjutant-General of the Division, Henry Havelock, forced their way into a palace which commanded three bastions of the Kaisar Bágh. Once in that position, they brought to bear upon the enemy's gunners below them a fire so withering that one by one the guns were deserted, the last to fire being an 8-inch howitzer, which was only abandoned under pressure not to be withstood. This daring act had the most important consequences. By it the second line of the enemy's defences, the line stretching from the Gúmti, in front of the Mess-house, to the Imámbárá, was turned. Its defenders, panic-stricken at seeing their position thus taken in reverse, had no thought but to save themselves. Abandoning, then, the second line, they ran into the

Book XI. Chapter IX.

1858. March 14.

buildings yet intervening between the Imámbárá and the Kaisar Bágh, and from behind the walls of these endeavoured to stay the further progress of our troops. Then it was that the engineers proposed to suspend operations for the day, and to proceed by the slower process of sap. But the men, the Sikhs of Brasyer's regiment especially, were not to be restrained. The joy of conquest had mastered every other feeling. Led by Brasyer and Havelock, they effected an entrance into a bastion by a vacant embrasure, and forced their way, cheering, under a terrible fire into a courtyard adjoining the Kaisar Bágh, driving the enemy before them.

Brasyer's Sikhs gain a courtyard adjoining the Kaisar Bágh.

Seeing the possibilities before him—the chance of gaining the Kaisar Bágh at a blow—Havelock ran back to the detachment of the 10th Foot, commanded by Captain Annesley, and ordered it to the front. Obeying with alacrity, the 10th dashed to the front and joined the Sikhs. A portion of these latter, led by Brasyer, diminishing by casualties as they went, pushed daringly on, nor did they halt until, expelling the enemy before them, they had penetrated to the Chíní Bázár, to the rear of the Tárá Kothi and Mess-house, thus turning the third line of the enemy's works.

The Sikhs and 10th Foot turn the third line of the defences.

The enemy, congregated in numbers at not less than six thousand in the Tára Kothi and the Mess-house, now finding themselves taken in reverse, evacuated these buildings, and endeavoured to re-enter the city by an opening in the further gateway of the Chíní Bázár. Had they succeeded in so doing, they would have cut off Brasyer and

The rebels evacuate that line.

his gallant band, which must then have been overwhelmed. But Havelock, advancing with sixty Sikhs, in support of Brasyer, promptly seized two adjoining bastions, and, turning the six guns found there on the enemy, so plied their masses, issuing from the positions above named, with round shot, grape, and musketry, that he stopped their dangerous movement and turned them back.

This action assured the posts won by the advanced party. Gradually Havelock's small body was strengthened by a company of the 90th, brought up by Colonel Purnell himself, and from that moment success was certain.

Supports arrive.

By this time the fourth note sent by Havelock urging him to come on reached Franks, and that gallant officer at once pushed forward with every available man to aid the advanced parties. His arrival shortly after with his supports, accompanied by the Chief Engineer, made the position of the attacking party completely solid. The only question now to be solved was, whether the advantages already so wonderfully achieved should or should not be turned to account by the storming of the Kaisar Bágh.

Shall the advantage be pursued?

Every consideration seemed to urge the attempt. Although that morning it had been intended to storm only the Imámbárá, events had moved so quickly, the assailants had displayed so much energy and daring, the enemy had been so mastered by panic, that it seemed advisable to push on whilst the stormers were still eager, the rebels still dejected.

Accordingly, after a brief consultation, Franks

Book XI. Chapter IX.

1858. March 14.

and Napier resolved to push on. Reinforcements were sent for from the rear, and an order was despatched to the troops at the Sikandar Bágh and the Shah Najíf on the right to push forward.

The Kaisar Bágh is stormed.

The reinforcements soon came up, and whilst the troops on the right advanced and occupied, with but little resistance, the Moti Mahal, the Chattar Manzil, and the Tárá Koti, Franks sent his men through the court of Sádat Ali's mosque into the Kaisar Bágh itself. The Kaisar Bágh is a rectangular enclosure, made up of a series of courts and gardens, interspersed with marble summer-houses. These were still full of sepoys, who, from the roofs and from the summits of the houses in the adjoining enclosure, poured a heavy musketry fire on the invaders. But the British once within the garden, the game for which the rebels were struggling was lost, and, in a comparatively short space, those of them who had failed to escape lay dead or in death's agony.

The plundering which followed.

Then began a scene of plunder, of which it is difficult to give an adequate description. The glowing words of an eye-witness, then in the zenith of a literary fame which still lives, mellowed by time and increased by experience, brings it, however, as vividly before the reader as words can bring a scene so rare and so terrible. "The scene of plunder," wrote Dr. Russell, "was indescribable. The soldiers had broken up several of the store-rooms, and pitched the contents into the court, which was lumbered with cases, with embroidered

Book XI. Chapter IX. 1858. March 14.

cloths, gold and silver brocade, silver vessels, arms, banners, drums, shawls, scarfs, musical instruments, mirrors, pictures, books, accounts, medicine bottles, gorgeous standards, shields, spears, and a heap of things which would make this sheet of paper like a catalogue of a broker's sale. Through these moved the men, wild with excitement, 'drunk with plunder.' I had often heard the phrase, but never saw the thing itself before. They smashed to pieces the fowling-pieces and pistols to get at the gold mountings, and the stones set in the stocks. They burned in a fire, which they made in the centre of the court, brocades and embroidered shawls for the sake of the gold and silver. China, glass, and jade they dashed to pieces in sheer wantonness; pictures they ripped up, or tossed on the flames; furniture shared the same fate. . . . Oh the toil of that day! Never had I felt such exhaustion. It was horrid enough to have to stumble through endless courts which were like vapour baths, amid dead bodies, through sights worthy of the Inferno, by blazing walls which might be pregnant with mines, over breaches, in and out of smouldering embrasures, across frail ladders, suffocated by deadly smells of rotting corpses, of rotten ghee, or vile native scents; but the seething crowd of camp-followers into which we emerged in Hazratganj was something worse. As ravenous, and almost as foul as vultures, they were packed in a dense mass in the street, afraid or unable to go into the palaces, and, like the birds they resembled,

Book XI. Chapter IX.

1858. March 14.

waiting till the fight was done to prey on their plunder."*

Result of the day's work.

The day's work was over. A work great, unexpected, and, in every sense of the word, magnificent. The line which in the morning had stretched from the Shah Najíf to Hazratganj now ran from the Chattar Manzil to the Residency side of the Kaisar Bágh. Two strong defensive lines of works, garrisoned by thirty thousand to forty thousand men, had been turned, and the great citadel on which the second of those two lines rested had itself been stormed!

It was a great, even a magnificent work, but it might, and ought to, have been greater. Its greatness and magnificence were due mainly to the Sikhs and the 10th Foot, to the gallant leading of Havelock and Brasyer, the confident daring of Franks, and the skill of Napier—its want of completeness is attributable solely to Sir Colin Campbell and Mansfield. How this was so I shall explain in a few words.

Outram proposes to cross by the iron bridge.

In a previous page I have narrated how, on the 13th, 14th, and 15th, Outram continued to occupy his positions on the left bank of the Gúmti commanding the direct approaches to the iron bridge, but restricted from further movement in that direction by the orders of the Commander-in-Chief. The iron bridge led across the river to a point not far from the Residency. Now, when, on the 15th, the stormers under Franks attacked the Imámbárá, and, pushing onwards, dashed

* *My Diary in India*, by William Howard Russell.

Book XI. Chapter IX.

1858. March 14.

against the Kaisar Bágh, the enormous effect which would have been produced by the crossing of the river and the penetrating into the very heart of the enemy by Outram's division, may be imagined. Outram wished to carry out such an operation, and applied to the Commander-in-Chief for permission to do so. In reply he was informed by the Chief of the Staff that he might cross by the iron bridge, but "that he was not to do so if he thought he would *lose a single man.*" A more extraordinary proviso never accompanied an order to advance given to a general in the presence of the enemy. It was tantamount to an absolute prohibition. Outram had that afternoon reconnoitred the enemy's position across the river. His plans were laid, his troops were ready to attack, but he saw that there was at least one gun on the bridge; that the bridge itself was commanded by a large mosque and by houses which had been loop-holed; and that the rebels, in anticipation of a forward movement on his part, had laid their batteries in such a manner as to render it difficult and dangerous. Not only, then, would he have lost one man, but probably very many. On the other hand, the passage of the Gúmti by Outram that afternoon would have been fatal to the enemy. It would have in a great measure intercepted their retreat. Their slain would have been counted by thousands, and, in all probability, the province of Oudh would have immediately succumbed. The rebels who escaped on the 14th were the rebels who fell back on the forts and strong places of the province, there to renew the re-

Unsatisfactory reply of the Commander-in-Chief.

Book XI. Chapter IX.

1858. March 14.

sistance which had broken down in the capital. Had they been cut off, that resistance would not have been !

Comments on the Commander-in-Chief's reply.

That they were not attacked in their retreat was due solely to Sir Colin's order to Outram not to advance if the advance would cost him the life of *one single man.* Why the hands of a gallant soldier like Outram were thus tied is a question which has not been answered. True it is that Sir Colin had only contemplated on the 14th an attack on the Imámbárá. The Kaisar Bágh, in his programme, was reserved for the day following. But he had sufficient experience of war to be aware that the unexpected is always possible, and knowing that, he committed a grave error when he restricted the action of a lieutenant occupying a position which, under certain circumstances, could be made fatal to the enemy. In the camp the order was attributed to the counsels of Mansfield; but the responsibility rested, and still rests, with Sir Colin.

To return. The 14th, as we have seen, had been a day devoted entirely to work, and to little but work. It was necessary to take early measures to consolidate the progress which had then been

The 15th on the right bank of the river.

made. To this end the 15th was devoted—on the right bank of the Gúmti. Under the orders of the Commander-in-Chief powder was removed, mines were destroyed, and mortars were fixed for the further bombardment of the positions still held by the rebels on the line of advance, up the right bank of the river, and in the heart of the city.

The 15th on the left bank.

On the left bank it was different, Here two movements were ordered, both of which would have been more effective if directed the previous day. Sir Colin, sensible now that the door of retreat had been left too open to the enemy, despatched Hope Grant, with eleven hundred cavalry and twelve horse artillery guns, to pursue them along the Sitápúr road. Brigadier Campbell was likewise directed to move with his infantry brigade, some guns, and fifteen hundred cavalry from the Álambágh on the Sandíla road. Neither of these operations came to anything. The rebels had taken neither the Sandíla nor the Sitápúr road, and the only effect of the two movements, combined with a third on the 16th, to which I am about to refer, was to leave open to them the road to Faizábád, by which more than twenty thousand of them eventually escaped.

Book XI. Chapter IX.

1858. March 15.

Hope Grant and Campbell are sent to pursue the rebels,

who, however, escape.

The third movement was made by Outram. That general was directed on the 16th to cross the Gúmti, near the Sikandar Bágh, with Douglas's brigade, the 5th, (23rd, 79th Highlanders, 1st Fusiliers), and join the Commander-in-Chief at the Kaisar Bágh, leaving Walpole's brigade still in its position on the left bank watching the iron and stone bridges.

Outram ordered to cross the Gúmti.

March 16.

Outram crossed the Gúmti by a bridge of casks, far removed from the fire of the enemy, near the Sikandar Bágh, and, joined by the 20th Regiment and Brasyer's Sikhs, marched towards the Kaisar Bágh by a road made the previous day by the sappers. On the way Sir Colin rode out to the force and gave his final instructions to Outram. These were to push on through the Residency, take the iron bridge in reverse, and

He crosses near the Sikandar Bágh

and moves on the Residency.

Book XI. Chapter IX.

1858. March 16.

then, advancing a mile further, to storm the Machhi Báwan and the great Imámbárá.

Contrast between the English and the Indian defence of the Residency.

Outram pushed on at once, passed through the Kaisar Bágh, and then moved straight on the Residency. As his little force neared the venerated and battered defences of that monument of British valour, the 23rd leading, it was assailed by a fire of musketry from the line of posts which Aitken and Anderson, Sanders and Boileau, Graydon and Gould Weston, and many noble men had defended so long and so bravely. But now the positions were inverted. Then the assailants were Asiatics, the defenders mostly Englishmen. Now Asiatics defended, Englishmen assailed. The difference showed itself in a remarkable manner. For whereas in the former case the Englishmen defended themselves, unassisted, for eighty-four days, in the latter the Asiatics were disposed of in less than half an hour. One charge of Outram's division, and the enemy fled, panic-stricken and panting, from the classic ground.

Outram, pushing forward,

The 23rd pursued the fleeing rebels, followed by Brasyer's Sikhs and the 1st Fusiliers. Two companies of the 23rd under Lieutenant-Colonel Bell, guided* by Gould Weston, pressed rapidly forward, and, taking the enemy's defences in reverse, captured the gun of which I have spoken as commanding the passage across the iron bridge. The force then pushed on, taking in reverse the batteries between the two bridges.

* Outram's despatch.— This was a duty often assigned to Captain Weston, one for which his knowledge of the localities peculiarly fitted him.

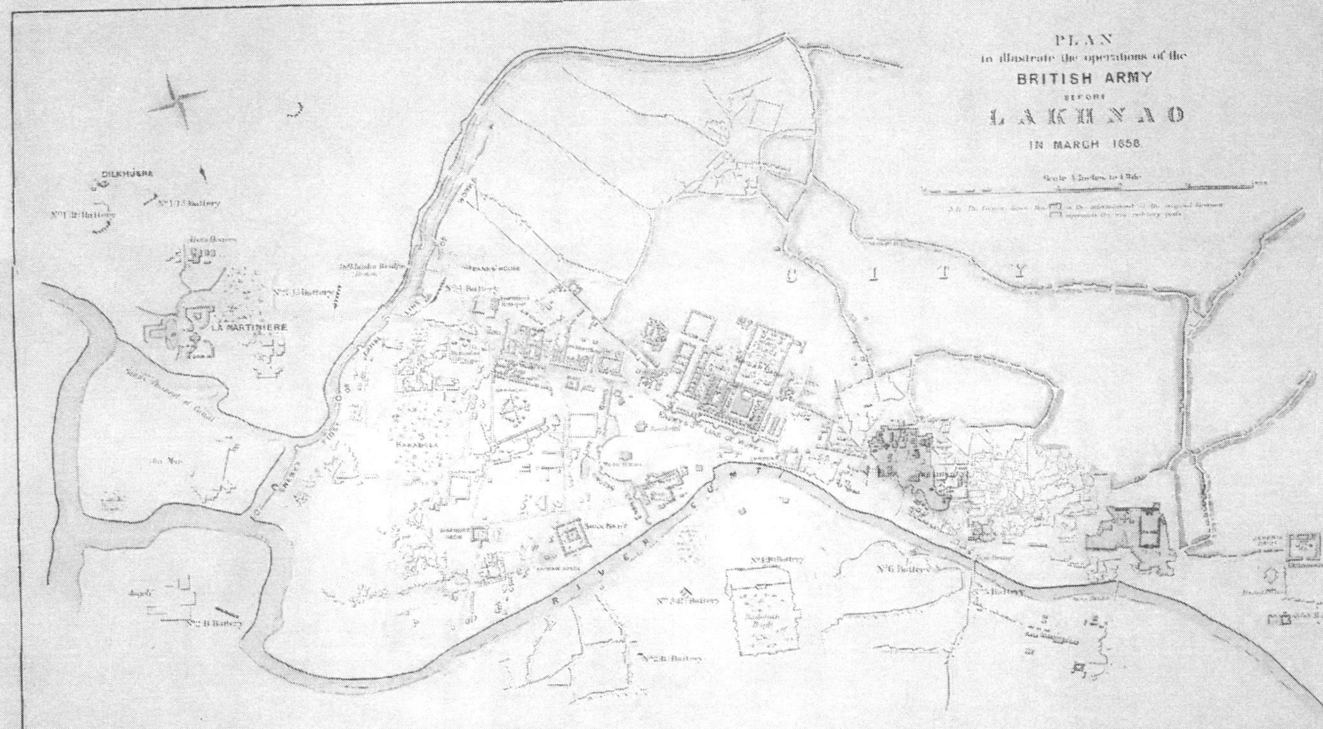
PLAN
to illustrate the operations of the
BRITISH ARMY
BEFORE
LAKHNAO
IN MARCH 1858.
CITY
RIVER GOOMTI
DILKHUSHA
LA MARTINIERE
No. 6 Battery

Book XI. Chapter IX.

1858. March 16.

Captures the great Imámbára and the Machhí Bawan.

Meanwhile Major Cotter crowned the Residency height with a field battery of Madras Artillery, and opening a heavy fire on the Machhi Báwan, maintained it till he was relieved by two 68-pounder guns of the Naval Brigade. After these had played with effect for some time on the devoted place, the 1st Fusiliers and Brasyer's Sikhs were sent forward to finish the work. This they did without difficulty, and the Machhi Báwan and great Imámbárá fell into their hands, the enemy abandoning seven guns. In this advance Captain Salusbury of the 1st Fusiliers and Lieutenant MacGregor,* doing duty with that regiment, greatly distinguished themselves.

The retreating rebels attack Walpole, but are repulsed.

Whilst these operations were successfully progressing on the right bank of the Gúmti, a number of the enemy, driven from the Residency and other places, poured over the stone bridge, and, the better to cover their design of retreating on Faizábád, made a strong attack on Walpole's pickets. The attack was repulsed, but the rebels made good their retreat.

A more serious counterblow had been attempted in another quarter.

Reduced garrison of the Alambagh.

The garrison of the Álambágh had been reduced by the number of troops withdrawn by Sir Colin to less than a thousand men of all arms. These were made up of about four hundred infantry, the Military Train, a small detachment of the 7th Hussars, and some artillery. The post was commanded by Brigadier Franklyn.

* Now Colonel MacGregor, C.B., C.S.I., C.I.E., author of *Narrative of a Journey through the Province of Khorassan*, &c. &c.

Book XI. Chapter IX.

1858. March 16.

The rebels attack it.

At 9 o'clock on the morning of the 16th the rebels came down in considerable masses, of the three arms. Whilst their infantry menaced the front of the British position their cavalry and artillery endeavoured to force back the left flank, and to get round it, with the view of giving their infantry the opportunity they were awaiting.

They are met,

To meet this movement Franklyn ordered four guns and the Military Train and cavalry, under Robertson, to the village in the rear of his position, whilst to Olpherts and the four guns which remained to him he entrusted the defence of his left.

and repulsed on the left and rear by Robertson and Olpherts,

These arrangements were made just in time. The rebels had been coming on boldly, but no sooner did Olpherts sweep the plain with his guns than their cavalry first halted, and then began to retire. A few of them did indeed make a sudden dash at the left front picket, and even entered the village in which it was, but eventually these, too, followed the example of their comrades.

Meanwhile the main body of the infantry attacked the front, throwing out skirmishers, and advancing beyond the British rifle-pits. But Vincent Eyre, who commanded the whole of the artillery, arranged his guns in such a manner as to rake their whole line from left to right, whilst the infantry brigade, commanded by Brigadier Stisted, waited for them to come on.

in the centre by Vincent Eyre.

The fire of the guns first checked the rebels and then drove them back; but the fact that the attack began at 9 o'clock and ceased only at half-past one will give some idea of its determined nature.

Book XI. Chapter IX.

1858. March 16.

Jang Bahádur covers the Commander-in-Chief's left.

Two days previously, the 14th, the Commander-in-Chief had requested Jang Bahádur and the Nipálese to move to his left, up the canal, and take in reverse the positions which, for three months, the rebels had occupied in front of the Álambágh, the garrison of which was now reduced to two regiments. Jang Bahádur carried out the instructions conveyed to him with ability and success. One after another the enemy's positions, from the Chár Bágh bridge up to the Residency, with their guns, fell into his hands. This operation, which effectually covered, as it was carried out, the Commander-in-Chief's left, occupied several days. The losses the Nipál chief experienced were inconsiderable.*

Outram continues

The 17th, Outram, pursuing his onward course,

* Jang Bahádur's successful advance was memorable for the recovery from captivity of two English ladies—Miss Jackson and Mrs. Orr. In the first volume of this history (note, page 389) I have given a sketch of the adventures of the Sitápúr fugitives, and have told how it was that on the 17th March only two of these, Mrs. Orr and Miss Jackson, survived. On the 20th March two British officers attached to the Nipál troops, Captain McNeill and Lieutenant Bogle, when exploring some deserted streets near the Kaisar Bagh, were informed by a friendly native of the place in which the two ladies were confined. They at once procured the aid of a party of fifty Nipálese, and after walking through narrow streets—about half a mile—they reached a house occupied by one Wájid Alí, an officer of the old Court. In a room within the house they found the two ladies dressed in Oriental costume. They at once procured a palanquin, and notwithstanding the opposition threatened by a body of ruffians who would have prevented the rescue, they conveyed the ladies in safety to the camp of Jang Bahádúr.

Book XI. Chapter IX.

1858. March 17.

his forward movements on the 17th

occupied, without resistance, in the morning, the Huséni Mosque and the Daolat Khána. In the afternoon he moved, with a brigade (Middleton's field battery, two 8-inch howitzers, one company native sappers, wing 20th Foot, wing 23rd Foot, wing 79th Highlanders, Brasyer's Sikhs), to occupy a block of buildings known as Sharf-u-Dáola's house. The enemy made no resistance, but hastily evacuated the place. The success, however, was marred by a deplorable accident. In the courtyard in rear of the Jamma Masjid, impeding the progress of the troops, nine carts, laden with gunpowder packed in tin cases and leather bags, were found. Outram directed Captain Clarke and Lieutenant Brownlow of the Engineers to remove the carts, and to dispose of the powder by throwing it into a large and deep well. If the order had been carefully carried out no accident could possibly have occurred. But it is supposed that in the course of the operation a tin case struck the side of the well near the surface and ignited. The fire communicated itself to the powder in the carts, and caused an explosion, which resulted in the death of the two officers and about thirty men. Others were also injured, more or less seriously.

An explosion causes loss of life.

Further progress on the 18th.

On the 18th, Outram's advanced post (a picket of the 20th under Lieutenant Gordon) cleared the houses and streets in front of it, though not without meeting a sharp opposition from the enemy. In carrying out this operation they captured a very fine brass 9-pounder gun, loaded to the muzzle with grape, and pointed down the street which they had to clear. The enemy, however, abandoned it on their advance, without discharging it.

Book XI. Chapter IX.

1858. March 18.

Sir Colin learns that a large number of rebels are still in the Músa Bágh.

It had become known during these last two days, to the Commander-in-Chief, that the rebels had occupied, to the number of from eight to nine thousand, the Músa Bágh, a large palace with gardens and enclosures, standing in the midst of an open country filled with trees, about four miles to the north-west of Lakhnao, near the right bank of the Gúmti. These rebels were believed to be animated by the presence of the Bégam and her son, and of the more desperate leaders of the revolt. Sir Colin Campbell was resolved, now that all the strong points in the city itself were in his hands, to expel them from this last stronghold.

Outram marches on the Músa Bágh. March 19.

On the morning of the 19th, therefore, Outram, under instructions from Sir Colin, marched against the Músa Bágh. His force consisted of two squadrons of the 9th Lancers; one company Royal Artillery; one company native sappers; Middleton's field battery; two 18-pounders, two 8-inch howitzers, four 8-inch mortars, under Captain Carleton, R.A.; three companies 20th Regiment; seven companies 23rd Regiment; 79th Highlanders and 2nd Panjáb Infantry. Whilst this force marched against the place from the advanced positions in the city, Sir Hope Grant, still on the left bank of the Gúmti, was directed to cannonade it, and, on the enemy being dislodged, to fall upon those who should attempt to cross the river; at the same time

Book XI. Chapter IX.

1858. March 19.

Brigadier Campbell of the Bays was ordered to take up, with a brigade of infantry, fifteen hundred cavalry, and a due proportion of guns, a position on the left front of the Músa Bágh, ready to pounce upon the rebels when Outram should expel them from their stronghold. The Nipálese troops were likewise directed to enter the city, from the Chárbágh line of road, towards the rear of the Húséni Mosque. This time it was hoped and believed there would be no fugitives. But again expectation was baulked.

Captures Ali Nakki Khán's house and the Músa Bágh.

Between Outram's advanced posts and the Músa Bágh there stood, near the Gáo Ghát, on the Gúmti, a house belonging to the last prime minister of Oudh, the Nawáb Ali Nakki Khán, at the time a prisoner in Calcutta. A company of the 79th, led by Lieutenant Evereth, attacked and drove the rebels from this place. Outram's further advance was delayed nearly two hours by the necessity of breaking through a thick wall. When at last this obstacle was removed, the troops pushed on through the suburbs to the Músa Bágh. Here the enemy appeared in great strength, but on Outram threatening their flanks, at the same time that his guns opened fire on their front, they hastily abandoned the place, leaving behind them two guns, which had been posted to protect the approaches to it.

They fled by the line which Campbell should have commanded. But where was Campbell? "With his large force of cavalry and artillery," writes Sir Hope Grant, "there was a splendid opportunity for cutting off the large masses of fugitive rebels, yet nearly all were allowed to escape." The gallantry of Colonel Hagart, splendid as it was, was far from atoning for the mistakes of his chief. I proceed to show the manner in which it was displayed.

Book XI. Chapter IX.

1858. March 19.

Close to the position taken up by Campbell was a village with a small mud fort, of which the enemy had taken possession. To dislodge them Campbell sent a troop of the 7th Hussars, some of Hodson's Horse, a few of the 78th, and two of Tombs' guns, the whole under the command of Colonel James Hagart of the 7th Hussars. A couple of shells had been fired into the fort, when the rebels, to the number of fifty, rushed out and made a dash at the guns. Hagart ordered the 7th to charge; but before they could be put in motion, the three troop officers, Slade, Wilkin, and Banks, were cut down, the latter mortally wounded. The loss of their officers took the men by surprise, when Hagart dashed at the rebels, who were hacking Banks as he lay on the ground, shot three with a revolver, and knocked over a fourth with the hilt of his sword, which was tied to his wrist by a silk pocket-handkerchief. His men quickly rallied round him, and killed every one of the enemy.*

Gallantry of Colonel Hagart.

* Hope Grant's *Sepoy War*. Sir Hope Grant further adds regarding Hagart's daring exploit: "Everything about him bore traces of his gallant struggle. His saddle and his horse were slashed about both in front and behind, his martingale was divided, his sword-hilt dented in, the pocket-handkerchief severed as clearly as with a razor, and a piece of the skin of his right hand cut away."—Sir Hope Grant recommended Hagart for the Victoria Cross.

Book XI. Chapter IX.

1858. March 19.

Remarks on William Campbell's inaction.

This was almost the solitary achievement of Campbell's fine brigade. No attempt whatever was made by him to cut off the fleeing enemy. His conduct was officially attributed to his having lost his way. "But," records an officer who wrote of these occurrences the year following that in which they took place, "his error appears to have partaken of wilfulness. He moved his force in utter disregard of the statement of his guides, in opposition to the protestations and explanations of all to whose information and advice he was bound to listen."* Consequently the greater number of the rebels escaped.

Splendid pursuit by the 9th Lancers

Not, however, all. Outram, keenly alive to the necessity of following up a victory, no sooner noticed that the rebels were abandoning the Músa Bágh, than he detached in pursuit two squadrons of the 9th Lancers, which had in anticipation taken up a position on the enemy's left flank.

Assuredly no man more deserved it. He alone rescued Banks, though in the end Banks died of his wounds; he gave the cue to his men when the sudden loss of the troop officers had for a moment staggered them. The reason why the recommendation was not attended to is, to say the least, curious. "Sir Colin Campbell," writes Sir Hope, "did not, however, forward the recommendation, as *he considered the reward an inappropriate one for an officer of so high a rank as Hagart.*" The italics are my own.

* *Calcutta Review*, March 1859; Art. "The Campaign of 1857-8." The writer continues: "But whatever may have been the cause of his erratic proceedings, whether they were accidental or whether they were worthy of blame, we believe that the mischief which resulted from them was incalculable; that to them is attributable such organization as the enemy were enabled to maintain, and the perseverance and pertinacity with which they still carried on a guerilla warfare with the British."

For four miles the men of this splendid regiment, despite of the obstacles offered by nullahs almost impassable and ravines difficult for horsemen, pursued the enemy, nor did they desist till they had captured six guns, and killed about a hundred of the foe.

Book XI. Chapter IX.

1858. March 19.

Nor were the 9th Lancers alone in the chase. The field artillery and infantry followed them in support as rapidly as possible, and captured the remaining four guns of the twelve possessed by the rebels that morning.

and the Artillery.

After this decided success Outram left the 2nd Panjáb Infantry in occupation of the Músa Bágh, and returned to his positions of the previous day.

The following day copies of Lord Canning's Oudh proclamation were received in camp. That proclamation professed to confiscate the whole proprietary right in the soil of Oudh, save in the case of six comparatively inferior chiefs. To rebel landowners who should at once surrender to the Government immunity from death and imprisonment was promised, provided only that they could show they were guiltless of unprovoked bloodshed. To those who had protected British lives special consideration was promised.

Lord Canning's Proclamation. March 20.

Of the proclamation itself I shall speak in another place. I will only refer here to the effect it produced in the camp. It arrived just when the city of Lakhnao had been gained, but when Oudh was still in insurrection, and when the rebel army, which had vainly defended the city, had cast itself on the provinces, there to

Effect of it in the camp.

Book XI. Chapter IX.

1858. March 20.

offer a fresh resistance. Every leading man who had taken a part in the campaign was struck with the impolicy, at such a moment, of disinheriting a whole people, that people being still armed and in the field. "I have not," wrote Dr. Russell,* who was attached to the headquarter staff, "heard one voice raised in its defence; and even those who are habitually silent, now open their mouths to condemn the policy which must perpetuate the rebellion in Oudh." Owing to the urgent remonstrance of Sir James Outram, authority was given to insert in the proclamation a qualifying clause, by virtue of which a further indulgence was held out to those who would throw themselves on British mercy, a claim to which would be strengthened by aid which might be given in the restoring of peace and order. But the other clauses remained.

A qualifying clause added to it on the suggestion of Outram.

March 21. The city is cleared of rebels.

Something remained to be effected even in the city itself. The Moulvi—the most obstinate of the rebel leaders—had returned to Lakhnao; he was still there, at Shádatganj, in its very heart, occupying, with two guns, a strongly fortified building, whence he bade defiance to the British. To dislodge him, Lugard was detached, on the 21st, with a portion of the division which had conquered the Bégam Kothi the first day of the attack. The troops employed were the 93rd Highlanders and the 4th Panjáb Rifles. Seldom did the rebels display so much pertinacity and resolution as on this occasion. They defended

by the 93rd and 4th Panjáb Rifles.

* *My Diary in India.*—W. H. Russell.

Book XI. Chapter IX.

1858. March 21.

themselves most bravely, and were not driven out until they had killed several men and severely wounded many others on our side. When at last they were dislodged, they were met by Brigadier Campbell's brigade of cavalry, this time on the spot, and were pursued, with considerable loss, for six miles. The Moulvi, however, effected his escape.

Hope Grant defeats the rebels at Kúrsi. March 22.

The following night, that of the 22nd, Hope Grant was ordered out at midnight with a strong force (two troops horse artillery, two 18-pounders, two howitzers, four Cohorn mortars, nine hundred cavalry, and four regiments of infantry) to attack the enemy, reported to be four thousand strong, at Kúrsi, a small town twenty-five miles from Lakhnao, on the Faizábád road. The mistake of a guide delayed the march, but at 4 A.M. on the 23rd Kúrsi was sighted. The enemy did not wait an assault, but, on the appearance of the British troops, began to evacuate the town. Upon this Hope Grant sent his cavalry at them. Two squadrons of the Panjáb Cavalry under Captain Browne,* and a party of Watson's Horse led by Captain Cosserat, dashed at them. "Captain Browne, who commanded," wrote Sir Hope Grant, in his diary, "seeing some guns moving off, charged the rebels in the most magnificent style. Five times he rode clean through them, killing about two hundred, and taking thirteen guns and a mortar. His unfortunate adjutant, Lieutenant Macdonald, was shot dead in the act

* Now Major-General Sir S. Browne, V.C., C.B., commanding in a portion of Afghánistán.

Book XI. Chapter IX.

1858. March 22.

of cutting down a sepoy. Captain Cosserat was shot through the face, and died shortly after."

The enemy having been pursued for some time, Hope Grant returned to Lakhnao.

Remarks on the campaign.

With this action the operations in Lakhnao and in its immediate vicinity ended. The city was captured. It had been gained at a loss—from the 2nd to the 21st March inclusive—of one hundred and twenty-seven officers and men killed, and five hundred and ninety-five wounded. Notwithstanding two errors which I have indicated—the one attributable to the Commander-in-Chief himself, the other, in the first instance, to one of his brigadiers—it is impossible to withhold admiration of the skill with which the operations were planned, of the courage with which they were carried out. The plans of the rebels, based on the conjecture that the British force would advance by the lines of the previous November, were entirely baffled by the masterly movement across the river. That movement, which placed an enemy on their flank, raking their defences, completely cowed them. It took all the heart out of them. Enfiladed from the opposite bank, they could not offer a stern or determined resistance to the foe advancing on their front. The weakness of their defence of the Imámbárá and the Kaisar Bágh was due in a very great degree to the moral depression which the position occupied by Outram had caused in their minds.

Claims of Sir Colin to a

But if, as has been well asserted,* the strategy

* Medley.

of Sir Colin Campbell in his attack on Lakhnao "must ever be the subject of admiration on the part of the military student of this campaign," it is fit that history should mark the blunder which prevented it from being decisive. Outram was a lieutenant to be trusted. He was cool and daring in action, always kept his troops well in hand, and carefully guarded his communications. No living man had a greater or more profound knowledge of the native character. If any man, in the circumstances in which he was placed, might have been trusted to act on his own judgment, that man was Outram. Yet when, at a critical period of the advance, Outram, firmly seated on the left bank, proposed to co-operate with the Commander-in-Chief in a manner which would have rendered the victory of the latter absolutely decisive, the proposal was refused in language totally unworthy of Sir Colin Campbell. He was forbidden to cross "if he thought he would *lose a single man*." The reasons for this prohibition have never been published. Dr. Russell, who was very much in the confidence both of Sir Colin and of Outram, whilst admitting the "blot" caused by Outram's compulsory inaction, does not explain the motive by which Sir Colin was actuated to make it compulsory.* Whether,

Book XI. Chapter IX.

1858. March 22.

high or to the highest rank as a general.

Reasons which are decisive against his claim to the highest rank.

* "The relations between Sir Colin and General Outram, though not unfriendly, are a little stiff, on account of past events, and Outram is not the man to act in opposition to the commands of his superior officer. Had Sir Colin not bound Outram's hands so tightly the advance would have taken place, and a tremendous slaughter of the enemy must have followed."—*My Diary in India*, W. H. Russell.

Book XI. Chapter IX.

1858. March 22.

The prohibition to Outram to cross the Gúmti.

as some assert, it was prompted by Mansfield, or whether it was the emanation of his own mind, Sir Colin, as the issuer of the order, was responsible for it, and he alone must bear the blame. That order derogates from his claim to be placed in the rank of the greatest commanders. He must be classed as a great general of the second rank, a general who could skilfully plan, carefully carry out that plan, who could achieve a victory, but who could not follow it up.

The appointment of William Campbell and the approval of his failure.

The second failure to pursue the beaten enemy is due likewise, though in a lesser degree, to Sir Colin Campbell. For the delicate operation he was bound to select an officer specially qualified, and if not acquainted with the country, yet ready to listen to the experienced officers at his elbow or to understand the language of the guides. He appointed, on the contrary, an officer new to the country, who would listen to nobody, who could not understand the guides, and who, consequently, let slip a golden opportunity. Yet this action, which allowed thousands of rebels to escape, was justified by Sir Colin Campbell.

"Brigadier Campbell, in command of the cavalry on the left," he writes, in his despatch, "performed his detached duty with much vigilance and judgment. His march round the city on the 19th inst., which was a running fight for the greater part of the day, was a very difficult one." What it really was has been recorded in these pages.

These errors, however, stood alone, and the capture of Lakhnao in March 1858 will remain to all time a splendid achievement of skill and daring.

Book XI.
Chapter IX.

1858.
March 22.

BOOK XII.

CHAPTER I.

Bengal.

It will be conducive to the clearness of the narrative, if, before recording the events in the north-west Provinces which immediately followed the capture of Lakhnao, I return for a moment to Calcutta, record the progress made towards the restoration of order in eastern Bengal and the Bihárs, and progress thence towards Allahábád by way of Ázamgarh and the adjacent districts. Then I propose to trace the action of Carthew in guarding the important line between Allahábád and Kánhpúr. Returning north-westward, I shall record the action of Seaton in the vicinity of Fathgarh, of Jones in Rohilkhand, of Walpole in Oudh, of Lugard, Rowcroft, and Douglas in the A'zamgarh and Gházipúr districts and in Bihár, of Jones and Coke in Rohilkhand, and of Sir Colin Campbell in Barélí. The book will close with an account in detail of the progress of events in Rajpútáná.

Reasons why Calcutta

When Sir Colin Campbell, on the 27th Novem-

Book XII. Chapter 1.

1857-8. Nov.-Jan.

ber, had left Calcutta for Kánhpúr, he carried with him the power of the country. For the moment the civil authority, though nominally existing, was in abeyance. The fate of India was in the hands, not of Lord Canning, but of Sir Colin Campbell; and although, as I have noted on one important occasion, the opinions of the Governor-General in Council exercised a potential influence on the general plan of campaign of the Commander-in-Chief, yet to the hands of the latter functionary its execution was committed. From the moment, then, when Sir Colin Campbell left Calcutta to direct the military measures for which he had been preparing, he became the chief centre of interest; and the capital, giving habitation though it did for a time to the Governor-General and his Council, was proportionately shorn of its importance. Thenceforward Calcutta deserves notice as the port for the reception of the troops, and the depôt of stores and supplies from England; the terminus whence the new arrivals started for the seat of war, and the invalids and wounded for Europe. The continuous attacks made upon the rebels satisfied the longings even of those who had been the severest critics of the tardy, the hesitating, and the half-hearted action of Lord Canning and his councillors; while the social tranquillity of the capital, no longer in real danger, was but once disturbed, and then by a panic which had for its foundation a want of confidence in the firmness of the Government.

Calcutta ceased, after the departure of Sir Colin, to exercise an all-absorbing influence on the campaign.

Lord Canning proceeds to Allahábád.

In the third week of January, 1858, Lord Canning quitted Calcutta and proceeded to Allah-

Book XII. Chapter I.

1858. Feb.-March.

ábád. A few days after his arrival at that place (9th February), he abolished the temporary office of Chief Commissioner of Ágra, till then held by Colonel Fraser, C.B., and drew the whole of the north-west divisions, that of Dehlí excepted, within one lieutenant-governorship. A few days later, Mr. J. P. Grant, who at a trying and critical period had governed with marked ability the Central Provinces, returned to Calcutta to take up the office of President of the Council, the Governor-General assuming the charge which Mr. Grant thus vacated.

Change in the administration.

Panic of the 3rd March in Calcutta.

It was after the return of Mr. Grant to Calcutta that the panic of which I have spoken occurred. Nothing happened, indeed, which ought to have alarmed men's minds, but in times of excitement the slightest causes often produce the most startling effects. The case was simply as follows. On the 3rd March, a telegraphic message from Barrakpúr was received in Calcutta to the effect that the sepoys of two native regiments stationed there were deserting in bodies of ten and twelve, and making their way to the capital. People did not stay to reflect that the sepoys had been disarmed; that in addition to regular troops there was a fine volunteer regiment—horse, foot, and artillery—in the city. The information conveyed by the telegram was circulated in exaggerated terms; and the inhabitants of the suburbs, consisting mainly of Eurasians, became much alarmed. Pickets of the volunteer guards were promptly posted at the points supposed to be threatened; the streets were patrolled by the volunteer cavalry; the artillerymen took post at their guns; the regular troops in the fort were placed under arms. But no enemy appeared. Some sepoys had indeed deserted, but with no intention of attacking Calcutta. The panic passed away more quickly even than it had been produced.

Book XII. Chapter I.

1858. March.

It passes away.

In eastern Bengal there had been some cause for anxiety. On the 18th November, the detachments of the 34th Regiment Native Infantry, stationed at Chátgáon, mutinied, plundered the treasury, released the prisoners from jail, burnt down their own lines, fired the magazine, and then left the station, carrying off with them three elephants, the property of Government, and the whole of the treasure they found in the collectorate, with the exception of three hundred and forty rupees in cash. These, as well as the stamps, the Government securities and records, they left untouched. They attacked none of the Europeans, and the only man who suffered at their hands was a native jailer who protested against their proceedings. Him they killed. They then made off in the direction of Tiparah, but at Sítákúnd they left the high road, and making for Hill Tiparah, endeavoured to make their way along the hills in a north-westerly direction, avoiding British territory.

Eastern Bengal.

1857. Nov. 18.

Mutiny of the 34th at Chátgáon.

Four days later an attempt was made by Lieutenant Lewis, Indian Navy, to disarm the detachments of the 73rd Native Infantry, and Native Artillery, stationed at Dháká, numbering about two hundred and fifty sepoys. Lewis had

Attempt to disarm the native troops at Dháká.

Nov. 22.

Book XII. Chapter I. 1857. Nov. 22.

at his disposal five officers and eighty-five men, English sailors, and two mountain-train howitzers. One of these was commanded by Lieutenant Dowell of the Bengal Artillery, who volunteered his services for the occasion. Three members of the Civil Service, Messrs. Carnac, Bainbridge, and Macpherson, and Lieutenant Hitchins of the Bengal Army, likewise accompanied the force, armed with rifles.

They resist,

Lewis disarmed, without resistance, the detached guards at the offices of the treasury, of the commissariat, and of the executive engineer. But when he marched down to the lines, he found the bulk of the sepoys drawn up close to their magazine, with two 6-pounders in their centre. Parties of them also occupied strong brick-built buildings in the vicinity, the walls of which had been carefully loop-holed. Lewis at once deployed his force, but the movement was not completed when the sepoys opened upon him with canister and musketry. Replying with one volley, Lewis then charged up the hill with his infantry, whilst the two mountain guns, taking up a position on the left rear of the enemy, opened upon them. The charge was most successful.

but are beaten;

The rebels, though offering a determined resistance, were driven, one by one, from their strong positions, until those who survived took refuge in

many are killed;

flight. Forty-one dead bodies were counted on the ground, eight men were brought in desperately wounded, three were drowned or shot in attempting to cross the river. This success was not attained without some loss. The list of killed and wounded contained one man killed, five dangerously, eight severely, and four slightly wounded, in all eighteen. The sepoys who escaped at once went off in a north-westerly direction, making, it was believed, for Jalpáigorí, the headquarters of the regiment. Prevented from reaching that place, they found a temporary refuge in Bhútán.

Book XII. Chapter I.

1857. Nov. 22.

the survivors escape.

The action of the local authorities at Chátgáon was prompt and effective. Whilst arrangements were made at the station for the security of European life in case the sepoys should return to it, the Commissioner communicated at once with the Rájá of Tiparah. This loyal feudatory at once directed his retainers and subjects to check the progress of the mutineers, and, if possible, to close the passes against them. The Commissioner called likewise upon the two principal zamindárs occupying the hill districts which it was thought the mutineers would traverse, to summon their men to arms and follow them up, and either to attack them or to shut them up in the defiles which lay before them. The manner in which this appeal was responded to, and the results it produced, will be related immediately.

Chátgáon.

The Rájá of Tiparah exercises his influence in favour of the British.

Nor was the action of the Government at Calcutta less satisfactory. Dealing with the cases of Dháká and Chátgáon as intimately connected the one with the other, they despatched, on the 26th November, by river from Calcutta, three companies of the 54th Regiment, and one hundred seamen; on the 27th, by the same route, another party of sailors. It was the intention of the Government that whilst the 54th detachment should proceed at

Prompt action of the Government of India.

Nov. 26-27.

Book XII. Chapter I.

1857. December.

first to Dákhá and thence pursue the Chátgáon rebels in the direction it would be ascertained they had taken, the Naval Brigade should move northwards to Rangpúr and Dínájpúr to protect the country towards which it was believed the mutineers from both stations were making their way. Their arrival at their destination on the 10th December contributed greatly to the preservation of order in the neighbouring districts.

The Chátgáon mutineers

The Chátgáon mutineers were, meanwhile, beginning to experience the drawbacks to a march across the hills, pursued and threatened by enemies. On leaving Sítákúnd, they had followed a northerly course, and, crossing the ferry at Rámgarh ghát, had pushed on towards Udaipúr, thence towards Ágartalá, the residence of the Rájá of Tiparah. That chief, hearing of their approach, despatched a considerable body of men, who stoppped them at Sankhola on the 2nd December. Turning then westward, they entered British territory at or near Mogra, and made their way towards Singár Hill—about one and a half day's journey north of Komillá, and on the direct route to Silhat. In their progress they had been much harassed; they lost the three elephants, and about ten thousand rupees of the treasure they had stolen; of the prisoners they had released from the jail, many were daily being captured; they found the mountain paths difficult, and though the hillmen were ready enough, for payment, to cut a way for them, their progress was necessarily slow. But worse things were in store for them.

traverse the hill ranges

and suffer much distress.

They attack a police

Harassed by the opposition of the Rájá of

Book XII. Chapter I.

1857. December.

Tiparah, and of the zamindárs of whom I have spoken, the mutineers resolved to make their way to Manipúr. On their way to that place, they descended from the hills, attacked and plundered, on the 15th December, a police-station in British territory. This attack gave to the British the information they had desired as to their position. Mr. Allen, the chief civil officer at Silhat, had the capacity to discern that the European troops would arrive too late to intercept the rebels. He took upon himself, then, the responsibility of ordering the Silhat Light Infantry, commanded by Major the Hon. R. B. Byng, into the field. That regiment left Silhat in pursuit of the rebels that very day, the 15th, and reached Partábgarh, a distance of eighty miles, by a forced march, in thirty-six hours. At Partábgarh, Byng received information from Mr. Dodd, who had accompanied the force for the special purpose of guiding it, that the rebels had changed their route, and would be at Látú, a place which they had passed through, on the night of that day, the 17th, or early the following morning. Látú was twenty-eight miles from Partábgarh; the men had made a forced march of eighty miles, but with one voice they expressed their willingness to return. The road led through jungles and swamps, but, setting out, they marched back cheerily. Dodd, who had ridden on in advance, met the column as it was entering the village of Látú at dawn on the 18th, with the information that the rebels were close at hand. Before line could be formed, they were seen advancing in good order. In the engagement which followed, the rebels made

station in British territory.

The Silhat Light Infantry are sent in pursuit of them.

After forced marches,

they encounter them at Látú.

Book XII. Chapter I.

1857-8. Dec.-Jan.

many efforts to seduce the men of the Silhat Light Infantry—one half of whom were Hindústánis—to make common cause with them. But their persuasions were answered by the cold steel of the bayonet. Notwithstanding their long march, the loyal soldiers of the Silhat regiment displayed a vigour and an energy which carried all before them. In the early part of the action their gallant leader, Major Byng, was killed. This occurrence only roused them to greater fury. The post he had held was filled by Lieutenant Sherer, an officer of rare merit—a son of the gallant soldier whose splendid audacity at Jalpaigori I have described in the preceding volume—and Sherer gave the rebels no breathing-time. After a loss of twenty-six men killed and a still larger number wounded, the enemy abandoned the field, and sought shelter in the close and difficult jungles which lie between Látú and Manipúr.

Byng is killed.

Sherer succeeds, and drives the rebels into the jungles,

where they cannot be followed.

Into these jungles it was impossible to follow them. Detachments having been sent to watch the issues from the jungle into Manipúr, the battalion returned to Silhat. The party of the 54th Regiment, which had been sent on to Silhat and had even marched towards Látú, was ordered back, first to Dháká, and a few weeks later to Calcutta.

The Chátgáon mutineers entering Manipúr,

After their defeat by Sherer, the Chátgáon mutineers marched north-eastwards, and entered the Manipúr territory. There they were joined by one of the Manipúr princes, with a few followers. The hopes they might have conceived from this accession of strength were, however, of short duration. On the 12th January they were attacked

Book XII. Chapter I.

1858. January.

by a party of the Silhat corps, under Captain Stevens, and after a fight which lasted two hours, they were driven into the jungles, with the loss of twenty men killed. Ten days later, the same officer, having learnt where they were encamped, succeeded in surprising them while their arms were piled, and putting them to flight, with the loss of all their arms and accoutrements. On this occasion they lost ten men killed. Eight days later another detachment of them was attacked and completely defeated, with the loss of thirteen men, by a small party of the Silhat regiment, led by a native officer, Jemadár Jaggathir. This was the finishing stroke. Since their departure from Chátgáon, the rebels had lost two hundred and six men in battle. The remainder were now blocked up in hilly country, the passes leading out of which were closed, and there the greater number perished miserably.

are attacked and beaten by Captain Stevens, who again surprises them.

The survivors are blocked up in the mountains.

Thus, by the firm attitude and the fearlessness of responsibility on the part of the civil authorities, especially of Mr. Allen, and by the daring leading of a few European officers and the gallantry of their native followers, order was re-established in the important districts to the east of Calcutta. All this time Colonel Sherer was nobly maintaining his position at Jalpáigorí, dominating, by the force of his character, the armed native regiment which he commanded.

Result of firmness and promptitude.

I pass on now to eastern Bihár, the division under the control of Mr. George Yule. Although the relief of Arah by Vincent Eyre, in the month of August, 1857, and the subsequent storming by

Eastern Bihár and George Yule.

Book XII. Chapter I.

1857. Nov.-Dec.

The normal difficulties in that province

that gallant soldier of the stronghold of Kúnwar Singh, had, for the moment, averted danger from eastern Bihár, the elements of revolt still continued to smoulder in that province. These elements were fostered by scarcity, caused by long-prevailing drought, and the temper of the people in the vicinity of Manghir was manifested as the year began to wane by an increased and increasing number of highway robberies and other crimes.

are increased by the outbreaks at Dháká and Chátgáon.

Under these circumstances the outbreaks at Dákhá and Chátgáon assumed a very threatening character. The station of Jalpaigori belonged to the division ruled by Mr. Yule. The headquarters and main body of the 73rd Native Infantry, commanded by Sherer, were at that station. The sepoys who had mutinied and resisted so stoutly at Dháká belonged to that regiment. It seemed only probable, then, that they would make their way to Jalpáigorí, and incite their comrades to revolt.

Yule marches with troops to Púrniá.

The Government had despatched a body of British sailors to Púrniá, midway between Bhágalpúr and Jalpáigorí, and these men were due at that station at the end of November. But this precaution did not seem to Mr. Yule to be sufficient. With the concurrence of the Government, then, he moved, on the 27th November, the small detachment of the 5th Fusiliers, then at Manghir, to Púrniá, accompanying them himself. He arrived there on the 1st December, and finding all quiet, marched on the next day towards Kishanganj, thirty-one miles distant.

The detachments at Madáriganj and Jalpáigorí mutiny.

He was not a moment too soon. On the nights of the 4th and 5th December the detachments of the

Book XII. Chapter I.

1857. December.

11th Irregular Cavalry at Madáriganj and Jalpáigorí mutinied, and went off, spreading alarm throughout the district.

The civil officers of the district.

The conduct of the civil officers in the district at this crisis was worthy of all praise. At many of the stations they had nought to depend upon but their own brave hearts. Not for a moment did their courage falter or their presence of mind fail them. Macdonald, the Collector of Rangpúr, placed all the moneys in the Government Treasury upon elephants, and moved with it into the jungle, hoping that the rebels, finding Rangpúr evacuated, would be too hardly pressed to search him out. The rebels, however, never went near Rangpúr, but made straight for Dínájpúr. The Collector of this place was Mr. Francis Anstruther Elphinstone-Dalrymple, one of the ablest men in the Civil Service, but whose prospects had been ruined by long years of persecution on purely private grounds by those wielding authority in Bengal. But if Dalrymple's worldly fortunes stood low, his courage was as high, and his determination was as unshaken, as they were when, a young civilian, he volunteered for and served in the first China war.* He had upwards of one

Macdonald.

Francis Anstruther Elphinstone-Dalrymple:

* Mr. F. A. Elphinstone-Dalrymple accompanied a party of soldiers sent during that war from the *Rustomjee* transport to attack a battery. As there appeared some chance that the party would arrive late, Dalrymple persuaded the mate to beach the boat at once in the centre of the battery, thus taking the lead of the whole force. He himself was the first man in the battery. At Chusan he accompanied the 55th Regiment in the storm of the steep hill and the intrenched camp. At Shanghai he was on the deck of H.M.S. *Nemesis* with Captain Hall, now an

Book XII. Chapter I. 1857. December. his splendid resolution.

hundred thousand pounds in his treasury, and he determined to fight for it. He packed off, then, by water, to Calcutta, the solitary missionary of the station and his wife. Then summoning Grant the judge, Drummond the magistrate, Brown the assistant, Harold Holm, a Dane, connected with indigo and well known and much liked in those parts, and a few other Europeans and Eurasians, he posted them, with their rifles and ammunition, in his official court, and, at their head, awaited there the coming of the rebels. Their arrival within twelve miles of the station was announced. Any moment, then, they might appear. But amongst Dalrymple and his companions there was but one thought—to defend the station to the very last, to die rather than abandon the trust confided to them. Fortunately for them, the rebels, when within a short distance of the place, received intelligence of the movements of the British seamen previously referred to. Instead, then, of marching on Dínájpúr, they hurried off to Púrniá, there to fall into the clutches of Yule. Dalrymple and his companions were not attacked. Not the less, however, did they deserve for their splendid resolution the praise and the credit which were never officially awarded to them!

The rebels move off to Púrniá.

Yule, meanwhile, marching northwards, had reached Kishanganj. There he heard of the

Yule returns to Púrniá,

admiral, better known as Nemesis Hall, fighting the batteries, and subsequently at the taking of Ningpo. He carried Sir Henry Pottinger's despatches to Lord Auckland.

revolt, and that the revolters had taken the road leading to Púrniá. No time was to be lost. He set out at once to return to Púrniá, and, marching all day, accomplished the distance, with the aid of his elephants, by sunset. He arrived in good time. The mutineers, ignorant of Yule's rapid march, were entering the town early the following morning with a view to plunder it, when they found themselves face to face with the Europeans. After an exchange of shots, they fell back a few miles, halted, and encamped. It was difficult for Yule, who had only infantry, to bring mounted men to action, but he resolved to try. That night he marched out his men, and at daylight came up with the enemy, just as they were preparing to set out. The rebels, putting on a bold face, charged, but were beaten back with the loss of thirteen of their number. They then fled to the north. Yule had saved Púrniá by his prompt action. He did more. Pushing on rapidly, the morning of the 12th, with his party, he succeeded, notwithstanding the obstructions offered by the numerous and extensive quicksands of the Kúsi, in crossing that river, and reaching Náthpúr before the rebels. Finding their onward progress thus checked; and cut off, by movements of which I shall speak immediately, from a retrograde movement; the mutineers took refuge for the moment in Nipál, only, however, to meet their fate at a later period.

encounters the rebels,

saves Púrniá,

and drives the rebels into Nipál.

Meanwhile, on the first news of the mutiny of the irregular cavalry, all the available troops, European and Gúrkah, amounting to one hun-

Jalpáigorí.

Book XII. Chapter I.

1857. December.

dred of the former and three hundred of the latter, had been sent down from Dárjíling to Pankibári, and thence on to Jalpáigorí. They served to strengthen the hands of Sherer. Acting on the principle that boldness is prudence, this firm and resolute officer had blown from the guns, in the presence of his armed native regiment, two troopers caught in the act of revolt.

The seamen reach Rangpúr.

Four days later the seamen of whom I have spoken as having been detached from Calcutta, on the news of the Dháká mutiny, to protect the districts of Rangpúr and Dínájpúr, arrived at Bagwah, thirty miles east of the former, and, pushing on quickly, reached their destination on the 15th December.

The rebels in the Nipál territory.

Yule, I have said, had, by his prompt and vigorous movements, saved the British districts on the right bank of the Kúsi from invasion, and forced the rebels to seek refuge in Nipál territory. There, at a place thirty-six miles from the British frontier, they were detained by the Nipálese authorities, pending instructions from Jang Bahádur. It was useless for Yule to wait any longer on the frontier, or to disquiet himself regarding the fate of men no longer able to plunder and destroy. And it happened that just at the moment his energies were required in another part of his division. In a previous page I have recorded how the Dháká mutineers, resisting the attempt made to disarm them, had set off from that station for Jalpáigorí, but finding it impossible to traverse the intervening country, had been forced to take refuge in Bhútán. Yule, as

The Dháká rebels threaten Jalpáigorí.

he lay with his small force at Náthpúr, received an express informing him that the Dháká rebels were threatening Jalpáigorí from the north-east, and urging him to march to that place.

Book XII. Chapter I.

1857. December.

Yule marches to meet them;

Yule at once set out, and, marching sixty-four miles in thirty-six hours, reached Kishanganj, thirty-one miles north-east of Púrniá. Another long march of thirty miles brought him, on the 22nd, to Titáliá. Here he received a despatch from Jalpáigorí recommending him to take up a position between Siligori and Pankabári, on the road to Dárjíling, there to await further intelligence. Yule complied, waited patiently till the 26th, but as the promised intelligence was still withheld, he determined to act on his own responsibility. The ideas he had formed on the subject were singularly clear and correct. Granted that the rebels intended to move on Dárjíling or on Jalpáigorí, they must of necessity cross the river Tístá. The Tístá is a river gradually increasing on the plains to a width of from seven to eight hundred yards, deep, rapid, and difficult. To the rebels scarcely any other option was offered than to cross at the Cháwa Ghát, where facilities existed. Now, Cháwa Ghát had not been occupied, and Yule, tired of waiting, resolved to act upon his own instincts, and occupy it. But the delay caused by waiting for intelligence which did not come had been fatal. As he approached the ghát through the jungle, his advanced parties discovered the enemy on the left bank of the river, occupying a position so strong and so favourable for defence, that it

forms correct ideas as to their movements.

He moves on Cháwa Ghát,

Book XII. Chapter I.

1857. December.

would have been madness for him, with his small force, to attack it. But there was still one way open to him to bar their progress. That was to occupy the only practicable road by which they could advance, and give them battle when they should attempt to move forward.

and occupies the road.

The rebels turn his position,

Yule accordingly occupied that road. But the rebels, more wily than he believed them to be, broke up their camp that night, and marching by an unfrequented by-path, turned his position, crossed the Mahánandá river, and made for the Dárjíling road. Yule discovered, early on the morning of the 28th, that he had been thus out-manœuvred. Promptly did he repair his error. Leaving his camp standing, he took up a position on the Dárjíling road, and awaited the approach of the enemy. He waited in vain all that day. As evening approached, there being no signs of the rebels, he determined to move back to the camp to allow his men to break their fast. But they had scarcely left the road when the enemy were seen emerging from the jungle by a path some little distance from the position he had held during the day. Yule at once sent his advanced party in pursuit. But so rapidly did the rebels rush across the road and the open country between the place of their issue and the next thick jungle that the British had only time to fire one volley, and although Captain Burbank and his sailors continued the pursuit for two or three hours, they failed to come up with the enemy.

and eventually escape.

The Jalpáigorí party, consisting of Europeans and Gúrkahs, commanded by Captain Curzon,

Book XII. Chapter I.

1858. January.

52nd Light Infantry, had been equally unsuccessful. False information had sent them to one ford of the Tístá whilst the rebels crossed by another.

But Yule follows them up,

But the failure he had encountered made Yule only the more resolved to follow the Dháká mutineers to the bitter end. Occupying as he did the inner line of communication, whereas the rebels, by their flight, had gained the outer line, it was still possible for him, by marching along the edge of the forests which skirt the Nipál frontier, to guard the British territories from incursion. This course he adopted. Marching westward, in parallel lines with the rebels, he having the inner line, he forced them to cross the Nipál frontier. Continuing within the British territory this parallel march, he again, on the 3rd January, crossed the Kúsi at Náthpúr. On that day the rebels were distant from him between forty and fifty miles, at a place called Chattra, at the foot of the hills at the point where the Kúsi issues from them, thirty-six miles within the Nipál frontier—the whole intervening space being jungle.

and marches parallel with them.

Major J. F. Richardson,

On the 11th Yule's party was strengthened by the arrival of Major Richardson, with the Bengal Yeomanry Cavalry. It was a great accession. Major Richardson was one of the most gallant men living. He had distinguished himself at the storming of Múltán in a manner which would have procured for him the Victoria Cross had that symbol of distinction then existed. As it was, his conduct in leading the stormers elicited

Book XII. Chapter I.

1858. January.

and the Yeomanry Cavalry

an expression of marked admiration from the then Commander-in-Chief, Lord Gough, and proved the stepping-stone to advancement in his profession. The Bengal Yeomanry Cavalry was composed of men, many of them Eurasians, some Europeans and well born, who had enlisted for that special service, on special terms, to aid in suppressing the mutiny in June and July 1857. When the corps was first raised Lord Canning was specially anxious to select as its commandant an officer who should possess alike the power of attraction and the power of command, who could rule as well as dominate, and inspire affection as well as fear. At the moment Richardson landed from furlough to Europe in Calcutta. He was at once recognised as the man for the situation. The choice was in all respects pre-eminently good.

join Yule.

Richardson joined Yule on the 11th January. The rebels were still at Chattra. Just about the same time the practical reply of Jang Bahádur to Yule's representations regarding the mutineers of the 11th Irregulars was received. That reply took the shape of an order to his lieutenant on the spot, Rattan Mán Singh, to attack the mutineers, in co-operation with the English. It unfortunately happened that the force at the disposal of Rattan Mán Singh consisted mostly of untrained infantry militia, and only a few trained artillerymen with their guns. The Nipálese commander was therefore unwilling to assent to any manœuvre which would necessitate division of his own force. After some discussion, then,

Jang Bahádur.

Orders his lieutenant to attack the rebels.

Book XII. Chapter I.

1858. January.

it was agreed between himself on the one side, and Mr. Yule and Major Richardson on the other, that whilst the Nipál troops should guard the roads leading eastward, and Richardson with his cavalry should watch the right bank of the Kúsí, Yule's infantry should attack Chattra. Yule and Richardson were aware that it would have been far better that the Nipál commander should watch the left as well as the right bank of the river, for the upper part of the left bank could not, from the nature of the country, be effectually guarded by cavalry. But, under the circumstances, it was the best thing to be done, and, after all, they both believed that the rebels would fight. To give time to the Nipál commander to make his arrangements, the 21st was fixed upon as the day for the attack.

Plan of the allied forces to hem them in.

Delay in its execution

This delay proved fatal to the success of the plan. Yule crossed the Nipál frontier on the 14th, and on the 19th reached Pirára, about ten miles from Chattra. Richardson meanwhile had advanced to Cháoría, a place which commanded the only path by which he believed the mutineers could possibly proceed westward, should they cross the river above it. But whether the mutineers had been warned, or whether they gained information from their scouts, it is certain that as soon as they heard that Yule had reached Pirára, they crossed the river, and marched westward. Yule and Richardson pushed after them, but as it was seen that the rebels were following a line of country totally impracticable for cavalry, Richardson proceeded by rapid marches to Dar-

proves fatal to its success,

and the rebels escape

Book XII. Chapter I.

1858. January.

into Oudh.

bangáh to cover Tirhút, whilst Yule * returned to his division—which was not subsequently disturbed. The mutineers succeeded in making their way into north-eastern Oudh, only eventually to fall by the bullet and the sword.

1857.

Before proceeding to western Bihár, I propose to say a few words regarding the extensive district known as Chútia Nágpúr. In a preceding page of this volume † I have briefly recorded how Major English had, on the 2nd October, inflicted a severe defeat upon the rebels at Chattra.‡ But this victory, important as it was in effecting the security of the grand trunk road, was far from restoring order to the country. From that period, and for several months following, the energies of Captain Dalton, Major Simpson, Lieutenant Graham, Lieutenant Stanton, R.E., of Colonel Forster and the Shekawáti battalion, and other excellent officers, were devoted to the arduous task of repelling attack, of checking petty risings, of suppressing pretenders to power, of hunting down armed freebooters, of recovering places which had been surprised, and of avenging the injuries, in some cases amounting to death, inflicted upon the unarmed and unoffending.

Chútia Nágpúr after October 1857.

Reasons why it is unneces-

To enter into full detail of the various marches

* In the month of May following, when the return of Kúnwar Singh had again thrown the affairs of Western Bihár into confusion, Mr. Yule offered to the Government the services of himself and twenty well-mounted gentlemen to act against the rebels in that province. The offer was declined.

† Page 141.

‡ Not to be confounded with the Chattra within the Nipál frontier.

and counter-marches of the companies and small detachments engaged for months in this desultory warfare, would require far more space than could be fairly allotted to a subject which, however important in itself, forms only an adjunct to the main story. No officers deserved better of their country than those who served in Chútia Nágpúr: none exhibited greater zeal, greater energy, greater self-reliance, greater devotion; but after the defeat of the rebels by English at Chattra, their action affected the course of events, not generally throughout Hindustán, but in Chútia Nágpúr alone. For this reason I shall be justified, I believe, if I recount in less detail than I have given to the actions of Sir Colin Campbell and his lieutenants, and to occurrences bearing directly on the main story, the principal events which marked the period of disturbance in the country forming the south-west frontier of Bengal.

sary to enter into full detail.

Palámao in November.

In the district called Palámao, affairs seemed, so late as November 1857, to be very critical. There Lieutenant Graham, with a handful of men, occupied a large house containing from three hundred to four hundred native women and children. The house belonged to a loyal Thákur, and was encircled by a strong wall. In this Graham was besieged by a body of rebels, whose numbers, amounting at first to two thousand, gradually rose to six thousand. Whilst a portion of these blockaded Graham, without daring to assault him, the remainder plundered the country all about.

The rebellion in Palámao collapses.

To relieve Graham two companies of the 13th

Book XII. Chapter I.

1857. Nov.-Dec.

Light Infantry, under Major Colter, were despatched from Sahasrám on the 27th November. Thither also was directed the Shakawáti battalion under Major Forster. Colter relieved Graham on the 8th December, but, though the presence of two companies of English troops in the rebellious district would have been invaluable, the necessity of guarding the grand trunk road was paramount, and Colter was ordered to lead back his men to Sahasrám. But though he was forced to leave, the good he had effected remained behind him. Graham had employed the first hours after his relief in seizing the person of Débi Bakkas Rái, a man suspected of being the real prompter of the rebellion. Graham's bold action proved the suspicion to be well founded, for the rebellion in Palámao at once collapsed. Then, too, did well-disposed chiefs, previously held in check by fear of the rebels, declare themselves in favour of the British; and Graham, though not strong enough without reinforcements to assume the offensive, was confident, notwithstanding the departure of Colter, to be able to hold his own.

Sambalpúr in December.

But by this time the spirit of insurrection had travelled to the southerly region of Sambalpúr. In this district large bodies of men assembled in the month of December and over-ran the country, committing excesses of every kind. Captain Leigh, who represented the civil authority of the Government in this district, had at his disposal a small party of the 40th Madras Native Infantry—too small even for proper de-

Book XII. Chapter I.

1857. December.

fensive purposes, and such was the demand for troops elsewhere, that Captain Dalton, the Commissioner, had been unable to comply with his request for reinforcements. But another officer, Mr. Cockburn, of the Civil Service, Commissioner of the neighbouring district of Katak, taking a clear view of the situation, saw the absolute necessity of supporting, at all risks, British authority in Sambalpúr. This able and zealous officer not only wrote to the Madras Government to transfer a body of its local troops for special service in that district, but nobly took upon himself the responsibility of ordering thither from Katak the remainder of the 40th Regiment Madras Native Infantry, with the guns and artillerymen posted at that station. Measures were likewise taken for the enlistment at Katak of two companies of sepoys known as Sibandis for the same service. These measures greatly tended to the ultimate success. Major Bates advanced with the 40th Madras Native Infantry into Sambalpúr, whilst, with a view to ensure prompt action, that district was temporarily transferred to the zealous and watchful superintendence of the Commissioner of Katak. Some time, however, elapsed before the disorder yielded even to his energetic action.

Mr. Cockburns farseeing conduct.

He sends Madras troops to Sambalpúr.

Singhbhúm.

The wave of insurrection passed then into the district of Singhbhúm. A large party, composed of the representatives of no less than three tribes, assembled at a place called Ayúdhya, and proclaimed the brother of one of the local rájás, the Rájá of Porahát, to be their ruler. Fortunately a party of Rattray's Sikhs, com-

Book XII. Chapter I.

1857. December.

manded by Captain Hale, was in the neighbourhood. Hale, supported by the followers of one of the local chieftains, attacked and dispersed the followers of the pretender. But for some time the insurrection remained unsubdued.

The rebels defeated in the Sambalpúr districts.

The unsatisfactory state of affairs in the three districts of which I have spoken, Palámao, Sambalpúr, and Singhbúm, continued without any important change until the 30th December. On the day immediately preceding that date, Captain Wood arrived in the Sambalpúr district with a squadron of the Nágpúr Irregular Cavalry, and drawing to him one hundred and fifty men of the Madras Native Infantry and fifty of the Ramgarh Infantry, he attacked the main body of the rebels the following morning, and completely defeated them, killing three of their chiefs.

Dangerous position of Mr. Lushington and his followers.

This victory was succeeded by a multitude of small affairs in the several districts, in most of which the advantage inclined to the side of authority. It was not, however, always so. On one occasion the Commissioner of the Mánbhúm and Singhbhúm divisions, Mr. Lushington, attended by Dr. Hayes and accompanied by Captain Hale, Lieutenant Birch, and fifty Sikhs, who had been engaged in seizing men convicted of murder, found themselves suddenly surrounded by not less than three thousand to four thousand infuriated Kóls, armed with arrows, who had stolen up unperceived. Nothing but the steady gallantry of the Sikhs extricated the party from their perilous position. They had to fight their way through their numerous opponents, and it

Book XII. Chapter I.

1858. January.

was only by great perseverance, and at the expense of a large casualty roll that they ultimately succeeded. Twenty-five Sikhs were wounded, one mortally; one was killed. Captain Hale was wounded in four places; Lieutenant Birch had his arm pinned to his side by an arrow: Mr. Lushington and Dr. Hayes were also wounded. Of the enemy one hundred and fifty are said to have fallen. The British party was, however, forced to abandon their camp equipage in order to effect a secure retreat.

He is extricated by the valour of the Sikhs.

After this affairs soon began to mend. On the 7th January Major Bates forced the Shérgáti pass; two days later Captain Shakespear stormed the Singhora pass and over-ran the country with his cavalry; on the 21st January Captain Dalton and Lieutenant Graham completely defeated the rebels near the Palámao fort; and about the same time Major Forster, with the Shakawáti battalion, restored order in Singhbhúm. These successes were followed by others of a similar character. Captain Dalton pursued the rebels from place to place. Ably seconded by Mr. Cockburn, and assisted by Major Forster, by Ensign Wardlaw, by Captain Moncrieff, and by other officers placed at his disposal, he re-established everywhere British authority. The embers of disaffection continued, however, to smoulder long after every enemy had disappeared from the field, and it was not before the close of 1858 that perfect tranquillity could be said to reign in every corner of Chútia Nágpúr.

Tranquillity is gradually restored.

BOOK XII.

CHAPTER II.

Retrospect of western Bihár.

Taking the reader with me north-westward, I propose to narrate now the state of affairs in western Bihár; to explain how the communications between Kánhpúr and Allahábád had been preserved; then, proceeding to the A'zamgarh districts, to show how insurrection triumphed there for a moment, only to be driven back to seek a refuge, destined to be of long duration, in the districts and jungles which owned the authority of the remarkable landowner, Kúnwar Singh.

I have told in the first volume how the important division of Western Bihár, saved by Mr. William Tayler during the dark and terrible days of June and July 1857, then exposed, by the wilful blindness of the Government, to dangers more acute, more vivid, more active, had been preserved from immediate destruction by the gallantry of Vicars Boyle, of Wake, of Colvin, and their companions, and finally, completely rescued by the splendid daring of Vincent Eyre. I have recorded the ingratitude with which one of

1857. July–Aug.

these gentlemen, Mr. William Tayler, had been treated by the Government he had served with an energy all-absorbing and a success most signal, and how the other principal actor in the drama, Vincent Eyre, after storming the stronghold of Kúnwar Singh, had been ordered to join the avenging army of Outram. From the hour of their departure a new era was inaugurated in western Bihár—an era in which truckling took the place of independence, and a desire to discover mistakes in Mr. Tayler's administration the determination to suppress, before all, the dangers threatening the State.

Patná under Mr. Tayler's successor.

For some weeks after his departure the effect of Eyre's victories continued to be felt in western Bihár. The Government, alive at last, after one revolt had been quelled, to the advisability of preventing another, had placed under the orders of Mr. Samuells, the successor of Mr. Tayler, two hundred Europeans, for the safeguard of Patná, and had despatched a gun-boat, under the orders of the Magistrate of Chaprá, to patrol the banks of the Ghághrá. But as time went on, the misguided spirits in the province began to be sensible that Eyre had left them, and that the spirit of William Tayler no longer inspired the administration. Though Patná, thanks to the presence of British troops, was reported to be quiet, strong precautionary measures were not the less taken. The opium godown was fortified, six guns were placed in position bearing on the town, and the most stringent measures were taken to avert a collision between the townspeople and the Europeans.

Book XII. Chapter II.

1857. Aug.-Sept.

The aspect in the district was even less assuring. Kúnwar Singh, with one thousand men, had taken up a position on the Són river, and it became known that dangerous and discontented characters, such men as his brother Ammar Singh, Nisban Singh, and Júban Singh, were flocking to his standard. At the same time, the 5th Irregular Cavalry, whose disarming Mr. Tayler had before ineffectually recommended, and whose mutiny in eastern Bihár I have already recorded,* were allowed to spread over the districts in the western province, and to plunder with impunity.

The difficulties in western Bihár aggravated by risings elsewhere.

The difficulties of the position in western Bihár were greatly aggravated by the evacuation of Gorákhpúr by the British civil authorities, one alone excepted,† on the 13th August, and subsequently by all; by the consequent pressure of rebels into British districts from Oudh; and by the exposure of the districts of Chaprá, Champáran, and Mozaffarpúr to the incursions of the leader of the Oudh rebels, Mehndi Husén.

The mutinous 5th Irregulars approach Gayá.

These difficulties soon came to a head. The mutinous 5th Irregulars, finding no one to oppose their course, destroyed the public buildings at Noáda, and marched in the direction of Gayá. Rattray, with a small force of Sikhs and Europeans, numbering about two hundred, had been posted to protect Gayá. But, learning that the rebels were approaching that place, he, acting on the strongly pressed advice of Mr. Alonzo Money, marched out on the 8th September to attack

Rattray marches to meet them,

* *Vide* page 133.

† The exception was Mr. F. M. Bird, the joint magistrate.

Book XII. Chapter II.

1857. Sept.-Oct.

and is defeated.

them. But the rebels, almost all mounted,* took advantage of Rattray's advance from his base to go round his position—inflicting upon him in his vain attempts to hinder them, a loss of twenty wounded—and to reach Gayá some hours before he could fall back. Arrived at Gayá, they liberated four hundred prisoners from the jail, and attacked the fortified house which the residents had prepared as a place of refuge. But in this attempt they were repulsed, owing mainly to the spirited conduct of Mr. Skipwith Tayler, son of the late Commissioner of Patná.

Two companies of the 32nd mutiny.

The disorder was subsequently further aggravated by the mutiny, on the 9th October, of two companies of the 32nd Native Infantry at Déogarh and by threatened movements on the part of Kúnwar Singh. The Commissioner had at his disposal Rattray's Sikhs, a portion of the Naval Brigade, under Captain Sotheby. Colonel Fischer's brigade of Madras troops entered the western Bihár districts early in October. Besides which, Lieutenant Stanton of the Engineers was at Sahasrám and its vicinity, and the energy, the zeal, and the activity of this officer compensated to a very great extent for the paucity of fighting men.

Forces at the disposal of the Commissioner.

Rattray was the first to come in contact with the rebellious sepoys. This officer had avenged his disaster of the 8th September by defeating a body of rebels on the 7th of the following month

* They consisted of the 5th Irregulars and other horsemen who had mutinied, amounting to six hundred. Accompanying them was a large party of marauders, some mounted on ponies, some on foot.

Book XII. Chapter II.

1857. November.

at Akbarpúr, and he now went in pursuit of the mutinous 32nd. On the 6th November he caught them at the village of Dhanchúa. The numbers on both sides were equal, and the contest was severe. Night fell whilst the combat was raging; then, covered by darkness, the rebels effected a retreat.

The events which followed each other in western Bihár until the formation of Colonel Rowcroft's force in November, present a constant succession of skirmishes, of movements against petty forts, and similar occurrences of a purely local character. To Rowcroft I shall return shortly. But before doing so it seems incumbent upon me, for the clearness of the subsequent narrative, to describe, as concisely as may be, the occurrences in the districts and on the grand trunk road between Allahábád and Kánhpúr during the period intervening between Sir Colin Campbell's battle of Kánhpúr and the final fall of Lakhnao.

The road between Kánhpúr and Allahâbâd.

Carthew at Fathpúr.

After the battle of Kánhpúr Brigadier Carthew was detached, with the Madras brigade, to command at Fathpúr. The command was an important one, as it was exposed to attacks from the districts south-west of Kánhpúr—from Kálpi, from Jhánsi, from Bandalkhand. Fathpúr, moreover faced—a narrow strip of land on the right bank of the Ganges alone intervening—the south-western frontier of Oudh, and was at any moment liable to incursions from flying parties of rebels. It devolved, therefore, upon Carthew, not only to thrust back attacks from these opposite quarters, but to guard intact the trunk road

—the line of communication between Kánhpúr and Alláhábád. The fact that troops and well-guarded convoys were constantly marching up the road doubtless facilitated his task, and enabled him to employ advantageously such passing troops to aid him in clearing the districts lining the road.

Book XII. Chapter II. 1857. December.

The task which devolved upon him.

Campbell at Allahábád.

The duties devolving upon the officer commanding at the south-eastern end of the line of which I am writing—the station of Allahábád—were of not less importance. Situated at the confluence of the great rivers the Jamná and the Ganges, abutting alike on Bandalkhand, on Oudh, and on the disturbed districts of A'zamgarh and Jánpúr, Allahábád was a place always threatened, and yet to be preserved at all risks. Allahábád was, in fact, at once the outlying frontier fortress of the province of Bihár, and its key.

At the time of which I am writing, December 1857 and January 1858, the officer commanding at Allahábád was Brigadier Campbell.

Fathpúr.

Carthew took up his command at Fathpúr on the 19th December. Just before he arrived (11th December) a small party under Colonel Barker, R.A., had made a raid amongst the disaffected villages in the district, had burned some, and had expelled the turbulent villagers from others. In this way the district had been purged of its disloyal citizens. The revenue returns and the supply of provisions to the headquarters proved, almost at once, how very beneficial had been these domiciliary visits.

The rebels assemble on

The expelled villagers had fled across the

BOOK XII. Chapter II. 1857-8. Dec.-Jan.

the right bank of the Jamná.

Jamná, and it was on the right bank of this river, from Kálpi down to Bandá, that mutineers from Gwáliár, Jhansi, and Bandalkhand, even fugitives from Fathgarh, now began to assemble. Amongst them were the Rájá of Chikáni and a brother and nephew of Náná Sáhib; some accounts even spoke of Náná Sáhib himself. Certain it is that the rebel leaders who had their headquarters at Julápúr on the Bétwa, near Kálpi, exercised the right of sovereignty by calling upon the landowners west of the Jamná to furnish money and recruits for the service of the representative of the Péshwá.

Carthew clears the country on the left bank.

Across the Jamná it was not possible to act. The Commander-in-Chief, however, deemed it especially advisable that the districts to the east of that river should be kept clear of the mutineers. In accordance, then, with instructions which he issued, Carthew marched on the 10th January with a small force (two horse artillery guns, four companies Rifle Brigade, two hundred 17th Madras Native Infantry) along the Kánhpúr road. On reaching Jahánábád, he turned westward towards Kálpi, communicated with the 34th Regiment, sent from Kánhpúr to co-operate with him, and then moved on Bhognipúr. The occupation of this place, the locality of which has already been indicated,* forced the several rebel parties who had come over from Kálpi to recross the river. Carthew then, in compliance with an order received from Brigadier Inglis, pushed on to Sikan-

* *Vide* page 228.

Book XII. Chapter II.

1858. January.

dra, and then returned leisurely, *viâ* Kánhpúr, to Fathpúr. He had thoroughly purged the district of rebels.

Brigadier Campbell clears the country across the Ganges.

About the same time (5th January) Brigadier Campbell, with a brigade composed of the 79th Highlanders, a regiment of the Rifle Brigade, some foot and horse artillery, and a newly-raised cavalry levy, the Banáras Horse, effectually cleared the districts near Allahábád, on the left bank of the Ganges. His operations were in every respect successful, and in three encounters which he had with the rebels the latter admitted a considerable loss.

Moveable columns patrol the district.

But the efforts of these columns occasionally despatched into the districts could not prevent a fresh appearance of the enemy after their departure. It was natural that so long as the Lakhnao question remained unsolved the delta west of Kánhpúr, that is the narrow strip lying between the two great arteries the Ganges and the Jamná, should be constantly threatened, and almost as constantly invaded. It was necessary, therefore, to patrol the entire district. In March a moveable column,* commanded by Lieutenant-Colonel Christie, engaged in this work, moved down to the village of Dhána, near the left bank of the Jamná, to prevent a threatened passage of the river at that point. Christie found the enemy occupying Siráoli, a town in the Hamirpúr district,

* One 12-pounder howitzer, one 6-pounder gun; seventy men, 8th Irregular Cavalry; two hundred and forty-four men, 80th Foot; two hundred and fifty-seven, 17th Madras Native Infantry.

Book XII. Chapter II.

1858. March.

on the right bank opposite Dhána, and engaged in firing on that village. By a judicious advance of his artillery, he drove the enemy from Siráoli, and set fire to the town, but the want of boats prevented him from crossing in pursuit.

Effect on the district of the fall of Lakhnao.

Occasional raids still continued. On the 26th March a corps of rebels crossed the Jamná near Hamirpúr, plundered and burned the village of Ghátampúr, and then returned. But this was an expiring effort. The fall of Lakhnao placed an overwhelming force at the disposal of the Commander-in-Chief, whilst, on the western side of the Jamná, another active leader, whose name will occupy a most prominent part in the succeeding volume, was pressing, with all the decision and enterprise of a great commander, the chiefs and leaders whose troops had so long been attempting to harass the British line of communications. It was just after the fall of Lakhnao that the action of Sir Hugh Rose and General Whitlock began to make itself felt. Just then, too, Sir Colin Campbell despatched a small force, under Colonel Maxwell, to Kálpi. The proceedings of these several forces will be narrated in their due course. Meanwhile it may be stated that the work of supervision and control exercised by Brigadier Carthew had been eminently useful to the Commander-in-Chief.

Rowcroft and Sotheby.

What Rowcroft and Sotheby had effected with their brigades up to the time of their occupation of Gorakhpúr, I have already narrated.*

* Pages 321 to 324.

I propose now to take up the story of their action from the point where I left them, and to show how it was that the Ázamgarh and Jánpúr districts fell again into extraordinary confusion.

Book XII. Chapter II.

1858. Feb.-March.

Sotheby defeats the rebels at Chandipúr.

Rowcroft, arriving at Gorákhpúr on the 19th February, had defeated the rebels on the 20th, and on the 25th had been left, by the departure towards Lakhnao of the Nipalese, in command at Gorákhpúr. Two days prior to his arrival, Captain Sotheby, R.N., of the Naval Brigade, who was escorting boats up the river Gághrá with a force of one hundred and thirty men of that brigade, thirty-five Sikhs, and sixty Nipalese, had attacked and captured the fort of Chandipúr, garrisoned by three hundred men. This fort was situated on the left bank of the river, in the midst of a dense bamboo jungle. Yet so well planned was Captain Sotheby's attack, that the capture of the fort and the guns and the property it contained cost his force a loss of only four wounded! Amongst these was Captain Charles Weston, of the 36th Native Infantry, a very gallant officer. It is due to add that the attack was most efficiently aided by the guns of a river steamer—the *Jamná*.

The intrenched camp of the rebels at Bélwá.

Within the British district of Gorákhpúr, sixty-eight miles to the west of it, and nine miles east of Faizábád in Oudh, is the town of A'mórha. Thither Rowcroft now marched, and on the 4th March took up a position not far from the intrenched camp of Bélwá, then occupied by a large rebel force. The rebel force alluded to was com-

Book XII. Chapter II.

1858. March.

posed of upwards of fourteen thousand men, led by the pseudo-Názim Méhndi Húsén, the Rájás of Gondah and Chardah, and other disaffected chiefs. Included in their ranks were two thousand five hundred trained sepoys, composed of the 1st, 10th, and 53rd Native Infantry, recently completed to five hundred men each, seven hundred men of the 2nd Oudh Police, and about three hundred of the 5th Regiment Gwáliár contingent.

They march to attack Rowcroft,

The approach of Rowcroft disconcerted the hopes which these rebel chieftains had entertained of taking advantage of the concentration of the main British army before Lakhnao to make a raid down into A'zamgarh and Jánpúr districts, and if possible to reach Banáras. But there was, it seemed to them, one mode—and a very certain mode—whereby to rid themselves of Rowcroft and his following, and then to prosecute their intentions. This was to attack him, with the vastly superior force at their disposal, as he lay at A'morha.

and are totally defeated.

Thus thinking, they acted. Early on the morning of the 5th March they marched towards the British camp, distant from them some seven miles. They had approached at half-past 8 within a mile of it when they were met by Rowcroft and Sotheby and Richardson. A severe contest ensued. The trained sepoys of the rebel force fought with great courage and determination, but they lacked the cool leading of the European officer, which, under other circumstances, had so often led them to victory. Sotheby's Naval Brigade greatly distinguished itself.

Book XII. Chapter II.

1858. March–April.

The charge of the Yeomanry Cavalry.

The enemy were already shaken when Richardson ordered the Yeomanry Cavalry to charge. The first charge caused the enemy to waver, another compelled them to give ground, a third drove them in headlong flight from the field. They were then pursued to their intrenchments at Bélwá, losing between four and five hundred killed and wounded, and abandoning eight guns on the field. The intrenchments at Bélwá gave them a safe refuge, for the cavalry could not penetrate within them.

Rowcroft remains at A'mórha.

Rowcroft remained at A'mórha waiting for reinforcements to enable him to attack the strong position of the rebels. Subsequently, on the 17th April, and again on the 25th, he met and defeated them in the plain between the two positions; but before this had happened, events had occurred in the districts to his left rear—the districts of A'zamgarh and Jánpúr—which compel me to return thither.

Kúnwar Singh in western Bihár.

I have already related how Kúnwar Singh, after his expulsion by Vincent Eyre from Jagdispúr, had hung about the districts of western Bihár to the terror of the successor of Mr. William Tayler and of the Government of Bengal. One of the three natives of India thrown up to the surface by the mutiny, who showed any pretensions to the character of a strategist—the others being Tántia Topi and the Oudh Moulvi—Kúnwar Singh had carefully forborne to risk the fortunes of his diminished party by engaging in a conflict which, however favourable might be its commence-

Book XII. Chapter II.

1858. March.

ment, must certainly end in his complete defeat. Shahábád, though the region of his birth, the district in which lay his confiscated estates, was too carefully watched, he felt, to present the chances which would alone justify in his eyes a departure from his system of reserve. His actual force was small. He had with him about twelve hundred sepoys, trained in the Indian army, and a few hundreds of untrained adherents, dependents of himself, his brother, and other discontented land-owners of the province. With such a force he could not hope to make a serious impression. But when he saw how British troops were being hurried up from every quarter to take part in the attack on Lakhnao, when he heard that the Nipálese and Franks had pushed on for that city, leaving the western frontier of the British provinces bordering Oudh comparatively denuded of troops, then he saw his opportunity, then he resolved to make a push for eastern Oudh, and combining with the numberless rebels still at large in that part, to make a dash on A'zamgarh, and, successful there, to avenge the storming of Jagdispúr by a dash on Allahábád or Banáras.

His policy.

His force.

He resolves to make a diversion in eastern Oudh.

Fortune greatly favoured him. At the moment when he crossed into Oudh, Rowcroft at A'mórha was confronting the intrenched camp of the rebels at Bélwá. His inability to storm that position had singularly encouraged the enemy. They, too, like Kúnwar Singh, had designs on A'zamgarh, and though their main plan had been for the moment baffled by the defeat inflicted upon their attacking columns on the 5th March, yet Rowcroft's inability to follow up his victory had incited them to pursue their original design by other means. Still holding the camp at Bélwá, they detached then a considerable force to the south-east, and this force, during its march, attracted to itself many detachments which had escaped the bayonets and horsemen of the victorious Franks. With these troops, Kúnwar Singh succeeded in effecting a junction at A'tráolia on the 17th or 18th March. Book XII. Chapter II. 1858. March 17.

The Ázamgarh district was then guarded by a small British force consisting of two hundred and six men of the 37th Regiment, sixty Madras cavalry, the 4th, and two light guns, under the command of Colonel Milman of the 37th. At the time when Kúnwar Singh and his rebel allies took up their position at Atráolia, Milman was encamped in the district at Koelsa, not far from Ázamgarh. The distance between Ázamgarh and Atráolia is twenty-five miles. The reader will recollect that Atráolia is the fortress which, on the 9th November preceding, had been captured by Colonel Longden, and by him partially burnt and destroyed. Dependent upon it was a small fort, comparatively insignificant. The fortress itself covered a number of strong buildings, all loop-holed. The outer wall was fifteen feet high. Atráolia.

On the afternoon of the 21st March, Milman received from Mr. Davies, magistrate of Ázamgarh, the intelligence of the vicinity of the rebels. He at once broke up his camp, marched all night, and at daybreak on the 22nd, came upon the advanced guard of the enemy's force, not occupying the forts, but posted in three or four mango- Milman beats the enemy near Atráolia,

Book XII. Chapter II.

1858. March.

groves, contiguous to each other. Without giving them time to recover from their surprise, he attacked and defeated them, the 4th Madras Cavalry behaving with great dash and resolution. The enemy being dispersed, Milman determined, before advancing further, to give the men their breakfasts. He accordingly halted in the mango-groves whence he had expelled the rebels, and his men, piling their arms, prepared to enjoy the matutinal meal. But the cup was dashed to the ground just as the hand was about to raise it to the lips. The breakfast was almost ready when information was suddenly brought to Milman that the enemy were advancing in great force!

then halts to breakfast,

when the rebels march on him.

It was too true. At last the opportunity for which Kúnwar Singh had longed through so many dreary months had come to him. An enemy, though European, yet vastly inferior in numbers; an enemy worn out by a long march, by deprivation of sleep, by fasting; an enemy twenty-five miles from his base and with no supports! What more could a general long for? Everything was in his favour. Kúnwar Singh, then, marched to a victory which he deemed assured. The imagination can almost picture him making to the confidant by his side an exclamation near akin to that which burst from the lips of Wellington when he noticed the false movement of Marmont which brought on the battle of Salamanca! *

Milman's position as Kúnwar Singh pictured it.

Yes, Milman was lost. Galloping forward, followed by some skirmishers, as soon as he re-

Milman endeavours to check the

* "Mon cher Alava, Marmont est perdu."

Book XII. Chapter II.

1858. March.

ceived the news of which I have spoken, the English leader beheld the enemy in great strength, some covered by a mud wall, others in fields of sugarcane and in topes of trees. Still, hoping that a daring movement on his part would check their further progress, he ordered an advance. But the numbers of the enemy exceeded his in the proportion of eight to one. Outflanked, it was impossible to advance. Forced back, he at least maintained a bold front. The enemy, never attempting to charge, contented themselves with a steady advance and a steady musketry fire. Once, indeed, as the British troops neared the camp at Koelsa, which they had quitted the previous evening, the rebels made a desperate effort to outflank them. But a timely charge of the 4th Madras Cavalry, which had shown remarkable steadiness, frustrated this movement. Then it was that, tired, worn out, wearied, having lost many men in killed and wounded, the survivors found their way into the encamping ground of Koelsa.

Advance of the rebels.

He falls back on Koelsa.

Not, however, to find a refuge there. The rumour of their mishap had preceded them. A panic had seized the camp-followers, most of whom had fled taking their bullocks with them. The foe was still near; the camp was not defensible; there was no food. Milman, then, abandoning the camp equipage, continued his retreat to Ázamgarh. He reached that place the same day, and whilst making every preparation to defend it in case it should be attacked, sent off expresses to Banáras, Allahábád, and Lakhnao for assistance.

Thence on A'zamgarh, whence he despatches messengers for aid.

Book XII. Chapter II.

1858. March.

Some reinforcements reach Ázamgarh.

The express despached to Banáras reached that station on the 24th March. Forty-six men of the Madras Rifles were instantly despatched to Ázamgarh. The following day one hundred and fifty men of the 37th Regiment from Gházipúr, and two days later one hundred and thirty of the same regiment, reached Ázamgarh, and penetrated within the intrenchment before it had been attacked by the rebels. Colonel Dames of the 37th then assumed the command. On the 27th he attempted a sortie with two hundred Europeans, two guns, and sixty Madras cavalry, and though successful at first, was repulsed with the loss of one officer and eleven men killed and wounded. He then retreated into the intrenchment, and thenceforward acted on the defensive.

Lord Canning hears of Milman's disaster,

The express despatched to Allahábád reached that place on the 27th. Lord Canning was at Allahábád. The news caused him anxiety. Knowing what sort of a man Kúnwar Singh was, that he possessed audacity and courage, and that he knew the value of time in military operations, he realised at once the danger of the situation.

and at once realises its magnitude.

He saw how possible it was for the Jagdispúr chieftain, reinforced as he daily was by troops who had escaped from Lakhnao, to overwhelm Milman at Ázamgarh, and then rapidly traversing the eighty-one miles which separated that place from Banáras, then almost ungarrisoned, to seize that important city, and thus sever the communications between Calcutta on the one side and the Governor-General of India at Allahábád and the Commander-in-Chief of the army at Lakhnao on the other.

Just then the headquarters and right wing of the 13th Light Infantry happened to be at Allahábád. The officer commanding that regiment was Colonel Lord Mark Kerr. Lord Canning at once ordered Lord Mark to proceed with all haste with his regiment to Banáras, and picking up there whatever troops might be available, to push on to Ázamgarh and check Kúnwar Singh.

Book XII. Chapter II.

1858. March–April.

He orders Lord Mark Kerr to push on to A'zamgarh.

Lord Mark Kerr, responding promptly to the call, set out that same evening, reached Banáras on the 31st March, picked up there a troop—fifty-five men and two officers—of the Queen's Bays, seventeen gunners and one officer, with two 6-pounder guns and two $5\frac{1}{2}$-inch mortars, and started thence for Ázamgarh at 10 o'clock on the night of the 2nd April. With the wing of the 13th were three hundred and seventy-two men and nineteen officers. His entire force consisted, then, of twenty-two officers and four hundred and forty-four men.

Lord Mark Kerr arrives within eight miles of A'zamgarh, and halts for the dawn.

Marching with all speed, Lord Mark Kerr reached Sarsána, eight miles from Ázamgarh, the evening of the 5th. There he received, and during the night continued to receive, most pressing letters from the staff officer at Ázamgarh, begging him to push on without a moment's delay. But to march a force of four hundred and forty-four men across a country utterly unknown to any of them, to relieve a place besieged by an army whose numbers certainly exceeded five thousand, and might amount to fifteen thousand, was an idea not to be entertained by a prudent commander. Defeat would

Book XII. Chapter II.

1858. April 6.

but precipitate the evil he had been sent to avert. Lord Mark Kerr, then, wisely resolved to defer his march till the day should approach its dawn.

He marches on the 6th and comes on the rebels

He set out at 4 o'clock on the morning of the 6th—a reconnoitring party of the Bays, with whom was Lord Mark, leading the way. After a march of two hours, Lord Mark observed some buildings and a mango grove to the left of the road, and the banked ditches of the fields to the right of it, to be crowded with sepoys lying in ambush and evidently on the look-out for him. Making as though he had not observed them, he made his cavalry dismount, and halted till his train of elephants, camels, and carts had closed up; he then despatched a company of the 13th to the right with the view of forcing back the enemy's left, and of thus opening a way for the progress of the train.

and fights them.

In this he so far succeeded, that the rebels fell back on the left, but almost at the same time a heavy fire opened from the buildings and the mango groves of which I have spoken, and which, on the left of the road from the British advancing line, constituted the enemy's right. Lord Mark threw out his men in skirmishing order and brought up the guns, which, at a distance of five hundred yards, began to throw shrapnel into the buildings.

Great difficulties of his position.

The enemy, however, were so numerous, and were so completely on all four sides of him, that it required all the soldierly skill of the British leader to keep them at a distance. His position was complicated by the necessity of defending the large train of animals accompanying the force, and the capture of which would, naturally, be a special object of the rebels. These animals, when the action had begun, had turned round with fright and bolted to the rear, the mahouts clinging to the elephants, whilst the drivers, descending from the carts, had run off, calling upon the trees and bushes to cover them. Everything now depended upon Lord Mark's ability to make head against the enemy. Up to this time, when the fight had lasted an hour, though he still held the position he had taken up, he had made no impression upon them; and just at the moment he could discern in rear of their skirmishers their reserves forming up in quarter-distance column, whilst a large body was being detached with the evident purpose of penetrating between him and the baggage animals. In this, before long, the rebels partly succeeded; for they set fire to many of the carts.

The rebels receive accession of strength.

The situation was critical. The two 6-pounders had been gradually brought to within sixty yards of the main building, without, however, producing the required effect. Lord Mark was anxious to try the effect of shelling, but the two mortars were so located, that, to use them with effect, it had become necessary to cause the gunners and their supports to fall back, and Lord Mark had noticed that the smallest retrograde movement caused the enemy to rise to their feet and, with loud shouts, display their numbers with a view to encircle him. But he felt the main building must be carried at any price. At last the two 6-pounders effected a small breach, and volunteers being called for, some thirty or forty men rushed to the storm. They found the breach not quite practicable, but,

Critical situation of Lord Mark Kerr.

The slightest hesitation would have lost him.

Book XII. Chapter II.

1858. March.

His splendid perseverance

far from falling back, they set to work vigorously to enlarge it. Their labours disclosing an inner wall yet uninjured, Lord Mark recalled them, and resumed practice with his guns. Before the men fell back, they set fire to the wooden portions of the building. The guns then re-opened fire, but the effect they produced was slight, since, to maintain his position, Lord Mark was forced to use one of them to throw shrapnel at the rebels in the rear of his right flank. Gradually, however, progress was made, and Lord Mark was meditating a second assault, when the flames, which, despite the efforts made to subdue them, had been gradually spreading, forced the rebels to evacuate the building. Instantly, a pursuit was ordered, the Bays rushed to the front, and the day was won!

is crowned with success.

The rebels are repulsed in an attack made, meanwhile, on the baggage.

But while the position of the rebels in front was being thus forced, they had completed the circle, and were now attacking the rear of Lord Mark's small force. In this part of the field a high embankment crossed the road. This embankment the enemy now seized. Captain Wilson Jones of the 13th, commanding the company of that regiment which formed the rear guard, at once faced about and charged them. He drove the enemy back, but lost his own life.

Lord Mark leaves the baggage with Major Tyler,

Lord Mark's position was now peculiar. He had pierced the enemy's centre; the way to Ázamgarh lay open to him; on his left, the rebels, terrified by the defeat in the centre, were rapidly falling back; but on the right, notwithstanding the success of the charge just narrated, they still occupied a menacing position. The drivers and the cartmen had run away, and the baggage remained exposed. Under these circumstances, Lord Mark resolved to leave a sufficient force to hold front to the right, whilst he should push on to Ázamgarh, and return with the Madras sepoys he might find there, who, on a pinch, would drive the carts. No doubt he calculated that the enemy, believing themselves threatened by the movement, would be glad to retreat while they could. Sending, then, Major Tyler of the 13th, a cool and capable officer, to command the rear and baggage guards, he pushed forward on the Ázamgarh road. The enemy's right wing, noticing the movement, beat a hasty retreat.

Book XII. Chapter II.

1858. April.

and moves on A'zamgarh.

No sooner had the enemy retreated than many of the carters and drivers and mahouts reappeared, and Major Tyler pushed on rapidly after his chief. No further opposition was offered. A village which had to be traversed, and which might have been easily defended with a few men, was abandoned. The bridge across the river leading to the intrenchment was reached at 11 o'clock. This bridge had been rendered impassable by the rebels, and after their flight they still continued to maintain a heavy fire on it. It was repaired under this fire by Lieutenant Colomb, R.A., acting under the orders of Lord Mark. As soon as it had been rendered serviceable, the Madras Rifles crossed it in compliance with a request made by Lord Mark, and the convoy was brought in in safety.

He is rejoined *en route* by Major Tyler,

and enters A'zamgarh.

This gallant little action reflects the greatest credit on the troops and the commander. Lord

Credit due to Lord Mark Kerr.

Book XII. Chapter II.

1858. April.

Mark was accompanied by Lieutenant-Colonel Longden of the 10th Foot and Mr. Venables, the daring indigo-planter, whose previous gallant achievements have brought him more than once before the reader; and no doubt the previous experience of these two gallant men was useful to him. But he was the leader; upon him it depended whether to advance against numbers or to retreat before numbers. Upon his shoulders rested the responsibility, and to him must be accorded the praise. When it was urged upon him to abandon the convoy and to make for the intrenchments, he merely replied "Wait a bit: we'll win yet," and persevered. The number against whom he contended did not, at the lowest computation, fall short of four thousand men, and probably greatly exceeded it. Against these, deducting his baggage guards, he could not put in line more than three hundred men. In the daring, the conduct, and the success of the achievement, Lord Mark Kerr's relief of Ázamgarh may be classed with Vincent Eyre's relief of Árah.

His prudence equalled his daring.

Nor, whilst awarding Lord Mark Kerr this high praise for his daring, can History deny him the not inferior merit of military prudence. The imploring letters he received for immediate aid on his arrival at Sarsána might have induced a less prudent commander to start that night on an errand, the accomplishment of which successfully might well be supposed to depend on the most absolute promptitude. There can be no more tormenting pressure on the mind of a commander than the knowledge that his countrymen within a few

Book XII. Chapter II.

1858. April.

miles of him may perish for want of immediate relief; that the few hours of the night, well employed, would bring them that relief; but that prudential considerations compel him not to use those hours. Lord Mark Kerr felt that pressure, and yet had the wisdom to resist it.

State of affairs in A'zamgarh.

The state of affairs at Ázamgarh was bad indeed. Milman's force, after its precipitate and disastrous retreat, had marched straight into the intrenchments within the jail, leaving the town to the mercy of the rebels. But these moved so cautiously that the reinforcements of which I have spoken * were able to enter. Two days later the rebels occupied the town and beleaguered the jail. Fortunately, this was surrounded by a deep ditch, and Kúnwar Singh did not care to risk an assault. He invested the place, and trusted to the effects of famine and an unremitting fire. He even had it in contemplation to blockade the jail and to march on Banáras, and there can be no doubt that this programme would have been carried out but for the splendid achievement of Lord Mark Kerr.

Defects in Kúnwar Singh's tactics.

The action fought by Lord Mark had cost the British a casualty list large in proportion to the number engaged, eight officers and men being killed and thirty-four severely or dangerously wounded. At such a price the defeat of Kúnwar Singh was cheaply purchased. That leader had showed himself greater as a strategist than a tactician. His plan of campaign was admirable, but

* *Vide* page 458.

Book XII. Chapter II.

1858. April.

in carrying it into execution he committed many serious errors. Milman gave him a great, an unexpected opportunity. He had that officer at his mercy. When Milman's men were waiting for their breakfast in the mango grove near Atráolia, it was in the power of Kúnwar Singh to cut them off from Ázamgarh. He preferred to attack them in front. Then the pursuit was not pressed on with sufficient vigour. A capable commander would still have cut them off. Once having seen them housed in Ázamgarh, he should have left a portion of his force to blockade them, pressed on with the remainder towards Banáras, and occupied a position in which he could have engaged Lord Mark Kerr with advantage. He had at his disposal, it subsequently transpired, about twelve thousand men. To oppose these the few men led by Lord Mark were alone available. Everything was within his grasp had he dared to stretch out his hand. The chances are that, capable man as he was, he saw all this. It was his misfortune to have under him many petty leaders, all wishing to be supreme!

Probable cause of his false tactics.

I have now recorded the result of the message sent from Ázamgarh to Banáras and Allahábád. Another result was produced by the message despatched to Lakhnao. What that was will be narrated when I return to the army still massed in the conquered city.

BOOK XII.

CHAPTER III.

I LEFT Sir Colin Campbell master, on the 21st March, of Lakhnao. I propose to narrate now the measures which he adopted to reap every possible advantage from his conquest.

Three main objects first presented themselves to his attention. The first was the strengthening of the weak places which had been threatened during his advance; the second, the formation of a moveable column for the reconquest of western and north-western Oudh; the third, the reconquest of Rohilkhand. Combined with this last was the necessity of holding out a hand to the brigade of Seaton, left at Fathgarh, and to the columns of Jones and Penny still accomplishing, or about to accomplish, the work which had remained to be carried out in the north-west. The action still remaining to be accomplished.

On the 24th March Sir Colin detailed a considerable force to constitute, for the moment, the

Book XII. Chapter III.

1858. March.

Sir E. Lugard is ordered to A'zamgarh.

garrison of Lakhnao.* The command of this force was entrusted to Sir Hope Grant.

On the 28th the Military Train, the 10th Regiment, and a field battery left for Allahábád. The same day Sir Colin received information of Milman's disaster near Ázamgarh, narrated in the previous chapter. His movement to repair the misfortune was as prompt as could be desired. On the 29th Sir E. Lugard was despatched, with a brigade of infantry (10th,† 34th, 84th), seven hundred Sikh sabres, and eighteen pieces of artillery, by the direct road to Ázamgarh, taking Atráolia *en route*. Whilst Lugard would thus relieve Ázamgarh, the advance of Jang Bahadúr's force towards Faizábád, on their return to Nipál, would, it was hoped, relieve Rowcroft, whom I left encamped at Amórah.

I propose, in the first instance, to follow the course of Sir E. Lugard. But before setting out with him I may state that there still remained at Lakhnao four regiments of cavalry and eight of infantry, with artillery in proportion, to be accounted for. These were constituted as a moveable column, at the head of which was placed Brigadier-General Walpole. To him I shall revert in due course.

* Two troops horse artillery; two field batteries; four garrison batteries; one company engineers; three companies pioneers.

The 2nd Dragoon Guards; the Lahór Light Horse; 1st Sikh Cavalry; Hodson's Horse; the 20th, 23rd, 38th, 53rd, 90th, 97th Regiments, and 1st Madras Fusiliers; Headquarters 27th Madras Native Infantry; 5th Panjáb Infantry.

† The 10th had started on the 28th *en route* to England, but were recalled by an express that night.

Book XII. Chapter III.

1858. March–April.

He sets out 29th March,

Lugard left Lakhnao on the 29th March. The distance to Ázamgarh was fifteen marches. Pushing on as rapidly as possible he reached Súltánpúr the 5th April. It had been his intention to cross the Gúmti at this place, and march direct on Ázamgarh. But to carry out this plan would have necessitated a week's delay. The bridge had been destroyed by fire, and there were no boats. Under these circumstances he resolved to continue his march down the right bank, and to make, in the first instance, for Jánpúr.

and defeats the rebels near Tigra.

A few miles only from Jánpúr, to the north-west of it, and on the direct road from Sultánpúr, lies the village of Tigra. Within four miles of this village a rebel force of three thousand men, one third of whom were trained sepoys, and two guns, under the command of Ghúlám Húsén, had appeared on the 10th April, threatening Jánpúr. The following day this rebel force attacked and burnt a considerable village within six miles of Tigra. The afternoon of that day Lugard reached Tigra, and heard of the vicinity of the rebels. He had made a sixteen-mile march, his troops were exhausted, the heat of the day excessive. He therefore resolved to remain where he was for the day. Towards evening, however, he received information that the rebels were on the move. He at once turned out his men, dashed after them, caught and attacked them. The rebels attempted for a moment to stand, but they could not resist the terrible onslaught of the cavalry. After a short resistance, they turned and fled, leaving eighty killed and

Book XII. Chapter III. 1858. April.

their two guns on the field. On the side of the victors six sowars were wounded. There was but one killed—but the loss was the loss of a most gallant officer, who had rendered excellent service during the mutiny. He who fell was Lieutenant Charles Havelock, a nephew of the renowned general.

Death of Charles Havelock.

Lugard marched on the next day to Didarganj, relieved the Gúrkahs at Jánpúr by three companies of the 37th Regiment, and then pushed on for Ázamgarh. On the 14th he was within seven miles of that place. Ázamgarh was still invested by the force under Kúnwar Singh, computed to be thirteen thousand strong; but if that leader had been unable to force his way into the British intrenchment when it was occupied by Milman's small force, still less was he capable of making an impression upon it after the reinforcements from Ghazipúr and Banáras had reached the place. Indeed, the British garrison had been so greatly increased that, had it taken the field, it might have ended the campaign at a blow. Colonel Dames, who commanded, was, however, restrained from action by the express orders of Sir Colin, and directed to await in his intrenched position the arrival of Sir E. Lugard. The rebels, therefore, still occupied the town, and still threatened the intrenchment. On the approach of Lugard, on the 15th, Kúnwar Singh drew up his forces along the banks of the little river Tons, commanding the bridge of boats across it, and resolved to dispute the passage. But the wily chieftain had matured plans far deeper than even

Á'zamgarh.

Plans of the British garrison.

Book XII. Chapter III.

1858. April 15.

those about him could fathom. He knew very well that the soldiers who had failed to stop the small force of Lord Mark Kerr would have no chance against the more considerable brigade of Sir E. Lugard. He therefore so arranged his forces that whilst those upon whom he could most depend should defend the passage of the Tons as long as possible, the great bulk, traversing the town, should march with all speed to the Ganges, and, crossing that river at or near Gházipúr, should endeavour to reach his native jungles at Jagdispúr, there to renew the war.

Plans of Kúnwar Singh.

Lugard attacked the rebels with great vigour. But for some time he failed to make any impression upon them. They held the bridge of boats with a resolution and perseverance worthy of veterans, and it was not until they had by their long resistance ensured the safety of their comrades that they fell back. Lugard then crossed the Tons, and at once detached half a troop of horse artillery, the Military Train, and two squadrons 3rd Sikh Cavalry in pursuit. In this action Mr. Venables, the indigo-planter, always to the front, always daring, and always, from his intimate acquaintance with the country, eminently useful, was severely wounded. To the regret of every soldier, he died of his wounds. He had rendered splendid and unpaid service to his country. In the earlier days of the mutiny, when all had been clouded and gloomy, he had set a noble example to everybody, and, when his station had been abandoned by the civilians, had

Lugard forces the passage of the Tons.

Death of Mr. Venables.

Book XII. Chapter III.

1858. April 15.

shown the power of preserving order which even one resolute Englishman can wield in India.

The rebels retreat, but are not beaten.

The rebels had taken every advantage of the firm resistance made by their comrades at the Tons, and the pursuers had a gallop of twelve miles before they caught sight of them. And when they did see them, the sight was far from reassuring. Instead of a defeated and scattered host seeking safety in flight, they came upon a body of men retiring unbroken and in good order. They were the men of the old Dánápúr brigade, of the 7th, 8th, and 40th Native Infantry. But the pursuers did not hesitate. They charged —to make, however, no impression. "It was all we could do," wrote one of the officers engaged, "to hold our own against such odds. Immediately our cavalry charged they stood and formed square, and used to abuse and tell us to come on."

The pursuers make little impression upon them.

The loss of the British was considerable. Hamilton of the 3rd Sikhs, a very gallant officer, was killed charging the squares. And although, by greatly daring, the British force succeeded in cutting off three of the enemy's guns, they found it useless to continue the pursuit. They therefore halted at Nathupúr, where they had fought, watched the enemy disappear in the direction of the Ganges, then sent their killed and wounded into Ázamgarh, with a request for reinforcements.

Lugard sends Douglas in pursuit.

Lugard, after crossing the Tons, had encamped at Ázamgarh, and drawing to himself the garrison of the place, was preparing to move actively against two rájás, allies of Kúnwar Singh—who, after the battle, had taken a northerly direction towards Oudh—and to watch the reuniting portions of Ghúlám Husén's force. But the moment he received the report of the pursuing column halted at Nathupúr, he detached Brigadier Douglas at the head of a wing of the 37th, the 84th, one company Madras Rifles, four guns Major Cotter's battery Madras Artillery, two 5½-inch mortars, to reinforce them. Douglas started at once, and reached Nathupúr that night (16th April). Book XII. Chapter III. 1858. April 16-17.

Meanwhile Kúnwar Singh had halted at the village of Naghai, near Ázamgarh, about fourteen miles from Nathupúr. The reasons which influenced Kúnwar Singh, at so critical a conjuncture, cannot be divined. It is fair to believe, however, that knowing, from the custom of his enemy, he would be pursued, he hoped to be able to strike him a blow so disabling as to permit him to continue his retreat without further molestation. Certain it is that he had occupied a strong position, and arranged his forces with considerable skill. Occupying groves of large trees, he had covered his front with breastworks, and had disposed his guns so as to reap the greatest possible advantage from their working. Here Douglas found him on the morning of the 17th, and here he attacked him. But again did Kúnwar Singh display great tactical ability. He kept Douglas at bay till he had secured two lines of retreat for his main columns, which he had divided. He then fell back leisurely, and though many of his men were cut up, they maintained to the end of the day their determined attitude. As soon as

Kúnwar Singh halts at Naghai.

Douglas attacks him there.

Kúnwar Singh falls back skilfully.

Book XII. Chapter III.

1858. April 17–20.

Douglas's pursuit—continued for four or five miles—relaxed, the two divided columns reunited, and took up a position for the night.

Douglas pursues,

Douglas lay that night at Ahúsi, within six miles of the rebels. Early next morning he started again in pursuit. But the rebels had been equally prompt, and marched that day without molestation to Nagra, eighteen miles distant. They were followed all day by the British cavalry and horse artillery, but the infantry did not come up in time to permit Douglas to engage. He encamped that night within three or four miles of the enemy's position. But Kúnwar Singh was well served by his spies. No sooner had he heard that the British had halted for the night than he broke up his camp, marched to Sikandarpúr, crossed the Ghágrá by the ford near that place, and pushed on to Mannahar, in the Gházipúr district. There he and his followers halted, wearied and hungry, hoping they might have time for sleep and food before their pursuers should appear.

and Kúnwar Singh retires.

Douglas tracks and at last reaches him.

But Douglas would allow them time for neither. At midnight on the 18th he heard of their move towards Sikandarpúr. At 2 o'clock in the morning he was on their track, and marching all day, picking up many stragglers as he proceeded, he bivouacked that night within four miles of Kúnwar Singh's position. He did not rest there long. Hoping to catch the enemy, he turned out his men at a very early hour on the 20th, and marching rapidly, found himself at daylight in front of his enemy.

That position was neither so strong nor so well

1858. April 20.

chosen as that at Naghai. The defence consequently was less determined, and the disaster was greater. Douglas advanced his infantry under cover of a fire from his guns, at the same time that he threatened the enemy's right with his cavalry. The rebels made no stand, but fled in disorder, leaving on the field a brass 9-pounder gun, several limbers and waggons, an immense quantity of ammunition, a large amount of treasure, a number of carts and bullocks, four elephants, and the colours of the 28th Regiment Native Infantry, which were found wrapped round the body of a Súbadár who was shot. The rebels were pursued for six miles, but, in pursuance of a preconceived plan, their several columns took different routes, to reunite again at a given hour of the night at some settled spot. What was this spot Douglas found it impossible to find out. Accordingly, when darkness set in, he bivouacked, prepared to move early on the morrow.

Douglas completely defeats the rebels at Mannahar.

But Kúnwar Singh had displayed his accustomed subtlety. His object was to cross the Ganges. He had impressed the country people and many of his own following that having no boats it would be necessary to cross the river on elephants, of which a certain number still remained. By this report he hoped to deceive the English general. But, meanwhile, he had, by means of his agents, collected a sufficient number of boats at Sheopúr Ghát, ten miles below Balliah. When, therefore, night fell, he marched off to this point, and outwitting Colonel Cumberlege, who with two regiments of Madras cavalry was waiting to

Kúnwar Singh eludes Cumberlege and crosses the Ganges into Bihár.

Book XII. Chapter III.

1858. April 21-22.

pounce upon him at Balliah, succeeded in embarking all his men except two hundred before the British appeared on the scene. Douglas, indeed, had started in pursuit at 2 o'clock in the morning, but misled by the false information circulated by Kúnwar Singh, he only reached the right track in time to cut off the two hundred men of whom I have spoken, to capture some elephants and another brass gun, and to sink one —the last—of the enemy's boats.

He retires to Jagdispúr.

Kúnwar Singh thus crossed the Ganges in safety. He made his way without delay to his ancestral domain at Jagdispúr. Here he found his brother, Ammar Singh, with several thousand armed villagers ready to support him. Kúnwar Singh posted these and the few men who, after crossing the Ganges, had adhered to his fortunes, in the jungles covering his castle—the same thick jungles which Vincent Eyre had forced on the 12th August of the preceding year.

But if, as I have already had occasion to remark, there was no William Tayler to exercise a vigilant supervision over the several districts of western Bihár, neither was there a Vincent Eyre to retrieve the errors of the Bengal Government. It happened that Árah was at this time occupied by a party of one hundred and fifty men of the 35th Regiment, one hundred and fifty of Rattray's Sikhs, and fifty sailors of the Naval Brigade, the whole under the command of Captain Le Grand of the 35th. Le Grand, knowing well what Vincent Eyre had accomplished in the same locality, how, with a smaller force at his disposal, he had beaten

Captain Le Grand resolves to attack him.

Book XII. Chapter III.

1858. April 23.

an enemy certainly not less numerous, and far better armed and disciplined, determined, if possible, to emulate his example. Accordingly, on the 23rd April, he marched from Árah with the force I have mentioned, and two 12-pounder howitzers. Early on the morning of the 23rd he came upon the little army of Kúnwar Singh. It consisted of about two thousand men, dispirited, badly armed, and without guns. It occupied the thick jungle, about a mile and a half in depth. Le Grand began the action with a fire from his two howitzers. These, however, seemed to make no impression on the enemy, and the infantry were then brought up to make the charge which, against Asiatics, has never failed. The exact course of the events which followed has never been clearly explained. But this is certain, that at a critical moment of the advance into the thick jungle, when the men in extended order were about to rush forward with a cheer, the bugle sounded the retreat. By whom the order to sound was given, or whether it was intended to sound the retreat, is not known. The effect of it on a scattered body of men unable to see each other was to cause irretrievable confusion. To repair it Le Grand used every means in his power, but in vain. The evil had been done. The men fell back in disorder, followed by the enemy, and abandoning the howitzers, fled to Árah. The 35th suffered very severely. Two-thirds of their number, amongst them Le Grand and two officers, were either killed*

He attacks him,

and is completely defeated.

* The casualties were in killed, 35th, one hundred and two men, sailors nineteen, Sikhs nine, officers three.

Book XII. Chapter III.

1858. April.

or died from apoplexy on the retreat. The gunners, refusing to retire, were killed at their guns. The disaster was complete.

Brigadier Douglas crosses into Shahábád.

This disaster threw the district once more into disorder. A panic ensued at the station of Chaprá, and expresses were sent from Danápúr to Brigadier Douglas, urging him to cross the river without delay. Douglas, whose incessant pursuit of Kúnwar Singh without tents had tried his men to the utmost, had been inclined, when the rebel chief had escaped his clutches, to wait till his heavy baggage should arrive. But on receipt of the expresses from Dánápúr, he crossed the Ganges, 25th April, at Sína Ghát, pushed on the 84th Foot and two guns to Árah on the 29th, and followed himself two days later.

Death of Kúnwar Singh.

But before Douglas could act against the rebels, a material change had taken place in their affairs. Whether Kúnwar Singh was wounded at the action fought at Mannahar, or, whether, as some of his followers aver, as he was crossing the Ganges, this is certain, that immediately on his arrival at Jagdispúr he underwent amputation of the wrist. He was an old man, and the shock was too much for him. He died three days after he had defeated Le Grand.

Ammar Singh succeeds him.

Kúnwar Singh was succeeded by his brother Ammar Singh. Though hardly the equal of his brother in military skill, Ammar Singh was not one whit behind him in energy and resolution, and the manner in which he conducted the operations which followed left little to be desired in a partisan leader.

The rebels, after defeating Le Grand, had followed up their victory by an attack on Árah. Though repulsed, they still continued to threaten it, and as their numbers were daily augmenting, Douglas thought it advisable to await the arrival of Lugard, who had warned him of his approach.

Douglas waits the arrival of Lugard,

Lugard, who, since I last spoke of him, had remained at Ázamgarh, occupied in clearing the surrounding districts, had no sooner heard of Kúnwar Singh's successful passage of the Ganges and the disaster of Le Grand, than he set off with a portion of his brigade, crossed the sacred stream on the 3rd and two following days of May, and marched at once to the neighbourhood of Árah.

who arrives early in May.

The news he received there led Lugard to believe that the rebels, who were reported to number eight thousand, were intrenching themselves in the jungle between Bihía and Jagdispúr. He resolved, therefore, to occupy with his main body a position in front of the western face of the jungle, guarding Árah with a detachment, whilst Colonel Corfield, commanding a small force at Sahasrám, should march from that quarter to his aid.

Plans of Lugard.

Lugard reached Bihía on the 8th, sent back thence the detachment to guard Árah, and then marched on the 9th to a plain a little to the west of Jagdispúr. Here he intended to halt to await the arrival of Corfield. But the enemy's movements forced him to change his plan. On the afternoon of that day Ammar Singh, covering his movement by a threatened attack on Lugard's camp, marched from the jungles with the bulk of

Lugard occupies Jagdispúr.

Book XII. Chapter III.

1858. May.

his following in the direction of Árah. Lugard resolved, then, to attack at once. Checking the advance on Árah with his cavalry and guns, he then divided his force into three columns, and driving the enemy before him, occupied Jagdispúr. In this operation he did not lose a single man killed, and only a few were wounded. The rebels fell back on Satwarpúr, a village in the jungle district.

Progress of the campaign.

The day following, Lugard, sensible of the necessity of following up his advantage, set out in pursuit. On the 11th he was joined at Pirú, seven miles south-west of Jagdispúr, by Corfield, who, fighting almost daily and always successfully, had made his way from Sahasrám. That same day he surprised and defeated the rebels at Hétampúr. From this day, skirmishes were of daily occurrence. On the 12th, he beat them at Jathin, whilst Corfield drove them from Dúvím. On the 20th they were again beaten, though they managed to kill an officer, Dawson, of the Military Train. Lugard, however, avenged his death on the 27th by inflicting a crushing defeat upon them at Dalilpúr, recapturing the two howitzers they had taken from Le Grand. On this occasion he did not lose a single man.

The persistent dispersion of the rebels,

But these victories did not crush the rebellion in the district. On each occasion the rebels, knowing every inch of the country, dispersed to reunite in nearly the same strength as before. Dividing themselves into small parties, they organised a system of freebooting, dangerous to life and property, and threatening to the stations, the peaceful villages, and the isolated posts all over

only to reunite.

Book XII. Chapter III.

1858. May.

the country. It was impossible to wage a war of extermination. Yet the jungles offered the rebels a means of defying for a series of months disciplined soldiers led by skilled and capable generals. In vain were their positions marked, encircled, and then marched upon from different quarters. The smallest delay on the part of one of the converging columns gave them the opportunity, of which they were ever prompt to avail themselves, to escape. Nor was it until the genius of a staff officer serving under Douglas devised a plan, based upon his experience of its efficiency elsewhere, that a certain means was attained for the extermination or expulsion of the persistent rebels. The nature of that plan will be developed in the pages which follow.

The defy pursuit, until a new scheme is devised by a staff officer with the force.

After the defeat at Dalilpúr on the 27th, the rebels broke up into small parties, and commenced their new trade of marauding on a large scale. One party attacked and destroyed an indigo factory near Dúmraon, another plundered the village of Rájpúr near Baksar, a third threatened the railway works at Karamnásá. These proceedings spread dismay and disorder throughout the Shahábád district.

They harry the district.

In the campaign up to the point which I have now reached, the British troops had suffered greatly from the heat and exposure to the sun. But in the presence of the occurrences just recorded, Lugard was compelled to keep them actively employed. To facilitate their movements and to lessen the chances of the escape of the enemy, he set to work to intersect the jungles by

Lugard again defeats them,

Book XII. Chapter III.

1858. June.

roads. On the 2nd June, he divided his force into two parts, the one at Késhwa the other at Dalilpúr, opposite points on the edge of the jungle. Between these he cut a broad road. Occupying this with a line of posts as a base, he attacked the rebels from the outside on the 4th, and defeated them with great slaughter, the 10th and 84th showing great dash and daring. But still many managed to escape.

but many escape.

Lugard resigns his command from ill-health.

It would be tedious to follow the course of every skirmish; to show how Douglas pursued the rebels with energy and vigour towards Baksar, and how the main body yet managed to elude his pursuit; how they again and again baffled Lugard. He could beat but could not clutch them. He had not, in fact, the means of maintaining a continuous and crushing pursuit. The rebels, therefore, though repeatedly beaten, were able to rally at a distance and return by a circuitous route to the corner of the jungle. But by the 15th June Lugard had so far succeeded that the rebels had been expelled to a further distance from the jungles than had ever been the case previously, and he was able to report that the task entrusted to him had been completed. Wearied and broken down by the unparalleled hardships of the contest, Lugard was then forced to resign his command and proceed to England. The troops were ordered into quarters. But they had scarcely retired from the field, when the rebels, strong in a conviction of real success in the past, and confident that the rainy season would secure them immunity for the four months to come, reoccupied their old positions, their numbers daily increased by recruits from all parts of the country.

Book XII. Chapter III.

1858. June–Sept.

Douglas succeeds him.

It was under these circumstances that Brigadier Douglas, C.B., was appointed to succeed Lugard. He had no sinecure. He had not even assumed command when he heard that owing to the manœuvres and intrigues of Ammar Singh, the rebel prisoners in the jail at Gayá had been released, and, joined by the police and the convicts, had driven the English into their intrenchment. This outrage—which was speedily repaired—was followed up by a raid into the station of Árah, the garrison of which had been cunningly enticed away, and by the burning of a gentleman's bungalow. The civil authority had, in fact, everywhere disappeared.

Difficulties of Douglas on first assuming his command.

Douglas devises means to baffle and subdue the rebels.

Under these circumstances stronger measures were resorted to. Douglas was placed in command of the whole of the disturbed districts as far as Dánápúr. The troops under his command were augmented to a numerical strength of seven thousand. He began at once to work on a system. He organised strong posts at easy distances from each other in all directions. He located his troops in such a manner that it would be easy to mass them at short notice on one particular point. He sent out trusted sepoys in disguise to penetrate the designs of the mutineers, and even to bring in their leaders, alive or dead. He continued with great effect the practice, initiated by his predecessor, of covering the jungles with roads. Finally, as a supreme remedy, he

Book XII. Chapter III.

1858. June–Sept.

elaborated a plan for driving the rebels into Jagdispúr, as a common centre, and for there finishing the campaign—as he had every right to expect—by the assault and capture of that stronghold.

Operations are necessarily deferred till after the rains.

This plan, it will be observed, involved the deferring of larger operations until October or November. Meanwhile it was necessary to secure the grand trunk road. On this road, which traverses the lower portion of the district from east to west, and the safety of which was of vital importance to Sir Colin Campbell and his army, large bodies of troops under Colonel Turner, C.B., 97th Regiment, were constantly employed. For the four months that followed Turner was unremittingly engaged on this arduous but necessary service.

The rebels continue active,

The rebels on their side were very persevering. Ammar Singh reoccupied Jagdispúr, and his adherents, in small parties, kept the districts in continued disturbance throughout July, August, and September. They seemed to be ubiquitous. Many places in opposite directions were attacked about the same time. Their principal depredations, however, were confined to the country south of the Ganges and west of the Són river.

in spite of frequent defeats.

It is true they met several reverses. On the 9th September, Colonel Walters defeated them at Rámpúr; on the 20th Captain French and a party of the 35th destroyed their boats on the Són; on the 14th October, Mr. Probyn, of the Civil Service, and twenty Sikhs, ran up a creek on the Shahábád side of the river and destroyed four large boats defended by three hundred and seventy-five sepoys

Book XII. Chapter III.

1858. October.

and one hundred horsemen—a most gallant performance. Not the less, however, did the rebels continue to threaten Árah; they even attacked the cavalry picket at that station.

Reasons for beginning operations on 13th October.

But the end was now approaching. The rainy season was passing away. In one point of view it would have been advisable to defer serious operations until it had actually passed. It was feared, however, and not without reason, that on the complete cessation of the rains, the rebels, thoroughly aware of the preparations made against them, would cross the Són and carry rapine and the sword into the districts which had up to the time been free from their presence. Consequently Douglas resolved to begin operations on the 13th October.

On the 13th October Douglas causes seven columns to converge near Jagdispúr.

On the 9th of that month he set out from Dánápúr to carry into execution the plan he had carefully and elaborately devised. The ground was still swampy, but, though this was likely to prove a material disadvantage in a campaign the success of which depended upon the exact punctuality of arrival at a given point of several converging columns, it was at least a guarantee that the rebels were still within the district.* From three opposite points of this district, Douglas set in motion, on the 13th October, seven different columns, the object of all being to drive the rebels before them to the common centre of

* It may be convenient to state that the district in question may be roughly described as a triangle, each side of which measured fifty miles. It was bounded on the north by the Ganges, on the east by the Són, and on the west and south transversely by the hilly districts of Mirzapúr.

Book XII. Chapter III.

1858. October.

Jagdispúr, there to fall upon them and finish the campaign at one stroke.

The rebels are pressed within the Jagdispúr jungles.

Success crowned his earlier combats. On the 14th Douglas drove the rebels out of Kárisát. On the 16th, Durnford, leading the Baksar column, defeated them, though after a determined resistance at Kámpságar. On the 17th Turner's column headed and defeated them at Pirú, and followed hotly in pursuit. These movements had been so thoroughly executed that the rebels, numbering four thousand five hundred, were pressed in on all sides towards the centre, and it was known on the evening of the 17th that they were all within the circle, the outlets on the outer ring of which were watched by the seven converging columns.

Douglas orders the columns to converge on Jagdispúr.

Douglas believed that he had them, and he had a right to believe it. Nothing but a mistake on the part of one of the leaders of the seven columns could save them, and he had impressed his orders so strongly on those leaders, and had made them see so clearly the issue at stake, that he had every reason to feel confident. He fixed the assault for noon of the following day. The result showed the mistake of reckoning with absolute certainty on the success of a manœuvre, the threads of which are in the hands of seven men, the failure of any one of whom, whether from accident or stupidity, would spoil the combination. The failure of one man out of the seven effectively ruined Douglas's well thought out plan. Six of the columns converged punctually to the common centre, only to find the place

Owing to Colonel Walter's mistake the rebels escape.

Book XII. Chapter III. — 1858. October.

evacuated. The seventh column, commanded by Colonel Walter of the 53rd, had been delayed five hours by inundation consequent on the cutting of embankments, and the rebels had escaped by the outlet he had given them!

Havelock's plan

It was at this period that the staff officer to whom I have alluded in a preceding page submitted to the general a plan which he believed would meet the difficulties of the case. The staff officer, who was no other than Major Sir Henry Havelock, Deputy Assistant Adjutant-General of the force, had, in his experience of Franks's advance without cavalry from the eastern frontier of Oudh to Lakhnao, noticed the enormous service which a few mounted soldiers of the 10th Foot, carrying rifles on horseback, had been able to render. Conceiving the idea, some time before Douglas had set out from Dánápúr, that the services of a few men might be advantageously utilised in a similar manner, he had caused forty riflemen of the 10th Foot to be hastily trained by Captain Bartholomew of that regiment. He now proposed to Douglas, and received permission, to employ the men so trained as mounted infantry—as men, that is to say, who could pursue and overtake the enemy, then, dismounting, hold them in check till the main force should arrive. He increased the forty men to sixty by volunteers from the 10th, and then, learning that the rebels were marching towards the Són, he set out to head them, having three troops of the Military Train and sixty cavalry as supports.

approved and adopted.

Havelock sets out.

The plan of his campaign.

The orders given to Havelock were to en-

Book XII. Chapter III.

1858. October.

deavour, by a forced march, to interpose between the rebels and the Són, whilst two columns of infantry should be despatched in the same direction, one north, the other south, of their line of flight, so that should he succeed in turning them they would find themselves surrounded.

Havelock heads the rebels;

Havelock set out from his post near Jagdispúr at a little past 8 o'clock on the night of the 18th; he reached Árah at 1 o'clock in the morning of the 19th, halted there for six and a half hours, and starting again at half-past 7, reached the Són before the rebels. The latter, finding themselves headed, halted, remained irresolute for twelve hours, and then retraced their steps south-westward.

who try to escape by pushing westward.

Havelock's mounted column followed, maintaining by patrols a constant communication with the infantry detachments, and guiding their movements. The mutinous sepoys, now fairly aroused to a sense of their danger, put forth their best efforts to out-march their pursuers, and, after an ineffectual attempt to re-enter the Jagdispúr jungle, pushed directly westward. But the mounted riflemen were sadly embarrassed by rice-fields, inundated to a depth of from one to two feet, making one continuous swamp for miles. These the rebels on foot avoided by moving along the "bands," or ridges used to confine the water. Still Havelock gradually gained on them. Overtaking their rear-guard of four hundred infantry on the afternoon of the 20th of October near Nonádí, he succeeded, by a dismounted rifle-fire on two faces, one towards the main body, one de-

The mounted riflemen overtake them,

1858. October.

taining the rear-guard, in cutting them off from the main body, and hemming them into that village till the arrival of Colonel Turner's infantry column. Turner then stormed the village, and slew three hundred rebels. About one hundred, desperately breaking out, were "ringed" in an adjoining field by Havelock's mounted riflemen, who shot them down till their numbers were so reduced that the supporting cavalry, bursting in on them, sword in hand, sabred almost every man. Only three or four, amongst whom was Ammar Singh himself, disguised, found safety in a neighbouring cane-crop. This was the most effective blow that had been struck against the Shahábád rebels. Its success is to be attributed solely to the new use of the mounted riflemen, without whose presence the enemy would, as on every former occasion, have escaped unscathed through their superior speed.

and cut them up.

The main body of rebels had meanwhile continued its flight, after several doubles, finally due west. Following on its track, Havelock again overtook it after a forty miles' march, on the afternoon of the 21st. The infantry column, under Brigadier Douglas's personal command, guided by reports from the mounted rifles, had been able to follow the foe in straight lines from point to point of his numerous twistings and doublings, so that when the sepoys, thoroughly fagged, halted on that afternoon to cook, it was sufficiently near to be expected to take part in the combat. Havelock's column came on the rebels while thus employed. Passing beyond

Havelock resumes pursuit, and overtakes the rebels,

Book XII. Chapter III.

1858. October.

them by a circuit, it again headed them towards the infantry, drove them from their cooking, and circling them in on three sides with skirmishers, kept them in check for three hours in the plain, waiting for the infantry to come up. There was now every hope that the success of the previous day would be repeated, but this expectation was not realised. By a mistake of the person guiding Douglas's infantry, they were brought up in the rear of Havelock's force instead of behind that of the rebels, who at once availed themselves of this error, and slipped out of the opening left for them. Evening, setting in at the same time, gave them ten hours' darkness to cover their flight. But, thoroughly terrified now at finding that they could not shake off their pursuers, they abandoned all attempt to do mischief in the district, and confined all their efforts to the one object of escape. Favoured by the long hours of darkness, and by the whole population of the district, who constantly and systematically misled the pursuers by false information, they marched in the next forty hours sixty-three miles further without being overtaken, making for a range of hills which bound the south-west of the district, and are accessible from the plain only by three difficult passes.

who escape, from the mistake of a guide, and get a ten hours' start.

Havelock a third time overtakes the rebels and punishes them.

But Havelock's mounted riflemen, not to be shaken off, again overtook the enemy on the evening of the 23rd. The horses were by this time so exhausted that it was impossible either to head or to charge the rebels, who, drawing up in two solid squares flanking each other, steadily continued

Book XII. Chapter III.

1858. October.

their way to the hills. But at every step men and horses fell in their very midst under the long-range rifles of the pursuers, who, while thus inflicting a severe punishment, were themselves beyond reach of the enemy's muskets. Not a minute but witnessed the capture of baggage-animals, including Ammar Singh's elephant, carrying a howdah containing his suit of chain armour. The rebels continued their hurried flight to the Kaimúr hills. But so great had been the terror inspired by the new arm, now for the first time in India employed against them, and from which escape seemed impossible, that even the telegraph wire, which it had always been their main object to destroy, remained uncut along the trunk road which they crossed in their flight; and the whole of the depôt establishments there—of vital importance to the regular supply of troops and stores to the army under Lord Clyde—remained uninjured. Havelock's loss in this singular pursuit, which covered two hundred and one miles in five days and nights, was only three men killed and eighteen wounded. But forty-three horses died of fatigue. The rebel loss in the three actions of the 19th, 20th, and 21st October was not less than five hundred killed, including those hemmed in and subsequently destroyed by Colonel Turner's column at Nonádí.

Terror of the rebels at the practice of the new Enfield rifle.

Thus sixty men, organised on a novel plan, and aided by a handful of cavalry, had effected, with almost nominal loss, in five days, what three thousand regular troops had for six months failed to accomplish—viz. the complete expulsion of four thousand five hundred rebels from the pro-

Success of Havelock's plan of mounted riflemen.

Book XII. Chapter III.

1858. Oct.-Nov.

vince, and the infliction on them of a punishment the impression of which has not to this day been effaced. When once the inhabitants of the district became aware that the enemy was opposed by troops against whom they could not only hope for no success in the field, and whom it was impossible for them to shake off in flight, their confidence in British power returned, and the restoration of order was an easy task.

Complete collapse of the rebels.

Meanwhile, the Jagdispúr jungle had been cut down and cleared away. The rebels were gradually driven from place to place, their hiding-places being occupied as the pursuers advanced. It is true that in the long pursuit the rebels managed once or twice to pounce upon the baggage of their enemies. But, in its results, the plan inaugurated by Havelock was most successful. On the 24th November Douglas surprised, by a night march, the main body of the rebels at Salia Dahár, in the Kaimúr hills, killed many of them, and took all their arms and ammunition. Before the year ended he could boast that the districts under his command had been completely cleared. The campaign had been more trying, more fatiguing than many which are counted more glorious in their results. Never had troops in India made longer, or more continuously long, marches. On one occasion, I may repeat, the British infantry marched twenty-six miles a day for five days; and the average daily march of Havelock's cavalry was scarcely less than forty miles.

BOOK XII.

CHAPTER IV.

I RETURN once more to Lakhnao. Of the army which conquered that city, one division, that commanded by Sir E. Lugard, has been disposed of in the preceding pages. There remain still the *corps d'armée* under Hope Grant, and the division under Walpole. I shall deal first with the former.

On the 9th April, Sir Hope Grant, commanding the force already noted,* received instructions in person from the Commander-in-Chief, to march at once with a column to Bári, twenty-nine miles from Lakhnao, to drive thence a body of rebels who had collected there under the famous Moulvi; then marching eastwards to Muhammadábád and following the course of the Ghágrá, to reconnoitre a place called Bitáoli, where it was rumoured the

Hope Grant is ordered to the districts.

* *Vide* page 468, note.

Book XII. Chapter IV.

1858. April.

Bégam of Lakhnao with six thousand followers had taken post; thence to march to Rámnagar to cover the march of the Nipálese troops on their return to Nipál.

Composition of its force.

To carry out these instructions, Hope Grant marched from Lakhnao on the morning of the 11th April. He took with him Middleton's battery, Mackinnon's troop of horse artillery, two 18-pounders, two 8-inch howitzers, two $5\frac{1}{2}$-inch Cohom mortars, the 7th Hussars, one squadron 2nd Dragoon Guards, Wale's Panjáb Horse, the 2nd battalion Rifle Brigade, the 38th Foot, the 1st Bengal Fusiliers, five hundred men of Vaughan's Panjáb Corps (the 5th), one hundred sappers and miners with a proportion of engineer officers—in all, about three thousand men.

Daring reconnoitring by the rebels.

A curious incident, emblematic of the progress made by the rebels in the art of daring yet crafty reconnoitring, occurred on the night of the following day. Hope Grant had encamped about three parts of the way between Lakhnao and Bári. As he lay there that night, a troop of irregular cavalry penetrated within the line of pickets, which at that point were drawn from Wales's Horse. When challenged, they replied, with the most absolute truth, that they belonged to the 12th Irregulars. They did not add that their regiment had mutinied so far back as July of the previous year, and murdered their commandant.* The pickets, replied to in this confident manner, suspected nothing, and allowed them to pass on. The

* Vol. i. page 72.

mutineers, having seen all they cared to see, quietly slipped out and returned to Bári. Book XII. Chapter IV. 1858. April.

The plan which the rebel leader, who was no other than the Moulvi, adopted on receiving the information which the men of the 12th had acquired, did credit to his tactical skill. He at once occupied a village about four miles on the Bári side of the British encampment with his whole force. This village was covered all along its front by a stream, the banks of which on the side nearest to it were high, and the ground leading up to which was honeycombed. It was a very strong position. The idea of the Moulvi was to hold the village with his infantry, whilst he sent his cavalry by a circuitous route to fall on the flanks of the attacking force. It was really a brilliant idea; for the British force, he was aware, would march at daybreak, entirely unsuspicious of his presence, and, could he but conceal his infantry from view till the British were well within range, and restrain his cavalry till the resistance from the side of the village had begun, the chances of success seemed to be all in his favour.

The Moulvi's plan shows great skill.

But the brilliant idea was spoilt by the mode in which it was executed. Hope Grant did indeed march at daybreak, unsuspicious of danger. The bulk of the enemy's cavalry, avoiding the line of march, was rapidly gaining a position on his rear, there to fall upon the six thousand carts which were carrying the baggage of the force, when their leaders were tempted by the sight of two guns in the British advance, lightly guarded

His cavalry are tempted to spoil it.

Book XII. Chapter IV.

1858. April.

by Wale's Horse, to throw to the winds the plan of their general and attempt to capture the guns. For a moment fortune seemed to favour them.

Their easy success

They surrounded the picket, wounded the officer commanding it, Lieutenant Prendergast, and had the guns in their power. Just as they were about to carry them off, however, they caught sight of a troop of the 7th Hussars, led by Captain Topham, on the point of charging them.

is changed into defeat.

Without awaiting the charge, they abandoned their prey, galloped off, and endeavoured to recur to the original plan. But they had spoilt it. The British were now thoroughly awake. Hope Grant made prompt arrangements for the protection of his rear guard, and though the enemy made two considerable efforts to capture the baggage, they were baffled, first by a splendid charge of the 7th Hussars troop under Topham, and secondly by a volley, delivered within thirty yards of them, by

The rebels are forced to retreat,

two companies of the 1st Bengal Fusiliers. Completely defeated in their plans, they then retreated.

Meanwhile, Hope Grant pushed forward with his infantry to the village. He noticed the strength of the position, the difficulty it might give him were it well defended. But the premature action of the cavalry, while it had ruined the plan of the Moulvi, had taken all the heart out of his followers. Prepared to surprise the British force and even to resist should the cavalry charge

and evacuate the village.

throw it into disorder, they did not care to meet the assault of the troops which had already repulsed the cavalry. Under the circumstances they preferred to wait for a more favourable opportunity, and evacuated the village without firing a shot.

Book XII. Chapter IV.

1858. April.

Pushing on to Bári and eastward from that place, Hope Grant reached Muhammadábád on the 15th, and Rámnagar on the 19th. Rámnagar was but six miles from Bitáoli, the spot where it was rumoured the Bégam and her followers had taken post. But the Bégam, wise in her generation, had not awaited the arrival of the English general, and Bitáoli was found evacuated.

Hope Grant rushes on to Rámnagar.

Bitáoli evacuated, Hope Grant proceeded to look after Jung Bahádur's Nipálese. He found them at Masáoli, midway between Rámnagar and Nawábganj. In his journal, the general gives a vivid description of the condition of our allies. "The European officer in command," he writes, "had great difficulties to contend with in marching through a country so filled with rebels. His force consisted of eight thousand men with twenty guns; yet he could only reckon on two thousand men for actual fighting purposes. He had two thousand sick and four thousand carts; and each of the latter being filled with tents, private property, and loot, required, according to the usages of these troops, a man to guard it."* From this place Hope

Jung Bahâdar's Nipálese.

Their condition described by Hope Grant.

* Hope Grant's *Incidents of the Sepoy War.*

As these troops took no further part in the war, it may be convenient to state here that they continued their retreat from Masáoli towards their own country and effected it without molestation. They reached Gorákhpúr early in May, and resumed their march thence on the 17th *idem.* In consequence of the number of their carts they experienced some difficulty in crossing the Gandak at Ba-

Book XII. Chapter IV.

1858. May.

Hope Grant returns to Lakhnao.

Grant marched suthwards to protect the road between Kánhpúr and Lakhnao, then threatened at Onáo. After some skirmishes of no great moment, in which the rebels were invariably dispersed, he reached the fort of Jallálábád, near Lakhnao, on the 16th May. Here, for the present, I must leave him to follow the plans of the Commander-in-Chief with respect to Rohilkhand.

Sir Colin's plans for the reconquest of Rohilkhand.

It had been determined by the Governor-General, the reader will recollect, that the reconquest of this province should follow the recapture of Lakhnao, and, in a flying visit paid by Sir Colin Campbell to Allahábád after the storming of Lakhnao, he had found Lord Canning still firm in this respect. He accordingly at once arranged to converge three columns, starting from different points, on the doomed province. One of these columns, commanded by General Penny, was directed to cross the Ganges at Nadáoli and march on Miránpúr Katra. At this place it would join Walpole's division, ordered to advance thither from Lakhnao along the Ganges, whilst Brigadier-General Jones, starting with another division from Rúrki and making for Morádábád, would penetrate into the province from the north-west. Connected, to a certain extent, with these operations was the force I have left at Fathgarh under Brigadier Seaton, guarding there the south-east entrance into Rohilkhand on the one side, and the districts between

gaha. Marching thence by way of Bhetiá and Sigáoli, they crossed the Nipál frontier early in June.

the two great arteries, the Ganges and the Jamná, on the other.

Book XII. Chapter IV.

1858. April.

Seaton at Fathgarh.

Seaton, left by Sir Colin Campbell, as previously narrated,* at the end of January, as Brigadier in command of the Fathgarh district, had employed the time which passed till the fall of Lakhnao in strengthening the fort of Fathgarh, in removing the bridge of boats to a point under the walls of the fort, and in practising his artillery at marks on the other side of the river near the positions which an advancing enemy would be likely to take up. The rebels meanwhile continued to threaten him from the Rohilkhand side of the Rámganga, though they took care to keep out of the range of his guns.

The rebels think of resuming the offensive.

But, as time went on, and Seaton made no move, whilst reinforcements flocked into the rebel camp, the situation became critical. Still more so when the rebel Rájá of Mainpúri, Téj Singh, entered their camp, and incited them to profit by the supineness of the British at Fathgarh to cross the Ganges and raise the Doáb.

Seaton watches their proceedings.

But Seaton, supine as apparently had been his action, had been neither blind nor indifferent to the proceedings of the enemy. He had held his hand so long as it seemed probable that they would remain on the left bank of the river; but the moment they showed a disposition to attempt to burst the door of the Doáb, he resolved to attack them.

Consequences had he

Hazardous as it was, with his slender force, to

* Page 311.

Book XII. Chapter IV.

1858. April.

remained supine.

assault a powerful enemy, he could not act otherwise. For the occupation of the Doáb by a large rebel force would close the grand trunk road, and cause the preparations, now about to be set in action, against Rohilkhand, to be indefinitely delayed.

He resolves to attack the central position of the rebels.

Seaton ascertained that the rebels occupied three strong positions: one at Álíganj, seven miles from Fathgarh, on the further bank of the Rámganga; a second at Bangáon, three miles from a ferry on the Ganges, twenty-four miles above Fathgarh; and a third at Kankar, in the same direction, twenty-two miles distant. Now, in the opinion of Seaton, Álíganj was so strong as to be proof against attack; Bangáon was too far off for a night's march. He resolved, then, to attack Kankar. Kankar being situated between Álíganj and Bangáon, he believed, to use his own expression, that "if he knocked out the middle post the upper one would collapse on the lower."

He defeats them

So, indeed, it proved. Leaving Fathgarh with his small force (one thousand infantry, three hundred cavalry, and five guns) at 11 o'clock on the night of the 6th April, Seaton reached Kankar by daylight, drove back the enemy's cavalry, and then stormed the villages occupied by the infantry, inflicting upon them a loss of two hundred and fifty killed and wounded, and taking three guns. In this action Lieutenant de Kantzow greatly distinguished himself. Seaton had only five men killed and seventeen wounded. The immediate effect was still more important. The

and baffles their main plans.

invasion of the Doáb was renounced, and so terrified were the rebels at Áliganj that they broke down the bridge across the Rámganga.

General Penny

Whilst Seaton was thus keeping fast the door of the province, Penny was moving down from Balandshahr to join in the operations contemplated by the Commander-in-Chief in Rohilkhand. His force consisted of two hundred of the Carabineers, three hundred and fifty-three of the 64th, three hundred and sixty Bilúch Battalion, two hundred and fifty Múltáni Horse, three hundred and twenty 2nd Panjábis, and six heavy and six light guns. Penny met Sir Colin Campbell at Fathgarh on the 24th, then crossed the Ganges, and pushed on to Úshait, a town on the further side of one of the confluents of the main stream. Úshait was found deserted, and Cracroft Wilson, the political officer with the column, brought the general information that the enemy had fled into Oudh, and that his march to Badáon would not be opposed. Penny accordingly started on the night of the 30th April to make a night march of upwards of twenty miles to that place. He had reached Kakráoli, riding with Cracroft Wilson at the head of the advanced guard, commanded by Captain Curtis, when some dusky forms and some lights were noticed a short distance ahead. It was quite dark, and before the nature of these appearances could be ascertained, a discharge of grape came into their midst. Penny was never seen again alive, and it was supposed that his horse, frightened by the sudden discharge, over-

occupies U'shait.

and marches to Badáon;

he is suddenly attacked by the rebels and killed.

Book XII. Chapter IV.

1858. May.

powered and carried him into the ranks of the enemy. Certain it is that his body was found there after the fight, shot, stripped, and sabred. When the discharge occurred the infantry were some distance in the rear. The Carabineers at once charged, took the gun, and then, it being dark, dashed forward into a trench full of Ghãzis (fanatics). A desperate contest ensued, many of the officers being cut down. As soon as they could extricate themselves, the village, which the enemy occupied in force, was shelled. When the guns had done their work, the infantry charged and carried it—the enemy retreating with but small loss. The column, falling under the command of Colonel Jones of the Carabineers, then continued its march, and joined the Commander-in-Chief at Miranpúr Katra on the 3rd May.

The rebels are eventually beaten.

Walpole's division.

Walpole's division had left Lakhnao for that place on the 7th April. He had with him the 9th Lancers, the 2nd Panjáb Cavalry, the 42nd, 79th, and 93rd Highlanders, the 4th Panjáb Rifles, two troops of horse artillery, two 18-pounders, two 8-inch howitzers, some mortars, and a few engineers and sappers.

Nature of the task entrusted to Walpole.

The name of General Walpole has been mentioned more than once in these pages, but once only as an officer holding independent command. The expedition upon which he was now about to enter was not one likely to test the qualities of a commander. It offered no difficulties. A fort here or there might require to be taken, a disorganised band of rebels to be dispersed. To carry it to a successful issue, then, demanded no more than the exercise of vigilance, of energy, of daring—qualities the absence of which from a man's character would stamp him as unfit to be a soldier.

1858. April.

Character of Walpole as a general.

Walpole, unhappily, possessed none of these qualities. Of his personal courage no one ever doubted, but as a commander he was slow, hesitating, and timid. With some men the power to command an army is innate. Others can never gain it. To this last class belonged Walpole. He never was, he never could have been, a general more than in name. Not understanding war, and yet having to wage it, he carried it on in a blundering and haphazard manner, galling to the real soldiers who served under him, detrimental to the interests committed to his charge.

Possible objections to such a delineation.

It may be remarked that this censure, however justly applicable, is out of place as a preface to a short campaign conducted by the commander in question—a campaign which I have already described as "offering no difficulties." If the campaign offered no difficulties, it may be urged, surely any man, even a Walpole, might have carried it to a successful issue. Thus to brand a commander with incapacity when the occasion did not require capacity, is as unnecessary as ungenerous!

The objections replied to.

It might be so, indeed, if the campaign, devoid of difficulty as it was, had not been productive of disaster. But the course of this history will show, that though there ought to have been no difficulties, Walpole, by his blundering and obsti-

Book XII.
Chapter IV.

1858.
April.

nacy, created them, and, worse than all, he, by a most unnecessary—I might justly say by a wanton—display of those qualities, sacrificed the life of one of the noblest soldiers in the British army—sent to his last home, in the prime of his splendid manhood, in the enjoyment of the devotion of his men, of the love of his friends, of the admiration and well-placed confidence of the army serving in India, the noble, the chivalrous, the high-minded Adrian Hope.

Walpole marches to Rúiya.

Walpole, I have said, set out from Lakhnao on the 7th April. His orders were to advance up the left bank of the Ganges, and so to penetrate into Rohilkhand. For the first week the march was uneventful. But on the morning of the 15th, after a march of nine miles, Walpole found himself in close vicinity to Rúiya, a small fort fifty-one miles west by north from Lakhnao, and ten miles east of the Ganges. The fort was enclosed by a mud wall high on its northern and eastern faces, loop-holed for musketry, and defended on those sides by a broad and deep ditch. It was provided with irregular bastions at the angles, and had two gates on the northern and eastern sides, where it was covered by a thick jungle. It belonged to a petty landowner named Nirpat Singh, a man who was a rebel as long as rebellion seemed profitable, but who had not the smallest inclination to run his head against a British force. Walpole had received information the previous day that Rúiya was occupied by rebels, and there can be no doubt that their number was, as usual, greatly exaggerated. The two or three hundred

April 15.

Description of Rúiya.

men who followed Nirpat Singh had been increased by report to fifteen hundred.

Book XII. Chapter IV.

1858. April.

Information given by a trooper of the state of affairs within Rúiya.

It happened that one of the troopers of Hodson's Horse, who, taken prisoner in some previous encounter, had been confined within the fort of Rúiya, found means that morning to escape, and to penetrate into the British camp. Taken to the general, he informed him of the state of affairs within the fort, and that Nirpat Singh was prepared, after making a show of resistance, sufficient to save his honour, to evacuate it that afternoon, leaving one gate open for the British to walk in.

Walpole disbelieves the story.

Walpole gave no credit to the man's story. What was worse, he would not even reconnoitre. He clung to the belief that the fort was garrisoned by fifteen hundred men, and, it would seem, he was anxious to win his spurs by driving them out of it.

Actual state of the southern and western faces of Rúiya.

He did not take the trouble to reconnoitre. The slightest examination would have shown him that whilst the northern and eastern faces were strong, covered by dense underwood and trees, the western and southern were weak and incapable of offering defence. These faces were approached by a large sheet of water, everywhere very shallow, and in many places dried into the ground, and the walls there were so low than an active man could jump over them. But, as I have said, Walpole made no reconnaissance. Without examining the fort at all, he sent his men in a blundering, haphazard manner against its strongest face!

He attacks it.

The rebels resolve to defend it.

The rebels were prepared to evacuate the fort,

Book XII. Chapter IV.

1858. April 15.

and they had intended to fire a few rounds and retreat. But when they saw the British general sending his infantry in skirmishing order against the face which could be defended, they changed their minds, and determined to show fight.

The attack on Rúiya is repulsed.

Two companies of the 42nd Highlanders and one hundred and twenty of the 4th Panjáb Rifles were sent, in skirmishing order and with no supports, to the front on this dangerous errand. The enemy meanwhile had not only manned the wall, but had sent skirmishers to mount the numerous trees within the fort. The fire from these men considerably annoyed the infantry as they advanced. When at length they neared the fort, they perceived the deep ditch, till then invisible, and at the same time encountered a concentrated fire from the loop-holed walls. The skirmishers still persevered, some of them even penetrated into the ditch; but their valour was useless, the enemy remained unseen, there was no breach, there were no ladders, and the hostile fire continued.

Gallantry of officers and men.

Several feats of splendid valour were performed. Edward Willoughby, a young officer of the 10th Bombay Native Infantry, now attached to the 4th Panjáb Rifles, though on the sick list, had left his dooly to join in the fight. Mortally wounded by a shot in the throat, he still pressed on up to the glacis, and there dropped dead. Of the one hundred and twenty men who composed his regiment that morning, forty-six were killed and two wounded. Nor was the gallantry and devotion of the 42nd less conspicuous. Lieutenants Douglas and Bramley and fifty-five of their following were killed; * and when, about 2 o'clock, as I shall presently relate, the order to retire from the scene of useless slaughter reached them, there were men amongst that following who could not resolve to leave there the bodies of the officers who had so nobly led them on. Conspicuous amongst these was the Quartermaster-sergeant of the regiment, Simpson by name. No sooner had this man heard the order to retire than he rushed back into the ditch, and brought back the body of Bramley safely in spite of the shower of musketry he encountered. He returned to do the same with Douglas, and then with seven other of his comrades. Not alone was he in this noble work. Private Davis was his able coadjutor at this point; whilst at another not remote, Lance-Corporal Thomson and Private Spence, all of the 42nd, brought back the body of the gallant Willoughby. It is a satisfaction to know that these men, Spence alone excepted, received the coveted Cross—and Spence was only excepted because he died two days later from a wound received in carrying out his gallant exploit.

Gallant conduct.

Before these gallant deeds had been performed, Walpole, alarmed at the consequences of his own rashness, had caused his heavy guns to open out on the wall; but as their fire seemed to make no impression, and the slaughter of the infantry continued, he ordered a retreat. This retreat was the signal for the display of the splendid devotion just recorded.

Walpole orders a retreat.

* Two other officers of the 42nd were wounded, and Lieutenant Harington of the Artillery was killed.

Book XII. Chapter IV.

1858. April 15.

Adrian Hope is about to ride up to Walpole,

All this time Adrian Hope had, after vain remonstrance against the madness of the mode of attack, seen, with grief and rage with difficulty suppressed, the useless sacrifice of his gallant soldiers. At last he could bear it no longer. Before the order to retire, of which I have spoken, was given, he had made up his mind how to act. He turned his horse in the direction where he believed Walpole to be, and was about to ride up to him, when one of the skirmishers in the trees within the fort marked him and shot him dead.*

when he is shot dead.

The communication Adrian Hope was about to make.

What was Adrian Hope going to say to Walpole? It can never perhaps be accurately known, but a general belief prevailed that he was about to take from him the command. That he would have been justified in virtually superseding him cannot be doubted. The image of helplessness, whilst his soldiers were being uselessly butchered, Walpole was then no more than a lay figure. It would have been kind to treat him as a lay figure.

Nirpat Singh evacuates Rúiya.

Adrian Hope fell. Then, the retreat having been ordered, Brigadier Hagart was directed to bring off the dead. Walpole rode back to camp. That same night the rebels evacuated the fort. Nirpat Singh kept his word. He marched out after vindicating his honour! But, thanks to Walpole, at what a cost to us!

The loss the country sustained by the deaths of Willoughby, of Douglas, of Bramley, of Har-

* I have received these particulars from an officer present on the occasion.

Book XII. Chapter IV.

1858. April 15.

ington, and of the hundred and odd men uselessly sacrificed before Rúiya was great—but the loss of Adrian Hope was a cause for national sorrow. His death was mourned on the spot by every man in the camp. Loud and deep were the invectives against the obstinate stupidity which had caused it.* Nor, though twenty-one years have since passed away, is he yet forgotten.

Mourning for Adrian Hope in the camp.

Adrian Hope was indeed a man to be loved. "A gentler, braver spirit never breathed—a true soldier, a kind, courteous, noble gentleman, in word and deed; devoted to his profession, beloved by his men, adored by his friends—this indeed is a sad loss to the British army." So wrote on the spot William Howard Russell. Nor was the testimony of the Governor-General and the Commander-in-Chief less genuine. "No more mournful duty has fallen upon the Governor-General in the course of the present contest," wrote Lord Canning, "than that of recording the premature death of this gallant young commander." "The death of this most distinguished

By the public and by the authorities.

* Dr. Russell writes: "I found the officers of the 42nd and 93rd in a state of furious wrath and discontent with their general. They told me they were afraid of mutiny, or worse, when poor Hope was buried! Nirpat Singh drew off his men in the night, and when Walpole was told the next morning that the place was evacuated, he said, 'Thank God!'"

It is a curious commentary on the principle, then, as now, in fashion, of conferring honours on men, not for the deeds they achieve, but for the high positions they occupy, that the general who lost more than one hundred men and Adrian Hope, in failing to take this petty fort, was made a K.C.B.

Though he failed to take the fort, he was yet a divisional commander!

Book XII. Chapter IV.

1858. April 22.

and gallant officer," wrote Sir Colin Campbell, "causes the deepest grief to the Commander-in-Chief. Still young in years, he had risen to high command; and by his undaunted courage, combined as it was with extreme kindness and charm of manner, had secured the confidence of the brigade in no ordinary degree."

Walpole expels the rebels from Sirsa,

Walpole pushed on the following day, and on the 22nd reached the village of Sirsa, forty miles beyond the fatal fort. Sirsa is a strong village on the right bank of the Rámganga, not far from Álaganj, the place occupied by the rebels who had so long annoyed Seaton. And, in fact, they were the same rebels, who had now crossed the river. The experience he had gained at Rúiya had made Walpole careful of his infantry. This time he brought his artillery to bear on the village in front, whilst he sent his cavalry to turn their flank. The manœuvre was so far successful that the enemy were driven out of the village, leaving their four guns behind them, and forced to cross the river in such disorder that they did not de-

but the bulk of them escape.

stroy the bridge which spanned it. But no proper arrangements had been made for following up the victory, and the great bulk of the rebels escaped.

The Commander-in-Chief joins.

Five days later, 27th April, Walpole was joined by the Commander-in-Chief on the Rohilkhand side of Fathgarh. The force then marched on Shahjahánpúr, which the enemy had evacuated. It then pushed on without opposition to Miranpúr Katra, where it united with the troops lately commanded by Penny, on the 3rd May.

I proceed now to trace the course of the Rúrki column, commanded by Brigadier-General Jones of the 60th Rifles.

A brigade formed at Rúrki.

Sir Colin Campbell had, in the first instance, decided that the force forming at Rúrki to march thence across Rohilkhand to Baréli should be merely a brigade force, and he had appointed Colonel John Coke, commanding the 1st Panjáb Infantry, to lead it.

Colonel Coke.

Colonel Coke was one of the best known and most distinguished officers of the Panjáb Frontier Force. To a thorough knowledge of his profession he added an acquaintance with the natives of India not to be surpassed, and a rare power of bending them to his will. He had seen much service. He had been with Sir Charles Napier in Upper Sind, with Gough at Chilianwála and Gújrat, with Gilbert in pursuit of the Sikhs. After the conclusion of the second Sikh war, he served continuously, up to the outbreak of the mutiny, on the frontier. There his name became a household word. Scarcely an expedition was undertaken against the wild border tribes but Coke bore a part in it. Twice was he wounded; but his unflinching demeanour, his power of leadership, whilst it gained the supreme confidence of his men, extorted respect and admiration from his enemies. Wherever he might be, his presence was a power.

His previous service.

Summoned to Dehlí early in August, Coke brought to the part assigned him in the siege all the qualities which had made his name on the

Book XII. Chapter IV.

1858. April.

frontier. He was always prominent in the fight, always daring and self-reliant.*

The troops composing his brigade.

The force into the command of which he suddenly fell was such as might well have inspired

* I may be pardoned if I relate here one special act, amongst many, which illustrated his conduct at this period. On the 12th August Coke received instructions from Brigadier Showers to turn out the European picket at the Metcalfe stables, and taking the men composing it with him, to proceed through the Metcalfe gardens and attack the guns which had been firing on the picket the preceding day. No information was given him as to the locality of the guns; but having been quartered at Dehlí before the outbreak, Coke imagined that he would find them in the vicinity of Ludlow Castle. He directed, then, the officer commanding the picket to extend the men on his right, and to follow the direction he should take. At the same time he ordered Lieutenant Lumsden, commanding his own regiment, to skirmish through the gardens on his left—the direction in which he expected to find the enemy in force. He then rode through the gardens towards Ludlow Castle. On reaching the boundary wall of the gardens on the main road leading to the city, he found that an embrasure had been made in the wall of the garden. At the same moment he saw the enemy's guns—two 9-pounder brass guns—in the road with horses attached, but no one with them, the enemy having apparently taken refuge in Ludlow Castle when driven out of the Metcalfe gardens by Lumsden. The horses' heads were turned towards the city. An alarm—a stray bullet—a discharge close to them—might start them off at any moment. Quick as lightning the idea flashed into Coke's brain that if he could but turn the horses' heads towards the camp, it would little signify how soon the horses might be alarmed: they would, of themselves, capture the guns for the British. On the instant he alighted from his horse, got down through the embrasure into the road, ran to the horses of the leading gun, and turned them up the road towards cantonments. Whilst doing this he was shot in the thigh by the enemy in Ludlow Castle, but the guns were captured. He had done his self-allotted task, and reaped his only reward in the admiration of all who witnessed his splendid audacity.

Book XII. Chapter IV.

1858. April.

him with the hope of gaining distinction as an independent commander. It was composed of a troop of the 9th Lancers, of Cureton's Múltáni Cavalry, of a wing of the 60th Rifles, of the 1st Panjáb Infantry, of the 1st Sikhs, and of the 17th Panjáb Infantry. The artillery portion of it was formed of Austin's light field battery and two 18-pounders.

Scarcity of carriage.

Coke had arrived at Rúrki on the 22nd February, but April was approaching, before, with the assistance of Baird Smith, who was then at that station, he had been able to complete his commissariat arrangements. The country, in fact, had been so thoroughly exhausted that but little carriage was procurable. In this dilemma Coke's practical knowledge and fertility of resource came into play. He had read how, in the olden days of Indian warfare, the Brinjáris —dealers who carry their grain on pack cattle, —had made themselves eminently serviceable. Calling to mind, then, that at the actual season these men were accustomed to pasture their cattle in the Terai, he sent thither, found them, and made such arrangements with their head men as enabled him to conquer a difficulty which many another man would have found insurmountable.

His practical knowledge causes the deficiency to be supplied,

Brigadier-General Jones supersedes him.

The carriage had been supplied, all the arrangements for the march of the force had been completed, the force was about to march, when Coke was suddenly superseded. It had seemed good to Sir Colin Campbell to make the command of the field force a divisional command. The other wing of the 60th Rifles was accordingly

Book XII. Chapter IV. — 1858. April.

added to it, and with that wing came Colonel John Jones, with the rank of Brigadier-General, to command the whole. Coke acted as brigadier and second in command under Jones.

The real command of the force

In reality the change was only in name. General Jones was a very brave man, but he was unwieldy in body, and incapable of very great activity. But he had no jealousy, and he was gifted with rare common sense. He saw at a glance that Coke was the man for the work, and he was content to leave it in his hands. In the campaign that followed, then, and of which he reaped all the credit, he never once interfered with Coke's arrangements. That officer continued to be supreme—in all but name.

is still with Coke.

The force crosses the Ganges at Hardwár.

General Jones—nicknamed at the time, from his habit of denouncing vengeance against the rebels, "The Avenger"—joined the force early in April. On the 17th of that month he opened the campaign by crossing, unopposed, the Ganges at Hardwár.

The position and hopes of the rebels.

The rebel troops were occupying the thick forest on the left bank of the river in considerable force. They were aware that the British force would be compelled to march through this forest, and, as it was traversed in many places by deep canals, they hoped to find opportunities for attacking them at advantage.

Jones had learned from Coke the general position of the enemy, and he had authorised that officer, as brigadier commanding the advance, to make the necessary arrangements for forcing it. When, then, he had crossed the Ganges,

Book XII. Chapter IV.

1858. April.

Coke pushes on and finds the rebels at Bhogniwála.

He completely defeats them.

Coke pushed on rapidly with the advance in the direction of the town of Nágal, near which it was known the enemy's main force was located. But he had marched only four miles when he fell in with a considerable body of rebels posted in a thick jungle, and their front covered by a canal, at a place called Bhogniwála. They had six guns, which at once opened on the British. But Austin, bringing up his field battery, promptly replied to them, whilst the infantry, in skirmishing order, steadily advanced. When they reached the canal, the water in which was nearly dry, they had a fair view of the rebels. At that moment Lieutenant Gosling, commanding a troop of the Múltáni Horse, let loose his men, and forced them back. This was the decisive moment. Coke, bringing the bulk of Cureton's regiment (the Múltáni Horse) and Austin's battery well to the front, charged the rebels whenever they attempted to form. The retreat soon, then, became a rout, the rebels abandoning their camp equipage and guns, casting away their arms, and even throwing off their clothes to facilitate escape. The Múltánis followed them for some miles, cutting up a large number of them, and capturing four guns. On this occasion Lieutenant Gosling killed eight men with his revolver. The loss of the victors was small, amounting to one man killed and sixteen wounded. That of the conquered was considerable.*

* That it was very great may be inferred from the saying of the natives, "that the spirits of the dead

Book XII. Chapter IV.

1858. April 18.

Brilliant feat of arms by a native officer.

The following morning a very brilliant and very daring feat of arms was accomplished, under the inspiration of Cureton, by a native officer of the Múltáni Horse, Jamadár Imám Bakhsh Khán. Conceiving that the rebels defeated on the previous day might have taken refuge in the thick jungle to the north of Najibábád, Cureton despatched the Jamadár mentioned and forty troopers to patrol in that direction. The Jamadár, in carrying out this duty, received information from villagers that a rebel Nawáb with five hundred followers was in occupation of a fort called Khót, a few miles distant. With happy audacity, Imám Bakhsh Khán proceeded at once to the fort, and summoned the garrison to surrender. He so imposed on them by his bearing and threats that they yielded unconditionally. Imám Bakhsh disarmed and dismissed the garrison, made prisoner of the Nawáb, and then returned to camp to report his brilliant exploit.*

The force pushes on to Naghína.

That day, the 18th, Jones pushed on first to Najíbábád, and, finding that place abandoned, to the fort of Fathgarh, also deserted by the enemy. In these two places he captured eight guns besides ammunition and grain. On the 21st, having in the interval been joined by four heavy guns and a squadron of the Carabineers, he

still haunt the scene, and that their groans may be heard in the night."—*Vide Cornhill Magazine* for January 1863, article "Indian Cossacks," containing a spirited account of this little campaign by an actor in it.

* He received the third class of the Order of Merit—an insufficient acknowledgment of such a deed.

Book XII. Chapter IV.

1858. April 21.

marched to Naghína, where, he had been informed, the rebels, numbering ten thousand infantry and two thousand cavalry, with fifteen guns, had taken up a strong position.

Position of the rebels near Naghína.

The position was strong. Its front was covered by the canal, guarded by ten of their guns; a bridge on the left was protected by a battery of five guns, whilst a tope of trees protected the right.

They are completely defeated.

The British force marched directly on to the canal. Whilst the guns on the right attacked the enemy's battery on the bridge, the 60th Rifles and the 1st Panjáb Infantry, with the Múltáni's on their left, crossed the canal and formed up to the right—the 1st Sikhs, under Gordon, clearing, meanwhile, its banks. By the time the canal had been cleared, the force which had crossed it had gained a position completely turning the enemy's right. The order was then given to charge. Never was a charge more successful. The rebels, panic-stricken, made no attempt to defend their guns, but fled in wild confusion. On this day Cureton rendered splendid service with his Múltánis. He pursued the enemy for five miles, and notwithstanding the resistance of despair which he and his followers encountered, he did not rest until he had slain their chiefs and captured their elephants and guns. It was a greater glory for him to rescue an unfortunate English telegraph signaller, who, previously taken prisoner by the rebels, had been brought into the field that he might witness the defeat of his countrymen!

Gallantry of Cureton.

Book XII. Chapter IV.

1858. April 21.

Cureton rescued this man at great personal danger to himself.*

Cureton defeats the remnant that had escaped.

But the toil of the day was not yet over. On returning from the slaughter of the chiefs with his two hundred mounted followers, Cureton descried approaching the main body of the defeated enemy, a compact force of eight hundred infantry five hundred cavalry, and some guns. The presence with him of the captured elephants of the Nawábs made it probable, he thought, that the rebels would regard the Múltánis as a party of their own friends. Cureton accordingly drew up into a grove by the roadside to await their approach. On they come, and the grove containing their supposed friends is almost reached. "Still not a sound issues from the trees, not a greeting strikes the ear, not a signal meets the eye. Suddenly a clear English voice rings out the word 'Charge!' and in an instant the Múltánis are in the midst of the panic-stricken foe. Taken by surprise, daunted by the fury of the onset, the rebels do not resist long, but flee in all directions, leaving upwards of one hundred dead on the ground, and a green standard and several guns as trophies."†

* "Indian Cossacks." — Vide *supra*.

† The *Cornhill Magazine*, January 1863, Art. "Indian Cossacks." The author of this article, who is believed to be a distinguished officer of the British army, thus proceeds: "With this feat of arms and the gallant deeds of Cureton and his Múltánis in the action of Naghína. They may well be proud of that day; for to defeat cavalry and artillery, then infantry, then again cavalry, artillery, and infantry combined, in the latter case contending against enormous odds, were exploits of which even a

1858. April 21.

Death of Lieutenant Gosling.

In the combat of Naghína the British loss was small in comparison with that of the rebels. The army had to regret, however, the death of Lieutenant Gosling, a gallant and meritorious officer, who fell in the final charge of which I have spoken. Where all so distinguished themselves it is difficult to single out any officer for special notice, but I cannot omit to record that the cavalry leading of Cureton * was talked of in camp at the time, and has been handed down to the new generation as a most brilliant example of the combination of skill, daring, readiness of resource, and practical ability.

How Cureton's feat of arms was regarded.

Mr. Hanna.

Amongst the volunteers present whose gallantry was marked was a young student of the Rúrki Civil Engineer College named Hanna. The desperate gallantry of this gentleman, who accompanied Cureton, procured him two serious wounds. It was then believed that he was a young officer, nor was it till after the fight was over that his real calling was discovered. Thanks to the strong recommendation of Cureton and his own intrepid spirit, Mr. Hanna obtained an unattached commission in the Indian army.

The force reaches Morádábád.

The victory was decisive. Thenceforward the progress of the column was not seriously opposed. Bijnor was reoccupied without opposition. Jones did not delay there, but pushed on rapidly to Morádábád.

veteran corps might boast. How much more, then, a young regiment only three months raised, and engaged that day in its second action!"

* Now Lieutenant-General Cureton, C.B.

Book XII. Chapter IV.

1858. April 21.

State of affairs in Morádábád.

The course of affairs at this station had not impressed the inhabitants with the advantage of the native rule of Khán Bahádur Khán,* and they had heard with anxious and beating hearts of the progress of the columns of the Avenger. The pent-up longings of their hearts had been confirmed and strengthened by the loyal attitude of a neighbouring native chieftain, the Nawáb of Rámpór, who had from the first exerted himself to maintain the authority of the British. As Jones advanced nearer and nearer these feelings displayed themselves in action. It happened on the 21st April, Firoz Shah, a prince of the royal house of Dehlí, who had cast in his lot with the Rohilkhand revolters, marched upon Morádábád, and demanded money and supplies. The townspeople refused, whereupon the prince, after some negotiation, endeavoured to take them by force. But the townspeople still holding out, the news of the approach of the avenging column forced Firoz Shah to beat an ignominious retreat. But the following day he returned secretly into the native part of the town.

The loyalty of the inhabitants is shown by the expulsion of Prince Firoz Shah.

April 26.

Jones arrived in the vicinity of Morádábád on the 26th April. His camp was there joined by Mr. Inglis, C.S., a gentleman thoroughly acquainted with the characters and doings of the rebel chiefs then figuring in Rohilkhand. Inglis informed Brigadier Coke that many prominent leaders of the revolt were at the moment in hiding in the city of Morádábád, and that it would not

Coke captures several rebel chiefs.

* Vol. i. pages 331, 332.

Book XII. Chapter IV.

1858. April 26.

be impossible, by the exercise of daring and prudence, to seize them. These two qualities shone conspicuously in the character of Coke. He at once made arrangements to effect the capture of these men. Placing the Múltáni cavalry to guard the outlets of the city, he entered with his infantry and proceeded to the houses indicated to him. The task was difficult and dangerous, but it resulted in success. Twenty-one notorious ringleaders of the revolt were actually taken. Others were slain defending themselves. In this affair Lieutenant Angelo greatly distinguished himself. Bursting open the door of one of the houses, he seized a prominent rebel leader and one of his sons. Whilst engaged in this work he was fired at from one of the upper rooms of the house. He at once rushed upstairs, forced the door of the room whence the firing had proceeded, and found himself face to face with seven armed men. Nothing daunted, he shot three of them with his revolver, and kept the remainder at bay with his sword till reinforced from below. Firoz Shah, unhappily, escaped.

The force moves on Barélí.

A few days later Jones again started to take part in the operations which the Commander-in-Chief was directing against Barélí, and to which I must now return.

The rebels evacuate Shahjahánpúr.

I have already stated that the Commander-in-Chief, with the force from Fathgarh joined to that of Walpole, had reached Shahjahánpúr on the 30th April, and had found it evacuated. It was not so much the evacuation of this important place as the escape of the rebel army

Book XII. Chapter IV.

1858. April 30.

which had held it, commanded by the notorious Moulvi, accompanied, it was believed, by Náná Sáhib* and his followers, in the direction of Oudh, which caused vexation to Sir Colin. It was a proof that, notwithstanding his great efforts, the campaign had failed in one important particular.

The consequent failure, to a great degree, of the plan of the campaign.

Though he had planned that four armies, starting from different points, should converge on Barélí and Shahjahánpúr, enclosing the rebels on four sides, their most formidable enemy had managed to break through the meshes, and to break through them, too, on the side for which he and Walpole were mainly responsible! However, there was no help for it. The Rohilkhand rebels were still in Barélí. They, at all events, he was resolved, should not escape him.

Sir Colin moves on Barélí.

Leaving at Shahjahánpúr five hundred men of the 82nd under Colonel Hales, De Kantzow's Irregular Horse, and four guns, Sir Colin pushed on, picked up Penny's column—commanded by Jones of the Carabineers—at Mìránpúr Kutra on the 3rd May, and on the 4th arrived at Faridpúr, a day's march from Barélí.

State of affairs in Barélí.

Khán Bahádur Khán was still holding sway in the capital of Rohilkhand. The exact amount of his force cannot be stated with certainty. Spies had rated it at thirty thousand infantry, six thousand horse, and forty guns, but it certainly did not reach anything like that number. The

* Before evacuating Shahjahánpúr, Náná Sáhib is said to have caused all the official buildings to be destroyed, in order that the Europeans, on their arrival, might find no shelter.

feeling that animated leader and men was the reverse of sanguine, for they knew that the town was threatened on both sides. Nevertheless there were amongst them a certain number of fanatics (Gházis) who were resolved to sell their lives dearly, neither to give nor to accept quarter.

Book XII. Chapter IV.

1858. May 4.

Defensive position of Barélí.

Barélí itself did not offer a strong defensible position. The town consisted of a main street, about two miles long, having occasionally narrow offshoots on both sides. Outside these streets were large suburbs formed of detached houses, walled gardens, and enclosures; outside these again were wide plains intersected by nullahs. One of these, called the Nattia Naddi, covered the town on the south side. Its banks were steep, and, if well protected, it was capable of presenting an obstacle to an advancing enemy. But it was bridged, and the bridges had not been broken.

Khán Bahádur Khán resolves to look Sir Colin in the face.

Khán Bahádur Khán heard on the 5th of the arrival of the Commander-in-Chief at Farídpúr. He was likewise aware that Jones was advancing from Morádábád. There was yet a way of escape open to him—the way he subsequently followed—in the direction of Pílíbhít. But the hot Rohilla blood of the descendant of Háfiz Rahmat forbade him to flee without striking a blow for his cause. He determined to meet the British force in the open plain outside the town.

He takes up a position.

On the evening of the 4th May he took up his position. Crossing the Nattia Naddi, he placed his guns on some rising ground—sand-hills—which commanded the line by which the British

Book XII. Chapter IV.

1858. May 4.

must advance, covered by his first line of infantry, whilst he guarded both his flanks with his cavalry. His second line occupied the old cantonments nearer to the town.

Composition of Sir Colin's force.

To force this position Sir Colin Campbell had under his orders a very considerable force. He had two brigades of cavalry,* the first commanded by Brigadier Jones, 6th Dragoon Guards, the second by Brigadier Hagart, 7th Hussars; Tombs's and Remmington's troops of horse artillery, Hammond's light field battery; two heavy field batteries under Francis; and the siege-train with Le Mesurier's company and Cookworthy's detachment, the whole commanded by Lieutenant-Colonel Brind; some sappers and miners under Colonel Harness; the Highland brigade under Leith Hay, consisting of the 93rd, 42nd, 79th, 4th Panjáb Rifles, and the Bilúch battalion; Brigadier Stisted's brigade, consisting of seven companies 64th Foot, 78th Highlanders, four companies 82nd, 2nd Panjáb Infantry, 22nd Panjáb Infantry.

Sir Colin marches on Barélí;

Very early on the morning of the 5th Sir Colin broke up from Farídpúr and marched on Barélí. As he approached the place the vedettes reported the presence of the enemy. It was 6 o'clock. Sir Colin halted his troops and formed them in two lines. In the first line he placed the High-

* The first cavalry brigade was composed of two squadrons 6th Dragoon Guards and Lind's Múltáni Horse; the second, 9th Lancers, 2nd Panjáb Cavalry, detachments Lahór Light Horse, 1st Panjáb Cavalry, 5th Panjáb Cavalry, and 15th Irregular Cavalry.

land regiments, supported by the 4th Panjáb Rifles and the Bilúch battalion, with a heavy field battery in the centre, and horse artillery and cavalry on both flanks. The second line, consisting of the remainder of his force, he disposed to protect the baggage and siege-train. The numerous cavalry displayed by the enemy seemed, in the opinion of Sir Colin, to render this precaution necessary.

Book XII. Chapter IV.

1858. May 5.

forms up his troops in order of battle.

It was striking 7 o'clock just as these dispositions were completed. Sir Colin then moved forward. He had not marched a hundred yards, however, before the enemy's guns opened upon him. But the British force advanced with so much steadiness and precision that the rebels promptly abandoned their first line, and made no attempt to defend the stream. Their infantry fell back on the old cantonments, covered by their cavalry and horse artillery, both of which occasionally made as though they would charge the British line. Nothing came of it, however. The British force still continued to press on, capturing as they reached the rivulet the guns which the rebels had failed to remove.

The rebels fall back before him.

The rivulet, not defended, offered but a slight obstacle to the advance of the British army. Whilst the left of their first line held the bridge, the right crossed it. The first line then advanced about three-quarters of a mile towards the town. The heavy guns were then rapidly passed over in succession, and were placed in a position to rake the enemy's second line. The troops then halted

Sir Colin crosses the Nattia rivulet,

and takes up a fresh position.

Book XII. Chapter IV.

1858. May 5.

to allow time for the siege-train and baggage to close up.

Whilst the troops formed up, thus halted, the 4th Panjáb Rifles in some old cavalry lines on the left, the enemy made a desperate effort to change the fortunes of the day.

The rebels make a counter attack.

In my description of the troops led by Khán Bahádur Khán I stated that there were amongst them a certain number who were resolved to sell their lives dearly, and neither to give nor accept quarter. I alluded to the Gházis, men who believed that the taking the life of an infidel opened to the slayer the gate of Paradise, and who were thus impelled by the most self-appealing of all motives to court, sword in hand and desperation in every act, the death which was to give them a glorious immortality.

The onslaught of the Gházis.

The line, formed up, was halting, when a considerable body of these fanatics, "fine fellows, grizzly-bearded elderly men for the most part, with green turbans and kammarbands, every one of them wearing a silver signet-ring, a long text of the Koran engraved on it," * rushed out from the right, and dashed at the village held by the 4th Panjábis. "They came on," wrote the eye-witness I have already quoted, "with their heads down below their shields, their talwars flashing as they waved them over their heads, shouting 'Dín, Dín!'" † dashed at the village, swept the surprised Sikhs out of it with the impulse and force of their rush, and then hurled themselves

* W. H. Russell. † Faith, Religion.

Book XII. Chapter IV.

1858. May 5.

against the 42nd Highlanders, who were moving to the support and to cover the re-formation of the Panjábis. Fortunately Sir Colin happened to be close to the 42nd. He had just time to call out "Stand firm, 42nd; bayonet them as they come on!" The 42nd did stand firm. The Gházis could make no impression upon their serried ranks. They killed some of them indeed; and they acted up to their professions. Not one of them went back. Killing, wounding, or failing to kill or to wound, every man of them who had flung himself against the Highland wall was bayoneted where he had fought.

Danger of Cameron,

But a portion of them had swept past the 42nd and had dashed to the rear, where were Cameron commanding that regiment, and, a little further back, Walpole, of Rúiya renown. Three of the Gházis dashed at Cameron, pulled him off his horse, and were about to despatch him, when Colour-Sergeant Gardner of the 42nd dashed out of the ranks and bayoneted two of them, whilst a private shot the third.* Walpole narrowly escaped death from a similar cause, and was delivered by men of the same regiment.

and of Walpole.

The British troops advance,

This attack repulsed, the 42nd, supported by the 4th Sikhs and a part of the 79th, advanced, sweeping through the empty lines and pushing forward for about a mile and a half into the old cantonments. The heat was intense; the men had suffered greatly from the heat, from thirst, and even from sunstroke, that Sir Colin thought

when Sir Colin suddenly halts them.

* Gardner received the Victoria Cross. I regret to be unable to record here the name of the private.

Book XII. Chapter IV. 1858. May 5.

it advisable to sound the halt for the day, even at the risk of leaving a door of escape to the enemy—for Barélí had not been entered.

The rebels attack the baggage, but are repulsed.

Another reason weighed to a certain extent with him in arriving at this conclusion. During the attack of the Gházis the enemy's cavalry, skilfully handled, had galloped round the British left, with a view to plunder the baggage. The amount of alarm, confusion, and panic created by this movement amongst the drivers and camp-followers is not to be described. A few rounds from Tombs's guns, and a threatened counter-attack from the Carabineers and the Múltáni Horse, soon dispersed the enemy. But Sir Colin deemed it nevertheless desirable that the *impedimenta* should close up with the main force. Directing, then, a portion of the 79th and 93rd to seize all the suburbs in their front, he placed the troops as far as possible in the shade, and halted for the day.

Sir Colin orders the baggage guards to close up.

Fresh encounter with the Gházis.

The attack thus made on the suburbs led to fresh encounters with the Gházis. One company of the 93rd—led by Lieutenant Cooper, whose gallant bearing at the Sikandar Bágh was the theme of admiring comment *—sent on this duty, arrived at a spot near the suburbs where some artillery guns under Lieutenant-Colonel Brind were posted. Brind pointed out to Cooper the position which he believed the Gházis were occupying. That officer, carefully noting the place, posted his men in some ruined houses and under cover of

* *Vide* page 183.

some walls to the left and left front of it. The guns then opened fire. After a few rounds the buildings occupied by the Gházis caught fire. The Gházis rushed out. Some five or six made a dash at Cooper. Two of these he shot dead, a third he killed after a brisk pursuit; with a fourth he then engaged in a sword fight, when the Gházi was shot dead by a private. The others were disposed of by the men.

Book XII. Chapter IV. 1858. May 5.

The halt ordered by Sir Colin, desirable as it was for the health of the troops, was, in a military point of view, fatal. It gave Khán Bahádur Khán a chance which he eagerly seized. No sooner had the shades of darkness fallen than the wily Rohilla quietly withdrew the bulk of his trained forces from the town and stole away to Pílíbhít, thirty-three miles north-east of Barélí, leaving only a rabble to maintain a show of resistance.

The halt enables Bahádur Khán to withdraw,

When, then, the following morning, the guns of Sir Colin Campbell began to play upon the city, they met with no reply. The sound of artillery fire was indeed heard on the opposite side, but that fire proceeded from the guns of Brigadier General Jones.

and the city is virtually evacuated. May 6.

I left that officer marching from Morádábád towards Baréli to attack that city on the side opposite to that by which Sir Colin Campbell had approached. The march was one long-continued skirmish. At Núrganj, twenty-one miles from Barélí, the Múltáni cavalry and Pathán horse again did admirable service, completely defeating the rebels, and capturing several guns. As he

General Jones closes in on the other side.

Book XII. Chapter IV. 1858. May 6.

approached with the advance of the force to Barélí, Coke could obtain no tidings of Sir Colin or his movements; but whilst waiting for information, some Hindú retail dealers announced to him that the rebels had deserted their guns placed at the entrance to the city. With a combined caution and daring adapted to the circumstances, Coke determined to proceed himself, and, should the story prove true, to take possession of the guns. He took with him a detachment of the Patháu cavalry. But he had hardly come within sight of the guns, barely within range, when the falsehood of the traders' tale became apparent—for the guns at once opened fire on his party. Fortunately the rebels were unable to control their impatience, or the consequences might have been disastrous. As it happened, one trooper only was killed. Coke at once sent back for the heavy guns and the infantry; then, placing a company of the 60th Rifles in a walled garden commanding the entrance to the city, ordered the guns to open fire. Ten minutes later the enemy's guns were silenced. Coke then led the Panjáb infantry regiments into the city and penetrated as far as the great mosque. Cureton's cavalry had meanwhile been sent to operate outside with the double view to cut off the rebels from their line of retreat to the north and to open out communication with Sir Colin. The action of the cavalry outside speedily made itself felt within the city, for the rebels, fearing for their line of retreat, evacuated the place with so much haste, that when Coke proceeded to make arrangements to

Coke presses on with the advance,

and effects a junction with Sir Colin.

force his way further, he discovered that none were required, as the city had been deserted. The next day, the 7th May, a junction was effected with Sir Colin.

Book XII. Chapter IV.

1858. May 7.

The town had indeed been conquered, but the bulk of the rebel army had escaped. This was the second occasion in this short Rohilkhand campaign in which the rebel leaders had outmanœuvred the British commander: on the first, the Moulvi had doubled back from Shahjahánpúr into Oudh; on the second, Khán Bahádur Khán had succeeded in escaping to a point not far from the Nipál frontier, along which it would not be difficult to penetrate into the same kingdom.

The second time the rebels had eluded Sir Colin.

But the Moulvi was influenced by motives nobler than those indicated by a mere avoidance of his powerful enemies. With the prescience of a capable general he had counted on the probability that Barélí would offer to the British army a certain resistance; and he had resolved to avail himself of the opportunity thus offered to make a raid upon Shahjahánpúr and overpower the small garrison which he hoped would be left there.

Skilful strategy of the Moulvi.

Sir Colin Campbell had left in Shahjahánpúr a wing of the 82nd, a detachment of artillery with two 24-pounders and two 9-pounders, and De Kantzow's Irregular Horse—the whole under the command of Lieutenant-Colonel Hale, C.B., of the 82nd. The habitable houses in Shahjahánpúr having been unroofed by order of Náná Sáhib, Hale had pitched his camp in a tope of trees near the jail, indicated to him by Sir Colin

Force left in Shahjahánpúr under Colonel Hale.

Book XII. Chapter IV.

1858. May 2.

as the place to be held should he be attacked. The enclosure round this building he at once proceeded to make defensible, placing in it his guns and as large a stock of provisions as he could procure. Working with great zeal and energy, Hale completed his preparations in one day—the day on which the Commander-in-Chief left him to proceed to Barélí—the 2nd May.

The Moulvi resolves to surprise Hale's force.

Meanwhile the Moulvi and his army had reached Mohamdi. There he found, eager to join him in any attack on the British, the Rájá of that place, and one Mián Sáhib, one of the old Lakhnao chiefs, each at the head of a considerable body of armed men, most of them mounted. Their plans were quickly formed. Learning that the bulk of the British force would leave Shahjahánpúr for Barélí on the morning of the 2nd, they resolved to attempt to surprise the place and cut up the detachment left to guard it the following morning.

His plan is ruined by a halt on the road.

They marched that day and part of the night of the 2nd to carry out this resolve. But again an excellent plan was spoiled by inefficient execution. Had the Moulvi pushed on he would have reached the town in the dead of night, and it is possible that he might have reaped all the advantage of a complete surprise. But, when within four miles of the place, he halted to rest his men. The halt was fatal to his complete success.

Hale is informed of his approach.

Native spies employed by the British were on the alert, and one of these flew with the intelligence of his dangerous vicinity to Colonel Hale.

Hale acted at once with the prudence which

Book XII. Chapter IV.

1858. May 3.

the circumstances required. He had been ordered to remain on the defensive. Instantly, then, he moved his stores and camp equipage into the jail, covering the transfer with four companies of the 82nd. He then went forward with De Kantzow's Horse to reconnoitre. The sudden apparition of vast bodies of cavalry, numbering about eight thousand, covering the plain, proved the truth of the spy's story. De Kantzow,* truly one of the heroes of the mutiny, always ready for action, always cool and resolute, was for a charge to check their advance. Hale, mindful of his orders, would not permit it, but falling back, brought all his men within the jail enclosure, thence to bid defiance to the enemy.

He reconnoitres, and then falls back on the jail.

Meanwhile the Moulvi and his allies, pressing on, speedily mastered the undefended town, seized the old fort, and then imposed a money requisition upon the wealthier inhabitants. In acting thus he simply conformed to the customs of war as practised in Europe. Simultaneously he placed his guns, eight in number, in position against the jail. From this day, the 3rd, till the morning of the 11th, he bombarded the British position incessantly, without, however, producing any other effect upon Hale and his comrades than an increasing resolve to hold out until assistance should arrive.

The Moulvi occupies and plunders the town.

Intelligence of the state of things at Shahjahánpúr first reached Sir Colin Campbell on the 7th. On that very day he had become master of Barélí, and had effected a junction with the Rúrki

Sir Colin learns of the state of affairs at Shahjahánpúr.

* *Vide* vol. i. pages 157–9, and page 500 of this volume.

Book XII. Chapter IV.

1858. May 7-11.

column under Jones. The news was like a message from heaven. Fortune gave him a chance to repair the error by which the Moulvi had been allowed to escape him on his march, and this time he was determined that there should be no mistake.

He orders Jones to march on Shahjahánpúr.

He at once sent for Brigadier John Jones, and directed him to march the following morning with a brigade, the nature and composition of which he indicated, to Shajahánpúr, there to deal with the Moulvi. He gave him further discretionary power to pursue his success, and, should he think it advisable, to attack Mohamdi.

Composition of Jones's force.

The troops composing the brigade ordered on this duty were the 60th Rifles, the 79th Highlanders, a wing of the 82nd, the 22nd Panjáb Infantry, two squadrons of Carabineers, the Múltáni Horse, with some heavy guns and some horse artillery. With this little force Jones marched on the morning of the 8th. Shortly after sunrise on the 11th he reached a point close to Shahjahánpúr, where the road branches out to the city and cantonments.

He advances on Shahjahánpúr,

Immediately afterwards the advance guard reported the presence of the enemy. Jones at once drew up his men, the heavy guns in the centre, and then moved forward. He soon came in sight of the enemy, huge masses of horsemen, formed up, and ready, apparently, to dispute the further progress of the British. A few shots from the heavy guns checked them, and, the Highlanders and Rifles pushing on in front whilst the horse artillery guns opened on their flanks, their hesitation developed into retreat, and, very soon after, by a continuance of the same tactics, retreat

Book XII. Chapter IV.

1858. May 11.

into flight. They still held the old fort, the bridge of boats over the river, the stone bridge over the Kánárat Naddi, the houses in the town, all loop-holed, and the position was in all respects formidable. But Jones was too quick for them. Pushing forward his skirmishers and horse artillery, he drove the enemy to the banks of the river opposite to the entrance to the city, and by a heavy and continuous fire forced them to abandon the idea they had attempted to put into execution of destroying the bridge of boats, and drove them within the city. Bringing up then his heavy guns and mortars, he compelled them to abandon, one after the other, the old fort, the stone bridge, and other commanding positions. He had now only the town to deal with. Made aware, by the reports which reached him, that all the houses in the main street had been loop-holed, and that the enemy counted upon his forcing an entrance through that street, Jones resolved to baffle them by avoiding the route indicated, and by taking the road which led through the eastern suburb. He met with no opposition as he traversed the suburbs, but no sooner did he emerge into a plain near the new schoolhouse, than he discovered a body of rebel cavalry. He at once attacked them, drove them back, and then quickened their movements by a few rounds of shrapnel. The Carabineers, who came up in the nick of time, were at once sent in pursuit. At first the rebels seemed inclined to measure swords with that gallant regiment, but second thoughts came to their aid, and they fled, leaving

and presses back the enemy.

Jones traverses the suburbs

and drives the rebels before him.

Book XII. Chapter IV.

1858. May 11-14.

a gun and ammunition waggon in the hands of their pursuers. Jones halted for a quarter of an hour in the open space I have mentioned, to allow his men to form up, and then pushed on by the church and across the parade ground to the jail, still held by the gallant Hale and his comrades. But there commenced the difficulties of the relieving force. The main body of the enemy was here found assembled. Their advanced positions —leading through the main street, and which could only have been forced at great risk and with enormous loss—had been turned by the skilful manœuvre of Jones. But in this open plain, where the masses of their cavalry could act freely, they were too strong to be attacked with any hope of success. Jones, therefore, was forced to maintain himself on the defensive until reinforcements should reach him from Barélí. To wait for these he established himself in a strong position, flanked on one side by the jail.

He effects a junction with Hale, and waits for reinforcements.

So passed the 11th. The 12th, 13th, and 14th were spent in preparations for the encounter looming in a very near future, Jones engaged in increasing his means of resistance, the Moulvi in welcoming fresh allies. And, indeed, those allies poured in with an alarming celerity. It was not alone the rabble escaped from previous fights, the discontented landsmen, the freebooters by profession, who flocked to his standard. There came, likewise, one after another, the Bégam of Oudh, the prince Firóz Shah, and although Náná Sáhib did not himself appear, he sent a body of his followers, whose presence gave colour to the rumour

Reinforcements, too, flock to the Moulvi.

Book XII. Chapter IV.

1858. May 14-15.

that he too was not afraid to meet in fair fight the countrymen of those whom he had murdered. Rumour lied. Náná Sáhib loved his life too well to risk it in a battle with the English.

The Moulvi attacks Jones.

By the evening of the 14th all these reinforcements had poured into the Moulvi's camp. On the 15th he struck his great blow. He attacked Jones with his whole force. But the troops led by Jones were men unaccustomed to show their backs to a foe. Charged and charged again, they repelled every assault. Jones's deficiency in cavalry would not permit him to retaliate, to carry the war into the enemy's camp. But at least they gained no ground from him. His men clung, then, with all the stubbornness of their natures, to the positions which they had been ordered to defend; and when evening fell, and the baffled enemy ceased their attack, they could boast that they had not lost so much as an inch. They could make the same boast when, three days later, the Commander-in-Chief appeared in person on the scene. To him I must now return.

Sir Colin, on detaching Jones to Shahjahánpúr, distributes his forces,

When Sir Colin Campbell had despatched Jones to Shahjahánpúr on the 8th, he imagined that he had certainly disposed of the Moulvi and had cleared the country as far as Mohamdi in Oudh. Regarding, then, the Rohilkhand campaign as virtually settled, he began at once to distribute his forces. He nominated General Walpole as divisional commander of the troops in Rohilkhand. Some regiments were ordered to remain at Barélí itself; some to proceed to Lakhnao; one or two to march to Mírath. A column, consisting of a

Book XII. Chapter IV.

1858. May 15–18.

wing of the 42nd Highlanders, the 4th Panjáb Rifles, the 1st Sikh Infantry, a portion of the 24th Panjáb Infantry, a squadron of the Carabineers, a detachment of the 17th Irregular Cavalry, and a considerable force of artillery, with three weeks' supplies for the Europeans and four weeks' for the natives, was directed on the 12th to proceed, under the command of Brigadier Coke, towards Pílíbhít, the line of retreat taken by Khán Bahádur Khán.

and sets out for Fathgarh.

Having made these arrangements, Sir Colin deemed that he might safely return himself to some central station on the great line of communication, whence he could more easily direct the general campaign. Taking with him, then, his headquarter staff, the 64th Foot, two troops of the 9th Lancers, the Bilúch Battalion, Tombs's troop of horse, and Le Mesurier's company of foot, artillery, he started from Barélí in the direction of Fathgarh on the 15th.

Hearing, on the march, of Jones's position, he turns towards Shahjahánpúr.

On the 16th, at Faridpúr, he received Jones's message. Sir Colin at once sent to Barélí for the remainder of the 9th Lancers, and the next day moved cautiously forward to Tilhar. That evening he received information that the Moulvi, whilst still pressing Shahjahánpúr, had withdrawn the bulk of his troops in the direction of Mohamdi, the entire length of the road to which he commanded.

He effects a junction with Jones.

The next morning, the 18th, Sir Colin marched towards Shahjahánpúr. As he approached the place, a strong force of the enemy's cavalry, calculated to number fifteen hundred men, with five guns, threatened to attack him. But it was little more than a demonstration, and Sir Colin, passing the ground on which he had previously encamped, made a partial circuit of the city to the bridge of boats. Crossing this, unopposed, he traversed the city, and effected a junction with Brigadier General Jones.

Book XII. Chapter IV.

1858. May 18.

His cavalry skirmish with the rebels,

But even then the British force was too weak in cavalry to encounter the enemy with any hope of a decisive result—a result, that is to say, fraught not only with defeat but with an annihilating pursuit. The truth of this presumption was fully shown that very day. Sir Colin had no intention whatever to engage the enemy. It happened, however, that a reconnoitring party of horse was fired on by the enemy from four guns posted in a fortified village called Panhat; the sound of the guns brought out the masses of the enemy's cavalry; and these again attracted to the field the Commander-in-Chief and his whole force.

which brings on an action,

The battle then partially engaged. The 82nd, pushed forward, occupied the village of Panhat, on the right front. They were followed by the horse artillery, and a field battery, and part of the 9th Lancers and the Irregulars. The 79th then took possession of a grove of trees in the centre of the position, near a small rising ground, on which were posted a couple of heavy guns; whilst a heavy field battery, supported by a wing of the Rifles, with parties of the Carabineers and Bilúchis, covered the left flank.

which, for want of cavalry, is indecisive.

It was a strong defensive position, on which the enemy could make no impression. In the artillery and cavalry

Book XII. Chapter IV.

1858. May 18-24.

skirmish which followed, the rebels displayed more than ordinary skill and courage, and although in the end they gave ground, no attempt was made to pursue them.

Sir Colin sends for Coke's brigade.

Sir Colin, in fact, was quite satisfied with the repulse of the enemy. He preferred to defer a decisive battle till he should have more troops, especially more cavalry. He sent off, then, a despatch to Brigadier Coke, directing him to bring down his brigade with all possible speed.

He then marches to attack the rebels,

Coke at once turned back, and joined the Commander-in-Chief on the 22nd. On the 24th the whole force marched to attack the enemy. But again the Moulvi baffled him. Whilst his light cavalry did their utmost to hinder the British advance on Mohamdi, retiring the moment the pursuers halted to discharge their guns, the Moulvi and his allies evacuated that place, after destroying the defences. They had similarly treated Katchiáni, the mud fort which had previously given shelter to European fugitives. The expulsion of the rebels from Rohilkhand was the one result of the campaign.

who fall back into Oudh.

Close of the summer campaign.

How they were followed up and hunted down in Oudh I shall tell in another chapter. The occurrences in Rajpútáná, long neglected, demand immediate attention. It will suffice here to state that on the expulsion of the Moulvi from Rohilkhand, the Rohilkhand and Rúrki field forces were broken up, the regiments of which they were composed being detailed for other duties. The Commander-in-Chief himself, and the headquarter staff, resumed his journey to Fathgarh; Brigadier

Book XII. Chapter IV.

1858. May.

Seaton, relieved by Colonel M'Causland in his command at that place, was appointed to Shahjahánpúr, having under him the 60th Rifles, the 82nd, the 22nd Panjáb Infantry, the Múltáni Horse, two squadrons of the Carabineers, and some artillery. Coke turned with his force to Moradábád, to act as Brigadier commanding the district; the 64th went to Miráth; the 9th Lancers to Ambála; the 79th to Fathgarh. The army was broken up. In south-eastern India, Oudh alone remained to be thoroughly subjugated.

The Moulvi.

But I cannot leave the scene of so many combats without recording events which, either from their historical interest, or from the deep personal sympathy they excited, demand special notice. The first of these, not in date, not in importance, not in the sympathy it excited, but in the connection which it bears to the contents of this chapter, is the death of the Moulvi of Faizábád. The Moulvi was a very remarkable man. Sir Thomas Seaton, who had many opportunities for arriving at a just opinion, has described him as "a man of great abilities, of undaunted courage, of stern determination, and by far the best soldier among the rebels." It has been surmised, and with great reason, that before the mutiny occurred the Moulvi was travelling through India on a roving commission, to excite the minds of his compatriots to the step then contemplated by the master-spirits of the plot. This at least is known: that such a commission was undertaken; that the Moulvi travelled to the parts of India which subsequently proved most susceptible to

Book XII. Chapter IV. 1858. May.

the revolt; that he was the confidential friend and adviser of a very prominent member of the deposed royal family of Lakhnao. If, as I believe, the mutiny was really caused not less by the annexation of Oudh than by the sudden and treacherous manner in which that annexation was carried into effect—that the greased cartridges were simply a means used by the higher conspirators to force to revolt men who could be moved only by violence to their faith—the story of the action of the Moulvi only seems natural. Certain it is that in April 1857 he circulated seditious papers throughout Oudh; that the police did not arrest him; and that to obtain that end armed force was required. He was then tried and condemned to death. But before the sentence could be executed, Oudh broke into revolt, and, like many a political criminal in Europe, he stepped at once from the floor of a dungeon to the footsteps of a throne. He became the confidential friend and adviser of the Bégam of Lakhnao, the trusted leader of the rebels.

His appearance and ability as a leader.

In person the Moulvi was tall, lean, and muscular, with large deep-set eyes, beetle brows, a high aquiline nose, and lantern jaws. Of his capacity as a military leader many proofs were given during the revolt, but none more decisive than those recorded in this chapter. No other man could boast that he had twice foiled Sir Colin Campbell in the field!

His death follows immediately the close of the summer campaign.

His death he owed, strange to say, not to his enemies, but to his *quondam* allies. After his retreat from Mohamdi, determined to use every means in his power to hinder the complete success of the British, the Moulvi started off, armed with the authority and money of the Bégam, for Powáin, a town on the frontiers of Oudh and Rohilkhand, thirteen miles north-east of Shahjahánpúr. The Rájá of this place was supposed to possess a certain amount of influence, and it was the Moulvi's object to induce him and others to join in a new league against the British. Book XII. Chapter IV. 1858. June.

The Moulvi started for Powáin, with a small following, on the 5th June, having previously sent forward a messenger to make known his wishes to the Rájá. The Rájá, Jaggarnáth Singh by name, was a fat unwieldy man, not given to martial feats, desirous to sit at home at ease, and particularly anxious to avoid giving offence to the British in the hour of their triumph. He, however, consented to grant the Moulvi a conference. Upon this the Moulvi pushed on to Powáin. The manner of it.

On reaching that place he found, to his surprise, that the gates were closed, the walls manned, and the Rájá, his brother, and his armed retainers, were lining the ramparts which overlooked the gateway. Amid these unpromising appearances the conference began. But the Moulvi soon satisfied himself that unless he could overawe the Rájá his eloquence would be wasted. To overawe him, then, he made the driver of the elephant upon which he was mounted urge the animal forward to burst open the gate. The elephant advanced, and applied his head with such force to the barrier, that in a second or two it must inevitably have yielded. In this crisis the Rájá's brother, inspired The Moulvi attempts to force an entrance into Powáin,

Book XII. Chapter IV.

1858. June.

by the urgency of the occasion, seized a gun and shot the Moulvi dead. His followers at once turned and fled. The Rájá and his brother at once cut off the Moulvi's head, and, wrapping it in a cloth, drove to Shahjahánpúr, thirteen miles distant. Arrived at the magistrate's house, they entered, and found that official and his friends at dinner. They at once produced the bundle, and rolled the bloody head at the feet of the Englishmen. It was at once exposed to view in a conspicuous part of the town, "for the information and encouragement of all concerned."*

and is shot dead.

His head is exposed.

Tribute due to the Moulvi.

Thus died the Moulvi Ahmad Úlla of Faizábád. If a patriot is a man who plots and fights for the independence, wrongfully destroyed, of his native country, then most certainly the Moulvi was a true patriot. He had not stained his sword by assassination, he had connived at no murders: he had fought manfully, honourably, and stubbornly in the field against the strangers who had seized his country, and his memory is entitled to the respect of the brave and the true-hearted of all nations.

Naturally enough, the British Government rejoiced to be rid of a formidable enemy. But another death, occurring a few weeks earlier, caused an outburst of the deepest sorrow in the heart of every Englishman serving in India—throughout the homes and the hearths of England. The reader who has accompanied me so far will

* The Government paid the Rájá a reward of five thousand pounds for killing the Moulvi.

have marked with pride and pleasure the record of the splendid achievements of the Naval Brigade under its gallant and accomplished leader, William Peel; they will remember that on the 9th March, when seeking a suitable place for the posting of some guns to breach the outer wall of the Martinière, William Peel was shot in the thigh by a musket-ball. The ball, however, was extracted, and the progress to convalescence after the extraction, if slow, was solid and hopeful.

Book XII. Chapter IV.

1858. April.

William Peel.

Reception designed for him and his brigade in Calcutta.

With the capture of Lakhnao the work of the Naval Brigade was regarded as completed. On the 1st April, then, the sailors struck their tents, and started for Kánhpúr on their way to Calcutta. Great preparations were made to receive them in that city. The Government had decided to notify their sense of their splendid services by giving them a public reception, and the Calcutta people, for once in accord with the Government, were resolved that the reception should yield, in heartiness, in sincerity, and in splendour, to none by which a body of public men had ever been greeted in their palatial city. No one foresaw that the daring leader, for whom the greatest ovation was reserved, would be called to his last home too soon to witness the admiration of his non-combatant countrymen.

Honours awarded to William Peel by the Crown.

One gratification, indeed, had been reserved for William Peel. On the 2nd March he had received the mark of the approval of his Gracious Sovereign, intimated by his nomination to be an Aide-de-Camp to the Queen, and by the bestowal of the Knight Commandership of the Bath. They

Book XII. Chapter IV.

1858. April.

were fit honours for his noble service, rewards of the nature he would prize the most, as constituting spontaneous testimony from his Sovereign of the efforts he had made to suppress the rebellion, the possible mischief of which, if unchecked, no one had recognised more clearly than had the First Lady in the Realm.*

He is attacked by small-pox, and dies.

William Peel reached Kánhpúr in safety. Though still weak, he was still slowly gaining strength, when, on the 20th April, he was attacked by confluent small-pox. His frame had been too much weakened to bear the shock. On the 27th he succumbed to the disease.

Universal grief at his death.

In him England lost one of the worthiest, of the noblest of her sons. How thoroughly he had impressed his spirit on the men whom he led may be gathered from the journal of one of them. "I cannot say," wrote Lieutenant Verney, on the 30th April, "what a sad loss we all feel this to be, and how deeply his death is felt and regretted by every officer and man; the mainspring that worked the machinery is gone. We never felt ourselves to be the *Shannon's* Naval Brigade, or even the *Admiralty* Naval Brigade, but always *Peel's* Naval Brigade." But the grief was not confined to the gallant men who had followed him. It was overpowering; it was universal; it was realised that England had lost a king of men.

General order issued on the occasion by Lord Canning.

The Government were not slow in giving expression to the universal feeling. On the 30th April Lord Canning issued a general order, in

* Life of the Prince Consort, vol. iv. chapter 78.

Book XII. Chapter IV.

1858. April.

which, after notifying the sad fact and recapitulating his services, he thus eloquently recorded his sense of the extent of the catastrophe, of the greatness of the man:—"The loss of his daring but thoughtful courage, joined with eminent abilities, is a heavy one to this country; but it is not more to be deplored than the loss of that influence which his earnest character, admirable temper, and gentle kindly bearing exercised on all within his reach—an influence which was exerted unceasingly for the public good, and of which the Governor-General believes it may with truth be said, that there is not a man of any rank or profession who, having been associated with Sir William Peel in these times of anxiety and danger, has not felt and acknowledged it."

Marble statue of him in Calcutta.

The memory of his great name and his great deeds still survives. In the Eden Gardens of Calcutta a statue in white marble recalls to the citizens, by whom those gardens are nightly thronged, the form and fashion of him who was indeed the noblest volunteer of this or any age, who was successful because he was really great, and who, dying early, left a reputation without spot, the best inheritance he could bequeath to his countrymen.

Venables.

I have already recorded the death of Venables. This gentleman, an indigo-planter, had, by his unflinching daring, saved the district of Ázamgarh in June 1857, when its natural guardians had withdrawn from it. Subsequently he had struggled bravely against the invaders from Oudh, and had ridden with Franks, as a volunteer, in his glorious

Book XII. Chapter IV.

1858. April.

march from the eastern frontier of Oudh to Lakhnao. Withdrawing thence to Allahábád, "broken in health and spirits, anxious for rest, looking forward eagerly to his return to England,"* he was persuaded by the Governor-General to return to Ázamgarh, once again seriously threatened. The reader will recollect how useful were the services he then rendered to the gallant Lord Mark Kerr. Nor were those subsequently given to Sir E.

* Letter from Lord Canning to the Committee of the Calcutta Chamber of Commerce, assembled in June 1858, to devise a fitting monument to Mr. Venables. The letter ran thus:—"It will be a satisfaction to me to join in this good work, not only on account of the admiration which I feel for the high qualities which Mr. Venables devoted to the public service, his intrepidity in the field, his energy and calm temper in upholding the civil authority, and his thoroughly just appreciation of the people and circumstances with which he had to deal, but also, and especially, on account of circumstances attending the last service which Mr. Venables rendered to his country. After the capture of Lucknow, where he was attached to Brigadier-General Franks's column, Mr. Venables came to Allahabad. He was broken in health and spirits, anxious for rest, and looking forward eagerly to his return to England, for which his preparations were made. At that time the appearance of affairs near Azimghar was threatening; and I asked Mr. Venables to forego his departure from India, and return to that district, with which he was intimately acquainted, there to assist in preserving order until danger should have passed away. He at once consented cheerfully; and that consent cost him his life. I am certain that the Court of Directors, who are fully informed of all particulars of Mr. Venables' great services and untimely death, will be eager to mark, in such manner as shall seem best to them, their appreciation of the character of this brave, self-denying English gentleman; and I am truly glad to have an opportunity of joining with his fellow-countrymen in India in testifying the sincere respect which I feel for his memory."

Book XII. Chapter IV.

1858. April.

The noble service he rendered to his country.

Lugard less remarkable. It was in the performance of "these great services," inspired by the highest sense of duty, that, on the 15th April, he was struck down. The wound was mortal. "A few days afterwards," wrote in eloquent language some years ago an able and conscientious historian,* "death, resulting from the wound, cut short the sufferings and belied the hopes of this 'brave, self-denying English gentleman,' one among many such who in those days of sharp trial proved their right to be held in equal honour with the best rewarded officers of the East India Company and the Crown."

* Trotter's *History of the British Empire in India.*

BOOK XII.

CHAPTER V.

Rajpútáná.

I HAVE brought the history of events in Rajpútáná up to the end of June 1857, and have shown how the foresight and energy of General G. St. P. Lawrence, had till then baffled all the efforts of the mutinous soldiers who had been sent to support British authority in that extensive country.

Continues tranquil.

The tranquillity restored in June continued throughout July. General Lawrence maintained his headquarters at Ájmir, but he moved thence occasionally, as his military and political duties required, to Biáór and Nasirábád. To show his confidence in the Mairs, he would have no other guard but a native officer's party of the Mairwárá battalion, and it is only fair to those loyal men to add that the events which followed, many of them peculiarly trying, fully justified that confidence.

Book XII. Chapter V.

1857. July.

Effect on the princes and people of the mild sway of the British.

It was a considerable evidence of the satisfaction felt by the princes and people of Rajpútáná with the mild but effective suzerainty of the British that they showed no sympathy with the revolted sepoys. The exactions of Amír Khán and the grinding tyranny of the Maráthás were not so remote but that the recollection of them could be entirely forgotten. The forty succeeding years of peace and prosperity, of protection against outer enemies, had been a proof of the advantage of the British connection too practical to allow the existence of a wish that the connection should be severed. They felt keenly, that whatever might be the result of such severance, even were it to be effected, it would not be to their advantage; and they knew from the experience of the past that complete success in the field of military hordes was the certain prelude to unbridled license, to a condition of rule without law.

The confidence bestowed by them in General Lawrence.

These sentiments of the people were fully displayed on more than one occasion during the months that followed the outbreaks at Nimach and Nasírábád. The air was infected with panic; the movement of a corporal's guard was magnified into a great military demonstration: rumours, slight in their origin, were multiplied by every mouth that repeated them, until the resemblance to the original disappeared altogether. In this state of affairs the merchants, the bankers, the trading community in the great centres of Rajpútáná, terrified by the reports, would send away their families for security, and then come to "their father," the Governor-General's agent, for

Book XII. Chapter V.

1857. July-August.

advice and protection. In every instance General Lawrence succeeded in calming their fears, and in inducing them to recall their families.

General Lawrence's demeanour.

His own example tended not a little to inspire them with confidence. When at Ájmir he never once allowed the routine of civil duties to be interrupted, but held open court, almost daily visiting the city, where, in spite of the fierce and sullen looks of the disaffected, he was always regarded with respect. Treating the people with a generous confidence, General Lawrence was nevertheless stern, even severe towards all wrongdoers, and never once relaxed the reins of strict and efficient discipline.

The disaffected few.

I have spoken of "the fierce and sullen looks of the disaffected." In all great cities, in all large countries, there must be some who hate restriction. The criminal class, the men who having nothing would live by other means than by labour, answer to this description. But above all, in the circumstances of 1857, were the soldiery. Throughout this period there was, there could not help being, a considerable amount of sympathy between the native soldiers of the Company and the native soldiers of the indigenous princes. They were of the same caste and the same class; they often came from the same recruiting-ground. The causes which impelled the British sepoys to mutiny could not fail to influence greatly their comrades in other services. These were the men whose looks were fierce and sullen, these the classes from whom danger was to be apprehended.

An émeute in the A'jmir

From these classes the danger came. On the

9th August an outbreak took place in the Ájmír jail, and fifty prisoners escaped—an outbreak of the criminal class. But General Lawrence was prompt. He sent out a detachment of the mounted police, previously warned by him to be in readiness, to pursue them, and rode after them himself. The fugitives were cut up or captured. It was a sign of the good feeling of the respectable classes, that when he set out on this pursuit, many leading Mahomedans of the city volunteered to accompany him.

Book XII. Chapter V.

1857. Aug. 9–10.

jail is suppressed.

On the day following, one of the other classes referred to—the military class—showed its teeth. One of the regiments accompanying the force for which Lawrence had made a requisition on Dísá, and which had reached Nasírábád on the 12th June, was the 12th Bombay Native Infantry. A trooper of the 1st Bombay Lancers, suddenly mounting his charger, had galloped in front of the lines of his regiment, endeavouring by cries and threats to induce his comrades to mutiny. The Bombay Lancers, however, were staunch, and some of them mounted their horses to pursue the rebel, whereupon, discharging his carbine at one of them, a native officer, he fled to the lines of the 12th, where he was received and sheltered. Meanwhile the Brigadier, Henry Macan, had come on to the parade ground. He at once ordered the men of the 12th to turn out. Only forty obeyed. Upon this the Brigadier called out the guns, and bringing up a company of the 83rd, proceeded to the lines of the 12th. The original mutineer, the trooper of the 1st Cavalry, fired at him but missed.

Slight outbreak at Nasírábád

is easily suppressed by Brigadier Macan.

Book XII. Chapter V. 1857. Aug. 10-12.

The rebel himself was then shot by an artillery officer. The men of the 12th were paraded, and all who had disobeyed the order to turn out were disarmed. Their muskets were found loaded. The ringleaders were then tried by court-martial, five were hanged and three sentenced to imprisonment for life. Twenty-five had previously deserted. To the remainder their arms, on their expression of contrition, were restored, and they behaved well in the field ever afterwards.

A similar occurrence at Nimach

A similar feeling displayed itself about the same time at another station. I have already stated* that after the revolt of the native troops at Nímach, General Lawrence, having no other soldiers at his disposal, had caused that place to be occupied by detachments from Méwa, Kotá, and Búndí. Subsequently, placing little trust in these men, he had ordered up a force composed of one squadron of the 2nd Bombay Light Cavalry, one hundred men of the 83rd, and two hundred of the 12th Bombay Native Infantry to relieve them. But some of the relievers were as bad as the relieved. About the 12th August some disaffected men of the 2nd Light Cavalry and the 12th Native Infantry endeavoured to promote a disturbance.

is successfully met by Colonel Jackson.

But Colonel Jackson, the commanding officer, acted with great promptitude. Before the mutiny had actually declared itself, he brought up the 83rd, and seized the ringleaders. Some of these were arrested, eight escaped, one man of the 83rd was killed, an officer and two men were wounded, but the mutiny was nipped in the bud.

* Vol. i. page 256.

But the mutinous feeling had been too widely spread over the province to be checked by one or two failures, nor had the officers at the out-stations at hand the same means of repression as those possessed by the commandants at Nímach and Nasirábád. Book XII. Chapter V. 1857. August.

The station of Mount Ábú, in the native state of Sirohí, was the summer residence of the Governor-General's agent, and generally of the wives and families of the officers serving under him. There, at this time, were congregated the wife and two daughters of General Lawrence, and the wives and families of many officers serving in the field. In the European barracks were likewise thirty convalescent soldiers of the 83rd. To protect the station was a detachment of sixty to seventy men of the Jodhpúr legion—whose head-quarters were at Írinpúrah—under the command of Captain Hall. Mount A'bú, the summer residence in Rajpútáná.

The Jodhpúr legion consisted of artillery, cavalry, and infantry. The artillery — two 9-pounders—was drawn by camels and manned from the infantry. The cavalry consisted of three troops, each having two native officers, eight non-commissioned officers, seventy-two troopers, and a trumpeter. The infantry was formed of eight companies of Hindústánis, each having two native officers, twelve non-commissioned officers, and eighty privates; and three companies of Bhíls, each counting seventy men besides native officers. The legion, especially the cavalry portion of it, had a good reputation for efficiency. Composition of the Jodhpúr legion.

On the 19th August a company of the infantry A company and a troop

Book XII. Chapter V.

1857. Aug. 19–21.

of the legion meet at Anádra.

portion of the legion, which had been sent with the view of holding in check a rebel chief in the neighbourhood, arrived at a place called Anádra, two miles from the foot of the mountain pass leading to Ábú. A troop of cavalry of the same legion had arrived there a few days previously, and had been distributed in small parties in the different villages to protect the road from Dísá to Ábú.

Captain Hall inspects them and finds them cheery.

The following afternoon Captain Hall arrived at Anádra to give orders for the occupation by the detachment of certain villages. The sepoys and their baggage had been soaked by heavy rain, but the men seemed cheery and well-disposed. Having given the necessary orders, he returned to Ábú. But on his way he met a havildár belonging to the detachment at that place, who, in reply to his question, said that he was going to see his newly arrived friends. This was true so far as it went: but the havildár deemed it unnecessary to add—what nevertheless was proved from subsequent inquiry to be the fact—that "he had been deputed to manage the attack which was to come off the following morning."*

The men at Anádra mutiny, climb the hill, and fire into the barracks.

The morning of the 21st was thick and hazy, and the people residing at A'bú, under the influence of murky atmosphere, kept their beds late. Not so the men of the Jodhpúr legion at Anádra. They rose very early, climbed the hill, and, under the cover of the dense fog, crept unseen to the door of the barracks, in which lay,

* Prichard's *Mutinies in Rajpútáná.*

buried in sleep, the thirty sick and invalid British soldiers. The native assassins then peeped through the window and saw their intended victims sleeping. Then raising their muskets, they poked the muzzles through the windows—and fired.

Book XII. Chapter V.

1857. Aug. 21.

Complete failure of the mutineers.

They aimed too high! The British soldiers starting from sleep at that sound, unwonted at Ábú, divine the cause, seize their muskets, and begin to load. But then another volley is poured in, harmless as its predecessor. By this time their muskets are loaded, they rush out, they reply. The result is "singular but satisfactory; one mutineer fell—the rest ran away."*

They fail also to kill Captain Hall,

While the main body were thus engaged at the barracks, another party of mutineers had crept round to Captain Hall's house, to dispose, if possible, of a man whom they knew to be capable and resolute, and whose influence they dreaded. Arrived in front of the house, they became aware that Captain Hall was asleep. They at once extended in line in front of it, and by word of command fired a volley within. Again was the result futile. Hall, awakened by the noise, managed to escape by a back door with his family into the schoolhouse, which had been fortified as a place of refuge. Leaving his family there, he took with him a small guard of four men of the 83rd, and, charging the assailants, drove them off. He was speedily joined by the remaining men of the 83rd, and the mutineers were driven from the hill. The state of the weather rendered pursuit impossible.

* Prichard.

Book XII. Chapter V.

1857. Aug. 21–22.

but wound Mr. Lawrence.

Only one European was wounded, and that was Mr. Alexander Lawrence, son of the General. Hearing the firing, he had started for Captain Hall's house, when the sepoys noted and shot him —in the thigh. The wound was severe, but he recovered.

The mutineers set out for I'rinpúrah.

The mutineers, baffled first by their own clumsiness, and secondly by the spirit of the men they had tried to murder, made at once for the head-quarters of the regiment—the station of Írinpúrah. The only Europeans at this station at the time were the adjutant, Lieutenant Conolly, two sergeants and their families. Early on the morning of the 22nd, a letter from one of the baffled mutineers was brought to Conolly by his orderly, Makdún Bakhsh by name. This letter, addressed to the men at headquarters, called upon them to

The Jodhpúr legion mutinies at that place.

revolt and join their comrades "who had been to Ábú, fought with the Europeans, and taken all precautions." Conolly immediately mounted his horse and rode down to the parade ground. A glance showed him that the spirit of mutiny had

Trying position of Lieutenant Conolly.

infected the troops. The gunners were running to their guns, shouting to Conolly, as they ran, to keep off. Conolly then determined to appeal to the Bhíls, who had no sympathies of caste, of kindred, or even of a common origin, with the men of the other branches of the legion. But to reach the Bhíls he was forced to pass the lines of the cavalry. These, too, he saw were mutinying, and though he stopped to order them to turn out under arms, but not to stir from their lines, his

He appeals to the Bhíls,

orders were not attended to. At last he reached

the Bhíls. He found them loyal and ready to obey him, except so far as to march against the loaded guns and muskets of their more numerous comrades. As a last resource, Conolly rode back to make an appeal to the infantry. He found them mad with excitement, and refusing to hear a word. He then tried the gunners. But, as he neared the guns, the men shouted to him to keep off; as he persisted in advancing, they wheeled their guns round, and pointed the muzzles at him, holding the portfires ready. Conolly then turned his horse's head, and changing his direction, rode again at the guns, taking them in flank. Upon this several troopers rode at him, between him and the guns, and pointing their carbines at him, exclaimed, "Go back, or we will fire." Conolly then called out with a loud voice that those on his side should join him. A few troopers rode over.

Book XII. Chapter V.

1857. Aug. 22.

then to the infantry,

then to the gunners,

and fails with all.

Meanwhile the sepoys had begun the work of plunder. The two English sergeants with their wives and families, two men, two women, and five children, unable to stem the tide, had abandoned their houses, and were seeking refuge in vain flight. Conolly sent for them to join him in the cavalry lines. They came. "Here, then," writes the chronicler of the story of the mutinies in Rajpútáná,* "the little band of English men and

The small English colony is in great straits;

* Lieutenant Iltudus Thomas Prichard, of the 15th Regiment Native Infantry, a soldier and a scholar of no mean capacity. The mutiny of his regiment disgusted Mr. Prichard with military service. He left the army after 1858, and devoted himself to literature, in which he played, in India, a conspicuous and honourable part. His work on the mutiny is styled *The Mutinies in Rajpútáná: a Personal Narrative.*

Book XII. Chapter V.

1857. Aug. 22.

women were collected, utterly helpless, surrounded by blood-thirsty villains, every instant plunging deeper and deeper into their career of crime, from which there was no drawing back, and becoming more and more intoxicated with the unbridled indulgence of their passion for plunder, lust, and rapine."

soon to become still greater,

It was indeed a terrible and a trying position. It was soon to become worse. Gradually the men who had responded to Conolly's call began to show a disposition to desert him. There were a few noble and loyal spirits, however, who in this dark hour dared to show that they preferred honour to life. A rasaldár,* Ábbás Áli by name, came forward, and taking off his turban in a solemn manner before the more infuriated of the rebels, declared to them that before they should offer violence to the English, they would have to pass over his body. His example was followed by another native officer, Ábdúl Áli. The orderly, too, Makdún Bakhsh, exerted himself to save his officer. Ultimately forty-five troopers swore to stand by Conolly or to die in his defence.

when a slight reaction occurs.

The "loyal" rebels are willing to spare Conolly and the children,

With a strange inconsistency, however, they would not ride off with Conolly and the sergeants and sergeants' families: they would not allow them to depart alone. They offered to allow Conolly to ride away, and to take charge of the children—but as for the parents, it was impossible, they said, to save them. With a spirit becoming a British officer, Conolly under those circumstances

but not the sergeants and their wives.

* A native cavalry officer—a squadron commander.

declined to leave. He resolved to save his comrades with himself, or to share their fate. Book XII. Chapter V.

Meanwhile the rebels had brought their guns to bear upon the cavalry lines. To prevent the escape of the Europeans and the loyal troopers, they then insisted that all the cavalry horses should be picketed close to the guns, and that the Europeans, now their captives, should be sent to occupy a small tent on the parade ground, carefully guarded. 1857. Aug. 22. The crisis continues.

So that long night passed. The next morning the Anádra mutineers, fresh from their baffled attempt on Ábú, marched into the station with a swagger scarcely consistent with their actual performances. However much minded they may have been to avenge their defeat on the prisoners, they were unable to do so without a fight with their own brethren. For the faithful "forty-five" still kept jealous guard. They contented themselves, then, with an outpouring of abuse. The Anádra mutineers arrive. Aug. 23.

The ways of the mutineers throughout the mutiny were inscrutable. They were so specially on this occasion. We have seen that on the day of the revolt of Írinpúrah, the revolters were willing to allow Conolly to go, but not the sergeants and their wives. On the evening of the second day they came to a resolution to permit the two sergeants, their wives and children, to depart, but to retain Conolly. In consequence of this resolve, the sergeants and their families were sent away. The mutineers then marched from the station in the direction of Ájmír, taking The rebels dismiss the sergeants and their families, and carry away Conolly.

Book XII. Chapter V.

1857. Aug. 23-24.

Conolly with them, a prisoner, mounted but carefully guarded.

The rebels allow Conolly to depart.

Conolly had given up all hope of life. But never was he in outward appearance more cheery. He has left in a letter to a friend a vivid account of the occurrences of that and the following day. On the third day he was allowed to depart, and he rode into Írinpúrah, followed by three faithful troopers.* The rasaldár who had first proved his loyalty, then wrote to Captain Monck-Mason, the political agent at Jodhpúr, offering to desert with a large body of the cavalry, and the guns, provided he and his comrades should be pardoned and reinstated in the service of the Government.

The "loyal" rebels offer to submit on promise of a pardon,

It may be convenient to state here that Monck-Mason was anxious to accept the offer, but his hands were tied by the order of Government, which prohibited all officers from making terms with rebels while they had arms in their hands. Monck-Mason therefore replied that though he was precluded by recent orders from accepting the terms offered, yet that if Ábbás Áli would act as a faithful soldier and servant of the British Government, and weaken the cause of the rebels by deserting in the manner he proposed, there was no doubt but that his case would be leniently

which the political agent has no power to grant.

dealt with by the Government, and he would probably receive an unconditional pardon and a suitable reward. Ábbás Áli, regarding this reply as a refusal, became an active leader of the rebel force. The results were serious to the British

* *Vide* Appendix C.

cause, and especially serious to Captain Monck-Mason himself.

Book XII. Chapter V.

1857. August.

The Rájá of Jodhpúr sends an army against the rebels.

The rebels, after dismissing Conolly, pushed on towards Ájmir with the intention of taking it. Their line of march lay through the Jodhpúr country. To stop them, and, if possible, to annihilate them, the Rájá, acting in conformity with the advice of Monck-Mason, despatched his own army, commanded by his favourite officer, a very daring and a very gallant man, who had given several instances of his courage—Anár Singh—to Páli, a place on the high road to his capital. To aid Anár Singh with his counsels, a British officer, Lieutenant Heathcote, was, by order of General Lawrence, despatched from the Rájpútáná field force, of which he was Deputy Assistant Quartermaster-General. The Jodhpúr troops intrenched themselves at Páli.

The Thákur of A'wah

Meanwhile the rebels, advancing towards that place, had arrived at Áwah. The Thákur or baron of this stronghold was in rebellion against his liege lord, the Rájá of Jodhpúr. The Thákur, a man of a long and proud lineage, of great repute throughout the country, was unwilling to enter into any bond of alliance with men whom he regarded as the revolted hirelings of the European. But revenge is sweet. And he, probably the second man in inportance in Márwár, believed that his wrongs cried out for vengeance. A rebel against his Rájá, he was likewise to that extent a rebel against the British suzerain of that Rájá. Before, however, he would consent to the terms which the rebel sepoys, in their anxiety to gain

Book XII. Chapter V.

1857. Aug.-Sept.

makes offers of submission to Monck-Mason,

him, pressed upon him with urgency, he despatched a messenger to the British agent, Monck-Mason, to tell him that if the British Government would accord him certain conditions, which he named, he would return to his allegiance, would keep the gates of his fort closed against the mutineers, and, if co-operated with either by a British force or by the troops of the Rájá, would open fire upon their camp, which was within gunshot of his walls.

which that officer has no power to accept.

Again was Monck-Mason tempted. Sound policy would have induced him to accept the Thákur's offer. The conditions named were of no great practical importance, relating as they did more to sentimental than to real grievances. But his hands were tied. He had no authority to treat with rebels still in arms. He had no authority at all to treat with this Thákur, whose first complaint lay against the Rájá. He was obliged to send a reply to this effect by the messenger; to inform him in addition that the Thákur's quarrel was with his own Rájá, and that the Rájá had frequently expressed his determination to hold no communication with him unless he should confess his error, throw himself upon his mercy, and pay up his arrears of revenue. The result of this reply was that the Thákur and the rebel sepoys came to terms, and together marched towards Páli.

He therefore coalesces with the rebels.

The rebels march on Pálí.

They marched towards Páli; but when they saw the intrenched position of the Jodhpúr troops, they did not care to attack it. The delay which ensued, trying as it was to men situated as were the Jodhpúr troops, might have been endured but for the evil effect it was sure to produce on the native courts and the native troops of Rajpútáná. These could not understand the utility of a Torres Vedras. Royal troops who would not advance were half beaten. The moment was especially full of anxiety for the officer responsible for the security of this important part of India, and General Lawrence was justified in the desire he expressed to the Rájá that some more active measures should be taken by his troops than those involved "in dancing attendance on the rebels, like orderlies."

Considera- which moved the Jodhpúr troops not to remain quiet.

But before General Lawrence's letter reached Jodhpúr, the commander of the royal troops, Anár Singh, had left his strong position and encamped in close proximity to the rebels. Here, on the early morning of September 8th, his camp was surprised by the enemy, his men gave way, and though he, with a few, a very few, kindred spirits, fought bravely to the last, giving their lives for their Rájá, he could not redeem the day. His camp, his guns, his military stores, fell into the hands of the rebels. Heathcote, after using every effort to induce the men to stand, had mounted his horse and galloped from the field.

The rebels attack and defeat the Jodhpúr troops.

General Lawrence was at Ájmir when the events I have recorded occurred. From the 21st to the 26th August he received no intelligence from Ábú, but on the 22nd a letter had reached him from Conolly at Írinpúrah, telling him of the anticipations he entertained of an outbreak at that

General Lawrence

Book XII. Chapter V.

1857. September.

station. Five days later he received the bare outline of the mutinies at both stations.

We have seen that the European forces at the disposal of Lawrence were all required for the maintenance of order at the great military centres in Rajpútáná, and that few, if any, could really be spared for service in the field. No one can wonder, then, at the anxiety expressed by the Governor-General's agent for the prompt and energetic action on the part of the Jodhpúr troops. But, after the defeat of those troops at Páli, Lawrence considering, and rightly considering, that the effect on the country would be very injurious if the course of the rebels were not promptly checked, assembled as soon as possible a small force at Bíáor for the purpose of co-operating with the Jodhpúr troops. This force was composed of one hundred and fifty men of the 83rd, a portion of the Mairwárá battalion, the 1st Bombay Lancers, two 12-pounders, three 6-pounders, and two mortars.

assembles a small force to coerce the rebels.

The rebels, after their victory over the Rájá's troops, had fallen back on Áwah, the fortifications of which they proceeded to strengthen. Áwah is surrounded by a high wall, and is only approachable through a dense jungle. Being well supplied with guns, it could claim to be defensible against the small force which Lawrence was marching against it.

The rebels fall back on A'wah.

He arrived before it on the 18th, and proceeded at once to make a reconnaisance in force. This had the effect of causing the enemy to bring a strong fire to bear upon his men from every

General Lawrence arrives before A'wah.

gun on their walls. It was seen that the place was strong and could scarcely be carried by an assault. Lawrence, then, hoping that the enemy would come out and attack him, fell back on the village of Chulawáss, about three and a half miles distant. Here he was to have been joined by Monck-Mason, but that officer, on arriving within three hundred yards of the place where the General was standing, was decoyed by the enemy's bugle-sound—similar to those of the British—and was shot dead. His death was a loss to the State, for he was a man of many and varied accomplishments, with a noble heart and a lofty mind—one of the old school of soldier-politicians who constituted one of the glories of the Company's rule.

Book XII. Chapter V.

1857. September.

Monck-Mason is killed.

Lawrence remained three days at Áwah. The rebels left him in peace, busily occupied in strengthening their position. Unable with his actual force to take the place, and having to a certain extent impressed the people of the country through which he marched, Lawrence then fell back leisurely on Ájmir and Nasirábád. Áwah bade him defiance, but with the exception of Kótá, the remainder of Rájpútáná remained for the three months that followed loyal and submissive. It may be convenient to add a word here regarding the proceedings at Áwah. Not many days elapsed before the proud Thákur and his rebel allies quarrelled. Instead of coming to blows, however, they sensibly agreed to separate. The Thákur remained at Áwah; the sepoys took their way towards Dehlí. They were en-

Lawrence falls back on A'jmir.

Ultimate fate of the Jodhpúr legion.

Book XII. Chapter V.

1857. October.

countered, completely defeated, and many of them cut up by a British force under Gerrard at Nárnúl on the 16th October following.*

Kotá.

Kotá, an offshoot from the more ancient principality of Búndí, is a native State bordering on the south-west frontier of Sindia's dominions, having an area of five thousand square miles, and a population of four hundred and thirty-three thousand souls. In 1857 the ruling chief was Maháráo Rám Singh. An auxiliary force of the three arms, commanded by European officers, had been maintained in the State since 1838. The entire cost of this force was maintained by the Maháráo. The political agent, representing the British Government, was Major Burton.

Troops from Kotá temporarily occupy Nímach.

The reader is aware that, when the troops of the regular army revolted at Nímach, Lawrence had caused that station to be reoccupied by detachments from the contingents of Mewár, Kotá, and Búndí, until such time as the Europeans he had sent for from Dísá should arrive.† Major Burton had accompanied the Kotá troops on that expedition. He did not, however, return with them, General Lawrence having requested him to remain at Nímach for some three weeks, as "in those unsettled times he could not have confidence in his troops."

Major Burton and his sons return to Kotá.

Major Burton, consequently, remained at Nímach. But, after the occurrences at A'wah to which I have adverted, deeming his presence at

* Page 112. I may add that the rasaldár, Abbás A'li, was ultimately pardoned by Lord Canning.

† Vol. i. page 256.

the capital of the State to which he was accredited necessary for the assurance of the policy of the Maháráo, he set out to return to Kotá, accompanied by two of his sons, the one aged twenty-one, the other sixteen, but leaving behind him, under the safeguard of the British troops at Nímach, his wife and four remaining children. He reached Kotá on the 12th October, was visited by the Maháráo in state the following morning, and returned the visit on the 14th. The Maháráo subsequently stated that at the return visit Burton gave him the names of some of his officers whom he knew to be disaffected, and impressed upon him the advisability of punishing or at least dismissing them. Whether Burton gave this advice can never be certainly known; but this is certain, that that same day the Maháráo caused the officers and men of the contingent to be informed that he had given it!

The Maháráo betrays Burton to the men whom he had denounced,

Officers and men were, in very truth, alike disaffected, and, being so, the communication made to them by order of the Maháráo determined them to take the law into their own hands. Accordingly they assembled the following morning, and killing Mr. Salder, the Residency surgeon, and Mr. Saviell, the doctor of the dispensary in the city, who resided in houses in the Residency grounds, attacked the Residency itself. The guards and servants fled from the premises and hid themselves in the ravines close by. Major Burton and his two sons, left with a single servant, a camel-driver, took refuge in a room on the roof of the house. The revolters then

who attack the Residency,

Book XII. Chapter V.

1857. October.

fired round shot into the Residency. "For four hours," writes General Lawrence in his graphic account of the mournful transaction,* "these four brave men defended themselves, till at length the Residency was set on fire, and Major Burton, feeling the case desperate, proposed to surrender on condition of the mob sparing his son's lives. The young men at once rejected the offer, saying they would all die together. They knelt down and prayed for the last time, and then calmly and heroically met their fate. The mob had by this time procured scaling-ladders, and thus gaining the roof, rushed in and despatched their victims, the servant alone escaping. Major Burton's head was cut off and paraded through the town, and then fired from a gun, but the three bodies were by the Maharájá's order interred that evening."

and murder Burton, his sons, and other Europeans.

The Maháráo excuses himself.

The Maháráo at once communicated the occurrence to General Lawrence, accompanying the communication with the expression of his regret and with the excuse that the troops had taken the law into their own hands and that he was powerless. He may have been powerless, but he had, perhaps unwittingly, set the troops on. The Government of India subsequently signified their opinion, that though innocent of fore-knowledge, the Maháráo had not wholly performed his duty, by reducing his salute from seventeen to thirteen guns.

* *Reminiscences of Forty-three Years' Service in India*, by Lieut.-General Sir George Lawrence, K.C.S.I., C.B.

Book XII. Chapter V.

1857. October.

The tragedy at Kotá was not the only outrage which disturbed the peace of the country during the month of October. About the same time that Burton was being besieged in the Residency of the former place, a party of rebels from Mandisúr, led by a chief who pretended relationship to the royal house of Dehlí, marched on and seized Jíran, a fortified town with a very strong defence, within ten miles of the cantonment of Nímach. It was impossible to allow such an outrage to pass unnoticed. On the 23rd October there was sent from Nímach to attack them a force of four hundred men, with two guns and a mortar. The men were chiefly Bombay native troops, cavalry and infantry, but they were headed by fifty men of the 83rd, the whole commanded by Captain Tucker. They found the enemy still at Jíran. Tucker at once opened fire with his guns, and when they had played some time upon the defences, he sent his infantry to attack the town. The rebels then sallied out in overwhelming numbers, drove back the infantry, and, pushing on, captured the mortar. Upon this the cavalry charged, recovered the mortar, compelled the enemy to re-enter the town, and silenced their fire. But the place itself was too strong for the efforts of a force so small and so lightly provided; the loss already incurred had been heavy, two officers, Tucker and Read, having been killed, and three wounded; a retreat was therefore ordered. Strange to say, the enemy evacuated Jíran that night.

Disturbances near Nímach.

The repulse at Jíran.

Their retreat, however, was only the prelude

The rebels advance

Book XII. Chapter V.

1857. November.

again in greater numbers and attack Nímach.

to an advance in larger numbers. On the 8th November a body of them, numbering four thousand, advanced on Nímach, occupied the station, and forced the European and native troops to take refuge within the fortified square. This they attempted, but vainly, to escalade; then, after a siege of fifteen days' duration, hearing that reinforcements were advancing to the aid of the British, they fell back.

Lawrence applies for reinforcements.

On receiving intelligence of the murder of Captain Burton and his sons, General Lawrence had made an urgent requisition to Bombay for troops. The first and smaller detachments of these began to arrive in Rajpútáná in January 1858, but it was not until March that the reinforcements assumed a sufficient strength to justify decisive action on a large scale.

1858. January.

On the arrival of some of them he besieges,

The detachments which arrived in January, however, enabled General Lawrence to throw off the quiescent attitude which he had till then deemed it politic to assume. In January he was able to detach a force of eleven hundred men, with a due proportion of guns, under Colonel Holmes, 12th Bombay Native Infantry, against A'wah. Holmes invested the place on the 19th, and the same day his guns opened fire. At the end of five days a practicable breach had been made, and the assault was ordered for the following morning. The garrison, perfectly cognisant of all that was going on in the British camp, resolved not to wait. Fortunately for them there raged that night a storm so fearful, and there ruled a darkness so intense, that sentries only a

and captures A'wah.

few paces apart could neither see nor hear each other. Under cover of these portents they evacuated the place in the night.

The fortifications of A'wah justify Lawrence's previous retirement.

The strength of the fortifications of A'wah, when it was occupied next morning by the British troops, were such as to justify to the full General Lawrence's determination regarding it in the previous September. It had a double line of defences, the inner of strong masonry, the outer of earthwork, both being loop-holed. Thirteen guns, three tons of powder, and three thousand rounds of small arms ammunition were found in the place. The keep, the bastions, and all the masonry works were blown up and destroyed, so as effectually to prevent the stronghold becoming a nucleus of rebellion for the future.*

This act of vigour had a very salutary effect. Order was maintained in the country; and in March, when the reinforcements from Bombay poured in, the difficulty of the task for which troops had been required in the previous November had in no way increased.

The main reinforcements arrive

The reinforcements numbered five thousand five hundred men of all arms. They were composed of the 92nd, 83rd, and 95th Regiments, the 10th Bombay Native Infantry, the 8th Hussars, the 1st Bombay Lancers, the Sind Horse, Brown's battery of artillery, eighteen field-pieces, of which ten were 8-inch mortars and howitzers, and a corps of sappers and miners. They were commanded by Major-General H. G. Roberts of the Bombay army.

* *Forty-three Years in India*, Sir G. Lawrence.

Book XII. Chapter V.

1858. March.

under General Roberts.

On the arrival of General Roberts in March, General Lawrence resigned the military command into his hands, and reverted to his civil and political functions as agent to the Governor-General. In this capacity he accompanied the force.

The state of Kotá after the murder of Burton.

The first operation to be attempted was the recovery of Kotá. Ever since the murder of Captain Burton disorder had prevailed in that State. The sepoys, having tasted the pleasure of revolt, drained the cup to the very dregs. They imprisoned the Maháráo in his palace. They then forced him to sign a paper consisting of nine articles, one of which was to the effect that he had ordered the murder of Major Burton. The Maháráo endeavoured by compliance to keep the rebels in good humour, but meanwhile he despatched secretly messengers to the Rájá of Karáolí, begging him to send troops to his aid. The Rájá complied, and his troops, faithful to their liege lord, drove the rebels from the part of the town of Kotá in which the palace was situated, and released the Maháráo. They were still occupying it, for the defence of that prince, when Roberts arrived in Rajpútáná. The rebels, however, occupied the other part of the town, reduced already by pillage and other excesses to extreme misery.

The road between Nasirábád and Kotá.

A military march from Nasirábád, the headquarters of Roberts's force, to Kotá, was not one which a general could regard as being necessarily a pleasure trip. Not only did the town of Kotá occupy a formidable position, covered by the river Chambal on one side and by a large and deep lake on the other, but the approach to it offered many positions capable of easy defence by a small force against one much larger. Chief amongst these was the Mokandára pass—a long and narrow valley between two ranges of hills.

Roberts penetrates to Kotá.

But once more the want of true military instinct was manifested. None of the difficult positions were defended. Roberts, marching from Nasirábád on the 10th, encamped on the north bank of the Chambal, opposite Kotá, on the 22nd March. He found the rebels in complete possession of the south bank, on which they had planted their guns, many in number, and some of them large in calibre. Roberts ascertained at the same time that the fort, the palace, half the city, and the ferry over the river, were held by the Mahá-ráo with the Karáoli troops.

He attacks and completely defeats the rebels.

Early on the morning of the 25th, information reached him that the rebels were making an assault on the palace with a view to seize the ferry. Roberts instantly sent across three hundred men of the 83rd, under Major Heath, to aid the Maháráo. The attack was repulsed. On the 27th he crossed over himself with six hundred of the 93rd, and two 9-pounders, and having placed the heavy guns in the fort in position to bear on the enemy's camp, he opened upon it on the 29th a heavy fire of shot and shell. On the 30th, whilst the remainder of the force cannonaded the rebels' position from the north bank, he, marching from the fort in three columns, moved on it on the south bank, and gained it with very small loss. By this brilliant manœuvre he not only

Book XII. Chapter V.

1858. March–April.

completely defeated the enemy but captured fifty guns! The cavalry, however, failed to intercept the rebels, and they almost all escaped.

The authority of the Mahárío is restored.

The British troops occupied Kotá for three weeks. At the end of that time, the authority of the Mahárío having been completely re-established, General Roberts evacuated it and returned to Nasirábád, despatching a portion of his force to garrison Nímach. With the fall of Kotá peace and order had been completely restored throughout Rájpútáná, and although, two months later, both were broken by Tántia Topi, the action of this famous leader was strictly an invasion. Tántia induced neither prince nor peasant to join his standard.

The reason why Rajpútáná was, by comparison, little affected by the mutiny.

Of all the large tracts of territory inhabited mainly by a people boasting a common origin, not one passed through the trying period of 1857–58 with smaller injury to itself, with less infliction of suffering and bloodshed, than the territory of Rájpútáná. Parcelled out into eighteen sovereign States, each ruled by its own independent chief, the circumstance may seem surprising. But the causes of it are not far to seek. I attribute the result mainly to the fact that no people in India had suffered so much or so recently as the Rájpúts from the lawlessness which characterised the sway immediately preceding the suzerainty of the British—the sway of the Maráthás. When the policy of Marquess Wellesley towards the Rájpút States was reversed in 1805 by Lord Cornwallis and Sir George Barlow, a system of oppression and misrule was inaugurated, under which the buffalo

Book XII. Chapter V. 1858.

was to the man who held the bludgeon, and the fair daughters of the land were to the strong arm of the marauder. For twelve years the sufferings of Rájpútáná cried to heaven for redress. That redress came only when, in 1817, the Marquis of Hastings reverted to the policy of his great predecessor. Under that policy the princes of Rájpútáná have been secured against invaders from outside and against each other. Once more has every man been able to lie down in his own mango-grove and to eat of his own date-tree. Security has prevailed throughout the land. The honour of every man and of every woman has been secured. It was the sense of this security, enjoyed under British suzerainty, that ensured the loyalty of the great bulk of the Rájpúts during the troublous times of the mutiny.

George St. Patrick Lawrence.

It is proper to add that this recollection of past and present benefits was stimulated and enforced by the choice made by the Government of India of the agents to carry out their policy. Foremost among these was George St. Patrick Lawrence. His tact, his energy, his fearlessness, his readiness of resource, when he had not a single European soldier at his disposal, stamp him as a man eminently fitted to rule in troublous times. The display of these qualities begat confidence in the minds of the native princes, fear and dismay among the adventurers who welcomed turmoil. His presence, thus, proved itself to be worth an army. But for his promptitude, Ájmir would have fallen, and with Ájmir occupied by two or three regiments of British sepoys, British authority

Book XII. Chapter V. 1858.

would have disappeared. The preservation of Rájpútáná, then, will ever be connected with the name of this gallant and distinguished officer.

The story reverts to Bombay.

The inroad of Tántia Topi into Rájpútáná, and the campaign in pursuit of that famous leader, will be treated of in its proper place in the next volume. Before dealing with him it will be my pleasing duty to record the statesmanlike measures by which Lord Elphinstone caused Bombay to become a strong wall of support to the threatened edifice of British rule in India, and to narrate how Sir Hugh Rose illustrated the highest genius of the inspired warrior by his daring and successful campaign in Central India.

APPENDIX A.

1.—(Page 39 of text.)

Major Reid's plan of attack on the strong position of Kishanganj has never been published. I therefore give it verbatim. On the 2nd February, 1858, after he had in a measure recovered from his wound, he wrote as follows:

"With regard to Kishenganj I can only say that were I ordered to attack the place to-morrow, supposing the enemy's heavy guns to be in the same position they were in on the 14th September last, my plan of attack would be just what it was then.

"You have seen the position, and know the localities and great strength of the place, and will therefore understand me when I say the hugging the garden wall on the left of the road before you come to the canal bridge, and then the loop-holed serai wall, as also the garden wall which runs parallel to it, places one, comparatively speaking, out of harm's way. The heavy guns in the two batteries could not be brought to bear, nor could the loop-holes be made use of for musketry, so long, mind you, as the column *hugged* the walls above alluded to 'four deep,' as I had my troops on the 14th September.

"I was just about to carry out this plan and make a feint in front of the heavy batteries whilst I made a *real* attack in rear of the serai,* when I was knocked over, but my intentions were to have attacked the strong works at the end of the road—their second line of defence—and had this been successful, I should have entered the serai through the breach which was made by my order in rear of the heavy batteries, as also through the gate, which I could have blown in, and through which I entered when I took the place on the 17th June.

"My object in detaching four hundred infantry, two hundred cavalry, and four guns of the Jammoo contingent to the Eedgar was to make a diversion and place Trevelyanganj between a cross fire, as also to watch the enemy and prevent my right flank being turned; and I had a still further object in view, namely, to make the enemy believe that our real attack was to be on the right! That they were deceived by this movement there can be but little doubt, otherwise they would not have reinforced Kishanganj in the way they did, for at the time I fell the enemy mustered at least fifteen thousand strong.

"After getting possession of Kishanganj I should have turned the four captured heavy guns, as also the two 8-inch mortars, on Trevelyanganj. Their fire, coupled with that of the four guns of the Jummoo contingent, would have made it too hot for them, and I calculated on their retreating into the city. Had they done so, I should have left half the reserve in the serai, and proceeded with my column along the dry bed of the canal up to the Kábul gate, which Nicholson would have opened for me after he had reached that point with his column inside the city walls.

* A loop-holed stone wall enclosure round a village.

"A good deal would have depended on circumstances, but certain it is I should not have attempted to enter the city so long as the enemy were in force on my right.

"My desire was to attack Kishanganj before daybreak, but I was over-ruled by the General, and it was decided that I should wait for the explosion—the blowing in of the Cashmere gate. But after all, I could not wait, as the detached party of the Jummoo contingent became engaged with the enemy. Had my orders been obeyed they would have got into the Eedgar without firing a shot long before daybreak, but the party was late in starting from the camp, and before getting half way to their destination the day had dawned, and the enemy were on the alert and at once attacked them, eventually driving them back and capturing their four guns."

2.—(Pages 42 and 43 of text.)

A great difference of opinion having been expressed at the time regarding the action of the fourth column after the fall of Major Reid, the matter was referred by Captain Lawrence, with the approval, I understand, of Major, now Lieutenant-General, Sir Henry Norman, to the late Colonel Sir Herbert Edwardes, K.C.B., for investigation. Sir Herbert Edwardes, after examining many witnesses who were present on the occasion, and giving to the subject the most patient attention, recorded his opinion in the manner stated below. It will be observed that, for reasons which seem to me sufficient, I have not adhered implicitly to Sir Herbert's conclusions, but I consider it only fair to General Richard Lawrence that they should be placed on record in this volume.

MEMO.: on a correspondence connected with the operations of the fourth column of attack on Delhi, on the 14th September, 1857, referred to me for arbitration by Majors Norman and Lawrence.

1. Major Lawrence complains of three passages, in a *Narrative of the Siege of Delhi*, published by Major Norman. The passages are as follows:

"No. 4 column, under Major Reid, advanced from the Subzee Mundi towards Kissengunge, the *Cashmere contingent* co-operating on its right. *The latter*, however, was so sharply attacked by the insurgents, who were in great force, that, after losing a great number of men and four guns, *they were completely defeated, and fell back to camp.*"

"Major Reid's column met with the most strenuous opposition, *greatly increased, doubtless, by the failure of the Cashmere contingent.*

"Captain Muter, 60th Rifles, *the next senior officer* (a) judiciously *withdrew the troops to their former posts* (b) at Hindoo Raos and in the Subzee Mundi."

2. The sentences in italics contain the statements objected to; and I proceed to express the opinions I have formed on the documentary evidence placed before me by Majors Lawrence and Norman, aided by conversation on the matter with Brigadier-General Chamberlain *previous* to my perusal of the papers; and a fuller personal inquiry made by me now from Captain Boisragon (who was in the action) *after* perusing the documents, for the sake of clearing up doubtful points.

3. The first passage is certainly very inaccurate, inasmuch as it conveys the impression that either the whole, or at all events the main body, of the Cashmere contingent was co-operating on the right of No. 4 column, and lost four guns; whereas the contingent on that occasion acted in two bodies. First, the main one (eight hundred strong, under Major R.

Lawrence) as reserve to No. 4 column in its attack on Kissengunge, which shared in the failure of that column, and lost no guns; and secondly, a detachment of four hundred, under Captain Dwyer, which acted separately against the Edgah at a distance of three-fourths of a mile on the right of No. 4 column, which *was* completely defeated, and *did* lose four guns. This inaccuracy is fully admitted by Major Norman in his reference to me, and it is unnecessary to discuss it farther than to mention that it arose apparently from the official report of Major Muter.

4. The second passage would similarly be admitted by Major Norman to be so far inaccurate as he spoke of the "Cashmere contingent" instead of a *detachment* of the Cashmere contingent; but with that exception he is still inclined to think that the passage is correct, that Captain Dwyer's detachment attacked the enemy at the Edgah before Colonel Reid attacked at Kissengunge, and that its defeat was sufficiently early to bring down a greater pressure on Colonel Reid's column, and so to contribute to its repulse. The evidence on these points is not always positive, and is very conflicting. Lieutenant Evans, who was in the Crow's Nest battery, evidently saw Captain Dwyer's detachment engaged with the enemy at the Edgah while No. 4 column was forming up; and I consider his testimony decisive upon that point. His evidence is not precise about the time of the retirement of Captain Dwyer's detachment, though it leans apparently to its having occurred previous even to Colonel Reid's assault. This cannot be the case, as Colonel Reid precisely states that some time after he had been wounded, and was making over the command to Major Lawrence, one hundred yards in rear of the canal, he told Major Lawrence "to support the four hundred Jummoo troops on the right, who were *becoming hotly engaged with the enemy.*" This establishes that the two engagements were going on simultaneously at Kissengunge and Edgah, and the inquiry

is thus narrowed to which of the two repulses occurred first. Major Muter says that No. 4 column attacked thus twice, and failed in being able to get up another attack, the loss was so heavy, the confusion so great, and the men so disheartened. This all occurred within a quarter of an hour of the fall of Major Reid, who was one of the first hit; in that quarter of an hour we lost two hundred men out of the seven hundred and fifty. Here it is precisely stated that No. 4 column had been finally repulsed a quarter of an hour after Colonel Reid was wounded; Colonel Reid describes himself as having been "for some time" insensible on the ground after being hit, and when he became conscious he was carried to the rear, where he met Major Lawrence. It would seem, then, that the second attack must have been about failing, if it had not failed, when Colonel Reid asked Major Lawrence to send aid to Captain Dwyer's detachment, which was then "becoming hotly engaged with the enemy"; but Colonel Reid goes on to say that "up to this time the troops were well in hand, and were as steady as possible, and I made sure of success," which would be irreconcileable with Major Muter's account, if we did not remember that Major Muter was in front engaged in the action, and therefore cognizant of the facts, while Colonel Reid was in the rear after having been some time insensible. Again, Captain Shebbeare is clear that one reason for the *retirement* of No. 4 column was the running in of Captain Dwyer's men upon the right flank of No. 4 column, which allowed the enemy to work round to the rear; on the other hand, Lieutenant Manderson, who was with Captain Dwyer's party, is equally clear that as he was returning he met two Cashmere guns coming back from No. 4 column, and the native officer in command related how No. 4 had been repulsed. The opinion I form upon these statements (which are perhaps not more conflicting than those of officers engaged in different parts of a field usually are) is that the two engagements at Edgah and Kissengunge were raging simultaneously, and that the repulse of neither was long enough before the other to have any effect on the result, considering that they were nearly a mile apart. The loss of more than one-fourth of No. 4 column, as described by Major Muter, sufficiently accounts for its repulse. It was obviously too weak for the operation, and I should say this alone was the cause of its failure.

5. The third passage contains two statements which Major Lawrence objects to.

1st. That Major Muter was "the next senior officer" after Colonel Reid's withdrawal.

2nd. That Major Muter "withdrew the troops to their former posts."

It is now acknowledged by all that the next senior officer in the field on the occasion was Major R. Lawrence, who was commanding the main body of the Cashmere contingent, which formed Colonel Reid's "reserve"; and Colonel Reid states that, on recovering his senses after his wound, he called out for Major Lawrence, and meeting him one hundred yards over the bridge, gave over the command to him: therefore, by military usage, Major Muter could not be described as "the next senior officer," though in point of fact he was the senior officer of all those who were in front with the troops which formed the column of attack, and, that being the case, in an affair wherein minutes were hours, while two desperate attacks had crowded themselves into one quarter of an hour, been overwhelmingly repulsed, and followed by hopeless confusion, Major Muter might fitly have retired with the attacking column, at all events as far as the reserve, and there have left the real senior officer to resume the attack or not. But I do not consider that he could fitly have withdrawn from the field the column which he knew was not under his command. But it does not appear in these documents that Major Muter ever assumed the command of the troops in front, or organised the retirement. Captain Shebbeare describes "all the officers in front as agreeing among themselves, in the absence of a commander, to retire, as the attack was a failure, and as having reported what they had done to Major Lawrence, when they found him after recrossing the canal, knowing him to be the next in command to Colonel Reid, on which 'he,' *i.e.* Major Lawrence, confirmed the order, but shortly after ordered an advance, which he again countermanded almost immediately. When he reached the serai in the Subzee Mundi, he, at my suggestion, ordered me to occupy the Crow's Nest and the line reaching right up to the battery. These are distinct acts of command amounting to this, that the final relinquishment of the attack, and the retirement of the majority of the troops in No. 4 column 'to their former posts,' were really carried out under the orders of Major R. Lawrence, who was also the proper person to issue them. Captain Wriford states that on Colonel Reid being wounded he considered Major Lawrence in command, but getting no orders from either him or Major Muter, he thought both were *hors de combat*, and withdrew his men, on his own judgment, to Subzee Mundi, where he found that Major Muter was present, and resigned the command to him as senior officer, *and some little time after this* Major Lawrence came into the Subzee Mundi picquet, when he of course became senior." This tallies with Captain Mocatta's account that he was sent by Major Lawrence to the posts in rear to bring up the European troops again, who had clearly been withdrawn without his authority, and, as he seems at first to have judged, without necessity (though in that matter I cannot agree with him). Major Muter himself puts the above testimonies beyond doubt, for in reply to a question whether during the day he received any orders, directly or indirectly, from Major Lawrence, he says he has "some recollection of a requisition for European soldiers *long after* the men had been reposted in our old position"; therefore Major Lawrence must have kept the field "long after" Major Muter, and he must have had troops with him. He could not have been alone. This is, in other words, what Captain Boisragon stated, that "the native portion of the column, Ghoorkas, Guides, and Sikhs, were in the field as long as I was present, hotly engaged with the enemy," and he explained that he was in the field for upwards of an hour after Major Reid was wounded. Farther, Doctor Corbyn, in a letter to Major Lawrence, testifies that he "went into the Subzee Mundi serai, where Parker and myself were of great assistance to the wounded Europeans. Here I found Captain Muter, Wriford also I think, and a number of Europeans. You did not retire with the Cashmeres, I know, for nearly an hour afterwards." And this brings me to the difficulty which I judge from the papers, more than anything else, prevented Major Norman from modifying the passages in his narrative; I mean the difficulty of understanding how the Europeans, Ghoorkas, and Sikhs of distinguished regiments, who were in the column of attack, could be repulsed, and retreat to their former posts, while the Jummoo reserve, consisting of troops of inferior discipline and armament, still kept the field. It seemed to Major Norman to involve an incredible reproach to the column of attack. But having very carefully analysed these papers, and corrected my notions of the localities by a published plan of the "City and Cantonments of Delhi," and by interrogating Captain Boisragon, who was in the action, it seems to me quite clear that the two statements are perfectly reconcilable with the honour of both corps. As I understand it, Colonel Reid disposed the Jummoo reserve on his right rear. The attack failed from being totally inadequate, Colonel Reid fell and was removed. The confusion in the column of attack, in consequence of the repulse, and of the enemy following hotly up, was very great. The next senior officer being in the rear with the reserve, could not possibly give any timely orders, or know that Colonel Reid had been wounded. No orders were consequently issued for retiring in good order, and the officers at the head of the column agreed together to withdraw, and did so to the best of their ability. Major Muter and Captain Wriford reached Subzee Mundi with the majority of their men without even meeting Major Lawrence, and Captains Shebbeare and Boisragon, commanding the Guides and Ghoorkas, both fell in with Major Lawrence, and placed themselves under his orders. A new advance was thought possible but abandoned, and Captain Shebbeare's party was ordered to occupy certain posts. But Major Lawrence remained out with the Jummoo reserve and Captain Boisragon's men, and (as Captain Boisragon informs me) fragments of almost every detachment, European or native, that had made up No. 4 column, for the following up of the enemy after the repulse of the column was very hot, and it became indispensable to check them ; and this was effectually done by our broken parties and the reserve lining the banks of the canal and occupying the jungle on the right of the road, while Lieutenant Evan's guns continued to fire over their heads, and completed the check of the enemy. Things seem to have remained in this position for a couple of hours at least, till the firing ceased and both sides withdrew. Thus the Jummoo reserve never renewed the attack on Kissengunge after the repulse of No. 4 column, and, as I understand, does not pretend to have ever advanced to the point between the first and second breastworks, where the column had been repulsed, and in no way puts itself in invidious comparison with any of the other troops, but did remain in the field with numbers of native and some European soldiers of No. 4 column, exchanging a hot fire with the enemy, and losing of its own number forty-three killed and wounded.

While, therefore, it shared in the general failure of the column of which it was the reserve, I cannot see that it in any way contributed to that failure; and, on the contrary, it took its full share in covering the retreat. Some opinions are offered in the correspondence that it was useless to keep the troops out a moment longer than could be helped after the main object of the column had failed; but in this I connot concur, for every rebel sepoy held engaged at Kissengunge was a loss to the garrison in the city. The siege of Delhi has been often compared with the siege of Sebastopol, and I should think that No. 4 column was to the other three columns at Delhi much what the English at the "Redan" were to the French at the "Malakoff."

6. The whole of the present misunderstanding has arisen, as it seems to me, from Major Muter taking the irregular course (as he admits to Major Lawrence) of reporting direct to General Wilson instead of through Major Lawrence. Had he pursued the regular military course, his due share of credit as the senior remaining officer of the attacking column would have accrued to him; Major Lawrence would have appeared as having done the best with a command to which he succeeded when the day was lost; Major Muter's mistake as to the two divisions of the Cashmere contingent (of which he seems to have only now become aware) would have been corrected in time; and no blame would have been attached to that contingent for sharing in the general failure of the fourth column which the disparity of numbers and artillery rendered perfectly inevitable.

(Signed) HERBERT B. EDWARDES,

Commissioner and Superintendent.

July 1st, 1879.

APPENDIX B.

Since I wrote the remarks in the text, a case of neglect, as remarkable as that of Cooper of the 93rd, has been brought to my notice. It is very curious that the neglect in this case should apply to an officer also of the name of Cooper—a near relative, I am informed, of Richard Cooper of the 93rd. I extract the case from Colonel Pack's Memoirs, published in 1878.

"As dawn approached, it became known that the guns were not to open, and that instead of our waiting for the signal to attack after two hours' bombardment, we were to look for it shortly after the French assault on the Malakoff. The Brigadier (Yea) came across from the Quarries and took post at the extremity of the Boyaus, that he might there watch for the commencement of the action. . . .

"Whilst watching the Malakoff, probably a few minutes, the Rifles, stationed close to the Quarries as a covering party, having evidently mistaken one of the French rockets for the British signal, commenced firing from their hiding-places, when round shot dropping about from the Redan proved our red jackets were observed. The error of the coverers was great, and considerably annoyed the Brigadier, who, pointing to a flagstaff near the 8-gun battery, said, 'A flag will be hoisted there when Lord Raglan stands.' He added, 'That fire,' (alluding to the covering party of the Rifles) 'must be stopped. Somebody must go across the open: it is no use attempting to get through the trenches.'

"Moments like these try the mettle of men and prove of what they are made. No mere bravado answers; for that always fails when actual and perilous deeds of cool and deliberate courage have to be performed. Whoever volunteered to fulfil the Brigadier's mission knew he must go as it were with his life in his hand. Not only every step, but every inch of the distance between the trenches and the covering party was strewn with peril, and carrying the message and escaping with his life was not for an instant to be looked for.

"A momentary silence ensued. The fire from all arms was pounding away in every direction, and the service was very perilous. To cross the open and reach the Quarries we saw and knew exposure to the fire from the Malakoff was certain, and the able marksmen and the guns of the Redan were also to be encountered. The duty was seen to be so momentous that all hesitated to undertake it, not from fear, but from the feeling of all but certain failure. Brigadier Yea then repeated his desire, saying, 'Who will go?' Then there was another pause, when every soldier who heard his leader's request felt his heart beat with intense rapidity, and every mental energy of his mind awakened. For a few moments there was intense silence amongst us, and then quickly and nervously Captain Cooper, one of his aides-de-camp, answered, 'I will, Sir!' And out this gallant officer went.

"Springing over the trench, commencing with a quick walk, he increased his pace gradually till he ran. His eyes were fixed upon the Rifles, all eyes were upon him. All expected to see him fall; but Providence guarded him. He reached the Quarries, and stopped the fire, his life most probably preserved by this courageous act of gallantry, for the crowd and confusion at the opening of the miserably small trench whence the stormers issued were so great, he never could have rejoined his lamented chief had he gone by the way of the trenches.

"Yet, though many an officer and many a man have received the Victoria Cross for the common act of humanity—aiding or assisting to bring in a wounded officer or comrade under circumstances of danger—acts which most of us at the time they happened thought little about, and certainly never regarded them as deserving the designation of 'distinguished,' *for the above gallant act, setting an example of the highest devotion to the service of his Queen and country in the face of hundreds, this officer received no reward.*"* The officer in question was Captain Joshua Cooper, 7th Fusiliers.—*Sebastopol Trenches, and Five Months in Them*, by Colonel Reynell Pack, C.B., 7th Fusiliers.

* The italics are Colonel Pack's.

APPENDIX C.

Page 562 of text.

Lieutenant Conolly thus wrote to Captain Black, regarding his escape: "Such a scene of confusion I never saw; some sepoys firing at Bhíls, they shot seven poor wretches on the parade-ground, who, I declare, were only looking at the novel scene. During the day we halted. The first day we marched to ——, and a greater rabble never crossed country than our once smart legion; not a sepoy hardly saluted me. I was taken to Abbas Ali's tent at ——, and the infantry were a little behind, when a tremendous row commenced. Some Mínas made a rush at the carts; the infantry thought it was an attack; away went the cavalry to see to matters, cut up a few Bhíls, and, seeing no one else, pulled up to look about them. Another row, and rush towards where I was standing near my saddled horse. I can't say I was desperately alarmed, for all hope of life I had cast aside some hours before, when we marched. The rush towards me was caused by some amiable sepoys taking the opportunity to make a run at me. Abbas Ali and his men saw it, and were soon between us; but I cannot enter into details of self;

once again they attempted to get at me at Doola. What made them so mad was, that my strenuous attempts to seduce the cavalry had been made known to Mihrwan Sing, and he swore I should die. At Doola they had three or four rows—councils they called them—about me. At last, Mihrwan Sing and the other beauties, seeing Abbas Ali would not give me up, said I might go solus. Next morning, they sent again to say, no, I should not go. However, Abbas Ali and his men surrounded my charpoy all night; we none of us slept, and on the morning of the 27th, when the force was ready, the guns were loaded, the infantry shouldered arms, and I was brought up. I was told to ride to the front; poor Dokul Sing, the havildar-major, and some others, ran out blubbering; Abbas Ali and Abdul Ali, rode up on each side, made me low salaams, and told me to ride for it; that not a sowar should be allowed to interfere with my retreat. My three sowars, who, I have forgotten to say, had stuck to me as if I had been their brother since the very beginning, by a preconcerted plan, were ordered to see me off a little way. I could not help giving a farewell wave of the hand to the infantry in irony; they shouted and laughed, the band struck up, and that is the last I saw of the legion. I rode right in to Erinpoora with three sowars; I came straight here, and the people seemed ready to eat me with joy. The names of the three sowars are, Nusseeroodeen, second troop; Elahu Bux, third troop (the man who used to ride my grey); and Momin Khan, first troop. They left everything behind, and, I must say, are three as fine fellows as I wish to see. By-the-by, the cavalry said if I would agree to turn Mussulman, to a man they would follow me. Very kind of them. They offered me money when I was coming away, and also on the march. I took twenty rupees from Abbas Ali; now I wish I had taken my pay; they twice offered it. Now is our time, the legion is divided. Jawan Sing, golundaz, and his party, about seven other golundaz (gunners), will play the infantry a trick if they can. I have told Jawan Sing I will myself give him five hundred rupees if he breaks with the infantry. Abbas Ali, the havildar-major, and Abdul Ali, are in danger on my account, and they are kept with their men under the guns night and day. I feel most glad to think I did them as much harm as I could. Makdun Bux had a musket put to his breast for letting me ride with my sword on. I was a bone of contention. I have this morning sent a sharp kossid to Abbas Ali, telling him, for his own sake, to try and communicate with Mason, who, I believe, is at Pali, and to whom I have written to try and communicate with Abbas Ali."

ERRATA.

Page 48, lines 15 and 16 from foot, *for* "to the hospital on the ridge," *read* "to his own tent."

Page 237, line 14 from top, *for* "a rebel army," *read* "the rebel army."

Page 352, head-line, *for* "12th January," *read* "16th January."

Page 365, line 10 from foot, *for* "Bégam Koti," *read* "Bégam Kothi."

Page 416, line 8 from foot, *omit* "of Jones in Rohilkhand."

Page 427, note, line 3 from foot, *for* "Shanghai," *read* "Chinhai."

DIRECTIONS TO BINDER.

WORKS BY THE SAME AUTHOR.

In Demy 8vo., Price 20s., Cloth.

HISTORY OF THE INDIAN MUTINY, 1857–58.

Commencing from the close of the Second Volume of Sir John Kaye's History of the Sepoy War. By Colonel G. B. MALLESON, C.S.I. Vol. I. Contemporaneous with Sir John Kaye's third volume. London: W. H. Allen & Co. 1878.

"Colonel Malleson is executing, in a manner deserving marked commendation, the task he has set himself. His research is untiring, and his love of his subject amounts to a passion. The equitableness of his judgments will rarely be challenged. Praise and blame he distributes very freely indeed; but he is judicially careful, while awarding his judgments, to justify them to the full; and his discrimination of character, in introducing or dismissing the various actors whom he brings on the scene, is marked by equal sagacity and thoroughness. Though a warm eulogist of sterling worth and merit, he leans, unquestionably, to the side of lenity, when called upon, as he is, ever and anon, to arraign and stigmatize incompetence."—*The Nation* (New York).

"If the literary quality of the rest of the work be equal to that of this volume, Colonel Malleson's history will in that respect be a worthy sequel to Kaye's. The style is always strong and vigorous, and the treatment characterised by that ease which thorough familiarity with the subject alone can give. It is probable that some of Colonel Malleson's statements and criticisms will provoke controversy, for he is no punctilious respecter of persons or reputations, and gives fearless expression to his views. Throughout his volume, however, there is abundant evidence that he has spared no pains to get at the exact truth about every transaction he describes; and, though he is sometimes strong in condemnation, he is never ungenerous."—*Scotsman.*

In one Volume, Crown 8vo., Price 10s. 6d., Cloth.

STUDIES FROM GENOESE HISTORY. By Colonel G. B. MALLESON, C.S.I. London: Longmans. 1875.

"These studies are very pleasant and interesting reading, and are fraught with information and matter for reflection."—*Standard.*

"To the political student such a book as Colonel Malleson's is invaluable, and it is invaluable for just the same reasons as those which make the investigation of the Republics of Ancient Greece the best of all preliminary disciplines for the historian."—*Hour.*

"A whole series of general propositions of universal and eternal truth might be formulated from this little book of Colonel Malleson's on the subject of the Genoese constitutions, as to the nature of oligarchies—a form of Government impotent against democratic usurpation on the one hand, or individual aristocratic despotism on the other. Colonel Malleson has done well in preferring to give us rather a series of pictures of the salient points in Genoese history, than a mere methodical narrative or a succinct epitome. The incidents selected by him are thoroughly typical, and their grouping genuinely dramatic. The sketches of Jacopo Bonfadio and of the Doria are specimens of literary work of a high order.—*The World.*

April, 1879.

BOOKS, &c.,

ISSUED BY

MESSRS. WM. H. ALLEN & Co.,

Publishers & Literary Agents to the India Office,

COMPRISING

MISCELLANEOUS PUBLICATIONS IN GENERAL LITERATURE. DICTIONARIES, GRAMMARS, AND TEXT BOOKS IN EASTERN LANGUAGES, MILITARY WORKS, INCLUDING THOSE ISSUED BY THE GOVERNMENT. INDIAN AND MILITARY LAW. MAPS OF INDIA, &c.

In January and July of each year is published in 8vo., price 10*s*. 6*d*.,

THE INDIA LIST, CIVIL & MILITARY.

BY PERMISSION OF THE SECRETARY OF STATE FOR INDIA IN COUNCIL.

CONTENTS.

CIVIL.—Gradation Lists of Civil Service, Bengal, Madras and Bombay. Civil Annuitants. Legislative Council, Ecclesiastical Establishments, Educational, Public Works, Judicial, Marine, Medical, Land Revenue, Political, Postal, Police, Customs and Salt, Forest, Registration and Railway and Telegraph Departments, Law Courts, Surveys, &c., &c.

MILITARY.—Gradation List of the General and Field Officers (British and Local) of the three Presidencies, Staff Corps, Adjutants-General's and Quartermasters-General's Offices, Army Commissariat Departments, British Troops Serving in India (including Royal Artillery, Royal Engineers, Cavalry, Infantry, and Medical Department), List of Native Regiments, Commander-in-Chief and Staff, Garrison Instruction Staff, Indian Medical Department, Ordnance Departments, Punjab Frontier Force, Military Departments of the three Presidencies, Veterinary Departments, Tables showing the Distribution of the Army in India, Lists of Retired Officers of the three Presidencies.

HOME.—Departments of the Office of the Secretary of State, Coopers Hill College, List of Selected Candidates for the Civil and Forest Services, Indian Troop Service.

MISCELLANEOUS.—Orders of the Bath, Star of India, and St. Michael and St. George. Order of Precedence in India. Regulations for Admission to Civil Service. Regulations for Admission of Chaplains. Civil Leave Code and Supplements. Civil Service Pension Code—relating to the Covenanted and Uncovenanted Services. Rules for the Indian Medical Service. Furlough and Retirement Regulations of the Indian Army. Family Pension Fund. Staff Corps Regulations. Salaries of Staff Officers. Regulations for Promotion. English Furlough Pay.

Works issued from the India Office, and Sold by Wm. H. ALLEN & Co.

Tree and Serpent Worship;

Or, Illustrations of Mythology and Art in India in the First and Fourth Centuries after Christ, from the Sculptures of the Buddhist Topes at Sanchi and Amravati. Prepared at the India Museum, under the authority of the Secretary of State for India in Council. Second edition, Revised, Corrected, and in great part Re-written. By JAMES FERGUSSON, Esq., F.R.S., F.R.A.S. Super-royal 4to. 100 plates and 31 engravings, pp. 270. Price £5 5s.

Illustrations of Ancient Buildings in Kashmir.

Prepared at the Indian Museum under the authority of the Secretary of State for India in Council. From Photographs, Plans, and Drawings taken by Order of the Government of India. By HENRY HARDY COLE, LIEUT. R.E., Superintendent Archæological Survey of India, North-West Provinces. In One vol.; half-bound, Quarto. Fifty-eight plates. £3 10s.

The Illustrations in this work have been produced in Carbon from the original negatives, and are therefore permanent.

Pharmacopœia of India.

Prepared under the Authority of the Secretary of State for India. By EDWARD JOHN WARING, M.D. Assisted by a Committee appointed for the Purpose. 8vo. 6s.

Archælogical Survey of Western India.

Report of the First Season's Operations in the Belgâm and Kaladgi Districts. January to May, 1874. Prepared at the India Museum and Published under the Authority of the Secretary of State for India in Council By JAMES BURGESS, Author of the "Rock Temples of Elephanta," &c., &c., and Editor of "The Indian Antiquary." Half-bound. Quarto. 58 Plates and Woodcuts. £2 2s.

Adam W. (late of Calcutta) Theories of History.
8vo. 15s. (See page 27.)

Advice to Officers in India.
By JOHN McCOSH, M.D. Post 8vo. 8s.

Allen's Series.
1.—World We Live In. (See page 30.) 2s.
2.—Earth's History. (See page 6.) 2s.
3.—Geography of India. (See page 8.) 2s.
4.—2000 Examination Questions in Physical Geography. 2s.
5.—Hall's Trigonometry. (See page 9.) 2s.
6.—Wollaston's Elementary Indian Reader. 1s. (See page 29.)
7—Ansted's Elements of Physiography. 1s. 4d.

Analytical History of India.
From the earliest times to the Abolition of the East India Company in 1858. By ROBERT SEWELL, Madras Civil Service. Post 8vo. 8s.

*** The object of this work is to supply the want which has been felt by students for a condensed outline of Indian History which would serve at once to recall the memory and guide the eye, while at the same time it has been attempted to render it interesting to the general reader by preserving a medium between a bare analysis and a complete history.

Ancient and Mediæval India.
2 vols. 8vo. 30s. (See page 17.)

Anderson's (P.) English in Western India.
8vo. 14s.

Andrew's (W. P.) India and Her Neighbours,
With Two Maps. 8vo. 15s.

Ansted's (D. T.) Elements of Physiography.
For the use of Science Schools. Fcap. 8vo. 1s. 4d.

Ansted's (D. T.) Physical Geography.
5th Edition. With Maps. Crown 8vo 7s. (See page 23.)

Ansted's (D. T.) World We Live In.
Fcap 2s. 25th Thousand, with Illustrations. (See page 30.)

Ansted's (D. T.) Earth's History.
Fcap. 2s. (See page 6.)

Ansted's (D. T.)
Two Thousand Examination Questions in Physical Geography. pp. 180. Price 2s.

Ansted's (D. T.) Ionian Islands.
8vo. 8s. (See page 14.)

Ansted's (D. T.) and R. G. Latham's Channel Islands.
8vo. 16s. (See page 14.)

Ansted's (D. T.) Water, and Water Supply.
Chiefly with reference to the British Islands. — Surface Waters. 8vo. With Maps. 18s.

Archer's (Capt. J. H. Laurence) Commentaries on the Punjaub Campaign—1848-49. Crown 8vo. 8s. (See page 6.)

Armies of the Powers of Europe, The.
Their Strength and Organisation, &c., with an Account of some of the Famous Regiments, their Composition, &c., &c.; also an Account of the Navies of the several Powers. By Captain H. B. Stuart. (*In the press.*)

At Home in Paris.
By Blanchard Jerrold. 2 Vols. Post 8vo. 16s

Atterbury Memoirs, &c.
The Memoir and Correspondence of Francis Atterbury, Bishop of Rochester, with his distinguished contemporaries. Compiled chiefly from the Atterbury and Stuart Papers. By Folkestone Williams, Author of "Lives of the English Cardinals," &c., 2 vols. 8vo. 14s.

Authors at Work.
By Charles Pebody. Post 8vo. 10s. 6d.

Bengal Artillery.
A Memoir of the Services of the Bengal Artillery from the formation of the Corps. By the late Capt. E. Buckle, Assist.-Adjut. Gen. Ben. Art. Edit. by Sir J. W. Kaye. 8vo. Lond. 1852. 10s.

Bernays, (Dr. A. J.) Students' Chemistry.
Crown 8vo. 5s. 6d. (See page 26.)

Binning's (R. M.) Travels in Persia, &c.
2 vols. 8vo. 16s.

Birth of the War God.
A Poem. By Kalidasa. Translated from the Sanscrit into English Verse. By Ralph T. H. Griffith. 5s.

Blanchard's (S.) Yesterday and To-day in India.
Post 8vo. 6s. (See page 30.)

Blenkinsopp's (Rev. E. L.) Doctrine of Development
In the Bible and in the Church. 2nd edit. 12mo. 6s. (See page 6.)

Boileau (Major-General J. T.)
A New and Complete Set of Traverse Tables, showing the Differences of Latitude and the Departures to every Minute of the Quadrant and to Five Places of Decimals. Together with

a Table of the lengths of each Degree of Latitude and corresponding Degree of Longitude from the Equator to the Poles; with other Tables useful to the Surveyor and Engineer. Fourth Edition, thoroughly revised and corrected by the Author. Royal 8vo. 12s. London, 1876.

Boulger (D. C.) The Life of Yakoob Beg, Athalik Ghazi and Badaulet, Ameer of Kashgar. 8vo. With Map and Appendix. 16s.

Boulger (D. C.) England and Russia in Central Asia. With Appendices and Two Maps, one being the latest Russian Official Map of Central Asia. 2 vols. 8vo. 38s.

Bowring's Flowery Scroll.
A Chinese Novel. Translated and Illustrated with Notes by Sir J. Bowring, late H.B.M. Plenipo. China. Post 8vo. 10s. 6d.

Bradshaw (John) LL.D. The Poetical Works of John Milton, with Notes, explanatory and philological. 2 vols. post 8vo. 12s. 6d.

Brandis' Forest Flora of North-West and Central India.
Text and plates. £2 18s. (See page 8.)

Briggs' (Gen. J.) India and Europe Compared.
Post 8vo. 7s.

Browne's (J. W.) Hardware; How to Buy it for Foreign Markets. 8vo. 10s. 6d. (See page 9.)

Canal and Culvert Tables, based on the Formula of Kutter, under a Modified Classification, with Explanatory Text and Examples. By Lowis D'A. Jackson, A.M.I.C.E., author of "Hydraulic Manual and Statistics," &c. Roy. 8vo. 28s.

Catholic Doctrine of the Atonement.
An Historical Inquiry into its Development in the Church, with an Introduction on the Principle of Theological Development. By H. Nutcombe Oxenham, M.A. 2nd Edit. 8vo. 10s. 6d.

"It is one of the ablest and probably one of the most charmingly written treatises on the subject which exists in our language."—*Times.*

Celebrated Naval and Military Trials.
By Peter Burke, Serjeant-at-Law. Author of "Celebrated Trials connected with the Aristocracy." Post 8vo. 10s. 6d.

Central Asia (Sketches of).
By A. Vambery. 8vo 16s. (See page 28.)

Cochrane, (John) Hindu Law. 20s. (See page 13.)

Commentaries on the Punjaub Campaign 1848-49, including some additions to the History of the Second Sikh War, from original sources. By Capt. J. H. LAWRENCE-ARCHER, Bengal H. P. Crown 8vo. 8s.

Cruise of H.M.S. "Galatea,"
Captain H.R.H. the Duke of Edinburgh, K.G., in 1867—1868. By the REV. JOHN MILNER, B.A., Chaplain; and OSWALD W. BRIERLY. Illustrated by a Photograph of H.R.H. the Duke of Edinburgh; and by Chromo-Lithographs and Graphotypes from Sketches taken on the spot by O. W. BRIERLY. 8vo. 16s.

Cyprus: Historical and Descriptive.
Adapted from the German of Herr FRANZ VON LÖHER. With much additional matter. By Mrs. A. BATSON JOYNER. Crown 8vo. With 2 Maps. 10s. 6d

Danvers (Fred. Chas.) On Coal.
With Reference to Screening, Transport, &c 8vo. 10s. 6d.

Doctrine of Development in the Bible and in the Church.
By REV. E. L. BLENKINSOPP, M A., Rector of Springthorp. 2nd edition. 12mo. 6s.

Doran (Dr. J.) Annals of the English Stage.
Post 8vo. 6s. (See p. 26.)

Down by the Drawle.
By MAJOR A. F. P. HARCOURT, Bengal Staff Corps, author of "Kooloo, Lahoul, and Spiti," "The Shakespeare Argosy," &c. 2 Vols. crown 8vo. 21s.

Drain of Silver to the East,
And the Currency of India. By W. NASSAU LEES. Post 8vo. 8s.

Drury.—The Useful Plants of India,
With Notices of their chief value in Commerce, Medicine, and the Arts. By COLONEL HEBER DRURY. Second Edition, with Additions and Corrections. Royal 8vo. 16s.

Earth's History,
Or, First Lessons in Geology. For the use of Schools and Students. By D. T. ANSTED. Third Thousand. Fcap. 8vo. 2s.

East India Calculator,
By T. THORNTON. 8vo. London, 1823. 10s.

Edinburgh (The Duke of) Cruise of the "Galatea."
With Illustrations. 8vo. 16s.

Edwards' (H. S.) Russians at Home.
With Illustrations. Post 8vo. 6s. (See page 25.)

Edwards' (H. S.) History of the Opera.
2 Vols., 8vo. 10s. 6d. (See page 10.)

Elementary Mathematics.
A Course of Elementary Mathematics for the use of candidates for admission into either of the Military Colleges; of applicants for appointments in the Home or Indian Civil Services; and of mathematical students generally. By Professor J. R. YOUNG. In one closely-printed volume. 8vo., pp. 648. 12s.

"In the work before us he has digested a complete Elementary Course, by aid of his long experience as a teacher and writer; and he has produced a very useful book. Mr. Young has not allowed his own taste to rule the distribution, but has adjusted his parts with the skill of a veteran."—*Athenæum.*

English Cardinals.
The Lives of the English Cardinals, from Nicholas Breakspeare (Pope Adrien IV.) to Thomas Wolsey, Cardinal Legate. With Historical Notices of the Papal Court. By FOLKESTONE WILLIAMS. In 2 vols. 14s.

English Homes in India.
By MRS. KEATINGE. Part I.—The Three Loves. Part II.—The Wrong Turning. Two vols., Post 8vo. 16s.

Entombed Alive, and other Songs and Ballads. (From the Chinese.) By GEORGE CARTER STENT, M.R.A.S., of the Chinese Imperial Maritime Customs Service, author of "Chinese and English Vocabulary," "Chinese and English Pocket Dictionary," "The Jade Chaplet," &c. Crown 8vo. With four Illustrations. 9s.

Final French Struggles in India and on the Indian Seas.
Including an Account of the Capture of the Isles of France and Bourbon, and Sketches of the most eminent Foreign Adventurers in India up to the period of that Capture. With an Appendix containing an Account of the Expedition from India to Egypt in 1801. By Colonel G. B. MALLESON, C.S.I. Crown 8vo. 10s. 6d.

First Age of Christianity and the Church (The).
By John Ignatius Döllinger, D.D., Professor of Ecclesiastical History in the University of Munich, &c., &c. Translated from the German by Henry Nutcombe Oxenham, M.A., late Scholar of Baliol College, Oxford. Third Edition. 2 vols. Crown 8vo. 18s.

Forbes (Dr. Duncan) History of Chess.
8vo. 7s. 6d. (See page 10.)

Forest Flora of North-Western and Central India.
By Dr. Brandis, Inspector General of Forests to the Government of India. Text and Plates. £2 18s.

Franz Schubert.
A Musical Biography, from the German of Dr. Heinrich Kreisle von Hellborn. By Edward Wilberforce, Esq., Author of "Social Life in Munich." Post 8vo. 6s.

Gazetteers of India.
Thornton, 4 vols., 8vo. £2 16s.
,, 8vo. 21s.
,, (N.W.P., &c.) 2 vols., 8vo. 25s.

Gazetteer of Southern India.
With the Tenasserim Provinces and Singapore. Compiled from original and authentic sources. Accompanied by an Atlas, including plans of all the principal towns and cantonments. Royal 8vo. with 4to. Atlas. £3 3s.

Gazetteer of the Punjaub, Affghanistan, &c.
Gazetteer of the Countries adjacent to India, on the north-west, including Scinde, Affghanistan, Beloochistan, the Punjaub, and the neighbouring States. By Edward Thornton, Esq. 2 vols. 8vo. £1 5s.

Geography of India.
Comprising an account of British India, and the various states enclosed and adjoining. Fcap. pp. 250. 2s.

Geological Papers on Western India.
Including Cutch, Scinde, and the south-east coast of Arabia. To which is added a Summary of the Geology of India generally. Edited for the Government by Henry J. Carter, Assistant Surgeon, Bombay Army. Royal 8vo. with folio Atlas of maps and plates; half-bound. £2 2s.

German Life and Manners
As seen in Saxony. With an account of Town Life—Village Life—Fashionable Life—Married Life—School and University Life, &c. Illustrated with Songs and Pictures of the Student Customs at the University of Jena. By Henry Mayhew, 2 vols. 8vo., with numerous illustrations. 18s.

A Popular Edition of the above. With illustrations. Cr. 8vo. 7s.
"Full of original thought and observation, and may be studied with profit by both German and English—especially by the German." *Athenæum.*

Glyn's (A. C.) Civilization in the 5th Century.
2 vols. post 8vo. £1 1s.

Goldstucker (Dr.) The Miscellaneous Essays of.
With a Memoir (*In the press.*)

Grady's (S. G.) Mohamedan Law of Inheritance & Contract.
8vo. 14s. (See page 13.)

Grady's (S. G.) Institutes of Menu.
8vo. 12s. (See page 13.)

Griffith's Ralph (T. H.) Birth of the War God.
8vo. 5s. (See page 4.)

Hall's Trigonometry.
The Elements of Plane and Spherical Trigonometry. With an Appendix, containing the solution of the Problems in Nautical Astronomy. For the use of Schools. By the Rev. T. G. Hall, M.A., Professor of Mathematics in King's College, London. 12mo. 2s.

Hamilton's Hedaya.
A new edition, with the obsolete passages omitted, and a copious Index added by S. G. Grady. 8vo. £1 15s.

Handbook of Reference to the Maps of India.
Giving the Lat. and Long. of places of note. 18mo. 3s. 6d.
**** This will be found a valuable Companion to Messrs. Allen & Co.'s Maps of India.*

Hardware; How to Buy it for Foreign Markets.
By, J. Wilson Browne. (See page 5.)
This is the most complete Guide to the Hardware Trade yet brought out; comprising all the principal Gross Lists in general use, with Illustrations and Descriptions. 8vo. 10s. 6d.

Hedaya.
Translated from the Arabic by Walter Hamilton. *A New Edition*, with Index by S. G. Grady 8vo. £1. 15s.

Henry VIII.
An Historical Sketch as affecting the Reformation in England. By Charles Hastings Collette. Post 8vo. 6s.

Hindu Law.
By Sir Thomas Strange. 2 vols. Royal 8vo., 1830. 24s. (See page 13.)

Historical Results
Deducible from Recent Discoveries in Affghanistan. By H. T. Prinsep. 8vo. Lond. 1844. 15s.

Histories of India.
Mill, 9 vols., cr. 8vo. £2 10s. (See page 22.)
Thornton, 6 vols., 8vo. £2 8s. (See page 27.)
Thornton, 1 vol., 8vo. 12s. (See page 27.)
Trotter, 2 vols., 8vo. 32s. (See page 28.)
Sewell (Analytical) Crown 8vo. 8s. (See page 3.)
Owen, India on the Eve of the British Conquest. 8s. (See page 22.)

History of the Indian Mutiny, 1857-1858. Vol. 1.
Commencing from the close of the Second Volume of Sir John Kaye's History of the Sepoy War. By COLONEL G. B. MALLESON, C S.I. 8vo. With Map. £1. Vol. 2 (*In the press*).

History of Civilization in the Fifth Century.
Translated by permission from the French of A. Frederic Ozanam, late Professor of Foreign Literature to the Faculty of Letters at Paris. By ASHBY C. GLYN, B.A., of the Inner Temple, Barrister-at-Law. 2 vols., post 8vo. £1 1s.

History of Chess,
From the time of the Early Invention of the Game in India, till the period of its establishment in Western and Central Europe. By DUNCAN FORBES, LL D. 8vo. 7s. 6d.

History of the Opera,
From Monteverde to Donizetti. By H. SUTHERLAND EDWARDS Second edition. 2 vols., Post 8vo. 10s. 6d.

History of the Punjaub,
And of the Rise, Progress, and Present Condition of the Sikhs. By T. THORNTON. 2 Vols. Post 8vo. 8s.

Horses of the Sahara, and the Manners of the Desert.
By E. DAUMAS, General of the Division Commanding at Bordeaux, Senator, &c , &c. With Commentaries by the Emir Abd-el-Kadir (Authorized Edition). 8vo. 6s.

"We have rarely read a work giving a more picturesque and, at the same time, practical account of the manners and customs of a people, than this book on the Arabs and their horses."—*Edinburgh Courant.*

Hough (Lieut.-Col. W.) Precedents in Military Law.
8vo. cloth. 25s.

Hughes's (Rev. T. P.) Notes on Muhammadanism.
Second Edition, Revised and Enlarged. Fcap. 8vo. 6s.

Hydraulic Manual and Working Tables, Hydraulic and Indian Meteorological Statistics. Published under the patronage of the Right Honourable the Secretary of State for India. By LOWIS D'A JACKSON. 8vo. 28s.

Illustrated Horse Doctor.

Being an Accurate and Detailed Account, accompanied by more than 400 Pictorial Representations, characteristic of the various Diseases to which the Equine Race are subjected; together with the latest Mode of Treatment, and all the requisite Prescriptions written in Plain English. By EDWARD MAYHEW, M.R.C.V.S. 8vo. 18s. 6d.

CONTENTS.—The Brain and Nervous System.—The Eyes.—The Mouth.—The Nostrils.—The Throat.—The Chest and its contents.—The Stomach, Liver, &c.—The Abdomen.—The Urinary Organs.—The Skin.—Specific Diseases.—Limbs.—The Feet.—Injuries.—Operations.

"The book contains nearly 600 pages of valuable matter, which reflects great credit on its author, and, owing to its practical details, the result of deep scientific research, deserves a place in the library of medical, veterinary, and non-professional readers."—*Field.*

"The book furnishes at once the bane and the antidote, as the drawings show the horse not only suffering from every kind of disease, but in the different stages of it, while the alphabetical summary at the end gives the cause, symptoms and treatment of each."—*Illustrated London News.*

Illustrated Horse Management.

Containing descriptive remarks upon Anatomy, Medicine, Shoeing, Teeth, Food, Vices, Stables; likewise a plain account of the situation, nature, and value of the various points; together with comments on grooms, dealers, breeders, breakers, and trainers; Embellished with more than 400 engravings from original designs made expressly for this work. By E. MAYHEW. A new Edition, revised and improved by J. I. LUPTON, M.R.C.V.S. 8vo. 12s.

CONTENTS.—The body of the horse anatomically considered. PHYSIC.—The mode of administering it, and minor operations. SHOEING.—Its origin, its uses, and its varieties. THE TEETH.—Their natural growth, and the abuses to which they are liable.

FOOD.—The fittest time for feeding, and the kind of food which the horse naturally consumes. The evils which are occasioned by modern stables. The faults inseparable from stables. The so-called "incapacitating vices," which are the results of injury or of disease. Stables as they should be. GROOMS.—Their prejudices, their injuries, and their duties. POINTS.—Their relative importance and where to look for their development. BREEDING.—Its inconsistencies and its disappointments. BREAKING AND TRAINING.—Their errors and their results.

India Directory (The).
For the Guidance of Commanders of Steamers and Sailing Vessels. Founded upon the Work of the late CAPTAIN JAMES HORSBURGH, F.R.S.

PART I.—The East Indies, and Interjacent Ports of Africa and South America. Revised, Extended, and Illustrated with Charts of Winds, Currents, Passages, Variation, and Tides. By COMMANDER ALFRED DUNDAS TAYLOR, F.R.G.S., Superintendent of Marine Surveys to the Government of India. £1 18s.

PART II.—The China Sea, with the Ports of Java, Australia and Japan and the Indian Archipelago Harbours, as well as those of New Zealand. Illustrated with Charts of the Winds, Currents, Passages, &c. By the same. (*In the Press.*)

India and Her Neighbours.
By W. P. ANDREW. 8vo. With 2 Maps. 15s.

Indian Administration.
By H G. KEENE. Post 8vo. 5s.

The India List, Civil and Military,
Containing Names of all Officers employed by the Indian Government, including those of the Public Works, Educational, Political, Postal, Police, Customs, Forests, Railway and Telegraphs Departments, with Rules for Admission to these Services, Furlough Rules, Retiring Pensions, Staff Corps Regulations and Salaries, &c., with an Index. Issued in January and July of each year, by permission of the Secretary of State for India in Council. 8vo. 10s. 6d.

Indian Code of Civil Procedure.
In the Form of Questions and Answers. With Explanatory and Illustrative Notes. By ANGELO J. LEWIS. 12s. 6d.

Indian Criminal Law and Procedure,
Including the Procedure in the High Courts, as well as that in the Courts not established by Royal Charter; with Forms of Charges and Notes on Evidence, illustrated by a large number of English Cases, and Cases decided in the High Courts of India; and an APPENDIX of selected Acts passed by the Legislative Council relating to Criminal matters. By M. H. STARLING, ESQ., LL.B. & F. B. CONSTABLE, M.A. Third edition. 8vo. £2 2s.

Indian Penal Code.
In the Form of Questions and Answers. With Explanatory and Illustrative Notes. By ANGELO J. LEWIS. 7s. 6d.

Indian and Military Law.

Mahommedan Law of Inheritance, &c. A Manual of the Mahommedan Law of Inheritance and Contract; comprising the Doctrine of the Soonee and Sheea Schools, and based upon the text of Sir H. W. MACNAGHTEN's Principles and Precedents, together with the Decisions of the Privy Council and High Courts of the Presidencies in India. For the use of Schools and Students. By STANDISH GROVE GRADY, Barrister-at-Law, Reader of Hindoo, Mahommedan, and Indian Law to the Inns of Court. 8vo. 14s.

Hedaya, or Guide, a Commentary on the Mussulman Laws, translated by order of the Governor-General and Council of Bengal. By CHARLES HAMILTON. Second Edition, with Preface and Index by STANDISH GROVE GRADY. 8vo. £1 15s.

Institutes of Menu in English. The Institutes of Hindu Law or the Ordinances of Menu, according to Gloss of Collucca. Comprising the Indian System of Duties, Religious and Civil, verbally translated from the Original, with a Preface by SIR WILLIAM JONES, and collated with the Sanscrit Text by GRAVES CHAMNEY HAUGHTON, M.A., F.R.S., Professor of Hindu Literature in the East India College. New edition, with Preface and Index by STANDISH G. GRADY, Barrister-at-Law, and Reader of Hindu, Mahommedan, and Indian Law to the Inns of Court. 8vo., cloth. 12s.

Indian Code of Criminal Procedure. Being Act X of 1872, Passed by the Governor-General of India in Council on the 25th of April, 1872. 8vo. 12s.

Indian Code of Civil Procedure. In the form of Questions and Answers, with Explanatory and Illustrative Notes. By ANGELO J. LEWIS, Barrister-at-law. 12mo. 12s. 6d.

Indian Penal Code. In the Form of Questions and Answers. With Explanatory and Illustrative Notes. BY ANGELO J. LEWIS, Barrister-at-Law. Post 8vo. 7s. 6d.

Hindu Law. Principally with reference to such portions of it as concern the Administration of Justice in the Courts in India. By SIR THOMAS STRANGE, late Chief Justice of Madras. 2 vols. Royal 8vo., 1830. 24s.

Hindu Law. Defence of the Daya Bhaga. Notice of the Case on Prosoono Coomar Tajore's Will. Judgment of the Judicial Committee of the Privy Council. Examination of such Judgment. By JOHN COCHRANE, Barrister-at-Law. Royal 8vo. 20s.

Law and Customs of Hindu Castes, within the Dekhan Provinces subject to the Presidency of Bombay, chiefly affecting Civil Suits. By ARTHUR STEELE. Royal 8vo. £1 1s.

Chart of Hindu Inheritance. With an Explanatory Treatise, By ALMARIC RUMSEY. 8vo. 6s. 6d.

Manual of Military Law. For all ranks of the Army, Militia and Volunteer Services. By Colonel J. K. Pipon, Assist. Adjutant General at Head Quarters, & J. F. Collier, Esq., of the Inner Temple, Barrister-at-Law. Third and Revised Edition. Pocket size. 5s.

Precedents in Military Law; including the Practice of Courts-Martial; the Mode of Conducting Trials; the Duties of Officers at Military Courts of Inquests, Courts of Inquiry, Courts of Requests, &c., &c. The following are a portion of the Contents:—

1. Military Law. 2. Martial Law. 3. Courts-Martial. 4. Courts of Inquiry. 5. Courts of Inquest. 6. Courts of Request. 7. Forms of Courts-Martial. 8. Precedents of Military Law. 9. Trials of Arson to Rape (Alphabetically arranged.) 10. Rebellions. 11. Riots. 12. Miscellaneous. By Lieut.-Col. W. Hough, late Deputy Judge-Advocate-General, Bengal Army, and Author of several Works on Courts-Martial. One thick 8vo. vol. 25s.

The Practice of Courts Martial. By Hough & Long. Thick 8vo. London, 1825. 26s.

Indian Infanticide.
Its Origin, Progress, and Suppression. By John Cave-Brown, M.A. 8vo. 5s.

Indian Wisdom,
Or Examples of the Religious, Philosophical and Ethical Doctrines of the Hindus. With a brief History of the Chief Departments of Sanscrit Literature, and some account of the Past and Present Condition of India, Moral and Intellectual. By Monier Williams, M.A., Boden Professor of Sanscrit in the University of Oxford. Third Edition. 8vo. 15s.

Ionian Islands in 1863.
By Professor D. T. Ansted, M.A., F.R.S., &c. 8vo., with Maps and Cuts. 8s.

Jackson's (Lowis D'A.) Hydraulic Manual and Working Tables, Hydraulic and Indian Meteorological Statistics. 8vo. 28s. (See page 10.)

Jackson (Lowis D'A.) Canal and Culvert Tables. Roy. 8vo. 28s. (See page 5.)

Japan, the Amoor and the Pacific.
With notices of other Places, comprised in a Voyage of Circumnavigation in the Imperial Russian Corvette *Rynda*, in 1858—1860. By Henry A. Tilley. Eight Illustrations. 8vo. 16s.

Jersey, Guernsey, Alderney, Sark, &c.
The Channel Islands. Containing: Part I.—Physical Geography. Part II.—Natural History. Part III.—Civil History. Part IV.—Economics and Trade. By David Thomas

ANSTED, M.A., F.R.S., and ROBERT GORDON LATHAM, M.A., M.D., F.R.S. New and Cheaper Edition in one handsome 8vo. Volume, with 72 Illustrations on Wood by Vizetelly, Loudon, Nicholls, and Hart; with Map. 16s.

"This is a really valuable work. A book which will long remain the standard authority on the subject. No one who has been to the Channel Islands, or who purposes going there will be insensible of its value."—*Saturday Review.*

"It is the produce of many hands and every hand a good one."

Jerrold's (Blanchard) at Home in Paris.
2 Vols. Post 8vo. 16s.

Kaye (Sir J. W.) The Sepoy War in India. (See page 25.)
Vol. 1. 18s.
Vol. 2, £1.
Vol. 3. £1.

Kaye (Sir J. W.) History of the War in Affghanistan.
New edition. 3 Vols. Crown 8vo. £1. 6s.

Kaye (Sir J. W.) H. St. G. Tucker's Life and Correspondence.
8vo. 10s.

Kaye's (Sir J. W.) Memorials of Indian Governments.
By H. ST. GEORGE TUCKER. 8vo. 10s.

Keene's (H. G.) Mogul Empire.
8vo. 10s. 6d. (See page 22.)

Keene's (H. G.) Administration in India.
Post 8vo. 9s.

Kenneth Trelawny.
By ALEC FEARON. Author of "Touch not the Nettle." 2 vols. Crown 8vo. 21s.

Lady Morgan's Memoirs.
Autobiography, Diaries and Correspondence. 2 Vols. 8vo., with Portraits. 18s.

Latham's (Dr. R. G.) Nationalities of Europe.
2 Vols. 8vo. 12s. (See page 22.)

Latham's (Dr. R. G.) Russian and Turk,
From a Geographical, Ethnological, and Historical Point of View. 8vo. 18s.

Law and Customs of Hindu Castes,
By ARTHUR STEELE. Royal 8vo. £1. 1s. (See page 13.)

Lee (Rev. F. G., D.C.L.) The Words from the Cross: Seven Sermons for Lent, Passion-Tide, and Holy Week. Third edition revised. Fcap. 3s. 6d.

Lee's (Dr. W. N.) Drain of Silver to the East.
Post 8vo. 8s.

Lewin's Wild Races of the South Eastern Frontier of India.
Including an Account of the Loshai Country. Post 8vo. 10s. 6d.

Lewis's (A. J.) Indian Penal Code.
Post 8vo. 7s. 6d. (See page 12.)

Lewis's Indian Code of Civil Procedure.
Post 8vo. 12s 6d. (See page 12.)

Leyden and Erskine's Baber.
Memoirs of Zehir-ed-Din Muhammed Baber, Emperor of Hindustan, written by himself in the Jaghatai Turki, and translated partly by the late John Leyden, Esq., M.D., and partly by William Erskine, Esq., with Notes and a Geographical and Historical Introduction, together with a Map of the Countries between the Oxus and Jaxartes, and a Memoir regarding its construction. By Charles Waddington, of the East India Company's Engineers. 4to. Lond. 1826. £1 5s.

Liancourt's and Pincott's Primitive and Universal Laws of the Formation and development of language; a Rational and Inductive System founded on the Natural Basis of Onomatops. 8vo. *12s. 6d.*

Lockwood's (Ed.) Natural History, Sport and Travel.
Crown 8vo. With numerous Illustrations. 9s.

McBean's (S.) England, Egypt, Palestine & India by Railway.
Popularly Explained. Crown 8vo., with a coloured Map. 4s.

MacGregor's (Col. C. M.) Narrative of a Journey through the Province of Khorassan and on the N. W. Frontier of Afghanistan in 1875. By Colonel C. M. MacGregor, C.S.I., C.I.E., Bengal Staff Corps. 2 vols. 8vo. With map and numerous illustrations. 30s.

Mahommedan Law of Inheritance and Contract.
By Standish Grove Grady, Barrister-at-Law. 8vo. 14s. (See page 13.)

Malleson's (Col. G. B.) Final French Struggles in India.
Crown 8vo. 10s. 6d. (See page 7.)

Malleson's (Col. G. B.) History of the Indian Mutiny, 1857–1858, commencing from the close of the Second Volume of Sir John Kaye's History of the Sepoy War. Vol. I. 8vo. With Map. £1.

Malleson's (Col. G. B.) History of Afghanistan, from the Earliest Period to the Outbreak of the War of 1878. 8vo. With Map. 18s.

Manning (Mrs.) Ancient and Mediæval India.
Being the History, Religion, Laws, Caste, Manners and Customs, Language, Literature, Poetry, Philosophy, Astronomy, Algebra, Medicine, Architecture, Manufactures, Commerce, &c., of the Hindus, taken from their writings. Amongst the works consulted and gleaned from may be named the Rig Veda, Sama Veda, Vajur Veda, Sathapatha Brahmana, Baghavat Gita, The Puranas, Code of Menu, Code of Yajna-valkya, Mitakshara, Daya Bagha, Mahabharata, Atriya, Charaka, Susruta, Ramayana, Raghu Vansa, Bhattikavia, Sakuntala Vikramorvasi, Malali and Madhava, Mudra Rakshasa, Retnavali, Kumara Sambhava, Prabodah, Chandrodaya, Megha Duta, Gita Govinda, Panchatantra, Hitopadesa, Katha Sarit, Sagara, Ketala, Panchavinsati, Dasa Kumara Charita, &c. By Mrs. Manning, with Illustrations. 2 vols., 8vo. 30s.

Manual of Military Law.
By Colonel J. K. Pipon, and J. F. Collier, Esq., of the Inner Temple, Barrister-at-Law. 5s.

Mayhew's (Edward) Illustrated Horse Doctor.
8vo. 18s. 6d (See page 11.)

Mayhew's (Edward) Illustrated Horse Management.
New edit. By J. I. Lupton. 8vo. 12s. (See page 11.)

Mayhew's (Henry) German Life and Manners.
2 vols., 8vo. 18s.

Also a cheaper edition, Post 8vo. 7s. (See page 8.)

Max Muller's Rig-Veda-Sanhita.
The Sacred Hymns of the Brahmins; together with the Commentary of Savanacharya. Published under the Patronage of the Right Honourable the Secretary of State for India in Council. 6 vols., 4to. £2 10s. per volume.

Meadow's (T.) Notes on China.
8vo. 9s.

Military Works—chiefly issued by the Government.
Field Exercises and Evolutions of Infantry. Pocket edition, 1s.
Queen's Regulations and Orders for the Army. Corrected to 1874. 8vo. 3s. 6d. Interleaved, 5s. 6d. Pocket Edition, 1s.

Musketry Regulations, as used at Hythe. 1s.

Dress Regulations for the Army. 1875. 1s. 6*d*.

Infantry Sword Exercise. 1875. 6d.

Infantry Bugle Sounds. 6d.

Handbook of Battalion Drill. By Lieut. H. C. SLACK. 2s; or with Company Drill, 2s. 6d.

Handbook of Brigade Drill. By Lieut. H. C. SLACK. 3s.

Red Book for Sergeants. By WILLIAM BRIGHT, Colour-Sergeant, 37th Middlesex R.V. 1s.

Handbook of Company Drill; also of Skirmishing, Battalion, and Shelter Trench Drill. By Lieut. CHARLES SLACK. 1s.

Elementary and Battalion Drill. Condensed and Illustrated, together with duties of Company Officers, Markers, &c., in Battalion By Captain MALTON. 2s. 6d.

Cavalry Regulations. For the Instruction, Formations, and Movements of Cavalry. Royal 8vo. 4s. 6d.

Cavalry Sword, Carbine, Pistol and Lance Exercises, together with Field Gun Drill. Pocket Edition. 1s.

Manual of Artillery Exercises, 1873. 8vo. 5s.

Manual of Field Artillery Exercises. 1877. 3s.

Standing Orders for Royal Artillery. 8vo, 3s.

Principles and Practice of Modern Artillery. By Lt.-Col. C. H. OWEN, R.A. 8vo. Illustrated. 15s.

Artillerist's Manual and British Soldiers' Compendium. By Major F. A. GRIFFITHS. 11th Edition. 5s.

Compendium of Artillery Exercises—Smooth Bore, Field, and Garrison Artillery for Reserve Forces. By Captain J. M. McKenzie. 3s. 6d.

Principles of Gunnery. By JOHN T. HYDE, M.A., late Professor of Fortification and Artillery, Royal Indian Military College, Addiscombe. Second edition, revised and enlarged. With many Plates and Cuts, and Photograph of Armstrong Gun. Royal 8vo. 14s.

Notes on Gunnery. By Captain Goodeve. Revised Edition. 1s.

Text Book of the Construction and Manufacture of Rifled Ordnance in the British Service. By STONEY & JONES. Second Edition. Paper, 3s. 6d., Cloth, 4s. 6d.

Handbooks of the 9, 16, and 64-Pounder R. M. L. Converted Guns. 6d. each.

Handbook of the 9 and 10-inch R. M. L. Guns. 6d. each.

Handbook of 40-Pounder B. L. Gun. 6*d*.

Handbooks of 9-inch Rifle Muzzle Loading Guns of 12 tons, and the 10-inch gun of 18 tons. 6d. each.

Treatise on Fortification and Artillery. By Major Hector Straith. Revised and re-arranged by Thomas Cook, R.N., by John T. Hyde, M.A. 7th Edition. Royal 8vo. Illustrated and Four Hundred Plans, Cuts, &c. £2 2s.

Military Surveying and Field Sketching. The Various Methods of Contouring, Levelling, Sketching without Instruments, Scale of Shade, Examples in Military Drawing, &c., &c., &c. As at present taught in the Military Colleges. By Major W. H. Richards, 55th Regiment, Chief Garrison Instructor in India, Late Instructor in Military Surveying, Royal Military College, Sandhurst. Second Edition, Revised and Corrected. 12s.

Treatise on Military Surveying; including Sketching in the Field, Plan-Drawing, Levelling, Military Reconnaissance, &c. By Lieut.-Col. Basil Jackson, late of the Royal Staff Corps. The Fifth Edition. 8vo. Illustrated by Plans, &c. 14s.

Instruction in Military Engineering. Vol. I., Part III. 4s.

Elementary Principles of Fortification. A Text-Book for Military Examinations. By J. T. Hyde, M.A. Royal 8vo. With numerous Plans and Illustrations. 10s. 6d.

Military Train Manual. 1s.

The Sappers' Manual. Compiled for the use of Engineer Volunteer Corps. By Col. W. A. Frankland, R.E. With numerous Illustrations. 2s.

Ammunition. A descriptive treatise on the different Projectiles Charges, Fuzes, Rockets, &c., at present in use for Land and Sea Service, and on other war stores manufactured in the Royal Laboratory. 6s.

Hand-book on the Manufacture and Proof of Gunpowder, as carried on at the Royal Gunpowder Factory, Waltham Abbey. 5s.

Regulations for the Training of Troops for service in the Field and for the conduct of Peace Manœuvres. 2s.

Hand-book Dictionary for the Militia and Volunteer Services, Containing a variety of useful information, Alphabetically arranged. Pocket size, 3s. 6d.; by post, 3s. 8d.

Gymnastic Exercises, System of Fencing, and Exercises for the Regulation Clubs. In one volume. Crown 8vo. 1877. 2s.

Army Equipment. Prepared at the Topographical and Statistical Department, War Office. By Col. Sir HENRY JAMES, R.E., F.R.S., &c., Director.

PART 1.—*Cavalry*. Compiled by Lieut. H. M. HOZIER, 2nd Life Guards. Royal 8vo. 4s.
PART 4.—*Military Train*. Compiled by Lieut. H. M. HOZIER, 2nd Life Guards. Royal 8vo. 2s. 6d.
PART 5.—*Infantry*. Compiled by Capt. F. MARTIN PETRIE. Royal 8vo. With Plates. 5s.
PART 6.—*Commissariat*. Compiled by Lieut. H. M. HOZIER, 2nd Life Guards. Royal 8vo. 1s. 6d.
PART 7.—*Hospital Service*. Compiled by Capt. MARTIN PETRIE. Royal 8vo. With Plates. 5s.

Text-Book on the Theory and Motion of Projectiles; the History, Manufacture, and Explosive Force of Gunpowder; the History of Small Arms. For Officers sent to School of Musketry. 1s. 6d.

Notes on Ammunition. 4th Edition. 1877. 2s. 6d.

Regulations and Instructions for Encampments. 6d

Rules for the Conduct of the War Game. 2s.

Medical Regulations for the Army, Instructions for the Army, Comprising duties of Officers, Attendants, and Nurses, &c. 1s. 6d.

Purveyors' Regulations and Instructions, for Guidance of Officers of Purveyors' Department of the Army. 3s.

Priced Vocabulary of Stores used in Her Majesty's Service. 4s.

Transport of Sick and Wounded Troops. By DR. LONGMORE. 5s.

Precedents in Military Law. By LT-COL. W. HOUGH. 8vo. 25s.

The Practice of Courts-Martial, by HOUGH & LONG. 8vo. 26s.

Manual of Military Law. For all ranks of the Army, Militia, and Volunteer Services. By Colonel J. K. PIPON, and J. F. COLLIER, Esq. Third and Revised Edition. Pocket size. 5s.

Regulations applicable to the European Officer in India. Containing Staff Corps Rules, Staff Salaries, Commands, Furlough and Retirement Regulations, &c. By GEORGE E. COCHRANE, late Assistant Military Secretary, India Office. 1 vol., post 8vo. 7s. 6d.

Reserve Force; Guide to Examinations, for the use of Captains and Subalterns of Infantry, Militia, and Rifle Volunteers, and for Serjeants of Volunteers. By Capt. G. H. GREAVES. 2nd edit. 2s.

The Military Encyclopædia; referring exclusively to the Military Sciences, Memoirs of distinguished Soldiers, and the Narratives of Remarkable Battles. By J. H. STOCQUELER. 8vo. 12s.

The Operations of War Explained and Illustrated. By Col. HAMLEY. New Edition Revised, with Plates. Royal 8vo. 30s.

Lessons of War. As taught by the Great Masters and Others; Selected and Arranged from the various operations in War. By FRANCE JAMES SOADY, Lieut.-Col., R.A. Royal 8vo. 21s.

The Soldiers' Pocket Book for Field Service. By Col. SIR GARNET J. WOLSELEY. 2nd Edition. Revised and Enlarged. 4s. 6d.

The Surgeon's Pocket Book, an Essay on the best Treatment of Wounded in War. By Surgeon Major J. H. PORTER. 7s. 6d.

A Precis of Modern Tactics. By COLONEL HOME. 8vo. 8s. 6d.

Armed Strength of Austria. By Capt. COOKE. 2 pts. £1 2s.

Armed Strength of Denmark. 3s.

Armed Strength of Russia. Translated from the German. 7s.

Armed Strength of Sweden and Norway. 3s. 6d.

Armed Strength of Italy. 5s. 6d.

Armed Strength of Germany. Part I. 8s. 6d.

The Franco-German War of 1870—71. By CAPT. C. H. CLARKE. Vol. I. £1 6s. Sixth Section. 5s. Seventh Section 6s. Eighth Section. 3s. Ninth Section. 4s. 6d. Tenth Section. 6s. Eleventh Section. 5s. 3d. Twelfth Section. 4s. 6d.

The Campaign of 1866 in Germany. Royal 8vo. With Atlas, 21s.

Celebrated Naval and Military Trials By PETER BURKE. Post 8vo., cloth. 10s. 6d.

Military Sketches. By SIR LASCELLES WRAXALL. Post 8vo. 6s.

Military Life of the Duke of Wellington. By JACKSON and SCOTT. 2 Vols. 8vo. Maps, Plans, &c. 12s.

Single Stick Exercise of the Aldershot Gymnasium. 6*d*.

Treatise on Military Carriages, and other Manufactures of the Royal Carriage Department. 5s.

Steppe Campaign Lectures. 2s.

Manual of Instructions for Army Surgeons. 1s.

Regulations for Army Hospital Corps. 9d.

Manual of Instructions for Non-Commissioned Officers, Army Hospital Corps. 2s.

Handbook or Military Artificers. 3s.

Instructions for the use of Auxiliary Cavalry. 2s. 6d.

Equipment Regulations for the Army. 5s. 6d.

Statute Law relating to the Army. 1s. 3d.

Regulations for Commissariat and Ordnance Department 2s.

Regulations for the Commissariat Department. 1s. 6d.

Regulations for the Ordnance Department. 1s. 6d.

Artillerist's Handbook of Reference for the use of the Royal and Reserve Artillery, by WILL and DALTON. 5s.

An Essay on the Principles and Construction of Military Bridges, by SIR HOWARD DOUGLAS. 1853. 15s.

Mill's History of British India,

With Notes and Continuation. By H. H. WILSON. 9 vols. cr. 8vo. £2 10s.

Milton's Poetical Works, with Notes.

By JOHN BRADSHAW, LL.D., Inspector of Schools, Madras. 2 vols. post 8vo. 10s. 6d.

Mogul Empire.

From the death of Aurungzeb to the overthrow of the Mahratta Power, by HENRY GEORGE KEENE, B.C.S. 8vo. Second edition. With Map. 10s. 6d.

This Work fills up a blank between the ending of Elphinstone's and the commencement of Thornton's Histories.

Mysteries of the Vatican;

Or Crimes of the Papacy. From the German of DR. THEODORE GREISENGER. 2 Vols. post 8vo 21s.

Nationalities of Europe.

By ROBERT GORDON LATHAM, M.D. 2 Vols. 8vo. 12s.

Natural History, Sport and Travel.

By EDWARD LOCKWOOD, Bengal Civil Service, late Magistrate of Monghyr Crown 8vo. 9s.

Nirgis and Bismillah.

NIRGIS; a Tale of the Indian Mutiny, from the Diary of a Slave Girl: and BISMILLAH; or, Happy Days in Cashmere. By HAFIZ ALLARD. Post 8vo. 10s. 6d.

Notes on China.

Desultory Notes on the Government and People of China and on the Chinese Language. By T. T. MEADOWS, 8vo. 9s.

Notes on the North Western Provinces of India.

By a District Officer. 2nd Edition. Post 8vo., cloth. 5s.

CONTENTS.—Area and Population.—Soils.—Crops.—Irrigation.—Rent.—Rates.—Land Tenures.

Owen (Sidney) India on the Eve of the British Conqnest.

A Historical Sketch. By SIDNEY OWEN, M.A. Reader in Indian Law and History in the University of Oxford. Formerly Professor of History in the Elphinstone College, Bombay. Post 8vo. 8s.

Oxenham (Rev. H. N.) Catholic Eschatology and Universalism. An Essay on the Doctrine of Future Retribution. Second Edition, revised and enlarged. Crown 8vo. 7s. 6d.

Oxenham's (Rev. H. N.) Catholic Doctrine of the Atonement. 8vo. 10s. 6d. (See page 5.)

Ozanam's (A. F.) Civilisation in the Fifth Century. From the French. By The Hon. A. C. GLYN. 2 Vols. post 8vo. 21s.

Pathologia Indica, Based upon Morbid Specimens from all parts of the Indian Empire. By ALLAN WEBB, B.M.S. Second Edit. 8vo. 14s.

Pharmacopœia of India. By EDWARD JOHN WARING, M.D , &c. 8vo. 6s. (See page 2.)

Physical Geography. By PROFESSOR D. T. ANSTED, M.A., F.R.S., &c. Fifth Edition. Post 8vo., with Illustrative Maps. 7s.

CONTENTS:—PART I.—INTRODUCTION.—The Earth as a Planet. —Physical Forces.—The Succession of Rocks. PART II.—EARTH —Land.—Mountains.—Hills and Valleys.—Plateaux and Low Plains. PART III.—WATER.—The Ocean.—Rivers. —Lakes and Waterfalls.—The Phenomena of Ice.—Springs PART IV.—AIR.—The Atmosphere. Winds and Storms.—Dew, Clouds, and Rain.—Climate and Weather. PART V —FIRE.—Volcanoes and Volcanic Phenomena.—Earthquakes. PART VI.—LIFE.—The Distribution of Plants in the different Countries of the Earth.—The Distribution of Animals on the Earth.—The Distribution of Plants and Animals in Time.—Effects of Human Agency on Inanimate Nature.

"The Book is both valuable and comprehensive, and deserves a wide circulation."—*Observer.*

Pilgrimage to Mecca (A). By the Nawab Sikandar Begum of Bhopal. Translated from the Original Urdu. By MRS. WILLOUGHBY OSBORNE. Followed by a Sketch of the History of Bhopal. By COL. WILLOUGHBY-OSBORNE, C.B. With Photographs, and dedicated, by permission, to HER MAJESTY, QUEEN VICTORIA. Post 8vo. £1. 1s.

This is a highly important book, not only for its literary merit, and the information it contains, but also from the fact of its being the first work written by an Indian lady, and that lady a Queen.

Pebody (Charles) Authors at Work. Francis Jeffrey—Sir Walter Scott—Robert Burns—Charles Lamb—R. B. Sheridan—Sydney Smith—Macaulay—Byron Wordsworth—Tom Moore—Sir James Mackintosh. Post 8vo. 10s. 6d.

Pollock (Field Marshal Sir George) Life & Correspondence.
By C. R. Low. 8vo. With portrait. 18s.

Practice of Courts Martial.
By Hough & Long. 8vo. London. 1825. 26s.

Precedents in Military Law;
By Lieut.-Col. W. Hough. One thick 8vo. Vol. 25s.

Prichard's Chronicles of Budgepore, &c.
Or Sketches of Life in Upper India. 2 Vols., Foolscap 8vo. 12s.

Primitive and Universal Laws of the Formation and Development of Language. 8vo. 12s. 6d. (See page 16.)

Prinsep's (H. T.) Historical Results.
8vo. 15s.

Prinsep's (H. T.) Thibet.
Post 8vo. 5s.

Prinsep's Political and Military Transactions in India.
2 Vols. 8vo. London, 1825. 18s.

Races and Tribes of Hindostan.
The People of India. A series of Photographic Illustrations of the Races and Tribes of Hindustan. Prepared under the Authority of the Government of India, by J. Forbes Watson and John William Kaye. The Work contains about 450 Photographs on mounts, in Eight Volumes, super royal 4to. £2 5s. per volume.

Red Book for Sergeants.
By W. Bright, Colour-Sergeant, 37th Middlesex R.V. Fcap. interleaved. 1s.

Regiments of the British Army (The).
Chronologically arranged. Showing their History, Services, Uniform, &c. By Captain R. Trimen, late 35th Regiment. 8vo. 10s. 6d.

Republic of Fools (The).
Being the History of the People of Abdera in Thrace, from the German of C. M. Von Wieland. By Rev. Henry Christmas, M.A. 2 Vols crown 8vo. 12s.

Richards (Major W H.) Military Surveying, &c.
12s. (See page 19.)

Russians at Home.
Unpolitical Sketches, showing what Newspapers they read, what Theatres they frequent; and how they eat, drink and enjoy themselves; with other matter relating chiefly to Literature, Music, and Places of Historical and Religious Interest in and about Moscow. By H. Sutherland Edwards. Second Edition, post 8vo., with Illustrations. 6s

Russian and Turk, from a Geographical, Ethnological, and Historical point of View. By R. G. Latham, M.A., M.D., &c. 8vo. 18s.

Sanderson's (G. P.) Thirteen Years among the Wild Beasts of India. Small 4to. 25s. (See page 27.)

Sepoy War in India.
A History of the Sepoy War in India, 1857—1858. By Sir John William Kaye, Author of "The History of the War in Affghanistan." Vol. I, 8vo. 18s. Vol. II. £1. Vol. III. £1.

Contents of Vol. I. :—Book I.—Introductory.—The Conquest of the Punjab and Pegu.—The "Right of Lapse."—The Annexation of Oude.—Progress of Englishism. Book II.—The Sepoy Army : its Rise, Progress, and Decline.—Early History of the Native Army.—Deteriorating Influences.—The Sindh Mutinies.—The Punjaub Mutinies. Discipline of the Bengal Army. Book III.—The Outbreak of the Mutiny.—Lord Canning and his Council.—The Oude Administration and the Persian War.—The Rising of the Storm.—The First Mutiny.—Progress of Mutiny.—Excitement in Upper India — Bursting of the Storm.—Appendix.

Contents of Vol. II. :—Book IV.—The Rising in the North-west. The Delhi History.—The Outbreak at Meerut. —The Seizure of Delhi.—Calcutta in May.—Last Days of General Anson.—The March upon Delhi. Book V.—Progress of Rebellion in Upper India —Benares and Allahabad.—Cawnpore.—The March to Cawnpore.—Re-occupation of Cawnpore. Book VI.—The Punjab and Delhi.—First Conflicts in the Punjab.—Peshawur and Rawul Pinder.—Progress of Events in the Punjab.—Delhi.—First Weeks of the Siege.—Progress of the Siege.—The Last Succours from the Punjab.

Contents of Vol. III. :—Book VII.—Bengal, Behar, and the North-west Provinces.—At the Seat of Government.—The Insurrection in Behar.—The Siege of Arrah.—Behar and Bengal. Book VIII.—Mutiny and Rebellion in the North-west Provinces.—Agra in May.—Insurrection in the Districts.—Bearing of the Native Chiefs.—Agra in

June, July, August and September. BOOK IX.—LUCKNOW AND DELHI.—Rebellion in Oude.—Revolt in the Districts.—Lucknow in June and July.—The siege and Capture of Delhi.

History of the Indian Mutiny, 1857-1858. Vol. 1. Commencing from the close of the Second Volume of Sir John Kaye's History of the Sepoy War. By COLONEL G. B. MALLESON, C.S.I. 8vo. With Map. £1. Vol. 2 (*In the press*).

CONTENTS. BOOK VII.—Calcutta in May and June.—William Tayler and Vincent Eyre.—How Bihar and Calcutta were saved. BOOK VIII.—Mr. Colvin and Agra.—Jhansi and Bandalkhand.—Colonel Durand and Holkar.—Sir George Lawrence and Rajputana.—Brigadier Polwhele's great battle and its results.—Bareli, Rohilkhand, and Farakhabad. BOOK IX.—The relation of the annexation of Oudh to the Mutiny.—Sir Henry Lawrence and the Mutiny in Oudh.—The siege of Lakhnao.—The first relief of Lakhnao.

Sewell's (Robert) Analytical History of India.
Crown 8vo. 8s. (See page 3.)

Social Life in Munich.
By EDWARD WILBERFORCE, Second Edition. Post 8vo. 6s.

"A very able volume. Mr. Wilberforce is a very pleasant and agreeable writer whose opinion is worth hearing on the subject of modern art which enters largely into the matter of his discourse."—*Saturday Review.*

Student's Chemistry.
Being the Seventh Edition of Household Chemistry, or the Science of Home Life. By ALBERT J. BERNAYS, PH. DR. F.C.S., Prof. of Chemistry and Practical Chemistry at St. Thomas' Hospital, Medical, and Surgical College. Post 8vo. 5s. 6d.

Sin: Its Causes and Consequences.
An attempt to Investigate the Origin, Nature, Extent and Results of Moral Evil. A Series of Lent Lectures. By the REV. HENRY CHRISTMAS, M.A., F.R.S. Post 8vo. 5s.

Starling (M. H.) Indian Criminal Law and Procedure.
Third edition. 8vo. £2 2s.

Strange's (Sir T.) Hindu Law.
2 Vols. Royal 8vo. 1830. 24s. (See page 13.)

"Their Majesties Servants":
Annals of the English Stage. Actors, Authors, and Audiences. From Thomas Betterton to Edmund Kean. By Dr. DORAN, F.S.A., Author of "Table Traits," "Lives of the Queens of England of the House of Hanover." &c. Post 8vo. 6s.

"Every page of the work is barbed with wit, and will make its way point foremost. . . . . provides entertainment for the most diverse tastes."—*Daily News.*

Textile Manufactures and Costumes of the People of India,
As originally prepared under the Authority of the Secretary of State for India in Council. By J. FORBES WATSON, M.A., M.D., F.R.A.S., Reporter on the Products of India. Folio, half-morocco. With numerous Coloured Photographs. £3. 5s.

This work—by affording a key to the Fashions of the People, and to the Cotton, Silk, and Wool Textiles in actual use in India—is of special interest to Manufacturers, Merchants, and Agents; as also to the Student and lover of ornamental art.

Theories of History.
An Inquiry into the Theories of History,—Chance,—Law,—Will. With Special Reference to the Principle of Positive Philosophy. By WILLIAM ADAM 8vo. 15s.

Thirteen Years among the Wild Beasts of India: their
Their Haunts and Habits, from Personal Observation; with an account of the Modes of Capturing and Taming Wild Elephants. By G. P. SANDERSON, Officer in Charge of the Government Elephant Keddahs at Mysore. With 21 full page Illustrations and three Maps. Second Edition. Fcp. 4to. £1 5s.

Thomson's Lunar and Horary Tables.
For New and Concise Methods of Performing the Calculations necessary for ascertaining the Longitude by Lunar Observations, or Chronometers; with directions for acquiring a knowledge of the Principal Fixed Stars and finding the Latitude of them. By DAVID THOMSON. Sixty-fifth edit. Royal 8vo. 10s.

Thornton's History of India.
The History of the British Empire in India, by Edward Thornton, Esq. Containing a Copious Glossary of Indian Terms, and a Complete Chronological Index of Events, to aid the Aspirant for Public Examinations. Third edition. 1 vol. 8vo. With Map. 12s.

*** *The Library Edition of the above in 6 volumes, 8vo., may be had, price £2. 8s.*

Thornton's Gazetteer of India.
Compiled chiefly from the records at the India Office. By EDWARD THORNTON. 1 vol., 8vo., pp. 1015. With Map. 21s.

*** *The chief objects in view in compiling this Gazetteer are:—*

1st. *To fix the relative position of the various cities, towns, and villages with as much precision as possible, and to exhibit with the greatest practicable brevity all that is known respecting them; and*

2ndly. *To note the various countries, provinces, or territorial divisions, and to describe the physical characteristics of each, together with their statistical, social, and political circumstances.*

To these are added minute descriptions of the principal rivers and chains of mountains; thus presenting to the reader, within a brief compass, a mass of information which cannot otherwise be obtained, except from a multiplicity of volumes and manuscript records.

The Library Edition.
4 vols., 8vo. Notes, Marginal References, and Map. £2 16s.

Thugs and Dacoits of India.
A Popular Account of the Thugs and Dacoits, the Hereditary Garotters and Gang Robbers of India. By JAMES HUTTON. Post 8vo. 5s.

Tibet, Tartary, and Mongolia.
By HENRY T. PRINSEP, Esq. Second edition. Post 8vo. 5s.

Tilley's (H. A.) Japan, &c.
8vo. 16s. (See page 14.)

Tod's (Col. Jas.) Travels in Western India.
Embracing a visit to the Sacred Mounts of the Jains, and the most Celebrated Shrines of Hindu Faith between Rajpootana and the Indus, with an account of the Ancient City of Nehrwalla. By the late Lieut.-Col. JAMES TOD, Illustrations. Royal 4to. £3 3s.

**** This is a companion volume to Colonel Tod's Rajasthan.*

Trimen's (Capt. R., late 35th Regiment) Regiments of the British Army chronologically arranged. 8vo. 10s. 6d.

Trotter's (L. J.) History of India.
The History of the British Empire in India, from the Appointment of Lord Hardinge to the Death of Lord Canning (1844 to 1862). By LIONEL JAMES TROTTER, late Bengal Fusiliers. 2 vols. 8vo. 16s. each.

Trotter's (L. J.) Warren Hastings, a Biography.
Crown 8vo. 9s.

Turkish Cookery Book (The).
A Collection of Receipts from the best Turkish Authorities. Done into English by FARABI EFENDI. 12mo. Cloth. 3s. 6d.

Vambery's Sketches of Central Asia.
Additional Chapters on My Travels and Adventures, and of the Ethnology of Central Asia. By Armenius Vambery. 8vo. 16s.

"A valuable guide on almost untrodden ground."—*Athenæum.*

View of China,
For Philological Purposes. Containing a Sketch of Chinese Chronology, Geography, Government, Religion, and Customs. Designed for the use of Persons who study the Chinese Language. By Rev. R. MORRISON. 4to. Macao, 1817. 6s.

Waring's Pharmacopœia of India.
8vo. 6s. (See page 2.)

Warren Hastings: a Biography. By Captain LIONEL JAMES TROTTER, Bengal H. P., author of a "History of India," "Studies in Biography," &c. Crown 8vo. 9s.

Water, and Water Supply, chiefly in Reference to the British Islands.—Surface Waters. By Professor D. T. ANSTED, M.A., F.R.S., F.G.S., &c. 8vo. With numerous Maps. 18s.

Watson's (Dr. J. Forbes) Textile Manufactures of India. Folio. £3. 5s. (See page 27.)

Watson's (Dr. J. F.) and J. W. Kaye, The People of India. A Series of Photographs. Vols. 1 to 8, £18.

Webb's (Dr. A.) Pathologia Indica. 8vo. 14s. (See page 23.)

Wellesley's Despatches.
The Despatches, Minutes, and Correspondence of the Marquis Wellesley, K.G., during his Administration in India. 5 vols. 8vo. With Portrait, Map, &c. £6. 10s.

This work should be perused by all who proceed to India in the Civil Services.

Wellington in India.
Military History of the Duke of Wellington in India. 1s.

Wilberforce's (Edward) Social Life in Munich. Post 8vo. 6s. (See page 26.)

Wilberforce's (E.) Life of Schubert. Post 8vo. 6s.

Wilk's South of India. 3 vols. 4to. £5. 5s.

Williams' (F.) Lives of the English Cardinals. 2 vols., 8vo. 14s. (See page 7.)

Williams' (F.) Life, &c., of Bishop Atterbury. 2 vols., 8vo. 14s. (See page 4.)

Williams' Indian Wisdom. 8vo. 15s. (See page 14.)

Wilson's Glossary of Judicial and Revenue Terms, and of useful Words occurring in Official Documents relating to the Administration of the Government of British India. From the Arabic, Persian, Hindustani, Sanskrit, Hindi, Bengali, Uriya, Marathi, Guzarathi, Telugu, Karnata, Tamil, Malayalam, and other Languages. Compiled and published under the authority of the Hon. the Court of Directors of the E. I. Company. 4to., cloth. £1 10s.

Wollaston's (Arthur N.) Anwari Suhaili, or Lights of Canopus Commonly known as Kalilah and Damnah, being an adaptation of the Fables of Bidpai. Translated from the Persian. Royal 4to., with illuminated borders, designed specially for the work, cloth, extra gilt. £3 13s. 6d.

Wollaston's (Arthur N.) Elementary Indian Reader.
Designed for the use of Students in the Anglo-Vernacular Schools in India. Fcap. 1s.

Woolrych's (Serjeant W. H.)
Lives of Eminent Serjeants-at-Law of the English Bar. By HUMPHRY W. WOOLRYCH, Serjeant-at-Law. 2 vols. 8vo. 30s.

World we Live In.
Or First Lessons in Physical Geography. For the use of Schools and Students. By D. T. ANSTED, M.A., F.R.S., &c. 25th Thousand. Fcap. 8vo. 2s.

Wraxall's Caroline Matilda.
Queen of Denmark, Sister of George 3rd. From Family and State Papers. By Sir Lascelles Wraxall, Bart. 3 vols., 8vo. 18s.

Wraxall's Military Sketches.
By SIR LASCELLES WRAXALL, Bart. Post 8vo. 6s.

"The book is clever and entertaining from first to last."—*Athenæum.*

Wraxall's Scraps and Sketches, Gathered Together.
By SIR LASCELLES WRAXALL, Bart. 2 vols., Post 8vo. 12s.

Yakoob Beg (the Life of), Athalik Ghazi and Badaulet, Ameer of Kashgar. By DEMETRIUS CHARLES BOULGER, Member of the Royal Asiatic Society. 8vo. With Map and Appendix. 16s.

Yesterday and To-Day in India.
By SIDNEY LAMAN BLANCHARD. Post 8vo. 6s.

CONTENTS.—Outward Bound.—The Old Times and the New.—Domestic Life.—Houses and Bungalows.—Indian Servants.—The Great Shoe Question.—The Garrison Hack.—The Long Bow in India.—Mrs. Dulcimer's Shipwreck.—A Traveller's Tale, told in a Dark Bungalow.—Punch in India.—Anglo-Indian Literature.—Christmas in India.—The Seasons in Calcutta.—Farmers in Muslin.—Homeward Bound.—India as it Is.

Young's (J. R.) Course of Mathematics.
8vo. 12s. (See page 7.)

A SELECTION FROM

MESSRS. ALLEN'S CATALOGUE

OF BOOKS IN THE EASTERN LANGUAGES, &c.

HINDUSTANI, HINDI, &c.

[*Dr. Forbes's Works are used as Class Books in the Colleges and Schools in India.*]

Forbes's Hindustani-English Dictionary in the Persian Character, with the Hindi words in Nagari also; and an English Hindustani Dictionary in the English Character; both in one volume. By DUNCAN FORBES, LL.D. Royal 8vo. 42s.

Forbes's Hindustani Grammar, with Specimens of Writing in the Persian and Nagari Characters, Reading Lessons, and Vocabulary. 8vo. 10s. 6d.

Forbes's Hindustani Manual, containing a Compendious Grammar, Exercises for Translation, Dialogues, and Vocabulary, in the Roman Character. New Edition, entirely revised. By J. T. PLATTS. 18mo. 3s. 6d.

Forbes's Bagh o Bahar, in the Persian Character, with a complete Vocabulary. Royal 8vo. 12s. 6d.

Forbes's Bagh o Bahar in English, with Explanatory Notes, illustrative of Eastern Character. 8vo. 8s.

Eastwick (Edward B.) The Bagh-o-Bahar—literally translated into English, with copious explanatory notes. 8vo. 10s. 6d.

Forbes's Tota Kahani; or, "Tales of a Parrot," in the Persian Character, with a complete Vocabulary. Royal 8vo. 8s.

Small's (Rev. G.) Tota Kahani; or, "Tales of a Parrot." Translated into English. 8vo. 8s.

Forbes's Baital Pachisi; or, "Twenty-five Tales of a Demon," in the Nagari Character, with a complete Vocabulary. Royal 8vo. 9s.

Platts' J. T., Baital Pachisi; translated into English. 8vo. 8s.

Forbes's Ikhwanu s Safa; or, "Brothers of Purity," in the Persian Character. Royal 8vo. 12s. 6d.

[*For the higher standard for military officers' examinations.*]

Platts' Ikhwanu S Safa; translated into English. 8vo. 10s. 6d.

Platts' Grammar of the Urdu or Hindustani-Language. 8vo. 12s.

Forbes's Oriental Penmanship; a Guide to Writing Hindustani in the Persian Character. 4to. 8s.

Forbes's Hindustani-English and English Hindustani Dictionary, in the English Character. Royal 8vo. 36s.

Forbes's Smaller Dictionary, Hindustani and English, in the English Character. 12s.

Forbes's Bagh o Bahar, with Vocaby., English Character. 5s.

Hindustani Selections, with a Vocabulary of the Words. By JAMES R. BALLANTYNE. Second Edition. 1845. 5s.

Singhasan Battisi. Translated into Hindi from the Sanscrit. A New Edition. Revised, Corrected, and Accompanied with Copious Notes. By SYED ABDOOLAH. Royal 8vo. 12s. 6d.

Robertson's Hindustani Vocabulary. 3s. 6d.

Eastwick's Prem Sagur. 4to. 30s.

Akhlaki Hindi, translated into Urdu, with an Introduction and Notes. By SYED ABDOOLAH. Royal 8vo. 12s. 6d.

Sakuntala. Translated into Hindi from the Bengali recension of the Sanskrit. Critically edited, with grammatical, idiomatical, and exegetical notes, by FREDERIC PINCOTT. 4to. 12s. 6d.

SANSCRIT.

Haughton's Sanscrit and Bengali Dictionary, in the Bengali Character, with Index, serving as a reversed dictionary. 4to. 30s.

Williams's English-Sanscrit Dictionary. 4to., cloth. £3. 3s.

Williams's Sanskrit-English Dictionary. 4to. £4 14s. 6d.

Wilkin's (Sir Charles) Sanscrit Grammar. 4to. 15s.

Williams's (Monier) Sanscrit Grammar. 8vo. 15s.

Williams's (Monier) Sanscrit Manual; to which is added, a Vocabulary, by A. E. GOUGH. 18mo. 7s. 6d.

Gough's (A. E.) Key to the Exercises in Williams's Sanscrit Manual. 18mo. 4s.

Williams's (Monier) Sakuntala, with Literal English Translation of all the Metrical Passages, Schemes of the Metres, and copious Critical and Explanatory Notes. Royal 8vo. 21s.

Williams's (Monier) Sakuntala. Translated into English Prose and Verse. Fourth Edition. 8s.

Williams's (Monier) Vikramorvasi. The Text. 8vo. 5s.

Cowell's (E B.) Translation of the Vikramorvasi. 8vo. 3s. 6d.

Thompson's (J. C.) Bhagavat Gita. Sanscrit Text. 5s.

Haughton's Menu, with English Translation. 2 vols. 4to. 24s.

Johnson's Hitopadesa, with Vocabulary. 15s.

Hitopadesa, Sanscrit, with Bengali and English Trans. 10s. 6d.

Johnson's Hitopadesa, English Translation of the. 4to. 5s.

Wilson's Megha Duta, with Translation into English Verse, Notes, Illustrations, and a Vocabulary. Royal 8vo. 6s.

PERSIAN.

Richardson's Persian, Arabic, and English Dictionary. Edition of 1852. By F. Johnson. 4to. £4.

Forbes's Persian Grammar, Reading Lessons, and Vocabulary. Royal 8vo. 12s. 6d.

Ibraheem's Persian Grammar, Dialogues, &c. Royal 8vo. 12s. 6d.

Gulistan. Carefully collated with the original MS., with a full Vocabulary. By John Platts, late Inspector of Schools, Central Provinces, India. Royal 8vo. 12s. 6d.

Gulistan. Translated from a revised Text, with Copious Notes. By John Platts. 8vo. 12s. 6d.

Ouseley's Anwari Soheili. 4to. 42s.

Wollaston's (Arthur N.) Translation of the Anvari Soheili. Royal 8vo. £2 2s.

Keene's (Rev. H. G.) First Book of The Anwari Soheili. Persian Text. 8vo. 5s.

Ouseley's (Col.) Akhlaki Mushini. Persian Text. 8vo. 5s.

Keene's (Rev. H. G.) Akhlaki Mushini. Translated into English. 8vo. 3s. 6d.

Clarke's (Captain H. Wilberforce, R.E.) The Persian Manual. A Pocket Companion.

PART I.—A concise Grammar of the Language, with Exercises on its more Prominent Peculiarities, together with a Selection of Useful Phrases, Dialogues, and Subjects for Translation into Persian.

PART II.—A Vocabulary of Useful Words, English and Persian, showing at the same time the difference of idiom between the two Languages. 18mo. 7s. 6d.

A Translation of Robinson Crusoe into the Persian Language. Roman Character. Edited by T. W. H. Tolbort, Bengal Civil Service. Cr. 8vo. 7s.

BENGALI.

Haughton's Bengali, Sanscrit, and English Dictionary, adapted for Students in either language; to which is added an Index, serving as a reversed dictionary. 4to. 30s.

Forbes's Bengali Grammar, with Phrasesand dialogues. Royal 8vo. 12s. 6d.

Forbes's Bengali Reader, with a Translation and Vocabulary Royal 8vo. 12s. 6d.

Nabo Nari. 12mo. 7s.

ARABIC.

Richardson's Arabic, Persian and English Dictionary. Edition of 1852. By F. Johnson. 4to., cloth. £4.

Forbes's Arabic Grammar, intended more especially for the use of young men preparing for the East India Civil Service, and also for the use of self instructing students in general. Royal 8vo., cloth. 18s.

Palmer's Arabic Grammar. 8vo. 18s.

Forbes's Arabic Reading Lessons, consisting of Easy Extracts from the best Authors, with Vocabulary. Royal 8vo., cloth. 15s.

Matthew's Translation of the Mishkāt-ul-Masābih. 2 vols in 1. By the Rev. T. P. Hughes, Missionary to the Afghans at Peshawur. (*In the press.*)

TELOOGOO.

Brown's Dictionary, reversed; with a Dictionary of the Mixed Dialects used in Teloogoo. 3 vols. in 2, royal 8vo. £5.

Campbell's Dictionary. Royal 8vo. 30s.

Bromn's Reader. 8vo. 2 vols. 14s.

Brown's Dialogues, Teloogoo and English. 8vo. 5s. 6d.

Pancha Tantra. 8s.

Percival's English-Teloogoo Dictionary. 10s. 6d.

TAMIL.

Rottler's Dictionary, Tamil and English. 4to. 42s.

Babington's Grammar (High Dialect). 4to. 12s.

Percival's Tamil Dictionary. 2 vols. 10s. 6d.

GUZRATTEE.

Mavor's Spelling, Guzrattee and English. 7s, 6d.

Shapuaji Edalji's Dictionary, Guzrattee and English. 21s.

MAHRATTA.

Molesworth's Dictionary, Mahratta and English. 4to. 42s.

Molesworth's Dictionary, English and Mahratta. 4to. 42s.

Stevenson's Grammar. 8vo., cloth. 17s. 6d.

Esop's Fables. 12mo. 2s. 6d.

Fifth Reading Book. 7s.

MALAY.

Marsden's Grammar. 4to. £1 1s.

CHINESE.

Morrison's Dictionary. 6 vols. 4to. £10.

Marshman's—Clavis Sinica, a Chinese Grammar. 4to. £2 2s.

Morrison's View of China, for Philological purposes; containing a Sketch of Chinese Chronology, Geography, Government, Religion and Customs, designed for those who study the Chinese language. 4to. 6s.

MISCELLANEOUS.

Reeve's English-Carnatica and Carnatica-English Dictionary. 2 vols. (Very slightly damaged). £8.

Collett's Malayalam Reader. 8vo. 12s. 6d.

Esop's Fables in Carnatica. 8vo. bound. 12s. 6d.

A CHRONOLOGICAL AND HISTORICAL

CHART OF INDIA,

Price, fully tinted, mounted on roller or in case, 20s. size, about 40 in. by 50 in.

Showing, at one view, all the principal nations, governments, and empires which have existed in that country from the earliest times to the suppression of the Great Mutiny, A.D. 1858, with the date of each historical event according to the *various eras used in India.*

BY

ARTHUR ALLEN DURTNALL,

Of the High Court of Justice in England.

By this Chart, any person, however ignorant of the subject, may, by an hour's attention, obtain a clear view of the broad lines of Indian History, and of the evolutions which have resulted in the dominion of Her Majesty as EMPRESS OF INDIA. It will be found invaluable for EDUCATIONAL PURPOSES, especially in Colleges and Schools, where an Indian career is in contemplation. It will also be found of PERMANENT UTILITY in all Libraries and Offices as a work of ready reference for the connection of events and dates. Besides the History of India, it includes the contemporaneous histories of AFGHANISTAN, CENTRAL ASIA, and EUROPE.

A RELIEVO MAP OF INDIA.

BY

HENRY F. BRION.

In Frame, 21s.

A map of this kind brings before us such a picture of the surface of a given country as no ordinary map could ever do. To the mind's eye of the average Englishman, India consists of 'the plains' and 'the hills,' chiefly of the former, the hills bein g limited to the Himalayas and the Nilgiris. The new map will at least enable him to correct his notions of Indian geography. It combines the usual features of a good plain map of the country on a scale of 150 miles to the inch, with a aithful representation of all the uneven surfaces, modelled on a scale thirty-two times the horizontal one; thus bringing out into clear relief the comparative heights and outlines of all the hill-ranges, and showing broad tracts of uneven ground, of intermingled hill and valley, which a common map of the same size would hardly indicate, except to a very practised eye. The plains of Upper India are reduced to their true proportions; the Central Provinces, Malwa, and Western Bengal reveal their actual ruggedness at a glance; and Southern India, from the Vindhyas to Cape Comorin, proclaims its real height above the sea-level. To the historical as well as the geographical student such a map is an obvious and important aid in tracing the course of past campaigns, in realising the conditions under which successive races carried their arms or settlements through the Peninsula, and in comprehending the difference of race, climate, and physical surroundings which make up our Indian Empire. Set in a neat frame of maplewood, the map seems to attract the eye like a prettily-coloured picture, and its price, a guinea, should place it within the reach of all who care to combine the useful with the ornamental."—*Home News.*

THE

ROYAL KALENDAR,

AND

COURT & CITY REGISTER

FOR

England, Ireland, Scotland, and the Colonies

FOR THE YEAR

1879.

CONTAINING A CORRECT LIST OF THE TWENTY-FIRST IMPERIAL PARLIAMENT, SUMMONED TO MEET FOR THEIR FIRST SESSION—MARCH 5TH, 1874.

House of Peers—House of Commons—Sovereigns and Rulers of States of Europe—Orders of Knighthood—Science and Art Department—Queen's Household—Government Offices—Mint—Customs—Inland Revenue—Post Office—Foreign Ministers and Consuls—Queen's Consuls Abroad—Naval Department—Navy List—Army Department—Army List—Law Courts—Police—Ecclesiastical Department—Clergy List—Foundation Schools—Literary Institutions—City of London—Banks—Railway Companies—Hospital and Institutions—Charities—Miscellaneous Institutions—Scotland, Ireland, India, and the Colonies; and other useful information.

HISTORY
OF THE
INDIAN MUTINY,
1857-1859.

HISTORY
OF THE
INDIAN MUTINY,
1857-1859.

COMMENCING FROM THE CLOSE OF THE
SECOND VOLUME OF
SIR JOHN KAYE'S HISTORY OF THE SEPOY WAR.

BY

COLONEL G. B. MALLESON, C.S.I.
AUTHOR OF "HISTORY OF THE FRENCH IN INDIA,"
"HISTORICAL SKETCH OF THE NATIVE STATES OF
INDIA," ETC., ETC.

VOLUME III.

GYAN

Published by

GYAN

Gyan Publishing House
5, Ansari Road
Daryaganj, New Delhi-110002
Phone: 011-47034999, 9811692060
E-mail: books@gyanbooks.com

Distribution Network
gyanbooks.com
India, USA, Canada, UK, Australia, France

ISBN : 978-81-212-3541-9 (Set)
ISBN : 978-81-212-4916-4 (PB)
First Published, 1880

2nd Impression 2020

Printed at: Gyan Press, Delhi.

History of the Indian Mutiny, 1857-1859.
Author: Colonel G. B. Malleson

HISTORY

OF THE

INDIAN MUTINY, 1857–1859.

COMMENCING FROM THE CLOSE OF THE SECOND VOLUME OF SIR JOHN KAYE'S HISTORY OF THE SEPOY WAR

BY

COLONEL G. B. MALLESON, C.S.I.

AUTHOR OF "HISTORY OF THE FRENCH IN INDIA," "HISTORICAL SKETCH OF THE NATIVE STATES OF INDIA," ETC., ETC.

VOLUME III.

LONDON:
W. H. ALLEN & CO., 13, WATERLOO PLACE,
PALL MALL. S.W.

1888.

I INSCRIBE THIS VOLUME TO THE MEMORY OF

THE LATE

Sir Henry Marion Durand,

K.C.S.I.

A MAN WHO COMBINED A RARE GREATNESS OF SOUL
AND A PERFECT GENIUS FOR AFFAIRS
WITH SIMPLICITY OF MANNERS, DIRECTNESS OF PURPOSE,
AND A DETESTATION OF ALL THAT IS MEAN AND FALSE.
AS WISE IN COUNSEL
AS HE WAS PROMPT AND DECIDED IN ACTION,
HE MET ALL THE STORMS OF LIFE WITH FORTITUDE,
RENDERING EVER, ALIKE BY HIS ACTION AND HIS EXAMPLE,
UNSURPASSED SERVICES TO HIS COUNTRY.

AFTER A SERVICE FULL OF HONOUR, EXTENDING OVER
FORTY-TWO YEARS,
HE DIED IN THE PERFORMANCE OF HIS DUTY.
"HE LEFT A REPUTATION WITHOUT SPOT—THE BEST
INHERITANCE HE COULD BEQUEATH TO HIS CHILDREN."

PREFACE.

The present volume concludes the history of the great Indian uprising of 1857.

The question whether that uprising was simply a military mutiny or a revolt of which that military mutiny constituted the prominent feature, was debated keenly at the time, and is to this day as warmly contested. In the concluding chapter of this volume I have endeavoured to throw some light on the dispute, by the simple process of tracing effect to its cause. There is not a line in that chapter which will not bear the most searching analysis. The conclusion I have arrived at is that the uprising of 1857 was not primarily caused by the greased cartridges; that it was neither conceived nor designed by the sepoys. The mutiny was in reality the offspring of the discontent roused by the high-handed measures inaugurated, or at least largely developed, by Lord Dalhousie, and brought to a climax by the annexation of Oudh. The greased cartridge was the opportune instrument skilfully used by a band of conspirators, for the most part men of Oudh, for the purpose of rousing to action the sepoys, already made disaffected by consecutive breaches of contract and of faith.

Of these acts, of the attempt, as I have termed it, to disregard the silent growth of ages and to force Western ideas upon an Eastern people, and in the course of that attempt to trample upon prejudices and to disregard obligations, the mutiny was the too certain consequence. It is remarkable that the decisive points of this great uprising were at two places, famous in Indian history, in both of which we had, by force or by the moral power engendered by the possession of force, displaced the former rulers. These places were Dehlí and Lakhnao. At the one we were the besiegers, in the other we were besieged. Dehlí and Lakhnao constituted, so to speak, the wings of the rebel army. Had the centre, represented by Gwáliár, gone with the wings, it had fared badly with us. But, for the reasons I have specially referred to in the concluding chapter, the centre remained sound long enough to enable us to concentrate the bulk of our forces on the two decisive points of the rebel line.

It was after Dehlí had fallen and a severe blow had been dealt at Lakhnao that we had to deal with the centre—a centre formidable indeed, but which the loyalty of Sindia had deprived of much of its power and prestige. It is with the contest with that centre, carried on by Colonel Durand, Sir Hugh Rose, Sir Robert Napier, Generals Stuart, Roberts, Michel, and Whitlock, Brigadiers Smith, Honner, Parke, Somerset, Colonel Holmes, Becher, and many others, that the military portion of this volume mainly deals; and I venture to affirm that no part of this history is more remarkable for the display of capacity and daring by the generals, of courage and endurance by the men. It is a page of history which every Englishman will read with pride and satisfaction—with pride because the deeds it records were heroic—with satisfaction because many of the actors survive, ready, when they are called upon, to repeat their triumphs in other fields.

But important and full of interest as are the military records of this volume, the political action it relates is certainly not less so. There was not a moment of more consequence to India than that in which Lord Elphinstone had to decide whether he would content himself with saving his own presidency, or, risking everything, would send every available man to the decisive points in the endeavour to save India. Not for a second did that illustrious man hesitate. It has been to me a task of no ordinary pleasure to demonstrate how the daring and generous conduct of the Governor of Bombay vitally affected the interests of England at the most critical period of the struggle.

Nor have I experienced less gratification in rendering justice to the character of Lord Canning, as that character developed itself, when, in the early part of 1858, he stood unshackled at Allahábád. I have entered in the concluding chapter so fully into this point and into others affecting the judgment passed upon his action in the earlier part of his Indian career, that it is unnecessary to allude to the matter further here.

I have devoted one chapter to five of the most important civil districts of the North-West Provinces, but little referred to previously, and one to the more prominent of the many gallant actions performed by the officers of the late Indian navy.

Although I have exerted myself to the utmost to ensure accuracy of detail in all the military operations, I am conscious that there are many gallant deeds the details of which have not reached me, and which are therefore unnoticed. I have found it impossible, even in a work so bulky as this, to mention every individual who deserved well of his country. When a small body of men attack and defeat a large number of enemies, every man of the attacking party is necessarily a hero. There may be degrees of heroism, but it is difficult to distinguish them. Napoleon, feeling this difficulty, announced to his army after one of his great campaigns that it would be sufficient for a soldier to declare that he had belonged to the army which had fought in that campaign for the world to recognise him as a brave man. That assurance is certainly not less applicable to the soldiers whose gallant deeds are recorded in this volume, and on whom the campaigns of Málwa, of central India, of the southern Maráthá country, and again of Málwa and Rájpútáná, have fixed the stamp of heroes.

Attached to this volume will be found a few amplifications and corrections of details given in the second volume. The services of the artillery during the street-fighting at Dehlí; the gallant conduct of Lieutenant Wilkin, 7th Hussars, at Lakhnao, and of Captain Middleton, 29th foot, during the pursuit of Kúnwar Singh; and the additional support of my statement regarding the part taken by Brigadier Napier in the plan for the attack on Lakhnao, come under the former category. Under the latter will be found the measures taken by Major, now General, Orfeur Cavenagh, to provide for the equipment of the army before the arrival in Calcutta of Sir Colin Campbell; an accurate version of the manner in which Adrian Hope met his death before Rúija; a corrected account of the storming of the Mess-house at Lakhnao, rendering justice to Captain

Hopkins, 53rd foot; and an extract from a letter from General Cavenagh regarding the cause of the panic in Calcutta on the 2nd of March 1858. I desire also to add that in my account in the second volume of the defence of Lakhnao, after the first relief of that place by Havelock and Outram, I have not given sufficient prominence to the services of Major, now Major-General, Crommelin of the Engineers.

The last appendix gives the story of Tántia Topi's career as related by Tántia Topi himself.

I cannot conclude without expressing the deep obligations under which I lie to the many gentlemen who have placed their journals and letters, all written at the time, at my disposal. The value of the information I have thus been able to obtain is not to be expressed in words. But especially do I desire to acknowledge the benefit I have received from the services of the gifted friend who read this volume in proof-sheets, and whose frank and judicious criticisms have greatly contributed to the clearness and accuracy of the military narrative.

G. B. MALLESON.

27, West Cromwell Road,
31*st July*, 1880.

CONTENTS

OF

THE THIRD VOLUME.

BOOK XIII.

CHAPTER I.

CHAPTER II.

CHAPTER III.

CHAPTER IV.

BOOK XIV.

CHAPTER I.

CHAPTER II.

CHAPTER III.

CHAPTER IV.

BOOK XV.

CHAPTER I.

CHAPTER II.

CHAPTER III.

BOOK XVI.

CHAPTER I.

CHAPTER II.

BOOK XVII.

CHAPTER I.

CHAPTER II.

BOOK XVIII.

CONCLUDING CHAPTER.

LIST OF MAPS.

LIST OF ERRATA.

Volume I.

page 405, line 24, *for* Sultánpúr *read* Chandah.

Volume II.

page 515, lines 14 from top and 5 from foot, *for* Gosling *read* Gostling.

Volume III.

page 119, line 4 from top, *for* Madras *read* Bengal.

HISTORY

OF THE

INDIAN MUTINY OF 1857.

BOOK XIII.

CHAPTER I.

Book XIII. Chapter I.

1857. May.

The Bombay Presidency.

THE western, or Bombay, Presidency of India comprises a long, narrow strip of country of varying breadth and irregular outline. Including the province of Sindh, the administration of which is subordinate to it, it occupies the western coast of the peninsula from the mouths of the Indus to the northernmost point of Goa, and from the south of that territory to the borders of Maisúr. It is thus bounded on the west by Balúchistán and the Arabian Sea; on the south by Maisúr; on the east by the Madras Presidency, Haidarábád, Barár, the central provinces, the states forming the central Indian agency, and Rajpútáná; on the north by Bhawalpúr, the Panjáb, and Balúchistán. The area of the British portions of the Presidency is one hundred and thirty-four thousand one hundred and thirty-five square miles, supporting fourteen millions of inhabitants; but

Its area and population.

Book XIII. Chapter I.

1857. May.

The native states contained in it.

in subordinate political relations to it, there are, or rather there were in 1857, native states comprising seventy-one thousand three hundred and twenty square miles with six millions of inhabitants. The principal of these were Barodah, Káthwár, Kachh, Kambhayat, Mahikánta, Réwakánta, Kohlapúr, Sáwantwári, and Khairpúr.

Lord Elphinstone.

In 1857 Lord Elphinstone was Governor of Bombay. A man of culture and ability, Lord Elphinstone had enjoyed more experience of India than generally falls to the lot of governors unconnected with the civil or military services. He had been Governor of Madras from 1837 to 1842; and although the records of the Madras Presidency throughout his incumbency had marked no stirring events within its borders, yet the first Afghán war, with its early success and its later collapse, had excited the minds of the natives throughout the country, and had called for the exercise of tact and judgment on the part of the

His previous career.

rulers. These qualities Lord Elphinstone was eminently qualified to display, and he had displayed them. He was called, however, to deal principally with administrative details. The manner in which he performed these duties gained for him the confidence of the natives. His measures for improving the resources of the country, and for establishing means of communication in all directions, are spoken of to this day.

His travels in India.

Lord Elphinstone revisited India at the time of the first Sikh war, 1845–6, and marched in company with the 14th Light Dragoons, then commanded by the late Colonel William Havelock, who had been his military secretary, from Bombay, through central India, to the head-quarters of the British army before Láhor. On the transfer of Káshmir to Gúláb Síngh, a proceeding following the treaty of 1846 with the Sikhs, Lord Elphinstone formed one of the party which first visited that famous valley. After a residence in it of nearly three months, he set out for Ladák by the Husora valley, and endeavoured to proceed thence up the Gilghit valley—in those days an utterly unknown country. Forced, perhaps fortunately, by the objections of the authorities, to renounce this expedition, Lord Elphinstone crossed the Hurpo pass to Rondu on the Indus, being the first Englishman by whom that journey had been attempted.

His qualifications for his post.

It will be seen, then, that when in 1853 Lord Elphinstone was called to the post of Governor of Bombay, he brought to that office experience such as few men, not trained in the Indian services, could command. His knowledge of men, his courtesy, his genial bearing, gave effect to that experience. Up to the outbreak of the mutiny in 1857 his conduct as Governor of Bombay was invariably marked by temper, judgment, and discretion. Calm and dignified in manner, courteous to his colleagues and to all with whom he was brought in contact, he evinced, on all occasions likely to test his action, the possession of a directing mind, of a will not to be shaken, a resolution that went direct to its aim. The crisis of 1857 was just one of those occurrences which Lord Elphinstone

Well fitted to encounter the crisis of the mutiny.

Book XIII. Chapter I.

1857. May.

was constitutionally fitted to cope with. He at once realised its difficulty and its danger, and rose equal to encounter the one and to neutralise the other. In the words of a contemporary writer, generally unfavourable to him, he displayed "the courage of the soldier who knows his enemy."*

Lord Elphinstone's action on hearing of the mutiny at Mírath,

The truth of this judgment was proved by the action taken by Lord Elphinstone when the news reached him of the outbreak of the 10th of May at Mírath. Lord Elphinstone was at Bombay when he heard of that event. It happened that General Ashburnham, commanding the expeditionary corps on its way to China, was staying with him. So greatly did the importance of the intelligence impress the Governor, so certain did he feel that the Mírath revolt would spread, and that it should be met at once by bringing large reinforcements of European troops without delay into the country, that he urged General Ashburnham to proceed immediately to Calcutta, and to offer his services, and the services of the China expeditionary force, to the Governor-General.

with reference to General Ashburnham;

It was a fortunate circumstance that the war with Persia had just been brought to a successful conclusion. Fortunate, likewise, that the disaffection had not spread to the native army of Bombay. Lord Elphinstone thus felt himself equal to the most decisive measures. He at once authorised the Commissioner of Sindh, Mr.

* *The Friend of India.*

1857. May.

Frere, to transfer the 1st Bombay Fusiliers from Karáchi to the Panjáb. He arranged that the 64th and 78th regiments, then on their way from Persia, should proceed forthwith, without landing at Bombay, to Calcutta. The more speedily to carry out this object, he caused vessels to be equipped and prepared for the reception of these regiments, so that on the arrival in the Bombay harbour of the transports which were conveying them from Bushír they might be transhipped without loss of time. This measure was duly and effectively carried out. The men moved from the one transport into the other, and reached Calcutta in time materially to influence the campaign. But Lord Elphinstone did more. He despatched on the instant to Calcutta a company of Madras artillery which happened to be on the spot, taking the duty of the Bombay artillery, then absent in Persia. He at the same time sent instructions to the officer commanding at Dísá to hold the 83rd Regiment and the troop of horse artillery at that station in readiness to march on Ájmír, on the sole condition that, in the opinion of the local authorities, the departure of the only European troops in the vicinity of A'hmadábád and Gújrát might be hazarded without the absolute certainty of an outbreak. And, still penetrated by the necessity to concentrate on the scene of the mutiny as many European troops as could be collected, Lord Elphinstone chartered, on his own responsibility, two steamers belonging to the Peninsular and Oriental Company, the *Pottinger* and the *Madras*, provided them with all

to Mr. Frere; regarding the regiments on their way from Persia;

regarding the Madras Artillery in Bombay.

He prepares to assist Rajpútáná,

Book XIII. Chapter I.

1857. May.

and sends to the Mauritius and the Cape for reinforcements.

necessary stores, and despatched them, under the command of Captain Griffith Jenkins of the Indian navy, to the Mauritius and the Cape, with letters to the Governors of those settlements, dwelling upon the importance of the crisis, and begging them to despatch to India any troops they could spare.

Result of his applications to the Mauritius,

I may here state that the result of these applications was such as might have been anticipated from the characters of the men to whom they were addressed. The Governor of the Mauritius, Sir James Higginson, embarked on board the *Pottinger* the head-quarters and as many men of the 33rd as that steamer could carry. Not contented with that, he took an early opportunity to charter and despatch another transport to convey the remainder of that regiment, a battery of artillery, and as much money as could be spared from the treasury of the island.

and to the Cape.

Nor was the Governor of the Cape, Sir George Grey, animated by sentiments less patriotic. It fortunately happened that an unusually large force of British regiments was, at the moment, concentrated at Cape Town. Sir George despatched, without delay, as many of them as he could spare. The 89th and 95th he sent to Bombay; the 6th, the 1st battalion 13th, the 2nd battalion 60th, the 73rd, 80th, and 31st to Calcutta. In subsequent vessels he despatched horses in as large a quantity as he could conveniently procure.

Responsibility nobly assumed by

The despatch of Lord Elphinstone to Sir George Grey had painted the urgency of India's needs in terms so glowing that that able governor considered himself justified to stretch his powers. He did not hesitate to direct the commanders of the transports conveying the China expeditionary army so far to divert from their course as to call at Singapor for orders. The result of this patriotic action was most happy. The intelligence which met these transports at Singapor induced their commanders, in every case, to bear up for Calcutta.

Book XIII. Chapter I.

1857. May.

Sir George Grey.

To return to Bombay. So important did it appear to Lord Elphinstone, that reinforcements should promptly be sent from England by the overland route—a route till then untrodden by British troops—that, telegraphic communication being open with Calcutta, he suggested to the Governor-General the propriety of sending to England a special steamer, which he had ready, with despatches, impressing upon the Home Government the urgency of the need. There can be no doubt that the suggestion was a wise one. A fast lightly-laden steamer, travelling at her highest speed, would have anticipated the ordinary mail steamer by three or four days at the least. This, too, at a time when the most important events depended on prompt and decisive action. But Lord Canning did not view matters in the same light. He refused to interfere with the ordinary mail service. The steamer, therefore, was not sent.

Lord Elphinstone suggests sending a special steamer to England,

but Lord Canning refuses.

Before I pass from the record of the precautionary measures taken in the early days of the revolt, to describe the actual occurrences in the

Book XIII. Chapter I.

1857. May.

various parts of the Bombay Presidency, I wish to advert for a moment to one material result which followed them. Those measures undoubtedly saved Bombay from serious outbreak. They did more. They secured an important base of operations against central India and Rajpútáná, and they preserved the line of communication between those provinces and the provinces beyond them and the seaboard. It is difficult to overestimate the importance thus gained, solely by the exercise of timely foresight.

Effect of the precautionary measures above recorded.

Lord Elphinstone meets a breach of law in Baroch.

A rather serious breach of the law at Baroch in the month of May, originating in a dispute between the Pársís and the Muhummadans, might have led to important consequences but for the firmness with which it was met, in the first instance, by the officer commanding on the spot, and, in the next, by the Governor. The spirit of Lord Elphinstone's action may be judged from the fact that, to prevent the spread of the riot, he despatched two hundred men of the 86th to Súrat—a movement of troops which left only three hundred European troops of all arms in Bombay itself.

He designs a policy of offensive defence;

The riot at Baroch was, for a time, the only indication of ill-feeling manifested in the western Presidency, and it was entirely unconnected with the great revolt then raging in the north-west. Lord Elphinstone, whilst carefully repressing it, did not abate a single effort to carry out the policy which he was convinced was the only sound policy—the policy of offensive defence. Almost from the very first he had designed to form, at a convenient point within the Presidency, a column to secure and hold the great line of road between Bombay and Ágra. Not only would the line thus secured form a base for ulterior operations, but a great moral advantage would be gained by its tenure. In the crisis which then afflicted India, it was not to be thought of that any portion of the empire would stand still. The attitude of folded arms was an attitude to invite danger. To check the approach of evil, the surest mode was to go forth and meet it. A column marching towards the north-west would encounter the elements which, having brewed there disturbance, were eager to spread it, and encountering, would annihilate them. The presence of such a column, marching confidently to the front, would, moreover, go far to check, perhaps even to suppress, any disloyal feelings which might have been engendered in the minds of the native princes whose states bordered on this line of communication. For these reasons, then, at a very early period of the crisis, Lord Elphinstone proposed in Council, and ordered the formation of a column, under the command of Major-General Woodburn, to open out communications with central India and the North-West Provinces.

to hold the line between Bombay and Agra,

and, by advancing to meet the evil coming from outside, to prevent it entering within.

With this view forms a column under General Woodburn.

The column formed in consequence, under the command of Major-General Woodburn, was but small in numbers. It consisted only of five troops of the 14th Light Dragoons, the 25th Bombay Native Infantry, Captain Woolcombe's horse-battery of artillery, and a pontoon train. It set out from Púna on the 8th of June, under

Composition of the column.

Book XIII. Chapter I.

1857. June.

It is ordered to march to Máu.

orders to march with all speed to Máu, with the view to save that place while there was yet time, and to prevent the spread of the insurrection in Málwa, and along the northern frontier of the Bombay Presidency.*

Possibilities before General Woodburn.

The state of affairs at Máu and at Indúr was such as to demand the most prompt action on the part of General Woodburn. It was just possible that, making forced marches, he might approach so near to Indúr as to baffle the plans of the discontented. The dread that he might do so for a long time paralysed their action.† Circumstances, however, occurred which baffled the hopes expressed by Lord Elphinstone, when, acting on his own unaided judgment, he pressed upon the military authorities the necessity for General Woodburn to advance.

Aurangábád.

The city of Aurangábád—once the capital of the kingdom of Ahmadnagar, and, at a later period, the favourite residence of the Emperor Aurangzéb—occupies a prominent and important position in the north-western corner of the dominions of the Nizám. The corner of which it was the capital, juts like a promontory into British territory. To the east and north-east it touches western Berár and the central provinces; to the south, the west, and the north-west, the northern portions of the Bombay Presidency. Beyond the northernmost part of that Presidency, and within easy distance of Aurangábád, lies Málwa.

* Lord Elphinstone's letter to General Woodburn.

† *Vide* vol. i. page 212.

Book XIII. Chapter I.

1857. June.

Garrison of Aurangábád.

Disaffection was known to reign in Málwa, and it was of the highest consequence that that disaffection should not spread southward to Bombay. But at Aurangábád, the capital of the small promontory I have described, almost touching Málwa on one side and running into Bombay on the other three sides, were quartered the 1st and 3rd Cavalry, the 2nd Infantry, and a battery of artillery, of the Haidarábád Contingent. These regiments, commanded by British officers, were composed chiefly of Muhammadans, and one of them—the 1st Cavalry—had, in the early part of June, displayed symptoms of disaffection.

Aurangábád is distant from Púna a hundred and thirty-eight miles, from Ahmadnaggar, about midway between the two, sixty-eight miles. In the ordinary course of events, General Woodburn, armed with positive instructions to push on with all speed to Máu, would not have entered the dominions of the Nizám. It happened, however, that the disaffection I have spoken of as prevailing at Aurangábád proceeded on the 13th of June to more open demonstrations, and in consequence General Woodburn received, not from Lord Elphinstone, instructions to deviate from the line urged upon him by that nobleman, and to march upon Aurangábád.

Disaffection of the garrison.

In explanation of the open demonstrations at Aurangábád, I may state that a rumour had reached that place that the cavalry regiment stationed there would be required to join General Woodburn's column and march with him on Dehlí. The rumour was founded upon truth, for

Reasons of the disaffection.

Book XIII. Chapter I.

1857. June.

it had been intended that the regiment in question should join General Woodburn's force. But to the minds of soldiers who were not British subjects, who lived under the rule of the descendant of a viceroy appointed by the Moghol, the idea of fighting against the King of Dehlí was peculiarly distasteful.* They showed their dislike on the moment. On the 13th of June the men of the 1st Cavalry openly expressed their dissatisfaction, and—it was stated at the time—swore to murder their officers if pressure to march against Dehlí were put upon them. Fortunately, the commanding officer, Captain Abbott, was a sensible man. He summoned the native officers to his quarters, and discussed the question with them. The native officers declared that, for their own part, they were ready to obey any lawful order, but they admitted that their men would not fight against the mutineers. Captain Abbott then, after communicating with the Resident, resolved to adopt a conciliatory course. He gave the men assurances that they would not be required to march on Dehlí. In this way order was restored. So little confidence, however, in the stability of the compromise was felt on both sides, that the officers proceeded to barricade themselves in their mess-house, whilst the mutinous cavalry boasted over their moral victory in every quarter of the city.

Judicious conduct of Captain Abbott.

Order is restored, but not confidence.

Matters were in this state when, on the morn-

* The splendid manner in which the Haidarábád cavalry atoned for this momentary disaffection will be found recorded in subsequent pages.

Book XIII. Chapter I. 1857. June.

Woodburn enters Aurangábád and disarms the mutineers.

ing of the 23rd of June, General Woodburn's column entered Aurangábád, marched at once to the ground occupied by the mutineers, and ordered the men to give up their arms. With the exception of one troop of the 1st Cavalry, all obeyed. The general gave the men of that troop six minutes to consider the course they would pursue. When the time elapsed, the men, instead of submitting, put on a bold front and attempted to ride away. In this attempt most of them succeeded. The next morning some three or four, convicted of attempts at assassination, were hanged, and order was restored.

Lord Elphinstone urges Woodburn to press on to Máu.

General Woodburn was under the orders of the Commander-in-Chief, Sir Henry Somerset. In the opinion of Lord Elphinstone, the danger at Aurangábád had not been so pressing as to necessitate the deviation of the field force from the direct road to Máu. He thought that in the presence of two dangers, that which would result from the mutiny coming down to Bombay from central India and Málwa was greater even than the disaffection of a portion of the troops of the Nizám. Forced, however, to accept General Woodburn's action at Aurangábád, he lost not a moment in urging him to press on towards Máu. "I am persuaded," he wrote to that officer on the 22nd of June, "that the local officers greatly exaggerate the danger of a rising in our own provinces. I have no fear of anything of the sort; and if it should happen, I trust that we should be able to put it down speedily. But I feel confident that it will not happen—at all events,

Book XIII. Chapter I.

1857. June.

for the present. If you allow the insurrection to come down to our borders without attempting to check it, we shall almost deserve our fate; but if by a rapid advance you are able to secure Mhow" (Máu), "you will also, in all probability, save Mehidpúr, Ságar, Hoshangábád," &c. Lord Elphinstone followed up these noble words, displaying the true conception he had formed of the situation, by a letter addressed, the same day, to Sir Henry Somerset: "I am very much obliged to you," he wrote, "for the perusal of General Woodburn's letter. I conclude that since it was written he has received his orders to continue his march to Mhow" (Máu) "with all possible expedition."

Woodburn, however, delays to try his prisoners.

But General Woodburn did not move forward. In reply to the letter I have just quoted, he wrote, on the 25th, to Lord Elphinstone, urging the various reasons which, he thought, would necessitate a long stay at Aurangábád. These reasons might, in the presence of the greater danger at Máu, be justly termed trivial. They consisted in the possibility of a fresh outbreak after his departure, and in the necessity of trying some sixty-four prisoners by court-martial.

Lord Elphinstone combats his reasons and still urges him onwards.

Lord Elphinstone answered the objections to advance urged by the general, in a very decided manner. "I wish you to remember," he wrote to him on the 27th of June, "that it was for the object of relieving Máu, and not for the purpose of chastising a mutinous regiment at Aurangábád, that the field force was formed. The latter is an incidental duty, which it was hoped would not

Book XIII. Chapter I. 1857. June.

interfere with the main object. I am perfectly aware that, in these times, circumstances may occur to divert your force from its original destination, but I do not think they have yet occurred." He then proceeded in a few forcible words to urge the folly of wasting unnecessary time upon trials,* and the necessity of disarming regiments which might show disaffection, instead of delaying a movement of the first importance from a fear that a revolt might take place after the departure of the British troops.

Lord Elphinstone is ordered further to diminish his strength.

This letter, I have said, was despatched to General Woodburn on the 27th of June. On the morning of the 28th Lord Elphinstone received a despatch from Calcutta, instructing him to send to Calcutta by sea the wing of the 12th Lancers then stationed at Púna. This diminution of his available European strength, already extremely small, following immediately upon the departure from the Presidency of General Woodburn's force, and accompanied by reports received from many district officers to the effect that rebellion was only watching its opportunity, so affected Lord Elphinstone, that for the moment he felt inclined to authorise General Woodburn to halt at Aurangábád. Indeed, on the spur of the moment he wrote that officer a letter, expressive of his deep regret and disappointment at having to request him to give up a measure which he believed to be of great importance. But the night dissipated his anxiety. In the morning

This order, for a moment, causes Lord Elphinstone to waver.

* "To allow twenty days for the trial of sixty-four prisoners is out of the question in these times."

Book XIII. Chapter I.

1857. June.

he had resolved to dare all, to risk all, for the supreme advantage of saving central India. On the 29th, then, he wrote again to General Woodburn, cancelling that portion of his previous letter which had given him authority to defer the projected movement.

But only for a moment.

Woodburn falls ill and is replaced by Major Follett.

But, before this letter could reach General Woodburn that officer had become incapacitated for command by ill-health. The Government promptly replaced him by Colonel C. S. Stuart, of the Bombay Army, then commanding the 3rd Regiment Native Infantry. Pending the arrival of that officer, the command of the field force devolved upon Major Follett, 25th Regiment Native Infantry.

Follett inherits Woodburn's opinions.

Major Follett had a grand opportunity before him. He had only to move forward. Unfortunately, he wrote to the Commander-in-Chief a letter in which he dwelt upon the impossibility of leaving Aurangábád in the then condition of the Nizám's regiments. More unfortunately still, Major Follett's representations were strongly supported by the head of the army.

Difficulty of Lord Elphinstone's position.

Lord Elphinstone's reasons and instincts still told him that the further delay thus proposed was the delay of red tape—the natural consequence of the absence of a clear mind and a firm will. But he was in a very difficult position. He was not a soldier. And although he would unhesitatingly have disregarded the scruples of Major Follett, unsupported by higher authority, he could not treat with contempt the weighty support given to those scruples by the officer who was

Commander-in-Chief of the armies serving in India. Unwillingly, then, and solely in deference to the strong opinion expressed by Sir Henry Somerset, Lord Elphinstone consented to the delay.

Book XIII. Chapter I.

1857. July.

Major Follett is converted to Lord Elphinstone's views.

A few days proved how true had been his judgment. On the 7th of July, Major Follett convicted himself and the chief who supported him of a hasty and premature decision. On the 7th of July that officer wrote to Lord Elphinstone,* declared that it was perfectly feasible to leave Aurangábád, and announced his intention to march for Máu on the 10th, leaving a troop of cavalry and two guns for the protection of the Aurangábád cantonment.

Lord Elphinstone promptly requested Sir Henry Somerset to confirm this change of feeling by cancelling his previous orders. This was, in effect, carried out.

Colonel Stuart comes to command the force, and sets out for A'sírgarh.

The force, led by Colonel C. S. Stuart of the Bombay army, who joined it on the 8th, quitted Aurangábád on the 12th, too late to prevent the mutinies at Máu and Indúr, but not too late, under the guidance of Colonel Durand, who joined it at Ásírgarh, to restore British authority in central India. To the further movements of this column I shall return in a subsequent chapter. Its march beyond the Bombay fron-

* It is probable that Major Follett's change of opinion was due to the receipt of a despatch from Colonel Durand addressed to Mr. Plowden, and sent through the officer commanding at Aurangábád. This letter contained convincing proofs of the necessity of promptly advancing.

Book XIII. Chapter I.

1857. July.

tier was due solely to Lord Elphinstone.* Had he been unfettered, and had its first commander been a man after his own heart, it would have taken place in time to prevent much evil in central India.

But the despatch of Colonel Stuart's column to central India was not the only aid proffered by the Bombay Presidency for the suppression of the mutiny. I have already alluded to the splendid self-abnegation by which the province of Sind was denuded for the benefit of the Punjáb. Again, the western Presidency was prompt to comply with the indent made upon it by Colonel G. St. P. Lawrence,

* "I quite agree with you," wrote Lord Elphinstone to Colonel Durand, the 27th of July, "in regretting the delay which took place in the advance of the force. You cannot have written more strongly than I have upon the subject, but there was a strong counter-prejudice on the part of the officers on the spot, everyone of whom declared that the departure of the column from Aurangábád would be the signal of a general rising. I from the first recommended that the mutinous troops should be disarmed and dismounted. But this was considered inexpedient. It was represented that it was not so much the troops but the whole population was against us. Mr. ——, the Deputy Commissioner in North Berár, who is reckoned a very good officer, said that there were, I am afraid to say how many, armed Musulmans in his district, who would rise the moment the column was ordered to move. Colonel ——, who commands the Madras cavalry regiment at ——, said it was utterly impossible to send half his regiment over to Aurangábád, as the people in that neighbourhood would attack the station." It is immensely to the credit of Lord Elphinstone that, in spite of these and many similar reports from district officers, and of the opposition referred to in the text, he should have persevered in urging the forward movement. He was, in fact, one of the few men in high position in India who realised how the mutiny should be met.

Book XIII. Chapter I.

1857. July.

the Governor-General's agent in Rajpútáná.* The greater part of the garrison of Dísá, consisting of a troop of horse artillery, one regiment and one squadron of native light cavalry, a detachment (four hundred men) of the 83rd, and a detachment of the 12th Native Infantry, was formed into a movable column, and placed at the disposal of George Lawrence, just then nominated Brigadier-General in Rajpútáná. Lord Elphinstone was prompt to confirm this arrangement—an arrangement which gave General Lawrence a power, exercised with remarkable ability and judgment, to maintain order in a country ruled over by the great Rajpút chiefs.† Further, on the 23rd of July, four companies of the 86th Regiment were sent from Malligám to join Colonel Stuart's column on its way to Máu. Marching direct by the Bombay road, they did not join till after that column had arrived at Máu.

Lord Elphinstone places a column at the disposal of Colonel Lawrence.

Whilst Lord Elphinstone was thus actively employing a policy of aggressive offence alike to keep the evil from his own borders and to crush it in the provinces beyond them, the spirit which had worked so much mischief in the north-west suddenly raised its head on his very hearth. The first symptoms of mutiny in the Bombay Presidency broke out shortly after the march of the columns whose movements I have just recorded.

First symptoms of mutiny in the Bombay Presidency.

The southern Maráthá country comprises the territory between Satárah and the Madras Presidency to the north and south, and between the

The southern Maráthá country;

* Vol. i. page 249. † *Vide* pages 245 to 260, vol. i.

Book XIII. Chapter I.

1857. May.

Nizám's dominions and the western gháts to the east and west. It has an area of fourteen thousand square miles and a population of about three millions, for the most part of pure Maráthá blood. Within this country are the two collectorates, Balgáon and Dhárwár, the native state Kolhapúr, and numerous small semi-independent states, each with an annual revenue rising up to, but in no case exceeding, fifty thousand pounds. In 1857 the principal of these were Sánglí, Míraj, Sávanúr, Kurándwár, Jámkhandi, Nargúnd, and Múdhol.

its area, and native states.

Character of Mr. George Berkeley Seton-Karr.

Of this important country the Collector and Magistrate of Balgáon, Mr. George Berkeley Seton-Karr, had political charge. Mr. Seton-Karr possessed remarkable natural abilities, and these had been developed by an education which had continued up to the date of which I am writing. He was a firm advocate for the rights of native princes, for continuing to them the power to adopt, for interfering as little as possible with their customs which, however little understood by Europeans, were harmless in themselves, and which were hallowed by the practice of ages. He was one of those men who, whilst possessed of a firm and decided character, yet preferred to try to their fullest extent the arts of persuasion before having recourse to intimidation or violence.

Internal condition of the southern Maráthá country.

The internal condition of the southern Maráthá country when Mr. Seton-Karr assumed charge of it in May 1856, just twelve months prior to the revolt, was one of brooding discontent. The

THE MARÂTHÂ COUNTRY
English Miles
0 50 100 150
Longitude East from Greenwich
W. H. Allen & Co. London. S.W.
INDIAN OCEAN
DAKHAN
Khandesh
Birâr
Aurangâbâd
Satpûrah Mts
Kâtiwâr
G. of Cambay
Cambay
Barôdah
Dabhâi
Broâch
R. Narbadâ
R. Tapti
SÛRAT
Sachin
Damân
Trimbak
Nâsik
Bassein
Salsette I.
Bombay
Kolâbah I.
Râjâpur
Jinjirah I.
Savarndurg
Jaigarh
Sangâmeshwar
Ratnagiri
Vishâlgarh
Gheriah
Malwân
Vingôrla
GOA
Sivadashagarh
Ankôlah
S. Warda
Malligâon
Chandûr
Ellôra
Dâolatâbâd
Jâlnah
Jafirâbâd
Asai
Akôla
Ellichpûr
Gâwilgarh
Barhanpur
Asirgarh
Baitûl
NÂGPUR
Manakdurg
Mâhûr
R. Wardâ (Northern)
Wain Gangâ R.
Sirôncha
R. Godâvari
Paithan
Ahmadnagar
Wargâon
Jawir
Kalyân
Khandâla
Châkan
Sirûr
Jaligâon
PÛNAH
Pûrandar
Sôpah
Bârâmati
R. Nira
Indâpur
Phaltan
Wâi
Mahâbalishwar
Sâtârâ
Tarla
Karâr
Kûrdlâ
Purinda
Ashtî
Pandarpur
Tûljâpur
Shôlâpûr
Akalkôt
Ûdghîr
Bîdar
R. Manjerah
Kalburgah
Golconda
HAIDARÂBÂD
R. Musî
R. Bima
Tôlapûr
BIJAPÛR
Kolâr
Miraj
Malkapur
Kolhâpur
Gokâk
Shâhpur
Sawant Wâri
Belgâum
Kittûr
Dhârwâr
Hublî
R. Malapûrba
R. Tûmbhadra
R. Hagri
Râichûr
R. Kistna
Karnâl

annexation by the Government of India of Berár and of Oudh had been in the one case followed, in the other preceded, by an Act known as Act XI. of 1852, under the operation of which an Inám Commission was empowered to call upon all landed proprietors to produce the title-deeds of their estates. A new tribunal had, under this Act, been invested with arbitrary jurisdiction over this vast mass of property. The holders of estates, careless and improvident, unacquainted with law, and accustomed to consider that thirty years' possession conferred an irrefragable title, had failed in many instances to preserve the most valid muniments of their estates. In some cases, indeed, no muniments had ever existed. Chiefs who, in the anarchy which prevailed in India subsequent to the death of Aurangzíb, had won their estates by the sword, had not been careful to fence them in with a paper barrier—in that age utterly valueless—but they had transmitted to their descendants the arms and the retainers who had constituted their right to possession, and with whose aid they had learned to consider mere titles superfluous, as without it they were contemptible. In other cases, men who had acquired land in the general scramble which preceded the downfall of the Péshwá's Government, had transmitted their acquisitions to their children, fortified by no better titles than entries in the village account-books. To both these classes the Inám Commission had been a commission simply of confiscation. In the southern Maráthá country the titles of thirty-five thousand

Book XIII. Chapter I.

1857. May.

The Inám Commission.

The manner in which that commission affected many of the chiefs and landowners.

Book XIII. Chapter I.

1857. May.

estates, large and small, had been called for by the new tribunal. In twenty-one thousand cases that tribunal had pronounced sentences of confiscation. Thousands of other landowners, still unevicted, looked on in dismay, tremblingly awaiting the sentence which was to add their wail of distress and resentment to that of their impoverished neighbours.* Can it be wondered at, then, that Mr. Seton-Karr, when he assumed charge under these circumstances in May 1856, found the native landowners of the southern Maráthá country in a state of moody discontent, which was prevented from bursting into open disaffection only by a sense of its utter hopelessness?

Their discontent.

* In writing thus of the feelings of the actual landowners, I am far from desiring to say a single word against the inquiries instituted by the Inám Commission. I wish to record only the discontent of the men who actually possessed the land when the inquiry was ordered. I admit not only that the Government was perfectly justified in ordering that inquiry, but that it was demanded by thousands who had been violently and, in some cases, fraudulently dispossessed of their hereditary acres during the period antecedent to the fall of the Péshwá. The Inám Commission rendered substantial justice to these men. On the other hand, it must be borne in mind that forty years had elapsed since the dominions of the Péshwá had been brought under British sway, and that during those years, and, in many cases, during many antecedent years, the landowners who felt aggrieved by the action of the Inám Commission, had enjoyed and transmitted to their children the estates which their fathers had gained. The long possession gave them in their eyes a better right than any which could be urged by the descendants of the men who had been dispossessed. No wonder, then, from their point of view, the Inám Commission was an instrument of tyranny.

Book XIII. Chapter I.

1857. May.

The right of adoption,

But another cause increased, even intensified, the discontent, and, by its connection with the religious feelings of all classes, added greatly to the danger of the situation. Of all the rights devolving upon a Hindú landowner, the right to adopt is at once the most cherished and the most sacred. It is an observance enjoined upon him by his religion. Should he fail to beget a child, he is bound to provide for himself an heir by adoption. On the child so adopted he bestows all the care and the affection ordinarily lavished on the offspring of love. Taught by his religion to believe that his own happiness in the other world depends upon the transmission to the adopted son of the inheritance of his fathers, he is ever careful to instil into his mind that he actually is of the family, and will be, after his death, the representative of its traditions and its honours. The idea that he might die heirless is to the Hindu landowner an ever-present canker-worm. It is sufficient to make him moody, despairing, miserable. The prohibition to find for himself such an heir might even make him reckless.

a religious rite necessary for the Hindú.

But the Anglo-Indian Government had, in many instances, pronounced such a prohibition. The policy of absorption adopted by Lord Dalhousie had shown no respect for the principle of adoption. Under its action large states had been absorbed, and the power to adopt had been denied to lesser landowners. This refusal had been extended to the landowners of the southern Maráthá country—amongst others, to the important chief of Nargúnd. The prohibition produced conster-

The policy of Lord Dalhousie

denies the exercise of this rite to many influential chiefs.

Book XIII. Chapter I.

1857. May.

nation. The effeminate training of the Hindú upper classes often rendered it absolutely necessary to employ the rite of adoption to prevent the extinction of a family. The custom had been hallowed by time. The prohibition of it by a paramount power, alien in race and faith, could be attributed only to greed for the land. When, then, the prohibition was extended, and the landowners saw family after family disappear, a great fear fell upon them. They felt, one and all, that their turn would come; that their names, too, would perish; that none would succeed to commemorate their deeds and the deeds of their ancestors, and to appease their *manes* by yearly celebrations. In the common despair old feuds were laid aside, hereditary enmity was forgotten. A common dread produced a common sympathy, and the indignation or alarm of each was supported and increased by the sense that it was shared by all. For the moment, indeed, no one thought to combine against the British Government. But though tranquillity prevailed, it was not the tranquillity which is based upon contentment. The landowners were tranquil simply because successful revolt seemed impossible. The British authority seemed too firmly fixed to be easily shaken. But, were it to be shaken, it was always possible, considering the intense and widespread discontent of the landowners, that their hopeless apathy might become the audacity of despair.

Effect produced by this refusal.

State of the southern Maráthá

Such was the state of the southern Maráthá country when, in May 1856, Mr. Seton-Karr as-country in May 1856.

sumed charge of it. But a few weeks elapsed before his experienced mind had mastered the causes of the discontent which he found everywhere prevailing. It was difficult, even for a man who condemned the policy of the Government and who sympathised with the native landowners, to allay it. He found, in fact, that in almost every instance the landowners had been grievously wronged. The influential chief of Nargúnd had been denied the rights of adoption in terms which—owing to the faultiness of the translation of the original English—added insult to injury. Other landowners of ancient lineage, and possessing weight in the country, were found by Mr. Seton-Karr estranged from their loyalty by the causes to which I have adverted—the Inám Commission and the withholding of the right of adoption—and plunged in moody mistrust of the Government. It was not in the power of Mr. Seton-Karr to carry out the only act which would have restored confidence—to moderate the action of the Inám Commission and to restore the right of adoption. Nor, conciliatory and sympathising as he was, was he more able to reconcile the native chiefs and landowners to the new order which had to them all the effects of a revolution. But all that an earnest and high-minded man could do he did. He visited every landowner. Their individual characters he carefully studied. To their complaints he listened with patience. He met them generally with such explanations of the policy of the Government as might remove misapprehension as to its general

Mr. Seton-Karr's powers, in respect of the grievances, restricted;

but he uses all his influence to soothe the discontented.

Book XIII. Chapter I.

1857. May.

intention; whilst, in cases of individual hardship—which he was powerless to remedy—he endeavoured to soothe the sense of hardness and injustice by kindly expressions of sympathy. In this way he won their confidence. He made the landowners feel that in the highest official in the province they had a real friend. More it was impossible for him to effect. Regard for the individual in no way obliterated resentment at the action of the Government. A sense of deep injury still continued to rankle in each breast.

He wins the confidence of the landowners.

Effect produced in the Maráthá country by the revolt at Mírath.

Such was the state of affairs when, on the 21st of May 1857, the news of the mutiny at Mírath and Dehlí reached Belgáon. The effect of this news, and of the worse tidings which continued to follow, upon the peoples of the southern Maráthá country was electric. The Muhammadans were at once aroused to an intense pitch of excitement. The Hindús, on the other hand, were far more reticent, and for some time concealed their inner feelings by an impassive exterior. British authority seemed so firmly rooted in the country that they hesitated to believe that it could be suddenly destroyed.

The means at Mr. Seton-Karr's disposal totally inadequate.

Mr. Seton-Karr was fully alive to the dangers of the crisis. The force at Belgáon consisted of one regiment of native infantry, the 29th, a weak battery of European artillery, and the depot of the 64th Foot, composed of about thirty men fit for duty, guarding upwards of four hundred women and children belonging to that regiment. Exclusive of the artillery, not more than one hundred Europeans fit to carry arms could be mustered in the place; whilst between Belgáon and Púna and Sholapúr there were more than two thousand native, and only one hundred and twenty European soldiers. The defences of Belgáon consisted of a fort nearly a mile in circumference, the ramparts of which, unrepaired for years, presented breaches in several places. In a military point of view the place was, in fact, untenable, but it had nevertheless to be regarded as the sole refuge for the European non-combatants, consisting of some five hundred including children. Belgáon was the head-quarters of the southern division of the army, and Major-General Lester had arrived there on the 11th of May to assume that command. Mr. Seton-Karr at once placed himself in communication with that officer, and, under his direction, such improvements as in so brief a time were practicable, were made to the defences.

Book XIII. Chapter I.

1857. May.

General Lester.

During the week or two following, the unusual exaltation of the Muhammadans alone gave evidence of the effect produced by the bad news from the north-west. But in the early part of June Mr. Seton-Karr discovered that an emissary from that part of India had arrived some days before, and that he had been in daily communication with the Muhammadan leaders. Prompt to act in the presence of real danger, as he was slow to use violence when the end could be accomplished by peaceable means, Mr. Seton-Karr caused this intruder to be arrested and confined. He did not act one minute too soon. The sepoys, many of them natives of Oudh, had for some days pre-

An emissary arrives from the north-west.

He is arrested.

Book XIII. Chapter I.

1857. May.

vious displayed an unaccustomed insolence. It had become hourly more and more evident that they sympathised with the action of their brethren in the north, and that they would grasp at an opportunity to follow their example. In the proportion in which their insolence increased did the peril of Mr. Seton-Karr's position increase. It was still further augmented by the action of Náná Sáhib at Kánhpúr towards the end of June.

Relationship of many of the southern Maráthá chiefs to Náná Sáhib.

To understand this it is requisite only to remember that Náná Sáhib claimed to be, and in the eyes of his countrymen actually was, the adopted heir of the last of the Péshwás; and that some of the most important estates in the southern Maráthá country—the estates of Sángli, of Jámkhandi, of Míraj, and of Kúrandwar—were held by branches of the great Patwardhan family, the most illustrious of the dependants of the Péshwá. The fact that Náná Sáhib was married to the first cousin of the chief of Sángli; that his most active lieutenant was that chief's uncle; and that the chief himself, on the verge of his majority, had evinced a taste for low and intriguing associates, did not certainly lesson the danger of the position.

The discontent of the Désáis of Nipáni,

There were other chiefs whose discontent was hardly less formidable. Prominent amongst these were the Désái of Nipáni, a small fortress built on the model of Bharatpúr, about forty miles from Belgáon—a chieftain who had lost a large portion of his estates under the operation of the Inám Commission, who was known to be disaffected, and whose disaffection would cut off communications with Bombay; the Désái of Jámboti—a chieftain whose family, settled for many generations amongst the forests which stretch onwards from the Gháts, had come to be regarded as the natural lords of the wild population of the jungles, and who, in his own person, had been reduced to penury by the action of the same arbitrary tribunal. The temper of this chieftain had been soured by his misfortunes. He had little to lose, everything to gain, by rebellion. It was in his power to draw after him a large portion of the jungle population, and by their means to sever the communications of the British with the sea. Not less dangerous was the adopted son of the late Désái of Kittúr. The retainers of this family, twenty-four years previously, had crowned a rash insurrection by a gallant defence of their fort, in the siege of which a political agent of that day had fallen. The last representative of the race was then living as a pensioner upon the bounty of his father-in-law, commanding in his fallen state the sympathies of the whole Lingayat population. He, too, had nothing to lose, everything to hope, from rebellion. His father-in-law, the Désái of Wantmúrí, though a cautious and prudent man, did not possess the strength of character to resist extraordinary pressure placed upon him by his co-religionists. Add to these the chief of Nargúnd, connected with some of the most powerful families in the southern Maráthá country, and known to be thoroughly disaffected; add, moreover, that the population, naturally turbulent and

of Jámboti,

of Kittúr,

and of Wantmúrí,

also of the chief of Nargúnd.

Book XIII. Chapter I.

1857. June.

causes apprehension.

warlike, had retained the arms which had all but gained empire for the Maráthás; and the reader may gather some idea of the position which, difficult in May, became dangerous in the early part of June, and threatening as every day witnessed a closer approach to the advent of July.

Mr. Seton-Karr applies for extended powers and responsibility.

For long Mr. Seton-Karr met the increasing danger from the resources suggested to him by his long experience, and by his thorough acquaintance with native character. But as time went on, each post bringing with it intelligence of further outbreaks in the provinces of the north-west, that gentleman deemed it at last his duty to bring the situation of the provinces under the eyes of the Government of Bombay. He did this on the 20th of June. Cognisant, however, of the great difficulties which Lord Elphinstone had to encounter, of the unselfish foresight which had induced that heroic man to denude his own presidency that he might crush rebellion upon its borders, Mr. Seton-Karr did not ask for aid, material or other. He merely asked that his own powers might be extended. He asked, in fact, that the entire responsibility of meeting and encountering the crisis might be cast on him alone. It was a noble request; especially noble at that crisis; especially noble considering the resources at his disposal—a native regiment in a state of veiled rebellion, a weak battery of artillery, about one hundred Europeans—to meet the rebellion which might occur at any moment. The request was complied with.

His request is complied with.

Book XIII. Chapter I.

1857. July.

Free now to act, Mr. Seton-Karr developed his plan. The use of force was out of the question. The only possible policy was conciliation. In carrying this out Mr. Seton-Karr enjoyed advantages which would have been denied to many men. During the year immediately preceding the mutiny he had carefully cultivated friendly relations with the chiefs. Over the minds of many he had acquired an extraordinary ascendancy. This ascendancy he now tested—and in the most cases with the happiest results. Valuable information was placed at his disposal; the intercommunication of the disaffected was prevented; a vigilant watch upon their movements was secured. In this way, and by a show of confidence towards all, by impressing upon each chief the idea that his neighbour was loyal, and by the expression of a confidence, really felt, that the scare would soon pass away, leaving the British complete master of the situation, Mr. Seton-Karr succeeded in staving off the fatal day and in averting the dreaded explosion.

He gradually unfolds his plans

and retains the confidence of the chiefs.

Difficulties, however, continued to increase. On the 31st of July the 27th Native Infantry mutinied at Kolhapúr, plundered the treasury, and after murdering such officers as fell in their way, set off for the Gháts. Kolhapúr is sixty-five miles from Belgáon. Communications between the 27th Regiment and the 29th at the latter place had been frequent. At Dhárwár, forty-two miles from Belgáon in a direction opposite to that of Kolhapur, the 28th Regiment had been for some time on the very verge of revolt.

Mutiny at Kolhapúr.

Its position with respect to Belgáon and Dhárwár.

Book XIII. Chapter I.

1857. July.

Mr. Seton-Karr was thus occupying a position between one station where the garrison had just mutinied, and another the garrison of which was on the verge of mutiny—the troops at the central point being also infected. It happened, however, that the native officer of the 29th—the regiment stationed at Belgáon—who was the secret leader of the disaffected, one Thákur Singh, was known to Mr. Seton-Karr. That gentleman at once, and before the news of the mutiny at Kolhapúr was generally known at Belgáon, entered into communication regarding this native officer with General Lester. To arrest him might have precipitated a calamity. It was more easy to devise a pretext to remove him honourably from the station. Such a pretext was soon found. Two companies of the 29th, that of Thákur Singh being one of them, were ordered on command to Badámi, a small town some ninety miles distant near the south-western frontier of the Nizám's dominions. The two companies set out on the morning of the 29th, still ignorant of the mutiny at Kolhapúr. When the tidings of that mutiny reached the sepoys left behind at Belgáon they were too disconcerted by the absence of their leader to act on the moment. The opportune seizure and the condign punishment of an emissary from Jámkhandi who had come to incite them to an immediate outbreak, awed them into still longer inaction.

Mr. Seton-Karr and General Lester adopt plans for preventing the spread of mutiny to Belgáon,

which succeed.

Conspiracy of the Muhammadan population at Belgáon

The danger, however, was by no means removed. Concurrently with the events I have just related, Mr. Seton-Karr discovered a plot of

Book XIII. Chapter I.

1857. August.

the Muhammadan population of Belgáon. He soon found that this conspiracy had its ramifications at Kohlapúr, at Haidarábád, and at Púna, and that its outbreak was to be signalled by the seizure of Belgáon itself. The arrest of one of the chief conspirators at Púna seemed likely to precipitate the outbreak. Mr. Seton-Karr, therefore, no sooner received information of this event, than he secured the local leaders at Belgáon, all of whom he had carefully watched. The evidence regarding some of these proved defective, and they were discharged. But the principal conspirator was convicted on the clearest evidence, and he was blown from a gun in company with the emissary from Jámkhandi just spoken of.

is baffled by Mr. Seton-Karr.

Three days before this execution—the 10th of August—a small detachment of European troops arrived to reassure the authorities at Belgáon. Another detachment went on to produce a similar good effect in Dhárwár. General Lester at once proceeded to repress the rising mutinous spirit of the 29th Native Infantry. Five men of that regiment were tried, one of them was condemned to death, the remainder were transported for life. Taking advantage of the good effect produced by these proceedings, Mr. Seton-Karr began the work of disarming the district, including the towns of Belgáon and Sháhpúr. On the 24th of August a further reinforcement arrived in the shape of a detachment of the 86th Foot. Their presence, combined with other precautionary measures taken by Mr. Seton-Karr, caused the great Muhammadan festival of the Muharram to pass off

The arrival of reinforcements enables General Lester to suppress the ill-feeling in Belgáon and Dhárwár.

Book XIII. Chapter I.

1857. August.

without disturbance—and, for a time, the Europeans in the southern Maráthá country felt that they could breathe freely.

Review of the success of Mr. Seton-Karr's measures and the reason of that success.

Mr. Seton-Karr had thus succeeded, by a combination of firmness and tact, the result of good judgment directing intimate acquaintance with the native character, in guiding the territories committed to his charge through the most dangerous crisis of the mutiny. Considering the previous discontent of the chiefs and landowners, the fact that he was supported by no force, that he had only his own energies upon which to rely, this result will ever be quoted as a marvellous instance of skilful management of men. It is not too much to say that a single false step would have produced the most fatal consequences. Not only would it have involved the southern Maráthá country in revolt, but it would have kindled a flame which would have spread throughout the dominions of the Nizám. Had Mr. Seton-Karr diverged, but for one day, from the line of vigilant forbearance which he had laid down as his policy; had he hurried the ill-disposed into open insurrection by any unguarded word of suspicion or slight; or had he encouraged their designs by supineness, a great calamity would have been inevitable. Unhappily, subsequent events proved only too truly the truth of this assertion. When in an evil moment, to be related hereafter, the charge of political affairs was removed from the hands of Mr. Seton-Karr to those of an officer distasteful, from his previous connection with the Inám Commission, to the chiefs and landowners,

The truth of the argument proved by subsequent events.

Book XIII. Chapter I.

1857. August.

one month did not elapse before the rebellion, controlled by good management, began its course with murder. All honour, then, to the wise and farseeing officer who kept it within bounds when its outburst would have been far more dangerous.*

Kolhapúr.

Before returning to Bombay, I must ask the reader to accompany me for a brief period to Kolhapúr. The state of this name, ruled over by the descendants of Sivaji, had up to the year 1842

* The Government of Bombay was not insensible to Mr. Seton-Karr's great merits. On the 14th of September 1857, he was informed that "the Right Honourable the Governor in Council considers that in a conjunction of great anxiety and danger you have displayed a calmness, an energy, and a foresight which entitle you to the thanks and commendations of Government." Again, "the judicious arrangements made by you have amply secured the future tranquillity of the southern Maráthá country." These and other commendations were repeated and confirmed by Lord Elphinstone in letters under his own hand, in which he alludes to "the marked ability and success" with which Mr. Seton-Karr had performed his duties. In his published minute on distinguished services rendered during the mutiny, Lord Elphinstone placed Mr. Seton-Karr's name third on the list of those who had deserved well of their country. The honour was the more marked, because, as Lord Canning observed, every recommendation from Lord Elphinstone carried double weight from the fact that out of the many who had rendered important services in western India, he selected only a few names for mention. Yet, strange as it may appear, when so many were decorated, Mr. Seton-Karr received neither honours nor reward. He returned to England towards the end of 1860, his proud nature suffering from the unmerited slight which had been cast upon him. In less than two years he died, conscious that he had performed a great service which his country had failed to recognise.

Book XIII. Chapter I.

1857. July.

Its previous history.

suffered from continuous disorder and misrule. To such an extent had the evil proceeded that in the year I have mentioned the British Government was forced to interfere and to nominate a minister to introduce order and good government. The efforts made in that direction by this enlightened man, a Brahman named Dáji Khrishna Pandit, to deprive the corrupt party in the state of their illicit gains, provoked a rebellion. This rebellion having been suppressed, the British Government assumed the direct administration of the state during the minority of the Rájá. Within this period, which did not expire till 1862, the forts of every description were dismantled, and the system of hereditary garrison was abolished; the native military force was disbanded, and a local corps, officered by three English officers, was substituted for it. These measures, especially those for the disarmament of their forts and the disbandment of their native force, though in view of the many previous rebellions absolutely necessary, had been regarded with great disfavour by the higher orders in Kolhapúr, and had tended not a little to the unpopularity of the paramount power.

Reasons for the discontent of the people.

Effect of the Miráth mutiny at Kolhapúr.

Such was the state of affairs in the province when the mutiny broke out at Miráth. Hopes and wishes similar to those which I have described as actuating the Muhammadan population of the Belgáon district, at once took possession of the minds of their neighbours in Kolhapúr. To a people accustomed to revolt, living on the memories of plunder and corruption, and hating good government, the occasion seemed singularly

Garrison of Kolhapúr.

favourable. The town of Kolhapúr is distant only sixty-five miles from Belgáon. It was garrisoned by one native regiment, the 27th, and by the local corps raised on the disbandment of the native force. There were no European troops nearer than Belgáon, and it was impossible to spare any from that place. Satárah was eighty-one miles to the north, and Púna, whence European aid was alone possible, seventy-one miles further. The political superintendent of Kolhapúr was Colonel Maughan. Major Rolland commanded the 27th Native Infantry, Captain Schneider the local corps.

The mutinous regiments at the various stations intercommunicate.

I have already stated* that communications between the 27th Native Infantry at Kolhapúr, the 29th at Belgáon, and the 28th at Dhárwár, had been frequent during the months of June and July. Supported, as they were, secretly, by discontented chiefs, almost openly by the disaffected Muhammadan populations, these three regiments had the game in their own hands. Concerted and simultaneous action was only necessary to their success. Happily on this, as on so many occasions at this eventful period, the conspirators failed in this essential particular. It would seem that they reckoned without the telegraph. Instead of deciding to rise on a settled date, they arranged that the example should be set by Kolhapúr, and followed at once by Belgáon and Dhárwár. The 27th Native Infantry accordingly rose on the 31st of July at Kolhapúr. But for the telegraph the

The one blot in their plan.

* Page 31.

Book XIII. Chapter I.

1857. July.

regiment at Belgáon would have received by express intelligence of the movement, and have followed the example. But the telegraph forestalled their express. And Mr. Seton-Karr, using his priority of news with judgment, averted, as we have seen, the calamity from that place.

Mutiny at Kolhapúr.

But the mutiny at Kolhapúr was a reality. During the night of the 31st of July the 27th rose in arms and detailed parties to attack their officers' bungalows. The native adjutant, a Jew, and a Hindú havildar ran to give warning only just in time to permit the ladies to escape from their houses before the sepoys came up and poured volleys into them. Some of the officers nobly endeavoured to bring back the rebels to their duty, but their efforts were vain. The treasury and the bazaar were plundered, and riot reigned supreme. Three officers who had escaped into the country were shot and thrown into the river. The remainder took refuge in the Residency, about a mile from the cantonment, but near the lines of the Kolhapúr local regiment, which happily remained loyal.*

Lord Elphinstone despatches Le Grand Jacob to Kolhapúr.

Character of Le Grand Jacob.

The news of this disaster reached Bombay by telegraph. Lord Elphinstone acted with promptitude and decision. It happened that Colonel G. Le Grand Jacob, a man of the old heroic type, ready in council, prompt and decisive in action, had but just returned to Bombay from a command in the Persian campaign. He was about to start for Púna under the orders of the Commander-in-

* *Western India before and during the Mutinies*, by Major-General Sir George Le Grand Jacob, K.C.S.I., C.B.

1857. August.

Chief, when the telegram from Kolhapúr was placed in the hands of the Governor. Lord Elphinstone at once sent for Jacob. He told him all that had occurred at Kolhapúr; that he would receive orders from the Commander-in-Chief to take command of the troops in that quarter. He added that he was well aware that there were no troops to be depended upon, except perhaps the local regiments; but that he would receive special powers, and was to do the best he could.*

Instructions given to him.

Colonel Jacob set out at once, saw the Commander-in-Chief at Púna, pushed on, then, to Satárah, and found there a troop of horse artillery and dragoons. The rainy season was at its height, the track between Satárah and Kolhapúr was composed of the black soil in which, during the monsoon, horses not unfrequently sank up to their girths, and wheels to their axles; there were several rivers and streams unbridged and unfordable. Still, time was everything. Colonel Jacob then pushed on two guns with double allowance of men and horses, and riding forward himself with a few men of the Southern Maráthá Horse, a loyal and capable regiment, reached

Jacob sets out,

and, despite of difficulties,

* The final orders to Colonel Jacob were not issued till the following day, as Lord Elphinstone wished, before their issue, to receive a reply to a telegram he had sent to Kolhapúr. As no reply came, the orders were at once issued. "They were," writes Sir G. Le G. Jacob, "brief and satisfactory. 'I am aware,' said Lord Elphinstone, 'that in a crisis like this, a person on the spot ought to be the best judge of any action that might be at once necessary; to wait for orders may allow events to become too strong to master. I have confidence in your judgment; do your best to meet the present emergency, and rely on my full support.'"—*Western India*, by Sir G. Le G. Jacob.

Book XIII. Chapter I.

1857. August.

Kolhapúr on the 14th of August, just before midnight.

reaches Kolhapúr.

The mutineers have, meanwhile, been checked by Colonel Maughan.

How, meanwhile, had matters been progressing in Kolhapúr? There, according to all probabilities, there would have been little to check the victorious progress of the rebels! Thanks to their delays and to the prompt action of Colonel Maughan, it had happened otherwise. The sepoys, greedy of plunder, went first to pillage the treasury and sack the station. Then, and then only, did they make their way to the town, fully expecting to find its gates open. But Colonel Maughan had closed those gates. The sepoys, not caring to attempt to force them, took up a rather formidable position outside, close to the gates, in a small outwork where the Rájá's horses and menagerie were kept. Here they maintained their position all night, repulsing Colonel Maughan in an attempt made by him to dislodge them.

Many return to their duty:

It would seem that from this time the greater part of the regiment returned to its allegiance. This movement was probably hastened by the knowledge, brought to the sepoys by some of their still recalcitrant comrades, that the passes to the coast had been occupied by Europeans landed on the coast by the splendid exertions of the Indian Navy. This is certain, that the recalcitrant sepoys were checked in this way; that the greater number betook themselves to the jungles; whilst the minority, about forty in number, returning to Kolhapúr, reoccupied the outwork close to the town. But the garrison of the town had in the

Book XIII. Chapter I.

1857. August.

meantime been reinforced. Lieutenant Kerr, of the Southern Maráthá Horse, had marched a detachment of that regiment from Satárah—a distance of eighty-one miles—without a halt. The rebels were at once attacked, on the 10th of August, in their outwork, some of their own comrades joining in the attack. They made a desperate defence—but a secret entrance to the outwork having been pointed out to Lieutenant Kerr, that gallant officer dashed in, followed by horsemen whom he had caused to dismount, and fought his way to the interior of the building. At the same time, Lieutenant Innes, with a party of the 27th, took the rebels in the rear. These two attacks decided the affair; but so desperate had been the defence, that of the forty rebels three only escaped wounds or death.*

the remainder are attacked and killed.

When, then, Colonel Le G. Jacob reached Kolhapúr, he found that the mutiny had been quelled. Some forty of the most rebellious men of the 27th Native Infantry had been killed in fair fight; a larger number was in the jungles; but still the great bulk of the regiment was doing its duty, and there was no evidence against any man of it.

Jacob determines to disarm the 27th Native Infantry.

Three days after his arrival, Colonel Jacob was reinforced by the two horse-artillery guns he had sent on from Satárah, and about a hundred men of the 2nd Europeans from the coast—the same who had so opportunely occupied the passes. With so small a force at his disposal, he felt it

* Jacob's *Western India*. Lieutenant Kerr received the Victoria Cross for his conduct on this occasion.

Book XIII. Chapter I.

1857. August.

would be impossible to act against the insurgents unless he should decide, before acting, to disarm the regiment whose conduct had been so suspicious. On the one hand was the danger of his being attacked before his force should gather further strength, or of the mutineers marching away with their arms; on the other, the chance of the men who were still loyal, those of the local corps especially, yielding to the temptation to join their countrymen. It was a balance of risks and probabilities. Many men would have preferred to wait. But Jacob was, as I have said, a man of the old heroic type, and, feeling the importance of striking the first blow, he determined to disarm the men of the 27th Native Infantry.

He disarms them.

He disarmed them on the morning of the 18th of August. Under his orders were twenty-five European gunners, with two guns and two howitzers; ninety men of the 2nd Europeans; one hundred and eighty men of the Southern Maráthá Horse; and three hundred and fifty men of the local corps. These were drawn up in a manner to command any movement tending to resistance on the part of the rebels.

But they made no resistance. They piled their arms in silence. The investigation which followed brought to light many hidden springs of the movement. It had been intended, it was discovered, to delay the mutiny till the 10th of August; but the action of the Jew native adjutant on the 31st of July, in sending away his family, aroused suspicion, and prompted a sudden and ill-matured rising. This premature movement

Remarks on the success of the prompt action of the Bombay authorities and officers.

Book XIII Chapter I. 1857. August.

ruined the plot. Acting hurriedly and without concert with their brethren at Belgáon and Dhárwár, the mutineers acted without plan or settled purpose. It required, then, only energy to baffle them, and that energy was conspicuous in the conduct of all the European officers concerned, in the conduct alike of Lord Elphinstone at Bombay, of Maughan, of Kerr, of Innes, in defence and attack, and of Colonel Jacob in striking the decisive blow.

Bombay.

I ask the reader to return with me now to Bombay. Until the approach of the great Muhammadan festival of the Muharram there had been no apprehensions of an outbreak in that city. The Superintendent of Police, Mr. Forjett, a gentleman who, born and bred in India, knew the natives thoroughly, had deemed it sufficient, when the news of the massacre of Kánhpúr reached Bombay, to obtain permission to incorporate into the police a body of fifty mounted Europeans. He reasoned justly that as the Muhammadan population of the city exceeded a hundred and fifty thousand, it would be folly to trust implicitly to the fidelity of the native police.

The police force there.

It may be fitting to describe here the officers to whom was entrusted the direction of the civil and military forces, upon whose conduct depended the safety of the important town of Bombay at this critical juncture.

The commander of the military forces was Brigadier-General Shortt of the Bombay army. General Shortt was an officer of capacity and intelligence. He thoroughly understood the native

General Shortt.

Book XIII. Chapter I. 1857. August.

soldier. He was quick to decide on an emergency and prompt to carry his decision into execution. In a word, he was an officer thoroughly to be depended upon in danger, a tower of strength to the Government in the crisis which was then impending.

Mr. Forjett.

The Superintendent of Police, Mr. C. Forjett, was* one of the most remarkable men brought to the front by the events of 1857. I have already stated that he was born and bred in India. When the mutiny broke out, he was in the very prime of manhood. He was so thoroughly acquainted with all the dialects of all the languages of western and southern India, that it was easy for him to pass himself off as a native upon the most astute of natives. Mr. Forjett gave an extraordinary proof of this talent immediately prior to his nomination to the office of Superintendent of Police. He had gained so great a reputation for ability, tact, and judgment in the performance of his duties in the southern Maráthá country, that in 1855 Lord Elphinstone sent for him to offer him the chief superintendence of police in Bombay. Mr. Forjett came to the presidency, saw Lord Elphinstone, and received the offer. He at once expressed his willingness to accept it, but requested that Lord Elphinstone would defer the nomination for a fortnight, so as to give him time to find out for himself the true character of the men he had been sum-

His large acquirements,

his tact, and judgment.

His answer to Lord Elphinstone when offered the office of Superintendent Police.

* I am happy to add that the imperfect tense is used only historically. Mr. Forjett still lives in the vigour of healthy life.

moned to command. The request was at once granted. Mr. Forjett then disguised himself as a native and went to places haunted by the police, passing himself off as the son of a subadar in search of a girl whom he loved. He so completely deceived the natives that men of the highest caste invited him to eat with them. He found out the character, the secret longings, of the natives, who, in a few days, would be his instruments. Nor did he neglect the European police. His experience with them was remarkable. He tried them all, and not a single man amongst them refused the bribe he offered. At the end of the fortnight he presented himself to Lord Elphinstone, and took up the office. I leave the reader to imagine the consternation of his native subordinates when they learned whom it was whom they had now to serve.

Mr. Forjett's experiment on the police.

He assumes the office.

But quickness, cleverness at disguise, readiness of resource, represented but a small part of Mr. Forjett's qualities. Small in person, endowed, according to all appearance, with no great strength, he united the cool courage of a practised warrior to remarkable powers of endurance. The courage was not merely the physical courage which despises danger; it was that, and much more. It was a courage set into action by a brain cool and clear—so cool and so clear that there never was a crisis which could blind it, never a danger which it was unable to parry. I venture to describe it as the highest form of intellectual courage.

His other remarkable qualities;

his intellectual courage;

I have spoken of his powers of endurance. These were often tested in the southern Maráthá

his powers of endurance;

Book XIII. Chapter I.

1857. August.

country prior to 1855. If to ride a hundred miles a day, on dismounting to partake of a rude meal of the natural products of the country, and then to lie on the ground, with a bundle of grass for a pillow, in the morning to wash in the stream or in the water drawn from the well, and pursue a similar journey in a similar manner, if this be a test of endurance, then Mr. Forjett may claim to be a passed master in the art. If, to the qualities I have recorded, I add an upright mind, a lofty sense of honour, a devotion to duty, I present to the reader an accurate portrait of the Superintendent of Police of Bombay.

his lofty character.

He gains Lord Elphinstone's entire confidence.

During the two years which had elapsed between his assumption of that office and the outbreak of the mutiny, Mr. Forjett had gained the complete confidence and esteem of Lord Elphinstone. Those who knew that high-minded noble are aware that he never bestowed his trust until he had assured himself by experience that the recipient was fully worthy of it.

Difference of opinion between General Shortt and Mr. Forjett.

There being thus two men so capable and in all respects so well qualified at the head of the departments regulating order, it would seem that the repressal of disturbance in Bombay would be easy. But there were two causes which militated against such a conclusion. The first was the great disparity between the numbers of European and native troops. Whilst there were three native regiments, the 10th and 11th Native Infantry and the Marine Battalion, of the former there were but four hundred men. The other cause affected the concert between the heads of the two departments.

General Shortt believed in the loyalty of his sepoys but mistrusted the native police. Mr. Forjett was confident that he could do what he would with the police, but mistrusted the sepoys. To use his own words, Mr. Forjett regarded the sepoys as "the only source of danger."

Book XIII. Chapter I.

1857. September.

The Muharram festival at Bombay.

The festival of the Muharram was a festival of a character the most dangerous of all. It was a religious festival, lasting many days, the excitement of which increased with each day. Lord Elphinstone had confided to General Shortt the arrangements for preventing disturbance during the whole of the time it lasted. Granted one premiss—that the sepoys were absolutely loyal—those arrangements were perfect. Mr. Forjett, when informed of them, declined, without pledging himself to the contrary, to admit this premiss, and he informed Lord Elphinstone of his doubts. Lord Elphinstone replied that he was sorry he had not known of his objections before, but that it was now too late to alter them. I may here state that the arrangements made by General Shortt involved the division into very small bodies of the European force under the orders of Mr. Forjett. The reply made by that gentleman to Lord Elphinstone's remark just referred to, is eminently characteristic. He intimated that he should, at all events, be obliged to disobey the orders of Government with respect to the police arrangements, because it was necessary for him to have them in hand in the event of a sepoy outbreak. "It is a very risky thing," replied Lord Elphinstone, "to disobey orders,

General Shortt's arrangements.

Forjett's interview with Lord Elphinstone.

Book XIII. Chapter I.

1857.

September.

but I am sure you will do nothing rash." Mr. Forjett construed this tacit permission in the sense in which it was doubtless intended.*

The last night but one of the Muharram.

Five days of the festival passed without disorder. The next night would see its conclusion. On the eve of that night an incident, accidental in its cause, almost produced an outbreak. A Christian drummer belonging to the 10th Regiment Native Infantry, whilst in a state of intoxication, insulted the carriers of a Hindú god which was being carried in procession by some townspeople, and knocked over the god. Two policemen, who witnessed the outrage, took the drummer into custody. It happened that the sepoys of the native regiments were possessed by an inner conviction that their loyalty was doubted by Forjett, and they replied to the feeling they thus imputed to him with one of hatred to himself and his subordinates. When, then, the men of the 10th heard that one of their comrades, albeit a Christian, caught in the act of offering an insult to a Hindú god, had been taken into custody by the police, some twenty of them turned out, broke into the lock-up, rescued the drummer, assaulted the policemen, and marched them off as prisoners to their lines. The European constable of the section at once proceeded with four native policemen to the lines, and demanded the liberation of their

A Christian drummer insults the Hindús. The police take him into custody.

The sepoys take the part of the drummer.

* "Happy was it for Bombay, happy for western India, and happy probably for India itself," wrote Mr. Forjett, reviewing at a later period these events, "that one so noble and clear-headed as Lord Elphinstone was Governor of Bombay during the period of the mutiny."

comrades. The demand was not only refused, but the new-comers were assaulted by the sepoys, and, after a conflict, in which two of the assailants were left for dead, and others were wounded, they were forced to retire. The excitement in the sepoy lines, increasing every moment, received a further impetus from this retirement, and the sepoys began to turn out in such numbers that a messenger was sent at full speed to Mr. Forjett, with the information that the native regiments had broken out.

The police try to rescue their comrades, but fail.

Forjett is sent for.

This was the one danger which Mr. Forjett had all along dreaded, and against which he had taken every precaution possible under the circumstances, already noted, of his limited sphere of action. He had, that is to say, disobeyed orders, and massed his European policemen. On receiving the news that the sepoys had broken out, Mr. Forjett ordered the European police to follow him as soon as possible, and galloped down to their lines at so great a speed as to outstrip all his attendants. He found the sepoys in a state of tumult, endeavouring to force their way out of the lines, their European officers, with drawn swords, keeping them back. The sight of Mr. Forjett inflamed the sepoys still more. They called out loudly that this was the man who had wished them all to be killed, while the European officers, seeing how the presence of Mr. Forjett excited their men, begged him in earnest language to go away. The fate of Bombay at that moment hung upon the conduct, at this critical conjuncture, of Mr. Forjett.

Forjett arrives alone.

Fury of the sepoys at seeing him.

The European officers beg him to retire.

Book XIII. Chapter I. — 1857. September.

Such are Asiatics, that had that gentleman obeyed the calls of the officers, the sepoys would have burst the bonds of discipline and dashed forward to pursue him. He was there, alone, seated on his horse, calmly daring them. His knowledge of natives made him feel that so long as he should remain there, facing and defying them, they would not move; but that a retrograde movement on his part would be the signal for a real outbreak. In reply, then, to the shouts of the officers and men of the native regiments,

He refuses,

Mr. Forjett called out to the former, "If your men are bent on mischief, the sooner it is over the better," and remained facing them. Two minutes later his assistant, Mr. Edington, galloped up, followed very shortly by fifty-five European policemen—the men he had kept massed in case of a disturbance. Then Mr. Forjett acted. Forming up and halting his men,

and crushes the incipient mutiny.

he called out, "Throw open the gates; I am ready for the sepoys." Again was displayed that complete acquaintance with the Asiatic character which was one of the secrets of Mr. Forjett's power. The excitement of the sepoys subsided as if by magic, and they fell back within their lines. Never had a nobler deed been more nobly done!

The Muharram, thanks to Mr. Forjett, is tided over.

The tide now turned. The evil-disposed amongst the sepoys—and that many were evil-disposed subsequent revelations fully proved—were completely cowed. Nevertheless, Mr. Forjett relaxed not one of his exertions. The Muharram was not yet a thing of the past, and it was

1857. September.

clear that an accident might yet kindle the mine. One night still remained, and Mr. Forjett, far from relaxing his precautions, bent himself to increase them. He so posted his police that the smallest movement upon the part of the sepoys would at once become known to the main body of his Europeans, forty-eight in number, located at a decisive point. His precautions were not only successful, they were the cause of success. To borrow the language, subsequently revealed, of the baffled conspirators, "it was the vigilance maintained that prevented the outbreak." The vigilance was the vigilance of the police personally directed by Mr. Forjett.*

* Mr. Forjett's great services were not left unacknowledged. On the 19th of June 1858, Lord Elphinstone thus recorded his sense of their value:—"The Right Honourable the Governor in Council cannot too highly praise the devoted zeal of this excellent public servant, upon whom such grave responsibilities were imposed during last year." Referring to Mr. Forjett's "very valuable services" in the detection of the plot in Bombay in 1857, the same high authority thus wrote: "His duties demanded great courage, great acuteness, and great judgment, all of which qualities were conspicuously displayed by Mr. Forjett at that trying period."

All classes combined to testify to the great services rendered on this occasion by Mr. Forjett. Couched in varying phraseology, every letter received from the members of the European community indicates that, in the opinion of the several writers, it was the vigilance of Mr. Forjett which saved Bombay.

I may add here that, for his services in the mutiny, the European and Native communities in Bombay presented Mr. Forjett with addresses, and, with the sanction of the Government, with testimonials and purses to the value of three thousand eight hundred and fifty pounds. It was still more gratifying to him that, after he had left the service and

Book XIII. Chapter I.

1857. October.

I have already stated that, thanks to the precautions taken and to Mr. Forjett's energetic action, the festival of the Muharram had passed off quietly. The discontented men amongst the sepoys still, however, cherished the hope that another opportunity more favourable to the execution of their projects would soon arise. The Hindú festival of the Diwáli, occurring towards the end of October, seemed to them to offer such an opportunity. During this festival the Hindús of the upper and wealthier classes are accustomed to collect all their wealth in one room of their dwelling, and assembling, to worship it. The discontented sepoys resolved, in many a secret council, to break out during the Diwáli, to pillage Bombay, killing all who should oppose them, and then to march out of the island. Had this plan been carried out, it is nearly certain that the contagion would have spread all over the presidency, and have even reached Madras.

The sepoys hatch a new conspiracy,

But again had the mutineers to reckon with Mr. Forjett. That gentleman was informed by

quitted India, the native cotton merchants sent him a handsome address and a purse of one thousand five hundred pounds, "in token of strong gratitude for one whose almost despotic powers and zealous energy had so quelled the explosive forces of native society, that they seem to have become permanently subdued. In addition, and likewise after he left India, the shareholders of a company, mainly composed of natives, presented Mr. Forjett with shares, which they subsequenty sold on his account, for thirteen thousand five hundred and eighty pounds.

Book XIII. Chapter I.

1857. October.

a detective that suspicious meetings were being held by disaffected sepoys at the house of one Ganga Parshád. Attempts to introduce a confidential agent of the police into those meetings having been baffled by the precautions of the sepoys, Mr. Forjett had Ganga Parshád conveyed to the police-office during the night, and obtained from him a complete revelation. Fertile in disguises, Mr. Forjett subsequently became an eye-witness—by means of holes made in the wall which separated the chamber where the conspirators assembled from the ante-room—of the proceedings of the sepoys, a listeuer to their conversation. More than that, aware of the feeling prevailing amongst the officers regarding himself, he induced Major Barrow, the officer commanding the Marine battalion, to accompany him, on four different occasions, to the meetings.* The information there obtained was duly reported to General Shortt by Major Barrow, and to Lord Elphinstone, through his private secretary, by Mr. Forjett. Courts-martial were in due course convened. The proceedings resulted in sentences of death being passed and executed on two, of transportation for life on six, native soldiers of

which is discovered by Mr. Forjett,

and revealed by him to Major Barrow,

by which means the conspiracy is nipped in the bud.

* "Major Barrow's astonishment when he saw some of his own men in Ganga Parshád's house was remarkable. He exclaimed, 'My God, my own men! Is it possible!' And his memorable words to me at the court-martial were: 'It is well I was present and saw and heard them myself, but for which I should have been here, not as a witness for the prosecution, but as one for the defence; *such was my confidence in these men.*'"—Forjett's *Our Real Danger in India.*

Book XIII. Chapter I.

1857. December.

various ranks. But the projected mutiny was nipped in the bud.

Recapitulation of events at Bombay.

With the story of the measures taken for the safety of Bombay closes the general sketch of events in the western Presidency up to the close of 1857. We have seen how, displaying at once a rare foresight and a remarkable self-reliance, Lord Elphinstone had denuded his own Presidency of European troops in order to crush the mutiny beyond its borders. No man in high position recognised more truly, and acted more conscientiously, on the maxim that the art of war consists in concentrating the greatest number of troops on the decisive point of the action. Now, the decisive point of the action in the early days of the revolt of 1857 was not in Bombay. To Lord Elphinstone it was clear that Dehlí could only be reached from Bengal, and that it was just possible he might save central India and Rajpútáná. Whilst, then, he sent every available European soldier to Calcutta, he formed, from the small remnant which was left, a number in reality not sufficient for his own needs—one column which should march on Máu, another which should restore order in Rajpútáná. Feeling that amidst the many dangers which threatened him the most fatal was that which would come from without, he sent to meet and to crush it before it should penetrate within. His defence of Bombay was an aggressive defence. It was a policy requiring rare courage, immense confidence in his own judgment, and great resolution. In carrying it out he exposed himself to the danger, only one

Lord Elphinstone's forethought, unselfishness, and decision.

His plan of aggressive defence.

degree less, of a rising within the Presidency. How nearly that was occurring I have shown in these pages. The southern Maráthá country was saved, in 1857, partly by the prudence and the judgment displayed by Mr. G. B. Seton-Karr, aided by the energy of General Lester, partly by the bungling and want of concert of the conspirators. How Bombay was saved I have just told. The reader will have seen that the danger was real, the peril imminent, that but for the unlimited confidence placed by Lord Elphinstone in Mr. Forjett—a man of his own selection—it might have culminated in disaster. That he dared that risk to avert a greater danger is one of the many proofs of Lord Elphinstone's capacity. Sufficient credit has never been given to him for his noble, his far-seeing, his self-denying policy. In the presence of the massacres of Kánhpúr and of Jhánsi, of the defence of Lakhnao, and of the siege of Dehlí, the attitude of Lord Elphinstone, less sensational though not less heroic, has been overlooked. Had there been an uprising attended with slaughter in Bombay, the story of its repression and the deeds of valour attending that repression would have circulated throughout the land. Instead of that, we see only calm judgment and self-reliance meeting one danger and defying another, carefully selecting the most experienced instruments, and by their aid preventing a calamity so threatening that, if it had been met by men less tried and less worthy of confidence, it must have culminated in disaster. It is an attitude which gains from being contemplated,

Mr. Seton-Karr. General Lester.

Mr. Forjett.

The attitude of Lord Elphinstone has never yet received its due meed of praise.

Book XIII. Chapter I. — 1857. December.

which impresses the student of history, in an ever-increasing degree, with admiration of the noble character of the man whose calm trust in himself made possible the success of the policy he alone inaugurated.

BOOK XIII.

CHAPTER II.

A'sírgarh.

Ásírgarh is a very famous fort, lying two hundred and ninety miles to the north-east of Bombay, one hundred and fifty miles from Maligám, and ninety-nine miles to the south-east of Máu. It is built on an isolated hill, detached from the Sátpúra range dividing the valley of the Tápti from that of the Narbadá. It has a history which has sent its name through the length and breadth of India. Alike in the times of the Hindú, of the Muhammadan, and of the British overlordship, it has been considered a place worth fighting for. After many changes of masters, it surrendered, on the 9th of April 1819, after a vigorous resistance, to a British force commanded by Brigadier-General Doveton, and it has, ever since, remained in the occupation of a British garrison.

Garrison of A'sírgarh.

In 1857 that garrison consisted of a wing of the 6th Regiment Gwáliár Contingent, lent by the Bengal Presidency to replace the 19th Bombay

Book XIII. Chapter II.

1857. June.

Native Infantry ordered on service to Persia, but which never embarked for that country. The commanding officer of the garrison was Colonel Le Mesurier, and the Fort Adjutant was Lieutenant John Gordon of the 19th Bombay Native Infantry.

Situation of the fort.

The hill on the summit of which Ásírgarh is perched rises abruptly to about five hundred feet above the jungle. Below it is a town of no real importance, inhabited by villagers mainly engaged in tending their flocks.

The men of the contingent evince symptoms of mutiny.

The men who formed the garrison of Ásírgarh belonged to a contingent which speedily asserted its right to a prominent place amongst the mutineers. The events at Nímach and at Gwáliár speedily convinced the European residents at Ásírgarh that their guardians were not to be trusted. Even before this discovery had been made, the fort adjutant, distrusting their demeanour, had enlisted some ninety men from the villagers of the town, and had charged them with the task of watching the behaviour of the sepoys. These men were known as Gordon's Volunteers.

Bad news reaches the Europeans,

On the 19th of June the Europeans of the garrison heard of the mutinies at Nímach and Nasirábád. From that day almost every post brought them distressful tidings. Every precaution was taken by Lieutenant Gordon. To relieve the fort, by fair means, of a portion of its real enemies, one company of the regiment was detached to Búrhánpúr, twelve miles distant. The anxieties of the ladies of the garrison

who send one company to Búrhánpúr;

were lessened about the same time by the intelligence, verified by a personal visit made by Lieutenant Gordon, that Captain Keatinge,* the political agent for that part of the country, had fortified a position fourteen miles distant from Ásírgarh.

From this time till the end of July good and bad news succeeded each other with strange rapidity. At times the Europeans were in great danger. The company sent to Búrhánpúr mutinied, marched on Ásírgarh, and was only prevented from entering it by the havildar-major of the regiment, whose loyalty had been appealed to, not in vain, by Lieutenant Gordon.

where it mutinies.

The following morning the four remaining companies obeyed, not without murmuring, the order given to them to march out and encamp below the fort, their places within being taken by Gordon's Volunteers. The next day a party of Bhíl infantry, commanded by Lieutenant Birch, surprised and disarmed the Búrhánpúr mutineers, and carried their arms into Ásírgarh. A few hours later that place was reinforced by two companies of the 19th Native Infantry under Captain Blair. The disarming of the Gwáliár men outside the fort—a work performed admirably and without bloodshed by Captain Blair and Lieutenant Gordon—completed the necessary measures to ensure the safety of the fortress pending the arrival of Colonel Stuart's column.

The remainder are disarmed.

That column, the earlier movements of which

* Now Colonel Keatinge, V.C.

Book XIII. Chapter II.

1857. July.

Arrival of Stuart's column and of Durand.

I have recorded in the preceding chapter, quitted Aurangábád for A'sírgarh on the 12th of July. Marching rapidly, it reached Búrhánpúr on the 21st and A'sírgarh on the 22nd idem. Here it was joined by Colonel Durand, who had reached Ásírgarh some days previously.

Summary of Durand's proceedings after leaving Indúr.

In another part of this history* I have shown how Durand, after the catastrophe of Máu, had fallen back on Sihor; how, staying there only one day, he had set out for Hoshangábád on the southern bank of the Narbadá, in the hope of being able to communicate there with General Woodburn; how, hearing at Hoshangábád of the safety of Máu, he heard also of the attempts made to change the direction of Woodburn's force from the line of the Narbadá to Nágpúr; how, not content with simply protesting against such a line of conduct, he had set off for Aurangábád with the intention of enforcing his arguments there, and, if necessary, of pressing on to Bombay; how, on his road, he received the gratifying intelligence that Woodburn's column, now commanded by Stuart, was advancing towards A'sírgarh; how he had at once hurried to that place. He had the gratification of meeting that force on the 22nd of July. From the moment of his joining it, he assumed his position as the Governor-General's representative, and became likewise, in everything but in name, the real leader of the column.

He assumes the real direction of the column.

The column pushed on for Máu on the 24th

* Vol. i. pages 242, 243.

with all practicable expedition. On the 28th it was joined by the 3rd Regiment Cavalry, Haidarábád Contingent, under the command of Captain S. Orr. On the 31st it ascended the Simrol pass, halted on its summit to allow the artillery to close up, and the following morning marched into Máu. The weather for the time of the year, the height of the monsoon, had been exceptionally fine; no rain had fallen to hinder the march of the guns over the sticky black soil. On the night of the 1st of August, however, the weather changed. Heavy rains set in and continued throughout August and September. But Durand was now at Máu, within thirteen and a half miles of the capital whence the mutinous conduct of Holkar's troops had forced him to retire just one month before. He had returned to vindicate British authority, to punish the guilty, to give an example which should not be forgotten.

Is joined by the 3rd Regiment Cavalry, Haidarábád Contingent.

Durand arrives at Máu.

Even before he had marched into Máu, whilst he was yet halted on the top of the Simrol pass, Durand had received a message from the Indúr Darbár. Maháráját Holkar and his minister sent to inform him that they were still in a state of alarm as to the conduct of their own troops, and to inquire whether aid could not be afforded to them. Durand replied that he was ready, if the Maháráján wished it, to march with the entire force into Indúr instead of into Máu. Apparently, this was not the end desired by the Darbár, for the messengers at once withdrew their requisition.

He offers to march on Indúr and disarm Holkar's troops;

but Holkar declines.

In deciding to march on Máu instead of Indúr,

Reasons why Durand

Book XIII. Chapter II.

1857. August.

marched on Máu instead of on Indúr.

Durand was mainly influenced by the fact that at the latter place there was no accommodation for European troops. He had with him, indeed, no European infantry,* but four companies of the 86th were marching up by the Bombay road, and would join in a few days. It was desirable also, after the events which had occurred, that the Indúr rabble should see in the British force the white faces of the unvanquished foot soldiers of England. Durand marched then on Máu.

He is joined by four companies 86th.

The four companies of the 86th having joined a few days later, the propriety of marching on Indúr to punish Holkar's guilty troops and the townspeople who had abetted the revolt again became a question for Durand's consideration. It was a very difficult question. That Holkar's troops had attacked the Residency on the 1st of July was a fact admitted by everyone. But Holkar had asserted that this act had been committed without his sanction or authority. Durand himself never believed this; but officers who had occupied the Máu fort in July, notably Captain Hungerford, had been penetrated with the conviction that Holkar was innocent, and, in his letters to Durand, Lord Elphinstone, the Governor of Bombay, had insisted on the same view. Under these circumstances Durand, duly weighing the difficulties presented by the case, deemed it advisable to defer all action, so far as

Circumstances which induced Durand to defer all proceedings with respect to Holkar.

* The force consisted of five troops 14th Light Dragoons, 3rd Cavalry Haidarábád Contingent, one horse battery of European artillery, the 25th Bombay Native Infantry, and a pontoon train.

Book XIII. Chapter II.

1857. August.

Holkar was personally concerned, until he should become acquainted with the views of the Governor-General regarding him. He accordingly made a complete reference on the subject to Lord Canning.

Probable reasons for Holkar's conduct.

Holkar, on his part, was naturally anxious to delay Durand's action as long as he could. He knew that, in his heart, Durand had condemned him. And, although it was well known that, in the excited state of native feeling throughout the country, he could not depend on the conduct of his own troops, and would have been glad to see them coerced by the British, yet, when he thought of the possible results of such action, he inclined to prefer the uncertainty of his actual condition. Could he, he felt, but stave off the critical moment for a few months, Durand would be relieved by Sir Robert Hamilton, and Sir Robert Hamilton, an old and much-regarded friend, would, he felt confident, accept explanations regarding the events of the 1st of July which Durand would utterly contemn.

Reasons why Durand determines to defer to a later period any movement against Holkar's troops.

The question of disarming Holkar's revolted troops, whilst the personal case regarding Holkar was still pending, opened out difficulties of another description. The force at the disposal of Durand was small, and, though sufficient to dispose of the revolted troops of Indúr, could these be encountered *en masse*, it was scarcely large enough to attack its several component parts in detail, holding the bulk in check whilst portion after portion should be destroyed. It must always be remembered, writing of this period, that the

Book XIII. Chapter II. — 1857. August.

revolt had at that time nowhere received a serious check. The force before Dehlí was almost as much besieged as besieging. Lakhnao was supposed to be at its last gasp; Havelock had made no impression upon Oudh; Bihar was surging with mutineers. The disaffected in central India might, then, well be excused if, regarding all these points, they were not only hopeful, but confident that resolute resistance on their part would serve the cause which they now regarded as the common cause of their co-religionists throughout India. Under these circumstances, it was to be apprehended that Holkar's troops, the three arms of which, each superior in numbers to the entire British force, were located in separate cantonments, might evince a strong disinclination to be disarmed; and that, morally supported as they were by a large party in the city of Indúr, and, as I shall presently show, by a strongly aggressive party in the districts lying between Indúr and Nímach, they might offer a resistance certain to entail great loss on the attacking party, and to cripple its future movements. This will be clear to the reader when, recalling the composition of the force at the disposal of Durand,* extremely weak in infantry, he calls to mind that a rainy season of unusual force was at its height, that the roads could be traversed by guns only with the greatest difficulty, that the bridges in many places had been carried away, and that any military opera-

* *Vide* page 62, note.

tion against the several cantonments occupied by Holkar's troops would have to be carried out on a swampy plain, on which, at that season of the year, it would be impossible for the three arms to work together.

But there were other reasons which impressed Durand with the necessity of dealing in the first instance with those rebels in the districts, of whose aggressive tendencies I have just spoken.

Mandisúr is a large and important town on a tributary of the river Chambal, about one hundred and twenty miles from Indúr. In the month of July this place had been occupied by some of Sindia's revolted troops, and these had been joined, and were being constantly further strengthened, by Afghán, Mekráni, and Mewáti levies. In August the insurrection at Mandisúr threatened not only to embrace all western Málwá, but Nímach as well. Impressed with a confidence in themselves, justified only by the prolonged immunity which had been allowed them, the rebels at this place began, in the month of August, to display an aggressive temper far more dangerous than the sullen disaffection of the compromised troops of Holkar. The more active and daring of the mutineers of Holkar's army had proceeded to Gwáliár after the insurrection of the 1st of July; the less energetic mass remained, sullen, dangerous, watching events, but to a certain extent paralysed, though not controlled, by the English party in power at Holkar's court. The progress of the Mandisúr insurrection was, however, so rapid that to uphold British supremacy in Raj-

Mandisúr becomes a centre of insurrection, aggressive in its nature,

Book XIII. Chapter II.

1857. October.

and requiring the most prompt attention.

pútáná and Málwá, and to maintain the line of the Narbadá, it became absolutely necessary to check its growth with the utmost promptitude. In the presence of this new danger, the disarming of Holkar's troops became, in every sense, a matter of secondary importance. An attempt to subdue the lesser evil might have augmented the greater, whilst a decisive blow struck at the greater could not fail to be fatal to the lesser.

The rains an impediment to prompt action.

Action in any shape was impossible so long as the heavy rains continued. But when, in the beginning of October, the monsoon passed away, and the country began to dry up, the Mandisúr rebels began to give proof of the possession of the aggressive nature with which I have credited them.

Composition of the Mandisúr insurgents.

The leader of the Mandisúr insurgents was Firoz Sháh, a Sháhzáda or prince connected with the imperial family of Dehlí. It was estimated in September that some fifteen thousand men with sixteen or eighteen guns, had rallied round his standard, and this estimate was subsequently found to have been below the actual number. To meet these, Durand, after deducting the sick and wounded, and a sufficient number of men to guard Máu, could not bring into the field more than one thousand five hundred men* and nine guns.

Durand's effective force.

Under these circumstances it was perhaps for-

* Thus composed: Artillery, one hundred and seventy; Dragoons, two hundred; 86th, two hundred and thirty; 25th Bombay Native Infantry, three hundred and fifty; 3rd Nizám's Cavalry, three hundred and fifty.

Book XIII. Chapter II.

1857. October.

Durand learns that central India is about to rise in revolt.

tunate that the aggressive movement was made by the rebels. Durand expected it. Towards the very end of September he had intercepted letters from Haidarábád, from Nágpúr, from Surát, from Újjén, from Gwáliár, and from Mandisúr, all telling the same tale. The tale was to the effect that, after the conclusion of the Dasahra festival,* a general rising would take place in Málwá, and that influential personages were coming from Nágpúr and Haidarábád for the purpose of giving life and strength to the insurrection. The close of the Dasahra corresponded with the setting in of the dry season. The result corresponded with the information Durand had thus obtained. Early in October the Sháhzáda's troops, who had previously occupied Dhár and Amjhéra, advanced to the Bombay road and threatened to interrupt Durand's communications with Bombay, to command the line of the Narbadá along the Bombay frontier, and to attack Nímach. They sent also a pressing invitation to Holkar's troops to join them.

The rebels attempt to cut off Durand from Bombay.

Everything depended upon the rapidity with which Durand would be able to strike a blow at this enemy. Failing it, it was quite possible that Náná Sáhib, who at that time was hovering in the vicinity of Kálpi, might transfer the whole of his troops to central India, and that the Maráthá war-

The vital importance of rapid action.

* A festival of ten days' duration, nine of which are spent in worship and religious ceremonies. The tenth day is the birthday of Gangá (the Ganges). Whoever bathes in the Ganges on that day is purified from ten sorts of sins. The festival occurs in September or October, the date varying with each year.

Book XIII. Chapter II.

1857. October.

cry might raise the whole of the country formerly acknowledging the supremacy of the Peshwá. Seeing the necessity, Durand struck. On the 12th of October he detached one bòdy of Haidar-ábád cavalry to defend Mandlésar, threatened by the rebels, and another to the village of Gújrí to intercept them on their way. On the 14th he sent three companies of the 25th Native Infantry and some dragoons to support this last-named party, and on the 19th, with all the men who could be spared from forming the garrison of Máu, he marched for Dhár.

Durand strikes at Dhár.

A'nand Ráo Púár, a lad of thirteen years, had succeeded to the chiefship of Dhár on the death of his brother, cut off by cholera on the 23rd of May 1857.* His minister, Rámchandar Bápoji, a shrewd and intelligent man, who, from his thorough knowledge of the English and from his large acquaintance with British officers, was supposed to be devoted to British interests, began, almost immediately after his assumption of office, to pursue a line of policy the very reverse of that which had been hoped from him. In direct opposition to the policy pursued by the Government of India ever since the settlement of Málwá, to prevent the employment of mercenary troops in native states, this man began to enlist large numbers of Arabs, Afgháns, and Mekránis. As soon as the news of the Indúr rising of the

History of Dhár immediately previous to the events of 1857.

Disloyalty of Rámchandar Bápoji.

* The formal recognition by the British Government only reached the young chief on the 28th of September, but he was acknowledged and treated as Rájá from the date stated.

He enlists mercenaries,

whom, after their plunder of British stations, he receives with honour.

Captain Hutchinson reports the complicity of the Rájás family, and of the Darbár.

Durand dismisses the Darbár's agent with a warning.

1st of July reached Dhár, a party of these mercenaries, four hundred in number, joined with the mercenaries of the rájá of Amjhéra, and plundered the stations of Bhopáor and Sirdárpúr, burning the hospitals over the heads of the sick and wounded. Returning to Dhár with their plunder, they were met and honourably received by Bhim Ráo Bhonslá, the young rájá's uncle, and three of the guns which they had captured were placed in the rájá's palace. On the 31st of August they were in possession of the fort of Dhár, with or without the consent of the Darbár was not certainly known. But on the 15th of October Captain Hutchinson, the political agent, reported that there was strong reason to believe that the rájá's mother and uncle and the members of the Darbár were the instigators of the rebellion of the Dhár troops, that the conduct of the Darbár was suspicious, that its agent had purposely deceived him regarding the negotiations entered into by its members with the mutinous mercenaries and the number of men they had enlisted, and that it had received with attention and civility emissaries from Mandisúr, the centre of the Muhammadan rising. It was this intelligence which decided Durand to dismiss the Dhár agent in attendance on him, with a message to the Darbár that its members would be held strictly responsible for all that had happened or that might happen,* and to despatch all his available troops to attack Dhár.

* Durand repeated this warning to the Rájá in person during the siege of the fort.

Book XIII. Chapter II.

1857. October.

The British troops arrive before Dhár.

On the 22nd of October the British force arrived before Dhár. The Arab and Mekráni levies who garrisoned that fort gave a signal instance of the confidence engendered by the long compulsory inaction of the British by quitting the protection of their lines of defence and coming to attack them in the open. Planting three brass guns on a hill south of the fort, they extended from that point along its eastern face in skirmishing order, and advanced boldly against the British.

The action.

But their confidence soon vanished. The 25th Bombay Native Infantry, a splendid regiment, often to be mentioned, and always with honour, in these pages, led by their most capable commandant, Major Robertson, charged the three guns, captured them, and turned the guns on the rebels. Almost simultaneously, the four companies of the 86th and the sappers, flanked by Woollcombe's (Bombay) and Hungerford's (Bengal) batteries, advanced against the centre, whilst the cavalry threatened both flanks, the dragoons, under Captain Gall, the left, the Nizám's cavalry, under Major Orr, the right. Baffled in their advance by the action of the 25th, and the play of the British guns on their centre, the enemy made a rapid movement to their left, and attempted to turn the British right. The dragoons, led by Gall, and the Nizám's cavalry, led by Orr and Macdonald, Deputy Quartermaster-General of the force, charged them so vigorously that they retired into the fort, leaving forty bodies of their companions on the field. On the British side

Gallantry of the 25th Native Infantry,

of the British troops,

Gall and Orr and Macdonald.

The rebels are beaten.

three dragoons and one native trooper were wounded, a jemadar and native trooper were killed.

Book XIII. Chapter II.

1857. October.

Dhár is invested.

The fort was now invested, but the British force had to wait for the siege guns, expected on the 24th. They arrived on the evening of that day; the next morning they were placed in position.

Description of the fort of Dhár.

The fort of Dhár is entirely detached from the town of the same name. Its southern angle rests on the suburbs, the road running between. It is situated on an eminence of thirty feet above the surrounding plain, and is built of red granite, in an oblong shape, conforming itself to the hill on which it stands. The walls are about thirty feet in height, and have at intervals fourteen circular and two square towers.

Investment of Dhár.

On the 25th a sandbag battery, two thousand yards south of the fort, armed with one 8-inch howitzer and one 8-inch mortar, began to shell the fort. Under cover of this fire the infantry pushed on to a low ridge, about two hundred and fifty yards from the southern angle of the fort, forming a natural parallel, and took possession of it. On this the breaching battery was at once constructed. Simultaneously, strong cavalry and infantry pickets were thrown out on the north and east faces of the fort, whilst the west face was covered by an extensive tank or lake which could not be forded. Durand was in hopes that the rebels, seeing themselves thus surrounded, would spontaneously surrender. But although, during the six days the siege lasted, they made many

Book XIII. Chapter II.

1857. October.

The rebels ask for terms.

efforts to obtain aid from outside, acting and writing in the name of the Darbár, under whose orders they professed to be defending the fort, they waited until, on the night of the 29th, the breach had been made so large that its practicability was only a question of a day or two, ere they sent a white flag to inquire the terms which would be granted. "An unconditional surrender," was the reply, upon which the firing continued.

The reply.

The breach practicable and

At sunset on the 31st the breach was reported practicable, and that night a storming party was detailed to assault the place. Never was a task easier. The breach was easily ascended. Almost immediately afterwards firing was heard on the plain. Whilst dragoons and irregulars were despatched in that direction, the storming party entered the fort. It was empty.*

the fort evacuated.

In fact the rebels, foreseeing the assault, had quitted the fort by the main gate between 9 and 11 o'clock, and escaped in the direction of the north-west. The firing heard on the plain at the moment the breach was entered was only a skirmish with the rear-guard of the retreating enemy and an outlying picket of the 3rd Nizam's cavalry. The main body had passed by them and the dragoons† wholly unobserved, and were well away before the alarm could be of any avail.

Escape of the rebels.

* Sindhia and Dhar. *Calcutta Review.* Lowe's *Central India.* Private papers.

† It had unfortunately happened that the European pickets, which had been there for some days and which knew the ground well, had been changed that very day. The trooper, sent by the jemadar of the native picket, fell with his horse on the way, and was disabled.—Lowe.

Book XIII. Chapter II.

1857. November.

Pursuit, though it could scarcely avail much, was attempted. It resulted, however, only in the capture of a few wretched stragglers.

Pursuit useless.

Durand demolishes the fort and marches towards Mandisúr.

Durand ordered the fort of Dhár to be demolished, the state to be attached, pending the final orders of Government, and charges to be prepared against the leaders and instigators of the rebellion.* The force then continued its march through western Málwá towards Mandisúr, in pursuit of the rebels. These latter, however, had by no means renounced their aggressive tendencies. On the 8th of November they attacked the cantonment of Mahidpúr, garrisoned by a native contingent of the three arms, officered by English officers. Major Timmins, who commanded the contingent, imprudently permitted the rebels, without offering opposition, to take up a strong position close round his guns and infantry. The men of the contingent, on their side, displayed mingled cowardice and treachery, the majority eventually going over to the rebels. Half a troop of the cavalry behaved, however, extremely well, and, after making a gallant but ineffective charge, in which their leader, Captain Mills, was shot dead, and their native officer severely wounded, escorted the remainder of their European officers to Durand's camp, where they arrived on the 9th.

The rebels attack Mahidpúr,

and plunder the station.

* Ultimately, owing to circumstances upon which it is unnecessary for me to enter here, they all escaped punishment. To the young Rájá himself, merciful consideration was shown, and he was restored to his title and position.

Book XIII. Chapter II.

1857. November.

The line of the Narbadá saved.

Two other affairs, which occurred during the pursuit of the rebels to Mandisúr deserve here to be recorded. The first was the capture and destruction of the fort of Amjhéra by a small party of Haidarábád cavalry and infantry under Lieutenant Hutchinson. There was, indeed, no opposition, but the fact of the occupation was satisfactory, as it proved that Durand's rapid action had saved the line of the Narbadá, and had maintained that barrier between the blazing north and the smouldering south.

The other action was one in which Major Orr and the Haidarábád Contingent was prominently engaged.

Reinforcements brought by the Haidarábád Contingent.

I have already stated* how one regiment of the Haidarábád Contingent had joined Brigadier Stuart's force on its march from Aurangábád. The remaining cavalry of the contingent and a large force of its infantry and artillery, had, about the same time, been formed at Edlábád, one of the chief outlets of the Dekhán, on the high road to central India. Here they remained until the monsoon had ceased and the roads had begun to dry up. They then marched with all speed into Málwá, and coercing on their way the refractory zamindárs of Pípliah and Rágugarh, reached Durand's force before Dhár.

Major Orr pursues the Mahidpúr plunderers.

Upon the news reaching camp of the successful action of the rebels at Mahidpúr, Major Orr, with a small force, consisting of three hundred and thirty-seven sabres drawn from the 1st,

* *Vide* page 61.

3rd, and 4th regiments Nizám's cavalry, was sent to follow on their track. The second morning after he had left camp, Orr, having marched some sixty miles, arrived before Mahidpúr. There he learned that the rebels had left the place the same morning, carrying with them all the guns, stores, and ammunition upon which they could lay hand. Orr stopped to water and feed his horses, and whilst thus halting had the gratification to receive Mrs. Timmins, the wife of the commandant already mentioned, who had been unable to effect her escape* with her husband. Having despatched that lady under a sufficient escort to rejoin her husband, Orr followed the rebels, and after a pursuit of twelve miles came up with their rear-guard, about four hundred and fifty men with two guns, about 4 o'clock in the afternoon, at the village of Ráwal. They were prepared to receive him. They had taken up a very formidable position, especially calculated to resist cavalry, their right resting on the village, and their front covered by a muddy nullah or rivulet. Occupying this position they hoped effectually to cover the retreat of their main body, conveying their stores, their ammunition, and the spoils of Mahidpúr. But they had not counted on the gallant spirit of their enemy. Orr and his officers, Abbott, Johnstone, Clark, Murray, and Samwell, led their men forward, crossed the nullah, charged the guns, and then fought

He catches them up.

Their strong position.

Orr gallantly and successfully assails it,

* This lady had been concealed by a faithful tailor, who frustrated all the efforts of the rebels to discover her hiding-place.

Book XIII. Chapter II. 1857. November.

hand to hand with the enemy. The contest was desperate and continued till the sun went down. Then the rebels gave way, and all their guns, eight in number, and stores, fell into the hands of the victors. The nature of the engagement may be gathered from the fact that the British lost nearly one hundred men killed and wounded. Amongst the latter was Lieutenant Samwell, shot through the abdomen. The rebels lost one hundred and seventy-five killed, and some seventy taken prisouers.

and carries it, though with loss.

Satisfaction of the 14th Dragoons at Orr's success.

When the despatch containing the account of this affair reached Durand, he handed it over to Major Gall to read to the 14th Dragoons and 86th Foot. By these men it was heard with more than satisfaction, for it dissipated any doubt which might have been caused by the escape of the garrison of Dhár.

Durand reaches the Chambal.

Durand now pushed on as fast as the baggage-carts and the roads would permit him, and on the 19th of November reached Hernia on the banks of the river Chambal. The crossing of this river, unopposed as it was, presented no inconsiderable difficulties. Its banks are rugged and almost perpendicular, its stream is deep and rapid, and its bed is broken by enormous boulders of basalt. The baggage of the force was carried almost entirely on carts drawn by bullocks, a few camels only having been obtainable, and to convey these carts and the artillery guns across a river presenting the difficulties I have described would, under no circumstances, have been an easy task. That the rebels, hitherto

Description of the river.

so aggressive, should have neglected the opportunity thus offered to them adds another to the many proofs in which this history abounds, that brave as they were in fight, they understood little of the art of war. As it was, nearly two days were spent in effecting the passage, nor was this possible until the sappers had cut a road down the bank for the artillery and carts, and another up the opposite bank.*

Book XIII. Chapter II.

1857. November.

The rebels foolishly leave it undefended.

The column halted the afternoon of the 20th on the east bank of the Chambal, and marching early the following morning, encamped four miles south of Mandisúr, in a position covered to the front by some rising ground, flanked on the left by a little village and gardens, beyond which again were several large topes, some cultivated ground, and another village surrounded by gardens and trees. On the right of the British position were hills and villages, and between these and the rising ground in front already

Durand approaches Mandisúr.

* "I never saw a more animated and beautiful picture in my life than when our brigade crossed this river. The steep, verdant, shrubby banks, covered with our varied forces, elephants, camels, horses, and bullocks; the deep flowing clear river, reaching on and on to the far east, to the soft deep-blue tufted horizon; the babble and yelling of men, the lowing of the cattle, the grunting screams of the camels, and the trumpeting of the wary, heavily-laden elephant; the rattle of our artillery down the bank, through the river, and up the opposite side; the splashing and plunging of our cavalry through the stream—neighing and eager for the green encamping ground before them; and everybody so busy and jovial, streaming up from the deep water to their respective grounds; and all this in the face, almost, of an enemy, formed a *tableau vivant* never to be forgotten." — Lowe's *Campaign in Central India.*

Book XIII. Chapter II.

1857. November.

Aggressive humour of the rebels.

referred to was an extensive plateau, covered here and there with acres of uncut grain. Beyond it, again, the city of Mandisúr.* A reconnaissance having indicated that all was quiet in front, the camp was pitched, and the men went to their breakfasts.

But the rebels were again in an aggressive humour. Rumours had been industriously spread in their ranks that the British force had been repulsed from Dhár and, in sheer desperation, was now meditating an attack on Mandisúr. The leaders knew better, but they used all their efforts to give currency to the story. Consequently, about mid-day on the 22nd, the rebels, confident that they had before them only a dispirited and beaten column, sallied forth from Mandisúr, and, marching gaily, took possession of the village surrounded by trees and gardens beyond the extreme left of the British line, and making that village their extreme right, occupied, with two considerable masses, the plateau connecting it with Mandisúr.

They threaten the British force,

Which turns out to receive them,

The men in the British camp were at their breakfasts when the news of the rebel movement reached them. Instantly they fell in, and the line formed; the dragoons on the extreme right, the Nizám's horse on the extreme left, Hungerford's and Woollcombe's batteries forming the right-centre, the bullock battery of the Haidarábád the left centre, the 86th and 25th Bombay Native Infantry the centre, and the Haidarábád

* Lowe.

Book XIII. Chapter II. 1857. November.

infantry with the Madras Sappers on the left of the Haidarábád guns, opposite the village occupied by the rebels. The British guns at once opened fire; and Woollcombe's guns, pointed by Lieutenant Strutt, to be again mentioned in these pages, firing very true,* the rebels wavered. An advance of the Haidarábád troops converted their wavering into flight. The cavalry then pursued and cut up a number of them. The remainder escaped into the city.

and beats them.

The next day, the 22nd, Durand crossed to the right bank of the Mandisúr river and encamped to the west of the town within two thousand yards of the suburbs. His object was to gain a position whence he could threaten Mandisúr with one hand, and the rebel force, which had occupied Nímach,† and which, he had learned from spies, was now hastening to the aid of their comrades, on the other. A cavalry reconnaissance showed the Nímach rebels to be in considerable force in the village of Goraríá on the high road to that place.

Durand interposes between the Mandisúr and Nímach rebels.

In that direction, then, Durand moved on the 24th. After a march of three miles, he espied the rebels about a mile distant, their right rest-

* "Lieutenant Strutt's shooting was very true. All the while this firing was going on at the village, a fine fellow, dressed in white, with a green flag, coolly walked out from the cover, and sauntered leisurely along the whole line of our guns, while round shot and shell were whizzing about him in awful proximity. He occasionally stooped down but never attempted to run; he then quietly retraced his steps, when a shot from Lieutenant Strutt struck him just before he regained the village."—Lowe's *Central India.*

† Vol. ii. pages 571, 572.

Book XIII. Chapter II.

1857. November.

ing on the village, their centre on a long hill, and their left well covered by fields of uncut grain, with broken ground and nullahs in their front, full of water and mud.

Attacks the latter at Gorariá.

The British guns, opening out on the rebels, soon overcame the fire of their five field-pieces, and forced their line to fall back. They clung, however, with great pertinacity to the village of Gorariá, and on this, retiring from the centre and left, they fell back very slowly. Whilst the British were endeavouring to drive them from this position, a strong party sallied from Mandisúr and attacked the rear. They were driven back after a very sharp contest by the Nizám's horse and the dragoons. In front, however, the British could make no impression on the village. The brigadier detailed the 86th and 25th Bombay Native Infantry to carry it with the bayonet, but

Desperate conflict.

the fire from it was so fierce that he countermanded the order, preferring to reduce it with his guns. When night fell the rebels still occupied Gorariá. The British loss had been considerable, amounting to upwards of sixty officers and men killed and wounded.

Gorariá is finally carried.

At 10 o'clock next morning the 18-pounders and the 24-pounder howitzer were brought to within two hundred and fifty yards of the village, and the firing recommenced. The place was shelled till it became a mere wreck; everything that could be burned in it was consumed. Still the rebels held out. At last, about mid-day, some two hundred and twenty came out and surrendered. Those that remained were Rohillas, and

Book XIII. Chapter II.

1857. November.

they stuck to the last brick in the place. About 4 o'clock firing ceased, and the 86th and 25th Bombay Native Infantry stormed it.

The gallantry of the Rohillas allows the Sháhzádah to escape.

The stern defence of the Rohillas did service to their cause. Whilst the British force was dealing with them the Sháhzádah and his two thousand Afgháns and Mekránis evacuated Mandisor and retreated on Nángarh. The cavalry, worn out by four days of unremitting exertion, was unable to pursue them.

The blow struck at Goraria is decisive.

Pursuit, however, was scarcely necessary. The blow struck at Goraria was a blow from which there was no rallying. The Afgháns and Mekránis, as panic-stricken as they had been bold, fled through the country, avoiding towns and villages, and endeavouring to seek refuge in the jungles. One party of them, more daring than their fellows, suddenly appeared at Partábgarh. The loyal chief of that state, summoning his Thákurs, attacked them, killed eighty of them, and drove the rest into flight. The others seemed, above all, anxious to place the Chambal between themselves and their conqueror.

The objects the campaign achieved.

The objects which Durand had in his mind when he set out from Máu on the 14th of October had now been accomplished. With a force extremely weak in infantry, he had crushed the rebellion on the plateau of Málwá, thus saving the line of the Narbadá, and cutting off the disaffected troops of Holkar from the supports on which they had rested. The campaign, brief as it was, had proved decisive, and had vindicated to the letter the prescience of Durand when, re-

Book XIII. Chapter II.

1857. December.

sisting every temptation to act otherwise, he resolved to allow Holkar's troops to rest in quiet until he should have disposed of the Dhár rebels and the mutineers of Mandisúr and Nímach.

Durand marches on Indúr,

He was now at liberty to turn his arms against Holkar's troops. This he did. Returning by Mahidpúr and Újjén, he reached the vicinity of Indúr on the 14th of December, fully prepared to encounter the troops of the Mahárájá should they offer opposition to his entrance into the city. But the spirit which had prompted the treacherous attack of the 1st of July quailed before the sight of a British force returning from victory over traitors. The Indúr troops, held in check during Durand's campaign by the Máu garrison, had been utterly disheartened by the defeat of their sympathisers at Mandisúr, and were as humble as some few weeks previously they had been boastful and defiant.

disarms Holkar's regular cavalry,

Near the ground on which Durand encamped on the 14th of December he met and disarmed Holkar's regular cavalry, and placed the men under the care of the Sikh cavalry of the late Bhopál Contingent. He sent likewise to Holkar's chief minister a letter, in which he insisted that the remainder of the troops should be promptly disarmed. Should this demand not be complied with immediately, he expressed his firm resolution to disarm them himself.

and engages Holkar to disarm the infantry.

The reply came that afternoon. The agent who brought it expressed the intention of the Darbár to disarm the infantry at once, and the request that whilst the operation was being carried into effect Durand would halt at a point one mile from the cavalry lines. Durand complied, and Holkar's infantry, one thousand six hundred in number, were quietly disarmed that same evening.

Book XIII. Chapter II.

1857. December.

After the disarming had been completed, Durand, accompanied by a large body of the officers of the Máu column, called upon the Maharájá in his palace in the city of Indúr. It was the first time since the month of June that Durand had seen Holkar. Regarding him in his own mind as an accessory to the attack made upon the Residency on the 1st of July, Durand had sent a report of all the circumstances of the case to Lord Canning, and pending a reply, had declined to renew personal relations with a prince who might possibly be adjudged by the English authority in India to be a rebel. But when, after the Málwá campaign, Holkar had acquiesced in the disarming of his cavalry and infantry, and his minister had promised that a suitable punishment should be meted out to the guilty, Durand, on the eve of being relieved by Sir Robert Hamilton, felt that the circumstances were not such as to warrant the omission of the ordinary courtesy required to be displayed on such an occasion. Holkar himself was anxious for the visit, and that it should be conducted with a ceremony and an ostentatious display of friendly intercourse such as would produce an impression on his people. Durand acceded. The visit went off well. Holkar was in good spirits, expressed him-

Durand visits Holkar,

prompted by reasons of courtesy.

Interview between Durand and Holkar.

Book XIII. Chapter II.

1857. December.

self delighted at the disarming of his troops, and a hope that the act would be regarded by the British Government as a proof of his loyalty. Durand quietly, but firmly, impressed upon him that something further was yet required—the punishment of the guilty, whether soldiers or citizens—and stated his confident belief that the British Government and the British people would expect that this remaining duty would be properly carried out. Holkar gave an assurance that a Commission, which he had previously appointed, would make full inquiries into the matter. The interview then terminated. The next day Durand was relieved by Sir Robert Hamilton.

Durand's "character created his career."

He had completed a noble task. His personal character had been the mainstay of British authority in central India. Had Durand not been there, the result had not been accomplished. This little sentence conveys to the reader more clearly than a multitude of words the vast value of his services. He was the representative of political power and, virtually, the general; the brain and the hand, in a most important part of India. He foresaw everything, and he provided for everything. He foresaw even—his own despatches and memoirs written at the time show it most clearly—all that was to happen in the few months that were to follow: how the pacification of the North-West Provinces would increase the pressure west of the Jamná; the action of Náná Sáhib and his nephews; the incursion of Tántia Topi. He saw equally clearly the line that should be, and that was, followed. "If affairs at Indúr

His great capacity;

his foresight.

are successfully arranged," he wrote on the 12th of December, "I shall lose no time in marching the bulk of the Máu column to Sihor with the view of concentrating Sir H. Rose's command, and enabling him to relieve Ságar, clear Bandalkhand, and advance on Jhánsi and Gwáliár." In these lines Durand foreshadowed the course which he would himself have pursued, and which Sir Hugh Rose did pursue. But it is his actual achievements which call for special commendation. In spite of his earnest entreaties, in spite of the pressure exercised by Lord Elphinstone, Woodburn had in June chosen to waste most precious moments at Aurangábád. Had that general not delayed at that Capua, it is more than probable that the insurrection of the 1st of July would never have been attempted at Indúr. But mark the conduct of Durand after that misfortune had happened. He hastens to meet Woodburn's column, now commanded by another officer; he meets it, quickens its movements, and brings it to Máu. He finds western Málwá in a state of aggressive insurrection, and the only line which had remained a barrier between the Central Provinces and Bombay—the line of the Narbadá—sorely threatened. Of all the political officers in central India he alone understands the enormous importance of that line. He finds Mr. Plowden from Nágpúr, Major Erskine from the Ságar and Narbadá territories, urging measures which would have lost it. Though pressed by many considerations to disarm Holkar's troops, he, receiving from no quarter a word of encou-

The value of his great achievements.

In spite of the incapacity and wrong-headedness of others,

Book XIII. Chapter II. — 1857. December.

ragement or support, risks everything to save that important line. Then what do we see? With a weak column of five hundred Europeans of all arms and eight hundred natives,* he sets out from Máu, and in five weeks takes a strong fort, fights several cavalry combats, gains three actions in the open field, takes more than forty guns, crushes the Mandisúr insurrection, saves the line of the Narbadá, and, marching back to Indúr, causes the disarming of the disaffected troops of Holkar. In four months he more than counteracts the evil effected by an army of conspirators.

he wins back in four months all that had been lost.

His greatness not appreciated by his contemporaries,

It was, I repeat, a noble work, nobly performed, and, like many noble works, left unrewarded. No man has been more calumniated than its author. No one more bravely fought the battle of life in face of calumny. I may add that of no man that ever lived will the career bear more acute and critical examination. Should the life of Henry Marion Durand be written with the fearlessness the occasion demands, his countrymen will realise alike the worth of the man who, at a most critical period, secured a line the loss of which would have produced incalculable evils. They will learn, too, something of the nature of the smaller beings who aided in the attempt to calumniate, to insult, and to depreciate him. They will learn that it is not always the truly great who occupy the most conspicuous position in the eyes of their contemporaries!

who were also rivals, though far below him.

* Reinforced at Dhár by the Haidarábád troops.

Book XIII. Chapter II.

1857. December.

Some of the men who served under him.

Many officers distinguished themselves in this campaign. One of these, who for his daring, his gallantry, and his brain power was specially noticed by Colonel Durand, requires mention here. "Much of the success in quelling this insurrection," wrote Durand to Lord Canning at the end of November 1857, "is due to the judicious daring, the thorough gallantry with which, whenever opportunity offered, Major Gall, his officers and men, sought close conflict with the enemy—a bold one, who often fought most desperately. I feel it a duty to Major Gall and H.M.'s 14th Light Dragoons, men and officers, thus especially to beg your Lordship's influence in favour of officers and men, who have merited, by conspicuous valour, everything that Her Majesty's Government may be pleased to confer. They deserve most highly." Durand also noticed with marked commendation the splendid services of Major Orr, Captain Abbott, and the officers and men of the Haidarábád Contingent and of the 25th Regiment Bombay Native Infantry. This regiment boasted a commanding officer, Major, afterwards Lieutenant-Colonel, Robertson, than whom no one rendered better service to the State. Captain Woollcombe, Lieutenants Strutt and Christie, of the Bombay Artillery, the last-named of whom was shot through the heart, also greatly distinguished themselves. But there were many others in the same category. The list is too long.

BOOK XIII.

CHAPTER III.

The Ságar and Narbadá territories.

THE territories known as the Ságar and Narbadá territories formed an extensive tract, bounded on the north by the British districts of Bandá, Allahábád, and Mirzapúr; on the south by Nágpúr and the dominions of the Nizám; on the west by Gwáliár and Bhopál. Within these boundaries is comprehended the state of Rewá, whose Rájá recognised the overlordship of the British. The other native feudatories, the feudatories of Kótí, Maihír, Uchéra, and Soháwal, held their lands under grants from the East India Company. Within the limits of those lands, however, they exercised a ruling authority, subject to the interference, when necessary, of the paramount power. The larger portion of the Ságar and Narbadá territories were directly British. This portion comprised the districts of Ságar, Jabalpúr, Hoshangábád, Sióni, Damoh, Narsingpúr, Baitúl, Jhánsi, Chandairi, Nagód, and Mandlah.

Book XIII. Chapter III.

1843.

Sketch of the later history of those territories.

When, in 1843, the Gwáliár Darbár commenced those hostilities against the British which culminated in the battle of Maháréjpúr, the chiefs and people of the Ságar and Narbadá territories, then ruled by Mr. Fraser, C.B., as Agent to the Governor-General, broke out into open rebellion. This rebellion was due partly to the great dislike felt by the people to the civil courts, and more particularly to the mode in which they were administered, and partly to the propaganda of the Gwáliár Darbár. When, however, the pride of that Darbár had been lowered by the battle of Maháréjpúr, peace was restored to the Ságar and Narbadá territories. Lord Ellenborough, who, throughout his Indian career, always displayed a marked detestation of proved abuses, inaugurated the newly-gained peace by making a clean sweep of the British officials serving in the territories, and by sending one of the ablest officers in the Indian services, the late Colonel Sleeman, to administer them on a new basis. Colonel Sleeman succeeded in pacifying the chiefs and in contenting the people. When, after a rule of two or three years, he was promoted to be Resident at Lakhnao, he handed over the territories to his successor, Mr. Bushby, in perfect order. Mr. Bushby's administration of five or six years was characterised by ability and good judgment; but when, at the close of that period, he was promoted to the Residency of Haidarábád, the Ságar and Narbadá territories were joined to the North-West Provinces, then ruled by Mr. Colvin, Major

Book XIII. Chapter III.

1855.

Erskine* receiving the appointment of Commissioner of Jabalpúr and becoming Mr. Colvin's representative in the territories. Subordinate to Major Erskine, were, amongst others, Captain Skene, Commissioner of Jhánsi, and Captain Ternan, Deputy Commissioner of Narsangpúr.

They fall under the rule of the A'gra Board of Revenue,

With their transfer to the North-West Provinces, the Ságar and Narbadá territories came under the Sudder Board of Revenue. In accordance with its traditions, that venerable Board at once proposed changes in the administration so startling that, if carried out, they would inevitably have caused a violent rebellion. Before finally deciding in favour of the proposed changes, Mr. Colvin had the good sense to ask the opinion of the officer who had served longest in the territories, a man of remarkable sense and strength of character, Captain A. H. Ternan. Captain Ternan replied by pointing out the inapplicability of the rules of the Sudder Board of Revenue to the needs of the province, and the certain consequences which would follow any attempt to enforce them. Mr. Colvin, struck by Captain Ternan's representations, withdrew nearly the whole of the proposed changes. It is a pity that he did not withdraw the whole, for the few that he allowed, relating chiefly to the subdivision of properties, roused a very bad feeling, and led to many agrarian outrages.

which proposes revolutionary changes.

On Captain Ternan's representation many of these are modified.

Sufficient remains to sour the temper of the people.

Such was the state of the territories in 1855. The temper of the people, kindled by the cause I

* Afterwards Earl of Kellie.

have mentioned, had not wholly subsided into its normal condition of contentment. The outbreak in the North-West Provinces came inopportunely to inflame it still more.

Book XIII. Chapter III.

1857. January.

Captain Ternan at Narsingpúr

The small station of Narsingpúr on the Narbadá, sixty miles to the west of Ságar, was garrisoned at the outbreak of the mutiny by four companies of the 28th Madras Native Infantry, under the command of Captain Woolley, an excellent officer. The Deputy Commissioner of the district, Captain Ternan, to whose calm and cool judgment I have already referred, had his head-quarters also at Narsingpúr. The district of which this town was the capital was largely inhabited by petty chiefs, who had gone into rebellion in 1843, and who had never submitted willingly to British jurisdiction. So early as December 1856 there were not wanting indications that some great event was looming before the eyes of these men, but no European could venture an opinion as to the form that event would take. It happened, however, that one evening in January 1857, Captain Ternan was sitting outside his tent, smoking a cigar, when the Kótwál* of the village came running to him, bearing in his hand some small chapatties or cakes of unleavened bread. On reaching Ternan, the Kótwál, out of breath and panting, stated that the cakes were the remnant of a large quantity he had received that morning, with instructions to leave them with the watchman of every village, to be

His first experience of the chapatties in circulation.

* A Kótwál is generally a chief officer of police.

Book XIII. Chapter III.

1857. January.

kept till called for; that he had so distributed them in the neighbouring villages, and that those which he held in his hand constituted the surplus. "What," he asked Ternan, "was he to do with them?"

Ternan divines the mystery,

Ternan, naturally shrewd, and that natural shrewdness sharpened by the experience of the rebellion of 1842–43, at once divined the truth. In those small unleavened cakes he saw the fiery cross sent through the land to unsettle the minds of the great mass of the people; that, distributed broadcast as the Kótwál had distributed them in his district, they would indicate a sudden danger that might come at any moment upon the people, threatening their caste and undermining their religion. He at once embodied these ideas in a report, which he transmitted forthwith to his official superior, Major Erskine.

and reports his views to Major Erskine.

Major Erskine

Major Erskine was an officer who had written a book of "Forms and Tables for the Use of the Bengal Native Infantry." That book was a reflex of his mind. His mind was a mind "of forms and tables." His mental vision commanded the line of strict and formal routine. Out of that line he saw nothing, he was incapable of seeing anything. When, therefore, he received Ternan's report and read the conclusions drawn by that officer regarding the unleavened cakes, he ridiculed them; he considered the idea far-fetched, absurd, impossible. He wrote back to Ternan to that effect, adding that it was simply a case of "a dyer's vat having gone wrong," and that the owner of the vat was

utterly declines Ternan's view.

propitiating the gods by the distribution of cakes!

Ternan's prescience is justified by events.

Subsequent events made it abundantly evident that Erskine was wrong and Ternan was right. Distributed broadly over the North-West Provinces and in Oudh, in the earlier months of 1857, these cakes were the harbingers of the coming storm. It is certain now that they originated in the brain of the Oudh conspirators, of the men made conspirators by the annexation of their country, and they were sent to every village for the very object divined by Ternan—the object of unsettling men's minds, of preparing them for the unforeseen, of making them impressionable, easy to receive the ideas the conspirators wished to promulgate.

I may record here a decision of the Government promulgated in the same district a year or two prior to 1857, and of the remarkable consequence it produced after the mutiny had broken out, as illustrative of the influence which an able and conscientious English officer can almost always bring to bear upon native chiefs. One of the most influential chieftains in the territories under Captain Ternan's supervision was the rájá of Dilhérí, the feudal lord of all the Gónd clans. This chief had ever been loyal. For his fidelity and good conduct in the trying times of 1842–43, the Government had presented him with a gold medal. Like many of the Gónd tribe, he had been somewhat too profuse in his expenditure, and had incurred debts. But by exercising a strict economy he had paid off those debts.

The rájá of Dilhérí

Book XIII. Chapter III.

1855.

Such was his condition in 1855, shortly after the Ságar and Narbadá territories had been brought under the government of the North-West Provinces. It had been a principle of that government, since the time when it was administered by Mr. Thomason, to discourage large landowners. One morning in that year Captain Ternan received instructions, emanating from Ágra, desiring him to inform the rájá of Dilhéri that, inasmuch as he was unfit to hold the title of rájá and had proved himself incapable of managing his estates, he was deprived of both; that his title of rájá was abolished, and that his property would be distributed among his tenants, he receiving a percentage from the rents! When this decision was most unwillingly announced to the rájá by Captain Ternan, the old man drew his medal from the belt in which it was habitually carried, and requested the English officer to return it to those who had bestowed it, as they were now about to disgrace him before his clan and before the whole district. With great difficulty Ternan pacified him. It was generally expected that he would break out into rebellion. He might well have done so, for every member of the clan felt insulted in his person. Ternan, fearing an outbreak, pressed on the Government the mistake they had committed, and urged them to rectify it. But the Government would not listen. The order was carried out. Ternan did all in his power to save the family from ruin; but even he could do little.

Falls under the displeasure of the Board of Revenue,

and is deprived of his title and estates.

He feels the insult bitterly;

but, despite Ternan's remonstrances, the decision is persisted in.

Before the mutiny broke out in May 1857, the

Book XIII. Chapter III.

1857. May.

When the mutiny breaks out, his grandson and his clansmen

old man had died; his son, too, had died. The next heir took the title—for, however the Government might order, the representative of the family was always rájá to the people. Then came the mutiny of May 1857. The Narsingpúr district felt its shock. Muhammadans from across the border invaded the district and pillaged the villages. The outlook became every day more gloomy. "Save yourselves while yet there is time," said the loyal officials to Ternan. But Ternan stayed. One morning, however, early in June, his house was surrounded by a considerable body of armed men, with lighted matchlocks. Ternan saw at a glance that they all belonged to the Dilhéri clan. He at once summoned the chief and asked him what had brought him and his clansmen in such numbers and in so warlike a garb. The chief replied that he would answer if he and the other chiefs were allowed a private audience with their interlocutor. Ternan admitted them into his drawing-room. The chief replied: "You behaved kindly to us and fought our battle when the title and estate were confiscated, and you were abused for so doing. Now we hear disturbances are rife, and we come to offer you our services. We will stick by you as you stuck by us. What do you wish us to do?" Ternan thanked them, accepted their offer, assured them they should be no losers by their conduct, and promised to do his utmost to see justice done them. The members of the clan remained loyal throughout the trying events of 1857–58, resisted the urgent solicitations made to them to join the

offer their services to Ternan, and continue loyal under every change of fortune.

1857. May.

rebels, and, what was of equal importance, they induced other clans to join them in rendering most valuable service to the British cause.

I turn now to the part of the territories the chief centres in which were more purely military stations.

Garrisons of the Ságar and Narbadá territories.

There were three military stations in the Ságar and Narbadá territories—the stations of Ságar, Jabalpúr, and Hoshangábád. Ságar was garrisoned by the 31st and 47th Bengal Native Infantry, the 3rd Regiment Irregular Cavalry, and sixty-eight European gunners; Jabalpúr by the 52nd Bengal Native Infantry, and Hoshangábád by the 28th Madras Native Infantry. The commandant of the Ságar district force was Brigadier Sage, who had his head-quarters at Ságar.

Brigadier Sage at Ságar.

Neither the news of the mutiny at Mírath nor the tidings of the nearer and more horrible events at Jhánsi,* affected, according to all appearance, the demeanour of the native troops at Ságar. Indeed, so conspicuous was their good conduct, that, early in June, Brigadier Sage, not trusting them, yet unwilling openly to display an opposite feeling, did not hesitate to send a detachment, consisting of five hundred infantry, one hundred and twenty-five cavalry, and two 9-pounders, against a rájá who had rebelled, promising them a reward of six thousand rupees for the capture of the said rájá, dead or alive. A few days later, however, the brigadier had reason to feel that the policy of concealing distrust was not likely to answer

* Vol i. page 190.

better in Ságar than in the places where it had been already tried and had failed. The station of Ságar was laid out in a manner which rendered it difficult for a commander with only sixty-eight European soldiers at his disposal, to exercise a general supervision over the whole. At one end of it were the fort, the magazine, and the battering train. At the other end, distant from it three miles and a quarter, was a commanding position known as the artillery hill. Both these points could not be retained. The artillery hill, though in many respects important as a position, wanted water and storing-room for provisions. There was no question, then, in the brigadier's mind, as to the position which should be abandoned. Yet he laboured under this great difficulty, that the sepoys possessed the fort and the treasury, and they took care to let it be surmised that they would yield neither the one nor the other. In a word, the station was at their mercy.

Book XIII. Chapter III.

1857. June.

The position at Ságar.

Affairs were in this position when, on the 13th of June, Brigadier Sage received an application for assistance in guns from Lallatpúr, a station in the Jhánsi district, garrisoned by three hundred men of the 6th Infantry, Gwáliár Contingent. The brigadier promptly despatched two 9-pounders, escorted by one company of the 31st Native Infantry, one of the 42nd, and seventy-five troopers of the 3rd Irregulars. The detachment never reached Lallatpúr. The very evening before it left Ságar, the three companies of the Gwáliár regiment at that station had broken out into mutiny, had plundered the treasury, and had

Mutiny at Lallatpúr.

Book XIII. Chapter III.

1857. June.

driven the European officers* to flee for protection to the rájá of Bánpúr, who, under the pretence of being a friend, had been for some days in the vicinity of Lallatpúr, exciting the sepoys to mutiny.

The Rájá of Bánpúr rebels.

For a moment I follow the action of this rájá. Finding that the rebel sepoys had taken possession of the Lallatpúr treasury, and were marching off with its contents, he attacked them, and was repulsed. Thus baffled, he sent off his European guests to the fort of Tehrí, there to be confined, and then marched in haste to meet the detachment coming from Ságar, with the view of inducing the sepoys composing it to join him.

Major Gaussen with a detachment from Ságar reaches Málthoni.

Major Gaussen, commanding that detachment, had reached Málthoni, thirty-seven miles from Ságar, when he heard of the mutiny at Lallatpúr and of the movement of the Bánpúr rájá. He at once halted and wrote for reinforcements. Sage replied promptly by sending four hundred infantry and one hundred cavalry. The night previous to the day on which those men were ordered to set out, great commotion reigned in Ságar, and it seemed as though mutiny might break out at any moment. The danger passed, however. Brigadier Sage, though urged by many of those about him to put an end to the terrible suspense by striking a blow with the few Euro-

* Captain Sale, commanding; Lieutenant Irwin, second in command, his wife and two children; Dr. O'Brien, and Lieutenant Gordon, Deputy Commissioner of Chandairi. They were made over to the rájá of Sháhgarh, by whom they were kindly treated. Ultimately they were all released.

Book XIII. Chapter III. — 1857. June.

peans under his orders, remained impassive. He had resolved to act only when the sepoys should commit themselves unmistakably to revolt.

His men revolt.

The detachment marched the following morning, the 19th of June, and joined Major Gaussen on the 23rd. Gaussen then marched with his whole force against the fort of Bálábét, held by the rebels, stormed it,* and took sixteen of the garrison prisoners. The sepoy stormers promised these men their lives, and two days later, on the return of the detachment to Málthoni, they insisted on their release. Major Gaussen being powerless to refuse the demand, they released the prisoners, and made them over to the Bánpúr rájá. No sooner had this act been accomplished than that rájá entered the British camp, and openly offered the sepoys a monthly pay of twelve rupees if they would leave their officers and go over to him with their arms and ammunition! The sepoys complied, dismissed their officers, and joined the rájá.

Sage prepares for a decisive movement.

The information brought by the returning officers to Ságar decided Sage to act promptly. He saw that if he were to wait till the rebel rájá should march on Ságar, he and his sixty-eight men would be surrounded and lost. According he at once, and in the most judicious manner, began his operations. He first moved the contents of the treasury to the fort; to the same place he next conveyed the contents of the

* In blowing open the gate, Ensign Spens of the 31st was accidentally killed. Lieutenant Willoughby of the artillery was wounded.

Book XIII. Chapter III.

1857. June.

expense magazine and the artillery magazine; and last of all, he removed thither the women, children, and baggage of the European artillery. As soon as this had been accomplished, he took a guard of Europeans and relieved the sepoy guard at the fort gate. He then marched into it the ladies and children. Thus, by a few decisive strokes, the one following the other with rapidity, Sage gained a place of refuge, secured the contents of the magazine, and saved the treasure.

He reasons with the native officers.

The second day after, the morning of the 30th of June, whilst the ordinary grand guard-mounting was progressing, Sage marched the Europeans and sixty cavalry, who remained loyal, into the fort. He then sent for all the native officers, and frankly telling them the reason of his action, added that they had suffered acts of mutiny to take place without opposing them, and had forfeited their character; that there was yet one method open to them of regaining it, and that was to have the leading mutineers seized and delivered up to justice. The native officers of the three regiments, apparently very much affected, promised everything. The next morning, however, the 3rd Irregulars and the 42nd Native Infantry broke into open mutiny and plundered the bazars and the bungalows of the officers. The 31st held aloof, professing loyalty; and on the 7th of July, one of their men having killed a trooper who had fired at him, a desperate fight ensued between the two native infantry regiments. The 31st being unable to make much impression on the 42nd, who had two guns, sent

The 3rd Irregulars and the 42nd Native Infantry break out into mutiny: the 31st Native Infantry remains staunch.

Book XIII. Chapter III.

1857. July.

into the fort imploring assistance. Sage sent them the sixty loyal troopers. A good deal of fighting then ensued, but, in the midst of it, forty of the 31st deserted to the 42nd. Still the bulk of the loyal regiment persevered, and, when evening fell, sent again to the fort to implore assistance in guns. Sage replied that it was too late to send them that night, but in the morning he would bring them victory. Information to this effect reaching the two belligerent parties fixed the 31st in their loyal resolves, whilst it so dispirited their opponents that during the night they fled, pursued for some miles by the loyal sepoys and troopers, who captured one of the guns. When the victors returned, it was ascertained that whilst the entire 31st, the forty above alluded to excepted, had remained loyal, fifty of the 42nd had followed their example, and the sixty loyal troopers had been joined by at least an equal number of the same temper from out-stations.

Battle between the loyal and disloyal sepoys.

Final victory of the loyal natives.

The brigadier now devoted himself to strengthening the mud fort. He had supplies and medical stores for six months, and a sufficiency of guns and ammunition. The able-bodied men of the Christian community were gradually drilled, and as they numbered about sixty, Sage soon had at his disposal a force of one hundred aud twenty-three fighting men. The number was not at all too large, for the duties were heavy; there were one hundred and ninety women and children to be guarded, and occasionally parties of Bandíla rebels, into whose hands the surrounding country had fallen, made known their pre-

Life in the Ságar fort.

Book XIII. Chapter III.

1857. August.

sence by a sudden volley. They fired, however, only to disappear in the jungles on the first appearance of pursuit.

The districts held by the natives.

The districts—in close vicinity to each other—of Jabalpúr, of Ságar, of Chandairi, of Jhánsi, and of Jaláun, continued, from this time until the arrival of the relieving force under Sir Hugh Rose, to be over-run by rebels, sepoy and other. These harried the country, captured forts, plundered villages, for a long time with impunity. Befcre I narrate the manner in which they were ultimately dealt with, it will, I think, be advisable to clear the ground by recording the events passing at the other stations in this part of India.

Jabalpúr.

Of Lallatpúr I have spoken. Jabalpúr, one hundred and eleven miles south-east from Ságar, has next to be noticed. This station was, in 1857, garrisoned by the 52nd Native Infantry, commanded by Lieutenant-Colonel Jamieson. It was the head-quarters likewise of Major Erskine, the chief political officer in the Ságar and Narbadá territories. For a few weeks after the news of the mutiny at Mírath had reached Jabalpúr the men of the 52nd showed no sign of disaffection, but it soon became clear that they, too, were only watching their opportunity. On the 16th of June one of the men attempted to murder the adjutant; and though the man in question was subsequently released on the ground of insanity, the conduct of his comrades a little later proved that there had been method in his madness. They assumed the usual airs of authority, treated their officers with patronising familiarity,

Dubious conduct of the 52nd Native Infantry.

1857. September.

and declared that they would only mutiny if a European regiment were sent to disarm them. One consequence of this conduct was that all the ladies and children were promptly despatched to Séoni and Narsingpúr.

For a time they do good work in the district.

The news that a native brigade was advancing on Jabalpúr from Kámpti would appear to have produced a good effect on the men of the 52nd, for in the interval between the period I have referred to and the arrival of the brigade, 2nd of August, they were usefully employed by Major Erskine in repressing disturbances in the district.

The Kámpti column arrives.

The Kámpti movable column—for it was no more—consisted of the 4th Madras Light Cavalry under Captain Tottenham, the 33rd Madras Native Infantry under Colonel Millar commanding the column, a battery of Field Artillery under Captain Jones, and one company Rifles, Nágpúr Irregular Force, under Lieutenant Pereira. This column marched into Jabalpúr on the 2nd of August. After a halt there of a few days, the larger portion of it was sent into the neighbouring districts to restore order. During its absence an old rájá of the Gónd dynasty, Shankar Sháh, his son, and some adherents of his house were convicted, on the clearest evidence, of plotting the destruction of the English at Jabalpúr, and the plunder of the station. On the 18th of September the father and son were blown away from guns, the adherents being reserved for the following day. But little doubt was entertained that the criminal rájá and his criminal son had made many efforts to seduce the men of the 52nd from their alle-

Rájá Shankar Shah and his son mutiny and are punished.

Book XIII. Chapter III.

1857. September.

giance. To allay, then, the excitement which, it was apprehended, their execution might create in the minds of the rank and file, Colonel Jamieson and other officers of the regiment proceeded almost immediately to the lines, and explained to the men that the rájá and his son had merely paid the penalty for proved misconduct. They judged, from the manner of the men, that they had removed all apprehensions from their minds.

The 52nd Native Infantry mutiny,

At 9 o'clock that night, however, the entire 52nd regiment marched quietly out of the station, without noise or alarm, and proceeded some twenty miles without a halt to the Tahsildári of Patan. At that place was stationed a company of their own regiment commanded by Lieutenant MacGregor. MacGregor, who naturally had had no intimation of the proceedings of the regiment, was surprised, and at once placed in confinement under sentries. The sepoys then sent in to their colonel a letter, most respectfully worded, in which they announced their intention of marching to Dehlí, and offered to release MacGregor in exchange for ten sepoys left behind in Jabalpúr. This offer not having been complied with, the rebels kept their prisoner till they were attacked, and then shot him.*

and kill one of their officers.

But long before the commission of this atrocity information of the high-handed action of the 52nd

* MacGregor's body was found by the officers of the Madras column with one ball through the neck, both arms broken, and his body perforated with thirty or forty bayonet wounds. Major Erskine had previously offered eight thousand rupees for his release.

Native Infantry, and orders to return to Jabalpúr, had been conveyed to the Madras column in the district. That column, consisting of four hundred men of the 33rd Madras Native Infantry, the rifle company of the 1st Madras Native Infantry, one troop of the 4th Madras Light Cavalry, and four guns, manned by European gunners, happened to be at Damoh, sixty-five miles to the north-west of Jabalpúr. It started at once, on the 21st of September. On the night of the 25th it encamped at Sangrámpúr, about twenty-five miles from its destination. Between this place and Jabalpúr, close to a village called Katanji, flows a navigable river, the Hiran, the passage across which, it was thought possible, might be disputed by the 52nd. To secure the means of crossing it, a party, consisting of the grenadier company 33rd Madras Native Infantry, under Lieutenant Watson, and a few troopers of the 4th, under Major Jenkins, left the camp at 2 o'clock in the morning of the 26th. At daybreak, as they were nearing Katanji, Jenkins and Watson, who were riding in front of their column, were suddenly fired at, and almost immediately surrounded. How they escaped it is difficult to imagine. But, notwithstanding all the efforts made by the sepoys, they fought their way through them and reached their men. These were not numerous enough to take the aggressive. Jenkins, therefore, drew them up on a hill difficult to escalade, and there awaited the arrival of the main column.

Book XIII. Chapter III.

1857. September.

A Madras column marches against the 52nd Native Infantry.

An advanced party meets them,

fights its way through them,

and waits for the main body,

To this column, on the point of starting about

Book XIII. Chapter III.

1857. September.

6 o'clock in the morning, information arrived, in an exaggerated form, of the events at Katanji. The two European officers were reported killed, and the rebels were said to be pressing on in force. Eager to avenge their officers and relieve their comrades, the gallant native soldiers of the coast army hurried forward. On reaching the mouth of the gorge leading to Katanji, they found the 52nd had taken up a very strong position, both flanks covered by thick jungle. Without hesitating, they opened fire from the guns, and then attacked the rebels with the bayonet and drove them before them. On reaching Katanji, they were joined by Jenkins and Watson. The pursuit was continued beyond that place. In Katanji the body of MacGregor, murdered that morning, was found. The rebels suffered severely. A hundred and twenty-five dead were actually counted on the field, and it is certain that many more were wounded. On the side of the victors one man was killed and fifty were wounded. The column then returned to Jabalpúr.

which totally defeats the rebels.

A force is sent from Ságar against the Bánpúr rájá.

This was not by any means the only skirmish which took place in the Ságar and Narbadá territories during the autumn of 1857. In my story of the transactions at Ságar, I have alluded to the conduct of the Bánpúr rájá. This rebel chief, still hoping to gain greatly by the downfall of the British, had, after a great deal of promiscuous plundering, taken up a position at Niráoli, about nine miles from Ságar, and had strongly intrenched it. Against this position a force was sent from the Ságar fort on

Book XIII. Chapter III.

1857. September.

the 15th of September, under the command of Lieutenant-Colonel Dalyell, 42nd Native Infantry. The expedition was not successful; for though the rebels suffered severely from the fire of the British guns, Colonel Dalyell was killed and the loss of the attacking party in killed and wounded was very severe. The intrenchment was not stormed.

It is repulsed with the loss of its leader, Colonel Dalyell.

This affair did not increase the chances of the restoration of order. The remnant of the 52nd native infantry, numbering some five hundred and thirty men, continued, after its defeat at Katanji, to ravage the country. Joining the adherents of rebel rájás, these men took advantage of the withdrawal of the Madras column from Damoh to plunder that place and to release the prisoners. They then took possession of a strong fort, about thirty miles from Ságar, called Garhákót, and from this they constantly sallied forth to plunder and destroy. In fact, as the year drew to a close, in spite of the fall of Dehlí, the daring of the rebels increased, whilst the handful of British, shut up in the stations at long distances from each other, and powerless to interfere effectually, could do little more than hold their own. Several skirmishes, indeed, occurred, but with no decisive result. In one of these, early in November, near Jabalpúr, the Madras troops defeated the enemy, but their commander, Captain Tottenham, was killed. In others, the defeat of the rebels merely signified a disappearance from one jungle to appear immediately in another.

The country is still ravaged by the rebels.

Book XIII. Chapter III.

1857. November.

Military operations in the Narsingpúr district.

Woolley.

Ternan.

Roberts.

Mayne.

In the preceding pages of this chapter I have alluded to the conduct of Captain Ternan in the Narsingpúr district. I must devote a few lines to the military operations in that quarter. The garrison of Narsingpúr consisted of four companies of the 28th Madras Native Infantry under Captain Woolley. These sepoys, unlike the bulk of their brethren in Bengal, continued throughout the period of 1857–58 loyal and true. In November 1857, led by Woolley and accompanied by Ternan, they restored order in the disturbed parts of the district, co-operating for that purpose with a detachment sent from Ságar under Captain Roberts of the 31st Bengal N.I. and Captain Mayne of the 3rd irregular cavalry. Its action was most successful. The districts north of the Narbadá were cleared of rebels; and in a hand-to-hand encounter with the largest body of them, the rebel leader, Ganjan Singh, a landowner of considerable consequence, was slain, and nearly all his followers were destroyed. Ternan, who had his horse shot under him in this encounter, then urged a rapid march upon Singpúr, a place held by a noted rebel called Dalganjan. His advice was followed, and Dalganjan was taken and hanged. The following month another fatal blow was dealt to the insurgents near Chírápúr. When Woolley reached this place it was found evacuated. Ternan, however, pushing on with a small party in search of the rebels, succeeded in surprising them, and capturing their tents, one 4-pounder gun, and many native weapons. This enterprising officer

Energy displayed by Ternan at Chírápúr,

followed up the blow in January 1858 by completely defeating the invading rebels from Rátgarh and Bhopál at Maddanpúr. By this vigorous stroke the Narsingpúr district was finally cleared of all rebels of consequence.

Book XIII. Chapter III. 1857. September. and at Maddanpúr.

Before describing the measures ultimately taken to reassert British authority throughout this part of India, it is necessary that I should take the reader for a moment to Nagód.

Nagód.

Nagód is a military station, in the Úchéra district, distant forty-eight miles from Réwah, one hundred and eighty from Allahábád, and forty-three miles from Ságar. The garrison in 1857 consisted of the 50th Bengal N.I., commanded by Major Hampton. Up to the month of September this regiment had displayed no mutinous symptoms, and the men were regarded by their officers as staunch and loyal. It happened, however, that at the time that the 52nd native infantry decamped from Jabalpúr in the manner already described, a rumour reached Nagód that Kúnwar Singh was marching on that place. The men of the 50th were accordingly ordered to prepare to march against that warrior. They appeared delighted at the order, made all the necessary preparations with alacrity, and marched. The regiment had not, however, reached the second milestone from Nagód when a voice from the ranks gave the order to halt. The regiment halted. Some of the men then told the officers that their services were no longer required, and that they had better go. Opposition was useless. A few faithful men escorted the

The 50th Native Infantry, appear staunch and loyal, but they mutiny,

Book XIII. Chapter III.

1857. September.

and ravage the district.

officers and their families to Mirzapúr, whilst the remainder, returning to Nagód, plundered and burned the place, and then inaugurated in the district a career similar to that of their brethren of the 52nd.

Réwah.

Réwah, I have already stated, is a small native state, ruled by a quasi-independent rájá, recognising the suzerainty of the British, bound to them by treaties, and having a British resident at his court. In 1857 the resident political agent was Lieutenant Willoughby Osborne, an officer of the Madras army, possessing great strength of will, a courage that never faltered, and resolute to do his duty to the utmost. Left unfettered, Willoughby Osborne almost always did the right thing; but, like many other men conscious of their powers, he writhed under the sway of self-appreciative mediocrity. Happily, at Réwah, he was unfettered.

Willoughby Osborne.

Description of the town of Réwah.

The town of Réwah lies little more than midway between Allahábád and Ságar, being one hundred and thirty-one miles south-west of the former, and one hundred and eighty-two miles north-east of the latter. It is built on the banks of a small river, the Bíhar, a tributary of the Tons. Around it runs a high and thick rampart, still nearly entire, flanked by towers, many of which have fallen into decay. Within this outer defence a similar rampart immediately environs the town; and still further inward a third surrounds the residence of the rájá. It is a decaying place, and the population in 1857 scarcely exceeded six thousand.

Book XIII. Chapter III.

1857. June.

Glance at the political situation of Réwah.

Tact and judgment displayed by Willoughby Osborne.

The residence of a rájá whose ancestors had been proud of their independence, surrounded by districts in which mutiny was rampant, lying many miles from the route of the British armies between Calcutta and the north-west, Réwah, in June and July of 1857, seemed utterly lost. Not, however, to Willoughby Osborne. The first point to which that able officer directed his efforts was to win the rájá. His character had, indeed, already gained the respect and admiration of the prince, but in such times as were then upon them it became necessary that the princes of India, especially the small rájás, should feel that they had everything to lose, nothing to gain, by the success of the mutineers. Osborne succeeded in instilling that feeling into the mind of the rájá. On the 8th of June he was able to announce that the rájá of Réwah had placed his troops at the disposal of the Government of India; that the offer had been accepted; and that eight hundred of those troops, with two guns, had been sent to Ammapatan—a place commanding the roads to Jabalpúr, Nagód, and Ságar—ready to oppose insurgents from any of those stations, and to intercept communications with the rebellious villages on the Jamná. He despatched, about the same time, eleven hundred of the rájá's troops and five guns to the Kattra pass, about midway to Mirzápúr, and whence a rapid advance could be made on that important commercial city, on Banáras, or on Chunár, as might be deemed advisable. A week later he obtained the rájá's sanction to send seven hun-

He gains the rájá,

and sends his troops to guard the districts.

Book XIII Chapter III. — 1857. June-Dec.

dred troops to Bandá, and he induced him to issue a proclamation promising rewards to any of his soldiers who should distinguish themselves by their gallantry and loyalty.

Excellent effect of these measures on Bandalkhand.

The measures taken by Willoughby Osborne had a very marked influence on affairs in Bandalkhand. There, as in the adjacent territories, the smaller chieftains, mostly men of impoverished fortunes, thought the opportunity too favourable to be lost. They, too, rose in revolt. But Osborne was incessantly on the watch. By the skilful disposition of the rájá's troops, and by the display of an energy which never tired, he baffled all the earlier efforts of the rebels. By the exercise of similar qualities he kept open the important line of road between Mirzápúr and Jabalpúr, a necessary part of the available postal route between Calcutta and Bombay. In a few weeks he was able to take an active offensive against the insurgents. He defeated them at Kanchanpúr and Zorah, then advancing on their stronghold—Maihír—he stormed that city on the 29th of December, pushed on to Jakhání, captured that place, thus opening thirty-six miles of road in the direction of Jabalpúr. At a date considerably later he, in the most gallant manner, captured the important fort of Bijérájúgarh. Owing solely to the indefatigable exertions of this gallant Englishman, the rebel cause not only found no footing in Bandalkhand, but it lost way in the adjacent territories.

He takes the field against the insurgents, and performs wonders.

Nágpúr.

Nágpúr, till 1853 the capital of the Bhonslá dynasty, and since that period the chief town in the Central Provinces and the head-quarters of the Chief Commissioner, is a large straggling city, about seven miles in circumference, having in 1857 a population somewhat exceeding a hundred thousand. Close to the city, on its western side, is a hilly ridge running north and south, known as the Sítábaldi, possessing two summits, one at each extremity, the northern being the higher, the southern the larger, but both commanding the city. Outside of but near the city were the arsenal—containing guns, arms, ammunition, and military stores of every description—and the treasury of the province, containing a large amount of cash. To protect these and the city, the Commissioner, Mr. George Plowden, had, of European troops, one company of Madras artillery, whose head-quarters were at Kámptí, eleven miles distant. The local native troops at his disposal were thus stationed: at Kámptí or in Nágpúr itself, the head-quarters of the 1st Infantry, the 1st Cavalry, and the artillery of the Nágpúr irregular force; at Chánda, eighty-five miles south of Nágpur, were the 2nd Infantry, and a detachment of the 1st, of the same force; at Bhandára, forty miles to the east, was another detachment of the 1st Regiment; the head-quarters and greater part of the 3rd Regiment were at Raipúr, one hundred and thirty-seven miles still further in the same direction; the remainder of that regiment was at Biláspúr. These, I have said, were local troops. Kámptí was likewise the head-quarters of a brigade of the Madras army. The troops stationed there in 1857 were the 4th Madras Light Cavalry,

Book XIII. Chapter III.

1857. June.

Description of its position.

Mr. George Plowden.

The local troops,

and those of the regular army at Kámptí.

Book XIII. Chapter III.

1857. June.

the 17th, 26th, 32nd, and 33rd Native Infantry, and the European artillery already alluded to. Brigadier H. Prior commanded the Nágpúr subsidiary force.

Ill-feeling amongst the local troops.

Very soon after the events of May 1857 at Mírath became known to the troops located in the Central Provinces, symptoms of disloyalty began to be manifested by the troops, especially by the cavalry portion, of the local force. In the position he occupied, ruling a large city, dependent for physical aid upon a few European gunners and five native regiments, Mr. Plowden could not afford even the symptoms of mutiny to pass unnoticed. Still less could he afford it when all the circumstances of the intended rising, to the extent even of the signal which was to set it in action,* were revealed to him.

Mr. Plowden and Colonel Cumberlege disarm the local troops.

Mr. Plowden resolved to act, and to act promptly. He arranged with Colonel Cumberlege, who entirely trusted the men of his own regiment—the 4th Light Cavalry—that the troopers of the local regiment should be disarmed on the 17th of June. Colonel Cumberlege performed the task with skill and tact, and without bloodshed. Mr.

Mr. Plowden prepares for eventualities.

Plowden followed up this blow by strengthening the two peaks on the Sítábaldi hill, that they might serve as a refuge for the residents of Nágpúr in the event of a mutiny. The residency

* The mutiny was to have broken out on the 13th of June; the signal to have been the ascent of three fire-balloons from the city. One of the ringleaders, caught in the act of seducing the men of the 1st local infantry, gave the first intimation of the plot.

Book XIII. Chapter III.

1857. June.

was at the same time converted into a barrack, in which the civil and military officers should congregate during the night.

Loyalty of the soldiers of the Madras army.

These precautions were effective. Notwithstanding serious alarms, no outbreak actually occurred. The Madras soldiers not only remained faithful, but when a column of them was despatched to Jabalpúr,* the departing men were replaced by others of the same army not less loyal and true.

Isolated position of Nágpúr

The position at Nágpúr was the more difficult in that the province of which it was the capital was isolated. No part of it was used as a high road for troops. No Europeans could be spared for it from their more pressing duties of crushing the revolt in Oudh and in the North-West Provinces. Its safety was in the hands of the Commissioner. For it he was responsible. It was his duty, with most inadequate means, to assure it. Fortunately, Mr. George Plowden, who represented the Government at Nágpúr, was a gentleman of lofty courage and imperturbable nerve. Without appliances, he acted as though he possessed them.

Great credit due to Mr. George Plowden.

Left without external resources, he regulated his conduct as though they were abundantly at his command. And he succeeded. Eventually, when the first fever-heat of mutiny had subsided, he restored their arms to the local troops. There is no truer test of a man than this capacity to meet dangers and difficulties when he is unarmed, to look them calmly in the face, to remain cool

* *Vide* page 103.

Book XIII. Chapter III — 1857. June.

and imperturbable in their presence. If to do this thoroughly, to cause disaffection to quail before the glance—if this be a proof of greatness, then most assuredly Mr. George Plowden deserves to be classed amongst the great men brought to the front by the mutiny.

BOOK XIII.

CHAPTER IV.

It will clear the ground if, before I record the action of the British generals which restored order throughout central India, I deal with the events in a part of the country already slightly touched upon in the first chapter of this book, and upon the issue of which depended, to a very considerable extent, whether the rebellion would or would not extend throughout the length and breadth of southern and western India. I refer to the dominions of the Nizám.

Haidarábád.

Those dominions — called after the capital Haidarábád, the abode of Haidar—occupy a portion of India south of the Vindhya range, and enclose about ninety-five thousand three hundred and thirty-seven square miles. Measuring from their extreme point in the north-east, they extend four hundred and seventy-five miles to the south-west, and in their widest part they produce almost a similar result. On the north-

Extent and boundaries of the Nizám's dominions.

Book XIII. Chapter IV. — 1857. May.

east they are bounded by the central provinces, of which Nágpúr is the capital; on the southwest by portions of the Madras Presidency; on the west by the Bombay Presidency; and on the north-west by a portion of the same presidency, by the dominions of Sindia, and by the Ságar and Narbadá territories. A consideration of this proximity to so many inflammable points will convince the reader how dangerous would have proved a Haidarábád in arms; how essential it was that tranquillity should be maintained within her borders.

The Nizám.

When the year 1857 dawned, the Nizám was Nasir-úd-dáolah. This prince died, however, on the 18th of May, and was succeeded by his son Afzúl-úd-dáolah. The minister, Sálar Jang, nephew of his predecessor, Súráj-úl-Múlk, had held the highest office in the state since the year 1853. He was a man of great ability, great intelligence, devoted to the interests of his country and his master. It was his pride to prove that the natives of India can be governed by natives, not only with justice, but with a regard to their habits and modes of thought, such as, he considered, was impossible under alien rule. But, holding these opinions, he was, nevertheless, a sincere admirer of the British character, and sensible of the absolute necessity of an overlordship, which, while interfering as little as possible with the internal affairs of a native state, should take from each the power to draw the sword against a neighbour. The British Resident at the Court of the Nizám in the early part of 1857

Sálar Jang.

Book XIII. Chapter IV. 1857. May–June.

was Mr. Bushby. This able officer, however, died in February of that year. He was succeeded by Major Cuthbert Davidson, an officer of the Madras army, who had at a previous period held the office temporarily, and who had then shown that he possessed all the qualifications necessary for discharging its duties in quiet times. Major Davidson took charge of the office of Resident on the 16th of April. In a very short time an opportunity offered for him to show the stuff he was made of. I have already stated that on the 18th of May the Nizám, Nasir-úd-dáolah, died. His son, Afzúl-úd-dáolah, was installed after the necessary ceremonies. But to the disaffected in Haidarábád the death of one ruler and the succession of another seemed to offer a mine of promise. The late Nizám had trusted Sálar Jang. It was quite possible that his successor might refuse his confidence to that powerful minister. At all events an attempt might be made to discover the actual lay of the situation. Accordingly, when the men of the city of Haidarábád rose on the morning of the 12th of June, they found the walls of the city covered with placards, signed or purporting to be signed by orthodox máulvis, calling upon the faithful to enrol themselves and murder the Europeans. Major Davidson was not the last to receive the intelligence. He acted promptly and with vigour. He requested the general to parade his entire force in full marching order, with forty rounds of ammunition per man. This parade impressed the disaffected immensely. On the morning of the 15th a

Major Cuthbert Davidson.

Tumult on the accession of the new Nizám

is suppressed by Major Davidson,

Book XIII. Chapter IV.

1857. June.

second parade, not less imposing, was ordered. At this the resident was present, and addressed the troops.* By that time it had become known that the influence of Sálar Jang was not less weighty with the new, than it had been with the late ruler.

and by Sálar Jang.

That loyal minister, on learning that a large mob had assembled near the mosque known as the Mekka mosque, and had hoisted there a green flag, sent down a corps of Arab mercenaries upon whom he could rely to disperse them. Subsequently he arrested the principal leaders of the movement, and for the moment the plague was stayed.

Bad feeling produced on the population by the news from the north-west.

Only, however, for the moment. The information which poured daily from the outer world into the city, often in an exaggerated form, made every day a deeper impression upon the minds of the more bigoted of the population. They argued that whilst their co-religionists had risen for the faith in the north-west, it was not becoming in them to sit idle in the south. They recalled to the minds of listeners, likewise impressionable and fanatic, that little more than half a century had elapsed since Dehlí, the capital of the Muhammadan world of India, had fallen into the hands of the infidel; that a supreme effort had now recovered it, and that if that effort were supported by the entire Muhammadan community

* The garrison at or near Haidarábád consisted of a battalion of artillery, the 7th Madras Light Cavalry; the 3rd Madras Europeans; the 1st, 22nd, 24th, 34th, 41st, 42nd, and 49th Native Infantry. The force was commanded by Brigadier, now Sir William, Hill.

of Hindustán, the recovery would be made complete, the gain would become permanent. These were no idle words. They sank deep into the minds of the people of Haidarábád—a people that had never known European rule, and that had never welcomed its approach to their borders. In a few weeks they produced corresponding acts.

Book XIII. Chapter IV.

1857. July.

Mutiny at Haidarábád.

A little before 5 o'clock on the evening of the 17th of July, five hundred of the Rohilla troops in the service of the Nizám, supported by some four thousand of the mob of Haidarábád, rose in insurrection and marched on the residency, demanding the release of thirteen mutineers and deserters, who, caught red-handed in revolt, had been made over by Major Davidson to Sálar Jang. That minister, who was not very well served by his agents, only heard of the outbreak just on the eve of its occurrence. He at once sent a special messenger to warn the resident. Major Davidson, however, in anticipation of some such movement, had improvised defences all round the residency, had mounted guns on the newly-erected bastions, and had warned his military secretary, Major Briggs, to arrange the troops at his disposal in the manner best calculated to meet a sudden attack. Seven minutes then sufficed to send every man in the residency to his post. The insurgents came on, in the manner of undisciplined fanatics, drunk with excitement, without order, and without leading, properly so called. A fire of grape from the ramparts sent them reeling back. They came on again, only similarly to be received, and

Sálar Jang warns the Resident.

Major Davidson's previous preparations.

Book XIII. Chapter IV.

1857. July.

Repulse and defeat of the rebels,

similarly to retire. Staggered by this reception, they were beginning to recover from their intoxication, when a charge of the Nizám's troops decided them to flee in confusion. Many of them then took refuge in a two-storied house, at the end of a narrow street. In this place it was resolved to allow them to stay till the morning. They did not, however, avail themselves of the permission. Mining under the floor, they escaped during the night. In their attack on the residency, several of the rebels were killed; in their flight from the Nizám's troops more were taken prisoners. Amongst the latter were the two ringleaders, Torábáz Khán and Maulvi Alla-úd-dín. The former, attempting to escape, was shot dead; the latter was tried, convicted, and transported to the Andamán islands.

and capture of their leaders.

Good effect produced at Haidarábád.

The manner in which this wanton attack terminated produced a very salutary effect on the minds of the Haidarábád population. It showed them very clearly that their own rulers, men of their own faith, sided with the British. It needed but one word from Sálar Jang to rouse the entire country. Not only was that word not spoken, but the fanatical Muhammadans were made clearly to understand that, in the event of their rising, they would have to deal, not with the British only, but with their own Government as well.

The situation still critical

Still the situation grew daily more critical. The city of Haidarábád had ever been filled with military adventurers. The custom of importing Arabs from beyond the sea, and of forming of them regiments of peculiar trust, had long prevailed. But in addition to the Arab, there used to come from every part of India those adventurous spirits to whom the sober administration of the British gave no avocation. From Rohilkhand, from the Panjáb, from Sindh, from Dehlí, and from the border-land beyond the Indus, men of this stamp had never been wanting. To them were added, in the autumn of 1857, adventurers more dangerous still. The mutinied and disbanded sepoys who had been unable to reach Dehlí, or whose offers had been rejected by Sindia, poured in shoals into Haidarábád. Combining with the other classes I have mentioned, and who gave them a cordial welcome, they helped to swell the ranks of the disaffected, and to impart to them a discipline in which the others were lacking.

Book XIII. Chapter IV.

1857. July.

by reason of the numerous adventurers

crowding into the city.

The presence of these men added not a little to the difficulties of Sálar Jang and the Nizám. Every rumour which reached the city of misfortunes befalling the British arms roused feelings which might at any moment prelude an outbreak. If we think of all that was happening in those provinces—of the massacre of Kánhpúr, of the long siege of Dehlí, of the leaguer of Lakhnáo, of Havelock's three retirements, of the events at Ágra, at Indúr, at Jhánsi, at Bandá—we shall cease to be surprised that this was so. It must be remembered, too, that every skirmish was magnified into a battle, every repulse into a catastrophe, that victories gained by the British were studiously concealed. When we think of the

The effect of rumours

Book XIII. Chapter IV. — 1857.

news of these disasters coming upon an inflammable people, hating the English, armed to the teeth, and chafing under their forced inaction, we may well wonder that peace was, on any terms, preserved.

upon an inflammable people.

Loyalty of the Nizám.

But peace was preserved—mainly owing to the excellent understanding between the Government of the Nizám and the British resident. Whilst the former used all those arts which a powerful native government has so well at command, to check the fanatical ardour of the disaffected, the resident, acting in concert with the Nizám, applied for a larger force of European troops to overawe the same class. In consequence of these representations Davidson received later in the year a reinforcement of a regiment of cavalry, a regiment of infantry, and some artillery.

Reinforcements arrive.

Davidson suggests the employment of the troops of the Haidarábád contingent in central India.

Whilst thus securing his base, Major Davidson was not unmindful of another means for employing the trained soldiers of the Nizám—the soldiers of the Haidarábád contingent, led by English officers—in a manner which might transfer the sympathies of the great bulk of the people, from whose ranks those soldiers were drawn, to the British cause. Acting in concurrence, then, with the Nizám and Sálar Jang, and with the full approval of the Government of India, he formed towards the beginning of 1858 a brigade from the regiments of the contingent, and sent it to act in central India. This brigade was composed of the 1st, 3rd, and 4th regiments of cavalry, of the 3rd and 5th regiments of infantry, and of three field-batteries of artillery. The splendid deeds of these troops will be recorded in their proper place. But I will not wait to record that the other purpose which had suggested this action to Major Davidson was entirely accomplished. The successes obtained by these soldiers elated the relations they had left behind them, and these came, in a very brief period, to regard as their own the cause for which their kinsmen were fighting. From that time forward all anxiety ceased in Haidarábád itself. In some parts of the districts the disturbances which arose were eagerly quelled, and with one exception, no chieftain of rank showed the smallest inclination to question the wisdom of the policy adopted by the Nizám and his minister.

Successful result of Davidson's policy.

That exception was the rájá of Shorápúr.* Shorápúr is a small territory situated in the south-west angle of the Nizám's dominions. The Hindú chief who had ruled it, had, fifteen years prior to 1857, fallen into pecuniary difficulties so great that he found himself unable to fulfil his obligations to his suzerain, the Nizám. Certain arrangements, unnecessary here to detail, followed, which ended, after the death of the rájá, in the administration of the country falling for a time into the hands of the British. This arrangement lasted till 1853, when the country

Shorápúr.

Its condition antecedent to the mutiny.

* For a most interesting account of the rájá of Shorápúr and the causes which led him to revolt, I refer the reader to the *Story of My Life*, by the late Colonel Meadows Taylor, one of the most charming of autobiographies.

Book XIII. Chapter IV.

1857.

was handed over to the native ruler in a very flourishing condition. The young rájá, however, soon dissipated his resources; he became so embarrassed as to be utterly reckless. He was in this state of mind when the events of 1857 occurred. With the record of the disasters attending the British came whispers of the advantages which must accrue to him from a successful rebellion. The rájá had not the strength of mind to resist the temptation. Intoxicated by the promises made him, he called together the men of his own clan, and began to levy Rohilla and Arab mercenaries.

Character and conduct of the rájá of Shorápúr;

he levies troops.

Davidson takes decisive measures,

Full intelligence of the doings of the rájá was quickly conveyed to Major Davidson. Well aware that to prevent an outbreak even by an extravagant display of force was far wiser and far cheaper than to allow it to come to a head, Davidson at once took decisive measures. Acting in concert with Lord Elphinstone, who displayed on this occasion, as on every other, a far-sighted policy and a rare unselfishness, he called up from the Bombay Presidency a force under Lieutenant-Colonel Malcolm, consisting of a detachment of European troops, the Maráthá Horse, the 15th Bombay Native Infantry, and a battery of artillery. This force he located at a point equidistant between the Shorápúr and the southern Maráthá country. At the same time he arranged that a force from the Madras Presidency, under Major Hughes, should watch the eastern frontier of Shorápúr, whilst he detached four hundred men and two guns of the Haidarábád contingent,

and surrounds the rájá's country.

Book XIII. Chapter IV.

1858. Jan.-Feb.

commanded by Captain Wyndham, to occupy Linsúgúr, ready to act in concert with either of the other forces, as necessity might require.

Detaches Rose Campbell to save him,

Before these preparations had been completed Cuthbert Davidson, hoping to save the rájá from his own folly, despatched to his court, early in January 1858, one of his own most trusted assistants, Captain Rose Campbell. Campbell, however, only wasted his efforts. The rájá had given himself to the fanatical party. Not only did he continue deaf to all entreaties, but he was, it is believed, prepared to connive at the murder of his guest. This, at least, is certain, that Captain Campbell received an intimation from the rájá's own relatives and servants that his life was in imminent danger.

but fruitlessly.

Wyndham moves on Shorápúr;

It would have been fruitless to temporise further. Captain Campbell proceeded to Linsúgúr and ordered Wyndham to march on Shorápúr. Wyndham started at once and reached Shorápúr on the 7th of February. As he approached, the rájá, as is customary in such cases, sent his own servants to indicate a proper encamping-ground. The servants led Wyndham to the place selected —a narrow valley, surrounded by lofty hills and rocks. But Wyndham, though but a captain, was too old a soldier to fall into the trap. He moved on to an open plain, where he was comparatively safe from danger of surprise.

sees through and avoids a snare laid for him by the rájá.

The rájá's troops attack Wyndham,

That night Wyndham was attacked by a force composed of the clansmen of the rájá, of Arabs and Rohillas, estimated at from five thousand to seven thousand strong. The attack continued all

Book XIII. Chapter IV. — 1858. February.

night, but its result was never doubtful. Wyndham, aided by Rose Campbell and the medical officer, Dr. Williamson, barricaded the position, and with the guns kept up a continuous fire. At 1 o'clock in the morning he was reinforced by one hundred cavalry of the Haidarábád contingent. The rebels then ceased their attack, and occupied the heights near the town.

who repulses them.

Meanwhile, expresses had been sent to Major Hughes and Colonel Malcolm. Major Hughes, with two companies 74th Highlanders and some Madras cavalry, arrived first, early on the morning of the 8th. Joining his troops to those of Wyndham, Hughes at once attacked the rebels. A squadron of the 8th Madras cavalry, commanded by Captain Newberry, led the attack, and charged a body of Rohillas. Unfortunately, Newberry and his subaltern, Lieutenant Stewart, better mounted than their men, dashed into the middle of the rebels before their men could follow them. Newberry was killed and Stewart was severely wounded. The enemy, however, were driven from the heights above the town. The city being very strong, the approaches to it difficult of access, and the walls and bastions crowded with defenders, Hughes thought it advisable to wait for Colonel Malcolm's force, which was expected that night, before attempting anything further.

Hughes arrives to the rescue, and defeats the rebels, who retire into the city.

But the rájá did not wait for Malcolm. Dispirited by the failure of his attack on Wyndham, and aware that reinforcements were approaching, he gave up the game as precipitately

The rájá flees in the night to Haidarábád,

Book XIII. Chapter IV.

1858. February.

as he had entered upon it, and, accompanied by a few horsemen, fled that night towards Haidarábád. Arriving there, with but two followers in his train, he made a fruitless attempt to gain the protection of the Arabs. Found, then, wandering in the bazar, he was apprehended and taken to Sálar Jang, who made him over to the Resident.

where he is taken prisoner.

The departure of the rájá led to the immediate evacuation of Shorápúr by the hostile bands. Colonel Malcolm, who arrived on the evening of the 8th, entered the town the following morning and found it almost deserted. Captain Rose Campbell assumed charge of the administration of the country.*

Malcolm enters the town.

So ended the only serious attempt made to disturb the tranquillity of the Dekhán. The preservation of that tranquillity was essential to the maintenance of the British power in India. There can be no question but that the rising of Haidarábád, headed by the Nizám, would have been a blow struck at the heart. The whole of western and southern India would have followed. Central India, the dominions of Holkar, and Rajpútáná could not have escaped; and it is more than probable that the communications between Calcutta and the north-west would have been severed. That this calamity did not occur is due

The tranquillity of the Dekhán assured in a great measure by

* The story of the rájá's end is tragical. He was sentenced to death, but the Governor-General commuted the punishment to four years' imprisonment for life, after which he might be restored to his territory. The very day the rájá received this news he shot himself, Colonel Meadows Taylor thinks accidentally.—Vide *Story of My Life*, vol. ii.

Book XIII. Chapter IV.

1858. February.

Lord Elphinstone, Lord Harris, Major Davidson and the officers acting under his orders,

to many causes. The far-sighted policy of Lord Elphinstone did much; the Governor of Madras, Lord Harris, contributed all that was possible for a man in his high position to contribute. Major Cuthbert Davidson displayed a skill, a tact, and an energy far above the average; he was well served by his subordinates: Colonel Malcolm, Major Hughes, Captain Wyndham, and their comrades executed with marked ability the tasks entrusted to them. But the efforts of these men, great and valuable as they were, would have been utterly unavailing had the Nizám and his minister not seconded them. For three months the fate of India was in the hands of Afzúl úd dáola and Sálar Jang. Their wise policy proved that they preferred the certain position of a protected state to the doubtful chances of a resuscitation of the Dehlí monarchy under the auspices of revolted sepoys.

but mainly by the Nizám and Sálar Jang.

BOOK XIV.

CHAPTER I.

In a previous chapter of this history* I stated that Colonel Durand had been appointed to act as agent for the Governor-General at Indúr in consequence of the departure of the agent, Sir Robert Hamilton, to Europe on leave. Sir Robert Hamilton, on hearing of the mutiny at Mírath, at once asked permission, though he had been but six weeks in England, to return and join his appointment. The application was granted, and Sir Robert arrived in Calcutta in August 1857.

Sir Robert Hamilton arrives in Calcutta.

Very soon after he had reached Calcutta, Sir Robert Hamilton was called upon by the Government to state the measures which he considered necessary for the restoration of tranquillity in central India. There were very many reasons why it was natural that the Government should be anxious to have his views on this important

* Vol i., book viii., chapter iii.

Book XIV. Chapter I.

1857. August.

Qualifications of Sir R. Hamilton to advise the Government regarding central India.

subject. Sir Robert Hamilton was a very eminent public servant. He had passed the greater part of his career in high official positions in central India. Not only had he traversed every inch of that territory, but he knew the exact distances between village and village throughout it, the lay of the ground, the disposition of the people, the peculiarities which constituted either a bond or a division between the several districts. Sir Robert had trained from his early youth the boy who, in 1857, ruled the possessions of his ancestors as Túkaji Ráo Holkar. The training and the connection—that between a guardian and a ward—had inspired both with similar feelings, feelings of the warmest regard. More than that—each thoroughly believed in the other. Each would have waged the possession he most valued on the question of the loyalty of the other. Sir Robert Hamilton was not less acquainted with all the courtiers of his charge, with their character, their dispositions, the influences they exercised. He knew to a scarcely less degree every man of note in the country.

Hamilton submits a plan for the pacification of central India to the Government.

When, then, the Government of India applied to Sir Robert Hamilton to state the measures which he considered necessary for the restoration of order in central India, they did that which it would have been in the highest degree unwise to omit. Sir Robert Hamilton responded to the call. He drew up a memorandum, which he submitted to the Governor-General. Lord Canning passed it on to Sir Colin Campbell, who was still in Calcutta.

Book XIV. Chapter I.

1857. December.

Nature of the plan.

Sir Robert Hamilton's plan was as follows. He proposed that whilst one column, coming from the Bombay Presidency, should make Máu its base of operations, and sweep thence the country between that point and Kálpi on the Jamná, reconquering Jhánsi in its course; another, coming from Madras, should form its base at Jabalpúr, clear the line of communication with Allahábád and Mirzápúr, and cross Bandalkhand to Bandá. Thus Kálpi and Bandá would constitute the points towards which the two columns would separately be directed.

The plan is, with one slight modification, approved of.

This plan was fully discussed between Sir Robert Hamilton, Sir Colin Campbell, and the Chief of the Staff—General Mansfield—and, in the end, was, with one slight modification in one of its details, adopted.* Sir Robert Hamilton calculated that if no delay were to occur in the formation of the several columns, the points indicated would be reached by the 1st of May 1858.

Sir Robert relieves Durand, and assumes political charge of the country to be traversed by the British forces.

This plan approved, Sir Robert Hamilton proceeded to Indúr, and arrived there on the 16th of December 1857, and not only resumed the appointment of Governor-General's Agent for central India, but took up likewise the political functions in respect of all the chiefs in the Ságar and Narbadá territories, which, till then,

* The modification was immaterial. Sir R. Hamilton had suggested that the two brigades of which the Máu column would be composed should, prior to their advance on Jhánsi, effect a junction at Sipri. Sir Colin Campbell substituted Gúnah for Sipri. Gímah is nearer to Jhánsi by seventy miles.

Book XIV. Chapter I. 1857.

had been exercised by the Commissioner of those territories.

The day that witnessed the return of Sir Robert Hamilton greeted likewise the arrival of the officer who had been nominated by Lord Canning to command the force which, having its base at Máu, was to work up to the southern bank of the Jamná. That officer was Major-General Sir Hugh Rose, K.C.B. Sir Hugh Rose bore, even then, a high character for ability, decision, and firmness. Entering the army in 1820, he had early given proof of those qualities, and when, in 1840, the Government of the Queen decided to detach several British officers to serve in Syria with the view of checking the progress of the rebellious Pasha of Egypt, Lieutenant-Colonel Rose proceeded thither in the capacity of Deputy Adjutant-General. Here he distinguished himself no less by his judgment than by his daring courage. In a hand-to-hand encounter with the Egyptian cavalry, in which he was wounded, Colonel Rose captured with his own hand the leader of the enemy, an exploit which procured for him a sabre of honour from the Sultan and the Order of the Nishán Iftihár set in diamonds. For his conduct in Syria, too, he was decorated with the companionship of the Bath. A little later he was nominated by Lord Palmerston Consul-General of Syria.

Character and antecedents of Sir Hugh Rose

in Egypt,

When, a few years subsequently, Russia was

* Now Field Marshall Lord Strathnairn, G.C.B., G.C.S.I., &c.

preparing to make her bid for the inheritance of the "sick man," Colonel Rose was nominated secretary to the embassy at Constantinople. Later on, just before the storm broke, Lord Stratford de Redcliffe proceeded to England, and Colonel Rose succeeded him as chargé d'affaires. Holding that office, he not only penetrated the designs of Russia, but detected that the one means by which only England could foil them was to put her foot down, and say, "One step further constitutes war." Impressed with this idea, when Prince Menschikoff endeavoured to impose upon the Sultan terms which would have annihilated the independence of Turkey, and the Sultan, turning to the British chargé d'affaires, implored him to give a material pledge of the support of England by bringing the British fleet into Turkish waters, Colonel Rose took the responsibility upon himself, and ordered the fleet to Besika Bay. The fact that such an order had been sent answered for the moment the purposes of the Sultan. Russia was checked; and, if she renewed her attack, it was because the same firmness and the same clear-sightedness were not apparent in the conduct of the British ministers who approved the admiral for refusing to comply with Colonel Rose's requisition.

at Constantinople,

Subsequently Colonel Rose served in the Crimean war. He was recommended for the Cross of the Legion of Honour for his conduct at Alma, was repeatedly mentioned for distinguished conduct in the trenches before Sebastopol, and had

in the Crimea.

Book XIV. Chapter I.

1857. December.

two horses shot under him at Inkerman. I cannot omit to add that Marshal Canrobert, then commanding the French army in the Crimea, recommended General Rose for the Victoria Cross for his gallant conduct on three different occasions, and that the claim was not preferred solely because general officers were expressly excluded from the decoration. For his services in this war General Rose received the Turkish order of the Medjidie, was nominated a Knight Commander of the Bath, and received a step in rank "for distinguished conduct in the field."

Sir Hugh lands in Bombay.

When the mutiny broke out in India, Sir Hugh Rose proceeded at once to that country. He landed in Bombay on the 19th of September, was brought on the general staff of the army from that date, and was shortly appointed to the command of the force acting in Málwa, the operations of which I have recorded in this volume.* He proceeded accordingly to Indúr in company with Sir Robert Hamilton, who had taken the only route then open, that *viâ* Bombay.

General Whitlock is appointed to direct the Madras column.

Simultaneously, almost, with the appointment of Sir Hugh Rose to command one of the columns indicated, Brigadier General Whitlock of the Madras army was nominated to direct the other. The proceedings of this officer will be related in the next chapter. This will be devoted to the operations of the Máu column.

Composition of Sir Hugh Rose's force.

The force, now called the Central India Field

* *Vide* Chapter ii. of the last Book.

Book XIV. Chapter I.

1857. December.

Force, of which Sir Hugh Rose took command on the 17th of December, consisted of two brigades—the first being at Máu; the second at Sihor. The brigades were thus formed. The first, under the command of Brigadier C. S. Stuart of the Bombay army, was composed of a squadron 14th Light Dragoons, a troop of the 3rd Bombay light cavalry, two regiments of cavalry Haidarábád contingent, the 86th Regiment, the 25th Regiment Bombay Native Infantry, one regiment infantry Haidarábád contingent, one troop of horse artillery, one light field battery, two field batteries Haidarábád contingent, and some sappers; the second, commanded by Brigadier Steuart, 14th Light Dragoons, of the head-quarters of the 14th Light Dragoons, head-quarters of the 3rd Bombay light cavalry, one regiment of cavalry Haidarábád contingent, the 3rd Bombay European Regiment,* the 24th Bombay Native Infantry, one regiment of infantry Haidarábád contingent, a battery of Bombay Horse Artillery, one field battery of artillery Haidarábád contingent, one company Madras sappers, a detachment of Bombay sappers, and a siege-train.

Antecedents of the troops composing the field force

From the second chapter of the last book the reader will have gathered some idea of the hard work which had already devolved upon this force; he will have seen how they had triumphed over obstacles, had beaten every enemy, had proved incontestably that they were made of the stuff which required only leading to conquer. They

* Now the 109th Regiment.

Book XIV. Chapter I.

1858. January.

had now once more a leader. Personally, indeed, that leader was a stranger to them, but his reputation had gone before him, and that reputation was of a nature to make the men grudge even the short period of repose which it was necessary to give them.

A short period of repose was necessary to enable Whitlock to move in concert with it.

That repose was necessary for the perfect carrying out of the plan devised by Sir R. Hamilton with Sir Colin Campbell in Calcutta by virtue of which a second force, that to be commanded by Whitlock, should start from Jabalpúr. Until tidings of Whitlock's movements should be received, Sir Hugh was forced to halt at Máu.

The period is not wasted.

The time was not thrown away. The two brigades were organised; the country was pacified; the line of advance was marked out; the men had time to recruit themselves. The country about Máu and Indúr is peculiarly suited to be a resting-place. It abounds with the necessaries of life; there is plenty of water and of fodder; the climate at that season is most enjoyable; the country, hilly and diversified, is pleasant to the eye. The halt there was but short; it scarcely exceeded three weeks—not too long to satiate the men with their rest, yet long enough to make them glad to be once more on the move.

The force enters upon the campaign.

On the 6th of January Sir Hugh Rose, accompanied by Sir R. Hamilton, started from Máu to join the 2nd brigade at Sihor. On the 8th the siege-train was despatched to join him there. It arrived on the 15th. On the following morning Sir Hugh, reinforced by about eight hundred Bhopál levies contributed by the loyal Bégam of

Book XIV. Chapter I.

1858. January.

that principality, started for Ráthgarh, a strong fort held by the rebels. The 1st brigade left Máu on the 10th, and then marched in a line parallel with the 2nd brigade upon Chandairi, a very famous fortress in the territories of Sindia. I propose first to follow the fortunes of the 2nd brigade.

Ráthgarh.

Ráthgarh, distant only thirty miles from Ságar, is situated on the spur of a long high hill, and commands the country surrounding it. The eastern and southern faces of the fortress are almost perpendicular—the rock being scarped. Round their base runs a deep and rapid river—the Bína—answering the purpose of a wet ditch. The north face is covered by a strong wall, facing a very thick jungle, between which and the wall is a deep ditch twenty feet wide. The western face overlooks the town and the road to Ságar, and its gateway is flanked by several bastions, round and square. Along each face and in the four angles were bastions commanding the only possible approaches. Altogether it was a most formidable position.

Sir Hugh disposes his forces before the place.

Sir Hugh Rose arrived before this place the morning of the 24th of January. He at once, with small loss, drove the enemy from the outside positions they had occupied in the towns and on the banks of the river, and then completely invested the place. Fronting the eastern face he posted the Bhopál troops; facing the northern the 3rd Bombay light cavalry and the cavalry of the Haidarábád contingent. With the remainder of the force he occupied the plain across which runs

Book XIV. Chapter I.

1858. January.

the road to Ságar. He then reconnoitred the ground preparatory to selecting sites for his breaching batteries.

The rebels make an offensive defence.

The enemy had reoccupied the town. Issuing from its walls into the thick jungle already spoken of, they made thence, during the 25th, several raids on the camp-followers and baggage-animals of the force, and at night even attacked the position held by the Bhopál troops. They were, however, repulsed with slight loss.

The rebels fire the jungle and force Sir Hugh to change his point of attack.

Early the following morning Sir Hugh Rose made a move forward. Crossing the Ságar road with the 3rd Europeans, followed by the 18-pounders, howitzers, and mortars, and the guns of the Haidarábád Contingent, he entered the jungle. He had no sooner reached a point well within its thick covering, than the enemy, who had been lurking near, fired the jungle grass on all sides. For a few moments the position was perilous, but Sir Hugh, turning back beyond the range of the flames, sent his sappers to cut a road up the height to the north of the town for the guns. This, and the getting up of the guns, occupied the greater part of the day.

Sir Hugh gains the town.

Meanwhile the remainder of the force had occupied the town, and driven the enemy within the fort.

Sir Hugh's mortar batteries open on the fort.

At 3 o'clock the summit of the hill fronting the northern face of the fort was gained. Sir Hugh at once selected sites for his breaching batteries, and set the sappers to work. By 8 P.M. the mortar battery was ready. Whilst it was being thrown up the 6-pounders of the Haidarábád contingent kept up a constant fire of shot and shell on the fort, whilst the 3rd Europeans employed their Enfield rifles to keep down the matchlock fire of the enemy. At 11 P.M. the mortar battery opened fire, and continued it all night. The breaching batteries were completed by daybreak.

The breaching batteries open.

These opened fire early on the morning of the 27th, and continued it all that day and the day following. At 10 P.M. on the 28th a large breach had been made, and two men went forward to examine it. They had just returned when a sudden rush of camp-followers and cattle-drivers from the rear gave intimation that something startling had happened. It transpired immediately that a rebel force was advancing to the relief of the place.

The rájá of Bánpúr marches to relieve the place,

It was so indeed. The rájá of Bánpúr, whose doings in the vicinity of Ságar I have already recorded,* was advancing on the rear of the besieging force with a considerable body of revolted sepoys and other levies. He came on with great boldness, his standards flying, and his men singing their national hymns. But if his appearance at this critical juncture was a surprise to Sir Hugh Rose, it was a surprise that did not embarrass him. Instead of ceasing his fire against the fort he redoubled it. As for the rájá of Bánpúr, Sir Hugh detached a small force, consisting of a detachment of the 14th Light Dragoons, the 3rd Bombay cavalry, the horse artillery, and the 5th Haidarábád infantry, to deal with him. It did

* *Vide* page 98.

Book XIV. Chapter I.

1858. January.

but vanishes on the approach of the British troops.

not require extraordinary exertion to effect this object. The confidence of the rájá and his followers vanished as they heard the tramping of the horses of the British and Indian cavalry. They did not wait to be charged, but throwing away their arms and ammunition, made off with such celerity, that, though hotly pursued, a few only were cut up.

Ráthgarh is thereupon evacuated.

The attempt at relief, apparently so formidable, was really a stroke of fortune for Sir Hugh. It had been made, evidently, in concert with the rebels within the fort, and its failure so disheartened them, that they silently evacuated Ráthgarh during the night, escaping by a path the precipitous nature of which would seem to preclude the possibility of its being used by man.* Their flight was not on the whole to be lamented, for Ráthgarh was found to be so strong as to make it tenable by a few resolute defenders against numbers greatly superior.

The rebels were pursued, but without much effect; they had gone too far before the evacuation of the place had been discovered. A little before noon on the 30th Sir Hugh received information that the rájá of Bánpúr, reinforced by

* "The most amazing thing was to see the place from whence they had escaped. To look down the precipitous path made one giddy—and yet down this place, where no possible footing could be seen, they had all gone—men and women—in the dead of night! One or two mangled bodies lay at the bottom, attesting the difficulty of the descent. Nothing but despair could have tempted them to have chosen such a way."—Dr. Lowe's *Central India during the Rebellion of* 1857-58" — a book to which I am much indebted.

1858. January.

The rebels take up a position near Barodia,

the garrison, had taken up a position near the village of Barodia, about fifteen miles distant. He at once ordered out the horse artillery, two $5\frac{1}{2}$-inch mortars, two guns of the reserve battery, the 3rd Europeans, the majority of the cavalry, and a section of the Madras sappers, and went in pursuit. About 4 o'clock he came upon them posted on the banks of the Bína, and prepared to dispute his passage. Sir Hugh at once attacked, and though the rebels fought well, he forced the passage of the river. The country on the other side was thick and bushy, and the rebels took every advantage of it. From the river to Barodia Sir Hugh had to fight his way step by step. He did not do this without loss. Two officers* were killed and six were wounded. The casualties among the men were likewise severe. In the end, however, the rebels were completely defeated, and though the rebel rájá was not captured, he owed his safety only to his acquaintance with the intricacies of the jungle. The force returned to Ráthgarh about 2 o'clock in the morning. It found there a supply of provisions sent from Ságar escorted by a detachment of the 31st Regiment Native Infantry.

where they are attacked and beaten by Sir Hugh.

Result gained by the fall of Ráthgarh.

The fall of Ráthgarh had effected two most important objects. It had cleared the country south of Ságar of rebels, had reopened the road to Indúr, and had made it possible for the general

* One of these was Captain Neville, R.E. He had joined the force only the day before. Captain Neville had served throughout the Crimean war, in which he had greatly distinguished himself.

Book XIV. Chapter I.

1858. February.

to march to the relief of Ságar, now beleaguered for nearly eight months.

Ságar, since the reader last visited it.

The state of Ságar has been recorded in a preceding chapter. Although during that period the garrison had made occasional sallies, more or less successful, it may be stated generally that the rebels had retained possession of the strongholds all over the district, and that, by means of these, they had possessed likewise the country. The manner in which they had used their usurped power had made the peasantry look earnestly to the time when the law-loving rule of the British should be restored.

Sir Hugh marches on Ságar,

That time had now arrived. Sir Hugh Rose marched from Ráthgarh direct on Ságar. He entered that place on the morning of the 3rd of February, escorted by the Europeans, officers and others, who had held the fort, and who had gone forth to welcome their deliverers.

and enters it.

The 31st Native Infantry.

The 31st Native Infantry was one of the very few regiments of the Bengal army which, retaining its arms, had remained faithful throughout that trying period. The greater honour to the 31st, for its companion infantry regiment had revolted, and it had been tempted on all sides.

The fort of Garhákót.

Some of those companions had now to be dealt with. Twenty-five miles to the east of Ságar stands, on an elevated angle of ground, the strong fort of Garhákót. The eastern face of this fort is washed by the wide river Sonár; the western and northern faces by the nullah Gidári, with precipitous banks; the south possesses a strong gateway flanked by bastions, and a ditch twenty feet in depth by thirty in width. So strong are the parapets of this fort, that when, in 1818, it was attacked by Brigadier Watson with a force of eleven thousand men, he was unable, in three weeks, to effect a breach in them, and was glad to allow the garrison to evacuate the place with all the honours of war! In February 1858 it was held by the revolted sepoys of the 51st and 52nd Native Infantry, and other rebels, well supplied with ammunition and provisions.

Book XIV. Chapter I.

1858. February.

Its great strength.

Sir Hugh Rose sent a small force to destroy the fort of Sanoda on the 8th, and on the 9th of February marched towards Garhákót. He arrived within sight of it and encamped at half-past 3 o'clock on the afternoon of the 11th. He at once made a reconnaissance, which was not concluded till 8 P.M. Sir Hugh found that the rebels had thrown up earthworks on the road to the south, by which they had expected him to arrive, and that they were occupying a position close to the village of Bassári, near the fort, in some force. Notwithstanding the lateness of the hour, he at once drove them from the positions they held, and occupied Bassári; nor, though during the night the rebels made repeated efforts, could they regain the posts they had lost.

Sir Hugh arrives before it and reconnoitres;

drives the rebels from the village of Bassári.

The next day Sir Hugh commenced his attack. He first caused a breaching battery to be thrown up opposite the western face. A 24-pounder howitzer working all day from this battery soon silenced the enemy's guns. Lieutenant Strutt of the Bombay artillery, already referred to in

Excellent effect of Strutt's fire

Book XIV. Chapter I.

1858. February.

these pages, succeeded in dismounting one of the enemy's guns which had been worked very successfully against the assailants. It was this shot, "one of the many good shots made under fire by Lieutenant Strutt," which, in Sir Hugh's opinion, made the sepoys reflect on the casualties which might befall them. Certainly after that they lost heart. In the night they consulted, and determined to escape if they could. Unfortunately Sir Hugh Rose's force was so small, a great part having been left at Ságar, that he had been unable to place a portion of it in a position which would guard the gateway. By this gateway the sepoys made their way into the country during the night of the 12th. They were, however, pursued early the following morning for twenty-five miles by Captain Hare, with his Haidarábád cavalry, a troop of the 14th Light Dragoons under Lieutenant Reed, and half a troop of horse artillery. Hare came up with them at the Biás river, near the village of Biár. The river not being practicable for guns, he led the cavalry across, fell upon the rebels, and cut up about a hundred of them.

impels the rebels to evacuate the place;

they are pursued by Hare and cut up.

Garhákót was found full of supplies. Sir Hugh had its western face destroyed, and returned to Ságar on the 17th.

The road to Jhánsi.

Jhánsi, one hundred and twenty-five miles to the north, was the next point to be aimed at. But between Ságar and Jhánsi lay the passes of Máltún and Maddanpúr, the forts of Sorai and of Maráora, the towns of Sháhgarh and Bánpúr. After overcoming the certain obstacles which

Book XIV. Chapter I.

1858. February.

would be offered by these places, Sir Hugh would have, before marching on Jhánsi, to effect a junction with his 1st brigade under Brigadier Stuart.

Considerations which demanded some delay.

Before setting out on this expedition, there were other considerations demanding attention. Sir Hugh could scarcely move from Ságar until he should receive certain information that Brigadier Whitlock's column had started from Jabalpúr for that place. Meanwhile he would have time to repair damages and to store supplies. The necessity for this was the more pressing inasmuch as it had been ascertained that the districts through which the force would have to march, still occupied by rebel sepoys or disaffected chiefs, would supply little or nothing in the way of commissariat. The hot season, too, was setting in, and it was certain that not a blade of grass would survive a few weeks of its duration. Sir Hugh foresaw all this, and employed the enforced delay in laying up supplies.

Excellent use to which the delay was put.

He caused to be collected sheep, goats, oxen, grain, flour, and large supplies of tea and soda-water. Much of the grain was sent by the loyal Bégam of Bhopal. The sick and wounded men he transferred to the Ságar field hospital, to be sent away or to rejoin as opportunity might offer. He resupplied the siege-train with ammunition, and strengthened it by the addition of heavy guns, howitzers, and large mortars from the Ságar arsenal. He obtained likewise an additional supply of elephants, and, what was of great cousequence, he secured summer clothing for his European soldiers.

Book XIV. Chapter I. 1858. February.

Hearing that Whitlock had left Jabalpúr, Sir Hugh takes the road to Jhánsi.

At length news came that Whitlock had left Jabalpúr. Sir Hugh's preparations were now as complete as they could be made. Accordingly a start was determined upon. On the evening of the 26th of February Sir Hugh detached Major Orr's column of the Haidarábád contingent to march on a route parallel with his own, and at 2 o'clock he set out with the remainder of the troops. The following day he took, after some shelling, the fort of Barodia. Pressing forward, he found himself, on the 3rd of March, in front of the pass of Máltún. This pass, of great natural strength, had been fortified, and was now held in force by a mixed army of sepoys and local levies. A reconnaissance having convinced Sir Hugh of the great loss of life which would inevitably attend a direct attack upon it, he determined then only to feign an attack in front, whilst, with the bulk of his force, he should gain the table-land above the hills by a flank movement through the pass of Madanpúr. With this view, early on the morning of the 4th of March, he detailed a force,* under Major Scudamore, to menace the pass, whilst with the remainder, now strengthened by the junction of the Haidarábád troops, he moved on Madanpúr.

The pass of Máltún.

Sir Hugh decides to attempt a flank march.

Madanpúr.

The Madanpúr pass

The pass leading to this town forms a narrow gorge between two ranges of hills, thickly covered with jungle and brushwood, and capable of offering a solid defence. The rebels had not only

* Consisting of the 24th Bombay N.I., three guns Bhopál artillery, one howitzer, a detachment 14th light dragoons, and the 3rd Bombay cavalry.

crowned the heights on both sides of the gorge, and planted guns in the gorge itself, but they had sent, to a considerable distance in advance, skirmishers, who, concealed in the jungle, would be able to harass an advancing enemy. The British troops, in making the turning movement contemplated, marched for about six miles along the foot of the hills, which they then began to ascend. Almost immediately the enemy opened fire. The crests seemed alive with their infantry, whilst their guns from the gorge opened a continuous fire. Sir Hugh sent the 3rd Europeans and the Haidarábád infantry to storm the heights, brought his guns to the front, and returned the enemy's fire.

is attacked by the British.

The British skirmishers drove back the rebel footmen, but as these retired another artillery-fire opened from a commanding position at the further end of the pass. So galling and so heavy was this fire that for a short time the British advance was checked. Sir Hugh even ordered the guns to retire some yards. Before this could be done Sir Hugh's horse was shot under him, and the artillerymen were forced to take refuge behind the guns. Bullets fell like hailstones, and the number of killed and wounded increased every moment.

Determined defence of the rebels,

The halt, however, was only temporary. The guns of the Haidarábád contingent coming up at this conjuncture opened with shell on the enemy's masses to the left of the pass in support of the guns in action. Under cover of this combined shower, the 3rd Europeans and

but it is overcome by a charge of infantry.

Book XIV. Chapter I. — 1858. March.

the Haidarábád infantry charged. Asiatics can stand anything but a charge of infantry. They had here a splendid position, and a large force of the three arms to hold it; but the sight of the charging infantry struck awe into them. Far from awaiting, with their superior numbers, the hand-to-hand encounter offered, they fled in disorder and dismay. They were followed through the pass by their enemy, and only halted to take breath when they found themselves within the town of Madanpúr.

Sir Hugh drives them likewise from the town.

That town, however, was to be no secure refuge to them. Sir Hugh Rose brought his howitzers to the front and opened fire upon it. For a few minutes the rebels replied, and then fled to the jungles behind. The cavalry, sent in pursuit, followed them to the walls of the fort of Sorai.

Great results obtained from the victory.

The effect of this victory was very great. It so daunted the rebels that they evacuated, without a blow, the formidable pass of Máltún, the fort of Nárút to the rear of it, the little fort of Sorai, the strong fort of Maráora, the fortified castle of Bánpúr—the residence of the rebel rájá called after it—the almost impregnable fortress of Tál-Bahat on the heights above the lake of that name. They abandoned also the line of the Bína and the Bítwa, with the exception of the fortress of Chandairi, on the left bank of the latter river.

The 1st brigade.

Leaving Sir Hugh Rose to reap the consequences of his victory at Madanpúr, I propose to return for a moment to the 1st brigade, under the command of Brigadier C. S. Stuart of the Bombay army, which, in pursuance of the instructions of Sir Hugh Rose, had left Máu on the 10th of January, and marched upon Gúnah, meeting on its route no serious opposition. About seventy miles to the east of Gúnah lies the important post of Chandairi. Chandairi is a very famous town. Its splendour in the prosperous times of the Moghol empire had made it notorious. "If you want to see a town whose houses are palaces, visit Chandairi," was a proverb in the time of Ákbar. In the reign of that illustrious prince it was described as a city possessing fourteen thousand houses built of stone, three hundred and eighty-four markets, three hundred and sixty caravansarais, and twelve thousand mosques. Since that period, it is true, the rule of the Maráthás had worked a great change in its prosperity. In later years, too, its manufactures had suffered from competition with Manchester. But its fort still remained—strong, menacing, defiant, with a long history, testifying alike to its prestige and to the valour of its defenders. Situated on the summit of a high hill, defended by a rampart of sandstone, flanked by circular towers, the fort of Chandairi, seen by an approaching enemy, looked worthy of its reputation. To this place, in February 1858, flocked the sepoys beaten in the actions already detailed by Sir Hugh Rose, to join there the men who had sworn to defend it successfully or to perish.

Chandairi.

Its former splendour.

Its later decay.

Great strength of its fort.

Against it Brigadier C. S. Stuart marched from Gúnah. On the 5th of March he reached a place, Khúkwásás, six miles from Chandairi. Between

Stuart advances against Chandairi.

Book XIV. Chapter I. 1858. March.

Khúkwásás and Chandairi the road lay through a dense jungle. Stuart, therefore, sent the 86th Foot and the 25th Bombay Native Infantry to the front in skirmishing order. After marching three miles, he arrived at a narrow pass between two high hills—a place offering splendid capabilities for defence. To the surprise of Stuart, none was offered. Two miles further, however, the road was found barricaded. The engineers began to clear away the barricades; but they had not worked long before the enemy were seen to climb the hill to the left. On reaching it they opened out a musketry-fire. From this point of vantage they were soon dislodged by a small party of the 86th, and the barricades having been removed, the artillery advanced, covered by the 86th on the right, and the 25th Native Infantry on the left. They had not gone far, however, before a very heavy fire opened upon them from the wall of an enclosure about one mile distant from the fort. The 86th dashed forward to gain this enclosure. One officer of the regiment, Lieutenant Lewis, and the political agent with the force, Captain Keatinge* of the Bombay artillery, outrunning the men, gained first the top of its wall, and jumping down, followed by a few men, drove out the enemy. Stuart pursued his advantage, and did not halt till he had occupied the hills to the west of the fort.

Opposition of the enemy.

Gallantry of Lewis and Keatinge.

Preparations for the storm.

The next few days were spent by Stuart in clearing the neighbouring villages, in reconnoi-

* Now Colonel Keatinge, V.C.

tring, and in planting his guns in a commanding position. On the 13th the breaching-batteries opened fire, and by the evening of the 16th effected a breach which was reported practicable. On the morning of the 17th Stuart sent his stormers, men of the 86th and 25th Native Infantry, to the attack. Their impetuous rush carried all before them. Captain Keatinge, who accompanied the party, and who led it into the breach, was struck down severely wounded. But his fall did not stop the stormers. The rebels hurled themselves over the parapets to avoid the rush they could not withstand, and most of them escaped. A letter which the brigadier had sent the previous day to Captain Abbott commanding a party of cavalry, and requesting him to invest the north side of the fort, reached that officer too late. But the place was taken with all its guns.*

Keatinge again distinguishes himself.

The storm.

Sir Hugh Rose heard of the storming of Chandairi on the 18th. Hearing that the garrison had escaped northwards, he sent a detachment of the Haidarábád contingent to intercept them. This force came up with a few stragglers only, but captured some camels and ponies. On the 19th he marched to Chanchanpúr, one march, fourteen miles, from Jhánsi. After a rest here of about two hours, he despatched the cavalry, horse artillery, and light field-guns of the 2nd brigade to reconnoitre and invest that place.

Sir Hugh marches on Jhánsi.

To the fall of Jhánsi Lord Canning and Lord

Great importance

* The casualties in the capture were twenty-nine, including two officers.

Book XIV. Chapter I.

1858. March.

attached to the fall of Jhánsi.

Elphinstone attached the greatest importance. They regarded that fortress as the stronghold of rebel power in central India, the main strength of the formidable rebel force on the Jamná. It was a place, moreover, in which the slaughter of English men and women had been accompanied by circumstances of peculiar atrocity, and where hatred to the English name had been illustrated by acts of the most wanton barbarity. Nevertheless, anxious as was Lord Canning, anxious as was Sir Colin Campbell himself, that the blow, the most effective of all to the rebel cause in central India, should be struck, they were both so little appreciative of the enormous value of delivering that blow at once, whilst the success of Sir Hugh Rose's brigades was yet fresh in the minds of the rebels, that, on the very eve of the crisis, they both sent orders to defer the attack on Jhánsi, to divert the force elsewhere. From the dangerous consequences of their own orders they were saved by the firmness and decision of Sir Robert Hamilton.

Causes which prompted Lord Canning and Sir C. Campbell to order the diversion of the force from Jhánsi.

Sir Hugh Rose and Sir R. Hamilton receive despatches

I have already stated that Sir Hugh had sent the cavalry and horse artillery of his 2nd brigade, on the afternoon of the 20th, to reconnoitre and invest Jhánsi. He was about, a few hours later, to follow with his infantry, when an express arrived in camp bearing two despatches. One of these was from the Governor-General to Sir Robert Hamilton, the other from the Commander-in-Chief to Sir Hugh Rose.

ordering the former to march on Chirkári.

The purport of these two despatches was identical. They represented that the rájá of Chir-

Book XIV. Chapter I.

1858. March.

kári, a man who, throughout the trying period of 1857–58, had shown unwavering fidelity to his British overlord, was being besieged in his fort by Tántia Topi and the Gwáliár contingent, and they ordered Hamilton and Rose to march at once to his relief, Whitlock's force not being near enough to do so.

Reasons why the order appeared devoid of sense to Hamilton and Rose.

Chirkári was about eighty miles from the ground on which Sir Hugh's force was encamped, on the direct road to Bandá. Jhánsi was within fourteen miles. To the mind of a soldier the idea would naturally present itself that the surest mode of saving the lesser and more distant place was to attack at once the more important and nearer fortress; that to act on the principle indicated in the despatches would be to act in defiance alike of the rules of war and of common sense. So it appeared to both Hamilton and Rose. But Sir Hugh was a soldier. He had received a positive order. Foolish though he knew that order to be, he was bound to obey it. He would be forced to obey it unless the means could be devised of superseding it by higher and more potential authority.

Sir Robert Hamilton takes upon himself the responsibility of ordering the continuance of the movement on Jhánsi.

Sir Robert Hamilton devised those means. How, I will relate in his own simple words. "Sir Hugh Rose considered the order of the Commander-in-Chief imperative: there was not anything left to my discretion in my letter from the Governor-General; it was clear to me it would be a great political mistake to draw off from Jhánsi, which our cavalry were investing, and our force within fourteen miles; moreover,

Book XIV. Chapter I.

1858. March.

supposing the force moved on Chirkári, it was not possible to march the eighty miles before the rebels had carried the fort, the rájá having no provisions, and having lost the outworks according to my intelligence. I, therefore, took on myself the responsibility of proceeding with our operations against Jhánsi, trusting to that course as the most effective to draw the enemy from Chirkári, and so I wrote to the Governor-General." *

Hamilton's determination gives a decided character to the campaign.

It was a responsibility which only a strong man would take, thus to act in direct opposition to the orders of the two highest officials in the country, but, under the circumstances, it was a responsibility which it was necessary to assume. It gave a decided character to the campaign, and enabled Sir Hugh Rose to carry to a glorious conclusion the task which he had taken in hand at Máu.

Sir Hugh moves on Jhánsi.

Freed by Sir Robert Hamilton from the necessity of pursuing the vicious course indicated by the Commander-in-Chief, Sir Hugh Rose set out at 2 o'clock on the morning of the 21st for Jhánsi. He arrived before that city at 9 o'clock, and halting his troops in the open about a mile and a half from the fort, proceeded with his staff to reconnoitre. He did the work completely, for it had struck 6 P.M. before he returned.

The lay of the ground before Jhánsi.

Between the open ground on which Sir Hugh had halted and the town and fortress of Jhánsi,

* Memorandum submitted by Sir Robert Hamilton to Lord Palmerston, dated the 20th of March 1862.

Book XIV. Chapter I. — 1858. March.

were the ruined bungalows occupied nine months before by Europeans, the jail, the "Star" fort,* and the sepoy lines. Near the town were several large temples and topes of tamarind trees. On the right of the halting-ground, stretching to the north and east of the city, was a long belt of hills, through which ran the Kálpi and Úrchah roads; to the left were other hills and the Datiah road; due north was the fortress on a high granite rock, overlooking, to the north, the walled-in city.†

Great strength of the fort of Jhánsi.

The great strength of the fort of Jhánsi, natural as well as artificial, and its extent, entitle it to a place among fortresses. It stands on an elevated rock, rising out of a plain, and commands the city and surrounding country. It is built of excellent and most massive masonry. The fort is difficult to breach, because composed of granite; its walls vary in thickness from sixteen to twenty feet. It has extensive and elaborate outworks of the same solid construction, with front and flanking embrasures for artillery-fire, and loop-holes, of which in some places there were five tiers, for musketry. Guns placed on the high towers of the fort commanded the country all around. On one tower, called the "white turret," recently raised in height, waved in proud defiance the standard of the high-spirited ráni.

The fortress is surrounded on all sides by the city of Jhánsi, the west and part of the south face excepted.

* Vol. i. page 185.

† Lowe's *Central India.*

Book XIV. Chapter I.

1858. March.

The steepness of the rock protects the west; the fortified city wall springs from the centre of its south face, running south-east, and ends in a high mound or mamelon, which protects by a flanking fire its south face. The mound was fortified by a strong circular bastion for five guns, round part of which was drawn a ditch, twelve feet deep and fifteen broad, of solid masonry.

The city of Jhánsi.

The city of Jhánsi is about four miles and a half in circumference, and is surrounded by a fortified and massive wall, from six to twelve feet thick, and varying in height from eighteen to thirty feet, with numerous flanking bastions armed as batteries, with ordnance, and loop-holes, with a banquette for infantry.*

Garrison of the town and fortress.

The town and fortress were garrisoned by eleven thousand men, composed of rebel sepoys, foreign mercenaries, and local levies, and they were led by a woman who believed her cause to be just, and who, classified according to Channing's definition of greatness, was a heroine, though of the third order.

Result of Sir Hugh's reconnaissance.

In his long reconnaissance of the 21st of March, Sir Hugh Rose had noted all the strong points of the defence, and had examined the lay of the ground. He noted the many difficulties presented to the attack, by the fort perched on a lofty granite rock, with its three lines of works, its

* Sir Hugh Rose's despatch, dated the 30th of April 1858, from which this description is taken almost textually. Sir Hugh adds, further on, "A remarkable feature in the defence was that the enemy had no works or forts outside the city."

flanking fire, its thick and solid walls. He had discovered that it would be necessary to take the city prior to assailing the fortress, a work involving double labour and double danger. In this reconnaissance, however, he had decided on his plan of attack. That night he was joined by the cavalry of the 1st brigade. The next day he completely invested the city and fortress with his cavalry. In this investment the defenders read the determination of the English general to capture not only the place but its garrison.

Difficulties of supplies.

One of the measures taken by the ráni might, under other circumstances, have caused considerable embarrassment to the besiegers. She had made the country all about bare. Not a blade of grass was to be seen. Thanks, however, to the loyalty of Sindia and of the ráni of Théri, the force was throughout the operations abundantly supplied with grass, firewood, and vegetables.

The siege begins.

The cavalry having invested the city on the 22nd, the siege began on the night of that day. At 9 o'clock a detachment of Madras and Bombay sappers, was sent with two 18-pounders, and a company 24th Bombay Native Infantry, to throw up a battery near the Úrcha road on the east side of the town wall; other parties were detached at the same time to positions which the general had selected. Working hard that night, the next day, and the night and day which followed, four batteries, constituting the right attack, were ready on the evening of the 24th. On the morning of the 25th they opened fire. That day, too, the bulk of the 1st brigade came

Book XIV. Chapter I.

1858. March.

up, and was at once posted south of the fort, constituting there the left attack.

Progress of the siege for seventeen days.

The siege now progressed in real earnest. For seventeen days the fire from the besieging batteries and from the walls of the city and fort was incessant. Shot and shell were poured into the city, and the enemy's guns never ceased to reply.

Labours and resolution of the besiegers

The labour entailed upon the small force of the besiegers was tremendous. During the period of which I have spoken the men never took off their clothes, nor were the horses unbridled except to water. Nor were the exertions of the besieged less determined. Women and children were seen assisting in repairing the defences of the walls, and in carrying water and food to the

and the besieged.

troops on duty, whilst the ráni constantly visited the troops and animated them to enthusiasm by her presence and her words.

For breaching purposes Sir Hugh had been able to employ only two 18-pounders, the remainder of the guns being laid so as to employ the enemy incessantly, and to damage the buildings inside the city. The progress made by these 18-pounders was, owing to the great strength of the walls, extremely slow. But on the 29th the parapets of the mamelon bastion were levelled by the fire from the left attack, and the enemy's guns there rendered useless. The two following days the cannonading continued with great spirit.

At length a breach is effected,

A breach had been effected, but it was barely practicable; the courage of the enemy continued unabated; danger seemed only to increase their resolution. Such was the state of affairs when a new danger arose for the besiegers. On the evening of the 31st of March intelligence reached Sir Hugh Rose that an army was advancing from the north for the relief of the fortress!

Book XIV. Chapter I.

1858. March.

when an army advances to relieve the place,

This was the army of Tántia Topi. The career of this able Maráthá leader will be told at fuller detail in a subsequent chapter. Suffice it to say that after his victory over Windham and his subsequent defeat by Sir Colin Campbell, Tántia had crossed the Ganges, and subsequently, in obedience to orders from Ráo Sáhib, the nephew of Náná Sáhib, had proceeded to Kálpi. Thence, complying with orders from the same quarter, he had, with a small force of nine hundred sepoys and four guns, moved on Chirkári, and, on the eleventh day, had taken it, capturing twenty-four guns and three lakhs of rupees. Just at this time he received a letter from the ráni of Jhánsi, begging him to come to her help. Again he asked for orders, and again received the full approval of his superior. His force, by this time, had been increased by the junction of five or six regiments of the Gwáliár contingent and the levies of rebel rájás to twenty-two thousand men and twenty-eight guns. Leading it himself, he marched on the English camp before Jhánsi.

Tántia Topi

captures Chirkári

and marches to relieve Jhánsi.

The position of Sir Hugh Rose was full of peril. Before him was an unconquered fortress, garrisoned by eleven thousand warriors, full of the ardour of battle; advancing against and close to him, an army of more than twenty thousand men led by a chieftain who hated the English, and

Danger of Sir Hugh Rose's position.

Book XIV. Chapter I.

1858. March.

who had twice revelled in their defeat at Kánhpúr. It was a position which required in a special degree great daring, a resolute will, the power to take responsibility. A single false step, a solitary error in judgment, might have been fatal. But Sir Hugh Rose was equal to the occasion. Rightly believing that to withdraw the troops then investing the fortress, for the purpose of meeting the new enemy, would give the besieged all the moral advantages of victory as well as the material advantages which they would derive from a virtual raising of the siege, the English general resolved still to press the siege with vigour, whilst at the head of all the troops not engaged in actual duty he should march against the new enemy. The extreme daring of this plan will be realised when the reader reflects that Sir Hugh was unable to assemble more than one thousand five hundred men of all arms for this purpose, that of these only five hundred were British, and that the enemy numbered, according to Tántia Topí's own admission, twenty-two thousand men. Sir Hugh's preparations* for the engagement were made on the evening of the 31st. He resolved to attack early the following morning.

He resolves to maintain the siege and to meet the relieving army.

Sir Hugh had drawn his covering force from both brigades, the detachment from the 1st being led by Brigadier C. S. Stuart, that from the 2nd by

* The preparations were witnessed with delight by the defenders of Jhánsi, who thought the English were marching to certain destruction. They shouted all night in a frenzy of joy.

Book XIV. Chapter I.

1858. April.

Sir Hugh meets Tántia Topi,

himself in person. The men slept in their clothes ready for immediate action. The precaution was necessary. At 4 o'clock in the morning of the 1st, Tántia Topi advanced towards the British encampment. Half an hour later, the falling back of his pickets warned the English general of his approach. In a few minutes the British guns opened fire, and almost immediately those of the enemy answered. But the fire of a few guns was powerless to check the onward march of an enemy whose line overlapped that of the British on both flanks. Tántia had but to move straight on to reach with his overlapping wings the troops besieging the fortress, who would thus, literally, be placed between two fires. Sir Hugh comprehended the position in an instant, and took measures to meet it. Massing his horse artillery on his left, and attaching to it a squadron of the 14th Light Dragoons, under Captain Prettijohn, he ordered them to attack the enemy's right, whilst he himself, on the other flank, should direct another squadron against their left. The plan succeeded admirably. The rebels were so surprised and intimidated by this double attack, that their centre, which up to that time had been advancing steadily, first halted, and then, as the men composing it discerned a movement on the part of the British infantry, broke up into disordered masses. The movement of the British infantry is easily accounted for. Sir Hugh Rose, in the moment of charging, had sent orders to his infantry to advance as soon as the cavalry attack should be well pronounced. This order

attacks their flanks with cavalry,

whilst the infantry attack their centre.

Book XIV. Chapter I.

1858. April.

The enemy's first line is defeated.

was now obeyed. The infantry sprang to their feet, advanced a few yards, then poured in a volley and charged. The result was magical. The first line of the enemy at once broke, and fled in complete disorder towards the second line, abandoning several of their guns.

Meanwhile, Stuart defeats a detached body of the enemy and threatens the second line.

The second line, commanded by Tántia in person, was occupying a position upon rising ground, its front covered by jungle, about two miles in rear of the first line. Tántia beheld in dismay the latter rushing helter skelter towards him, followed by the three arms of the British in hot pursuit; but he had scarcely realised the fact when another vision on his right flank came to add to his anguish. Whilst Sir Hugh Rose had been engaged in the manner I have described, Brigadier C. S. Stuart, with the detachment of the 1st brigade, had moved round the hill into the plain on the right of the enemy, in order to check a large body of them, who were taking advantage of the battle raging in front of the line to move off towards Jhánsi. Stuart attacked, defeated them, and drove them back, hotly following them. So close, indeed, was the pursuit, that they had no time to reform, but fled in confusion, leaving gun after gun in the hands of the victors, and leaving numbers of their own men dead or dying on the field. This was the vision that came to add to the dismay of Tántia Topi.

It had the effect of forcing upon him a prompt decision. The day, he saw, was lost, but there was yet time to save the second line and his remaining guns. I have said that the ground upon which he rested was covered to the front by jungle. This jungle was dry and easily kindled. He at once set fire to it, and under cover of the smoke and flames, commenced a retreat across the Bétwah, hoping to place that river between himself and the pursuers. His infantry and horsemen led the retreat, his guns covered it. Right gallantly and skilfully they did it, and he did succeed in crossing the Bétwah with his reserve and guns and some of the fugitives of the first line. But he was not the safer for the passage. The British horse artillery and cavalry had dashed at a gallop through the burning jungle, and they were resolved not to cease the pursuit till they had captured every gun that had opened against them. They carried out their programme to the letter. The pursuit did not cease till every gun had been taken. Fifteen hundred rebels were killed or wounded on this day. The remainder, with Tántia Topi at their head, fled towards Kálpi.*

Book XIV. Chapter I.

1858. April.

Tántia fires the jungle

and flees,

pursued across the Bétwah by the British.

Whilst this battle had been raging, the besieged had redoubled their fire. Mounting the bastions and the wall, they had shouted and yelled, and poured down volleys of musketry, seemingly threatening a sortie. Never, however, did the besiegers' batteries ply with more vigour or with greater effect. The sight from the wall, moreover, did not long continue to inspire.

The besieged, first jubilant,

are afterwards discouraged.

* Tántia states that four or five guns were saved, but these must have been additional to the twenty-eight field-pieces accounted for. He adds that he was followed in his flight by only two hundred sepoys.

Book XIV. Chapter I.

1858. April.

Suddenly the yells and the shouts ceased—a sure sign that the garrison had recognised that the hour of deliverance had not arrived for them.

The victorious army, returning from the pursuit, its *morale* strengthened as much as that of the enemy had deteriorated, resumed its former positions the same evening. Sir Hugh Rose determined then to take the promptest advantage of the discouragement which, he was well aware, the defeat of Tántia Topi could not fail to produce in the minds of the garrison. He poured in, then, a heavy fire all that night and the day following. On the 2nd the breach in the city wall having been reported practicable, though only just practicable, Sir Hugh determined to storm the place the following morning. He made his preparations accordingly. His plan was to make a false attack on the west wall with a small detachment under Major Gall, 14th Light Dragoons; as soon as the sound of his guns should be heard, the main storming party was to debouch from cover, and enter the breach, whilst on the right of it attempts should be made to escalade the wall. The right attack, composed of the Madras and Bombay sappers, the 3rd Bombay Europeans, and the infantry of the Haidarábád contingent, was divided into two columns and a reserve. The right column was commanded by Lieutenant-Colonel Liddell, the left by Captain Robinson—both of the 3rd Europeans—the reserve by Brigadier Steuart, 14th Light Dragoons. This attack was to attempt to gain the town by escalade. The left attack, composed of the Royal Engi-

Sir Hugh pours in a heavy fire on the fort all the night

and prepares to storm.

neers, the 86th Foot, and the 25th Bombay Native Infantry, was similarly divided. Its left column, commanded by Lieutenant-Colonel Lowth, 86th Regiment, was to storm the breach; the right led by Major Stuart, 86th Regiment, to escalade the rocket-tower and the low curtain immediately to the right of it. The reserve was commanded by Brigadier C. S. Stuart.

Book XIV. Chapter I.

1858. April.

At 3 o'clock on the morning of the 3rd of April the storming parties marched to the positions assigned to them, to await there the signal from Major Gall's party. No sooner was it given than the stormers dashed to the front. On the left, Captain Darby, 86th, led the stormers of Colonel Lowth's column up the breach in the most gallant manner, driving the enemy before him. At the same time Major Stuart attacked the rocket-tower, and though met by a strong opposition, forced his way by it into the town. Lowth then collected his men, and detached a portion of them against that section of the rebel forces which were engaged in opposing the right attack. Taking these in flank and rear, this detachment forced them to let go their hold on the defences, thus greatly facilitating the difficult task of the right attack. With the remainder of his troops, Lowth prepared to march on the ráni's palace.

Storming of Jhánsi.

Success of the left attack.

The right attack, on hearing the signal, had marched silently from their cover in three bodies. No sooner, however, had the troops composing it turned into the road leading towards the gate which was the object of their assault than the

The right attack

Book XIV. Chapter I. — 1858. April.

enemy's bugles sounded, and a very heavy fire opened upon them.* Through this fire the stormers had to march upwards of two hundred yards. Steadily they pushed on, and planted the ladders in three places against the wall. For the moment, however, it was impossible for the stormers to ascend. "The fire of the enemy waxed stronger, and amid the chaos of sounds of volleys of musketry and roaring of cannon, and hissing and bursting of rockets, stink-pots, infernal machines, huge stones, blocks of wood, and trees—all hurled upon their devoted heads—the men wavered for a moment, and sheltered themselves behind stones."†

is momentarily checked.

Notwithstanding this momentary check, the sappers, animated by their officers, kept firm hold of their ladders, and in spite of the superhuman efforts of the enemy, maintained them in their position against the wall. How long this lasted it is difficult to state. Minutes seemed hours, when, happily, Major Boileau, Madras Engineers, who had gone back to report the state of affairs to the brigadier, brought up a reinforcement of a hundred men of the 3rd Europeans. The stormers then rushed to the ladders led by their engineer officers. Some were found too short, others, from weakness, broke down under the men; but Lieutenant Dick, Bombay Engineers, gained, by means of one of them,

The ladders too short, or too weak.

Gallantry of Dick,

* "For a time it appeared like a sheet of fire, out of which burst a storm of bullets, round shot, and rockets, destined for our annihilation."—Lowe's *Central India.*

† Lowe, *ibid.*

the summit of the wall, and fighting against enormous odds, called upon the men to follow him. Lieutenant Meiklejohn of the same noble regiment mounted by another, and then boldly jumped down into the seething mass below. Lieutenant Bonus, also of the Bombay Engineers, reached the wall by a third. The men pressed on from behind; but before they could, in any number, join their officers, Dick had fallen from the wall, dying, pierced with shot and bayonets; Bonus had been hurled down, struck in his face by a log or stone; Fox of the Madras sappers, who had also reached the wall, had been shot in the neck; Meiklejohn had been cut to pieces. But the stormers pushed on, and in streams from some eight ladders, at length gained a footing on the rampart, dealing and receiving death from the enemy, who still continued fiercely to contest every point of the attack.

of Meiklejohn, of Bonus, of Fox.

The right attack gains a footing on the ramparts.

It was at this crisis that the stormers of the left attack made the charge upon the flank and rear of the defenders, of which I have spoken. Its effect was marvellous. The defenders relaxed their hold, the opposition ceased, and the stormers of the right attack jumped down and mingled with their comrades.

The left attack renders timely aid.

The defence having thus given way, the stormers made their way through the city to the palace, Lowth leading the way. The palace had been prepared by the rebels for a resistance in the last resort. The conflict, as the stormers forced their way through the streets, was severe. At the palace it was desperate. The houses on

The stormers march on the palace,

Book XIV. Chapter I.

1858. April.

both sides of the street leading to it had been set on fire, and the heat was fearful. When even the courtyard of the palace was reached, it became apparent that the resistance had only begun. Every room was savagely contested. Fruitlessly, however. From chamber to chamber the enemy were driven at the point of the bayonet. At length the palace itself was gained. The opposition, however, had not even then entirely ceased. Two hours later it was discovered that fifty men of the ráni's bodyguard still held the stables attached to the building. These men defended themselves to the last before, after a desperate encounter, they were disposed of. But the men who accomplished this task, the 86th and the 3rd Europeans, were compensated for their toil and danger by recapturing a British flag.*

which, after a desperate contest, they gain.

Terrible scene in the stables.

This occurrence had but just happened when Sir Hugh, who had been present throughout with the left attack, received information that a body of the rebels, numbering about four hundred, driven from the town, after having vainly tried to force the pickets of one of the cavalry camps, had taken up a position on a hill to the west of the fortress, where they had been surrounded by the cavalry. Sir Hugh instantly sent against the hill the available troops of all arms under Major Gall. This gallant officer sent to storm the hill a

The rebels driven from the town, occupy a strong position outside of it,

whence they are driven

* This was a Union Jack of silk, which Lord William Bentinck had given to the grandfather of the ráni's husband, with the permission to have it carried before him, as a reward for his fidelity."—Sir H. Rose's despatch.

detachment of the 24th Bombay Native Infantry. The 24th went at the rebels with a will, and killed all but about twenty, who retreated to the summit and there blew themselves up. The 24th lost an officer and several men in this attack. Another body of about one thousand five hundred who had collected in one of the suburbs of the town, declaring they would defend it to the last, were driven out, about the same time, with a loss of three hundred of their number.

by the 24th Bombay Native Infantry; another body is similarly treated.

All that night, and throughout the following day, desultory fighting continued, the enemy being either slaughtered or driven under the shelter of the fort guns. Sir Hugh was meanwhile engaged in organising measures for an attack on the fortress. But the ráni saved him further trouble on that score. On the night of the 4th, despairing of a successful defence of the fortress, and hoping that her presence at Kálpi might induce Tántia Topi once more to aid her, that princess evacuated the fortress with all her remaining followers. She rode straight for Kálpi, and arrived there the very evening on which Tántia, who had travelled more leisurely, reached that place. Sir Hugh sent a cavalry force in pursuit of her, but the start had been too great. A few of the fugitives were, however, cut up.

Desultory fighting continues during the night.

The ráni evacuates the fortress and rides for Kálpi.

The fortress of Jhánsi was occupied by Sir Hugh Rose on the morning of the 5th of April. The loss sustained by him during the operations against it, including the action on the Bétwah, amounted to three hundred and forty-three killed and wounded, of whom thirty-six were officers.

Sir Hugh occupies the fortress.

Book XIV. Chapter I.

1858. April.

The enemy's loss was computed at five thousand. One thousand dead bodies were actually burned or buried in Jhánsi itself.

Credit due to Sir Hugh Rose.

The mode by which Jhánsi was captured attests the merits of the noble soldier who planned and carried out the attack. Never was there a more complete combination of daring and skill, of foresight and resolution. The result was worthy of the plan, and of the genius which formed the plan.*

Importance of capturing Kálpi.

Sir Hugh's object now was to march on Kálpi, to drive the rebels from that stronghold on the Jamná whence they had so constantly menaced the communications of the British. Kálpi was the arsenal of the rebels, the head-quarters of the nephew of Náná Sáhib, and was extremely well provided with artillery and warlike stores. It lies on the Jamná, one hundred and two miles to the north-east of Jhánsi, and only forty-six to the south-west of Kánhpúr. The occupation of this place would enable Sir Hugh to touch the left rear of Sir Colin Campbell's army, and, in co-operation with him, to clear the triangle the angles of which were Jhánsi, Kálpi, and Ágra—Gwáliár being nearly midway in the line uniting Jhánsi and Ágra.

* The following extracts from Sir Hugh Rose's despatch attest the great strength of the town and fortress: "It was not till Jhánsi was taken that its great strength was known. There was only one part of the fortress, the south curtain, which was considered practicable for breaching. But, when inside, we saw this was a mistake, there being at some distance in rear of the curtain a massive wall fifteen or twenty feet thick, and immediately in rear of this a deep tank cut out of the live rock."

For seventeen days Sir Hugh's little army had known no repose. The halt at Jhánsi of nearly nineteen days which followed the capture of the place was, however, in no sense devoted to repose. Much had to be done in Jhánsi itself: the arrangements for a fresh campaign had to be organised, provisions had to be laid in, the magazines to be replenished. At length all was ready. Leaving at Jhánsi a small garrison consisting of the head-quarter wing of the 3rd Bombay Europeans, four companies 24th Bombay Native Infantry, left wing 3rd Bombay Light Cavalry, one hundred troopers Haidarábád contingent, half a company Bombay sappers, and three guns Bhopál contingent—the whole under the command of Colonel Liddell, 3rd Europeans—Sir Hugh detached, on the night of the 22nd of April, a detachment under Major Gall to watch the rebel garrison of Kotá, reported to be at a place called Máu in the neighbourhood, and set out himself with the 1st brigade at midnight on the 25th, leaving directions for the 2nd brigade to follow two days later. Major Orr had been previously detached with the bulk of the Haidarábád force to prevent the rájás of Bánpúr and Sháhgarh and any other rebels from crossing the Bétwah and doubling back southwards.

Book XIV. Chapter I.

1858. April.

Sir Hugh halts at Jhánsi to arrange for a march on Kálpi.

Dispositions made by him with that object.

Leaving for a moment these several officers engaged in carrying out the orders entrusted to them, I propose to return for a moment to the ráni of Jhánsi and Tántia Topi.

These two important personages had arrived, as I have said, at Kálpi the same day. The first

Book XIV. Chapter I.

1858. May.

The ráni of Jhánsi at Kálpi.

Her appeal to Ráo Sáhib,

act of the ráni had been to implore the nephew of Náná Sáhib, known as Ráo Sáhib, "to give her an army that she might go and fight." The following morning Ráo Sáhib ordered a parade of all the troops at his disposal. These consisted of some regiments of the Gwáliár contingent, several regiments of the regular native army recruited to nearly full strength, the contingents of various rebel rájás, and the remnant of the Jhánsi garrison. Ráo Sáhib reviewed these troops, addressed them, and then directed Tántia to lead them against the English. Tántia obeyed, and hoping to meet them when possibly all their forces were not reunited, marched to Kúnch, a town forty miles from Kálpi on the Jhánsi road, and there took up a strong position, covered by woods and gardens, with temples at intervals between each of them, surrounded by a strong wall, and there threw up intrenchments.

who holds a review, and orders Tántia Topi to march against the English.

He marches on Kúnch.

Meanwhile the English force was advancing on Kúnch. Major Gall, harassed by the enemy on his march, had reached the town of Pútch, sixteen miles from Kúnch, on the 1st of May. Here he was joined the same day by Sir Hugh Rose and the 1st brigade. Major Orr, on his side, had crossed the Bétwah, attacked the rájás of Bánpúr and Sháhgarh at Kotra, and had taken one of their guns. He had, however, found it impossible to cut them off, and they had succeeded, for the time, in escaping southwards, supplies and carriage being furnished them by the treacherous rájá of Jigni. By Sir Hugh's direction, Major Orr then marched on Kúnch.

Movements of Gall, of Rose, and of Orr.

Book XIV. Chapter I.

1858. May.

The rebels concentrate on Kúnch.

The country between Pútch and Kúnch was studded with little forts, which, up to the time of which I am writing, had been occupied by the enemy. From these they could undoubtedly cause considerable annoyance to small detachments; but, in the presence of the large force now collecting at the former place, they deemed it advisable to abandon them and concentrate at Kúnch.

Sir Hugh sends Gall to capture Lohári,

Sir Hugh was joined by his 2nd brigade, strengthened by the 71st Highlanders, on the 5th of May. He at once marched on Lohári, ten miles nearer Kúnch, thence to put into action the plan of attack which he had matured. Before this, however, hearing on his arrival at Lohári that the rebels were in possession of the fort of the same name close to it, he detached Major Gall, with a wing of the 3rd Europeans, some artillery and dragoons, to attack it. Gall took the fort, losing two of his officers and some men; but of the garrison not one escaped. Sir Hugh meanwhile had matured his plans.

and makes a flank march to turn the rebels' position.

An Asiatic army, Sir Hugh was well aware, always expects a front attack. He had also noticed that nothing disturbs such an army as a turning movement. Instead, therefore, of sending his troops against a position which the rebels had carefully prepared, Sir Hugh resolved to make a flank march with his whole force on the 6th to a position at once facing the unfortified side of the town of Kúnch, and threatening seriously the enemy's line of retreat from that place to Kálpi.

Book XIV. Chapter I.

1858. May.

He reaches the assigned point,

With this view Sir Hugh broke up from his encamping-ground early on the morning of the 6th, and making a flank march of fourteen miles, brought his force into the position contemplated. His 1st brigade, forming his left, rested its extreme left on the village of Nágupúra; his 2nd brigade, forming the centre, occupied the village of Chomair; Major Orr's Haidarábád force, forming the right, occupied the village of Úmri. This position was two miles from Kúnch.

gives his men their dinners,

sends Gall to reconnoitre,

The sun was high in the heavens before the troops had taken up the posts assigned to them. Sir Hugh, who had marched with the 1st brigade, ordered them to eat their dinners, whilst he galloped to inspect the arrangements made in the centre and on the right. In an hour he returned, and ordered Major Gall, with a detachment of cavalry, to reconnoitre the wood, garden, and temples which lay between him and Kúnch, covering that advance by a fire of shot and shell. At the same time he directed the siege-guns to take up a position whence they could play upon the town.

receives Gall's report,

Gall soon returned with a report that the enemy had retreated through the wood to the part of it near the town, having in their rear a body of cavalry; that the siege-guns had had the effect of driving the rebels on the right of the wood into the town, but that some outworks were still occupied by them.

and marches to storm the town.

Sir Hugh determined at once to clear the wood and the outworks with his infantry, and then to storm the town. Covering his left wing with a wing of the 86th, and the whole of the 25th Bombay Native Infantry, in skirmishing order, and supporting their flanks with cavalry and horse artillery, he sent them into the wood. Advancing in perfect order, the gallant sepoys of the 25th Native Infantry cleared the wood, temples, and walled gardens in front of them, whilst the 86th, making a circuit to their left, carried all the obstacles in their front, and then, bringing their left shoulders forward, advanced, despite a heavy fire of artillery and musketry, through the north part of the town and took the fort. This operation, performed by the 1st brigade, drove the enemy's right on their centre.

The 1st brigade drives the rebel right on its centre,

Meanwhile, Brigadier Steuart, commanding the 2nd brigade, having observed a body of rebel infantry strongly posted in cultivated ground threatening the line of attack of his brigade, marched to dislodge them. The rebels contested their position with great valour, and it was not until the 1st brigade, establishing itself in the manner already described, threatened their flank, that they gave way. It had been intended that Brigadier Steuart should then march straight into the town, but, with the view of cutting off the rebels, he moved to the south of it and missed them.

and affords aid to the 2nd brigade.

Major Orr's force had, whilst this was going on, advanced through the wood, round the town, to the plains traversed by the road to Kálpi.

Major Orr moves to cut off the rebels.

Although the operations of which I have given an outline had taken only an hour, and the rebels in that short period had been completely defeated, they managed, nevertheless, to gain with the bulk

Book XIV. Chapter I.

1858. May.

The enemy, nevertheless, gain the Kálpi road in full retreat.

of their forces the Kálpi road in advance of their pursuers, and on both sides of this road they were now endeavouring to restore some sort of order in their masses, so as to check by every means in their power the ardour of the pursuit. When Sir Hugh Rose, then, emerging from the narrow streets of the town, formed up his brigades for a renewed attack, he beheld the enemy retreating in a long irregular line, covered by skirmishers at close distances, the skirmishers supported by groups who acted to them as a sort of bastions.

The heat of the sun forces Sir Hugh to halt his infantry,

The terrific heat of the day, and the power of the sun, which had made itself felt with fatal effect on many of his European soldiers,* forbade him further to risk the soldiers of that arm in a pursuit which could not fail to entail a sacrifice of many valuable lives. He, therefore, halted them, whilst he launched in pursuit the cavalry of both brigades and of Major Orr's force,† and the horse artillery and field guns.

but he launches the cavalry in pursuit.

Masterly retreat of the rebels.

Then was witnessed action on the part of the rebels which impelled admiration from their enemies. The manner in which they conducted their retreat could not be surpassed. There was no hurry, no disorder, no rushing to the rear. All was orderly as on a field-day. Though their line of skirmishers was two miles in length it never wavered in a single point. The men fired, then ran behind the relieving men, and loaded. The relieving men then fired, and ran back in

* Many of the sepoys were also struck down by the sun.

† Except a party left to watch the Jaláon road and the rear.

their turn. They even attempted, when they thought the pursuit was too rash, to take up a position, so as to bring on it an enfilading fire. Their movement was so threatening that Sir Hugh ordered Prettijohn, 14th Light Dragoons, to charge the enfilading party, an order carried out by that most daring officer with great gallantry and success. Still, however, the rebels maintained the order of their retreat, nor was it until many of them had been killed, and all their guns had been captured, that the survivors were driven in on the main body. Then, for the first time, they lost their nerve; then they crowded into the Kálpi road, a long and helpless column of runaways. But the pursuers were completely tired; they were unable to move faster than at a walk; the cavalry horses were knocked up; and whilst the guns could not approach near enough to fire grape, the cavalry could only pick up an occasional straggler. When, then, a few hundred yards further, broken ground, over which the rebels scattered, supervened, the pursuit came to an end. It had produced great results. The rebels lost nine guns, a quantity of ammunition and stores, and five or six hundred men in killed and wounded. The mutinous 52nd Bengal Native Infantry, which covered the retreat, was almost annihilated. The English loss was three officers and fifty-nine men killed and wounded, in addition to many struck down by the sun.

Book XIV. Chapter I. — 1858. May.

Gallantry of Prettijohn.

The rebel covering force is at last driven on the main body.

The victors, completely exhausted, cease the pursuit.

The defeat at Kúnch sowed great mistrust among the rebels. The infantry sepoys taunted the cavalry troopers with having abandoned them,

Bad effect on the rebels of the defeat at Kúnch.

Book XIV. Chapter I.

1858. May.

and the men of all three arms brought the same accusation against Tántia Topi, who had disappeared at Kúnch even more rapidly than he had galloped away on the Bétwah. The Jhánsi horsemen, too, came in for their share of abuse, and when they excused themselves on the plea that they had felt bound to escort their ráni* to a place of safety, they were only vilified the more. To such an extent did the animosities among the several parties who constituted the rebel force proceed, that on the morrow of their reaching Kálpi, the rumour that Sir Hugh was advancing by forced marches against that place, sufficed to induce them to disperse. It is believed that shortly after that rumour arrived there were only eleven sepoys left in the town and fort of Kálpi. This dispersion was, however, soon remedied in a manner to be hereafter described.

Sir Hugh pushes on

The report which had so disquieted the rebels at Kálpi was not baseless. Despite the fact that his ammunition was well-nigh exhausted, Sir Hugh, determined to give the enemy no breathing-time, had pushed on with all practicable speed from Kúnch. On the 15th he established himself at Goláoli, on the Jamná, six miles from Kálpi. Goláoli is not on the direct road between Kúnch and Kálpi, but two reasons had prompted Sir Hugh to march on it in preference to taking the direct route. In the first place, he had heard from the Commander-in-Chief that Colonel G. V. Maxwell had been detached with the 88th Foot,

and establishes himself at Goláoli near Kálpi.

* The ráni fled to Kálpí after the defeat: Tántia Topi to Chirki, near Jaláor, the residence of his parents.

some Sikhs, and the Camel corps, to co-operate with him; and Maxwell having reached the left bank of the Jamná opposite Goláoli, Sir Hugh was able to hold out his hand to him at that place. In the second, by marching on Goláoli, Sir Hugh turned the fortifications which had been thrown up to impede his advance, and threatened Kálpi from an unexpected quarter.

Book XIV. Chapter I.

1858. May.

His reasons for taking that route.

Sir Hugh's march from Kúnch to Goláoli, though unopposed by the enemy, was in all respects most trying. The terrible heat, and the rays of the sun told upon his men with deadly effect, and admissions to the hospitals and deaths increased at an alarming rate. This fact was well known to the rebels, and they did their utmost to reap full advantage from it. An intercepted general order by their general-in-chief, issued about this time, directed that no attack should be made upon the European infidels before 10 o'clock in the day, as fighting in the sun either killed them or sent them to their hospitals. But in spite of the heat Goláoli was reached on the 15th, communications were opened with Maxwell, and Sir Hugh, in accordance with his invariable custom, made prompt arrangements for engaging the enemy.

Trying character of the march to Goláoli.

Who now constituted the enemy? I have related how, in the panic caused by the rumour of Sir Hugh's onward march, only eleven rebel sepoys had been left in the town and fort. A few days later, however, the unexpected arrival of the nawáb of Bandá with two thousand horse, some guns, and many followers—the remnant

The rebels are reinforced by the nawáb of Bandá.

Book XIV. Chapter I.

1858. May.

of the force defeated by General Whitlock at Bandá, in the manner to be told in the next chapter—and his energetic exertions, backed by those of the ráni of Jhánsi, produced one of those changes from despair to confidence which mark the Indian character.* The sepoys who had left returned, and, exhorted by their leaders to hold to the last Kálpi, their only arsenal, and to win their right to paradise by exterminating the infidel English,† declared their resolution to defend it to the last.

Their confidence returns.

Strong position of Kálpi.

Although as a fortification Kálpi had but little to boast of, its position was unusually strong. It was protected on all sides by ravines, to its front by five lines of defence, and to its rear by the Jamná, from which rises the precipitous rock on which stands the fort.

Nature of the country between the British camp and Kálpi.

Between the British camp and Kálpi, indeed, existed a most extraordinary labyrinth of ravines, over which artillery and cavalry could make no progress, but which furnished an interminable cover of the most formidable description for infantry. On the, so to speak, tongues of land formed by the prolongation of the ravines, the rebels had rapidly thrown up intrenchments, and had cut trenches near to these in a manner rendering it impossible that they should be turned. Even if driven out of the intrenchments, it was within the power of the rebels to fall back on eighty-four temples, built, as well as the walls round them, of the most

* Sir Hugh Rose's despatch, the 24th of May 1858.
† Intercepted letter, *idem*.

Book XIV. Chapter I.

1858. May.

solid masonry. These temples constituted a second line of defence; the outwork of ravines a third; the town of Kálpi a fourth; another chain of ravines a fifth; and the fort the last.

Skirmishes between the two armies.

On the 16th, 17th, 18th, 19th, and 20th, constant skirmishes occurred between the two armies, the enemy being the attacking party. On all these occasions they were repulsed, but the British suffered much from the sun, as well as from the incessant toil, anxiety, and heat. On the 19th a mortar battery, established on the right front of the British position, opened on the town. On the 20th a detachment from Colonel Maxwell's brigade, consisting of two companies of the 88th, one hundred and twenty Sikhs, and the Camel corps, crossed the river, and joined Sir Hugh Rose. On the 21st the batteries from Maxwell's camp opened on the fort and town. On the 22nd Sir Hugh determined to deliver his long-meditated blow.

Maxwell reinforces Sir Hugh.

The British plan of attack.

Sir Hugh had, from the first, determined that whilst Maxwell's batteries should shell Kálpi, he would clear the ravines and the other obstacles and attack the left face of the fort. Resolved to keep his men for this great blow, he had contented himself with simply repulsing the attacks I have mentioned. But when he received information that the rebels were meditating an attack on the 22nd, which should be fatal to one of the contending parties, he, now ready for them, resolved to second their views.

The rebel plan of attack.

The rebels had prepared a plan so skilful, that, if carried out with courage and resolution, it

Book XIV. Chapter I.

1858. May.

seemed to offer several chances in its favour. Whilst making, with great demonstrations, a false attack on the British left, they were to steal up the ravines with their main body, and try and overwhelm the right, weakened, they hoped, by detachments sent to support the left.

It must be understood that the British force occupied the ground situated between the river Jamná and the road running from Kálpi to Bandá, that its right rested on the ravines near the river, whilst its left nearly touched that road.

The rebels open the battle,

In pursuance of their plan, the rebels marched out in masses at 10 o'clock on the 22nd along the Bandá road, and threatened the British left, opening fire simultaneously with their guns on its centre. This attack, headed by the nawáb of Bandá and by Ráo Sáhib, nephew of Náná Sáhib, though intended only as a feint, soon made itself felt, and the British left became heavily engaged.

and attack the British left,

Still Sir Hugh, confident as to the real object of the enemy, did not move a man from his right. He contented himself with replying to their guns with his guns in a style which soon forced the rebels to limber up and fall back. The attack on his left not only continued, but became very real indeed, but still Sir Hugh did not move a man from his right. It was well he did not.

with great severity.

Suddenly, as if by magic, the whole line of ravines became a mass of fire; the enemy's left batteries opened, and their infantry, climbing from below, poured in an overwhelming musketry-fire on the right of the British line. The suddenness of the attack, their superior numbers, and

Maintaining that attack they suddenly direct their main energies against the British right.

Book XIV. Chapter I.

1858. May.

the terrible heat of the day gave the rebels a great advantage. Another point, too, was in their favour. Many of the Enfield rifles had become clogged by constant use in all weathers, and the men, after a few discharges, had found it very difficult to load them. The sun, too, had struck down an unusual number of the Europeans. When, then, the rebels, starting up in great numbers from the ravines, poured in volleys which the British reply to only feebly, when they saw that each discharge from the thin red line became weaker than that preceding it, they began to gain a confidence they had never felt before. They pressed on with loud yells, the British falling back, until they approached the British light field-guns and mortar-battery. Then it was that Brigadier C. S. Stuart, dismounting, placed himself by the guns, and bade the gunners defend them with their lives. The 86th and 25th Native Infantry, in thin extended line, disputed step by step. Still the rebels pressed on, and it seemed as though from their very numbers they must prevail, when Sir Hugh, to whom news of the attack had been conveyed, brought up the Camel corps at their best pace; then, dismounting the men, and leading them forward himself at the double, charged the advancing foe, then within a few yards of the British guns. For a moment the enemy stood, but only for a moment. A shout, a dash forward from the whole line, and they went headlong into the ravines below. Not only was the attack on the right repulsed, but the victory was gained! The attack

The confidence of the rebels increases.

Gallantry of Brigadier C. S. Stuart.

Sir Hugh brings up the Camel corps at the critical moment,

and gains the day.

Book XIV. Chapter I.

1858. May.

on the left collapsed when that on the right failed, and the guns, gaining the rebels' flank, inflicted great loss on them as they fled. Sir Hugh followed them up so closely, that he cut off a number of them from Kálpi. The fire from Maxwell's batteries made those who reached that fort feel that it was no secure place of refuge. They evacuated it accordingly during the night.

The rebels evacuate Kálpi.

The rest of their force, pursued by the horse artillery and cavalry, lost their formation and dispersed, losing all their guns and baggage. Even the ráni of Jhánsi, who fled with them, was compelled to sleep under a tree!

Trials to which the English troops were subjected during this campaign.

The position of the troops, their sufferings, the feelings that animated them, are thus graphically described by an eye-witness who, throughout its duration, took part in the campaign, and who subsequently gave to the world an eloquent record of the achievements of his comrades. "This was," writes Dr. Lowe,* "a hard day's work, and a glorious victory won over ten times our numbers under most trying circumstances. The position of Kálpi; the numbers of the enemy, who came on with a resolution and a display of tactics we had never before witnessed; the exhausted, weakened state of the general's force; the awful suffocating hot winds and burning sun, which the men had to endure all day, without time to take food or water, combined to render the achievement one of unsurpassed difficulty. Every soul engaged in this important action

* Lowe's *Central India during the Rebellion of* 1857–58.

Book XIV. Chapter I.

1858. May.

suffered more or less. Officers and men fainted away, or dropped down as though struck by lightning in the delirium of a sun-stroke; yet all this was endured without a murmur, and in the cool of the evening we were speculating upon the capture of Kálpi on the morrow."

Their unmurmuring endurance.

Before daybreak the following morning, Sir Hugh marched on that place. His 1st brigade, under Brigadier C. S. Stuart, he sent through the ravines, following the course of the Jamná, whilst he led the 2nd himself,* along the Kálpi road.

The fort of Kálpi is evacuated.

Colonel Maxwell's batteries still continued to shell the fort and the villages in front of it. As the two brigades advanced, however, these villages were abandoned by the rebels, and it soon became apparent that no serious resistance was contemplated. When the two brigades, having overcome all obstacles in their path, united near the town, and advanced into it, they were not opposed; the rebels had fled, quitting for ever the arsenal which had served them so long and so well.†

* Brigadier C. Steuart, C.B., commanding the 2nd brigade, had reported sick after the battle of Kúnch, and the command had devolved upon Lieutenant-Colonel Campbell, 71st Highlanders.

† The following description, given by an eye-witness, proves how the rebels had used the position of Kálpi, and the good stead in which it had stood them. After enumerating the quantities of ammunition, lead, iron, brass, gun-carriages, gun-moulds, &c., found in the fort, Dr. Lowe adds:—"The enemy had erected houses and tents in the fort, had their smiths' shops, their carpenters' shops. Their foundries for casting shot and shell were in perfect order, clean and well con-

Book XIV. Chapter I.

1858. May.

The capture of Kálpi completes Sir Robert Hamilton's plan.

The capture of Kálpi completed the plan of the campaign for the column having its base at Máu, which Sir Robert Hamilton had submitted to the Governor-General and the Commander-in-Chief towards the close of the preceding year. In all respects that plan had been carried out. Marching from Máu in November Sir Hugh Rose had, in five months, traversed central India, crossing its numerous rivers, storming strong forts, taking many towns, defeating armies vastly superior in numbers, led by men and by a woman whose hatred to the British name incited them to efforts not to be surpassed in the annals of the mutiny. He and his gallant comrades had accomplished these great deeds during a season the terrible heat of which far surpassed the heat of the corresponding season of previous years, and under a sun which proved scarcely less deadly than the enemy.* Yet moving steadily onwards,

Summary of the campaign.

structed; the specimens of brass shell cast by them were faultless. . . . In the arsenal were about sixty thousand pounds of gunpowder, outside it were large heaps of shot and shell ranged after the fashion of our own. . . . It would appear . . . . that the enemy had prepared for a long stand here."—Lowe's *Central India.*

* Dr. Lowe thus describes the condition of officers and men from the effects of the sun, when they entered Kálpi. "Most of the officers and men were sick, and the whole force needed rest. The general himself was very ill; his chief of the staff, Colonel Wetherall, C.B., was in a raving fever; his quartermaster-general, Captain Macdonald, was worn out, and among the list of those going away; the chaplain of the force, the Rev. Mr. Schwabbe, had lost his reason and was apparently sinking fast; and other officers, wounded or exhausted by their long and arduous duties and disease, brought on by these and the terrible sun, had been ordered to England."

Book XIV. Chapter I.

1858. May.

regarding difficulties as only obstacles to be overcome, keeping in view the goal at which he aimed, Sir Hugh had marched from victory to victory. It may be said of him that it was his character which created his success. Careless of himself, he conducted every reconnaissance, he planned every action, he was foremost in every attack, he courted danger and exposure. At the same time, no leader ever paid greater attention to the soldiers. To look after their comforts, to see, after a hard-fought action, that the wounded were attended to, and, after a long and tedious march, that provisions were abundant, was with him a sacred duty. It was this which endeared him to the troops; this that made them fight cheerily against numbers, endure the killing rays of the fierce sun. If he demanded all their energies on the battle-field, they saw that their wants were attended to when the battle was over; that he never spared himself; that with all the cares of command upon him, he managed to find time to attend to them. It was that sympathy which evoked the enthusiasm which enabled the soldiers of Sir Hugh Rose to equal the achievements of any warriors of whom history makes record.

Sir Hugh Rose's "character created his success."

The campaign now appeared over. Its every object had been accomplished. Sir Colin Campbell, sharing that opinion, wrote to Sir Robert Hamilton a letter explaining the mode in which the several corps of the Central India Field Force were to be cantoned, and adding, with regard to Whitlock's force, that "it would be otherwise em-

The campaign appears concluded.

Book XIV. Chapter I.

1858. May.

ployed as a movable division." The general who had conducted the campaign was about to dissolve the force and to proceed to a cooler climate for the recovery of his health. How all these arrangements were suddenly altered I shall tell in another chapter. Meanwhile it is my duty to record the operations of the other column, which, with Jabalpúr as its base, had been directed to move on Bandá, subduing the rebel rájás on its route.

BOOK XIV.

CHAPTER II.

On the 16th of November 1857 Brigadier-General Whitlock of the Madras army was appointed to the command of a division for service in the Nágpúr, Ságar, and Narbadá territories. His force was to consist of an artillery brigade composed of two troops of horse artillery and three companies of foot artillery, with two light field-batteries attached, commanded by Lieutenant-Colonel W. H. Miller; of a cavalry brigade composed of the 12th Lancers and the 6th and 7th Madras Light Cavalry, commanded by Colonel A. W. Lawrence; of one brigade of infantry composed of the 3rd Madras Europeans and the 1st and 5th Madras Native Infantry, commanded by Colonel Carpenter, M.A.; of a second infantry brigade composed of the 43rd Light Infantry and the 19th and left wing of the 50th Madras Native Infantry, commanded by Colonel McDuff, 74th Highlanders. There were also

The composition of General Whitlock's force.

Book XIV. Chapter II.

1858. Jan.-Feb.

details of sappers and miners. The force was to be massed at Jabalpúr, and to march thence towards Bandá.

The force at Jabalpúr is directed

A small force, previously detached from the Madras Presidency or serving in the central Provinces, was already at Jabalpúr.* This force consisted of six hundred and fifty men of the 33rd Madras Native Infantry under Colonel Miller; one hundred and twenty men 28th Madras Native Infantry, under Lieutenant Standen; one hundred and twenty men of the 1st Nágpúr Rifles†; three hundred men 4th Madras Light Cavalry under Lieutenant-Colonel Cumberlege; three hundred men 6th Madras Light Cavalry under Lieutenant-Colonel Byng; one hundred and fifty men 2nd Nizám's Cavalry under Captain Macintire; a total of eight hundred and ninety infantry and seven hundred and fifty cavalry. This small column had orders to halt at Jabalpúr pending the arrival of General Whitlock and his force.

to halt pending Whitlock's arrival.

General Whitlock reached Kámpti on the 10th of January. He was unable, from various causes, to leave that place till the 23rd of the same month. Setting out on that date, he arrived at Jabalpúr on the 6th of February.‡ Part of his 1st brigade reached on the 6th, the remainder a few days later.

Whitlock reaches Jabalpúr.

On the 17th of February General Whitlock,

* *Vide* page 103 of this volume.

† The Nágpúr local force had been rearmed by Mr. Plowden.

‡ The distance is one hundred and forty-eight miles.

Book XIV. Chapter II.

1858. Feb.-March.

leaving a small garrison in Jabalpúr, soon to be increased by the arrival of Brigadier McDuff's brigade to a tolerable strength, set out for Ságar. He moved in the direction of Jakháni with the object of overawing the mutinous landowners in the Réwah district. He reached that place, previously captured by Willoughby Osborne, on the 24th, and was there met by the loyal rájá of Úrchah. Halting here one day, he set out on the 26th for Damoh, and arrived there on the 4th of March. It is worthy of remark that during this march of fifteen days General Whitlock, though strongly urged by Major Erskine, the political officer accompanying his force, to drive the rebels from the strong places they occupied, and from which they still continued to harass the districts between Jabalpúr and Damoh, refused to send a single detachment for that purpose from his force. He preferred, he said, to keep it massed in his hand. The result was that, although Whitlock's column secured the ground on which it encamped, scared into submission the villages through which it marched, and even recovered Damoh, it left the population of the districts still occupied by rebels astonished at the regard paid to the latter.

He sets out with part of his force for Ságar.

His movements are characterised by extreme caution.

On the 5th Whitlock rode into Ságar accompanied by some horse artillery and cavalry. Ságar had previously been relieved by Sir Hugh Rose, but on reaching it Whitlock at once sent an express to Damoh for two hundred European and seventy native infantry to come in by forced marches; he also detached a small body of Europeans to

Whitlock reaches Ságar.

Book XIV. Chapter II. — 1858. March.

escort treasure from Jabalpúr, whilst the remainder of the force he kept halted at Damoh under the command of Brigadier Carpenter. He, however, returned and resumed command on the 12th.

Whitlock is ordered to march on Nagod, and to communicate with Sir Hugh Rose.

On the 17th Whitlock, still halted at Damoh, received the Governor-General's orders to march on Nágód and Pannah by way of Hattah, and to afford aid to the loyal rájás of Bandalkhand, notably to the rájá of Chirkári. Lord Canning's despatch further directed Whitlock to communicate his movement to Sir Hugh Rose so as to enable that officer to work in concert with him.

Whitlock reaches Pannah, and halts to obtain information.

In compliance with this order, Whitlock left Damoh on the 22nd of March, and entering Bandalkhand, arrived at Pannah without molestation on the 29th. Evidently a man of extreme caution, Whitlock halted here to obtain information regarding the position of the enemy and the practicability of the roads. The reader, if he refer to the preceding chapter, will see that this was the precise period when the Government would have diverted Sir Hugh Rose from his attack on Jhánsi in order to succour Chirkári, then besieged by Tántia Topi; and that activity on the part of General Whitlock was specially desirable. But none was displayed. The force remained halted at Pannah till the 2nd of April. Whitlock, having by that time come to a resolution, marched it by Marwá Ghát, a road almost impossible for guns and vehicles. So difficult was the road that on reach-

His extreme caution.

Proceeds by a difficult road towards Bandá,

ing Mándalá, at the foot of the pass, Whitlock had to halt for three days to repair damages. Whilst thus halted he received (3rd of April) a despatch from Sir Hugh Rose directing him to move with all expedition upon Jhánsi. The very day on which this despatch reached Whitlock, Rose stormed Jhánsi. Whitlock was unable to leave Mándalá till the 6th of April. He then marched, by way of Chattarpúr, on Bandá, reached Chattarpúr on the 9th, surprised the rebels the following night whilst evacuating the fort of Jhigan, then marched on Mahoba, and thence on Bandá.

still slowly and cautiously,

and eventually reaches Bandá.

The rebel nawáb of Bandá was playing the part of an independent prince in the district which took its name from the chief town. The nawáb had been well supplied with information regarding Whitlock's movements, and judging him to be a man of a cautious and anxious temperament, determined to attempt to lead him into a trap. No sooner, then, had he been certified of the advance of the English general than he directed the troops he had stationed at Mahoba, and which consisted of eight hundred and fifty men of the mutinied 50th Bengal Native Infantry, two hundred men of the 23rd Native Infantry, the 2nd Regiment Irregular Cavalry Gwáliár contingent, and half a battery of guns, to evacuate that place and take up a position in ambush at Kabrai, whence they should fall upon English troops as they would pass it before dawn. At the same time the nawáb took care that Whitlock should be informed that he would encounter no enemy south of Bandá.

The nawáb of Bandá endeavours to draw Whitlock into a trap,

Book XIV. Chapter II.

1858. April.

Had the courage of his troops equalled the cleverness of the nawáb, the plan would have succeeded. Whitlock so far fell into the trap that he believed there were no rebels before him. His troops were actually marching through Kabrai an hour before daybreak when the enemy opened upon them a heavy fire. The surprise was but for a moment. The Horse Artillery, the Lancers, and the Haidarábád Irregulars galloped forward, and soon compelled the rebels to retreat. Unfortunately, in the pursuit which followed, the principal body of the British force took, in the dark, a wrong direction, so that but few of the enemy were cut up. The attempt, however, clearly indicated to Whitlock what was in store for him at Bandá. He pushed on, however, and on the early morning of the 19th found the rebel forces, headed by the nawáb, occupying the plain south of the town, and barring his entrance into it. The nawáb's forces consisted of seven thousand men, of whom rather more than one-third were regular troops. The position he had taken up was strong. The ground was very much intersected by ravines and watercourses, and of these the rebels had taken skilful advantage.

and succeeds. The nawáb's troops surprise the English, but the latter, soon recovering, defeat them.

The nawáb's troops take up a strong position in front of Bandá.

Whitlock had broken up his camp at 4 o'clock on the morning of the 19th. At 5 o'clock his advance guard, commanded by Colonel Apthorp, and consisting of three companies 3rd Madras Europeans, two guns Mein's troop Horse Artillery, some Haidarábád Irregulars under Macintyre, a few of the 12th Lancers, and a detachment 1st Madras Native Infantry, came upon

Where he is attacked by Whitlock.

Book XIV. Chapter II.

1858. April.

the enemy. Apthorp was at once directed to turn the right of the rebel position, whilst the main body should threaten it in front. These orders were carried out to the letter. Apthorp's men had, however, no easy task. It was difficult to get at the rebels. One ravine carried, they were found in force in the next. There must have been much in the nature of the ground to screen human life, for though the fight lasted six hours, from 5 o'clock till noon, the casualties on the British side amounted only to thirty-nine, of whom four were officers. Several deeds of heroism were performed. The coolness of Apthorp was the admiration of everyone. Young Colbeck of the 3rd Europeans met a glorious death leading his men to the charge of the first nullah. Captain Macintire of the Haidarábád cavalry—which lost twenty killed and wounded—greatly distinguished himself, as did likewise Brigadier Miller, M.A., Sergeant-Major Alford of the same regiment, and Captain Clifton, 12th Lancers. At length the position was forced, and the nawáb fled, with two thousand followers, to Kálpi, leaving behind him seventeen guns, the town of Bandá, and a palace filled with property of great value. The rebel loss in the battle was variously estimated at from four to six hundred men. General Whitlock established his head-quarters in Bandá, to wait there till the remainder of his force should join him.

Gallantry of Apthorp, Colbeck, Macintire, Miller, Alford, and Clifton.

The nawáb is completely defeated.

The second brigade, under Brigadier McDuff, reached Jabalpúr on the 18th of March, and set out for Ságar on the 24th. In order, however, to prevent the mutineers from heading backwards

Whitlock is joined by McDuff's brigade.

Book XIV. Chapter II. 1858. May.

into the Mirzápúr district, Whitlock sent instructions to this brigade to change its course and to proceed to Nagód. McDuff, therefore, only reached Bandá on the 27th of May. He found Whitlock still halted there.

Whitlock, on being joined by McDuff's brigade, resolved to march to the assistance of Sir Hugh Rose at Kálpi, and had indicated the 29th as the day of departure on that errand. But Sir Hugh Rose, as we have seen, had completely defeated the rebels before Kálpi on the 23rd, and had entered that place on the 24th of May. Information of this reached Whitlock in time to change his plans regarding Kálpi.

In every particular Sir Hugh Rose had cleared the way for Whitlock.

The reader who has followed me through this and the preceding chapter will not have failed to see how, in every particular, the action of Sir Hugh Rose had cleared the way for the action of General Whitlock. It was Sir Hugh who at Garhákót and on the Bétwah, had disposed of the enemies with whom, but for that, Whitlock would have had to deal. The defeat of Tántia Topi on the Bétwah alone made it possible for Whitlock to march on Bandá. Yet—extraordinary perversity of Fortune!—whilst Sir Hugh and his force endured all the hardships of the campaign and did by far the most important part of the fighting, Whitlock and his little army, up to the time of the capture of Bandá, gained all the substantial advantages. The spoils of Bandá, which would not have been gained but for the action of Sir Hugh Rose, were allotted to Whitlock's force alone!

Perversity of fortune.

The same blind goddess, not content with one perverse distribution of her favours, now set about to perpetrate another. Whitlock had but just renounced his intention to march to the assistance of Sir Hugh Rose at Kálpi, when he received orders from Lord Canning to march against the Ráos of Kírwí.

Whitlock is ordered to march on Kírwí.

Kírwí, formerly better known as Tiróhan, is forty-five miles from Bandá and seventy from Allahábád. The two ráos, who lived there—Náráin Ráo and Madho Ráo—were descendants by adoption of the Péshwá Ragonáth Ráo. On the fall of the Péshwá's dynasty in 1818, Amrat Ráo of Tiróhan, a son of the Péshwá Ragonáth, had entered into an agreement with the British, under which a provision of seven lakhs a year was guaranteed to himself and his son. He selected Tiróhan (Kírwí) for his residence, and there an estate (jaghír) of four thousand six hundred and ninety-one rupees was conferred upon him. On the death of Amrat Ráo's son, Banaik Ráo, the pension of seven lakhs per annum ceased. Banaik Ráo left no natural heirs, but in accordance with the obligations imposed upon him by his religion, he had adopted two boys, Naráin Ráo and Madho Ráo. Though these lads succeeded to considerable accumulations of wealth, they regarded as a grievance the cessation of the pension, authorised though that cessation was by treaty, and these feelings were fostered by the courtiers who fattened upon them, especially by their dewán, Rádho Govind, a man of considerable ability and utter want of scruple. It is

Sketch of Kírwí.

The two ráos of Kírwí.

Their adviser, Rádho Govind, stimulates their disaffection,

Book XIV. Chapter II.

1858. May.

scarcely to be wondered at, under these circumstances, that when the earlier occurrences of the mutiny in the vicinity of Bandalkhand seemed to presage the fall of the British and the resuscitation of the dynasty of the Péshwá, these young Maráthá nobles should have thrown themselves heart and soul into the cause of their relative, Náná Sáhib, and have joined him in his revolt against the British.

who declare for Náná Sáhib.

Causes which prompted the ráos still to hope after Bandá had fallen.

Up to the third week of May 1858, the two young ráos had enjoyed blissful visions of a fortunate future. Kírwí was for a long time covered from attack by the nawáb of Bandá, and although Bandá fell on the 19th of April, the two ráos saw Whitlock halting at that place, they knew that Tántia Topi was at large, and they believed that Kálpi was impregnable, and would baffle even Sir Hugh Rose. It is true that they wrote to Sir Robert Hamilton, professing loyalty to the British and offering to surrender. But they did not surrender, and the intelligence which reached them shortly afterwards from Bandá, that Whitlock was about to march to join Sir Hugh, confirmed them in their disinclination to take that step.

On hearing that Whitlock is marching on Kálpi; they ride out and surrender.

But when the ráos heard that Sir Hugh, unaided by Whitlock, had taken Kálpi, and that a second brigade had joined Whitlock, they began to tremble. They trembled still more when they learned that, on the 2nd of June, Whitlock had left Bandá to march on their palace. At once their resolution was taken. Resistance they knew to be impossible. On learning, then, that Whit-

Book XIV. Chapter II.

1858. June.

lock had reached Bharatkúp, ten miles from Kírwí, they rode out and surrendered.

By this act the spoils of Kírwí devolve, without fighting, on Whitlock's force.

Whitlock's march on Kirwi had been made possible by the annihilation of the forces of the nawáb of Bandá at Kálpi. That chieftain fled from Bandalkhand, never again, during the war, to reappear within its borders. In him the two ráos lost their only protector, the more important as under his orders had been serving many of their own retainers. Thus it was that once more Fortune had given to Sir Hugh Rose the toil, the exposure, the danger; to General Whitlock the bloodless conquest and the spoils of war!

Enormous amount of treasure found at Kírwí.

For Whitlock, moving from Bandá on the 2nd June,* entered Kírwí without opposition on the 6th, and found there alike proofs of the complicity of the ráos in the rebellion, and enormous treasure. In the palace-yard were more than forty pieces of cannon, of calibres between 18 and 3-pounders; an immense quantity of shot, shell, and powder; two thousand stand of arms with accoutrements complete; muskets and belts belonging to several regiments which had mutinied. The gun-foundries and powder-manufactories had been, up to two days prior to the surrender, working full tides. But in the palace itself was stored the wherewithal to compensate soldiers for many a hard fight and many a broiling sun, but in this case gained without a shot. In its vaults and strong-rooms were specie, jewels, and diamonds of priceless value!

* The very day on which, it will be seen, one of Sir Hugh's columns started to encounter more dangers at Gwáliár.

Book XIV. Chapter II.

1858. June.

The right to the booty subsequently argued before the High Court of Admiralty.

The question of the proprietary right in this booty, declared to be prize-money, was ultimately argued before the High Court of Admiralty. By this court the claim of Sir Hugh Rose's force to share in the prize, which had come into British possession mainly in consequence of his action, was rejected; the claims of the commanders of other co-operating but independent divisions and columns were rejected; the claims of the Commander-in-Chief in India and of his staff, who were hundreds of miles from the spot, and whose action did not influence the capture, and the claims of the officers and men of General Whitlock's force, were admitted to an exclusive right in the prize of Bandá and Kírwí.

Its decision.

After the capture of Kírwí, Whitlock's force was distributed so as to maintain order in the Bandalkhand and Jamná districts. A portion was sent to Kálpi on the requisition of Sir H. Rose; one was left at Kírwí, other portions were sent to Mohába, Jaláon, Bandá, Kirka, Ságar, Damoh, and Hamirpúr. The general's head-quarters were fixed at Mahóba. Here we must leave him, to return to Tántia Topi and Sir Hugh Rose.

BOOK XIV.

CHAPTER III.

Movements of Tántia Topi, the ráni of Jhánsi, and Ráo Sáhib after the fall of Kálpi.

It has already been related that Tántia Topi, after his defeat at Kúnch, had fled to Chirki—about four miles from Jaláor—where his parents resided. He remained there during Sir Hugh Rose's march to Kálpi, and the events which led to the capture of that place. Learning that Ráo Sáhib and the ráni of Jhánsi had fled, after their defeat at Galáoli, towards Gopálpúr, forty-six miles south-west of Gwáliár, Tántia girded up his loins and joined them at that place.

Desperate condition of their affairs.

Their affairs seemed desperate. Not only had they lost their hold on central India, on the Ságar and Narbadá territories and on Bandalkhand, but their enemies were closing in on every side; Roberts had already detached from Rajpútáná a brigade under Colonel Smith to co-operate with Sir Hugh Rose; the force under that officer was at Kálpi, about to be distributed n the territories west of the Jamná; Whitlock,

Book XIV. Chapter III.

1858. May.

having conquered Bandá, had Kírwí at his mercy. On three sides, then, on the south, the east, and the west, they were encompassed by foes. Nor towards the north did the prospect look brighter. There lay the capital of Maharájá Sindia, overlooked by a wall-girt and almost inaccessible rock. Sindia was not less their enemy than were the British. In the darkest hour of their fortunes, at a time when hostility seemed to promise him empire, Sindia had remained faithful to his suzerain. It was not to be thought of, nor was it thought possible, that in the mid-day of their triumph he would turn against them.

Surrounded by enemies.

Desperate remedy suggested,

The situation then seemed desperate to the rebel chieftains. But desperate situations suggest desperate remedies; and a remedy which, on first inspection, might well seem desperate, did occur to the fertile brain of one of the confederates. To which one it is not certainly known. But, judging the leading group of conspirators by their antecedents—Ráo Sáhib, the nawáb of Bandá, Tántia Topi, and the ráni of Jhánsi—we may at once dismiss the two first from consideration. They possessed neither the character nor the genius to conceive a plan so vast and so daring. Of the two who remain, we may dismiss Tántia Topi. Not that he was incapable of forming the design, but—we have his memoirs—and in those he takes to himself no credit for the most successful act with which his career is associated. The fourth conspirator possessed the genius, the daring, the despair necessary for the conception of great deeds. She was urged on by hatred, by

probably by the ráni of Jhánsi.

desire of vengeance, by a blood-stained conscience, by a determination to strike hard whilst there was yet a chance. She could recognise the possibilities before her, she could hope even that if the first blow were successful the fortunes of the campaign might be changed; she possessed and exercised unbounded influence over one, at least, of her companions—the Ráo Sáhib. The conjecture, then, almost amounts to certainty that the desperate remedy which the confederates decided to execute at Gopálpúr was suggested and pressed upon her comrades by the daring ráni of Jhánsi.

Book XIV. Chapter III.

1858. May.

Her plan.

The plan was this. To march on Gwáliár by forced marches, appeal to the religious and national feeling of Sindia's troops, take possession of his capital, by force if it were necessary, and, gaining over his army, bid defiance to the British from the precipitous rock of the Gwáliár fortress!

The confederates accept it, and march on Gwáliár.

The scheme was no sooner accepted than acted upon. Emissaries proceeded in advance of the column to tamper with and, if possible, to gain over Sindia's troops; the column followed more leisurely, yet with a celerity adapted to the occasion, and reached the Morar cantonment, formerly occupied by the contingent, in close vicinity to Gwáliár, during the night of the 30th of May.

Mahárájá Sindia.

Mahárájá Sindia was informed that night of the arrival of his dangerous visitors. Probably no prince had ever been placed in circumstances of stronger temptation than was Jaiaji Ráo Sindia during 1857–58. The descendant by adoption and the representative of the family of the famous

Book XIV. Chapter III.

1858. May.

His great influence.

Mádháji Ráo Sindia, of the Dáolat Ráo Sindia who had fought for the possession of India with the two Wellesleys, he was still the most considerable chief of the Maráthá race; and his word, if spoken for religion and race, would have found a response all over central and western India.

For four months he had the fate of India in his hands.

For four months he had probably the fate of India in his hands. Had he revolted in June, the siege of Dehlí must have been raised, Ágra and Lakhnáo would have fallen; it is more than probable that the Panjáb would have risen. That, under such circumstances, possessing strong military instincts and chafing under a great ambition, Sindia should have remained loyal, is most weighty testimony to the character of the English overlordship, and to its appreciation by the princes of India.

Probable reasons for his loyalty.

That Sindia was greatly influenced in the course he followed by his shrewd minister, rájá Dinkar Ráo, and by the appeals from the fort of A'gra of the able British representative at his court, Major Charters Macpherson, may be admitted. But neither Sindia nor Dinkar Ráo liked the English personally. Both the one and the other would have preferred an independent Gwáliár. But though they did not like the English personally, they had great respect for the English character. Recollecting the state of north-western and central and western India prior to the rule of Marquess Wellesley, they could feel, under the English overlordship, a sense of security such as their fathers and their fathers' fathers had never possessed. They had, at least, secure possession of their holdings. No one from outside would venture to molest

Book XIV. Chapter III.

1858. May.

them as their ancestors had been molested. The question, then, would rise—and it was in answering this that the influence of Major Charters Macpherson came most beneficially into play—"Granting that, by joining the mutineers, we could confine the English to Bengal, would Gwáliár gain by their expulsion? It is doubtful: there would be many competitors for supremacy, and—who knows? The King of Dehlí might, with the aid of the sepoys, become supreme, or the Sikhs of the Panjáb, or Náná Sáhib, or perhaps even Holkar! The risk is too great, for, adhering to the English, we shall be safe in the end."

In some such manner reasoned Sindia and Dinkar Ráo. They argued the question in the light of the interests of Sindia, and in that light, held ever before them by the steady hand of Charters Macpherson, they cast in their lot with the British.

The same reasons do not affect the bulk of the Maráthá people.

But not in this manner reasoned many of the great families of Gwáliár, the bulk of the army and of the people. These men could recognise only what was passing before their eyes. They never attempted even to open the book of the future. They could only see, in 1857, the British power struck down, and an opportunity offering itself to their master such as the great Mádháji would have given half his years to have had a glimpse of. They could not understand Sindia's inaction, his attempts to befriend the British in the hour of their adversity. They sympathised with the men of his contingent when they revolted and

Book XIV. Chapter III.

1858. May.

Who, in consequence, vent their discontent on Sindia.

murdered their officers. The higher and more influential amongst them assailed Sindia with persuasions and entreaties; and when they found these fail, they began even to talk of dethroning him and setting up another mahárájá in his place.

The fall of Dehlí, the British successes in Lakhnao and in north-western and central India, had by no means changed these sentiments. The irritation caused by lost opportunities had produced a state of mind eager to grasp at any chance to mend the situation or to be rid of it.

Sindia hears of Tántia Topi's arrival at Morár,

Such was the state of general feeling in Gwáliár when, on the night of the 30th of May, information was brought to the mahárájá that Tántia Topi, the ráni of Jhánsi, and other chieftains, with a force estimated at seven thousand infantry, four thousand cavalry, and twelve guns, had reached Morár. No one knew better the general state of feeling about him than the mahárájá.

and resolves to do battle with him.

But he never wavered. The conviction of the ultimate triumph of the English was never stronger within him than at this apparently inauspicious moment, and, notwithstanding the ill-concealed hostility of many of his adherents, he determined to seize the offered opportunity and do battle with the rebels.

He marches to meet Tántia,

Accordingly, at daybreak on the 1st of June, he marched out and took up a position about two miles to the eastward of Morár. He had with him six thousand infantry, about one thousand five hundred cavalry, his own bodyguard six hundred strong, and eight guns. These he ranged

Book XIV. Chapter III.

1858. June.

in three divisions, his guns in the centre, and waited for the attack. About 7 o'clock in the morning the rebels advanced, covered by mounted skirmishers, with camels carrying guns of small calibre. As they approached, Sindia's eight guns opened on them. But the smoke of the discharge had scarcely disappeared when the rebel skirmishers closed to their flanks, and two thousand horsemen, charging at a gallop, carried the guns. Simultaneously with their charge, Sindia's infantry and cavalry, his bodyguard alone excepted, either joined the rebels or took up a position indicative of their intention not to fight. The rebel cavalry, pushing their advantage, then attacked the bodyguard, with which was Sindia himself. A portion of the guardsmen defended themselves with great gallantry, and did not cease to fight till many of their number had fallen. It becoming more and more apparent that it was useless to continue the unequal contest, Sindia turned and fled, accompanied by a very few of the survivors. He did not draw rein till he reached Ágra.

is completely defeated,

and flees to A'gra.

The first part of the ráni's bold plan had thus succeeded. She and her confederates delayed not a moment to carry it out to its legitimate consequences. They entered Gwáliár, took possession of the fortress, the treasury, the arsenal, and the town, and began at once to form a regular government. Náná Sáhib was proclaimed as Péshwá, and Ráo Sáhib as governor of Gwáliár. Plentiful largesses were distributed to the army, alike to the Gwáliár troops as to those who had come

The rebels enter Gwáliár,

and form a government there,

Book XIV. Chapter III.

1858. June.

and prepare to hold the place and the surrounding territories.

from Kálpi. Rám Ráo Govind, one of Sindia's disgraced courtiers, was appointed prime minister. The royal property was declared confiscated. Four Maráthá chiefs, who had been imprisoned by Sindia for rebellion, were released, clothed with dresses of honour, and sent into the districts to raise troops to oppose the British in any attempts they might make to cross the Chambal. The command of the bulk of the troops, encamped outside the city, was entrusted to the ráni of Jhánsi. Those within the town obeyed the orders of Tántia Topi. Letters were at once despatched to the rebel rájás still in the district, notably to the rájás of Bánpúr and Sháhgarh, to join at Gwáliár.

The story returns to Sir Hugh Rose.

The intelligence of the success of this audacious enterprise reached Kálpi on the 3rd of June. Before I refer to the action taken by Sir Hugh Rose, it is necessary that I should state the exact positions of the various portions of the force with which he had conquered Kálpi on the 24th of May.

His action after the defeat of the rebels at Kálpi.

As soon as, by the occupation of Kálpi on the 24th of May, Sir Hugh Rose had discovered the flight of the rebels, he sent out parties to discover the line they had taken. Information was soon brought to him that whilst a few had crossed the Jamná into the Doáb, whilst a few more had been checked in attempting the same course by Colonel Riddell,* the main body had bent their

* Colonel Riddell, who was moving down the north bank of the Jamná with the 3rd Bengal Europeans, Alexander's horse, and two guns, caught sight of a body of the rebels escaping from Kálpi, a few miles above that place, on the

Book XIV. Chapter III.

1858. June.

steps in almost a south-westerly direction to Gopálpúr. To pursue these latter he at once organised a column composed of the 25th Bombay native infantry, the 3rd Bombay light cavalry, and one hundred and fifty Haidarábád cavalry, and despatched it, under the command of Colonel Robertson, on the track of the rebels.

Robertson pushes on in pursuit of the rebels.

Robertson set out from Kálpi on the 25th of May, the rain falling heavily. This rain, which continued throughout that day and the day following, much impeded his progress. He pushed on, however, as fast as possible, and traversing Mahona and Indúrki, found that the rebels were but little in advance of him. At Iráwan, reached on the 29th, supplies ran short, and as none were procurable in the district, the column had to wait till they could be sent up from Kálpi. On the 2nd of June, Robertson received these and was joined by two squadrons of the 14th light dragoons, a wing of the 86th foot, and four 9-pounders. The following day he reached Moházar, fifty-five miles from Gwáliár. Here he was startled by information of the attack made by the rebels on Gwáliár and of its result.

south bank of the river, on the 25th of May. He instantly sent the 3rd Europeans across, who captured their camp equipage, the enemy not waiting to receive them. Colonel Riddell's force had previously had several skirmishes with detached parties of insurgents. A small party of his troops had proceeded to Kálpi in boats, joining there Sir Hugh Rose. On their way they were threatened by a numerous body of rebels near Bhijalpúr. Lieutenant Sherriff, who commanded the party, had at once landed 150 men, defeated the rebels, and captured four guns.

Book XIV. Chapter III.

1858. June.

Sir Hugh learns that the rebels are moving on Gwáliár, and at once despatches Stuart's brigade in that direction.

An express from Robertson, sent from Iráwan, and which reached Kálpi on the 1st of June, gave Sir Hugh the first information that the rebels had taken the road to Gwáliár. Instantly Sir Hugh despatched General Stuart with the remainder of his brigade, consisting of the other wing of the 86th foot, a wing of the 71st Highlanders, four companies of the 25th Bengal native infantry, one squadron 14th light dragoons, No. 4 light field battery, two 18-pounders, one 8-inch howitzer, and some sappers, to join Robertson, and to march on Gwáliár. Stuart reached Attakóna on the 3rd—the day on which Robertson had reached Mohárar—and there he too received the first information of the startling occurrences at Gwáliár.

No one divined that the daring of the rebels would be successful.

The order which had sent Stuart to Gwáliár was dictated by a sound military instinct. But no one, not even Sir Hugh Rose, had imagined the height of daring to which the ráni of Jháusi would carry her audacious plans. The rebels might march on Gwáliár, but no one believed they would carry it by a *coup-de-main*. It seemed more likely that they were marching into a trap, to be kept there till Stuart's force should fall on their rear.

The effect of its success upon Sir Hugh Rose.

How the impossible happened has been told. The information of it reached Sir Hugh on the 4th of June, after he had resigned his command and applied for leave on medical certificate. In a moment he realised the full danger of the situation. Gwáliár had fallen into the hands of the

Book XIV. Chapter III. 1858. June.

rebels at the time of year most unfavourable for military operations. Another week, and the monsoon rains would render the black soil untraversable by guns, and would swell the rivers. Under those circumstances, the transport of siege-guns, in the absence of pontoons, which Sir Hugh did not possess, would be most difficult if not impossible. He realised, moreover, the great danger which would inevitably be caused by delay. No one could foresee the extent of evil possible if Gwáliár were not promptly wrested from rebel hands. Grant them delay, and Tántia Topi, with the immense acquisition of political and military strength secured by the possession of Gwáliár, and with all its resources in men, money, and material at his disposal, would be able to form a new army on the ruins of that beaten at Kálpi, and to provoke a Maráthá rising throughout India. It might be possible for him, using the dexterity of which he was a master, to unfurl the Peshwá's banner in the southern Maráthá districts. Those districts were denuded of troops, and a striking success in central India would probably decide their inhabitants to pronounce in favour of the cause for which their fathers had fought and bled.

He realises the enormous issues at stake.

Thus reasoning, Sir Hugh considered, and rightly considered, that the time for ceremony had passed. He at once resumed the command which he had laid down,* and leaving a small garrison

He resumes his command

* It is said that for this breach of red tape rules Sir Hugh was severely reprimanded by Sir C. Campbell. Undoubtedly strict routine required the previous sanc-

Book XIV. Chapter III.

1858. June.

at Kálpi, set out on the 5th of June with a small force* to overtake Stuart's column.

and sets out for Gwáliár.

The Commander-in-Chief places other columns at Sir Hugh's disposal.

With a view to aid Sir Hugh in his operations against Gwáliár, the Commander-in-Chief placed at his disposal, by telegraph, Colonel Riddell's column previously referred to, and Brigadier Smith's brigade of the Rájpútáná field force. The only other troops of which it was possible for Sir Hugh to avail himself, were those composing the small garrison of Jhánsi, under Lieutenant-Colonel Hicks of the artillery; and the Haidarábád contingent, commanded by Major Orr.

Noble conduct of the Haidarábád contingent.

The Haidarábád contingent, after their hard and splendid service, had received orders to return home. They had already started; many of them, indeed, were far advanced on their road. But the moment the intelligence of the events passing at Gwáliár reached them, they one and all expressed their earnest desire to take part in the operations of their old commander.

Sir Hugh's plan of operations against Gwáliár.

Whilst Sir Hugh Rose himself proceeded by forced marches to join Stuart, he directed Major Orr to move to Paniar, on the road between Sípri and Gwáliár, to cut off the retreat of the rebels to the south; and Brigadier Smith, who was near Chandairi, to march with his brigade direct to Kotah-ki-serai, about five miles to the south-east of Gwáliár. To Colonel Riddell,

tion of the Commander-in-Chief. But there are circumstances which require that strict routine must be laid aside; and this was one of them.

* 1st troop Bombay horse artillery; one squadron 14th light dragoons; one squadron 3rd Bombay light cavalry; Madras sappers and miners.

Book XIV. Chapter III.

1858. June.

escorting a large supply of siege-guns, he sent instructions to move with his column by the Ágra and Gwáliár road. He hoped that all the column of operations would be at their posts by the 19th of June.

Sir Hugh overtakes Stuart and reaches Morar;

Setting out, as I have said, on the 6th of June, and making forced marches in spite of a heat which occasionally rose to one hundred and thirty degrees in the shade, Sir Hugh overtook Stuart at Indúrki on the 12th, and still pushing on, reached Bahádurpúr, five miles to the east of the Morár cantonments on the 16th. There he was joined by Brigadier-General Robert Napier, whom we last heard of at the storm of Lakhnao, and who at once assumed command of the 2nd brigade.*

is joined by General Napier;

Sir Hugh had reached Bahádurpúr at 6 o'clock in the morning of the 16th of June. He at once directed Captain Abbott with his Haidarábád cavalry to reconnoitre Morár. On receiving Abbott's report that the rebels were in force in front of it, Sir Hugh galloped forward himself to examine the position. He noticed that the side of the cantonments fronting the British position was occupied by strong bodies of cavalry, flanked to the right by guns, supported by infantry in considerable numbers.

reconnoitres the rebel position.

The position offered strong temptations to a commander who knew the value of time and promptitude in war, and who considered that

Reasons which decided him to attack,

* Only a small portion of this brigade was present; the bulk of it having been left at Kálpi.

Book XIV. Chapter III. — 1858. June.

minor difficulties must give way when a chance should present itself of overcoming a great obstacle. The effect produced on Sir Hugh Rose by his examination of the position of the rebels before Morar, I shall tell in his own words.

told in his own words.

"My force had had a long and fatiguing march, and the sun had been up for some time. Four or five miles' more march in the sun, and a combat afterwards, would be a great trial for the men's strength. On the other hand, Morar looked inviting with several good buildings not yet burnt; they would be good quarters for a portion of the force; if I delayed the attack until the next day, the enemy were sure to burn them. A prompt attack has always more effect on the rebels than a procrastinated one. I therefore countermanded the order for encamping and made the following arrangements to attack the enemy." *

The battle of Morar.

He attacked them accordingly. Placing his cavalry and guns on his flanks, and the infantry in the centre, he took ground to the right, the 86th leading the way, with the view of coming upon the road leading to cantonments, and the occupation of which would have turned the left of the rebels. Sindia's agent, however, who had promised to lead the troops to this road, lost his way, and Rose found himself in front of a masked battery in the enemy's centre. This at once opened upon the assailants, and its fire was rapidly

The guide loses his way, and the army debouches on the wrong front;

* Despatch of Sir Hugh Rose dated the 13th of October 1858.

followed by a musketry and artillery fire from both sides of it. Sir Hugh answered with his guns, at the same time pushing forward his infantry to gain the required turning position on the right. This once gained, he formed to the front, and, re-inforcing his left, which bore for a moment the whole weight of the enemy, pushed forward. The advance was decisive. The enemy limbered up and gave way on all sides. The gallant Ab-bott with his Haidarábád men had, meanwhile, galloped across the nullahs, further to the right, and dashing through the cantonments at a more northerly point, endeavoured to cut off the retreat of the rebels. But the broken ground he had had to traverse had enabled these to take their guns across the stone bridge which spans the river at the back of the cantonment on the road to the city. The main body of the enemy, driven through the cantonments, fell back on a dry nullah with high banks, running round a village, which they had also occupied. Here they maintained a desperate hand-to-hand struggle with the British. The 71st Highlanders suffered severely, Lieutenant Neave, whilst leading them, falling mortally wounded; nor was it till the nullah was nearly choked with dead that the village was carried. On this occasion Lieutenant Rose of the 25th Bombay native infantry greatly distinguished himself. The victory was completed by a successful pursuit of the rebels by Captain Thompson, 14th light dragoons, with a wing of his regiment. The wing of the rebel force which he destroyed

but, by a masterly movement, gains a firm position.

The rebels fall back,

and continue the contest in a village,

which is at length carried;

and the victory is completed by a successful pursuit of the rebels.

Book XIV. Chapter III.

1858. June.

had been turned by Abbott's advance already spoken of; Thompson, following them up, caught them in the plains and made a great slaughter of them. The guns were splendidly commanded during the day by Strutt, always to the front, and by Lightfoot.

Result of the battle.

The result, then, had justified Sir Hugh's daring. Not only had he dealt a heavy blow to the rebels, but he had gained a most important strategical point.

Brigadier Smith advances from the south-east,

Sir Hugh Rose's success was speedily followed by an exploit on the part of Brigadier Smith, fruitful in important consequences. That gallant soldier, coming up from the south-east, had to make his way through the difficult and hilly ground on that side of Gwáliár before he could reach Kotah-ki-serai. Picking up on his way the small field-force from Jhánsi, he reached A'ntri, with his brigade,* on the 14th of June, and was joined there the following day by Major Orr and his Haidarábád men. Under orders from Sir Hugh Rose, Smith marched from Ántri early on the morning of the 17th of June, and reached Kotah-ki-serai, five miles to the south-east of Gwáliár, at half-past 7 o'clock that morning.

and reaches Kotah-ki-serai;

Smith had met no opposition in marching into Kotah-ki-serai, but on reaching that place he observed masses of the ememy's horse and foot

discovers the rebels massed between him and Gwáliár.

* The brigade was thus composed: a wing 8th hussars, a wing Bombay lancers, H. M.'s 95th foot, the 10th Bombay native infantry, and a troop of Bombay horse artillery.

1858. June.

occupying the hilly ground between himself and Gwáliár. As these masses showed a strong disposition to attack him, and as, hampered with a large quantity of baggage, Smith did not regard his position as a very secure one, he determined to take the initiative. Reconnoitring the ground in front of him, he found it very difficult, intersected with nullahs and impracticable for cavalry. He discovered, moreover, that the enemy's guns were in position about one thousand five hundred yards from Kotah-ki-serai, and that their line lay under the hills, crossing the road to Gwáliár. Notwithstanding this, Smith determined to attack. First, he sent his horse artillery to the front, and silenced the enemy's guns, which limbered up and retired. This accomplished, Smith sent his infantry across the broken ground, led by Raines of the 95th. Raines led his men, covered by skirmishers, to a point about fifty yards from the enemy's works, when the skirmishers made a rush—the rebels falling back as they did so. Raines then found himself stopped by a deep ditch with four feet of water, and having banks so steep that it was with difficulty the men could cross in single file. The rebels took advantage of the delay thus caused to move off with their guns and to retire up the ravines and across the hills. Raines found them so retiring when, after surmounting the difficulty I have recorded, he gained the abandoned intrenchment. Whilst he was continuing his advance across the broken and hilly ground, Smith moved his cavalry across the river Úmrah, close to Kotah-ki-serai. They

Difficult nature of the ground before him;

he nevertheless resolves to attack.

Raines leads the infantry to the front,

and, after overcoming many obstacles,

gains the intrenchment abandoned by the enemy.

Meanwhile Smith moves forward the cavalry.

Book XIV. Chapter III.

1858. June.

had hardly crossed when they came under fire of a battery which till then had escaped notice. At the same time a body of the enemy threatened the baggage at Kotah-ki-serai. Matters now became serious. But Smith sent back detachments to defend the baggage and rear, and pushed forward. The road, before debouching from the hills between his position and Gwáliár, ran for several hundred yards through a defile along which a canal had been excavated. It was while his troops were marching through this defile that the principal fighting took place. Having gained the further end of the defile, where he joined Raines, Smith halted the infantry to guard it, and ordered a cavalry charge. This was most gallantly executed by a squadron of the 8th hussars, led by Colonel Hicks and Captain Heneage. The rebels, horse and foot, gave way before them. The hussars captured two guns, and continuing the pursuit through Sindia's cantonment, had for a moment the rebel camp in their possession.

Serious natnre of the action.

At length Smith is victorious,

and drives the rebels before him.

Death of the ráni of Jhánsi.

Amongst the fugitives in the rebel ranks was the resolute woman who, alike in council and on the field, was the soul of the conspirators. Clad in the attire of a man and mounted on horseback, the ráni of Jhánsi might have been seen animating her troops throughout the day. When inch by inch the British troops pressed through the pass, and when reaching its summit Smith ordered the hussars to charge, the ráni of Jhánsi boldly fronted the British horsemen.

When her comrades failed her, her horse, in spite of her efforts, carried her along with the others. With them she might have escaped but that her horse, crossing the canal near the cantonment, stumbled and fell. A hussar, close upon her track, ignorant of her sex and her rank, cut her down. She fell to rise no more. That night her devoted followers, determined that the English should not boast that they had captured her even dead, burned the body.

Book XIV. Chapter III.

1858. June.

Thus died the ráni of Jhánsi. My opinion of her has been recorded in a preceding page. Whatever her faults in British eyes may have been, her countrymen will ever remember that she was driven by ill-treatment into rebellion, and that she lived and died for her country.*

Smith falls back for the night on the head of the defile.

The charge of the 8th hussars was the last effort of Smith's force. "Upon the return of the squadron, the officers and men were so completely exhausted and prostrated from heat, fatigue, and great exertion, that they could scarcely sit in their saddles, and were, for the moment, incapable of further exertion."† But the enemy, recovering, were again threatening. Smith then determined to content himself with holding the defile, the road, and adjoining hills for the night. He drew back his cavalry accordingly, and brought up his baggage. The enemy held their ground on the heights on the other side of the canal.

* *Vide* pages 158, 204–5 of this volume, and pages 181–82 of volume i.

† Brigadier Smith's report.

Book XIV. Chapter III.

1858. June.

Dangerous nature of his position.

Sir Hugh reinforces him.

The position taken up by Brigadier Smith was still far from satisfactory. It left his left and rear threatened, his baggage within range of the enemy's guns, and his whole force cramped. Sir Hugh, on receiving an account of the action, with characteristic promptitude, despatched Colonel Robertson, with the 25th Bombay native infantry, three troops 14th light dragoons, and four guns, to reinforce him.

The 2nd brigade joins Sir Hugh, who resolves to "finish" with the rebels.

The next day Sir Hugh was reinforced and his 2nd brigade brought to its full strength by the arrival of the Kálpi garrison. This arrival left him free to act.

Leaving Napier in Morar with the troops he could spare,* he marched in the afternoon with the rest of the force to join Smith. The distance was long, the heat terrible, the march harassing in the extreme. No less than a hundred men of the 86th were struck down by the sun.† Nevertheless, Sir Hugh pushed on, and bivouacked for the night on the rocky ground between the river and Smith's position.

Harassing nature of his march.

He opens communications with Smith.

* These were—One troop Bombay horse artillery, three troops 14th light dragoons, three troops 3rd Bombay light cavalry, fifty men 1st Haidarábád cavalry, 3rd Haidarábád cavalry, two squadrons Meade's horse, 21st company Royal Engineers, wing 3rd Bombay Europeans, four companies 24th Bombay native infantry, three guns Haidarábád artillery.

† Of these men, Sir Hugh reports that they "were compelled by sun-sickness to fall out and go into dhoolies. These same men, the next day, unmindful of their illness, fell in with their companies, and took part in the assault of Gwáliár." These men, be it remembered, formed part of the unreformed British army, an army never equalled by any other in the world.

Book XIV. Chapter III.

1858. June.

Resolves to anticipate the rebels' attack and to cut them off from Gwáliár.

The first thing that struck Sir Hugh on reconnoitring the following morning was the possibility of cutting off the main body of the enemy from Gwáliár by forcing their left; the next, the extremely cramped and dangerous nature of his own position. The rebels, too, showed every indication that they intended an attack, for with the early dawn they began a heavy fire from their guns, whilst masses of their infantry were seen moving to positions from which they could manœuvre with advantage against the British position. On the principle, then, that an attack is the best defence, Sir Hugh resolved to become the assailant.

Sir Hugh sends Stuart to turn the left of the rebels,

whilst Raines makes a diversion.

The rebels, as we have seen, were occupying the heights separated by the canal from those gained by Brigadier Smith. That they meant to attack was evident. They spent the early hours of the morning in strengthening their right with the view of attacking the weakest point of the British line, the left. Soon an express arrived from Sir Robert Hamilton to say that he had received certain information that an attack was intended that day. There was no time for further consideration. Sir Hugh then directed Brigadier Stuart to move with the 86th regiment, supported by the 25th Bombay native infantry, across the canal, to crown the heights on the other side of it, and to attack the left flank of the rebels. As a diversion in favour of this attack he sent Colonel Raines with the 95th regiment from his right front, across the canal in skirmishing order over the shoulder of

Book XIV. Chapter III. — 1858. June.

the hill on which the rebels had intrenched some guns. This movement was supported by the 10th Bombay native infantry. Sir Hugh at the same time ordered up the 3rd troop Bombay horse artillery, supported by a squadron of the 8th hussars, to the entrance of the pass towards Gwáliár. The remainder of the force he disposed in support of the attacking columns and for the defence of the camp from the rear.

Stuart's attack

Lieutenant-Colonel Lowth led the 86th, in accordance with the orders he received, against the left of the rebels. These fell back rapidly on the battery; while the 86th pressed them so hard that they made no stand even under their guns. The 86th gave them no time to rally,

succeeds.

but dashing with a cheer at the parapet, crossed it, and took the guns which defended the ridge,

Three guns are captured,

three excellent English 9-pounders. Leaving a party with these guns, they pushed on after the fleeing enemy.

which Raines turns on the enemy.

Almost immediately afterwards Raines, advancing with the 95th, came upon the captured guns. Noticing the enemy's cavalry and infantry in detached parties in the plain below at a distance of about a thousand yards, he turned the guns on them and made excellent practice. Meanwhile the 10th Bombay native infantry, led by Lieutenant Roome, moving up in support of the 95th, and protecting the right of the assailing force, found itself exposed to a fire of musketry and artillery from the heights on the enemy's extreme left. Roome was equal to the occasion.

Wheeling to the right, he advanced with half his regiment in skirmishing order, the other half in support, cleared the two nearest heights of rebel infantry, and captured two brass field-pieces and three mortars which were in the plain below.

Book XIV. Chapter III.

1858. June.

Gallantry of Roome and the 10th Bombay native infantry.

The day was now won, the heights were gained; Gwáliár lay, as it were, at the feet of the British. "The sight," writes Sir Hugh, "was interesting. To our right was the handsome palace of the Phúl Bágh with its gardens, and the old city, surmounted by the fort, remarkable for its ancient architecture, with lines of extensive fortifications round the high and precipitous rock of Gwáliár. To our left lay the Lashkar or new city, with its spacious houses half hidden by trees." In the plain between the heights and the city was a great portion of the rebel forces, just driven from the heights, and now, under the influence of panic, endeavouring to seek a refuge in one or other of the walled enclosures or fortified places towards which they were moving.

Gwáliár lies at the feet of the British.

The sight of these men at once suggested to Sir Hugh that it would be possible to complete his work that day. "I felt convinced," he wrote in his despatch, "that I could take Gwáliár before sunset."

Sir Hugh resolves to occupy the city at once.

He at once, then, ordered a general advance. Covering his extreme right with the 3rd troop Bombay horse artillery and a troop of the 8th hussars, he ordered Colonel Owen, with the 1st Bombay lancers, to descend the heights to the rear, make his way into the road which led

Orders a general advance.

Book XIV. Chapter III.

1858. June.

through the hills to the south, and thence attack the grand parade and the new city. Covering his advance, then, with No. 4 light field-battery, and two troops 14th light dragoons, he moved forward his infantry from the left, the 86th leading from that flank, the 95th forming the right.

The British carry the Lashkar.

This prompt advance completely paralysed the rebels. Their guns, indeed, opened fire, but the main object of their infantry seemed to be to escape. The British infantry were approaching the plain, when Owen's lancers, who had gained the point indicated, charged across the grand parade, and, carried away by their ardour, followed the rebels into the Lashkar. In this charge a gallant officer, Lieutenant Mills, was shot through the heart. Raines followed up this charge with a dash on to the parade-ground with two companies of the 95th, and took two 18-pounders and two small pieces. The British line pushing on, the rebels retreated through the town. Before sunset, as Sir Hugh had divined, the Lashkar or new city was completely in his possession. That night, too, Sir Hugh rested in the regained palace of Sindia.

Smith takes the palace of Phill Bágh.

Meanwhile Brigadier Smith had taken the garden palace, the Phúl Bágh, killing great numbers of the rebels. He then, in pursuance of orders, followed up the retreating enemy, and continued the pursuit long after dark, inflicting great loss on them, and capturing most of their guns.

As soon as it was clear the day was won, Sir Hugh sent an express to General Robert Napier, directing him to pursue the rebels as far and as closely as he could. How this order was carried out I shall have to relate presently.

Sir Hugh sends an express to Napier to pursue,

The Lashkar and palace occupied, Sir Hugh, ever careful even of the vanquished, made arrangements for the security of the city. This task he found comparatively easy, for the shopkeeping class has always been on the side of its best paymaster, the British.

and then arranges for the security of the city.

Thus, on the night of the 19th of June, Sir Hugh had, with a loss of eighty-seven men killed and wounded, regained all Gwáliár, the formidable fortress alone excepted. But the exception was a grave one. The rock fortress, completely isolated, having a length of a mile and a half, and a breadth at its broadest part of three hundred yards, its face presenting a perpendicular precipice, might, if well defended, still give some trouble. The guns from its ramparts had maintained, during the operations of the 19th, a continuous, though not very effective, fire on the British troops. The fire recommenced on the morning of the 20th. It was then, early on that morning, that two officers of the Indian army and their Bombay sepoys performed a deed of unsurpassed daring.

The rock fortress defies him.

On the morning of the 20th Lieutenant Rose, 25th Bombay native infantry, was in command with a detachment of his regiment of the kotwáli,

Daring feat of Lieutenants Rose and Waller,

Book XIV. Chapter III.

1858. June.

or police-station, not far from the main gateway of the rock fort. As the guns from its ramparts continued to fire, Rose proposed to a brother officer, Lieutenant Waller, who commanded a small party of the same regiment near him, that they should attempt to capture the fortress with their joint parties, urging that if the risk was great, the honour would be still greater. Waller cheerfully assented, and the two officers set off with their men and a blacksmith, whom, not unwilling, they had engaged for the service. They crept up to the first gateway unseen. Then the blacksmith, a powerful man, forced it open; and so with the other five gates that opposed their progress. By the time the sixth gate had been forced the alarm was given, and when the assailants reached the archway beyond the last gate, they were met by the fire of a gun which had been brought to bear on them. Dashing onwards, unscathed by the fire, they were speedily engaged in a hand-to-hand contest with the garrison. The fight was desperate, and many men fell on both sides. The gallantry of Rose and Waller and their men carried all before them. Rose especially distinguished himself. Just in the hour of victory, however, as he was inciting his men to make the final charge, which proved successful, a musket was fired at him from behind the wall. The man who had fired the shot, a mutineer from Baréli, then rushed out and cut him across the knee and wrist with a sword. Waller came up, and despatched the rebel; too late, however, to

who, with a small following, *attempt to storm the fortress,* *and succeed.* *The success is dimmed by the death of Rose.*

save his friend.* But the rock fortress was gained.

Book XIV. Chapter III.

1858. June.

I have said that when Sir Hugh saw that success was certain, he sent a despatch to Brigadier-General Robert Napier requesting him to pursue the rebels as far and as closely as he could.

Napier, receiving Sir Hugh's order to pursue,

Napier started on this service at half-past 5 o'clock on the morning of the 20th, with about five hundred and sixty cavalry, of whom sixty were dragoons, and Lightfoot's battery of artillery, and pursuing the rebels rapidly, came up with them, at least four thousand strong, at Jáora-Álipúr, on the 22nd. Napier, reconnoitring, found them strongly posted, their right resting on A'lipúr, guns and infantry in the centre, and cavalry on both flanks; but he resolved to attack them.

pursues, and finds the rebels at Jáora-A'lipúr.

Finding the ground to his right open, Napier directed Captain Lightfoot to take up a position on the left flank of the enemy, about six hun-

* Sir Hugh Rose, in his despatch, thus alludes to this officer: "But the gallant leader, Lieutenant Rose, who has been twice specially mentioned by me for good and gallant conduct, fell in the fort, mortally wounded, closing his early career by taking the fort of Gwáliár by force of arms."

His brigadier, Brigadier C. S. Stuart, thus referred to him in his brigade orders: "Brigadier Stuart has received with the deepest regret, a report of the death of Lieutenant Rose, 25th Bombay native infantry, who was mortally wounded yesterday, on entering the fort of Gwáliár, on duty with his men. The brigadier feels assured that the whole brigade unite with him in deploring the early death of this gallant officer, whose many sterling qualities none who knew him could fail to appreciate."

Book XIV. Chapter III.

1858. June.

His guns rake their line.

dred yards from them, and to enfilade them. He then ranged his cavalry behind a rising ground, which afforded partial concealment, ready to act as soon as the fire from Lightfoot's guns should be felt.

The fire causes them to waver,

This soon happened. After a few discharges, a rapid thinning and wavering of the rebels' ranks took place. Lightfoot then limbered up and advanced at a gallop, whilst the 14th dragoons, led by Prettijohn, and the Haidarábád cavalry, by Abbott, dashed into their ranks.

and, when charged, break and flee.

The result was decisive. Prettijohn's distinguished valour and Abbott's gallant leading were especially conspicuous. The dash of Lightfoot's horse artillery was superb to look at. "You cannot imagine," writes an eye-witness, a cavalry officer, "the dash of the artillery: it was wonderful. We could scarcely keep up with them." But, in fact, every man behaved like a hero: each vied with his comrade. After a brief resistance the rebels broke and fled, hotly pursued. They lost twenty-five guns, all their ammunition, elephants, tents, carts, and baggage, and had three to four hundred men killed. Never was a rout more complete.*

Close of the campaign.

The capture of Gwáliár and the dispersion of the rebel army closed the campaign which will for ever be associated with the name of Sir Hugh

* Tántia Topi, who was present on this occasion, thus describes the affair: "We reached Jáora Alipúr and remained there during the night. The next morning we were attacked and fought for an hour and a half. We fired five shots and the English army fired four shots, and we then ran off, leaving all our guns."

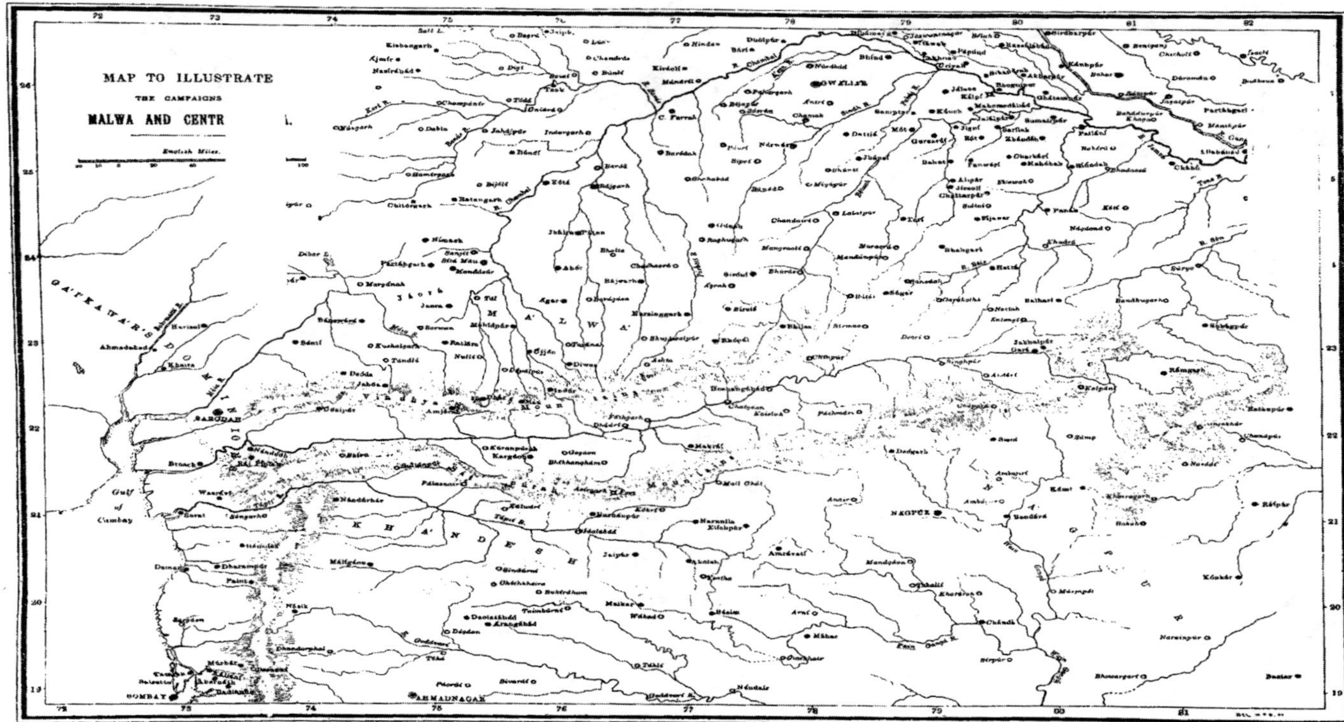
MAP TO ILLUSTRATE
THE CAMPAIGNS
MALWA AND CENTR
English Miles.
GWALIOR
NAGPUR
BOMBAY
AHMADNAGAR
BARODAH
Gulf of Cambay
KHANDESH
MALWA

Rose. In a previous chapter I have alluded to the personal character, strong and firm as iron and yet singularly sympathetic, which had chained success to all the incidents of that most eventful campaign. I may be pardoned if I briefly recapitulate here all that had been accomplished in a period falling somewhat short of six months. On the 6th of January 1858 Sir Hugh Rose had left Indúr; on the 24th he laid siege to Ráthgarh; on the 28th he defeated in the field the rájá of Bánpúr; on the 29th he took Ráthgarh; on the 3rd of February he relieved Ságar; on the 13th he took the strong fort of Garhákót; on the 4th of March he forced the pass of Maddanpúr; on the 17th his 1st brigade stormed the fort of Chandairi; on the 22nd he invested Jhánsi; on the 31st he defeated Tántia Topi on the Bétwah; on the 3rd of April he stormed Jhánsi; on the 6th of May he defeated Tántia Topi and the ráni of Jhánsi at Kúnch; on the 23rd he beat the rebels at Galáoli near Kálpi, and occupied that fort the following day. In this chapter I have told how, roused from a bed of sickness by the news of the capture of Gwáliár by the rebels, he pursued them with unremitting vigour, and stayed not his hand till he had recovered all that they had temporarily gained. In every undertaking he was successful, and he was successful because, careless of himself, he thought of the great end he had in view, and spared no means to attain it.

Recapitulation of its results; real cause of his success.

After the victory at Gwáliár, Sir Hugh Rose proceeded to Bombay to assume command of the

Sir Hugh proceeds to Bombay,

Book XIV. Chapter III.

1858. June.

army of that Presidency.* The force with which he had won so many victories was, to a great extent, broken up. The 95th regiment was ordered to occupy the rock fortress. The 71st Highlanders, the 86th regiment, and the 25th Bombay native infantry, with detachments of cavalry and artillery, remained at Morár. The 3rd Bombay Europeans, the 24th Bombay native infantry, with cavalry and artillery, were sent to Jhánsi. Of these troops the command devolved

* The following farewell general order was issued on this occasion by Sir Hugh Rose:—"The Major-General commanding, being on the point of resigning the command of the Puná division of the Bombay army, bids farewell to the Central India Field Force; and at the same time expresses the pleasure he feels that he commanded them when they gained one more laurel at Gwáliár. The Major-General witnessed with satisfaction how the troops and their gallant comrades in arms—the Rajpútáná brigade under General Smith — stormed height after height, and gun after gun, under the fire of a numerous field and siege artillery, taking finally by assault two 18-pounders at Gwáliár. Not a man in these forces enjoyed his natural health or strength; an Indian sun and months of marching and broken rest had told on the strongest; but the moment they were told to take Gwáliár for their Queen and country they thought of nothing but victory. They gained it, restoring England's true and brave ally to his throne, putting to rout the rebel army, killing many of them, and taking from them in the field, exclusive of those in the fort, fifty-two pieces of artillery, all their stores and ammunition, and capturing the city and fort of Gwáliár, reckoned the strongest in India. The Major-General thanks sincerely Brigadier-General Napier, C.B., Brigadier Stuart, C.B., and Brigadier Smith, commanding brigades in the field, for the very efficient and able assistance which they gave him, and to which he attributes the success of the day. He bids them and their brave soldiers once more a kind farewell. He cannot do so under better auspices than those of the victory of Gwáliár."

upon Brigadier-General Robert Napier. Brigadier Smith's brigade was distributed in three portions, respectively at Gwáliár, at Sipri, and at Gúnah. It seemed as though they were about to enjoy the rest they had so gloriously earned. But appearances were deceitful. Though one bitter enemy, the ráni of Jhánsi, had disappeared, there had escaped another, not less implacable, perhaps even more fertile in resources than that resolute lady. Though beaten at all points, that other adversary had never despaired. Not many weeks elapsed before the cities, the villages, and the jungles of central India once more resounded with the name of Tántia Topi.

Book XIV. Chapter III.

1858. June.

and the regiments of the force are distributed.

The prospects of peace are illusive.

BOOK XIV.

CHAPTER IV.

The southern Maráthá country.

In the first chapter of this volume I have brought the record of affairs in the southern Maráthá country up to the spring of 1858. In Belgáon and the neighbouring districts the crisis had passed away. It needed only the continuance of the same firm and conciliatory rule to ensure that it should never return.

Mr. Seton-Karr, applying to be relieved of a portion of his duties,

It happened, however, at this period (March and April 1858) that Mr. G. B. Seton-Karr, exhausted by the double labours which had devolved upon him, applied to the Government of Bombay to be relieved of portion of his overwhelming duties. Mr. Seton-Karr had, unquestionably, reason to believe that the Government, should it accede to his request, would grant him an option in the matter, or, at all events, would relieve him of the less important routine duties appertaining to the administration. But he was mistaken. The Government, in sanctioning Mr.

Seton-Karr's request, desired him to retain in his own hands the civil administration of the territory, and to transfer the charge of the political agency to his assistant, Mr. Charles Manson.

is directed to transfer the political agency to Mr. Manson.

Character of Mr. Manson.

Than Mr. Manson there was not a more high-minded, a more generous, or a more earnest officer in the Bombay Civil Service. He was devoted to his profession, he gave to it his whole soul and his undivided energies. He was in the prime of life, intelligent, energetic, decided. But—he had been employed on the detested Inám Commission—and he belonged to a school of politics differing in one essential point from that of which Mr. Seton-Karr was a leader. The reader will have already discovered the title of that school. Mr. Seton-Karr was strongly in favour of the maintenance of the native aristocracy, an upholder of the rights and customs held and enjoyed by native land-owners at the time that they came under British rule. He believed that so long as the British respected those rights and customs, it would never be necessary to employ force; that persuasion and management would effect the required end. How he had tried, and tried successfully, that policy, I have already shown. The success had proved to him its efficacy. Mr. Manson belonged to a more modern school. In one of the letters which Mr. Seton-Karr addressed to him before the transfer of the political duties, he is jestingly referred to as "an admirer of Lord Dalhousie." This, at least, is certain, that in a crisis such as that which was then prevailing, he gave his pre-

School to which Mr. Seton-Karr belonged.

School of which Mr. Manson was a partisan.

Book XIV. Chapter IV.

1858. May.

ference to measures stronger than those which Mr. Seton-Karr deemed suited to the occasion.

Reasons adduced by the Bombay Government for the change.

Mr. Seton-Karr was greatly disappointed by the decision of the Government, but the reason adduced by that Government was one to which he could take no exception. Lord Elphinstone desired that the whole of the southern Maráthá country should be placed under the control of one officer as commissioner, and, in the circumstances of the time, he deemed it further advisable that that officer should be a soldier. Now Colonel Le Grand Jacob already exercised political authority in one part of the territory. On the 6th of December he had suppressed a mutiny in Kolhápúr, and had, by his firmness and strength of character, impressed the Bombay Government with the conviction that he was peculiarly qualified to wield political power in troublous times. Lord Elphinstone, then, transferred to him in the new arrangement a similar authority in the other part, with Mr. Manson as political agent under him.

Colonel Le G. Jacob is appointed supreme political agent for the entire territory.

If, however, the reason for the transfer was sufficient in that it cast no slur upon Mr. Seton-Karr, it did not the less cause considerable misgivings to that gentleman, for, knowing as he did the native chieftains, he felt that a change would create suspicion in their minds, a change more especially which transferred political action from himself to an officer who had been engaged in the Inám Commission, and that if that change were followed by a tension of the tie which bound them to the suzerain power, it might even produce a catastrophe.

Reasons why Mr. Seton-Karr augured ill of the change.

Previous to the assumption of the charge of the political duties of the Belgáon districts, Mr. Seton-Karr had been gradually engaged in disarming the country—a work in which he had been most ably assisted by Colonel George Malcolm, commanding the Southern Maráthá horse, and holding military charge of the southern Maráthá territory. It would be difficult to overestimate the services rendered by this able and gallant officer. His regiment mainly preserved order in that excitable country. In a previous chapter I have referred to his services at Shorápúr. Prior to that event, on the 29th of November 1857, he had led his cavalry, supported by one company 28th native infantry, against the fortified village of Halgalli, which had become the head-quarters of the disaffected. For some days previously these men had been held in check by detachments of the horse, first under Kerr, subsequently reinforced by La Touche, of the same regiment. These officers had, by spirited charges, driven the enemy into the town, and were struggling with them desperately in the streets when Malcolm, with a fresh party, arrived. His men at once dismounted, and, assisted by the sepoys of the 28th native infantry, scrambled over the flat-roofed houses of the village, dashed upon the rebels, and decided the victory. The country, however, was still uneasy. Both above and below the gháts British authority had met with resistance, but, except that in some cases the guns and the arms had not entirely been delivered up, the danger from such disturbances was considered

Colonel George Malcolm.

Kerr and La Touche attack Halgalli.

Malcolm arrives and the place is stormed.

State of the country generally.

Book XIV. Chapter IV.

1858. May.

to have passed away when Colonel Jacob took charge. Within a very short time of that event, however, a new peril appeared in another quarter.

Nargúnd.

Of the chief of Nargúnd I have spoken in the first chapter of this volume.* That this chief was thoroughly disaffected there can be no doubt. Mr. Seton-Karr had even suspected him of treasonable correspondence with the chief of Shorápúr.† But up to May 1858 he had been managed. He had even, under the gentle pressure exercised by Mr. Seton-Karr, sent in a correct list of the guns and ammunition he possessed, and very recently, urged by Mr. Manson, had even begun to despatch them to Dhárwár. Those who are aware of the reverence and affection with which a native chief regards his guns, will realise the sacrifice which the rájá made to meet the expressed wishes of the Government.

Pressure exercised upon its chief by Seton-Karr and Manson.

The chief hears that Seton-Karr has been replaced by Manson.

Matters were thus progressing, the chief doubtless secretly disaffected, yet complying under gentle pressure with the orders of the Bombay Government, when, about the 25th of May, intelligence reached him that Mr. Seton-Karr had been removed from the political charge of his country, and that Mr. Manson had been gazetted his successor.

Reasons why the chief of Nargúnd dreaded Mr. Manson.

This intelligence changed all the good dispositions of the chief of Nargúnd. Although he did not personally dislike Mr. Manson, he regarded him as the living representative of the hated system of Inám examination—a system which, as I

* *Vide* pages 23, 25, and 29. † *Vide* page 126.

Book XIV. Chapter IV.

1858. May.

have said, had worked with most disastrous effects on the chiefs of the southern Maráthá country. At that moment, too, Mr. Manson was specially obnoxious to him, for, only few a weeks previously, whilst still serving under Mr. Seton-Karr, he had arrested and carried off as a prisoner his own dearest friend, the chief of Jamkhandi.* The conviction at once took possession of him that the change was aimed against himself, that he was to be arrested, as his friend had been arrested, and thrown into a dungeon.† In his fear and trepidation, the chief sent a confidential agent to Dhárwár to inquire of the magistrate the meaning of the portentous change.

He fears to be arrested.

But before he could receive an answer, those about him had begun to work on a nature constitutionally timid and nervous. His habitual advisers and companions had not even then despaired of receiving a summons to join the victorious standard of the heir of Péshwá. All seemed yet possible. Tántia Topi was confronting the British in Bandalkhand, Kálpi was yet held, and one good victory might give them all they desired. These men took advantage of the consternation caused in the chief's mind by Mr. Manson's appointment to inspire to resist, to

Influences which work on the chief of Nargúnd.

* Only a short time previously the rájá of Nargúnd had met Mr. Manson at the chief of Jamkhandi's house, visiting him apparently on friendly terms.

† So penetrated was he with this idea, that he despatched that day a letter to his brother at Rámdrúg, in which occurs the passage: "I had rather die than be arrested as Jamkhandi was."

Book XIV. Chapter IV.

1858. May.

cast defiance in the teeth of the foreigners who had persecuted themselves and their brethren.

The greatest influence of all,

These men were not alone in their endeavours. The chief's wife, a lady of great personal attractions, and twenty years younger than he was, had renounced all hopes of a natural heir. She loved power, and the chance of her possessing power after her husband's death rested on the prospect of her becoming the adoptive mother of a reigning boy. And the British Government having refused to the chief the right to adopt, this prospect was possible only in the event of the British rule being supplanted by that of the Maráthá. This favoured counsellor added, then, her entreaties to those of the chief's companions.

produced by the refusal of the Government to allow the chief to adopt an heir.

The chief of Nargúnd submits to those influences, and revolts.

The chief of Nargúnd gave way. That day he recalled the guns which had progressed only a few miles on the road to Dhárwár, began to store provisions, and on the 27th of May, possessing only three obsolete rusty cannon and a swivel gun, declared war, with all the formalities used by the Maráthás, against the British Government!

Manson has set out for the northern districts,

Mr. Manson had taken up his duties as political agent on the 16th of May. From that date till the 26th he had remained with Colonel Jacob at Kohlapúr, transacting business with him. On the 26th he set out for the northern states of the territory, with the view of judging for himself of the state of the country and of using his influence with the chiefs. Four hours after he had set out, Jacob received a telegram from General Lester, commanding at Belgáon, stating that an insurrection had broken out near to Dhárwár, and that the Nargúnd chief was believed to be supporting it as he had recalled some of his guns on their way to be given up. Jacob at once sent a horseman with this news to Manson, informing him also that he had telegraphed to the general to send, if the report were true, a sufficient force to Nargúnd, and recommending him to return to Kohlapúr.

Book XIV. Chapter IV.

1858. May.

when Jacob hears of the revolt.

He sends to warn Manson.

Jacob's messenger reached Manson at Kúrandwár. Englishmen in India are so accustomed to authority and to all the incense which waits on authority, that, except in rare cases, they judge men and affairs not as they are, but as to their complacent minds they seem to be. Now Manson had always been on the most friendly terms with the chief of Nargúnd. He had no adequate conception of the depth of bitterness and the dread his connection with the Inám Commission had roused in the mind of that Maráthá noble. It was not possible, then, that he should imagine for a moment that his nomination to the control of political affairs in place of Mr. Seton-Karr would rouse the chief to madness. Still believing, then, in the friendly professions of that chief and in the persuasive powers of his influence over him, he sent back word to Jacob that from Kúrandwár he could reach Nargúnd by a cross road; that he would arrive there in time to prevent, probably, the development of the intended mischief; but that if too late to prevent such development, he was confident of being able to prevent the chief's half-brother, the lord of Rámdrúg, from joining the rebellion. Having de-

Manson, confident in himself,

determines to push on to Nargúnd,

Book XIV. Chapter IV.

1858. May.

spatched this reply, Manson posted horses along the road to Rámdrúg, and sent off by a horseman a letter to Colonel George Malcolm, commanding at Kaladji, requesting him to join at Rámdrúg with a body of his regiment, the Southern Maráthá horse.

and sends to Malcolm for military aid.

Malcolm, meanwhile, had taken the field.

But before this missive reached Malcolm, that able and daring officer had taken the field with two hundred and fifty horsemen to attack the insurgents, who had already plundered the treasury of one of the district stations of Dhárwár. Mr. Manson, then, though he rode hard, reached Rámdrúg to find it unoccupied. He had with him the twelve troopers who had accompanied him from Kohlapúr, and these were as fatigued as he himself was. There he learned from the chief the treason of his half-brother; he read the compromising letters from the latter, urging the Ràmdrúg chief to follow his example; and, entreated by that chief not to pursue his journey to Nargúnd, he resolved to join the force in the field under Malcolm.

Manson reaches Rámdrúg,

and resolves to endeavour to join Malcolm.

He sets out that evening,

Tired as he was, Manson set out in a palanquin, escorted by his troopers, that evening. Better had he taken his rest at Rámdrúg and made the journey to Malcolm in one day, for, exhausted by the long day's work, he and his followers stopped about 10 o'clock at a temple near a little village on the way and slept.

and, tired, stops, near a temple, to sleep.

The chief of Nargúnd is made acquainted with Manson's movements,

A report of all Manson's movements had been duly carried to the chief of Nárgúnd. When the news reached him of the halt at the temple, he reasoned as a Maráthá will always reason. His

1858. May.

enemy was in his power; he would slay him.* He conceived that, having declared war against the British, he had a perfect right to destroy the members of that nation wherever he might find them. Accordingly, about midnight, he sallied forth with some hundreds of followers, and approaching the spot, poured in a volley, which killed the sentry, and then sent in his men to finish the work with the sword. Manson, roused from his sleep, fired his revolver at his assailants, but he was immediately overpowered, his head was cut off, and his body thrown in the fire, still burning, which had been kindled by his followers. Having killed as many of these as he could find, the chief returned with Manson's head to Nárgúnd, and suspended the bloody trophy over a gateway.†

and has him murdered.

Meanwhile, the insurgents who had plundered the treasury, had marched southwards and joined Bhim Ráo, the chief of Kopaldrúg. There they were attacked by a Madras force from Bellárí, under Colonel Hughes, already mentioned for his soldier-like conduct at Shorápúr, and who, in daring and manly qualities, in the capacity to manage men and to direct operations, yielded to none who came to the front in the mutiny. This gallant soldier pushed forward with an energy

One body of the insurgents marches to Kopaldrúg,

where they are attacked and beaten by Hughes.

* It was the reasoning of Jael, wife of Hebor the Kenite, whose conduct was infinitely more treacherous.

† Read also Sir George Le Grand Jacob's *Western India before and during the Mutinies*. The account of the suspension of the head over a gateway rests entirely on native testimony. When the place was taken it was found floating in a well.

Book XIV. Chapter IV. — 1858. May-June.

surpassing that of the rebels, caught them, as I have said, at Kopaldrúg, and stormed the place, killing Bhim Ráo, the chief of Hémbaji, and many of the defenders.

Malcolm hurries towards Nargúnd.

Malcolm, on his side, had no sooner heard that Nargúnd was in revolt than he felt that a moment's delay would provoke the rising of the entire Maráthá country. With only two hundred and fifty cavalry at his disposal he marched, then, immediately against the place, assisted by the wily Brahman officials, who believed he was marching on destruction.

He is reinforced by infantry and guns.

At the same time he wrote to Belgáon asking for some infantry and some guns. The authorities there sent him two companies of Europeans, one of native infantry, and two guns under Captain Paget. Riding on with these, only five days after the insensate declaration of war, he appeared before Nargúnd. He had scarcely dismounted before news reached him that the rebels were marching to attack him. His heart bounded with joy. "I have them now," he said. Mounting his troopers as quickly as possible, he went to the front. It was true, they were advancing. But when they saw Malcolm and his horsemen they hesitated, then halted, and, in the manner of natives, began to close in on their centre. Then, wavering, they fell back. By this time Malcolm had collected his men. Riding at their head, he charged, overthrew the rebels—who, however, fought well in groups—drove them back, followed them up into the town, and forced the surviving combatants to take refuge in the fort.

The rebels march to attack him.

Malcolm charges and defeats them,

and captures the town.

1858. June.

There remained now only the fort, a very strong one, so strong, that if defended, it would have defied the efforts of the small assailing force. But Malcolm knew the natives well. "Give them a quiet night," he said, "and they will save us the trouble." He was right. On the morning of the 2nd of June the strongest fort in the southern Maráthá country was found deserted.

The rebels evacuate the fort in the night.

The chief, accompanied by six of his principal advisers, attempted, in the guise of a pilgrim, to escape the fate he had provoked. Every possible ruse was had recourse to by the fugitives to baffle the pursuit which, they soon learned, had been instituted after them. The man who had been deputed for that task, Mr. Frank Souter,* possessed qualities which did not permit him to be easily baffled. He met ruse with ruse, and after a hot pursuit, captured the chief on the night of the 3rd.†

The chief attempts to escape in disguise,

but is captured by Frank Souter.

On learning of Mr. Manson's death, Colonel Jacob had taken the promptest measures to control the northern states of the territory. He forced the chief of Miraj, the best fortified town in the country, to give a pledge of his fidelity by

Colonel Jacob controls the country.

* Now Sir Frank Souter, Superintendent of Police in Bombay.

† The chief of Nargúnd was tried at Belgáon on the 11th of June. He pleaded guilty, and in his plea stated that it was the fear of arrest that had caused him to commit the bloody deed. He was executed, in the presence of all the troops and of a large number of natives, on the 12th. It remains only to add that the bodies of the wife of whom I have spoken and the chief's mother were found in the Málparba river on the night of the 3rd. Sir G. Le Grand Jacob states, in the work already referred to, that they drowned themselves, unable to bear up against the disgrace.

Book XIV. Chapter IV. — 1858. November.

surrendering his ammunition. Shortly afterwards, the death of General Lester led to the nomination of Colonel Jacob as Brigadier-General in military command in the southern Maráthá country.

Measures taken by him for its pacification,

Under General Jacob's firm rule the country above the gháts soon subsided into quiescence, but below the mountains, along the Goa frontier, the Sáwant rebels still continued to keep a large number of Madras, Bombay, and Portuguese troops, regular and irregular, in the field. Want of concert, however, naturally resulted from the action of troops serving under commanders independent one of the other. Eventually, in November, the Portuguese Viceroy, at a conference with General Jacob, consented to place the whole of his field detachments under the command of the officer who should unite that of the Bombay troops. Under this agreement Brigadier-General Fitzgerald of the Madras army took command of the united forces, and an organised plan was arranged. This was to hem in the track occupied by the rebels, and to inform them that unless they surrendered by the 20th of November, they would be hunted down without mercy. On that date the band had dwindled to the number of eighty persons. These surrendered to the Portuguese commander on the night of that day, and their ringleaders were subsequently transported to the Portuguese possessions in Taimor.

in concert with the Viceroy of Goa,

are eminently successful.

Thenceforward the peace of the southern Maráthá country was assured.

BOOK XV.

CHAPTER I.

In the preceding volume* I referred to the proclamation issued by Lord Canning regarding the tálúkdárs of Oudh, and of its reception in the victorious camp of Sir Colin Campbell; and I promised to deal with the subject more fully later on. I proceed now to redeem that promise. **Oudh.**

Purport of Lord Canning's Oudh proclamation.

The Oudh proclamation, despatched by Lord Canning to Sir James Outram in his capacity of Chief Commissioner of Oudh, with a letter bearing date the 3rd of March 1858, directing that it should not be published until Lakhnao had fallen, or at least lay at the mercy of the British commander, was at once a sentence, a warning, and a threat addressed to the inhabitants of the rebellious province. That proclamation announced that Lakhnao, after defying and resisting the power of the British for nine months, now lay

* Vol. ii. pages 409, 410.

Book XV. Chapter I. 1858. March.

at the mercy of the conqueror; that in that defiance and resistance the mutinous soldiery who had begun the revolt had been greatly aided by the inhabitants of the city and the province, even by those who owed their prosperity to the British Government; but that the hour of retribution had now arrived. Acting on the principle that before pronouncing sentence on the guilty, it was just and proper to reward the innocent, the proclamation proceeded to name six men—three of whom were rájás, two zamindárs, and one a tálúkdár—who had remained faithful amid great temptations, and who were not only declared "the sole hereditary proprietors of the lands which they held when Oudh came under British rule," but were promised additional rewards. Rewards and honours in proportionate measure were likewise promised to others in whose favour similar claims should be established to the satisfaction of the Government. But, with these exceptions, the proprietary right in the soil of the province was confiscated to the British Government, which would dispose of that right in such manner as might seem fitting. To the chiefs, tálúkdárs, and landowners, however, who should make immediate submission, surrendering their arms and obeying the orders of the Chief Commissioner, the proclamation promised the safety of their lives and of their honour, provided that their hands were "unstained with English blood murderously shed." For any further indulgence, the proclamation added, and with regard to the condition in which such men might thereafter be

Rewards it promises to the innocent,

punishment to the remainder.

Conditions of commutation of punishment.

placed, "they must throw themselves upon the justice and mercy of the British Government." The proclamation promised, in conclusion, that to those amongst the classes referred to who should come forward promptly and give the Chief Commissioner their support in the restoration of peace and order, the indulgence would be large, and that the Governor-General would be ready to view liberally the claims which they might thus acquire to the restoration of their former rights. Further, that whilst participation in the murder of Englishmen and Englishwomen would exclude those who had participated in it from all mercy, those, on the other hand, who had protected English lives would be specially entitled to consideration and leniency.

Participation in the murder of Englishmen and English women to exclude from mercy.

In the letter to which I have referred as accompanying the proclamation the Foreign Secretary, Mr. G. F. Edmonstone, was, as I have already stated, careful to lay down that it should not be published until Lakhnao had either been conquered or lay at the mercy of the conqueror. It further prescribed that, when published, the proclamation was to be addressed only to the non-military inhabitants of the province, and in no sense to the mutinous sepoys. It expressed likewise the conviction of Lord Canning that the tone of apparent severity which characterised the proclamation was necessary, inasmuch as the announcement in such a state paper of a liberal and forgiving spirit would be open to misconstruction; and it added that, in reality, the spirit of the proclamation was merciful and even

Mr. Edmonstone's accompanying letter

fully explains the mercy that underlay

Book XV. Chapter I.

1858. March.

the apparent severity of the terms of the proclamation.

lenient, in that it promised exemption, almost general, from the penalties of death and imprisonment to rájás, tálúkdárs, and zamindárs who had conspired and fought against the Government; that even the confiscation of estates was rather a merciful commutation of a severer punishment than a harsh measure of justice. The letter concluded with suggestions to Sir James Outram regarding the manner in which it might be requisite for him to deal with mutineers of varying grades of guilt.

Outram reads the proclamation in a sense different to that intended by Lord Canning,

Sir James Outram received the letter and the proclamation on the 5th of March. Reading the latter by the light of its actual contents, apart from the commentary furnished by the letter, he arrived at a conclusion regarding it the very reverse of that which Lord Canning had endeavoured to impress upon him. Lord Canning, when sending him the proclamation, had said in so many words, by the mouth of his Foreign Secretary, "Do not judge the proclamation simply by itself, as a paper dealing out stern justice to conquered revolters. Rather, looking at the measure of punishment which those revolters have brought upon themselves, see whether the proclamation does not in every case, except the case of atrocious murder, pronounce a mitigation of punishment, capable of still further mitigation." But Outram, disregarding this exhortation, looked at the proclamation without sufficient reference to the circumstances which had made it necessary, and condemned it. In a letter to the Foreign Secretary, dated the 8th of March,

and condemns it.

1858. March.

Embodies his views in a letter.

he declared his belief that there were not a dozen landowners in Oudh who had not, in some way or other, assisted the rebels, and that, therefore, there would be but few exceptions to the sweeping confiscations proposed by the Governor-General; he expressed his conviction that as soon as the proclamation should be made public nearly all the chiefs and tálúkdárs would retire to their domains and prepare for a desperate resistance. He proceeded even to urge extenuating circumstances for those of them who had revolted, by declaring his opinion—which, it must be admitted, was founded on fact—that the landowners had been very unjustly treated in the land-settlement after the annexation; that, apart from this, their sympathy with the rebels had been, in the actual circumstances, only natural; that it was not until the British rule in Oudh had been brought to a virtual end by the mutineers that they had sided against the Government; that they ought to be treated rather as honourable enemies than as rebels; that they would be converted into relentless enemies if their lands were confiscated, maintaining a guerilla war which would "involve the loss of thousands of Europeans by battle, disease, and exposure"; but that if their lands were insured to them they would at once aid in restoring order, and would so co-operate with the paramount power as, before long, to render unnecessary the further presence of the enormous army then occupying Oudh.

Lord Canning's first reply

To this letter Lord Canning replied, on the 10th, in a brief despatch, the nature of which

Book XV. Chapter I.

1858. March.

renders still clearer the really merciful intentions of his proclamation. Referring to the promise of safety of life and honour to the tálúkdárs, chiefs, and landholders, unstained with English blood murderously shed, who should surrender at once and obey the orders of the Chief Commissioner, Lord Canning authorised Sir James to amplify it by an addition which, if not very wide in itself, intimated as clearly as possible the merciful intentions of the Governor-General. "To those amongst them," ran this addition, "who shall promptly come forward, and give to the Chief Commissioner their support in the restoration of peace and order, this indulgence will be large, and the Governor-General will be willing to view liberally the claims which they may thus acquire to a restitution of their former rights."

renders his merciful intentions still clearer.

His second and more elaborate letter

Three weeks later Lord Canning replied at greater length to Outram's remarks. In Mr. Edmonstone's despatch, dated the 31st of March, Lord Canning admitted that the people of Oudh occupied a different position, with respect to their allegiance to the British Government, to that of the inhabitants of the provinces which had been longer under British rule. But, in the Governor-General's opinion, that difference constituted no valid ground for treating the chiefs and tálúkdárs in the lenient manner suggested by Outram. Arguing in the spirit of the letter of the 3rd of March, he again insisted that, in the presence of a great crime, exemption from death, transportation, and imprisonment were great boons, and that to have offered more lenient terms would

gives ample reasons

Book XV. Chapter I.

1858. March.

have been to treat the rebels—not, as Outram contended, as honourable enemies—but as enemies who had won the day. With respect to Outram's contention that the injustice of the land-settlement after the annexation had impelled the landowners to rebel, Lord Canning simply declined to recognise the hypothesis. Admitting that the policy of introducing into Oudh a system of village settlement in place of the old settlement under tálúkdárs might not have been altogether wise, Lord Canning declined to believe that the conduct of the landowners was in any respect the consequence of that policy. He attributed that conduct rather to the repugnance they had felt to suffer any restraint of the arbitrary powers they had till then exercised; to a diminution of their importance by being brought under equal laws; and to the obligation of disbanding their armed followers and of living a peaceful and orderly life. For these reasons, Lord Canning adhered to his proclamation.

for adhering to the proclamation.

Real similarity in the objects at which Lord Canning and Outram alike aimed.

That Sir James Outram did not at once realise the statesman-like nature and the really merciful tendencies of Lord Canning's proclamation may at once be admitted. The end of the two men was really the same; the difference was in the manner by which that end should be attained. Sir James would have carried leniency to a point at which leniency would have missed its aim. Lord Canning, maintaining the right to be severe, was prepared to be as merciful as Outram whenever the exercise of mercy was politically desirable.

Book XV. Chapter I.

1858. March.

The real character of Lord Canning's statesmanship at this period might have remained long generally unknown but for the action taken with respect to the proclamation by the then President of the Board of Control, the Earl of Ellenborough. That nobleman had but recently taken over the seals of that office from his predecessor, a member of the Whig Cabinet, Mr. Vernon Smith. In due course he received, about the 20th of March, a copy of Lord Canning's proclamation, unaccompanied by any explanatory document. In point of fact, Lord Canning, in transmitting the proclamation, had written to Mr. Vernon Smith, a member of his own party, and who, in his belief, still held the office of President of the Board of Control, a letter in which he stated that the proclamation required an explanatory despatch which he had not had time to prepare. Unfortunately Mr. Vernon Smith neglected to pass on that letter to his successor. He thus allowed Lord Ellenborough to believe that the proclamation stood alone, that it required no interpretation, and was to be judged on its merits as an act of policy.

Lord Ellenborough receives Lord Canning's proclamation without the letter addressed to his predecessor, explanatory of the reasons which justified it.

It is not surprising that, reading the proclamation in this way, Lord Ellenborough arrived at a conclusion not very dissimilar to that with which Sir James Outram, possessing all the advantages of proximity to, and personal communication with, Lord Canning, had been impressed. He condemned it as likely to raise such a ferment in Oudh as would make pacification almost impossible. In accord with Outram, of whose views,

Lord Ellenborough arrives at a conclusion similar to that formed by Outram,

Book XV. Chapter I. 1858. March.

however, he was ignorant, Lord Ellenborough believed that the mode of settling the land tenure when the British took possession of Oudh had been in many ways unjust, and had been the chief cause of the general and national character of the disaffection in that province. He concluded—agreeing in this also with Outram—that the people of Oudh would view with dismay a proclamation which cut them off, as a nation, from the ownership of land so long cherished by them, and would deem it righteous to battle still more energetically than before against a government which could adopt such a course of policy. Lord Ellenborough embodied these views in a despatch to be transmitted to Lord Canning in the name of the Secret Committee of the Court of Directors, added to them an argument—also an argument of Sir James Outram—to the effect that the people of Oudh ought to be regarded as legitimate enemies than as rebels, and concluded it with these stinging words: "Other conquerors, when they have succeeded in overcoming resistance, have excepted a few persons as still deserving of punishment, but have, with a generous policy, extended their clemency to the great body of the people. You have acted on a different principle. You have reserved a few as deserving of special favour, and you have struck with what they will feel as the severest of punishment the mass of the inhabitants of the country.

and embodies his views in a despatch.

Concluding paragraphs of this despatch.

"We cannot but think that the precedents from which you have departed will appear to have been conceived in a spirit of wisdom su-

Book XV. Chapter I.

1858. March.

perior to that which appears in the precedent you have made. We desire, therefore, that you will mitigate in practice the stringent severity of the decree of confiscation you have issued against the landowners of Oudh. We desire to see British authority in India rest upon the willing obedience of a contented people; there cannot be contentment where there is general confiscation.

"Government cannot long be maintained by any force in a country where the whole people is rendered hostile by a sense of wrong; and if it were possible so to maintain it, it would not be a consummation to be desired."

He sends this despatch to Lord Canning, without previously submitting it to the Queen or to his colleagues.

Lord Ellenborough was not content with penning these severe and galling strictures. Without submitting the despatch for the approval of the Queen, without even showing it to his colleagues, he transmitted it direct to Lord Canning. Nor was he content even with that. Three weeks later he allowed it to be presented to the House of Commons!

This action, when known, compels Lord Ellenborough to resign.

So far as Lord Ellenborough was concerned, the three mistakes he committed—the penning of an acrimonious despatch without waiting for an explanation, the transmission of that despatch before it had been submitted to the Queen or had received the approval of his colleagues, the disclosure of its contents to Mr. Bright with a view to its being presented to the House of Commons—were fatal to his tenure of office. The matter having come under the cognisance of the House of Commons, Lord Ellenborough taking upon himself the sole responsibility of the despatch, resigned his office.

Book XV. Chapter I.

1858. June.

Effect produced by the despatch on Lord Canning.

Far different was the effect produced by the receipt of the despatch upon Lord Canning. He received it at Allahábád on the 13th of June. Before its contents became known, rumours circulated that the Government of Lord Derby had written a disagreeable letter to the Governor-General. "I asked him," wrote, at the time, one deeply in his confidence, "if it was true that he had received something disagreeable. He said, almost indifferently, that it was impertinent; but he did not care much; he would answer what they wrote." He then entered into a conversation regarding his Oudh policy. The next day, when the despatch had been read by others, the prevailing feeling regarding it was that it was offensively impertinent, with a look of epigrammatic point in the concluding sentences—those which I have quoted—of which the writer was evidently proud. But, above all, there arose a feeling of indignation that a despatch so insulting should have been published for the benefit of the natives, many of them still in revolt, as well as of the Anglo-Indians.

Indignation it causes in the minds of his *entourage*.

Lord Canning is urged from England not to resign.

But Lord Canning had, at this crisis, a support not less grateful than the confidence of the friends about him. The same mail brought him a copy of a resolution of the Court of Directors expressing continued confidence in their Governor-General. Letters were received from Mr. Sidney Herbert, from Lord Granville, from Lord Aberdeen, and from many other leading men, express-

Book XV. Chapter I.

1858. June.

ing sympathy and regard. In almost all these Lord Canning was urged not to resign, but to carry on his own policy calmly, and to leave to the Government the odium of recalling him. Lord Canning never thought of resigning. He regarded Lord Ellenborough's despatch as Achilles would have regarded a javelin "hurled by the feeble hand of Priam," and far from allowing it to disturb his equanimity, he sat down coolly and calmly to pen a vindication of his policy.

He had no thought of doing so.

Curiously enough, ten days after that vindication was drafted and despatched—on the 27th of June—Lord Canning received a long private letter from Lord Derby himself on the subject of the point of difference. In this letter Lord Derby expressed a general confidence in Lord Canning's policy: he attributed Lord Ellenborough's despatch to the conduct of Mr. Vernon Smith in withholding the covering private letter which accompanied the Oudh proclamation, and which gave the only intimation that further explanations would be forwarded. Lord Derby concluded by virtually asking, almost pressing, Lord Canning to stay on, and spoke of the probability of Lord Stanley going to the Board of Control. To one in Lord Canning's position such a letter from the chief of the cabinet of which Lord Ellenborough had been a member was most satisfactory. It might almost be said that his policy was vindicated by his enemies.

He receives a letter from Lord Derby, virtually asking him to stay on.

Lord Canning's own vindication was dated the 18th of June. It began by alluding in a dignified manner to the fact that the despatch cen-

Lord Canning's reply to the despatch.

suring himself had been made public in England three weeks before it reached his hands, and that in a few days it would be read in every station in Hindustán. Dwelling then upon the pain which the censure of his conduct by the Court of Directors would cause him, and upon the manner in which the publication of it would increase his difficulties, he declared that no taunts or sarcasms, come from what quarter they might, would turn him from the path which he believed to be that of public duty. Expressing, then, his conviction that a change in the government of India at that time, taking place under circumstances which would indicate a repudiation of the policy pursued towards the Oudh rebels, would seriously retard the pacification of the country, he proceeded to declare his belief that that policy had been from the first merciful without weakness, and indulgent without compromise of the dignity of the Government; that it had made manifest to the people of reconquered districts all over India, including Oudh, that the indulgence to those who should submit, and who should be free from atrocious crime, would be large; and that the Oudh proclamation, thoroughly consistent with that policy, offered the best and earliest prospect of restoring peace to that province on a stable footing.

Book XV. Chapter I.

1858. June.

Preliminary.

Stating then, in dignified language, that although in a time of unexampled difficulty, danger, and toil, he would not lay down of his own act the high trust which he had the honour to hold, yet that if, after reading the vindication of his

Preliminary.

Book XV. Chapter I.

1858. June.

policy, the Court of Directors should see fit to withhold their confidence from him, he then preferred his respectful yet urgent request that he might be relieved from the office of Governor-General, Lord Canning proceeded to reply to Lord Ellenborough's strictures, and to assert the grounds upon which his convictions of the soundness of his policy rested.

Retorts upon Lord Ellenborough,

With respect to the former, Lord Canning referred to the extraordinary manner in which Lord Ellenborough's despatch had almost justified the people of Oudh, as if they were fighting in a righteous cause—a manner quite legitimate in a member of the legislature, but quite unjustifiable in a minister of the Queen of England, who herself was actually Queen of Oudh also. He declined to discuss the policy which, in 1855–56, had dictated the annexation; it was not his act, nor had he ever been empowered to undo it. But he felt it incumbent upon him to point out the disastrous results which might follow, should the people of Oudh be encouraged, by such reasoning as that contained in the despatch, to continue their resistance. At the actual moment, the chiefs of the various sections of rebels in Oudh were united neither by a common plan nor by a common sympathy, but, he added, if it should become manifest that the British Government shrank from a declaration of its right to possess Oudh, the Bégam, as the representative in the field of the late reigning family, would draw to herself all the sympathies of the country, and all the other factions would merge in hers.

and points out the mischief his despatch might have caused in India.

Book XV. Chapter I.

1858. June.

Defence of his proclamation.

Lord Canning prefaced the defence of his proclamation by stating that he had early in the year proceeded to Allahábád chiefly that he might be able to investigate the state of Oudh; that he soon determined to make a difference, in the measures to be adopted for the pacification of the country, between the mutinied sepoys and the Oudh rebels; that the latter should not be put to death for appearing in arms against the authorities, unless they had committed actual murder; that the general punishment for rebellion in Oudh should be confiscation of estates, a punishment recognised by native states as the fitting consequence of the offence, and one which in no way affected caste nor the honour of the most sensitive Bráhman or Rajpút; a punishment which admitted of every gradation according to the severity or lightness of the offence, which would enable the Government to reward friendly tálúkdárs and zamindárs, and which, in point of fact, would, in many cases, constitute a kind of retributive justice—many of tálúkdárs having acquired their estates by spoliation of the village communities; that, as a matter of abstract justice, it would only be right to restore those estates to the village communities; but that as there would be insuperable difficulties to such a course, it would be better to take the forfeited estates of the rebellious talúkdárs as Government property, out of which faithful villages and individuals might be rewarded.

Final result on Lord Canning of

With this vindication ended practically the crisis caused by Lord Ellenborough's hasty act.

Book XV. Chapter I. 1858. June. the Ellenborough letter.

The result was to seat Lord Canning, in the presence of a ministry of an opposite party, more firmly in the saddle, and to give him greater strength to carry out the policy which he believed to be adapted to the circumstances. In another way his hands had been strengthened at this crisis.

The nomination of Sir James Outram to the Supreme Council enabled Lord Canning to place at the head of the Oudh province a man who, imbued with his own views, was certain to carry out his policy with the vigour arising from conviction.

Mr. Robert Montgomery.

The new Chief Commissioner of Oudh was Mr. Robert Montgomery.* Mr. Montgomery was a man who, with a thorough acquaintance with administrative duties, combined great decision of character, a sound judgment, and a rare knowledge of native character. He had been the right hand of Sir John Lawrence in the Panjáb, had been the firm advocate of those resolute measures which made the fall of Dehlí possible, and, in the earlier stages of the mutiny, when Sir John Lawrence was absent from Láhor, had himself directed the measures for disarming the native troops, which, carried out in time, had unquestionably saved the province. In questions of administrative policy, Mr. Montgomery, as I have said, agreed in principle with Lord Canning.

His character and antecedents.

Mr. Montgomery's action

Such was the man to whom, in the month of May 1858, Lord Canning entrusted the carrying

* Now Sir Robert Montgomery, K.C.S.I., a member of the Council of India.

Book XV. Chapter I.

1858. June.

out of the policy towards Oudh embodied in his famous proclamation. Mr. Montgomery, without ignoring the proclamation, did not put it into rough action. He used it rather as a lever, by the judicious employment of which he could bring about the results at which the Governor-General professedly aimed. The situation was, for the first three months of his tenure of office, in many respects remarkable. The larger number of the relations, adherents, and dependants of the deposed royal family had their dwellings in, or belonged, by family association extending over many years, to the city of Lakhnao. Considering, moreover, the part which that city, and more especially the classes of its inhabitants to which I have referred, had played in the rebellion, it was especially necessary to exercise over it a strict supervision. In the provinces an entirely different feeling prevailed. There the rule of the king of Oudh had planted no seeds of loyalty or devotion. Alien in religion and in race to the great bulk of the people of Oudh, the king and his courtiers had been tolerated, first, because they were there, and, secondly, because they had exercised no strict supervising power, but had been content to be the nominal rulers of the great landowners, permitted to carry on, very much in accordance with their own wishes, their feudal rule. The central power, as exercised by the kings of Oudh, had interfered to put a stop to rapine and oppression only when that rapine and oppression had attained a magnitude so great that to ignore them would have produced a national

regarding the proclamation.

The situation in Oudh.

Lakhnao.

The provinces.

Feeling of the people towards the king.

Book XV. Chapter I.

1858. June.

rising. The sentiment felt, then, by the great body of landowners towards the royal family of Oudh was not loyalty; it was not affection; it was not sympathy; it was scarcely contentment. Perhaps the term that best describes it is the term toleration. They had been content to tolerate that family as exercising a kind of nominal suzerainty which permitted them to do just as they liked.

Their feeling regarding British rule very hostile.

Towards the British rule, exercised as it had been by the civilians who had immediately preceded Sir Henry Lawrence, they entertained a different feeling. In strong contrast with the selfish sway of the Muhammadan kings of Oudh, the British rule had made itself felt in every corner of the province. The reforms it had introduced, the inquiries which it made, had been so sweeping, that an almost universal feeling had risen amongst the landowners that it was not to be endured. If the king of Oudh had been king Log, the British rule was the rule of king Stork. The landowners of Oudh, then, had hailed the mutiny, not from affection towards the deposed dynasty, but from hatred of its successor. Indifferent as they were to the persons and the race of their Muhammadan kings, they would have gladly ejected the British to restore them.

But they have no central rallying point.

When, then, Lakhnao had fallen, the tálúkdárs and the landowners generally were as far as they had ever been from submission to the British authority. Could the Bégam show a strong front, they might yet combine with her for the restoration of the ancient dynasty in the person of one of its members. But as there did not appear in the field any force sufficiently strong to rally round, the landowners and other rebel leaders fought each for himself, each hoping that some great benefit would accrue to him out of the general turmoil.

Book XV. Chapter I.

1858. July.

This disunion greatly diminished the difficulties which Montgomery might otherwise have had to encounter had there been unity of purpose or concentration of action among the malcontents. But still the task before him was no light one. He met it with all the skill, the temper, and the judgment which might have been expected from so experienced a ruler of men. He exhausted every means of persuasion at the same time that he brought clearly to the view of the landowners the fixed determination of the British Government. He was thus able to restore in some few districts the lapsed British authority. To reorganise that authority in those deaf to his persuasions, he was content to wait until the forcible measures inaugurated by his military coadjutor, Sir Hope Grant, should produce their natural results.

This fact diminishes Montgomery's difficulties, which are, nevertheless, great.

He meets them;

restores British authority in some districts.

What those measures were I shall relate in the next chapter.

BOOK XV.

CHAPTER II.

Hope Grant

WHEN I last referred to General Hope Grant,* he was marching to the fort of Jallálábád near Lakhnao. The date was the 16th of May. Leaving his force to enter that place, the general, just then nominated a Knight Commander of the Bath for his services in the field, rode into Lakhnao to consult with Mr. Montgomery, just then appointed Chief Commissioner. Montgomery informed him that the Kánhpúr road was again endangered by Béni Mádho, an influential tálúkdár, who had likewise caused proclamations to be distributed in Lakhnao, warning the inhabitants to quit that city, as it was to be attacked. On receiving this information, Hope Grant, taking with him the 53rd foot instead of the 38th, and substituting Mackinnon's battery for Olpherts's,

* Vol. ii. page 498.

Book XV. Chapter II.

1858. June.

returned to Jallálábád, and started thence in pursuit of Béni Mádho on the 25th of May.

follows up Béni Mádho.

For some time Béni Mádho was invisible. Hope Grant followed him to Jassandá, eight miles from Bani, where he had been reported to be "with a force of eighty-five thousand men"; but the tálúkdár and his men had vanished. On the 4th of June the Sikh rájá of Kappartola joined Sir Hope with nine hundred Sikhs and three brass 6-pounders.

Then, leaving the pursuit, marches against a rebel force at Nawábganj.

Hope Grant posted this reinforcement at the Banni bridge, and leaving the pursuit of Béni Mádho, marched against a body of rebels, less fabulously numerous, but more really formidable—being fifteen thousand strong—who had taken up a strong position at Nawábganj, on the Faizábád road, eighteen miles from Lakhnao. Grant's division was tolerably strong.* Leaving, then, a small force at the other Nawábganj (on the Káuhpúr road), he marched on Chinhat. There he found another column, one thousand two hundred strong, under Colonel Purnell. Leaving his baggage under charge of that officer, he left Chinhat at 11 o'clock on the night of the 12th of June to march against the rebels.

* It consisted of the 1st and 2nd battalions Rifle Brigade, the 5th Panjab infantry, five hundred Hodson's horse, under Lieutenant-Colonel Daly; one hundred and fifty Wales's horse, under Prendergast; two hundred and fifty Bruce's horse police, under Hill; the 7th hussars, under Colonel Sir William Russell; two squadrons Queen's Bays; Mackinnon's horse artillery; and Gibbon's and Carleton's batteries. The whole of the cavalry was commanded by Colonel Hagart.

Book XV. Chapter II.

1858. June.

Strong position of the rebels.

These latter had taken up a position exceptionally strong. They occupied a large plateau, surrounded on three sides by a stream, crossed by a bridge at a little distance from the town. On the fourth side was jungle.

Grant halts near the rebels,

Hope Grant's force, led by a trustworthy guide, crossed the complicated country between Chinhat and the plateau during the night, and reached the bridge mentioned about half an hour before daybreak. He halted his column to allow his men to rest and get their breakfast, and then marched on the rebels. His plan was to turn their right and interpose between them and the jungle. His men would do the rest.

and surprises them.

At daylight Hope Grant crossed the bridge and fell on the rebels. He took them completely by surprise. Their forces, divided into four parts, each commanded by a separate leader, had no time then either to concentrate or to act with unanimity. Hope Grant had struck at their centre, and this move had greatly contributed to their confusion. Still, they fought very gallantly. "A large body of fine daring zamindári men," wrote Sir Hope in his journal,* "brought two guns into the open and attacked us in rear.

Gallantry of the rebels,

I have seen many battles in India, and many brave fellows fighting with a determination to conquer or die, but I never witnessed anything more magnificent than the conduct of these zamindáris." They attacked Hodson's horse, who

* *Incidents of the Sepoy War*, by Sir Hope Grant and Captain Knollys.

Book XV. Chapter II.

1858. June.

could not face them, and by their unsteadiness imperilled the two guns attached to their regiment. Grant at once ordered up the 7th hussars, and directed one of the batteries to open on the zamindáris. The fire from four guns of this battery mowed them down with terrible effect, but did not force them to retire. After they had played upon them some time, the 7th hussars came up, and charging through them twice, forced them to give way. The fact that round the two guns of Hodson's horse there lay, after the combat was over, a hundred and twenty-five rebel corpses, testifies to the valour of these gallant zamindáris. After three hours' fighting, the rebels fell back, leaving on the field six guns and about six hundred dead. The British lost sixty-seven in killed and wounded. In addition, thirty-three men died from sunstroke, and two hundred and fifty were taken into hospital.

who, after a desperate contest, are defeated,

This victory had very important results. The rebels had from all sides been flocking to Nawábganj to swell the formidable column already there. But Hope Grant struck dismay all around. The defeat was so crushing, that the fugitives left the vicinity of Lakhnao, each of the four parties taking a different direction. The concentrating movement was also efficiently stopped.

and disperse.

Sir Hope left his force at Nawábganj and returned to Lakhnao to consult with Montgomery, whom this victory had allowed for the first time to breathe freely. From Lakhnao he was ordered by Sir Colin Campbell, in the third

Sir Hope is sent to relieve Mán Singh.

Book XV. Chapter II.

1858. July.

week of July, to march to the relief of Mán Sing, a famous rájá,* who, having at one time taken part with the rebels, had listened to the advice of Mr. Montgomery, and returned to his allegiance. For this he had been denounced by his former associates, and at the moment was attacked in his fort by a body of them twenty thousand strong with twenty guns.

Hope Grant starts to carry out the order.

It being of great importance to retain the adherence of so powerful a chieftain, Hope Grant at once despatched the 90th regiment, the 1st Bengal fusiliers, Brasyer's Síkhs, Mackinnon's troop of horse artillery, and four hundred cavalry to Nawábganj to supply the place of the troops he should take on thence, and with these latter† he set out on the 22nd of July.

The position of the rebel parties in Oudh.

Before starting with Sir Hope on this expedition it may be convenient to the reader to realise the exact position at the moment of the several rebel parties in Oudh. Of these, counting as one the forces of the Bégam and her alleged paramour, Mammú Khán, there were nine of great, besides many of smaller dimensions. These nine disposed at the time of sixty or seventy thousand armed men, with forty or fifty guns. More than half of these were said to have their head-quarters under the command of the Bégam and Mammú Khán at Chaoká ghát, on the Gághrá, not far from Faizábád; but a con-

* Vol. i. page 398.

† The 1st Madras Europeans, the 2nd battalion Rifle Brigade, the 1st Panjáb infantry, the 7th hussars, five hundred Hodson's horse, twelve light guns, and a train of heavy guns.

siderable body of them were besieging Mán Singh. The remainder—led by such men as Rámbakkas, Behúnáth Singh, Chandabaksh, Gholáb Singh, Narpat Singh of Rúiya notoriety, Bhopál Singh, and Firoz Sháh—were scattered all over the province, never long at the same place, hoping that a chance blow might give them victory or plunder.

The rebels abandon the leaguer of Sháhganj on Sir Hope's approach,

Hope Grant, urged by letters from Mán Singh to the effect that unless speedily relieved he could not answer for the consequences, pushed on rapidly, so rapidly, indeed, that the rumour of his advance had all, or almost all, the effect of the advance itself. When within a day's journey of Mán Singh's stronghold of Sháhganj he learned that the besieging force had melted away!

and break up into three divisions.

It was perfectly true. On hearing that the English army was advancing by rapid marches the besiegers took fright, and broke up into three divisions. One of these fled towards Gonda, a second to Sultánpúr on the Gúmti; a third to Tándá on the Ghágrá.

Hope Grant moves on to Faizábád,

Hope Grant moved then, not the less rapidly, on Faizábád; thence he proceeded to the ghát of Ajúdhiá, and found a considerable body of rebels pushing forth in boats to the opposite side of the river. He opened on these and sank all but one. The crews for the most part escaped. The next day he had an interview with rájá Mán Singh.

and sends Horsford to Sultanpúr.

But he did not rest idle at Faizábád. Sultánpúr having been indicated to him as the next

Book XV. Chapter II. 1858. August.

point of attack, Hope Grant detached thither a column composed of the 1st Madras fusiliers, the 5th Panjáb rifles, a detachment of 7th hussars, three hundred Hodson's horse, and a troop of horse artillery under the command of Brigadier Horsford. Horsford was delayed by heavy rain, but at last, on the 7th of August, he set out, and on the 12th arrived within four miles of the town, separated from it by the river Sái.

Hope Grant learns the strength of the rebels at Sultánpúr,

Horsford having ascertained by means of a reconnaissance that the enemy were in force, that the river was peculiarly favourable for defence, and that his passage would be disputed, reported that state of affairs to Hope Grant. Almost simultaneously with the arrival of that report, Hope Grant received a telegram from the Commander-in-Chief, informing him that the Sultánpúr rebels numbered fourteen thousand men, that they had fifteen guns, and that it was advisable that he should reinforce Horsford with the Rifle Brigade.

and pushes on to aid Horsford.

Nothing loth, Hope Grant ordered up the 53rd from Dariábád, and taking the rifles with him pressed forward to reinforce Horsford. He reached that officer on the 24th of August, and at once changing the position of the British camp, resolved to cross the following morning. The remainder of that day he employed in making rafts. On these, early on the morning of the 25th, he sent over the 1st Madras fusiliers, and the 5th Panjáb infantry. Then, though with great difficulty and after one or two mishaps, he landed on the opposite bank two 9-pounder guns. This force, commanded by Colonel Galwey, then gallantly attacked and carried two villages in his front, at a point where the river forms a bend and where the rebels had a picket. The rifles were sent over in support of this advanced party.

After crossing the river, and a series of combats, the rebels abandon Sultánpúr.

It was not till the 27th of August that the main body had completed the passage of the river, and even then the heavy guns, artillery park, hospital, and a wing of the 53rd were left on the further bank. Nor did the British force even then attack. On the evening of the 28th, however, the rebels assailed that force, and after a sharp fight were repulsed. They then fled and abandoned Sultánpúr to the conqueror.

The marches and counter-marches of the rebels.

It is difficult to follow the Oudh rebels in their continuous marches and counter-marches. But few of the old sepoys, the men who had been the backbone of the mutiny, were now among them. Their fluctuating numbers were composed almost entirely of the adherents and vassals of the tálúkdárs and landowners of the province, aided by the scum of the population, the refuse of the jails. Their movements were extremely irregular. One day they appeared to retire into Ámethi, a fort twenty-five miles from Sultánpúr, seven miles in circumference, composed of mud walls and surrounded by a jungle, the residence of Lál Madho Singh, a young chief determined in his hostility to the British; then they were heard of near Mozaffarnaggar, then at Rámpúr Kassia.

Sir Hope Grant determines to postpone further operations

It became evident to Sir Hope that nothing would drive them to submission but force, and he had full instructions to use it. The season, however, was unhealthy, and, having gained Sul-

Book XV. Chapter II.

1858. August.

till after the rainy season.

tánpúr, he resolved, with the concurrence of Sir Colin Campbell, to postpone further operations till the middle of October.

The story returns to Rohilkhand.

Whilst the gallant soldiers of Sir Hope Grant's force are waiting, with anxious hearts, for the period of renewed action, it may not be inopportune to take a rapid glance at the events which had been occurring in the meanwhile in other parts of the disturbed province.

In the last volume* I recorded the close of the Rohilkhand campaign and the death of the Moulvi, the daring Ahmad Ulla of Faizábád. But although the campaign was terminated, some time elapsed before the border-lands of Oudh and of Rohilkhand were completely pacified. Many landowners on both sides of the border resented the conduct of the rájá of Powáin, and took up arms to punish, if they could, an act which they regarded as treachery in its basest form. It soon appeared, however, that the rebels could not agree amongst themselves, and they soon began to act independently of each other. One leader,

Nizám A'li Khán.

named Nizám Áli Khán, with a considerable following, threatened the station of Philibít. Then there appeared in the field the whilom pseudo-viceroy of the province, the treacherous pensioner

Khán Bahádur Khán, the Farakhábád nawáb. Wiláyat Sháh.

Khán Bahádur Khán, with about four thousand followers; the nawáb of Farakhábád with five thousand; and a third under Wiláyat Sháh with three thousand. The authorities, however, were on their guard. They sent a small force, including

* Vol ii. pages 540–44.

Book XV. Chapter II.

1858. August.

the cavalry commanded by the gallant de Kantzow, to protect Powáin, and they stimulated the corpulent rájá of that place to keep his levies, two thousand strong, in constant training. This measure saved Powáin; but in other parts of Rohilkhand it was found difficult to put down disorder. Towards the end of August, indeed, Áli Khán Mewáti, acting in concert with the Nizám Áli Khán above alluded to, approached so near Philibít as to menace Núriah, a large village ten miles only from that British military post.

The rebels menace Núriah.

The force at Philibít was commanded by Captain Robert Larkins, 17th Panjáb infantry. It consisted of the 2nd Panjáb cavalry under Captain Sam Browne,* the 17th Panjáb infantry† under Captain Larkins, the 24th Panjáb pioneers‡ under Ensign Chalmers, and a detachment of Kemáon levies under Lieutenant Cunliffe. Both Captain Larkins and the chief civil officer, Mr. Malcolm Low, considered that the occupation of Núriah by the rebels was at all hazards to be prevented. Larkins accordingly detached one hundred men of the 24th pioneers and one hundred 2nd Panjáb cavalry, under Lieutenant Craigie, to hold that village, Mr. Low accompanying the party.

Larkins sends a body of men under Craigie to hold the village.

Craigie—who, as senior officer commanded—reached Núriah on the 28th of August. On the

* Now Lieutenant-General Sir Samuel Browne, V.C., K.C.B.
† Now the 25th native infantry.
‡ Now the 32nd native infantry.

Book XV. Chapter II.

1858. August.

Craigie encounters the rebels,

following morning the rebel chiefs I have named came down with three guns, three hundred infantry, and one hundred cavalry to attack the place. Craigie made excellent dispositions to meet them outside the town, and checked their advance. So well did the rebels fight, however, that when nineteen of their cavalry met in a hand-to-hand encounter a party of the 2nd Panjáb cavalry, under Rassaidár Hakdád Khán, fourteen of the nineteen were killed fighting.

and compels them to fall back.

This occurred on the left flank. On the right flank Craigie repulsed them in person. They then fell back on Sirpúrah, three miles distant.

Larkins, hearing at Philibít the enemy's fire, thought it advisable to reinforce Craigie. Accordingly he directed one hundred and fifty 2nd Panjáb cavalry, one hundred and seventy-five 17th Panjáb infantry, and one hundred Kamáon levies to proceed at once, under the orders of

Browne is sent to reinforce Craigie.

Captain Sam Browne, to Núriah. Browne set off at once, and reached Núriah at 4 o'clock that evening.

Browne reconnoitres,

He at once reconnoitred the rebel position. It was on a rising ground or mound, amid the débris of the ruined village of Sirpúrah, separated from Núriah by an inundated tract of country nearly a mile in width, the inundating water varying from one to two feet. From that side

and resolves to make a détonr and attack the rebels.

Browne saw that it was impossible to attack. It was possible, however, to assail the position from the other side. The energetic magistrate, Mr. Malcolm Low, having procured him guides in the persons of an old woman and a boy, Browne started at midnight to make the détour necessary for the success of his plan.

Book XV. Chapter II.

1858. August.

Taking with him two hundred and thirty Panjáb cavalry, one hundred and fifty 17th native infantry, one hundred 24th pioneers, and one hundred Kemáon levies, Browne worked round the enemy's right flank, and by daybreak reached a position on his left rear admirably adapted for his purpose. The fatigue had been great, and Browne halted for a few minutes to refresh men and horses. Whilst so halting the rebels discovered him, and at once made preparations to resist him, bringing three 9-pounders to bear on his advance, and having one on their proper right flank. There was no time for further rest, so Browne at once moved forward.

He gains a position on the left rear of the rebels, when he is discovered.

He then advances.

Covering his front with skirmishers, and giving them strict orders not to fire, but to use the bayonet only, Browne pushed his infantry forward through some grass jungle which served to screen their movements. Very soon, however, the enemy's guns began to play on his cavalry on the left, which were marching on the open road. Browne, who was with that cavalry, seeing the effect which one of them, fired with grape at eighty yards, was producing, galloped up to it, accompanied only by an orderly, and at once engaged in a desperate hand-to-hand encounter with the gunners, hoping to prevent them working their piece till the skirmishers should come up. Surrounded by the enemy, who attacked him with great fierceness, Browne attained his object. He did prevent the working

The enemy's gun annoying the advance,

Browne charges the gunners,

Book XV. Chapter II.

1858. August.

of the gun until the skirmishers came up and relieved him. In the fight, however, he was first wounded on the knee; immediately afterwards his left arm was severed at the shoulder. As he received this terrible wound, his horse, struck in the face, reared up and fell back on him. Just then the Wúrdi major of his regiment, followed by two or three others, rushed in, and, though the former was severely wounded, these men kept the rebels at bay, and saved their commanding officer. Immediately afterwards the infantry came up, bayoneted the gunners, and secured the gun which Browne had captured.*

and is severely wounded,

but gains his point.

Meanwhile, the infantry push on.

To go back for a moment. Whilst Browne was thus engaging the gunners, the skirmishers had advanced steadily without firing a shot until close to the position, when a body of the enemy's infantry lying in the grass jumped up and fired. On this the skirmishers, firing a volley, dashed

* Few more gallant deeds than this were performed during the war. Mr. Malcolm Law, who was near Browne at the time, considered the daring act of prowess to have been the means of preventing the rebel gunners reloading and firing upon the infantry at the most critical period of the whole action. Sir William Mansfield stated that in his opinion and in that of Sir Colin, the affair was "very brilliant," and as "quite one of the best things we have seen of the sort, the attack by you having been made in a most soldierly manner and *secundum artem.*" Captain Browne received the Victoria Cross for his daring. The reputation of this gallant officer as a man of great ability and conduct had already been made, and he has subsequently shown himself as qualified to conduct large operations in the field as he was willing to risk his life in the cause of duty.

on, secured the gun, and, aided by the supports and reserve, carried the position.

Complete defeat of the rebels.

The cavalry on the right, meanwhile, had pushed on and, simultaneously with their comrades on the left, attacked the enemy's flank, and captured one gun. This completed their discomfiture. They broke and fled into the jungle, followed, as far as it was possible to follow them, by the victorious horsemen. Their loss had been heavy, amounting to three hundred men killed, their four guns, their ammunition, and their stores. The two rebel leaders escaped, though one of them, Nizám A'li Khán, had been wounded.

Eastern Oudh.

In eastern Oudh, near Allahábád, there were about this time many bold and daring tálúkdárs, the men who had already caused trouble to Longden at Ázamgarh, and who were at this time exerting themselves to the utmost to stimulate opposition to the British. They went so far, indeed, as to threaten with condign punishment any member of their class who should submit to or accept the friendship of the common enemy. On these threats they acted. Bábú Rámparshád Singh, a tálúkdár of Soráon who had displayed British sympathies, was attacked by some of these confederated rebels, who burned his house, sacked the town, and took himself and his family prisoners. On the intelligence of this outrage reaching Allahábád Lord Canning hastily organised a small force, to be designated the Soráon field force, composed of two hundred and sixty of the 32nd foot, eighty of the 54th foot, the 7th

Soráon is sacked by the rebels.

Book XV. Chapter II.

1858. July.

A British force is sent under Berkeley to clear the district.

Panjáb infantry, seventy men Brasyer's Sikhs, fifty-two troopers 6th Madras light cavalry, sixty sabres Láhor light horse, detachments of horse and foot artillery, and nine guns and mortars, and placed them under the command of Brigadier Berkeley, C.B., with directions to reassert British authority in that part of the country.

Dahâin

Berkeley crossed the Ganges on the 12th of July, and on the 14th came in sight of a body of rebels at Daháin. Daháin was not properly a fort. It was rather a large area of jungle surrounded by a dilapidated earthen wall and ditch, and fenced with a thorny abattis. In the centre of the enclosure was a square brick-house. On Berkeley's approach the rebels retired within the enclosure, allowing the British to occupy the village and the jungle outside without opposition. Berkeley waited for the arrival of his heavy guns, and then opened fire; but the result, owing to the dense nature of the jungle, not being satisfactory, he sent on his infantry to storm. The result was entirely successful. About two hundred and fifty rebels were killed in the ditch alone; as many more, chased through the jungle, were cut down by the cavalry and the horse artillery.

is captured by Berkeley.

Description of Saráon.

Resting on the 15th, Berkeley proceeded on the 16th to the fort of Tirúl, seven miles north of Soráon. He found this fort in the middle of an impenetrable thorny jungle, through which a few paths were cut in directions only known to the natives of the place; and it had walls, bastions, ditches, escarps, like a miniature fortress, with a stronghold in the centre, into which the garrison could retire on being closely pressed. There were only three guns on the bastions, but the walls were loop-holed for musketry. So thick was the jungle around, that Berkeley could scarcely gain a view of the fort; he therefore deemed it prudent to employ his mortars and a 24-pounder before sending in his infantry. This plan succeeded. The enemy evacuated the place during the night, leaving behind them their three guns and their gun-ammunition. The fort was then destroyed.

Under pressure the rebels evacuate it.

By a somewhat similar train of operations, Berkeley captured and destroyed a fort at Bhairpúr. Having thus completed the work entrusted to him, he returned with his field force to Allahábád. After a brief interval, he was again sent out to demolish other forts in Oudh at distances accessible from Allahábád. In this manner he extended his force as far as Partábgarh. Pushing on, then, to Sultánpúr, he touched Hope Grant's force, and they united the line of posts direct from Allahábád to Lakhnao.

Berkeley clears the forts of Oudh as far as Partábgarh, and touches Hope Grant's force at Sultánpúr.

The force under Rowcroft, and the *Pearl* brigade acting with it under Captain Sotheby, whom we left at A'mórha at the end of April, had fallen back on Captainganj. In the interval there was occasional sharp fighting. On the 9th of June a detachment of both services, led by Major Cox, the sailors commanded by Lieutenant Turnour, and some twenty marines by Lieutenant Pym, marched on A'mórha, where, it had been ascertained, Muhammad Husén had arrived in

Rowcroft's force and the Pearl brigade

Book XV. Chapter II.

1858. June–Aug.

force. Cox divided his detachments into two parts; one led by himself, the other—to which were attached the sailors and marines—by Major J. F. Richardson. Setting out at 2 o'clock in the morning, and arriving at daybreak within a mile of Ámórha, they were suddenly met by a heavy fire from skirmishers thrown out by the rebels. Pym and the marines drove these in: Cox then opened fire with his guns. Then foiling an attempt made to outflank him, he drove the rebels out of the place.

defeat the rebels at A'mórha

and Harriah.

Nine days later a larger detachment of Rowcroft's force again attacked the same rebel leader at the head of four thousand men at Harriah, and inflicted on him a defeat so crushing that he fled from that part of the country. A little later Rowcroft moved with his force to Hír, in the Gorákhpúr district, to guard the frontier until the advance of Sir Hope Grant in force should sweep the districts below him.

Rowcroft then falls back on Hír.

Isolated actions in the more western part of the province produced results not less beneficial. It happened that on the 7th of August a rebel band, the advance of the force of the rebel Firoz Sháh, attacked the station of Mohan, on the river Sái, seventeen miles from Lakhnao on the road to Fathgarh. Mohan was one of the places in which British rule had been re-established, and was at the time the head-quarters of the Deputy Commissioner of the district, Mr. Pat Carnegy, already mentioned in these pages.*

The rebels attack Mohan.

* Vol. ii. page 339.

At Mr. Carnegy's disposal was a native police battalion. The river Sái, close to Mohan, was traversed by a bridge. On the evening of the 7th of August the rebel band referred to, numbering two hundred infantry and one hundred and fifty cavalry—the advance guard of a larger force—drove in the police pickets, crossed the bridge, and made every preparation to attack the town the following morning.

Evelegh marches against them,

Information of this attack reached Colonel Evelegh, C.B., commanding at Nawábganj, at 5 o'clock on the morning of the 8th. An hour later Evelegh set off with three hundred Sikh cavalry under Godby, two horse-artillery guns, twenty-five gunners mounted, to support the guns, and twelve rank and file of the 20th foot, mounted on limbers, and reached a point three miles from Mohan. Conceiving that were he to continue his direct advance the rebels would acquire information of his approach, Evelegh turned off from that point to the village of Husénganj—a village between Mohan and Rassúlábád, the general headquarters of Firoz Sháh, and the occupation of which would cut the rebels' line of retreat. His foresight was justified; for on coming within a mile of Húsénganj, he perceived the rebels falling back on that place from Mohan. He immediately pursued them with his small force, but finding that his guns could not travel fast enough to overtake them, he pushed forward his cavalry under Godby. The result was satisfactory. Godby laid low forty-five of the rebels and

and defeats them.

Book XV. Chapter II.

1858. July.

captured their only gun, a brass 3-pounder, together with one elephant and two camels.*

Nearer to Lakhnao, between the Rohilkhand frontier and that city, a gallant deed performed by the Kavanagh whose immortal heroism was recorded in the last volume,† tended greatly to the pacification of the district in which it occurred.

Kavanagh and Dawson capture Sandéla.

Of the district of Malhiábád, twelve miles north-west of the capital, Mr. Kavanagh was Assistant Commissioner. Eighteen miles further to the north-west, lay the town of Sandéla, occupied chiefly by Patháns, possessing many brick-built houses and a small mud fort, and situated in a level plain. The Patháns of this place had displayed a determined hostility to the British, and had lost no opportunity to threaten their posts and to intercept their communications. It occurred to Kavanagh, a daring man, fertile in resources and full of the love of adventure, that it would be possible to put an end to these excesses by the capture of the town. He proposed, therefore, to Captain Dawson, commanding one of the new police levies, to attack Sandéla. Dawson agreed. The place was stormed on the 30th of July, the rebels were driven out, and the town remained in the occupation of the British. Kavanagh displayed great daring on this occasion. Nor was his tact inferior to his courage. By a ready display of that quality, he won over several

* This action had the effect of clearing the rebels from many of the districts of Unáo and Malláon.

† Vol. ii. page 163.

Book XV. Chapter II.

1858. July–Sept.

zamindárs to the British cause, and even engaged them to maintain a number of matchlockmen at their own expense for its support.

The Oudh banks of the Ganges.

The banks of the Ganges in Oudh, even so far down as Allahábád, required during these three months of July, August, and September, very close watching. They were infested by bands of rebels, some of whom pillaged the villages in Oudh; others, crossing the river, attacked and plundered those in British territory. To remedy this evil, river steamers were employed during the rainy season, when the river was navigable. On one occasion, information having reached the authorities, towards the end of July, that the rebels had collected many boats, ready, whenever a favourable opportunity should offer, to cross into British territory, a force of one hundred and twenty Sikhs and two guns was despatched in a steamer to destroy the boats. They did destroy some twenty boats, but the forts which the rebels occupied were too well armed and too strong to be attacked. The expedition against these was deferred, but on several occasions in August and September small detachments were sent up the river to check the predatory instincts of the rebels, and in most cases this object was accomplished.

Position in Oudh occupied by the rebels.

At the period at which we have arrived, the end of September 1858, the position occupied by the British in Oudh was very peculiar. They held a belt of country right across the centre of the province, from east to west; whilst the districts north and south of that belt were

Book XV. Chapter II.

1858. October.

either held by the rebels or were greatly troubled by them. North of the belt were the Bégam, Mammú Khán, Firoz Sháh, Hardat Singh, and leaders less notorious, with their followers; south of it were Béni Mádhú, Hanmant Singh, Harichand, and others. Besides these, in the north-eastern corner of the province, near the Nipál frontier, Náná Sáhib and his adherents were believed to rest.

The rebels attack Sandéla,

In October the cessation of the rains made the movement of troops again possible. The rebels were the first to take advantage of the change of season. On the 3rd of October Harichand with six thousand men and eight guns, crossed the Gúmti ten miles north of Sandéla. His force, increased by the junction of several zamindárs and their following to twelve thousand men and twelve guns, arrived within three miles of that post on the morning of the 4th. Sandéla was occupied by the Captain Dawson already spoken of with his newly raised police battalions and other infantry levies, one thousand four hundred strong, and five hundred irregular cavalry levies. On the approach of the rebels in such overwhelming force, Dawson placed his infantry in the small mud fort and sent his cavalry to Nalliábád. He kept the rebels at bay till the 6th, when Major Maynard, with a detachment of the 88th foot, two 9-pounder guns, two $2\frac{1}{2}$-inch mortars, two hundred and fifty police cavalry, and six hundred police foot, joined him, taking up the five hundred cavalry on the way. Maynard at once attacked the rebels and drove

are held in check by Dawson,

driven back by Maynard,

Book XV. Chapter II.

1858. October.

them to Pannú, about four miles distant, where they took up a very strong position. On the evening of the 7th, Brigadier Barker reached Sandéla with a strong column,* attacked the rebels on the morning of the 8th, and, after a desperate battle, completely defeated them. His loss, however, was severe, being eighty-two of all ranks killed and wounded. Major Seymour, Queen's Bays, Major Maynard, whose charger was hacked to death with tulwars when in the thick of the fight, and Lieutenant Green, of the Rifle Brigade, who received thirteen wounds, including the loss of his left arm and the thumb of his right hand, greatly distinguished themselves on this occasion. The rebels lost a large number, especially in the pursuit, which promptly followed on the victory. A few days later, after a hard day's fight, accompanied by many casualties, the fort of Birwah fell into the hands of the victors.

and completely defeated by Barker.

Gallantry of Seymour, of Maynard, of Green.

About the same time, the 5th of October, Brigadier Evelegh defeated the rebels at Miánganj, between Lakhnao and Kánhpúr, took two guns, and put about two hundred of them *hors de combat;* and on the 8th Sir Thomas Seaton added to his former laurels by intercepting a large body of the rebels on the frontier near Shahjahánpúr, killing three hundred of them, and taking three guns. The same day an attack

Successes of Evelegh and Seaton.

* Two field batteries, two squadrons Queen's Bays, six hundred and seventy native cavalry sabres, two hundred and fifty 88th foot, one hundred 3rd battalion Rifle Brigade, 900 police battalion.

Book XV. Chapter II.

1858. October.

upon Powáin was repulsed by the rájá of that place, though with trifling loss.

Lord Clyde's plan of pacification

These were the small actions which indicated the reopening of the campaign. The comprehensive plan which the Commander-in-Chief, now become Lord Clyde, had drawn up during his stay at Allahábád, came into operation only on the 15th of October. This plan was devised on the principle of acting by columns in all the districts simultaneously, so that, driven out of one district, the rebels might not be able, as they had previously, to take refuge in another. Thus, by Lord Clyde's plan, one column was drawn from Rohilkhand for operations in the north-west of

in general.

Oudh, clearing Mohamdi, Náorangábád, and similar places of importance, and proceeding then to establish itself at Sitápúr. For operations in the Baiswára country four brigades were detailed. Another column was posted to guard the Doáb; another to guard the Kánhpúr road; whilst other smaller columns starting from Lakhnao, Nawábganj, Dariábád, and Faizábád were ordered to be kept movable.

The plan more in detail.

The reader will at once conceive the general purport of the plan. The brigades detailed for duty in the Baiswára country would occupy the whole of the Faizábád district between the Ganges and the Ghághrá. Pushing then northward they would reconquer the country between the Ghághrá and the Rápti, holding out a hand to Rowcroft's force, on their right, in the Gorákhpúr district. Simultaneously the Rohilkhand force would reconquer Sitápúr and the places in the

Khairábád division. Then, with his right firmly fixed, as a pivot, at Balrámpúr and a point beyond the Rápti, Lord Clyde would wheel his main force round to the right till its left point should touch the Rohilkhand column, when the whole, sweeping onwards, would clear the northernmost parts of the province, and drive the surviving rebels, who should refuse to surrender, into the jungles of the kingdom of Nipál.

Instructions sent to Hope

On the 23rd of October Lord Clyde despatched instructions in the same spirit to Sir Hope Grant. That officer was directed, in co-operation with Brigadiers Pinickney and Wetherall, to make a circuit, moving up the Gúmti as far as Jagdispúr, then turning sharp to his left and moving southward by Jáis, place himself between Parsidápúr and A'methi, dispersing any rebels on his way. The brigadiers mentioned received at the same time detailed instructions as to their action so as to make it co-operate with Sir Hope's movement and to ensure the success of the general plan.

Wetherall marches on Rampúr Kussia.

Hope Grant, in obedience to these instructions, started immediately, arranging with Brigadier Wetherall, who was marching up from Sariám to join him on the 4th of November, and attack the fort of Rámpúr Kússia, held by an active partisan named Rám Ghúlám Singh. But Wetherall, reaching the vicinity of Rámpúr Kússia on the morning of the 3rd, resolved, despite of the orders he had received to wait for Sir Hope, to assail the place at once. Fortune greatly favoured him. Rámpúr Kússia was in very deed a stronghold.

Book XV. Chapter II.

1858. November.

Description of the place.

Its outer fortification, formed of mud ramparts, was three miles in circumference. Within this, surrounded up to the outer works by a dense jungle, was another fort, and within this again a stone building. So much for the interior. But beyond, and surrounding the outer ramparts, there was again a dense jungle in every direction save in that of the north-west; and beyond the ramparts was a formidable abattis. The ditch was deep but narrow, and there were rifle-pits in the part which, in fortification, would correspond to the berm.* It happened, however, that on one side the ditch and ramparts had not, for a very small space, been completed, and it fortunately happened that Wetherall lighted on this particular spot. At any other point he would certainly have been repulsed, but at this he effected an entrance, and carried the place and its twenty-three guns, with a loss of seventy-eight men killed and wounded. The rebels lost about three hundred.

Wetherall lights upon an unguarded point and takes the place.

Hope Grant first heard of Wetherall's success on the afternoon of the 3rd. He at once joined him at Rámpúr Kússia. Thence, in pursuance of instructions, he proceeded to A'methi. This fort likewise was almost covered by jungle. It was garrisoned by four thousand men, one thousand five hundred of them sepoys, and thirty guns. Grant arrived within two miles of its north-eastern face at 2 o'clock on the afternoon of the 7th of November. A reconnaissance

A'methi surrounded by the British,

* Sir Hope Grant's *Incidents in the Sepoy War.*

Book XV. Chapter II.

1858. November.

promptly made, assured him that the rebels were bent on resistance. On returning from this reconnaissance he found a messenger from Lord Clyde, stating that he was encamped three miles to the east of the fort. The Commander-in-Chief, in effect, having failed to induce the rájá of A'methi to come to terms, had marched from Pertábgarh on the 6th, to bring him to reason. This active measure succeeded. The rájá rode into camp on the morning of the 8th, and tendered his submission, yielding his stronghold.

surrenders to Lord Clyde.

A'methi taken, Grant, carrying out the orders of Lord Clyde, proceeded to Shankarpúr to attack it from the north, whilst Wetherall and Pinckney should invest it on the east and south, and Eveleigh on the west. In performing his part of the combined movement Evelegh was delayed by the bad roads and the opposition of the rebels. He defeated these on the 8th at Morar Máu, and on the 9th he took the fort of Simri, but these operations so delayed him that he was unable to arrive in time to take up a position to cut off the retreat of the chief of Shankarpúr and his followers.

Shankarpúr is invested on three sides.

This chief was no other than Béni Mádho, and he had with him a following estimated at fifteen thousand men. The Commander-in-Chief, anxious to avoid bloodshed, had offered him very favourable terms if he would surrender. Béni Mádho had returned the proud reply that he would yield his fort as he could not defend it, but that he would not yield himself as he belonged to his king! That night he and his followers evacu-

The fort surrenders,

but Béni Mádho escapes,

Book XV. Chapter II.

1858. Nov.–Dec.

ated the fort by its uninvested face. Not, however, with the freedom from molestation they had hoped for. Fleeing hastily to Dúndia Khéra they were encountered on the way by Eveleigh and defeated, with the loss of three of their guns.

and is encountered and beaten by Evelegh on his retreat.

Converging marches of Grant,

Shankarpúr was at once occupied by Grant, who then marched on the Ghághrá, which he crossed in face of the rebels, led by the rájá of Gonda and Méhndi Húsén, on the 27th of November, pursued the enemy twenty-four miles, and captured four guns. Marching thence towards Rái Baréli, he beat the rebels again at Machlígáon on the 4th of December, taking two guns, reached the fort of Banhassia, whence he extracted five guns, on the 5th, Gonda on the 9th, and Balrámpúr on the 16th. Lord Clyde, meanwhile, having learned the direction taken by Béni Mádho, took Evelegh's brigade with him, and marched on Dúndia Khéra, and attacked the chief on the 24th of November and completely defeated him, taking all his guns. Béni Mádho, however, escaped. The other columns had by this time formed a complete cordon round the circumference of eastern Oudh. They now closed in, and marching from their different points of departure, and on a common centre, traversed the whole territory, demolishing forts and strongholds, and re-establishing the civil power as they advanced.

Lord Clyde,

and the other columns.

The colnmn from Barélí

Whilst the east was being thus pacified, the Barélí column, commanded by Colin Troup, employed all its efforts to bring about a similar

Book XV. Chapter II.

1858. Nov.–Dec.

result on the western side. Crossing the Rohilkhand frontier in the end of October, Troup advanced on Sitápúr, dispersed the talúkdárs who attempted to oppose him in the vicinity of that place, captured Mitháoli on the 8th, and gave a final defeat to the rebels at Méhndi on the 18th of November. Columns, meanwhile, under Gordon, Carmichael, and Horsford, were engaged in clearing the country south of the Ghághrá, and before these the irreconcileable chiefs, men of the stamp of Béni Mádho, and Béni Mádho himself, fell back.

takes up its position in the converging line,

and sweeps chiefs before it.

Hope Grant, I have said, had reached Balrámpúr on the 16th of December. There he learned that Bálá Ráo, brother of Náná Sáhib, had taken refuge in the fort of Túlsipúr, twelve miles distant, with a number of followers and eight guns, and that he had been joined there by Muhammad Húsén, and his adherents. Grant at once directed Rowcroft to move from his position at Hír, and, reinforcing him with the 53rd, directed him to attack Túlsipúr. Rowcroft obeyed orders, found the enemy drawn up to receive him, beat them after a feeble resistance, but could not pursue them for want of cavalry. Hope Grant, fearing lest the rebels should escape into the Gorákhpúr country, then took up the pursuit himself, and cutting off Bálá Ráo from Gorákhpúr, ascertained that he had retreated with six thousand men and fifteen guns along the margins of the jungle to a place near Kandakót, where there was a half-ruined fort at the confluence of two rivers. Manœuvring with great

Hope Grant touches Rowcroft,

and sweeps the rebels into Nipál.

Book XV. Chapter II.

1859. January.

skill, and placing his columns in a position so that escape to any other quarter but Nipál was impossible, Grant moved against them on the 4th of January 1859, and drove them across the border, taking all their guns.

Whilst Grant was thus engaged, Lord Clyde, sending Evelegh to the west to join Troup, was engaged in sweeping the country from the points occupied by his troops towards the Nipál frontier.

On his side,

Moving on to Sikrora, with Grant's force forming his right, touching, as we have seen, Rowcroft's force on the extreme right, and which formed, as it were, the pivot, Lord Clyde drove the Bégam and Náná Sáhib before him from Bondi and Baraitch; then advancing on Nanpára, cleared the country between it and the Ghághrá; then marching on Bánki, close to the Nipál frontier, he surprised the camp of the rebels, defeated them with great slaughter, and drove them into Nipál. This action and that of Hope Grant at Túlsipúr, referred to in the preceding paragraph, cleared of Oudh the last remnants of the rebels. Sir William Mansfield wrote that he considered the mutiny crushed out; and Lord Clyde, sharing that opinion, left the province under the military care of Sir Hope Grant, instructing him to keep the frontier of the border of Nipál closely shut up, so as to prevent, if possible, the escape of any rebels into the lower country.

Lord Clyde sweeps the remaining rebels into Nipál.

Considering the mutiny crushed, he makes over command to Hope Grant and leaves.

The spirit of the rebels is not, however, extinguished.

The spirit, however, which had animated the rebel chieftains to sustain against the British a struggle which, during six months at least, had offered not a single ray of success, was not entirely extinguished.

Danger of fording Indian rivers.

Sir Hope Grant, taking leave of the Commander-in-Chief, proceeded to join Brigadier Horsford's force on the Rápti. An incident had occurred just before his arrival, which showed the great care required in attempting to ford Indian rivers. Horsford had driven a strong rebel force across that river, and in fording it in pursuit of them, many men of the 7th hussars and the 1st Panjáb cavalry had been swept away by the force of the current and were lost. Amongst these was Major Home of the 7th hussars. After some search his body was drawn out of a deep hole, his hands having a fast grip of two of the rebels, whilst the bodies of two troopers who perished with him were found, each with his hands clutching a rebel sowar! *

The Nipál frontier.

From one side only, from the side of Nipál, was further danger to be apprehended. On this side the frontier had a length of about a hundred miles, and a hundred miles of mixed hill and jungle; and with such a frontier it was always possible that, despite the best dispositions on both sides, the strictest precautions would be evaded.

Loyalty of Jang Bahádur.

At this crisis the real ruler of Nipál, the Mahárájá Jang Bahádur, behaved with the loyalty that had throughout characterised his dealings with the British. Not only did he inform the armed rebels who had crossed the border that he would afford them no protection, but he allowed British troops

* Grant's *Incidents in the Sepoy War.*

Book XV. Chapter II. 1859.

to cross the border to disarm any considerable body there assembled. Under this permission, Brigadier Horsford, early in the year, entered the Sonar valley, and crossing the Rápti at Sidonia ghát, came upon a body of rebels and captured fourteen guns; and, later on, Colonel Kelly, of the 34th, caused the surrender of six guns, after having chased the rebels with great loss under the hills. Under the pressure thus exercised, a moiety of the fifty thousand who had crossed into Nipál, one by one threw away their arms, and returned to their homes, trusting they would be allowed to settle down unmolested.

Gradual dispersion of the rebels.

A few more hardened

A few, more hardened in crime and therefore more hopeless of mercy, still continued to hold out, and some of these—the regiments which had perpetrated the Kánhpúr massacre, the 1st, the 53rd, and the 56th native infantry, led by Gújádar Singh, a rebel whose hate to the British had not been lessened by the loss of an arm when fighting against them—succeeded in crossing the border, in marching on Sikrora, and filching thence two elephants, and finally, when pursued from that place by Colonel Walker and the Queen's Bays, with two guns, in taking up a position at Bangáon, a small dilapidated fort on the river Naddi, at the entrance of the Ghúnglé jungles. There, at the end of April 1859, Colonel Walker, reinforced by four hundred men of the 53rd, and sixty of the 1st Sikh cavalry, attacked and completely defeated them.

invade Oudh

and are defeated.

Grant drives the remainder

Notwithstanding that the hot weather had set in, Sir Hope Grant deemed it of pressing impor-

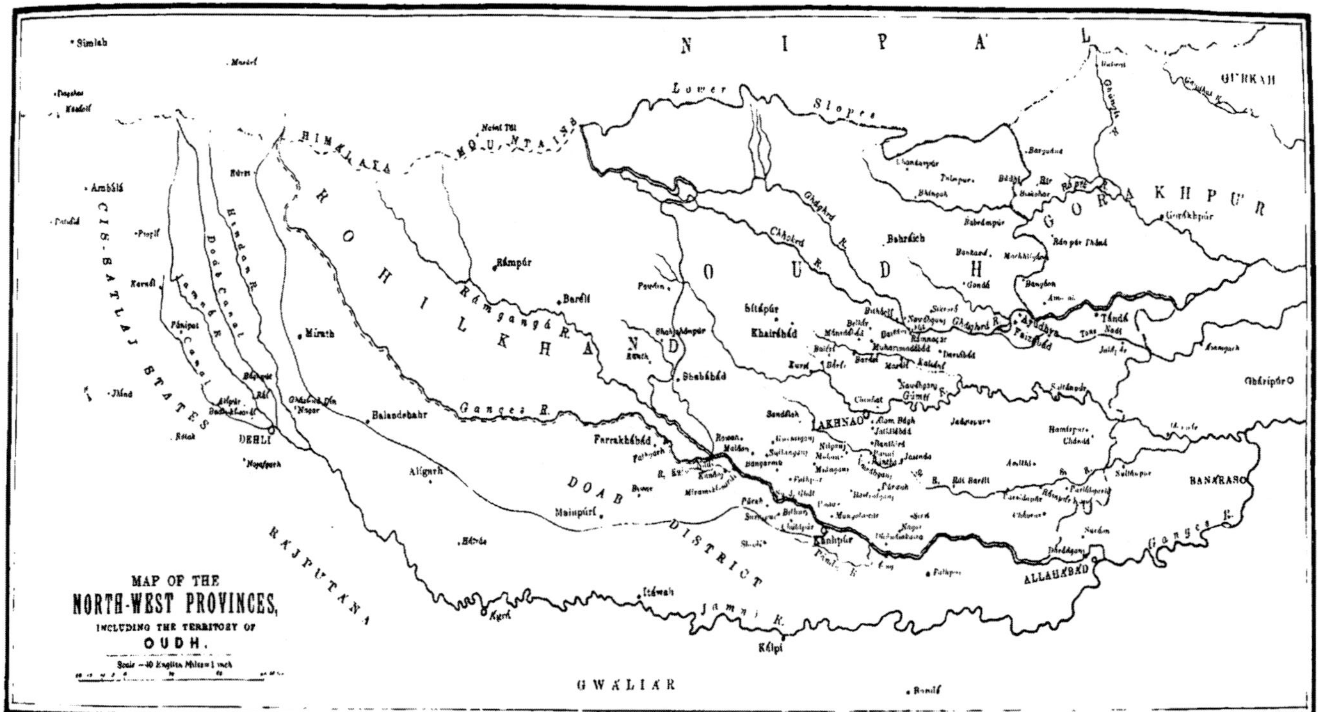
MAP OF THE
NORTH-WEST PROVINCES,
INCLUDING THE TERRITORY OF
OUDH.
Scale — 40 English Miles = 1 inch
NIPAL
Lower Slopes
HIMALAYA MOUNTAINS
ROHILKHAND
OUDH
GORAKHPUR
CIS-SATLAJ STATES
RAJPUTANA
DOAB DISTRICT
GWALIAR
GURKAH
Simlah
Ambálá
Mírath
DEHLI
Balandshahr
Alígarh
Rámpúr
Bareli
Farrakhábád
Maipúrí
Itáwah
Kálpi
Kánhpúr
LAKHNAO
Khairábád
Shahábád
Bahráich
Gondá
Faizábád
Gorakhpúr
BANARAS
ALLAHABAD
Ganges R.
Jamna R.
Ghághrá R.
Rámgangá R.

Book XV. Chapter II. 1859.

tance to drive the remainder of the rebels from the jungles. Learning that the last remnant of their disorganised forces was at the Sérwa pass, Grant moved against them in person, dislodged them by a turning movement, and then pursued them across the hills. The pursuit gave ample evidence of the state of exhaustion to which the enemy had been reduced. Without food and without arms and without money—for they lost here their last two guns—they were thenceforth powerless. Pursuit ceased, and Grant contented himself with posting troops at different points along the frontier as a precautionary measure. His only regret now was that Náná Sáhib and his brother Bálá Ráo had found refuge in Nipál. To the last the former had been defiant and daring as became his assumed position. Bálá Ráo, on the other hand, had expressed penitence and denied participation in the Kánhpúr massacre.

of the rebels from the jungles.

State of destitution to which they had been reduced.

At last, then, Oudh was at peace. The province had become British by a right far more solid and defensible than the pretext under which it had been seized in 1856. Then, the country of the ruler who had ever been true to his British overlord, was, in disregard of treaty, seized in the dead of the night, against the wishes alike of the sovereign and the people. Fifteen months experience of British rule, administered by doctrinaires who preferred the enforcement of their own theories to considerations of justice and policy, far from reconciling the people to their new master, had caused them to regret the sovereigns whom the British had expelled because of their mis-

Oudh finally becomes British.

Defect of the first title.

Book XV. Chapter II.

1859.

Its consequences.

government of that very people. They hailed, then, the opportunity, ingeniously fomented by the more influential of their countrymen, which seemed to promise them a relief from regulations which perplexed and from changes which irritated them. They joined in the revolt inaugurated by their brethren the sepoys—the majority of them Oudh men—and fought for independence. How pertinaciously they waged the contest has been told in these pages. No other part of India gave an example of a resistance so determined, so prolonged, as did Oudh. Throughout the struggle, the sense of the injustice perpetrated in 1856 steeled the hearts of its people and strengthened their resolution. If on some occasions they too precipitately fled, it was in the hope of renewing the struggle another day. When, finally, the sweep made over Oudh by Lord Clyde forced the remnant of the fighting class to take refuge in the jungles of Nipál, the survivors preferred starvation to surrender.* The agricultural population, the tálúkdárs, the landowners, the traders, accepted the defeat when, after that long struggle, they felt that it was final. Thenceforward Great Britain possessed Oudh by a title far sounder than that which she had set up in 1856, the title of conquest. She holds

The title of 1859 better,

* "Further on," wrote Sir Hope Grant, describing his last pursuit, "we discovered two of the rebels in a state of helpless exhaustion, dying from their wounds and from starvation. It was sad to see many of the poor wives of the sepoys, who had accompanied their husbands, deserted and left to die on the bare ground," and more to the same effect.

it now on a basis even stronger, on the basis of the affections of a people whom she has conciliated and of a territorial aristocracy whose rights, whilst defining, and, in some instances, curtailing, she has made inalienable.

Book XV.
Chapter II.

1857.
December.

that of 1880 the best of all.

BOOK XV.

CHAPTER III.

The Panjáb.

BEFORE proceeding to recount the other great military measure with which the story of the mutiny fitly closes, it is necessary that I should ask the reader to accompany me to the Panjáb to see how the fall of Dehlí, made possible by the noble self-denial of Sir John Lawrence, affected that border province. From the Panjáb the reader will return through the pacified provinces of the north-west to Ágra, in close vicinity to that Gwáliár but just reconquered by Sir Hugh Rose. In the succeeding book I shall record the most romantic episode in the history—the pursuit, from many starting points and by many independent columns, of the famous Tántia Topi.

Sir John Lawrence's position early in September 1857.

The decision at which Sir John Lawrence had arrived at the end of July 1857, to denude the Panjáb of troops in order to reinforce General Wilson's army before Dehlí, had not been arrived at without most serious and anxious considera-

Book XV. Chapter III.

1857. July.

tion. On the one side he had had before him General Wilson's letter announcing that unless he were reinforced from the Panjáb he would not be able to maintain his position, still less to assault the city; and the inner certainty that if General Wilson were to raise the siege of Dehlí the Panjáb would rise in insurrection. On the other he had the knowledge that the effective force of Europeans at his disposal, including the sick and convalescent, but not including the force under Nicholson, did not exceed four thousand men, and that these were not more than sufficient to maintain order in the Panjáb, even whilst the general feeling of the Panjábis should remain loyal; most insufficient should a striking reverse of fortune, such as the raising of the siege of Dehlí, turn the Panjábis against him. He had before him, in fact, a choice of two risks—the risk of a general rising in the Panjáb, caused by the effect which would certainly be produced in the minds of the Panjábis by a retreat from Dehlí; and the risk of rebellion induced by the knowledge that the Panjáb had been denuded of British.

Comparison of the two risks, one of which he was obliged to run.

Of the two risks, the second was undoubtedly really the lesser. To a nervous man, to a man fearing responsibility, however, the second risk would present dangers affecting to such a degree his position, that he would certainly shrink from incurring them. A man of that stamp would have argued that his primary duty was to protect the Panjáb, and that he dare not, for the sake of the uncertain chance of conquering Dehlí,

Book XV. Chapter III.

1857. July–Sept.

risk the safety of that province. "True," he would have said, "true it is that if the march of Nicholson's column enable Wilson to take Dehlí our situation will be ameliorated. But, Wilson might be repulsed; Wilson himself thinks it is quite a toss-up whether he will succeed or whether he will fail. And if he fail, the situation of the Panjáb without Nicholson's column will be a thousand times worse than if I were to retain it. Everything, then, depends upon a very doubtful 'if'; and, responsible for the Panjáb as I am, I dare not incur the risk." But Sir John was not a nervous man, and he had no fear of responsibility. He saw clearly that the one chance of preventing the further spread of the mutiny was to strike a blow at its heart. That heart palpitated at Dehlí. Every risk, then, which strengthened the blow to be struck at Dehlí was a prelude to safety.

Reasons for his decision in favour of the bolder policy.

How Nicholson's column successfully worked out the great result aimed at has been already recorded in these pages. Dehlí fell. But in the interval Sir John Lawrence had to meet the other risk of which I have spoken. He at once made preparations to face it. Nicholson's departure at the end of July had left in the Panjáb about four thousand European troops, including those sick and convalescent. Of these, three regiments were in the Pasháwar valley, but so reduced by sickness, that for the active work of a campaign they could not muster more than a thousand bayonets; one regiment, the 24th, held Láhor; one, sent from Sindh, held Múltan and Firozpúr; another

The Panjáb when Nicholson left it at the end of July.

1857. July–Sept.

How Sir John prepared to encounter the possible evil.

furnished detachments to hold Ráwal Pindi, Amritsar, and Jalandhar. Sir John first formed a movable column. For this purpose he drew from the 24th foot two to three hundred men, and joined with them four hundred Panjáb infantry and a few horsemen. The other troops alluded to being required for the purpose of watching, as at Pesháwar, the frontier, and elsewhere, the disarmed native troops, eighteen thousand strong, this column really constituted the only force which could be used in the event of an insurrection provoked by the hopes which the march of Nicholson's column might inspire in the minds of the disaffected.

Disaffection in the lower Hazára country.

The doubts which Sir John Lawrence had entertained regarding a prolonged continuation of the loyalty of the Panjábis were quickly justified. Nicholson had crossed the Satlaj on the 30th of July. Early in September it was discovered that the inhabitants of the lower Hazára country had conspired to revolt. Mostly Muhammadans, the people of that tract and of the adjoining hills had been tempted by the long successful resistance of Dehlí to plot the downfall of their English masters. They had evidently been close observers of the state of affairs, for they had arranged that their continued loyalty should depend on the turn affairs should take at Dehlí. If that royal city should not fall before the 10th of September, on that day they would revolt.

Their plot is discovered and baffled.

In this case to be forewarned was sufficient. Lady Lawrence, who was then at Marri, received the first intimation of the intended revolt. She

Book XV. Chapter III.

1857. December.

quickly entered into communication with Mr. Edward Thornton, Commissioner of Ráwal Pindi. That gentleman concerted at once with the other officials to baffle the conspirators. In a few hours their leaders were arrested, and the plot was thus nipped in the bud.

Rising in the country between Láhor and Múltan.

A few weeks later, a conspiracy of a similar nature actually came to a head in the country between Láhor and Múltán. On the evening of the 14th of December, the very day on which the assault on Dehlí was delivered, a Muhammadan official of the postal department arrived at Láhor from Goghaira, and making his way to Sir John Lawrence, reported "with somewhat of a malicious twinkle of the eye,"* that all the wild tribes inhabiting the jungle country between Láhor and Múltán had risen. Questioned further, he declared that the insurgents numbered one hundred and twenty-five thousand. Though he knew this number to be greatly exaggerated, Sir John, well aware of the wild and reckless character of the tribes to whom the tale referred, felt certain that a rising of a formidable character had taken place, and that it was a case to meet which it was necessary to take prompt and decided action. Within three hours, then, of the receipt of the message, one company of European infantry, two hundred Sikh cavalry, and three guns were on their way to the head-quarters of the insurgents. Small though the force was, totally inadequate to deal with any

Sir John meets

* *Panjáb Military Report*, page 16.

large body of rebels, the celerity with which it was despatched compensated for every disadvantage. The very rumour of their advance struck terror into the insurgents. They at once took refuge in the almost impenetrable jungles which formed their normal habitation. Their retreat did not in the least relax Sir John's endeavours to crush them. He sent reinforcement after reinforcement to his small column, and very speedily ensured the submission of the disaffected tribes.

Book XV. Chapter III.

1857-8.

and suppresses it.

This was the last attempt made by any portion of the population of the Panjáb to rise in revolt. The fall of Dehlí occurred about the same time to convince even the most disaffected that the star of England was still in the ascendant. The occurrences that followed seemed to add daily confirmation to this opinion. The relief of Lakhnao, the capture of that place, followed by the reconquest of Rohilkhand, and accompanied, almost, by Sir Hugh Rose's splendid campaign in central India, came as proof upon proof that the power which had won India was resolved to maintain it. In the latter half of the year 1858 one or two disturbances occurred which, by their exception to the general rule and by their easy suppression, served to prove the real tranquillity of the province.

Thenceforth, order throughout the Panjáb

is disturbed but slightly.

In July 1858 a portion of the 18th Panjáb infantry, stationed at Dĕra Ishmáil Khán on the Indus, planned a mutiny. The portion referred to was composed of Sikhs, known as the Malwái Sikhs, and numbered about a hundred. For

First at Dĕra Ishmáil Khán.

Book XV. Chapter III. — 1858. July.

some cause unknown, they proposed, it was said, to murder their officers, to seize the magazine and the fort, and to re-arm the 39th regiment native infantry, which had been disarmed some time previously. Fortunately, on the 20th of July, the plot was discovered. Major Gardiner of the 10th Panjáb native infantry, and Captain Smith of the artillery, proceeded, at 10 o'clock in the evening of that day, to the lines of the regiment and summoned two of the Malwáis. One, a sepoy, came out at once, when Major Gardiner ordered him to be confined. On hearing the order he ran off, at once pursued by the guard. Just as the foremost men of the guard had reached him a Malwái jemadar rushed out, cut down one man and wounded another, and fled with the sepoy. A few days later they were captured, and the revolt, of which they had been the ringleaders, was suppressed.

Suppressed by Major Gardiner.

Múltán.

At Múltán an attempt made, the following month, to dispose quietly and peaceably of some of the disbanded regiments, terminated in bloodshed. At that station there were the 62nd and 69th native infantry and a native troop of horse artillery. These men were a source of great embarrassment to the authorities, for it was considered unsafe to re-arm them; whilst, disarmed, they required European troops to guard them. It was resolved, as a middle course, to disband them by fractions, and allow them to depart quietly to their homes. The sepoys acquiesced in the decision when the decision was made known to them. Subsequently, however, they conceived

Embarrassment caused to the authorities there by the disarmed regiments,

the impression that it was intended to attack and destroy them piecemeal on their way home. Imbued with this idea, they rose in revolt. When the mid-day gun fired on the 31st of August, they seized clubs and whatever else they could find in the shape of weapons, and rushed to attack the European and Sikh troops. Those troops consisted of one hundred and seventy artillerymen, a wing of the 1st Bombay fusiliers, the 11th Panjáb infantry, and the 1st irregular cavalry. These men were taken by surprise, and five of their number were beaten to death with clubs. Lieutenant Miles, Adjutant of the Bombay fusiliers, was dragged from his horse and killed in the same manner. As soon, however, as the Europeans and Panjábis realised the state of affairs, they came up in strength, and showed no mercy to the assailants. The 11th Panjábis were especially furious at the unprovoked attack. Of the thirteen hundred men who made it, few lived to return to their native land.

the men of which, under the impression that they are about to be massacred, rise in revolt.

Suppression of the revolt.

Passing downwards through the territories of the loyal chieftains of the Cis-Satlaj states—of the rájá of Patiálá, who, at the very outset, cast in his lot with the British, protected the stations of Ambála and Karnál when the British army marched on Dehlí, guarded the grand trunk road from Karnál to Philor, co-operated with Van Cortlandt in Hissar, and maintained a contingent of five thousand troops for service with the British; of the rájá of Jhínd, who, emulating his brother rájá in loyalty, left his own country undefended to march against Dehlí, and in many

The reader traverses the loyal Cis-Satlaj states

and the Dehlí districts,

Book XV. Chapter III.

1858.

other ways rendered assistance to the good cause; and of the rájá of Nabhá, who aided in holding Lodiáná, supplied an escort for the siege-train, gallantly opposed the Jalandhar mutineers, and performed various other excellent services—the reader will traverse the pacified Dehlí territory till he reaches the district of Itáwah. Here he will make a short sojourn before proceeding to A'gra.

to Itáwah.

The position of Itáwah.

The Itáwah district had, in common with other districts in the Jamná Doáb, been included in the brigade command assigned to Sir Thomas Seaton.* The attention of that gallant soldier was, however, more constantly directed to the side of Rohilkhand than to the more peaceful districts to the south of him. In those districts order had been restored, and the civil administration generally re-introduced. The only chance of a renewal of disturbance in them arose from the possibility of some fugitive rebel from the country west of the Jamná endeavouring to restore the fortunes of his followers by a raid into a settled but little-guarded country. It was this possibility which occurred in the Itáwah district.

Inundated by rebels from across the Jamná.

The defeat of Sindia's rebellious troops at Gwáliár by Sir Hugh Rose had let loose on the country a number of turbulent partisans, who, escaping from the battle, had sought refuge in the ravines of the Jamná. Prominent among these was an adventurer named Rúp Singh. This man, followed by a few soldiers of the regular Gwá-

* Vol. ii. page 310.

Book XV. Chapter III.

1858.

liár contingent, a certain number of the fugitives of Sindia's army, and other rabble, crossed the Jamná and made his appearance at A'jítmal, twenty-five miles from Itáwah, in the month of July. Though he was routed by a force sent from Itáwah and forced to flee, he did not abandon the district. And, what was of more consequence, other adventurers, animated by similar aims, sprang up about the same time, and rivalled him in his endeavours to harass and plunder the newly pacified districts. Amongst all these marauders, however, Rúp Singh maintained the pre-eminence. Often beaten, he always managed to elude his pursuers. During long periods he was not heard of in the districts. But whenever that occurred, daily accounts of robberies and stoppage of traffic on the Jamná reached the authorities. It was then discovered that Rúp Singh had taken possession of a fort at Barhi, near the junction of the Chambal with the Jamná, and that from this place he levied contributions on travellers by land and water.

Rúp Singh

and his river piracy.

The exactions of this adventurer and of others like him reached at last so great a height that, in the month of August, a small force was despatched from Itáwah to destroy or disperse them. This force, commanded by Captain Gordon and accompanied by Mr. Lance, the able and energetic magistrate of the district, embarked in boats, and proceeded down the river towards Barhi. It had reached Garhá Kúdúr, a fortified village three miles from that place, and was still in the boats, when Rúp Singh attacked it.

A force proceeds against him from Itáwah,

Book XV. Chapter III.

1858.

Gordon's men at once disembarked, in spite of opposition, drove away the rebels, re-embarked, dropped down to Barhi, and took the place. After destroying three of the bastions of the fort and rendering it generally indefensible, Lance pushed on to Chakarnaggar, the resort of another rebel chief, completely defeated the rebels there, and fixed that place as the head-quarters of a small detachment to control the country. This prompt action for a time pacified the districts. But in October Rúp Singh reappeared on the Kúári with a following of four hundred men, and attacked a British picket on the Itáwa side of that river. Mr. Allan, in command of a few levies — one hundred and forty infantry and twenty-five sowars—happened to be at the moment at Sahson, not very far from the point of Rúp Singh's action. He at once went in pursuit of him, caught him near the village of Kúári, completely defeated him, and captured all his camels and pack-cattle. The band of the rebel leader then dispersed, and from that time the Itáwah district was undisturbed.

destroys Barhi,

and occupies Chakarnaggar.

Allan beats Rúp Singh on the Kúári,

when the band disperses.

In A'gra, since the relief of that place by Greathed, matters had remained fairly tranquil. In the early part of 1858 Brigadier Showers had been sent to command the district and to perform in its vicinity the work which he had so successfully accomplished in the Dehlí districts after the capture of the imperial city.* One of Showers's first acts was to work vengeance on some local

Showers at A'gra.

* Vol. ii. page 108.

rebels who had plundered the town of Báh and murdered the authorities. This was done on the 20th of March. Showers, making a long night-march, surprised the rebels at Kachrú and captured the ringleaders. But the task allotted to him and to the civil authorities in the fort was long and difficult. Not only were the districts swarming with small bands of insurgents, but the whole of the country west of the Jamná was in a state of complete insurrection. Gwáliár lies but sixty-five miles from A'gra, and it is no exaggeration to state that until the capture of Gwáliár by Sir Hugh Rose in June 1858, the influence of Mahárájá Sindia over his own people was not to be counted upon, and that A'gra was at any moment liable to an attack in force from any number of rebels.

Disturbed state of the districts.

This situation was entirely appreciated in A'gra. The guns of the fort remained pointed at the native town—the *focus* of a rebellion which might at any moment break out. Every precaution was, indeed, taken to prevent, or rather to ward off, such an event; but the fact that no European living beyond the range of the guns of the fort felt his life secure for a moment, shows how deep was the impression that a revolt was a mere question of opportunity. The slightest event might bring it on. The news of a disaster in the Doáb or in central India, the appearance on the Jamná of any one of the mutinied contingents or of Tántia Topi—any one of these eventualities would most certainly precipitate a catastrophe.

Apprehensions at A'gra.

Book XV.
Chapter III.
—
1858.

Colonel Fraser and Mr. E. A. Read.

Throughout this crisis the civil authorities at A'gra—Colonel Fraser, Mr. E. A. Reade, and their colleagues—displayed a coolness of judgment and a readiness of resource which left nothing to be desired. The self-denying energy with which they devoted themselves to the task of reorganising where reorganisation was possible, of meeting great and pressing wants from exhausted resources, of providing all the military and civil requirements day by day, and of infusing their own brave spirit into those whose fortunes were at the lowest, deserve a far longer and a fuller notice than I am able to give them in these pages. The history of the occupants of A'gra is the history of men who, deprived of the stimulus of action, of the excitement of the camp, of the joyous sound of the clash of arms, devoted all their energies to their country, and deserved fully the credit and the glory always assigned to deeds more showy but not more meritorious.

Their great deserts.

Meade's horse.

Amongst the useful measures carried out during the period of which I am writing was the raising of a corps of cavalry, subsequently known as Meade's horse. At the end of the year 1857 the want of native troopers and mounted orderlies at A'gra had been greatly felt, and as there were in the fort officers whom the mutiny had deprived of their employment, it was considered advisable to raise a regiment on a military footing. The task of raising it was, in December 1857, committed to Captain R. J. Meade.

Captain R. L. Meade.

This officer, who will occupy a conspicuous

figure towards the close of the next chapter, had been for some years brigade-major of the Gwáliár contingent, and in that office had won the confidence of the officers under whom he had served. He possessed a thorough acquaintance with the language of the people, and he invariably gave all his energies to the duties confided to him. It would have been impossible for a general in command to have had under his orders an officer who would more resolutely carry into execution the orders he received.

Process of formation of Meade's horse.

A body of a hundred Sikhs and Panjábi Muhammadans formed the nucleus of this new regiment. To them Meade added some forty odd Eurasians and native Christians, chiefly drummers and bandsmen, taken from the disbanded native regiments. These were ultimately increased to eighty-five, and were formed into a Christian troop. As none of these men had ever previously crossed a horse, some of Meade's difficulties may be imagined.

At the end of January 1858 Meade obtained an accession of forty-five mounted Játs, sent from Rohtak under a jemadar of good family by Mr. J. Campbell, collector of that district; and a little later the new commandant induced Baldéo Singh Thákur of Jhárra to raise, from men of his class in the neighbourhood of the Chambal, a troop of seventy horsemen. In this manner the regiment was formed, and Meade was, in a short time, able to form it into six class troops.* The labour

* 1. Sikhs; 2. Panjábi-Muhammadans; 3. Játs; 4. Christians; 5. Gwáliár Thákurs; 6. Mixed.

Book XV. Chapter III.

1858. Jan.-June.

of drilling the men and teaching many of them to ride may be imagined when it is considered that none of the men had served in the cavalry or as soldiers at all. Working incessantly himself, and aided by such men as Sergeant Hartigan, V.C., of the 9th Lancers, and who subsequently gained a commission in the 16th, by Cockburn, whose gallantry has been referred to in a previous volume, and by others, Meade was able, by the beginning of March, to show a fair proportion of his regiment fit for service. Brigadier Showers, who inspected them during that month, expressed himself well satisfied alike with men and horses.

The regiment is formed,

From this time up to the beginning of June Meade's horse were constantly employed in maintaining order in the neighbourhood of Ágra, and it would be difficult to exaggerate the services they rendered in this respect to the administrative and military authorities in the place.

and renders good service in the vicinity of A'gra.

But in June the aspect of Ágra suddenly changed. How on the 1st of that month Mahárájá Sindia was attacked and driven to flight by the rebels under Tántia Topi, I have recorded in a previous chapter. The mahárájá, abandoned by all but a few faithful men, fled to Dholpúr, intending to push on to Ágra. The news of his misfortune had, however, preceded him. Showers instantly despatched a squadron of Meade's horse to escort the fleeing sovereign with all honour into the capital of the north-west provinces. The mahárájá, who reached Ágra on the 2nd of June, remained there till the 14th and left it that day,

Sindia, after his defeat, is escorted to A'gra.

Book XV. Chapter III. 1858. June.

escorted by two squadrons of Meade's horse to Dholpúr, thence to proceed to join Sir Hugh Rose, expected to reach Morár on the 16th. News of Sir Hugh's arrival on that day having reached the maharájá, he set out on the morning of the 17th, still escorted by the two squadrons and made the march, fully sixty-five miles, within twenty-four hours. The events which followed have been recorded in the preceding book.

Showers moves to prevent Tántia Topi from fleeing northward.

Returning to Ágra, I have only to record the fact that on the defeat of Tántia Topi on the 17th and 19th of June at Morár and at Gwáliár Brigadier Showers sent out a detachment consisting of the 3rd Europeans and a battery of guns, to cover Bharatpúr, upon which place he believed the rebels to be marching. The demonstration was successful, inasmuch as the presence of the detachment induced Tántia Topi to bend his steps southwards. As soon as his march in that direction was definitively known, the detachment returned by way of Fathpúr Sikri to Ágra. Thenceforward that city and the districts east of the Jamná experienced the full relief caused by the crushing defeat, at a point so close to the British districts, of the one chieftain whose name up to that time had been a beacon of hope to the marauder.

Relief felt at A'gra by the recovery of Gwáliár.

Tántia Topi had fled from Gwáliár; had fled from Napier at Jáorá Alipúr; but whither? All that was known was that when he had fled from the battle field he had taken a southerly direction. Who could say how long he would

Book XV. Chapter III.

1858. June.

maintain that direction? It is time now that we should follow him, and recount in some detail the measures adopted by his pursuers to overtake him.

BOOK XVI.

CHAPTER I.

TÁNTIA TOPI, accompanied by Ráo Sáhib and the nawáb of Bandá, had fled from the field of Jáora Alipúr on the 22nd of June. The information which had induced Brigadier Showers to send a detachment to cover Bharatpúr was perfectly correct, for Tántia, as soon as he had ascertained he was no longer pursued, had turned his steps north-westwards. On reaching Sarmathurá, however, he learned the dispositions made by Showers. Foiled on one side, he pushed on directly westwards, hoping to gain Jaipúr, in which place he believed a strong party was prepared to rise in his favour.

Tántia Topi, baffled by Showers,

pushes towards Jaipúr.

On this route I propose to leave him, whilst I trace the positions taken up by the several British columns upon whom his pursuit was to devolve.

I have already shown how on the 29th of June Sir Hugh Rose made over the command of his

Book XVI. Chapter I.

1858. June.

force to Brigadier-General Robert Napier, and proceeded to Bombay to assume command of the army of that presidency. The season for active military operations on the black and spongy soil of central India had now passed away, and Napier hoped before the country should harden he would be able to afford some rest to his overworked soldiers. With this object he made arrangements for comfortably housing a portion of them at Gwáliár itself. Here he quartered three squadrons of the 14th light dragoons, Meade's horse, a wing of the 71st Highlanders, the 86th foot, the 25th Bombay native infantry, a company of Bombay artillery, a company of Royal Engineers, and a light field battery. To rest at and to hold Jhánsi he detached a squadron of the 14th light dragoons, a wing of the 3rd Bombay cavalry, the 3rd Bombay Europeans, the 24th Bombay native infantry, a company of Bombay sappers, and three guns of the late Bhopál contingent. Brigadier Smith's brigade—which, it will be remembered, took an active part in the operations against Gwáliár—consisting of two squadrons of the 8th hussars, two of the 1st Bombay lancers, the 95th foot, the 10th Bombay native infantry, and a troop of Bombay horse artillery, marched to occupy Sipri, whilst Mayne's irregular cavalry took up their position at Gúnah.

Napier cantons his force at Gwáliár

and at Jhánsi.

Smith's brigade occupies Sipri and Gúnah.

Roberts' Rajpútáná field force

But these were not the only troops which, in the month of July 1858, occupied positions overlooking the area on which only it was likely Tántia Topi would act. In a previous page I have recorded how General Roberts, commanding the Rajpútáná field force, had detached a column under Brigadier Smith to cover and to aid in the operations of Sir Hugh Rose. Roberts's force, diminished by the departure of that column, consisted of the 83rd foot, a wing of the 72nd Highlanders, wings of the 12th and 13th Bombay native infantry, two squadrons 8th hussars, two of the 1st Bombay lancers, three hundred Bilúchi horse, a light field battery, and a siege-train of six pieces. At the end of June Roberts lay with this force at Nasirábád.

at Nasirábád.

Roberts marches to cover Jaipúr.

Upon him it fell to strike the first blow against the fugitive leader. On the 27th of June Roberts learned from Captain Eden, the political agent, that Tántia Topi had sent emissaries to the disaffected party in Jaipúr assuring them that he was marching on that place, and begging them to be in readiness to join him. Roberts took his measures accordingly. On the 28th of June he set out from Nasirábád, and marching rapidly, reached Jaipúr before Tántia.

Tántia moves on Tonk followed by Holmes's light column.

Tántia, again foiled, turned southwards, and made a raid on Tonk, followed by a light column under Colonel Holmes.* The nawáb of this place, Vizir Muhammad Khán, was by no means disposed to submit to the dictation of a Maráthá fugitive with an English army at his heels. He, therefore, shut himself in his citadel with the men he could depend upon. The remainder of his force, with four guns, he left outside with orders to face the rebels. Instead of facing them

* Consisting of the cavalry and horse artillery, some native infantry, and two hundred 72nd Highlanders.

Book XVI. Chapter I. — 1858. June.

this force received them as brethren, and made over to them the four guns. With this addition to his army Tántia started off southwards to Madhopúr and Indragarh, still pursued by Holmes, and at a longer interval by Roberts.

Tántia takes four guns at Tonk and moves off.

The flight and the pursuit were alike retarded by the rains, which fell during this month with remarkable force, so much so that the river Chambal, swollen to a torrent, barred Tántia's passage from Indragarh to the eastward. Changing his course, then, he took a south-westerly course to Búndi, capital of the native state of the same name. The maháráo of Búndi, Rám Singh, had more than once displayed a disposition to strike for independence, but even he was not prepared to link his fortunes with those of Tántia Topi. He shut, therefore, the gates of Búndi in the face of the fugitive. Tántia, pursued, as he thought, by Holmes, had no time to stop to use force, but marched a few miles southward, then making a sudden tour westward, crossed the Búndi hills by the Kína pass, and made for the fertile country between Nasirábád and Nímach, a country which had already been the scene of warlike operations, and the larger towns in which had more than once shown a disposition to favour the rebellion. Tántia was able to change his course without fear of being disturbed by Holmes, for on leaving Búndi he had loudly asserted his intention to continue his course due south, and he counted that information thus disseminated would deceive his pursuers.

Tántia baffled by the rise of the Chambal, moves towards Búndi,

then turns to the country between Nímach and Nasirábád.

Tántia, pushing on, took up a position between

Book XVI. Chapter I.

1858. August.

the towns of Sánganír and Bhilwárá on the Nasírábád and Nímach road. Roberts, meanwhile, had been obliged, in consequence of the continuance of the heavy rain, to halt at Sarwár, an elevated plateau about thirty miles from Ájmir. On the 5th of August, however, the roads having been reported passable, Roberts broke up and marched towards Nímach. On the 7th, when at Dábla, ten miles from Sánganír, he received information regarding the position taken up by Tántia close to that place.

Roberts follows on his track,

The town of Sánganir is on the left bank of the little river Kotária. On the other side, and more than a mile up the stream, is the town of Bhilwára, in the front of which Tántia lay encamped.* Roberts was well aware that all his cavalry and a portion of his infantry under Holmes were following on the track of the rebels. He himself was in front of them. The opportunity was too good to be thrown away. He resolved, though he had no cavalry, to attack.

reaches, and determines to attack him.

The rebel infantry and guns had taken up a position in front of Bhilwára. Their horse, however, were thrown forward on the left, across the Kotária up to Sánganir, and on the right to the other side of that town, the whole forming a horse-shoe figure of about a mile and a half, connected by skirmishers. Their elephants and

Position occupied by Tántia.

* *Blackwood's Magazine*, August 1860. This number contains an admirably written account of the operations of Generals Roberts and Michel against Tántia Topi. It is difficult to exaggerate the obligations under which the author lies to the writer of this article, himself an actor in the scene.

Book XVI. Chapter I.

1858. August.

baggage were in the rear on the line by which they would retire if beaten.

Roberts attacks,

Roberts advanced his infantry, covered by skirmishers a short distance in front, cleared Sánganir of the few rebels who had penetrated within it, forced the rebel horse across the river, and bringing his guns to the river-bank, opened on the enemy's right. Under this fire his infantry, played upon by the rebel batteries, crossed the river, and took up a position on a rising ground, their right on a village, their left on a small tank. The guns then also crossed the river.

and forces him to retreat.

Seeing this, Tántia attempted no further resistance; he withdrew his guns and infantry, massing his cavalry on the intervening plain to cover the retreat. He retired unscathed, except by the guns, for Roberts had no cavalry to send after him,* and proceeded to a village called Kotra in the Údaipúr country.

Roberts is joined by his cavalry, and pursues

The next day Roberts was joined by his much-required cavalry, who had made a march of thirty miles. He then set out in pursuit of the rebels, doing twenty miles daily till, on the afternoon of the 13th, he came up with their advanced guard at Kankráolí,† a town situated on a lake not far

and overtakes Tántia.

* Tantia merely records of this action: "We were there" (Bhilwára) "attacked by the English force, and I fled during the night accompanied by my army and guns."

† The excellent information obtained by General Roberts enabled him, in more than one instance, to traverse the chord of a circle whilst the rebels had gone round by the arc. The method employed by Roberts to obtain this accurate information is thus succinctly described by the author of the article in *Blackwood*, already referred to. "The method which General Roberts adopted for

from the A'rávalli hills. On driving in the rebel outposts, Roberts learned from prisoners and villagers that their main force was occupying a position on the Banás river, seven miles distant.

Book XVI. Chapter I.

1858. August.

Tántia Topi, who was, according to his lights, a religious man, had devoted that 13th of August to a visit to the shrine of Náthdwára, reputed one of the most sacred in India. On his return at midnight he heard for the first time of the close vicinity of the English. Dreading an attack, he determined to decamp at once. But his infantry refused to move. They said that they were worn out by the long marches, and must rest; that they would march in the morning, and the guns should march with them; that the cavalry might act as they pleased. Under these circumstances, Tántia had no other alternative but that of fighting.

Tántia loses an important day in religious exercises.

His infantry refuse to move.

At daybreak, then, he ranged his men as skilfully as the nature of the ground would allow. His position was strong. In front of him flowed the Banás, which, covering his centre, then made a bend which protected his right; his left rested on some steep hills. The ground he occupied

He takes up a strong position.

obtaining information was to have about twenty cavalry in advance, close to the rebels. They left connecting links of two or three men every few miles, so as to keep up the chain of communication. The advance party was composed, half of Bilúch horse, who had no sympathy with the rebels, but could not communicate very well with the villagers, and half of horsemen belonging to the rájá of Jaipúr, who were supposed, as Rájpúts, to be on good terms and able easily to communicate with the villagers, but not to be very warm partisans of the British. By this mixed party, correct and immediate intelligence was constantly supplied."

Book XVI. Chapter I.

1858. August.

was a low, steep ridge, which formed the bank of the river. Before him, on the opposite bank, was an open plain, eight hundred yards wide, across which his enemy must march.

Roberts attacks,

At 7 o'clock on the morning of the 14th Roberts marched across it. In vain did Tántia's four guns, well protected by a natural parapet, sweep that plain. In spite of the effect they produced—and it was considerable—the British and native infantry reached the left bank, forded the river, and scaled the heights on the enemy's left and centre. The right, where the guns were posted, being thus left unsupported, abandoned the pieces under a volley from the 13th Bombay native infantry. The cavalry, led by Colonel Naylor, then dashed across the stream, and came upon the rebels scattered over the plain. Naylor pursued them for two miles, his men dealing and receiving death. He then collected his men, and, under orders from the general, kept up a steady pursuit for fifteen miles, killing numbers of stragglers, and capturing three elephants and a quantity of baggage. Two miles further on the rebels, having reached a village surrounded by jungle, determined to make a stand. Naylor, finding that the number of men whom he could then muster amounted only to a hundred and fifty, and that the country was quite unfit for cavalry, upon this abandoned the pursuit.*

defeats,

and pursues him for seventeen miles.

* *Blackwood's Magazine*, August 1860. Tántia Topi writes thus of this action: "The next morning we moved towards Patun, and after proceeding about one mile, the English army arrived and an action took place. We left our four guns and fled."

Book XVI. Chapter I.

1858. August.

Tántia Topi, having shaken off his pursuers, pressed, now without guns, eastward, hoping to find the Chambal fordable, and to place that river between himself and the English. Roberts, divining his intention, followed in that direction, and the fourth day after the action reached Púnah, a town north of Chitor, not far from the high road between Nímach and Nasirábád. Here he met Brigadier Parke, commandant of the Nímach brigade, who, some days before, had started from that place in anticipation of orders to cut off Tántia from the south. Roberts now made over to him the 8th hussars and the Bilúchis, and begged him to continue the pursuit.

Tántia flees towards the Chambal,

pursued by Parke.

Parke set out at once, but some of the horses of the 8th hussars being knocked up, he deviated from the exact course followed by Tántia to proceed to Nímach, where he knew he could obtain about fifty fresh horses. Here he was met by conflicting news regarding the fugitives. On the one side he was assured by experts that it was absolutely impossible that Tántia could cross the Chambal at that season of the year, and that he was bent on pushing southwards; on the other, Captain Showers, the political agent at Údaipúr, who was then at Nímach, had received information from the spot that Tántia was determined to cross the river. Unfortunately, Parke believed the experts. Proceeding to Morássa, fifteen miles from Nímach and thirty from the Chambal, he halted there a few hours to obtain more exact information. When it came it told him that the informant of Captain Showers was right, and

Parke makes a divergence to Nímach for fresh horses,

and is deceived by false information,

Book XVI. Chapter I. 1858. August.

that Tántia was attempting the Chambal. Parke hurried after him, reached the river after a hard march, only to find it just fordable, but rising rapidly; to see "a few disabled ponies standing on the left bank, and the rebels disappearing among some mango-trees in the west horizon." Tántia had escaped. Parke returned to Nímach to refit.*

in consequence of which Tántia escapes.

Tántia moves on Jhálra Patan.

Tántia, meanwhile, having crossed the Chambal, pushed for Jhálra Patan, thirty miles distant. Jhálra Patan is a handsome town in the Jhálá-war state built on the model of Jaipúr. The ráná of that state, Príthi Singh, great grandson of the famous Zálim Singh, the founder of the principality, was loyal to his British overlord. He had no idea of yielding without a struggle. But his troops, when drawn up to repel the Maráthá invader, behaved precisely as Sindia's troops had behaved at Gwáliár on a similar occasion. They at once fraternised with the rebels. Tántia at once took possession of the ráná's guns, more than thirty in number, his ammunition, bullocks, and horses, and surrounded the palace. The next morning he visited the ráná, and demanded a contribution in money. The ránás offered five lakhs; but this sum not being deemed sufficient, Ráo Sáhib, acting as representative of the Péshwá, sent for him and demanded twenty-five. Ultimately the ráná agreed to give fifteen. Of these he actually paid five, but having been insulted and ill-treated, he escaped that same night and

The ráná, loyal to the British, is deserted by his troops.

Tántia takes possession of Jhálra Patan and levies a heavy contribution.

* *Blackwood's Magazine*, August 1860.

fled to Máu, leaving some barrels of powder handy for his wife and family to blow themselves up if threatened with insult.*

Book XVI. Chapter I.

1858. August.

Tántia conceives the idea of marching on Indúr,

Tántia, freed by the rising of the Chambal from all chance of pursuit, halted five days at Jhálra Patan. He states that he employed the money taken to issue three months' pay to his troops, at the monthly rate of thirty rupees to each trooper, and twelve rupees to each foot soldier. Whilst so halting, he and his comrades, Ráo Sáhib and the nawáb of Bandá, conceived a very bold idea. This was no less than to march on Indúr, and summon Holkar's troops to join the representative of the liege lord of the Maráthás. Could he succeed in reaching the capital of Holkar before the small body of troops which the news of his approach would probably bring to the same spot from Máu, the fraternisation would be certain, and the result would spread to all Holkar's subjects. Impressed with this idea, he marched with his army, now reinforced by the Jháláwar levies and all the ráná's guns,† nearly direct south to Rájgarh.

and tries to carry it out.

But, whilst Tántia had been resting at Jhálra Patan, the officer commanding in Málwá, Major-General Michel, had, as if reading his thoughts,

* This account is taken mainly from Tántia's memoirs. The writer in *Blackwood* states that the war contribution amounted to sixty thousand pounds, whilst forty thousand pounds more was collected from Government property. As Jhálra Patan was a very rich town, this was very likely the case.

† Tántia says eighteen, but as three were abandoned and twenty-seven captured a few days later at Rájgarh, he must have taken all.

Book XVI. Chapter I.

1858. August.

Lockhart moves on the line on which Tántia is advancing.

despatched from that place a force,* under Colonel Lockhart, to cover Újjén, due north of Indúr. Lockhart proceeding further northwards, reached Súsnér, a place about seventeen miles to the west of Rájgarh. Not believing himself strong enough to attack Tántia, he intrenched himself, to await the arrival of a small reinforcement under Colonel Hope coming from Máu. He met this reinforcement at Nálkéra, about three miles to the south of Súsnér. At the very time of this junction Tántia was marching on Rájgarh, within a few miles of him.

Michel succeeds Roberts.

At this period, the end of August 1858, a change took place in the *personnel* of the British command. Major-General Roberts, who had up to that time commanded in Rajpútáná, was transferred to the military and political control of the Gújrát division. His place was taken by Major-General Michel of the Royal army, commanding in Málwa, a command which he was now to hold in conjunction with that in Rajpútáná. Michel was a zealous, active, resolute, and capable officer, thoroughly impressed with the necessity of pursuing the fugitive chieftain without cessation.

Takes command at Nálkéra,

Michel joined the united columns of Lockhart and Hope at Nálkéra. He had no information regarding Tántia Topi, but a vague rumour prevailed that he was moving in a north-easterly direction. Marching was, in every sense of the

* Three hundred and fifty 92nd Highlanders, four hundred and fifty 19th Bombay native infantry, one squadron Bombay 3rd light cavalry, and two guns Le Marchand's battery Bengal artillery.

word, difficult. Although the month of September had arrived, heavy rain, the precursor of the break-up of the monsoon, was falling, and the saturated cotton soil of Málwa resembled a sea of black mud. Still it was necessary to move, and Michel moved in the right direction. With great difficulty he transported his little army to Chápérá, about midway to Rájgarh. The following day, the rain having ceased, Michel pursued his march towards that place. The heat was so great and the sun's rays were so terrible, that some of the artillery-horses dropped dead in the traces. Still Michel pushed on, and about 5 o'clock in the afternoon, halting on a rising ground, he had the gratification of beholding Tántia Topi's army encamped near the walled town of Rájgarh.

and, pursuing,

finds Tántia at Rájgarh.

To traverse three miles of black soil and then, at the approach of night, to attack with a tired army a fresh body of men in the position they had chosen, was not for a moment to be thought of. Michel, then, waited for the morning. But when morning dawned, Tántia and his men had disappeared. Michel at once sent his cavalry on their track. This track was distinguished, first, by the marks of the gunwheels and the elephants, then, more decidedly, by three guns lying abandoned on the road. A little further on the rebel force was descried, drawn up in two lines, the second on higher ground than the first, and the guns on ground above both. The cavalry then halted to await the approach of the infantry and guns.

Tántia flees in the night.

Michel tracks him, finds him again,

Book XVI. Chapter I.

1858. September.

and completely defeats him.

The infantry and guns did not let them wait long. As soon as they came up the action began with an artillery fire from both sides. Then the English infantry, deploying, went at the rebels. The latter did not wait the conflict, but gave way and fled. Getting entangled in intersecting roads, they fell into inextricable confusion. The British horse artillery, galloping forward in alternate divisions of two guns, kept up a fire on the retreating masses, whilst the cavalry, threatening their left flank, forced them to incline towards the north.* In the pursuit, twenty-seven guns were taken.

The pursuers gather round Tántia.

Tántia, driven towards the north, wandered about for some time in the jungly country on both sides of the Bétwah, and eventually made for Sironj—in an easterly direction. But whilst thus seeking a place of security, new enemies were gathering round him. To Brigadier Parke, who had left Nímach on the 5th of September, was entrusted the duty of covering Indúr and Bhopal, thus leaving Michel's force to follow Tántia from the west, whilst Smith's brigade should advance

* Of this action, Tántia writes: "On reaching Ráj-garh the English army came up and attacked us. We left our guns and fled." It would be incredible, were it not true, that a force so large, numbering at least eight thousand, with thirty guns, should allow itself to be defeated by less than one-sixth of its number in men and guns, without drawing a drop of blood. Yet, so it was. It is the more strange, as about half the rebels had been trained and disciplined by Europeans; their guns were effective pieces of larger calibre than the English 9-pounders, their muskets bore the Tower mark, and their swords were excellent, yet not one man of the British force was killed or wounded!

Book XVI. Chapter I.

1858. September.

from the north, and the Jhánsi column under Colonel Liddell from the north-east.

The story reverts to Napier and Smith.

With this disposition opens a new phase of the pursuit. The defeat of Tántia Topi at Rájgarh almost coincided in time with the conclusion of the rainy season; for, although rain continued for some days to fall, further operations had become impossible. We are now entering upon the cold-weather campaign. In this new actors appear upon the scene. The Central India field force once more invites the attention of the public. It seems fitting, then, that before describing the events of that cold-weather campaign, I should trace the operations of General Napier and of Brigadier Smith from the period when we left them up to the middle of September. Meanwhile we must suppose Tántia Topi making the best of his way, by circuitous paths, from Rájgarh to Sironj.

The situation at Gwáliár apparently peaceful.

We left General Napier's division at Gwáliár and Jhánsi at the beginning of July, Brigadier Smith's brigade at Sipri, and Mayne's irregulars at Gúnah, all resting after the extraordinary fatigues and exposure of the central India campaign. To the superficial glance, order had been restored in Sindia's dominions. The mahárájá, grateful to the English, more fervent than at any previous period in his desire for their success, was doing his utmost to forward the views of the army administrators for the success of the troops. Sir Robert Hamilton, located in Gwáliár, was engaged in re-establishing political relations with the petty states

Book XVI. Chapter I.

1858. August.

around. The situation was full of promise; and yet, all the time, it was hollow and unsound.

Revolt of Mán Singh, rájá of Narwár.

During the whole of July the European troops had rest. The comparatively trifling matters which required attention in the districts were easily disposed of by the employment on detached duty of the men of Meade's horse, a regiment daily rising in estimation. But on the 3rd of August an incident occurred which led to very serious complications. A chief of Sindia's territory, named Mán Singh, rájá of Narwár, had quarrelled with his liege lord. To avenge the wrong which, he conceived, had been inflicted upon him by Sindia, and which will presently be related, and encouraged possibly by Tántia's action in the south, this chieftain, summoning his followers, twelve thousand strong, surprised on the 2nd of August the strong fort of Páori, eighty-three miles by the Sipri road south-west of Gwáliár, and eighteen to the north-west of Sipri, but recently supplied with six months' provisions and ammunition. Now, Smith's brigade was at Sipri. On the 4th he learned of the act of rebellion perpetrated by Mán Singh. On the 5th he started from Sipri with a force composed of two squadrons of the 8th hussars, two of the 1st Bombay lancers, a wing of the 95th, and three field-guns, and, marching as rapidly as the roads would permit, reached the vicinity of Páori early on the morning of the 7th. On approaching the place, Mán Singh sent a messenger with a flag of truce to the brigadier, to assure him that he had no quarrel with the English;

He seizes Páori.

Smith starts from Sipri to recover the place.

Book XVI. Chapter I. — 1858. August.

that his contention was with the mahárájá alone, and to supplicate earnestly for an interview. Smith granted the request and saw the chief that day. In an earnest manner, totally devoid of pretension, Mán Singh told his story to the brigadier. He and his family, he said, had ever been loyal servants to the mahárájá. During the lifetime of his father, nothing had occurred to mar the good feeling which had previously existed. But on his father's death, the mahárájá had insulted and robbed him by refusing to recognise his right to succeed to the principality of Narwár,* and the estates adjacent. It was to recover these, or, at all events, to avenge himself on the mahárájá, that he had drawn the sword and seized Páori, which formed a part of his ancestral possessions, but, he added earnestly, "I have no connection with the rebels and no quarrel with the English." The plea, though true, and convincing the listener of its truth, was not of a nature which, in those times, could be accepted by an English commander. Smith was responsible for the peace of the country near Sipri; that peace had been violated by Mán Singh, and Smith had but one plain duty, to see that the violaters were punished and that peace was maintained. He informed Mán Singh of this necessity.

Interview between Smith and Mán Singh.

Grievances of the latter.

Smith rejects his plea,

and prepares to besiege Páori.

* Narwár is a very important place, with an interesting history. It lies forty-four miles south of Gwáliár. In 1844, Narwár, with the lands pertaining to it, was assessed by the Gwáliár Government at 2,25,000 rupees annually. Little wonder, then, that the despotic ruler of the native state in which it lay should covet it.

Book XVI. Chapter I.

1858. August.

Mán Singh prepared, then, to take the consequences.

Strength and garrison of Páori.

Páori was strong, well supplied with provisions and ammunition, and its garrison, originally only two thousand, had been increased during the few days since the capture to nearly double that number. Amongst the new-comers was a chief, A'jhit Singh by name, uncle of Mán Singh. Smith's force amounted only to eleven hundred men of all arms, and his three pieces were field-pieces. He was thus far too weak to undertake a siege; and the place was too strong to be carried by a *coup-de-main*. Under these circumstances he deemed it prudent to maintain his position near the place, while he sent to Gwáliár an earnest request for reinforcements. On receiving this requisition Napier felt the enormous importance of settling the matter with as little delay as possible. Examples of that sort in a country long under Maráthá rule are apt to be contagious, and there was every probability that if Mán Singh were allowed for any length of time to parade his defiance of the British, chieftains more powerful than he might follow his example. Napier, then, determined to take the matter into his own hands. He started accordingly on the 11th with five guns and four mortars, escorted by six hundred horse and foot, reached Sipri on the 17th, and joined Smith on the 19th of August. He began operations the next day. For twenty-four hours he poured a vertical fire into the fort from his mortars, and then began to use his breaching batteries. This demonstra-

Smith sends to Gwáliár for reinforcements.

Napier sets out from Gwáliár to reinforce him.

tion quite satisfied Mán Singh. On the night of the 23rd he, A'jhit Singh, and their followers evacuated Páori, and made their way southwards through the jungles. Napier entered Páori the following morning, then equipped a light column under Robertson, 25th Bombay native infantry—an officer whose gallantry and soldier-like conduct have often been mentioned in these pages—and sent him in pursuit of the rebels. Napier himself having destroyed the fortifications of Páori and burst the guns, retired to Sipri to make arrangements for the further pursuit of Mán Singh should Robertson fail to capture him.

Book XVI. Chapter I.

1858. Aug.-Sept.

Mán Singh evacuates the place.

Robertson pursues.

That zealous officer left Páori on the 26th of August, on the track of Mán Singh. He had with him a squadron 8th hussars, a squadron Meade's horse, two 9-pounders, one 6-pounder, one 5½-inch howitzer, one hundred men of the 86th, one hundred and twenty of the 95th, two hundred 10th Bombay native infantry, and two hundred 25th Bombay native infantry. Pushing on by forced marches through the jungles, crossing difficult rivers, and conquering every obstacle, Robertson on the 3rd of September ascertained that the rebels were at Bijápúr, near Gúnah, twenty-three miles distant. His determination was instantly taken. Leaving the remainder to guard the camp and baggage, he mounted on elephants and camels seventy-five men of the 86th, ninety of the 95th, and one hundred each of the 10th and 25th native infantry, and with these and fifty men of the 8th hussars and one hundred and fifty of Meade's horse, he set out

Robertson overtakes A'jhit Singh's force at Bijápúr,

Book XVI. Chapter I.

1858. September.

that night. At daybreak the following morning he came in sight of the rebels occupying a rising ground on the opposite bank of the Párbati river. They had no scouts, and, the light being still grey, Robertson was able to cross the river unperceived and to send his cavalry round to take up a position in rear of the rebel camp. These movements were executed with so much care and precision, that, when the cavalry were taking up the position indicated, the rebels were actually preparing to bathe in the river, preparatory to their morning meal. The surprise was complete. Of organised resistance there was none; but the casualty list showed that the rebels, though taken unawares, defended themselves bravely. Lieutenant Fawcett, 95th, was killed; Captain Poore and Lieutenant Hanbury, 18th hussars, and Lieutenants Stewart and Page, of Meade's horse, were wounded. The remaining casualties in killed and wounded amounted to eighteen.

surprises them,

and cuts them up.

Composition of the routed force.

It was discovered after the action that it was not Mán Singh's but A'jhit Singh's band which had been routed. The astute Mán Singh, on learning that he was pursued, had divided his partisans into three divisions, with instructions to traverse a separate road and to combine at an appointed place. It was one of these divisions, six hundred strong, and composed, as was ascertained after the action, of men from the mahárájá's bodyguard, from the Gwáliár contingent, and from the 3rd, 40th, 47th, and 50th regiments native infantry. They were all dressed in red, and had percussion firelocks. About three-fourths of them were killed,* but A'jhit Singh escaped.

Book XVI. Chapter I.

1858. September.

Close of the rainy season campaign.

Robertson marched from the scene of action to Gúnah, where he arrived the middle of September. With this march may be said to terminate the campaign of the rainy season in the districts to the west and south-west of Gwáliár bordering on Rajpútáná. It is now fit that we should follow the various columns in the cold-weather campaign against Tántia Topi and his allies. Of these, that against Tántia Topi demands precedence.

The story reverts to Tántia Topi,

who rests at Sironj.

I left that chieftain making his way about the jungly country on both sides of the Bétwa towards Sironj. He duly reached that place about the middle of September, he and his men utterly exhausted. A rest of eight days, made sweeter by the absence of all fear—for the heavy rain that was falling would, they well knew, make the roads impassable to their enemy—set them on their legs again, and even restored to them their former audacity. On the conclusion of that period, the rains having ceased, Tántia led his men, with the four guns he had taken at Sironj, against Ísáogarh, a town with a fort, belonging to Sindia, in the hilly and difficult country south of Sipri. Here he demanded supplies; but the townspeople refusing them, Tántia stormed and plundered the place, and took seven guns. He and his associates halted there for a day to con-

Takes guns and supplies from I'sáogarh.

* The number of killed is often exaggerated, but on this occasion between four and five hundred dead bodies were actually counted on both sides of the river.

Book XVI. Chapter I.

1858. September.

sider their further plans. Their deliberations then culminated in a determination to divide their forces, Tántia proceeding with the bulk of them and five guns to Chandairi, the Ráo Sáhib with six guns and fewer followers making his way to Tál Bihat by Lalatpúr: this plan was carried out.

Tántia is repulsed at Chandairi,

What Chandairi was, the reader will recollect who has followed the history of Sir Hugh Rose's central Indian campaign.* It was now held for Sindia by a loyal soldier, a man who had no sympathy with rebels. He repulsed, then, Tántia Topi's appeals, and when the Maráthá chief attempted to storm the place he repulsed his attacks. Tántia wasted three days in an attempt to gain a place the possession of which would have been of incalculable use to him, and then, baffled though not dispirited, made for Mangráoli, about twenty miles south of Chandairi. He was marching, though he knew it not, on defeat, for the English were to meet him there!

and moves on Mangráoli.

I must now return to his pursuers. I have already stated the position of the several English columns; how Brigadier Parke was covering Indúr and Bhopál; how Colonel Liddell with the Jhánsi force was covering the country to the north-east. I have now only to add that Brigadier Smith, released by the capture of Páori, had taken up a position north of Sironj. In the inner part of the circle, the outer rim of which was occupied by these columns, General Michel was acting.

Positions of his pursuers.

* Page 151.

Book XVI. Chapter I.

1858. October.

Michel marches on Mangráoli.

Enabled at last, towards the end of September, by the cessation of the heavy rains, to act freely, Michel, believing he should find Tántia in the Bétwah valley, went in pursuit of him in a north-easterly direction. As he marched, he heard of the various depredations committed by the fugitives, and he felt sure he should find him. On the 9th of October, marching towards Mangráoli, information reached him that Tántia had occupied the high ground near the place, and was waiting for him.

Tántia resolves to risk an action.

Tántia had arrived there that very morning. He had not sought a battle, but as the ground was favourable he resolved to risk one. His position was strong, and the five guns he had placed in front of his line commanded the ground along which the English must advance. When, then, Michel sent his men forward, Tántia's guns opened a destructive fire. Grown bolder by despair, Tántia at the same time sent his cavalry to menace both flanks of the few assailants. For a moment the position of these seemed critical, the more so as some of the outflanking horsemen penetrated between the main body and the rear-guard. But whilst they still hesitated to come on, to risk a hand-to-hand encounter, the British troops advanced steadily, and gaining the crest, charged the guns. Then all was over. Tántia and his men abandoned their guns and fled. The want of sufficient cavalry did not allow Michel to pursue them.*

Possibilities before Tántia, who, however, is beaten, and flees.

* Of this action Tántia writes: "On our march to Mangráoli we met the English army. Shots were fired for a short time, when we left all our guns and fled."

Book XVI. Chapter I.

1858. October.

Tántia and Ráo Sáhib separate.

Tántia crossed the Bétwah and fled first to Jáklóm, and then, next day, to Lalatpúr, where he rejoined Ráo Sáhib, who, it will be remembered, had six guns. Tántia remained here, but Ráo Sáhib, with the bulk of the troops and the guns, set off the following day, and marched in a south-easterly direction. Michel, meanwhile, ordering Smith to watch the left bank of the Bétwah, followed Ráo Sáhib, and making his way with great difficulty through the dense Jáklón jungle, came suddenly upon him at Sindwáho, about thirty miles east of the Bétwah. Warned by the inopportune sound of a bugle in the British camp, Ráo Sáhib had time to draw up his men on a rising ground, with the guns in front. Then followed a scene almost similar to that at Mangráoli. The English, threatened on both flanks, advance and capture the guns, when the rebels flee. In their flight, however, they were, on this occasion, less fortunate than at Mangráoli. Michel had his cavalry handy; the ground, too, was unfavourable for rapid flight. In a pursuit which covered twelve miles, the rebels then suffered severely. Ráo Sáhib, however, escaped. The English lost five officers and twenty men in killed and wounded.

Michel totally defeats Ráo Sáhib,

who, however, escapes.

The rebel chiefs unite and resolve to cross the Narbadá.

Ráo Sáhib rejoined Tántia at Lalatpúr, and again the two held counsel as to the future. The country north of the Narbadá seemed about to close on them. The circle was gradually lessening, and in a few days they would be in the folds of the destroyer. They saw this clearly, saw that their only chance was to break through the

Book XVI. Chapter I.

1858. October.

circle and march to the south, putting the enemy, if possible, on a false scent. This was the difficult part of the programme, but they laid their plans to attempt it.

Retreat of Tántia towards the Narbadá.

It is impossible to withhold admiration from the pertinacity with which this scheme was carried out. Leaving Lalatpúr, Tántia and the ráo, whose design was to escape southwards, marched to Kajúria, with the intention of recrossing the Bétwah near that place and turning thence southward. But the ford being guarded by Colonel Liddell, Tántia turned north-eastward, and made for Lál Bahat. There he halted to rest his men. The following day, moving direct southwards, he penetrated into the Jáklón jungles, still to the east of the Bétwah. He halted one day at Jáklón, and the next at Itaia. There he heard that the English army was on his track, so he at once broke up and pushed on towards Khorai.

Michel learns that Tántia is marching southwards and follows in pursuit.

Whilst he is making that march I must return to General Michel. From the field of Sindwáho that general had marched to Lalatpúr, keeping always to the westward of Tántia with the view of baulking the intention he believed he might entertain of breaking through to the south. On reaching Lalatpúr, however, a messenger from Brigadier Smith reached him with the information that Tántia had been met marching southwards, and had probably gained the west side of the general. No time was to be lost. Michel, sending off an express to warn Parke, and pressing southwards by forced marches

Book XVI. Chapter I.

1858. October.

Catches him at Khorai. Whilst he annihilates Tántia's left wing, the right wing escapes.

came upon Tántia by a cross road just as that chief was approaching the village of Khorai. Instantly the battle joined. The British cavalry separated one wing of the rebels' force from the other. Whilst the British forces were engaged in annihilating the left wing, the right, with which were Tántia and Ráo Sáhib, favoured by the jungle, managed to escape westward. Not that the left wing fought to save their comrades; they had fled in the direction from which they had advanced, and the whole of Michel's force had pounced upon them, leaving the other wing to escape. Tántia and Ráo Sáhib, in fact, purchased their retreat with the sacrifice of one-half of their followers.*

Tántia, molested on the way by Becher,

This happened on the 25th of October. Tántia pushed on to Rájgarh, molested on his way, four miles from Bagrod, by Colonel Charles Becher, one of the most gallant officers of the Indian army, who, at the head of a newly-raised regiment,† did not hesitate to attack his whole force. Becher inflicted considerable loss (upwards of forty men killed), but Tántia pressed on, and

crosses the Narbadá.

proceeding *viâ* Rájgarh, crossed the Narbadá into the Nágpúr territory at a point about forty miles above Hoshangábád.

Effect which would have been pro-

Thus in the dying agony of the mutiny was accomplished a movement which, carried out

* Tántia writes of this action: "The English force came up in the morning and our army became separated, I accompanied the Ráo Sáhib," &c. Not a word about the sacrifice of the wing.

† Now one of the regiments Central Indian horse.

Book XVI. Chapter I.

1858. October.

twelve months earlier, would have produced an effect fatal for the time to British supremacy; a movement which would have roused the whole of the western presidency, have kindled revolt in the dominions of the Nizám, and have, in its working, penetrated to southern India. It was the movement to prevent which Lord Elphinstone had adopted the policy of aggressive defence till then so successful, which Durand had exerted all his energies, had used entreaties of the most urgent character with the Government of India, had stretched to the utmost the powers entrusted to him, to hinder. And now it was accomplished! The nephew of the man recognised by the Maráthás as the lawful heir of the last reigning Péshwá was on Maráthá soil with an army!

duced by the act twelve months earlier.

I have said that had that event occurred but fifteen months previously, British authority in western India would, for the time, have succumbed. As it was, the event happening in October 1858, when the sparks of the mutiny in every other part of India, Oudh excepted, had been extinguished, and when, even in Oudh, they were being surely trampled out; as it was, the event caused alarm of no ordinary character to the Governments of Bombay and Madras. Although Lord Elphinstone had shown, to a remarkable degree, a true appreciation of the character of the rebellion and of the manner in which it should be met, even he could not view without grave concern the arrival of Tántia Topi and Ráo Sáhib in the country of the Bhonslás, that

Alarm which it caused even in October 1858,

in Bombay.

Book XVI. Chapter I.

1858. October.

country the annexation of which but a few years previously had moved the Maráthá heart to its core. He could not but remember that a large proportion of the population of the Bombay presidency was Maráthá, and he could not foresee — who, indeed, could foresee? — the effect which might be produced on the easily kindled minds of a susceptible people by the presence amongst them of the representative of the man whom many amongst them regarded as their rightful ruler.

In Madras.

Nor could Lord Harris, who, throughout the trying times of 1857–58, had shown himself prompt to meet every difficulty, listen with an indifferent ear to the tidings that the Maráthá leader had crossed the Narbadá. True it was that the Madras Presidency was separated from the country now chosen by Tántia as his campaigning ground by the vast territories of the Nizám. True it was that the Nizám, guided by his able and far-seeing minister Sálar Jang, had displayed to the British a loyalty not to be exceeded. But the times were peculiar. The population of the Nizám's territories was to a very considerable extent Hindú. Instances had occurred before, as in the case of Sindia, of a people revolting against their sovereign when that sovereign acted in the teeth of the national feeling. It was impossible not to fear lest the army of Tántia should rouse to arms the entire Maráthá population, and that the spectacle of a people in arms against the foreigner might act with irresistible force on the people of the Dekhán.

Book XVI. Chapter I.

1858. October.

The people of the central provinces manifest a marked antipathy to Tántia and his followers.

Fortunately, these fears were not realised. Six years' experience of British rule had produced a remarkable effect upon the people of the central provinces. Whatever might be the feelings of the landowners, of the courtiers, and of those Bráhmans who, by means of their influence in a court where Bráhmanical influence was supreme, were able to live a life of luxury, of intrigue, and of pleasure without having recourse to industry and toil, this at least is certain, that the peasantry had no desire to recur to their old masters. In this respect the central provinces presented a remarkable contrast to Oudh and Bandalkhand. With all its faults, the people of this part of India preferred the substantial justice of the rule of their alien lords. It is, indeed, a remarkable fact that whilst, in the dominions of Sindia and in the principalities governed by Rájpút princes, Tántia and his followers enjoyed the sympathy of the villagers, and always obtained from them, without pressure and without payment, supplies in abundance, in the Maráthá country beyond the Narbadá the peasantry regarded them as pests in whose face the door was to be closed and the gates were to be barred, who were to receive no supplies without payment, and, if it could be managed without injury to themselves, no supplies at all.

To return to the story. Tántia, crossing the Narbadá forty miles above Hoshangábád, proceeded *viá* Fathpúr to Múltái in the direction of Nágpúr, but learning that a British force from that place had anticipated him, he turned sharp

Book XVI. Chapter I.

1858. November.

Tántia finds the country to the south and west barred against him.

westward, hoping to penetrate to the country southward by an unguarded pass in the hills. He found this impossible, for Brigadier Hill of the Haidarábád contingent was watching at Máilghát and Asirgárh; further westward, Sir Hugh Rose had made preparations to prevent Tántia from crossing into Khándésh, and, further westward still, General Roberts was bringing up troops to bar Gujrát against him. Nothing could have been more tantalising, for south of the Tápti river, from the banks of which he was separated only by the narrow Sátpúra, range lay the country to which Náná Sáhib laid claim as his rightful inheritance.* Across this, under the circumstances, Tántia dared not venture. Shut out, then, from further progress west or south, Tántia made a turn north-westwards into Holkar's possessions, south of the Narbadá, hoping to recross the Narbadá unperceived and to penetrate thence into the territory of the Gáikwár. On the 19th of November he reached Kargún, a decayed town in Nimár. Here was stationed a detachment of Holkar's troops, consisting of two troops of cavalry, a company of infantry, and two guns. These Tántia forced to joined him, and then pushed on westward. On the 23rd he crossed near Thán, the great high road from Bombay to Ágra, just as it was being traversed by carts laden with mercantile stores for the use of the English. Plundering these, taking with him the natives who had been escorting the carts, and

He turns to the north-west with the intention of recrossing the Narbadá and marching on Barodah.

* *Blackwood's Magazine*, August 1860.

destroying the telegraph wires, he pursued his course, feeling confident of success if only he could reach the Narbadá before the English, whom he believed he had outmanœuvred, should molest him.

Michel,

But fortune did not favour him. Michel, indeed, after defeating Tántia at Khorai, had pushed on in pursuit, though not on the same track, and, with his cavalry, had reached Hoshangábád on the 7th of November. There he joined Parke, whom he had previously ordered to meet him. Leaving Parke at Hoshangábád, Michel crossed the Narbadá and found himself in the wild country about Baitúl, with no accurate maps, no information of his own regarding the movements of the rebels, and with no prospect of obtaining any from the local authorities. Left thus to the resources of his own intelligence, Michel came to the conclusion that the roads to the south and due west would certainly be barred to Tántia, and that although there was little prospect of his attempting to recross the Narbadá, yet that it would not be wise on his part to move too far from that river. Impressed with this idea, he ordered Parke to cross the Narbadá at Hoshangábád, to march in a direction south-west by west, and take up a position at Chárwah, a town forming the angle nearest the Narbadá of a triangle of which Máilghát and A'sirgárh, both occupied by British troops, formed the other angles. In that direction, though more slowly, he moved himself.

left without information,

divines Tántia's intentions,

and takes steps to baffle them.

Whilst the general was making these preparations south of the Narbadá, the British authori-

Book XVI. Chapter I.

1858. November.

The British authorities at Máu

ties at Máu, to the north of it, were receiving disquieting rumours regarding the continued and persistent movements of Tántia westward. Dreading lest that chief should get possession of the grand trunk road, intercept supplies, and destroy the telegraph wire, Sir Robert Hamilton and Brigadier Edwards, who commanded at Máu, deemed it advisable, before Tántia had pillaged the carts in the manner already related, to post two small infantry detachments to watch the fords above Ákbarpúr. A day or two later, when intelligence was received that the westerly movement was being prolonged, Major Sutherland, who commanded one of these detachments, consisting of a hundred men of the 92nd Highlanders and a hundred of the 4th Bombay rifles, received instructions to cross the river at Ákbarpúr and keep clear the grand trunk road. Sutherland obeyed his orders, and passing through Thán—the village already spoken of—seventeen miles from Ákbarpúr, proceeded to Jilwána, thirteen miles further on, nearer to Bombay. There he was when, on the afternoon of the 23rd of November, Tántia and his troops passed through Thán, plundered the carts and cut the telegraph wires, as already described.

post parties to watch the fords of the Narbadá.

Sutherland crosses the Narbadá to a point below that traversed by Tántia.

Tántia having taken the precaution to carry off with him all the men accompanying the carts, Sutherland remained for some hours ignorant of this occurrence. He had been reinforced on the morning of the 23rd by fifty Europeans, sent on camels from Máu. The evening of that day, the report regarding the plundering reached him.

Book XVI. Chapter I.

1858. November.

The next morning Sutherland, taking with him one hundred and twenty Europeans and eighty natives, riding alternately on camels, proceeded to Thán, and inspected the damage done.* Learning there that the rebels had taken a westerly direction, he followed hastily and came in sight of them as they were passing through the town of Rájpúr, nearly midway between Thán and the Narbadá. Pushing on, his men in advance still riding camels, disregarding the enemy's stragglers and the quantities of abandoned baggage and baggage-animals, Sutherland, in half an hour, had approached near enough to force a battle. He ordered, then, his men to dismount; but the delay thus caused gave Tántia an opportunity, of which he availed himself, to retire. Before Sutherland could set out in pursuit, he had the satisfaction of being joined by his rear-guard—the men who had not been mounted, and who, in their desire for combat, had marched at a great pace. Keeping the whole of his force dismounted, Sutherland resumed the pursuit, and after marching two miles came up with the rebels, formed in order of battle on a rocky

Sutherland learns the vicinity of Tántia and pursues him.

Catches him only to see him retire.

Resumes the pursuit.

Comes upon them formed in order of battle,

* "The road for eight miles was strewed with articles, taken by the rebels the previous day from some merchants' carts on the main road; several carts had been brought on and abandoned when the bullocks got tired. The soldiers filled their water-bottles with port or sherry, of which there was enough to have stocked a large cellar, but not a man got intoxicated. A cart-load of books had been opened by the rebels during a halt—the contents were torn up and strewed in a circle, with a Walker's Pronouncing Dictionary left intact in the middle."—*Blackwood*, August 1860.

Book XVI. Chapter I. — 1858. November.

ridge, thickly wooded, with their two guns, the guns of Holkar found at Kargún, pointing down the road. Tántia had with him from three to four thousand men. Sutherland had just two hundred. After a little skirmishing, the smaller number charged the larger. Dashing up the road under a shower of grape, they captured the guns, Lieutenant Humfries, adjutant of the 92nd, receiving a sword-cut from their commandant, who was killed at his post. The rebel infantry then fled. The casualties on both sides were trifling.* Sutherland encamped on the ground he had gained.

attacks and puts them to to flight.

Tántia, relieved of his guns, resumes his flight,

The presence of the two guns with Tántia's force had necessitated that slow march over rough ground which had allowed Sutherland to overtake him. Now that the guns were lost his men were able to display that capacity for rapid marching in which the natives of India are unsurpassed, I might almost say unequalled, by any troops in the world. So quickly did they cover the ground that when at sunset the following day Sutherland reached the banks of the Narbadá, he beheld the rebel force comfortably encamped on the opposite bank. Between him and their camp flowed the waters of the Narbadá, at that point five hundred yards broad, its banks high and difficult. To cross it in the face of an enemy twenty times

and places the Narbadá between himself and his pursuers.

* Regarding this action, Tántia writes (after referring to the capture of the carts): "We then left the high road and proceeded westward. The next day we were surprised by the English force, and leaving our two guns, we fled and reached the Narbadá."

Book XVI. Chapter I.

1858. November.

his strength would have been an impossibility even for the troops he commanded.

How it was that Tántia had been able to cross the Narbadá.

That Tántia had been able to cross the Narbadá can only be accounted for by the fact that he had marched the previous afternoon, and the whole of the night, and had thus had at least twelve hours' start of his pursuers. It was well for him that he had that start. When he reached the left bank of the Narbadá Tántia had beheld on the bank opposite a party of a hundred sowars under an officer.* Under other circumstances the sight of these men might have made him hesitate. But he knew that Sutherland was behind him. He, therefore, plunged boldly in. The sowars then took flight.

Tántia pushes towards Barodah

At midnight Tántia, having plundered a village called Chickla, broke up his camp on the Narbadá, and marched in the direction of Barodah. It was his last chance, but it was a great one could he but arrive before the English. Barodah was the seat of a Maráthá dynasty, and it was known that a large party at the court sympathised deeply with Náná Sáhib. There were in the city only one company of Europeans and two native regiments, besides the troops of the Gáikwár, who were almost sure to join the rebels.

full of hope:

Full of the hope raised by the prospects before him, Tántia pushed on rapidly, marching from the banks of the Narbadá thirty-four miles straight

* So states Tántia himself, and I have usually found his statements corroborated by other writers. But I have been unable to ascertain who were these troopers or who was the officer. Probably he was a native officer.

Book XVI. Chapter I.

1858. Nov.-Dec.

arrives within fifty miles of Barodah.

on end. He halted at Rájpúra, took three thousand nine hundred rupees and three horses from the chief of that place, and marched the next day for Chota Údaipúr, only fifty miles from Barodah and connected with it by a road. Could he arrive at and leave that unmolested his future, he thought, would be assured.

Michel discovers Tántia's intentions,

But his pursuers were too many. I left General Michel and Brigadier Parke, in the second week of November, at Chárwah, south of the Narbadá, confident that Tántia's progress to the south was barred, and that he would endeavour to seek some means of recrossing into Malwá. Some days elapsed before an accurate account of his movements reached Michel. There was not a moment's hesitation as to the course to be followed. Michel recrossed the Narbadá at the Barwáni ford, and marching himself on Máu, despatched Parke with a flying column of cavalry, mounted infantry, and two guns, with orders to conduct the pursuit with the utmost speed that was possible.

and despatches Parke in pursuit of him.

Parke carried out these instructions to the letter. Marching, in nine days, two hundred and forty-one miles, for the last twenty of which he was forced to thread his way through a dense jungle, he came up with the rebels on the morning of the 1st of December, at Chota Údaipúr, just an hour or two after they had reached that place. Considering the climate, the nature of the country, and the other difficulties of the route, this march must be considered as rivalling any of which history makes record.

Parke catches Tantia at Chota U'daipur.

Book XVI. Chapter I. — 1858. December.

Force under Parke.

The force commanded by Parke consisted of two 9-pounder guns Bombay artillery, fifty men 8th hussars, fifty of the 2nd Bombay cavalry, a party of the Maráthá horse under Kerr—which, after having disarmed the southern Maráthá country, had been sent from the west to join Michel—Moore's Aden horse, one hundred of the 72nd Highlanders, mounted on camels, and one hundred and twenty-five Gujráti irregular horse. For the last twenty miles before reaching Chota Údaipúr, this force had, as I have stated, threaded its way through a dense jungle, skilfully piloted by Moore with his Aden horse. On emerging from the jungle Moore perceived the rebels. He instantly surprised their outlying picket. The ground beyond the jungle was covered with large trees, brushwood, and tents still standing,* and was so broken as to be very difficult for cavalry and artillery. As Parke's troops debouched on to it, he deployed his force, placing some of the 8th hussars, of the Maráthá horse, and the Aden horse on his right; the rest of the Maráthá horse, under Kerr, on his left, the 72nd Highlanders flanking the two guns in his centre; the remainder of the cavalry in the rear. His whole front scarcely covered two hundred yards. The rebels, meanwhile, roused to action, had formed up about six hundred yards distant. They numbered three thousand five hundred men and outflanked the British force on both sides. Tántia first endeavoured to turn

Discovery of Tántia's force.

Parke sets his force in battle array.

Tántia's aggressive

* Tántia admits that he was surprised on this occasion.

Book XVI. Chapter I.

1858. December.

action is checked.

the British left, but Kerr, changing his front, charged with great impetuosity, and driving the rebels from the field, pursued them for a considerable distance, laying sixty of them low. A similar attempt on the British right was met with equal success by the cavalry stationed there, Bannerman, of the southern Maráthá horse, greatly distinguishing himself and killing four men with his own hands. In the pursuit a standard of the 5th Bengal irregulars, borne by the rebels, was captured. Whilst the wings were thus engaged, the two British guns had kept up a heavy fire from the centre. But it was not long needed. With the repulse of the flanking attacks the action terminated. A pursuit along the whole line then followed.

Tántia defeated and cut off from Barodah.

This engagement was fatal to Tántia's hopes regarding Barodah. Leaving his route to the westward he fled northwards into the jungles of Bánswárá, the southernmost principality of Rajpútáná. These jungles, extremely dense in their character, are inhabited principally by Bhíls, a wild and uncivilised race, much given to plunder. Hemmed in on the south by the Narbadá, now for ever abandoned, on the west by Gujrát, now completely guarded by General Roberts, and on the north and east by difficult ranges which separate it from Údaipúr and Sirohi, and the passes across which are few and difficult, Tántia might have been excused if he had despaired of escape. But he did not despair. Ráo Sáhib was now his only companion, the nawáb of Bandá having in November taken advantage of the royal procla-

Flies to the Bánswárá jungles.

Desperate position of Tántia and Ráo Sáhib.

mation to surrender.* But these two men were, in this hour of supreme danger, as cool, as bold, as fertile in resource, as at any previous period of their careers.

Book XIV. Chapter I.

1858. December.

They remain undaunted.

And yet the British commanders had done their utmost to hem him in. They really believed that at last they had him. The troops of Roberts's division were echelonned along the roads and paths and passes leading from Bánswárá to the west. On that side escape was impossible. A force detached from Nímach under Major Rocke guarded the passes to the north and north-west. Another column sent from Máu, under Colonel Benson, commanded at the moment by Colonel Somerset, watched the passes leading eastward and south-eastward whilst Tántia was cut off from the south by his recent pursuers, greatly strengthened by flying detachments from Búrhánpúr and from Khándêsh. To add to his difficulties the Bhíl inhabitants of the jungles of Bánswárá, far from aiding him, followed his track as the vulture follows the wounded hare, anxious for the moment when she shall lie down and succumb.

The cordon about them is apparently complete.

But, undaunted, Tántia pressed deeper into the jungles. On reaching Déogarh Bári he found that but a small portion of his force was with him. He halted there two days, to allow his men to reunite. This result having been obtained, he, on the 10th of December, entered Bánswárá. Here he halted a day, his men plundering sixteen or seventeen camel-loads of cloth from

Tántia, after many movements in the jungles,

* To be hereafter referred to.

Book XVI. Chapter I.

1858. December.

Ahmadábád. He probably would have halted here longer but that information reached him that Colonel Somerset's brigade was closing up from Ratlam. Disturbed by this information, he marched in a nearly north-westerly direction to Salúmbar, an isolated fort belonging to the ráná of Údaipúr, encircled by hills, in the heart of the A'rávalli range. It was a strong position, commanding the approaches to Údaipúr. Here Tántia obtained some supplies, of which he was greatly in need, and set off the following day in the hope of surprising Údaipúr. But the British had received information of his movements, and Major Rocke's column had taken up a position at Bhánsrá, whence it would be easy for him to cover Údaipúr or to fall on Tántia as he emerged from the northern passes. Discovering this obstacle before he had committed himself too far, Tántia turned sharply to the north-east and took up a position at the village of Bhilwára,* in the densest part of the jungle. Here, it is said, Tántia and his followers debated the advisability of surrendering. But the intelligence which reached them during their deliberations that Mán Singh was at hand, and that Prince Firoz Sháh was advancing to their assistance, induced them to persevere in their resistance, to give one more chance to Fortune.

marches to surprise U'daipúr,

but discovers Rocke at Bhánsrá,

moves back into the jungles, and deliberates regarding surrender.

Decides against it.

Tántia halted two days at Bhilwára and then made for Partábgarh, the capital of the rájá of the state of that name. His probable line of

The English movements somewhat disarranged by the news

* Not the town of the same name on the road between Nímach and Nasirábád.

Book XVI. Chapter I.

1858. December.

route had been well divined by the English general. But he, too, had received information of Firoz Shah's movements, and it was necessary to arrange to meet him also. For this purpose, Somerset had been despatched with a light column to A′gar, Rocke had been moved to take his place at Partábgarh, whilst Parke, plunging into the jungles from the westward, was rapidly following on the track of the fugitives.

of the approach of Firoz Shah.

Tántia emerges from the jungles,

It thus happened that when, at 4 o'clock in the afternoon of the 25th of December, Tántia and his followers emerged from the jungles close to Partábgarh, he found himself face to face with Major Rocke. That officer, not having a sufficient number of men at his disposal to close the three passes, had taken up a position about two miles from the jungles, whence he could march to any point at which the rebels might threaten to debouch, provided he had any information of their movements. On this occasion he had no such information. His force, too, was, as I have said, small, consisting only of two hundred infantry, two guns, and a handful of native cavalry. He had no chance, however, of assuming the offensive. Tántia marched straight at him, and kept him engaged for two hours, a sufficient time to enable his elephants and baggage to clear the pass. Seeing this result gained, Tántia, who had thus, in spite of his many foes, escaped from the trap, marched in the direction of Mandisor, and halted for the night within six miles of that place. Thence he marched very rapidly—in three days—to Zirápúr, a hundred miles east-south-east of

baffles Major Rocke,

and marches towards Mandisor and Zirápúr.

Book XVI. Chapter I.

1858-9. Dec.-Jan.

Nímach, thus returning to the part of the country almost directly south of Gwáliár.

But the English were at his heels. Benson, who had resumed command of the Máu column, had received excellent information regarding Tántia's movements from Captain Hutchinson, one of the assistants to Sir Robert Hamilton. He pushed on after Tántia, then, marching thirty-five miles a day, caught him up at Zirápúr the very day he had arrived there. Tántia, completely surprised, fled without fighting, leaving six of his elephants behind him, and pushed northwards to Baród. Here another surprise followed him. Somerset had reached Zirápúr the morning after Tántia had left it. He had two horse-artillery guns with him. Taking fresh horses from the ammunition wagons, he attached them to Benson's two guns. With these four guns, and the ammunition contained in the limber, Somerset started at once, and marching seventy miles in forty-eight hours, came upon Tántia at Baród. After an action fought in the usual Tántia Topi style, the rebels fled to Náhargarh in the Kotá territory. Here Tántia was fired at by the Kiladár. Moving out of range, he halted for the night. Ráo Sáhib then sent a messenger to summon Mán Singh, who had appointed to meet him at this place. On Mán Singh's arrival the rebels moved to Parón, where they halted two days. They then pushed northwards towards Indragarh. On reaching the banks of the Chambal, Mán Singh, for some unexplained reason, left them. On the 13th of

Benson catches him at Zirápúr. Tantia flies to Baród:

is caught there by Somerset and beaten.

Tántia meets Mán Singh

January they reached Indragarh, where Firoz Sháh, with his bodyguard and the 12th irregulars, met them. To ascertain how this had been possible, I must return to the movements of General Napier and the Central Indian force.

Book XVI. Chapter I. 1858. December. and Firoz Sháh.

I left General Napier just after he and his lieutenants had, at the end of September, expelled Mán Singh from the Gwáliár territory. His detached parties still continued to operate in the districts to the west and south-west of Gwáliár, bordering on Rajpútáná, and the work which those parties accomplished was of a most useful character. In this manner passed the months of October and November, but in December Gwáliár was invaded by a new enemy.

The story reverts to General Napier.

The pseudo-prince, Firoz Sháh, already mentioned in these pages, had, after his expulsion from Mandisor by Durand in November 1857, proceeded with his followers to Rohilkhand to try conclusions with the British in that quarter. Expelled from Rohilkhand by Lord Clyde, he entered Oudh and cast in his lot with the irreconcilables who, to the last, refused submission to the paramount power. It was only when the native cause was absolutely lost in that province that Firoz Sháh, reading the glowing accounts of his achievements which Tántia Topi regularly transmitted from the Chambal and the Narbadá, determined to march to the assistance of one whom he could not but consider as a worthy ally. At the time that he arrived at this resolution he was at a place called Bisúah, not far from Sitápúr. Marching rapidly from that place, he crossed the

Firoz Shah, baffled in Oudh and Rohilkhand, resolves to join Tántia Topi;

Book XVI. Chapter I.

1858. December.

leaves Oudh, baffles pursuit,

Ganges on the 7th of December, cut the telegraph along the grand trunk road, and spread the report that he was about to proceed northwestwards. Instead of that he took the road to Itáwa, baffled a gallant attempt made by Mr. Hume and Captain Doyle—who lost his life—to stop him, out-marched a column led by Brigadier Herbert from Kánhpúr to pursue him, crossed the Jamná on the 9th, and moved off in the direction of Jhánsi. He marched with such speed that on the 17th he had arrived in the vicinity of Ránód, a large town fifty miles north-east of Gúnah. It was here he encountered his first check.

and crosses into Sindia's country.

Napier is informed of his movements,

General, now become Sir Robert, Napier had received timely intimation regarding the course pursued by Firoz Sháh, and he had sent out detachments to watch the roads which that chieftain would probably follow. On the morning of the 12th of December he received from the commander of one of these, Captain McMahon, 14th light dragoons, located near the confluence of the Jamná, Chambal, and Sindh rivers, information to the effect that the rebels had passed into the Lohar district of Kachwázár. Believing, from this, that their course would be up the jungles of the Sind river, Napier marched at 2 o'clock that day with a lightly-equipped force,* intending to

and pursues him.

* Two Bombay light field-battery guns, Captain G. G. Brown; one hundred and fifty men 14th light dragoons, Major Prettijohn; one hundred men 2nd Gwáliár Maráthá horse, Captain Smith; one hundred and seventeen men 71st Highlanders, Major Rich; fifty men 25th Bombay native infantry, Lieutenant Forbes; forty camels, Gwáliár Camel corps, Captain Templer.

proceed to Dabrá on the Jhánsi road, thence, according to the information he might receive, to intercept the enemy.

Napier's accurate conceptions regarding the enemy's movements

Napier halted that evening at A'ntri. At 2 o'clock the following morning, however, he was roused by an express message from the political agent at Gwáliár, Charters Macpherson, to the effect that information he had received led him to believe that the rebels would pass by Gohad, north of Gwáliár. Instead, then, of pushing on to Dabrá, Napier halted till the post should arrive with letters containing the grounds for the belief expressed by Macpherson. He did well not to act upon it without due caution, for at half-past 10 o'clock the tahsildár of A'ntri came to him to state that he had just ridden in from Dabrá, and had seen there the smoke of the staging bungalow which the rebels were then burning, and that they were taking a south-westerly direction. The express from Gwáliár had just come in time to baffle the accurate conceptions of Napier's brain, for had it not arrived, he would have caught them at the very spot he had selected.

are baffled for the moment by a despatch from the political agent.

There was nothing for it now but to march southwards. Leaving A'ntri, then, immediately, Napier proceeded with great rapidity in that direction. At Bítáor, which he reached on the 14th, he learned the rebels were only nine miles in front of him. Indeed, at this place the Gwáliár Maráthá horse, for the first time under fire, came in contact with the rear-guard of the enemy and greatly distinguished themselves.

Napier pursues, and approaches the rebels.

Book XVI. Chapter I.

1858. December.

Napier continued the pursuit through Narwár, and leaving there the greater portion of the infantry and all the artillery, who could not keep up with him, took with him only thirty-eight men of the 71st Highlanders on camels, all his cavalry, including twenty-five of the Balandshahr horse he found halted at Narwár, and proceeding with the utmost speed, reached Ránód on the morning of the 17th before the rebels had arrived there. His divination that they would make their way through the jungles of the Sindh river had proved to be perfectly accurate.

Catches them at Ránód.

Firoz Shah, ignorant that Napier is at Ránód,

Firoz Sháh, indeed, had preferred the more circuitous and difficult road through the jungles to the easier but more open route followed by Napier. Naturally he wished to make his way unseen, and thus to effect, with an unbeaten force, the contemplated junction with Tántia Topi. As it was, he had marched on a line almost parallel to that followed by the English leader, and it was only the temptation to leave the jungle cover to sack Ránód which had saved him from an attack the previous day. But Napier had now reached Ránód before him, and the sacking of the place was likely to be more difficult than he had anticipated. Full, however, of confidence, and utterly ignorant of the arrival of the English, Firoz Sháh marched on that eventful morning against Ránód, guided by a zamindár of the locality, his army forming an irregular mass extended in a front of nearly a mile.

marches on that places.

Napier's force.

Napier had scarcely time to form up the 14th light dragoons, when the rebels were within a

Book XVI. Chapter I.

1858. December.

few yards of him. The Gwáliár Maráthá horse had been impeded in crossing a deep ravine by the riding-camels, and were a little behind. The force actually engaged consisted of one hundred and thirty-three 14th light dragoons under Major Prettijohn, sixty of the Maráthá horse under Captain F. H. Smith, and thirty-eight of the 71st Highlanders under Captain Smith, mounted on camels, and guided by Captain Templer.

Prettijohn charges them, and

As soon as the rebels had arrived within charging distance, Prettijohn and his hundred and thirty-three light dragoons dashed into their midst. The blow completely doubled them up. Though individuals amongst them fought bravely, the mass made no stand whatever. Their one thought seemed to be to try and escape. They were in full flight before the Maráthá horse could come upon the scene, in time only to participate in the pursuit. That pursuit was continued for seven miles, the rebels losing six elephants, several horses and ponies, and many arms. They left one hundred and fifty dead bodies on the ground before Ránód, including those of some native officers of the 12th irregulars, the murderers of the gallant Holmes. Prettijohn having been severely wounded before the pursuit began, the command of the dragoons devolved on Captain Need, and that officer estimated the loss of the rebels in the pursuit at three hundred. On the British side the wounded amounted to sixteen; one of these died subsequently of his wounds.

completely defeats,

and pursues them.

Firoz Shah makes for the A'rói jungles.

Firoz Shah led the fugitives in the direction of Chandairi. Learning, however, that one British

Book XVI. Chapter I.

1858. December.

force* had moved towards Ránod from Jhánsi, and another† from Lallatpúr to Chandairi, he suddenly turned westward, passed Ísáogarh and Púchar, and made for the jungles of A'róni. Passing near Rámpúr, between Gúnah and Sironj, he came suddenly upon forty men of the 1st Bombay lancers, under Lieutenant Stack, escorting clothing and remounts to Brigadier Smith. The rebels had captured the clothing of the detachment and one trooper when Stack gallantly brought up the rest of his men, and, skirmishing with the rebels, carried the remainder of his charge to Gúnah. The rebels then pushed on to Áróni. Meanwhile, Captain W. Rice, 25th Bombay native infantry, a noted tiger-slayer, had been ordered with a small column‡ from Gúnah to intercept their retreat. At Baród, on the 22nd of December, he learned from a horse-dealer, who had been robbed by them, that the rebels were encamped near the village of Sarpúr, eleven miles distant. Leaving his camp standing under charge of forty-two men, Rice set off that night, and outmarching the guns with his infantry, surprised the enemy at 11 P.M. The surprise was so complete that the rebels made no resistance, but ran off at once, leaving a hundred horses, several camels, many arms, and much clothing. From this point Firoz Sháh made the best of his way, unmolested, to Rájgarh, hoping to meet there Tántia Topi. He

Gallantry of Stack.

Rice marches from Gúnah against Firoz Shah,

and drives him off.

Firoz Shah then makes for Indragarh, where he joins Tántia Topi.

* Under Brigadier Ainslie.

† Under Colonel Liddell.

‡ Two 9-pounders, ninety Royal Engineers, fifty-five 86th foot, one hundred and fifty 25th native infantry, one hundred and forty Meade's horse.

lingered there for a few days waiting for his ally, but learning that Brigadier Smith was on his track, he made for Indragarh, where, on the 9th of January, he effected the junction in the manner already related.*

Book XVI. Chapter I.

1859. January.

Disposition of the British columns.

I left Brigadier Somerset at Baród, having, after his march of seventy miles in forty-eight hours, driven Tántia from that place. Brigadier Smith, who had been posted at Sironj, had, after Napier had driven Firoz Shah southwards, moved in pursuit of him from that place and had been near Baród when Somerset beat Tántia there. He was now moving on Indragarh in pursuit of Firoz Sháh. General Michel was, at this time—early in January 1859—at Chaprá, ten or twelve miles due north of Baród. Thence he directed Colonel Becher to join him with all the cavalry under his command. He had previously ordered Brigadier Honner, commanding the Nasirábád brigade, to march in a north-easterly direction towards Indragarh, watching whilst he did so the fords between that place and Kotah. To complete the investment of the rebels, Brigadier Showers, moving with a light column from Ágra, had taken up a position at Kúshalgarh, north-east of the Banás river.

Desperate position of the rebels.

Escape now seemed absolutely impossible. Hemmed in by Napier on the north and north-east, Showers on the north-west, Somerset on the east, Smith on the south-east, Michel and Benson on the south, and Honner on the south-west and

* Page 359.

Book XVI. Chapter I. 1859. January.

west, how was it possible for the man who had so long defied pursuit to break through the net closing around him? It did, in very deed, seem impossible. It will be seen, nevertheless, that the resources of the rebel leader were not yet entirely exhausted.

Tántia, knowing himself to be almost surrounded,

Tántia had joined Firoz Sháh at Indragarh on the 13th of January. But Indragarh was no safe resting-place. He had sure information that two English columns were marching on it. Strange it was, however, that whilst he received the fullest details regarding the movements of the various columns which had so long pursued him, and of Napier's troops, he had heard not a word of Showers's movement. Believing, then, that a way of escape in a north-westerly direction lay before him, he made a forced march to Dewássa, a large fortified town about midway between Jaipúr and Bharatpúr.

endeavours to creep ont by a north-westerly path.

Showers surprises him at Dewássa.

Showers heard of Tántia's arrival at Dewássa as soon as the speed of his scouts could convey the news. A similar message was conveyed, over a longer distance, to Honner. Both brigadiers set out immediately. But Showers, starting from Kúshalgarh and having the shorter road to traverse, arrived first. Showers entered the town on the morning of the 16th, just as Tántia, Ráo Sáhib, and Firoz Sháh were holding a council of war. How they escaped was a miracle. They were completely surprised. "The English force surprised us there," writes Tántia in his journal. About three hundred of his followers were killed or disabled, the remainder fled.

Book XVI. Chapter I.

1859. January.

Whither? Every pass seemed closed to them. But the English columns from the south-west closing too rapidly on Dewássa, had just left one opening—the opening which, turning as it were the Jaipúr territory, led into Márwár. Of this Tántia and his followers availed themselves, and marched with all the speed of which they were capable towards the city which gives its name to the principality. Passing by Alwar, they turned westwards, and reached Sikar on the 21st. They were encamped there that night when Holmes, who had been sent from Nasirábád with a small party of the 83rd and the 12th Bombay native infantry and four guns, fell upon him, after marching fifty-four miles through a sandy country in twenty-four hours. The surprise was complete. The rebels abandoned horses, camels, and even arms, and fled in the utmost confusion. A few days later six hundred of them surrendered to the rájá of Bikanír.

Tántia avails himself of one loop-hole to escape to Sikar, where Holmes catches and defeats him.

This defeat inaugurated the break-up of Tántia's army. On that very day Firoz Shah and the 12th irregulars separated from him. Since his wanderings in the Bánswárá jungles, Tántia had been on very bad terms with Ráo Sáhib, and the day after the defeat their quarrel came to an issue. "I told him," writes Tántia, "that I could flee no longer, and that whenever I saw an opportunity for leaving him, I would do so." Some Thákurs related to Mán Singh had joined Tántia that morning, and with them Tántia left the force to proceed in the direction of Parón, having as followers only "two pandits to cook

Book XVI. Chapter I. 1859. February.

his food, and one sais* (groom), two horses, and a pony." In the Parón jungle Tántia met rájá Mán Singh. "Why did you leave your force?" asked the rájá, "you have not acted right in so doing." Tántia replied, "I was tired of running away, and I will remain with you whether I have done right or wrong." In fact, after the long chase, he was beaten.

Meanwhile, Ráo Sáhib, still with some three or four thousand followers, pushed first westwards, then to the south, and reached Kosháni, west of Ajmir, and about eighty miles east of Jodhpur, on the 10th of February. But the avenger was on his track. Honner, who had arrived too late for the rebels at Dewássa, had, after some inevitable delay, discovered their track. He set out in pursuit on the 6th, and, marching very rapidly, reached Kosháni on the morning of the 10th, having accomplished one hundred and forty-five miles in four days. Finding Ráo Sáhib there, he attacked and defeated him, killing about two hundred of his followers. Ráo Sáhib fled southwards to the Chatterbúj pass and reached it on the 15th. Somerset, coming from the east, arrived within a few miles of it the same day. Unfortunately, no one with him knew the country, and many precious hours were spent in reconnoitring, hours which the ráo utilised in threading the pass. Finding, however, that the British were still close to him, the ráo turned

* "The grooms," adds Tántia, "left me and ran off after coming two stages."

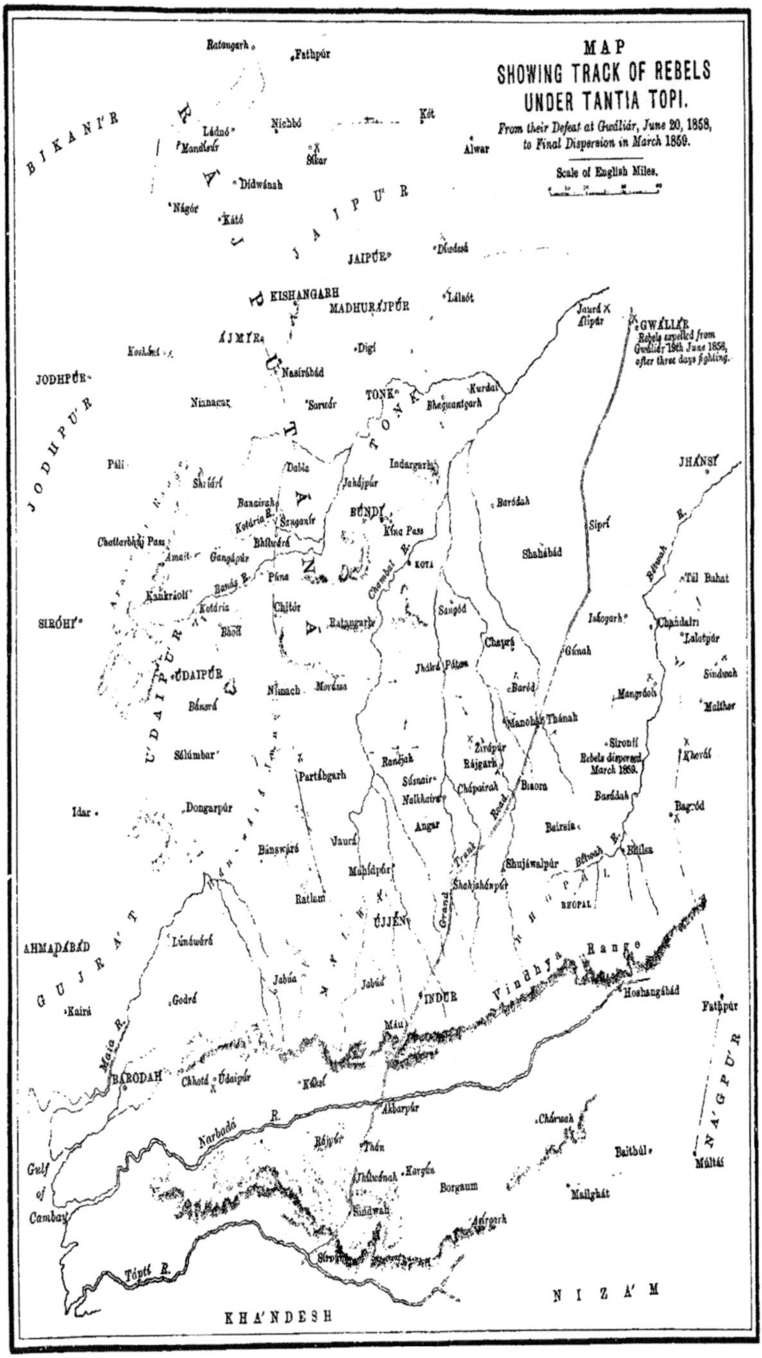
MAP
SHOWING TRACK OF REBELS
UNDER TANTIA TOPI.
From their Defeat at Gwáliár, June 20, 1858,
to Final Dispersion in March 1859.
Scale of English Miles.
Ratangarh
Fathpúr
BIKANI'R
Nichbó
Kót
Alwar
Sikar
Dídwánah
Nágór
JAIPU'R
JAIPÚR
KISHANGARH
MADHURÁJPÚR
Lálsót
Jaurá
Alipúr
GWÁLIÁR
Rebels expelled from Gwáliár 19th June 1858, after three days fighting.
JODHPÚR
Nasírábád
Digí
TONK
Kurdai
Bhagwantgarh
JODHPU'R
Páli
Dabla
Indargarh
JHÁNSI
Barodah
Sipri
BUNDÍ
Kína Pass
Chattarbhúj Pass
Gangápúr
KOTA
Shahábád
Kankraoli
Púna
Chambal R.
Betwah R.
Tál Bahat
SIRÓHI
Kotária
Chitór
Ratangarh
Sangód
Isáogarh
Chandairi
Lalatpúr
Chaprá
Gúnah
UDAIPÚR
Jhálrá Pátan
Sindwah
Nímach
Mangróli
Malthor
Bánsrá
Manohar Thánah
U'DAIPU'R
Sálúmbar
Sironj
Rebels dispersed March 1859.
Khorái
Partábgarh
Rájgarh
Biaora
Chápairah
Baródah
Idar
Dongarpúr
Angar
Bagród
Bairsia
Bánswárá
Jaurá
Shujáwalpúr
Bhilsa
Mahidpúr
Shahjahánpúr
BHOPAL
Ratlam
UJJEN
Grand Trunk Road
AHMADÁBÁD
Lúnáwárá
Vindhya Range
Jabúa
Hoshangábád
INDUR
GUJRA'T
Kairá
Godrá
Fathpúr
Máu
Mahi R.
BARODAH
Chhotá Udaipúr
Akbarpúr
Narbadá R.
Chárwah
Rájpúr
Thán
Baithúl
Múltái
Gulf of Cambay
Borgaum
Mailghát
Sindwah
Tápti R.
NA'GPU'R
NIZA'M
KHA'NDESH

Book XVI. Chapter I.

1859. February.

The rebels break up and disperse.

down to the Bánswárá jungles, closely pursued. Finding the passes leading to the south and east closed, the ráo turned to the north-east and passed by Partábgarh, where Tántia had encountered Major Rocke only a few weeks before. As he fled before Somerset, who followed closely on his track, there occurred a great diminution of his followers. Like Tántia, these were "tired of running away." The majority of them fell out of the line during the retreat, threw away their arms, and quietly took the road to their homes. Some of them, Muhammadans from Kánhpúr and Baréli, about two hundred in number, gave themselves up. The chiefs and the other irreconcileables made their way to the Sironj jungles, where, sometimes disguised as mendicants, sometimes acting as marauders, they tried to obtain food from the villagers. Their organised opposition to the British Government had disappeared.

Ráo Sáhib.

Of the chiefs of this long campaign, five still remained in whose fate the reader is naturally interested. These five were Ráo Sáhib, Firoz Sháh, Mán Singh, and Ájhit Singh, and last and greatest of all, the leading spirit of the drama, the Maráthá Tántia Topi. Of Ráo Sáhib I can relate nothing. He disappeared and was never heard of after. Firoz Sháh was equally successful in eluding the vigilance of his pursuers, and was never heard of afterwards. But it was not so with the others. Their case constitutes in itself an episode.

Firoz Sháh.

Mán Singh.

The Párón jungles, in which Tántia Topi and Mán Singh were hiding, constituted a portion of

Book XVI. Chapter I. 1859. February.

the large family estates of Narwár, of which Sindia had unjustly deprived the latter. Here they were safe, safe absolutely, so long as each should remain true to the other, for no mere retainer of Mán Singh would betray his master or his his master's friend. The clear and acute intellect of Sir Robert Napier had recognised this fact the moment he received the report that the two chiefs in question had separated themselves from their army and taken refuge in the jungles. He had at once felt certain that to capture Tántia Topi the preliminary step was to gain Mán Singh. No star of lesser magnitude would suffice. Now, there were strong grounds for believing that it might be possible to gain Mán Singh. He was a chief of ancient lineage, of lofty birth, born to great possessions. To avenge himself on Sindia for confiscating a portion of those possessions, he had lost everything except the affection of his dependants, and the ground on which he slept; he had imperilled his head. Thenceforward, so long as he remained unreconciled to his liege lord, there was no prospect in the present, no hope in the future. On such a man, driven to desperation, become from a feudal lord an outcast, what might not be the effect of an offer of free and absolute pardon, with the prospect of intercession with Sindia for the restoration of some portion of his property?

Sir Robert Napier endeavours to gain Mán Singh.

Impressed with this idea Napier resolved to try the experiment. It happened that on the 27th of February Sir Robert had directed Meade, of Meade's horse, who then commanded a detach-

Napier sends Meade to Sirsimáo

to open the jungles.

ment* at Bijráon to proceed to Sirsimáo, to dislodge thence any party of rebels in the vicinity, to keep open his communications with Gúnah, and, in conjunction with Major Little's force at Párawant, to clear the roads to Amroa, Agár, Thánnah, Rájgarh, and Sipri. Napier further instructed him to attack Mán Singh and Tántia Topi, then wandering in the jungles, whenever opportunity should offer.

Meade gains the confidence of an influential friend of Mán Singh.

Meade reached Sirsimáo on the 3rd of March, found the place deserted, opened a communication that evening with Little, and, in co-operation with him, was engaged from the 5th to the 8th of March in clearing a roadway up the rugged and densely-wooded pass. But, before leaving Sirsimáo, Meade had ascertained that the old thákur who held that village, Niraiyan Singh by name, was connected with Mán Singh and possessed much influence in the neighbourhood. On the morning of the 8th this man and his followers came to a village some four or five miles distant from the pass up which the English troops were working, and showed an evident desire to communicate with Meade. Meade, feeling the great importance of obtaining the submission of so influential a personage, proceeded to the village, reassured the old man, who was at first nervous and alarmed, by his tact and kind manner, and induced him to return to Sirsimáo with his followers. He saw the thákur again that evening

* One hundred men 3rd Bombay Europeans, one hundred men 9th Bombay native infantry, one hundred men 24th Bombay native infantry, fifty men Meade's horse.

Book XVI. Chapter I. — 1859. March.

at the village, and drew from him a promise to bring the dewán or confidential agent of Mán Singh to him within two or three days, and to do all in his power to induce Mán Singh himself to surrender.

Meade offers terms to Mán Singh,

The old man kept his word. On the 11th Meade had a long interview with the dewán. Through him he offered to Mán Singh the conditions he was empowered to offer—a guarantee of life and subsistence. He further requested the dewán to find out the rájá's family and household, to invite them to come to his camp, to promise them, should they comply, to do everything in his power for their comfort, to assure them that they should not be molested by the officials of the Gwáliár's darbár or by anyone else. With the dewán he likewise sent one letter addressed to the family, reiterating his invitation and his promise, and another addressed to Rájá Mán Singh himself, inviting him to surrender. He impressed, moreover, upon the dewán the primary necessity of bringing in the ladies first, feeling sure that the rájá would follow.

and assures him of safety and honour for his family.

Sir Robert Napier

It is at this point of the story that the action of Sir Robert Napier comes in. That officer, acquainted with Meade's proceedings in the matter just described, and fully approving of them, had become naturally impatient when day followed day and no result issued from a beginning so promising. He waited a week after the interview with the dewán, and when, at the expiration of that time, no tidings had been received regarding the ránís or the rájá, he determined to

Book XVI. Chapter I.

1859. March.

put greater pressure upon the latter. He wrote, then, on the 18th of March to Meade, directing him to leave his road-work, as "it is of great importance that the pressure upon Mán Singh should not be relaxed, till he comes in. Your letter of the 11th inst. gave hopes of certain parts of Mán Singh's family coming in, but as your letter of the 13th makes no allusion to the subject the brigadier-general concludes that the proposals have not been renewed." *

urges upon Meade

Sir Robert added that, notwithstanding that Meade had no information on the subject, he had grounds for believing that Mán Singh had frequently been in the vicinity of the British force; that he had frequented places called Gárla, Hátri, Bhirwán, and Mahúdra; that he had been supplied with provisions from the last-named place. He accordingly directed Meade to move on Ágar, and to make a road up the Múshairi pass through the jungles from that place by Gárla and Hátri to Mahúdra; and at the same time to exercise pressure upon the dewán at Sirsimáo by threatening to quarter his force there.

to put pressure on Mán Singh's dewán.

In conformity with these instructions Meade marched to the Múshairi pass. He found the people in that part of the country extremely hostile to the British. Not a man would give him information. His surprise was great, then, when, on the 25th of March, the rájá's dewán and his own confidential servant conducted into camp the ladies of the rájá's household and their at-

Mán Singh's family surrender to Meade.

* From Assistant Adjutant-General to Captain Meade, dated 18th March 1859.

Book XVI. Chapter I.

1859. March–April.

tendants, some seventy persons. Meade received them kindly, and sent them on to one of the rájá's villages near Sipri. His servant likewise informed him that he had seen Mán Singh four times, and that he had expressed his intention to give himself up in two or three days—a statement which was confirmed by the dewán.

Mán Singh agrees to Meade's conditions,

Meade continued his march to Mahúdra, sending a party of horse in front of him with the rájá's dewán and a múnshi, whom he instructed to open at once a communication with Mán Singh. On the 31st he received, at Mahúdra, the rájá's final offer to surrender on certain conditions. To some of these Meade declined to agree. Finally he induced him to come in on the following conditions:—1st, that he should be met at some distance from the camp by a native of position—a ceremony the omission of which is an insult; 2nd, that he should not be made over to the Gwáliár darbár, but should remain in the English camp; 3rdly, that after staying two or three days in camp he should be allowed to proceed to his home at Máori near Sipri, whither the females of his family had gone, to re-equip himself in a manner befitting his rank. On the 2nd of April Mán Singh entered the British camp.

and surrenders.

Feelings which coursed through the mind of Mán Singh.

Tántia Topi was still at large. But Tántia without Mán Singh, Mán Singh reconciled to his enemies, was assailable. Now had arrived the time to play upon the more selfish instincts of the rájá. He had life, and security for his life. But what was life to a born feudal chieftain

Book XVI. Chapter I.

1859. April.

without consideration, without esteem, without position? What was life to a vassal lord of Sindia, disowned and hated by his sovereign? The first feeling of satisfaction at escape from death passed, and life to such a man in such a position would become a burden. But could not the position be ameliorated? Yes—a signal service—a deed for which men would be grateful—that would remove the still remaining obstacles to a return to his position among the nobles of his country.

Meade works upon those feelings.

On feelings such as these Meade worked with tact and skill. In many conversations which he had with the rájá during the 2nd and 3rd of April he urged him to perform some service which should entitle him to the consideration. His reasoning had so much effect that when, at 11 o'clock on the night of the second day, the 3rd, information reached Meade that the uncle of Mán Singh, A'jhit Singh, already mentioned in these pages, lay, with a band of men, fifteen miles distant, in the jungle, Mán Singh volunteered to accompany the force of one hundred and fifty men at the head of which Meade immediately started. The little force reached, at daybreak, the place where A'jhit Singh had been marked down, only to discover that he and his band had moved off during the night. Meade pushed on in search of him some seven miles further, to a place where the jungle was so dense that cavalry were useless. A'jhit Singh and his men were actually in this jungle, but before Meade could surround them they became aware

Mán Singh volunteers to accompany Meade in an attempt to capture his uncle.

Book XVI. Chapter I.

1859. April.

The uncle escapes, to Mán Singh's mortification.

of the presence of enemies, and succeeded in getting away.* No one was more mortified than Mán Singh. A'jhit Singh was his uncle; A'jhit Singh had been his comrade on the battle-field, his abettor in his revolt against Sindia, and although, in his fury at Mán Singh's apostasy, as he regarded it, in surrendering to the English, he had threatened to take his life, yet he stood to Mán Singh in a relation than which there can scarcely be a closer between man and man—friend, comrade, uncle, and yet Mán Singh grieved bitterly that this man had not been captured by his enemies. It was a first step in moral debasement, a prelude to one still lower!

His first step in moral debasement.

The second step.

During the three days which followed, close observation satisfied Meade that Tántia Topi was in the Parón jungles, and working daily on Mán Singh's longing desire for restoration to his former position† he persuaded him to acknowledge that he knew where Tántia was. From this moment he had made up his mind to betray him. His only anxiety now was lest Tántia should slip through his fingers. At that very time, to his

* A'jhit Singh and his band were so terrified by their narrow escape, that they marched seventy or eighty miles on end, not halting till they joined the other rebels near Sironj.

† "I have done all I could by kind and encouraging counsel to urge him to establish, by so signal an act of service" (the betrayal of Tántia Topi), "his claim to the consideration of Government, promised him by Sir R. Hamilton in his telegram of the 27th ultimo."—Major Meade to Sir R. Napier, the 8th of April 1859. Sir R. Hamilton's telegram was to the effect that if Mán Singh surrendered his life would be spared, and his claims would receive consideration.

knowledge, Tántia was debating whether or not he should rejoin Firoz Sháh. Tántia had even sent his emissaries to Meade's camp to consult him on the subject. Were Tántia to go the chance would be lost. No thought of old comradeship, of the ties of honour, weighed with him for a moment. He would at once betray him, if——

Book XVI. Chapter I.

1859. April.

He resolves to betray Tántia Topi,

Yes,—if he could himself recover his position. That was his one thought. "In the course of this forenoon" (the 7th of April), wrote Meade, "I learnt from Pribhú Lál that he thought Mán Singh would do as I wished, but that he was desirous of having Sir R. Hamilton's general assurance of 'consideration' for such a service reduced to some specific promise, and that his ambition was to have Sháhábád, Páori, or some other portion of the ancient ráj of Narwár, guaranteed to him in the event of his efforts to apprehend Tántia Topi being successful."

for a consideration;

It was quite out of Meade's power to make any such promise; he could only assure him that he "might rely on any claim he might establish being faithfully considered by Government." Unable to extract more, Mán Singh clutched at the prospect which this vague promise offered, and consented to betray his friend.

even for the chance of a consideration.

Then came Meade's difficulty. To seize such a man as Tántia Topi, great caution was required. Tántia had many spies in the British camp, and to have sent a European on such a duty would have been sufficient to warn the victim. Eventually Meade decided to send a party of the 9th

Meade sends a party of sepoys accompanied by Mán Singh.

Book XVI. Chapter I.

1859. April.

Bombay native infantry on the service, under an intelligent native officer. The orders he gave them were simply to obey the directions of Mán Singh, and to apprehend any suspicious characters he might point out. The name of Tántia Topi was not mentioned, and the men had no idea of the actual duty on which they were proceeding.

Tántia Topi, all the time, reposes absolute faith in Man Singh.

Whilst Meade was thus negotiating with Mán Singh, Tántia Topi had lain quiet in the Parón jungles. Shortly after his arrival there, and some days before Mán Singh had surrendered, Tántia had, with the approval of that rájá, sent to obtain information regarding the position of his old comrades. The reply brought to him was that to the number of eight or nine thousand men they were in the Sironj jungles; that Ráo Sáhib had left them, but that Firoz Sháh, the Ámbapáni nawáb, and Imám Áli, Wúrdi major of the 5th irregulars, were there. The last-named also sent him a letter begging Tántia to join them. It was on the receipt of this letter that, on the 5th of April, Tántia sent to consult Mán Singh as to the course he should adopt. Tántia was well aware that Mán Singh had surrendered, yet he trusted him implicitly. He had placed himself quite in his power, and had chosen his actual hiding-place on the recommendation of the retainer to whose care Mán Singh had consigned him with these words: "Stop wherever this man takes you!"

Man Singh surprises Tántia asleep,

To Tántia's message Mán Singh replied that he would come in three days to see him, and that then they would decide on the action to be taken. Mán Singh more than kept his word. At midnight on the third day, the 7th of April, he came to the hiding-place—followed at a distance by the Bombay sepoys. Tántia was asleep. Asleep he was seized, roughly awakened, and conveyed to Meade's camp. He arrived there by sunrise on the morning of the 8th.

Book XVI. Chapter I.

1859. April.

and conveys him to Meade's camp.

Meade marched him into Sipri and tried him by court-martial. He was charged with having been in rebellion and having waged war against the British Government between June 1857 and December 1858, in certain specified instances. No other charge was brought against him.

Tántia is brought to a court-martial.

His defence was simple and straightforward; it ran thus: "I only obeyed, in all things that I did, my master's orders, *i.e.* the Náná's orders, up to the capture of Kálpi; and afterwards, those of Ráo Sáhib. I have nothing to state except that I have had nothing to do with the murder of any European men, women, or children; neither had I, at any time, given orders for anyone to be hanged."

Tántia's defence.

The defence displayed the existence of a feeling very common among the Maráthás. To many of these men the descendant of the Péshwá was their real lord, they knew no other. Tántia Topi was born and bred in the household of Báji Ráo, who had been Péshwá of the Maráthás. From his earliest childhood he had been taught to regard the adopted son of Báji Ráo, Náná Sáhib, as his master, his liege lord, whose every order he was bound to obey. Of the English he

Position, in his own eyes and in the eyes of the natives of India, of Tántia Topi, with respect to the English.

Book XVI. Chapter I.

1859. April.

knew nothing, except they were foreigners who had robbed his earliest master of the country he had inherited, and his son of the pension guaranteed to his first master in lieu of his ancestral dominions. To them he was bound by no ties. The English Government, by leaving the heir of the Péshwás on the world, had forced that heir to be a conspirator and had compelled all his dependants to be free-lances.

Tántia is sentenced to be hanged, and is hanged.

Notwithstanding this reasoning, which was not put before the court, and which probably did not present itself to the minds of any of its members, Tántia Topi was sentenced to be hanged. The sentence was carried into effect at Sipri on the 18th of April.

Reflections on the sentence.

Public opinion at the time ratified the justice of the sentence, but it may, I think, be doubted whether posterity will confirm that verdict. Tántia Topi was no born servant of the English rule. At the time of his birth—about the year 1812—his master was the independent ruler of a large portion of western India. He was under no obligation to serve faithfully and truly the race which had robbed his master. When that master, unbound equally by any tie to the English, saw the opportunity of recovering the territories of the Péshwá, Tántia Topi, who was his musáhib, his companion, obeyed his orders and followed his fortunes. He declared that he committed no murder. He was not charged with committing any. He, a retainer of the ex-Péshwá's family, was charged with fighting against the English. On that charge alone he was convicted and hanged. Surely, under the circumstances of the case, the punishment was greater than the offence. The clansman had obeyed his lord, and had fought with fair weapons.

Doubts whether a reflecting posterity will confirm it.

Tántia Topi and Hofer.

Posterity has condemned Napoleon for causing Hofer to be shot. There is considerable analogy between the cases of Hofer and Tántia Topi. Neither was born under the rule of the nation against which he fought. In both cases the race to which each belonged was subjugated by a foreign race. In both cases the insurrection of the subdued race was produced by causes exterior to its own immediate interests. In both cases the two men cited rose to be the representatives of the nationality to which each belonged. In both—Hofer in the one, Tántia Topi in the other — they resisted the dominant race in a manner which necessitated the calling forth extraordinary exertions. In both cases the leader was a hero to his own countrymen. The one, the European, is still a hero to the world. The other, the Maráthá—well—who knows that in the nooks and corners of the valleys of the Chambal, the Narbadá and the Párbati, his name, too, is not often mentioned with respect and affection?

Tántia Topi as a general;

One word, before we dismiss him, regarding his character as a general. For nearly nine months, from his defeat at Jáora Alipúr by Sir Robert Napier, to his capture by an officer serving under that general, Tántia Topi had baffled all the efforts of the British. During that period he had more than once or twice made the tour of Rájpútáná and Málwá, two countries pos-

Book XVI. Chapter I.

1859. April.

sessing jointly an area of one hundred and sixty-one thousand seven hundred square miles, had crossed the Narbadá, and had threatened the more vulnerable parts of western India. The qualities he had displayed would have been admirable, had he combined with them the capacity of the general and the daring of the aggressive soldier. His marches were wonderful; he had a good eye for selecting a position, and he had a marvellous faculty for localities. But when that has been said, everything has been said. Unable to detect the weak points of his adversaries, he never took advantage of their mistakes or their too great daring; he never exposed himself in action, and he was the first to leave the field. On many occasions a judicious use of his cavalry, always superior in numbers, would have so crippled the English that further pursuit by them would have been impossible. With a little more insight and a little more daring he could, whilst retreating before them, have harassed the flanks and the rear of his pursuers, have captured their baggage, and cut up their camp-followers. But he never attempted anything of the sort. Provided he could escape from one place to harass them in another, with the chance of striking at Indúr, at Barodah, at Jodhpúr, or at Jaipúr, a blow similar to that which he had struck successfully at Gwáliár, he was satisfied.

his merits; his demerits.

Then, again, the fact that the enemy marching against him were English sufficed, no matter how small their numbers, to scare him. A striking

The fact that his enemies were English scared him.

proof of this occurred when Major Sutherland attacked him with two hundred men, three-fifths of whom were Highlanders. Tántia had a strong position, two guns, and three to four thousand men. Had the natives been well led, their numbers must have prevailed. But fighting was repugnant to Tántia. He did not understand it. He was a guerilla leader, content to fire at his enemy and then to run away. For the lives of his followers he cared nothing.

The English leaders,

Too much praise, on the other hand, can scarcely be awarded to the English generals and officers who conducted the pursuit. Sir Robert Napier, first defeating Tántia, drove him into Rájpútáná, and then shut him out from the north. Roberts, then in Rájpútáná, and later, Michel, in Rájpútáná and Málwa, pursued him in a circle, bounded on the south by the Nizám's territory or by Khándésh, and on the west by Gujrát. His attempts to break the rim of that circle were baffled by General Hill, by Sir Hugh Rose, and by General Roberts. Finally, all but surrounded as the circle became smaller, he broke away to the north and penetrated once more into the territories guarded by Sir Robert Napier. The English officers who pursued him showed, on more than one occasion, that they could march as quickly as he could. Witness the remarkable performances of Brigadier Parke, two hundred and forty miles in nine days; of Brigadier Somerset, two hundred and thirty miles in nine days, and, again, seventy miles in forty-eight hours; of Holmes, fifty-four

Napier; Roberts; Michel.

Remarkable marches of Parke, of Somerset, of Holmes,

Book XVI. Chapter I.

1859. April.

of Honner.

Daring of Becher and Sutherland.

miles through a sandy desert in little more than twenty-four hours; and of Honner, a hundred and forty-five miles in four days. Becher's daring, too, in assailing Tántia's whole army with a newly-raised regiment of troopers, and driving it before him, was a glorious act, vying with Sutherland's attack above referred to.

But these acts, daring as they were, do not stand out markedly from the achievements of other officers engaged in this pursuit. Where all did nobly it is impossible to draw a contrast. The historian, however, is bound to call attention to the skilful strategy which gave to the pursued no rest, which cut them off from the great towns, and which forced them to seek the jungles as their hiding-place. This result General Michel accomplished in Rajpútáná and Malwá, by distributing his forces in lightly equipped columns at salient points in those two divisions, with orders to pursue the rebels without intermission.* It has been calculated that the whole distance they were pursued between the 20th of June 1858 and the 1st of March 1859 exceeded three thousand miles; that Michel himself marched one thousand seven hundred and Parke two thousand.† There can be no doubt that this system, thoroughly well carried out, was the cause of the break-up of the rebel army. When Honner beat it at Kosháni on the 10th of February, and the pursuit was

Use of Michel's light columns.

---

* *Blackwood's Magazine*, August 1860.

† Captain Flower's troop 8th hussars was with Parke the whole time.

Book XVI. Chapter I.

1859. April.

taken up at once by a fresh force under Somerset, the campaign was virtually over. The rebels lost heart, abandoned their standards, and crept to their homes. It will be understood that these rapid pursuits were made without tents. These followed in the rear under charge of a small guard. They did not often come up for days, during which time the troops had to bivouac under trees.

With the surrender of Mán Singh tranquillity returns to the country.

To return. Tranquillity was restored. With the surrender of Mán Singh the rebellion collapsed in central India. So long as he was at large and hostile, the entire population held aloof from the British. The rebels could always find security in jungles in which they could not be tracked. The sense they had of security was so great, that at one time Tántia Topi and Mán Singh remained for days withing five miles of the English army, then searching for them, their position known to the natives, not one of whom would betray them. But with the surrender of Mán Singh an entire change was inaugurated. The people of central India surrendered with him.

BOOK XVI.

CHAPTER II.

The capture of Mán Singh and Tántia Topi produced all over western and southern India an effect similar to that realised by the pacification of Oudh in the North-Western Provinces. The mutiny was now stamped out. The daring of the soldier had to give place to the sagacity and breadth of view of the statesman.

The Queen's proclamation.

Some months before the final blow had been struck, when the rebels had lost every stronghold and been driven to take refuge in the wooded hills and the dense jungles which abound alike on the northern frontier of Oudh and in central India, Her Majesty the Queen had deemed it advisable to issue a proclamation to her Indian subjects, a message of mercy to those who still continued to resist, of promise to all. Before referring more particularly to this proclamation, it will be advisable to refer to some of the events which rendered its issue at the end of 1858 particularly advisable.

Book XVI. Chapter II.

1858. January.

Trial and sentence of the King of Dehlí.

The titular sovereign of India, the King of Dehlí, had been brought to trial in the Privy Council Chamber of the palace, the Díwán-i-Khláss, on the 27th of January 1858. Four charges were brought against him. The first accused him, when a pensioner of the British Government, of encouraging, aiding, and abetting the sepoys in the crimes of mutiny and rebellion against the State; the second, encouraging, aiding, and abetting his own son and other inhabitants of Dehlí and the North-West Provinces of India, to rebel and wage war against the State; the third, of having proclaimed himself reigning king and sovereign of India, and of assembling forces at Dehlí, and of encouraging others to wage war against the British Government; the fourth, of having, on the 16th of May, feloniously caused, or of having been accessory to, the death of forty-nine people of European and mixed European descent, and of having subsequently abetted others in murdering European officers and other English subjects. After a trial conducted with great patience, and which extended over forty days, the king was found guilty of the main points in the charges, and sentenced to be transported for life. Eventually he was taken to Pegu, where he ended his days in peace.

A scape-goat required.

Meanwhile it had been necessary in England to find a scape-goat for all the blood which had been shed in crushing the mutiny—an event, which, though it seemed at first to give a shock to the prestige of England, had been the means of displaying a power greater and more concen-

Book XVI. Chapter II. 1858.

trated than that with which the world had credited her. If India had at that time been under the rule of the Crown, the natural scape-goat would have been the Ministry of the day. As it was, the blow fell upon the grand old Company which had nursed the early conquests on the eastern coast of Hindustan until they had developed into the most magnificent empire subject to an alien race which the world has ever seen.

The East India Company,

The East India Company had not deserved its fate. Its rule had been better and purer, more adapted to the circumstances of the great dependency than would have been possible had its acts and orders been subject to the fluctuations of party feeling. True, it had committed some faults; but it is a remarkable fact, especially in later years, that it had been driven into the commission of those faults by the Ministry of the day. This remark especially applies to the "crime," so to speak, of the mutiny. I call it a crime, because the Court of Directors were summoned before the bar of public opinion to answer for it, and were condemned upon it. Now, if, as I believe, the mutiny was due in a great measure to the acts of the Government of Lord Dalhousie, to the denial of the right to adopt, to the shock to public morality caused by the annexation of Oudh and especially by the manner in which that annexation was carried out, then, the Government of England was equally guilty with the Court of Directors, for it was that Government which more than sanctioned the annexation and the antecedent acts to which I have referred. But

though the faults she had were more than shared in by the Ministry of the day, in times of excitement justice almost always sleeps. The scape-goat was of the very kind which suited the public humour. He was old-fashioned, pursy, and defenceless. Against him every interest was arrayed. The Ministry, which wanted his patronage; the outsider, who saw an opening to the 'covenanted' services; the doctrinaire, on whose mind the idea of a double government grated harshly; these and other classes combined to cast stones at the scape-goat. The great Company was unable to withstand the pressure. It fell, but it fell not without regret and an honoured name. On the 2nd of August 1858 the Queen signed the act which transferred its functions to the Crown.

is made that scape-goat,

and doomed to death.

No sooner had this act been accomplished than it devolved upon the First Minister of the Crown, the late Earl of Derby, to draw up for submission to the Queen a proclamation, forthwith to be issued by Her Majesty in Council, in which should be set forth the principles on which the government of India should, for the future, be conducted. The circumstances which followed the preparation of the first draft of the proclamation by Lord Derby have been given to the world on the highest authority, in a work which has brought home to every Englishman and every Englishwoman the enormous loss sustained by the country in the premature death of the illustrious prince whose noble life it so touchingly and so gracefully records.* There were

Lord Derby draws up a proclamation for submission to the Queen.

* *Life of the Prince Consort*, vol. iv. page 284.

Book XVI. Chapter II.

1859. August.

Objections taken to the original draft by the Queen and Prince Albert.

expressions in that draft which seemed to Her Majesty and to Prince Albert, in one case to invert, in another to express feebly, the meaning they were anxious to convey. In the memorandum with which the objections to these points were conveyed to Lord Derby, Her Majesty expressed in noble language the sentiments by which she was animated towards the great people of whom she was about to become the Empress, Empress in reality, though not then actually in name. "The Queen would be glad," continued the memorandum, after referring to the objections taken to the original draft of the proclamation, "if Lord Derby would write it himself in his excellent language, bearing in mind that it is a female sovereign who speaks to more than a hundred millions of Eastern people on assuming the direct government over them, and, after a bloody war, giving them pledges which her future reign is to redeem, and explaining the principles of her government. Such a document should breathe feelings of generosity, benevolence, and religious toleration, and point out the privileges which the Indians will receive in being placed on an equality with the subjects of the British Crown, and the prosperity following in the train of civilisation."

Those objections anticipated by Lord Derby.

Before the memorandum containing these noble words had reached Lord Derby, that minister, warned by a telegram from Lord Malmesbury, then in attendance on the Queen, that Her Majesty was not satisfied with the proclamation, had turned his attention to the draft, and discovering in it instinctively the faults which had been noticed by the Queen and Prince Albert, had recast it. In its amended form it met every objection, and corresponded entirely to the wishes of the august Lady in whose name it was to be issued to the people of India.

Book XVI. Chapter II.

1857. September.

The Queen's Proclamation.

The proclamation, as finally approved by Her Majesty, ran as follows :—

"Victoria, by the Grace of God, of the United Kingdom of Great Britain and Ireland, and of the Colonies and Dependencies thereof in Europe, Asia, Africa, America, and Australasia, Queen, Defender of the Faith.

"Whereas, for divers weighty reasons, we have resolved, by and with the advice and consent of the Lords Spiritual and Temporal, and Commons, in Parliament assembled, to take upon ourselves the government of the territories in India, heretofore administered in trust for us by the Honourable East India Company:

"Now, therefore, we do by these presents notify and declare that, by the advice and consent aforesaid, we have taken upon ourselves the said government, and we hereby call upon all our subjects within the said territories to be faithful and to bear true allegiance to us, our heirs and successors, and to submit themselves to the authority of those whom we may hereafter from time to time see fit to appoint to administer the government of our said territories, in our name and on our behalf.

"And we, reposing especial trust and confidence in the loyalty, ability, and judgment of our

Book XVI. Chapter II.

1859. September.

right trusty and well-beloved cousin and councillor, Charles John Viscount Canning, do hereby constitute and appoint him, the said Viscount Canning, to be our First Viceroy and Governor-General in and over our said territories, and to administer the government thereof in our name, and generally to act in our name and on our behalf, subject to such orders and regulations as he shall, from time to time, receive from us through one of our principal Secretaries of State.

"And we do hereby confirm in their several offices, civil and military, all persons now employed in the service of the Honourable East India Company, subject to our future pleasure, and to such laws and regulations as may hereafter be enacted.

"We hereby announce to the native Princes of India that all treaties and engagements made with them by or under the authority of the Honourable East India Company are by us accepted, and will be scrupulously maintained; and we look for the like observance on their part.

"We desire no extension of our present territorial possessions; and while we will permit no aggression upon our dominions or our rights to be attempted with impunity, we shall sanction no encroachment on those of others. We shall respect the rights, dignity, and honour of native princes as our own, and we desire that they, as well as our own subjects, should enjoy that prosperity and that social advancement which can only be secured by internal peace and good government.

"We hold ourselves bound to the natives of our Indian territories by the same obligations of duty which bind us to all our other subjects; and those obligations, by the blessing of Almighty God, we shall faithfully and conscientiously fulfil.

"Firmly relying ourselves on the truth of Christianity, and acknowledging with gratitude the solace of religion, we disclaim alike the right and the desire to impose our convictions on any of our subjects. We declare it to be our Royal will and pleasure that none be in anywise favoured, none molested or disquieted, by reason of their religious faith or observances, but that all shall alike enjoy the equal and impartial protection of the law; and we do strictly charge and enjoin all those who may be in authority under us that they abstain from all interference with the religious belief or worship of any of our subjects, on pain of our highest displeasure.

"And it is our further will that, so far as may be, our subjects, of whatever race or creed, be freely and impartially admitted to offices in our service, the duties of which they may be qualified, by their education, ability, and integrity, duly to discharge.

"We know and respect the feelings of attachment with which the natives of India regard the lands inherited by them from their ancestors, and we desire to protect them in all rights connected therewith, subject to the equitable demands of the State; and we will that, generally, in framing and administering the law, due regard

Book XVI. Chapter II. — 1859. September.

be paid to the ancient rights, usages, and customs of India.

"We deeply lament the evils and misery which have been brought upon India by the acts of ambitious men, who have deceived their countrymen by false reports, and led them into open rebellion. Our power has been shown by the suppression of that rebellion in the field; we desire to show our mercy by pardoning the offences of those who have been thus misled, but who desire to return to the path of duty.

"Already in one province, with a view to stop the further effusion of blood, and to hasten the pacification of our Indian dominions, our Viceroy and Governor-General has held out the expectation of pardon, on certain terms, to the great majority of those who, in the late unhappy disturbances, have been guilty of offences against our Government, and has declared the punishment which will be inflicted on those whose crimes place them beyond the reach of forgiveness. We approve and confirm the said act of our Viceroy and Governor-General, and do further announce and proclaim as follows:—

"Our clemency will be extended to all offenders, save and except those who have been or shall be convicted of having directly taken part in the murder of British subjects.

"With regard to such, the demands of justice forbid the exercise of mercy.

"To those who have willingly given asylum to murderers, knowing them to be such, or who may have acted as leaders or instigators in revolt,

Book XVI. Chapter II.

1859. September.

their lives alone can be guaranteed; but in appointing the penalty due to such persons, full consideration will be given to the circumstances under which they have been induced to throw off their allegiance, and large indulgence will be shown to those whose crimes may appear to have originated in a too credulous acceptance of the false reports circulated by designing men.

"To all others in arms against the Government we hereby promise unconditional pardon, amnesty, and oblivion of all offences against ourselves, our crown and dignity, on their return to their homes and peaceful pursuits.

"It is our Royal pleasure that these terms of grace and amnesty should be extended to all those who comply with their conditions before the first day of January next.

"When, by the blessing of Providence, internal tranquillity shall be restored, it is our earnest desire to stimulate the peaceful industry of India, to promote works of public utility and improvement, and to administer its Government for the benefit of all our subjects resident therein. In their prosperity will be our strength, in their contentment our security, and in their gratitude our best reward. And may the God of all power grant unto us, and to those in authority under us, strength to carry out these our wishes for the good of our people."

The proclamation published throughout India,

On the 1st of November 1858 this noble proclamation was published to the princes and people of India. At Calcutta, at Madras, at Bombay, at Láhor, at A'gra, at Allahábád, at Dehlí, at Rán-

Book XVI. Chapter II.

1859. November.

gún, at Lakhnao, at Maisúr, at Karáchi, at Nágpúr, and at every civil and military station in India it was publicly read on that day with every accompaniment of ceremonial splendour which could give importance to the occasion in the eyes of the natives. Translated into all the languages and many of the dialects of India, it was, at the same time, transmitted to all the native princes, and was distributed by thousands for the edification of those of lower rank and position. The first Viceroy of India used all the means in his power to acquaint the native princes and people that, transferred to the suzerainty and rule of the Queen, they might rely upon the strict observance of all engagements entered into with them by the Company; that her Majesty desired no extension of her dominions, but would respect the rights, the honour, and the dignity of the princes of her empire; that while their religion would not be interfered with, the ancient rights, customs, and usages of India would be maintained; that neither caste nor creed should be a bar to employment in her service. Lord Canning took every care, at the same time, that the rebels still in arms should have cognisance of the full and gracious terms offered them, terms which practically restored life and security to all those who had not taken part in the murder of British subjects.

And distributed.

Communications made to the native princes,

and to the rebels still in arms.

Its reception in India by princes and landowners;

The proclamation was received by all classes throughout India with the deepest enthusiasm. The princes and landowners especially regarded it as a charter which would render their possessions secure, and their rights—more especially the right, so precious to them, of adoption—absolutely inviolate. The people in general welcomed it as the document which closed up the wounds of the mutiny, which declared, in effect, that bygones were to be bygones, and that thenceforward there should be one Queen and one people. Many of the rebels still in arms—all, in fact, except those absolutely irreconcileable—took advantage of its provisions to lay down their arms and to submit to its easy conditions. In the great towns of India, natives of every religion and creed, the Hindús, the Muhammadans, the Pársis, met in numbers to draw up loyal addresses expressive of their deep sense of the beneficent feelings which had prompted the proclamation, of their gratitude for its contents, and of their loyalty to the person of the illustrious Lady to whose rule they had been transferred.

by rebels.

The natives draw up loyal addresses expressive of their gratitude.

With the issue of the proclamation the story of the mutiny should fitly close. But those who have accompanied me so far will have seen that in Oudh and in central India the work of warfare was prolonged for six months after its promulgation. In this there is, however, only a seeming misplacement. In the jungles on the Oudh frontier and of central India there survived for that period men who were more marauders than soldiers—men whose continued rebellion was but remotely connected with the original cause of the mutiny, who had offended too deeply to hope for forgiveness. In one notable instance, indeed, that of Mán Singh, the quarrel was in no sense a conse-

The mutiny had really terminated when the proclamation appeared.

Book XVI. Chapter II. 1859. November.

quence of the mutiny. It was a quarrel between a noble and his feudal lord. Yet it was that quarrel, not the mutiny, nor any fact connected with the mutiny, which kept the dominions of Sindia in continual disturbance for more than six months. When Mán Singh surrendered, those disturbances ceased.

The proclamation the beginning of a new era.

As far as related, then, to the actual mutineers, with but a few exceptions to the sepoys, and to all the landowners in British territories, the proclamation of the Queen was, in very deed, the end and the beginning—the end of a conflict which had deluged the country with blood, the beginning of an era full of hope, alike for the loyal and the misguided, for the prince and the peasant, for the owner and for the cultivator, for every class and for every creed.

BOOK XVII.

CHAPTER I.

THE record of military events has necessarily almost monopolised the pages of a work the object of which was to deal with the rise, the progress, and the suppression of a mutiny. I use the word mutiny advisedly, for although, as I shall show in a subsequent chapter, the disturbances of 1857 were primarily excited by men who were not soldiers, yet, had the native army remained faithful, these men would have been powerless for much evil. When, however, they succeeded in inducing the native army to revolt, the mutiny became the great factor in the disturbance. It was mainly the mutiny of the sepoys which demanded all the attention of the English. And as mutiny, both as regards the acts of its fomentors and in those who strive to subdue it, is the form of contest which of all others provokes the worst passions of mankind, the story of the rise, progress, and suppression of this par-

The civil districts have necessarily attracted less attention than was their due.

Book XVII. Chapter I. 1857.

ticular uprising has necessarily dealt almost entirely with marches and battles, with deeds of treachery and the punishment they call forth, with the clang of arms and the bustle of the camp. I am well aware that even in this particular subject many details of great interest, but not affecting the main issue at stake, have been omitted. Still more am I conscious that the civil districts and the heroic exertions of the officers who administered, have not in many cases received the attention which those exertions demanded. It is not easy to provide a perfect remedy for this perhaps unavoidable omission. To illustrate, however, the difficulties the civil officers encountered and the heroic way in which they met them, I propose to devote this chapter to a brief consideration of the events which occurred in five important civil districts, each with a character of its own, and to ask the reader to form his own opinion regarding the manner in which the members of the Civil Service of India, placed in circumstances of exceptional difficulty and danger, performed their duty to their country.

The omission to be partly remedied.

Bijnor.

The first district I take is that of Bijnor. Bijnor is a district in Rohilkhand, containing an area of one thousand eight hundred and eighty-two square miles, and a population of nearly seven hundred thousand souls. It is bounded on the north-east by the hill district of Gahrwál; on the east and south-east by Morádábád; on the west by Mírath, by Mozaffarnagar, and by Saháranpúr. In 1857 the magistrate and collector of this district was Mr. A. Shakespear; but at the station of

Bijnór, which gave its name to the district, were likewise Mrs. Shakespear; the joint magistrate, Mr. G. Palmer; the civil surgeon, Dr. Knight, and Mrs. Knight; Mr. Robert Currie, C.S., on his way to the hills; Mr. Lemaistre, the head clerk; Mrs. Lemaistre and three children; Mr. Johnson, a clerk; Mr. Murphy, a clerk; Mrs. Murphy and four children; and Mr. Cawood.

Book XVII. Chapter I.

1857. May.

Mr. Shakespear and the European residents of Bijnor.

Though Bijnor was but forty miles distant from Mírath, the news of the terrible events there of the 10th of May did not reach Mr. Shakespear till the 13th, and then only through natives. That officer at once endeavoured to ascertain the real facts of the case by communicating with Mírath. But the whole country was up. The hereditary instincts of a marauding section of the population, extremely prolific in those parts, known as the Gújars, had been thoroughly roused, and their appetite for plunder had been whetted by the rivalry of the convicts escaped from the Mírath jail, who, spreading over the country, stopped and plundered everyone, not excepting the meanest traveller. It seems probable, also, that they stopped the communications near Míráth, for it is a curious fact that the horsemen sent by Shakespear to that station on the 13th of May, took the first intelligence of the mutiny of the 10th to the police station of Baisúna, which was on the high road between Mírath and Bijnor.

The mutiny of the 10th of May

rouses the districts to plunder.

The indiscriminate plunder of which I have spoken attained in a few days so alarming a proportion, that Shakespear found it was necessary

Shakespear invites the aid of the chiefs, land-owners,

Book XVII. Chapter I.

1857. May.

for the retention of British authority to take stringent measures to repress it. He accordingly called on the principal landowners of the district to afford him all the aid in their power, at the same time that he sent a notice to all native soldiers on leave at their homes to come to the station and give their services to the State. Both these appeals were responded to fairly well. The cháodris* of Haldáor and Tájpúr responded on the 23rd, and a few non-commissioned officers and men, chiefly belonging to the irregular cavalry, came on a few days later. At the same time the police was considerably strengthened. But events were marching too fast even for these precautionary measures. On the 19th of May the jail at Morádábád was broken open, and the worst prisoners connected with the Bijnor district were released. The freedom of these men added enormously to the insecurity of life and property in the neighbourhood. To add to the general danger, three hundred of the sappers and miners who had mutinied at Rúrki entered the Bijnor district and entered into negotiations with Mahmúd Khán, nawáb of Najibábád, with the view, as it was then suspected, and subsequently transpired, to making an attack on the chief station. Eventually, however, these mutineers preferred to proceed to Moradábád, plundering on their road the town of Naghína.† On the very day, however, the 21st, on

(Margin: and of soldiers on leave.)

(Margin: The insecurity increases.)

* A cháodri is the head man of a village.

† Being short of ammunition, they hoped at Moradábád to obtain the co-operation of the 29th native infantry, but, instead of co-operation, that regiment robbed them of their spoil.

Book XVII. Chapter I.

1857. May.

which they entered that town, the prisoners broke out of the jail in Bijnor itself. Mr. Shakespear hurried to the spot followed by some horsemen, and succeeded in stopping further egress, some of the prisoners falling under the fire of his followers. Whilst thus engaged, he despatched the joint magistrate, Mr. G. Palmer, to pursue the fugitives. The result would in all probability have been satisfactory but for the accidental refuge afforded to the malefactors by a sand-bank in the river, on which they had collected. To secure them here foot-soldiers were necessary, and before these could arrive night had set in. Under cover of darkness, two hundred and fifteen of them managed to escape.*

The prisoners at Bijnor break out.

But they are pursued and partially recaptured.

It was evident to Mr. Shakespear that the love of liberty had far less prompted this outbreak than a lust for plunder, for the news of the disordered state of the districts had penetrated even within the jail. Under his charge, in the treasury, within a short distance of the jail, were the moneys belonging to Government, the collections of the district, amounting to a considerable sum. In a station, the capital of a surging district, where the number of the Europeans could be counted on the fingers, this treasury could no longer be considered safe from the greed of the disorganised rabble. It certainly could not be defended against a determined attack. Under these circumstances the happy thought occurred to Shakespear to throw all

Shakespear secures the moneys of the State

* Seven had been killed, and one hundred and twenty-six, of whom twelve were wounded, were recaptured.

Book XVII. Chapter I.

1857. May.

in a well.

the coin, except the small amount necessary for current expenses, into a well, the mouth of which could be defended from the roof of the treasury building. He carried out this measure. The result showed his prescience. Even the most covetous felt that the abstraction of the rupees had become a service fraught with certain death to those who should be foremost in the attempt.

Mahmúd Khán arrives to give trouble.

The precaution had not been taken one hour too soon. That very evening Mahmúd Khán, the nawáb of whom I have already spoken, arrived with a number of empty carts, and announced his intention to carry off the money to Najibábád. Even he quailed before the prospect of extracting it from the well. Yet the station seemed at the mercy of this man and his Pathán followers, evidently unsettled and dangerous, disappointed, too, in their hopes regarding the rupees. The two days that followed were very critical. On the third day, fortunately, the retainers of the Hindú zamindárs arrived, and having in the interval raised some horse and taken measures for the protection of the station, Shakespear felt able to think of offensive measures. He was further confirmed in this view by the arrival, on the 28th, of fourteen sowars, nearly all leave men, under the command of a rassaldár of the Gwáliár contingent, followed by twenty-five sowars of the new Moradábád levy, and forty sepoys of the 29th native infantry—a regiment which, though mistrusted, had not then mutinied.

The station is relieved by the arrival of loyal Hindú landowners and others.

Palmer quiets one district.

Shakespear's first act was to send Mr. Palmer,

with the 29th sepoys and thirty sowars to coerce a large body of marauders near Mandáwar, a large and wealthy town which they were threatening. Palmer struck the rebels most successfully, and quieted the district. The next person to deal with was the nawáb. This man, baffled in his hopes regarding the rupees, had returned, on the 23rd, with his carts still empty, to Najibábád. A week later, however, he returned, uninvited, accompanied by upwards of two hundred stalwart Patháns, armed with matchlocks. His demeanour showed that he meant mischief, but that he was prepared to wait for the opportune moment. To get rid of him was difficult yet most necessary. Shakespear attempted the task, and after some trouble, persuaded the nawáb to move to a little distance to settle some Mewáti marauders, hoping, during his absence, to be able to do much to restore confidence.

The nawáb returns to Bijnor,

but is persuaded to retire.

These hopes were doomed to be disappointed. The mutiny at Barélí on the 31st of May* produced effects which were felt all over Rohilkhand. Shakespear had heard rumours of the event on the 1st, but rumours in those days were common. He received authentic information only on the 3rd. The danger was indeed imminent. The Nawáb's Patháns were close at hand, and it was but too clear that the forty men of the 29th native infantry would follow the example set them by their brethren at Barélí. But in this conjuncture Shakespear displayed both judgment

The mutiny at Barélí changes the situation for the worse.

* Vol. i. page 310.

Book XVII. Chapter I.

1857. May.

Shakespear faces the difficulty.

and decision. He at once recalled Palmer, under whose orders the men of the 29th native infantry were serving, and on their arrival despatched them instantly, before they could communicate with anyone, to rejoin their head-quarters.

By the exercise of judgment Shakespear saves some of the state moneys.

At this time a party of the 4th irregulars, commanded by Lieutenant Gough, arrived from Mírath with a string of camels to carry off a portion of the Government money at Shakespear's disposal. The roads were unsafe; a long string of camels carrying coin could not be guarded efficiently by nineteen men, and everyone in the district was aware of the purpose for which the camels had arrived. Again did Shakespear display his judgment. For camels he substituted elephants. He loaded these animals with fifty thousand rupees, and Gough was thus enabled, by making a forced march, to accomplish his journey in safety at the same time that he relieved Bijnor of that which most tempted the miscreants of the period.

Communication with the outer world ceases.

But darker times were approaching. The revolt at Barélí had, as I have said, produced a ferment all over Rohilkhand. From the 2nd of June communications between English authorities elsewhere and Bijnor ceased. That place was cut off from the outer world.

The nawáb returns to Bijnor.

Affairs were in this darkened condition when Mahmúd Khán, nawáb of Najibábád, suddenly returned from the district. That return was occasioned solely by a report which had reached him that Shakespear was about to make over the remainder of the money under his charge to the loyal Hindú cháodris. Mahmúd Khán arrived evidently resolved to take strong measures. To men of his class and country, placed in the extraordinary position in which they found themselves in 1857, the proverb, *ce n'est que le premier pas qui coûte*, is specially applicable. Accustomed from their earliest childhood to respect British authority, habit had become a second nature, and it was not without a very extraordinary effort that they were able to break through the iron bar by which it bound them. But that bar once broken, there remained no extreme of villainy of which they would not be capable. The memory of the old bond, indeed, incited them to extreme measures. They felt, when they had committed themselves, that a return to the former condition was impossible; that thenceforth their safety required the death of those against whom they had lifted their hands. Shakespear was thoroughly cognisant of this feeling. He deemed it, therefore, of the utmost importance to soothe the nawáb, to persuade him not to take a step which would be irrevocable, which would commit him to murder. Fortunately he had at his hand an instrument for the purpose—a Muhammadan official of proved loyalty and trust named Saiyid Áhmad Khán. This man, sent by Shakespear to the nawáb, succeeded, by dint of smooth words and assurances, in inducing him to remain still on the further bank of the Rubicon. He continued, however, in a dogged and perverse humour, and declined to go and see Mr. Shakespear.

Feelings which animated men like the nawáb.

Shakespear manages him.

Book XVII. Chapter I.

1857. June.

Bad news from Barélí.

That evening, the 7th of June, news reached the station of the assumption of authority by the rebel Khán Bahádur Khán, and of the murders committed at Barélí and Morádábád. It was now clear that a sentence of death had been pronounced against every European, every Christian in Rohilkhand.

Shakespear makes over charge of the district to the nawáb,

Under these circumstances, the pressing character of which was increased by the rumour that the detachment of the 29th native infantry was on its way to Bijnor, there remained no hope of saving the station. Mr. Shakespear determined, then, as a first measure of precaution, to place the ladies in safety by escorting them to a point beyond the province. But such an operation could not be undertaken without the consent of the nawáb. With the nawáb, then, Shakespear entered into an accommodation, by virtue of which that nobleman agreed to take charge of the district during the ten days for which Shakespear and his companions proposed to absent themselves. The nawáb was not authorised to collect revenue, but as he would have to meet heavy charges, the money in the treasury was placed at his disposal, and he was required to keep a regular account of its expenditure. In common with almost every other Englishman in India, Shakespear believed that Dehlí would fall as soon as the English force appeared before it, and that, within the ten days he had covenanted for, he would be able to return with a sufficient force to put down all disturbance.

and marches with the

He and his companions—those whose names

Book XVII. Chapter I.

1857. June.

have been already given,* had intended to start early on the morning of the 8th for Rúrki, forty-three miles distant, and, marching all night, to reach it the same evening. The party, was, however, so much delayed in crossing the Ganges, that they were obliged to make for Mozaffarnagar instead. Here doubts arose regarding the fidelity of the escort. The travellers, then, after resting one day, pushed on for Rúrki, escorted by twelve troopers of the 4th irregulars, a detachment of which regiment was stationed at Mozaffarnagar.† Here they arrived on the night of the 11th of June.

ladies and Europeans to Rúrki.

It now became Shakespear's great object to return to his district. He made numberless efforts to organise a small party of Gúrkhas or Europeans or other men who could be depended upon to effect this object. But Dehlí had not fallen, and every soldier was required to aid to contribute to its fall. Not a man, then, could be procured.

He finds it impossible to return.

Meanwhile Mahmúd Khán was carrying all before him at Bijnor. His first act was to proclaim himself ruler of the district under the king of Dehlí. He next fished up the remainder of the money from the well, and sent it to his own house at Najibábád. Then, having stopped the posts, placed guards at the ferries, and increased his forces as much as possible, he despatched a confidential servant to Dehlí to endeavour to

The nawáb at Bijnor

* Page 401.

† This detachment rose a few days later and murdered the adjutant, Lieutenant Smith.

Book XVII. Chapter I.

1857. July.

accepts the king of Dehlí as his lord.

obtain authority from the king to hold the district in his name. He proceeded at the same time to alter the weights and measures, substituting for those of the Company others of a different character, bearing the imperial stamp of Dehlí.

Character of his rule in Bijnor.

The cause which, perhaps, more than any other contributed to the downfall of the Moghol dynasty was the system of persecution for religion, inaugurated by Aurangzib. It is remarkable that, whenever and wherever the Muhammadans in India obtained supremacy during the period of the mutiny they showed the same inclination. The nawáb was no exception. He had scarcely consolidated, as he thought, his usurped authority than he began to use it against the Hindús, leaguing himself with that object with co-religionists without birth and without character, and whose co-operation under other circumstances he would have spurned. His first operations were successful. Umráo Singh, cháodri of Shérkot, was compelled to flee the country with the loss of a great part of his property. This success was, however, fatal. It impelled the Hindú village chiefs, who had hitherto stood aloof from each other, to combine. An opportunity soon offered which enabled them to make their combination felt.

The Hindús rise and expel him,

To carry on his plans against the Hindús the nawáb had weakened his own forces at Bijnor, where he himself remained. Taking advantage of this circumstance, the younger of the cháodris of Haldúr, combining with the cháodris of

Book XVII. Chapter I.

1857. August.

Bijnor, suddenly attacked the nawáb on the morning of the 6th of August and drove him in precipitous flight to Najibábád. The immediate result was not altogether satisfactory. It is true that the town was saved; but the public and private property outside it fell into the hands of the rabble, who had joined the cháodris simply with the hope of plunder, and who were altogether beyond control.*

but the place is plundered.

Before the events of the 6th of August could be made known to Mr. Shakespear, that gentleman, satisfied that the nawáb was not to be trusted, had resolved to cancel the written authority he had given him to administer the district. He wrote a letter to that effect on the 7th, and by the same opportunity directed the cháodris to consider themselves responsible for their respective properties and the quiet of the district. But when, a little later, information of the events of the 6th reached him, he saw that more decisive measures were required. It happened that there were on the spot two Muhammadan gentlemen of conspicuous loyalty—Muhammad Rahmat Khán the deputy collector, and Saiyid Ahmad Khán, already referred to. Shakespear then directed these gentlemen to assume charge of the district. They obeyed his orders, assumed the office on the 16th of August, and devoted to it the loyal zeal and true-hearted decision by which their conduct had been always characterised.

Shakespear transfers the charge of the district to loyal Muhammadans.

* A type of the proceedings which would certainly take place all over India if the protecting hand of England were to be withdrawn.

Book XVII. Chapter I.

1857. Aug.–Sept.

Fresh complications arise,

But every day now saw a fresh complication. The quarrel between the Muhammadans and the Hindús became so embittered that the nawáb sounded the religious war-cry of the former, and, at the head of an infuriated band, marched to the vicinity of Bijnor on the 23rd. He first burned and plundered a Ját village, and then marched on Bijnor. There there were no defenders. The Hindús had gone to Naghína to oppose there an anticipated attack from another party of Muhammadans. Under these circumstances the two loyal officials above cited deemed it advisable to retire to Haldúr. Meanwhile the Muhammadans had taken and sacked Naghína. They then advanced on Haldúr, defeated the Hindús who moved from that place to meet them, and were only prevented from destroying it by the outbreak of fires in all directions, which hindered their advance. Bijnor, however, fell into their hands. The two loyal Government officials fled across the river, and one or two of the Hindú cháodris quitted the district which no longer offered them a safe habitation.

and the loyal Muhammadans are forced to flee.

The Hindús are finally defeated,

From this time the district was a prey to civil war between the members of the opposite faiths, each alternately gaining some advantage. Some attempts were made at reconciliation, but neither party had sufficiently felt its inferiority to the other. At length, on the 18th of September, the Hindús experienced a decisive defeat, and another attempt was made to induce them to submit to Máhmúd Khán and his followers. Nothing, however, could tempt the younger cháodris to place

and flee.

themselves in the power of the Muhammadans, and towards the end of the month they escaped across the Ganges to Mírath.

Disputes arise amongst the victors.

Just about this time a wanton massacre of unoffending Hindús confirmed the supremacy of the Muhammadans. But as always has happened in such cases—as, till the race greatly changes, always will happen—no sooner was their supremacy uncontested than disputes broke out amongst themselves. Finally, these disputes were arranged by the conferring on the nawáb the chief authority, with an allowance of twelve thousand rupees a month, having under him Márah Khán, a noted bad character, his own eldest son, and his nephew. The two first were to contribute two-thirds, the last one-third, of his salary. This arrangement lasted till the 22nd of February 1858.

The Muhammadans carry their raids across the river.

The Muhammadans now became so strong that notorious freebooters from neighbouring districts gathered to their party; they even attracted three princes of the imperial family of Dehlí! They then began to make successful raids across the border, and to burn and plunder at their will. They did this on several occasions in December 1857 and January 1858. On the 5th of the latter month they crossed the Ganges with a large force and two guns, burned the station of Mîránpúr, proclaimed the nawáb, and retreated before the British troops could intercept them. Two days later they carried out the same programme at Kankhal and Hardwár. On the 9th, emboldened by their success, they again crossed

Book XVII. Chapter I.

1858. January.

the Ganges—this time only to repent their audacity, for they had the misfortune to fall in with a party sent from Rúrki under Captain H. Boisragon. This affair, which redounded greatly to that officer's credit, merits special notice.

As soon as the news regarding the three raids into British territory, just referred to, reached Rúrki, the officer commanding at that place, Captain Read, directed Lieutenant T. Boisragon, commanding at Manghúr, to proceed ot once with his detachment* towards Maiapúr. Lieutenant Boisragon received this order at 8 o'clock on the evening of the 8th of January. He set out at once, and marching across a country, very indifferent for guns, reached Maiapúr at 9 o'clock the next morning. There he was joined by his brother Captain H. Boisragon, the district staff officer, accampanied by Captain H. Drummond, B.E., Lieutenant Thomason, B.E., Mr. Melville, B.C.S., and a few sowars. Captain Boisragon at once took command.

Boisragon marches to check the rebels.

Accompanied by the gentlemen named and three or four sowars, Captain Boisragon proceeded down the bank of the river in search of the enemy. After a ride of between two and three miles he came suddenly upon their camp, pitched within a few feet of the water, opposite to the ford of Anjon, a distance of about three miles in a direct line from Khankal. Owing to inequalities in the ground, Boisragon could not

He ascertains their position.

* Consisting of fifty Gúrkahs, fifty Sikhs, and two 6-pounder guns under Lieut. St. George, B.A.

gain a clear view of the position, but he ascertained that they numbered certainly five hundred, and that they had at least one gun. Boisragon and his party then fell back leisurely on their camp, to wait till the movement of the rebels should be more pronounced.

His patience was not long tried. The following afternoon, about 2 o'clock, Boisragon received information that the rebels were crossing the river in force, and that a great number had established themselves to the south of Khankal, which they were about to enter. Leaving a small party to protect his camp and watch the ford, Boisragon marched with the rest of the detachment to Khankal, entered it from the north side, traversed the main street, and went out from the south gate, just in time to prevent the entrance of the rebels. Detaching his few mounted men (sixteen men 1st Panjáb cavalry) to cover his flanks, Boisragon, with his small force,* advanced to cut off the rebels from the town of Jowálápúr, in which he had reason to believe they had many sympathisers. Posting the guns between that town and a large building, he sent the Gúrkahs on the extreme right, under Lieutenant Boisragon, to attack their left flank, whilst the Sikhs, who were next the guns, should charge their front. The attack was irresistible. One of the rebel leaders fell by the hand of Lieutenant Boisragon; their rank and file were thrown back on the river, and sought refuge either in the stream or by

Marches to Khankal,

attacks,

* Eight Europeans, thirty Gúrkahs, thirty Sikhs, and two guns.

Book XVII. Chapter I.

1858. January.

and completely defeats them.

flight along its banks. In their flight they were followed by the cavalry and considerably cut up. Captain Boisragon ascertained that they numbered about a thousand and that they had two guns. This little affair was the more important as it was the first decisive blow struck at the rebellion so long rampant in Rohilkhand.

Terror of the nawáb.

To return to Bijnor. The effect of Boisragon's victory was immediately felt in that district. No people traverse more quickly than the natives of India the space between exalted elation and bitter despondency. To conciliate the small landowners, the nawáb's nephew at once announced that all rent-free holdings resumed under British rule would be released; but this helped him but little, and the declension of the fortunes of the usurpers was followed by a renewal of their quarrels. Some bitter disputes terminated in a new agreement, in virtue of which the nawáb's monthly salary was reduced to eight thousand rupees; his eldest son was declared his heir-apparent; his nephew was nominated as his representative; two other Muhammadans were promoted to be generals, and assignments of lands were made to provide for their salaries; a third was appointed to be commander-in-chief; stipends were set apart for all the members of the nawáb's family, and an engagement was taken from the nephew that he would not aspire to the succession, or interfere in any way with the claims of the eldest son on his father's death.

The disputes between him and his coadjutors are readjusted.

Jones's force enters Rohilkhand.

This tinsel fabric was shattered at the very first push. Even whilst it had been building there was being prepared at Rúrki a British force whose very appearance in Rohilkhand would be sufficient to shake it to its very foundations. On the 17th of April that force, accompanied by Mr. Shakespear and others crossed the Ganges near the head of the Ganges canal, and in five days effectually cleared the Bijnor district in the manner described in the second volume of this history.*

Book XVII. Chapter I.

1858. April.

Shakespear resumes his duties.

From the date of the crossing of the avenging force into the Bijnor district, Mr. Shakespear resumed his duties as the representative of the Government. His responsibilities were extremely onerous. He was the only officer of the column who had any acquaintance with the country, so that matters connected with the department of the Quartermaster-General were mainly dependent upon his opinion and advice, and, added to this, it devolved upon him to decide the measures which should be taken for the punishment of offenders and for the restoration of order. In a sketch such as this is, it is impossible to render full justice to all that Mr. Shakespear in a very brief period was able to accomplish. The principle upon which he acted was to mark in an effective manner the displeasure of the Government, whilst opening to all, except to actual murderers, a way of reconciliation and pardon. Thus —even before the fight at Naghína—to leave a lasting symbol of the sentiments entertained by the British Government regarding the nawáb, the

Services rendered by him to Jones's force.

He reorganises the district.

* Vol. ii. pages 513 to 519.

Book XVII. Chapter I.

1858. April.

hall of audience at Najibábád was destroyed; the district was at the same time dominated by the occupation of the fort of Pattargarh in the vicinity. These acts accomplished, Mr. Shakespear fixed his headquarters at Najibábád, re-established the collectorships and police posts in the districts, and endeavoured, by conciliatory measures, to induce the rebel Muhammadans, who had not been engaged in any distinct crime in connection with the rebellion, to return to their peaceful avocations. His measures were so far successful that his police were able, even at that early period, to enter the jungles and capture without opposition some relatives of the nawáb. When, after Naghína, he returned, escorted only by the loyal Hindús and accompanying the guns captured at that fight, to Bijnor, he ascertained that the population were returning to their normal avocations; that traffic was being reopened, and that the collection of rebels in the jungles was rapidly diminishing. Mr. Shakespear subsequently visited every part of his district, and by his firm, conciliatory, and judicious measures, speedily removed the very last remnant of discontent. As he, at the beginning of the disturbances, had clung to his district longer than any other officer in Rohilkhand, so on their subsidence he was able to bring back the normal routine earlier than was found practicable in the other districts of the same province.*

His tact and conciliatory measures

speedily restore order and confidence.

* The nawáb Mahmúd Khán was sentenced to be transported for life. His property was forfeited to the State.

The "energy and sound judgment" displayed by Mr. Shakespear were noticed by the cordial approval of Lord Canning. With other civil officers, likewise, he was thanked for his services as a volunteer with the Rúrki force; but there the public acknowledgments ended. In the circumstances in which he was placed, no one could have accomplished more than Mr. Shakespear. It must have been trying for him to notice, when the honours were apportioned, that others who had done less were substantially rewarded.

Book XVII. Chapter I.

1858. May.

Dehrá Dún.

Dehrá Dún is another typical district which seems to deserve special mention.

In the beginning of May 1857, this district consisted of a valley measuring about sixty miles by fifteen, partly forest and partly tea-plantations, a hill-tract of less extent, and a sanitarium and convalescent depôt, containing invalids, women, and children, to the number of about two thousand. It was bounded on the north by native states, on the west by native states, on the south by the district of Sahāranpúr, on the east by the district of Bijnor. The chief civil authority was the superintendent, Mr. H. G. Keene, his assistant being Mr. J. C. Robertson. The garrison consisted of the Sirmúr regiment of Gúrkahs under the command of Major Charles Reid. The Trigonometrical Survey had its head-quarters there under Colonel Scott Waugh of the Bengal Engineers. There was a small establishment under the American Presbyterian Board of Missions. There were also some old

Mr. Keene and the European population of the district.

Book XVII. Chapter I.

1858. May.

officers of the retired list resident at Dehrá, and a very few rich natives, the most prominent of whom was a political *détenu*, the rájá Lál Sinh, formerly regent of the Panjáb.

Mr. Keene is in the heart of the hills when the mutiny breaks out.

When the news of the Mírath outbreak reached Mr. Keene—which was on the 16th of May—he was in the heart of the hill subdivision, engaged in a survey preliminary to the settlement of the land revenue. The tracts were being swept by epidemic cholera, and there was considerable difficulty in moving the camp. He came in, however, as quickly as he could, met on the way with further alarms. On arriving at Dehrá he found that Reid's Gúrkahs had marched to join the main body of troops about to move from Mírath upon Dehlí. A depôt of eighty men constituted the total force left with him to maintain order. He accordingly lost no time in raising recruits to guard the passes by which his district could be entered from the plains. Rájá Lál Sinh also placed some of his armed retainers at Mr. Keene's disposal. In a few days news arrived of the fall of Bijnor, brought in by the civil officer of that district. Sahâranpúr still held out under Mr. R. Spankie. The tract to the westward, under the Sirmúr rájá, was fairly peaceful. The hill tracts to the north were quiescent, except in the British subdivisions already mentioned, where petty outrages occurred which could not just then be punished.

He returns and organises exterior defensive measures,

also for the maintenance of internal order.

Having made such provisions as appeared proper for his outward defences, the superintendent turned his attention to the maintenance of internal order. For this purpose he appointed the mess-house of the absent Gúrkah officers as a rendezvous in case of alarm, and enrolled a number of European volunteers whose names he placed upon a roster, and with whose aid the town of Dehrá and its environs were patrolled every night at unfixed hours. By this device it was calculated that the native police would be kept on the alert by their ignorance of the exact hour when they might be visited. The success was complete, no post having been found deserted, no beat unkept, during the whole time of trouble.

Book XVII. Chapter I.

1858. June.

Bad news from the exterior.

Matters were in a state of tension, but all remained quiet—with the exception of one or two fires, probably accidental—till the middle of June. Then, one evening, a runner came in from the Sirmúr territory, bringing news that four hundred infantry and two hundred cavalry from the Jalandhar brigade were in full march upon the district. The messenger brought these tidings in a note from a British officer, and they were strictly true. The contents of the treasury were at once sent up to Masúrí (the hill sanitarium) with a note to the officer commanding the convalescent depôt, requesting his aid. The next day was occupied with preparing carriage and provisions, for the men of the Gúrkah depôt were to be marched out on elephants and the invalids on horseback. That evening the force started, about one hundred and fifty men in all,* and marched

Measures taken in consequence.

A force marches against the rebels,

* Mr. R. Forrest, of the Canal Department, the Rev. D. Herron, American Missionary, and some sick officers from Masúri, accompanied Mr. Keene, as also did his assistant.

Book XVII. Chapter I.

1858. June.

thirty-six miles during the sultry June night. In the morning they arrived at Bádsháh Bágh the outer end of the Timli pass, and found that their prey had escaped them. Like snakes in the grass, the sepoys had slipped away during the hours necessarily given to preparation. The force could not go farther out of the district without draining it of its administrators and defenders; and the rebels had to be left to such obstacles as they might encounter in other districts.

who escape,

This was the most serious military occurrence that took place, with one exception, to be hereafter noticed. It had no important results. Still, it was well planned, showing spirit in all concerned. The enemy were well armed and equipped, and the cavalry superbly mounted on stud-bred horses. With a motley force, of which only a small portion was British, and that composed of convalescents, the task of bringing them to book, though a serious one, would probably have succeeded but for circumstances which no one could control or avoid.

The next trouble that arose was from the lawless state of the Sahāranpúr district. Mr. Spankie kept such order as the times admitted. His coadjutor, Mr. H. D. Robertson, was actively engaged in scouring the district for the same purpose. But their efforts were much paralysed by the protracted defence and prolonged attack going on at Dehlí; and marauders of the old type who had given so much trouble in Shore's days, thirty years before, began to appear. One gang

The protracted length of the siege of Dehlí foments disorder.

of these men came across the border and drove off a herd of cattle after killing the herdsman. They were pursued and arrested, brought to trial, condemned, and hanged within less than three weeks from the commission of their crime. The example proved sufficient; the forays ceased.

Book XVII. Chapter I.

1858. June.

The difficulty which next supervened was as to food and money, neither of which are sufficiently produced in the valley, even in common times. Now, when agriculture was almost suspended by war's alarms, when the roads were almost entirely closed for traffic by the disturbed state of the country, the difficulties may well have appeared almost insurmountable. And the population never was so large. The wives and families of officers in the field thronged to the hills, followed by flocks of servants; and the officers—unable to do anything else with their pay—drew it chiefly in the form of orders upon the treasuries of places where their wives were harbouring. Of these the most frequented was that of Dehrá, where a run consequently occurred to meet which the resources of the Panjáb were laid under requisition. John Lawrence and Donald Macleod, the strong rulers of that province, sent in several supplies, which were loyally escorted to Dehrá by the yeomanry of the Dún to whom Mr. Keene entrusted the duty. On one occasion, Mr. Spankie sent a small sum from Sahárанpúr, to fetch which the Rev. J. Woodside, an American missionary, and Mr. R. Currie, a young civilian, went over and brought the cash

Difficulties regarding food and money

how partly surmounted.

Book XVII. Chapter I.

1858. June.

safely through one of the most disturbed parts of the Sahāranpúr district.

These resources proving insufficient, Keene issues bank-notes.

These resources proving insufficient Mr. Keene —adopting a suggestion made to him by Captain Tennant, of the Engineers—determined to issue paper money on his own responsibility. He, therefore, prepared forms of acknowledgment for sums running from one rupee to fifty (which he marked with a crest press to prevent forgery). He then registered these in his treasury office, and issued them under his own signature in part payment of the drafts that were presented; so much paper and the balance in cash.*

The Dún passes through the ordeal.

Food was also procured through local merchants, and by these expedients the troubles of the time, though they could not be neutralised, were reduced to a minimum. The result was that of all those tender beings confided to the superintendent's care, not one hair of the head of any suffered wrong. The cattle-lifting above mentioned was the only damage that property sustained in the Dún up to the fall of Dehlí. After that date, when a military officer had been sent to take charge, the Dún was once invaded at its extreme corner; but the invasion was repulsed with considerable loss by a party from Rúrki before the Dún force could come to the spot.

Of an entirely different character to the foregoing were the proceedings of Mr. R. H. W. Dun-

* *Vide* extract from Accountant to Government, quoted in *Letters on Indian Administration*, 1867 (p. 2).

lop, magistrate and collector of Mírath. Mr. Dunlop was travelling in the Himálaya mountains when the mutiny broke out.* He heard of that event at the village of Naggar near the source of the Biás river on the 31st of May. He at once pushed for the plains, passed through the Simla sanitarium, the inhabitants of which he found "either in the hot or cold fit of panic," and reached Ambála on the 9th and Karnál on the 10th of June. At the latter place he received a letter from his commissioner, Mr. Greathed, who was with the English army before Dehlí, in reply to one from himself asking for active employment, summoning him to the camp. It was just after the action of Badli-ki-sarái had been fought—an action considered by everyone as a precursor to the immediate storming of the imperial city. As Dunlop and Speke rode across that plain, still strewn with the bodies of the dead sepoys, the only anxiety they felt was the anxiety lest they might arrive too late for the great event, to attempt which, in fact, the army had still to undergo three months' toil, fighting, and privations.

Dunlop in the Himalayas when the mutiny breaks out.

Hastens to Dehlí.

On the very day of his arrival in camp, Dunlop was informed by the commissioner that the gentleman who had acted for him at Mírath was dead, and that as it was of great importance

He is ordered to Mírath,

* His companion was Speke of the 65th native infantry, brother of the African traveller. Speke was a few months later mortally wounded at the storming of Dehlí. He was a gallant soldier and a noble-hearted man. His dying words were: "Thy ways are not our ways, but they are just and true."

Book XVII. Chapter I.

1858. June.

that someone possessing local experience should take charge of that district, it was incumbent upon him to proceed thither at once, and that, owing to the scarcity of cavalry, he must find his way without an escort. Dunlop started that night on a hired horse, accompanied by one mounted orderly* belonging to his district who happened to be in camp, and rode straight for Bhágpat on the Jamná.

And rides through the disturbed districts to Bhágpat.

Thence he rides for Mírath.

Having travelled three consecutive days and nights Dunlop was overcome with fatigue when he reached Bhágpat. Received with apparent cordiality by the two senior native officials of that place, he threw himself down and slept. When he awoke he found himself surrounded by natives; learned that the Muhammadans were ripe for rebellion, and that the country was becoming every day more dangerous. He devoted a portion of the night that followed to write a report of all that he had heard, accompanied by suggestions from himself to the commissioner, and the following afternoon rode for Mírath which he reached the same night.

Peculiar position of Mírath.

Dunlop at once took charge of his duties. Under ordinary circumstances they would not have been very different from those devolving upon civilians in other large military stations held throughout the period of the mutiny by British troops. But the circumstances of Mírath were not ordinary. Only forty miles from

* There were four orderlies in camp, but one only could be spared.

Dehlí, and surrounded by districts in which mutiny was rampant, it constituted, in June 1857, the one spot on the grand trunk road running from Allahábád to the north-west which might serve as an effective rallying-point for loyal natives. Dunlop had early experience of this truth. The morning of the day or the second day after he had taken charge nine Sikh horsemen, without arms, rode to his house to report their arrival to him as district officer. They represented themselves as belonging to the detachment of the 1st Oudh cavalry which had murdered Fletcher Hayes and two other Englishmen, and had then ridden for Dehlí. They had declined to accompany their mutinous comrades, had surrendered their arms to Mr. Watson, magistrate of Aligarh, and had then ridden to Mírath, there to proffer their services to the British authorities. Dunlop was only too glad to engage them.

Book XVII. Chapter I.

1858. June.

Dunlop takes loyal Sikhs into his service.

Passing over an expedition into the neighbouring district, in which Dunlop served as a volunteer, I come to that part of his conduct which gives a special mark to his proceedings as district officer, and of which the incident regarding the enrolment of the nine Sikh horsemen may be considered as the foundation-stone.

To meet the difficulties of the time,

Dunlop had not only found the civil treasury of Mírath almost empty, but that means of replenishing it were wanting. He had no men at his disposal to aid in collecting revenue in the district. Military aid could not be counted upon; whilst the native bankers and merchants of the

Book XVII. Chapter I.

1858. June–July.

Dunlop resolves to raise volunteers.

city, under the circumstances of the time, positively refused to advance a loan to the Government. In this crisis Dunlop, availing himself of the ready co-operation offered by the brigade-major, Colonel Whish, resolved to organise a volunteer troop of European civil and other officers then refugees at Mírath.

Formation of the Khâki Risála.

The corps was speedily organised. Major Williams, superintendent of police, was nominated commanding officer, Captain Charles d'Oyly* as second in command, and Lieutenant Tyrwhitt† as adjutant. Volunteers flocked in, and so actively were the drilling, mounting, and arming proceeded with that within three days one troop, composed of Englishmen, Eurasians, and a few Sikhs, was fit for duty. The uniform chosen was a suit of dust-coloured cloth called kháki, and this cloth gave the name of the Kháki Risála to the corps.

The Khákí Risála pacifies one district.

The Kháki Risála began its career as a regiment by proceeding, towards the end of June, to attack some villages only five miles from Mírath, which the Gújars had occupied. Accompanied by two guns and a few of the Carabineers, they drove out the Gújars, burned three of the villages, killed several Gújars, and took forty of them prisoners. From the date of this successful attack the revenue collections in the district began. At first the task was not easy, but other expeditions followed that just recorded, and it was found that every fresh ex-

* Now Major-General Sir D'Oyly, Bart.

† Now Major-General Tyrwhitt.

pedition increased the facility of realising the revenue.*

Book XVII. Chapter I.

1858. July.

It may be interesting to record some of these expeditions.

Atrocities of the Gújars

On the 8th of July news of the burning of Bégamábád, an important village about twelve miles distant on the road to Dehlí, reached Mírath. The atrocity had been committed by a large body of Gújars, and had been accompanied by circumstances of singular atrocity, the victims being a number of loyal men of the Ját tribe who had bound themseves together to resist Gújar incursions. On this occasion, greatly outnumbered and despairing of success, the Játs had made a feeble resistance, and had succumbed. Within a few hours of the news reaching Mírath, Dunlop set off, accompanied by the Kháki Risála, fifteen of his armed retainers, twenty armed native Christians, and two mountain-guns, manned by native artillerymen. Pushing on with vigour, this column reached the ruins of Bégamábád by grey dawn of the morning of the day following the commission of the atrocity. The fires were still smouldering, the walls were blackened, the flooring in many places was dug up, and a few miserable fugitives were seen wandering here and

* "Every fresh expedition added to the facility of realising our revenue, and in a few months, amidst the wreck and disorganisation of surrounding districts, the entire government had been collected, with a rapidity and completeness hitherto unprecedented."—*Service and Adventure with the Khakee Ressalah;* a book upon which that portion of this chapter relating to that Risála is mainly based.

Book XVII. Chapter I.

1858. July.

are punished by the Risála.

there in the fields. The village of Sikri, two miles distant, was known to be the head-quarters of the Gújars. Thither the Kháki Risála proceeded, and before the alarm could be raised surrounded it. The Gújars defended themselves with great obstinacy, and five hours elapsed before the victory was gained. But when gained it was complete.

Devastations of Sáh Mall.

One of the most enterprising and daring of the Gújar leaders was Sáh Máll, zamindár of Bájrúl, a man who had conquered, and who had since maintained, a kind of semi-independence in the town of Baráuth, capital of the district of the same name in the Mírath division, but in close proximity to Dehlí. From this district and from Bájrúl, Sáh Mall had been for some time in the habit of sallying to carry fire and the sword into the neighbouring villages. The proximity of Baráuth to Dehlí seemed to promise him immunity from assault. Not so, however, thought Dunlop. This gentleman, angered at the ruthless destruction wrought by this brigand and his followers upon an unoffending people, sketched a plan for attacking the southern village of the Baráuth district by a rapid advance of the Kháki Risála and of such assistance as the general would afford him from Mírath. He laid his plan before the general, and obtained his assent to its execution. Dunlop knew well that considerable danger would attend the attempt, as forces would certainly be sent after him from Dehlí; but he trusted to the rapidity of his movements, to the increasing distance from Dehlí, as he should ap-

Dunlop resolves to check them.

His plans for that purpose.

proach Sáh Mall's stronghold of Bájrúl, and to the prestige inseparable from audacity.

Book XVII. Chapter I.

1858. July.

Towards the end of July the expedition, composed of two mountain-guns, fifty men of the Risála, forty men 60th Rifles, two sergeants, and twenty armed bandsmen, and twenty-seven armed native retainers, marched to the village of Dalháora, on the Hurdan, little more than twenty miles from Dehlí. There they heard heavy firing in the direction of Déolah, seven miles distant. The cháodri of Déolah, who was with the British force, was despatched at once to learn the cause of the firing. He returned during the night with information that Sáh Mall and his friends were lying at the Muhammadan village of Basáod, with the intention of attacking Déolah the next day. Early next morning the small British party marched on Basáod. Their approach was sufficient. Sáh Mall and his followers evacuated the place, leaving large supplies in it. Basáod, long used as a store-house for the rebels, was burned; the prisoners taken were shot. The force then marched for Baráuth. No revenue had been collected from this subdivision since the commencement of the mutiny. In fact, the civil establishments had been driven out in May, and the country had been more or less over-run by the rebels. Dunlop now devised and carried out a daring plan to remedy the evil. Whilst the force marched away along the course of the east Jamná canal he, taking with him a tahsildár*

The expedition sets out

and marches on Basáod,

and thence on Baráuth.

Dunlop's daring plan to restore order.

* A native collector of revenue. The party was three days later joined by a native officer.

Book XVII. Chapter I. — 1858. July.

and two mounted orderlies, visited all the villages on the left bank, moving parallel with the force, collecting sheep and supplies for the force as he went aloug, and trusting to his prestige as district officer for immunity from attack.

The plan at first successful,

The experiment was at first most successful. From the first two villages, indeed, the inhabitants had fled, and Dunlop's care was to send out to reassure the zamindárs. The third village, Bichpúri, was a Gújar village, the inhabitants of which had taken a leading part in plunder and destruction. Dunlop, nevertheless, entered it; and here his prestige served him, for, he records, "numbers of armed men were leaving it as I arrived." In the four villages next visited his reception was not unfriendly; the inhabitants "appeared glad to see the tahsildár." From each he carried off one or two of the principal landowners as security for the Government revenue. The people of the next village, Barká, were known to be friendly. To his surprise, then, on arriving before it, Dunlop found the gates closed and the people swarming from their houses. A whisper from one of them sufficed to give the information that they were expecting an attack from Sáh Mall.

but, on reaching Barká, signs of disturbances are apparent.

Dunlop stayed for a few minutes, endeavouring to calm the fears of the villagers, when a tremendous noise of shouting and bellowing from a neighbouring village convinced him that they were well founded. In a few seconds Sáh Mall, at the head of two thousand men, came in sight. Very soon their matchlock-balls were flying

Sáh Mall

amongst the small party, only one of whom was an Englishman. Dunlop would willingly have faced them—but *cui bono?* One or two hundred Englishmen might, as they did in the pursuit of Tántia Topi, face, and even successfully attack, four or five thousand. But one man against two thousand! The odds were too great. Dunlop and his five companions unwillingly fell back, leaving the fifteen landowners and twelve sheep he had collected, unguarded, as a prey to the rebels.

Book XVII. Chapter I.

1858. July.

forces Dunlop to retire.

But the danger was not over. A horseman, armed with a matchlock and drawn sword—subsequently ascertained to be Bagdá, nephew to Sáh Mall—rode at Dunlop. Under ordinary circumstances the combat would probably have been short. But Dunlop was riding that morning, for the first time, a horse which had an insane dread of fire-arms. His position would have been ludicrous but for its danger. "The animal," he writes, "proceeded to the charge alternately tripping along sideways, or waltzing round on its hind legs, springing clear off the ground at every discharge of my revolver." Ultimately, however, Dunlop succeeded in depriving Bagdá of his thumb and in mortally wounding his charger. He then rode after his friends, leaving his pith helmet, which had fallen off in the fight, as a trophy on the field.

Dunlop meets in single combat the nephew of Sáh Mall;

danger of bestriding a timid horse.

Dunlop deprives his antagonist of his thumb and his horse;

but loses his own helmet.

Dunlop now made, with his small escort, for Baráuth. There he found that the column had had that morning an engagement with, and had put to flight, a body of rebels who were then being

Book XVII. Chapter I.

1858. July.

Defeat of Sáh Mall,

pursued. The cavalry had scarcely returned from the pursuit, when Sáh Mall led the men who had chased the small party in the morning to the attack. But it was Dunlop's turn now. The rebels, their flanks turned, soon broke and fled.

who is slain,

This affair proved to be most important. In the pursuit Sáh Mall was overtaken and killed by a young volunteer, by name Tonnochy, assisted by a native trooper. His head, stuck on a pole, materially influenced the decision of a third attack, which the remainder of the rebels, unaware of Sáh Mall's death, ventured to deliver the same afternoon. It was repulsed with ease.* I should not omit to add that in the second fight of the day Dunlop's lost helmet was recovered.

and Dunlop's helmet is recovered.

Great results of Sáh Mall's death.

The effect of Sáh Mall's death was shown by the freedom with which the native dealers at once brought grain and other supplies into the British camp. That evening, too, the officers and men of the force enjoyed the gratification of encamping in and around a bungalow which Sáh Mall had set apart for himself as a hall of justice.

From Baráuth the little column marched for Sirdhána, famous as the residence of Bégam Samrú. Here Dunlop made arrangements for

* In this affair, and indeed throughout the campaign of the Kháki Risála, a young civilian made himself particularly distinguished for his coolness in danger and his courage in the field. This was Mr. A. C. Lyall, now Foreign Secretary to the Government of India, as remarkable for his ability now as he was for the sterner qualities in those troublous days.

Book XVII. Chapter I.

1858. July.

the payment by the neighbouring villages of arrears of rent. But one village, Akalpúra, was refractory. This village belonged to one Narpat Singh, a notorious rebel. Under his auspices, then, the men of the place sent back Dunlop's messengers with the inquiry, "Who is the district officer and who is the tahsildár that they should demand revenue from Akalpúra?" and threatened the messengers with death should they return on a similar errand. In consequence of this message, it was deemed advisable to pay the refractory villages a visit. The Khákis, then, started before daybreak, reached Akalpúra before the alarm had been sounded, surrounded and stormed it, Narpat Singh being among the slain. This prompt and successful action produced a marvellous effect on the turbulent spirits in the neighbourhood. The force then returned to Sirdhána.

Insolent message of Nirpat Singh, for which he atones with his life.

An act of justice such as the natives of India would thoroughly appreciate was performed about this time. There were two villages in the Rájpút portion of the Mírath division, known as Solána and Dháolána. The inhabitants of both were Rájpúts. The native official of the district was a Muhammadan, Toráb Áli, loyal to the British. As the district, however, was in close proximity to Muhammadan districts which had rebelled, the inhabitants of Dháolána, thinking to earn the praise of the court of Dehlí, declared against the English, attacked the police station, and took prisoner Toráb Áli. Upon this the people of Solána, loyal to the English, attacked Dháolána and released Toráb Áli. The Dháo-

Dunlop metes out justice which can be understood and appreciated.

Book XVII. Chapter I.

1858. July–Sept.

lána men, knowing they had sinned beyond forgiveness, incited other villages to revolt. Whereupon Dunlop visited the district with the little column, defeated the rebels, and gave their lands over to the loyal people of Solána.

Other successful expeditions

Shortly after this, the 21st of July, the little column, somewhat strengthened, proceeded to Hauppar, thence to defeat the rebels at Galáoti—an achievement gallantly and successfully performed.

of the Kháka Risála.

An expedition on the 18th of September to Morwána was so far successful, that the report of its approach was sufficient to scare the rebels. It was followed by one of greater importance—to drive some rebels from Bhowan, eighteen miles beyond Mozaffarnagar—a place whence they had repulsed the district officer and a strong force. Dunlop's force, joined at Mozaffarnagar by that previously repulsed, was successful on this as it had been on every other occasion.

With the fall of Dehlí the necessity for its labours ceases.

With the fall of Dehlí the necessity for such detached expeditions in the Mírath division practically ceased. The army, released from the labours of the siege, proceeded, as we have seen, to free the country in all directions. It is impossible to exaggerate the services which in the interval had been rendered by the little band of volunteers, of whom Mr. Dunlop was the original organiser, the constant companion. Who were these volunteers? The best answer to that query is that given in the work in which their deeds are recorded, and which tells in eloquent language of the results they accomplished.

"Few of those," wrote Mr. Dunlop at the time, "who so gallantly volunteered for a life of peril and adventure in lieu of patient anticipation while awaiting the issue of the struggle at Dehlí, had any military experience to assist them, and their drill had to be commenced; but they possessed the hereditary courage of their race; they could all ride; many of them were sportsmen, some of them crack shots and admirable swordsmen. Made of such material, is it to be wondered at that they traversed the most distracted portions of the district in the height of the revolt; that they fearlessly faced, with the support of two little mountain-train guns, manned by native artillery-men of doubtful loyalty, forty native najibs, and forty of the rifle regiment, the assembled hordes of one of the most enterprising leaders this rebellion has produced, and, with little or no loss to themselves, routed and destroyed in hundreds the same class of men as those whose unbridled villainy produced such mischief in the station on the night following the outbreak; that, maddened by the insults and massacres inflicted on their own relations, on their own brothers and sisters, they executed, if let loose on a rebel village, a vengeance which made it a terror and a fear to the country around?" It is impossible to show more clearly how it was that, in the most critical times of the mutiny, the Mírath division was prevented from falling a prey to the rebels.

Book XVII. Chapter I.

1858. September.

Who and what were the volunteers?

I turn now to Allahábád—a name familiar to the readers of this history. The situation of

Allahábád.

Book XVII. Chapter I.

1857. May–June.

Allahábád had many things common with that of Mírath. It was an important military station held throughout by the British, yet surrounded by districts and divisions in full revolt. Immediately to the north lay Oudh, to the north-east the districts of Ázamgarh and Gorákhpúr, to the west and south Bandalkhand. At the confluence of two great rivers, it was a most important strategical point, especially during the rainy season, when it formed the river terminus for the steamers from Calcutta. The military events occurring at Allahábád have been related in these volumes, but the heavy duties which devolved upon the members of the civil service have been but incidentally referred to. Yet those duties were of a nature to tax all the energies even of men accutomed, as are the members of the Indian Civil Service, to give themselves, heart and soul, to their country.

Importance of its position.

Early days of the mutiny at Allahábád.

When the mutiny broke out, the Commissioner of the Allahábád division was Mr. C. Chester; the magistrate was Mr. M. H. Court, a glorious specimen of an Englishman, a good sportsman, a generous friend, and one whose hospitality was famous even in India. The news of the mutiny at Mírath reached Allahábád on the 12th of May; on the evening of the 5th of June the 6th regiment native infantry mutinied. That mutiny was the signal for a general revolt. That very night the rabble of the city, the whole of the native police, joined in the outbreak; the jail released its prisoners, two thousand in number, and the inhabitants of several adjoining villages, men renowned for lawlessness and plunder, sprang forth, and the work of incendiarism, riot, and plunder commenced.* The Europeans and Eurasians, men, women, and children, all who could escape the fury of the revolters, had, meanwhile, taken refuge in the fort, where they remained beleagured till the 11th of June.

Book XVII. Chapter I.

1857. June.

How, on the afternoon of the 11th of June, the gallant Neill relieved the anxieties of the garrison, has formed a portion of the military history of the mutiny. It will suffice here to state that from the date of his arrival Allahábád formed the base of military operations undertaken against Kánhpúr, the most eastern part of Oudh, and the Ázamgarh districts. My subject now relates solely to the civil officers and their duties.

The arrival of Neill gives the first check to the rebels.

No sooner had Neill restored the British power in the fortress and the city, than the European residents returned to the smoking ruin of their houses. In the city it was comparatively easy to restore matters to the condition antecedent to the mutiny. From the date of the 11th of June, Allahábád itself was never in danger. European troops were constantly arriving and passing through, and the inhabitants of the city were thoroughly aware that any other course but submission to the law would bring upon them sure and swift destruction. But in the districts the case was quite different.

Position of Allahábád after Neill's arrival.

* "A District during the Rebellion"—*Calcutta Review.* This article forms one of many about to be published in a separate volume by its accomplished author, Mr. R. N. Cust, C.S.

Book XVII. Chapter I.

1857. June.

The three natural divisions of Allahábád.

The effect of the junction of the streams of the Ganges and Jamná just below Allahábád has been to form three great natural divisions of land. These divisions contain more than one thousand villages and towns, and a population of nearly a million. Now in the centre division, that between the left bank of the Jamná and the right bank of the Ganges, no vestige of police remained. The villagers had everywhere commenced the career of plunder, and led on probably by some notorious criminal escaped from jail, had "commenced reprisals on their neighbours, paid out old scores, removed old boundary-marks, and ejected purchasers of land." * In this division disorder was rampant; Europeans were hunted down, the telegraph posts were torn up, the iron sockets converted into rude cannon, and the wire into slugs.

The centre division utterly lawless.

In the division on the right bank of the Jamná order is maintained by the landowners.

In the division on the right bank of the Jamná a far different order prevailed. There one or two large proprietors exercised great influence, and they were wise enough to see that their interests were bound up in the maintenance of the dominant power which had ever afforded them protection. They therefore at once offered to undertake the protection of their own villages if the Government would give them a subsidy. The Government complied, and the result was that in this division order was maintained. In due course, when the back of the mutiny had been broken,

* Cust, who enters into much fuller details than I have space for.

the magistrate was able to re-introduce his own police. But not the less was he thankful to those who, when he was powerless, had taken the initiative to maintain order.*

From the third division British authority had disappeared.

From the third division, again, on the left bank of the Ganges, British authority had disappeared. The vicinity to Oudh, now in full revolt, had proved fatal to that authority. The neighbouring districts of Jánpúr, of Azimgarh, and of Gorakhpúr, had fallen into the hands of rebels, to be recovered only by the sword.

Means taken to maintain order.

To maintain order in the first and third of these divisions, very considerable powers of life and death were given by the Government to the commissioner, the judge, the magistrate, the deputy magistrate, and the assistant magistrate; and so great was the panic at Calcutta, that, as if this had not been sufficient, similar powers were conferred upon two private individuals and the civil surgeon. No doubt some examples were required. Most certainly they were given. "Zealously," writes Mr. Cust, "did the three volunteers use their new powers, and in the short time which elapsed before their recall, one of the private individuals had sentenced sixty, the second sixty-four, and the civil surgeon fifty-four, to the gallows. No record remains of the crime or the evidence, but we gather that one man was hung

The lawlessness of amateur authority.

* Mr. Cust well says:—"This opens out another and a serious question whether our established policy of cutting off the heads of all the tallest poppies, and leaving nothing betwixt the Imperial Government and the cultivating owners of the soil, is a wise one."

Book XVII. Chapter I. 1857. June-July.

for having a bag of new copper coin in his possession, presumed to have been plundered from the treasury, or, most probably, abandoned by the mutinous sepoys, who were surfeited with silver. More than a month after our power had been restored in the city, we find fifteen sentenced one day and twenty-eight the next, for rebellion and robbing the treasury; but it does not appear that they were sepoys. Thirteen were hung another day for a similar offence. Six were hung for plying a ferry for the convenience of the rebels." It is a relief, after the perusal of this disgraceful record, to find Mr. Cust declaring that "the investigations of the officers of Government, men trained to the consideration of evidence, and conscious of the necessity of supporting the character, as well as vindicating the authority, of the Government, were more deliberate." They had, indeed, need to be so; but the question occurs, how it was that the same Government which refused to disarm the sepoys at Dánápúr, and thus imperilled the safety of Calcutta, delayed the advance of Havelock, and caused an enormous amount of slaughter, should have complacently invested the three untrained gentlemen referred to with the terrible powers of life and death!

The measured justice of trained officials.

Responsibility resting on the Government.

The measures enforced regarding property.

To return. In addition to power over life, the magistrate was entrusted with authority to confiscate property, real and personal. In the hands of Mr. Court this authority was used with judgment and discretion. Mercy was tempered by judgment. But, nevertheless, the amount of property which changed hands was considerable.

Some men had died, their relatives were not forthcoming; some had absconded; some had openly joined the rebels. But there is reason to believe that in every instance justice was meted out with a hand more inclined to leniency than to its opposite.

It devolved upon Mr. Court likewise, in his capacity of collector of revenue, to furnish money and collect it. I cannot do better than transcribe the graphic account given by Mr. Cust of the manner in which these duties were performed.

The monetary arrangements of the division.

"All this time the executive officer of the district was not idle in his duties of collector. Money poured in by every steamer from Calcutta and poured out like water, leaving the tale of unadjusted items to be told in tens of thousands of pounds. There was constant payment of sums for saving European life or distinguished bravery, for it was then no light service for a native to stand by an Englishman, as he was liable to attack by the rebels for so doing. The terrorism of the rebels is scarcely appreciated by us to its full extent. There were compensations for losses or for wounds, or advances made to starving Christians or faithful natives, driven with only the clothes on their backs from out-stations. There were rewards to be paid for the arrest of notorious rebels and criminals escaped from gaol; spies and messengers to be paid handsomely for their services generally, by dipping their hands into a bag of silver, and securing as much as they could grasp; advances to be made to officers

Book XVII. Chapter I. 1857-8.

engaged in raising regiments of low-caste men; and reward for the restoration of Government horses, cattle, and stores. State-prisoners had to be maintained. Supplies of cash had to be furnished to every advancing column, or placed at the disposal of the commissariat and the ordnance department. No wonder that in these hasty remittances the tale of rupees ran short, that boxes of treasure were found violated, and, in one instance, a box of five hundred pounds was found missing. In the general moral debasement, we cannot be surprised that the European sentry was not always trustworthy. In the treasure chamber also was stowed away the plunder belonging to the army, the spoil of captured cities, valued at hundreds of thousands of pounds, and fastened down in beer-barrels until the end of the war. Among these spoils were the crown jewels of sovereigns, the gold plate of princes, ear-rings, and nose-rings, and jewels of women, ornamented daggers and diamond necklaces, all the pomp and wealth of oriental monarchs, wrung from a plundered and oppressed people, and now captured by the English army.

Duties devolving on the collector.

"At the same time the collector had to look after the revenue of those parts of the district in which his orders were respected. He had to suspend collections from such villages as had been plundered, burned, or deserted. He had to determine where he should remit and where enforce the demand; as it is a grave moral question how far a government is justified in demanding the payment of taxes, when it has notoriously failed in its duty of protection, owing to no fault of the people. No sooner was the danger past than red tape raised its head again, and a gentleman, sitting in comfort and ease at Calcutta, reminded the excited collector of unattended-to forms and discontinued returns. With hundreds of boxes of stationery and stamps in his charge, directed to districts in the hands of the rebels, the collector, without a pen or sheet of paper belonging to him, dared not use the consignment of his neighbour without special authority. As he returned to his half-ruined home from his morning-duty of hanging rebels, flogging rioters, and blowing up temples, he found letters from the Head of the Finance Department, reminding him that he was personally responsible for every rupee missing in a treasury guarded by European soldiers in a fort three miles off. On his table he found notes from an officer with the force of Jang Bahádur, requesting a daily supply of a hundred he-goats for the hungry Gúrkah; from the post master, requesting him to hunt for a missing mail-cart; from the commanding officer, requesting him to close the grog-shops; from a cavalry-commandant to know whose grass was to be cut, and where a farrier was to be found; from the pension-paymaster requesting him to attend a committee on the confiscation of pensions. Telegraphic messages up and down were tumbling in all day long, sometimes announcing a victory, sometimes heralding a traveller, for, in addition to his other duties, he had to keep a "Red Lion" tavern for strangers, examine the passport of

The red-tape of Calcutta.

Difficulties of the collector.

Book XVII. Chapter I.

1857-8.

every native traveller, and ascertain the contents of every native letter.

The collector's reward.

"Thus passed six months away, and if some gray hairs had shown themselves in his beard (for since his razors were plundered, he had remained perforce unshorn), if his heart sometimes palpitated from over-excitement, and his liver sometimes troubled him, no wonder. If his temper was somewhat soured, if he hated the natives with a deep hate, if he talked too lightly of cutting the thread of human life, and scoring the backs of poor devils, no wonder. He had had much to bear, and the rebellion had fallen heavily on his estate, his family, and his health. He was mentioned in no despatches; the thanks of Government reached him not; and, when he saw that the tide had turned, and that the country was saved, he hurried to England, on the chance of quiet restoring tone to his body, and change of scene bringing back equanimity to his mind."

The picture somewhat overdrawn.

The concluding portion of the description appears to me to be somewhat overdrawn. No; though he had lost many friends, probably some relations, though he had worked hardly under difficulties, and had earned the thanks and the honours which he did not receive, the magistrate and collector harboured no hatred against the natives. I shall never forget the last exhortation of one of those noble servants of the East India Company, a man who had served many years at that very Allahábád, on my return to India in 1858; they were words of exhortation to be kind, to be mindful of the many excellent qualities possessed by the natives of India. And that man was, I believe, a type of his class.

I pass on now to Gorákhpúr.

Position and extent of Gorákhpúr.

The district called, after the chief town within its borders, Gorákhpúr, is bounded on the north by Nipál; on the east and south-east by the district of Sáran; on the south by Ázamgarh; on the south-west and west by the kingdom of Oudh. It includes an area of seven thousand three hundred and forty-six square miles, and possessed in 1857 a population somewhat exceeding three millions.

Mr. Wynyard, Mr. Paterson, Mr. Bird.

In 1857 the judge of Gorákhpúr was Mr. William Wynyard, already mentioned in these pages *; the magistrate and collector was Mr. Paterson; the joint magistrate was Mr. Bird. In such times as those of 1857 the lead taken was never dependent on the rank of the officer. Sometimes, as at Patná, the senior officer directed affairs; at others, as at Banáras, the second in rank came prominently to the front. At Gorákhpúr Mr. Wynyard at once took the reins in his hands.

Wynyard, seeing the storm, takes the responsibility

Mr. Wynyard joined to great activity of body and a love of field-sports, a cultivated mind and a thorough acquaintance with native character. The station of Gorákhpúr being off the main line of postal communication, Wynyard did not hear of the events of the 10th of May till a week later,

* Vol. ii. page 318.

Book XVII. Chapter I.

1857. May.

the 17th. It happened that Mr. Paterson, the magistrate, was just on the point of quitting the station on leave of absence, for which he had applied and which had been granted. In the presence of the crisis then impending, and which he saw could not fail to bear with particular severity upon a place so near the Oudh frontier as was Gorákhpúr, Wynyard took it upon himself to delay Paterson's departure. I mention this fact not because in itself it was of great importance, but because it produced from the commissioner of the division a reply which indicated a belief common to almost all the high officials in India. Mr. Tucker thanked Wynyard for his action in having delayed Mr. Paterson's departure "till he has heard of the annihilation of the rebels." It was evidently not thought that the delay would be long!

to retain Mr. Paterson.

Mr. Tucker's opinion regarding the duration of the mutiny.

The troops at Gorákhpúr.

The troops of Gorákhpúr consisted of two companies 17th regiment native infantry and a small detachment 12th irregular cavalry. The head-quarters of the former were at Azamgarh, of the latter at Sigáoli. Very few days after the news reached him of the mutiny, Wynyard received information that the 17th native infantry could not be depended upon. The 12th irregulars bore then a good character, and their commanding officer, Major Holmes, whose name was a household word in the army, was known to trust them implicitly. But, even granting that they were loyal, their numbers were few, and Wynyard felt that it would be necessary for him to look elsewhere for sure support.

Happily, at this conjuncture, the commissioner, Mr. Tucker, placed Wynyard in civil charge of the district, warning him that trouble might be on him at any moment, that Banáras was shaky, recommending him to act boldly and on his own judgment, and giving him authority to assume any amount of responsibility, civil or military. The way thus made plain to him, Wynyard proceeded to act. He enlisted recruits for the jail and other local guards; he caused similar enlistments to be made in the districts; he wrote to the well-affected native landowners and to the Europeon planters, authorising them to enlist well-affected natives for the Government service; he appointed a place of rendezvous in case of attack; and he despatched one hundred and twenty-five of the 17th native infantry and a detachment, thirty-four men, of the 12th irregulars to Banáras in charge of treasure. This still left him burdened with one hundred and twenty sepoys and sixty sowars.

Book XVII. Chapter I.

1857. May-June.

Wynyard receives from the commissioner powers,

which he uses judiciously.

From that day forth for a long time to follow every post brought bad tidings from outside. One day it was the mutiny at Firozpúr, the next the outbreak at Lakhnao, then those at Nímach and Nasirábád. But the news received on the 5th of June was still more ominous for Gorákhpúr. It told of the mutiny at A'zamgarh of the 17th native infantry, a detachment of which regiment was, as we have seen, on duty at Gorákhpúr.

Continued arrival of bad tidings.

That detachment was commanded by Captain Steel, an excellent officer. He at once paraded his men, Paterson having disposed the cavalry

Steel addresses the men of the 17th native infantry,

Book XVII. Chapter I.

1857. June.

and local levies so as to attack them if they should mutiny. Steel then addressed them, apparently with effect. They displayed no outward sign of discontent. But this apparent loyalty lasted only for the day. The very next morning Steel endeavoured to march the sepoys to

who, nevertheless, refuse to obey his orders.

A'zamgarh, but they refused to obey his orders, and one of them, whom the rest were evidently disposed to follow, was heard to declare that the money in the treasury should not leave the station without a fight.

The prisoners attempt to break out, but are baffled.

The day following, the 7th of June, the prisoners attempted to break out from the jail, but they were baffled by the jail-guard, energetically led by Mr. Bird the joint magistrate and Mr. Desmazures an indigo-planter. Eight of the prisoners were killed in the attempt, and ten or twelve were wounded. That night the sepoys, apparently, resolved to join their comrades. They seized empty carts, and with these marched, armed, the following morning, towards the treasury. Their purpose was evident. They had determined to go, but not without the money. In this crisis

Another attempt at mutiny is checked.

Steel and Wynyard, who, from the verandah of the former's bungalow, saw them approaching, came to meet and harangued them. Their arguments were effective, for the sepoys returned to their lines. Still business was at a standstill. Everyone felt that one day, sooner or later, the trial would come. There seemed no means of averting it.

Major Ramsay offers to send a rein-

Next morning, however, Wynyard received from Major, now Major-General the Honourable

Book XVII. Chapter I.

1857. June.

Sir Henry, Ramsay, the British resident at the court of Khátmándu, a letter, in which he promised to send him two hundred Gúrkahs from Pálpa, just across the border. This was cheering news. With the aid of that number of trustworthy troops, it seemed possible still to maintain the district.

forcement of Gúrkahs.

The sepoys in the district mutiny.

But the following day showed that events were marching too fast for the Gúrkahs. I have already told how, towards the end of May, Wynyard had sent money to A'zamgarh escorted by one hundred and twenty-five of the 17th native infantry and thirty-four men of the 12th irregulars. On the morning of the 11th the irregulars returned, telling how, after leaving A'zamgarh, the sepoys had mutinied and had seized the money; how the Gházipúr district was in revolt, and how the loyalty of Bahár depended upon the power of the commissioner of Patná to maintain order in that turbulent city.

Great and successful measures adopted by Wynyard.

Nevertheless Wynyard did not lose heart. Trusting to the 12th irregulars, whose loyalty had, up to that time, been proof against seduction, he sent detachments to A'zamgarh, to Basti, and to other parts of the district, under his own officers or European residents, to restore order. And he succeeded. He proclaimed martial law in the district, suspended the ordinary forms of trial, and showed a zeal, an energy, and a resolution which had an extremely deterring effect upon the disaffected. They argued that no man would act with such boldness unless he had resources of which they knew nothing.

Book XVII. Chapter I.

1857. June.

The commissioner attempts to prevent the coming of the Gúrkahs.

And yet, all this time, Wynyard had not only no resources, but his superior officer was doing his best to deprive him of those whose timely arrival would still have saved the district. Mr. Tucker, the commissioner of Banáras, wrote at this crisis to tell him that no troops could be spared from that city. This was true, and was probably anticipated. But what was not anticipated, what in its result was fatal to many European lives, was the fact that at the same time Mr. Tucker was exerting all his efforts to prevent the arrival of the Gúrkahs, whose number was now swollen to three thousand, in British territory. To accept the aid of Jang Bahádur was, in Mr. Tucker's opinion, an evil; but surely it was a lesser evil than that involved in the occupation of British territory by rebels! Yet that was, as the result proved, the only alternative.

Fugitives from Oudh arrive.

On the 17th and on the 19th fugitives from Oudh arrived in Gorákhpúr. On the 20th Wynyard sent off all the ladies in the station—the wives of the clerks, who at the last moment refused to leave, excepted—to Banáras under an escort of twenty-five men of the 12th irregulars, seventy men belonging to the rájá of Bánáres, and accompanied by six officers and a sergeant who had escaped from Oudh. This party reached Jánpúr in safety; but the districts were swarming with rebels; all the landowners were up. Some of these stopped the party near Jánpúr and diverted their course to Gházipúr.

Two hundred Gúrkahs reach Gorákhpúr.

On the 28th the two hundred Gúrkahs originally promised by Ramsay arrived from Pálpa. It must have been a satisfaction to Wynyard thus to have saved for seven weeks a district on the borders of revolted Oudh, contiguous to other districts in which the torch of mutiny had been lighted, and whose landowners had followed with light hearts the example set them by the sepoys. If, in the presence of adverse circumstances which he saw rising around him, Wynyard could not feel very sanguine as to the immediate future, at least he had grounds for hope. It needed but a decisive blow struck at some rebel centre to pacify the district, and it always seemed possible that any day might bring the good news.

Book XVII. Chapter I.

1857. June-July.

The one thing requisite to pacify the district.

It was encouraging to Wynyard at such a crisis that he should feel that his conduct had been approved not only by his local superior, but by the Governor-General. Mr. Tucker, just at this time, wrote him a letter fully approving of his arrangements and of the manner in which he had carried them out, and on the 28th of June Lord Canning sent him an autograph letter expressive of his gratitude for the excellent service which, in conjunction with Mr. Paterson, Mr. Wynyard had rendered at Gorákhpúr, and concluding with a hope that he might be still able to hold his ground; "if not," wrote Lord Canning, "have no scruple as to retiring in time. You have long ago saved your honour."

Wynyard receives an autograph letter of thanks and commendation from the Governor-General.

It was known on the 25th of July that more Gúrkahs were approaching. The districts, however, were greatly disturbed. During the preceding three weeks many untoward events had

Despite the arrival of news,

Book XVII. Chapter I.

1857. July.

happened. The slaughter of Kánhpúr had become known; the mutinies at Gwáliár and Barélí; the Ázamgarh district had been the scene of warfare, marked by the splendid gallantry of the daring Venables. The only counterbalancing news was that of the victories obtained by Havelock over the rebels and of his arrival at Kánhpúr. But Wynyard still kept his hold on the district; the Nipál army was near, and having accomplished so much Wynyard was still hopeful that he might accomplish more.

Wynyard maintains his hold on the district.

News of the mutiny of the 12th irregular cavalry arrives.

But on the 28th of July the fatal news of the mutiny of the 12th irregulars at Sigáoli, of the murder of Holmes and his noble wife, and of the doctor, and the intelligence that the regiment was marching on Gorákhpúr reached him. Instantly he sent off an express to the first division of Gúrkahs to push on. They pushed on and arrived that evening.

The Gúrkahs march in.

The arrival of the Gúrkahs produced a double effect. It saved the lives of the Europeans, but it necessitated the evacuation of Gorákhpúr. How this was so is capable of easy explanation. The Gúrkahs were under orders to march, by way of Ázamgarh, for Allahábád. At that time Ázamgarh had again fallen into the hands of the rebels. The officer commanding the Gúrkahs, Colonel Pahlwán Singh, declined to leave a detachment at Gorákhpúr, or in any way to divide his forces. Information had been received from English sources that the 12th irregulars, red with the blood of their own officers, were marching on Gorákhpúr. For the few English officials to re-

The colonel of the Nipál troops imposes the necessity of abandoning Gorákhpúr.

main there after the Gúrkahs should have left it, and to meet alone the 12th irregulars, accompanied by all the rabble of the districts, seemed indeed to be madness utterly wanting in method.

Book XVII. Chapter I.

1857. August.

Troops at Gorákhpúr are disarmed.

Two or three days were left for Wynyard and his colleagues to consider the course to be adopted. These days were well employed. On the 1st of August the men of the detachment 17th native infantry were peaceably disarmed. The few men of the 12th irregulars were less successfully dealt with. These men gave up their arms, it is true, to their own commandant, Risáldár Muhammad Bakhsh; but they had scarcely done so when some of them made a rush at the arms, recovered them, mounted their horses, and galloped off. They were pursued by their own comrades under Captain Warren; six of them were killed, one was wounded and died of his wounds. The eighty-three loyal men remained staunch to the end.*

Mr. Wynyard and all the officials but one quit Gorákhpúr.

The news which arrived two days later of the defeat of Captain Dunbar's detachment near Árah, and the receipt the following day of a letter containing Mr. Tucker's approval of a retirement upon Ázamgarh and Jánpúr, decided Mr. Wynyard and the other gentlemen of the district to accompany the Gúrkahs. The district was no longer tenable. "Have no scruple," Lord Canning had written, "in retiring in time—you have

* These men did good service in the mutiny, and marched with Havelock and Outram to the relief of Lakhnáo. The Risáldár, Muhammad Bakhsh, was made extra Aide-de-camp to the Governor-General.

Book XVII. Chapter I.

1857. August.

long ago saved your honour." Mr. Wynyard and his companions then, on the 31st of August, made over charge of the district to the loyal landowners and rode that evening into the Gúrkhá camp.

The official who remained

One, and one only, remained behind. This was the assistant magistrate, Mr. Bird. Mr. Bird was a great sportsman, affected the society of natives, and believed he could trust them. He, therefore, declined to accompany his countrymen. He soon had reason to repent it. Gorákhpúr, after the departure of the Gúrkhás, was contested for by the zamindárs of the neighbourhood, and Muhammad Husén, calling himself the Nazím, from Oudh. Eventually the latter took possession of the place. But before this happened one of the zamindárs, the rájá of Gopálpúr, entered the town and released the prisoners. One of these, a man whom Bird himself had committed for forgery, forced his way into the presence of his old committing officer, and seated himself on the table. The native guards declined to remove him. Bird then wrote to his European comrades for assistance, but it could not be given. The Gúrkah commandant declined to send a man. After four or five days of stirring adventure, going about with his life in his hand, he eventually escaped into the jungle. Muhammad Husén, who had by that time occupied Gorákhpúr, offered a reward of five thousand rupees for his head, and whilst he despatched two hundred men to cut him off, sent as many more on his track. But Bird, a sportsman who knew thoroughly the bye-ways

insulted,

and forced to flee for his life, with a price upon his head.

of the jungle, succeeded in baffling both and in reaching Bétiah in the Champáran district, eighty-two miles from Gorákhpúr, in safety.

Book XVII. Chapter I.

1857. August.

The Gúrkah force, meanwhile, proceeds to A'zamgarh.

Meanwhile the Gúrkah force, accompanied by Wynyard and his comrades, marched towards Ázamgarh. On the 20th of August they repulsed a spirited attack made upon their camp by the rebels at Gagha. On the 21st the force crossed the Ghághrá river and marched without further interruption on Ázamgarh, which was reached on the 27th. Mr. Wynyard was then nominated chief civil officer of the Ázamgarh district. How that district was fought for and maintained has been told in a previous volume.*

The maintenance of Gorákhpúr for three months redounds to the credit of Wynyard and the other officials,

The state of Gorákhpúr immediately upon the departure of the English officials fully justified that departure. In few parts of India did the districts become more infested with men thirsting for European blood than in the districts bordering on Oudh. To have maintained Gorákhpúr for three months without assistance, in the presence of disaffected sepoys, and surrounded by turbulent landowners, was a feat worthy of the highest praise—a feat which testified to the courage, the tact, the judgment of those by whom it was accomplished, and which redounded greatly to their honour. But, notwithstanding Lord Canning's emphatic declaration in this respect, notwithstanding the services subsequently rendered, Mr. Wynyard and his companions were not admitted within the favoured circle of official

who are, nevertheless, left unrewarded.

* Vol. ii. pages 317 and following.

Book XVII. Chapter I. 1857-8.

approbation. The more necessary is it, then, that admiration should be accorded to them by their countrymen.

The civil servants of India.

Here I must pause. The history of the other civil districts of India during the crisis of 1857–58 would present the same tale of gallantry, of devotion, of energy, of zeal, as has the history of those I have recorded. The circumstances, it is true, were not precisely similar in all. Not only did the incidents vary, but the localities, the distances from one important central point, the temper of the people, the amount of aid to be counted upon, varied also. But in one respect there was a striking similarity. In every case the English officials, members of the Indian Civil Service, untrained to arms as they were, displayed the characteristics of the island home of their birth—the cool courage, the firm resolution, the devotion to duty, well becoming the descendants of the men who had made an empire on which the sun never sets, and which their children now found themselves called upon, under the most dangerous and difficult circumstances, to maintain. How well they performed that duty these pages have shown. Not in this chapter only; for the names of John Lawrence of the Panjáb, of William Tayler who saved Patná, and, conjointly with Vincent Eyre, Calcutta; of Frederic Gubbins, who saved Banáras; of Seton-Karr, who saved the southern Maráthá country; of Montgomery, of Barnes, of George Ricketts, of Ross Mangles, and of many others—stand out in a manner which will cause them to live for ever in the memory of those who love cool and calm heroism, who value true and noble action more than the tinsel decoration which so often rewards subservience and self-seeking.

BOOK XVII.

CHAPTER II.

The officers of the Indian navy.

In another part of this history* I have recorded the gallantry of a young midshipman of the Indian navy, Arthur Mayo—a gallantry which was rewarded by the bestowal of the Victoria Cross. This display of courage and conduct was emulated by very many of the profession to which Mayo belonged, and I feel it is only due to the members of a service which no longer exists, but whose bright and brilliant deeds form an important part of the story of English adventure and English rule in India, to devote a short chapter to the more prominent of those services.

Lewis and Mayo at Dháká.

The gallant service of Lieutenant Lewis, Mr. Mayo, and their comrades at Dháká, has been already related. It has been truly remarked† that "if the Indian naval detachment had been repulsed in their attack on the mutineers' posi-

* Vol. ii. second edition, page 420.

† Low's *History of the Indian Navy.*

Book XVII. Chapter II.

1857. November.

tion, and had been obliged to retreat, a general massacre would probably have ensued, for in their rear lay the city of Dháká with a large fanatical Muhammadan population in a very excited state." The gallantry of the sailors was thus mainly instrumental in saving eastern Bengal from pillage and slaughter.

The officers and men who saved Dháká distinguish themselves again in 1859.

The same officers, accompanied by others, took a very leading part in an expedition against the Abor hillmen in February 1859. This operation, though occurring before the mutiny had been finally crushed in central India and in Oudh, cannot properly be brought within the range of its events. I refer to it here only to mention that the officers who were prominent at the Dháká affair in 1857 were again well to the front on this occasion, and, with Lieutenant Davies, I.N., were most favourably mentioned by the military officer commanding.

Lieutenant Carew;

In the Jagdispúr jungles, Lieutenant Carew, I.N., rendered excellent service. I have related* how, on the 23rd of April 1858, Captain Le Grand of the 35th foot had been defeated in those jungles by Kúnwar Singh with the loss of two guns; how this disaster had thrown the district once more into disorder; how the safety of Árah was threatened, and how a panic had reigned at Chaprá. I have recorded, also, how for the time the arrangements made assured the safety of these stations, and that a few days later Sir E. Lugard and Colonel Corfield had beaten the rebels con-

* Vol. ii. pages 477 to 480.

Book XVII. Chapter II.

1858. May.

his services under Corfield in the Jagdispúr jungles.

tinuously. In these contests Lieutenant Carew, serving under Corfield, took a prominent part. Carew, after making several most earnest requests, had been allowed to serve in that part of the country in command of a battery which he had formed himself. His battery was supplied with two 9-pounders and two $5\frac{1}{2}$-inch mortars, and was manned by one hundred and ten sailors. Serving under him were two midshipmen, Brownlow and Cotgrave. In Corfield's action with the rebels on the 11th of May at Hétampúr, Carew's battery took a very prominent part. They "worked their guns admirably."* And yet that very day they had marched fourteen miles, and before they had time to take a meal had to march against the rebels under a sun which struck dead seven men of the 6th regiment marching with them. Though the Indian navy sailors were more acclimatised than their brethren of the royal army, yet even they lost three of their comrades that very day from the effect of exposure. The same cause compelled, a little later, Carew to resign his command to Mr. Midshipman Cotgrave.

Lieutenant Batt;

Lieutenant, afterwards Commander, Batt did splendid service in the same district. Batt had distinguished himself by his activity in the Gangès between Allahábád and Kánhpúr, in July and August 1857, by shelling the rebels out of their position in the fort of Káli Kanki. Subsequently he commanded at Baksar where he

* Corfield's despatch.

Book XVII. Chapter II.

1858. July-Sept.

repaired the fort, made gun-carriages, and trained his men. Later on, in the autumn of 1858, he assisted in the measures taken to drive the followers of Kúnwar Singh from the jungles of Jagdispúr, being always to the front. On one of the many occasions in which he was in action, an officer serving under him, Acting-Master George Chicken, gained the Victoria Cross. The force to which Chicken was attached was engaged with and had driven back the rebels near Pirú on the 4th of September 1858. In the pursuit Chicken suddenly came alone upon a group of twenty preparing to rally and open fire on their scattered pursuers. He at once charged them. Surrounded on all sides, Chicken fought most desperately and killed five of the rebels. He would, however, have succumbed had not four native troopers arrived in the nick of time to his rescue. He escaped with a severe wound.

His gallant and useful services.

Mr. Chicken gains the Victoria Cross.

In the western Bihár division, Lieutenant Duval, Midshipmen Wray and Scamp, and later Lieutenant Barron, rendered good service after the mutiny of the sepoys at Dánápúr had introduced disorder there, In the repression of the mutinies in Chutiá Nágpúr,* Captain Burbank of the Bengal Marine and Lieutenant Windus, I.N., and the seamen under them, were most efficient and useful. The latter received the special thanks of the Government, and it is clear that he was a man who was equally at home when at work in the field and when engaged in organising arrange-

Duval, Wray, Scamp, and Barron,

Burbank of the Bengal Marine, Windus.

* Vol. ii. pages 436 to 441.

Book XVII. Chapter II.

1858. July-Aug.

ments for that work. There was nothing he could not turn his hand to. Captain Burbank's services with Mr. Yule in pursuit of the Dháká rebels have been already recorded.*

The Indian navy on the western coast.

On the western coast the services of the Indian navy in the suppression of the mutiny were invaluable. "In the months of July and August," writes Mr. Low, "though in the height of the south-west monsoon, the *Berenice*, Lieutenant Chitty, and the *Victoria*, Lieutenant Sweny, were engaged carrying troops from Bombay to Karáchi, and landing them on that open and storm-beaten coast, sixteen miles below Jargarh near Ratnaghari, and at Goa. . . . These officers made several voyages with troops, including portions of the 33rd and 86th regiments and the 2nd Bombay Europeans.† The services of Griffith Jenkins have been previously referred to in connection with the despatch by Lord Elphinstone to the Cape and to the Mauritius for reinforcements, but it is due to that gallant sailor to add that he possessed all the qualifications necessary to ensure the success of a delicate negotiation, and that Sir George Grey and Governor Higginson alike expressed their sense of the admirable man-

Chitty, Sweny,

* Vol. ii. pages 426 to 435.

† These were the troops landed on the coast referred to in pages 40 and 41 of this volume, whose opportune arrival disconcerted the mutineers of Kohlapúr. Lord Elphinstone specially thanked Lieutenants Chitty and Sweny for the "good services they rendered in carrying the different detachments of European troops down the coast at the height of the monsoon, by which movement, under Providence, the peace of the Southern Maráthá country and of the presidency was preserved."

Book XVII. Chapter II.

1858.

ner in which he discharged his duties. Captain Jenkins had the gratification of receiving from the highest quarter an official acknowledgment of his services. "I have been commanded," wrote Sir C. Wood to him from the India Office, "to convey to you the gracious approbation of Her Majesty of your conduct during that critical period."

Griffith Jenkins.

"The cold shade of officialism."

With regret I confine myself to this short notice of the services of the officers of the Indian navy. Those officers knew well, when in Bengal they gave their fullest energies to a service which was not properly their own, that they were serving under the cold shade of officialism, that though the brows of their brethren in the army might be crowned with laurels, their modest deeds would remain comparatively unnoticed. Knowing this, they yet vied with the bravest in daring, with the most zealous in energy and devotion, and when the mutiny came to an end they had the satisfaction of knowing that they had deserved well of their country. They had little more. Besides the war medal, which the detachments engaged with the rebels received in common with the army, and two Victoria Crosses gained by personal valour, not a decoration was bestowed upon any one of them. Shortly after the mutiny the noble service with which they had been connected was abolished, the survivors were pensioned, and nothing remained but the consolation of heroes—the conviction of duty performed, of honour unsullied, of great services rendered to their country!

Book XVII. Chapter II.

1858. May-June.

One final episode.

With one episode, slight though it may be as compared with others recorded in this history, yet reflecting, in the story of one officer, the conduct of many placed in circumstances not altogether dissimilar, this chapter will fitly conclude.

When the mutiny broke out at Mírath on the 10th of May 1857 two companies of the 53rd native infantry, then at Kánhpúr, were on detached command duty at Orai, on the right bank of the Jamná, about eighty miles from Kánhpúr. The officers commanding these companies were Captain Alexander and Lieutenant Tomkinson. The native regiments stationed at Kánhpúr surpassed all the other regiments of the native army in the cruelties and barbarities they perpetrated; but the men of the detachment at Orai, free from the contamination produced apparently by the close vicinity to the wronged province of Oudh, displayed a spirit far more amenable to reason. Everything remained quiet at Orai till the end of May. On the 3rd of June, however, the deputy commissioner of that station received orders to send to Gwáliár the money he had in the treasure-chest. The sepoys, on hearing of this order, evinced a great inclination to dispute it. However, they did not do so, and on the 4th Tomkinson started for Gwáliár with the treasure and a detachment of his men. Leaving him for a moment, I may mention that on the 6th of June the regiments at Kánhpúr mutinied. When this news reached the men stationed at Orai, they provided Captain and Mrs. Alexander with a

Alexander and Tomkinson at Orai.

Tomkinson escorts treasure to Gwáliár.

camel, and recommended them to make the best of their way to Ágra, which they eventually succeeded in doing.

Book XVII. Chapter II.

1858. June.

Meanwhile Tomkinson and his men arrived safely with the treasure, on the 12th of June, in the vicinity of Gwáliár. At that time the troops at Gwáliár were very shaky; it was known that Tomkinson's regiment had mutinied at Kánhpúr; fear and distrust were in every man's mind. Major C. Macpherson, then, the political agent at Gwáliár, on hearing of Tomkinson's approach, sent out a party to relieve him of the treasure, but at the same time forbade him to enter Gwáliár, and directed him to proceed to A'gra. Tomkinson would have obeyed had it been possible, but meanwhile Mr. Colvin had been communicated with at A'gra, and Mr. Colvin, as distrustful as Macpherson, had telegraphed that no native troops were to proceed thither.

Tomkinson's party is forbidden by the political agent to enter Gwáliár,

and A'gra is barred to them by Mr. Colvin.

Left to himself, Tomkinson stayed with his men until the state of the country forced them into action. They made no attempt on his life; on the contrary, they expressed on parting with him the greatest regret that they were forced to take the line they were about to follow.

Tomkinson is forced to separate from his men.

Left alone, it would seem that the villagers, intent on plunder, deprived him of his horse and his gun, and it would have gone hard with him but for the kindness of a native. Hungry and destitute, having nothing but the clothes on his back, he was seen by a Muhammadan villager wandering in the fields in apparent distress. The poor man took him to his home in the village of

His life is preserved by a Muhammadan.

Book XVII. Chapter II.

1858. October.

Amain, concealed him there till the month of October. A man of substance in the village supplied him with clothes and paid for his food. Tomkinson apparently chafed under this life, and longed for active work; but the country around him was in revolt. He persuaded his host on one occasion to take a letter into Kánhpúr, but the news that met the poor man on the way so frightened him that he destroyed the letter. At length, towards the end of October, an opportunity of rendering service to his country seemed to offer. Information reached the village that a body of rebels, with a large quantity of ammunition, was about to pass in its vicinity. If he could only explode the ammunition, Tomkinson thought, he would perform an act which would paralyse their movements. He resolved to attempt to explode it. Accordingly, on the 23rd of October, he crept out, reached the rebel camp, and made the effort. He was, however, discovered and killed.

I hope that a story which paints the devotion to duty of an Englishman, and the kindness and fidelity of a Muhammadan, may be considered a fitting close to this somewhat desultory chapter.

BOOK XVIII.

CONCLUDING CHAPTER.

What caused the mutiny?

EVEN before the last embers of the mutiny had been trampled out, the question which had from the first puzzled every man, from the Governor-General in Council to the subaltern in his modest bungalow, the question as to the original cause of the mutiny, became the burning question of the day. It was a question which required a complete and accurate reply, because prompt reorganisation was necessary, and to carry out a complete scheme of reorganisation a knowledge of the circumstances which had caused the collapse of the system to be reorganised was indispensable.

Anxiety to know the opinion of Sir John Lawrence.

On this question the opinion of no man was looked forward to with so much eagerness, so much anxiety, and, I may add, with so much curiosity, as the opinion of the great Indian official whose daring and unselfish policy had made possible the storming of Dehlí. It was

Book XVIII. Concluding Chapter.

Reasons why his opinion should be,

and why it might not be,

sonnd.

very natural that this should be so. Few men had associated more with the natives than Sir John Lawrence; few men had more thoroughly pierced to the core the national character, and few men possessed a more complete power of mental analysis. People, for the most part, did not stop to remember that, with all his gifts, Sir John Lawrence had ever been the partisan of a school—a school opposed to the tenure of land by great families; that he had favoured Lord Dalhousie's policy of annexation; and that although he was thoroughly acquainted with the feelings of the agricultural class, he contemned those of the large proprietors, and that he knew little of the sepoys. Furthermore, and especially, that he possessed no personal knowledge of Oudh and of its people.

He attributes the mutiny to the greased cartridges, only.

It will readily be believed, then, that when the opinion of Sir John Lawrence was published it gave absolute satisfaction to the many, none at all to the thinking few. After an exhaustive argument, Sir John Lawrence arrived at the conclusion that the mutiny was due to the greased cartridges, and to the greased cartridges only. The public applauded a result so beautiful in its simplicity, so easy of comprehension. It chimed so entirely with the ideas of men who never take the trouble to think for themselves, that by the masses, which are mainly composed of such men, it was promptly and thankfully accepted. With them it remains still the unanswerable reason for the mutiny of the Indian army. They did not stop to consider that to declare that

Reasons why the conclusion cannot be accepted.

the greased cartridges caused the mutiny was in all respects similar to the declaration of a man who if asked what causes a gun to discharge, should reply—the powder. True it is that the powder, when exploded, forces out the bullet: but who ignites the powder? That the greased cartridges were the lever used to excite the sepoys is incontestable; they were explosive substances. But, though explosive, they had been perfectly harmless had the minds of the sepoys not been prepared to act upon them in the same manner that the percussion-cap acts upon gunpowder. It should never be forgotten that the greased cartridges were not the only instrument employed to create discontent in 1856–7. Before a greased cartridge had been issued the chapatties had been circulated by thousands in many rural districts. The chapatty was, it is true, a weapon far less perfect than the greased cartridge. It was, nevertheless, sufficiently adapted to the comprehensions of the class to whom it was addressed—the class given to agriculture. To minds, simple, impressionable, suspicious, prompt to receive ideas, the chapatty acted as a warning of an impending calamity. A Hindú can conceive nothing more dreadful than a violation of his caste and his religion. The conclusion was a foregone one. The receipt of the chapatties foreshadowed a great attempt to be made to upset the national religion.

The greased cartridges not the only instrument employed to create discontent.

The chapatties.

Though we might even grant, then, for the sake of argument, that the greased cartridges were not in themselves harmless, yet the chapatties cer-

The cartridges and the chapatties alike a means to an end.

tainly were so. But it was these harmless chapatties which stirred up the rural populations, especially those in Oudh and in Bandalkhand, to participate in the rebellion. What becomes, then, of Sir John Lawrence's conclusion? It simply vanishes. The greased cartridges became dangerous only when used by others as a means to an end. Before the plans of the leaders of the revolt were ripe the cartridges and the chapatties were nothing more than gunpowder stored in a magazine. When the opportune moment arrived, when the minds of the sepoys and the agricultural classes had been instructed to receive any ideas, however absurd, then the cartridges and the chapatties were rammed into them, and were exploded.

The real cause of the mutiny.

But what was it that made the minds of the sepoys, what was it that made the minds of the agricultural classes prone to conceive suspicions alike regarding the greased cartridges and the chapatties? The answers to these two questions will bring us to the real cause of the mutiny. Sir John Lawrence's conclusions were not pushed to their legitimate issue. He named only one of the means. I must go back to the cause.

Bad faith, and the attempt to force western ideas on an eastern people.

The real cause of the mutiny may be expressed in a condensed form in two words:—bad faith. It was bad faith to our sepoys which made their minds prone to suspicion; it was our policy of annexation, of refusing to Hindú chiefs the permission to adopt—with them a necessary religious rite—of suddenly bringing a whole people under the operation of complex rules to which they were unaccustomed, as in Oudh, in the Ságar and Narbadá territory, and in Bandalkhand, and our breaches of customs more sacred to the natives than laws, which roused the large landowners and the rural population against the British rule.

Bad faith towards the sepoys;

The bad faith towards the sepoys goes back so far as the period immediately succeeding the first Áfghán war. In that war the sepoys had behaved splendidly; they had fought well, they had suffered privations without a murmur, they had borne with cheerfulness absence from their country and their families, in a cause which was only theirs because it was the cause of their foreign masters. I recollect well meeting in 1844 at Allahábád a political officer whose conduct during his mission at Herát can never be mentioned without admiration—the late d'Arcy Todd. Speaking to me of the difficulties of his position at Herát, d'Arcy Todd stated that but for the zeal, the energy, and the fidelity of the few sepoys who were with him he could not have stayed at Herát; he added, "When properly treated the Bengal sepoy will go anywhere and do anything." Well, these men returned from Afghánistán. Immediately afterwards we annexed Sindh. The Bengal sepoys were sent to garrison a country then notoriously unhealthy. How were they treated? The time-honoured rule which provided that they should receive a fixed extra food allowance on proceeding to certain localities was rescinded, in one instance after the men had reached one of the

their devotion when properly managed.

Breach of faith towards them in the double batta question.

Book XVIII. Concluding Chapter.

indicated localities, in another instance when the regiment was in full march to it. Is it to be wondered at that the men grumbled and then actually refused to march? They committed no violence. They simply said, "You are guilty of bad faith; we contracted to enter your service and to perform all the duties entrusted to us on certain conditions, of which the payment to us of food allowance under certain circumstances was one. We have fulfilled our share of the contract, and now you refuse to fulfil your share. We decline to work until you fulfil it." In equity the sepoys were right; but the Government, instead of soothing them, acted in a high-handed manner: disbanded one regiment and severely punished the men of another.

The Government punish the sepoys for declining to fulfil a contract which the Government had broken.

Bad effect produced on the Indian army.

This conduct produced a very bad effect throughout the Indian army. It was felt in every regiment that the word of the Government could no longer be depended upon. Nevertheless no open indignation was manifested. The Satlaj campaign ensued, and again the sepoys fought well. The annexation of the Panjáb followed. Then succeeded a long period of quiescence—a period during which seeds, sown some time before, took root, sprang up, and blossomed into regulations fraught with danger to the discipline of the Indian army.

Gradual progress of the weakening the power of commanding officers.

The natives of India serve a master well when once he has shown himself capable of wielding authority. But should that authority slacken, or, worse still, should they find out that the Government they serve has placed at their disposal

Book XVIII. Concluding Chapter.

the means not only of shaking but even of upsetting it, then the nominal master wielding it ceases to be their real master; the substance of his power vanishes; the shadow only remains. The occurrences in the Indian army during the several years immediately preceding 1857 completely illustrate this assertion. In former days, in the time of Lake, in the time of Hastings, and even later, the commanding officer of a native regiment was supreme in all matters of discipline. Responsible immediately to his divisional commander, he could prómote, he could reduce, he could punish. But as time passed on, men were appointed to the general staff of the Indian army whose visions became clouded and whose brains became turned by the air of the new regions to which they had been transferred. Forgetting their own regimental experience, not caring to know that the routine system which suits a British regiment formed of men taught to obey the law, no matter by whom administered, is not applicable to a regiment composed of Asiatics bred to obey the man in whose hands they see authority centred and him only, these men began, step by step, to introduce the British system into the native army. It would take too long to tell how gradually the real power of the commanding officer was undermined; how the sepoy was, by degrees, taught to look upon him, not as a superior who must be obeyed, but as a very fallible mortal, peculiarly liable to err, and against whose lightest exercise of authority he had the right to appeal to the one central power, the

Book XVIII. Concluding Chapter.

Commander-in-Chief. Suffice it to say that this process of sapping the powers of the commanding officer was carried to so great an extent that immediately prior to the mutiny the sepoys had lost all respect for the authority he only nominally wielded. Nor had the sepoy imbibed for the Commander-in-Chief the feeling which he had ceased to entertain towards his commanding officer. To him the Commander-in-Chief was but a name; he was a lay figure, living in the clouds of the Himálayas, rarely, often never, seen, but whose interposition enabled him to defy his own colonel and to set discipline at nought! The extent to which this interposition was exercised before the mutiny was dangerous in the extreme. It succeeded before 1857 in weakening the influence of all the regimental officers, and in undermining the discipline of the army.

Disastrous result of this policy.

It undermines the discipline of the army.

I have said that the refusal of the Government of India in 1843 to act up to their contract with regard to the sepoys sent to occupy Sindh, had been felt throughout the Indian army. Immediately subsequent to that event, the process of undermining the powers of commanding officers had made swift progress. When, then, in 1852, the Government most unadvisedly again attempted another breach of contract, the sepoys, demoralised by the process I have alluded to, were even more inclined to resent it.

The progress of demoralisation between 1843 and 1852.

The breach of contract referred to occurred in this manner. With the exception of six or seven regiments, the sepoys of the Bengal army are enlisted for service in India only; they were

A proportion of the regiments of the Bengal army alone enlisted for service never to be required to cross the sea. But with the view of supplying the necessities of the state in A'rakán and the Tenasserim provinces, six or seven regiments had been specially raised for general service, and these regiments were invariably sent across the sea whenever their services were there required. Lord Dalhousie, however, who had ridden roughshod over so many native customs, considered that he might set aside this one also. Accordingly, when, during the Burmese war, he wanted to send an additional regiment to Burma, instead of despatching a general service regiment or of inviting a regiment to volunteer, he ordered a regiment stationed at Barrákpúr to proceed thither. The men of the regiment refused to go. "You ask us," they said, "to embark upon a service for which we have not enlisted, and which many of us regard as imperilling our caste. We will not do it." Lord Dalhousie was forced to submit. He was very angry, but there was no help for it.

across the sea.

Lord Dalhousie attempts to break contract with the sepoys.

But the result on the minds of the sepoys was most disastrous. For the first time in the history of India the orders of the Governor-General had been successfully resisted. It was little to the purpose to argue that the Governor-General had exceeded his powers: the blow to the discipline of the native army was not the less deadly.

The result most disastrous to discipline.

The minds of the sepoys were under the influence of this blow, and by the insane action of the head-quarter staff they were becoming more and more released from the bands of dis-

The annexation of Oudh.

Book XVIII. Concluding Chapter.

cipline towards their own officers, when the annexation of Oudh took place. How this affected them I shall state as briefly as possible.

Reason why service in the Company's army was popular with the men of Oudh, when Oudh had her own king.

A very large proportion of the army of the Bengal presidency, and a smaller proportion of the army of the Bombay presidency were recruited from the kingdom of Oudh. It is scarcely too much to affirm that there was not a single agricultural family in that country which was not represented by at least one of its members in the Indian army. Service in that army, in fact, offered no inconsiderable advantages to the subjects of the king of Oudh. It made them clients of the paramount power. Every sepoy was, so to speak, represented at the court of Lakhnao by the British resident. His commanding officer was authorised to frank any petition he might present addressed to the resident, and the fact that the resident had received such petition ensured substantial justice to the claims of the petitioner at the hands of the court of Lakhnao. Everyone familiar with the workings of a native court will at once recognise the value at which service in the Indian army was rated by the natives of Oudh. By accepting such service they obtained an all-powerful advocate at their sovereign's court.

Persistent loyalty to the paramount power of the nawábs and kings of Oudh.

The nawábs and kings of Oudh had from the time of Warren Hastings shown a loyalty to the British Government not to be surpassed. During the Afghán disasters, the Gwáliár campaign, the battles on the Satlaj and in the Panjáb, Oudh had been the milch-cow of the suzerain power.

She had lent that power money, she had given her her best sons as soldiers, she had done all that she could do to maintain unimpaired the relations between the prince independent only in his own country and the paramount overlord.

The plea of misgovernment one not to be sustained as a justification for annexation.

"But," exclaimed the advocates for annexation, "she had misgoverned." Misgovernment is a relative term. There can be no question but that in the English sense of the term there had been no good government in Oudh. But a kind of administrative system had, nevertheless, prevailed which induced the sepoys, after the term of their service under the British flag had expired, to settle in their native country. More than that, after the natives of Oudh had had one year's experience of British government as administered by Mr. Coverley Jackson and Mr. Martin Gubbins, they, one and all, evinced a strong preference for the native government which had been superseded.

Disastrous effect produced on the minds of the sepoys by that annexation.

It is necessary to take all these circumstances into consideration when one analyses the effect which the annexation of Oudh produced upon the sepoys of the Bengal army. In my belief that annexation gave them the greatest shock they had felt since the occurrences, already adverted to, of 1843. It was the last and the most fatal blow to their belief in British honesty. It made them ready to become the tools of any adventurer.

They regarded it as another breach of faith.

It was not only that they beheld in that annexation a lowering of their own position as men represented at their sovereign's court by a British

Book XVIII. Concluding Chapter.

resident, though that was a blow under which the Indian army yet reels. They beheld in that act, and in the manner in which it was carried out, a deliberate infringement of promises they had ever looked upon as sacred, a repayment for the good services of nearly a century such as even the most abandoned amongst their own princes would have hesitated to enforce.

Fury of the sepoys stationed at Kánhpúr when Outram crosses into Oudh to annex it.

These are not statements made at random. It devolved upon the officer of the Commissariat Department of the Kánhpúr division to supply carriage and provisions for the force which, under Outram, crossed the Ganges into Oudh at the end of 1855. Over that officer's house and office, which were in the same compound, was a sepoy guard—a sergeant's party. Contrary to custom and to departmental instructions, no written orders were given to that officer for the requisitions. The expedition was to be a secret, he was told, and he must obey verbal orders. But, in spite of this mystery, the destination of the force became known before it set out to every sepoy in the cantonment, to every native in the town. The effect was alarming. The natives had no doubt whatever as to the real meaning of the demonstration. For the first time in the memory of man an English regiment was about to march on Lakhnao, and an English regiment would march on Lakhnao with but one object.

The authorities are warned,

The agitation of the sepoys of the guard was a circumstance never to be forgotten. They were with great difficulty controlled, and the subordinates of the Commissariat Department assured their officer that a similar feeling was manifesting itself in every regiment in the place. The officer made no secret of these manifestations. He reported them in the proper quarter. He communicated them even to one of the officials, a man of remarkable gifts, who had accepted a high post in Oudh; but his warnings found no more credence than did the warnings of Cassandra. They were remembered afterwards.

but in vain.

The annexation of Oudh, keeping in view the way in which it was carried out, was, in very deed, the act which finally broke the trust of the sepoys in their English masters. The perpetration of that deed prepared their minds to receive and to believe any matter, however absurd in itself, which might betoken English perfidy. How their minds were played upon I shall show presently. Meanwhile it is necessary that I should indicate how it was that the landowners and agricultural classes of India became impressed with the 'bad faith' of their rulers.

The annexation of Oudh removes the last remnant of confidence in the British.

The internal annexation policy inaugurated by Lord Dalhousie was, in many instances, based upon his refusal to recognise a right which the Hindús hold as an essential part of their religion—the right to adopt an heir on the failure of children lawfully begotten. In the early part of this volume I have spoken of the disaffection, the terror, the hatred of the English which this policy produced in the southern Maráthá country. Carrying out this principle Lord Dalhousie had annexed the territory of the Bhonslás, he had annexed the state of Jhánsi, he had endeavoured

The mode in which the princes, chiefs, and landowners, of India lost faith in the British.

to annex the state of Karáuli, and had only been prevented by the interference of the Home Government on a threatened motion in the House of Commons. Still he continued to hold the principle *in terrorem* over the heads of the princes and chiefs of India, and the fact that such a principle was held in esteem by the paramount power, and might, on the occurrence of death without natural heirs, be applied, produced, it is not too much to say, "a terror" in the minds of the Hindú princes throughout India.

The principle of granting a life annuity in exchange for a kingdom.

But in another and a far more guiltless manner the Government had sown the seeds of hatred in the minds of the representatives of great families whose ancestors they had deprived of their dominions. Two instances of the action of this policy will occur at once to the reader—Náná Sáhib and the ráo of Kirwi. Náná Sáhib was indubitably the lawful representative, according to Hindú law, of the last of the Péshwás. When, in June 1818 Báji Ráo surrendered to Sir John Malcolm, the Court of Directors considered that a life annuity of eighty thousand pounds was more than an adequate compensation for the loss of an empire. Báji Ráo lived in the enjoyment of this pension nearly thirty-five years. When he died, in January 1853, Lord Dalhousie refused either to recognise his adopted son or to continue the pension.

Totally repugnant to Hindú ideas.

According to European ideas this ruling was perfectly just. It strictly carried out the agreement made by Sir John Malcolm in 1818. But it was, nevertheless, totally repugnant to the ideas and opposed to the customs of the races of Hindústán. With them it was a point of honour to recognise in the son, whether begotten or adopted, the successor to the titles of his father. Whether the English recognised him or not, Náná Sáhib was still Péshwá in the eyes of every true Maráthá.* The refusal to recognise him and the stoppage of the pension forced the heir of the Péshwá to conspire. It can easily be conceived how readily such a man, occupying a fortified palace close to the Oudh frontier, would hail and encourage the discontent which the—in the minds of the natives—nefarious annexation of Oudh could not fail to produce.

Book XVIII. Concluding Chapter.

That principle made Náná Sáhib a conspirator.

The story of the ráo of Kirwi† is similar in character and in application.

* I recollect well when I was at Banárás in 1851-52, the Governor - General's agent, Major Stewart, a man of great culture and information, told me that there was living then, in extreme poverty, in the Mirzápúr jungles, near Banáras, a man recognised by the natives as the lineal descendant of Chéit Singh, rájá of Banáras, expelled by Warren Hastings in 1781, and that to that day the natives salaamed to him and treated him with the respect due to the rájá.

† *Vide* page 199. I may be permitted to note here another instance in which the British Government has applied the same unjust principle. When in 1845 and 1848-49 England waged war with the Sikhs, the King of Láhor was a minor, under the tutelage of his mother, and in no respects responsible for the occurrences which in either instance led to the war. Yet in 1849, although his irresponsibility was officially admitted, he was treated as though he was in all respects the guilty party. The British annexed his kingdom and gave him in exchange a life pension. The matter has only to be seriously examined for the injustice to become apparent. Most of the nobles of the Panjáb, who secretly fomented the wars of 1845 and 1848, were secured in the possession of their estates, and their posi-

Book XVIII. Concluding Chapter.

The Western principle pushed to its logical extreme alienates an Eastern race.

We see, then, how many of the princes and the chiefs of India in possession, and all the chiefs not in possession, were predisposed to view with at least indifference any troubles which might assail their British over-lord. Incidents like that of the rájá of Dilhéri* came at uncertain intervals to add to the general mistrust. Such incidents affected alike chieftain and retainer, noble and peasant, for in many parts of the country the latter considered their interests as bound up with those of the former.

The annexation of Oudh is made doubly odious

It was when the minds of all were thus distrustful that the annexation of Oudh—of Oudh which had ever been faithful, always true and loyal—came to startle them still more. It is just within the bounds of possibility that if the system introduced by the English into Oudh had been administered in a conciliatory manner the result might have been similar to that which was produced in a few years in the central provinces.

by the principle of forcing Western notions on an Eastern people.

But the Englishmen to whom the administration of the newly annexed province was intrusted were men with fixed ideas, which they rode to death; the slaves of a system which they carried out without regard to the feelings and previous habits of those with whose lands and property they were

tion, under English rule, has become trebly secure. But Maháràjá Dhulip Singh, who was a mere child, innocent of intrigue, was awarded in exchange for his kingdom and its princely revenues a life annuity only — an annuity which will expire with his life. Yet his children are the children of one who was once King of Láhor! Can we wonder that treatment of this sort sinks deep into the hearts of the natives?

* Page 93.

Book XVIII. Concluding Chapter.

dealing. In less than twelve months the result was disaffection and dismay. The new settlement made the men of Oudh rebels at heart.

At the close of 1856 all classes are ready for the machinations of conspirators.

With Oudh thus disaffected, the chiefs and the territorial interest doubting and trembling, with the sepoys alienated and mistrustful, there needed but one other element to produce insurrection. The country, the army, the newly-annexed province were alike ready for the machinations of conspirators.

The authors of the mutiny.

The conspirators, too, were ready. Who all those conspirators were may never certainly be known. Most of them died and made no sign. It is, however, a fact beyond question that the Moulvi of Faizábád—the man who was killed at Powáin—was one of them. I have already given a sketch of the previous career of this man.* I have shown how, after the annexation of Oudh, he travelled all over the north-west provinces on a mission which was a mystery to the Europeans; how he was suspected even then of conspiring. Abundant proofs were subsequently obtained that a conspiracy had been formed by some influential people in Oudh in the interval between the annexation and the outbreak of the mutiny. Of this conspiracy the Moulvi was undoubtedly a leader. It had its ramifications all over India—certainly at A'gra, where the Moulvi stayed some time, and almost certainly at Dehlí, at Mírath, at Patná, and at Calcutta, where the ex-king of Oudh and a large following were residing.

The Moulví of Oudh.

* Vol. ii. page 541.

Book XVIII. Concluding Chapter.

The one thing wanting to the success of the conspiracy

For some time there was one thing wanting to the conspirators—the means, the instrument—with which to kindle to action the great body of their countrymen. Especially were they at a loss how to devise a scheme by which the minds of the sepoys serving throughout the Bengal Presidency should be simultaneously affected. They

is found in the greased cartridge.

were in this perplexity when they heard of the new cartridge—a cartridge smeared with animal fat and which they were told was to be bitten.

It was easy for them to make this discovery. Their spies were everywhere. The cartridges

When the cartridge is found

were openly manufactured at Damdam. Eagerly looking out for a novelty to be introduced from Europe into the native army, they were the most likely men of all to hit upon the greased cartridge. They had no sooner found it than they felt they

the chapatties are circulated.

had the weapon required. Instantly the chapatties were distributed by thousands to the rural population, whilst means were employed to disseminate in every military station in Bengal the information regarding the cartridge.

Natural effect on the minds of Hindú and Muhammadan sepoys.

To tell a body of Hindús already suspicious of their foreign master that they would be required to bite a cartridge smeared with the fat of their sacred animal, and to tell Muhammadans that they would be required to bite a cartridge smeared with the fat of an animal whose flesh was forbidden to them, was tantamount to tell them that their foreign master intended to make them break with their religion. Certainly that result was produced. When the new cartridges were issued suspicion and calumny had done their work. The sepoys even believed that cartridges made of paper had been feloniously tampered with; and, when they were issued to them, they broke into revolt.

The cartridge only the instrument.

In this lesser sense, then, and in this only, did the cartridges produce the mutiny. They were the instrument used by conspirators; and those conspirators were successful in their use of the instrument only because, in the manner I have endeavoured to point out, the minds of the sepoys and of certain sections of the population had been prepared to believe every act testifying to bad faith on the part of their foreign masters.

The exceptions who proved the rule.

I have said that the mistrust of the British faith had, towards the year 1857, become as great in the minds of the princes and chiefs and landowners of India as in the minds of the sepoys. There were, however, a few exceptions, and, when the country rose, those exceptions saved us. I will briefly refer to the most prominent amongst them.

The provinces which rose against us.

In four great provinces of our empire—in Oudh, in Rohilkhand, in Bandalkhand, and in the Ságar and Narbadá territory—the great bulk of the people rose against British rule. In western Bihár, using that geographical expression as inclusive of the districts subordinate to the Commissioner of Patná, in many districts of the Allahábád division, in the A'gra division, and in many parts of the Mírath division, the risings of the people and the sepoys were almost simultaneous in point of time. Had the revolt been universal, had the chiefs, the people, and the sepoys

Book XVIII. Concluding Chapter.

risen at one and the same moment, India could not have been held. Fortunately for British interests, the great prince who occupied the most important position in India, and whose action, had he risen, would have been felt to the extremities of western India, was, throughout the crisis, loyal to his suzerain. Throughout the period between the 12th of May and the 1st of September 1857 Sindia held the fate of India in his hands.

The loyalty of Sindia.

In another volume* I have described very briefly how it was that in an unexampled crisis in the fortunes of the people with whom his ancestors had contended for empire, Sindia did remain loyal. I have shown that the loyalty did not proceed from affection towards the English. His minister and confidant, Dinkar Ráo, had no love for our nation. Sindia's people were, almost to a man, against us. Yet Dinkar Ráo used all his great influence in favour of a loyal policy, and his representations, backed by the solid arguments of the able representative of the British power at the court of Sindia, Major Charters Macpherson, prevailed over national sentiment, the solicitations of other courtiers, and the boisterous demonstrations of the people. The importance of the result to English interests cannot be over-estimated. Sindia's loyalty alone made possible Havelock's march on, and the retention of, Kánhpúr. It acted at the same time on the rebels like a wedge which pierces the centre of

His loyalty was not based upon affection for the British as a people.

Yet it saved us.

* Vol. i. pp. 151, 152.

an army, dividing the wings, and preventing concentrated action. Nor, when, after the back of rebellion had been broken, Sindia's army revolted against himself, was the effect much lessened. Sindia's great influence was still used for the English.

The loyalty really based on the fact that we had dealt faithfully and generously with him.

In considering Sindia's loyalty in connection with the risings of others—of all, or almost all, the rájás and tálúkdárs of Oudh, of the chiefs in Bandalkhand, in the Ságar and Narbadá territory, in the southern Maráthá country, and in western Bihár—it is impossible to shut our eyes to the fact that there had been a marked difference in the behaviour of the British Government towards Sindia on the one side, and towards the rájás and landowners of the countries mentioned on the other. Under circumstances of a peculiarly tempting character, Lord Ellenborough had behaved with the greatest generosity and forbearance towards Sindia in 1844. The Government had kept faith with him ever since. The reader of this volume will see that towards the rájás and landowners of the other provinces mentioned the British Government had shown neither generosity nor forbearance. In some instances they had not even kept faith. It is scarcely necessary to point the moral.

The remarkable instances in which the behaviour of the people of India corresponded to the faith we had kept with them.

It is, indeed, a very remarkable fact, and one which the rulers of India at the present moment would do well to bear in mind that in the several provinces and districts traversed by our troops in 1857-8-9, the behaviour of the people corresponded to the character of our rule. Thus, in

Book XVIII. Concluding Chapter.

the Central Provinces, to which the regulation system had never penetrated, the people were loyal and contented, and refused all aid to Tántia Topi. In the Ságar and Narbadá territories, in Oudh and in the districts bordering on that province, in the A'gra division—in all of which the British hand had been heavy, and the British acts opposed to the national sentiment—the people showed a spirit of opposition, a resolution to fight to the last, and in many cases a detestation of their masters, such as no one would before have credited. Cases similar to that of the rájá of Dilhéri referred to in the earlier part* of this volume, had sown far and wide the seed of disaffection and revolt.

The mutiny the result of a rude attempt

If these facts are, as I believe them to be, correct, we have not to go far to seek the conclusion. The mutiny of the army and the insurrection in the provinces I have named were the natural consequences of an attempt to govern a great Eastern empire according to pure Western ideas.

to govern an Eastern people according to puro Western ideas.

The civilisation, over-refined though it might be, of thousands of years was ridiculed by the rougher race which, scorning sentiment, regarded utilitarianism as its foundation-stone. The governing members of that race failed to recognise the great truth upon which their forefathers had built their Indian empire, that the Western race can gain the confidence of the Eastern only when it scrupulously respects the long-cherished cus-

* Page 93.

toms of the latter, and impresses upon it the conviction that its word is better than its bond. This is just the conviction which, during the thirty years immediately antecedent to 1856, the majority of the Hindús and Muhammadans of India had been gradually losing, and which in 1857 they had lost.

Lord Canning,

If Lord Canning had had any idea in the early part of 1857 that the isolated outbreaks which then disturbed the general serenity were part of an organised plot, he would, I believe, have at once taken measures to meet the difficulty. Not that, at any time in 1857, he could have prevented a mutiny, but he could easily have made better arrangements to meet one. I am far, however, from imputing any blame to Lord Canning in this respect. He had but recently arrived in India. His predecessor, when making over to him charge of the empire, had expressed his conviction that never had the country been in so satisfactory condition. All the time the ground was undermined, the train was being laid, the miners were at work. But how was Lord Canning to know this? He inherited Lord Dalhousie's councillors. They were as satisfied, and as ignorant of the real state of the country, as was Lord Dalhousie. Lord Dalhousie had quitted India in a blaze of glory; and the new Governor-General, unused to the currents of Indian thought, could for some months only steer the vessel by the advice of the officers who had helped to bring to Lord Dalhousie a renown far-reaching and seemingly well-deserved.

new to India,

inherits Lord Dalhousie's councillors.

Book XVIII. Concluding Chapter.

The councillors of Lord Canning.

But, in fact, upon no men did the news of the mutiny descend with so startling a surprise as upon the councillors of Lord Canning. They could not comprehend it. Weeks and weeks elapsed before they could bring themselves to believe that it was anything more than a fortuitous explosion at various points, each having no concert and no connection with the other. The Home Secretary's assurances that the apprehensions expressed regarding its nature were "a passing and groundless panic," that "there is every hope that in a few days tranquillity will be restored throughout the presidency," testify to the ideas that filled the minds of these men. The admission at least is due to them that they were honest—they believed what they said. But those sayings betrayed a complete ignorance of the country and of the situation. This ignorance, this blindness to the fact that it was more even than a mutiny of the Bengal army, and not merely a series of isolated revolts, with which they had to cope, was illustrated in a thousand ways, but in none more strongly than in the refusal to disarm regiments which were known to be mutinous. The consequences of this refusal were most serious. In the case of the regiments at Dánápúr, the reader will have seen that it brought revolt into western Bihár, added enormously to the dangers of Havelock, and even imperilled Calcutta.

Their utter ignorance of the India outside Calcutta.

Lord Canning's real greatness evident when he stood unshackled at Allahábád.

How great Lord Canning really was, how small were his councillors, was shown when, having completely shaken off their influence, he stood alone and unshackled at Allahábád in the early party of

Book XVIII. Concluding Chapter.

1858. A different man was he then from the Lord Canning of April and May 1857. His nature then displayed itself in its real nobility. His grasp of affairs, at Calcutta apparently so small, excited at Allahábád the admiration of all who came in contact with him. He showed a truer insight into the military position than the Commander-in-Chief himself. It was entirely owing to Lord Canning's insistance that the campaign in Rohilkhand followed close upon the capture of Lakhnao. Sir Colin Campbell would have postponed it. But Lord Canning was too convinced of the danger of allowing a province to continue to flaunt rebellion, unchecked, in the face of the Government to permit the delay. He insisted with all the determination of a man whose resolution, based on the logic of facts, was not to be shaken. It was Lord Canning at Allahábád who gave his fullest support to Sir Hugh Rose, and to the generals engaged against Tántia Topi; and if, in one respect, to which I have adverted, his judgment was faulty, his companion in error was the Commander-in-Chief, and the error was a solitary one.

His military acumen.

Nor is lesser praise due to him for the measures inaugurated at Allahábád to heal the wounds caused—he must have seen—in a great measure by the mistakes of his predecessors. His Oudh proclamation, despite of the apparently harsh terms which it contained, was intended as a message of mercy, and, in its application, was a message of mercy. It gave every landowner in Oudh a title better, safer, more valid than the

His legislation in regard to Oudh.

Book XVIII. Concluding Chapter.

title he had lost. It ensured mercy to all except to those who by their crimes had forfeited all right to it. Interpreted, as Lord Canning meant it to be interpreted, by one of the ablest administrators in India, it became the charter upon which the position now occupied by the people of Oudh has been built up and secured.

His reception of Lord Ellenborough's strictures.

Never was the real greatness of Lord Canning's character more completely displayed than when the galling strictures of Lord Ellenborough's despatch were published to the world. At the moment the insult, the breach of etiquette, were lost sight of in the fear lest the condemnation of his policy proceeding from so high a quarter should afford encouragement to the rebels or weaken the attachment of the native tributaries. As soon as he ascertained that the despatch had not produced that result he was calm. He could not help seeing that it was designedly impertinent, that it was intended to provoke him to resign. Conscious of the rectitude of his motives and of the soundness of his views, he laughed at the pettiness of the display. In his calm and statesmanlike answer, he sought neither revenge nor triumph. But both soon came to him. The news that Lord Ellenborough had been hoisted with his own petard, the receipt of Lord Derby's almost imploring letter not to resign, followed the insulting missive with a rapidity almost startling.

His conduct towards his colleagues and subordinates.

Towards the men who served under him, Lord Canning displayed generosity, kindness, and forbearance. He knew that in many departments he had been badly served, yet he would rather

Book XVIII. Concluding Chapter.

bear the burden himself than dismiss the incapable minister. But so low did he rate the abilities of the men about him, that when he had resolved to appoint Mr. Edmonstone Lieutenant-Governor of the North-West Provinces, he cast his eyes far from the men surrounding him to select a successor to that official. He had actually resolved to offer the post to Herbert Edwardes when the publication by that officer of a letter, violently polemical, caused him to reconsider his resolve. For the moment he was cast back upon the clique about him, but finally he made an admirable choice in Durand.

The lofty-minded English gentleman, the trained statesman.

Judging Lord Canning's conduct after his arrival at Alláhábád, it is difficult to find a fault in it. He was then the lofty-minded English gentleman, the trained and skilful statesman. Every day made it more clear that the mistakes of the Calcutta period, mistakes which have been fully recorded in these volumes, were due to the inexperience of a generous nature guided by men whom he had been told to look upon as masters of the situation, but who were in fact hopelessly ignorant and incapable. That Lord Canning came to know this himself was evidenced by the generosity he displayed, after the mutiny had been quelled, to those who had ventured to express very boldly their disagreement with his policy of 1857.

Lord Elphinstone

But if Lord Canning was to be admired from the time of his arrival at Allahábád, Lord Elphinstone deserves the fullest meed of praise that can be accorded to him from the very first.

Book XVIII. Concluding Chapter.

Lord Elphinstone possessed this advantage over Lord Canning—his previous experience in India had given him a thorough knowledge of the country and the people. When the mutiny broke out at Mírath he saw it as it really was; he saw that it was no isolated outbreak, no local discontent, but part and parcel of an organised rebellion which had its main roots, indeed, in the North-West Provinces, but the development of which, especially in the direction of Bombay, was certain, unless it could be promptly stopped. The Bombay Presidency, in fact, with an army partly recruited from Oudh, and composed mainly of a conglomeration of Maráthá states, was in a peculiar degree, susceptible. Lord Elphinstone understood the situation at once. He dealt with it in a manner possible only to a statesman of high and lofty courage, of a clear intellect and of far-seeing views. The idea of waiting for the mutiny within his own borders, if, indeed, it ever occurred to him, came only to be promptly rejected. To mass the greatest number of men on the decisive point of the scene of action—that Napoleonic motto became at once his principle. For that purpose he denuded his own presidency, highly sensitive as it was, of European troops, and despatched them as fast as he could force them to move to the threatened points outside of it. He, too, like Lord Canning, had colleagues in his government, but here again his previous experience saved him from the mistakes which marred Lord Canning's administration during the first seven months of the mutiny.

comprehended the full extent of the mutiny from the very outset.

His policy of offensive defence.

Knowing his counsellors thoroughly, he listened to them with courtesy—but he acted on his own convictions. To the men who were the instruments of his policy he gave the most complete and generous confidence. How large was his trust when he once gave it Mr. Forjett is a living evidence. Mr. Frere in Sindh, Mr. Seton-Karr and afterwards Colonel Le G. Jacob in the southern Maráthá country, Mr. John Rose in Satárah, and Colonel Malcolm, are instances of a similar import. When, in spite of all his measures to keep the mutiny from Bombay by a policy of offensive defence, the poison crept in and infected the regiments of the regular army in the southern Maráthá country, how vigorous, how decided is his policy! We see here none of the hesitation, of the half-heartedness, the halting between two extremes, which enabled the mutinous regiments of Dánápúr to disturb all the plans of the Government and to imperil the safety of the empire. Promptly, without an hour's delay, Lord Elphinstone sent for the fittest man at his disposal and told him to go to Kolhapúr and at all costs quell the mutiny. Le Grand Jacob went and disarmed the rebellious sepoys. How Lord Elphinstone was occasionally thwarted by men not immediately under his orders has been shown in the case of Woodburn. But his firmness was proof even against opposition of this description, and, after some vexatious delay, he carried out his policy.

Book XVIII. Concluding Chapter.

The generous confidence he placed in his subordinates.

His quick decision.

Only those who have enjoyed the privilege of reading his voluminous correspondence during 1857-58 can form an idea of the remarkable per-

His correspondence evidences his foresight.

Book XVIII. Concluding Chapter.

spicacity which characterised Lord Elphinstone's views on every point connected with the stirring events of those years. The strong and the weak points of a case, the true policy to be pursued, the proper time for putting it in action, when to withhold the blow, when to strike, the reasons for withholding or for striking, are laid down in clear and vigorous language in his letters. Reading them after the event, it seems marvellous how a man standing alone should have judged so clearly, so truly. Many of the military movements which tended to the pacification of the country had their first inspiration from Lord Elphinstone, and the smallest of the tardy tributes that can be paid him is this—that no man in India contributed so much as he contributed to check the mutiny at its outset; no man contributed more to dominate it after it had risen to its greatest height.

Lord Elphinstone is appointed by three successive secretaries of state to succeed Lord Canning.

In the glory of the victory, amid the bestowal of well-merited rewards for military services, the great deserts of Lord Elphinstone received but small notice from the public. But it is a remarkable fact that after the death of Sir Henry Lawrence he was nominated by three successive secretaries of state—by Mr. Vernon Smith, by Lord Ellenborough, and by Lord Stanley—to be successor to Lord Canning in the event of a vacancy occurring in the office of Governor-General. It now becomes the duty of the historian to place him on the lofty pedestal to which his great services and his pure and noble character entitle him.

Book XVIII. Concluding Chapter.

Lord Harris

The southern presidency was never invaded by the mutinous spirit. But not the less is a large share of credit due to its governor, Lord Harris. The responsibility which weighed upon this nobleman was very great indeed. The immunity of Madras depended upon the loyalty of the Nizám, and, at the outset, the Nizám had much to apprehend from his own people. It was in the height of the crisis that Lord Harris denuded his own presidency to send troops to Haidarábád, and it cannot be doubted but that their opportune arrival tended greatly to the pacification of the Nizám's dominions. The formation of the Kámpti column, of Whitlock's force, of the brigade which fought under Carthew at Kánhpúr, the despatch to Bengal of the regiments which kept open the grand trunk road in western Bihár and who afterwards co-operated against Kúnwar Singh, of the troops who rendered good service in Chútia Nágpúr, testify to the energy, the foresight, the devotion of the Governor of Madras. He used all the resources of his presidency to crush outside the rebellion which never penetrated within his own borders.

displays foresight, energy, and devotion.

Of other actors in the rise, progress, and suppression of the rebellion I have written in the body of this history, not always, perhaps, in as full detail as their splendid services demanded, but, I hope, in full proportion to the scope and requirements of the work entrusted to me. It may be that some incidents have escaped me. I shall regret much should such prove to be so, for my chief anxiety has been to render full justice

The deserts of Englishmen in the crisis of 1857-8-9.

to every man. This, at least, I may say, that, however ineffectively the history of the Indian mutiny may at any time be told, the character of our countrymen must be seen to emerge from the terrible ordeal of 1857-58 in a form that would gratify the most exacting people. We are, fortunately, as a nation, accustomed to success in the field, but on no occasion in our history has the nerve and fibre of our troops, or the fortitude and manliness of our countrymen of all ranks, been more conspicuous—often in the face of death itself, or under circumstances which would have seemed to justify despair. But with life they never despaired. They endured all that had to be endured, with a patience and cheerfulness never to be surpassed, and sought victory when it was possible with a determination before which the strongest opposition had to yield. And in all this they were sustained and animated by our countrywomen, who, in positions and under trials to which few gentle-nurtured women have been subjected, showed all the noblest and most loveable aspects of a woman's character. The history of the Indian mutiny is, in fact, a record of the display of all the qualities for which Englishmen have been famous—of the qualities which enabled the inhabitants of a small island in the Atlantic to accumulate the noblest and largest empire in the world, and which, so long as they remain unimpaired in their descendants, will maintain it.

APPENDIX A.

Reference to pages 38 to 67, Volume II.

The Services of the Artillery during the Street-fighting at Dehlí.

WHEN the third column entered the city through the Káshmir gate, it was followed by Major Scott's light field battery (No. 14). Heavy fighting was going on in the streets. Two guns, under Lieutenant M. M. FitzGerald, were at once sent to Ahmad Alí Khán's house on the right of the College gardens, to support the 60th regiment, which was soon after joined by the 52nd. Two guns, under Lieutenant Minto Elliot, joined the Bilúchis and 61st regiment in the College gardens, where Lieutenant Elliot was soon dangerously wounded. The remaining two guns, under Lieutenant Aislabie, joined Nicholson's column just as it had been compelled to retire to the Kábul gate, and assisted in all the subsequent fighting of that column until the capture of the Láhor gate. FitzGerald's and Elliot's guns were more or less actively engaged in all the street-fighting that took place on the left and centre, including the capture of the magazine and bank. The losses of the battery in men and horses were considerable, but not greater than were to be expected when manœuvring in narrow streets under constant musketry-fire from the houses. They remained in the city, horses in harness, without relief until late on the 17th of September, when they were sent back to Ludlow Castle very used up. A detachment of the gunners, under Lieutenant Aislabie, was retained in the College gardens until the 20th of September. They manned some heavy mortars and howitzers there, and shelled the palace and the bridge of boats.

The 5th troop 1st brigade (native) Bengal horse artillery was the only battery of native artillery which remained faithful to us when it had the chance of mutinying. It was quartered at Jalandhar when the mutiny occurred there. Lieutenant Renny then marched it to Dehlí. On the 9th of July, after the fanatic attack by the rebel cavalry on the right of our camp, it was thought advisable to take away its guns and horses as a precautionary measure. The native officers and men begged to be allowed to prove their loyalty, and were placed in charge of the mortar battery on the ridge, which they manned and worked without relief until the end of the siege

On the 14th of September Lieutenant Renny took some of these native gunners into the city with him. They carried by hand a couple of 12-pounder mortars, and were usefully employed in shelling the houses and streets in front of our attack. Lieutenant Renny himself earned the Victoria Cross for gallant conduct at the attack on the magazine, and the loyalty of his troop was a striking proof of his personal influence. When the city had fallen, guns and horses were restored to him, and the 5th troop 1st brigade did gallant service in the Rohilkhand campaign.

APPENDIX B.

Reference to page 122 of Volume II.

I REGRET that, in describing somewhat in detail the stimulating effect on the provision of means for the epuipment and progress of the army produced by the arrival of Sir Colin Campbell in Calcutta in August 1857, I should have seemed to undervalue the services of a most distinguished officer, Major, now General, Orfeur Cavenagh. I take the earliest opportunity of endeavouring to supply the omission. The Government of India had not under its orders in Calcutta an officer more deserving, or who rendered in that city such excellent service as did Major Cavenagh. In the early stages of the mutiny, and before the arrival of Sir Colin Campbell, it was Major Orfeur Cavenagh who, as town and fort-major of Fort William, had officially represented to the Government the necessity for being prepared to receive the expected reinforcements. He had suggested that he should be allowed an assistant who should superintend all disembarkations, render any assistance to commanding officers on their arrival, and have under his charge a staff of servants to be kept complete and allotted to troops on their arrival. As usual, Cavenagh's suggestions were negatived, though permission was given him to entertain the servants should he consider it necessary to do so. On this permission he acted, and, throughout the mutiny, under his own superintendence, he kept up a body of native servants. Eventually a disembarkation officer was appointed, not, however, as assistant to the town-major. To enable this officer to carry out his duties successfully, Cavenagh directed his own subordinates to recognise him and afford him every aid as though he were his assistant.

APPENDIX C.

Reference to pages 201, 202, 203, Vol. II.

FROM the sixth line from the bottom, page 201, beginning at the words "He ordered" to the word "Moti Mahal," in the second line from the top on page 203, the text in subsequent editions will, in lieu of the present text, which is cancelled, run as follows:

"He ordered on this duty a company of the 90th foot, under Captain Wolseley, and a picket of the 53rd, sixty strong, under Captain Hopkins, Major Barnston's battalion of detachments, under Captain Guise of the 90th, and some of the 4th Panjáb rifles, under Lieutenant Powlett.

"The feat of arms devolving upon these men to attempt was no light one. The Mess-house, a building of considerable size, was surrounded by a loop-holed mud wall, covering a ditch about twelve feet broad, scarped with masonry. The ditch was traversed by drawbridges, but whether these were up or not was unknown to the storming party.

"I must deal first with Hopkins. Leading his men at the double across the intervening space, exposed to a hot fire from the neighbouring buildings, that most daring officer reached the mud wall of which I have spoken, dashed over it, crossed the drawbridge, fortunately left down, and entered the Mess-house. Shortly after Hopkins had thus gained the place, Roberts of the Artillery—now Sir Frederic Roberts of Afghán celebrity—galloped up, handed him a Union Jack and requested him to hoist it on one of the turrets. Followed by one of his men, Hopkins ran to the top of the roof, and giving three cheers, planted the Union Jack on the summit. The cheers were responded to by a shout from the men, but the flag had not been up ten minutes before a round shot cut it and sent it down into the garden. Again did Hopkins plant it and again was it knocked down. He wished to hoist it again, but an order from the Commander-in-Chief arrived forbidding its further display. Whilst searching for the flagstaff in the garden Hopkins met Sir Colin and, after a brief colloquy, was at once placed in command of the Mess-house by the Chief of the Staff. He never left it till relieved the following afternoon by Captain Rolleston, 84th regiment. Wolseley, on his side, assaulting the place from a different point, had attacked the houses on the right of the building, whilst Irby, with a company of the supports, attempted to clear those on the left. Both attacks were successful, and the rebels, driven out, fled in panic to the Moti Mahal."*

* "About 5 P.M., when it was considered that men might be sent to storm it" (the Mess-house), "it was taken by a company of the 90th under Captain Wolseley and a picket of H.M.'s 53rd under Captain Hopkins, supported by Major Barnston's battalion of detachments under Captain Guise H.M.'s 90th, and some of the Panjáb infantry under Lieutenant Powlett. The Mess-house was carried with a rush." —*Sir Colin Campbell's Despatch.*

APPENDIX D.

Reference to page 364 of Volume II.

THE statement made by me in the first edition of the second volume regarding the part taken by Brigadier Napier in the plan for the attack on Lakhnao having been taken objection to, I drew attention in the second edition to the official papers on the subject extracted from Volume X. of *Professional Papers of the Corps of Royal Engineers.* I now attach extract from a letter, dated the 4th of February 1858, addressed by Brigadier Napier to Sir Colin Campbell containing his proposals for the attack—all of which were accepted and carried out.

"MY DEAR SIR COLIN,—

"I am afraid you will be disappointed at not receiving the projects, but our people have been bringing a considerable amount of intelligence to fill up our plans, which have tempted me to enter into details. I may, however, briefly state that, notwithstanding the enemy has made a good many defences and thrown up a ditch and rampart round the north side of the Kaisár Bágh, and has endeavoured to cut away all the passages across the canal, I do not apprehend any great difficulty.

"I would propose to encamp the force sufficiently far behind the Dilkusha to be out of fire; to establish a bridge on the Gúmti to pass over artillery and cavalry, to cut off the enemy's supplies, and to deter them from bringing out guns on the north side of the river to annoy us.

"To cross the canal in the first instance at Banks's house, under cover of our artillery, and to place guns in position to bear on the mass of buildings which flank the European infantry barracks, the hospital, the Bégam's house, and the Hazratganj—the places which rendered the European barracks so barely tenable—and to take that mass of buildings with the barracks.

"This position takes in flank all the defences of the north side of the Kaisar Bágh, and from them we may penetrate gradually to the Kaisar Bágh with the aid of the sapper and gunpowder, at the same time that we will occupy your old ground between the Kaisar Bágh and the Gúmti, to have positions for our artillery of all kinds to play on the Kaisar Bágh and its surrounding buildings. We shall, during this time, be steadily penetrating through the buildings on the left of the European barracks, making irresistible progress until we reach the Kaisar Bágh.

"Until we take that place we shall have as little street-fighting as is possible, and I hardly expect they will await an assault. But if they should do so, and defend the remainder of the city, we must advance, under cover of our mortars, until we occupy the bridges, which will certainly clear off the remainder, or they will starve.

"Jallálábád will be our depôt, and when we have got the enemy's guns driven off, we may bring our park up to the Dilkusha.

"I should have chosen your old passage across the canal but the enemy have cut a new one across the neck of a loop, and have put guns behind it, so that, as far as the intelligence guides us, Banks's house will be easier."

APPENDIX E.

Reference to page 407 of Volume II.

For the sentence beginning "Hagart ordered the 7th to charge," the following will be substituted in subsequent editions:—"Hagart ordered the 7th to charge. Before they could get well in motion, Slade, who commanded the party, was severely wounded, and Bankes and his charger were cut down. Wilkin charged to his side, but in warding off the attack from his wounded comrade, his horse reared. This caused him to miss his aim, and at the same time he received a severe wound in the foot. Wheeling again to the rescue, he cut down the rebel who was on the point of killing Bankes. The loss of their officers had taken the men by surprise, but Wilkin, though wounded, rallied them, and, joined by Hagart, who came up opportunely, once again charged the rebels, and cut down nearly all those who remained. These two officers particularly distinguished themselves."

To be added in a note: "For his gallant conduct Wilkin was twice recommended for the Victoria Cross, but he received neither recognition nor reward."

APPENDIX F.

Reference to page 418 of Volume II.

On the subject of the panic in Calcutta of the 3rd of March 1858, the following particulars have been furnished me by General Orfeur Cavenagh:—"On the 2nd of March, about 6 P.M., I received a note from General Ramsay stating that he had received information that arms had been collected in the suburbs of Calcutta for the purpose of being distributed amongst the men of the Reserve guard, on their march down to the fort, to enable them to make an attack on the European residents. The general begged me to be on the alert, and to cause a search to be made for the arms. Mr. Dorin was then President of the Council, and I rode over to his house and showed him the note. He requested me to instruct the civil authorities to make the requisite search for the arms, and to quietly intimate to commanding officers, including Turnbull, who commanded the volunteers, that it was possible that the services of the troops might be required, so that they might be ready to turn out if necessary. No orders were given for any pickets to be posted, nor was the garrison guard under arms. It was late before I returned to the fort, as I had to ride over to A'lipúr to see F., who was the magistrate by whom orders for the search had to be made. Only a few muskets were discovered. This was the real cause of the alarm to which you refer. I was rather surprised at hearing of the excitement that had taken place in Calcutta."

APPENDIX G.

Reference to page 472 of Volume II.

For the sentence, "Hamilton of the 3rd Sikhs, a very gallant officer, was killed charging the squares," the following will be substituted in subsequent editions:—"Hamilton of the 3rd Sikhs, a very gallant officer, was wounded and unhorsed when charging the squares. As he lay on the ground, the rebels cutting at him, Middleton of the 29th Foot and Farrier Murphy rushed to his assistance, and succeeded in rescuing his body from being cut to pieces. The wounds Hamilton received were, however, mortal. A little later, when a body of rebels, who had re-formed, left their ranks with drawn talwárs in their hands to cut down a dismounted wounded trooper of the Military Train, Middleton dashed at them, drove them back, dismounted, and placed the wounded trooper on his horse. The rebels fell back, leaving only three guns on the field. The British found it impossible to pursue. They therefore halted," &c. &c.

APPENDIX H.

Reference to pages 507 and 508 of Vol. II.

SINCE the second edition of the second volume of this history was published I have ascertained that the account of the death of Adrian Hope given in that volume was not quite accurate in some of its details. It will be seen from the amended account, which I subjoin, and which in future editions will occupy its proper place on pages 507 and 508 of the second volume, that, notwithstanding the rumours of the camp, Adrian Hope never had the smallest intention of taking the command from Walpole. The amended account will immediately follow the paragraph in page 507 concluding with the words "his gallant exploit," and will displace the now cancelled paragraphs in page 507 beginning "Before these gallant deeds," and in page 508, beginning with the words "All this time Adrian Hope" and "What was Adrian Hope going to say to Walpole?"

"Before these gallant deeds had been performed, Walpole, alarmed at the consequences of his own rashness, had caused the heavy guns to open on the wall from the side opposite to that occupied by the skirmishers. Soon after they had opened fire, a report was made to Adrian Hope that the shots from the heavy guns were going over the fort and dropping amongst his men. Adrian Hope at once rode to Walpole. What passed between them cannot with any certainty be known, but it seems probable that Walpole doubted the truth of the report, for on his return from the conversation Adrian Hope declared to his aide-de-camp, Lieutenant Butter, that he would go and see for himself. Dismounting from his horse, and closely followed by the brigade-major and Butter, Hope walked to the advanced line of skirmishers and crept up the glacis to look over. He had scarcely shown himself before he fell back, shot dead. Before, during, and for a short time subsequently to this event occurred those deeds of daring on the part of Willoughby, Douglas, Bramley, and their men which I have spoken of. At last Walpole, unable to make any impression on the fort, and seeing that every minute added to the slaughter of his infantry, ordered a retreat. This retreat was the signal for the display of the splendid devotion recorded in the preceding paragraph."

The next paragraph will begin, "Adrian Hope had fallen. Then, the retreat having been ordered, Brigadier Hagart," &c. &c.

APPENDIX I.

Translation of Tántia Topi's Voluntary Deposition or Statement taken in Camp Múshairi on the 10th of April 1859, in presence of Major Meade, commanding Field Force.

My name is Tántia Topi; my father's name is Pándurang, inhabitant of Jolá-Pargannáh, Patoda-Zillah, Nagar. I am a resident of Bithúr. I am about forty-five years of age, in the service of Náná Sáhib in the grade of companion or aide-de-camp.

In the month of May 1857 the collector of Kánhpúr sent a note of the following purport to the Náná Sáhib at Bithúr, viz. that he begged him (the Náná) to forward his wife and children to England. The Náná consented to do so, and four days afterwards the collector wrote to him to bring his troops and guns with him from Bithúr (to Kánhpúr). I went with the Náná and about one hundred sepoys and three hundred matchlockmen and two guns to the collector's house at Kánhpúr. The collector was then in the intrenchment, and not in his house. He sent us word to remain, and we stopped at his house during the night. The collector came in the morning and told the Náná to occupy his own house, which was in Kánhpúr. We accordingly did so; we remained there four days, and the gentleman said it was fortunate we had come to his aid, as the sepoys had become disobedient, and that he would apply to the general in our behalf. He did so, and the general wrote to A'gra, whence a reply came that arrangements would be made for the pay of our men. Two days afterwards the three regiments of infantry and the 2nd light cavalry surrounded us and imprisoned the Náná and myself in the Treasury, and plundered the magazine and Treasury of everything they contained, leaving nothing in either. Of the treasure the sepoys made over two lakhs and eleven thousand rupees to the Náná, keeping their own sentries over it. The Náná was also under charge of these sentries, and the sepoys who were with us also joined the rebels. After this the whole army marched from that place and the rebels took the Náná Sáhib and myself and all our attendants along with them, and said, "Come along to Dehlí." Having gone three coss from Kánhpúr, the Náná Sáhib said that, as the day was far spent, it was better to halt there then, and to march on the following day. They agreed to this and halted. In the morning the whole army told him (the Náná) to go with them towards Dehlí. The Náná refused, and the army then said, "Come with us to Kánhpúr, and fight there." The Náná objected to this; but they would not attend to him, and so, taking him with them as a prisoner, they went towards Kánhpúr, and fighting commenced there. The fighting continued for twenty-four days, and on the twenty-fourth day the general raised the flag of peace, and the fighting ceased. The Náná got a female who had been captured before to write a note to General Wheeler to this effect, that the sepoys would not obey his orders, and that, if he wished, he (the Náná) would get boats and convey him and those with him in the intrenchment, as far as Allahábád. An answer came from the general that he approved of this arrangement, and the same evening the general sent the Náná something over one lakh of rupees, and authorised him to keep the amount. The following day I went and got ready forty boats, and having caused all the gentlemen, ladies, and children to get into the boats, I started them off to Allahábád. In the meanwhile the whole army, artillery included, having got ready, arrived at the river Ganges. The sepoys jumped into the water and commenced a massacre of all the men, women, and children, and set the boats on fire. They destroyed thirty-nine boats. One, however, escaped as far as Kolá Kankar, but was there caught and brought back to Kánhpúr, and all on board of it destroyed. Four days after this the Náná said he was going te Bithúr to keep the anniversary of his mother's death; they (the sepoys) allowed him to go, and some of them also accompanied him. Having kept the anniversary, they brought him back to Kánhpúr, and they took for their pay the money they had first made over to the Náná's charge, and made arrangements to fight against Hussan Fathpúr, where they heard some Europeans had arrived from Allahábád, and they told the Náná to accompany them there. The Náná refused. I and the Náná remained at Kánhpúr, and sent Joala Parsad, his (the Náná's) agent, along with them to Fathpúr. Having arrived there and been defeated, they retreated to Kánhpúr, and the aforesaid European force pressed them the whole way to Kánhpúr, when there was a battle for about two hours, and the rebel army was again defeated, and ran away from Kánhpúr. Under these circumstances the Náná and I fled to Bithúr, arriving there at midnight, and the rebel army followed us. The next morning the Náná, taking some cash, &c. with him, went to Fathpúr. The rebel army followed, and looted the place. The Náná, Bálá Sáhib, Ráo Sáhib, and myself, with all our wives, crossed the Ganges in boats, and arrived at Fathpúr in the Lakhnao territory, and put up with the cháodri Bhopal Singh. Some days passed, when the 42nd native infantry arrived at Sheorájpúr, and wrote to the Náná to send them someone to take them to him. I went and told them that the Náná had sent for them. In the meanwhile the English army arrived, and the said 42nd regiment native infantry went to Bithúr, and fought there. I accompanied the said regiment, and having been defeated, we fled from Bithúr and crossed the Ganges, and came to the Náná. Some days after, I received orders from the Náná to go to Gwáliár, and to bring back with me to fight the English such of the contingent as were at Morár. According to his order, I went to Morár, and brought back the contingent with me to Kálpi. The Náná had sent his brother, the Bálá Sáhib, to Kálpi, and according to his order, I went with the army to fight against Kánhpúr, leaving a small force and magazine at Kálpi. Having arrived at Kánhpúr, there was a battle which lasted eleven days. After eleven days the rebel army was defeated, and we all ran away. The next day after this we fought at Sheorájpúr, and there also having been defeated, we ran away, having with us fifteen guns (including one horse-artillery gun). I and the Bálá Sáhib and the Ráo Sáhib, who had been sent by the Náná to Kánhpúr, all crossed the Ganges at Nana Máu-ki-Ghát. We remained at a place called Kheyra for the night. I got orders from the Ráo Sáhib to go and take charge of the small force and magazine left at Kálpi, in obedience to which I went there. After my arrival at Kálpi, I received orders from the Náná to go and attack Chirkári, and that the Ráo Sáhib should be sent after me. Accordingly I, with nine hundred sepoys, two hundred cavalry, and four guns, went to Chirkári, and fighting commenced. Four days afterwards the Ráo Sáhib came to Kálpi. I fought at Chirkari for eleven days, and took it. I took twenty-four guns and three lakhs of rupees from the rájá. The rájás of Bánpúr and Shahgarh, and Dewán Despat and Daolat Singh, the Kuchwaya Kharwála, and a great gathering of people joined me there at this time. I received a note from the queen of Jhánsi to the effect that she was waging war with the Europeans, and begging me to come to her aid. I reported the news to the Ráo Sáhib at Kálpi. The Ráo came to Jaipúr, and gave me permission to go to the assistance of the queen of Jhánsi. Accordingly I went to Jhánsi, and halted at

Burrua Ságar. There rájá Mán Singh came and joined me. The next day, about a mile from Jhánsi, the whole of our army had a fight with the English army. At this time we had twenty-two thousand men and twenty-eight guns. In this battle we were defeated. A part of the rebel army, with four or five guns, fled to Kálpi, and I went to the same place, *viâ* Bhánderi and Kúnch, with two hundred sepoys. The queen of Jhánsi arrived there the same evening as myself, and begged the Ráo Sáhib to give her an army that she might go and fight. The following morning the Ráo Sáhib ordered a parade of all the troops, and told me to accompany the queen to battle. Accordingly I, with a force, accompanied the queen, and there was a battle at Kúnch which lasted till noon. We were again defeated, and fled, and I fled to "Chirkí," which is about four miles from Jalaur, and where my parents were. The queen of Jhánsi and the force which fled with her arrived at Kálpi. The Ráo had a battle afterwards at Kálpi and was defeated, and he and his whole army arrived at Gopálpúr. I also left Chirkee, and joined him at Gopálpúr; we all marched thence towards Gwáliár. We had one day's fight with Mahárájá Sindia, and defeated him. Three days afterwards all Sindia's army joined the Ráo Sáhib, and having procured from the Gwáliár treasury, through Amarchand Batia (the mahárájá's treasurer), the requisite funds, pay was distributed to the army. Rám Ráo Govind was also with us. Some days afterwards the English army arrived at Gwáliár from Kálpi, and a force also came from Sirpúr. Fighting again took place, and continued for four or five days, during which the Jhánsi ráni was killed. Rám Ráo Govind had her corpse burnt, and we were all defeated and fled, taking twenty-five guns with us. We reached Jaora Alipúr and remained there during the night. The next morning we were attacked, and fought for an hour and a half. We fired five shots, and the English army fired four shots, and we then ran off, leaving all our guns. We crossed the Chambal; and reached Tánk *viâ* Sirimuthia. The nawáb of Tánk fought with us, and we took four guns from him. With these guns we proceeded to Bhilwára *viâ* Mahdípúr and Indragarh. We were there attacked by the English force, and I fled during the night, accompanied by my army and guns. At that time I had eight or nine thousand men and four guns with me. We all proceeded to a village called Kotra (about four miles from Nathduwarra) and halted there for one night. The next morning we moved towards Patan, and after proceeding about one mile, the English army arrived, and an action took place. We left our four guns and fled, reaching Patan as fugitives. (The nawáb of Bándá, who had come with us from Kálpi, and the nawáb of Kumona, who had joined us at Indúrkí, were both with us.) On our arrival at Patan fighting commenced between us and the rájá of that place; we conquered, and got possession of all the rájá's guns and magazines, and surrounded his palace, in which he was. The next day I went and told the rájá to give some money to pay the expenses of my army. He said he could give five lakhs of rupees, but not more. I returned and told the Ráo Sáhib this. The next day the Ráo Sáhib sent for the rájá and demanded twenty-five lakhs from him. The rájá declared he could not give more than five lakhs; but, after some discussion, it was settled that he should pay fifteen lakhs. The rájá said he would go to his palace and send this sum. He went accordingly, and sent two and a quarter lakhs in cash, and promised that the rest should follow. By the next day he had paid up five lakhs.

Imám Alí, Wúrdi-major 5th irregular cavalry, ill-treated the rájá very much, and the latter fled during the night. We remained there five days, and issued three months' pay to our troops at the rate of thirty rupees each sowar, and twelve rupees to each foot-soldier per mensem.

We then marched for Sironj, taking eighteen guns with us. On reaching Rájgarh the English army came up and attacked us. We left our guns and fled, and reached Sironj *viâ* Nija Killa. We halted at Sironj eight days, and having taken four guns from the Tánk nawáb's agent at Sironj, we proceeded thence to I'sághar. On arrival there we demanded supplies; but the I'sáogarh people would not give them. We therefore attacked I'sáogarh, and plundered it. The following day we halted, and the Ráo Sáhib told me to go to Chandairi, and that he would come round by Tál Bahat. I accordingly went to Chandairi, and the Ráo Sáhib came to Lallatpúr from (or by) Tál Bahat. On my reaching Chandairi, four shots were first fired on us from the fort, which we attacked and fought with Sindia's agent. After three days we marched from Chandairi towards Mangaulí, taking with us eleven guns, viz. seven which we had brought from I'sáogarh and the four we had got from Sironj. On our march to Mangráuli, we met the English army. Shots were fired for a short time, when we left all our guns and fled. (Of the eleven guns five were with me and six with the Ráo Sáhib. I lost my five in this fight, but the Ráo kept his six.)

(Note.—It would appear that the Ráo was not in this action.)

I reached Jaklom, and the next day went to Sulantpúr, where the Ráo Sáhib also arrived. After three days the English force arrived, and the Ráo Sáhib took his army to Jaklom (about five miles from Lallatpúr), and some firing took place there. I was not present in this fight. The Ráo Sáhib returned to Lallatpúr, and the following day proceeded to Kajúriá (ten miles from Sulantpúr) and halted there. The next day the English army came up just as we were going to march, and an action commenced which lasted an hour and a half. We then left all our guns and fled, and reached Tál Bahat. We halted there, and the following day went to Jaklom, and thence to a village called Itaia, twelve miles distant, where we stopped. We there heard that the English army was coming to surprise us, and marched at night. The English force came up in the morning, and our army became separated. I accompanied the Ráo Sáhib, and we proceeded, *viâ* Rájghar, and crossed the Narbadá, and got to Kaogáon Battís *viâ* Kandula. The troops who were with us burned the Government thanna and bungalow at Kandula. The Ráo Sáhib forbad their doing so, but they would not obey him. This was about four months ago. At Kaogáon Battís there were some of Holkar's troops—one hundred and forty sowars, one company of infantry, and two guns. These we forced to join us, and took them with us when we marched the following day towards Gujrát, crossing the high road where the telegraph-wire ran. The sepoys broke the wire and plundered seven hackeries which were on the road proceeding with Government property towards Gwáliár, and seized the chuprassis and chaukídárs who were with the hackeries, and took them with them. Some of the chaukídárs belonging to the chaukí were hanged by them. We there left the high road and proceeded westward. The next day we were surprised by the English force, and leaving our two guns, we fled, and reached the Narbadá. An officer, with one hundred men, was on the opposite bank. Our force commenced to cross, and this officer and party of sowars ran off. We plundered a village there called Chikla, and marched thence at midnight. After proceeding thirty-four miles, we halted at Rájpúra. The next day we took three thousand nine hundred rupees and three horses from the rájá of that place, and from it went on to Chota Udaipúr. The following day the English force surprised us; some of them were killed, and some of ours. From Chota Udaipúr we went on to Deogarh Bári, and our army became separated. There was jungle at that place, and I halted there two days. Our troops having been collected again, we started, and went to Bánswára. Our men plundered there sixteen or seventeen camel-loads of cloth (some of Ahmadábád) belonging to a mahájan which they ound there. We thence went to Salomar, and I called on

Kaisar Singh, agent for the Udaipúr rájá, to furnish us with supplies. He sent us some, and the following day we again started with the intention of going to Udaipúr. However, *en route* we received tidings of the English force, and retraced our steps to Bhílwárá. We remained there two days and then proceeded to Partábgarh, where we fought for two hours with a body of English troops which had come from Nímach. About 8 o'clock P.M. we ran off, and proceeded about six miles to the east of Mandisor and halted there. We then went on to Zirápúr, making three stages *en route*. An English force surprised us there, and we were again surprised by another force at Chaprá Baród. We fled thence to Nahargarh, the agent of the Kotah rájá, at which place nine shots were fired at us from guns. We moved out of range, and halted there during the night; and the Ráo Sáhib sent Risáldár Nannú Khán to call rájá Mán Singh. The rájá came and accompanied us—*i.e.* the Ráo Sáhib, myself, and our force—to a place about two miles from Parón, where we halted. We remained there two days, and on the third went on to a place about eight miles beyond Kilwarrí, whose name I do not remember. Rájá Mán Singh accompanied us as far as a river which we crossed *en route*, and then left us. We made two stages thence to Indragarh; and Firoz Shah with the Khás Risálá (body-guard) and 12th irregulars met us there. The next day we went on, making two stages to Dewás, which is fourteen miles from Jaipúr. The English force surprised us there; some men on both sides were killed, and flying thence towards Márwár, we reached a village about thirty koss from Márwár, whose name I do not remember. At 4 o'clock that night we were surprised by the English force, and the 12th irregular cavalry separated from the Ráo Sáhib's army. The next day Thákur Naráyan Singh, Ajhít Singh, uncle of rájá Mán Singh, and Thákur Gangá Singh joined us at that place (? to which the Ráo's army had fled). They were coming in this (the Parón) direction. I had been quarrelling with the Ráo Sáhib all the way from Deogarh Bárí, and told him I could flee no longer, and that whenever I saw an opportunity for doing so, I should leave him. The opportunity for doing so here offered, and I left him and accompanied the (three) above-named parties in this (the Parón) direction. When I left the Ráo Sáhib he had about six thousand men with him. But three men (two Pandits to cook my food and one sais) and three horses and one tattú accompanied me. The names of the two pandits were Rám Ráo and Naráyan. The sais's name was Gobind, but he left me and ran off after coming two stages. We reached the Parón jungle and met rájá Mán Singh. Ájhít Singh took leave of rájá Mán Singh, and went to his home. Naráyan Singh and I remained with rájá Mán Singh. The rájá said, "Why did you leave your force? You have not acted right in so doing." I replied that I was tired of running away, and that I would remain with him whether I had done right or wrong. I heard after this that the Ráo Sáhib's army had gone to Patan, and thence towards Sironj. I told rájá Mán Singh I would send a man to get intelligence of them, and he approved of my doing so. I sent accordingly, and got information that the Ráo Sáhib was not there; but Imám Alí, Wúrdí-major, Firoz Sháh, and the Ambapáni-wala Nawáb, Adíl Muhammad, were there with eight or nine thousand men. Imám Alí, Wúrdí-major of the 5th irregular cavalry, wrote to me to come and join them. I had lost my master's (the Náná's) seal, and had another made up at Parón.

When I heard, as above, from the Wúrdí-major, I sent a man to rájá Mán Singh, who was at Mahúdia in Major Meade's camp (he had then been there three days), to inform him that I had received a note of this purport, and to ask him if I should go or remain. Rájá Mán Singh had consulted me before giving himself up to Major Meade, and had left one of his men with me, saying, "Stop wherever this man takes you." Rájá Mán Sing replied to my message that he would come in three days to see me, and we should then settle what to do.

He came accordingly on the third day, at night, and spoke a great deal to me, and told me that he had met Major Meade, and that his disposition was good. When I asked him what he advised—whether I should go or remain—he said he would reply in the morning. I then went to sleep, and during the night some sepoys of the Government came and seized me, and took me to Major Meade's camp.

Signature of Tántia Topi,
Agent of the Náná Sáhib.

Question by Major Meade.—Have you made this statement of your own free will and without compulsion; and has any promise been made, or hope held out, to you to induce you to give it?

Answer.—I have, of my own free will, caused this statement to be written; and no one has forced me to do so, or held out hope or promise of any sort to induce me to do so.

Signature of Tántia Topi,
Agent of the Náná Sáhib.

Signature of Witnesses.
(Signed) Gangá-prasád Múnshi, Meade's horse.
Rubhúlál-Naibo Kamasdor of Siprí.

The above deposition or statement was made by the prisoner Tántia Topi in my presence on the 10th of April 1859, at Camp Múshairi, of his own voluntary act and without compulsion of any sort, or promise made, or hope held out to him as an inducement to make it.

(Signed) R. J. Meade, Major,
Commanding Field Force.

Certified that the above is a true and correct translation of the original deposition or confession of Tántia Topi appended hereto.

(Signed) J. J. M. Gibbon, Lieutenant,
Adjutant Meade's horse.

(True copy.)

R. Meade.